THE WEIGHTLIFTING ENCYCLOPEDIA

A GUIDE TO WORLD CLASS PERFORMANCE

THE WEIGHTLIFTING ENCYCLOPEDIA

A GUIDE TO WORLD CLASS PERFORMANCE

By ARTHUR J. DRECHSLER

A IS A COMMUNICATIONS, FLUSHING, N.Y.

THE WEIGHTLIFTING ENCYCLOPEDIA:
A Guide To World Class Performance
By ARTHUR J. DRECHSLER
Published by:
A IS A COMMUNICATIONS
P.O. Box 680
Whitestone, NY 11357-0680   USA

WARNING—DISCLAIMER

Weightlifting, like all strenuous sports, can be dangerous. You should consult with a physician before beginning to practice weightlifting and learn and practice the sport guided by a knowledgeable coach.

This book is meant to inform and entertain. The information contained herein is based on information from various sources, published and unpublished and merely represents literature and practice as summarized by the author. The author and publisher make no warranties, expressed or implied, regarding the currency, completeness or scientific accuracy of this information, nor do they warrant its fitness for any particular purpose. No book can address all aspects of weightlifting This book is meant to complement, amplify and supplement other information that is available and should be pursued.

The author is neither a health professional nor an attorney. Although a variety of legal, dietary, medical and pharmaceutical concepts, and descriptions of injuries and their treatments, are presented in this book, they are for informational purposes only and do not represent legal, health or medical advice. They are merely reported on the basis of the experiences and/or observations of the author. None of them should be applied without the knowledge and supervision of an appropriate professional.

While the author has been associated with the United States Weightlifting Federation (doing business as USA Weightlifting/USAW) and the International Weightlifting Federation for many years, the opinions expressed here are the author's and are not necessarily representative of either of these organizations.

We have tried to assure that this book is accurate and complete but there may be typographical and content mistakes, so this book should be used as a general guide. The author and publisher have neither the liability nor responsibility for any loss of damage caused, or alleged to be caused, directly or indirectly, by the information contained in this book. **If you do not wish to be bound by the above conditions of purchase and use of this book, you may return it to the publisher for a full refund.**

Publisher's Cataloging In Publication
(Provided by Quality Books, Inc.)

Drechsler, Arthur
     The weightlifting encyclopedia : a guide to world class
performance / by Arthur J. Drechsler. -- 1st ed.
     p. cm.
     Includes bibliographical references and index.
     Preassigned LCCN: 97-93857
     ISBN: 0-9659179-2-4

     1. Weight lifting--Handbooks, manuals, etc. 2. Weight lifting--
Rules.   I. Title. II. Title: Weight lifting encyclopedia

GV546.3.D74 1998   796.41
                                QBI97-40958

The photographs introducing Chapters 1, 4 and 11 are courtesy of the York Barbell Co.. Lower right cover photo is courtesy of Joseph Byrd & Associates. The other cover photos, photos introducing Chapters 2, 5, 8 and 9 and Figs. 1-4 and 10-11 and 35 were provided by Bruce Klemens. The photo introducing Chapter 3 is courtesy of Glenda Anderson and the Paul Anderson Youth Home. All other photographs are courtesy of James Curry Sr. The art work in Figs. 5, 13 and 50-58 was created by Nicholas Curry.

DEDICATION

This book is dedicated to all who search for mental and physical strength, but especially to the World Record holders of the future—they set the standards for the development of weightlifting performance and are truly the immortals of the Iron Game!

CONTENTS AT A GLANCE

CONTENTS

FOREWORD

My acquaintance with the author, Artie Drechsler, dates back over a quarter of a century. Little did I suspect this teenager, who I first met at Lost Battalion Hall in New York in 1968, would become so intensely interested in the sport of weightlifting that he would groom himself to establish world records shortly thereafter.

Artie is a rare type of person, unique among all my friends. He likes and accepts challenges. When he was told he could not be a good weightlifter, it made him all the more determined to succeed.

He lived and breathed weightlifting and read all of the weightlifting journals and books he came across. He collected back issues of the sport's magazines, so he became knowledgeable about the history of weightlifting. He wanted to capture the essence of the sport, not just the veneer that most lifters see.

And, when he could no longer continue in weightlifting competition, he spent much of his spare time researching and combining that research with his experiences so that he could write the first encyclopedia on Olympic weightlifting!

While he was conducting research for his book, Artie spent time compiling the 16 mm movie films made of weightlifting during the 1940s through the 1960s; he created a series of video tapes that is now available to all weightlifting enthusiasts.

A man of great patience and thoroughness, Artie took more than seven years to write this book that you are about to read. It is the most comprehensive book in the English language on Olympic weightlifting that I have seen. It covers all aspects of Olympic weightlifting, from the novice to the world-class level, from technique to training programs.

It is a "must" book for coaches and elite athletes to have. I also recommend it highly for novices who want to understand the finer points of training and lifting and to shorten the time it takes for them to reach their full potential.

Read, study, and apply the information you find within these covers and you will be richly rewarded with rapid improvement on your Olympic lifts. I wish this book had been available when I started the sport of weightlifting!

Tommy Kono

PREFACE

I have admired strength for as long as I can remember. When I was very young, I always looked for the movie and television characters who displayed the greatest physical strength. Whenever we went to the circus, most of my friends went to see the acrobats or animals. I went to see the strongman. My favorite biblical character was Samson and my favorite mythological character was Hercules. John Henry was the American folk hero I admired most. In my father's boiler business, where I worked many summers from an early age, the men I respected the most were those who had the greatest physical strength. The examples could go on and on.

One of the reasons for my admiration of strength was my own lack of it. Mental activities came more easily to me than physical ones, and for that reason I never seemed to focus on the importance of mental activities as much—I took mental processes as a given when I was younger (something I learned never to do as I grew older). Physical strength didn't come naturally to me, so I always coveted it.

All of my pent-up desire for strength came to fruition in three major steps in my life. The first step was taken on a warm, sunny, day, at the end of the summer of 1961, just a few months before my eleventh birthday. I was walking down one of the busiest streets in town where I live, right in front of a large newsstand that stood on the sidewalk. Among the dozens of magazines on display was one with a man on the cover who seemed to have chest muscles of freakish proportions and an overall muscular development of his upper body that almost matched the muscularity of that chest. My immediate reaction was "This guy must be really strong; maybe this magazine will give me some clue as to how he got that way." The magazine was the September 1961 issue of the now defunct Strength & Health (for more than 50 years the leading strength publication in America, and one of the leading publications in the world covering weightlifting and weight training).

After pouring through the magazine, I was initially disappointed to discover that no information on the cover man was given, but the wealth of other information offered was more than enough to make up for that initial disappointment. There were pictures of various bodybuilders and weightlifters, results from weightlifting and bodybuilding competitions, and an article about the

1960 Olympic Champion weightlifter from Poland, Ireneusz Palinski.

In those early stages of my discovery of the iron game, I shared the common misconception of many beginners that outward muscle size (that which is apparent to the naked eye) and strength were closely correlated. Though weightlifting was clearly regarded as the true measure of strength by the magazine's writers, it seemed esoteric. What, after all, was a snatch or clean and jerk (C&J)? Why did some of the men doing these lifts have their feet placed with one well forward and the other well behind? Why were others sitting in a deep squat position? Surely these could not be positions for exerting maximal strength.

It took a significant amount of additional reading for me to begin to piece together the differences between weightlifting and bodybuilding (there was no competitive powerlifting to speak of in those days) and to realize that if what I really wanted was the maximum in strength, weightlifting was the sport for me. Some months later, I started to train with a set of weights that my father made for me out the steel that he used in his boilermaking business. My early efforts were rather crude and when others heard what I was doing, they began to bombard me with stories of hernias, stunted growth, back injuries and other sorts of catastrophes that supposedly happened to all weightlifters. Some of these "experts" even suggested that weightlifting and bodybuilding publications consisted of propaganda issued by barbell manufacturers and that their advice therein was therefore not to be trusted. Since I could find no one who could give me any advice from real experience, my parents were really against my lifting weights and since I wasn't sure (from the little reading that I'd done) that I knew what I was doing, or that the voices of doom weren't correct, my participation in the sport came to a temporary halt. However, I continued to learn what I could about weight training and the development of strength.

With my weightlifting placed on hold, I directed my energies to my other athletic loves of swimming, handball, wrestling and football, finally deciding to concentrate on football as I entered my teenage years. It was at this time that I first tried to see how much I could lift. With a great struggle, I managed to clean and press 95 lb., at a bodyweight of approximately 135 lb..

Once I turned my full attention toward football, I realized that added strength and size could be of great value on the gridiron and that weight training could develop such strength. So once again my interest in weight training grew and I started to train with some degree of regularity. I searched every magazine and book I could find for items about weight training and football. But I couldn't help but read about the sport of weightlifting itself. Little by little, my desire for strength began to return to the foreground and I began to agonize over whether to become a weightlifter and to give up my football career. A series of events that transpired in a matter of weeks put an end to the false starts that had stretched across a period of nearly four years (from age 11 to age 15).

First, immediately after my initial season of high school football (during which I had taken time off from weight training because of the demands of daily football practice and some fairly rigorous academic studies) I tried myself out on the military press and found that I could make only 140 lb.. (as compared with my pre-season best of 165 lb..). I had worked hard to get my press up to 165, and such a drop-off was a bitter disappointment. Suddenly football seemed unproductive. I had trained long and hard to get in shape for football and then I had torn myself down by playing the game. Weightlifting, by contrast, seemed like a much more direct athletic activity—both the training and the performance in competition contributed toward the overall development of the body. This really made me think.

The second event that pushed me toward a career in weightlifting was a weightlifting exhibition given at my high school given by a former local champion and then administrator in the NYC school system, Julie Levy. At that exhibition, it was announced that there would be a weightlifting competition conducted at the school in several weeks. I went home to do some more hard thinking. Eventually, the combination of my love of strength, my disappointment over the strength loss I had suffered during the football season, the excitement caused by the exhibition and the anticipation of the coming competition virtually made the decision for me—weightlifting was to be my sport.

It was then, when I was just about to be presented with my first varsity "letter" by the football coach, that I told him and my teammates that my football career was over. They were shocked. I had been one of the hardest workers on the team and many of the older and bigger players had become impressed with my strength. A number of them had gotten interested in weight training as an adjunct to football at my encouragement, an influence not appreciated by the coaches, who abhorred weight training, believing that it would make a player musclebound, whatever that is (thirty years ago, weight training was not accepted in athletics in the

way that it is today). Most of my former teammates were quite supportive of my decision, but I was told by the coaches "If you quit football you will quit a everything in life." I didn't care what they thought; I was embarking on a new career and my enthusiasm couldn't be restrained.

At this point, I had my goals set, but, unbeknownst to me, I lacked two key ingredients needed to achieve success in weightlifting—the knowledge and the emotional support needed to perform the arduous training required to become top notch. Then, quite by accident, the key to these important ingredients that I lacked appeared in the person of Danny Ruchames.

My first meeting with Danny was rather confrontational. I was standing in one of the basement hallways of my high school, in front of a flyer that announced the upcoming weightlifting competition. A friend and I were speculating about my prospects. Danny happened to overhear my claim of having in the past succeeded with a 165 pound military press and he challenged that claim. I was appalled at his allegation of dishonesty and offered to show him that I could indeed do 165 if he was willing to come to my house to watch me. It happened that he lived near my home, so he agreed to visit me the next day after school.

That next afternoon, to my chagrin, I was only able to press 155. Waiving off my embarrassed apologies, Danny indicated that he recognized one could not always perform ones best—but he felt that the 155 demonstrated the validity of my claim of 165. Impressed with my ability, he then offered to introduce me to his former weightlifting coach, a man named Morris Weissbrot (a congenital spinal defect had halted Danny's otherwise promising career some years earlier). Morris Weissbrot! I was in awe. Morris had recently written a series of articles in Strength & Health. The thought of training with such a famous authority was a dream come true. Danny and I agreed to make the trip to Lost Battalion Hall, the gym where Morris coached, later that week.

On Friday, January 14, 1966, I walked into the gym at Lost Battalion hall. There, I met Morris Weissbrot for the first time. He was a big man, warm, enthusiastic and friendly. I demonstrated my technique (or lack thereof) on the "Olympic" lifts. Morris quickly pointed out some of my numerous flaws, but he indicated that with hard work they could all be corrected. He showed me some exercises for developing my technique and had me practice them on the spot. I literally practiced until my hands bled, with little sign of improvement. But as I left the gym that night, I knew that a lifelong search had come to an end. I had truly discovered the sport of weightlifting—the premier sport of strength and power. It was the end of one journey and the beginning of another.

It has been more than 30 years since I began my weightlifting journey. There have been plenty of bumps, detours and disappointments along the way. But, on balance, it has been a journey of unbounded joy. With all of the years that have passed, I am in as much in love with the sport as I was on the first day. This book is an outgrowth of that continuing love.

Weightlifting is truly one of the greatest sports ever conceived by the mind of man or woman. It is my profound hope that this book will help to make someone else's journey to weightlifting mastery smoother, more direct and more far reaching than mine has been. If what is here is of value, it is because I have had the advantage of standing on the strong shoulders of those who have come before me—a position where it is much easier to see the realities of weightlifting. For sharing what I've learned, I expect little in return,* except that you do the same as I have done, along with so many before me. Once you have learned it, share the secrets of strength and weightlifting with all who will listen—keep the flame burning. It is in meeting the myriad challenges of weightlifting that we can discover and develop what is truly the best within us, the strength of mind and body that will help us to become the masters of our fates. Use the challenge of weightlifting to mold your own characters into something far stronger than the steel you strive to overcome. Good luck in your own personal journey!

*I am a good enough businessman to realize that I am highly unlikely to make a great deal of money from a book on competitive weightlifting. Moreover, a share of the profits from the sale of this book (assuming there are any) will be used to pay for copies of the book that are donated to individuals or libraries throughout the country, or to subsidize the purchase of this book by organizations that are promoting the sport of weightlifting. Therefore, the price you have paid for the book is in part a contribution to the future of weightlifting.

ACKNOWLEDGMENTS

Over my years in weightlifting, many people have taught me many things about the sport. They have taught me freely and with no motive other than the pleasure they derived out of seeing someone else succeed in the sport they love so much. With the same motive, I have volunteered countless hours to help others master the sport, with the same motive.

The greatest contributors to my success have been my training partners, fellow athletes who have graciously shared all they know, not self-sacrificially, but for the very personal pleasure of watching still another person triumph over our indefatigable adversary, the barbell. To Danny, Joe, Ted, Alex, Dave, Mark, Stan, Carl, John, Denis, Ben, Bud, Mike, Jerry, Victor, Charlie and so many others who have helped so much over the years I want to say once more that I can't thank you enough. And I thank the athletes that I coach today for helping to make my current training sessions the pleasure that they remain.

During my career, for better or for worse, I have been my own coach most of the time. But there were two people who coached me for a time and taught me much for which I will be eternally grateful. The first of these is Morris Weissbrot. He started the Lost Battalion Hall weightlifting club more than 30 years ago. If Morris had not done that, I, and so many others, would have never had the chance to experience the wonderful sport of weightlifting in the way we did. Morris was a great facilitator at LBH, and he continues to be a great promoter or weightlifting wherever he travels. He provided an atmosphere where everyone could progress and improve, where seriousness was fun and where one felt that the continued existence of weightlifting was as certain as Morris's devotion to it. I owe Morris a great debt of gratitude, as do many others, for the good work that he has done for weightlifting for so many years.

My other coach was Dave Sheppard. Dave is not only one of the greatest lifters ever to represent the United States in international competition, he also has one of the sport's great analytical minds. He has devoted more than half a century to weightlifting and his enthusiasm is as great today as it ever was. He is an unsung hero who pioneered many of the techniques and training methods of his day, methods that became the underpinnings of many of today's approaches to training. I don't think that there are many of us who have known Dave who haven't felt that we could always lift a little more when he was in the gym—certainly I always did. Dave has taught me much and encouraged me much over these many years—these are gifts I can never repay.

There is also a debt of gratitude that, I, along with virtually every other weightlifter in the US, and much of the world, owes to Bob Hoffman. For more than 50 years, his magazine, Strength & Health, informed the world about the benefits of weightlifting and the achievements of its great athletes. I learned much from reading that magazine over the years. Perhaps more importantly, with its inspirational biographies and exciting accounts of great weightlifting competitions, Strength & Health fueled my desire to become a weightlifting champion and a lifelong contributor to the sport . We who grew up from the 1930s to the 1980s are all, as Bob liked to refer to us, "Bob Hoffman boys grown up." And those of you who have never heard of Bob were probably introduced to the sport by someone who was touched by him.

I want to thank Tommy Kono, Dr. John Garhammer, Rudy Sablo, Jack Hughes, Lynne Stoessel-Ross, Nicholas Curry, Dan Nugent, Dan Peck, Ben Green and Bud Charniga for their comments on parts or all of the third draft of this book. Any errors that may remain in it exist despite, not because of, their assistance. They are my sole responsibility.

I want to thank James Curry Sr., for taking most of the exercise photos and some of the chapter introduction photos for this book. During his career, Jim has taken some of the best photos ever made of weightlifters. I want to thank Nicholas Curry for providing most of the line art for this book—he is a young man of many talents.

I also want to thank my former secretary, Janette Moore, whose patience in making corrections to the second draft of this book made the difficult process of bringing it to its final form much easier. I also want to thank Susan Heath and her assistant, Kelly Jewett, who edited this volume with such skill and respect for the author's style and message.

Finally, I want to thank my wife, JoAnne. She has been a constant source of encouragement in my training and my efforts to improve the sport of weightlifting. Her unflagging support throughout the preparation of this book made the entire process a great deal easier than it would have otherwise been. I can never thank her enough. I can only marvel at how great her patience and understanding are.

What Weightlifting Is All About —

It May Not Be What You Think!

Welcome! You hold in your hands a comprehensive guide to the most exciting strength and power sport ever developed—Olympic style weightlifting. Weightlifting is a sport that challenges its participants in a way that no other sport can—making them strong mentally as well as physically. Yet weightlifting is one of the most misunderstood sports in the world.

Mention the word "weightlifting" to anyone you meet and that person will probably affirm that he or she knows what weightlifting is. However, in my experience, most people do not understand the difference between those who participate in the actual sport of weightlifting and the millions of people who lift weights for a variety of other reasons. Moreover, an even larger majority of people harbor at least one major fallacy regarding the sport of weightlifting. Therefore, it is appropriate to begin this book by briefly explaining what weightlifting is, why one would want to participate in it and what major fallacies people often hold about the sport.

What Is Weightlifting?

Weightlifting is a sport that involves lifting a barbell overhead. Formally, the sport has existed on an international level in something resembling its current form for more than 100 years. Today, the sport is practiced in more than 130 countries around the world. It is the only event involving the use of heavy weights that is part of the Olympic Games (which is why the sport is often called "Olympic Lifting").

The sport of weightlifting consists of two events (which is why it is sometimes referred to as a biathlon). The first event, the snatch, involves lifting a barbell from the floor to arm's length overhead in one continuous motion. It is one of the most difficult, explosive and elegant events in sport. The second event is called the clean and jerk

(C&J). It involves lifting a barbell from the floor to the shoulders in one continuous motion and then, in a second motion, bringing the weight to arm's length overhead. It is by far the single greatest test of strength in all of organized athletics (see Figs. 3 & 4 on for examples of the snatch and C&J, respectively).

Weightlifting: A Sport That Is As Wonderful As It Is Misunderstood

There may be no sport ever conceived by the mind of man or woman that is as misunderstood or underappreciated as the sport of Olympic-style Weightlifting - the sport that tests how much weight a man or a woman can lift from the ground to arm's length above his or her head.

That the strongest men and woman in the world compete in weightlifting is understood by some people (although many still believe a falsehood—that other athletes are stronger than weightlifters). But most people think weightlifting is far more dangerous than it is, underestimate the speed, flexibility and coordination that is required to be a champion weightlifter, and are completely unaware of the sheer pleasure that there is in mastering the technique of weightlifting.

There is literally no other sport that challenges your strength, skill and mental powers more fully than weightlifting. All of these factors and others make weightlifting the uniquely fascinating and unbelievably rewarding sport that it is for men and women of all sizes and ages.

Why Become a Weightlifter?

While the reasons that people fall in love with the sport of weightlifting are all different, the most

1

important reason to become a weightlifter is that it's fun to be strong, but there is much more.

Those who have acquired a proficiency in weightlifting, acknowledge that they've never participated in a sport that they enjoyed as much. There is a feeling that comes from executing a perfect lift with a maximum weight that almost defies description. Amazingly, a limit lift performed in perfect style feels almost weightless to the lifter. This feeling of effortlessness gives one a sense of triumph over the weight that is something akin to the way baseball players feel when they hit a home run, what basketball players feel when they "swish" a challenging jump shot, or what golfers feel when they've sunk a perfect put. But most athletes who have experienced the joys of other sports as well as weightlifting feel that weightlifting provides the biggest thrill of all.

Why? No one knows for sure. Perhaps it is because knowledge of your success is immediate and certain. In baseball, basketball, or golf, you have to wait for the ball to travel before success is assured. In football you may make a good "hit," but your opponent's response may still not be as desired. In gymnastics or diving an athlete receives a certain degree of immediate feedback, just as one does in weightlifting. However, the athlete must then wait to see if the judges agree with his or her own impression. In weightlifting there are judges too. But these judges are there merely to rule on marginal performances. When a lifter does a clean lift there is no doubt the lift is good (there are no points awarded in weightlifting competition for technique per se). In my more than thirty years in the sport, I have almost never seen a totally clean lift turned down by competent officials have only seen marginal lifts judged inconsistently. When you make a lift properly, you know it, and you know it in a split second.

Perhaps another reason for the pleasure that you get out of weightlifting is the certainty that comes from being at your best. If you shoot a hole in one in golf, roll a strike in bowling or hit a home run in baseball, there can never be any certainty that the result truly came from your own best ever performance. The hole-in-one may have resulted from a gust of wind or a bump in the green. To be sure, you must have hit a very good shot, but other factors may have played a role. In rolling a strike you could have been assisted by a groove in the alley. In baseball, the distance of a hit can be influenced by the speed with which the pitcher threw the ball or the liveliness of the ball itself.

In weightlifting, the barbell is the barbell. It is manufactured to exacting specifications and its weight is precise. Moreover, in competition, everyone uses the same one. There is generally little doubt that when you lift a new personal best you are at your all time best. The combination of training, diet, rest and mental preparation was just right to make it happen. Strength, speed and coordination were all at a peak. The reward was to hold aloft the greatest weight that you have ever lifted and to savor the fruits of your hard earned success. There is simply no other thrill like it in all of sport.

Another reason for the satisfaction that weightlifting provides. One reason is that there is probably no sport for which the training is harder. The training is not necessarily harder than that of other sports in terms of the calories expended, the time spent or even the total weight lifted in a training session (some manual laborers lift more total tons in a day than even top weightlifters). Rather, it is the intensity of the physical and mental effort that goes into a single maximum lift that makes weightlifting such a tremendous challenge. Because the challenge is so great, the satisfaction that one gains from success in weightlifting is great as well—you truly must give your all to succeed.

Still another reason for weightlifting's appeal is that while it can have a limited element of "team" competition, it is first and foremost an individual sport. Your success in weightlifting depends on you and you alone. Teammates can offer many kinds of indirect help. Coaches can provide valuable feedback on your performance. Friends, relatives and teammates can lend their moral support. But the ultimate outcome of competition depends on you. If you fail, the agony is yours. When you succeed, the glory belongs to you. If everyone on your team goes out to party the day before the competition, that is their problem. If you are the only one left in the gym late at night, gutting out the last few lifts on an exercise that you know you need, only you will benefit. Everyone else may have showered and gone home long before. Their lack of discipline cannot hinder your success, your extra effort cannot help them when they are on the platform, alone with the barbell. You are the master of your fate.

Officials are at competitions for only one purpose in weightlifting: to assure that you comply with the rules of the competition. They are not there to judge your strength, your technique or your character. The weights you lift are the measure of your competitive success. The officials don't have to know you or like you for you to succeed. Your race, religion, nationality or economic status have no bearing on your treatment in competition. This is not because of rules or laws, but because there is a strong tradition of judging people solely on their ability in the sport of weightlifting. All of the peoples of the earth have their strongmen and strongwomen. It has always been that way and so it will always be. It is no accident that arguably the four greatest weightlifters who ever lived (John Davis, Tommy Kono, Naim Suleymanoglu and Vasili Alexseev) were, respectively, of African, Asian, Asian/European (Turkish) and European heritage.

2

All of mankind is welcome in weightlifting and has always been.

In competition nothing matches the drama of weightlifting. Each athlete, regardless of his or her level of ability, gets his or her moment in the spotlight. This is partly because weightlifting is an individual sport where the focus is on the efforts of the individual. But it is more than that. Unlike most individual sports, weightlifting is conducted one lift at a time. There are no multiple events going on at the same time (as in gymnastics or track and field). The focus is on each lifter as he or she performs. From the standpoint of the audience, this can make for a somewhat slow moving event as each athletes takes a turn. For the athlete, however, it means that each will have a moment to achieve his or her own personal glory with complete concentration. In addition, there is a natural build up in excitement as the competition progresses. Weightlifting competitions open with the lightest weight requested by any athlete and end with the heaviest, so even though every athlete has his or her moment in the spotlight, the "best" is saved for last. However, the astute audiences of weightlifting love a courageous battle with the barbell, so regardless of the weight on the bar, a lifter who has fought well—win or lose—is greatly admired, respected and applauded, as he or she should be.

Finally, one of the most endearing features of weightlifting is the camaraderie that is so much a part of the sport. Since there are so few weightlifters in the United States, we cherish each other's friendship all the more. We converge often to hold local competitions and several times a year to hold national competitions. There, beyond the competitions themselves, we have an opportunity to renew friendships that seem to last forever. We are friends bound by the powerful adhesive of a deep love and admiration for the sport and those who engage in it. Looking at each other, we know that there is only one reason for our being at the event: our love of weightlifting. The essentially "amateur" nature of weightlifting has its drawbacks, but surely one of the overwhelming virtues of this amateur approach is that those of us who participate do so because our love for the sport is pure and deep. No one ever looks at another competitor or contributor and wonders: "Is he or she in it primarily for the fame or fortune?" In weightlifting, there is only one fundamental coin of the realm: devotion to, and love for, the sport.

Some Common Fallacies About the Sport of Weightlifting

So many fallacies exist about the sport of weightlifting that a very lengthy book, could be written about them. While I want dwell in this book on the realities of weightlifting rather than the fallacies surrounding it, I believe that the process of learning about the sport will be greatly enhanced if some of the most common and most mistaken myths regarding it are addressed at the outset.

Fallacy #1: Bigger "muscles" are stronger muscles.

Intuitively, people believe that bigger "muscles" (what they can observe merely by looking at a person) are stronger muscles. Exercise physiologists acknowledge that larger muscle fibers are able to contract more forcibly than smaller muscle fibers. Logic therefore suggests that the athlete with the biggest muscles is the strongest athlete. Unfortunately, this simple rule of thumb is simply untrue.

When you look at what we commonly refer to as a "muscle" with the naked eye, what you see is a combination of muscle fibers; tissue and chemical substances that are involved in energy storage and transport within the muscles; blood vessels; and fat. Those tissues are surrounded by several layers of skin and connective tissue. While you can get a limited sense of the degree of fat that is underneath your skin by a visual inspection, there is no way to tell how much of what remains is attributable to true muscle tissue versus the other types of tissue. Fortunately, research done by exercise physiologists can help us to understand the rest.

The research merely confirms and explains what experts in the area of weight training have known for many years—that there is little correlation between visible "muscle" size and muscle strength. Moreover, there is a fundamental difference between the large, unnatural looking, muscles of bodybuilders and those of weightlifters. Science has helped to explain that difference as well.

It seems that the high volume and relatively high intensity (terms that will be explained later in the book) training that most bodybuilders do tends to stimulate more muscle fiber types than the training that weightlifters perform. (Muscle fiber types, some of which are better suited for intense efforts and others suited for repetitive efforts are discussed fully in Appendix 2.) In addition, the kind of training that bodybuilders do increases the blood supply going to the muscles (capillarization), as well as the effectiveness of the portion of the muscle tissue that furnishes energy to the muscles. Stated rather crudely, under a weightlifter's skin are maximally developed muscle fibers of the type that are best suited for all out efforts of muscular contraction when supplied with enough energy for brief and intense efforts and just enough blood circulation to make this all happen. (Not visible is the ability that the weightlifter has developed through specialized training to contract more muscle fibers in a highly coordinated way to accomplish higher results with the same muscle fibers than could an athlete without such training.) In contrast, under a bodybuilder's skin is a combination of highly developed muscle fibers of different types and energy transport tissue richly supplied with blood, ready to do great deal of work over an extended period of time but not as well equipped to explode as quickly or forcefully as the muscles of a weightlifter. Therefore, while the muscles of a bodybuilder may appear larger and more well developed than those of a weightlifter (although the muscles of a weightlifter can also be very large), the greater size visible in bodybuilders is due to greater development of muscle fiber types that are not of great help in maximum efforts, capillarization of the muscle tissue and more effective energy transport systems. Consequently, the muscles of two athletes can appear to be very similar in development yet have a very different functional capacity. So, in the usual sense of the phrase, bigger muscles are not necessarily stronger muscles (although, all other things being equal, an increased diameter in muscle fibers themselves leads to an increase in their contractile power).

Fallacy #2: Everyone who lifts weights is a "weightlifter".

The general public assumes that exercising with weights of any kind is synonymous with the sport of "weightlifting." While it is true in the broadest sense that anyone who lifts an object that has any weight at all can be called a "weightlifter," those who truly understand the "iron game" (the entire realm of activities that are performed with weights or exercising against "resistance" of any kind) reserve a special meaning for the term "weightlifting" (i.e., the sport of competitive weightlifting - which will be identified shortly).

If we were to include the lifting of any object under the term "weightlifting," then bricklayers would be weightlifters, then bricklayers would be weightlifters, as would be mothers and fathers who lift their children. In fact, even pencils weigh something, so the proverbial "pencil pushers" of the world would be weightlifters too.

What separates those who exercise with "weights" from bricklayers and pencil pushers is really the purpose of their activity and/or the specific objects that they lift. Pencil pushers are seeking nothing in terms of added strength, muscle size or endurance from their efforts with the pencil. Mothers and fathers who lift babies seek only to care for their children, and bricklayers are concerned only with laying their bricks as planned. None of these groups can be said to be "training with weights," both because they are not interested in stimulating the muscles of the body toward an enhanced level of functioning and because the objects they are lifting are not there for the purpose of pure exercise.

In contrast, those who lift weights, or exercise against resistance in any of its many forms are taking advantage of the body's ability to make its muscles larger and stronger when the muscles are made to contract more and more forcefully. What separates those who lift weights (all of whom are properly called "weight trainers") from one another is their purpose for using the weights. Those who train with weights generally fall into one of four functional categories: weight trainer, bodybuilder, power lifter and weightlifter. The last three categories all involve competitive sports. While these categories can and do overlap to an extent, the essential nature of each is quite different.

Weight trainers are those people who lift weights with a purpose other than competing in one of the three weight sports. Some are training with the purpose of improving their proficiency in a particular sport (such as swimming, football or golf). Others are merely trying to improve their overall level of muscular fitness (ability to perform work) or to improve or to retain the firmness and outward shape of their muscles.

Bodybuilders (such as Arnold Schwarzenegger, Lou Ferrigno, Lee Haney and Dorian Yates) train with weights for the purpose of developing the size and overall appearance of their muscles. Bodybuilders use "free weights" (like dumbbells and barbells) and weights or other resistance devices that are part of "exercise machines" (which are lumped into category "machines") in their training. Many bodybuilders train to get stronger and or to improve their overall fitness, but the fundamental purpose of bodybuilding is to build and display the skeletal muscles of the body (see Fig.1).

Powerlifting is a sport designed to test pure strength. It is really just another way, besides the sport of weightlifting, to test physical strength (just as weight throwing ability is tested in one of several field events, such as the discus and shot put). Powerlifting involves three events: the squat, the bench press and the deadlift. The squat involves placing a barbell on the shoulders behind the neck, and lowering the body by bending the legs until the top of the thigh, near the hip, is at the same level as the top of the knee (roughly where the thigh is parallel to the floor) and then standing up. The bench press consists of pushing a barbell from a position against the chest to straight arms, while the body is lying in a supine position on a bench. The deadlift consists of lifting a barbell from the floor until the body is standing erect with the barbell approximately at a level just below the hips (see Fig.2).

Fig. 1

Fig. 2

When you understand the differences between the activities that involve the use of weights, you realize that calling all of those who exercise with weights or weight machines "weightlifters" is somewhat like calling all doctors "surgeons." All doctors practice medicine and many could become surgeons if they were willing to undergo the extensive and rigorous training that is necessary to become a surgeon. However, not all doctors become surgeons, nor could all doctors become surgeons. In fact, the majority of doctors are not surgeons.

Similarly, all of those who exercise with weights are weight trainers. Many of these weight trainers could become weightlifters if they were willing to perform the extensive and specialized training necessary to master the sport of weightlifting (as was defined in the section "What Is Weightlifting" at the beginning of this Introduction). However, not all of those who train with weights are weightlifters, nor could all become weightlifters. In fact, the vast majority do not. It takes great dedication and much hard work to become a weightlifter, and many of the benefits of weightlifting can be achieved through mere weight training, which is why many weight trainers never take the step to weightlifting. Unfortunately, by so

choosing, they miss the opportunity to participate in the most challenging and rewarding activity that can be performed with weights. Those who have become proficient in the sport of weightlifting, most of whom have been proficient in a number of other sports, almost without exception regard weightlifting as the most challenging and rewarding athletic event in which they have ever participated.

Fallacy #3: Bodybuilders, football players, wrestlers, powerlifters, etc. are stronger than weightlifters.

Accomplished bodybuilders have large, well defined and symmetrically proportioned muscles. They represent the ultimate in the development of maximum muscle size with minimum bodyfat. They are strong people, far stronger than athletes engaged in most other activities. Men like Reg Park, Bill Pearl, John Grimek and Dorian Yates (some of the strongest bodybuilders in history) are all extremely strong. Yet, with all of their strength and despite the amazing appearance of their muscles, they are simply no match for the best weightlifters in the world in terms of pure strength or power.

This is not meant to be a criticism of bodybuilders; their objective is to develop the appearance of their muscles as fully as possible. Their primary objective is not strength. Muscular development is the basis on which they are judged. If one bodybuilder's appearance is only slightly better than another's, and the one who looks slightly better is only half as strong as the other, the weaker bodybuilder will win. Strength delivers no advantage whatsoever in bodybuilding competitions.

Some incredibly strong athletes are to be found in the ranks of football, wrestling, field events and other sports in which strength plays a major role. But the strength performances of those athletes do not compare to the performances of elite weightlifters, whose special focus is on the development of pure strength and power (as compared with athletes who must focus more on the skills and all around conditioning needs of their respective sports than on strength and power development).

Powerlifters are generally not quite as impressive in terms of muscular appearance as bodybuilders. Powerlifters may be very well developed in certain areas of the body, but they will seldom have the kind of balanced development of each muscle group that bodybuilders have. Bodybuilders have an incentive to achieve all around muscular development, since symmetry (well balanced muscular development throughout the body) is one of the bases on which they are judged. In some instances, the muscles of a powerlifter may be as large as those of a bodybuilder, but a powerlifter's muscles are almost never as well defined as those of bodybuilders; since their bodyfat is not as low, their muscles cannot be seen as readily. Consequently, the powerlifter's appearance is not as striking. What they give up in appearance, powerlifters more than make up for in terms of pure strength. Powerlifters are incredibly strong. They are undoubtedly among the strongest men walking the earth. But today, weightlifters, as a group, have the strength edge.

Many powerlifters will reject this notion out of hand. They will argue that weightlifting involves technique and powerlifting does not. They will argue that this distinction has three important consequences. First, since powerlifting only requires pure strength, the training of powerlifters is concentrated in that area. It makes sense, they reason, that training concentrated in a given area will lead to superior results. Second, the powerlifts themselves are designed to measure only pure strength, whereas the events that comprise the sport of weightlifting involve technique as well. Therefore, the champion weightlifter may not even be the strongest man in his sport, let alone the world. Finally, powerlifters will argue, powerlifting competitions consist of three events as compared with weightlifting's two, therefore powerlifters must have greater all around strength than weightlifters.

While these arguments have merit, none is as telling as it first appears, and all are refutable. Moreover, there are a number of arguments that can be made for the superiority of weightlifters that are not so easily dismissed.

For example, while the training for powerlifting is oriented more toward strength development than is the training for weightlifting, the argument about concentrated training fails on three grounds. First, while powerlifters concentrate on the development of strength, many powerlifters devote considerable training time to bodybuilding exercises to improve the support that some muscle groups give others during the performance of the

powerlifts. For instance, many powerlifters argue that increasing the size of the biceps muscle will have a positive affect on one's bench press, because when the arms are folded up in preparation for beginning the bench press, a muscular cushion will be provided by the biceps. Many powerlifters also bodybuild for the sake of appearance and because they believe that increased muscular size will contribute toward the ultimate development of muscular strength. Regardless of the rationale, a large percentage of powerlifters (like weightlifters) devote at least some of their training to goals other than the development of pure strength. Second, even if it were true that weightlifters devoted a larger percentage of their training time to exercises other than those used for pure strength development, it would not prove that powerlifters spend more time on the development of strength. This is because top weightlifters train much longer and harder that top powerlifters—probably at least two to three times longer and in many cases four to five times longer. For example, Eastern European weightlifters generally train six days a week and most train at least twice a day. The average lifter squats at least once a day, while many top powerlifters squat once a week! Clearly, frequency of training is not proof of its effectiveness, but the argument that powerlifters devote more energy to strength development is patently false.

Finally, let us look at the percentage of training time spent on strength development. Top weightlifters spend almost no training time on bodybuilding exercises. There is virtually no one in the sport of weightlifting who argues that the leverage needed for weightlifting is improved by the development of certain muscles, that muscle size developed through bodybuilding will improve strength or that appearance should be achieved at the expense of developing non-functional muscles. More importantly, it is a myth that top weightlifters spend any significant degree of time on pure technique development. Most top weightlifters develop their technique at an early stage in their training. Once they have advanced from the novice ranks, they devote very little time to pure technique. It is true that top lifters spend a great deal of time practicing the lifts they perform in competition. In fact, the lifters from some countries, most notably Bulgaria, spend more of their time doing the competitive exercises (i.e., the snatch and clean and jerk) than anything else. However, they are not performing these exercises solely for the purpose of developing technique (although they always perform the lifts with the best technique possible and make every effort to improve upon their execution of the lifts at every opportunity). Rather, they choose to do the snatch and clean and jerk (C&J) because they believe that these are the best exercises available for developing functional strength in the competitive lifts. Like many powerlifters who perform the bench press, squat and deadlift with the best form possible when they practice the lifts, weightlifters' primary objective in performing these exercises is to develop strength.

What about the arguments that the snatch and clean and jerk involve more technique than the powerlifts and that the strongest weightlifter does not always win? It is true that weightlifting involves considerably more technical skill than the powerlifts. In fact, as was noted earlier, one of the great sources of satisfaction in weightlifting, beyond the development of incredible strength, is that of the mastery of a difficult skill. However, this skill tends to be developed at an early stage in a lifter's career, and by the time a lifter has reached the advanced level, it is nearly second nature. Consequently, at a high level of competition, most competitors are relatively equally matched in terms of technique. Therefore, victory goes to the stronger and more determined athlete. Similarly, at advanced levels of powerlifting, the technique differences tend to be small, and the stronger and more determined athlete will tend to be the victor. Naturally, at the very highest levels of competition, even small differences in technique can mean the difference between success and failure. This is true in powerlifting as well as weightlifting. In powerlifting there is the added technical consideration of who has the better bench shirt or knee wraps, items that support lifters while they perform. No comparable supportive items are permitted or are even of any use in weightlifting. Therefore, in powerlifting, the strongest lifter may not always win either. However, overall, in both sports, the strongest athletes tend to win.

The argument that powerlifting is a better measure of strength than weightlifting because it consists of three events is also unconvincing for a number of reasons. First, weightlifting really consists of three (arguably four) separate tests of strength: the pull (which can be further subdivided into the snatch pull and the clean pull); the recovery from the deep squat position (more of a challenge from the low position in the clean than from the low position in the snatch;) and the jerk. Each event requires different kinds of strength in differing degrees.

The test of leg strength in powerlifting is the squat; in weightlifting, it is recovering from the deep position in the clean. In squatting, heavier weights are handled than in cleaning. However, the squat performed in powerlifting is not nearly as low as the squat position in the clean, so recovery from the lowest position in the squat in powerlifting is much easier than recovery from the low position in powerlifting. In addition, the bar is not in as favorable position on the body in the clean as it is in the squat (i.e., while squatting with the weight behind the neck, on the shoulders or below, considerable weight can be shifted toward the back

so that the strain on the legs is far less). Finally, it is not possible for weightlifters to wear the kinds of supportive devices that powerlifters do (e.g., power suits and belts) because they would be unable to move as quickly and as freely as is necessary in the sport of weightlifting. All things considered, the recovery from the deep squat position in the clean is at least as great , if not a better, test of pure leg strength as the squat performed in powerlifting competition. Both the squat in powerlifting and the recovery from the low clean position in weightlifting are ultimate tests of leg strength.

The second event in powerlifting competitions is the bench press. The bench press is the best all around test of a lifter's strength in the muscles in the chest (pectorals), in the back of the arms (triceps) and in the front of the shoulder (the anterior deltoids). A heavy bench is an awesome display of upper body power. However, in weightlifting, upper body power is tested in a different direction (overhead) by the jerk. In the jerk, the legs and arms combine to drive the bar upwards from the shoulders, then the triceps and deltoids (not just the anterior part, as in bench pressing, but the medial and even the posterior parts as well) take over to help secure the bar overhead. (The same muscles are used in holding a snatch overhead as well.) Overhead lifting does not tax the chest muscles in the way that the bench press does, so the bench press has the clear advantage in that respect, but it does tax muscles (in addition to the side and rear deltoids) that are not tested at all in the bench press. In holding a weight overhead, all of the supportive muscles of the trunk (e.g., the abdominals and obliques) are tested to the extreme. Getting a weight overhead and bringing it under control are also displays of awesome strength in the upper body. However, just as there is no guarantee that the strength garnered from overhead lifting will translate into the bench press, so there is no assurance that an accomplished bench presser will have significant overhead strength. Therefore, both the bench press and the jerk test the muscles of the upper body to the extreme. Who has a more powerful upper body overall, the powerlifter or the weightlifter? In a way, it is really like comparing apples to oranges; both sports are wonders of nature and both are sweet to those who partake in them. Similarly, both sports are to be admired and respected.

Finally, let's compare the deadlift in powerlifting with the pull in weightlifting. Both involve lifting the barbell from the same position on the floor. In powerlifting, the object is merely to straighten up with the load. In weightlifting, it is to impart enough force to the bar so that it will go high enough, with sufficient speed, to permit the lifter to catch it on the shoulders (in the clean) or overhead (in the snatch). The mechanical positions used in the deadlift as opposed to the snatch and clean are somewhat different because of the ultimate purpose of the lifts; for example, in the deadlift the back is generally permitted to "round" or hunch, at least somewhat, while in weightlifting it is generally kept arched or at least quite straight. In weightlifting the muscles of the upper back (and sometimes even the arms) are used more than they are in powerlifting, because the bar is being lifted much higher. Which lift is a greater test of back strength? It is hard to judge. Both test the muscles of the back and hips to the maximum, but in somewhat different ways. Clearly, no other sports test the back and hips nearly as much.

Overall, which sport is a better test of strength? Obviously, there is no clear answer. Both weightlifting and powerlifting are wonderful tests of human strength. The athletes of both sports are admired and respected by everyone in the iron game. However, for the athlete seeking the ultimate challenge in terms of competition, overall athletic ability and physical courage, weightlifting has the clear advantage. Weightlifting today presents the superior challenge. How can such a sweeping statement be made? Let's look at a few telling points.

First, there are far more athletes training for weightlifting today than powerlifting (probably at least 50 to 100 times as many and perhaps many more) and they are training in many more countries of the world. Not only are the number and distribution of athletes in weightlifting much greater than in powerlifting, but there are also far more full time weightlifters in the world than powerlifters, so the real differences in terms of the number who are training seriously (i.e., under professional conditions) are even greater than the ratios of 50 or 100 to 1 suggest. In addition, weightlifting is a much older sport, so it is far more developed in terms of technique and training methods. Finally, no top flight powerlifter has ever become a truly top weightlifter (among the current group of powerlifters, Shane Hamman looks like someone with the potential break that barrier). In contrast, weightlifters, even some who were not at all exceptional in weightlifting, have become successful powerlifters (several have become world champions). Therefore, I think there is little question that when the title of the world's strongest man is awarded today, it clearly belongs to the world champion in weightlifting, not powerlifting.

None of the above is meant to demean the sport of powerlifting. Powerlifters are heroic athletes, men and women who are building a new sport devoted to testing strength in a different way from the sport of weightlifting. Someday the level of competition and performance in powerlifting may rival or even surpass that of weightlifting, but that day is still a long way off, and it may never come. I truly wish powerlifting well in its struggle for advancement and recognition. However, the fact remains that today, for the athlete who is looking for the ultimate challenge in the world of strength competition as well as all around athletic ability, weightlifting has no rival.

This is not to say that an individual powerlifter may not be as strong as his or her counterpart in weightlifting at a particular moment in time. For example, Ed Coan is an incredibly strong man, who, in his strongest condition, might have been stronger than the best 100 kg. weightlifter in the world at the time. But overall, comparing the best weightlifters in the world with be best powerlifters (the latter without wraps and other supportive devices and performing comparable movements to the weightlifters - e.g., full squats) the weightlifters will win.

The superiority of weightlifters over powerlifters in terms of power is even more pronounced. It should be noted that while laymen often use the terms strength and power interchangeably, from the scientific standpoint, power and strength are entirely different concepts. Strength has been defined in many ways, but in the context of athletics it can be defined as the maximum force which muscles can develop. In the laboratory it is often measured directly as the amount of force an athlete can generate against resistance. In the gym, it is generally measured by the amount of weight an athlete can lift one time (and no more than one time) in a given exercise.

Power is formally defined as the rate at which work is performed. For example, if athlete A requires one second to deadlift 250 pounds, while athlete B requires two seconds to perform the lift, athlete A would be considered twice as powerful as athlete B. In short, power is a measure of speed and strength.

Because powerlifters move heavy weights slowly, they develop relatively low levels of power when they perform. In fact, powerlifting is a poor name for that sport; it would be more appropriate to refer to it as strength lifting. Weightlifters, in contrast, lift weights as rapidly as possible (for technical reasons that will described in later chapters of this book). In contrast to powerlifters, they develop incredible rates of power when they perform—among the highest rates ever measured by sports scientists. There is absolutely no comparison between powerlifters and weightlifters with respect to power outputs; the weightlifters are far superior in terms of developing power when they lift.

When athletes are measured on a combined basis of strength and power, weightlifters are without question the winners. Powerlifters may come close to weightlifters in the area of strength, sprinters and weight throwers (e.g., shot-putters and discus-throwers) may come close to weightlifters in terms of the power outputs that they are capable of, but no athletes in any other sport possess the combination of strength and power of competitive weightlifters. They are hands down the strongest and most powerful athletes on earth.

Fallacy #4: Weightlifting "stunts" your growth and has a very high injury rate.

Long years of experience have proven that weightlifting is far safer than most people believe. There are fewer injuries in the sport of weightlifting than in most major sports, probably fewer than in casual weight training, where the number of "do-it-yourselfers" is high and the instruction one is likely to receive in many gyms is extremely variable in terms of its quality. In addition, in the sport of weightlifting, the injuries that do occur tend to be far milder than in many other sports. For example, head and spinal chord injuries are practically nonexistent in weightlifting. Serious contusions, ligament damage and broken bones are also quite unusual.

Contrary to popular belief, hernias are extremely rare among weightlifters, and, when they do occur, they are almost uniformly the result of non-weightlifting activities. There are several reasons for this. First, weightlifters carefully condition themselves for maximum effort. Well conditioned athletes are unlikely to be injured by their activities. Second, proper technique is of vital importance in weightlifting, and it is the first thing taught by qualified coaches. When an athlete uses proper technique, injuries like hernias are unlikely to occur. Finally, the apparatus used in weightlifting—the barbell—has been meticulously designed and carefully balanced to facilitate safe lifting. That design, developed and refined over the course of more than a century, helps to assure safety.

The same general rules apply to bad backs, knees and other kinds of injuries. Proper conditioning, proper technique and safe equipment minimize the risk of injury and the proof of this is in the relatively low rate of injuries suffered by weightlifters. Therefore, the need for proper conditioning proper coaching and using good equipment cannot be overemphasized.

While no amount of skill, care in training and proper equipment can eliminate the risk of injury in a strenuous sport like weightlifting, the situation in weightlifting is not different from that in other sports, and in many ways it tends to be better.

Fallacy #5: Drug usage is rampant in the sport of weightlifting.

Drug usage pervades our society. Few would disagree that drugs pose a major threat to our culture. Weightlifting is not immune from the influences of the culture around it. Nevertheless, weightlifting has acquired an unfortunate association in the public mind with drug usage, principally because of the presence of a particular kind of drug usage that is common in virtually all sports: the use of anabolic steroids.

There are a number of popular fallacies about anabolic steroids. We will examine just a few. First, anabolic steroids are not—at least primarily—mind altering drugs. They are not taken by serious athletes for their mind altering effects. There is no steroid "high" that corresponds to that of drugs like cocaine or heroin. Second, steroids have no effect on people who do not train for sport (you do not become a "superman" merely by ingesting anabolic steroids, regardless how much you take or for how long). Third, steroid use does not confer any instant competitive advantage on an athlete. Instead, anabolic steroids have a performance enhancing effect that occurs over time and only in conjunction with the training process. Even those who are training intensely will experience a positive effect from the use of anabolic steroids only if their use is maintained for at least several consecutive weeks, and many months or even years of use are required in order to achieve the full effect of the drug. Finally, the health risks attributable to steroid use are not in the same category as those attributable to drugs like heroin and cocaine. To be sure, anabolic steroids have negative health effects, effects which should discourage all athletes from using them. However, such effects are on a very different level of magnitude from the negative effects of many "recreational" and "hard" drugs, and those effects have been overstated (at least in relation to any actual scientific evidence) by the media.

With the exception of anabolic steroids, drug use among weightlifters is probably lower than among most other athletes and the weightlifting public at large. Why? One reason is that most athletes who choose the sport of weightlifting do so at least partially because they want to enhance their health and well being through sport. They engage in the sport not only because they enjoy it (although that is a very important motivation), but also because they prefer a sport that is non-combative, leads to an aesthetically pleasing level of muscular development, builds high levels of strength and power and challenges the mind and character to the limit. These objectives are not consistent with activities that harm the mind or body.

A second powerful reason why most weightlifters reject drug use is that weightlifting, perhaps more than any other sport, is a measurement sport. Weightlifters are constantly testing themselves against the barbell in a way that measures strength, speed, flexibility and coordination. If you are doing something that is deleterious to your health, it will soon become obvious. When you are competing directly against other athletes in sports like football or wrestling (particularly when competing against other athletes who might also have been out "partying"), it may be difficult to tell whether you are having a good or a bad day; athletes can mistakenly think they are having a "good day" in spite of the fact that the previous night's activities have hurt their performances, because their competitors have also indulged in activities that have had a negative effect on their performance. The bar permits no such speculation. It weighs the same amount regardless of how you feel. It is an unrelenting reminder of reality. If you have done something injurious to your mind or your body, the barbell will not let you delude yourself for long.

If weightlifters tend to avoid the use of most drugs, then what about anabolic steroids? Anabolic steroids can have a positive effect on strength. Since strength is an asset in most sports, many athletes, not just weightlifters, have resorted to their use. It is not unfair to criticize weightlifting for this fact, but it is unfair to single out weightlifting. This is especially true because weightlifting has been a leader in its advocacy of the elimination of performance enhancing drugs from all sports. The governing body for international weightlifting competition (the International Weightlifting Federation, or "IWF") banned a number of performance enhancing drugs in 1968 and began to test for stimulants (then the prevalent category of performance enhancing drugs) shortly thereafter, long before most other sports even began to address issues of drugs in sports. Extensive anabolic steroid testing began at the 1976 Olympic Games, and testing for steroids, as well as other performance enhancing drugs, has been performed with greater vigor by weightlifting's national and international governing bodies (the United States Weightlifting Federation, which now does business as USA Weightlifting or the "USAW" and the IWF, respectively) than by any other sport. Moreover, the penalties applied by these federations have generally been greater than those recommended by either the United States Olympic Committee and the International Olympic Committee, the organizations that govern overall Olympic sports

Why has the eradication of anabolic steroids from weightlifting competition not been accomplished thus far? Very simply, because a method for completely eliminating the advantage of using anabolic steroids in athletic competition has not existed. Until recently, athletes could take the drugs up until several weeks before an event, discontinue their use prior to the event and still perform at an elevated level. Since anabolic steroids take several weeks to several months to deliver their advantage to the user, it also takes an equal period for the performance enhancing effects of these drugs to wear off.

Now a method for greatly reducing anabolic steroid use has been developed. As usual, it has been deployed first within the sport of

weightlifting, in particular by the USAW, the sole governing body for weightlifting in the United States In 1990 the USAW began random testing of its athletes several weeks before major competitions, as well as at the competitions themselves. Consequently, any athlete who uses steroids is forced to stop taking them two to three months before any major event in order to pass the random tests. Since major competitions take place every few months, this process makes it difficult for most top athletes to find a period when they would be able to take the drugs without being subject to testing.

More recently, the USAW has gone much further. Now the highest level athletes in the United States must agree to be tested on a random basis throughout the year—without any notice. An athlete is merely approached by a representative of the United States Olympic Committee (the organization that performs the drug testing for the USAW) and asked to produce a urine sample. An athlete who has been using anabolic steroids or any other kind of banned drug will not find it possible to mask the presence of that drug or have the drug clear his or her system before the test. US Weightlifters who are caught using steroids in competition or random testing are subject a four year suspension from competition for a first offense and a lifetime suspension for the second offense. Therefore, on a practical level, the advantages of taking anabolic steroids have been virtually eliminated.

Some weightlifting federations in other countries have adopted programs similar to that of the USAW and it is hoped that all other national weightlifting federations will soon follow suit (the IWF has a limited program of worldwide out-of-competition testing at present). Once this occurs, steroid usage, by and large, will become a thing of the past for weightlifting competitions. It has already been greatly reduced. For example, there were no weightlifters who were found to be taking any banned substance at the most recent Olympic Games in Atlanta, while some athletes in other sports were found to be doing so.

Testing in weightlifting competition will not eliminate our societal problem with anabolic steroids or with drugs in general. Education is the key to that process. However, testing will assure that weightlifters can compete on an even, drug free, playing field. The champions of weightlifting, the strongest men and women in the world, may once again be drug free. That fact will help to return weightlifting to its deserved position as one of the most highly respected sports worldwide, and its champions will serve as leaders in showing our youth what can be accomplished by hard training and dedication alone. Can any sport do more?

Fallacy #6: Weightlifting muscles make you "musclebound."

The musclebound myth has probably survived as long as it has for only one reason; its proponents have never been willing to define clearly what they mean by the term. However, while musclebound "theorists" hate to be pinned down in their definitions, they would probably have to agree that wrapped up in the vague notion of "muscleboundedness" is the idea that those with large muscles are less flexible, slower moving and more poorly coordinated than the general population. In truth, none of these assumptions is supported by the facts. Unfortunately for those who hate, envy or fear those with large muscles, resistance trained muscles not only look better, they also perform better than untrained ones.

The musclebound myth has been losing ground on several bases. First, it has slowly been eroded by the millions of athletes worldwide who utilize weight training. They have gotten bigger, stronger and <u>faster</u> by training with weights. For example, most, if not all, of the world's top sprinters and jumpers use weight training extensively; it does not seem to be slowing them up! Second, no loss of flexibility has been noted by those athletes who train properly with weights. Quite the contrary, many athletes have experienced improvements in their mobility through weight training. Scientific studies support this empirical finding in that they have generally found no decrease in flexibility as a result of weight training.

Finally, there is the issue of lack of coordination. Surely no one who has trained with weights has noted a diminution in their coordination associated with such training. In many cases, stronger muscles help one to perform a particular skill better because a certain level of strength may be needed in addition to skill. What then is the basis of the accusation that those with larger muscles are less coordinated? Perhaps it stems from the recognition that while a person who trains with weights will tend to have muscles that look "athletic" (i.e., well developed), such persons are not necessarily able to apply their muscle capacity successfully toward a particular activity with any less practice than a person who has not trained with weights. Consequently, while people expect those with an athletic appearance to be more skilled at moving their muscles than people who do not have such an appearance, there is no reason to believe that weight trainers or other athletes are able to dance better or to hit a baseball more skillfully than the average person. Weight training develops skills in performing the weight training activities that the weight trainer practices and it develops muscles that are more fit to perform certain activities, but it does not develop (or hinder the development of) the skills necessary to perform a particular activity (other than the aforementioned advantage that stronger muscles can make the performance of certain skills an easier process).

What about competitive weightlifters? Is the flexibility of weightlifters hindered by their intense training with weights? A study of Olympic athletes done in the late 1970's found that weightlifters were second only to gymnasts in all around flexibility. In addition, weightlifters have been found to be among the very fastest athletes in the Olympic Games. Finally, with respect to coordination, you have only to observe the sport of weightlifting to realize that snatches and clean and jerks are among the most complex and exacting movements in sport. Weightlifting is hardly a refuge for the uncoordinated. Let us hope that the musclebound myth has finally been put to rest, especially as it pertains to competitive weightlifters.

Fallacy #7: The athletes of any one country (e.g., the US) can't beat the athletes from another (e.g., Russia).

There is a widespread feeling in American weightlifting circles today that we cannot beat the athletes from the area that was formerly the Soviet Union, Bulgarians and athletes from any country whose lifters seem to be on the rise at any time.

One reason often cited for this state of affairs is that the athletes in certain other countries (we'll use Eastern Europe as an example because that is probably the area most often named by US athletes) use drugs and that their drugs are superior to those available to athletes in other countries. This argument overlooks the relatively primitive state of science in general and the pharmaceutical industry in particular in the Eastern European countries. Even if it were true that they have "better" drugs, the discussion about drug testing presented earlier should serve to convince people in this country that arguments of this type are becoming less persuasive.

Another argument often given is that sports science in the Eastern European countries is far superior to that of the United States. In view of the dismal record of Eastern European science overall, it is extremely doubtful that sports science in these countries is the equal of, let alone superior to, the sports science that is available in Western countries. Political repression simply does not contribute to an environment in which science flourishes. Moreover, a centrally planned economy does not lead to the kind of economic well being that permits well rounded spending on scientific research or to the development of the kinds of technology that assist in scientific research. To look at just one area, in an age where computer aided research is inextricably intertwined with modern biological research, is it likely that countries with weak computer facilities would lead the world in

11

research in a biological area? Western superiority in medicine, biology, chemistry and engineering strongly suggests that sports science should be better in the West than in Eastern Europe (an advantage that may not long continue if the countries of Eastern Europe move toward Westernization).

How then can we explain the outstanding performances of Eastern European countries in the area of amateur sports in general and weightlifting in particular? Sports have long been in the realm of clinicians, not theoretical or research scientists. The best scientists are rarely the best coaches. This does not mean that the best coaches do not employ the so called scientific method (i.e., setting up a hypothesis and then testing it). Coaches employ their techniques in the real world, where double-blind verifications and the isolation of all variables that can affect outcomes are not normally possible. In this realm, the inferential thinker is king, not because of his or her sophisticated laboratory but because of his or her special ability to observe complex events and to identify the essential elements. This is something anyone living anywhere can do without a lot of high-tech equipment.

The legendary Bulgarian weightlifting program of the 1970s and 1980s was a case in point; Bulgarian coach Ivan Abadjiev built his team under difficult conditions (and with very limited formal "scientific" support). He certainly did not the human, economic or scientific resources of the neighboring Soviet Union of that era, but his team defeated the Soviets on many occasions.

Many European coaches excel in practical training analysis, and many more coaches are applying themselves to weightlifting in Eastern European countries than in the United States. Moreover, many coaches work full time with their athletes in Eastern European countries, where coaching weightlifting is regarded as a true and honorable profession. Consequently, in the course of a lifetime, an Eastern European weightlifting coach may have opportunities to observe many more athletes than his American counterpart. This gives such coaches the potential for enjoying a significant experience edge.

Does this mean that he <u>necessarily</u> knows more? No, because coaching 1,000 athletes can simply mean making the same mistake 1,000 times, while a thoughtful coach who handles ten athletes can learn many valuable lessons. Experience surely makes it more likely that one will learn more, but what a coach learns depends as much on the mental habits of the coach as it does on the coach's experience. When you combine experience with an active mind you get a great coach and I have had the good fortune to meet and learn from some of them.

Finally, the training of Eastern European coaches is far more organized than in the United States In Eastern Europe, coaching is a profession which can be studied in a university with a major in a particular sport. In the United States a prospective coach might major in physical education and then gain practical experience coaching his or her sport. There are few academic degrees in coaching (and there are none in weightlifting coaching). Therefore, it is only reasonable to expect that some terrific coaches have developed under the Eastern European sporting system. However, while the advantages that Eastern European coaches have in many areas are significant, but they are certainly not insurmountable by the coach and athlete who wish to apply themselves by reviewing the published literature, learning from other athletes and coaches and to honing their knowledge and experience in the gym.

Is there another reason for Eastern European superiority? Yes, but it does not lie in the psychological training of the Eastern bloc athlete, although an Eastern European weightlifter, unlike many Americans, may have the advantage of believing he or she can be a champion. It does not lie in the mud at the bottom of the Dead Sea (recently touted as a health food) or any of the other forms of "snake oil" peddled by many would be entrepreneurs in this country. The answer lies in another realm entirely: the economic. In Eastern Europe enormous economic resources have historically been devoted to "amateur" sports, to the point where such sports are hardly amateur. Young athletes are selected by the state. And other than politics, there is really no other game in town for the youngster who wishes to free himself or herself from grinding poverty and the travel restrictions that have been part of Eastern European life for so long. Notice that the nations that have tended to perform best in amateur sports have been the most closely tied to the former Soviet Union. A sports system that offers total support to athletes they are competing and thereafter is going to attract the talented individuals of a nation and will permit them to train with a complete focus on their sport. In the United States there has been nothing comparable. As lucrative as big time collegiate and professional sports can be, they cannot compare with athletics in Eastern Europe, because youngsters can make it big in many ways in the United States, not just through sports. In addition, a lower income person in the United States tends to live more comfortably than a professional athlete in the former Soviet Union. The economic drives for athletic success are simply not as great here.

As a case in point, it is estimated that before the fall of communism there were 300,000 to 400,000 weightlifters in the Soviet Union as compared with fewer than 3,000 in the United States. There are those who argue that numbers do not tell all because there are only two to three times the number of weightlifters in Bulgaria as in the United States. However, what is neglected in such an analysis is that the thousands of athletes training in Bulgaria are the cream of the school system and are enrolled in nearly full time programs with constant professional supervision. In the United States more than one-fourth of our participants in weightlifting are masters (athletes aged 40 or above) and another fourth, or more, are transient young athletes who may compete only once or twice with little training and preparation and then disappear. Only a very small number of the remaining U.S. weightlifters are training for international competition, and none of them are truly "professionals" who do nothing but train for weightlifting competition (except, perhaps, the handful of athletes who are in the USAW Resident Athlete program in Colorado Springs or individuals who find themselves in similar conditions in other parts of the United States) . Moreover, the professional weightlifters in other parts of the world have often been "selected" from many candidates on the basis of their particular talents for weightlifting. Therefore, the real differences between the number of talented and devoted weightlifters who are training in the United States today and the number of athletes who are training in other countries are truly staggering.

Today, there is significant evidence that many of the competitive advantages that Eastern European athletes have long enjoyed are beginning to erode. For one thing, the Eastern European nations are on their way toward Westernization. With that will come a broader focus in the athletic and general tastes of the nation. The youth of these nations will not be forced exclusively into amateur sport, with an emphasis on weightlifting. Another consideration is that the citizenry is unlikely to support amateur sport as fully as the communist regimes did. The need for propaganda will be reduced, and the general population may well put other needs ahead of sport. Still another major phenomenon that will level the playing field is the final elimination of hypocritical amateurism from sport. For many years Western athletes have been denied the opportunity to support themselves through sports or have had to go through ridiculous gyrations to maintain the aura of amateurism while making a living. Today athletes all over the world are moving toward increasingly fairer forms of competition, competition aimed at deciding who is the best athlete rather than who is better at passing a drug test or disguising his or her income.

In short, the opportunities for athletes of all nations to compete in weightlifting are better than they have been in at least a generation. Many people have forgotten or never knew that before state sports became entrenched in Eastern Europe, the United States fielded World and/or Olympic championship weightlifting teams from 1947 to 1952 and from 1954 to 1956, finishing second or

third several times before and after that period of dominance, having two individual male world champions as late as the World Championships of 1969. Women from the US have won medals in all but one World's championship from 1987-1996.

A Time Of Unprecedented Opportunity In Weightlifting

Today there are many athletes in all of the countries of the world who, with the proper dedication and intelligent training, have the potential to become the champions of the future. Perhaps the only real obstacle that Americans (and athletes from other nations who have not been leaders in weightlifting in recent years) now face is the possibility of inheriting a massive inferiority complex from many of their immediate predecessors. Athletes who believe they cannot win will not win. They will not train the way they must to be champions and they will not be inspired by the infinite energy that comes from the dream of being a champion. But to those few who dare to be great, to undertake the challenge of meeting the best in the world on their own terms and with all of their advantages, will go the highest accolades and the greatest personal sense of achievement.

It took great courage for the first American international lifters to venture to Europe in the 1930s and to return victorious (the myth of European invincibility was at least as strong then as was the myth of Eastern European invincibility until recently - when weightlifters from other parts of Europe and Asia mounted a serious challenge to the Eastern Europeans). Men like Tony Terlazzo and John Davis will forever be remembered in the history of American weightlifting as those who led the way - those who had the courage to challenge the World's best and to win.

Now the opportunity presents itself for a new generation of Americans and other athletes from all of the nations of the world to take up a similar challenge, to bring themselves and their nations to positions of glory in the world of weightlifting. It will not be easy and it will not come quickly, but for those few who have the courage to accept the challenge of that glorious effort, victory will be all the sweeter. They will be the weightlifting heroes of the new millennium.

This book is dedicated to the athletes of all nations who wish to accept the challenge of becoming the best in the world, the best who have ever lived!

There is another sense in which there is unprecedented opportunity in weightlifting today—the prospect of making a living as a weightlifter. Until recently, weightlifting, along with many other Olympic sports, was considered an amateur sport. Athletes who earned money (directly or indirectly) from their sport could be banned from competition. Today those limitations are a thing of the past. And, while there are no formal professional weightlifting leagues in which athletes earn large sums of money for winning competitions (there is at least one "semi-pro" league), there are countries in which high caliber athletes can earn a comfortable living. It is rumored that in at least one country in Europe, athletes who won the Olympic Games received several hundred thousand dollars as a reward for their victories. The USAW presently has a system for rewarding its top athletes which makes it possible for those athletes to concentrate on their weightlifting (though certainly not to become wealthy).

But there are many other opportunities for weightlifters to earn money. Many have become personal trainers. Although it is true that there is a "glut" in the personal trainer market today, it is also true that most personal trainers are people who like exercise and take a quick exam to become certified. When the expertise of such people is compared with that of a competitive weightlifter it generally pales by comparison. Consequently, the weightlifter who knows how to promote himself or herself can achieve great success in this field.

Similarly, a number of top weightlifters have become strength coaches for college and professional sports teams. This is another field in which people can take an exam and become certified. But there is no comparison between the expertise of someone who has merely studied to pass an exam and someone who has devoted his or her life to developing strength and power.

Finally, unlimited opportunities are available to those who can conduct effective seminars, secure endorsements and break into advertising. The world's strongest man or woman who knows how to promote himself or herself has fantastic potential today (as compared with their predecessors—who could be, and were, banned immediately from competition for promoting themselves). This is truly an era of unprecedented opportunity in weightlifting!

Some Advice On Reading "The Weightlifting Encyclopedia"

In creating this book I have tried to provide the most comprehensive resource on the sport of weightlifting that has ever been published. There are nearly 400,000 words in this book, nearly 90 photos or illustrations and more than 100 references (many of them annotated) in the Bibliography. Hundreds of topics are covered, some at a level of detail that has never been available before, hence the term "encyclopedia" in the title.

Because this book is so large and complete, reading the book straight through may appear to be a daunting task. But such an approach to reading this book is no more necessary than reading a typical encyclopedia at one sitting.

For the person who likes to read, absorbs much of what he or she reads on the "first pass" and has the time to devote to the reading process, this encyclopedia builds progressively on what has been presented previously (unlike the typical encyclopedia, which is arranged alphabetically by topic). This permits the reader to go through the book from cover to cover with great benefit.

But beginners and novices, particularly those who are anxious to quickly apply what they have learned, will be better served by utilizing something like the following sequence in their reading:

Introduction (the part preceding this section of the Introduction as well as this section)
*Chapter 1 (through the section entitled "An Analysis of the Technique of the Snatch and Clean and Jerk"–studying the sequence photos in particular–it is not necessary to read the details of each phase at this point)
Chapter 2, the following sections:
*Proper Breathing While Lifting
*Selecting an Optimal Hand Spacing
*Selecting an Optimal Foot Spacing
Returning the Bar to the Platform...
*Practice and Feedback: The Foundations for Learning a Motor Skill
*Teaching Technique (the entire section)
*Perfecting An Athlete's Weightlifting Technique (the entire section)
Methods of Identifying Technique Faults (the entire section)
*The Selection of Reps...
*The Selection of Weights...
Chapter 3, the following sections:
The Training Effect
*Guidelines Regarding Repetitions
*Guidelines Regarding Sets
*Developing Flexibility For Weightlifting (the entire section—unless you test your flexibility as suggested on pages 170-2 and find that it is sufficient without any special training, in which case you can skip that section for now)
*Chapter 4 (the Personal Equipment section, through the section on "tape", then skip to the portion of the Gym Equipment section that focuses on the: Bar, Plates, Platform, Power Rack, Squat Rack, then the section on The Training Facility—the first two pages and the section on Spotters.
*Chapter 5, descriptions of the: power snatch, power clean, power jerk, dead hang snatch, snatch and clean pulls, squat (back, front and overhead), presses (especially behind the neck and military).
*Chapter 6, (the sections on the Workout Plan, Training Log and the Process of Developing Training Programs (particularly the description of "Cindy's" program). You should also read the section on "The Special

Needs of Powerlifters and Other Strength Athletes..." if you are converting to weightlifting from powerlifting or another sport for which you have done extensive strength training.

Chapter 7,(through the section on Positive Mental Attitude, then the section on Goal Setting through the section on the Importance of Concentration.

*Chapter 9, (if you are a woman, a lifter 40 or above, or an athlete under the age of 18—read the appropriate section of this chapter—which addresses each of these groups)

Chapter 10, the sections on achieving your "Ideal Bodyweight" and "Pre-Game Meals".

*Chapter 11, the opening section on Prevention of Injuries and, under, Dealing With Injuries the initial section on first aid.

Appendix 1 (the section on the Technical Rules of Weightlifting through the section on Incorrect Movements Particular to the Clean and Jerk)

Appendix 4 (the section on Selecting a Coach (if you are a lifter who is beginning without a coach or who is looking for one).

Read the asterisked sections noted above before you walk into a gym and the other ones as soon as possible after you have begun training.

Another thing you should consider very early on is purchasing some video footage of weightlifters in action. The USAW has an instructional video on the subject of "pulling" and for its Club Coach's course. Both videos have limitations, but both provide useful information for the beginner. Another important source of video information is Iron Mind Enterprises (for more information on the USAW and Iron Mind see the Organizations and Publications... section at the end of the Bibliography of this book). Iron Mind offers videos of top international events (purchase the two part tape of the Atlanta Olympic Games and you'll have a good idea of what good technique looks like).

Join the USAW and ask them if they can supply you with the name of some weightlifting clubs that are near you. Visit several, if possible, to determine which most fits your needs. Every club has a different atmosphere and no one club is for everyone. If there is no club nearby, consider starting your own (see the section on Starting a Club in Chapter 4).

Borrow a video camera and get someone to film your workouts. You'll then be able to see what you are doing and make appropriate modifications. Using a mirror is a good idea to study static positions—you should not be looking in a mirror when you are actually performing the lifts (especially the competitive lifts).

Go to a weightlifting competition (the USAW will be able to tell you about the events nearest you). At those events you will see the sport in action and can meet other lifters and coaches. Weightlifters and coaches are generally only too happy to help you get into the sport. Naturally, you do not want to approach a top lifter or coach during the heat of the competition, but well before or after the contest most athletes and coaches are happy to be of help (remember someone helped them when they were beginners too).

Read the other sections of the book as they make sense and interest you (e.g., read about competition about 8 weeks before your first meet so that you will understand what you will need to do there).

More advanced readers and those with limited time at any one sitting may prefer to read The Weightlifting Encyclopedia by selecting sections from the table of contents or topics from the extensive index. Most of the many sub-sections of the book have been written in such a way that they can be read by themselves with a high level of understanding (especially with the use of the index at appropriate points).

Whatever your approach to reading "The Weightlifting Encyclopedia", I hope you will find it to be as interesting and enjoyable to read as it was to research and write. Most importantly, I hope it is helps you to achieve your goals in weightlifting, whatever they may be. Good reading, good training and successful competition!

STRENGTH
and HEALTH   35¢

OLYMPIC STANDARD YORK

DAVE SHEPPARD

By virtue of his sheer mastery of what was then a new style of lifting, perhaps no other athlete helped to popularize the modern squat style to a greater extent than Dave Sheppard.

The Technique Of The Snatch And The Clean And Jerk

Why begin a book about weightlifting with a chapter on weightlifting technique? After all, weightlifting is first and foremost a sport designed to test strength and power. Why not begin, then, with a discussion of those subjects? The reason is that you cannot participate in an activity until you understand how it is performed, and you cannot properly measure your strength or train to increase it until you know how to execute the basic movements of weightlifting. Only when you understand what good technique is (i.e., the correct means of executing the two competitive lifts) can you begin to fully appreciate the sport of weightlifting.

In this chapter we will focus on understanding weightlifting technique, first on a very basic and then on a more advanced level. In the next chapter we will focus on how to learn and teach weightlifting technique. We will begin our discussion of technique by examining three major controversies that surround the subject. In the process of that examination, we will develop a framework within which it will be easier to understand various principles of sound weightlifting technique.

Some Controversies And Concepts Of Modern Weightlifting Technique

The Technique Versus Strength Controversy

Whenever weightlifters and their coaches get together, there is bound to be a discussion about the importance of technique. Some coaches see technique as virtually all important. Members of this school judge a weightlifter almost completely on his or her technical ability. They view technique as not only very necessary to be a good weightlifter

but also as sufficient. To these coaches and athletes, the amount lifted is secondary to how beautifully and efficiently a lift is performed. These extremists show little respect for the champion who has serious technical flaws in his or her lifting performance. Top athletes who make errors in technique are seen by the technique purists as reprehensible "freaks" who were blessed with strength but never took the time to learn how to lift properly and therefore are wasting their gift. These purists overlook several obvious facts.

First, the sport of weightlifting was devised as a test of strength. Techniques for performing the snatch and C&J have evolved over the years as part of the constant effort to improve performance. It is certainly true that the lifter who fails to master technique will perform at a lower level, in a less consistent way and at greater risk of injury than the athlete who has excellent technique. Nevertheless, the athlete who exhibits great strength is to be admired for that single capacity that weightlifting is fundamentally about.

Second, the athlete who fails to develop good technique should not be any less well regarded than an athlete who fails to put in the hard and consistent training that is necessary in order to develop his or her enormous strength potential. Developing strength is at least as hard as developing technique, and even harder in certain ways. The strong lifter should be given his or her due for all of the hard work that was required to develop that strength. I have met many people who have told me that "it's easy to get strong," but none of these individuals has actually achieved the strength of a top international weightlifter. Anyone who has acquired truly great strength understands the enormous effort required too well to take his or her strength for granted.

Third, the athlete with poor technique may have lacked the proper coaching at the outset. He or she may have worked very diligently on technique during his or her formative years. However, for a variety of reasons, the requisite

17

skills may not have been developed. One should not immediately assume that the poor technician is guilty of sheer sloth or stupidity. Rather, one should at least consider the possibility (unless it is proven otherwise) that the athlete in question is trying just as hard as any technique specialist to fulfill his or her potential.

Unfortunately, the technique fanatics sometimes use their technical skills to protect their delicate egos. They have mastered technique. Of their mastery there can be no doubt. It is easy enough to claim a genetic deficiency with respect to the ability to develop strength and then to say: "If I had Jack's strength, I'd lift twice as much as him." Such lifters ignore the fact that the challenge of developing strength is as least as great as that of developing technique and is more fundamentally linked to the reason behind the sport of weightlifting. For such people the frustration caused by failing to develop strength is like that felt by the strong lifter who is unsuccessful in developing technique. It is no more or less painful.

At the other extreme are the advocates of pure strength. They seem to hate technique, almost to wish it had never been invented. They view good technique as an intrusion into the purity of a sport that was devised to test strength. They long for the "old days" when technique was a secondary consideration in lifting big weights. There is nothing that pleases these lifters more than to be told: "You are so strong, you are not using even half of your great strength. If you would just develop proper technique, you would lift twice as much." What could be more gratifying? In reality, if that lifter were to develop perfect technique, he or she would not lift twice as much, probably not fifty percent more, and perhaps not even twenty-five percent more. Why then would a person with unrealistically "optimistic" appraisals of his or her strength develop proper technique, only to discover that the accolades that were once received are no longer as grand?

Today many strength purists gravitate toward powerlifting, a wonderful sport. I thin , however, that many of the powerlifters of today would prefer the sport of weightlifting if they could just see how to do it. I have yet to meet one powerlifter who has mastered Olympic-style lifting, and whose body can withstand the rigors of training on the Olympic lifts, who does not prefer it. A great deal of satisfaction comes from being amazingly strong and at the same time capable of producing extremely powerful and efficient motion. There is a unique thrill that comes from controlling the motion of a very heavy object and in the end holding it aloft in celebration of a "victory" over gravity.

In conclusion, strength may be more fundamental to the sport of weightlifting than technique, but in order for an athlete to fulfill his or her maximum potential, it is absolutely essential to develop both qualities to their highest potential. Obviously, maximum efficiency is needed to maximize performance. But there are two more subtle and perhaps more important reasons for perfecting technique. One reason is that correct technique is generally safer. An athlete who lifts correctly greatly reduces the risk of injury. A second reason to master technique (perhaps the most important of all) is to minimize frustration. All weightlifters miss lifts from time to time, and beginners will miss fairly often, but unskilled lifters and those who have serious flaws in technique will miss again and again unnecessarily. They will miss in training and in competition far more than is necessary, and their joy in lifting will suffer greatly as a result. More careers in weightlifting have ended due to frustration than any other cause. Don't let technique flaws frustrate you; learn to lift properly from the outset, no matter how long it takes.

Is There Only One "Best" Weightlifting Technique?

A second major controversy with respect to weightlifting involves two groups that I will call the absolutists and the relativists. In their purest version, the absolutists maintain that: 1) there is only one proper technique for lifting weights; and 2) they know what it is. Absolutists are easy to spot at a competition; they are the ones who contort their faces and snort in disgust whenever someone fails to perform a lift in accord with their own model. They simply "know" that their method is best and that everyone not using it is wasting their potential. How they have come to know this is not always clear, often not even to them.

In contrast, the relativists, in their most extreme version, maintain that proper technique merely involves "doing what comes naturally." They maintain that the body has its own most efficient and "natural" way to perform the lifts and that each person has merely to search his or her soul for guidance and then do whatever the subconscious seems to say. There is a second school of relativists who accept the notion of proper technique but who maintain that a lifter can only do what is natural, even if another technique is preferable. You can spot relativists because they exhibit a perpetual grin of resignation while observing virtually any lift, a grin that grows even wider when an obvious fault occurs, as if they are affirming the irony that the harder you try, the more likely it is that nature and whatever it holds in store will emerge.

As is normally the case in such controversies, both sides have some valid basis for their claims, but both sides are also dead wrong in a number of important ways. The absolutists fail to recognize that each human body is unique. Bodies are different with respect to the size and shape of the bones that are the levers and the joints that are the fulcrums in the mechanics of human movement. The muscle-tendon units that move the skeleton vary in their structure and capacity as well. Moreover, even if the infinite variety in humankind were not present, even if everyone were built in the same way, there would be a variety of ways in which the human body could develop a given force, each with its own advantages and disadvantages. This is not to say that there are not a significant number of absolutes with respect to technique that we can state; there surely are, and we will identify them in this chapter. But absolutes are far harder to come by, and the variety that is possible while still achieving good technique is far richer than the absolutists would have us believe.

Perhaps an even greater weakness in the argument of the absolutists is that they know what the optimal technique is. (How they come to know is often not clear, even to them, but when it is, the reason(s) given rarely stand up to serious analysis.) While we know a great deal about human movement in general and the scientific principles of weightlifting technique in particular, there is also a great deal that we have been unable to measure, analyze or understand. It is very likely that at least some, and perhaps a great deal, of what we believe to good technique today may be abandoned and replaced with something better in the future. The fact that the champions of today do something deserves our attention. However, their utilization of a particular technique is not proof that it is "the" optimal one, any more than the technique of the great champions of yesteryear has always withstood the test of time (although much can be learned from the old champions).

The relativists are not safe from criticism either. They are often unwilling to work with their lifters to develop proper technique or to confess their own lack of understanding of what is known today. They recognize the importance of biological individuality. Instead of using it as a basis for further study and learning, however, they use it as an excuse for whatever their athletes do. Clearly humankind was not born with proper weightlifting technique etched deeply within the recesses of the brain. The mechanics of weightlifting technique are not intuitive in nature. When you are doing a snatch or a clean and jerk, you are not moving in the way that most people think. Many lifters cannot explain the mechanics involved in weightlifting, even after observing and practicing it for many years. Therefore, the intuitive approach has great shortcomings. Correct technique needs to be taught by the coach and learned by the athlete.

As you might conclude from the preceding discussion, the development of technique is a process based on firm principles applied within the context of the individual characteristics of the athlete being trained. It is a difficult process at best, yet virtually everyone can develop a technique that is suitable for them with a well planned, consistent and flexible effort.

Oversimplification Versus Unnecessary Complexity

A third major controversy with respect to technique stems from the tendency of those who analyze and teach it either to oversimplify, or to add artificially to the complexity of, the sport of weightlifting.

The oversimplifiers revel in offering some simple fact as justification for a given technique, while appearing to be shocked that no one else sees how simple it all is. An example would be the person who says that you should always lift a bar straight up because "the shortest distance between two points is a straight line." While no one can argue with the accuracy of this statement, its application to the sport of weightlifting is not as straightforward as the advocate of such a point would have you believe.

For instance, in order to perform the snatch, the first lift in weightlifting competitions, the bar needs to be raised from the floor past the shins and knees (which are in the way of the vertical path of the bar when the lifter bends down to lift the bar from the floor). The bar's motion must be accelerated so that it picks up enough speed to carry it to a sufficient height for the lifter to "catch" the bar overhead, and this must take place while the lifter's center of gravity is shifting first in a rearward and then in a forward direction as the bar is being lifted. In addition, although the bar begins the lift at a point in front of the lifter, it must reach a point above and to the rear the lifter's head. This kind of relative motion on the part of the bar and the athlete suggests that a straight line, while undoubtedly the shortest distance for the bar to travel, will not necessarily be the best path to meet all of the requirements of performing an efficient lift.

While it is clear that oversimplification is a mistake, so is making lifting unnecessarily complex. Teaching and analysis only need to be complex enough to impart understanding. Unfortunately some coaches seem to think that pointing out each of the manifold elements that go into the lifting process demonstrates their level of expertise. This may be true, but it also can hinder the learning process if the complexity is introduced before it is appropriate.

For example, one popular book on weightlifting devotes an entire section to the concept of the combined center of gravity of the lifter and bar. The first problem with the way the writer handles the issue is that the concept of the center of gravity is not well explained before the concept of the combined center of gravity of the lifter and bar is introduced. As a result, the subject becomes quite confusing. Nevertheless, the concept of combined center of is presented, and an example of its application to the lifting process is given (an example which does not offer any illumination regarding the importance of the concept). After the reader has struggled to grasp the concept (probably with only limited success), the writer goes on to explain weightlifting technique at length across several short chapters. During that explanation, the concept of the combined center of gravity is mentioned only twice, and both of those times the author only repeats the initial example. No further use of the concept is ever made. Why did the writer bother to explain the concept if no important application of it is ever used thereafter? This is unnecessary complexity at its worst. (In this chapter we will explain the concept of a center of gravity, but then we will use it as well.)

A Proper Context for the Study of Weightlifting Technique

On the basis of the preceding discussion, we can identify several key concepts regarding weightlifting technique. First, in order to reach his or her potential in the sport of weightlifting, an athlete must master technique, but technique alone is not sufficient to become a high level performer. Second, there are definite principles of good lifting technique, but there is also more than one narrow way to perform the two Olympic lifts effectively. Third, weightlifting is a learned activity performed by athletes who have individual differences, and no amount of pure introspection or a priori reasoning will lead to the best technique for all athletes in all respects. Proper principles must be applied within the context of the characteristics of a given athlete in order to optimize technique. Fourth, weightlifting technique is neither absurdly simple nor so complex as to defy the understanding of those who do not have a graduate degree in biomechanics. Finally, perfecting technique is an absolute necessity. It makes weightlifting safer, more pleasurable to participate in and more aesthetically pleasing to behold. The purpose of the balance of this chapter is to provide you with an understanding of proper technique, a crucial first step on the road to becoming a weightlifter's weightlifter.

The Basics of the Technique of the Snatch and the Clean and Jerk

We will begin our analysis of weightlifting technique with an explanation of what the athlete is doing when he or she performs two Olympic lifts, the snatch and the clean and jerk (C&J). These are the lifts performed in weightlifting competitions (the winner being the athlete who lifts the most weight in both lifts combined). The snatch is a one stage lift and the C&J a two stage lift in which greater amounts can be added.

This overview will be more easily understood if you examine the sequence photographs that appear in Fig. 3 and Fig. 4 before reading further and then refer to them freely as you read descriptions of the lifts. (Fig. 4 omits the starting position from the floor and the "recovery" from the split position in which the athlete takes one step back with the front foot and then a step forward with the rear foot to bring the feet in line with one another and complete the lift).

As can be seen in the first photo of the snatch sequence, the lifter begins by gripping the bar with the hands significantly wider than the shoulders. From this position the lifter uses the muscles of the legs to lift the bar from the floor and then uses the muscles of the legs, hips and back in an extremely powerful (i.e., explosive) fashion to accelerate the upward motion of the bar. When the bar has been lifted to a level approximately at the height of the lifter's hips (at which point the lifter has generally extended his or her legs and risen somewhat on the balls of his or her feet.) the lifter begins to descend under the bar while the bar continues to rise, primarily as a result of the explosive force that the lifter has applied to the bar before the descent commenced. The lifter then "catches" the bar at arm's length and allows the legs to continue to bend after the catch to absorb the downward force exerted by the bar in much the same way a fielder in baseball "gives" with his or her glove as a ball is received. Finally the lifter stands up from the low squat position that was assumed in order to catch the bar. (Catching the bar in a low position means that it does not have to be lifted as high and that more weight can therefore be lifted.)

Methods similar to those used in the snatch are used to lift the bar in the clean and jerk. The lifter initially raises the bar through the use of the leg muscles; then, as the bar rises to the level of the knees, the lifters uses the muscles of the legs, hips and back to straighten the body in an explosive fashion, accelerating the upward motion of the bar.

Once the bar is approximately at hip level, the lifter begins to descend under the bar in order to catch it when it reaches its highest point. (The bar continues to rise because of the explosive effort the lifter made with the legs, hips and back.) The lifter permits the legs to bend further after catching the bar in order to absorb the force of the downward descent of the bar. The lifter then stands up and prepares for the jerk.

In order to propel the bar overhead during the jerk portion of the lift, the athlete bends his or her legs into a position similar to one that would be used to jump vertically. The legs are then very forcefully extended in order to thrust the bar upward.

Figure 3 — Snatch Sequence

Figure 4 — C&J Sequence

Just after the bar leaves the lifter's shoulders as a result of the leg drive the lifter has generated, the lifter typically moves one foot forward and the other foot backward in order to lower the body as the bar is rising and to prepare to catch the bar at arm's length. The front foot is placed flat on the floor and the back foot is balanced on the ball of the foot and the toes. This "split" position gives the lifter both stability and the ability to move forward or backward slightly to maintain balance. After the bar has been brought to a stop, the lifter returns to a standing position, first bringing the front foot back a step and then bringing the back foot forward until the feet are in line with one another.

Two important principles can be learned from the preceding discussion together with careful study of the photos. First, contrary to what most people think when they see Olympic-style lifting for the first time, the process is not merely one of lifting the bar. It involves a combination of raising the bar and lowering the body quickly enough to catch the bar at nearly the maximum height to which the lifter has been able to raise it. In order for the lifter to catch the bar successfully, the bar must have acquired enough upward speed to continue to travel upward for that very brief period while the lifter is moving under the bar (otherwise, as soon as the lifter tried to descend under the bar, the bar would fall and the lifter could never catch up to it). It is important to understand that the lifter does not lift the bar to its maximum height and then, when the bar stops, jump under it. Rather, the movements of raising the bar and lowering the body are taking place simultaneously. Consequently, the lifter must possess sufficient power to throw the bar, not just lift it. In addition, the lifter must possess considerable finesse in order to catch a heavy moving object at its maximum vertical height.

Second, the role of the arms in lifting is much smaller than you might initially assume. The arms do not lift the bar to its maximum height. Instead, the muscles of the legs, hips and back are primarily responsible for this action, generating an explosive force that creates upward velocity of the bar sufficient to cause it to continue to rise for at least a portion of the time the lifter is descending under the bar, permitting the lifter to catch the bar successfully. This is not to minimize the role of the muscles of the arms and shoulders. These muscles do interact with the bar, applying force to it as the lifter descends under and catches the bar. Moreover, strong arms and shoulders are needed to support the bar overhead. However, the role of the arms is not primary. The strength and explosive power of the lifter's leg, hip and back muscles, the strongest muscles in the body, form the foundation for championship lifting.

Analyzing The Snatch And Clean & Jerk Via The "Six Phases" And The Trajectory Of The Bar

The technique of modern weightlifting has been studied quite extensively, particularly in Eastern Europe, and most particularly by researchers within the former Soviet Union. As a result of the methods used to perform the analysis, some aspects of technique are quite well understood, while others remain only incompletely explained. Let us review what has been learned about the technique of today's high level athletes.

We will analyze the snatch and clean first. We will use a method similar to that advocated by A. Lukashev of the Soviet Union in 1972 (for the snatch) and further developed by B. Podlivayev in 1975 (for the clean). This method consists of breaking down these lifts into six phases or stages. (Lukashev and Podlivayev also group the six phases into three pairs of phases which they refer to as "periods"; we will refer primarily to the six phases or stages.) Breaking the lifts down into phases makes it easier to understand what is occurring when each lift is being performed. I have taken the liberty of framing the explanation of the jerk into six phases as well, because such a procedure fits well with what has been done by the aforementioned Soviet writers. The translations of the Soviet literature that I have reviewed refer to only five phases in the jerk. Much of the information that is presented in the next several sections about what lifters are doing in the various phases of the snatch, clean and jerk draws on work done by Robert Roman, a world renowned Soviet weightlifting analyst who specialized in the area of technique. (See the Bibliography for a listing of some of his fine works.)

There are at least four important limitations to using the six-stage kind of analysis. The first limitation is that this kind of analysis focuses on the snatch, clean and jerk up to the point where the bar is caught or fixed. There is little or no coverage of how the lifter stands up or "recovers" from the position in which the bar is fixed. The second point to remember is that the six phases used in the Lukashev/Podlivayev analytic method, while useful for purposes of analysis, are somewhat arbitrary. Their segments are easily visible to the external observer and are very useful for the purposes of film analysis. However, further refinements in the method of analysis will probably occur with the application of better technology. While the six phases described are easy to see and discuss, they are not really crucial in analyzing the effectiveness of a particular style. For example, the point at the which the maximum application of force to the bar occurs is neither the beginning nor the end of the explosion phase of the snatch or clean. Rather, the maximum force is applied between these two points. Similarly, the position and balance of the lifter at the point of exerting maximum force have an important influence on the outcome of the lift, perhaps more so than what goes on at the beginning or end of the phase (the major focus of the Lukashov/Podlivayev analytical approach). Yet, little research has been done, and even less has been widely published, in these and other vital areas of analysis of the dynamic aspects of technique (such as the rate of bar acceleration throughout each of the phases of the lift).

The third limitation of this analytical method is that it is simply an analysis of what the lifter is doing, not what he or she is thinking or feeling. You do not normally teach a lifter how to lift by saying "place your back at an angle of between 25 and 50 degrees in relation to the floor" or " move into the squat under when the bar reaches the height of the hips." Athletes do not think in terms of angular measurements and reaction time is a factor in movement control. (There is a necessary delay between the moment when lifter directs his or her body to do something and when the body actually executes the desired motion.) Therefore, if proper technique calls for the lifter to begin squatting under when the bar has reached the level of the hips, the lifter must think of moving when the bar is in an even lower position if the actual motion is to begin at the appropriate point. In addition, many of the motions that a lifter makes are a natural reaction to the actions that have preceded it. Consequently, it is those precursor actions that are crucial to teaching and learning certain aspects of proper technique, not necessarily the patterns of motion that follow. By merely attempting to assume certain positions during the lift, the lifter may be imitating the appearance of good technique without actually using the mechanics necessary to achieve an efficient lift.

The final caveat to the analysis that follows is that what is being presented is not necessarily an endorsement of the techniques described. It is simply an explanation or what is being done by the average, highly qualified lifter. Some champions perform in a manner very close to the one described while others do things quite differently. The important thing at this point in our analysis of technique is to gain an overall understanding of what most high level lifters are doing when they perform the snatch or C&J. A subsequent discussion in this chapter will address the issue of individual variations within the model presented.

While much of importance can be learned from the basic analysis presented, it should not be viewed as "the" method to be used. The proper evaluative approach to the "average" lifting technique used by high level athletes and to what a particular champion lifter is doing is to say: "There may be a very good reasons for the majority of

lifters (or the champion) to be doing things that way, but I need to understand and to experiment with their methods before I can accept their approach, even conditionally. It must be remembered that most lifters, even the champions, are often victims of "me too approaches to training and lifting (whether developed by their coaches or themselves).

It is prudent not to ignore the lessons that many before you have learned the "hard way" or to overlook the insights of those who have carefully studied technique. However, it is also prudent to remember that throughout mankind's history the masses have often agreed on what later turned out to be a complete falsehood. As the saying goes in the study of logic: "Fifty million Frenchmen (or Americans or Russians) can be wrong."

An Explanation of the Six Phases of the Snatch and Clean "Pull"

The six phases of the snatch and clean set forth by Lukashev and Podlivayev are explained in this section. Each phase will be analyzed in some detail in the next section. During the discussion we will often refer to the "pull". In the context of this discussion, pull means the lifting of the bar from the floor to the point at which the lifter brings to the bar to a stop on his or her shoulders (in the clean), or overhead (in the snatch). Pull always refers to both lifts unless otherwise specified.

The first phase of the snatch and clean starts from the point where the lifter begins to interact with the bar. This includes such actions as the placement of the lifter's feet and body in relation to the bar, the setting of the lifter's grip and any rocking or other motions the lifter may make in preparation for lifting or separating the bar from the platform. The first phase ends at the moment when the bar "separates" (is lifted) from the platform by the athlete.

The second phase of the snatch and clean, also called the "preliminary acceleration" phase, begins where the prior phase ends (i.e., when the bar leaves the platform) and ends when the legs have straightened to their maximum extent for the first time during the pull (i.e., approximately at the point when the bar has reached knee level in the clean and the bar is at the level of the lower third of the thigh in the snatch). This also marks the end of the first "period" in the pull.

The third phase of the snatch and clean, also called the "adjustment " phase, begins when the athlete starts to flex the knees again and to move them under the bar. It ends when the knees have reached their maximum point of flexion.

The fourth phase of the snatch and clean, also known as the "final acceleration" or "explosion" phase, begins when the knees have reached maximum flexion and ends when the knees are fully straightened, or nearly so, and the athlete is at the highest point that he or she will reach on his or her toes (i.e., the point where the lower extremities of the body reached their maximum amplitude in the pull before they begin to relax so that the body can be lowered to catch the bar). This point also marks the end of the second period of the pull.

The fifth phase of the snatch and clean, also known as the "unsupported squat under," starts once the athlete's lower limbs have reach their maximum amplitude of extension and ends once the bar has reached its maximum height.

The sixth and final phase of the snatch and clean begins when the bar has reached its maximum height and ends when the bar has been "fixed" (i.e., the downward progress of the bar has been halted and the lifter has some degree of control over it).

An Analysis of the Six Phases of the Snatch and Clean Pull

A detailed analysis of the snatch and clean is presented in this section. This analysis includes a number of technique metrics. The figures provided for those metrics are representative of an athlete with an average, mesomorphic physique who is 170 cm tall (approximately 5' 7"). Athletes who are significantly taller or shorter will generate different numbers. For example, athletes who are taller will tend to move the body and bar greater distances and will tend to move the bar at higher speeds.

It should also be noted that in many areas of the analysis differences are noted in the patterns of movement that occur in the snatch and the clean. These differences are believed to exist primarily because of the differences in the grip widths and weights that are used in the snatch and the clean. A narrower grip (as is used in the clean) places the shoulders at a greater distance from the bar than does a wider grip, generally resulting in the torso being held more upright during the pull for the clean than in the pull for the snatch. This grip also produces in a greater deformation (bending) of the bar during the pull for the clean because the force applied during the pull is applied more toward the center of the bar. The heavier weights used in the clean also contribute to the greater deformation of the bar.

Some interesting trade-offs occur in the clean as opposed to the snatch. For example, the amortization phase is longer in the clean than in the snatch because of the heavier weights lifted in the clean. However, the final acceleration phase in the clean is shorter than in the snatch because the torso is straighter at the beginning of that phase.

Before we begin our analysis, the reader should have at least a basic understanding of the concepts of the line of gravity (LOG) and center of gravity (COG). It is important to understand these basic

concepts of mechanics because they are used in the analysis of technique that follows. In the simplest terms, an object's line of gravity (when it is viewed from a given perspective) is the point at which the object would balance if a straight edge were placed under the object. For example, if we were trying to balance a ball on the edge of a steel ruler, we would have to place the ball in such a way that the ruler was under the exact center of the ball (i.e., under an imaginary vertical line that divided the ball into two halves). Alternatively, if we were trying to balance a flat wooden map of the United States that was 1" thick in a upright position, we would place the ruler near the center (east/west), but the point of balance would be unlikely to fall in the exact center measured from side to side, because the map is not perfectly symmetrical. Since the eastern and western parts of the country do not have the same shape, the left and right halves of the map would not weigh the same and would not balance along a line in the exact center. The line would be somewhat off to one side. In contrast, if we viewed such a map from the side, the line of gravity would be 1/2" from the front of the map or 1/2" from the back because the map is flat and made of wood that is 1" thick. Finally, if we laid the map down flat and then found the balance point between the western and eastern sides, a line drawn through the map at that point would represent its third line of gravity. The point at which all three lines of gravity intersect is the map's center of gravity.

Finding the center of gravity of the human body is much more difficult than finding the center of gravity of a ball or a map of the United States, because the human body can change its shape at any time by simply moving a part of the body; such a movement will change its balance points. For example, when a body is viewed from the side (the perspective that is used for much of the analysis of lifting technique that follows), the center of gravity runs approximately along a line that divides the body in half from front to back. However, if the body bends forward from the waist, the center of gravity will shift forward. If one leg is then lifted to the rear, the center of gravity will shift back toward the middle of the body. In contrast, the center of gravity of the bar is always at its exact center (as measured from all directions) since the bar is symmetrical. When two objects are connected to one another, a combined center of gravity is created. For instance, if a lifter who weighs 100 kg. holds a 100 kg. bar at waist height, the combined center of gravity of the two objects will be toward the front of the lifter's body and the rear of the bar.

The concept of the center of gravity has a number of implications for the weightlifter, and it is discussed in greater detail in Appendix 2. It should be noted that while from the technical standpoint the line of gravity concept is appropriate only for discussions of a single dimension, and the center of gravity is appropriate for discussions of three dimensions, the term center of gravity is used for single and multiple dimensions throughout this chapter, both for simplicity and because in the contexts in which it is used the difference in the terms is not material.

Its primary importance in the discussion that follows is in describing the general motion of the athlete and the bar during the performance of the snatch and C&J. For instance, during the second phase of the pull, the lifter's center of gravity shifts toward the rear, but during the fourth phase of the pull, it moves forward.

The lifter's center of gravity can be thought of as his or her balance point. When the center of gravity shifts back, so does the lifter's balance and vice versa. An important principle of mechanics is that at no time may the center of gravity go outside the base of support of an object (in the case of the weightlifter the base of support is the athlete's feet). If the center of gravity of the lifter does go forward or to the rear of the furthest edge of the foot (the toes or heels, respectively), the lifter will topple over. Since the athlete's feet represent the base of support of both athlete and bar once the bar leaves the platform, the combined center of gravity of bar and lifter may not exceed the limits of the lifter's feet or the entire system will fall over (with the lifter going one way and the bar the other).

In the analysis that follows, the centers of gravity of the lifter and bar and their combined center of gravity are often referred to in order to convey a sense of how these objects are moving and interacting and where the lifter's balance is at various points during the lift.

Now let's look at the six stages of the snatch and clean.

The First Phase of the Pull: "Pre-Lift-Off

In both the snatch and the clean, today's lifters typically begin to exert force on the bar with their feet placed approximately at the width of the hips and turned out slightly. The bar is positioned roughly over the juncture of the metatarsal/phalangeal joints (the juncture of the toes and the foot). The torso is typically inclined at an angle of 25-50 degrees in relation to the ground or "platform"; the angle tends to be larger in the clean than the snatch, i.e., the torso is more upright. The shoulders are positioned directly over or slightly forward of the bar (a few lifters start with the shoulders slightly behind the bar, but this is generally considered to be a mistake). The shins are inclined forward and slightly outward and are close to or touching the bar.

There is typically an arch in the lumbar region of the spine (the lower back), with the rest of the spine held relatively straight (i.e., the curve that normally exists in the thoracic region of the spine is reduced in most athletes at the start of the pull).

The shoulders are slightly back but are not shrugged upward toward the neck and the arms are straight. The hips are at approximately the same horizontal level as the knees but are often somewhat above or below the knees. (The hips tend to be higher in the clean than the snatch.)

The differences in hip position and torso angle in the clean and the snatch are due in part to the wider grip that is used in the snatch (causing the lifter to have the torso closer to the bar and hence often to lower the hips further at the start) and in part to the difference in the weights used in the snatch and the clean. It is harder to start the bar from a lower hip position, so when heavier weights are lifted, as they are in the clean, the hips tend to be placed in a higher position. The angle of the knees in the starting position is between 90[degree] and 45 ° (the smaller the angle the more fully the athlete's knees are bent).

At the start of the pull, the position of the head typically ranges from being in line with the torso to being held in a vertical position. Having assumed this position the lifter begins to exert force against the bar. When the force exerted on the bar reaches a level that exceeds the combination of the bar's weight <u>and</u> inertia (the resistance of a body to change in what it is doing, in this case not moving), separation of the bar from the platform takes place. At this point the center of gravity of the athlete is typically at the middle of the foot or somewhat behind that point.

The Second Phase of the Pull: Preliminary Acceleration

Most athletes separate the bar from the platform in a relatively smooth fashion and then begin to accelerate the upward motion of the bar. During this phase of the pull, the bar travels toward the lifter, and the center of gravity of the lifter shifts toward the heels. Throughout most of the preliminary acceleration phase, the angle of the back in relation to the platform remains essentially the same as at the moment of bar separation, an average of 30 ° in relation to the platform in the snatch and 32 ° in the clean; toward the end of this phase, the angle of the torso begins to increase (i.e., the torso begins to straighten). The hips rise, while the torso of the lifter travels upward and forward so that the shoulders move well in front of the bar. If the head did not begin in a vertical position it often begins to assume such a position during this phase of the pull. The acceleration phase typically begins with the knees at an angle of between 80 ° and 110 ° and ends when the knees have reached an angle of 145 ° to 155 °. The angle in the snatch tends to be at the higher part of this range, and the angle in the clean at the lower part of this range; athletes with a longer torso and shorter legs tend to have the lower knee angles in these ranges and athletes with the opposite conformation have larger knee angles. Because the legs straighten more in the clean than in the snatch, the torso shifts forward more in the clean. The shins achieve an essentially vertical position at the end of this phase. The bar is usually at about 31% of the athlete's height in the clean and at 35% in the snatch (just above the knees in the clean and approximately at the lower third of the thigh in the snatch).

As the preliminary acceleration is executed, the centers of gravity of the bar and athlete move closer together than they were at the start of the pull. The bar moves toward the athlete less in the clean than in the snatch, but the athlete moves toward the bar to a greater extent. (The further apart the centers of gravity of the body and the bar are at the start, the more the bar will shift at this stage in the pull.) This phase of the pull generally takes about half a second (the time involved in the snatch is usually very slightly less than for the clean). The velocity achieved by the bar at this point is approximately 1.5 meters per second in the snatch and 1.2 meters per second in the clean (taller lifters tend to generate somewhat greater bar speeds and shorter lifters somewhat lower). By the end of this phase, the bar has shifted as much toward the athlete as it will at any point in the pull (4 to 12 cm in the snatch and 3 to 10 cm in the clean, the bar shifting a greater distance for taller lifters).

The Third Phase of the Pull: Adjustment

The third phase of the pull is called the amortization or adjustment phase. This phase is used to position the bar and body appropriately in order to properly execute the fourth or "final explosion" phase of the pull. During the adjustment phase, less force is applied to the bar than during either the preceding or succeeding phase. In effect, the lifter is relying on the acceleration developed during the second phase of the pull to keep the bar moving upward while the body assumes a favorable position for the final acceleration (though the lifter is normally not consciously doing this). This movement is often referred to as a rebending of the legs or a "double knee bend" (since the knees have been bent once to lift the bar from the floor and then rebent after the bar has passed the knees).

During the third phase, the lifter continues to straighten the torso (a process that was begun at the end of the previous phase). However, this straightening is carried out more forcefully and extensively in the third phase of the pull. If the head is not held in a vertical position at the start of the pull or during the second phase, it will often assume that position during this phase of the pull. Partially as a consequence of the torso moving in an upward and backward direction, an opposite reaction occurs in the knee and hip joints (i.e., they move forward and down). The combined actions of the legs hips and torso place the body in a position favorable for expressing the all important force of the final explosion. In addition, this process keeps the center of gravity of the body close to the bar (as compared to a position that would have been well behind the bar had the hips and knees remained in the same position while the torso straightened).

The forward and downward movement of the knees take about .1 to .2 seconds (toward the lower part of this range in the snatch and the higher in the clean) and ceases when the knees reach an angle in the range of 125 ° to 135 ° (the lower half of the range in the snatch and the upper half in the clean). The average torso inclination at this point is 58 ° in the snatch and 60 ° in the clean.

During this phase the feet normally remain flat on the platform, though some exceptional lifters do begin to rise on the balls of the feet. The bar reaches approximately the lower third of the thigh in the clean and the middle of the thigh in the snatch. The bar is typically just over the middle of the foot (a little closer to the ankle in the snatch). The center of the shoulder joints is typically equal to 3% to 4% of the athlete's height in front of the bar. The speed of the bar has dropped by an average of .08 to .1 meters per second during this phase (toward the higher end of this range in the clean and the lower in the snatch).

The Fourth Phase of the Pull: Final Acceleration

The fourth phase of the pull is the one in which the athlete applies the maximum and most critical force to the bar. This is accomplished by explosively straightening the legs and torso, lifting of the shoulder girdle upward and backward and rising on the balls of the feet and toes. It should be noted that not all lifters straighten the legs fully during the explosion phase of the pull or jerk and that some high level lifters do not rise on the toes to any significant extent at all. Some coaches believe that this lesser amplitude of body straightening is an advantage.

During this fourth phase of the pull , the bar describes a forward arc as the combined center of gravity of the bar and athlete shifts toward the toes of the athlete (upon which the athlete is typically balanced at this stage) until, ultimately, the bar finds a nearly vertical direction. This stage takes approximately .1 to .25 seconds to complete (the clean requiring less time than the snatch). At the end of this phase, the athlete's center of gravity has moved up and back as the bar has moved forward, and the body assumes a straightened position with the entire body generally having a slight backward lean. A straight but slightly backward leaning line passes through the bar , the lifter's shoulders and the balls of the feet. The combined center of gravity of the bar and lifter is at approximately the same vertical line as the feet of the lifter, which are now supported on the balls of the feet (on average the bar is actually of 2 to 4 cm forward of the base of the toes). The bar reaches speeds of 1.65 to 2.05 meters per second in the snatch and 1.2 to 1.6 in the clean (taller athletes tending to achieve greater speeds than shorter athletes).

The Fifth Phase of the Pull: The Unsupported Squat Under

The unsupported squat under begins with the lower limbs of the athlete at their most extended position and continues while the athlete is moving into position for the squat under. It ends when the feet make forceful contact with the platform once again. Once the final acceleration has been completed, the bar continues to rise, primarily as a result of the momentum gained during the final acceleration phase. However, the speed gained during that phase is not sufficient to account for the total height that the bar ultimately reaches (68% to 78% of the athlete's height in the snatch and 55% to 65% in the clean). Several explanations have been offered for the extra height that the bar achieves. One is the interaction of the arms and the bar while the athlete begins to descend into the squat or split position (i.e., while the athlete's feet still are in contact with the floor, a period of .05 to 1 second in the snatch and .1 to .15 of a second in the clean).

A second factor cited is the thrusting of the feet from the platform during the descent under the bar (because the bar's velocity is higher after this thrust). In a way, the body collides with the bar after the maximum effort has been exerted in the explosion (the body goes up and then bounces down away from the bar), adding some impetus to the bar.

A third factor is the interaction of the arms and bar as the athlete descends in the unsupported and supported phases of the squat under. The action of the arm flexors and the muscles of the shoulder girdle (in the latter part of the snatch descent and during the jerk, the arm extensors come into play) after the feet have left and then returned to the ground can generate an upward reactive force on the bar, resulting in additional acceleration. This acceleration occurs when the force of the body returning to the platform is transmitted back to the bar thorough the arms.

During the unsupported phase the center of gravity of the lifter typically shifts forward somewhat as the athlete descends under the bar while it moves upward and then downward and backward. After the feet are thrust from the platform, they typically remain out of contact with the platform for between .15 and .33 of a second in the snatch and .1 and .2 of a second in the clean.

The Sixth Phase of The Pull: The Supported Squat Under

Once the lifter's feet have landed on the platform in a flat footed position after being thrust from it during the unsupported squat under, the lifter quickly assumes a squat position if the lifter uses this style (and most do). In this position the heels are under the hip joints, the toes are turned out to the sides, the back is arched and the torso is tilted slightly forward (more so in the snatch than in the clean). The combined center of gravity is in the middle of the foot. In the snatch the arms are straight, with the shoulder blades pulled together. In the clean the bar rests on the shoulder muscles, and the elbows are up, preferably at or near the level of the bar.

During the lowering of the body, the bar moves backward and then down. The downward motion is typically 5% to 9% of the athlete's height in the snatch and 14% to 18% in the clean. The bar is actually fixed (i.e., its downward progress is stopped) at 62% to 70% of the athlete's height in the snatch and 40% to 48% in the clean.

Roman and many other analysts believe that if the pull is performed correctly overall, the combined center of gravity of the bar and athlete will shift forward slightly during the pull. As a result the athlete must jump slightly forward in the squat under. Next best, according to Roman, is when the bar shifts only very slightly backwards during the pull, in which case the feet are jumped straight out to the side as the athlete squats under the bar. In the least desirable instance the lifter pulls the bar significantly back, causing the lifter to jump back. Roman suggests that this makes it more difficult for the athlete's movement to be precise and for the bar to be brought under control. A number of the Bulgarian coaches, however, are very persuasive defenders of the latter style. It should be noted that many world records have been established by lifters using all of these styles.

An Analysis of the Six Phases of the Jerk

The technique of the jerk, like that of snatch and the clean, can be broken up into six phases: the start (the motions the lifter makes and the position the lifter assumes prior to bending or "dipping" the legs to thrust the bar overhead); the initial dip; the braking portion of the dip; the thrust; the unsupported part of the squat or split under; and the supported phase of the squat or split under. As was the case in the analysis of the snatch and clean, these six phases exclude the recovery from the receiving position of the bar in the jerk (e.g., the split position). Although there are important differences between the phases of the pull and the jerk, in some respects the six phases of both movements have much in common. Both the similarities and differences will be explained below.

The same caveats that applied to the description of the snatch and clean also apply to the description of the jerk. In brief, they are: a) the analysis, in the main, ignores the recovery of the body to a standing position once the bar has been fixed; b) the segments analyzed are somewhat arbitrary, but they are the segments upon which the greatest amount of data has been gathered; c) the analysis describes what the lifter is doing but not necessarily what he or she is thinking or feeling;, and d) the descriptions are of what is being done by high level athletes today, not necessarily what athletes should be doing.

In both the pull and the jerk, the alignment of the body at the start has an important influence on the performance of the subsequent parts of the movement. The pull and the jerk share a preliminary phase of motion (in the snatch and clean the bar moves up during that phase, in the jerk it moves down) followed by an amortization phase that brings the body and the bar into proper position for the important final explosion that imparts the majority of the force needed to lift the bar to the proper height. Finally, two phases of the squat under in the snatch, the clean and the jerk have characteristics that cause the bar to be lifted higher than the bar velocity at the end of the explosion would suggest, characteristics that enable the athlete to fix the bar in preparation for a recovery to the final position of the lift.

The First Phase of the Jerk: The Start

At the start of the jerk, the shoulder and hip joints of the lifter and the bar all form a vertical line with, or slightly behind, the middle of the foot. The feet are placed approximately at the width of the hips, either straight or with the toes turned out slightly.. The arms are relaxed. The elbows are in front of the bar (if the bar were viewed from the lifter's left side as the center of a clock, the elbows would be anywhere between the seven o'clock and nine o'clock positions). Lifters who keep the elbows relatively low (i.e., at the seven o'clock position) because they find a higher elbow position is uncomfortable or impedes their breathing at the start, sometimes raise the elbows just before the second part of the jerk begins. The head is normally tilted slightly back, and the line of sight is generally looking slightly up. The combined line of gravity of the bar and athlete, viewed from the side, is in the middle of the foot. The balance of the lifter can be anywhere in the middle third of the foot with a weight that is 150% of the athlete's weight, though it is generally recommended that the weight of the lifter and the bar should be felt toward the rear portion of the middle of the foot, rather than toward the front. However, as the bar gets heavier, the point of balance through which the lifter can control the bar grows smaller. For a weight that is 275% of the lifter's bodyweight, the range of balance is cut roughly in half, and most of the range lost is from the front half of the range that exists with 150% of bodyweight. The first phase of the jerk ends when the lifter begins to bend the knees for the initial dip.

The Second Phase of the Jerk: The Dip

When the lifter executes the initial dip, assuming that dip is perfectly vertical, the lifter's balance (technically, the lifter's "center of gravity"—a term explained in Appendix 2) shifts slightly forward because the knees move forward of their starting position and all other parts of the bar and body remain essentially in the same vertical line. It is considered preferable to have the combined center of gravity of the bar and lifter remain in the same position, or even to travel slightly backward during the dip, therefore; some lifters let their pelvises travel slightly back during the dip to counteract the small shift in the lifter's center of gravity that takes place when the knees move forward during the dip. This does not necessarily mean that the shoulders of the athlete and the bar move forward more than is normal (although there is a school of thought that advocates dipping slightly forward, though not beyond the front of the foot, and then tilting the torso backward as the athlete drives up out of the split). During the initial dip the bar normally shifts forward by 1 to 2 cm (such forward movement should be avoided).

The average time for the initial dip is just over .25 of a second, and this time does not vary with the height of the athlete (taller athletes tend to execute the initial dip more quickly than shorter athletes). The distance covered by the initial dip is typically just under two-thirds of the distance that will ultimately be covered by the lifter during both the initial and second parts of the dip. At that point the knee angle of the lifter is typically between 114° and 132°. The initial dip ends when the lifter begins to resist the downward progress of the bar in order to stop it.

During the preparatory dip for the jerk, the speed of the bar can vary from one that is faster than a pure free fall of the bar (because the lifter is pulling down on the bar to accelerate its downward speed) or to a speed that is much slower than a free fall (because the lifter is resisting the downward movement of the bar). Most analysts suggest a speed close to the free-fall speed or slightly slower (i.e., the lifter should neither rush into the dip nor substantially resist the bar's downward motion). This "natural" kind of dip speed not only enables the lifter to maintain control over the bar but also permits the optimization of the lifter's use of the elastic qualities of the leg muscles and the bar. (This issue will be discussed further later in this chapter.)

The Third Phase of the Jerk: The Braking Phase

The braking phase normally takes about .12 of a second and encompasses a little more than one-third of the overall depth of the first and second phases of the dip. At its conclusion the downward progress of the center of the bar has stopped. The knees are typically at an angle of between 99° and 111°. Overall, between the first and second portions of the dip, the bar has typically been lowered between 8% and 12% of the height of the lifter. At the lowest point of the dip, the athlete normally pauses for between .01 and .04 of a second (i.e., there is virtually no detectable pause, but, rather, an immediate rebound).

The Fourth Phase of the Jerk: The Thrust or Explosion

The recovery from the lowest point in the dip for the jerk to the starting position of the dip takes approximately .02 of the second, or about half time it took to get from the starting position to the lowest point in the dip. The lifter is actively influencing the bar for about 85% of the time that it takes to perform the upward thrust, and acceleration is only taking place for 75% of the thrust. Maximum velocity of the bar is achieved at a point a little less than 1% higher than the initial position of the bar before the dip. At this point the athlete has shifted his or her area of support to the toes (and has risen somewhat on the toes), and the knees are nearly straight (and they appear to be straight). The velocity of the bar is between 1.45 and 1.8 meters per second (the lower figure is more common for shorter athletes, the higher for taller athletes). This velocity only accounts for about half of the height the bar reaches at its highest point in the jerk. It is hypothesized that the balance of the force that causes the bar to reach its ultimate height is generated by the force of the lifter's feet being replaced on the platform in the split—force delivered to the bar by the lifter's arms pushing up on the bar as the feet make contact with the platform—and the force generated by the arms and shoulders once the feet have been replaced on the platform. The thrust ends when the legs of the lifter have reached their maximum point of extension in the drive.

The Fifth Phase of the Jerk: The Unsupported Squat Under

After the thrust is executed, the athlete's feet begin to leave the ground. (The back foot is slightly ahead of the front foot when the lifter uses the split style in the jerk, as does the vast majority of lifters.) The athlete pushes against the bar with the arms and shoulders to push the body down. During this time the lifter's balance is moving slightly forward and down while the bar is moving up for 70% to 80% of

its upward path and then upward and backward slightly for the rest. The unsupported squat under phase ends when both feet have made contact with the platform again.

The Sixth Phase of the Jerk: The Supported Squat Under

As noted, the back leg lands before the front in the split. That leg is nearly straight (typically at an angle of 160°, and the foot is balanced on all of the toes. Therefore, the heel of the back foot is turned out slightly. The front leg in the split has a knee angle of 90% or more, the thigh is angled from 10° to 20° from the platform, and the shin is vertical or inclined slightly in the direction of the lifter. The front foot is flat on the platform. The bar is typically in a position slightly behind the athlete's head, at about the same vertical plane as the shoulder blades of the athlete. The hips, shoulders, elbows and wrists are all in the same vertical plane, the head is vertical and pushed forward somewhat and the back is arched. The front foot is typically a little more than one foot-length in front of the hip, and the back leg is a little less than two foot-lengths to the rear of the hip. Altogether, the torso has been lowered a total of 15% to 20% of the height of the athlete. During the amortization of the bar in the jerk, it typically drops between 3 cm and 8 cm.

The Movement of the Bar During The Pull and the Jerk

The Trajectory of the Bar During The Pull

Perception of the pattern of bar movement during a snatch or clean is affected by your position in relation to the bar and lifter. If you are watching a lift from the front, the bar will be perceived as moving vertically and evenly, i.e., the bar will be parallel to the ground during the pull. However, if the lifter is viewed from the side, the observer can see that the bar travels backward and forward during the lift, as well as upward.

At first glance, this pattern of bar movement may seem odd. After all, science tells us that the shortest distance between two points is a straight line and that a strictly vertical trajectory will give a projectile its greatest height. It also tells us that once horizontal motion is imparted to an object, the object will continue to travel horizontally until it meets a force that interrupts that motion. These principles clearly suggest that the straighter the pull, the better. However, considerations other than the three mentioned above influence the most effective pattern of bar movement. For example, the lifter's line of gravity travels forward from the heels to the toes during the third and fourth phases of the pull. This generates a tendency to apply a forward force to the bar during the amortization and final explosion phases of the pull. More important, the lifter typically makes contact with the bar at the middle to top of the thighs during the pull. The combination of these factors (which are more pronounced in the snatch) drives the bar forward.

Much work has been done in Eastern Europe and the United States to analyze the pattern of the bar's travel during the pull. (In the United States most of this work has been done by Dr. John Garhammer, who has been active as an athlete, coach and sports science advisor in the USAW for many years.) The evidence provided by this research is quite conclusive in certain respects. It is clear that for most accomplished lifters the pattern of bar movement very roughly approximates the shape of a somewhat flattened S. The bar first moves in a backward curve toward the lifter in the second and third stages of the pull; then and in the final explosion phase, it moves in a curve away from the lifter. Finally, during the unsupported phase, the bar loops backward and down toward the lifter again. The curves traveled by the bar tend to be flatter in the clean than in the snatch. The shape of the trajectory in the pull tends to be much more consistent among lifters during the third through fifth stages of the pull than during the second stage of the pull. During the third stage of the pull, virtually all lifters pull the bar toward the body; during the fourth stage there is almost always some movement of the bar away from the body; and at the end of the pull for a successful lift, the bar nearly always travels in a downward loop

backward toward the lifter. In contrast, during the second phase of the pull, many lifters pull the bar toward the body while some pull the bar in an almost perfectly vertical pattern; some actually cause the bar to move away from the body during the first phase of the pull (although this pattern can hardly be considered good technique).

Although the pattern of the bar's movement generally describes the shape of a flattened S, the S can be slanted from the vertical, and its shape can deviate rather dramatically from the curves of the letter S (see Figs. 5 a-c). Figure 5(a) represents the fairly conventional kind of bar pattern, with the overall S-curve being positioned vertically and the curves within the S being rather significant. Figure 5(b) depicts an S-curve in the same general shape, but it is essentially tilted somewhat backward. This type of pattern indicates that the lifter is pulling with his or her bodyweight, and/ or the bar itself, too far back toward the heels at the start of the pull, or soon after the start, and that the lifter is exploding upward and rearward instead of primarily upward during the final explosion phase of the pull. Figure 5(c) shows the bar pattern of a lifter who has the hips very high during the early phases of the pull and who begins with the bar forward of the juncture of the toes and the foot. Such a lifter may produce a curve that tilts somewhat forward and may actually finish with the bar forward of its initial position on the floor.

While studying the pattern of bar movement during a lift can be very useful to both lifter and the coach, it should be remembered that bar

Fig. 5

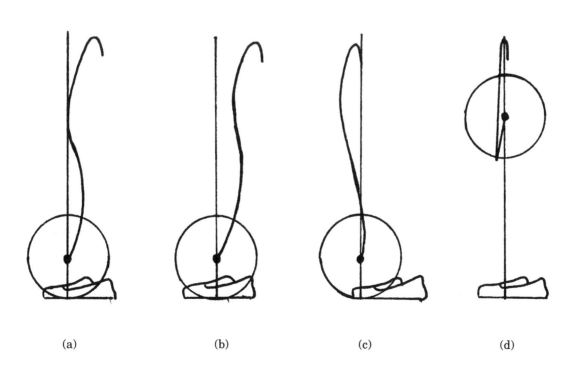

(a)   (b)   (c)   (d)

movement is more appropriately viewed as an effect rather than a cause. It is true that if the bar moves significantly forward or back of its initial point during the course of the pull, it can cause the lifter to lose control of the bar while trying to fix it in the low position of the squat or split. Therefore, in a sense, it is this pattern that causes the lifter to miss. However, the faulty movement pattern of the bar is only a symptom of improper positioning of the joints of the body and/or the bar and body in relation to one another during one or more preceding phases of the pull. It can also result from improper timing of force application during the pull. These faults must be corrected if the pattern of the bar's movement is to be corrected. This is not to say that it is not possible for the athlete and coach to use the bar trajectory as a means for correction in the pulling style. For example, the lifter could be given feedback on the curve at the top of his or her pull, learn to associate certain feelings with the desired curve and thereby correct the pull. Nevertheless, it is the correction of the positions and force patterns of the body that correct the curve, not the reverse.

It is important to understand that each of the three styles depicted in the illustrations of bar trajectory have been used with success by some very accomplished athletes. The real problems develop when the lifter does one of two things. The first happens when the bar does not travel backward towards the lifter during the initial stages of the pull. Such a bar pattern is indicative of the lifter who begins with the bar too far behind the juncture of the foot and toes, with the combined weight of the bar and body toward the rear of the foot, and who keeps the back too upright or attempts to straighten it too early in the pull. Occasionally, forward movement of the bar during the second stage of the pull is seen in the lifter who begins with the correct balance but shifts the body weight toward the toes and/or uses the arms to direct the bar forward during that stage of the pull.

The lifter who holds his or her torso too upright or tries to straighten it prematurely will tend to have shins that are abraded (although abrasion can occur with lifters who are pulling more of less correctly as well) and will tend to exhibit a lack of both consistency and smooth movement during the second stage of the pull. There will also be a tendency for the bar either to move away from the lifter or to have too little horizontal movement toward the lifter during the second half of the S. This is because the bar is too far forward of the lifter's point of balance during the final explosion for the lifter to direct it back over his or her body by the end of that explosion. Typically the bar will end up over its original position on the platform, the lifter will either jump back or remain in place, and the bar will be left forward of the lifter.

A second major fault occurs when the combined weight of the lifter and bar is shifted toward the rear of the foot to a greater degree or for a longer period than is appropriate during the pull. The result is that the lifter's balance is in the middle or even toward the rear of the foot as the final explosion of the pull commences. In addition, the athlete's shoulders will travel to a position behind the bar earlier than is appropriate. This will cause the athlete to apply a rearward as well as an upward force to the bar during much of the pull. This kind of bar pattern results in a rearward displacement of the bar from the starting point and hence a need to jump back during the squat under in order to be in a position to control and ultimately fix the bar. If this fault is pronounced, it can lead to less consistency in lifting performance and greater stress on the joints and muscles as the lifter attempts to bring the bar under control.

The Bar's Relative Speed at Various Points in the Pull

The bar typically achieves its greatest upward velocity during the second and fourth phases of the pull. However, lifters generally create different relative bar speeds in the second and fourth phases of their pulls. The bar speed generated during the fourth phase of the pull is almost always greater than the speed achieved during the second phase. The difference in speed between the second and fourth phases of the pull tends to be greater in the snatch than the clean. The ranges of the relative speed differences between the second and fourth stages of the pull are as follows (for purposes of comparison, it is always assumed that the speed during the second phase of the pull is 1.00): 1.00 to 1.50 in the snatch and 1.00 to 1.40 in the clean. This means the bar always moves at least as fast in the fourth stage of the pull as in the second, but it may move up to 50% faster.

Now that we have described the movements of the body and the bar during the snatch and clean, let us evaluate these movements during the jerk.

The Trajectory of the Bar During the Jerk

The trajectory of the bar during the jerk is very different from that of the pull. The bar travels down in a virtually straight line as the lifter dips and then goes nearly straight up until the lifter moves under the bar into the split or squat. At that point the bar describes a backward and downward loop similar to that seen during the snatch or clean but typically a little less extreme in terms of the amount of backward loop. This straighter overall path is not surprising when one considers the relative simplicity of the jerk drive as compared with the pull (e.g., the knees do not have to be brought out of the way or back and only the legs are imparting force). See Figure 5 (d).

General Guidelines For Sound Technique

Although the six-stage analysis of technique presented above conveys some important issues regarding technique, many aspects of technique are ignored in such an analysis. The section that follows will explain a number of important aspects of technique that have not yet been covered. These represent some fundamental aspects of sound technique that come more as a result of experiencing and coaching technique than from observing the grosser features of technique via film analysis.

Guidelines For All Lifts

Apart from the aspects of technique that have already been covered, there are some additional principles of weightlifting technique that apply to all lifts in nearly equal measure. These principles are discussed in the next several sections.

Proper Breathing While Lifting

While not technically part of the subject of weightlifting technique, proper breathing is an important part of weightlifting. Although weightlifting is considered to be an anaerobic activity, it does increase the body's need for oxygen far more than most activities that are considered to be aerobic. What makes it anaerobic is that the activity of weightlifting is not sustained for a long enough period to use up the body's anaerobic energy supply. Therefore, a lifter could simply not breathe at all during a lift and still execute it without difficulty most of the time. Consequently, there is a tendency for some athletes to attempt to hold their breath throughout a lift. This should be avoided for at least two reasons.

One reason is that if a lift takes a long time to complete, the lifter may run out of oxygen, much in the same way a resting person holding his or her breath for a minute without exercising might do. An example of this would be a C&J during which the lifter struggled for balance in the squat position, remaining there for several seconds, then arose from the squat position, took some time with the weight at the chest preparing for the jerk and then struggled to control the jerk overhead; this process could all take from 15 to 30 seconds and would result in one very breathless lifter. Another example would be a lifter who was doing several repetitions or "reps" (lifting the weight several times in succession without resting) in a simpler exercise.

Another important reason to breathe properly is to avoid unnecessary increases in blood pressure when lifting. There can be a twofold or greater increase in blood pressure when the major muscle groups of the body are involved in a substantial muscular effort. However, at least one group of researchers has found that this increase is due as much to the lifter's making an effort to expel air against a closed glottis (a portion of the larynx through which air flows during breathing) as to the exertion itself. Therefore, proper breathing can reduce this component of the increase in the pressure.

There is considerable evidence that the overall issue of elevated blood pressure during exertion should not cause great concern. Empirically there have not been any instances of strokes occurring during weightlifting competitions. (I know of at least one instance in which a lifter over the age of forty had a heart attack while warming up for a competition, but this athlete had existing coronary artery disease of which he was apparently unaware.) If heightened blood pressure were a very significant risk, we would expect to see more evidence of it when the strain was greatest.

On a more scientific level, researchers have argued that a difference in pressure across the walls of the heart and its large blood vessels can occur. This is because the pressure outside increases at least as much as the pressure inside. The brain is protected in a similar fashion in that any increase in intrathoracic pressure is transmitted to the cerebrospinal fluid, counteracting the increase in the pressure within the blood vessels that supply the brain. The peripheral vessels are more subject to the increased pressure, but their smaller diameter makes them more able to accept the increased pressure. There is actually more concern among some researchers about breathing too deeply and frequently (hyperventilation) before a heavy exertion than about breathing too little. This is because it has been discovered that hyperventilation before heavy exercise can lead to convulsions or even fainting. In short, extremes in breathing patterns are to be avoided.

As a general rule, proper breathing consists of inhaling just before or as a weight is lowered and breathing out while it is raised. During complex motions like the snatch and C&J, there are actually several points where breathing generally occurs. In the snatch there is usually some exhalation during the pull, particularly in conjunction with the final explosion of that pull. The lifter often does not inhale again until he or she recovers from the squat or split position but may exhale the rest of the air that was not expelled during the pull as the recovery to a standing position occurs. However, if the lifter remains in the low position for more than a few seconds, he or she may inhale at the low position and then exhale during the recovery to a standing position.

In the C&J, as in the snatch, there is often a partial exhalation during the pull, with the remaining exhalation occurring during the recovery from the low position . If the lifter remains in the low position for some time, there may be some breathing while in that position and exhalation during the recovery, but this is unusual. After the recovery from the clean, the lifter generally takes several quick breaths in preparation for the jerk, then ceases breathing during the actual dip for the jerk, sometimes exhaling as he or she lowers the body to catch the bar at arm's length. Some lifters move so quickly into the jerk that they do not take any additional breaths after the clean, but this is the exception rather than the rule.

In preparation for any lift (the snatch, clean, or jerk), the lifter should at least partially inflate the lungs and use the air that has been taken in to thrust the chest out just before the lift begins. This elevation and expansion of the rib cage give the lifter important assistance in achieving the rigidity of the torso that is so necessary during the pull and jerk. It is certainly not necessary to expel air with a great deal of force or an accompanying shout while lifting, but some lifters feel that such an action improves their concentration and power.

When the lifter performs exercises other than the snatch and C&J (or related movements), the general rule for breathing is to breathe in just before lowering the weight or while it is being lowered and to exhale toward the completion of the lift. For instance, when one is squatting, one typically takes one or more shallow breaths before the squat, then lowers the body into the squat position. A partial exhalation occurs as the lifter rises, at or just past the most difficult part of the squat.

Locking Body Parts

A number of elements of technique are difficult to describe verbally. They are things that you can feel, but not easily explain. The concept of locking body parts while lifting is one such notion.

The need to lock or make rigid a given body part stems from the need to use that part of the body as a means of transmitting force (rather than its acting as a source of that force). One example is locking the back in the pull. When a lifter properly locks his or her back, or any other body part, only a part of that lock arises out of the actual position of the back or other body part. In the case of the back, it is difficult to hold it rigid if the back is in certain positions (e.g., rounded or greatly bent at the waist). It is easiest for most people to lock their backs when the back is in a fairly natural position, the kind of position the back is in when the lifter stands in a good posture. That is, the shoulders are slightly back, the chest out just a little so that the normal curve in the thoracic area of the spine is reduced (though not eliminated) and the normal curve in the lumbar area of the spine is maintained. The exact position will vary somewhat with the anatomy of the lifter. For example, some lifters will find that their normal curve in the

thoracic region of the spine as well as a curve in the opposite direction in the lumbar spine are conducive to keeping the back rigid. Others will find that virtually eliminating the arch in the thoracic area of the spine helps them to solidly lock their backs. It is most important that the lifter find a position in which the rigidity of the back can be maintained, even under great stress.

Apart from the lifter's assuming a strong position, the key to maintaining the back in a rigid position is increasing the level of tension in selected muscles of the torso to the point where the back has the feeling of being locked. The lifter will know he or she is in the correct position when it feels as though the back simply cannot be moved from its locked position, no matter how large an external force is applied to it. The ideal position must be rigid and yet comfortable enough to be sustained as the lifter prepares to pull and during the pull itself. Maintaining the torso in a rigid position during the pull and jerk is easier when the lifter makes an effort to push the chest out by inflating and lifting the rib cage. The ultimate test of whether the back is in its proper position is its performance during the pull. If the back "gives" at any point (if the position of the curves in the spine changes or the muscles are felt to lose their tension), then the position needs further attention.

If the lifter is having difficulty achieving the locked position, there are several possible causes. The most likely is that the position chosen initially is not the ideal one for that lifter. A larger or smaller curvature in both areas of the spine can be tried, but any changes should be very gradual. For example, if the thoracic region of the spine experiences an increase in its curvature during the pull, it may be a result of the lifter's assuming a position that has reduced the normal curvature so much that the lifter cannot sustain the position. On the other hand, the lifter may have allowed the starting curvature to be so great that it placed the back in a weakened mechanical position, and the lifter could not sustain that position when force was applied; the result was that the back gave even further. Once that standard back position has been tried, the lifter needs to experiment and to pay attention to his or her body in order to find the most secure position.

Another possible reason for the problem is that the lifter has inadequate flexibility in the hips or legs. A lack of flexibility can make it difficult for the lifter to assume a correct starting position or make that position so difficult to assume that the position is lost as soon as force is applied. An example of this kind of problem is when the hamstrings are so tight that the lifter cannot maintain an arch in the back during the pull. The obvious solution here is to improve flexibility so that the lifter is able to assume and maintain a proper position.

Still another possible cause of failure to lock the back is the lifter's inability consciously (at the early stages of learning) and unconsciously (at the later stages of learning) to maintain proper tension in the muscles of the back. A tension that is too small will cause the back to lose its position when force is applied; an excess of tension will make it impossible for the lifter to execute the pull smoothly. A related problem is the failure to relax the muscles that pull the trunk forward. For example, if the lifter unnecessarily contracts the abdominal muscles during the pull, it can cause the spine to round out.

The final major cause of failure to lock the back is relative weakness in the back muscles; weak back muscles cannot withstand the force that is applied from the legs during the pull. The strength of the lagging back muscles can be improved through special exercises for the back, such as hyperextensions. Perhaps the best method to strengthen the back is to practice deadlifts with the back in perfect position. These assistance exercises are explained in detail in Chapter 5.

In general, the portions of the lift that call for rigidity in any body parts are those in which the greatest force is applied or received. These moments are: the second stage of the pull; reaching the bottom of the dip in the jerk; beginning the final explosion in the pull and jerk; catching the bar on the shoulders in the clean; and fixing the bar overhead in the snatch or the jerk. ·

Finding a Focal Point

Many sports teachers emphasize the importance of a specific kind of visual focus or attention. Baseball players and golfers are taught to "keep their eyes on the ball." Skaters, divers and gymnasts are taught to maintain a "focal point." This means that while spinning or somersaulting, they try to keep their eyes on a fixed object for as much of the movement as possible. Doing so helps them both to understand where they are during a movement and to maintain their balance.

The emphasis on finding a focal point tends to take a back seat in coaching lifting, but it is a point of some importance nonetheless. Focusing his or her eyes on a fixed point will help the lifter to maintain his or her balance (especially important in the large arenas in which competitions are often held) and to understand his or her body position at any point during the overall movement. It will also help the lifter to control unwanted head movement since it is difficult to move the head wildly while maintaining visual contact with a specific point.

In the snatch I recommend that the lifter begin by maintaining visual contact with a point on the wall in front and slightly above eye level when in the squat position. This point of focus, which can be used during both the pull and the squat under, is relatively comfortable during the pull, and it tends

to keep the head well up and the spine in good position while the lifter is in the squat position. If the suggested focal point brings the desired results, it can be maintained. If the lifter feels uncomfortable or unbalanced after giving the suggested point of focus a fair trial, then modifications can be experimented with. As with so many aspects of technique, the lifter will find that general principles (here, the need for a focal point) must be adapted to his or her own circumstances; the lifter must decide where the points should be and when they are used.

In the clean the lifter can use a focal point similar to that used for the snatch. In the jerk the eyes should be are focused on a position that is similar in principle but different in application (because the lifter is standing instead of being in the full squat position). The line of sight should be slightly above eye level when the body is in a standing position.

For the lifter who elects to pull in a style that keeps the rear of the head aligned with the spine (a technique discussed in further detail in the next section), there will need to be two focal points during the snatch and the clean. The first point will generally be on the floor several feet in front of the lifter during the early stages of the pull. Contact with a fixed point will generally be lost during the third and fourth stages of the pull, but in the fifth and sixth stages the lifter will find a point of focus appropriate for controlling the bar in the squat position.

Positioning the Head

What is inside a lifter's head is his or her most vital tool for weightlifting success. But the physical position of the head is also an important part of weightlifting technique. Since the head is not an inconsequential portion of a lifter's bodyweight, its position affects the center of gravity of the lifter. In addition, the proper position of the head tends to align the spine properly, making transmission of force from the lower body and torso to the bar more effective. Finally, the proper positioning of the head can facilitate the lifter's using his or her vision to maintain his or her balance while moving.

There is some controversy over the positioning of the head during certain phases of the pull. Virtually all analysts believe that the head should be aligned with the body at the end of the pull. Years ago it was believed that throwing the head backward during the final explosion of the pull aided the lifter in fully extending the legs and back and thereby imparting maximal force to the bar. Today it is generally accepted that the lifter can impart just as much vertical force to the bar without throwing the head and at the same time speed up the transition from the final explosion to the squat under. Most theorists also agree that head has a neutral function once the pull has commenced (i.e., it does not direct the body but rather serves as a relatively motionless extension of the body). However, there are considerable differences of opinion about how the head should be positioned during the early stages of the pull.

One group of theorists believes that the head should be held in line with the spine throughout the lift. This means that the lifter will be looking forward and down during the early stages of the pull. Advocates of this pulling style argue that the lifter will tend to keep his or her shoulders over the bar to a greater extent during the second and third stages of the pull when the head is in line with the spine. In addition, they believe that any tendency to shift the body and bar too far towards the rear of the lifter will be reduced with the head-in-line position. Finally, they assert that holding the head in line with the spine early in the pull facilitates keeping the head in that position at the end of the final explosion and during the unsupported squat under. As a result, advocates of this style argue, the lifter will be able to elevate the shoulders more easily, which will assist both in imparting force to the bar with the trapezius muscles and in using those muscles to assist in the descent under the bar.

Advocates of maintaining the head in an upright and vertical position throughout the pull argue that the head-up position at the start of the pull assists the lifter in maintaining an arch in the back. In addition, they believe that with the head in a vertical position, the lifter will be able to maintain a focal point throughout the first four stages of the pull and most of the squat under, which helps the lifter to maintain his or her balance.

I find the arguments made by this latter group to be more persuasive, and most lifters seem to agree, but there have been some outstanding champions who have used the head-in-line positioning technique very effectively. There is certainly no harm in a lifter giving both methods a try.

Before leaving the subject of head positioning, a few points should be made about the position of the head in the jerk, a subject that is far less controversial than that of the head position while pulling. In the jerk the head is generally tilted slightly backward during stages one through four of the lift. More importantly, the lifter also pulls the chin in toward the neck and moves the head backward in relation to the spine. This is done primarily so that the lifter can keep the chin out of the way of the bar during the drive. During the squat under phases of the jerk, the rear of the head is brought forward to align itself with the spine or is even placed somewhat forward of it.

Moving Under the Bar Rapidly and Immediately

During the fifth and sixth stages of the snatch, the lifter works to gain control over a bar that has effectively been "launched" into the air during the fourth stage of the pull. The faster the lifter's feet regain contact with the floor and the faster the lifter assumes a position in which he or she is able to receive force, the better able the lifter will be to catch a bar so launched,.

Rapid movement under the bar can be facilitated by a conscious effort to lower the body quickly. In the snatch and clean the lifter needs to think of pulling himself or herself under the bar once the squat under has begun. In the snatch and jerk the lifter needs to push out forcefully with the arms and in the clean to raise the elbows as vigorously as possible as the bar nears its final position.

A conscious effort to place the feet against the platform as quickly as possible after the final explosion is extremely important, as such an effort can significantly shorten the unsupported squat under phase, enabling the lifter to apply upward force against the bar as quickly as possible after the squat under has commenced. Hundredths of a second are important here. Some coaches advocate that the lifter actually stamp the feet against the platform as the feet make contact. They believe that a conscious effort to stamp the feet will result in a more rapid placement of the feet. This does seem to help in certain cases, but an overemphasis in this area can lead to the lifter's unnecessarily lifting the feet well above the platform to make a stomping noise, thereby jarring the body when the bar is caught (and actually making it harder to control). It also increases the time that the bar is unsupported by the athlete—which means there is more time for the bar to gain downward velocity. Vigorously replacing the feet on the platform and immediately exerting force downward against the platform transfer upward force rapidly to the bar, making it easier to control. The key is to make solid contact rapidly, not to make as much noise with the feet as possible.

Bulgarian Antonio Krastev, former World Superheavyweight Champion and world record holder in the snatch, has told me that the Bulgarians emphasize a rapid placement of the heel of the front foot in the jerk, with both feet remaining very close to the floor during the movement into the split position. He also points out that any unnecessary rising on the toes during the final explosion in the jerk is to be avoided. As a group, the Bulgarians are probably the surest jerkers in the world, so this advice, in addition to squaring with theory, has yielded excellent results.

Some of the Bulgarian coaches actually teach their lifters to jump back at the end of the fourth stage in the pull. They believe that if the lifter explodes with the trunk upward and backward, the bar will travel rearward at the end of the pull and that the lifter will therefore need to jump back. As this tends to be an individual matter, I do not subscribe wholesale to the idea. Nevertheless, thinking of moving the feet forward or backward as well as sideways during the squat under may well be valuable for some lifters.

One final point on a rapid and precise squat under. Lifters who truly master technique develop an ability to use a rebound from the effort of the final explosion of the pull to propel them under the bar. This is a very difficult feeling to describe, but when a lifter applies a very explosive effort to the bar during the final explosion phase, he or she will feel a point of extreme resistance on the part of the bar. This is natural, as the lifter is attempting to accelerate the bar and the upward force applied to the bar is experienced by the body as a downward force on it (see Newton's third law of motion as explained in Appendix II). If the lifter's upward effort against the bar is rapid and strong enough the lifter can use the downward force against the body as a mechanism to drive the body rapidly downward. Lifters who master this nuance of technique will find an immediate improvement in the crispness with which the bar is locked out or racked at the shoulders and an increase in the poundages that can be lifted.

Moving with the Greatest Possible Speed Consistent with Maintaining Control

One general principle of technique is that the lifter should always endeavor to move both the bar and himself or herself with the greatest speed that is consistent with maintaining proper body positioning and balance. Weightlifting is a sport where speed matters and, therefore, speed must be focused on at all times. This is not to say that speed is always achieved (it is hard to move the bar very quickly while pulling on a limit clean), but the lifter must strive for speed in the context of what he or she is trying to accomplish during a given stage of the lift. For example, it is not crucial that the lifter move with maximum speed during the first stage of the pull. At this stage, as was noted earlier, proper grip and body positioning are of foremost importance. Nevertheless, once proper body position and grip are established and concentration on what is to follow is achieved, the lifter's overall results are influenced by how quickly he or she carries out the first stage of the pull. In the context of the first stage of the pull, for the lifter who pull from a static start, this would mean getting set quickly. It would mean pumping quickly for the lifter who uses that style and "diving" quickly for the lifter who uses the dive style (all of this within the context of assuring grip and proper starting position first).

Speed is most critical from the third through the sixth stages for the pull and jerk. Speed in amortization, speed during the explosion and speed in moving under the bar are all absolutely essential. Therefore, throughout a lifter's career, speed must be emphasized, and the lifter must always be endeavoring to move the bar and body faster and faster. Doing this during any workout (regardless of the intensity of that particular workout) can provide the lifter with a continual mental challenge. Naturally the emphasis on speed must be increased gradually in order to permit the lifter's body to adjust to the stress that additional speed can place on the muscles and connective tissue. There are exceptions to the speed rule, such as when a lifter is training with slow movements to stimulate greater muscle tension.

The Value of Limited Bar Drop

When you watch lifters at top international events like the World Championships, you cannot help but be struck by the variety of techniques used by the very top lifters. However, upon closer study a number of common characteristics can be identified. One of the most important is a minimal bar drop. What is bar drop? I define it as the distance the bar travels from its highest point in the lift before it is brought under control by the lifter. The distance tends to be shortest in the jerk, longer in the snatch and longest in the clean. Generally speaking, the shorter the bar drop, the more efficient the technique on a number of levels. The issue of bar drop is harder to detect and less important in the clean because the bar must be allowed to drop over a relatively long distance in order to amortize the downward force of the bar. Because heavier weights are used in the clean than in the snatch (thereby reducing the distance the bar can be thrown during the later stages of the pull), the bar will fall a greater in the clear distance before the lifter can bring it under control. But there is a significant difference among lifters as to how long this descent takes in the same lift.

What are the variables that affect the distance a bar drops? One variable is the velocity at which the bar is traveling when the lifter begins to descend under the bar. If the bar has a greater velocity, it will rise for a relatively longer period and the athlete has a better chance (longer time) to get under the bar and "fix" it before it drops a great distance. The second factor affecting the drop in the bar is the time it takes the lifter to drop into the receiving position. That time interval is a function of the distance the lifter has to travel; the speed of the switchover from the explosion to the squat under phase, the speed with which the lifter executes the squat under and the speed with which the lifter can begin to exert upward force against the bar in the squat or split position so that the weight can be caught. The higher the lifter's body before the drop begins and the deeper the position to which the body descends, the greater the distance the lifter needs to travel. Whatever that distance, the faster a lifter switches from the explosion to the squat under phase and the faster the lifter moves into the catch position, the less time the bar will have to drop. One of the surest signs that the body has been overextended or held too long in the extended position during the pull is that there is a "pressing out" in the snatch or the bar "crashes" on the lifter in the snatch or clean; the bar seems to be moving falling very quickly by the time to lifter is in a position to receive it, making the catch more difficult to execute and placing undue strain on the joints. This crashing motion is proof that the bar has picked up too much downward speed before the lifter was in a position to stop the bar's downward descent. Another indicator of this problem is when the coach is able to clearly see with the naked eye the lifter fully extend his or her body during the final explosion phase of the pull. Lifters with proper timing appear to barely reach a position with the body fully straightened before they squat under (although film analysis may show the lifter fully straightened and somewhat on his or her toes).

A third factor that affects bar drop is the amount of force that is applied to the bar as the lifter drops, which can occur as a result of the interaction of the bar and body (e.g., the force applied to the bar as the body makes first contact with the ground). As was mentioned above section in "Moving Under The Bar," there is also a point toward the end of the explosion in which the lifter can feel a reaction from the explosion, a force which seems to push the body back down from the bar. If the lifter can learn to align the timing of the squat under to coincide with that reaction force, its speed and effectiveness will be significantly enhanced.

The shorter the bar drop, the better is the athlete's performance in the technique variables described above. Therefore, bar drop is one important measure of how far a lifter has traveled in terms of technical mastery. In addition, the shorter bar drop is much easier on the body in terms of the effort needed to decelerate the bar. All things being equal, the longer the bar drops, the greater speed the it gains. More speed means more force will be required to stop the bar's downward travel. At the very least this will tire the lifter more quickly, and at the worst it can lead either to acute injury or to a chronic accumulation of microtrauma, making the body susceptible to injury over time. Consequently, the lifter is well advised to master the shorter bar drop.

One final advantage of a shorter bar drop is that the lifter can fix the bar at a lower point. For example, if a lifter pulls the bar so that he or she requires a 5" drop before the bar can be brought under control, the bar will have to be pulled 2"

higher than if the lifter needed only a 3" drop to fix the bar.

How can the lifter minimize bar drop? There are four basic means. First, the greater the momentum the lifter can apply to the bar before descending under it, the more time the lifter will have before the bar begins to fall. This momentum is achieved both by improving the lifter's explosive power through training and by making sure that the lifter is performing the final explosion at a point where the body's capability for delivering maximum force is greatest. For example, if a lifter can achieve the same bar height by exploding violently with the bar at mid-thigh or by accelerating the bar more gradually and pulling longer, the former approach is preferred. Consequently, the timing of the switchover between the final explosion and its follow through and the squat under must be both optimal and precise.

A second important factor in minimizing bar drop is to shorten the distance the lifter has to drop. This is accomplished primarily by avoiding overextension of the body (e.g., by not going unnecessarily high on the toes or leaning back excessively at the top of the pull, from which position the lifter has to travel a greater distance to get under the bar in a position that is suitable for receiving the weight). Another is method is to assure that the lifter goes no lower than is necessary to fix the bar. This does not mean that the lifter should not gain control over the bar and then use a comfortable stopping distance to decelerate the downward motion of the bar. Rather, it means that the lifter should not jump into the lowest possible squat under position immediately, whether or not the bar's position requires it. Some lifters actually pull the bar down on themselves in a race to beat the bar down to the bottom position. This movement both increases the bar's downward velocity and places the lifter in a weaker position in which to catch the bar.

A third way to reduce bar drop is to minimize the time spent in the unsupported squat under phase, which means that he or she must cover the necessary distance in the smallest possible time. This generally involves focusing on moving under the bar as quickly as possible, interacting energetically with the bar so as to use it as a basis for increasing the speed of the descent and using the forces generated by the body itself in order to increase the speed of the descent (e.g., whipping the elbows quickly to create an opposite downward force on the body).

The last way to minimize bar drop is to exert upward force on the bar as early as possible in the squat under phase of the pull or jerk. This helps to transmit force from the floor to the bar and to cause the bar to achieve greater height than it would merely through the force applied during the explosion phases of the pull or jerk thrust.

Returning the Barbell to the Platform After a Successful Lift

When a lifter succeeds in lifting the bar and has completed a "set" (one or a series of lifts preceded and followed by a rest period), he or she needs to return the bar to the platform. In the days when weights were made solely of cast iron, there was little choice for most about how the bar was replaced on the platform. The bar had to lowered with some care lest it damage the flooring beneath (dropping the bar was restricted solely to instances in which a lift was missed). Since rubber "bumper" plates were perfected, the practice of dropping the bar after a lift has come into vogue.

Dropping the bar, especially immediately after the lift has been completed, is a poor habit. It can create a tendency for the lifter to lose control of the bar at earlier and earlier stages in the lift. Then, at competition time, it is possible to fail to control the bar long enough to satisfy the rules of the game. To prevent this, athletes should hold every heavy (90% or better) lift in training just a bit longer than is necessary to gain control of the bar and make an effort to control the bar to a certain extent on the way down (the methods for doing this will be explained shortly).

Apart from the fact that dropping the bar tends to cause some lifters to lose the ability to control it, dropping the bar with unnecessary frequency and force hastens the destruction of the equipment you are training with. Bars will be bent and come apart more easily. "Bumper" plates will lose their spring and become damaged prematurely. The flooring on which the lifts are done will become damaged and the sub-flooring or structure of the building in which the lifting is performed can become undermined.

Weightlifting has not historically been a moneymaking sport for those who sponsor it, so finding a facility at which weightlifters can train for weightlifting competition is often not a simple task. Unfortunately, many weightlifters have made the sport even more unappealing to gym owners because they have cultivated a reputation for destroying equipment and facilities. Therefore, the facilities that do exist for weightlifting practice and competition should not be abused. If lifters limit dropping the bar to missed lifts, or at least to lifts with 90% or more, I would estimate that the rate of equipment wear and destruction could be reduced by 75% to 90%. A bar's life could be increase from several months or years (depending on the quality of the bar) to several decades or more. It also means that lifters would be far more welcome in gyms, Y's and other facilities. Weightlifting would then become more popular and widespread.

Whenever you discuss this topic with weightlifters and coaches, you will always hear the counterargument that "lifters are unnecessarily injured by having to lower the bar." In my experience, this is a half-truth. While lifters do sustain occasional (and generally very minor) injuries as a result of lowering the bar, almost all of those injuries occur as a result of the lifter's failure to lower the bar under reasonable control. Moreover, it has been my experience that many more lifters have been injured as a result of dropping the bar unnecessarily (such as when the bar bounces up and hits the lifter's hands or shins) than by lowering it under control.

Irrespective of whether or not dropping the bar is advisable, there is absolutely no excuse for a behavior that some lifters cultivate: throwing the bar down. When an athlete lowers a bar somewhat and then lets it fall to the platform (or misses a lift and very appropriately lets in fall), the bar travels a limited distance, gaining speed solely as a result of the pull of gravity. Such a fall will have limited force. When a lifter throws the bar down from his or her full height, the bar not only falls further (i.e., from a greater height); it also falls with the added downward force supplied by the lifter. This kind of behavior is unnecessary, dangerous and destructive. It should not be tolerated.

Athletes who complain that lowering the bar hurts have probably never received instruction in the proper technique for lowering the bar. That technique varies slightly among the snatch, the clean and the jerk, but the principles used in each are the same: the bar and body are rendered motionless, the centers of gravity of the bar and body are lowered together, the arms then offer some resistance to the bar as the center of gravity of the body is raised and the descending bar is then brought under control and returned to the platform.

In the jerk the method used is to bend the legs into approximately the quarter squat position while still holding the bar overhead. From that position the bar is lowered toward the shoulders with some resistance from the arms, while at the same time the legs are returned to a nearly straightened position (which raises the lifter's shoulders). As the bar comes in contact with the lifter's shoulders, the lifter allows the legs to rebend to absorb the shock of the descending bar. (The torso is kept strictly vertical during this process; it is particularly important not to permit the torso to lean back when the bar is received on the shoulders.)

A similar process is followed in the snatch, except that the bar is caught at the top of the lifter's thighs instead of the shoulders, with first the arms and then the thighs offering the primary resistance to the descending bar. In the clean the shoulders are lowered by bending the legs; then the arms offer some resistance as the bar descends, and the legs nearly straighten once again to stop the bar at the mid-thigh position. Once the bar has been lowered to mid-thigh after a snatch or clean, it is lowered with the legs and arched back to the floor. Following these steps will make lowering the bar a relatively easy process and will actually make the lifter stronger by providing some eccentric muscle action training. (See Appendix 2 for an explanation of eccentric muscle action.).

Irrespective of the issues raised above, there will be times when the lifter will want or need to drop the bar after a successful lift. In such situations, certain safety rules must be followed. First, the platform must be clear of any plates or other objects that make it anything but perfectly flat. When the bar is to be dropped, it must be on a surface that is free of objects from which the bar can ricochet. Dropping the bar at the edge of a raised platform should be avoided, as the bar can rebound against the corner of the platform and travel horizontally with great force.

Second, before dropping the bar the lifter should lower the body as much as is comfortably possible (e.g., by bending the legs) so that the length of the bar's fall is reduced. Third, the lifter should keep all parts of his or her body behind the falling bar (including the wrists, which should never be above the bar). When a lifter has his or her legs near the bar or the wrists above it, any rebound of the bar when the it hits the platform, can cause an injury. When the hands are in contact with the bar but the palms are facing the floor and the wrists are behind the bar, any rebound of the bar will simply push the hands up. If the lifter lets the bar go entirely before it hits the platform, he or she should keep the entire body well behind the bar; even if the bar travels in a somewhat horizontal direction when it rebounds, it will not hit the lifter. Following these procedures should make lowering the bar a safe procedure in all cases. A description of how to drop the bar after a missed lift is provided in the next chapter.

Guidelines for the Snatch and Clean "Pull"

The Importance of the Starting Position in the Snatch and Clean

The importance of the starting position in the snatch and clean cannot be overemphasized. While a good starting position does not assure a successful lift, it is very difficult, if not impossible, to exhibit proper technique without a good starting position, and many lifts have been lost due to a failure to achieve an optimal starting position. This is particularly tragic when you consider that the skill required to assume a functional starting position is minimal and the opportunity to assume it greater than for any other portion of the lift because timing is not necessarily an important issue, particularly if the athlete starts from a static position. (Bar timing is a very important issue in all other phases of the lift.) Even if a lifter uses a

"dynamic" start (which will be discussed shortly), precision is easier to achieve in the starting position than in any other phase of the lift because the lifter need only control the movement of his or her body, not the bar and the body, as is required at other stages in the lift.

The starting position can be viewed from two perspectives: from he position of the various joints of the body in relation to the bar and one another and from the tension of the various muscle groups at the moment of starting the lift (separating the bar from the platform). You can use the position of the joints relative to one another, as described in the Eastern European literature, as a guideline for a good starting position. Ranges for the angles of each of the key joints were given in the description of the six stages of the pull. These ranges will be appropriate for the vast majority of lifters, but occasionally a lifter will find it necessary go outside these ranges in order to find the optimal position. This is reasonable if the positions in the normal range have been given a fair trial and it is obvious that some facet of the lifter's structure makes a different position more advantageous. However, regardless of the position assumed, certain basic principles should be followed in assuming the starting position in the snatch and clean.

1. The lower back should be slightly arched and the upper back should have a minimal curve in the thoracic region of the spine (one that can be sustained throughout the pull). In addition, the chest should be out (in the classic military "at attention" kind of position) and the shoulders slightly back, and the latissimus dorsi muscles should be somewhat flexed. This kind of positioning and muscle tension assures that the power of the leg and hip muscles will be transmitted directly to the bar during the most explosive parts of the pull. In addition, they provide the athlete with protection for the spine; when the spine is in the position described, it is relatively strong and stable. The tension in the latissimus dorsi muscles arises from a slight backward pressure on the arms. This pressure continues during the second and third phases of the pull, when it aids in keeping the bar close to the lifter's body.

Lifters who have trouble achieving a sufficient arch in the back at the start may find it helpful to employ one of three techniques to assure proper back positioning. One approach is for the lifter to begin with the hips higher than they will be when the bar leaves the floor and to align the back properly while in that position. Then the lifter can set the back in the proper position and lower the hips (maintaining that back position) just before commencing the pull. A second option is for the lifter to prepare for the pull by standing fully erect at a position of strict attention. The lifter lowers the body by bending the legs and hips and inclining the torso while maintaining the arched position of the torso. The lifter must guard against looking down for the bar as his or her hands near the bar, since the effort to do so often results in losing the arch. Once the bar has been grasped and the initial arched back position maintained, the lifter can look down, with as little head movement as possible, to assure an even grip. The third option is for the lifter to position the feet and hands properly, then to lower the hips while arching the back, pulling the shoulders back and looking up. This action helps many lifters to achieve a proper position. Then the lifter can raise the hips to their proper starting position for the pull.

2. The arms should be straight and the trapezius and related muscles should be relatively relaxed. Premature contraction of the arms makes the pull more difficult, both off the floor and at the point where the bar passes the knees. Premature tension in the traps makes the final explosion in the pull more difficult (the need to keep these muscles relaxed does not contradict the advice given in the prior section to keep the chest out and the shoulders back, because that can be done with the trapezius muscles in a relaxed state).

It should be noted that a very small number of some very high level lifters have extended the concept of relaxing the upper body well beyond what is suggested above. Bob Giordano, a US Olympic Team member in 1980, used to advocate relaxing the thoracic region of the spine and even the lower back somewhat, (i.e., employing a slightly rounded back) during the early stages of the pull. His reasoning was that if the back was held in a relaxed position, it could impart force more effectively at the top of the pull with a powerful contraction of his back muscles. Bob feels his unconventional method helped him to become one of the strongest pullers in the country, if not the world. Bob is not alone. Yordan Mitkov, the Bulgarian Olympic champion and world record holder of the 1970s, used a rounded back style in the pull, (although I do not know if it was intentional in his case). While I would not go so far as to recommend the use of a rounded back during the early stages of the pull (or at any other time while executing the classic lifts or related exercises—because I believe it exposes the athlete to an increased risk of a back injury) I must admit that the styles used by these men underscore the value of relaxing the muscles of the upper back during the early stages of the pull.

3. The balance of the lifter should be felt in the middle area of the foot. If the weight is felt toward the heels, it means that the overall position of the body in relation to the bar is too far towards the rear. This will almost invariably cause the lifter to have less control of the motion of the bar during the pull and to make the motion of the body and the bar less fluid. It is also likely to cause the lifter to sacrifice some ability to apply force to the bar.

If the weight and the lifter's balance is toward the front of the lifter's foot as the bar comes off the floor, there will be a tendency for the hips to rise faster than the shoulders as the bar travels towards the knees. The athlete may also be forced to jump forward to catch the bar as it travels in that overall direction during the pull. Added strain is placed on the knee and ankle joints bar if the bar is somewhat forward when it is "caught " by the lifter, and added strain is placed on the back when it is too far forward in the pull (the latter because the lifter is in an unfavorable mechanical position in which to exert force on the bar when the bar is unnecessarily forward of the lifter's body).

When the weight is too far back on the heels from the start, the center of the shoulder joint is behind the bar as the bar comes off the floor and/or the shoulders assume that position during the pull to the knees. In contrast, when the bar, and/or the athlete's balance, is too far forward as the bar leaves the platform, the shoulders move backward in relation to their starting position as the lifter reaches the end of the second phase of the pull.

The coach and lifter must be careful to distinguish between positions and feelings before the bar clears the platform and while it is being raised from the platform. It matters little where the balance is felt prior to the liftoff, as the lifter adjusts the position of his or her body and its relationship to the bar. What matters is where those positions, balance points and tensions are felt as force is being applied to take the bar off the floor.

Joe Mills (a national champion weightlifter in the 1930s and coach of hundreds, if not thousands, of lifters over the years including world champions) and I were so convinced of the importance of the starting position and the related position of the body during the first and second phase of the pull that we decided one year to conduct an informal experiment at the Philadelphia Open (in its day probably the premier annual open competition in the United States). We observed a lengthy series of lifts to see how accurately we could predict the outcome of snatches and cleans solely by observing the pull from the floor to the knees. We found that our predictions were accurate approximately two-thirds of the time. Perhaps we were just lucky that day, but I think not. The early stages of the pull are critical, and the first stage is the foundation for much of what follows.

The Importance of Gripping the Barbell Securely

The degree to which the subject of the grip is ignored in weightlifting circles is a continual source of amazement to me. In sports such a bowling, golf and baseball, sports in which no special grip strength is required, a proper grip seems to be discussed more widely. In weightlifting, where the grip is in direct contact with the projectile to be launched and the forces involved are so close to the lifter's maximum ability, little is said beyond "get a sure grip" or "always use the hook grip." Perhaps this is because most lifters feel, "I've never lost my grip so why make and issue out of it?" I would argue: do not assume that because you have never lost your grip, it has created no problems. We must remember that the subconscious mind is always aware of subtle changes in a lifter's body and the bar. If the grip is subconsciously felt to be loose, the nervous system will tend to reduce the force it applies to the bar to a point where the grip will not be lost. This reduction may not be noticeable to the lifter, but it can result in a significant decrease in the force that is applied to the bar. If lifters who are blessed with large hands and good grip strength find this argument unconvincing, they can skip the next section. For those who want to learn to maximize their gripping strength and confidence, please read on.

Before going on to the subject of assuring a secure grip, the reader should recognize that a secure grip is only important when the lifter is pulling. When the bar is supported overhead or at the shoulders, it is advisable to have all of the fingers securely around the bar, but the grip should not be tight. A tight grip while flipping a snatch overhead, racking a clean or driving a jerk overhead is a recipe for disaster. The speed that is so crucial during these stages of the lifts will be greatly hampered by any attempt on the part of the athlete to grip the bar tightly.

Techniques For Maximizing the Effectiveness of the Grip

There are several techniques for maximizing the force of your grip on the bar. One of the simplest and most direct methods is to strengthen the grip. This subject is covered in Chapter 5, but a few comments on the subject are in order. First, since the strength required of the lifter is that of isometrically gripping a bar, the best form of training for the grip is to do just that, to hold the bar isometrically. The lifter can practice holding with and without a hook grip for variety; the weights used should sometimes be ones which nearly cause the grip to loosen slightly. When the lifter does singles in the lifts and some pulls (at least during the first repetition or when doing singles), grip aids (such as straps) should not be used. However, when the lifter is performing repetition lifts or pulls, using "straps" (see Chapter 4 for a definition) is a good idea, particularly when these movements are being executed from the hang.

Since the strength of the grip is affected by the position of the arm (e.g., the grip is stronger with the arm bent than with the arm straight), there may be special circumstances in which bending the

arms in the pull might actually assist the lifter in holding onto the bar, if such bending can occur in such a way as not to adversely affect other aspects of the lifter's pulling style. This is very difficult to accomplish and is a complex technical issue, somewhat beyond the level of this book.

A special means of gripping the bar called a "hook" grip is perhaps the greatest method ever developed for improving a lifter's grip and is used by virtually every high caliber lifter. The technique of the hook consists of wrapping the thumb around the bar and then placing the first, second and third fingers of the hand around the thumb and the bar. Why is this technique so effective? I am aware of no scientific research on the subject, but several reasons can be discerned with some thought. First, the hook grip places the thumb (easily the strongest finger on the hand) in a better position to apply force to the bar than with the normal grip (fingers around the bar and thumb on top of the fingers going in the opposite direction). With the normal grip, the thumb is not in direct contact with the bar, and its only contribution to holding the bar is that of pressing on the index finger with the last joint of the thumb, a rather poor position for the thumb in terms of applying force. With a hook grip, nearly the entire thumb is in direct contact with the bar; more importantly, the first joint of the thumb (a joint which is directly connected and is in close proximity to the powerful pollicis muscles at the base of the thumb) is in contact with the bar, giving the thumb better leverage in applying their force. Another advantage of the hook grip is that while the thumb is in a stronger position, the other fingers press against the thumb while they are still in a good position to exert their strength (the second segment of the fingers presses against the thumb and bar— not the last, as is the case with the thumb when a normal grip is used). Finally, when the hook grip is used, the lifter is able to harness the force of friction more effectively than is possible with the conventional grip, since the normal friction between the thumb and the bar is augmented by the pressure of the fingers on the thumb.

In terms of applying the hook properly, there are several guidelines. However, these guidelines vary with the needs of the lifter. For example, for the small handed lifter, it is useful to spread the hand (i.e., to hold the fingers apart as much as possible) before gripping the bar. This stretches the skin and soft tissues of the hand and enables the lifter to assume a grip with the bar deeper into the hand, a more secure position overall (particularly for the lifter with a small hand). Another pointer for the small handed lifter is to begin the grip by pressing the spot between the thumb and forefinger deeply into the bar and then roll the hand until the rest of the fingers are gripping the bar, again, to get the bar deeper into the hand (perhaps enabling the thumb to contact an extra finger or to be in better contact with the same fingers). All lifters, regardless of the size of their hands, should employ the hook grip by wrapping the fingers snugly around the thumb and/or bar, with as many fingers covering the thumb as securely as possible.

Two final comments need to be made about the hook grip. One is that the lifter will experience considerable discomfort, even significant pain, when first using the grip. Usually, the peak of the pain occurs just after releasing the hook. The lifter may also notice a discoloration on the thumbs from minor internal as a consequence of the pressure of the bar and fingers against the thumb (i.e., a black and blue mark). In most cases, both the pain and any discoloration will pass, usually after a few weeks. The only residual effect will be a more secure grip. If the fingers develop a soreness that continues unabated from one workout to the next, the lifter should slow the breaking-in process. This is done by performing only some lifts with a hook or skipping a workout with the hook to allow the soreness of the fingers to abate. Many lifters find that wrapping surgical tape around the thumb before the workout lessens any irritation of the skin of the thumb as a result of hooking.

Another issue that is related to the hook is when to release the grip. Many lifters, perhaps the majority, automatically release the hook and assume a normal grip as the hands are turned from the palms-down position to the palms-up position during the squat under. Other lifters continue to maintain the grip until they replace the bar on the platform after the snatch. Almost all lifters jerk with a normal grip (which means they switch from the hook to the regular grip either during the hand turnover or during or after the recovery from the clean).

Fig.6

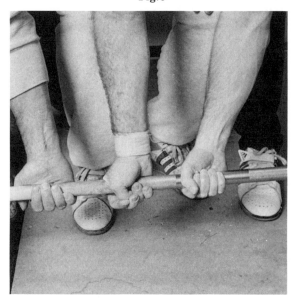

It should be noted that some lifters jerk with a "thumbless" grip. With the thumbless grip, the thumbs go around the bar in the same direction as the other fingers (instead of in the opposite direction as they do in the regular and hook grips). Advocates of this style feel that it makes their position stronger and more comfortable overhead. Most lifters do not notice any improvement with this style. Only personal experimentation will help a lifter to determine whether the thumbless grip is of any benefit. However, I do not recommend the thumbless grip, because it is far more likely for the bar to slip completely out of the hand (an extremely unlikely event with either a normal or thumbless grip but much more of a possibility with the latter grip). Fig. 6 depicts, from left to right, the thumbless, hook and regular grips.

Still another strategy for improving the grip is to increase the friction between the hand and the bar. The most common way of doing this is to use chalk (magnesium carbonate) on the hands. Magnesium carbonate dries the hands and considerably improves the grip. Another strategy is to remove oils from the hands with a skin drying agent before applying chalk. Special cleansers (such as "Pernox") used to treat oily skin conditions are available at any drug store and will serve this purpose well.

Finally, there is the strategy of growing the nails a little (particularly the thumbnail) so that at least 1/16 "of white area is visible. This gives the skin at the tips of the fingers something to push against when the they are compressed against the bar. In the case of the thumb, an even longer thumbnail presents a greater surface area for the fingers to press against when they are engaged in the hook grip. A better grip can be achieved in the area of the thumbnail by taking the sheen off the nail with fine sandpaper and then actually scoring the nail with coarse sandpaper.

How much can these techniques add to gripping strength? There has been no scientific study of this issue, but, as an experienced practitioner of all of the above techniques, I can assure you that they do work.

The Importance of the Position and Effort in the Final Explosion

Although the position of the body and the bar is crucial throughout the lift (particularly because an incorrect position in any part of the lift often creates a tendency to assume incorrect positions at later stages), the position just prior to the final explosion is perhaps the most crucial. If that position is off, it almost assures that difficulties will arise during the amortization and recovery phases. Therefore, both athlete and coach should devote a significant share of their attention to this issue. What is the correct position?

It is a position with the shoulders directly above the bar (not significantly in front of it or behind it, when viewed from the side): the arms straight or nearly so; the outside of the elbows turned to the side and not toward the back; the knees well bent (sometimes the athlete is beginning to rise on the toes as well); the back flat or arched; and the shoulders back but not yet shrugged upward (see the 3rd photo in the sequence in Figure 3): Ideally, the lifter's balance is toward the front of the full foot; if the lifter's balance is significantly toward the rear at this stage, the lifter will necessarily accelerate the bar in a rearward as well as an upward direction during the explosion. This wastes energy (a straighter bar trajectory is more efficient) and causes an excessive degree of bar motion that will be difficult to control when the bar is caught (i.e., excessive horizontal motion). As the lifter rises on the toes, shoulders, the base of the toes and the bar should line up vertically; mispositioning of the shoulders relative to the bar at this point reduces the ability of the athlete to exert maximal force and increases the likelihood that the bar will be directed further forward or backward than is optimal.

Regardless of whether the athlete pulls as quickly as possible during the entire pull or accelerates during the later phases, the lifter must make a special effort to apply a maximal explosive force to the bar at the beginning of the final explosion of the pull. This explosive effort serves to accelerate the bar, raising it and giving the athlete time to squat under the bar. Most lifters find it helpful to think of an explosive effort with the leg, hip and back extensors. Some coaches talk about "hitting" the bar with the traps at the last stage of the final explosion. Others talk of a jumping motion with the bar in the hands and an explosive shrug.

Many lifters think of making violent contact with the bar at the level of the thighs or hips at the finish of the pull; some lifers make such an effort to "hit" the bar explosively with the hips that they wear a pad over their pubic bone— arguably an illegal piece of equipment. While this works for some lifters, it has been my experience that significant contact with the thighs or hips can misdirect the bar, particularly when it is intentional. When the lifter is thinking of an explosive extension of the legs, hips and back, the noticeable contact of the bar against the lifter's body occurs as a result of the rapid extension. If the contact occurs as a result of a conscious effort to hit the bar with the body, the lifter has wasted valuable energy and attention on a horizontal rather than vertical motion. There is horizontal motion of the hips and back during the explosion phase of the pull, to be sure, but, it is much more beneficial when that motion is a result of an effort to explode upward than when the objective is to move the hips or thighs forward into the bar (or to move the bar back into the hips).

There are, however, exceptions to the preceding guidelines. Some lifters have a tendency to extend the trunk upward and backward, with their hips held in a stationary position during the final explosion of the pull. These lifters actually seem to freeze the position of the hips and to simply rotate the trunk around that fixed point. Clearly this can lead to a horizontal misdirection of the bar. For such lifters, the instruction to drive the hips forward at the finish of the pull will often lead to a correction of the problem caused by the rotation of the trunk around fixed hips and will result in the lifter effecting the proper combined contraction of the leg, trunk and hip extensors.

Explosiveness and following a proper sequence in the use of the athlete's muscles go hand in hand in making the final acceleration phase of the pull as effective as possible. This is because a lack of explosiveness or an improper sequence of muscle utilization will result in less than optimal acceleration. The proper sequence is legs and back together, followed by the calves and the muscles of the shoulder girdle (the arms are not really used at all during the acceleration phase of the pull). Although the combined action of the muscles of the shoulder girdle and the calves follows that of the legs, hips and torso, they do not wait until the action of the first set of muscles has ceased. Rather, the contraction of the calf and trapezius muscles begins while the legs and hips are finishing their effort, so that there is a continual application of force.

One final point should be made about the final explosion phase. From the 1950s through the 1970s, much discussion appeared in the weightlifting literature regarding the importance of fully stretching the body at the end of the final explosion phase of the pull. Athletes were pictured on their toes like ballerinas, with the legs fully locked—the more extreme the stretch the better. As more modern methods of technique analysis became available, research findings disclosed that the power developed by the lifter at the point before the legs were locked and the lifter rose high on the toes was primarily responsible for the ultimate height attained by the bar. The force applied by the lifter in the extended position was far less important. Moreover, it was discovered that many elite lifters did not lock their legs completely at the end of the final explosion. This failure to lock the legs meant that the lifter had a shorter distance to drop under the bar after the completion of the final explosion and it enabled them to drop faster (spared the time of unlocking the legs while squatting under). It has been rumored that Soviet researchers have also discovered that a snap of the legs to a completely straight position at the end of the final explosion causes the feet to be displaced in a rearward direction just after the final

44

explosion— still another reason to avoid the legs-locked position. This in no way means that the lifter should straighten the legs at the end of the final explosion stage; it merely means that being rigidly locked high on the toes may have negative consequences that offset any advantages of an extreme stretch of the body.

In view of the complexity of the above considerations, a specific lifter's approach to the body's position in the final extension needs to be worked out on the basis of individual needs and through experimentation.

Balance in the Squat Position

In most cases the accomplished lifter is very comfortable in the squat position. In the snatch, most lifters find that the best position for them has the bar in line with the back of the head and with the rearmost portion of the hips slightly behind the bar. The arms are straight and the lifter is pushing up on the arms and thinking of stretching the bar as well. In the clean the bar rests on the tops of the shoulders and the elbows point straight forward, with the upper arms held parallel to the floor. Regardless of how comfortable the lifter is in the bottom position, it is important to stand up from that position as quickly as possible. The lifter should remain in the bottom position of the squat only long enough to halt the bar's downward progress. If an adjustment needs to be made, it is better to make it in a partially recovered position (e.g., the lifter can step forward to move his or her base of support in that direction when the bar has traveled in front of that base and as the lifter sits in the bottom position). Driving up against the bar also gives the lifter more control over the motion of the bar than when the lifter merely sits passively in the bottom position.

A position with the feet wider than the hips provides for greater stability and generally makes it easier for the lifter to keep the torso upright and the lower back slightly arched than does a position with the feet narrower than hip width. The feet are generally best kept at an angle of 45° to 75° relative to one another (although some lifters find that a smaller of greater angle is more appropriate for them). The more upright the shins, the smaller the pressure on the knee joints, but the more difficult it is for the lifter to keep the torso upright and the lower back arched. A higher heel in the weightlifting shoe enables the lifter to assume a more upright position and to keep the lower back more arched than does a lower heel, but it tends to place more strain on the knees as the knees are pushed forward of the toes in the deep squat position. A higher heel also changes the lifter's balance to a forward direction during other phases of the pull and jerk. In addition, it shifts the lifter's knees forward to a greater extent at the start of the pull, which means that the lifter will have to move the knees further to remove them from the path of the bar as it rises upward. Therefore, it is an advantage if the lifter can achieve the flexibility necessary to in order to assume a more correct low position and lower his or her heels,.

An Alternative Means for Lowering the Body: The Split Style

Today virtually all lifters at an international or national level employ the squat style in the clean and snatch. This was not always the case. In the early years of weightlifting, the split style was the predominant method of lowering the body to catch a weight at arm's length or on the shoulders. Even as late as the 1950s there were more World Champion splitters than squatters, and many top lifters of the 1960s were splitters. (By the 1970s the style was almost extinct among international competitors, and it remains so today.)

Although the squat style was used by a number of notable lifters at least as early as the 1930s, the American lifting superstars, Pete George, David Sheppard and Paul Anderson, probably did more to convert the world to the squat style than any other influence: Pete George as a result of his great success with a relatively slight musculature and youthful appearance; Dave Sheppard because of his prolific recordbreaking and the sheer mastery and majesty of his technique; and Paul Anderson because he proved that even large and somewhat inflexible men could employ the squat style successfully. Before these great Americans, the squat style was viewed as too risky, too hit and miss and suited only to the few who were blessed with natural flexibility in the squat position.

As is so often the case when styles in weightlifting, or anything else, change, some very useful technologies fall into disuse or are actually lost in the process. This was certainly the case when the split style was abandoned. While it is true that the squat style is both easier to master and more efficient for the majority of lifters, the split style is still appropriate for some. It has the advantage of not requiring the flexibility of the shoulders, elbows and ankles that is required by squat style. Less rotational strain is typically experienced in the shoulder and elbow joints when a lifter uses the split style in the snatch and jerk. In addition, it requires less leg strength than the squat style, and it enables a lifter to execute the lowering of the body under the bar 30% to 50% faster than in the squat style. The time is reduced by one-third in the snatch and by approximately one-half in the clean (the bar is fixed at a somewhat higher position however). The split style also places less strain on the knee of the leg that is thrust back in the split than happens with the squat style. On the negative side, the split style tends to place more strain on at least some portions of the front leg and on the groin muscles of the rear

Fig. 7

leg than is placed on either leg in the squat style. There is also a tendency to twist the hips, with the hip on the side of the body of the forward leg being held higher than the hip on the side with the leg thrust backward. Finally, it is tougher for many lifters to master the split style because lowering the body into a deep split rapidly requires great precision with respect to foot placement.

When a lifter employs the split style, the pull is the same as in stages one through four of the squat style. A difference begins to show up during the unsupported squat under. (The Eastern Europeans refer to any lowering of the body in order to fix the bar on the shoulders or straight arms as a squat under, regardless of whether the athlete actually ends up in a split or squat position.). In the split style, instead of bending the legs while keeping the feet in contact with the platform and pulling with the arms, the athlete begins to move the back foot as soon as the legs have reached their fullest point of extension. Almost immediately thereafter, the front foot begins to move forward and the lifter is descending into the split position. In the split style the dividing line between the support and nonsupport phases is regarded by Soviet theorists as the point where the front foot lands on the platform (i.e., when both feet have made contact).

The front foot is placed approximately one and one-half foot-lengths forward, and the back leg goes back more than two foot lengths. (The actual spread of the feet will vary with the lifter, but the ratio between the movement forward and back is approximately 1:1.4, front leg movement to back.). In the split position the thigh of the front foot rests on the calf muscle, and the back leg is straight or nearly so, with the heel turned out (toes in) so that the foot is at approximately a 45° angle with the platform (when viewed from the side) and is resting

on all of the toes; the front foot should either point straight ahead or be turned in slightly. The bar should be vertically in line with the hip joints, with the torso upright and the back arched (see figures

Figure 7 depicts the low position of a split clean by one of the great masters of that style, two time Olympic champion Waldemar Baszonowski of Poland. For a picture of a similar position in the snatch see the photo at the beginning of Chapter 11 - a world record performed by the legendary Norbert Schemansky, winner of 4 medals in four separate Olympic Games (one gold, one silver and two bronze - the last at age 40).

In recovering from the split position, the lifter straightens the front leg while shifting the hips, torso and bar toward the back leg (i.e., the lifter is pushing back as well as up with the front leg). At the end of this motion, when the body has risen nearly as high as possible without moving the feet, the lifter (with the weight shifted toward the rear leg) slides the front foot back to a position approximating its starting position; when a deep split is used for the jerk, two backward steps may be needed. Then the back foot is brought forward to a position in line with the front foot. The only exception to this sequence might occur when the bar is forward of the lifter's hips when the lifter is in the full split position. In such a case the lifter might rise with the combined effort of both legs and then push off the back leg in order to run forward under the bar part way through the recovery. This is an act of desperation to save a lift, not a technique to be utilized under normal circumstances.

Guidelines for the Snatch

The Proper Position for Receiving the Bar in the Snatch

In the snatch, as was noted in the detailed analysis of snatch technique earlier in this chapter, the torso of the lifter typically assumes a nearly upright position while in the deep squat. However, in the snatch some lifters assume a position in which the body is inclined forward more than in the clean. This reduces the height to which the bar must be pulled relative to an upright position and tends to give the lifter a little greater ability to maintain his or her balance in a forward and backward direction while in the bottom position. An important factor in bar control in the full squat snatch is adequate rigidity in the arms and shoulders. Such rigidity is fostered by correct shoulder position and proper pressure against the bar. Most lifters will find that a strong support position is facilitated and stress on the elbow joint is minimized if the arms are rotated at the shoulders so that the crook of the elbows points somewhat forward and not directly upward while the lifter endeavors to bring the shoulder blades together. Proper tension in the arms and shoulders is essential both for controlling the bar and protecting the joints of the shoulders and elbows. If the muscles are relaxed, the bar can be dropped unnecessarily (even after it has achieved the proper bar height and speed for it to be caught by the lifter in the low position). If the lifter tries to extend the elbows too much or rotates the arms in too extreme a fashion, undue strain can be placed on the elbow and/or shoulder joints. The way to maintain proper tension is to think of pushing up on the bar somewhat with the arms and shoulders and to think of stretching the bar (pulling on it in a sideways direction). This simple act brings the arms, shoulders and trapezius muscles of the upper back into a well coordinated balance of tension. The result is that the pressure of the bar is distributed over more muscles and less stress is placed on any single area. If, despite the above advice, the lifter experiences undue strain in the elbows or shoulders, different relative tensions of the aforementioned muscle groups and positions involving greater or lesser rotation of the arms should be tried.

While proper positioning of the foot is an important prerequisite for receiving the weight of the bar effectively in the snatch, it is of even greater importance in the clean. This is because the bar weighs more and has fallen further by the time the lifter is able to catch it in the clean. Therefore, the subject of proper foot positioning in the squat position is covered in detail in the section on receiving the bar in the clean. When reading that section, it should be remembered that the same basic principles apply to the snatch as well as the clean, except that because standing up from the full squat position in the snatch rarely tests the leg strength of an athlete (but it often does so in the clean) the lifter can go lower in the snatch (e.g., using a wider foot stance and/or simply squatting lower) than he or she does in the clean.

Balance in and Recovery from the Squat Snatch

In recovering from the squat snatch, the lifter raises the hips up and somewhat back while permitting the shoulders to travel forward with the torso inclining forward. However, the direction of the bar is as vertical as possible throughout the process, because the line of gravity of the bar must remain within the middle of the lifter's feet in order for the lifter to maintain his or her balance. There is a tendency for the balance to shift from the middle of the foot towards the rear of the foot as the hips travel back during the recovery. Subsequently, the balance shifts in a forward direction as the extension of the legs progresses, but it always remains toward the center of the lifter's foot.

In his once pathbreaking book, <u>Secrets Of The Squat Snatch</u>, Larry Barnholth (a pioneer in teaching the squat style snatch and coach of Pete and Jim George) provided some very useful advice on recovering from the low position of the squat snatch. He advised the lifter to drive up out of the bottom position as quickly as possible after stopping the bar's downward progress—even before the lifter feels completely balanced. As was discussed earlier, he reasoned that a lifter would be far more likely to be able to save a lift from a partially recovered position than from the deep squat.

An additional point not mentioned by Barnholth was that by immediately pushing upward on the bar, the lifter exerts control over the bar by applying a force that influences its direction. I have witnessed many lifts in which athletes merely sat in the bottom position after essentially arresting the downward, but not horizontal, motion of the bar. The bar ultimately traveled outside the lifter's base of support and the lift was lost. Had the lifters continued to exert upward force against the bar, they would have had much better chances of gaining control.

Barnholth also recommended procedures for saving squat snatches that are quite correct but seldom discussed in today's literature. If the lifter feels the bar drifting backward, he or she should lower the head and torso, or at least maintain his or her position while raising the hips backward. If the bar is traveling forward, the lifter should lower the hips, raise the head and then immediately drive up from the squat. These reactions may feel unnatural, but so is turning into the direction of a skid when you lose control of an automobile. Nevertheless, these movements work.

Barnholth was saying in a non-technical way that once the bar and body are outside their base of support (in this case the middle of the lifter's foot), there is no chance to save the lift unless the lifter has risen high enough out of the squat position for the support (feet) to be moved under the bar quickly. Some lifters are so comfortable under the bar that they can move their feet while in the deep squat position, but this is an extremely rare ability, one which can lead to damage to the knees.

Guidelines for the Clean

The Proper Position for Receiving The Bar in the Clean

Raising the elbows high and with substantial speed (a movement known as "whipping the elbows") and landing with the torso, feet and knees in proper position are the keys to receiving force in the clean. The elbow whip helps to keep the upper body properly rigid .(This subject is covered in greater detail in a later section of this chapter.) Proper foot positioning consists of placing the feet so that the best combination of stability and strength is achieved. This will normally be a position with the feet at an angle between 30° and 60°, although some use an angle that is considerably longer or smaller with great success. The distance between the lifter's heels is typically between 10" and 18".

The correct foot position for a given athlete is one in which the lifter's lower back can remain arched, or at least relatively flat, and the upper body can be held upright (i.e., nearly perpendicular to the floor). Some lifters have no difficulty in achieving such a position with virtually any foot position. But for most lifters a wider stance and/or a greater angle between the feet help them to achieve an upright position of the torso with the back arched. A wider stance also lowers the lifter's center of gravity and provides the lifter with a wider base of support. These factors lead to a more efficient and stable receiving position.

If a wider foot position is so advantageous, why don't all lifters place their feet as wide as possible? The primary disadvantage of a wide foot position and/or a large angle between the feet is that this kind of position can place extra stress on the hip joints. This will be experienced by the lifter either as sort of an "unhinging" at the hips or as actual discomfort. The unhinging is somewhat difficult to describe, but the lifter feels as though all or most of the strain of the supporting effort is on the hip joint and the muscles, tendons and ligaments of the knees and ankles are under relatively little stress. Another sure sign is that the lifter feel a rotation of the femur in the hip joint during the early stages of rising from the squat position. Healthy hip joints play a major role in weightlifting success and in general human locomotion. It is extremely important to protect the hip joint from undue strain. Therefore, it is a good idea to place the feet wide enough to achieve as solid and upright torso position but no wider.

For the lifter who is extremely flexible, there is one other constraint on foot spacing. Such a lifter can find that with the feet in a wide position his or her hips actually travel well past the heels in the deep squat position, particularly when the bar is coming down with substantial force. This causes the lifter's lower back to lose its arch and generally places the lifter in a unstable position for receiving the weight of the bar. Placing the feet in a narrower position (one in which the lifter's buttocks touch the lifter's ankles in the deep squat position) will enable the lifter to control the bar more effectively.

As was suggested earlier, turning the feet outward (i.e., increasing the angle between the feet) tends to cause the lifter to spread the knees and to attain a more upright position and arched back with the same spacing between the heels. The correct knee position is generally directly over the foot; placing the knees too far outside the feet will

place a great strain on the hip joint and adductor muscles of the legs, and turning the knees too far inside the feet will tend to place a twisting kind of strain on the knee joints.

Apart from discomfort reported by the lifter, the clearest indicator of improper foot and leg positioning is lateral movement of the knees and/or feet when the bar is received by the lifter. The knees should be functioning essentially as a hinge when the bar is received by the lifter, and the feet should be flat on the platform. Lifters who are on their toes at any point during the supported squat under should be carefully observed in terms of foot positioning. There are several causes for the lifter being on his or her toes during the squat under, but the possibility of improper foot positioning should be ruled out. Lifters whose feet are supported on their inner edge of the foot (i.e., the outer edge of the foot is raised from the platform) while descending into the squat position or while receiving the force of the bar are almost certainly positioning their feet and legs improperly. Similarly, when the lifter's knees are seen to wobble while the bar is being received (when they move laterally in addition to merely bending), the lifter's positioning needs to be improved. Improvements in the lifter's receiving position can be achieved through conscious repositioning of the feet. If that fails to achieve a satisfactory result (it almost inevitably yields an improvement of some kind), attention needs to be paid to the lifter's flexibility and the height of the heel in the lifter's shoe.

Apart from body positioning, the key to receiving and controlling the force of the bar lies in the action of the legs. In the squat position the lifter's arms and torso play a relatively small role in stopping the downward progress of the bar. They must be held in a proper position so that they do not give when the bar is received, but their primary role is to transfer the force of the bar to the lifter's legs. The legs function like shock absorbers when the bar is being received. Therefore, the arms and torso should assume a rigid position as soon as possible during the squat under, and the legs should assume the crucial role of stopping the downward progress of the bar. The legs should begin to interact with the bar as soon as possible because every split second during which the bar has no support causes it to pick up downward speed and become more difficult to control. Nevertheless, if the lifter attempts to apply a braking force too vigorously or while he or she is in an unfavorable anatomical position, the muscle-tendon unit of the thighs will be subjected to unnecessary trauma, and the elastic qualities of those muscles will not be effectively utilized in assisting the lifter to recover from the low squat position.

In short, the lifter should use the legs early and actively to bring the bar under control but should then use a sort of natural rebound from the low position to assist in the lifter's recovery. No effort to stop short or even to significantly slow down the bar should be made unless the lifter is at or near his or her lowest position in the squat. At that point the knee, hip and ankle joints of the body and all of the muscle-tendon units that support them are being used in concert to stop the bar and to support one another (e.g., the pressure of the back of the thighs against the calves). If, in contrast, the lifter catches the bar with the thighs and calves at a near 90° angle and attempts to stop immediately, great and unnecessary stress will be placed almost exclusively on the muscle-tendon unit at the front of the thighs. In addition, while the lifter could have employed the elastic qualities of the quadriceps muscles to stand up from the squat position, he or she will be recovering from a dead stop.

The preceding discussion is not meant to suggest that he lifter "crashes" into the deep squat position at all times, offering little or not resistance to the bar. Each lifter will need to learn the proper balance of control and using the natural flow of the muscles in order to feel a relatively smooth receiving of the bar's force and an almost seamless transition into the recovery from the squat position.

Elbow "whip" (the rapid movement of the elbows from a position above the bar during the pull to a position for receiving the bar in the clean) is a very important element of receiving the bar effectively in the clean, and a number of aspects of it are often neglected when it is taught. If you are observing a lifter from his or her left side, elbow whip consists of a rapid clockwise turning of the elbows around the bar from a position above or just behind the bar to one in which the elbows are well forward of the bar, preferably so that the underside of the lifter's upper arm is at or near the nine o'clock position, or even above it (e.g., at ten o'clock). Coaches often talk about keeping the elbows over the bar during the later stages of the pull so that the bar will remain close to the body while the elbows are turned from the pull to the racking position on the chest. I have never been persuaded of the usefulness of this method of describing the motion of the arms to the lifter, because the elbows never bend while they are positioned over the bar in the pull for the clean (or the snatch for that matter). The arms do not bend until the lifter is descending under the bar, and at that point the elbows are behind the bar. Sometimes telling the lifter to keep the elbows over the bar will prevent a tendency to "reverse curl" the bar (i.e., keep the elbows at a fixed position near and in line with the torso and simply pull the bar to the shoulders with the arms), so this instruction is certainly worth a try. But it should be understood that this is what some lifters think, not what is actually occurring.

An approach that I have found to be much more effective in correcting a "reverse curl" kind of pull is one taught to me by Joe Mills. The Mills method was essentially to have the lifter run his or her thumbs along the front of the torso and to flip the hand over to a palms up position at the end. This movement is extremely simple and can be executed with great speed after very little practice. It teaches the lifter that the hands need not travel in front of the body (as compared with along it) in order for the hands and elbows to turn over quickly, although the elbows do necessarily go behind the bar during this process. Naturally the position cannot be precisely duplicated with the bar, because the bar will remain in front of the lifter to a certain extent. However, the lifter will quickly feel how close the bar could be and that the reverse curling motion is unnecessary and inappropriate.

With the bar, the lifter must concentrate on whipping the elbows fast and high (above the level of the shoulders if possible, to the same level at least). Most coaches and athletes understand that speed in the elbow whip is essential, so that the lifter keeps the elbows away from the knees while going under the bar and settling into the rack position. They recognize that in the clean a high elbow position in the squat helps the lifter to maintain an upright position, with the back (particularly the upper part) properly arched. Therefore, good coaching leads to assuming the correct position in the squat and to assuming it quickly. However, what is often overlooked by coaches is that the speed and force of the elbow whip are important in maximizing the lifter's speed in descending under the bar and therefore are of immense help in improving the efficiency of the lifter's clean. When a very forceful elbow whip is executed, it requires a powerful contraction of the shoulder muscles (which drives the elbows up). The elbows and shoulders create an equal and opposite downward force on the lifter's body, driving the body down under the bar. Dave Sheppard intuitively recognized this principle when he told me and many others over the years to "whip the elbows like mad." Dave had one of the fastest and greatest cleans in the sport of weightlifting, no doubt due in part to his commitment to elbow speed.

One last point on the subject of elbow whip: when a lifter has a shoulder width grip, thinking of pushing the elbows up is sufficient to get the elbows to a position of maximum height with maximum speed. However, when the grip is significantly wider than the shoulders, the lifter must think of pushing in as well as up with the elbows (i.e., think of pushing the elbows toward one another as well as up). This little trick, which was taught to me by a fine lifter named Mark Gilman, has enabled many who have tried a wide grip but have been unable to get the elbows up to master the elbow whip with a wide grip after a little practice.

Recovery from the Squat Clean

The recovery from a squat clean is quite different from the recovery from a squat snatch. First, the torso cannot lean forward as much and the hips cannot travel backward to anywhere near the same degree as in the snatch because the bar's final position rests on the torso at the shoulders (as compared with overhead in the snatch). In the snatch, if the shoulders travel forward and the hips back, the bar can still go straight up. In the clean, if the shoulders go forward, so does the bar, and the lifter will not be able to control it. Therefore, the hips and legs must go up more than back, with the hips having a greater ability to travel back than the shoulders to travel forward (with the lifter still maintaining control).

The limitations inherent in moving the shoulders and hips front and back while rising out of the clean prevent the body from assuming positions that are mechanically the most favorable for such a process. Compounding this problem is the fact that the bar is much heavier in the clean than the snatch (so it is harder to recover from the deep squat position). Moreover, once the lifter recovers from the low position in the snatch, the lift is more or less completed. After the clean, the lifter must perform the jerk.

While there is simply no substitute for strong legs in recovering from a clean, lifters have developed several strategies for making the recovery as easy as possible. First, lifters will lean forward and let the hips travel back to the greatest extent possible while maintaining control of the bar (not only the hips but the entire body and even the combined center of gravity of the bar and lifter can shift somewhat back in the most difficult point of the recovery). Some lifters also round the thoracic region of the spine somewhat to permit the legs to continue to extend without the bar rising because the torso shortens. (Some of these lifters drive the hips forward somewhat toward the end of this process so that the are in a more balanced position to finish the recovery.) Other lifters actually shift their pelvic region to one side while they are recovering from a clean. This rounding and shifting cannot be recommended because rounding places a great deal of strain on the spinal column and sideways shifting places a great strain on the knee joints and spine, but it can be marginally effective. A much better strategy, indeed the only safe strategy, is to strengthen the legs and to use both muscular and bar rebounds to aid in the recovery from the squat position.

It is well accepted in both the coaching and scientific communities that a muscle that is stretched to any extent before it is contracted contracts with greater force. On a practical level this means that an athlete can jump higher if he or she bends the legs and then immediately jumps than if the body is lowered to the starting position for the jump, the athlete pauses and then jumps. The same basic principle applies when an athlete recovers from the deep squat position. If the lifter recovers immediately upon reaching the full squat position, virtually rebounding in a controlled fashion from the bottom (i.e., maintaining control of the torso in an upright and arched position), the recovery will be stronger than if the athlete pauses in the full squat and then recovers. Therefore, the lifter should learn to catch all cleans as quickly as possible after lowering the body into the squat position and to recover as soon as the muscular rebound is felt. The only exception to the preceding rule would be a situation in which the lifter is off balance or otherwise not in control of the bar when the squat position is reached and he or she requires a moment to assure that position. There would be a loss of the elastic potential for muscle contraction with the pause, but that loss might be offset by the lifter's gaining greater control of the bar. Lifters who find themselves in this kind of situation sometimes find it helpful to drive the body up just slightly from the full squat and then to lower it smoothly to catch a muscular rebound and then to attempt the recovery.

Still another point to consider in the recovery from the squat is one that was made to me many years ago by Bob Bednarski, former World Champion, many time world record holder in both the 110 kg. and 110+ kg. classes and one of the greatest American lifters of all time. Bob, who was known for getting the maximum efficiency out of his leg strength, told me that he used to time his rebound from the low position in the squat with the flexing of the bar. Bob would wait until he felt the downward pressure of the bar peak and then would rebound up immediately. Since the maximum downward pressure would be felt at just about the time the bar reached its maximum bend, Bob was timing his upward muscular explosion so that it would work together with the elastic qualities of the bar to facilitate the recovery from the clean. This kind of bar reaction tends to be felt only with heavier weights and with more flexible bars.

One final note on the important point of recovering from the low position in the clean: leg strength, a good mechanical position, a muscular rebound and the spring of the bar can all be invaluable in facilitating the recovery from the clean. However, perhaps the most significant factor is applying volitional effort as one recovers from the squat. Concentrating on driving hard out of the squat and continuing that upward pressure until the weight of the bar is overcome is a critical element in recovering successfully. Even lifters with very strong legs can experience difficulty during the recovery stage of the clean if they don't apply sufficient volitional effort.

The Period Between the Recovery from the Clean and the Start of the Jerk

While considerable attention has been devoted in weightlifting literature to the clean and the jerk, little has been said about the period between the clean and the jerk. This is unfortunate, because the transitional moments and movements between the clean and the jerk often spell the difference between a successful jerk and an unsuccessful one. For purposes of this discussion, we will define this period as beginning immediately after the lifter has gotten through the hardest point in the recovery from the clean (but the legs are still well bent) and ending the moment before the dip for the jerk. Several mistakes are common during this period.

The first mistake is a mental one, and it consists of celebrating the successful completion of the clean, rather than focusing on the jerk that lies ahead. For lifters who tend to have trouble with their jerks relative to their cleans, the sooner they begin to focus on the jerk the better; they can begin to do so after the most difficult point in the recovery from the clean has been passed.

The next points to consider are the speed achieved and the force applied during the final part of the clean recovery. During a difficult recovery, the spine will often lose its arched position, the hands or elbows will assume a position that is not the most favorable for the jerk and the bar will slide slightly on the shoulders or will press on the windpipe, the nerves and/or large blood vessels in the neck, threatening the athlete's clearheaded performance in the jerk. All of these conditions can be corrected, at least in part, by driving the bar up with the legs at the end of the clean so that the bar leaves the shoulders very slightly. This slight thrust of the bar off the shoulders requires very little energy and momentarily leaves the body without the pressure of the bar. During this period, the arms and shoulders can be repositioned (the grip width changed if necessary), the spine can regain its arched position, pressure on the neck can be relieved and the bar can be caught again on the shoulders in the correct position from which to execute the jerk. The key to using this maneuver successfully is to drive the bar just high enough for the necessary corrections and/or preparation. Then the legs are bent very slightly to absorb the force of the bar as it contacts the body on its way down.

While this slight lifting of the bar off the shoulders after the clean can be a key element in preparing for the jerk, there are some hazards that must be avoided in executing this motion. First, if the bar is driven too far off the chest, the lifter will have wasted strength that could have been used for executing the jerk. Second, driving the bar up too much can cause the bar to crash on the lifter's body when it falls, causing a minor trauma and perhaps forcing parts of the body into positions that are unfavorable for executing the jerk. Therefore, it is necessary for each lifter to find just the right minimum height of the drive. For some few lifters that may be none at all, and for others it may be a couple of inches above the shoulders while in a standing position. For most lifters it will be to a position just above the shoulders when standing.

If any lifting of the bar from the shoulders is to be done before the jerk, it is advisable to do it at the end of the recovery from the clean and not after the recovery is complete (i.e., not after the legs are locked and the body has become motionless in preparation for the jerk). If the lifter becomes motionless after the clean and then rebends the legs to drive the bar off the shoulders and to assume a more comfortable position, the referees may consider this preparatory motion as an attempt at the jerk. There have been some very successful lifters who systematically rebend the legs after the clean to adjust the bar and then do a separate motion for the jerk without the referees questioning the maneuver (e.g., Mario Martinez, silver medalist in the 1984 Olympics). But those lifters usually have a reputation that is well known to the referees and perform such an adjustment after every clean. However, these lifters run the risk of losing the lift because a referee can interpret the lifter's motion as an attempt to jerk the bar (only one such attempt is permitted under the current rules). Therefore, it is better for the lifter to perform any adjustment at the last stage of the clean, when no disqualification is possible.

An additional point to consider in the transition from the clean to the jerk is the length of the time that the lifter should wait before beginning the jerk. Many coaches recommend that this wait be as brief as possible. A lifter who is not comfortable with the bar at the shoulders will certainly want to follow this advice and to move into the jerk as quickly as is reasonably possible (although a lifter who does not feel capable of holding the bar on the shoulders without undue fatigue should attempt to correct this problem). All things being equal, minimizing the time between the end of the clean and the beginning of the jerk is good advice. Unfortunately, as is so often the case, all things are not always equal. For example, some lifters can focus their concentration so that they are mentally prepared for the jerk immediately after the clean. While this is a desirable ability, not all lifters have it. For those who do not, it is important to take enough time to compose themselves after the clean and before the jerk. For those lifters who are very comfortable holding the bar on their shoulders, spending some extra seconds concentrating in preparation for the jerk presents no problem.

Another consideration is the spring of the bar that is experienced after the recovery from the clean. If the bar has a significant amount of spring, it may be flexing for some seconds after the clean. Most lifters will want to wait for this motion to cease before attempting to dip for the jerk (otherwise, the oscillation of the bar may negatively affect the precision of the dip). Moreover, the technical rules of lifting prohibit a lifter's using the oscillation of the bar to assist him or her in performing the jerk. This rule requires that the lifter wait for the bar to stop moving before the dip for the jerk begins, or at least that the lifter does not add to any movement that is already taking place as a result of recovering from the clean. With a springy bar the lifter will need to pause for at least several seconds between the clean and the jerk.

Now that we have examined some of the fundamentals of technique in the snatch and clean and what is to be done in preparation for the jerk, let us look at some important aspects of the execution of a successful jerk.

Guidelines for the Jerk

Maintaining a Stable and Balanced Position During the Dip and Thrust of the Jerk

When the lifter prepares for the dip and thrust of the jerk, it is important to address at least three key factors. First, the lifter should have the bar resting on the shoulders and clavicles as close to the neck as is possible, with the elbows raised as high as possible and without interfering with his or her breathing or putting pressure on the arteries of the neck (either of which can lead to a light head or even to blacking out). Using these three points of support (shoulders, clavicles and hands) provides for maximum control of the bar (although the clavicles are the least important support point and are avoided by some lifters who experience discomfort with such support). In such a position it is virtually impossible for the bar to move in relation its starting position as the dip and drive are performed. The lifter should also pull in or tuck in the chin, bringing it close to the neck; lifters who leave the chin forward may actually hit their chins with the bar but are more likely to push the bar forward during the drive, out of a subconscious desire to avoid hitting their chins or noses. During the dip the elbows should never move to a lower position than that in which they started; some lifters find it helpful to raise the elbows slightly as they dip to assure that the bar does not roll forward on the shoulders as the dip progresses. The hands, while providing some support to the bar, are not being pushed up forcefully against the bar with the arms but, rather, are being used as a mechanism to assure that the bar does not roll forward on the shoulders as the dip progresses.

The second key factor in preparing for a good jerk is the positioning of the torso. There are two important elements to such positioning. First, the torso should be kept absolutely vertical during the dip and thrust (except in the special style recommended by Nechepurenko, which is discussed below). Second, the torso must be positioned so that it can maintain a rigid position during the dip and thrust. This means that curvatures in the spine should be minimized and the torso should be held rigid by the entire muscular "corset" of abdominal, oblique and spinal muscles and by the action of raising and expanding the rib cage. These muscles need not consciously be held as tensely as possible, but they should have an athletic sort of tension, strong yet flexible and ready for movement. If the torso is felt to give during the dip or drive, the lifter will need to experiment with spinal curvatures and relative muscle tensions until a stable position is discovered.

The third key factor in preparing for a good dip and drive is the lifter's balance on the feet at the start of the dip. Since there is a tendency for the combined center of gravity of the lifter and bar to shift forward slightly during the dip, it is a good idea for the lifter to shift the weight of the body and bar toward the rear of the foot as the dip begins. In this way, even if a slight forward shift of the center of gravity occurs during the dip, there is some margin for error in terms of remaining over the lifter's balance point. Such a position also helps to keep the bar behind the lifter's head later in the jerk.

Another approach to assisting the lifter in maintaining proper balance during the dip and thrust was recommended by V. Nechepurenko of the Soviet Union in 1972. He advised the lifter to allow the torso to incline forward slightly and the hips to travel slightly rearward during the dip, while maintaining the lifter's balance over the feet. Then, during the beginning stages of the thrust, the torso is straightened and the hips are brought forward so that they are directly under the torso. While this technique requires a more complex set of actions from the body than the conventional dip, it has the advantage of helping some lifters to keep both the bar and their bodies balanced over the middle of the foot throughout the first four stages of the jerk. This technique can be especially helpful for lifters with relatively stiff ankles and/or sore knees and lifters who find it difficult to keep from inclining the torso forward during the dip for the jerk.

Maximizing the Upward Thrust During the Jerk

As in the explosion in the pull, it is important that the lifter achieve an explosive thrust during the jerk. Several factors influence the generation of such a thrust. One factor is leg strength. All other things being equal, the lifter with stronger legs will be able to drive the bar higher than a lifter with weaker legs. A second factor in generating upward thrust is the lifter's ability to reverse the direction of the downward motion of the bar during the dip; the more rapidly and powerfully the lifter is able to do this, the more force he or she will be able to generate during the upward thrust. A third major factor which influences the height to which the bar will rise is the elasticity of the bar itself. A more elastic (springy) bar can be used by the lifter to generate greater height in the thrust.

Interestingly, the one factor that will not help the lifter to generate greater jerk drive is to use the arms during the drive. Using arms will not generate significant additional upward thrust to the bar but, rather, will keep the lifter fixed against the platform when he or she should be splitting under the bar. Alternatively, it will tend to push the lifter backward and away from the bar, which will lead to the lifter's being backward and leaning back when the bar arrives at arms length—a disaster.

The Importance of Elbow Positioning in the Jerk

Several years into my lifting career I noticed that if I permitted the outside or rear portion of the elbow to point in a forward direction, I had less strength in supporting the bar than if I made sure the outside or rear of the elbow pointed to the side with the bar overhead. Years later, Naum Kelmansky, the coach of the Lost Battalion Hall weightlifting club in New York City, gave me a even more useful tip in this area. Naum was a very promising young lifter in the Ukraine, and later a high level coach in the Soviet Union, before he emigrated to the United States. He is one of the most knowledgeable Eastern European coaches that I have met and has many valuable insights about weightlifting, particularly with respect to technique.

Naum pointed out that a rotation of the elbow

beyond the point that I was using (so that the crook of the elbow is rotated somewhat forward) improves even further the strength of the overhead position. This is an especially important point for lifters who have poor arm lock or some other problem that makes holding the bar overhead difficult. Although attempting this kind of elbow positioning will normally result in the lifter's placing the bar further behind the head than he or she has heretofore, this is a bonus and is not as important for all lifters as is the elbow rotation. A number of lifters with poor elbow lock have found this tip to be invaluable. Figures 8 and 9 depict good and mediocre (respectively) elbow rotation.

The Proper Position for Receiving the Bar in the Split Jerk

The keys to a strong lock position in the jerk are similar to those for the snatch, except that the narrower arm position generally leads to less shoulder rotation and places less strain on the elbows. Nevertheless, the need to rotate the arms, to push up on the bar, to stretch the bar sideways and to pull the shoulder blades together is just as great. In fact, many lifters who have difficulty in locking the arms in the jerk could overcome their instability in that exercise simply by turning the crooks of their elbows forward more distinctly and pulling the shoulder blades together. For most lifters the resulting position will have the bar just over the back of the head or behind it. This position is not only powerful, but it also gives the lifter something of a margin of error.

If for some reason the lifter has difficulty getting the bar behind the head in a given attempt, the effort to get the bar there will at least place it directly above the head, where the lifter may have a chance to move the body under the bar and take

Figure 8

Fig. 9

control. If the lifter's normal position is with the bar just above the middle of the head or in front of it, any failure to get the bar into that position, even by a small margin, will make it difficult to get the bar under control.

It should be noted that there have been some famous and highly successful practitioners of styles which place the bar toward the front of the head. Bob Bednarski and Yuri Vardanian, both former World Champions and world record holders, jerked very successfully when they positioned the bar near the front of the head. They found this to be a strong and comfortable position and it saved time in getting into position under the bar. This is because the body does not have to travel as far under the bar while moving into the split with the bar forward position as it does when the upper body comes through and ends up under the bar. Most lifters are able to move the upper body under at the same time the rest of the split is taking place and so do not give up much in terms of time (and any loss of time is generally compensated for by having the bar in a safer position). Nevertheless, Bednarski, Vardanian and a number of others have demonstrated that an alternative position can be very effective.

In terms of stability in the torso in the jerk, the most important point is to keep the torso absolutely straight or inclined slightly forward. This position places minimal strain on the back and puts the lifter in a favorable position from which to adjust his or her balance. Any leaning back of the torso is to be avoided. Such a position is weak and unstable and subjects the spine to great stress. On occasion a high level lifter has emerged with a backward leaning of the torso in the jerk. Such a position does lower the torso and thereby permit the lifter to fix the weight at a lower position, allowing the lifter to hold the bar in front of the head. However, this position cannot be recommended because of the inconsistency it fosters (if the lean back is only slightly too great the torso will lose its rigidity and the lift will be lost) and because of the dangerous stress it places on the lower back; most lifters would be well advised to avoid lay back at any cost.

The keys to stability in the split position are: turning the feet inward slightly (or at least placing them parallel to one another), placing the feet at least at shoulder width and maintaining proper balance on the feet. Maintaining the feet in a position strictly parallel to one another or turning the feet inward slightly (i.e., to a slightly pigeon-toed position) assists the maintenance of balance and the safety of the split position in several ways. First, while in the split position, there is a tendency for the feet to be pulled in toward the body. Among the various muscles that are contracting in the legs in order to support the body while it is in the split position are those that pull the legs in toward the body (e.g., the adductors).

This inward pressure is placed toward the heel of each foot (which is where the legs connect with the feet via the ankles). Consequently, there is a tendency for the heels to be pulled in toward the body while friction keeps the toes where they are. The result is that the feet turn out.

The very act of the feet turning out causes the body to lose its balance and stability, making loss of control of the bar more likely. In addition, any significant turning out of the foot of the front leg places the knee of that leg in a very unstable position, putting great strain on the ligaments of the knee instead of the thigh muscles. When the back leg turns in, force is transmitted to the adductor muscles of the thigh and the ligaments of the knee instead of the quadriceps and hip flexors. The knee ligaments and adductor muscles are far less able to withstand pressure than the quads and hip flexors, so the chance of losing a lift and/or being injured in the process are greatly increased. The lifter is also better able to adjust the position of the body forward and back with the feet turned inward or at least held in a parallel position. A further advantage of assuming a slightly pigeon-toed position, or at least strictly straight foot position, is that the rear leg will tend to be balanced on all of its toes and the entire ball of the foot instead of primarily on the big toe and the portion of the ball of the foot that lies behind that toe. This position provides a much larger base of support and thereby improves the lifter's stability.

The Recovery from the Low Position in the Split Jerk

The recovery of the lifter from the low split position in the jerk is similar to the process described for the recovery from the low split position in the snatch described earlier; the lifter straightens the front leg while shifting the hips, torso and bar toward the back leg (i.e., the lifter is pushing back as well as up with the front leg). At the end of this motion, when the body has risen nearly as high as possible without moving the feet, the lifter (with the weight shifted toward the rear leg) slides or slightly lifts the front foot back to a position approximating its starting position. The back foot is then brought forward to a position in line with the front foot.

The Power Style of Jerking

The power style of jerking involves lowering the body into a partial squat during the fifth and sixth stages of the jerk (usually accompanied by a small sideways jump of the feet as well). While the split style in the jerk is acknowledged as offering the lifter greater stability and capacity to lower the body in the jerk than does a half squat, users of the power style of jerking have appeared periodically on the international platform over the past several decades. Paul Anderson used a modified push jerk during the 1950s. He merely drove the bar with his legs and then pressed it up quickly with his arms the rest of the way, never bothering to rebend his legs (today the technical rules are interpreted in such a way that a second bend of the legs is required). A. Nemessanyi, an Olympic medalist in the 1960s, V. Sots, a Soviet World Champion and world record holder in the C&J in the early 1980s, and two time Olympic Champions (both in 1992 and 1996) P. Dimas and A. Kakhiashvilis are among the most famous practitioners of the true power jerk style. Figure 10 illustrates the power jerk style as performed by Kakhiashvilis.

In analyzing V. Sots' technique in the power jerk, the Soviets found that he had a shorter braking phase in the dip, did not bend his knees as much as is normal in the dip and drove the bar a little longer as well. The bar dropped approximately 5 cm when Sots caught it in the half squat. Sots claimed to be better in the power jerk than the split jerk, hence his use of this style in competition. Since the sample of lifters doing the power style jerk in competition is so small, it is not possible to tell whether Sots' technique is typical of an athlete who would find the power jerk more effective or whether it is peculiar to Sots.

Fig. 10

One of the most consistent characteristics of the successful power jerker is shoulder mobility sufficient to permit the athlete to incline the torso forward and lower the hips to a receiving position that requires the power jerker to lift the bar no higher that the typical split jerker

While practicing the power jerk can develop the jerking power of most lifters, it can obviously be used by some lifters as their primary style of jerking. The fledgling lifter would be wise to remember the technical advantages of the split jerk and to master it. The lifters who use the power style successfully will continue to impress audiences with their superior strength. However, most audiences and competitors will be far more impressed by superior ability in the jerk, not by whether a lifter uses the power jerk style or the split style (and the official records of the competition do not indicate which style was used).

The Squat Style of Jerking

He Yingqiang of China registered an historic moment at the 1986 World Weightlifting Championships. He executed a successful jerk by lowering the body into a full squat position during the squat under. After the clean, which was performed with the normal slightly wider than shoulder width grip, He lowered his body into a full squat position to fix the bar overhead and then recovered from that full squat position without difficulty to complete the lift. Analysis of He's technique showed that he drove the bar only a little less high than the average lifter during his lift and really only needed to lower the body into a half squat position in order to catch the bar. However, when the lifter catches the bar with such a heavy weight and with the knees bent at such an angle, a combination of balance difficulties and mechanical weakness seems to require an extremely long amortization phase. As a result, He Yingqiang traveled all of the way into the full squat before recovering.

He's lift was interesting for several reasons. First, it proved beyond a shadow of a doubt that a full squat jerk could be successfully performed with top poundages. (He finished second overall and third in the jerk that day.) Second, it supported the contention that recovery from a deep squat position is assisted by the fore-aft movement of the shoulders and hips (a degree of movement that is not possible when the bar is resting on the shoulders instead of at arm's length). This point was made when He made a relatively difficult recovery from the squat clean and seconds later made a far easier recovery from the squat position in the jerk.

The reaction to He's style was varied. Some viewed the performance as essentially a one-time event, and others saw it as the kind of style that would someday become predominant. He's performance in the C&J remained at relatively the same level in subsequent years. Since that time a number of other world class athletes have employed the squat style in the jerk (perhaps most notably the 1996 Olympic Champion in the 70 kg. class, Zhan Xugang). Figure 11 depicts Zhan performing the squat style jerk.

Fig. 11

However, it generally takes a combination of technical superiority and outright superiority for a lifter's performance to motivate people to consider changing technique on a grand scale. While it seems very unlikely that the squat style jerk will ever emerge as the dominant style, it is a virtual certainty that before that could ever occur, more lifters will need to achieve a level of clear superiority using that style and it is probable that at least one lifter will have to achieve outright dominance it the jerk for this style to achieve true popularity).

Nevertheless, He and his successors have shown that another style is available in the jerk, at least for lifters who have special needs and abilities. He has offered us a clear demonstration of the point that there is still much room for technique innovation in the sport of weightlifting.

The Trade-Offs In Technique And Their Role In Individualization

Although there are obviously many basic principles that must be followed by all lifters to achieve optimal technique, there are also a number of judgments that every lifter must make about the technique that he or she will employ in the snatch and C&J on the basis of general weightlifting principles <u>and</u> his or her individual characteristics. It is easier to understand the need for these kinds

of choices regarding technique if we realize that many aspects of technique involve trade-offs. As an example, consider the trade-offs that exist with respect to selecting the width of you grip for the snatch. The wider the athlete grips the bar in the snatch, the higher the bar is lifted merely by the athlete's standing erect with the bar in his or her hands. As a result, less effort is needed in order to lift the bar to the required height from the point where the body reaches a straightened position (after which it is not possible to apply any significant amount of additional force to the bar). In addition, a wider grip in the snatch means that the bar does not have to be lifted as high with a narrower grip (the bar is closer to the top of the lifter's head and the trunk in the overhead position).

The advantages of a wider grip are offset by several disadvantages. First, the athlete will find it harder to lift the bar from the floor with a wider grip (because the torso must lean forward more and/or the legs must be bent to a greater degree to reach the bar). Second, it is generally harder for the athlete to hold onto the bar securely with a wider grip (unless the lifter's hand are actually in contact with the inside collars of the bar). Third, a wider grip can place more strain on the shoulder muscles, while the stress on the shoulder joint itself will be of different nature with a wide as opposed to a narrow grip (e.g., the shoulders are generally twisted more with a narrow grip).

Which grip is better? That depends on the interaction of these various aspects as they present themselves to a specific athlete at a specific stage of that athlete's development. The athlete must work to find the grip that incorporates the most and most significant advantages while presenting the fewest and least important disadvantages for that athlete. The trade-offs in technique variables must be weighed and properly balanced. To further illustrate this point, consider the issue of selecting a proper grip in the snatch in more detail. We will then examine other areas of technique which involve choices.

Selecting an Optimal Hand Spacing

Hand Spacing for the Snatch

Optimal hand spacing in the snatch is dependent on a number of factors, and, as stated earlier, there are trade-offs in the selection of a grip width. There are often "rules of thumb" given in various weightlifting manuals for selecting the width of the snatch grip. For example, one text suggests that the distance between the hands be equal to the distance between the lifter's elbows when they are held out to the sides at a position level with the shoulders. Such rules of thumb are of very limited value because they take into account only the length of the lifter's arms and the width of his or her trunk. They fail to consider an even more important relationship: the relationship between the length of the lifter's trunk and the length of his or her arms. A more precise measure has been suggested by a number of Eastern European writers. They recommend a grip width in which the angle of the arms in relation to the bar is between 49° and 63°. However, even such a measure does not take into account such factors as the length of the lifter's torso in relation to the arms.

One simple technique that does take this relationship into account is to have the lifter hold the bar with straight arms while pushing the chest out and pulling the shoulders back but not up. Next the lifter should bend forward slightly at the waist (with the back arched) and bend the thighs several inches. The lifter then adjusts the width of the grip so that the bar contacts the top of the thighs or the crease of the hips (the area where the most solid bar contact will occur during the pull of most lifters). However, even this is just a beginning point for selecting a grip width. The lifter should fine tune the width of the grip by considering and experimenting with the following factors.

1. Shoulder flexibility, strength and joint structure: A lifter with very flexible shoulders will be able to grip the bar comfortably at virtually any width (i.e., from shoulder width to a position in which the outside of the lifter's hands touch the inside collar of the bar). As a general rule, the narrower the grip in the snatch, the smaller the strain on the shoulder muscles. However, a narrower grip in the snatch tends to place more of a twisting force on the shoulder joint than does a wider one. On the other hand, a grip that is extremely wide places an enormous strain on the shoulder muscles and the shoulder joints when they are supporting the weight. Lifters who have snatch grips that are either very wide or very narrow have tended to have more shoulder problems than lifters with more moderate grip positions. When experimenting with grip width, it is essential that the lifter make any changes very gradually. This is particularly true of more experienced lifters who have been using a particular grip for some time. They are strong enough to lift very heavy weights and are conditioned to handle a certain grip width. Any significant change can result in an injury. I know at least one nationally ranked lifter who virtually ended his career as a result of a shoulder dislocation that occurred when (on the advice of a well known coach) he widened his grip significantly after many years of lifting and tried a near maximum weight shortly thereafter.

2. Elbow joint stability: The majority of lifters have arms that lock in a straight position when they straighten their arms to the greatest extent possible. However, some lifters are able to hyperextend their elbows (i.e., to have an angle between the forearm and upper arm, measured at the crook of the elbow, that is greater than 180°) and others cannot straighten their arms fully. The lifter with the hyperextended elbow will need to exercise care in finding the arm position in which the elbow is most stable when the bar is overhead. If the grip is too narrow and the shoulder is rotated too much, a shearing force can be placed on the ligaments of the elbow, exposing them to injury if the bar becomes mispositioned while it is supported overhead. If, on the other hand, the grip is too wide, the arm can be placed in a position where the ligaments of the elbow joint are put under a great direct strain, and that can expose the elbow joint to injury.

Another factor affecting elbow stability is the position of the elbow in relation to the ground when the bar is overhead. If the crook of the elbow is facing directly up to the ceiling, there is more direct strain placed on the elbow joint than if the crook of the elbow points forward and up. However, if the crook of the elbow is rotated too much (i.e., the crook points only forward, or even down), there can be sufficient shearing force on the elbow to expose it to danger.

Fortunately, few lifters ever have any elbow problems, and it is rare for an elbow to act up without warning (so any such warning should be heeded). Moreover, elbow problems can nearly always be eliminated with appropriate corrections in technique. The only exceptions to this are some lifters who have some anatomical lack of stability in the elbows or shoulders, such as a significant hyperextension of the elbow. Even these lifters are likely to be able to minimize their physical limitations with careful experimentation.

It should be noted that perhaps the greatest risk to elbow and shoulder integrity arises out of the movement of the bar and body as the weight is received in the overhead position rather than the position of the elbow alone. If the bar has a long distance to drop in the unsupported squat under phase, it will pick up more downward speed and will therefore place more of a strain on the elbows, the wrists and the shoulders when it is caught. In contrast, if the distance over which the bar is brought to a stop in the supported squat under is lengthened, there will be less force at any particular point and the strain on the elbows and shoulders will be minimized. Similarly, when the bar and lifter are moving horizontally, in opposite directions as the bar is caught (e.g., the shoulders of the lifter are moving well forward and the bar is moving backward), strain on the arms and shoulders is increased more than when the movements of the lifter's body and the bar are more vertical. Consequently, a large "swing" of the bar (i.e., a horizontal motion) and/or a significant movement of the torso forward when the lifter is executing the squat under place the lifter at greater risk. Grip width can affect the degree of relative horizontal motion of the body and bar, so the individual lifter will need to experiment to determine the best grip.

3. Thigh contact and pulling strength: In the snatch most lifters make thigh contact with the bar at a point that is approximately one-third to one-half of the way up the thigh from the knee. However, others do not have any contact until the bar is nearly at the top of the thighs. The bar loses contact with the body of some lifters about one-third from the top of the thigh, and others have solid contact until the bar reaches the height of the hips. Different lifters are more efficient with one approach or another (because of differences in the relative strength of their leg and back muscles and because of differences in the lengths of the body links and positions from lifter to lifter). Clearly, if the grip is so wide that the lifter does not contact the bar until it is above the level of the hips or the grip is so narrow that the bar contacts the thighs just above the knees and leaves the thighs before the bar reaches mid-thigh level, the lifter should at least try a more mainstream grip and body position.

4. Achieving a correct starting position in the pull: Some lifters will note that if the grip is too wide, they will have difficulty maintaining an arched back when they take the bar off the floor. Since a correct starting position is important, lifters who find themselves in this situation should either become more flexible or narrow the grip.

5. The height necessary in order to fix the bar: There is no question that the bar will not have to be lifted as high with a wide grip as with a narrower grip. All things being equal, a wider grip places the bar closer to the ground and to the lifter's body. This lower position also gives the lifter greater stability (a lower center of gravity yields greater stability).

6. Grip strength and hand size: Most lifters will find that the wider their grip, the more difficult it will be to hold onto the bar. With a wide grip the arms exert a horizontal as well as vertical force on the hands (in contrast with the more purely vertical pull against the fingers that occurs when the forearm is in line with the hand, as happens during the clean). This causes the outer fingers of the hand to open slightly and the forearm to be placed in a diagonal position relative to the hand. This position is somewhat less secure for holding the bar in the hand. The lifter with large hands will be less affected by this positioning because his or her fingers can grip the bar effectively even if they are opened slightly. The lifter with a small hands can experience a significant problem if the grip of the outer fingers is affected sufficiently. Naturally grip strength is also a factor, as the lifter with a surplus of grip strength will have little difficulty in holding onto the bar even if the hands are placed at a less favorable angle. Any hand position that results in the lifter losing his or her grip (or loosening it sufficiently to cause the lifter

to reduce the explosiveness of his or her pull) is too wide for the lifter at that point in time. The option is either to strengthen the grip or to move it in. The correct solution may be difficult to determine early in a lifting career as almost anyone can hold onto the bar with light weights (although even relative beginners may notice a grip problem stemming from the wide grip when doing reps).

Hand Spacing for the Clean

The common advice given to the beginning lifter with respect to grip width in the clean is that the grip should be "shoulder width." This generally means a grip that is wide enough to position the inside of the hand just outside the shoulders when the bar is resting on the lifter's shoulders. Individual grip widths vary from approximately 16" to 26" between the insides of the hands (with most lifters being between 17" and 22"), although there have been some international level lifters who have used grips that were even wider or narrower. Most lifters execute the clean and the jerk with the same grip width, but there have been some very successful lifters who have switched their grip widths after the clean, almost invariably widening the grip after the clean.

As noted earlier, a narrower grip (up to the point of being shoulder width) generally makes it easier for the lifter to start the bar from the floor. In general it also tends to make bar contact with the thighs and body steadier during the lift. Most lifters find it easier to place their elbows in a high position when they receive the weight on the shoulders in the clean with a narrower grip. A wider grip in the clean leads to greater difficulty for the lifter in taking the bar from the floor than does a narrower grip, but the bar is generally more easily lifted to a greater height with a wider grip. A wider grip will also force the lifter to lean forward at the torso during the pull to a greater extent than happens with a narrow grip. This places a greater strain on the muscles of the spine an the hip extensors, with the result that the lifter will have a greater tendency to shift the body further back toward the heels and perhaps to straighten the torso prematurely during the pull than he or she would with a narrow grip. This results in the lifter's pulling and jumping back. Most lifters find it somewhat more difficult to get the elbows up in the bottom position of the clean with a wide grip (a problem that can be overcome to a certain extent by pushing in as well as up when whipping the elbows (a tip I learned from a very analytical coach and lifter named Mark Gilman).

Hand Spacing for the Jerk

As indicated above, most lifters use the same grip for the clean as for the jerk (i.e., a width between the insides of the hands from 16" to 26", with most lifters using a grip in the 17" to 22" range). A narrow grip in the jerk places less strain on the muscles of the shoulders than does a wider grip and generally permits the athlete to thrust more forcefully with the arms in the later stages of the jerk. However, with a wider grip, the bar does not need to be lifted quite as high, and many lifters feel that with a wider grip they can both get the bar further behind their head and rotate their shoulders to a greater degree (a position considered to be more stable by many lifters). In addition, a wider grip generally enables the lifter to get his or her chest out while preparing for the jerk and to support the bar more solidly on the shoulders. As with other technique issues, the trade-offs between wider and narrower hand spacings will need to be considered and experimented with.

One final factor to consider in choosing a grip for the jerk is the grip that is used in the clean. While it is possible to move the grip between the clean and the jerk, doing so adds another variable to preparing for the jerk. It is a relatively easy to straighten the torso or to rearrange the position of the bar in relation to the neck after the clean. Rearranging the spacing of the hands is more difficult because each hand may move to a different degree, thereby creating an uneven grip. Therefore, where it is possible to select a grip that is relatively effective for both the clean and the jerk, that should be done.

Selecting an Optimal Foot Spacing

Foot Spacing for the Pull

Athletes will often ask about the correct foot stance for the pull. The answer given by most coaches is that the best stance is the one from which the athlete can jump the highest since, they argue, the final explosion in the pull is like a jump. There is a lot to be said for such advice. The final explosion in the pull is like a jump in many ways, and position that is functional for a jump may well be best for executing the final explosion in the pull. In addition, the jumping position (which is generally with the feet spaced at approximately at shoulders' width) permits the lifter to assume his or her full height when standing. In contrast, if the lifter stands with the feet wider, he or she will be slightly shorter. This will result in the bar being at a lower position than is usual when the lifter is performing the final explosion or assuming the extended position. Consequently, the bar will need to travel higher in relation to the position of the body with a stance that is wider than shoulders' width.

Despite the advantages of pulling with the feet in a jumping position, some lifters will find it hard to assume a correct starting position in the pull with the feet so placed. Their flexibility and body proportions may cause them to round their backs, to raise the hips faster than the shoulders, or to

make some other important error in the start of the pull If the trade-offs a lifter must make in order to keep his or her feet in a jumping position are too great, any advantages of such a position are overcome by the disadvantages. If a lifter has trouble finding a strong starting position in the pull, widening the stance and/or turning the toes out more than usual will often help. Something may be given up in the explosion, but that may be worth giving up in order to gain a correct and secure position at the start or in any of the first three phases of the pull. Only the coach and lifter can decide this, and it must be done case by case. The main point is that blind obedience to the generalities of technique can result in less than optimal performance for at least some athletes.

An Uncommon Foot Position for the Pull: The Frog-Leg Style

From the 1960's through the mid 1970's seven Japanese lifters set a total of 30 world snatch records. Two of those lifters, Yoshinobu Miyake and Masashi Ohuchi, astounded the weightlifting world with their prowess in the snatch: Miyake with eleven world records and Ohuchi by snatching a world record in the 82.5 kg. class weighing only a little above the 75 kg. class limit!. The Japanese lifters of this era used the "frog" style in the pull—the most distinctive characteristic of which is a starting position with the lifter's heels together and the toes and knees at an angle of approximately 75 degrees or more in relation to one another. In this position the hips are closer to the bar at the start of the pull than in the conventional style. Figure 12 illustrates the frog leg position in the snatch (the angle of the feet is normally greater in the snatch) than the clean).

Fig. 12

Most of the frog style lifters (Miyake in particular) started their pulls with their hips lower than was typical in their day. (Miyake's habit of sitting with his hips in a low position in preparation for the pull and then raising them as he applied force to lift the bar from the platform made the starting position of his hips appear to be even lower than it really was.) In addition, they held their torsos at a greater angle to the platform (i.e., in a more upright position) than did their contemporaries, who used a conventional pulling style. It was from this unusual starting position, which has some resemblance to the position in which a frog sits, that the style probably got its name.

From their starting position, most of the frog stylists drop their hips momentarily and then, while rebounding slightly from this low position, begin their pull (many froggers pull as hard as possible from the start, although there are some who pull more slowly). The combined weight of the bar and lifter is felt on the middle of the foot or even slightly forward of the middle. The Japanese frog stylists suggest that the angle of the back should remain the same during the pull from the floor to the knees and that the hips should move upward and not back. Once the bar has passed the knees, the hips are driven forward toward the bar. Advocates of the frog style generally recommend beginning the final explosion of the pull with the bar at or above the height of the middle of the thigh. They recognize that the foot position assumed during the first stage of the pull inhibits the forward drive of the hips during the final explosion but feel that there is an offsetting advantage in that the hips move more directly upward, yielding a straighter final pull. In addition, the froggers feel that because they begin their final explosions in the pull later than most lifters, the chance of "swing" (a horizontal as well as vertical movement of the bar) is reduced.

The Soviets studied the style during the 1970s and concluded that: a) it was suited for the peculiarities of the "oriental physique" more than the occidental; and b) the turned-out feet meant that the anterior/posterior balance point on the foot was smaller than in the conventional style, making the pull less stable and reducing the athlete's ability to use the back muscles properly during the pull. By the time this analysis was made, the Japanese lifters and their defenders had faded from the international scene, and the long dominance of the Eastern Europeans had begun. Just as the frog may have received too much attention when Miyake, Ohuchi and other Japanese were breaking records, it may have been too quickly dismissed once they departed the competitive platform.

Two criticisms of the Soviet analysis are apparent today. First, the analysis was primitive by today's standards. Therefore, any conclusions reached at that time bear some re-examination in a more modern era. After all, it was during this same period that many Soviet theorists predicted the "modern" (post-press) lifter would be leaner and more athletic in appearance than the lifters of earlier years. The days of the stocky little man were over, they said. (Fortunately, the great World and Olympic Champion, Naim Suleymanoglu, was either unaware of or unwilling to accept such a hypothesis). The linking of an "oriental" body type to the frog was a crude explanation even then. Any observer could have seen that Miyake's and Ohuchi's body types were quite different (as were the bodies of other Japanese lifters). Consequently, the effectiveness of the style was not related to one body "type," at least as defined by the analysts who made the claim.

Second, the arguments that the frog style is more precarious than the conventional style because of the athlete's foot position or that the back muscles can be used less while employing the frog style are a classic case of oversimplification. Such oversimplification arises out of the focus on one or two aspects of technique to the exclusion of all others. It is true that the athlete has a smaller base of support when pulling with the frog style, but the frog has advantages that tend to offset that disadvantage. Since the knees are spread wider in the frog style than in the conventional style, partly due to the foot position that is used in the frog style, the bar can pass the knees with less need for the knees to move backward and then forward. The result is that less fore-aft instability is produced during the pull, and the length of the transitional phase of the pull can be shortened. Hence the body is able to balance in a smaller area. In addition, since the back works differently in the frog than in the conventional style, the need for strength in the muscles that straighten the torso is diminished in the frog style.

The success of the Japanese lifters with the frog does not necessarily prove the efficacy of that style. Champion lifters can certainly be wrong about technique, and they often are. However, the frog style does have some special things to recommend it. First is the outstanding ability of the Japanese who mastered it. Beyond the famous ones, there are several reports of even more remarkable feats performed with the frog-leg style by less well known lifters, including cases of Japanese lifters who improved dramatically when they converted to the frog style from the conventional style.

There have been many success stories from American lifters who have tried the frog style as well. Eight-time United States national champion Mike Karchut had significant success with the style, as did Chuck Nootens, a former American record holder in the snatch. Former World Champion Joe Dube, who for many years struggled with a relatively poor snatch, became a multi-time American record holder and world class snatcher when he switched to the frog. On a more personal note, while hardly known as a great snatcher, I used both the frog and various more conventional styles during my career and was more consistent with the frog. Even if I abandoned the frog style for years at a time (which I did several times during my career), I was always able to snatch as much or more with the frog as with the conventional style on my first try (not a wise practice, but it did prove a point to me).

None of this is to say that everyone, or even anyone, should go out and master the frog tomorrow. Today's conventional style is well proven, likely to be better coached and probably better suited for most lifters. Instead, the evidence regarding the frog style suggests that the style may have been inappropriately dismissed and that at least some new research (focusing on more aspects of the lift than the balance on the feet) should be conducted. It is a style that clearly has value for at least some lifters. In addition, the story of the frog style offers us all a valuable lesson about style. All that can be known about style has not yet been learned, and some of what we have learned along the way may have been forgotten as fashions changed. Alternative techniques that are superior to anything that is used today may still be out there. Neither the coach nor the athlete should assume there is no need to think about or to experiment with new techniques. The science of weightlifting is still young.

Foot Spacing for the Jerk

Most lifters assume a foot position in the jerk that is similar to the one they use in the pull. The most common position is the so called "jumping" position, the same position that the lifter would assume in order to achieve a maximum standing-jump height (usually about the width of the hips with a minor turning out of the toes). This position may promote application of maximum force during the explosion phase of the jerk, but, in the jerk as in the pull, some lifters will find this position ineffective overall.

For example, in the jerk some lifters have a tendency to lean forward at the torso when they are dipping with a jumping stance. This can often be corrected by shortening the lifter's dip and asking the lifter to focus on a strictly vertical dip. Despite these efforts, the lifter may persist in dipping forward. In such a case, many lifters will find it easier to keep the back in an arched position and to dip straight with a wider and/or more turned-out foot position (particularly if the knees travel over the toes during the dip). If the lifter uses such a position, something may indeed be given up in terms of the power developed in the drive, but improved control over the direction of the drive may well make such a loss acceptable.

Optimizing Various Aspects of the Pull

Executing the Second Stage of the Pull with the Hips Low Versus High

Some lifters perform a portion of the first phase of the pull with their hips in a relatively low position (e.g., with the hips joints at, below or slightly above the level of the knees). Others prepare to lift the bar with their hips significantly higher than the knees. Observers of athletes who begin with their hips low often make the mistake of assuming that the lifter is actually lifting the bar from that position. In fact, the lifter with the low hip preparatory position typically moves his or her hips up considerably as force is applied to the bar, so that at the actual moment of liftoff the hips are well above the bar. In contrast, the lifter who sets his or her body with the hips high typically does not move the hips until the bar moves as well. Therefore, the lifter who executes stage one of the pull with the hips low may actually lift the bar from the platform with his or her hips in a higher position than the athlete who finishes the first stage of the pull with the hips higher; any argument that a lifter is starting with the hips too low is an incorrect one. While this point may obvious, it is often not easy to determine just where a lifter's hips are as the bar leaves the platform, even if the lifter's hips are moving slowly. In such a case, a little slow-motion film will prove to be enlightening.

Among lifters with sound technique, differences with respect to starting hip position have to do with anatomical differences. In assuming a correct starting position, different lifters will have their hips in different positions in relation to the bar. These differences are incidental from the standpoint of effective technique as long as the lifter's balance is over the middle area of the foot, the shoulders are held in a position directly over the bar , the shins are touching the bar, or nearly so, and the proper muscle tensions are maintained (e.g., the back is solidly locked into position).

Actually entering stage two of the pull with the hips low can be a problem if the hips are so low that: a) the weight of the athlete and bar combined are positioned toward the back of the foot as the bar is started from the platform; or b) the back, particularly the lower back, is rounded; or c) the shoulder joints are behind the bar. If one or more of these conditions exists, the bar will almost certainly be directed improperly during some or all of the rest of the lift (e.g., the bar may travel forward from its starting position instead of back during the early phases of the pull, or the bar may be misdirected rearward at later stages in the pull). This is unfortunate, since errors or this type are among the easiest ones for the lifter and coach to correct. The lifter need only be aware of where the weight is distributed on his or her foot to correct the first problem. Immediate feedback from the coach is needed to correct errors in back or shoulder positioning. They tend to arise simply from the athlete having no feedback on his or her position and failing to associate the feelings he or she is experiencing with faulty positioning.

One other issue with regard to hip positioning at the start of the actual liftoff has to do with the trade-off between hip position and torso angle. The lower the hips at the start of the pull, the more upright the torso will tend to be as the bar is lifted from the platform and during the balance of the lift. A more upright torso tends to reduce the strain that is placed on the torso muscles during the pull, but it also reduces the distance over which those muscles can operate to raise the bar.

Different Methods of Executing the First Phase of the Pull

Perhaps the majority of beginning and intermediate lifters begin to exert the force necessary to separate the bar from the platform from a stationary position. That is, these lifters carefully assure their starting positions while holding onto the bar, setting their position and then pausing before beginning to exert the force necessary to separate the bar from the platform. Since there is a high probability that as a will finish as he or she starts, it makes sense to start the bar very carefully.

Although care in positioning the body for the start of the pull is laudable, it is not the only consideration in finding an optimal starting technique. Offsetting the advantages of a start from a stationary position are two well known physiological principles. First, a muscle which is stretched before it is contracted will contract more forcefully than one that is not. Second, as the lifter "sits" in the starting position, the muscles of the hips, legs and back contract isometrically to support the body, which fatigues the muscles somewhat. (It is true that the muscle fibers involved in supporting the body in this position tend not to become easily fatigued and that they are assisted by other more rested fibers in lifting the bar; this phenomenon is explained in Appendix II, which discusses muscle physiology.) In order to minimize muscle fatigue, many lifters attempt to relax the leg, hip and/or back muscles just prior to exerting force against the bar. Some lifters simply sit in a fairly deep squat position with the hands on the bar and then straighten the back and legs to begin the contraction of those muscles, ultimately lifting the bar when the legs and torso have been raised to the position from which the lifter normally begins the liftoff. This style was particularly popular with the Bulgarians of the 1980s and is still used by many lifters today.

Other lifters get their bodies more or less positioned for the start of the pull, except that their hips are higher than their starting position. Then, just before they begin to pull, they lower the hips to the starting position and then start the pull. Some lifters even raise and lower the hips several times in a sort of pumping motion.

A very small number of lifters (including some of very high ability) use what is called a "dive" style. In this style, the lifter slowly lowers the body in a manner that is approximately the reverse of the pulling motion. As soon as the hands are in a position to grip the bar the athlete does so and begins the pull. In using the dive style, the lifter probably gains, in the most effective way possible, some of the advantages available to an athlete who pre-stretches the muscles of the body, but there is a trade-off in that the athlete does not have much time to set his or her grip or to be sure that the body is in just the right position to begin the pull.

Which technique is the best? That will depend on the lifter and the lift. The lifter who relies on a rapid pull from the floor to accelerate the bar will tend to benefit from some form of dynamic start that is between the extremes of the stationary start and dive style, and some may even find the dive style to be useful (this is more likely to be the case in the clean, where the acceleration in the second part of the pull tends to be smaller than in the snatch and the start from the floor more difficult). The dive will be most attractive for the athlete who pulls rapidly from the floor, can time the start of the pull correctly and has no trouble with a fast gripping of the bar.

A lifter who pulls relatively slowly from the floor and has trouble concentrating if the body is moving needs to be stationary before the pull begins; one who has trouble finding the correct starting position may be better served with a stationary position than a more dynamic one. A compromise position for a lifter who has trouble with a dynamic start is a static start that is held as briefly as possible. Whichever style is chosen, the method of the start tends not to be a "make or break" matter since most lifters rely more on the explosion that take place during phase four of the pull than the preliminary acceleration of phase two to get the bar to the necessary height with the required momentum, particularly in the snatch.

A Fast Versus a Slow Pull From the Floor

Lifting circles have probably debated the relative advantages of a slow and fast pull from the floor as long as there have been lifters, and that debate is likely to continue for many years to come. The controversy stems from the failure by each side to see the full arguments of the other side and to acknowledge that individual differences influence the value of each technique and that trade-offs in both styles tend to cancel each other out so that the issue is not one of "night and day." However, there are some relevant principles that should help each lifter and coach decide what is best for the individual lifter.

Physics tells us that the longer a net force is applied to an object, the greater will be the acceleration imparted to that object. Taken at face value, this principle suggests that a lifter should pull as long and as hard as possible in order to impart maximum acceleration to the bar (i.e., tear the bar off the floor with maximum force and continue to increase the force with each passing split second). However, before you reach such a conclusion, it is important to reexamine precise meaning of force as it applies to acceleration. Acceleration is a change in the speed of an object. Acceleration only occurs when an unbalanced force (a force that is greater than any other counterforces that it encounters, such as friction or an opposing force like gravity) acts on an object. When a force is applied in a way that only involves the movement of a single lever or series of levers in a given direction (such as a vertical jump of the drive in the jerk), the athlete need think only of applying maximum force to the ground throughout the movement . Since the object is traveling in a straight line, the only acceleration arises out of a change in the speed of the object.

In pulling a bar from the floor, the situation is different. The body does not simply straighten; first the legs straighten, then the back straightens and the legs rebend, then both the back and legs straighten. This is, needless to say, a very complex motion. Some lifters who attempt to move too fast, particularly when they are learning the motion, will tend to omit certain parts of necessary movement or to time their movements improperly (e.g., to straighten the torso prematurely). In addition, no matter how much acceleration the lifter achieves during the first part of the pull, a deceleration will occur during the amortization phase of the pull (i.e., the body will apply no net force). Then the application of force will resume during the final explosion. This is not because the lifter is not trying to apply force, but rather because some of that force is being used to reposition the body during the amortization phase of the pull. If a fast second stage of the pull leads to a greater reduction of speed during the adjustment phase, such a style is probably not very efficient for the lifter; the lifter either needs to move faster during the adjustment phase or to perform the second phase of the pull a little more slowly, so that the combined second and third phases of the pull are better coordinated.

One problem that often arises in connection with a fast pull as opposed to a slow pull from the floor (really an 80% to 90% effort versus an all out effort) is that when the lifter exerts maximum force during the first stage of the pull, there is a greater tendency for the athlete to lose the rigidity of his or her body links or the proper positioning of those links (e.g., for the spine to lose its arched position or the shoulders to be pulled forward or to contract the arms or traps prematurely). Another reason for not pulling with 100% effort during the second phase of the pull is that some athletes have a greater tendency to misdirect the movement of the body and the bar or to contract certain muscle groups when maximum force is applied as the bar leaves the platform prematurely than when the effort expended is more moderate during this stage. Still another reason for exerting less than maximum speed off the platform is that such an effort may fatigue the pulling muscles somewhat, thereby making them less able to exert maximum force during the crucial fourth phase of the pull. Finally, the joints of the body are at their most acute angles as the bar comes off the platform and thereby are most vulnerable to injury. Exploding off the platform places great stress on these joints at their weakest positions. Injuries from this kind of effort are rare, but if the explosive technique off the platform is applied over a period of many years, its effects may accumulate and eventually cause overuse injuries to the athlete.

Because a relatively greater weight is used in the clean than in the snatch, the effort that the lifter must exert during the second phase of the pull for the clean is greater than in the snatch. However, this does not necessarily translate into a proportional increase in the difficulties faced by the lifter during the second phase of the pull in the clean. Because the athlete grips the bar with the hands closer together in the clean than in the snatch, the lifter's torso tends to be in a somewhat more upright position and the legs are a little straighter in the starting position. This is a more favorable mechanical position for the athlete so the effort required is smaller than it would be if the athlete lifted the same weight with the snatch grip. Misdirection of the bar is also a little less of a problem in the clean as a heavier bar is harder to misdirect. However, it is more difficult to accelerate the bar in the clean, due both to the greater weight that is on the bar in the clean and the shorter distance that the lifter has to accomplish any acceleration. (A lesser degree of acceleration is acceptable because the athlete does not need to raise the bar as high in the clean as in the snatch.)

Given all the aforementioned considerations, it is generally preferable to exert a low to medium degree of force in the snatch during the second phase of the pull and then to exert maximum force during the fourth phase. In the clean, a medium or even greater effort in the second phase of the pull and then a maximum effort in the fourth phase are the most appropriate tempo for most lifters. Nevertheless, it should be noted that certain lifters make every effort to exert maximum force throughout the pull. Many of the Bulgarians appear to be doing this. Certainly there are many World Champions who seem to have pulled with a maximal effort all of the way.

Why are different tempos in the pull effective? One reason may be the bodily proportions of the lifter (e.g., athletes whose proportions enable them to apply force to bar for a longer period of time may be able to increase the force they apply more gradually than athletes who do not have the same ability). Another reason may lie in the trade-off between lifters who have a longer adjustment phase in the pull and those who have a shorter one; the former may lose so much speed during that phase that a rapid second phase of the pull is not very helpful overall. Still another reason may be that lifters have different compositions of muscle (e.g., fast twitch vs. slow twitch) and different abilities to activate those muscles explosively. A lifter who can reach a maximum level of force quickly may be better able to pull smoothly and then accelerate the bar suddenly. The lifter who does not have such a capacity may have to begin applying maximum effort earlier in order to achieve maximum force output at the desired stage in the pull.

All of these issues should be considered in determining the best style for a given lifter, at least at a given stage of his or her career. Often, experimentation is the only way for the lifter to determine what is best for him or her. If such experimentation suggests that a lifter can achieve maximum results with more than one tempo, the one that leads to the greatest consistency in performance and causes least strain on the joints is to be preferred.

Whether the lifter begins the pull slowly or as rapidly as possible, it must be remembered that several things should be occurring during the second phase of the pull. First, the knees joints straighten and go backward, out of the way of the bar. Second, the angle of the torso in relation to the floor should not change significantly during the second phase of the pull (the torso may straighten somewhat during the end of this stage). Third, the shoulders should move forward to a position in front of the bar as the second phase of the pull progresses. Fourth, the bar should move rearward toward the lifter's body from its initial position on the platform (this process continues during the third phase of the pull).

Degree of Leg Bend During the Adjustment Phase of the Pull

There are two different schools of thought regarding the amount of rebend that a lifter should achieve during the adjustment stage of the pull. Some authors argue that the smaller the rebend, the less time and speed the lifter will lose in the transition from the second to fourth stages of the pull (the two stages during which the greatest force

is exerted on the bar). Others argue that deeper the rebend, the greater the lifter's ability to exert force during the fourth stage of the pull.

Both arguments have merit. Obviously the lifter who achieves significant bar speed during the second stage of the pull and not much greater speed during the fourth will want to maintain as much speed as possible during the adjustment stage (i.e., use a lesser knee bend). On the other hand, the lifter who relies of the fourth stage of the pull to impart most of the force to the bar will want to achieve the most functional position from which to create maximum force (i.e., to achieve a relatively greater knee bend). Some experimentation with both styles is generally useful.

One principle that applies to either style is that the adjustment phase should be conducted as quickly as possible. It is generally desirable to retain as much of the bar speed achieved during the second stage of the pull as possible. A faster adjustment will enable the lifter to move the body as much as possible while the bar is in a relatively weightless stage (i.e., the body can move freely while momentum continues to keep the bar rising) and a rapid rebending of the knees will activate the elastic properties of the leg extensors, fostering a more powerful final explosion in the pull. (See Appendix II for further details.)

There are a number of weightlifting analysts who believe that the degree of leg bend achieved by the lifter during the adjustment stage of the pull cannot be influenced by the coach or athlete. Indeed, it has been argued that the rebending of the knees that occurs during the second stage of the pull cannot be taught at all! I find such a position untenable for several reasons. First, if a rebending of the knees could not be taught, it would follow that any lifter who does not automatically generate such a rebending ought to give up any hope of a weightlifting career. In reality, many lifters who do not rebend their knees when they first begin to lift ultimately learn to do so. Second, I know at least one elite level lifter, Cal Schake, who learned to consciously modify the degree of his knee bend in the pull after having lifted for many years. Moreover, Cal points to that modification (in his case increasing the degree of leg rebending) as one of the key reasons for his becoming the first American ever to snatch double his weight. Third, why would the knee bend during the pull be so unique a movement that it could not taught?

In reality, the coach who says that the knee bend during the adjustment stage cannot be taught or the lifter who says that it cannot be learned simply does not know how to make the knee bend happen. In fairness to such coaches and lifters, that knee bend can be quite difficult to learn and to teach. A lifter who consciously focuses on rebending the legs faces two difficult challenges:

achieving the correct rebent position and doing so quickly enough so that the overall rhythm of the pull is not broken. While the lifter can learn to do both these things on a conscious level and then automate the process with enough practice, there is an easier way for most lifters to achieve the same end. That method is related to the modification of other aspects of the lifter's technique that are likely to be causing the lack of or the improper rebending of the knees.

The failure of a lifter to achieve a proper second bending of the knees most often stems from one or more of several causes. One of the most common is improper balance on the foot before and during the adjustment stage. Another common cause of a less than optimal knee bend is the improper positioning of the lifter's torso relative to the legs during the second and third phases of the pull. For example, if the lifter begins to straighten his or her torso prematurely during the pull <u>and</u> shifts his or her weight too far rearward, that lifter will be unlikely to drive the knees forward and under the bar properly during the adjustment phase. Similarly, the more upright the lifter's torso during the second stage of the pull, the smaller the displacement of the torso when it is straightened and the smaller the rebending of the knees.

One final common cause of a failure to properly rebend the knees during the third stage of the pull is improper timing during that stage. If the lifter attempts to slow or stop the pull in order to reposition the knees, the bar will tend to stop or even to fall. This is illegal; the rules of weightlifting do not permit the lifter to stop the upward progress or to lower the bar during the execution of the pull. It is also inefficient, as any upward momentum of the bar is lost during such a transition. The lifter is much better served if the movement of the knees under the bar is a part of the overall flow of the pulling movement.

If a lifter corrects these flaws, the knee bend is likely to be improved. To summarize, the keys to a proper knee bend are: a) proper positioning of the shoulders relative to the bar at the completion of the second stage of the pull (shoulders forward of the bar and shins nearly vertical and proper balance on the feet); and b) a well timed and explosive effort to straighten the torso. Some lifters achieve the best result in the latter respect by thinking about raising the torso upward and, somewhat backward. Others achieve a better result by thinking of driving the hips toward the bar. Whatever the case, the focus on straightening the torso and bringing the hips closer to the bar causes the legs to bend and the knee to move forward and under the bar, because the same muscles that extend the hip joint also cause the legs to bend. (See the section on two joint muscles in Appendix II for a further explanation of this concept.) By applying these methods and without a conscious effort to bend the knees in a certain way, the proper bending of the knees can be "learned." Nevertheless, some lifters who are having difficulty in this area may need to think consciously of rebending the knees, at least for a time, in order to achieve the optimal motion in this aspect of the pull. They should not be discouraged by those who say that the second knee bend cannot be learned. Every lifter can learn it; it is merely a question of selecting the proper means for the learning process to occur.

Other Common Style Variations in the Early Phases of Pulling

Lifters vary significantly with respect to certain fundamental aspects of their starting position other than those already mentioned. For example, most lifters begin the pull with the bar over the juncture of the toes and the ball of the foot. However, many athletes place the bar in front of the base of the toes at the start of the pull (though never altogether in front of the toes), and others place the bar over the ball of the foot, behind the toes.

When the bar is placed further away from the body than the base of the metatarsals, it will travel toward the lifter to greater extent during the early stages of the pull than when the bar begins directly over the metatarsals. The distance of this additional movement toward the lifter approximates the added distance between the lifter and the bar at the start of the pull (e.g., if the bar is 1" in front of the base of the metatarsals at the beginning of the pull, the bar will travel an additional inch toward the lifter during the second stage of the pull). Its movement during the later phases of the pull will be similar to the pattern of movement that occurs when the bar starts in a more conventional position.

When the bar is placed behind the base of the toes at the start, it will tend to shift toward the athlete to a lesser extent, by an amount approximately twice the distance that the athlete's feet are placed forward of the conventional position in the start; e.g., if the base of the metatarsals is 1" forward of the bar, and the bar would normally have traveled 4" toward the lifter during the early stages of the pull, it will now travel only 2" toward the lifter. If the bar is brought still closer to the lifter, it may actually travel away from the lifter during the early stages of the pull. Placing the bar too close to the lifter at the start will also require the lifter to lean back more than is usual during the explosion phase of the pull in order to keep the bar moving in a vertical path. If the placement of the bar is very extreme in terms of placement behind the base of the metatarsals, the bar may actually travel forward at the end of the pull.

Another common variation in pulling style among lifters involves differences in the angles assumed by the major joints of the body at various phases in the pull. What are the reasons for these differences? The Eastern Europeans often refer to three basic body types in their literature, and they have identified certain technique characteristics which they feel are correlated with those physique types. The mesomorphic type is considered "normal." An athlete with longer limbs and a shorter torso is generally referred to as the dolichomorphic type. The third type is the brachimorphic, characterized by shorter than average limbs and a longer than average torso.

An example of the kinds of technical differences that exist among lifters with different body types occurs in the starting position. In this position, lifters with shorter legs and longer torsos tend to hold their torsos more upright and to bend the legs more at the start. However, when starting positions vary because of physical characteristics (as compared with technical mistakes), the differences among the positions athletes assume tend to be minimized during the middle stages of the pull (there are differences in the squat position, just as there are in the starting position). Differences that are created by technical errors are not ironed out during the middle stages of the pull. In some cases, the differences grow smaller but in others they grow even larger than they were at the outset.

Naturally, there are an infinite number of variations that extend within and across these fundamental types. All of these major differences in technique and body proportions and many smaller ones can lead to variation in the overall pattern of movement that lifters generate during the lifts.

Some analysts have argued that lifters who are mechanically better suited than the average lifter to use the back in the pull (this could be the result of stronger back and hip muscles, a shorter back or both) will tend to have a greater than normal incline in the torso (i.e., a smaller angle relative to the platform) during much of the pull. As a result, the bar will be lower in relation to the platform than is normal, at least through the second phase of the pull and perhaps later. This results in the lifter being able to exert force over a longer distance in subsequent stages of the pull. However, this is only an advantage if the lifter is not too fatigued to exert force over the entire distance or is not in a mechanical position that lessens the amount of force that can actually be applied, an unlikely set of conditions.

Similarly, some analysts have argued that lifters who have legs that are mechanically better suited than average to lift the bar tend to begin the pull with the torso more upright than normal and to straighten it earlier during the pull than is normal. This results in the height of the bar being greater in relation to the platform than is normal prior to the final acceleration so that the lifter can exert the force during the final acceleration over a

shorter distance than is normal. There is also an tendency for the lifter with a more upright torso to straighten the torso faster than the legs during the explosion phase and therefore to generate excessive lean-back at the finish of the pull, with the result that the bar is pulled backward from its starting point on the platform. Roman has suggested that when the bar travels up to 3 cm forward or 5 cm behind the base of the metatarsals after the final explosion has been executed, the bar will end up in an area that is controllable by the athlete. (These distances are guidelines for the athlete of average height; taller athletes have larger tolerances and shorter athletes have smaller ones.) Horizontal movement beyond that point will make it difficult for the athlete to control the bar during the squat under. While this would seem to be a disadvantage, there are some very good lifters who lift in this manner. Therefore, there may be some compensating mechanisms that overcome, at least to some extent, the disadvantage of a shorter distance to accelerate the bar. (For example, since the bar is already higher, it needs to be accelerated less to reach its ultimate height, or the body is in a stronger mechanical position for the shorter explosion than it is for a longer one so that the shorter duration is compensated for by a greater force generation over that shorter distance.)

Jumping Forward or Backward When Receiving the Bar

For many years there has been discussion in weightlifting literature about whether the lifter should jump forward, jump back or simply jump down when performing the squat under in the squat style. Most lifters simply place the feet sideways relative to their position or jump them back slightly during the pull when they perform the squat under. However, some great champions have either jumped forward an inch or two or backward to even a greater extent while the feet are being replaced. A few lifters have even placed the feet closer in the squat position than during the pull (though this is extremely rare and is generally a mistake). The Soviet analysts tend to encourage only moderate forward or backward motion of the feet during the unsupported phase of the squat under, while some Bulgarian theorists believe that a significant backward displacement of the feet is appropriate because they believe that the bar is displaced rearward during a proper execution of the pull.

As a general rule, the less the degree of forward or backward floor movement, the better. Most lifters will experience inconsistency if they move the feet too far forward or backward during the squat under. Moreover, the perceived need to jump forward or backward generally results from a fault during the pull, a fault which causes the weight of the body to be shifted too far towards the front or rear. Every effort should be made to correct such errors. However, in the end, if proper pulling mechanics are employed, the need to place the feet forward or backward relative to their initial position is an individual matter. The key, as Dave Sheppard told me many years ago, is to "go wherever the bar is." If the lifter needs to jump forward or back somewhat in order to receive the bar in a balanced position, then that is what must be done and done appropriately and consistently.

Optimizing Various Aspects of the Jerk

A Long Versus a Short Dip In The Jerk

The dip for the jerk is essentially a preparatory motion for imparting maximum vertical velocity to the bar. It is much like the bend in the knees that an athlete makes when he or she prepares to make a vertical jump, and therefore the same essential principles apply to both motions. The preparatory bending of the legs accomplishes a number of things. First, it lowers the center of gravity of the jumper's body (or the combined center of gravity of the lifter and the bar). This creates a distance over which the jumper or lifter can apply force and achieve acceleration. All things being equal, the longer the jumper/lifter can generate force, the greater the velocity achieved by the time the jumper or lifter loses contact with the ground.

In addition to the benefit of achieving a longer distance for and time of acceleration, a longer dip of the legs tends to increase the activation of the elastic properties of muscle tissue. When a muscle is made to contract in an eccentric manner immediately before it contracts concentrically, that muscle will contract with greater force than if it had not received the preliminary external force. Up to a point, a greater external force will elicit a greater eccentric contraction and hence greater subsequent concentric contractile force. Therefore, the preparatory bending of the legs both positions the legs so that a maximum duration of acceleration can take place and "charges" the muscles with elastic energy so that the upward thrust will be greater than if the athlete had started from a dead stop.

Taken to their ultimate extreme, the preceding formulations imply that the greatest possible jumping height can be generated by dropping into a full squat position with maximum force and then jumping up. Clearly a drop into a full squat can both provide maximum stimulation of the downward force against the muscles that will subsequently contract and give the legs an opportunity to accelerate the body and bar over the greatest distance. Not surprisingly, the deep squat position is not the best method of achieving a maximum jumping height (or thrusting height in

the jerk). This is because offsetting factors begin to overcome the advantages of a longer period of thrust and a greater elastic muscle "charge."

One problem with too long a dip is that while muscles can only achieve maximal contractile force if they are given sufficient time to do so; after a certain period of time the force of muscle contraction begins to diminish as a result of fatigue. Therefore, there is an optimum time of muscle contraction, and after that period force diminishes rather than grows. Another problem is that as the legs bend ever further in preparation for a jump or jerk drive, the amount of force required to straighten the legs increases, placing the muscles at a disadvantage. Still another problem is that as the depth of the bend grows, the extent of the movement of various joints increases, which tends to destabilize the pattern of movement and make it more difficult to maintain balance and control as the upward thrust is performed. Finally, greater downward force generated in the dip also means greater effort is required to reverse the direction of the bar.

Given these considerations, the depth of the dip will vary somewhat with the strength of a lifter's muscles, his or her body proportions and the style he or she uses to perform the drive (e.g., the speed of the dip and the speed with which the downward force is reversed). A faster dip and reversal can elicit the elastic properties of the leg muscles as much as a slower but deeper dip and reversal of the downward motion of the dip. For most lifters this depth will range from 8% to 12% of the lifter's height.

Unlocking the Knees in Preparation for the Dip

The rules of weightlifting generally require that the athlete straighten his or her legs fully at the conclusion of the clean. Many lifters begin the dip from this position (i.e., with the legs straight). Other lifters and coaches believe that the knees should be unlocked slightly before the dip for the jerk commences. They argue that doing this makes the dip smoother and straighter that when the lifter first unlocks the knees while dipping.

The advantage of the locked leg position is that it minimizes the development of fatigue in the quadriceps while the lifter is preparing for the dip. For a lifter who takes some time in preparation for the dip, maintaining a straight leg position can be very important (at least until just before the lifter begins the dip proper). For most lifters this is a minor issue, and either approach will work. For those lifters who are having trouble controlling their dips, it is probably a good idea to experiment with both styles and to adopt the one that is most successful.

A Fast Versus A Slow Dip in the Jerk

The speed of the dip in the jerk is another area of variation among lifters. As noted above in the discussion of the dip, a faster dip will create a greater elastic contraction in the leg muscles and therefore facilitate the generation of a greater upward force. However, it is also true that, carried beyond a certain point, a fast dip will create so much downward acceleration that the muscles will actually become fatigued from the effort of stopping the downward motion of the bar, lessening the ability of the legs to generate an upward thrust. Carried to an extreme, the lifter may actually lose control of the bar if the downward speed used in the dip is too great. This can result from inadequate muscle strength, n inability to effectively coordinate the motion or loss of balance. In addition, if the lifter dips too fast, he or she can lose contact with the bar by opening a gap between the body and the bar. As a result, the bar and body will collide at some point; because the body and bar are not in contact, the collision can result in the lifter and bar traveling in different directions after contact is made. There will also be a loss of upward thrust energy; these are not desirable effects, to say the least. Even if there is no deflection of the bar and body during a collision, timing and the process of developing maximum thrust can be thrown off. Therefore, the correct balance, in terms of the depth of the dip, must be found so that the elastic properties of the muscles are activated to their maximum extent while the lifter maintains control.

One additional factor that affects the determination of the optimal speed of the dip is the elastic properties of the bar itself. When a lifter dips his or her legs, he or she is effectively removing the support of the legs from the upper part of the body and the bar, allowing both objects to fall. When the lifter applies leg force once again to stop the fall, the upper body stops almost immediately, causing it, in effect, to collide with the bar. The collision occurs at the center of the bar, a point some distance from the bulk of the weight of that bar. Since the bar is constructed of a material with elastic properties (steel), the plates will continue to travel downward after the bar collides with the body, and the bar will convert the kinetic energy expended by the plates during their fall into elastic energy in the bar. Once the kinetic energy of the plates has been absorbed, the bar will release elastic energy in order to return to a straight position, driving the plates upward (and ultimately imparting more elastic energy to the bar, which is released as the bar begins to slow somewhat in its vertical rise). If this upward rebound of the plates is timed correctly and occurs at the correct position in the drive, it can help the lifter to raise the center of gravity of the bar to a height sufficient for the lifter to fix the bar overhead. If the rebound is permitted to occur too early, the bar will have a chance to spring back down on the lifter before he or she has assumed a strong position in which to catch the bar. All other things aside, a shorter stopping time will therefore elicit the greatest elastic properties of both the bar and the muscles of the leg.

Consequently, the optimal depth of the dip, the optimal speed of the dip and the speed with which the downward motion of the bar is reversed are all interrelated. If two dips are executed with the same downward acceleration, the longer dip will have a greater terminal speed. This will generate a greater elastic response in the muscles and the bar. Of course, it will also place a greater force on the muscles that must stop the descent of the bar and place the joints of the leg in a weaker mechanical position from which to stop the downward acceleration of the bar and to reverse that direction. Therefore, the faster the dip, the less depth is required to activate the same elastic properties of the legs and bar and the stronger position the legs will be in order to overcome the downward force of the bar. (A faster switchover from the dip to the explosion will also more vigorously activate the elastic properties of the leg muscles.) However, a shorter dip will give the leg muscles a shorter period in which to accelerate the bar upward. A deeper dip will give the lifter a longer period during which upward acceleration can be accomplished.

Therefore, the lifter is always better off dipping as long and as fast as is possible and reversing the direction of the dip as rapidly as possible. However, all three things cannot be achieved at once. The lifter dipping deeper will need to dip more slowly and will not be able to reverse direction as quickly, but will be able to exert muscular force on the bar over a longer period of time. The shallower dipper will be able to dip more quickly and stop more rapidly, but will not be able to exert muscular force on the bar for as long a period of time. The lifter should also be aware that regardless of the length and speed of the dip, it must be straight up and down, and the lifter's body must not sag or give in any other way as he or she reverses direction from the dip to the drive upward.

Each lifter must find his or her own balance of speed, depth and amount of time reversing the downward direction of the bar in the jerk. Regardless of the speed, depth and reversal time of the dip, the lifter must be careful to remain on the flat foot until the latter stages of the final explosion (i.e., from the start of the dip to the point where the lifter has nearly straightened the legs once again). Going on the toes too early can preclude a thrust of maximum power and make the lifter subject to a loss of balance arising out of a smaller base of support. Using the arms prematurely can cause the bar to separate from the shoulders during the dip or thrust or to push the lifter down against the platform before a full split position has been assumed. With respect to what the lifter thinks about during the dip, Roman advises that a slight resistance by the leg muscles during the dip will provide a correct downward speed for most lifters, while Vorobyev suggests that the lifter attempt to apply no resistance at all and simply let the bar fall to the appropriate depth. While these are starting points t may be helpful for the majority of lifters, the process must be individualized for each lifter.

When to Terminate the Jerk Drive

There are a number of issues to consider when determining when the active thrusting of the lifter against the bar should be completed and when the movement into the squat under should begin in the jerk. All things (e.g., launching speed) being equal, the higher the bar is when force ceases to be applied to it, the greater height the bar will ultimately achieve. Therefore, if the lifter could achieve an identical launching speed with the legs bent at an angle of 150° or standing on the toes, it would be to the lifter's advantage to release the bar while on the toes. The bar would then travel higher, and the lifter would not have to lower the body as much to catch the bar in the jerk. As a practical matter, this is simply not the case, since the lifter applies maximum force with the thigh extensors and not the gastrocnemius muscle (the muscle that is primarily responsible for extending the foot when the body rises on the toes).

Offsetting the consideration of the height of the bar is the consideration of how quickly the lifter can move from the extended position in the final explosion to the necessary split or squat position. If the position on toes leads to the lifter's taking longer to get into the split, it might offset any advantages that could accrue from a higher absolute drive. A longer time getting into the split leads to a greater bar drop. This means both that some of the added height advantage could be lost because the bar will descend from the highest point it has reached before it can be caught and that the bar will take longer to control because it will have had time to build up a greater downward speed than if its descent had been arrested earlier. Therefore, the decision about where to terminate the drive must be balanced on three considerations: a) the means by which maximum bar speed can be achieved; , b) the height of the bar at release; and c) the time it takes to get into position to catch the bar from the position at which the drive has been completed. Most lifters stay with the drive too long. Significant additional force cannot be applied once the thighs have reached a nearly straightened position. Lifters who extend the body much further than this are wasting valuable time which could be better used to move under the bar. The telltale sign of this is the lifter driving the bar to a relatively high position but then catching the bar on bent arms with the feet positioned in a relatively narrow split. This has occurred because the lifter has wasted valuable time in the drive, time that contributed little to the upward progress of the bar and that could have been used to reposition the feet and body under the bar.

The Depth of the Split Position

The depth of the squat or split position should be based on several considerations. There are at least two advantages to assuming a lower position. First, the lower the split, the less height the lifter will need to achieve in the drive in order to get the bar overhead. Second, a lower position is actually more stable than a higher one (see Appendix 2 for an explanation of this concept). Offsetting the stability and efficiency of a lower center of gravity is the fact that a lower split generally places the body in a weaker anatomical position than a higher split position and can make it more difficult for the body to stop the downward progress of the bar. In addition, a lower position takes longer to assume. This gives the bar more time to accelerate in a downward direction, placing more stress on the joints (and making it more difficult to stop the downward movement of the bar). Some analysts have argued that placing the front foot further out in the split it indicates that the lifter is using the legs more energetically and so is indicative of better technique. While this argument is worth considering, there are other reasons for the front foot being placed well forward of its starting position (e.g., as compensation for a forward dip), reasons which suggest that it cannot be used in isolation as in indicator of effective technique. One final point for the lifter to keep in mind is that he or she should distribute more of his or her weight on the front foot than ton he back in the split. The back foot offers considerable support and stability to the overall position but is clearly subservient to the front foot in terms of supporting the bar and body.

Summary

In this chapter, I have spent a great deal of time explaining weightlifting technique and its importance. An analysis of technique, guides to good technique and explanations of many of the trade-offs that exist with regard to technique have been presented. If you have studied the chapter carefully, you now have a better conceptual understanding of technique than do many athletes and coaches who have been involved with the sport for many years. But reading about technique does not substitute for practical knowledge. That can come only from practicing it and teaching it: the focus of the next chapter.

One of the greatest lifters of all time, 3 time Olympic Champion Naim Suleymanoglu's technique is virtually perfect for his body type.

CHAPTER 2

Teaching And Learning Weightlifting Technique

In this chapter, we will focus on how to teach, learn and evaluate technique. But before we address the practical aspects of teaching and learning technique, it is useful to establish a foundation for that discussion through the presentation of some basic principles of human motor control and motor learning theory. The first part of this chapter contains such a discussion. The second section deals with practical issues in teaching and learning technique. The last section focuses on the evaluation and correction of technique errors and on the process of optimizing technique.

Basic Concepts Of Human Motor Control And Motor Learning Theory

Motor control is the way in which we control our movements, using our neuromuscular and skeletal systems. Motor learning is the acquisition of the skills of physical movement through practice; it refers to relatively permanent increases in a person's ability to respond and is therefore not directly observable while it is taking place. This is contrasted with motor performance, which is the pattern of movement that is achieved in a specific moment, without considering an ability to reproduce that movement effectively. Motor performance can be enhanced through a variety of techniques, but the permanent ability to reproduce such a performance (i.e., motor learning) may actually be hindered by those very same techniques. The way in which we control and learn to control our bodies has been the subject of a great deal of research over the last several decades. While there is still much that we do not understand about how we control movement and how we acquire our motor skills, much of what we have learned can be directly applied by coaches and athletes to the teaching and learning of weightlifting technique.

The Stages of Motor Learning

Anyone mastering a new skill progresses through three stages of motor learning: cognitive, associative and autonomous. The cognitive stage involves gaining an understanding of what is to be done, how it is to be done and how some early approaches to the skill will be attempted. During this phase performance gains are dramatic, but performance is also erratic. The associative phase involves determining the best way of performing the task in question via subtle adjustments in performance. By the time the learner has reached the autonomous stage, the skill has become automatic. Performance is consistent and the skill is so well learned that other kinds of processing can often take place while that task in being performed. It is believed that as a skill is mastered, fewer and fewer abilities are used to produce the skill. The mind and body become more proficient at performing the skill with fewer and fewer mental and physical resources; from the vantage point of the nervous system, the task has gotten simpler.

It is now thought that unskilled performers use different abilities than skilled performers. For example, when learners were exposed to a complex task, it was found that the learners who were believed to have a good level of sensitivity to spatial orientation performed better during early trials. However, later in the skill development process, it was discovered that learners who had a better native ability to sense tensions applied to their body performed better. Therefore, early performance apparently relied more on a sense of spatial orientation and later performance relied more on a sense of the tensions that the body was experiencing. This suggests that even the results of a test that is thought to test "pure" athletic ability, like the vertical jump, might be influenced by differences in the previous practice of related skills by the subjects and that ample practice before testing would increase the likelihood that the test would be a good predictor of performance. In addition, early success in performing a skill does not assure that true mastery will occur at a more rapid rate.

The Stages of the Motor Control Process

Most motor activities take place in several stages. First a stimulus (i.e., something that provokes a reaction) presents itself. Next the stimulus is identified. Then, we select a response. Finally, we direct the response. There are two important qualifiers to this sequence. One is that if we initiate an action (like deciding to lift a bar), the first two stages are bypassed and we only select and direct the action. The second qualifier is that some or all of the stages may take place on a subconscious level. In fact, in most movements, at least one stage is subconscious.

The current evidence on motor control suggests that when skillful performers are executing many movements as an apparently single action, they have really learned to string separate actions together into what the mind conceives of as one action (as compared with the novice who sees several actions taking place in sequence). This is not unlike the difference between a novice chess player, who can only remember the position of a few chess pieces at a time, and the grand master, who may be able to retain the positions of all of the pieces placed on several different chess boards at the same time. There is no evidence that the advanced chess player's neurological capabilities—or those of the skilled athlete— are any greater than those of novices in the same field. Rather, the chess master sees the placement of the pieces as one, or perhaps a few, patterns, while the beginner sees each piece's position separately.

During the learning process, actions that will ultimately be performed on a subconscious or automated level often require conscious attention. In order to properly direct conscious attention during the learning stage, it is important to understand that there is a lag or "response time", between the time one perceives the need to act (i.e., senses a stimulus), selects an action and executes that action.

The Lengths of the Various Response Phases

Scientific study has enabled us to understand the length of the stages of the motor control process under varying conditions. For example, the clarity and intensity of a stimulus affect identification time (the greater the clarity and intensity of the stimulus, the shorter the reaction time). The time required to choose a response is influenced by the number of alternatives from which the responder can select and how "natural" the stimulus and response are to each other (e.g., it might take longer for a person to begin writing a nonsense syllable after hearing a gunshot than to begin running). Response direction time is greater when a the reaction called for is more complex or longer in duration.

It appears that when a stimulus presents itself, the mind has a "window" of approximately one-twentieth of a second in which to absorb all stimuli. That is, if a stimulus to which a person will respond presents itself, there will be a period of approximately 50 milliseconds (msecs) during which the person can notice other stimuli and consider them in the response). After that period the mind begins to process the information received for a period of approximately one-fifth of a second. During that processing period, reaction to a new stimulus cannot take place. Reaction time to a stimulus can be lengthened when someone is either physically or mentally occupied doing something else, so concentration is critical when reaction time is a factor in performance. Anticipation can shorten this reaction time because you can plan for a response and then execute it more efficiently. This is particularly true when the periods preceding a called for reaction are short. In such situations, these periods can be used as a technique "cue," and the response time can almost be eliminated. Under cued conditions, reaction times can drop to as low as 120 msecs.

The implications of reaction time for weightlifters are numerous, but perhaps the most important relates to what the lifter is told to focus on at various stages in the lift. It is not uncommon for a coach to describe what actually happens during a lift and then to expect the lifter to think about that sequence while performing it. A common example is what occurs when some coaches teach the jerk. These coaches instruct the lifter to drive the bar to the top of the head in the jerk and then to split. The most obvious problem with such an instruction is that while the bar does reach or approach such a height during the execution of the jerk, the skilled lifter begins to move into the receiving position while the bar is between the level of the shoulders and the chin. If the lifter waits until the bar reaches the top of his or her head before splitting, the bar will be falling before the lifter can get into position. A more subtle problem arises out of the limitations placed on the lifter by reaction time. Although the typical lifter is actually moving into the split when the bar is at throat level, if he or she waits until the bar is felt to reach that level, actual movement into the split will be delayed by two-tenths of a second, and the timing of the lifter's movement will thereby be inappropriate. The lifter needs to think of splitting earlier in the movement, so that his or her body has time to react and execute the movement into the split at the correct moment. Failure to account for reaction time is a major and common coaching mistake.

The Mechanisms of Motor Control

There are a number of physical mechanisms that assist in the control of movement. The eyes assist the body in understanding its position (some of this understanding occurs on a subconscious level), and the vestibular apparatus of the inner ear gives feedback on the position of the head. At one time it was thought that groups of nerves housed in the joint (called joint receptors) gave the body information on the joint's position. However, it is now believed that these receptors are probably best at sensing only extreme ranges of joint motion and that they must work in concert with other sensory capabilities in order to give the body useful information on the positions of its joints. In contrast, the golgi tendon organs, which are located at the junction of the muscle and tendon, were once thought only to serve as protectors of the muscles and tendons from overexertion. Now it is believed that they are also sensitive to low levels of tension in the muscles and that they therefore assist in motor control operations that are unrelated to maximal efforts. It is known that the muscle spindles (small combination of muscle and nervous tissue that lie between the muscle fibers of major muscles) are responsible for the stretch reflex, and it is believed that they also have a role in sensing limb position and velocity. Finally, the skin is sensitive to pressure, so it can provide vital information with respect to movement and forces as well. The combination of all of these systems assists in bodily control. Sensitivity to the body and its movements is called kinesthesis or proprioception.

Early motor control theorists hypothesized that the body controlled its movement on the basis of the feedback it received about the body's position. Now it is generally accepted that only slower and more deliberate movements are performed in this way. Faster movements are probably controlled by combinations of reflexive and conscious actions. The faster reactions are reflexive in nature. (These range in time from 30 msecs to 80 msecs; actions in the lower end of this range involve the spine and actions in the higher end of this range involve the brain as well.) Reaction times between 80 msecs and the standard 200 have been observed, and, as a result, some theorists have posited the existence of another category of reactions that they refer to as "triggered reactions." These reactions, believed to occur when there is only one alternative, are characterized by restructured, coordinated actions of the same or closely related musculature and typically take from 80 msecs to as long as 200 msecs. In terms of length of reaction time, the next actions are those for which there is some degree of anticipation, and these range in duration from 120 msecs to 200 msecs. As was indicated earlier, where there is no appreciable degree of anticipation, reaction time returns to 200 msecs.

Research in the area of motor control has discovered that performance decreases, but does not completely, collapse without feedback. Therefore, feedback alone (regardless of the nature and speed of that mechanism) cannot be the controlling method of movement. Although the mechanism through which motor programs operate is not well understood, it is at least known that something other than normal unrehearsed movement is in operation. It is also known that some generalization in terms of motor learning must be occurring; otherwise the body could not make novel moves smoothly as it does when reactions are quick (such as when running down the field in soccer or counterpunching in boxing).

An athletic activity like weightlifting probably involves all or nearly all of the preceding variations of feedback based motor control. Some movements that lifters make utilize reflexive actions (such as when the elastic properties of muscles are employed). Other motions probably involve triggered and/or anticipated reactions arising out of practice and the similarity in tempo that lifters experience in performing a relatively constant or "closed" skill. More normal reaction times are used to adjust to situations in which the weight is not where the lifter expects it to be, which is probably the reason that an observer notes the bar being out of position in relation to the lifter and wonders why it is taking the lifter so long to adjust (even though that period involves only a fraction of a second). An example of this situation occurs when the lifter catches the bar in a full squat snatch position and it is slightly forward of the point at which the lifter can sustain balance but is still in a position that permits the lifter to modify his or her position slightly and thereby to save the lift. Unfortunately, there is a delay (the reaction time) before the lifter notices this problem, and often, by the time the lifter can respond, the bar has moved even further out of position, with the consequence that the lifter cannot regain control and misses the lift.

Despite the use of feedback controlled movements in weightlifting, it is also likely that because the activity involves complex and rapid movement patterns that cannot possibly be controlled consciously, or even at a reflexive level, motor programs are relied upon heavily. These motor programs (learned patterns of movement) have the advantage of overcoming the slowness of processing information during conscious control of movement, but they cannot be stopped once started. Creating, refining and automating motor programs are what skill development seems to be all about.

The Relationship Between Speed, Force and the Accuracy of Motor Control

It was once accepted as a fundamental law of human motion that the more complex a movement, the more slowly it must be performed; conversely, the faster it is performed, the less accurate it will be. While generally true, this theory has been modified on the basis of further study. For example, recent research has suggested that faster movements are more consistent in terms of timing when movement time is shorter, although they are not necessarily spatially more accurate. Consequently, going faster will not necessarily hamper technique as it is often assumed to do.

Research has also shown that accuracy is sacrificed as the amount of force required to execute a certain motion is increased (e.g., it is less difficult to control the motion of a basketball than a medicine ball, because less force is required to launch the basketball). However, the loss of accuracy as force increases seems to have a limit. As the force required reaches approximately two-thirds of maximum force, the loss of accuracy appears to slow, stop, or even to reverse itself (i.e., performance consistency may even improve). The important implication of this for weightlifting is that the heavier the weight, the less likely it is (for skill reasons alone) that performance will vary (although a breakdown in technique due to arousal or fear may occur).

Weightlifters and their coaches should also so note that the longer the duration of a movement, the more variability it tends to have. In addition, movements with a greater amplitude are subject to nearly proportional increases in errors of spatial movement, but the effect on timing errors is not appreciable (other than due to the increased time it takes to execute the movement). One obvious implication of this is that if the lifter can to achieve a certain result through two methods (e.g., adequate bar height), the method which is shorter in duration and employs a smaller amplitude of movement is to be preferred, because such a movement will tend to be more consistent.

The Specificity of Motor Control

Like so many other kinds of skills or abilities, motor control and the ability to learn motor skills tend to be specific in nature. Extensive research has shown that there are few, if any, "natural" athletes (individuals who are gifted at learning any motor skill that they are shown). People clearly have different levels of ability with respect to learning specific skills. However, movement scientists believe that these differences are due more to previous development of certain general motor programs than to any inherited ability. The only exception to this rule is that individuals who are developmentally handicapped will tend to have lesser abilities in developing all motor skills than those who are "normal" in their abilities.

Thus far scientists have had poor results in identifying general kinds of motor abilities and in predicting success at a particular task from any such identified skills. For example, one of the problems with skills tests is that the very abilities that may enable an athlete to perform well on early trials can have little bearing on high level performance. Results appear to be improved when those tested have had an ample period to practice the test itself. So general selection methods cannot be expected to be at all fruitful (as least in terms of measuring potential ability to acquire certain specific skills).

Basic Principles Of Motor Learning

As was noted earlier, there is a distinction between performance and learning. Certain external influences may have very different effects on performance versus learning. For example, for many years one of the foundations of motor learning theory was that immediate feedback about performance should be given to an athlete. That advice was based on the results of early studies which showed that the more rapidly feedback was provided after a performance, the better the athlete's performance on the next trial (s) that he or she performed. Now it has been recognized that the process and value of providing feedback are not that simple. Giving subjects immediate feedback on their performance may have a positive effect on their performance during the next trial, but it may not have much of an effect on their ability to learn the improved skill in the long run. Amazingly, performance and skill learning do not appear to be as closely linked as was once believed.

Many early studies in the area of motor learning made no distinction between performance and learning. Consequently, a number of erroneous conclusions were drawn with respect to the effect of various kinds of practice on the development of motor skills (such as the conclusion that immediate feedback was always desirable). The concepts presented below reflect some of the more modern research findings.

The Effectiveness of Massed Practice Versus Distributed Practice

Massed practice has no strict definition, but is generally considered to be relatively continual practice. Distributed practice is practice divided in to several separate sessions (e.g., with two hours of rest between practice sessions). Many experiments have been conducted to determine whether massed practice or distributed practice is superior in terms

74

of learning. It is relatively clear the distributed practice leads to better performance than massed practice. This may be due to the athlete's becoming fatigued with massed practice, and it may also be due to some processing that takes place during the intervals between distributed practice sessions, processing which improves performance in subsequent trials.

Surprisingly, it has been found that massed practice is often at least as effective as distributed practice, and is sometimes more effective in fostering learning of a skill. This may be because practicing while fatigued forces one to focus more on the practice (which fosters subsequent learning). It may also be that the deterioration of performance while fatigued injects variability into the practice session, which has been shown to enhance learning. The positive aspect of this finding with respect to coaching weightlifting is that when time constraints force a coach to have an athlete go through massed practice, that athlete can hope for a rate of learning that is at least equal to that of athletes who are able to practice more than once per day (assuming overall practice time is the same).

Skill Transfer

When practice at one skill leads to better performance in another, it is called a positive transfer. When practice of one skill leads to poorer performance in another, it is called negative transfer. Transfer can either be prospective or retrospective in nature. If the practice of one activity affects your performance of a subsequent activity, it is said to have a prospective transfer. If the practice of one skill causes a previously learned skill to improve or deteriorate, the influence is said to be retrospective.

The bad news is that very little in the way of practice of one skill results in a positive transfer to another, even quite similar skill. Skills are very specific, and unless two skills are very similar, it is unlikely that practicing one will transfer to another. The good news is that it is very unusual for the learning of one skill to have a negative influence on the learning of another.

The basic exception to the negative transfer rule is when activities involve opposite timing and coordination. For example, if skill A requires you to push with the right arm while pushing with the left foot, practice of skill B (a movement that requires pulling with the right arm while pushing with the left foot) might have a negative effect on the learning of skill A. There appears to be little in terms of modern learning theory to suggest that technique patterns learned for the snatch will have a negative on technique in the clean (even though the tempo and amplitude of movement in the clean are clearly different) as long as the athlete is not mentally associating the two movements. It should be noted that some weightlifting theorists in Eastern Europe have a dissenting opinion in this area, believing that the snatch and clean do interfere with one another.

Overlearning

Practicing a skill after it has been mastered leads to a phenomena known as overlearning. Overlearning is the incremental, often barely visible or even invisible (to the naked eye) learning that continues to take place after a skill has apparently been mastered. When overlearning has occurred, the efficiency with which the movement is performed improves, as does the consistency with which the skill is executed. In addition, the athlete is able to sustain the correct pattern of movement even under stressful conditions. Therefore, it is very important for an athlete to practice a skill long after it has apparently been learned.

Other Factors That Aid Motor Learning

There are several basic factors that aid (though often indirectly) in the acquisition of motor skills. Motivation is important in learning motor skills (not so much because it will help you to learn more from a given practice session as because it will tend to lead to more practice, which in turn contributes to more learning). Seeing the advantages of mastering a particular skill (intellectually, as well as emotionally) is a key factor in creating motivation to learn. Observing role models is another powerful source of motivation. Social approval, competition, working as a team and the presence of an audience can all increase motivation as well. It should be understood, however, that these factors can actually hurt early learning by raising the athlete's arousal level too much.

Many motor learning theorists contend that the body's level of excitation, its arousal level, affects learning and performance in what is called an inverted U pattern. As arousal increases, learning and performance are enhanced. However, at a certain point, the rate of improvement that occurs as the performer becomes aroused begins to diminish, until it finally begins to decline as arousal continues to increase. Therefore, if arousal is too low, the person will not function optimally, but if it is too high, learning and performance will actually be hampered.

The optimal level of arousal is related to the athlete's mastery of a given skill. A more highly skilled lifter, one for whom the process of lifting is relatively automatic, will be able to perform effectively with a higher level of arousal. Similarly, when an athlete is first learning a skill, his or her arousal should be only enough to provide the energy of enthusiasm to the task. If any higher level of arousal is developed, the motor performance and learning of the lifter will diminish. It is generally unwise, therefore, to admonish a lifter at the early stages of learning or to permit any significant peer pressure. Peer pressure may increase the athlete's level of excitation to the point at which learning is hampered (to say nothing of the athlete's displeasure at being embarrassed).

The First Steps in Teaching an Athlete a New Skill

Before the learner attempts to perform a certain movement for the first time, he or she should be given the idea of the movement through the use of films, demonstrations (lower skilled performers tend to respond more favorably to peer demonstrations while the highly skilled tend to favor a demonstration by a more skilled performer or a teacher), verbal instructions on how to move the body and verbal explanations of the reasons for the particular pattern of movement that is being taught. It should be noted that verbal instructions tend to be overused. Words are often only a rather crude method of communicating movement patterns and you can only remember a limited number of words at one time (often many fewer words than are required to talk through the movement). One means that has been suggested for improving the effectiveness of verbal instructions is to use them to give the learner a pre-practice reference to corrections (e.g., "if you are doing it correctly, you will feel..." or "if your feet land properly in the split jerk, you will hear...").

Once an understanding of the movement has been acquired and the learner is ready to attempt it, guided movement in which the instructor physically assists the learner to move his or her body through the correct pattern of motion can be helpful. A variation of this is to have the learner "walk through" (perform the movement at a slower than normal speed or only perform some aspects of the movement) while focusing on what he or she is feeling; asking for some explanation of what is being felt or experienced tends to cause the learner to focus more fully during the walk through.

Practice and Feedback: The Foundations for Learning a Motor Skill

There are two fundamental requirements for learning a motor skill: practice and feedback about the practice. In order for a person to acquire a skill, he or she must practice that skill. This means the person must consciously direct his or her nervous system through the required movement, and the person must experience feedback with respect to the success of that effort. As noted earlier, it is possible and often desirable to help a person

experience a particular movement passively, so that the learner can gain an understanding of how the body feels when it goes through the appropriate motion (this can help a beginner to understand what is required in order to perform a movement properly). In order for the person to learn to perform that movement him or herself, however, the experience of putting the body through the motion must occur; the correct muscle tensions (a critical aspect of motor skill) will not be learned otherwise. In addition, the person must have a sense of what is occurring when he or she directs the body through the movement or little or no learning will take place. Much as the mind and body must generate maximal voluntary muscular contractions if the muscles are to become strong (passive contractions via electrostimulation do not work as well), so conscious effort at movement is required to acquire a skill.

Kinds of Feedback and Their Value

Feedback on our movements comes via the senses of touch, sound and sight and from the observation of results; the three senses give direct input about the movement of the body, and the last feedback mechanism provides information about the performance of the body or an implement relative to the desired end. Feedback can be intrinsic or extrinsic. Intrinsic feedback is sensory feedback inherent in the performance itself (what the athlete sees, hears and feels during the activity). Extrinsic feedback is feedback supplementary to the intrinsic type. It may be received during the activity, immediately afterwards or at some interval after the activity. It can be verbal or nonverbal, separate (i.e., feedback after each performance) or accumulated (summarized after a number of trials). Within each category of feedback there are two varieties: knowledge of performance and knowledge of results. Knowledge of performance is information about the nature of the body's movement. Knowledge of results is information about the outcome of the movement with respect to the environment.

Without knowledge of results, little or no learning occurs; knowledge of results also helps performance. However, giving feedback on results too often can actually hinder learning. The reason for this is not completely understood. but it is thought that the learner becomes so reliant on the motivating and guiding properties of the feedback that when it is withdrawn, he or she has trouble producing the movement effectively. Therefore, knowledge of results should be given frequently at the early stages of learning and then should progressively be diminished as performance improves.

There appears to be little difference in learning between situations in which there is a one-second or a six-second delay in providing feedback, but immediate extrinsic feedback may actually hinder learning by diverting the performer's attention from his or her own feedback mechanisms and processing.. In addition, any period of delay between the performance and the feedback should be kept free of other movements that could be confused with the desired ones (which is why practicing cleans and jerks separately when learning to perform them as well as later makes sense). It also appears that delays between trials actually help learning (perhaps because the delay requires one to recall the movement, which is an aid to learning). It is fairly clear that very short intervals (less than a few seconds) between trials are not helpful. Consequently, the use of repetitions with no delay between them may not be proportionally beneficial for learning (e.g., five trials that consist of five rapid reps may not be as effective as five singles in terms of the learning).

When separate feedback (e.g., feedback after each rep) was compared with summary feedback (e.g., after a set), it was found that summary feedback had a slight advantage overall (as long as the summary did not take place after more than about five trials, e.g., reps).

Information on either the direction or magnitude of a movement improves performance (direction is typically of more help than magnitude and feedback on both appears to be the most effective). Quantitative feedback is more effective than merely qualitative (e.g., "one inch to the front" is better than "not good" or "too much to the front"). Up to a point, the more precise the feedback, the better (older learners can deal with greater precision than younger ones). In adults, the unit of measure does not seem to matter (e.g., three "quotarks" forward is as effective a description as three inches forward once an adult has mentally calibrated a quotark). Children seem to require more concrete measures, ones that they are familiar with.

Video replays have been disappointing in terms of their effect on learning (perhaps because they provide too much information). However, directed viewing of videos (e.g., "look at how the arms are bending too early in the pull") appears to improve their effectiveness. In some studies, learners who observed a model performing a simple task and who received the model's feedback performed those tasks quite well.

Kinematic feedback pertains to positions, times, velocities and patterns of movements. Studies involving this type of feedback showed dramatic improvements in learning. The key seemed to be that the subjects were given feedback about some aspect of movement that they could not ordinarily perceive. Kinetic focuses on the forces which produce kinematic variables. Such feedback is very effective in helping a person to acquire motor skills. For example, a force/time curve shown to runners after their starts in a series of sprints enabled them to improve their performance significantly.

It is posited that feedback works by assisting the learner in developing an internal representation of what it feels like to be on target. The feedback thus offers a reference of correctness that would not have been as easily obtained, or obtained at all, without the feedback. This internal representation gets stronger with each trial near the target and provides an increasingly effective means for detecting errors. In short, more skilled performers are more capable of evaluating their own performances.

The performer's own mechanism for detecting error can be, and often is, a substitute for knowledge of results. In at least one experiment, learners were required to give an estimate of their performance without being given any knowledge of their results. When later tested on their learning of the skill involved, the learners who gave performance estimates maintained high scores, but the learners who had not given estimates during earlier practices regressed systematically as no feedback trials progressed.

The Effect of Variability in Practice on Learning a Skill

It might be assumed intuitively that the more precisely the practice of a skill approaches what is desired in performing the skill, the better will be the motor learning; as indicated earlier, this is true— to a point. It appears that some variability in practice aids in motor learning (although perhaps not performance). To be effective, the variability should be limited (it is not reasonable to expect that stiff-legged deadlifts will help in learning the clean pull, but cleans from the blocks certainly may). It also appears that variability is more effective when it is random in nature rather than placed into blocks of time during which the differing activity is performed. This suggests that doing snatches from the floor, then doing a few snatches from the blocks and then returning to snatches from the floor may be more effective for learning than doing all of your snatches from the floor, followed by all of your snatches from the blocks (although performance during the workout might well suffer).

The reasons for the effectiveness of variability are not well understood. Apparently, however, similarity in the underlying processes going on internally, not necessarily the conditions of practice, is the key to learning.

The Warm-up Decrement

When a performer is practicing skill, a relatively large decrement in performance is produced after rest periods of even several minutes, but that decrement is typically eliminated by a few practice trials. One explanation for this performance decrement is that the performer has "forgotten" or gotten out of the mental "groove" of how to perform the movement during the rest interval. Another theory is that the skill loss is related to the loss of some temporary internal state(s) or "set" that underlies and supports the skill in question. Support for the first theory comes from introspection, while support for the second theory has come from experimental evidence. For example, when subjects rested from a right handed task but performed a similar left handed one, there was very little decrement in performance when the right hand was again brought into action. Some studies have shown some loss of the "set" after as little as twenty-five seconds.

Another test found that when the interval between trials of an activity included the performance of another activity that used the same muscles but was very different in nature, the performance deterioration from the first trial was quite significant. This could be due to differences in timing, arousal or feedback sources used during the differing activities. While the readjustment of the mental "set" may take only a few seconds, inferior performance even for a few seconds can be disastrous (in weightlifting even a split second of worsened performance can lead to a miss). Therefore, it is important to learn what kinds of physical and mental practice are required by each athlete to maintain and/or restore his or her mental set.

The Value of Lead Up Activities in Learning New Skills

The value of learning "lead up" skills (the preparatory movements that take place just before or at the beginning of the actual task, such as a walk up and jump to a swing on the high bar in gymnastics) is probably threefold. First, there are many lead ups that teach a universal skill for that sport (such as the kip in gymnastics). Second, the lead up actually prepares you mentally as well as physically for the activity to come. Third, lead ups can play a role in overcoming any fear of the movement. Therefore, weightlifting lead ups, such as practice at assuming the starting position of a lift, can be of value to the lifter, particularly the beginner. This is one of a number of the learning sequences described later in this chapter.

Learning Segments of a Skill Versus the Entire Skill

Virtually all complex movements can be broken down into segments or stages. Many coaches believe that teaching skills segment by segment is more effective than trying to teach the entire skill at once. There is considerable empirical and experimental evidence that learning a new skill in segments and then putting those segments together is a more effective way of learning than attempting to practice a skill in its entirety. Yet many experiments have shown relatively poor results when activities are broken down into segments.

Why the contradictory results? The key seems to lie in the nature of both the segmental practice and the activity. An activity with distinct points of separation (e.g., the clean versus the jerk) will tend to benefit more substantially from segmented practice (in this case, separate practice of the clean and the jerk) than will an activity that is essentially one motion, such as the clean. In the latter case the transition from one phase of the lift to the next is in many ways as important as any one segment of the pull itself. This is not to say that learning a motion like the clean in segments may not have value. (Indeed such an approach may be very helpful for some lifters because the overall complexity of the movement may make it difficult for the beginner to practice the complete movement effectively, at least initially.) However, the segments need to be carefully linked together before overall learning can be completed, and the time spent in learning the segments and linking them together may be greater than the time that would have been needed to master the full movement at the outset. In all cases, it appears that the sooner practice of the full movement (or important segments of it) can occur in the learning sequence, the better.

In summary, it appears that learning in segments can be helpful if four basic conditions are met.

1) The segment practiced must be similar to the performance of that segment during the lift. If the practice of the segment of a lift is to have any significant carryover into the complete lift, it must virtually duplicate what takes place during that segment when it is performed as part of the total lift.

For example, during one portion of my career, I practiced a considerable number of snatches from the blocks. While I gained a relatively high level of proficiency in that lift and soon exceeded my best snatch from the floor, the carryover to the snatch was very disappointing. My snatch had actually declined somewhat, despite the improvements I had made in the snatch from the blocks. I later discovered that the primary reason for the disappointing result was that the position of my body relative to the bar when I snatched from the blocks was not the same as the one that I assumed during the corresponding point in the full motion of the pull. In addition, the speed of the bar was not the same (because it was being started from a static position as compared with being in motion), and the balance on the feet was different as well. When I started to eliminate as many differences as possible between the technique used for the snatch from the floor and the snatch from the blocks and began to practice more regular snatches and fewer snatches from the blocks, my snatch from the blocks declined somewhat, but my snatch from the floor improved.

2) The sequence practiced must involve all activities that are being executed simultaneously during the actual task. Much evidence suggests that when one aspect of a motion involving a number of body parts is practiced, there will be little carryover to the complete motion.

For example, if a lifter wishes to improve the effectiveness of his or her trapezius contraction during the explosion phase of the pull, it is not a particularly good idea to practice regular shrugs (elevating the shoulder girdle with the rest of the body remaining motionless). This is because the contraction of the trapezius never takes place in isolation during the explosion phase of the pull. Rather it occurs in concert with contractions of the leg and hip extensors. Therefore, more forceful contraction of the trapezius muscles needs to occur in the context of an explosive effort of the leg extensors and in the same position the body will be assuming during that phase of the pull. As a result, practicing the explosion phase of the pull (via the performance of pulls and shrugs with the bar beginning in a position above the lifter's knees), while emphasizing the motion of the traps, is far more likely to carryover to the full pull than the practice of merely shrugging the shoulders with a bar held in the hands. This is not to say that the practice of pure shrugging may not build strength in the traps and that one might not want to practice the exercise for that purpose. However, it should be understood that any gain in strength will not necessarily be fully carried over into the actual pull unless the body has learned to perform the skill of incorporating the traps into the pulling motion at the proper point in the pull and with the appropriate motion in other parts of the body. The latter skills will not be acquired by practicing regular shrugs alone.

Similarly, practicing front squats will improve leg strength, but unless you practice squat cleans and learn to incorporate the added leg strength into the cleaning motion, the affects of improving your front squat may be disappointing. (Obviously, once the lifter has learned the coordination of the pull and recovery from the clean, any gain in functional leg strength would be carried over almost immediately and completely.)

3) Practice in parts must eventually be combined into the full movement. Once practice has been performed in parts, it is important to string the parts together into the whole. One common and effective means for doing this is "backward chaining." This process consists of beginning the learning process by learning the last motion in a sequence and then gradually adding earlier and earlier stages. For example, in the snatch this might mean learning the snatch from the explosion phase of the pull on. Then you might move back to the amortization phase in the pull and practice the lift from that point forward. Finally, the lift would be practiced from the floor. This approach would probably be more effective than first practicing the pull to the explosion and then the pull from the explosion on, because it would involve incorporating the transition from the amortization phase to the explosion phase earlier in the practice.

4) The practice of a segment should involve the most difficult or weakest part(s) of the lift for the individual athlete. As was indicated earlier, practice in parts has been shown to be most effective when it involves distinctly separate motions (such as the clean and the jerk) which need only be performed later, with one lift following shortly after the other, not nonstop in one continuous lifting motion. When the part(s) practiced are the more difficult ones in the motion, practice in parts has actually been shown to be more effective than practice in the whole For example, if you are having more difficulty with the jerk than with the clean, you are more likely to improve the C&J overall by practicing the jerk for one hour than by practicing the C&J for one hour, as long as some practice on the C&J is included in the overall training as well.

Mental Practice

There is considerable evidence that many skills can be acquired, at least partially, through mental practice. This is particularly true in the early stages. In fact, it has been found that mental practice can be nearly as effective as actual practice in terms of motor learning (at least at early stages of skill acquisition). Just what is meant by mental practice? There is no universal definition, but it generally involves imagining or visualizing the activity to be learned. The most common form of such visualization is that of imagining yourself going through the motion required. The subject is generally told to experience the activity as fully as possible in his or her imagination. This involves feeling the body go through the motions and seeing any motion that you would ordinarily see if you actually performed the motion. For example, if you were bowling, you might "feel" the texture, temperature and weight of the ball in your hand. You would imagine being at the starting line ready to bowl and then feel yourself go through the approach and release, then watch the ball roll down the alley into the pins and see the reaction of the pins. There are also those who suggest that "seeing" yourself as if you were an observer is useful, but the effectiveness of this kind of mental practice appears not to have been as carefully researched as the former kind.

It is clear that mental practice is very effective for beginners. It enables them to plan (i.e., anticipate) their motion. Mental practice also helps the beginner to run through any cognitive elements involved in the task and to think through what might be done in a variety of circumstances. In his autobiography, Second Wind, the basketball great Bill Russell tells of the endless nights that he spent traveling on buses early in his career. He used that travel time to envision various situations that might occur on the court and to imagine how he would handle each. Then, when actual situations of the kind he had imagined did occur, he was ready to react quickly and appropriately.

There is some disagreement in the literature with regard to the effectiveness of mental practice at teaching true motor skills. However, many high level athletes have reported that they believe such visualization is very effective for them. In experimenting on myself and athletes I have coached, I have found it to be effective, at least in improving performance. Even if mental practice is better at helping performance than learning, it is a worthwhile activity. Performance counts, even if it a performance that has only temporarily been enhanced. Similarly, even if visualization is merely a way to focus attention and to build confidence, it can play an important role. Moreover, mental practice has the advantage of facilitating learning while the muscles rest and at any time and place. The only significant disadvantage appears to be

that mental rehearsal may fatigue the nervous systems of some athletes and that some athletes may practice the wrong motion mentally (especially because there is an absence of the kinds of feedback that are available when the athlete actually practices the motion in question). A further discussion of mental rehearsal is presented in Chapter 7.

Teaching Technique

There Are Many Approaches that Work

There are probably nearly as many different philosophies of teaching weightlifting technique as there are weightlifting coaches. However, several countries have developed general models for teaching technique. While it should not be assumed that all, or even most, coaches in a given country are using that country's general model, those models have been used by at least some coaches in those countries with success. Therefore, they are useful to examine as a starting point for teaching of technique. During the discussion of the various technique learning models, reference will often be made to specific exercises that are used to teach technique. Most of these exercises are described in some detail in Chapter 5. Therefore, if you encounter an exercise that you are unfamiliar with while you are reading this chapter, refer to Chapter 5 for a clarification

The Soviet Model

Coaches in the former USSR extensively studied the best methods for teaching technique, and while, as was noted above, different coaches and writers promote different methods, the general direction of their thinking in this area is as follows. First, they argue that it is useful to teach the lift in parts before having the lifter attempt to perform the entire movement. Second, they believe in teaching the snatch before the clean and jerk.

The idea of teaching parts of the lift instead of the entire lift at once is grounded in motor learning theory that says: a) learning parts is easier for the mind to handle than attempting to learn all aspects of a movement at once; and b) once one or more parts are learned, it is easy either to add another stage to the sequence or to add the separate parts together. The Soviet approach is essentially a modified version of the "backward chaining" method of motor skill development that was referred to earlier in this chapter (i.e., learning the last sequence in a movement and then adding each previous segment, segment by segment).

The notion that the snatch should be learned before the clean is supported by several arguments.

First, some theorists feel that faster movements place less of a strain on the body than do slower ones and therefore attacking faster movements first is more natural and gentler on the body's adaptive mechanisms. Another argument is that the timing of the snatch is more delicate than that of the C&J; as a consequence, learning the clean first might inhibit learning of the snatch.

One influential Soviet author, former World Champion and national team coach A. Medvedyev, recommends the following sequence of learning: power snatch (a version of the snatch in which the lifter bends his or her legs to a limited degree to catch the bar overhead instead of lowering the body into a full squat position);, snatch; jerk from rack (an apparatus which supports the barbell at chest height and from which the barbell is removed in order to perform the exercise—see the section of Chapter 4 which refers to "Squat Racks" for a further description); power clean (a lift in which the body is only lowered into a partial squat); and clean. When teaching each exercise, he recommends that the lift be broken into sub-categories. The athlete first learns the power snatch by starting with the bar in a position similar to the one reached at the end of the third stage of the snatch. Then a power snatch in which the bar begins from a position just below the knees is mastered. The athlete then practices properly lifting the bar from the floor to the knees. Then a full snatch pull from the floor is learned. Next the athlete learns the power snatch from the floor and then adds an overhead squat after the power snatch (i.e., the athlete lowers his or her body into a full squat position while holding the bar overhead on straight arms). Finally, the athlete learns the full squat snatch from the floor. A similar sequence is followed for learning the clean.

Medvedyev thinks the jerk should be learned between the snatch and the clean, and the sequence he recommends is: the front squat, the power jerk and the split jerk. The sequence used to learn the clean is similar to the sequence used to learn the snatch (i.e., power clean from the hang above the knees, power clean from just below the knees, etc.).

The USAW Model

The United States Weightlifting Federation, which recently started doing business as the USAW, has recommended two approaches in its official literature. The first approach, which was disseminated in the early 1980s as part of a series of coaching manuals, employed a learning sequence that was similar to that of the Soviets in certain respects (such as teaching the snatch before the clean), but the nature and sequence of the exercises was significantly different. The USAW suggested that the lifter first assume the starting position in the snatch without attempting to move the bar

from the floor. The emphasis was on assuming the correct position of the body while maintaining proper balance and a proper relationship of the body to the bar. Next the lifter learned the push press behind the neck with a snatch grip and then the overhead squat. Next the athlete performed a drill that consisted of standing with the hands on hips with the feet in the starting pull position and then jumping the feet to an ending position (presumably the position used for the overhead squat). After learning the foot movement and position, the lifter learned the wide grip upright row, the hang-above-the-knees position, and then jumps with the bar in hand from that position. After this preparatory work, the USAW recommended that the lifter learn the power snatch from above the knees, the power snatch from below the knees and then the power snatch from the floor. Following this, the lifter practiced the drop snatch and what some lifters call the dead hang snatch (and others call the "going under the bar exercise") and, finally, the squat snatch.

A similar sequence was recommended for the clean, except that the width of the grip was for the clean, there was no counterpart for the push press behind the neck or the drop snatch (so these steps were eliminated), and the front squat was substituted for overhead squat. For the jerk, the USAW recommended the following learning sequence: the push press; push jerk; moving into the split after holding an empty bar at the top of the head; the jerk behind the neck; and then the regular jerk.

More recently the USAW has published a Club Coach Manual that outlines a teaching sequence that differs from the original USAW guidelines in a number of ways. This revised method is currently taught in USAW clinics and coaching seminars. This sequence can be summarized as follows. First, the lifter masters a series of "basic" exercises. These include: the power clean; presses behind the neck with a clean and snatch grip (with the body held motionless, the bar is pushed over head with the arms); front squat (a squat with the bar held in front of the neck—see Chapter 5 for further details); back squat (a squat with the bar held on the shoulders but behind the neck); and the power snatch. The power clean is learned in the following sequence: the power clean from mid-thigh; power clean from knee level; power clean from mid-shin level; and, finally, power clean from the floor. While the lifter is proceeding through the power clean learning stages, he or she is taught the press behind the neck with the clean grip and the same exercise with the snatch grip. The lifter is also taught a squat sequence at this time, with the front squat taught first. Once the front squat has been mastered, the lifter learns the back squat. Once the power clean has been learned, the lifter learns the power snatch, following a sequence comparable to the one that was used for the power clean.

After the basic exercises have been learned, the lifter begins a learning progression that will lead to the mastery of the snatch and C&J. The coaching guide suggests that the lifter who has learned the power clean and front squat can learn to squat clean simply by making sure the feet jump into a proper position for executing the front squat at the end of the power clean. Then the lifter allows himself or herself to sink into the full squat after the power clean. Over time the lifter learns to sink deeper and more quickly until a command of the full squat clean is attained. It is further suggested that the squat clean will typically be learned as the lifter is working on the squat snatch and as jerk learning segments are being practiced, so that the squat clean will be learned before the lifter begins actual practice of the squat snatch or completes the learning of the split jerk. Once the lifter has learned both the split jerk and the squat clean, the two are combined into the C&J.

The sequence followed in learning the full squat snatch is the same as that for the full squat clean except that before attempting to sink into a full squat position after the power snatch, the lifter must learn another sequence of exercises. The first exercise is the overhead squat. That is followed by the pressing snatch balance exercise, the heave-pressing snatch balance exercise and the regular snatch balance exercise (these exercises are described in Chapter 5).

The sequence used for learning the jerk is as follows: push press behind the neck, power jerk behind the neck, push press, power jerk and split jerk. These exercises are also described in Chapter 5).

The Unofficial IWF Model

Several years ago, the International Weightlifting Federation (IWF) published a book called Weightlifting: Fitness For All Sports by Dr. Tamas Ajan and Mr. Lazar Baroga.. Dr. Ajan is General Secretary of the IWF and Mr. Baroga is a member of its executive board. While the book did not specifically state that the material therein was representative of a position taken by the IWF, the foreword, written by the President of the IWF, Gotfried Schodl, clearly stated that the book was part of the IWF effort to foster education regarding weightlifting worldwide. The teaching sequence presented there was reportedly based primarily on one that was used in Romania (Baroga's home). In this sequence the snatch is taught first, followed by the clean and then the jerk. The teaching sequence itself differs from those that have already been discussed in a number of significant respects.

First, the lifter is taught the correct positioning of the body for the first stage of the pull, then the second and third stages of the pull are taught together through the use of a partial deadlifting motion (i.e., from the floor to above the knees).

Then the lifter is taught the concept of creating an explosive upward force to the bar through a reaction force with the ground. This is done by having he lifter experiment with creating an explosive downward force into the platform by bending and then sharply extending the legs. The lifter stands on a force plate (a device which measures the forces generated by the feet against the floor) or platform scale and observes the effect of various efforts at explosive leg thrusting on the measuring device (seeking the technique which generates the greatest force). Next, the third and fourth stages of the pull are combined with snatch pulls with the bar resting on a support that places it at knee height. This is followed by power snatches from the same level. Then the lifter learns the power snatch from the floor. The next stage is to teach the overhead squat and that is followed by drop snatches. Finally, all of the movements are combined into the snatch. A similar sequence is used in the clean.

In the jerk, the lifter is first taught to support the bar in the proper position on the chest (the first stage of the jerk), then to execute the dip (the first through the beginning of the fourth stage of the jerk, using a sort of partial front squatting motion). The next stage is to teach the lifter the power jerk. This is followed by teaching the lifter the movement of the body into the split position without weight. Finally, the entire jerk is attacked and mastered.

There is much merit is this teaching sequence particularly because of its emphasis on mastering some fundamental body positions that are critical for success and because of its unique focus generating optimal explosiveness via performance feedback versus pure modeling of good technique.

The Bulgarian Model

The Bulgarian teaching model is quite different from those which have already been discussed. The Bulgarians teach the clean before the snatch, and they do not break up the lifts into as many or the same kinds of components.

The Bulgarians teach the back squat before anything else because they believe that the squat position is the fundamental position for lifting and because they believe that it teaches the lifter to achieve the appropriate tensions in the legs and back muscles during the lifts (the use of a belt is encouraged). They then teach the front squat with an emphasis on keeping the elbows up and the trunk upright. This is followed by teaching the clean pull from the floor to the fully extended position. Finally, the lifter is taught the squat clean.

After a lifter has mastered the squat clean, he or she is taught the proper movement of the feet in the split for the jerk without weights. This is done by having the lifter perform an exercise in which the feet are jumped into the split position with the hands on hips. Once the lifter has perfected the footwork necessary for the split jerk, the lifter is taught the entire movement.

In the snatch the lifter first learns the snatch pull, then the overhead squat. This is followed by practice in the power snatch, and then the lifter attempts to gradually lower himself or herself into the squat snatch position. The lift is considered mastered only when the lifter has both the timing and the movement right. The Bulgarians emphasize active and energetic placement of the feet in the full squat or split as the bar is caught (the lifter "stomps" the feet briskly against the floor while squatting down).

The Bulgarians believe that the clean should be taught first because it is less complex than the snatch and therefore easier for most lifters to learn. The argument that the snatch should be taught first because the smaller loads handled in the snatch versus the clean place less stress on the beginner is overcome by the use of only light weights in teaching the clean. The Bulgarian coaches also believe that there is no need for the lifters to break the pull into parts when it can be learned as one motion and when it should be thought of as one only movement.

Which Approach To Teaching Is Best?

There are at least two basic approaches for evaluating the teaching sequences used by the Soviets, the Americans, the Bulgarians and the IWF/Romanians. The first approach is to examine how each sequence squares with the latest thinking in terms of motor learning. The second approach is to examine the concept of an "ideal" sequence. We will use both approaches in the analysis provided below.

The Five Technique Teaching Models Viewed from the Perspective of Motor Learning Theory

In terms of motor learning theory, all of the teaching methods described above have merit. This is not surprising when one considers that all of these methods, on a combined basis, have probably been used to teach technique to hundreds of thousands, if not millions, of weightlifters. There are some fundamental similarities among the methods and some fundamental differences as well. Essentially, all of the approaches share the method of breaking a complex motion (the snatch and C&J) into relatively simple segments, teaching the segments and then combining them gradually until they are mastered. The Bulgarians use fewer segments and teach the C&J first. Overall, the Bulgarian method has the advantage of using the smallest number of segments; learning theory

suggests that the smaller the number of segments that can be used effectively, the better (except when teaching movements as unrelated as the clean and the jerk). The IWF/Romanian approach is interesting for its emphasis on teaching proper starting positions and on teaching the all important explosion, and using a focus on the action of the legs early on in the teaching process. The newer U.S. method has eliminated a number of the exercises in the original sequence, exercises that were highly questionable in terms of their carryover into learning the lifts. (Exercises such as the upright row had the dual disadvantage of resembling little that was done during the actual performance of the lift; what little was similar was done in a way that isolated the contraction of muscles that normally operate in concert with others during the actual lift, such as the trapezius muscles.)

All of these sequences have been used with success and the can be used in exactly the way they were formulated. But most of the coaches who formulated or use the sequences described are well aware that modifications to them are necessary from time to time. Unfortunately, those who learn about the sequences by reading descriptions of them often follow them far too rigidly.

It must be recognized that in the group teaching environment in which many of the methods of the Eastern European coaches were developed and applied, the coaches (of necessity since they were teaching many lifters at once) needed to follow a similar learning sequence with all lifters (much as lectures to large classes in schoolrooms all over the world target the "average" student). But when technique instruction is done one on one (as it often is in the United States), the notion of a single "ideal" sequence for teaching is open to examination and serious doubt.

An Individualized Approach to Teaching Technique

I believe that there is an approach to teaching weightlifting technique, that can be more effective than any of the aforementioned technique teaching models. The approach is what I will call the "contextual" method. The underlying principle of the contextual method is that the sequence to be used in teaching weightlifting technique to each lifter be determined by the readiness or starting state of that individual lifter. No two lifters begin lifting with the same background, physical characteristics or mental attitude. Therefore, the sequence of learning must be tailored specifically for that lifter.

For example, it is true that it is easier for many athletes to learn the power snatch and/or power clean than the squat snatch or clean. The former are simpler movements, and some beginners do not have the flexibility to assume the proper squat position initially. However, in teaching the power clean, I have experienced a number of instances in which the beginning leans back considerably finishing the pull and/or catching the bar at the shoulders. In other cases lifters jump their feet too wide when they catch the bar. It has been my experience that such lifters may benefit from learning the squat clean before the power clean. In so doing, leaning back is reduced or eliminated, and proper foot positioning is more likely to be achieved.

It has also been my observation that most beginners grasp either the movements of the snatch or the clean more quickly. It seems rather wasteful to me not to use such information as a basis for planning the early learning sequence rather than adhering to one prescribed sequence or another. If a lifter is able to perform a certain movement correctly the first time out, why follow a rigid sequence that requires mastery of a sub-skill that appears to be more difficult for that athlete to perform?

It must be remembered that in countries in which there is (or was) state supported weightlifting on a grand scale, the athlete has no choice but to learn in the prescribed sequence. Boredom or frustration is not a major issue for the coach to contend with, as the lifter is effectively a member of a captive audience. In addition, most athletes tend to have adequate readiness to learn all of the lifts (e.g., flexibility, etc.), or they would not be selected to participate in weightlifting. In countries where weightlifting is more voluntary, the situation is quite diffcrent. Fledgling lifters vary greatly in terms of their previous preparation and aptitude. If the lifter becomes bored or frustrated, you may lose him or her. If the lifter cannot experience some early joy in the execution of at least parts of the lifts, he or she may move into another weight or strength sport.

One of the key factors in getting young athletes to stay with weightlifting is helping them to experience the joy of lifting with proper technique (in at least some exercises). While it is true that the beginning lifter who becomes easily frustrated will never grow to champion caliber, it is also true that if training is not at least a somewhat pleasurable experience, retention of the athlete in the sport becomes far less likely. Giving the lifter several things to work on, each in the proper point in the learning sequence, makes a great deal of sense, as compared with blindly putting them through a routine sequence, no matter how well conceived that sequence may be.

It is my contention that if more athletes experienced the thrill of a properly coordinated snatch or clean and jerk there would be far fewer athletes doing bodybuilding, powerlifting, or other sports that attract people who are interested in sports as a test of their power and athletic skills. Therefore, by getting an athlete to master one lift,

regardless of what the "ideal" sequence might be, you have a better chance of retaining that athlete long enough for him or her to master the technique of all the lifts and thereby to have a better chance of achieving a full appreciation of the sport. Moreover, nothing in modern learning theory suggests that learning one skill truly interferes achieving proficiency in another. This is because the snatch, the clean and the jerk are sufficiently different from one another that the likelihood of one interfering with the learning of the other is remote, as long as it is not suggested to the athlete that the lifts have identical techniques. In short, there are no good reasons for not teaching the lifts concurrently or in the order dictated by the individual athlete's readiness, and there are a number of very good practical reasons for doing so.

Perfecting An Athlete's Weightlifting Technique

Once obvious faults have been corrected and major areas for improvement have been identified and pursued, the athlete enters a new stage of learning, that of refining and perfecting his or her technique. This process is often referred to as overlearning. The road to overlearning can be a difficult one. The athlete who is undergoing the overlearning process has already achieved a good or even excellent skill level and must motivate himself or herself to strive for further improvements. Improvement at this stage tends to be both slow and difficult to measure, and as a result, the athlete who is in the overlearning mode may find his or her motivation waning.

In order to overcome problems with motivation, the athlete must find reasons for practicing. Perhaps the most engaging reason is the pursuit of perfection and consistency. The athlete must learn to covet each perfect lift and to discover what means of mental preparation for each lift is the most effective in eliciting perfect execution. The athlete can make a game of seeing how many perfect lifts he or she can make in a row. Alternatively, the athlete can attempt to make a perfect lift overall while concentrating on making a slight improvement in one particular area. The athlete must be careful that he or she is not giving up performance in some other area in order to achieve improvement in the new area. It is not worth giving up technique that is already sound in order to pursue some minor improvement elsewhere, but an athlete must never lose the hunger for improvement, no matter how minor.

Robert Roman, the Soviet technique analyst and theorist who contributed so much to the modern understanding of weightlifting technique, recommended several methods for perfecting technique. One method is to lift a bar with 85% to 100% of a lifter's maximum to the same height.

Specifically, he recommended doing three singles with the 100% weight and lifting 85%, 90%, 95% and 100% weights, all to the same height. He believed that the ability to lift a weight to the same height consistently is one key to effective technique, and I tend to agree.

Another method which Roman recommended (though he did not think it as effective as the same height-of-pull approach) is to have the lifter lift the same weight to different target heights. After ten to twelve workouts using the varying heights approach, the lifter's level of precision in achieving the target heights should be much improved. Once this has occurred, the lifter is instructed to lift the bar and then to specify the height that was achieved. Once accuracy has been gained in this exercise, the lifter's sense of control and mastery should have improved significantly.

Finally, Roman recommended lifting without the faculty of sight for a lifter who has already mastered the basics of technique. He felt that such practice helps the lifter to learn and reproduce joint angles and muscle tension better than lifting with visual feedback. He urged the lifter to work up from light to medium weights with the sightless method. He believed that the best method of such practice is in a darkened room; the second best method is with a blindfold (made of a soft and dark material and placed so that there is as little tension on the eyelids as is possible); the least preferred method is simply to close the eyes. Obviously, the darkened room is the least convenient and most dangerous (as well as a method which prevents the coach from observing the outcome). The blindfold is better for the coach and allows others to warn the lifter from any impending disaster (like running off the platform or into a foreign object). The closed eyes are the safest and most convenient means for creating sightless lifting because the lifter can always regain his or her sight in an instant, and others can observe the performance of the athlete in the usual way.

Another interesting approach to perfecting technique (which comes from and entirely different sport than weightlifting) is one outlined in a book called "Free Throw", by Tom Amberry. Amberry is a retired podiatrist who in his college days was a top basketball player. After retiring from his podiatry practice in his late 60's, Amberry began to practice his free throws (foul shots) again as a hobby. At age 71 he set a world record for the most consecutive free throws without a miss - 2750. Although he is not a weightlifter, Amberry's advice for perfecting ones free throws can be applied to many other activities.

Amberry believes in establishing a ritual to improve and stabilize ones performance in addition to having sound mechanics that facilitate accuracy and consistency "built-in" to the technique (e.g., for free throws he recommends keeping the elbow against the body as one prepares to shoot).

He then urges the athlete to use a "mantra" to focus and calm the mind (in his case pre-viewing the steps one will go through during the throw) and ending with the visualization of a perfect success.

He uses seven steps in his shooting, some of them directed at assuring proper mechanics during the shot and the rest at focusing the mind properly. He recommends that the athlete does not even begin the ritual until he or she is ready to perform.

For a lifter, the readying steps in the snatch might be: place the feet carefully under the bar, set the grip, lock the back, pump the legs three times, look at your focal point, pull and catch the bar, recover from the low position and wait for the down signal.

Amberry believes in completely "emptying" the mind of the details of the skill prior to executing it. He feels that consciously controlling a performance as it is being carried out is a recipe for disaster.

If one makes an error during a performance, the focus should be on making the next performance perfect. This is quite different from trying to "correct" for the previous mistake. For instance, if a lifter misses a lift behind, he or she should focus on doing it perfectly the next time rather than trying to place the next lift a little further forward.

Amberry also recommends that the athlete establish goals for technique performance and that he or she measure improvement continually.

Neither Roman's nor Amberry's methods for perfecting technique are the only tools available, but they can be very useful ones.

One Skill That Should Be Taught Early On: How To Miss

Regardless of the method a coach uses to teach an athlete how to lift, there is one skill that should be taught during the very first workout (if not at the beginning of that workout). That skill is how to miss safely. Why is the skill of missing so fundamentally important? It is crucial to protecting the physical and mental well being of the athlete. Perhaps an analogy is the best way to demonstrate this point.

When I was quite young, I took a course in judo that was given at the local YMCA. Those were the days before karate and the other martial arts systems based on striking an opponent became the rage in this country. In those days the appeal of judo to many youngsters was similar to that of the popular martial arts today. That appeal was in developing the ability to reduce the most evil, powerful and aggressive foe to a state of absolute harmlessness with but one spectacular move (though the emphasis in judo is on rendering an opponent temporarily harmless, not unconscious or injured). Much to my dismay and that of the other youngsters in the class, the instructor said that we would have to spend our early lessons learning how to fall! We were mortified and we voiced our dissatisfaction. The entire objective of our study (to us) was to make the opponent fall, not ourselves. Surely, if we were skilled enough, a fall would never occur. Why focus on the subject of falling? Our wise instructor was steadfast in his position but patient in his explanation. He reasoned that when we were practicing, someone would have to fall, and that person could only do so safely if he or she knew how to do it properly. Moreover, in the unlikely event that we did have a temporary lapse in our own technique and were thrown by an opponent, our skill in falling would render that fall harmless to us.

I have a similar theory in weightlifting. There the lifter has one opponent and one opponent only: the bar. When a well trained and determined lifter battles with the bar, the battle will nearly always be won by the athlete. In the event it is not, the lifter should be prepared to get out of harm's way quickly, effectively and automatically. Therefore, the method of missing safely should be learned on day one.

Learning to miss has one added bonus beyond injury prevention. An athlete who knows how to miss, one who knows he or she knows, will not be afraid to try. Therefore, learning to miss does not introduce a negative (i.e., the concept of a miss) into the learning process. The lifter who is well equipped for a miss can be as aggressive as possible in attacking the bar, bolstered by the knowledge that in the event of any emergency, the falling bar can be easily escaped.

The good news about misses on the classical lifts is that the equipment is designed to prevent and minimize injury. The proper lifting platform is constructed with a non-slippery surface so that the lifter's feet will have a sound footing. Nothing but the bar and the lifter is on the platform during the lift; all plates that are not being used for that attempt are stored safely off the platform. Plates that fit tightly on the bar and collars that hold the plates in place assure proper balance of the bar and guarantee that the plates will tend to be a safe distance from the lifter should they fall (the lifter will be under the bar and not the plates).

The 45 cm diameter of the all plates 15 kg. and up (and even some plates as light as 5 kg. or even 2.5 kg.) is sufficient so that if the lifter is lying flat on his or her back with the head turned to the side when the bar falls, the bar will be clear of the body in the vast majority of cases (i.e., unless the lifter's head or body is unusually large). Assuming the lifter has the proper equipment and is using it in the correct manner, he or she can then focus on the proper principles of getting out from under the bar in the event of a miss.

One principle is that the lifter should generally remain between the plates of the bar. This should not be misinterpreted to mean the lifter should

remain under the bar. Rather, the principle is that the lifter should not try to move the body or feet sideways in an escape, because doing so can place the foot or another part of the body under the falling plates. A second principle is to use the potentially harmful downward force generated by the bar to force the body out of the way of the bar when it falls. This is accomplished by the lifter's always using the hands and arms to push the body away from the bar, generally in a backward direction. In the snatch and jerk, it means that the lifter should always push out on the arms as vigorously as possible when performing the squat under in order to reach a straight arm position by the end of the squat under phase, no matter what the height of the bar. When the bar has not been lifted to a sufficient height to complete the snatch or jerk, pushing out on the arms will usually result in the body's being pushed backward (sometimes forward), but always away from the bar. The lifter should add to this by pushing forward and up when the bar is felt to be both short of the necessary position and forward of the body (up and back when the bar is short and behind), allowing the body to jump or fall in the opposite direction of the push (e.g., if the athlete is pushing the bar forward, he or she should be jumping backward).

In the clean effort should be made to rack the bar on the shoulders with elbows well up. If the bar then falls short, its force in contacting the shoulders will generally drive the hips down and back, causing the lifter to fall backward and away from the bar. The lifter should assist this motion by pushing forward with the hands against the bar and forward with the feet against the floor to drive the arms, shoulders, hips and knees out from under the bar's falling path. If the elbows are forced down when the bar is caught, the lifter can assure that no wrist injury will occur via contact of the elbows and thighs or knees by pushing in on the elbows as they fall while also pushing back with the arms and legs as described above .

In the unlikely event that the lifter cannot push the bar forward beyond the knees and move the body back when a clean is missed, the lifter may feel himself or herself falling back with the bar on the shoulders. Should this occur, the lifter should push the bar away from the shoulders as he or she falls back and let the bar fall between the knees and shoulders (i.e., at waist level). As a last resort (but a reasonably safe one), the lifter should keep the elbows pointing up toward the ceiling during the fall and turn the head to the side as it nears the platform so that it there is ample room between the falling bar and the head. This kind of positioning assures that no part of the body is between the bar and the platform as the bar falls, decreasing the potential for catching the full force of the falling bar on that body part, rather than by the platform and the plates.

Some early practice at missing and occasional drills thereafter will be well rewarded because the lifter will have acquired a clear knowledge of what to do when the going gets tough. Knowing how to miss, committing to alertness and selecting poundages correctly are the keys to eliminating fear and avoiding traumatic injuries in weightlifting. Weightlifting is inherently safer than many of the most popular sports practiced in the United States today. When safety is stressed, it becomes a very safe sport in which traumatic injuries will be rare. Therefore, safe lifting should always be the first rule in any gym.

Some other things that should be taught to the beginning lifters are the basics of gym safety and etiquette. For example, a lifter should never stand in front of, or too close to, another lifter while that lifter is lifting. Lifters should share equipment freely and load the bar for one another (e.g., lifter A, who is about to lift, prepares mentally to do so while the lifter B, who will lift next after lifter A, and the lifter who has just completed a lift on that bar, lifter C, load for lifter A). Further aspects of safety are discussed in a number of other chapters of this book, particularly in Chapter 4.

What the Athlete Should Be Thinking About While Learning the Lifts

There are several important concepts to consider when an athlete is learning technique. The first concept is that there is a limit to what the mind can hold in its focus at any one point in time. Therefore, the athlete cannot be expected to remember too many things when performing the lift. The coach who shouts a stream of instructions is having little positive effect. If the athlete tries to focus on them all, he or she will either forget the earliest ones or fail to capture the later directions. Strategies and instructions for correcting faults must recognize the need for economy in terms of what the lifter must retain in the process of fault correction.

A second concept is that while the athlete can be expected to feel certain things while lifting, particularly at the early stages of learning, the ultimate goal is to make the lifting so automatic that those feelings are not as acute. Therefore, while the athlete can be told how doing a certain technique correctly will feel, the ultimate goal is to perform the motion without feeling a great deal on a conscious level along the way that can be used as a cue; rather, the aim is to execute one "seamless" motion.

A third basic concept is that there is a difference among what a lifter appears to be doing, what the lifter is actually doing and what the lifter is experiencing as he or she is doing a lift. The coach needs to know what the athlete is actually doing in order to counsel the lifter. However, it is also crucial for the coach to be able to tell the lifter

what to think of accomplishing in order to achieve the desired results.

In order to understand this distinction, it is helpful for the coach to recall the pattern of development through which our understanding of weightlifting technique has evolved to the present day. When weightlifting began, athletes experimented with techniques that could improve performance, often without the benefit of a coach. These lifters were the explorers, those who conceived and tested various aspects of technique, mastering their activity by trial and error. In the next stage, those who observed an athlete performing a new technique analyzed it and adopted the athlete's actions as a sort of model. They then taught the model to fledgling athletes, thereby saving the athlete the effort of having to experiment with many techniques and perhaps never discovering the most effective one. A still later development in weightlifting technique occurred when scientific tools of gross observation (e.g., high-speed film analysis) enabled us to overcome the limitations of human perception to understand what athletes are doing vs. what they appear to be doing. It was through such analysis that we learned lifters were beginning to split in the jerk as soon as the bar cleared their shoulders, not once the bar reached the top of the head (as was once believed when only the raw powers of observation were available to coaches).

In the next step in the development of learning technique, findings from other fields were integrated with the improved understanding of weightlifting technique. Knowledge of such areas of science as mechanics and motor learning were brought to bear on technique issues. For example, when an understanding of the concept of reaction time was obtained, it was realized that what a lifter is doing is not necessarily what he or she should thinking of doing when trying to employ proper technique.

Therefore, if the lifter wants to assure that the split will begin when the bar just clears the shoulders in the jerk, the athlete may have to focus on what occurs just before that happens in order to react fast enough for actual motion to begin at the correct time. If the lifter thinks of beginning the split just as he or she feels that a maximum effort has been applied to the bar in the drive (i.e., near the bottom of the dip), he or she will actually split one-fifth of a second later, about when the actual beginning of the split should take place.

Today, with sophisticated scientific equipment, we are able to provide athletes with feedback about their performance that would have been impossible to obtain only a few years ago. For instance, through the use of force plates and computer aided analysis, we are able to tell an athlete what his or her power output is during various phases of the lift, thereby helping the lifter to attain a more correct power output or to reinforce one that is already correct.

With all of the sophistication that is available in regard to weightlifting technique today and the far greater sophistication that will develop in the future, the basic need to learn the movement is still the key to becoming a weightlifter. The coach and athlete must always bear this in mind. As a consequence, the focus should always be on advising the athlete with regard to what he or she should be thinking, feeling and doing before and during the lift, as compared with describing in great detail what they are doing wrong.

Different phases of the lifts lend themselves to different approaches. Lifters can learn the starting position by thinking of how the various parts of the body feel in terms of tension and position. Since the start of the pull and the jerk are static positions, the lifter has plenty of time to assume the proper position and to assure that everything is in order. The lifter must practice this position until he or she can, at will and almost unconsciously, assume a correct starting position.

The Starting Position

The starting position was described in detail in the previous chapter, but some additional comments, which are more from the athlete's perspective, can be given here. In the starting position of the pull, the upper arms are relaxed, and the lower arms have the tension created by the lifter's assuming a firm grip. (Thinking of the arms as ropes that are stretched slightly taut sometimes helps the lifter to assume the correct arm position.) The elbows are positioned so that the outside point of the elbow is pointing out to the lifter's side, and the crook (inside) of the lifter's elbow is pointing toward the lifter's side; the lifter can simply look at his or her arm position in order to assure that it is correct. Tension in the muscles of the mid-back pulls the shoulders back, but the shoulders are not pulled upward (are not shrugged in any way), and the chest is out (i.e., thrust forward or inflated). Tension in the lower back muscles is sufficient to hold the lower back in an arched position when the bar is separated from the platform. Many lifters find it helpful to tense and even spread the latissimus dorsi muscles of the back in preparation for the separation of the bar from the platform. Tension in these muscles, as well as some tension in the rear deltoids, helps to keep the bar close to the lifter in the early stages of the pull.

This concept of tension in muscle groups should not be misunderstood. A sprinting coach will encourage a sprinter to run at 90% speed rather than to push to 100%, because by thinking about maximum speed, the athlete will tend to "tie-up," to tense his or her muscles to the point at which they inhibit the production of speed. Similarly, the tension that we are speaking about here is enough to hold the body links rigid but is not necessarily the maximum tension the athlete is capable of generating in that muscle group or groups.

Preparing to assume the starting position by standing at attention and then, while maintaining that positioning of the upper body, bending the legs and leaning forward with the torso to grip the bar are good ways to maintain the chest-out, flat-back position. The lifter's balance is over the middle of the foot (helping the lifter feel weight on the heels and the toes enables the lifter to feel the middle by contrast), and the feet are flat on the floor. When the lifter is practicing the start, the coach can assist the lifter by giving corrective instructions and (with the lifter's consent) moving the body to the correct positions or by using the hands as a means for directing the lifter's attention to areas that have insufficient or excessive tension.

In the starting position for the jerk, the feet are flat on the floor, the legs are straight and the legs muscles have an athletic tension; they are ready for activity and supporting the bar and body comfortably, but they are not tense. The torso is in a strictly vertical position with the spine held in as straight a position as possible (both the lumbar and thoracic arches are reduced to the greatest extent possible). There is sufficient tension in the muscles all around the torso to assure that the torso will not "give" in terms of its angle or rigidity during the dip or drive. The angle of the upper arm to the floor varies from 45° to as high as 90°. (The higher it is, the greater the security of the bar on the chest, but too high a position causes some lifters to experience a sensation of choking or lightheadedness as the bar presses on the windpipe or the blood vessels of the neck.) The arms should have just enough tension to hold the bar in the proper position, but they should not be actively pushing the bar upward off the chest. The head is tilted back slightly with the chin pulled in toward the neck (which keeps the face out of the direction of the bar's upward path).

The Lift-Off

The muscles of the legs are used to separate the bar from the platform. To avoid a tendency to straighten the torso immediately as the bar is separated from the platform, some coaches encourage lifters to think of pushing the feet into the floor (as compared with lifting the bar). Some lifters pull nearly as hard as they can from the floor, particularly in the clean, while others rely on a more explosive effort later in the pull, but all lifters must explode during the final explosion phase. At no point in the lift is the lifter thinking of lifting the bar solely through the action of the torso. In the final explosion of the pull, the torso, legs and hips are all working together to impart force to the bar.

Ultimately the lifter pulls and then pushes the body under the bar by using his or her arms and by jumping down vigorously. At the end of the effort, as the body is preparing to receive the bar, the arms are pushing up in the snatch and jerk, and the elbows are whipping in the clean. An effort is made to tighten the torso and, to a very limited extent, the lower body. Finally, catching the muscular rebound that is generated from the downward force of the legs in receiving the bar, the lifter pushes up with the legs so that recovery from the bottom position is almost automatic and uses the elastic energy of the legs effectively.

In the jerk the lifter thinks of a natural speed dip (but of dipping as fast of possible) while maintaining solid contact with the bar; the bar must not be permitted to lose even the slightest contact with the shoulders. At the end of the dip, the lifter thinks of reversing the downward motion of the bar as rapidly and vigorously as possible. This is followed by an effort to make a sharp upward thrust and an immediate and vigorous downward movement into the squat under while pushing up hard on the arms. There is an emphasis on keeping the feet close to the platform and replacing them as quickly and vigorously as possible. Foot placement must also be correct (slightly pigeon toed, especially with the back foot), and the lifter must be careful to move the hips slightly forward from their original position (in no event should they be permitted to travel rearward). Perhaps the single most important technique issue in the jerk is the instantaneous movement from the drive into the split (thinking of jumping immediately from the low point in the dip to the split approximates to correct timing).

In all three lifts, the lifter must keep in mind two explosive efforts, one during the final explosion phase of each lift and the other in squatting under and fixing the bar. Far too many lifters simply explode to hurl the bar upward and then simply "float" under the bar. The lifter must make two explosive efforts in virtually immediate succession in order to reach his or her maximal capabilities.

Using Goals, Pictures and Feelings To Guide You

Most lifters benefit by thinking of goals rather than the specific movements of body parts (i.e., "seeing" or "feeling" the correct position as opposed to thinking that they will move their legs in a certain way). Mental pictures or projections of how a certain movement will feel are also generally more effective than thinking in words in eliciting an optimal outcome. For example, in the jerk the lifter needs to think of landing in the split with both feet turned in, the arms turned so that the crooks of the elbows are pointing toward the front of the head, and the torso vertical or leaning slightly forward and with the bar placed at or somewhat behind the

rear of the head. The lifter can think of a very small number of details, but a mental picture of a position subsumes many details. Once the lifter has a picture and is failing to assume the position that is in his or her mind's eye, the coach can explain what is not being achieved, and the lifter can focus on the overall picture as well as the detail that must be corrected. In most cases the lifter is limited to thinking of a few things: assuring a proper starting position, exploding at the proper point and catching the bar with an explosive effort. The easiest way to do that is to picture or think of the entire effort. See the body in the correct position. If some incorrect result occurs, visualize a new picture (one that is clearer, more precise or more exaggerated than the one before). One of the biggest road blocks to proper technique is failing to understand that your image and feeling of a certain position assumed are not correct. By learning to associate a new feeling and/or image with the proper technique, you can achieve correct performance and set about the process of automating that performance.

There are some generic objectives that lifters should have during each stage in the lift. During the first phase there should be a focus on developing a solid link between the bar and the platform through the body. The lifter in effect endeavors to take any "slack" out of the body's kinetic chain. Just as a tractor trying to pull a trailer through a slack rope will waste power at best and snap the rope at worst, so the body must serve as the taut conduit through which force from the support (platform) is transmitted to the bar.

During the second stage of the pull, the lifter should try to achieve correct bar direction and generate sufficient velocity to carry the bar through the adjustment phase effectively. During the jerk it is important to achieve optimal speed (not so fast as to foster a loss of control and not so slow as to tax the leg muscles unnecessarily or lessen the elastic reaction that the muscles stretched before a contraction can deliver). In all of the lifts it is critical to maintain correct positioning of the bar in relation to the body and to maintain proper balance during the second phase. It is particularly important to keep the shoulders ahead of the bar during this phase (and the next as well). In many ways the second phase of the pull sets the stage for the rest of the lift, and errors here can have dire consequences throughout the rest of the lift.

In the execution of the third phase of the lift, the athlete should focus on correct positioning and a rapid movement into the correct execution of the fourth phase. Most coaches urge the athlete to keep the feet flat and in solid contact with the platform at this stage of the pull, but many top athletes begin to rise on the balls and toes of the feet during this stage of the pull. Correct positioning is critical for the optimal execution of the fourth phase, but, all things being equal, the shorter the duration of this phase, the smaller the loss of acceleration that the bar suffers and the more effective the elastic reaction of the muscles. It is important to make the transition from the this phase to the fourth phase of the pull as quickly as is consistent with maintaining proper positioning. Doing so will serve the dual purpose of minimizing the drop in velocity that occurs during this stage in the pull and maximizing the use of muscle elasticity in moving from the rebending to the ultimate straightening of the legs at the end of the final explosion phase of the pull.

During the fourth, or final explosion, phase, the lifter must endeavor to accelerate the movement of the bar as much as possible without remaining with the pull so long that the squat under is compromised. Many lifters find that focusing on raising the shoulders vertically and as explosively as possible helps them generate maximum power at this critical stage of the pull.

During the fifth, or unsupported squat under, phase, the athlete should be concentrating on moving through the phase at utmost speed by regaining contact with the platform as soon as possible and by interacting with the bar (pulling himself or herself under it and then pushing away from it to get the bar to arm's length as rapidly as possible, using the bar to propel the body downward).

The focus of the sixth phase is on interacting with the bar and bringing it under control by exerting force against it to control any horizontal or downward movement. It is also important to recover from this position as quickly as is consistent with maintaining control of the bar.

"Freeing" the Mind to Lift Effectively

Before leaving the subject of what the athlete should be thinking during practice it should be noted that there has been much discussion in the scientific and popular literature in recent years about such notions as letting the "intuitive", "right brain" and "inner" aspects of the mind direct bodily movement. The main premise behind these notions is that the body has an existing "intelligence" about movement, an intelligence that, if left undisturbed by conscious thought, would enable us to perform most new skills much more quickly and easily than we would if we had to rely on a conscious effort to master the same skills.

The advocates of this theory generally argue that animals, many of whom have highly developed and graceful movement patterns, lack the conceptual faculty of man. Therefore, they reason, such a faculty adds little or nothing to skill development. Similarly, children, they argue, are often quite adept at learning and executing certain skills, and they have limited conceptual development. In addition, top performers rarely think of specific movements of the body in carrying

out their skills (perhaps, the "inner" theorists argue, that is why they are top performers). Still further, there have been stories of top athletes who have analyzed their own performances to the point where they have lost the natural rhythm that they once had and have suffered diminished performance as a result. Finally, there have been reports of coaches in various sports who have used new, intuitive and non-verbal techniques of teaching with a success rate that exceeds anything that has been achieved through more conventional methods.

An indirect argument has also been made in favor of non-conscious control of the body during practice on the basis that conscious evaluation can have a negative effect on performance. This argument essentially states that conscious thought regarding physical performance necessarily leads to self-criticism and analysis, which can contribute to a negative attitude on the part of the learner, and, hence, to poor overall learning progress.

While these arguments have some legitimacy, it is clear that at a conscious understanding of a skill is essential for truly mastering it. What is also clear is that there is an interplay between conscious and unconscious learning as one moves from awareness to mastery of a particular technique. Therefore, the athlete should practice at times with the mind focused on how one is trying to achieve something and at other times on what one is trying to achieve. If things are not going well in practice when a "how" focus is being used, it may be appropriate to switch to a "what" focus for a time and vice versa.

There are many intuitive approaches to skills development, but the essentials are to picture or feel the desired movement (and/or outcome) and then to relax the mind during the performance to permit the unconscious mind to take over and carry out the movement. This lack of conscious direction of a movement may seem hard to accomplish for a person who has been practicing conscious direction for some time. But with practice, the athlete can learn to "let go" with the conscious mind and simply let the unconscious take over. This kind of practice should be in the arsenal of every athlete and coach

A Commitment to Being Alert

A commitment on the part of the athlete to being alert when receiving the bar on the shoulders and overhead is critical to safety. Some lifters, out of fear of a heavy weight, actually execute the final explosion and then purposely blank out their minds during the squat under. The implicit belief here is: "If I just explode and go under the bar, maybe I'll wake up again with the bar safely over my head or on my shoulders." This is a practice that one of my early weightlifting buddies, Al Conde, used to describe as "a pull and a prayer."

A careful distinction must be made between the blanking out above described and a fearless attitude toward attempting a heavy lift. The former is a dangerous habit, the latter is an absolutely necessary characteristic of the elite lifter. The lifter who is blanking out suspends his or her awareness of the bar until hitting his or her lowest receiving position and then, in effect, opens his or her eyes to see what has happened. The fearless weightlifter goes under the bar with the expectation that the lift will be made and with the understanding that in the blinding speed of the squat under a complete and conscious awareness of the body in relation to the bar may not be available to the lifter at all times. Consequently, the lifter must rely on learned skills and habits to move under the bar and to catch it. However, such a lifter is fully committed to being aware of the bar's position as soon as such conscious awareness is possible and to interacting with the bar as necessary when full awareness is available. The lifter who blanks out is denying reality as long as possible. The fearless lifter's focus is on reality, because such a lifter is confident that, whatever the situation, he or she can deal with it. The commitment to reality delivers to the lifter an awareness of the bar's position only a split second before it is delivered to the lifter who avoids such knowledge, but in that split second resides the moment of truth for the weightlifter, the difference between success and failure, between safety and risk.

The Selection of Reps When Learning Technique

There are differences of opinion among coaches about the optimal number of reps for learning technique. Some coaches advocate the use of three to five (or more) repetitions, and others believe that singles— doubles at most—are best for learning. Scientific research and practical experience have shed significant light on this area.

Certainly there is a correlation between the number of trials an athlete completes in a certain activity and the degree of learning that the athlete experiences. Since repetitions permit more practice in a given time frame, they can therefore enhance learning within a specified practice period. In addition, learning is enhanced in an environment in which the athlete can experiment and adjust the technique used with ever greater refinement, and repetitions facilitate this process. However, it is also well known that fatigued muscles cannot perform motor skills as well as muscles that are not in such a state. Moreover, there is a difference between a miss that occurs when an athlete is fatigued, and one that occurs when the weight is too heavy. Fatigue may cause the last rep in any set to emulate a rep with a heavier weight in terms of perceived effort, but it is unlikely that exactly the same muscle fibers are being used in the same way as they would be with a heavier weight.

Given the conflicting advantages and disadvantages of higher and lower reps for the purpose of learning, a reasonable approach to the prescription of repetitions for an athlete learning an Olympic lift is to consider the load to which the lifter will be subjected. If a lifter is using a light bar to experiment with a particular aspect of technique (e.g., foot position in the split, or balance in the low position of the snatch), there is no reason why the lifter cannot perform three to five or even more reps, as long as the athlete does not feel real muscular fatigue by the last rep of set. With a heavier weight, it is important that the number of reps attempted does not result in a significantly fatigued lifter attempting another rep (and doing different things due to fatigue).

In my early days in the sport, five reps were the rage for most exercises in my gym. It was my experience, and that of most of the lifters that I observed on such a program, that maximum sets of five reps could be performed effectively only in very simple exercises (e.g., squats, good mornings and perhaps even partial pulling motions). And five repetitions were very effective in such exercises. However, where more complex movements were involved (e.g., on the snatch and C&J themselves), this number of reps was not effective, because while they may have stimulated growth in muscle strength and size, they tended to lead to a breakdown of technique arising out of fatigue.

Once the lifter has gone past the early stages of learning, with its frequent need for experimentation and correction, singles emerge as the preferred method for perfecting technique. Singles permit the load to approach maximal levels more often, levels at which the patterns of movement, tempo and force application resemble most closely those to be used in competition. Singles also permit greater precision in movement, the ultimate objective of weightlifting mastery.

In addition, sets of two to three reps with weights in the 80% to 90% range can be very effective for the practice of technique under sub-maximal conditions. When performing such sets, a lifter is handling sufficient weight to make error detection reliable but not so much weight that technique cannot remain the primary focus. Even higher reps can usefully be employed to introduce variety into workouts for warm-ups and in simpler assistance exercises (particularly when the object of performing these exercises is to stimulate muscle growth as well as strength). For example, when an athlete is performing power versions of the Olympic lifts (e.g., the power snatch and power clean, exercises described in Chapter 5), three and even as many as five reps may be employed consistently because they are simpler and involve less strenuous movements per repetition than the full versions of the Olympic lifts. However, singles should be the foundation for the advanced lifter while performing the classical exercises (the snatch and C&J), with doubles and triples being employed intermittently with sub-maximal weights.

The Selection of Weight When Learning to Lift

Weight selection is one of the most important decisions the coach or athlete can make during the learning process. The use of too little weight for too long can result in the athlete's receiving very limited feedback on performance and in a loss of motivation, but these risks are small compared to the risks of using too much weight. When an athlete lifts too much weight too early, he or she risks outright traumatic injury. He or she also assures that technique mastery will never occur; skills cannot be learned or materially improved by beginners when they lift heavy weights. Over the long term, early application of heavy loads will lead to inconsistency, frustration and unnecessary overuse injury; because poor technique is mechanically unsound, it subjects the body to unnecessary stress. It is almost impossible to overemphasize how important it is for beginners to train with moderate weights. To do otherwise is to virtually ruin an athlete's career at its start.

I always begin teaching the lifter how to perform the Olympic lifts with a stick, a light (10 kg. to 15 kg. bar or a standard 20 kg. Olympic bar; weaker athletes are better off with a stick and stronger athletes with a 20 kg. bar. Some aspects of the lift will be impossible to experience with a bar or stick, but some of the basic patterns of movement can be amply modeled with minimal resistance. Once the athlete has grasped the basics of the movement with the stick or empty bar, he or she can begin to add weight gradually. The perfect weight for beginners provides the athlete with barely enough resistance to feel how the bar is responding to technique variations. If the weight is too light, the lifter cannot feel any resistance and hence any difference between the efficient and improper application of force. At the same time the weight must be light enough so that the lifter does not have to worry about whether or not he or she can make the lift. Such worries force the athlete to put technique on autopilot and hope for the best, instead of permitting the athlete to focus on the process with the assurance that success will occur automatically as long as he or she does it properly.

The correct weight is relatively easy for the experienced coach to see, but for the newer coach there a few guidelines regarding what to look for. First, the weight should not be flying forward or back with a flick of the lifter's shoulders or arms (e.g., traveling in front of the lifter on one rep and behind on another merely because the lifter flexes the arms and/or shoulders in a certain way). Second, the lifter should not be able to perform more than five to eight reps with the weight (and the lifter should never do more than three reps with a weight that can be made for five and no more than five reps with a weight that can be made for eight when he or she is learning technique). The athlete should look nearly as fresh on the last rep of the set as the first. If there is a noticeable slowing down or declining precision with later reps in the set, the weight is too heavy for that number of reps (so either the weight or the number of reps must be reduced).

The general principle of not using a weight that causes the athlete's technique to decline materially holds true throughout the athlete's career. In the beginning the athlete's technique will decline when the lifter is further from his or her maximum. A beginner's technique may deteriorate with much more than 60% or 70% percent of maximum; an advanced lifter's technique will not deteriorate until maximum loads are reached. In either case, attempts with weights that lead to any material decline in technique cannot be recommended and must be carefully guarded against.

The good news is that the athlete can improve his or her power with virtually any resistance in the beginning. In fact, research performed in Eastern Europe, as well as practical experience, have demonstrated the young athletes improve more rapidly using lighter loads than heavier ones. Therefore it is ridiculous to have beginners train with maximum weights. It is not until later in the lifter's training that heavier weights are needed in order to cause the lifter to improve. Heavy weights in the beginning are both counterproductive from the standpoint of building technique and unnecessary for building strength and power.

It will generally take an athlete anywhere from several to a dozen or more workouts to exhibit basic technique in the Olympic lifts done in power style. It will take several months for the lifter to handle even close to maximum weights with sound technique and years for the lifter to handle maximum weights with little or no technique breakdown. Again, this presents no problems in terms of the athlete's enjoying the benefits of the Olympic lifts, because improvements will come at first through handling only very modest weights (this issue is discussed further in Chapter 3).

Methods Of Identifying Technique Faults

There are two basic approaches to identifying technique faults. One method involves comparing the technique of a given athlete to some idealized model of technique and noting any differences. Implicit in this "ideal" approach is the assumption that some model or perfect technique has been identified, typically on the basis of what one or more champions or some group of accomplished lifters does when lifting. The analysis of technique presented in the previous chapter is an example of what many coaches would use as the basis for an "ideal" model of weightlifting technique. Deviations from such a model in the technique of a given lifter can be noted, and the lifter can be then be asked to reduce or eliminate those deviations.

The second basic method for identifying technique faults is more proactive in nature. It consists of identifying and examining each of the factors that affect performance in at effort to determine which factors can be changed to yield the largest improvement in results with the smallest amount of effort. For instance, you can examine the degree to which the bar descends between the final explosion of the pull and the point at which it is fixed overhead in the snatch. By reducing the amount of that descent, the lifter can reduce the height to which the bar must be pulled in order to snatch it. The distance which the bar descends during the squat under depends on a number of factors (as were illustrated in the qualitative analysis section of the previous chapter): the length of time the bar travels upward after the final explosion phase (the longer it travels upward, the longer the athlete has to move under the bar and bring it under control before the bar falls back toward the platform); the distance the lifter must travel in order to get under the bar (this is affected by the starting height of the lifter during the final explosion phase and the height of the position reached when the lifter brings the bar under control); and the speed at which the lifter travels in descending under the bar.

If the athlete can achieve greater bar velocity during the final explosion, reduce the distance which he or she must travel to get under the bar or go under the bar faster, performance can be improved. The coach and/or athlete must decide which factor(s) will be the most amenable to correction and then arrange for training interventions which will lead to the desired improvements.

This second method of identifying areas of improvement should be an ongoing process throughout a lifter's career. It requires ingenuity on the part of the coach and daring on the part of the athlete to persist in identifying and correcting areas of improvement when others would say that your technique is already almost perfect. It also requires persistence to continually improve the consistency of technique that is already very sound. The more immediate problem for less accomplished lifters is no identify current and significant technique errors and to eradicate them. That effort will be the focus of the next several sections of this chapter.

The Kinds of Technical Mistakes that Are Made in Weightlifting

It is fairly common for books on weightlifting to have a section on the correction of technique faults. Such sections normally identify a series of faults in outcomes (e.g., "the bar is forward of the lifter during the squat under"), along with their possible causes, and recommended corrective measures. There are at least two major problems with such approaches to error correction. The first problem is that the list of faults identified and the corrective measures offered tend to be incomplete. This is because the range of possible errors is nearly infinite (there are many individual errors and many more possible combinations of errors). The second problem is that the remedies suggested are necessarily applied in a random fashion. Since the author is not in a position to evaluate a specific lifter, he or she must merely say: "The problem may be A, B or C. D and E are possible corrective measures if the cause is indeed A, but corrective measures F, G or H must be employed if the problem is B." Naturally, such a system leads to hit or miss solutions to problems, and a great deal of time is wasted experimenting with inappropriate corrective means.

We will attempt to overcome these difficulties at least partially with a somewhat different method of fault identification and correction. The emphasis will be on the proper identification of faults and the effective analysis of their causes. Once the real cause of a given fault has been identified, developing a prescription for its correction becomes far easier and far more systematic. In this section we will first explain the basic kinds of faults that exist. The next step will be to give guidance with respect to how those faults can be uncovered. Finally, some case studies in fault correction will be provided.

Five basic kinds of errors can occur when executing the two Olympic lifts and their variations. They are errors of : a) balance; b) body positioning; c) relative muscle tension; d) timing; and e) effort. While these errors can occur at virtually any stage of a lift and in nearly any combination, almost every fault in weightlifting technique can be traced to one or more of these five basic errors. If you can learn to identify and address these mistakes, then you are well on your way to perfecting your technique or your coaching.

It must emphasized that while the errors listed above have been identified separately, they are often interrelated. For example, inappropriate tensions in various muscle groups can result in an improper sequence of muscle contractions during an explosive effort, and improper positioning can lead to improper tension. Therefore, while these faults should be viewed as separate when errors are first being identified, it is important to understand that once identification has been accomplished, the possible interrelationships between the errors (especially in terms of cause and effect) must be considered before any attempt at correction is made. If this is not done, the coach and athlete can be frustrated by efforts to correct causes that are more fundamentally effects.

Errors of Balance

Errors of balance are among the most common and serious in all of weightlifting, yet they are relatively easy to correct. Why are they so common? Perhaps it is because improper balance can be difficult to detect. Moreover, it is often difficult for the coach to explain proper balance, particularly if that coach has never experienced the sensation of a heavy lift (in relation to his or her body weight). The most common instances of this error are situations in which the athlete's weight is centered over the wrong part of the foot.

In the pull the lifter is most often shifting his or her body backward too early (i.e., shifting the center of gravity of his or her body and the bar backward at the same time). This generally results in the lifter's getting his or her shoulders too far behind the bar too early in the pull (thereby hampering the lifter's ability to impart force to the bar) and/or generating excessively rearward force during the final explosion phase of the pull (which leads to the lifter's jumping back and pulling the bar back, often to a different degree). It is possible for the lifter's balance to be too far forward during the pull (at the early stages of the pull this is characterized by the balance being felt toward the toes rather than toward the middle or rear of the foot). This error can cause the lifter to be unable to properly apply force to the bar and/or cause the lifter to throw the bar forward unnecessarily during the final explosion phase of the pull.

In the jerk there is a tendency for the athlete transfer his or her balance toward the front of the foot during the dip. This will hamper the athlete's ability to impart force to the bar, make it more difficult for the athlete to split forward under the bar enough to support it overhead and cause the force generated during the explosion phase to be forward as well as upward. Improper balance in the split undermines the lifter's ability to control the bar and can place undue stress on the front of the back leg (depending on the direction in which the balance is misdirected).

It will take careful observation to uncover minor errors in balance. Major errors are telegraphed during the pull by the positioning of the athlete's shoulders relative to the bar, particularly when the bar reaches the height of the knees. If the shoulders are behind the bar at this point, there is most assuredly a balance error; there can be a problem even when the shoulders are directly over the bar. Input from the lifter can be very helpful because he or she can feel his or her balance.

While a thorough discussion of balance problems could itself require at least a chapter of a book to discuss, the main point for the beginning coach and lifter is to understand where the balance should be at each stage of the lift (based on the technical descriptions that were provided in the prior chapter) and to check that aspect of technique on a regular basis. If the lifter's balance is improper, it will difficult for that lifter to do anything else very well.

Errors in Body Positioning

Errors in body positioning often appear in concert with errors in balance, but they can be rather independent of balance issues as well. Errors in positioning the body prevent it from exerting maximal force. Often an error in positioning can make the bar feel lighter at a certain stage of the lift, which is one reason why lifters so frequently assume an improper position. The problem arises when the lifter proceeds to a subsequent position in the lift. The very position which has made a preceding stage in the lift easier has compromised the athlete's position in a subsequent and more crucial stage in the lift. Common errors in positioning are: permitting the shoulders to travel behind the bar at too early a stage in the pull (i.e., before the later portions of the final acceleration stage); raising the torso or hips prematurely during the pull; and not assuming a sufficiently upright position during the squat under to receive the force of a heavy weight.

In order to diagnose errors in positioning, the coach will want to compare the athlete's positions throughout the lift to some model of a lifter who is performing correctly. The analysis of technique presented in the previous chapter provides ranges of positioning that have been employed successfully by high level athletes.

Errors in Tension

In order to perform a correct lift, the tension in each muscle group must be optimal at each stage in the lift. Any unnecessary tension can hamper the application of force, place the bar and body in an improper relation to one another or greatly inhibit the athlete's speed. Errors in tension are among the most intractable. Until a lifter grasps a virtually new concept of the kind of force that he or she must apply, the correct approach often cannot be achieved. For example, if the athlete "sees" the power clean as an exercise in which the bar is lifted to the shoulders using the arms, at least in part, he or she is likely to use the arms improperly. If, in contrast, the lifter understands that he or she is really throwing the bar vertically into the air, using the legs and back and then catching it on the shoulders, the likelihood of using the arms improperly is diminished.

Premature contraction of the upper trapezius muscle and the biceps are among the most common errors of this kind during the second through fourth stages of the pull. Premature contraction of the upper trapezius muscles will reduce the effectiveness of the athlete's final explosion. In contrast, a lack of sufficient tension in the back muscles will express itself as an inability to hold the torso rigid during the pull.

During the latter part of the squat under, unnecessary tension in the biceps can hamper proper elbow positioning in the clean. Undue tension in the legs during any part of the squat under can slow the athlete's descent under the bar in any of the lifts.

In weightlifting, as is so many other sports, the most problems result from excessive rather than inadequate tension. I often hear coaches exhorting their lifters to be tight during some phase of the lift. While there are certainly some lifters who compromise their positioning as a result of inadequate tension, the far more likely result of such as exhortation will be for the athlete to create unnecessary tension in his or her muscles, compromising their ability to explode effectively later in the pull.

The primary area in which tension is required in weightlifting during the first four stages of the lift is the torso (the rear torso, except the upper trapezius muscles, during the pull and virtually the entire torso in the jerk). The torso transmits power from the legs during the early stages of the lift. If it "gives" during the application of force, that force application will be compromised.

During the squat under phases of lifting, tension in the arms and torso is necessary in order to control the bar. In the snatch and jerk the athlete should be pushing out with the arms and pulling inward on the shoulder blades while pulling outward slightly on the bar (as if to stretch it). There should not be unnecessary tension in the shoulders or any effort to shrug the shoulders up. In the snatch, the clean and the jerk, the athlete should be endeavoring to puff the chest out. In the clean the focus is on driving the elbows up as well. The legs are always acting as shock absorbers, so they should not be consciously tightened to receive the bar.

None of the preceding discussion should be interpreted to mean that tension is not or should not be generated by muscles during the lifts. The legs, for example, are contracting vigorously during most of the lift. But the lifter is not trying to generate tension per se. He or she is attempting to generate an explosive effort (which will necessarily lead to an appropriate level of tension in the muscles that are needed in order to generate the explosive effort that is required).

Errors in Timing

It has often been said that "timing is everything in life." While that is not entirely true in weightlifting, or in life, timing is extremely important in both. You can have all of the explosive power and correct body positioning that is required to perform a given lift, but if your timing is off, your performance will suffer significantly.

Perhaps the most common timing error is weightlifting is premature straightening of the torso during the pull. This error is caused primarily by the athlete's anticipating the next stage of the lift. It also occurs because the lifter's back is weak relative to his or her legs, so he or she straightens the torso because it feels less strain in a more upright position. To correct the former problem the lifter needs to focus on performing each stage of the lift in its entirety without rushing on to a subsequent phase. To correct the latter problem, the lifter needs to increase his or her strength in the lagging area.

The opposite side of the coin from the lifter who rushes through a sequence is the lifter who hangs up in a sequence, devoting too much time to a certain phase. This is particularly common in lifters who are relatively poor in a particular lift or a portion thereof. Because the lifter feels inadequate in part or all of the lift, he or she tries to correct any perceived problem by an effort to apply force to the bar for a longer period. For instance, poor jerkers tend to drive the bar longer during the explosion phase than good jerkers. Such a lifter is attempting to correct a perceived problem of not driving the bar high enough when the actual problem is that the lifter is not able to assume a solid position for receiving the bar because he or she has insufficient time to get into the split once the drive has been completed. Such a lifter needs to emphasize rearranging the feet rapidly and replacing them vigorously during the squat under phase of the jerk rather than remaining with the drive phase for a longer period of time.

Another common example of this error occurs in new lifters who are learning to power clean or power snatch. An athlete performing a power clean often believes that he or she needs to pull the bar all the way up to the shoulders. The only way to do that is to keep pulling with body and arms right up to the point at which the bar is racked on the shoulders. An effort to pull the bar up to the shoulders will result in the lifter's catching the bar in a poor position because the athlete had no time to assume a correct one. The classic case is when the lifter catches the bar while leaning back with the torso and with the legs nearly straight. What has happened here is that the lifter has had virtually no time between completing the final explosion phase of the pull and catching the bar on the shoulders. The torso has not had time to return from a position in which it was leaning back slightly (at the completion of the explosion phase), and the legs have not had an opportunity to rebend properly. By pulling too long, the lifter has added a small amount of additional force to the bar during the final explosion phase, in return for which he or she has given up much of his or her ability to impart force to the bar during the supported squat under phase and the time necessary to assume an effective position in the squat under. What has been gained is less than what has been lost. The result is that the lifter lifts less and places himself or herself at greater risk or injury. Perhaps the surest indicator of a failure to move under the bar soon enough or quickly enough is a lack of speed or sponginess in the lifter's lockout in the snatch and jerk and a tendency for the bar to "crash" on the lifter during the clean.

Errors in Effort

Failure to apply maximum effort at the appropriate point in a lift will lead to less than optimal use of the power that an athlete can generate. On the other hand, application of maximal effort at the wrong stage in the lift will tend to compromise the application of maximal effort at a subsequent stage. It is indispensable for a lifter to explode as powerfully as possible during the final explosion phase of a lift. Such an effort will impart maximum force to the bar, causing it to reach the height necessary to execute the lift and giving the lifter time to move under the bar and catch it. Many lifters can lift effectively without generating a great deal of effort during the other stages in the lift, but maximum effort during the final explosion is a necessity for high performance.

In contrast, the lifter who concentrates on creating loud stamping noises with his or her feet by jumping into the air at the end of the lift and stamping his or her feet down when landing in the split or squat, rather than moving his or her feet immediately and vigorously into a correct position for receiving the bar, is likely to jar unnecessarily the body and ultimately the bar. Alternatively, the force that is created when the lifter contacts the platform will be dissipated through the lifter's body rather than being transmitted into the bar.

Analyzing Human Motion With Limited Scientific Training and Equipment

Many experienced coaches simply observe an athlete, sense what is going wrong and offer some corrective advice, all without a conscious and detailed analysis of what the athlete is doing. The advantage of such an approach is that it is simple and often effective. However, when a problem is relatively subtle, or the typical advice of the coach does not result in a correction, the intuitive method breaks down. For newer coaches and for problems

that are difficult for even experienced coaches to solve, there are several techniques that can be used to systematically analyze an athlete's technique and to explain that analysis to the athlete. The first and simplest technique described in this section is the development of the coach's powers of observation. The other techniques described do not require specialized scientific equipment or skills but do require some extra effort on the part of the coach.

Evaluating Performance Effectively by Using the Sense Organs

When observing the performance of an athlete for purposes of evaluating the athlete's technical mastery, it is important to establish the appropriate conditions for observation. The athlete should warm up fully, and then the observer should watch as many as fifteen to twenty trials (accomplished in sets of one to three repetitions), taking notes but making no comments. Generally, a 45° angle from the front or back affords the most favorable view of the largest number of technical factors. Many sports analysts prefer a 90° angle, but in weightlifting such an angle, while useful in a number of ways, allows the plates on the bar to block the observer's view. The further away the observer is from the lifter (to a point), the better the opportunity the observer has to look at the entire athlete-barbell system. Most coaches have a tendency to get too close to the athlete (i.e., a few feet away). There is nothing wrong with this method if only one aspect of technique is being focused on, but for a more general view of technique a distance of several yards is much better.

After a general observation of a few trials has taken place, the observer will want to focus on one or more areas that appear to need attention. Once this decision has been made, a suitable vantage point should be selected. Such a vantage point must afford an unobstructed view of the aspect of movement that is to be studied. In addition, if at all possible, it is very helpful to assure that a proper background is in place (i.e., one that provides a reference against which performance can be compared). For example, if the observer wishes to study the shape of the bar's trajectory for a given lifter during the snatch, a background that has some vertical lines to which the movement of the bar can be compared is invaluable. Similarly, when studying foot movement in the split, it is very useful to have straight lines drawn on the platform, some parallel and others at right angles to the lifter's feet when they are in the split position.

In addition to having points of reference below or beside the lifter, the use by the observer of a mask or other object that restricts the visual field to the area of the lifter or bar in question may be of help. With very fast movements, closing the eyes quickly at the moment of interest can help to preserve the desired image.

A chalk mark on the lifter's uniform from contact with the bar, the development of the lifter's muscles and wear on the lifter's uniform or shoes can also provide some evidence of technique factors that may be at work (although such evidence should be confirmed more directly before any advice is given to the lifter with respect to technique). Audible information can and should be used to evaluate technique as well. Certain aspects of lifting technique can be analyzed very well by using such information. For example, if the lifter makes virtually no sound with the feet while lifting, this suggests, but does not prove, that the athlete's foot movement is not vigorous enough when the squat under phase of the lift is being performed. There is a distinct temporal relationship between the hip or thigh contact that occurs during the lifter's pull and the sound of the feet landing on the platform; if these sounds are placed too far apart, the lifter is probably staying with the bar too long in the extended position of the pull.

Even tactile evidence (e.g., feeling the tension in a given muscle during the lift) can be useful for the coach. Unfortunately, such a hands on approach usually gets in the way of the lift and can be a distraction to the lifter (it can also be interpreted in the wrong way by the athlete). Therefore, it is almost never appropriate to touch an athlete during the execution of a lift (except when an athlete is being guided through a partial lift by the coach—a method called "guided movement," which is discussed later in this chapter). However, a proxy for feeling tension is to have the lifter bare the body part in question so that muscular tension can be observed. Alternatively, immediately prior to a lift the coach can touch the muscle (or muscle group) that he or she wants the athlete to focus on contracting. Finally, the observer should seek information from the athlete about such issues as what the athlete is thinking and feeling during the performance of the lift.

On the basis of all of the data so gathered, the coach can then begin to make recommendations for the lifter. Naturally, this process applies primarily to the lifter and coach who are new to one another. Where this is not the case, many of the steps can be bypassed because the coach can merely compare what the lifter was doing when her or she was performing well to the current technique. However, even when the coach and lifter are well acquainted, going through the process described above on occasion can yield some valuable insights since familiarity can make things a little too comfortable for the coach and athlete and hinder the observation of the obvious.

Evaluating Performance Through the Use of a Movie or Video Camera

With the advent of high quality video cameras at reasonable cost, relatively sophisticated methods of technique analysis are available to the average trainee. Dr. John Garhammer, a professor of biomechanics at California State University, a veteran weightlifter and coach and someone who has probably done more biomechanical analysis of weightlifting than any other person in the United States explained how simple video analysis of technique could be performed most effectively in , International Olympic Lifter (IOL) magazine several years ago.

Garhammer recommends that the video camera be placed to the side of the platform at its center (front to back). The camera is set at the height of the average lifter's waist and placed on a tripod (it should remain in the same position throughout the filming session). The camera is adjusted so that the screen displays the lifter's feet and the bar at its highest point overhead. This is the optimal position for analyzing bar trajectories and other aspects of bar movement that will be very useful for many coaches. The camera should be level and pointing straight toward the platform from its position and clearly focused.

It is then recommended that a measuring device like a yardstick be held in both horizontal and vertical positions at waist height above the bar (presumably when the bar is at the center of the platform). This assists the analyst in getting a spatial sense of what is going on with the movement of the bar and lifter. Garhammer points out that if the photographer fails to do this, the plates of the bar, the largest of which measure 45 cm in diameter, can always be used to provide a spatial perspective. Recording speed should always be the one that permits the clearest slow and freeze frame analysis. A log of each lift should be kept (lifter and weight). Once the filming has taken place, the coach is prepared to perform an analysis.

The coach or athlete should compare the perspective of the monitor with that which was captured during the event. For example, if the plates measure 4.5" on the monitor, the analyst knows that 1" equals 10 cm (because the diameter of the plates is 45 cm). Tracing paper or plastic wrap can then be placed over the monitor and taped in place. After that, you can move the film frame by frame through the lift, placing a dot on the plastic or paper at each point of the body or bar on the screen. When tracing the movement of the bar, Garhammer recommends that the dot be placed at the center of the plates, not the end of the bar. It is also a good idea to trace around some fixed object in the background at the beginning of the analysis to assure that the each frame of the picture is placed at the same point on the screen. If you are careful to note the speed at which you are filming (30 frames per second is common), you will be able to calculate the speed at which the bar is moving during the lifts filmed.

The method suggested by Dr. Garhammer is very robust in that a significant amount of analysis can be performed with this arrangement of equipment. For example, a given lift can be played back one frame at a time with tracing paper placed over the monitor screen. During the first playback sequence the trajectory of the bar can be drawn on the tracing paper. During the second playback the position of the bar at various points in the pull can be noted on the tracing paper, such as the position of the bar at lift off and at knee level. Then, during the third playback, the number of frames between the two positions can be recorded and the duration of the pull can be calculated (e.g., if the camera speed was 30 frames per second and 15 frames were used, then .5 seconds elapsed). Finally, bar velocity can actually be calculated by measuring the distance the bar has traveled in a given interval (if a yardstick had been placed in the background before the filming it would be possible to determine that the bar moved at a rate of 9 inches in .5 seconds, or at a rate of 18 inches per second). Still further analysis is possible if one uses a little ingenuity (e.g., calculating the maximum bar velocity).

The coach will find that other methods of video analysis can be useful. This is because there are limitations to the side angle of filming. As noted above, such a perspective is critical for the measurement of bar trajectories and other quantitative aspects of lifting performance, but it places some limits on the coach. The plates block the camera from observing a number of important aspects of the athlete's movement. In addition, even if the plates and bar were invisible, certain aspects of the lifter's movement would not be well observed from the side. One example would be the opposite side of the lifter's body, and another would be whether both arms were locked. Therefore, the best overall angle for the coach who is filming, as well as merely observing the athlete is at a 45° angle from the front or back of the lifter. However, there is no one position that can give the coach a perfect view of every aspect of the lifter. Therefore, points of observation and filming should be established in the context of the purpose of the analysis. Clearly, if the movement of the lifter's body is the most important consideration, then any obstruction of the view of the body by the plates should be avoided. If the coach wants to see such things as whether the bar is level or the arms straight the lift must be observed from the front or back.

Some years ago analysts in the former Soviet Union began performing multi-camera analyses of the same lift (the lifter was simultaneously filmed by cameras placed at different positions, so that the lift could be evaluated from several perspectives).

Using the multi-camera method, these analysts were able to determine that the bar trajectory for the same lifter could be significantly different depending on the side from which it was viewed. When a significant difference of this kind is noted, it is typically in the athlete who twists or turns during the lift.

In recent years, with the assistance of the biomechanics staff of the United States Olympic Committee (USOC), USAW have cooperated to do some interesting work in the area of multi-camera, force-plate assisted, computer aided lifting analysis. Lifters were simultaneously filmed with three cameras while a force plate under the platform was used to measure the force that the lifter was applying to the bar during the course of the lift. A vast amount of information was collected with respect to the lifter's body positions, the trajectory of the bar and the forces involved at various points in the lift. This kind of research will undoubtedly add important new dimensions to our understanding of technique.

For those who do not have such sophisticated technology available to them, the simple one-camera kind of analysis explained above will help athletes and coaches immeasurably in the process of acquiring lifting mastery.

A very recent advance in analytical technology for weightlifting has been the development of the V-Scope by an Israeli firm. Using a PC, the V-Scope can numerically analyze and graphically plot (to a screen or printer) bar trajectories, bar velocities and bar acceleration patterns. At a cost of approximately $15,000 (including the computer) at the time this is being written, the V-Scope cannot be characterized as highly affordable. However, it does represent perhaps the first computer application designed specifically for the analysis of weightlifting. No doubt the capabilities of the V-Scope and other analytical tools will improve in time, and the costs of these tools will fall. We are not far from the day when quantitative analysis will no longer be available only to the sports scientist.

The approaches to perfecting technique are limited only by your imagination. The only commandment in this regard is to constantly seek improvement in some respect.

Simple Techniques of Mechanical Analysis

Methods of analyzing technique are generally placed in one of two categories: qualitative or quantitative. Qualitative analysis is based on simple observation of performance, whereas quantitative analysis is based on measurements recorded during the performance. Experts in biomechanics who have sophisticated tools at their disposal can perform wonderfully interesting quantitative technique analyses. But an athlete and/or coach using a pencil and paper can analyze from a qualitative standpoint a number of key aspects of technique which can lead to significant performance improvements.

In one such approach a mechanical model of performance factors is constructed. In essence, the model diagrams the major factors which can affect performance and their interrelationships. In the model, boxes contain the factors identified. The position of those boxes in the diagram and lines drawn between the boxes portray the various interrelationships among the factors. Factors over which the performer has little or no control are generally ignored (e.g., in weightlifting, air resistance has an effect on the lifter's speed in the squat under, but that effect is very minor and virtually impossible to affect significantly, so it is not even depicted). A complete list of the ways in which performance can be enhanced via improvements in appropriate factors is thus created. The advantages of this kind of mechanical modeling method are that it is comprehensive and systematic and does not rely fundamentally on an ideal form (although some aspects of existing technical methods may be implicit in certain portions of the analysis).

In building the model that is the basis for this kind of qualitative analysis, the coach must first identify the desired result (in the case of weightlifting, lifting a weight in a certain way). Next, the factors that produce the desired result are identified and placed underneath the desired result. If possible, factors should be mechanical quantities (velocities, masses, etc.). Beneath those direct factors should be the factors that influence them. Each factor should be determined completely by factors linked to it from below. As an example, I am providing an analysis of the jerk (the analysis can be created for the snatch and clean with minor adjustments—see Fig. 14 on the next page).

Once the diagramming process has been completed, the coach should find boxes at the ends of various paths. Circles should be drawn around end boxes for each factor, and a line should be drawn through the factors over which the performer has little or no control or which are negligible. (For example, the weightlifter has no control over the force of gravity at any given point on earth and although air resistance has an effect on the lifter's ability to squat under the bar, it is so minor and so difficult to affect as to be considered negligible.) Finally, the coach should examine the remaining boxes and note ways in which performance can be improved by improving the performance of these factors.

Generally, in these kinds of diagrams, relationships between factors which are at the same level are not shown. Consequently, while forces exerted by muscles crossing at various points are related with each other, no effort is made to indicate the relationship between these factors in the model (but it is important to remember they exist and can be important).

The Construction of a Free Body Diagram

There will be times where the coach or athlete will want and need to systematically analyze the key forces that are acting on the lifter and/or the bar during a given segment of a lift. A free body diagram is a very useful tool for such an analysis of human motion. It is created by drawing a simple sketch of the body as if it were totally removed from its surroundings. The next step is to sketch arrows that represent all of the external forces acting on the body, including the weight of the athlete's body acting down through the athlete's center of gravity and the various reaction forces acting through the body's points of contact with other bodies. It is often helpful to represent one or more forces as components rather than as a single force. Curved arrows are used to show external torques on the body at points where contact is made with other bodies. If you are unsure whether a torque is actually applied at that point, it is a good practice to draw in the curve and then see whether is actually has a value later. The final step is to label all arrows with the forces that are applied there (if those forces are known). A simple example appears in Fig. 13

Fig. 13

The details of constructing such a diagram are beyond the scope of this book, but the example provided above (which depicts a lifter at the start of the jerk) should give you an idea of how one is constructed. For more information consult Anatomy, Biomechanics and Human Motion by J. Hay, (see the Bibliography)..

99

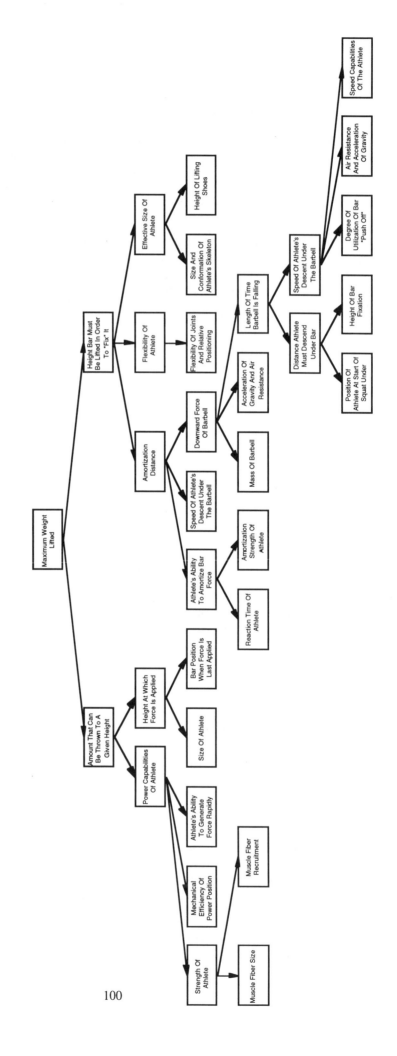

Fig. 14 — Qualitative Mechanical Analysis
A Generic Model For The Classic Lifts

How To Correct Technique Problems

The Technique of Teaching the Lifts by the Progressive Elimination of Faults

Since it is well established that athletes who are learning how to perform an activity (or learning anything) cannot focus on too many items at once, my approach to teaching technique (once the basic movement has been learned) has always been to target one or two faults and to work on those faults until they are eliminated. Naturally, in order for this approach to be effective, one must identify the most fundamental and significant faults and then communicate those faults to the lifter, along with suggestions about how the errors can be corrected.

I have often been approached by one of my lifters with a question like: "Joe Quads just told me that my head is in the wrong position in the jerk; if that's true, shouldn't I be correcting that fault?" My answer is usually something like: "You do have your head too far down, but you are also dipping forward, your dip is too fast and your back foot is positioned improperly and your elbows should be turned out more." The lifter is usually shocked at this point because at that point the only faults that I have emphasized are the fast dip and the dipping forward. Once the lifter recovers his or her composure, he or she usually asks: "Why haven't we been working on all of that?" My answer is that the lifter can only concentrate on a limited number of items at one time, so we cannot emphasize all of them at the same time. Moreover, some of the faults that a lifter exhibits are effects and not causes. I have tried to select the most fundamental of the errors to be corrected, so that if they are corrected some other problems will be eliminated as well.

How can the process of correcting faults be properly prioritized? There are several guidelines. First, safety always comes first. If a fault presents a direct danger to the lifter, it must be corrected immediately, to the exclusion of all other faults. For example, if a lifter is bouncing the elbows off the knees when he or she squat cleans, there is a danger that lifter will damage his or her wrists. Either the fault must be corrected immediately (if the lifter's flexibility permits), or the lifter cannot be permitted to squat clean.

A second factor that needs to be considered is the severity of each fault. Severity is a function of two qualities. One is the extent to which the pattern observed deviates from the desired one. The second quality is the amount of damage the fault is causing. For example, a lifter may be dropping his or her elbows rather significantly during the dip for the jerk. The amount of this drop might clearly identify the action as a significant mistake. However, the lifter is dipping in a very

upright position, the bar is well back on the lifter's shoulders and the hands and wrists are supporting the bar only moderately, so there is no movement in the bar when the elbows are lowered. Therefore, the fault represents a significant difference from the desired pattern, but in the context of the lifter's overall technique, it is not causing any serious harm at this time. Consequently, the fault should be corrected, but it can be to be placed fairly low on the list of priorities if other more significant faults have been identified as well.

Another consideration is when in the sequence of the performance of a lift a given fault appears. Faults that appear at earlier stages of the lift are obviously in a position to cause subsequent faults. Therefore, when two faults appear to be of equal severity and importance, it is generally appropriate to correct the earlier one first.

The last and least important consideration of the prioritization process is the ease with which a fault can be corrected. This can often be learned by having the athlete attempt to correct the mistake. If it appears that the correction will occur quickly, it may be worthwhile to focus on such a fault in order to eliminate it from the list (assuming that the previously mentioned prioritization standards have been applied and two or more errors are thought to be of equal importance on the basis of these standards). An added advantage of this approach is that the correction of such a fault will also tend to enhance a lifter's confidence that other faults can be corrected as well.

Communicating About Faults

Once technique faults or areas of potential improvement have been identified and a determination of which areas need to be attacked first has been made, the task of the coach is to talk about the areas which need improvement so that the athlete has a thorough understanding of what needs to be done in order to improve.

Language is an amazingly powerful means of communication. However, when it comes to using language to communicate about matters of physical movement, only certain specialists who are highly trained in biomechanics are able to communicate with any real degree of precision by using language alone (and then only with one who is similarly trained). To maximize the communicative power of language, the coach should talk about the full range of technique factors (body positioning, the tensions of various muscles, balance, timing, degree of effort and overall feel). Obviously, all of these factors should not be discussed at the same time, to avoid overloading the lifter, but they demonstrate the range of factors that can and should be communicated verbally tot he lifter to assure that all elements of technique are covered at one time or another and to increase the likelihood that good technique will be understood.

In utilizing verbal communication, you can try to convey information with an instructions such as, "keep the body erect as you dip for the jerk." or with a question such as, "how can you maintain your balance most effectively during the dip for the jerk?" The first approach tends to be more effective for athletes and the second tends to be more effective for coaches, but either approach can help both the athlete and coach improve his or her understanding. Another alternative to stating "keep body erect" is to have the athlete focus on something that will cause the body to assume and maintain an erect position (e.g., "drive the head up").

When training athletes, especially beginners, it is often useful, even crucial, to supplement language with visual means of communication, such as demonstrations. Demonstrations must be carefully performed, because the uninitiated may find it hard to derive much in terms of understanding by merely observing a complex motion. The demonstrator should direct the attention of the observer so that the observer is focused on the appropriate aspect of the activity. Special care should be taken to assure that the observer is not focusing on the results of the motion to the exclusion of the motion itself.

Guided movement can be useful in certain circumstances. With guided movement, the coach places his or hands on the bar or the lifter's body to move the lifter through the correct pattern of movement. For instance, if the coach is trying to teach the lifter to pull the bar closer to the body during the second phase of the pull, the coach might have a person stationed on either side of the bar to push the bar toward the lifter during the second phase of the pull. (Naturally, the lifter would only be executing the first and second stages of the pull during this kind of teaching phase, not the full lift). Another example would be one in which the coach stands to the rear of the lifter, placing one hand between the lifter's neck and shoulder on one side and the other hand on the lifter's belt. The coach would then have the lifter execute the first four stages of the pull very slowly. During the lift the coach would use upward and backward pressure of the upper hand combined with forward pressure on the lower hand (the hand on the lower back) to assure that the lifter is using the leg and back muscles in proper sequence and amplitude during the pull. Still another example would be the coach's moving the arms to an appropriate position while the athlete is supporting the bar on the shoulders or overhead after a lift. Naturally, very light weights are used during these demonstrations, and guided movement should not be used while the lifter is actually performing a lift under his or her normal power (a serious injury could result from such an action).

A model of an athlete's body can be employed to explain various aspects of technique to athlete or coach. A complex model has the advantage of being able to duplicate virtually any aspect of human movement. However, a simple model that resembles a stick figure can be used to demonstrate many concepts of technique and has the advantage of helping the athlete to focus on only very limited aspects of technique at one time. Coaches can construct a simple model of the lower leg, the upper leg, the torso and the head with four pieces of cardboard and three brass fasteners available in any stationary store. Such a model can be used to demonstrate to the lifter the relative positions of the legs torso and head during nearly any phase of the lift. While such a model permits analysis and demonstration only from the side view of the lifter, it can be very useful in the majority of coaching situations.

It is critical to remember that the volume and nature of any information that is communicated to the athlete cannot exceed the level and rate of the lifter's comprehension. It is important to focus on one or two points at a time (or figure out a way to convey more than one point with a single statement). If a slower than normal speed is being used to demonstrate a point, the lifter should return to a normal tempo as quickly as possible.

After explanation, demonstration and/or actual trials efforts (whether guided or not), the coach should check the athlete's understanding of various technique concepts with questions and observations of the athlete's attempts to implement what has been communicated.

If It Doesn't Work, Try Something Different

When you've been to as many weightlifting meets as I have, you tend to see many of the same coaches and athletes in action over and over again. To me, one of the most surprising things that one learns from these continued observations is how often the same athletes and coaches make the same mistakes over and over again, particularly in the area of technique. In fact, in some cases, I have heard the same coach saying the same thing to the same athlete over a period of decades, with the same lack of effect.

For example, the coach might say, "keep it close." The lifter will then proceed to pull the bar several inches away from the body, miss the lift and shake his head in resignation. The coach will then describe the fault in an animated fashion, coupled with a frustration that borders on disgust. Then the lifter and coach will reconcile, and the process will begin anew, a continual cycle of failure.

Why are faults often not corrected by shouting the same commands over and over again (even if they are seemingly correct)? The problem is at least partially one of language. We all learn language in a specific context. The concept "dog" is pretty clear to most of us. However, you learned the word dog from Spot (a Dalmatian) and Rover (a Labrador), and I learned it from Spike (a bulldog) and Rex (a German Shepherd). Therefore, when you think of dog, you see Spot and Rover in your mind's eye while I see Spike and Rex in mine. Similarly, when a coach says "step through" as an athlete is getting ready to split for a jerk, the coach may be seeing the back foot land a split second before the front foot and driving the body forward under the bar. In contrast, the lifter may be visualizing the process of rushing through a door while leaning forward to get the head through first. Obviously, this difference in meaning will result in frustration for both parties. The coach will not understand why the athlete is not stepping through properly, and the lifter will not understand why the coach is not happy with what he or she is doing.

Not surprisingly, the only way to break a cycle of failure is to try something new. There are several effective approaches to this, but they all have a common goal: to change the athlete's concept of the correct technique. If an athlete "sees" a clean as a motion in which the arms help to lift the bar up to the chest, he or she will tend to bend the arms to accomplish the desired motion. Sometimes a lifter will consciously accept the notion that a clean is a powerful shrugging and jumping motion, followed by an explosive combination motion of pulling of the body under the bar and jumping down into the squat. Nevertheless, when the pressure is on, the lifter will instinctively (i.e., subconsciously) lift and pull with the arms. It is very difficult to keep the lifter from pulling with the arms by saying, "don't pull with the arms." It is like telling a person "don't think of pink elephants." Just telling someone not to think of a pink elephant causes most people to do it. Therefore, the lifter must think of what to do. The concept of what the lifter is to do must be inculcated at the very deepest levels. The more clearly a lifter grasps the concept, the more likely it is that he or she will be able to execute the desired movement properly. If the lifter can understand the concept on a verbal level, can visualize the correct performance and can hear the correct tempo, he or she has a far better chance of executing the proper motion than if he or she has simply been told what to do.

Regardless of the specific methods that are used to educate the lifter, the real issue is having the lifter understand what is being done and why, not just on an intellectual level but on experiential one. The athlete must ultimately feel what it is like to do the movement correctly. More than that, the athlete must understand on a feeling level why the "correct" technique is really more effective. He or she must feel that the bar is going higher, or that it is going straighter, faster etc., before the new technique will be fully accepted and used. It is only at this point that the lifter can begin to work on the long term and challenging task of automating the movement he or she has learned.

Examples Of Specific Errors And Methods For Correcting Them

The human genius for solving problems is virtually limitless, as is evidenced by the phenomenal achievements that have been made by humankind through the course of history. However, the ingenuity that humans exhibit in finding ways to commit performance faults is also quite impressive. Athletes are no exception. They discover myriad ways to make mistakes when they perform. Often, when I think I have seen all the technical errors that a weightlifter can make, some athlete is gracious enough to put me in my place by committing an error I would have never dreamed possible.

Despite the variety of errors that athletes make, certain mistakes occur most often in weightlifting. I have chosen several of these for the purpose of illustrating the process of error correction. An entire book could certainly be written on the subject, and perhaps someday one will. The purpose of this section is to provide the coach and athlete with some examples of how the error correction process can be developed. Armed with the basic principles outlined in this chapter and some sense of how to apply those principles in the real world the athlete and coach should be able to correct most of the errors that they encounter.

The Lifter Who Drives the Bar Forward in the Jerk

It is not at all uncommon for a lifter to get into the habit of driving the bar forward during the explosion phase of the jerk, instead of in a completely vertical fashion. There are several factors that can create a tendency for the lifter to drive the bar forward. First, in the act of dipping, because the knees move forward as the dip progresses, the combined center of gravity of the bar and body shifts forward. This forward shift in the balance of the body can be continued or can worsen during the drive.

A second problem is that many lifters (especially those who tend to position the bar too far forward when they are in the split position) think about assuring that the head, torso and front leg are placed ahead of the bar as it goes overhead. Since these lifters tend to end up with their torsos and hips behind the bar and/or with the arms slightly bent when they attempt to catch the bar in the split, they worry about getting into the split quickly and consequently begin a forward movement of their bodies as they are coming out of the dip. This forward movement of the body drives the bar forward by adding a horizontal component to the drive for the jerk (instead of there being

103

solely a vertical component). The result is that the lifter feels that the bar is too far in front of the balance point and redoubles his or her effort at getting forward and under the bar early, which leads to a still earlier and more vigorous forward drive. Naturally, a vicious circle is created , one out of which many lifters never escape. This tendency can be eliminated by having the lifter think of the dip and split as two separate movements that occur in immediate sequence (a straight dip and drive followed by a quick downward and only slightly forward motion into the split) or merely by having the lifter think of driving the bar straight up (or even backward) during the explosion phase. It also important for the lifter to understand that the problem is in the dip and not the split. A vertical dip and drive will help to assure correct positioning in the split.

Still another cause of a forward drive is that the lifter descends to a position in the dip that is too low for the flexibility that the lifter has in the Achilles tendon (the tendon at the rear of the ankle) and/or the strength of his or her quadriceps (frontal thigh) muscles. If the dip is too deep for the Achilles tendons to handle, the lifter will tend to rise on the toes and/or lose his or her balance forward. If the legs are not strong enough to handle the depth of the dip, the legs may actually give way, causing a loss of balance forward. The means for correcting this error are to have the lifter shorten the depth of the dip and/or change the position of the feet and/or knees so that the legs are traveling in an outward as well as downward direction. For example, if the lifter stands with the feet in a parallel position in preparation for the drive, the probability of a loss of balance is greater than if the lifter turns the toes out somewhat and the knees are made to travel both forward and sideways over the feet. Similarly, if the lifter lets the knees travel slightly to the sides as well as forward, the dip will tend to be straighter; too much sideways motion can lead to knee strain, so it is unwise for most lifters to permit the outside of the knee travel sideways beyond the outside of the foot.

Another mechanism for correcting this fault is to have the lifter consciously shift his or her weight toward the heels prior to the commencement of the dip. This action reduces the likelihood of a forward dip and gives the lifter a margin for error; a slight forward movement will not hurt the jerk as much if the lifter began the dip a little to the rear of center. Still another means for dealing with this fault is to have the lifter perform one or two "practice" dips with no movement into the fifth and sixth phases of the jerk. These practice dips give the athlete an opportunity to concentrate on a straight dip and to receive immediate feedback from the coach on that single aspect of the jerk. When the athlete has performed one or two correct practice dips in several sets, he or she can move into a jerk on the next rep (assuming he or she has warmed up first). Doing so carries over what has been learned immediately into the jerk. Over time, the practice dips can be phased out.

Bending the Arms Excessively While Pulling

It is almost an article of faith among lifting technicians that bending the arms in the pull is an error. Countless words of lifting analysis have centered around this point, and the example given is often one of a lesser lifter with the arms bent, with the author ascribing at least a portion of the lifter's ineptitude to the premature bending of the arms.

While it is true that bending one's arms during the pull is usually a serious fault, the reality is that this issue is not quite as simple as some analysts would have us believe. Bending the arms before the bar separates from the floor means that the body will have to be placed in a lower position than would otherwise have been required in order to get the bar off the floor. A lower position is generally less advantageous for the muscles of the legs, hips and back. As a result, the lifter places greater strain than necessary on his or her legs and back at the start of the pull. Therefore, pulling with bent arms from the floor is almost always a disadvantage.

If the arms are bent after the bar is separated from the floor, the lifter is spared some or all of the extra effort required to lift the bar from the platform when the arms are bent at the moment of separation. However, bending the arms after the moment of separation tends to cause the lifter to lose proper position during the pull; the angle of the back in relation to the floor will grow smaller when it should remain the same or increase, or the arch in the back may be reduced or lost. In addition, the bar can collide with the shins and/or knees, impeding its upward motion. As a result, it is likely that bar speed and/or control will be lost unnecessarily during the execution of the pull if the arms are bent.

Although a lifter may bend his or her arms, he or she is not necessarily accomplishing the arm bend with the muscles of the arms (or at least not solely with the arms). The shoulder muscles, and muscles or the upper back, are often the primary factors contributing to the arm bend. If the bent arms are sustained during the first three stages of the pull, it means the height of the bar in relation to the floor will be greater than usual. This can position the bar higher on the thighs or hips as the final explosion stage of the pull is executed. For some lifters, a higher point of contact with the bar can lead to a more explosive finish to the pull. In addition, holding the arms bent also tends to strengthen the gripping force that the lifter can apply to the bar.

Offsetting these advantages is the likelihood that the transmission of force to the bar during the all important final explosion phase of the pull will be compromised by the lifter's bent arms. It will be difficult for the lifter to maintain the arms in the bent position while force is exerted via the legs and hips. If the arms give, some of the force developed by the legs and hips will be dissipated by the arms, and a less forceful final explosion will be the result. This is one reason why many coaches are completely against any bending whatsoever of the arms during the first four stages of the pull. While this is generally a sound position, the coach would be wise to consider the tradeoff aspect of technique that was mentioned at the outset of this chapter. In some cases, the advantages that lifters get by bending the arms somewhat may offset the disadvantages (though this is the exception rather than the rule and occurs much less frequently than most of those who bend their arms think).

In my experience, a bend in the arms during the pull is more detrimental to the clean than the snatch. There have been a number of record holders in the snatch who bend their arms somewhat during the pull, but these lifters are generally not as proficient in the clean as they are in the snatch.

Correcting an inappropriate bend in the pull can be a difficult process, particularly when a lifter has had this fault for some time. That is why every effort should be made to address this problem as soon as it occurs. This problem is generally caused by a subconscious (and sometime conscious) belief that pulling with the arms is necessary in order to achieve maximal height in the pull. If the athlete can be convinced that he or she will pull more effectively with the arms straight, it will greatly hasten the process of correcting the fault. Shrugs, partial pulls and complete pulls employing a height gauge can be used to prove to the lifter that his or her pull is actually better with relaxed arms. In order for this to occur, it will often be necessary for the lifter to acquire a fundamentally different understanding of the pulling process. The body and not the arms must do the work. It helps some lifters to visualize what happens when one pulls explosively on a slack rope in order to move a heavy object. The rope will straighten with a snap, but the object will not move. If tension is put on the rope first, it will transmit force directly to the object; so it is with the arms in pulling.

Performing a rep or two in the pull with straight arms before cleaning can help eliminate arm pulling as well, because the lifter gets into a correct "groove" before attempting a clean (of course the lifter must warm up the body for cleans before switching from a pull to a clean).

If the arm bending is caused by the lifter's remaining with the bar too long in the pull (the lifter pulls with the arms straight most of the way but then bends them before going under the bar),

the emphasis should be placed on applying the maximum explosive effort in the pull a little earlier, so that the arm bending and squatting under the bar are taking place at the same time.

Premature Contraction of Various Muscle Groups

It is important that all of the muscles that are used to impart force to the bar be activated in the proper sequence (generally beginning with the muscles closest to the lifter's physical center and then moving outward, away from the center, from hips and back outward toward the limbs). In the final explosion of the pull, this sequence is essentially the hip extensors and quadriceps, followed by the trapezius and perhaps the gastrocnemius and finally the arms and shoulders (the latter only as the lifter begins his or her descent under the bar). It should be noted that while these contractions are occurring in the aforementioned sequence, the contraction occurring in each muscle group does not begin after the previous one ends. Rather, there is a degree of overlap in the contractions that facilitates the continuous application of force to the bar. If a particular muscle group is activated too early in the sequence, it interrupts the smooth progress of motion, attenuates the force applied by the right muscles at the same stage and makes the muscle group contracted early unable to assist in imparting force to the bar at the proper moment.

An example of this is when the trapezius muscles (the muscles which raise or "shrug" the shoulders) are contracted early in the pull, raising the shoulders. The lifter will find that such a motion upsets the pattern and/or the rhythm of some earlier stage for the pull (e.g., it makes the moment of separation more difficult or upsets the flow of the movement of the hip extensors and quads outward). In addition, the traps are not strong enough to hold their position when the legs explode into action. Therefore, the traps will tend to give during the final explosion, perhaps almost imperceptibly, thereby acting as a shock absorber for the force of the pull. Finally, the traps will be fatigued from their early involvement and will already be partially contracted when it is their turn in the sequence to impart force It is unlikely that the weakened traps will be able to play any meaningful role in pulling the bar up or the body down.

I encountered a classic case of this problem when I was working with a national level lifter who was making a comeback from a serious injury. He had run into a sticking point on his snatch. While his recovery was progressing steadily in the C&J and most of his assistance exercises, his snatch would not budge. He had even reached a point where he was having trouble making weights that he had done consistently at earlier stages of his comeback. I noticed in his first rep in his first snatch workout with me that he was contracting his traps prematurely. When this was pointed out, he corrected the problem rather quickly, and within a few weeks he easily overcame the weight that had stymied him for so long. A similar correction with respect to any muscle that is contracting early can yield similar positive results.

Perhaps the most common form of premature contraction involves the hip extensors during the pull. The proper pattern of motion during the pull is to move leg extensors concentrically and hip extensors isometrically during the second phase; hip extensors concentrically and leg extensors eccentrically during the amortization phase; and hip extensors concentrically and then isometrically during the explosion phase, with the leg extensors contracting concentrically. Many lifters attempt to contract the hip extensors throughout the pull. This causes the lifter to significantly increase the angle of the torso in relation to the platform (i.e., straighten it) during the second phase of the pull (instead of simply maintaining its position or straightening it slightly during the latter portion of this phase). It also causes the lifter to incline the torso rearward and not to drive the hips sufficiently forward during the final explosion phase of the pull, misdirecting and lessening the force generated during that stage of the pull.

Naturally, before a premature contraction can be corrected, it must be noticed. This can be difficult when an athlete wears oversize garments on the upper body and trains in long sleeved shirts. But even when a lifter is covering up the premature contraction with clothing, the possibility of premature contraction should be at least considered when a lifter begins to look sluggish and loses any "snap" in his or her pull or when the entire pull seems to be proceeding at one speed. If the contraction is occurring at the start of the lift, this problem can often be corrected merely by having the lifter become aware of unnecessary tension in the wrong muscle groups as he or she prepares to lift. In other cases approaches similar to those used for correcting the bent arm problem (which is primarily a premature contraction problem) can be employed.

Extending the Body Too Much and/or Holding the Extended Position for Too Long a Period

One of the most frustrating technique flaws in weightlifting is that of applying maximum force to the bar through a complete range of motion, only to find that the bar is nowhere near completion, It is a frustrating phenomenon because you can lift the same or a lesser weight easily and then, through a mistake of timing, miss the next weight you attempt with it feeling "like a ton." This can certainly happen when you are trying a weight that is simply beyond your means. But when a lifter

finds that jerks are rather routinely caught on bent arms while the body has not reached a deep position or snatches are often pressed out or the bar "crashes" on the lifter in the clean (i.e., seems to fall on the lifter from a point well above the lifter's bottom position, the culprit is often the practice of staying with the bar too long in the final explosion: that is, after exerting maximum force, the lifter stays in the extended position for too long a time without being able to generate any significant additional acceleration to the bar. In such a case, the lifter is wasting valuable time that could be used for going under the bar. The result is that the bar begins to descend at almost the same time as the lifter, giving the lifter no time to set his or her body in the low position and catch the bar. Instead, the lifter has only just arrived at the catch position and finds that the bar is already there (and is moving with considerable downward speed).

The flaw tends to compound itself because the heavier the lifter perceives the bar to be and the greater the shortfall between the bar height and where the bar is felt to be, the more and longer the lifter tries to follow through in the explosion phase. Obviously, the more and longer the lifter follows through, the worse the problem becomes. I was a victim of this problem early in my lifting career (then intermittently thereafter when I lapsed into my old ways), particularly in the jerk. It was not until I studied films of my lifting and compared it to that of other lifters that I found I was driving my jerks higher than most lifters but was being caught with the bar on bent arms and in a relatively shallow split. Once I got into the habit of driving hard but then moving into the split more quickly, the problem was at least partially resolved.

Awareness of this problem prompted me to point out a similar flaw to one of the United States' best lifters of the 1960s and 1970s. This lifter had a habit of pressing out his snatches (although his timing was fine in the jerk). When I analyzed his snatch technique, it became obvious to me that he stayed the extended position on the pull longer than virtually any other lifter of his caliber. This led to the bar's falling on him by the time he reached the squat position, Although I actually demonstrated the problem to him on film, he did not completely accept my analysis and never did correct the problem. Ultimately, it was in attempting to press out a snatch that he tore a triceps muscle, an injury that eventually ended his career.

Another version of this problem exists when a lifter achieves too great an amplitude of body extension while pulling. This kind of problem can be seen when the shoulders shrug in a pronounced fashion before the legs rebend or the lifter rises very high on the toes at the completion of the explosion phase of the pull or jerk. This kind of excessive amplitude makes it difficult for the lifter to descend under the bar (the body has to move various body levers through a greater range of motion and the entire body through a greater distance in order to achieve the squat under). And since the lifter has traveled further than necessary into the extended position, he or she has wasted precious time that could have been used to begin the descent under the bar.

Cures for both of these related problems consist of learning to complete the final explosion phase earlier and making the transition from the explosion to the squat under more crisp. It is often helpful for a lifter to think of rebounding downward, virtually bouncing off the resistance offered by the bar. Thinking of a lift as both an upward and then a downward explosion as well is often helpful. Visualizing the lift as one complete movement up and down is also often helpful.

Some coaches believe in teaching the lifter to perform the pull "flatfooted" so that the tendency to overextend is reduced. And while I have never been convinced that pulling flatfooted is not more of an effect than something to strive for, this approach does seem to work for some lifters. If the lifter thinks of descending under the bar at the right point in the pull, a ballet like rise on the toes will be avoided. One thing is clear, however; one of the most powerful explosions that the body can make (and certainly the most powerful it can make in the pull) occurs before the knees reach their fully extended position. Therefore, there is good reason at least to question the value of any extension past that point (the longer the extension, the greater the question).

The Lifter Who Splits Backward or Forward in the Jerk

During the split for the jerk, it is important that the hips be positioned directly under the bar; they must not travel in front or to the rear of the bar. In order to avoid these errors, therefore, the motion of the back foot and leg cannot be permitted to pull the hips backward at all, and the motion of the front foot cannot be permitted to pull the hips forward excessively (some forward movement of the hips is often desirable).

A tendency to throw the rear foot backward can be corrected in most cases by simply thinking of jumping down with the body (as the famous coach Joe Mills used to say) instead of either jumping forward or backward. In cases where the lifter is has gotten into the habit of splitting back, two tricks taught to me by the great champion Dave Sheppard virtually never fail. First, Dave taught the "camel hop" (a style named after the Egyptian greats of the 1930s, 1940s and 1950s who were kiddingly associated with the camels that their countrymen presumably rode). They believed in striking the rear foot first in the split and then using that rear foot to push their bodies forward under the bar. Reportedly, you were able to hear a distinct slap-slap noise emanating from the feet of such lifters as the back foot hit before the front foot. If the lifter hits the back foot first and not too far back, he or she can certainly use the frictional force applied to the platform by the rear foot (more accurately the forward force applied to the body by the floor via friction) to drive the body forward (or at least prevent it from traveling backward).

A second technique is to have the lifter do some light workouts in the jerk standing near enough to a wall so that the back foot will strike the wall if the lifter splits too far rearward. Banging into the wall a few times will get even the most ingrained backward splitter to end his or her erroneous ways. Naturally, care must be taken to position the lifter far enough from the wall so that only a slight touch will occur if a mistake is made. In addition, only light weights can be used, so that the lifter is not danger of missing the lift and having the bar crash into the wall (perhaps damaging the wall and/or rebounding off the wall to injure the lifter). Interestingly enough, practice with light weights in this exercise often proves sufficient to eradicate the problem with heavier weights and without the wall; this is unusual because some drilling with fairly heavy weights is usually required to eliminate most technique flaws.

The tendency to drive the hips too far forward under the bar arises less frequently than the tendency to step back. However, when the former does appear, it can be just as difficult a problem to correct. One method is to get the lifter to practice movements that do not require a forward movement of the hips, like the power jerk. Jerks behind the neck can help because the lifter begins with the hips under the bar. Therefore, the need to split slightly forward, as required in the regular jerk, is diminished. Contrary to popular belief, jerks behind the neck are often not very helpful for those who find the bar to be forward of the body in the split because the bar is generally there due to either a forward dip or backward split, neither of which tends to benefit from practicing jerks from behind the neck.

A more direct approach is to have the lifter hit both feet in the split at the same time, eliminating any possibility that the back leg will drive the body forward when it hits. In addition, the lifter can use the arms to push the body directly downward. This arm action will tend to prevent the body from going forward.

The Fine Art of Automating the Correction

Regardless of the methods that are used to correct a given technical error, once the lifter has grasped the nature of the correction to be made (cognitively and via the correct execution of the skill), the athlete must then undertake the process of automating the correction. The lifter will not be able to exert conscious control of his or her movements with maximum weights. With such weights, the lifter must focus on moving the weight and the body with great speed and no hesitation. In addition, movements occur with great speed when heavy weights are being lifted. There is simply no time for thought or hesitation.

The process of automation takes place partly as a consequence of many practice sessions. But no amount of practice of the movement with light weights or through imagery will obviate the need for making attempts with progressively heavier weights. The lifter must ultimately perform with heavy weights, and the only way to be certain that learning has extended to that level is to try such weights.

In very rough terms, the lifter learns the correction with light weights, practices through mental imagery and is supplied with constant feedback by the coach. Then the lifter needs to practice with heavier weights. When a lift can be performed consistently with a given weight, the lifter then needs to add more weight. When a weight is reached that causes a breakdown in technique, the weight must be reduced until correct practice can again be achieved. Some practice sessions will be limited solely to those weights with which correct movement is extremely consistent. Other workouts will involve flirting with a weight that permits correct movement on most lifts but leads to a miss or an incorrect movement if there is any lapse of concentration or effort. By gently pushing the correct technique, the athlete will eventually automate the correction. However, the lifter must be cautioned that overlearning is necessary before the correction becomes automated and that constant vigilance will be required if the correction is to be maintained. Correcting flaws that advanced lifters make is not an easy process. That is why correct patterns should be emphasized so strongly at the outset.

Summary

In the previous chapter, the focus was on the nature of good weightlifting technique. In this chapter we focused on the basic concepts of motor learning: how those concepts can be applied to learning weightlifting technique, how faults can be identified and eliminated and how technique can be perfected. The development of sound technique should be the area of primary emphasis during an athlete's early months and years in weightlifting. It is he foundation upon which the athlete's success will be built. Having great technique will not make an athlete a champion, but not having it will virtually preclude success. Moreover, if it is not learned early on, it will be difficult, if not nearly impossible, to learn later on. Finally, since the beginning weightlifter will advance most rapidly in terms of strength by handling light to moderate weights, there is every reason to focus on technique and no good reason not to.

Everyone wants a shortcut to success. My advice is that no shortcuts be taken in the area of technique. Any attempt at taking one will end up as a short circuit or at least a detour on the road to weightlifting success.

Although technique is one of the most important foundations for weightlifting success, the development of unlimited strength and power is the key to high performance. Weightlifters are the strongest and most powerful men and women in the world. Their achievements are simply unmatched by the athletes of any other sport. It is the pursuit of strength and power that attracts most athletes to weightlifting, and it is the achievement of those qualities that will make a beginner of average strength a superman or superwoman. Another physical quality essential to success in weightlifting is a considerable degree of flexibility. Such flexibility is required in order to attain technical proficiency in weightlifting. It is on the development of strength, power and flexibility that the next chapter of this book is focused.

No weightlifter has ever dominated the sport more completely on the basis of pure strength than the 1956 Olympic Champion, Paul Anderson.

CHAPTER 3

The Development Of Strength, Power And Flexibility

Merely learning the technique of the Olympic lifts with light to moderate weights will lead to an improvement in an athlete's strength, power and flexibility during a lifter's early training. As was noted in the previous chapter, the use of light to moderate weights actually leads to the fastest improvements in strength and power possible during the early stages of training. Therefore, the beginner does not generally need to devote special effort to developing his or her strength and power; early practice on the classical lifts alone will be nearly sufficient in this regard (a few strength building exercises are generally added to round out the program). However, the beginning lifter may well need additional training in the area of flexibility just to assume the positions that are required for the proper execution of the classical Olympic lifts.

In fact, it is vital for the athlete to have a certain degree of flexibility even to begin to learn all of the technique elements of the Olympic lifts. This does not mean that lifters (those generally not limited by lack of flexibility) deficient in certain aspects of flexibility cannot begin to learn, however. On the contrary, at least some elements of the classic lifts can and should be practiced immediately. But it is important for the coach to determine what the athlete has the flexibility to do and then not to go beyond the lifter's capabilities in that area until his or her flexibility has improved. For example, the athlete may be flexible enough to execute the third and fourth phases of the snatch and clean but be unable to assume the proper starting position in the pull from the floor or to perform a full squat with the weight over his or her head. Such a lifter requires a crash course in flexibility while he or she is learning the limited stages of the snatch and clean, so that once adequate flexibility has been cultivated, the athlete

will be able to move on to the squat version of the snatch with the bar being lifted from the floor.

In essence, the first two chapters of this book were about what to do with the body while lifting. This chapter is about how to condition the body to achieve maximum strength, power and flexibility. The chapter begins with a discussion of the role of strength and power and explains how those capacities are developed. The latter part of this chapter presents a discussion of how to develop flexibility.

Strength And Power And Their Importance In Weightlifting

Another Look at Strength Versus Technique in Weightlifting

The shared root of all weightlifting and weight throwing sports is the desire to measure strength. The elegant techniques described in earlier chapters have evolved to maximize the performance of weightlifters. Similar techniques exist in all of these weight sports, making the application of strength to the object being lifted or thrown as efficient as possible. There can be no doubt that, even in the purest of strength events, technique makes a difference. However, in focusing on the importance of developing proper technique, many people get carried away with the role of technique in the sport of weightlifting, as in other weight sports, to the point where they forget about the foundation of the sport: its function as a measure of strength. Surely the athlete who wishes to achieve success in weightlifting without technique is foolish, but the athlete who thinks that technique will make him or her a champion is engaged in pure fantasy.

There have been world champions in weightlifting who had relatively poor technique (though winning a world championship today with poor technique is all but impossible, due the high levels of strength and technique possessed by most top competitors today). But there has not ever been, nor will there ever be, a world weightlifting champion who is not incredibly strong, and the strongest man generally wins. How do weightlifters get so strong? It is the mission of this chapter to answer that question.

It is important to remember that while many who are involved in weightlifting are overly concerned with strength or technique, both are inextricably interrelated. Lack of strength makes the execution of proper technique all but impossible. If you are not properly conditioned, you cannot assume the correct positions during the execution of the lifts. For instance, if the lower back is not strong enough, an athlete will tend not to position his or her shoulders properly in front of the bar during the second phase of the pull and will tend to prematurely straighten the torso, a serious technical mistake.

Similarly, using proper technique assures that functional strength (strength that can be applied to the competitive lifts) will be developed. It will also assure that the lifter can execute maximum efforts with the lowest possible risk of injury (as we shall see, a key to developing maximal strength). So there is no choice between strength and technique. The athlete must have strength and technique, not only because they are each important in and of themselves, but also because they are important to one another.

What Is Strength?

Strength can be defined as the maximal force or torque a muscle can generate at a specific velocity and in a specific position. The velocity and positions are important because the same muscle will have a very different ability to generate force at different angles and different speeds. For an explanation of why muscle strength varies with the speed and position of contraction, see Appendix II. In this chapter we will say only that a muscle can generally generate greater force at slower speeds (the greatest force being delivered during an isometric contraction). We will also say that muscles can generate greater force at longer lengths. (However, when muscles are at their full natural length, the levers (bones) that they move are generally in a mechanically disadvantageous position in terms of translating the force they develop into functional force that can be supplied to external objects.)

What Is the Difference Between Strength and Power?

While the terms power and strength are often used interchangeably, the two are fundamentally different (although there is an area in which the two concepts can virtually overlap). Strength is simply the ability to generate force. It is a measure of that one capacity. The rate at which force can be applied is not a primary issue in measuring strength; nor is the amount of work that can be accomplished by that strength. In contrast, power is a measure of the ability to accomplish units of work within a defined period (e.g., the ability to move an object of a given weight through a specific distance within a given interval of time). It is a measure of the rate at which work can be done, not the force needed to perform that work (although it is clear that a certain amount of force is required to move an object of a given weight at a certain speed).

Since force is required to move any object, there is an element of strength involved when any animal generates power. However, both a given object's resistance to movement (i.e., the force required to move it) and the rate of the object's movement have an equal effect on the amount of power that is generated during a particular motion. An equation for calculating power is: weight x distance / time utilized in performing the work = power). Therefore, an athlete who moves 10 lb. at a rate of 10 feet per second (10 x 10 / 1 = 100 units of power) is just as "powerful" as the athlete who moves 100 lb. at a rate of 1 foot per second (100 x 1 / 1). However, the maximum strength and speed of these two athletes may be very different. Not surprisingly, both sprinters and weightlifters are among the athletes who generate the greatest power outputs in all of sport, sprinters because of the rate at which they move a relatively light object (the body) and weightlifters because they move heavy objects relatively quickly.

Ironically, powerlifters, who move heavier objects more slowly than weightlifters, do not generate anywhere near as much power as do weightlifters when they are performing their competitive lifts. Because of this, there are those who have argued that powerlifting should be called strength lifting instead of powerlifting, because the main function of that sport is to test strength and not power. Power is less important than strength in powerlifting. However, these are differences of a very limited degree. Both sports test and rely very much on strength.

Speed Strength and Its Importance in Weightlifting Success

In Eastern European sports circles a great deal of discussion has occurred in recent years over the characteristic of "speed strength." Some have argued that "speed strength" is almost a separate characteristic of human ability derived completely from (neither speed nor strength) and that it may be more closely related to speed than to strength. Much of this discussion has taken place with respect to the sport of weightlifting. Weightlifters, some argue, require not just strength but also the ability to move heavy objects quickly. Therefore, the argument goes, activities that concentrate on the development of speed, not just pure strength, are critical for the training of weightlifters. As a consequence of this reasoning, some coaches have their lifters sprinting and jumping at a level that rivals track and field athletes.

Clearly the sport of weightlifting requires speed. In weightlifting an athlete needs to move the bar that is being lifted fast enough for the lifter to enjoy a split-second respite from exerting force against the bar while it continues to travel upward. This enables the lifter to get into a split or squat position under the bar and to be ready to "catch" the weight at arm's length or on the shoulders. If a vertical bar velocity is insufficient to continue the upward movement of the bar while the lifter moves under it (and is unable to exert upward force), the bar will begin to fall as soon as the athlete stops exerting force against it, and the lifter will not be able to get into position to catch the bar.

However, a certain amount of speed is utilized in executing virtually all exercises with free weights, even when performing very simple weight training exercise, such as the ubiquitous bar curl. Yet few would argue that the bodybuilder who does curls needs to develop his of her speed strength in order to improve his or her curl. How does speed play a role in the performance of the curl? When a lifter executes a curl at a relatively slow and constant speed, he or she experiences a point at which the lift is the most difficult (referred to in the weightlifting vernacular as the "sticking point"). The lifter experiences a varying amount of difficulty at different points in the lifts because of a combination of factors: a) the joint angle; b) the direction of the resistance; and c) the length of the muscles being contracted relative to their resting length. Even the novice weight trainer discovers early on that by thinking of contracting the muscles forcefully, even explosively (as compared with contracting the muscles with just enough effort to keep the bar moving), performance in virtually every exercise, including the curl, is improved (in terms of the amount of weight lifted). This is because a certain amount of speed is built up as a result of the lifter's greater than required effort at the early stages of the lift. This speed permits the bar to pass through the sticking point to a more favorable position in the lift before maximal difficulty is experienced.

Therefore, all things being equal, the greater the velocity of the bar when it reaches the most unfavorable mechanical point in the movement, the further away from that point will be the point at which the athlete experiences the greatest difficulty in completing the exercise. Unfortunately, all things are never equal, and the there is a point of diminishing returns in terms of generating bar velocity to get through the most difficult point in the movement.

For example, the effort required to get the bar moving at maximum speed before it reaches the worst mechanical position can be so great as to tire the muscles somewhat. In such a case, the bar is moving faster than it would have done if a little less effort had been expended at the outset of the lift, but the ability of the athlete to generate maximal force mechanically at the worst point in the movement has been compromised by the onset of fatigue. Another possibility is that the athlete has gotten the bar moving so quickly at a certain point that the muscles are unable to keep up with it and to exert their greatest force when it is most appropriate. (It is well accepted by sports scientists that it is harder to apply force to a faster moving object than to a slower moving one.) Still another problem arises if an athlete sacrifices technique when he or she tries to move the bar too fast at a point where the body is in an unfavorable biomechanical position. In such a case, greater speed may sometimes be achieved at the expense of altering the body's position in an unfavorable manner (e.g., allowing the back to round in order to get the bar moving quickly between the floor and the height of the knees during the pull and placing the back in a less efficient position for moving the bar quickly later on in the lift) or generating an improper bar trajectory.

This discussion suggests that for every lift there is an optimal timing of the application of force to the bar. This concept of optimal timing helps to explain why there is generally a limited degree of carryover in performance from the training on one form of resistance training to another (e.g., isometric strength training does not have a complete carryover to regular weight training). Isometrics may train the muscles to contract with great force at a certain point in the movement, but the exact lines of force required during the isometric may not be the same as the lines of force required to move the bar. Moreover, the successful completion of the bar lift requires optimal timing in the application of force on the bar and the contraction of muscle groups in the proper sequence, a combination of factors that are not significant during an isometric contraction. Because of the differences in the relative import of factors that determine performance in isokinetic, isometric, variable resistance and eccentric contraction exercises, their effectiveness in enhancing the ability of an athlete to perform an exercise concentrically (i.e., lifting a bar up as a muscle contracts) is limited.

When training to improve performance in a given exercise, you must train the correct muscles through the correct range of motion, against the appropriate lines of resistance, in the right sequence and at the right tempo to get the desired effect. Generally, there is no better way to accomplish this than to perform the lift you want to improve with weights that are relatively close to what you will lift in an all out effort. The principle that muscles get better at doing exactly what they practice to do is known as "specificity of training." Specificity of training is one of the keys to success in strength training, as it is to the training for any sport.

As was indicated earlier, weightlifting requires the athlete to get a bar moving fast enough to move under the bar before it falls very far. But faster is not necessarily better, except in terms of the body's speed in moving under the bar ; naturally, the faster you go under the bar, the less time you spend in the unsupported phase. If a bar moves faster, it will go further before it begins to fall. Therefore, you do not need to go as low and/or to have more time to descend to get the bar. However, once an optimal speed for raising the bar has been discovered, the object is to achieve that speed, and no more, with heavier and heavier weights. It is true that increasing the speed of contraction is one important way to maintain the same bar velocity with heavier weights; in order to increase the speed of contraction, the athlete must think of attaining maximum speed, but in terms of actual bar movement, once speed in excess of that needed to get the bar to the necessary height at the necessary velocity is achieved, the athlete will simply add more weight to the bar (enough weight so that only the required speed is achieved). Since weightlifting involves the moving of heavy objects, the ability to generate force is more critical than the ability to generate velocity (though both are important).

In moving heavy objects, the speed that is achieved is more a function of strength than speed. If an object is light to a given athlete, then that athlete can move the object faster. If it is heavy, no matter how fast or springy, etc., the athlete may be, he or she will be unable to move the object, or at least unable to move it quickly over time. What a weightlifter needs is strength enough to move a heavy bar quickly enough to catch it in the desired position.

There are weightlifting analysts who argue that the proof speed is more important than strength in weightlifting is the existence of athletes who can move very heavy weights slowly but who are often unable to perform the snatch and clean and jerk with any degree of success concomitant with their demonstrated strength level (i.e., these athletes lack that elusive and desirable quality of "speed strength"). However, these arguments miss several important points. First, while it may be true that some athletes with remarkable strength may not

be able to perform either the snatch or C&J at a level suggested by their strength, these results can be explained in a number of ways other than a lack of speed strength. The most obvious explanation is that such athletes lack the skill (i.e., technique) to convert their strength into outstanding performances in the competitive exercises. Another reason might be a lack of flexibility, which would preclude an athlete from employing efficient technique. Still another reason for a lack of carryover in strength is that the exercise which is regarded as an indicator of strength actually demonstrates enormous strength in muscle groups and at joint angles that do not approximate those used in the competitive lifts. Finally, there is an element of courage involved in weightlifting. While there is little real danger to a skilled lifter who misses a heavy snatch or C&J (actually far less danger than when an athlete misses a squat or bench press), many athletes are fearful of missing a snatch or C&J, because they perceive a danger. Naturally, this significantly hinders performance.

Unfortunately the 1956 Olympic weightlifting champion Paul Anderson is often cited as an example of an athlete who is classified as lacking in "speed strength." This conclusion was reached because it has been reliably reported that Anderson performed a squat with more than 900 lb. and perhaps as much as 1200 lb. (without any of the supportive devices used by powerlifters today) and his best official C&J was "only" 440 lb.. (Today most athletes who C&J 440 lb. can only squat with between 550 lb. and 600 lb.)

The example of Paul Anderson (and that of similar athletes) is unfortunate because the "evidence" on which it is based, the logic used in the argument and the conclusion are all incorrect. Paul Anderson never squatted with anything like 1100 lb. or 1200 lb. during his competitive weightlifting career. Reports made during the period when Anderson clean and jerked 440 lb. indicate that his squat was probably somewhere in the area of 800 lb. to 900 lb. (the higher squats came later in his professional career). He never really got a chance to try the strength that he developed later in his life on the competitive platform (although he did claim a 475 lb. to 485 lb. clean in later years despite having little reason to train on the snatch or clean when he was a professional athlete). In addition, Anderson's technique was not very efficient, even by the standards of his day. He trained by himself during most of his rise to weightlifting prominence, and his competitive career was scarcely long enough for him to develop proper technique skills. Moreover, even if Anderson had employed efficient technique, the technique of his day was far less efficient than it is today and the equipment was not as sophisticated. One of the reasons for Anderson's not lifting more at his competitive prime in 1956 is that he already held all of the world records and had broken the world record for the total by more than 100 lb. in his brief competitive career. (It is psychologically difficult to keep pushing up the world record when you are so far ahead of the competition and lifting more than anyone ever has.)

Perhaps the most compelling argument against the example of Paul Anderson is that Anderson was exceptional by any standard of "speed strength." At a body weight of between 320 lb. and 370 lb., Anderson was reportedly capable of broad jumping 11 feet! He raced the world record holder in the 440 yard dash in his day in a short sprint (50 yards) and lost by only two strides (without proper track shoes). His lighter weightlifting teammates, many of whom had outstanding speed in their own right, have verified Paul's surprising speed. His schoolmates remember him not as the strongest but rather as the fastest athlete on the football team. Therefore, if Anderson's performance in the weightlifting events was not what some think it should have been, a lack of speed strength was almost certainly not the reason. What made Paul Anderson great, what makes any weightlifting champion of today great, is his or her strength and the ability to generate high power outputs at relatively moderate speeds.

If the preceding discussion is not enough to convince you of the overwhelming importance of strength in weightlifting, then you should be aware that research suggests that speed can only be improved relatively modestly with training. You can improve the speed of your reaction to stimuli and improve on other factors which give the appearance of faster movement, but raw speed is not subject to dramatic improvements over an athlete's career. Why would an athlete devote a great deal of energy to the development of a quality that has a limited influence on performance and is only moderately trainable?

This should not be interpreted to imply that weightlifters should not always endeavor to move the bar as quickly as possible in keeping with the application of sound technique. In fact, such an effort is critical. Research and practical experience have shown that when an athlete is thinking of moving the bar as quickly as possible, he or she is simultaneously developing strength and power (whereas pushing up a weight with no attempt at speed will build strength more than power). Rather, an athlete should understand that much of the speed he or she possesses is inherited, and the emphasis in weightlifting is on developing strength (and power at relatively low velocities).

If high strength levels and high power outputs at low velocities are appropriate goals of a weightlifter's training, how do you get strong and powerful? That is the subject of this chapter, perhaps the most important one in this book (along with the next chapter, which deals with mental preparation for weightlifting).

How To Become Strong

There are two fundamental ways to become strong: a) to be born with a hereditary predisposition toward strength and then just let the biological processes unfold as one matures, or b) to train. Just as there are people who seem to have a great deal of natural endurance or superior memories, so there are those who are "naturally" strong. However, the stories about natural abilities, when they pertain to any faculty possessed by human beings, tend to be greatly overblown. Often, when hears of a person with an especially good memory, that person has merely found the proper ways to store information effectively, ways that can be learned by anyone else. Similarly, many naturally strong people have engaged in hard physical work or play of some sort that has developed their strength. They were often complimented on their strength at some point, then began to "test" it or to employ it in a work environment, both of which often had the effect of further improving that strength.

We will not spend any further time on the subject of being born strong for two reasons. First, you are either born strong or you are not. There is nothing you can do about natural strength except to use it. Someone who is "born" strong need not read a book about how to get that way (unless he or she wants to get strong enough to be a weightlifting champion). Second, being born strong does not seem to matter much in terms of your potential for success as a weightlifter. Why not? Born strong or not, there is only one way to become strong enough to win high level weightlifting competitions. That is to train to become strong. No one has ever been born strong enough to defeat the trained athlete (although there have been some remarkable naturally strong men and women)

It may be true that those who were born strong have at least an initial advantage in terms of developing strength. However, the good news for those who were not born strong is that nature seems to have its compensating mechanisms. Those who are naturally the weakest seem to have the greatest capacity for the development of strength. Training appears to be the great equalizer. Those who start strong are often not as highly motivated to use their gifts as those who are not naturally gifted (and motivation is far more important in terms of success in weightlifting than natural strength).

One of the goals of this book is to make strength happen for anyone who wishes to develop it. It has often been said of running that anyone can run a marathon if they are willing to train for it. I will say something similar about weightlifting. Anyone (other than persons with certain serious medical conditions that attack the muscles and/or nerves) can become very strong through proper training. (Even many people with the kinds of medical conditions mentioned above can grow stronger, or at least not lose ground as quickly if they train properly.) Perhaps more importantly, everyone can build character and self-esteem in the process of training, and that is something that, everyone , born strong or not, needs to train to develop. Let us now begin the adventure of getting strong.

The Training Effect: The Key to Developing Strength and Power

Strength is developed through generating what is known as the training effect on skeletal muscles (the muscles used to move the skeleton of the body). The concept of the training effect is better understood if you look at the more general process of biological adaptation (of which the training effect is a class or category).

The human body is constructed in such a way that it is able to expend a certain level of physical effort or be exposed to a certain kind of stimulus (e.g., stress, excitement, irritation, infection) without that effort or stimulus having any lasting material effect on the body. (For example, the body will adapt to the demands of running very slowly for a short period of time by speeding up the heart and breathing rates and by using the body's energy stores more quickly than it would if the body were at a state of rest; then it returns to its "normal" state when the running stops, with no lasting effect on the body.) However, when the effort the body expends or the stimulus that it encounter is of a sufficient magnitude, the body often reacts by adapting itself in a way that will enable it to perform at a higher level or to withstand the stimulus more effectively with less disruption to the body's functioning in the future.

Examples of this kind of adaptation process are endless. Let us look at just a few. When aerobic activities (endurance related activities like long distance running or cycling) are performed strenuously enough and for a long enough period, the body will adapt itself in such a way as to use oxygen and certain energy supplies within the body more effectively (e.g., by making changes in the heart muscle and the efficiency with which energy for muscular contractions is delivered). Exercise that involves intermittent muscular effort, like occasionally lifting heavy objects or frequently moving moderate weight objects will cause skeletal muscles to become larger and stronger.

The body's ability to adapt is not limited to muscles in the heart, arms and legs. The skin adapts. Exposure to the sun (though it may have long term negative effects on the skin) reduces the tendency of the skin to burn (although not necessarily to be damaged). Similarly, many of us have had the experience of developing a callus after performing manual labor of some kind. That callus

is the body's attempt to adapt to the stress it has experienced on the skin as the result of the manual labor performed.

The body's ability to adapt varies with the organ or function involved. For example, the iris of the eye adjusts to the level of light it encounters relatively quickly. However, it does not appear that the ability of the iris to adjust to light changes significantly upon continual exposure to light. Muscles, in contrast, have a great ability to adapt, growing larger, stronger and/or more enduring as adaptation to the stimulus encountered requires. Sometimes the body's adaptations are not positive. Cancer is the body's reaction to certain kinds of stimuli, as are auto-immune diseases. Unfortunately, these are adaptations that can threaten the existence of the organism.

All areas of the body that can and do adapt to a stimulus of some kind seem to have two characteristics in common. First, in order for adaptation to occur, the stimulus must be of sufficient strength. Minor disturbances in the body's equilibrium do not seem to cause it to change, because, as was indicated earlier, the human body has the capacity for certain ranges of activity built into it. Activities and/or stimuli within those ranges are apparently "ignored" by the body. Second, stimuli beyond those necessary to cause an adaptation can have negative effects (even if a positive adaptation occurs). Working with garden tools for half an hour may stimulate the body to create calluses on ones hands. Working for three hours will also stimulate the body to form calluses, but it may also cause blisters to form on the hands. This blistering may prevent or make difficult further activity, and it may preclude (or at least delay) the formation of calluses. Similarly, the administration of a vaccine to the body (a substance that generally has a weakened form of some kind of infectious agent) will not cause the body to become outwardly ill, but it will cause the immune system of the body to alter itself in such a way that the introduction of the full strength infectious agent at a later time will have little or no negative effect on the organism. In contrast, the exposure of the body to the full strength infectious agent can threaten the body's very survival (although if it survives, the body may not be subject to the illness again).

From this discussion of the kinds of reactions that the body can have to a stimulus, we can understand one final and crucial aspect of the body's adaptive mechanisms. In some instances the body adapts as completely as it can (or nearly so) upon a single exposure to a stimuli that is of sufficient strength. In other cases the adaptation is incremental in nature. For example, in the case of the body's adaptation to an infection like the measles, one exposure seems to be sufficient for the body to adapt itself in a way that prevents a person from contracting the disease for a lifetime. In contrast, retaining resistance to other kinds of diseases may require the reintroduction of the stimulus at certain intervals (e.g., the need for inoculation against tetanus infections every ten years). Further, it seems that in some cases repeated stimuli can lead to increasing levels of adaptation and in other cases adaptation can only take place to a general level (a sort of "all or nothing" kind of adaptation).

The adaptive capabilities of the body present us with the proverbial double-edged sword: the "all or nothing" side of the sword and the incremental side of the sword. The "all or nothing" side of the sword achieves complete adaptation after only one stimulus of sufficient strength. That is positive in that the stress of the stimulus need only be suffered once in order to achieve the full benefit of an adaptation. The negative aspect of the "all or nothing" side of the sword is that there is no hope of achieving a further improvement in the adaptation. The incremental side of the sword presents a dilemma of another kind. It offers the potential for repeated and ever increasing adaptations, with all of the existing potential that such progressive adaptation embodies. On the other hand, there is a need for continued exposure to the stimulus, so that any adaptations already achieved are not lost.

Skeletal muscles fall primarily on the incremental side of the sword. Adaptations to exercise tend to require relatively frequent reintroduction of stimuli in order for those adaptations to be sustained. However, progressively higher levels of adaptation can be achieved through repeated introductions of training stimuli. On a very intuitive level, the need for continual stimulation in order to maintain muscle size and function can be seen in the muscles when a limb is immobilized by a plaster cast (as when a bone has been broken). In such a case, muscles that have been used for a lifetime diminish greatly in size, strength, flexibility and endurance. When the cast is removed and activity is reintroduced, the size and exercise capacity of the muscles that move that limb tend to return to their previous level. Over time the increase in a muscle's capacity to perform work is seen in the person who suddenly discovers, after undertaking a new kind of strenuous muscular activity, that his or her muscles have grown, stronger, larger and harder (the latter most likely from the increase in muscle size along with a decrease in the amount of body fat). As has been noted, incremental adaptation is a two way street. If stimuli of sufficient strength are not introduced often enough, the adaptations that have already been made by the body will not be maintained. Incremental de-adaptation will occur. It is interesting to note that the body seems to have a sort of internal clock that recognizes the difference between stimuli and/or adaptations that have been shorter and longer

lived (this difference has been noted both in the coaching and scientific literature). This training "memory" suggests that if the body has noted repeated stresses of a certain strength, it is more reluctant to reverse its adaptation than if the stimuli has been repeated a smaller number of times.

When activity is undertaken with the express purpose of causing the body to adapt in a way that is favorable for that activity, the process is called training. In following the general principles of adaptation to a stimulus, for any kind of training to be effective, it must provide a stimulus of sufficient strength to cause an adaptation, yet not be so strong as to cause the body harm (which may come in the form of a threat to health and/or an actual barrier to the process of adaptation).

In strength training, the training effect is both measured and achieved through the manipulation of two very fundamental exercise variables: intensity—our way of talking about the strength of the stimulus—and frequency—how often the stimulus is administered. ("Volume" is often cited as the second primary training variable, but volume is only meaningful within the context of a given frequency or time interval.) These variables are in keeping with the general nature of adaptation as discussed above. The level of intensity is what gives the muscle a sufficient stimulus to cause it to adapt. A certain frequency in the application of a training stimulus is required to achieve the training effect. There are at least three reasons for this. First, a certain frequency is needed merely to maintain muscle capacity that already exists. Muscle strength will tend to return to its pre-training level unless the muscle is "reminded" to maintain its existing strength level occasionally. Second, a certain frequency of stimulation is required to catch successive peak levels of adaptation. Third, a certain frequency of stimulus is necessary to maintain the muscle's work capacity. A training stimulus of sufficient strength to cause a positive adaptation might only be needed or accepted by the body once a week or once a month, but a failure to train at all between the periods when a new stimulus can be accepted and adapted to would be likely to result in a muscle's losing at least some of its existing work capacity. Such a loss might result in the body being unable to withstand the training necessary to generate further adaptations without breaking down in some way in the process. The ability of the body to perform a given amount of work is related, but not identical, to its maximum capabilities. For example, while two lifters may both have the ability to lift 300 lb., one athlete may be able to lift 285 lb. 10 times with a one-minute rest between each lift while the other lifter might be able to perform the lift five times before fatiguing.

It has been established that the stimulus necessary to maintain a certain level of muscular strength is lower in frequency and/or intensity than the stimulus necessary to cause the muscle to become stronger. (The stimulus to readapt must be at least as strong as, though not necessarily greater than, the stimulus that caused the previous adaptation. Therefore, a training stimulus must be stronger than that which is necessary to maintain a given level of strength if one wishes to improve. However, the training must not so intense and/or frequent that it overcomes the body's capacity to adapt, thereby preventing a positive adaptation and/or causing actual harm to the organism. In short, if you wish to improve your strength, you must not overtrain or undertrain.

It sounds simple. To get stronger, you must simply exercise intensely enough (i.e., provide a strong enough stimulus) and often enough to stimulate your muscles to make successive adaptations (i.e., to get stronger). Fortunately, in principle it is simple. And you should never forget that simplicity when it seems that the subject of how to design your training seems to be getting overly complex. Unfortunately, there is complexity in the process of training for strength, and it arises out of the difficulty we have in measuring the activity of training and its effects. Frequency is relatively easy to measure simply by dividing any training activities performed by time involved; an exercise session with content X done once a week has half the frequency of exercise session X done twice a week. However, no one has yet come up with a truly complete definition of intensity, and it will undoubtedly be many years before this is accomplished (despite the claims made by many experts that they have already completely or even satisfactorily defined and measured intensity).

Contributing further to the complexity of the training process is the fact that frequency and intensity interact. If intensity could be perfectly measured, the effects of exercise sessions conducted at different intensity levels but with identical frequency would be easy to compare. But how do we compare the training effects of two exercise session per week at intensity X with three session at intensity Y?

Why is the issue of intensity such a difficult one? The human body is an extremely complex organism. It operates through the interaction of many systems (e.g., nervous, endocrine), all of which operate in a somewhat different fashion, all of which possess different potentials for adaptation and all of which affect and are affected by the actions of the other systems. Moreover, no two human bodies are precisely the same. They share certain characteristics and basic methods of functioning, but they all possess inherent biological individuality. And as if these differences weren't complicated enough, each body has already adapted to its environment in innumerable ways, so that even if two organisms started out on an identical biological basis (e.g., as identical twins),

varying interactions with the environment would cause certain qualities of these organisms to diverge over time.

In my view, the failure to focus fully on the individual and that individual's unique nature (not ignoring his or her success) limited the development of weightlifting and other sports in the heralded sports science institutes of many former Eastern bloc countries. (Their approach rested to a certain extent on a moral and political philosophy that downplayed the role and very existence of the individual.) As great as many Eastern European countries are in weightlifting, their results in a number of areas of sports science are relatively disappointing when compared with the resources they expended. In many cases sports science contributed relatively little to the success of those sports programs. More often than not, it was the individual coaches working in local areas, generally without highly sophisticated scientific equipment, who attained the best results and pointed the sports scientists in the direction of fruitful areas of study. It appears that many of the sports research institutes concentrated on merely collecting and disseminating such results (an important function but not often one that requires any significant level of scientific sophistication).

This is not to say that such studies have no value. On the contrary, carefully performed and interpreted studies can provide us with invaluable information about the human body's responses to training. Good coaches follow and apply research as soon as results become available. However, research cannot substitute for more basic scientific study or for judgment, creativity and experience.

Returning to the issue of intensity, while the measurable intensity may be the same from athlete to athlete and year to year, the training effect of that intensity may be different from individual to individual, within the same individual over time, and on mental and physical levels (via the differing strengths of the effect that one stimulus may have on different systems of the body). Therefore, it can be said that there is an external (and measurable) intensity, but there is also an internal component of intensity. It is this latter intensity that is so difficult to measure. There are certain objective indicators of "internal" intensity, but we are surely far from being able to know and to measure it fully.

For example, doing a certain number of snatches with a certain weight may have a training effect on several bodily mechanisms. Such training may stimulate the muscles of the legs and back to become stronger and may cause an adaptation of the connective tissues of the knees (e.g., cartilage, ligaments and tendons) to the stresses they receive. At age fifteen, the muscles and connective tissues might recuperate at the same rate from that heavy snatch. At age thirty-five, the muscles may recuperate at a rate that is 25% slower than at age fifteen. The soft tissues, on the other hand, might now require 50% longer to recuperate (or simply be stressed more than the muscles by the same workout). Therefore, when the muscles are demanding another snatch workout in order to stimulate them to further improvement or even to prevent a return to lower level of development, the soft tissues may require three more days of rest.

This difference may exist with respect to athletes of the same age for a variety of reasons. One athlete might employ a technique that creates more stress on certain tissues. Even with identical techniques and connective- tissue characteristics, one athlete, upon hitting a certain position in the lift, might experience a greater stress on the joints because of anatomical differences, resulting in different rates of stress and recuperation.

Biological differences between lifters can be equally confounding within muscles. Different blends of white and red fibers (muscle fiber "types" are explained in Appendix II) may react differently to the same training stimuli (when those stimuli are quantitatively at the same level). Different patterns of rest and levels of nutrition (and absorption of nutritional elements introduced into the body) affect lifters differently. Some lifters just seem to recuperate faster than others, and still others seem to require a lesser stimulus to respond.

Compounding the complexity presented by the various biological mechanisms that are at work when training is undertaken are psychological and emotional factors. One lifter may require a great deal of mental preparation and/or effort to perform a maximal lift, while another is able to prepare almost instantly. Similarly, one lifter may have a tendency to relax immediately after a workout while another may be "up" for hours. Therefore, one lifter may be emotionally drained for several days or even weeks after a heavy workout. Other lifters take their heavy workouts in stride. Even within the same athlete, a different approach to a workout will have different effects. I have gotten stronger going up to an absolute physical maximum more than once a week, as long as I did not become emotionally involved in the workout (i.e., I was exerting force maximally against the bar, but I could have exerted even more force if I had gotten more emotionally aroused). On the other hand, I have gotten stronger going heavy less frequently but getting emotionally worked up when I did (and of course lifting more).

One final issue that makes it difficult to track the true training effect of a given stimulus is the lag between the application of a training stimulus and the adaptation of the body to that stress. There is always some interval that separates the moment when a training effect is generated and the time when the body adapts to that stimulus. Moreover, the length of this lag is different for different bodily capacities. While this may seem like an obvious point to some trainers, it is often overlooked entirely, or the full implications of this issue are not fully considered when an athlete or coach is analyzing a response to training.

For example, the practice of a certain exercise may teach the athlete to exert his or her muscles in a particular way (i.e., sequence, force and angle) and train those muscles to become stronger as well. The learned ability to exert high levels of force through your muscles in a particular way may be fairly rapid, but the adaptation that is taking place in the muscles in response to that stimulus may take from several days to several weeks or even longer to occur. Therefore, that athlete may be able to repeat the exercise the following day with equal or greater success because of the learned ability to exert force more effectively, even though the full capacity of the muscles has not been restored.

The conclusion from the experience described above might then be "that exercise made me stronger right away, therefore I'll do it the night before my next competition." The magic exercise is thus performed and the athlete is not able to perform well at the competition. What has happened is that the neurological effect of the exercise is not as profound as it once was, while the effect of the bout of exercise in terms of reducing the short term capacity of the muscle is now greater. As a result, what the athlete feels on the day of the event is a temporary loss of muscle capacity but only a minor offsetting benefit in terms of neurological improvement: hence the poor performance (though the stress placed on the muscle before the competition might lead to a positive adaptation at a later date).

A similar case would be one of changing the exercises, sets and reps performed in a series of workouts, enjoying an immediate improvement and then concluding that it was the new training program that had a positive effect on performance. Instead, the muscles may still be adapting to the stresses imposed by the prior routine, with the dividend not appearing until the athlete is some weeks into the new routine. Another possibility is that the combination of the residual effects of the old routine and the effects of the new routine are causing the improvement and that one or the other of the routines alone (or in a different sequence) would not achieve the same effect.

Still another case would be an athlete concluding that his Saturday workout is going poorly because he or she has not fully recuperated from the workout done on Thursday. In fact, the body may not have had much of an opportunity to react to Thursday's workout because it is still trying to adapt to the stimulus imposed by the workout done on the previous Saturday (an adaptation which would have been fully accomplished had the workout done on Thursday not been so severe).

The general point being made here is that the effects of lag must always be considered and must never underestimated. Calculating the lag in an athlete's responses to specific regimens is one of the most significant steps that the coach or athlete can make in terms of learning to design effective exercise prescriptions for that athlete.

Does all of this complexity make planning a workout impossible? Of course not. What it does mean is that the same workout (measured by existing external means, such as the weight on the bar) will almost provide exactly the same benefit to two different lifters, or even to the same lifter at different times if conditions within that lifter change over time (e.g., the degree of psyche used in the workout, the age of the athlete). While the same training program or "routine" may work for a number of athletes, you should not be lulled into thinking that even similar rates of improvement mean that athletes are reacting to the workout over time in the same way in all respects (e.g., it may take a long time for differences in the effects of training to manifest themselves in terms of observable reactions or symptoms of trauma).

The purpose of this discussion is not to confuse or discourage the coach or lifter with the complexity of it all. Rather, its purpose is to alert athlete and coach to the fact that training needs to be monitored individual athlete by individual athlete. The effects of that training need to be analyzed on as many levels as possible. Adjustments must then be made as necessary in order to adapt the routine to that particular lifter at that point in time. In effect, the development of an optimal training method for each athlete is based on viewing each athlete as a unique laboratory in which experiments will be performed over time. The results of those experiments will be monitored carefully and then analyzed at length. Through this effort the most effective training methods for that particular athlete can be formulated. This is why slavishly following "cookbook workouts" (generalized workouts that prescribe a certain set of exercises, frequencies and intensities for all athletes) or computerized training plans precludes optimization of training for a particular athlete (though such approaches may produce as least some improvement in most athletes and can expand the knowledge of how to apply training principles to athletes under practical conditions by providing examples).

The need for individualization and adjustment does not diminish the importance of planning your workouts. But that planning must be done carefully and must always be the product of the best information that is available based on previous adaptive reactions to training experienced by that athlete. Therefore, the effects of any planned training on the athlete must be carefully monitored, both because such monitoring facilitates adjustments during the training session (if this is necessary) and because monitoring makes possible the development of even better training plans in the future.

A great deal has been learned about strength training over the last century. While precise individual prescriptions for optimal training cannot be made on the basis of the general knowledge thus far accumulated, our ability to make individual prescriptions has improved as general knowledge of strength training has grown. Sufficient information is now available to enable the athlete to narrow the range of his or her search for effective training methods, to begin at a point where optimal training techniques for him or her can be discovered in a relatively short time. In addition, the likelihood of making major errors while the search is on has been reduced. Consequently, substantial progress can be made while movement toward true optimization of the training process continues. Let us now turn to what is known about measuring frequency and intensity.

Three Key Variables Generate the Training Effect: Frequency, Intensity and Specificity

Three key variables act in concert to generate a training effect—frequency, intensity and specificity. Frequency is the measure of how often the training stimulus is administered and intensity is the level of the stimulus. A certain threshold intensity is required in order to generate a training stimulus and a certain level of frequency in the administration of the training stimulus is necessary in order to maintain and build on any prior training stimulus. These two concepts are very much interrelated in that within certain ranges of training frequency and intensity, the two variables complement on another. In general, as the intensity of a stimulus increases it needs to administered less frequently in order for it to achieve the same training effect. Similarly, as the frequency of the administration of the stimulus increases a lower intensity is required to generate the same training effect. However, the effects of intensity and frequency are not fully interchangeable. For example, the training effect of a maximal effort made every few days will not be identical to the effect of a lesser level of intensity repeated every day. But the effects are similar enough within certain ranges that one can often be exchanged for another.

Frequency and intensity control the level of the training stimulus but specificity controls the direction (i.e., what qualities are trained). More will be said regarding specificity in a later section of this chapter in the section the discusses the "SAID" principle. Now, let's turn to a discussion of frequency and intensity.

Frequency

Frequency of resistance training is measured in several kinds of units. The first and most fundamental unit is the repetition. A repetition can be defined as a single completed effort at a particular exercise (although a single "repetition" sounds like a contradiction in terms). With free weights (the tools of weightlifting training and competition), there is normally a concentric and an eccentric contraction of the muscles being exercised in each repetition. The concentric contraction occurs when the resistance (weight) is being lifted, and the eccentric contraction of the exercise occurs when the resistance is being lowered. It may seem contradictory to call the lowering of the resistance an eccentric "contraction" since the muscle is not actually shortening in length (contracting) during that process. Nevertheless, the muscles are working to control the weight during the lowering process; hence the convention of calling such a process a contraction. It should be noted that there has been a relatively recent movement in the scientific community to change the convention from "muscle contraction" to "muscle action" for this very reason. (Under this system, concentric and eccentric actions would replace the terms concentric and eccentric contractions.)

When they exercise, weightlifters sometimes do what are known as "partial movements or lifts" because these exercises represent only a portion of the range of motion that is achieved by doing the full exercise. In such a situation, a repetition consists of moving the weight through the entire partial movement that was intended.

Putting aside the technical rules of competition, a lift is considered completed when a weight has been raised in the desired way. (Most exercises involve lowering the weight as well, whether in preparation for raising it, as in a bench press or squat, or by lowering the bar after raising it to prepare for another repetition, to replace the weight on the floor, or to replace it on a supportive device that holds the weight in preparation for lifting it.) A repetition in other kinds of resistance training (e.g., isometric, isokinetic) is defined somewhat differently. (Those kinds of training are described in a later section of this chapter.)

As noted earlier, calling a single effort a repetition may seem incongruous, but resistance training often involves repeating an exercises two or more times, so the nomenclature of "repetitions" has simply become part of worldwide weightlifting language. Almost everyone in the weightlifting culture uses the abbreviation rep(s) for repetition(s). Often one lift is referred to as a "single.," two reps as a "double" and three reps as a "triple." Beyond three reps, the lifter usually refers to a series of repetitions by the actual number of reps performed, e.g., "five reps" or "a set of five,"

However, repetitions have a broader meaning than just how many times a lift was performed. They imply that a relatively short period time has elapsed between the performance of each repetition. For example, if a lifter raised and lowered a bar from the shoulders to arm's length overhead using only arm strength (in an exercise called the press), that would be considered a repetition. If he or she repeated the lift instantaneously or within a few seconds of lowering the bar to the chest, everyone would agree that two reps had been performed. Even if the lifter waited as long as ten or twenty seconds, with the bar on his or her shoulders between repetitions, the lifter would generally be credited with two repetitions. In contrast, if the lifter performed the lift once, placed the bar on a holder (usually referred to as a "rack") and then returned some minutes later to repeat the lift, that lifter could not claim to have performed two repetitions with the weight in question in lifting circles. Rather, the lifter would be regarded as having performed two "singles" or two "sets" of one repetition each.

What is the distinction between a set and a rep? When a lifter talks about having performed a certain number of reps, the lifter is referring to a series of lifts done with little or no rest in between. "I did four reps with 300 lb." is shorthand for "I lifted 300 lb. four times without giving my muscles any significant time to rest in between those lifts." A series of repetitions performed without significant rest is called a "set.." For example, while training, a lifter might perform four lifts with a given weight. Those lifts could be performed in one series of four repetitions, two sets of two repetitions, a combination of a single rep and one set of three reps or four sets of single repetitions. Why is the distinction important?

There are at least two reasons. One reason is that performances are judged partially by whether an athlete has lifted a weight a certain number of times in one as opposed to several sets. The second reason is that different physiological effects arise from lifting the same weight for several repetitions as compared to several sets with one repetition each. The muscles become fatigued during exercise that exceeds a certain level of difficulty, thereby temporarily losing their ability to function to some extent. After a maximum effort at lifting a weight, a significant percentage of muscle function can be recovered within thirty seconds and nearly all of muscle function in two to three minutes. If a lifter says that he has lifted 300 lb. for five singles in a row without a miss, it suggests that the lifter has mastered that particular amount of weight to the point that it can be repeated without missing. The ability to perform singles with a given weight suggests that this weight may be somewhat below the lifter's maximum, in that it is difficult to perform an all out effort five times in succession with or without a miss. On the other hand, many lifters have achieved such technical proficiency and superior conditioning that they are able to handle weights that are in the range of 97% to 99% of their maximum in such a way. In contrast, in order for a lifter to perform an exercise with a particular weight for five repetitions (i.e., without a rest between lifts), the weight in question can be no more than 85% to 90% of that lifter's all out maximum single lift. If the percentage were any higher, the fatigue of each rep would build to a point where no more repetitions would be possible before five repetitions were achieved. Consequently, it is generally far more meritorious for a lifter to perform five reps with a weight than five single lifts.

Naturally, the longer the rest a lifter takes between repetitions, the more chance there is for the lifter to recuperate fully unless the lifter is supporting the weight between repetitions. If the lifter takes very long between repetitions, and particularly if the lifter is in a state of rest between repetitions (e.g., the weight has been returned to a resting position on the floor or a rack in between repetitions), the repetitions become more like sets. Where is the dividing line between sets and reps? There is no formal definition, but most lifters perform their repetitions with only one to a few seconds in between. When the rest period gets any longer than seven to ten seconds, the nomenclature "repetition" becomes suspect. By thirty seconds, virtually everyone would agree that repetition is no longer the proper term, or that the nature of such a repetition is so different from the ordinary definition of the term as to render it unrecognizable as a rep. In other words, any lifts done would be classified as part of different set.

The intervals between sets generally fall between two to five minutes, but the interval can be shorter if the weights being lifted are sub-maximal (or the lifter is warming up or training primarily to build muscle size, as in bodybuilding) and/or if the number of repetitions in each set are low (usually one or two). The time span between sets can also be longer than five minutes when exercise is particularly intense and if the repetitions in each set are relatively high (ten or more, but more often twenty or more). Also, the purpose of training governs the rest periods to a certain extent. Those athletes whose ambition is to achieve maximum muscular size find that shorter rests between sets seem to facilitate acquisition of muscular size, while longer rests seem to develop more strength without size. In short, bodybuilders tend to seek the aching and swollen feeling (the now famous "pumped" feeling) that comes from more repetitions in a set and shorter rest intervals in between the sets performed. Weightlifters and powerlifters tend to avoid feeling "pumped" because pumping a muscle has at least he immediate effect of compromising that muscle's ability to lift maximum poundages. Moreover,

while there also appears to be some correlation between the pumped feeling during a workout and the muscle growth that a workout stimulates, there appears to be little or no such relationship between the pump and the development of strength.

When sets are punctuated by rests of more than five or ten minutes, there tends to be a subjective feeling (that appears to be supported to an extent by research) of no longer being warmed-up (more will be said about warming up later in this chapter). Therefore, lifters rarely rest more than five minutes between sets. When some unusual situation necessitates a longer rest, the lifter will often take a set with a lighter weight than was previously being used, in order to prepare for a heavy exertion once again.

One way to increase the intensity of a workout with the same weight is to decrease the rest taken between sets and reps over time. When an athlete can perform a certain weight with virtually no rest between reps and only one to two minutes between sets, the weight can be increased and the rest between reps and sets increased to permit the lifter to handle the increased load. When this approach is used, it should be carefully recorded so that the lifter will be able to compare training intensities achieved in different periods and under different timing conditions.

When the rest between exercises grows to be in the thirty-to-sixty minute range or longer, most trainees consider the next time a weight is lifted to mark the beginning of a new training session or workout. Many advanced weight trainers have two or more workouts per day. The advantage of such training is not so much that the athlete works out more overall (although this is certainly true in most cases), but rather that by dividing a day's training in such a way, the lifter can be "fresh" for each session. As a practical matter, it is difficult for an athlete who is exercising intensely to be able to perform with his or her full energy and attention for hours on end. By dividing what would otherwise be a three or four hour workout into two or three sessions of an hour or an hour and a half, the athlete tends to be able to perform at a higher level overall. Some research in Eastern Europe has even suggested that exercise aimed at increasing muscle strength and size is better performed during periods when certain hormones (notably testosterone) are elevated (which, they argue, begins fifteen or twenty minutes into a hard workout but seldom lasts an hour). The existence of this precise pattern of hormone elevation has yet to be confirmed by experiments in the West (where equipment tends to be substantially more accurate); nor has a link between the timing of any hormone elevation and a training effect been demonstrated scientifically. Regardless of the true link between hormone variations and the training effect, this theory may have some merit, because brief and intense workouts seem to be of significant practical value.

It should be noted that repetition, set and workout are far from the only intervals used to measure frequency. You often see frequency measured in terms of days, weeks, months and years. And these intervals do not exhaust the possibilities.

Now that we have defined exercise frequency in terms of the intervals of repetition, set and workout or session, etc., how can we define and measure intensity?

Intensity

While proper training frequency plays a major role with respect to maintaining and improving long term results from training, the intensity of an exercise session is perhaps the most important key to how a particular bout of exercises affects the organism, both in terms of the extent to which it stimulates an adaptation (from not at all to substantially) and the nature of that adaptation.

Consider how the intensity of an exercise effort controls its training effect. If a muscle experiences great resistance in contracting, it may not be able to move the limb to which the muscle is attached. If the effort made to move the limb is great, it cannot be sustained for very long. However, that effort will have a training effect on the muscle that will cause it to become stronger in positions similar to the one in which the limb is placed during the contraction effort. There will no discernible training effect on the endurance capabilities of the muscle (other, perhaps, than its ability to exert considerable effort for a longer period of time than before). There will also tend to be little effect on the size of the muscle.

If, in contrast, a exercise performed by a given muscle is very difficult and is accompanied by movement, the muscle will tend to become stronger as a result of the exercise, but if the effort is such that it cannot be repeated more than one or two times, the primary effect of that exercise on the muscle will be to make it stronger (throughout a greater range of motion than the effort in which the limb could not move). Training accompanied by a full range of limb movement tends to stimulate a greater increase in muscle size than the contractile efforts with the limb fixed.

In terms of exercise performance, differences in the speed with which individual reps are performed can yield different results. Moving a given weight as fast as possible requires a greater volitional effort than moving the same weight at a more "comfortable" speed. Maximizing the speed with which each rep is performed also improves power more effectively then training at more moderate speeds. However, in contrast, moving a weight at slower than normal speed can cause create greater tension in a muscle group than does moving that same weight at a more comfortable speed, thereby

affecting intensity. (Developing greater tension in a muscle that is being exercised appears to increase the training effort generated by that training session.)

If the resistance during the contraction is reduced to the point where ten or fifteen repetitions can be performed, the effect on strength, as expressed by one all out effort, will be smaller than when more resistance is used, but the effect of the exercise on the size of the muscle will be more profound. If the resistance is lowered still further, to the point where 100 repetitions are possible, the set of exercises will tend to develop muscular endurance more than size or strength. Finally, if the resistance is lowered enough to perform thousands of repetitions, the effect of the training, if it is strenuous enough, is essentially aerobic (the ability of the heart and lungs to withstand sustained exercise will be enhanced, as will muscular endurance). Of course if the body is not required to perform at a certain threshold of effort (e.g., if the athlete lifts a weight that could be lifted fifty repetitions for one or two reps), no training effect on any of the body's capacities will occur. So it is intensity, as much as or more than any other element of exercise, that determines its training effect. How are the combined efforts of frequency and intensity measured?

In the real world, frequency and intensity cannot be isolated. Every rep of every set contributes both intensity and frequency to an athlete's training. Moreover, frequency and intensity interact to constitute the overall training stimulus. How is the training stimulus measured?

Measuring the Training Stimulus

Over the years the strength of a given training stimulus has been measured in a number of ways. Early strongmen tended not to attempt to measure the strength of the training stimulus in a very scientific way. They simply learned that in order to get stronger, you must continually attempt to lift more. These pioneers realized that by attempting to lift a certain weight over and over again, you could eventually overcome weights that seemed entirely intractable at an earlier point. Depending on their philosophical premises, some of these men interpreted ultimate success purely as a triumph of the will and others as an adaptation of the body, while still others (the ones who were closer to the truth) saw improvements as a combination of both of these elements. Some of these early strongmen tried to develop "routines" or patterns of exercise that were repeated at specific intervals (e.g., certain exercises might be performed every day). Others trained less systematically, performing the exercises that they felt like doing on a given day.

Regardless of their approach to training, early strongmen also recognized that you could not be at your best every day, nor should you try. Some took off long periods from their training from time to time. Others merely had easy periods of training. Still others made a practice of changing their training regimens periodically to avoid stagnation. During the 1930s and 1940s, perhaps earlier, the weight training literature began to talk with regularity about the need for lighter and heavier days in training. However, more often than not, workouts were varied by focusing on different repetition schemes and/or exercises. For example, a lifter might lift bars on Monday, Wednesday and Friday and dumbbells on Tuesdays and Saturdays. In addition, the athlete might work on sets of ten repetitions on Monday, five repetitions on Wednesday and try heavy single efforts on Fridays. In this way, both the nature and strength of the training stimulus were varied in some way from workout to workout.

Early weight trainers also recognized the need to avoid working on the basis of "nerve." It was recognized that by exciting the nervous system you could lift more on a given day and that such all out efforts might have a beneficial effect on the development of strength. Yet it was also recognized that if an athlete trained that way during every workout, he or she would eventually become exhausted, and progress would cease (or the athlete might even regress).

When the Eastern Europeans began to take a more "scientific" approach to analyzing training in the postwar years, they began to focus on measuring more effectively the strength of the training stimulus. Unfortunately, as with so much "science" of the time, the focus on measurement led to an assumption that if it could not be measured, it was not real or important. This fallacy became common in the social sciences and in business during the same period, hurting development in these areas at least as much as it helped.

The Soviets (the overall leaders in studying the sport of weightlifting in Eastern Europe) began by measuring what they called the "volume" of training. This was done simply by adding up the total amount of weight that was lifted during a given period. The Soviets hypothesized that the amount of total work done would correlate with the training effect and that, eventually, patterns of successful training volumes would emerge and could then be duplicated. It took a number of years for them to conclude that the total tonnage lifted in training had a very limited relation to improvements in an athlete's performance (something less quantitatively oriented analysts had concluded many years before). After all, a man who loads a truck with fifty-pound sacks of sand all day lifts far more in terms of total tonnage than the hardest training weightlifter, yet he is not nearly as capable of lifting heavy objects (technique aside).

The next method that became popular in measuring the strength of the training stimulus

was calculating the average weight on the bar, referred to as the absolute intensity. It was felt that there was a correlation between the average weight lifted and the performance of the athlete. This average weight was later used to measure the intensity of the training of Olympic lifters by comparing the average weight on the bar to the biathlon result of the lifter (the result was called a K value). It was believed that if one lifter was training with an average weight that was equal to 40% of his biathlon result while another was training with an average of 35%, the former was training more intensely (i.e., at a greater level of training stimulus) than the other.

Subsequently, some analysts began to realize that even average and relative intensities were of limited value as a measure of the training stimulus because the exercises that athletes performed varied so much. For example, in Olympic lift training, the average weight on the bar could be very high if an athlete happened to perform many exercises in which there was a potential to lift more than in the snatch and clean and jerk (e.g., squats and pulls, exercises that are described fully in Chapter 5). To overcome this problem, analysts began to measure the percentages of the workouts that were devoted to various exercises. It was assumed that if two athletes were performing similar exercises for similar percentages of their workouts, the intensities of their workouts could be validly and reliably compared.

Over time, the weaknesses of those "average" (whether in terms of average weight on the bar or relative to some other value) measures of intensity began to be understood. Even if averages were adjusted in some way to recognize the blend of exercises that was done, the problems with using averages could not be fully overcome. For example, a lifter could attain the same average training loads by handling only the average weight, by performing equal numbers of lifts with a weight that was 10% above and 10% below the average weight or by performing a nearly infinite number of other combinations that resulted in the same average weight. When it was realized that the distribution of the training load was important, perhaps as important as the average training poundage, pure average measures of training intensity began to lose favor. In recent years such averages have come to be regarded as a less important indicator of the training stimulus than was previously thought.

It is interesting to note that a relatively recent major publication by a very well known coach from the Soviet Union suggests that the average poundage lifted is a measure of training quality that is inappropriately overlooked. The argument made by the author is that there is perhaps no measure that correlates more closely with a lifter's progress than the increase in the average weight on the bar during training. The limitations of the "average weight on the bar" measure of training intensity have already been discussed, but this coach's argument is fallacious for still another reason. While there is no doubt that there is a correlation between the average weight on the bar that a lifter uses in training and his or her maximal performances, the reasoning that the author has used is a classic non-sequitur (an argument that does not follow from the facts). His argument is analogous to saying that there is a correlation between the amount of money made by a Wall Street investor and the increase in the amount that he or she invests. The end prescription would then be: "to make more, simply invest more." Instead, the real question is what is increasing the amount that the investor has to invest? It is more likely to be the judgment of the investor than the mere quantity of the money invested, both because the investor has more money to invest as a result of previous gains and because he or she has attracted new investors on the basis of his or her previous record of success. Similarly, to lift more, a lifter does not necessarily try to increase the average weight on the bar during training. Rather, the athlete focuses on improving functional capacity, and this results in the lifter's capabilities improving sufficiently to enable him or her to train with a higher average weight on the bar.

The mainstream Soviet response to the deficiencies in the "average weight on the bar" method of measuring intensity was to begin to measure workouts in terms of "zones of intensity." Zones of intensity generally involve the counting of the number of repetitions performed at 90% or more of the athlete's maximum in that exercise, 80% to 89%, 70% to 79%, 60% to 69% and 50% to 59%. (Weights below 50% of maximum are not considered to be worth measuring because they seem to be unable to stimulate strength gains and because comparatively little overall training time is spent with them today ; in fact, weights below as much as 80% of maximum are excluded from consideration by some coaches.). The coaches count the number of reps in each zone and compare workouts in terms of the number of lifts done with weights in each zone. (Zones based on an athlete's best performance in that exercise are set up for each classical exercise.)

While the use of zones is clearly an advance in training measurement, such a measurement system still leaves much to be desired. One problem with such a system is that there is no distinction between lifts that are performed with substantial rest in between and those that are performed in immediate succession (e.g., five singles versus five reps with the same weight). This difference in performance method has a great influence on both the degree of stimulus provided by exercise in a given zone and the specific adaptive mechanisms in the muscles influenced. A

second limitation of the zone method of measurement is that is does permit us to draw conclusions about the overall training process of all exercises combined (e.g., ten squats performed in zone 1 will not affect the body in the same way as ten cleans performed in the same zone). While the zone method does enable us to compare the workouts of two athletes more effectively than many other methods, for reasons mentioned earlier, the same pattern of relative intensity will have different effects on the organisms of different lifters (and even on the same lifter over time).

A further difficulty in quantifying the training stimulus is that no intensity measure has yet been devised which can quantify the effect of a given training session on technique. A lifter could be performing a certain number of lifts in a given zone, but due to improper technique, the training session could be stimulating the muscles to perform in a sequence and a direction that will never be useful while the lifter is performing a correct lift. Therefore, the training effect will be virtually useless in terms of advancing competitive performance (which is one reason why two lifters can appear to train at the same intensity and one will improve while the other does not). Finally, no measure that currently exists and no method is likely to be developed for a long time to come to quantify the mental effort that goes into a given lift.

In recent years the Bulgarians have made what they consider to be an advance in terms of measuring and planning the amount of stimulus to apply in a given training session. They reportedly no longer measure percentages or plan workouts using percentages or zones (at least in the traditional sense). Instead, they plan each workout session as it unfolds by having the athlete work up to a maximum for that day. When it is clear to the coach just what that maximum is (the lifter may be allowed to miss several times in attempting to establish that day's maximum), the coach then prescribes a series of sets and reps (usually doubles and singles) that involves working within 5 kg. to 20 kg. of the maximum and working up to it again once or twice. In this way the athlete is always working with a weight that is near his or her maximum for that day. The Bulgarians then simply look at the total number of reps performed in a session, a day, a week, a month or a year in comparing workouts. Since workouts are always similar in content (the Bulgarians only use a few exercises in their training and generally use only one or two reps), they feel that comparisons of this type are sufficient.

We are probably at least some years away from being able to measure accurately the training effect of different exercises on the body. We are also some time away from being able to compare precisely the training of two different athletes because of the different effect that the same program of exercises, frequencies and intensities will have on two different athletes. Breakthroughs in these areas will probably not occur until we are able to measure accurately the response of the entire organism (or at least most of it) to a particular training effort. It will be a much longer time before we are able to quantify the training effect of a particular routine when the technique employed in that routine is not precisely the same as the technique used in the competitive exercises when they are perfectly performed. However, I believe that some improvements can be made in the measurement of training intensity without any sophisticated technological improvements.

First, instead of using zones as they are today, these zones could be further refined by subdividing them in accordance with the number of reps performed in a given exercise. Today, an athlete who performed a set of 5 in the squat with 87% of his or her best single would be credited with having performed 5 lifts with 87% of his or her maximum. If the same athlete were to perform 5 singles in the squat with the same weight, he or she would get the same "credit" under the zone system. Clearly, the merit and the training effect of the two exercise sessions would be completely different. Five singles with 87% of the lifter's best would at best maintain his or her present condition. A set of 5 with 87% would constitute something close to an all out effort, which might well stimulate the body to improve. Here is why. When a lifter is performing a set of 5 repetitions, each rep gets progressively more difficult because the body is becoming more and more fatigued from the previous reps done in that set. Therefore, the first rep in a set of 5 with 87% would indeed require the same effort as a single with that weight. However, the second rep, because of the fatigue caused by the first rep, might have a perceived effort (and perhaps a concomitant training effect) equivalent to performing a single with 88.5%; the third rep might be like a single with 90.5%, the fourth rep like a single with 95% and the last rep like a single with 100%. Is it reasonable to treat such a set like five singles with 87%? In addition, is it reasonable to consider five singles and five reps synonymous when the degree of mental preparation for a set tends to be greater than the amount of preparation that takes place between reps?

There are those who will argue that comparing different patterns of reps is pointless because doing five reps with 87.5 kg. does not prove that a person can do one rep with 100 kg, and they have a point. The technique used with the 87.5 kg. (at least on some of the reps) might be such that if any weight had been added to the bar, the lifter would have failed. In addition, some lifters are either very efficient at doing reps (learning to rest just the right amount between reps to maximize their performance, etc.) or are very poor at doing singles

(being intimidated by heavier weights, having trouble concentrating prior to the lift, etc.).

Critics of comparing reps with singles also argue that while the perceived effort on the last rep of a set of five might be 100%, the training effect on the muscles and/or the exact fibers used is not the same as that which would be used to do a single with 100%. Again, these critics have a point. However, I would argue that any inaccuracy that exists in comparing performances done with reps and singles is substantially smaller than the inaccuracy that exists in ignoring the differences altogether.

Moreover, most of the shortcomings of comparing sets with different numbers of reps can be controlled once you know a particular athlete reasonably well. For example, most athletes have relationships between reps and singles that fall within the following ranges: 5 reps with 85% to 90% of best single; 4 reps with 86% to 91%; 3 reps with 89% to 92%; and 2 reps with 94% to 97%. There is a tendency for these relationships to remain constant for the same athlete over time, at least with respect to the same exercises. An exception to this tendency occurs when the athlete specializes in one pattern of reps to the exclusion of most others (in which case he or she will tend to become relatively more efficient at the practiced rep pattern). The argument that the training effect of reps vs. singles is not identical is simply a further reason for measuring the two kinds of exercise separately, instead of aggregating them all into a zone. This does not preclude aggregating all lifts (whether singles or reps) into all sets in order to gain some overall measure of the work done. Rather, it suggests that separate records should be kept for purposes of analysis of the content of a lifter's training.

In order to perform the proper analysis, records should be kept of the full range of zones for each pattern of repetitions from 1 to 6, with perhaps one additional zone assigned to the unusual instances in which repetitions in excess of 6 were employed. If an athlete did a single with a weight that was equal to 90% of his or her best single, the lift would be assigned to the 90% zone of the "singles" set of zones. If that same athlete did a triple with 90% of his or her best triple, the lift would be assigned to the 90% zone of the triples set of zones.

As long as separate reps are tracked, the coach can evaluate workouts on the basis of "equivalent" reps and actual reps. That is, the coach can convert an actual set of 5 reps to five equivalent singles. This is done by dividing by the percentage of that lifter's one-rep maximum in that exercise being lifted in by a decimal representing the percentage of a single rep maximum that can typically be performed by that athlete in that exercise for that number of reps.

As an example, consider an athlete who has the relationship of reps to singles in the squat described earlier (i.e., the athlete can generally perform 87% of his or her single rep maximum for 5 reps, 88.5% for 4 reps, 90.5% for 3 reps and 95% for 2 reps). In such a case, the fifth rep in a set of 5 is divided by .87, the fourth rep by .885, the third rep by .905 and the second rep by .95. (The first rep is equivalent to a straight single, so it is divided by 1.0, i.e., it remains the same). Therefore, if this athlete performed a set of 5 reps with a weight equal to 87% of his or her best single, it would convert to the equivalent of 5 singles, one each with 87% (the first rep), 88.5% (the second rep), 90.5 % (the third rep), 95% (the fourth rep) and 100% (the fifth rep). Similarly, a set of 5 reps performed by this athlete with a weight that was 80% of his or her maximum would convert to equivalent singles of 80%, 84.2%, 88.9%, 90.4% and 92%, for the first through fifth reps, respectively.

Another important area in which current methods of workout intensity measurement are very poor is in comparing different exercises. While perfect comparisons cannot be made at present (due to our inability to measure the effect of a given exercise on all of the bodily systems), we can do a much better job than we are currently doing. For example, it is clear that a squat clean has several components to it. One is the pull (the first four stages of the lift), another is the squat under and finally there is standing up from the position. In order to simulate (though not duplicate) the training effect with other exercises, you would need to do a clean pull, a front squat with a bounce at the bottom and some kind of technique exercise (such as a dead hang clean or "going under" exercise from the standing position); these exercises are explained in Chapter 5. While most lifters and coaches recognize that a set of high pulls and a set of cleans are not the same, few take the time to analyze the differences and to plan their training so that the correct blend of pulling, moving under, catching and front squatting up is substituted for cleans. It may well be true that the coach prescribes a certain exercise because he or she feels that the lifter requires more work in one element of the clean than another, but often the full implications of changing exercises are not thought through, and something is overlooked in the transition. (For example, the coach may prescribe pulls and front squats instead of cleans to save the lifter a respite from catching cleans in the squat position but fail to prescribe an exercise to preserve practice in moving under the bar, even though the coach would agree that the lifter needs the practice.) In planning and analyzing training, the athlete and coach must therefore carefully break down all of the components of an exercise in order to understand better its effects on the organism of the athlete.

Different Responses to Training in Different Muscle Groups

One final area of training stimulus and response that deserves attention is that of the different responses of different muscle groups to the same kind on training. Muscle groups vary in terms of their ability to return to maximal performance levels after a given bout of exercise. It is not clear whether this is true because some muscle groups are less easily torn down than others or because there are differences in the speed of recovery from a stimulus, or because both of these factors are at work. It is also not clear whether the degree of rest that each muscle group enjoys in the natural course of events between workouts is a factor in recovery time. We do not know all of the answers, but it clear is that there are differences and that some guidelines regarding those differences do exist.

As a rule, smaller muscle groups recover more quickly from a workout session than larger muscle groups. Muscle groups that are activated more frequently in daily life appear to recuperate more rapidly from a training session than those that work less often. For instance, the calves and forearms appear to recuperate more quickly than the thighs. There is some evidence that white muscle fibers recover from a bout of exercise more slowly than red muscle fibers. In addition, the body appears to recover more rapidly from high and low rep sets than from sets in the middle range of reps (a maximum single or set of twenty will not impair an athlete's strength level for as long as a maximum set of five reps). Partial movements appear to require less recovery time than full movements. Finally, the muscles of the lower back and thighs appear to be among the muscle groups that are the slowest to recover from a training session.

The degree to which these differences exist will vary from lifter to lifter, but it is unlikely that lifters recover at an equal rate in all areas of the body. Therefore, a pattern of frequency and intensity that works well for the arms may have limited value for training the shoulders, and if both muscle groups were exercised solely with a lift that used both muscle groups equally, one group would might not be trained hard enough and another might be trained too hard. Similarly, a pattern of sets and repetitions that worked well for training the press of a particular lifter might have no positive effect on that lifter's squat. As a result, training sessions for each muscle group need to be planned individually if the optimal training effect for the entire body is to be achieved.

In addition, the overall intensity presented by a given training session needs to be evaluated for each muscle group, because different exercises may affect the same muscle group (albeit in different ways). To say that an athlete has performed a given load in the squat with varied degrees of success does not address the issue of whether the athlete has been exposed on these different occasions to varying loads on the leg muscles because of the presence of other exercises that worked the legs (e.g., on one occasion the athlete was doing a large load in the squat clean and on another the athlete was not). If the lifter repeated the same loading scheme in the squat without performing the same workload in the squat clean, perhaps the results would not be as good. Alternatively, if more deadlifts were added to the routine, the lifter's lower back might be so fatigued as to cause an injury (a phenomenon which was not previously encountered with the use of the same squat routine in the past).

Another reason for differences in the response of different muscles to the same exercise is that different physical qualities are trained with different exercises. For example, the full squat is training the concentric capacity of the quadriceps muscles through a full range of motion and the eccentric capacity of those same muscles at a lower level of effort. (You can descend in the squat with more in the squat than you can stand up with). In addition, the lower back muscles are being isometrically contracted, generally at a sub-maximal level during both the concentric and eccentric portions of the squat.

The snatch is training the concentric contractile power of the quadriceps (but generally through a different range of motion and with maximal stress of the quadriceps muscles at a different joint angle than in the squat). It is also training the spinal extensors in a sub-maximal isometric fashion; when the bar moves from the floor to knee level, the position of the back remains essentially the same, and there is a partial concentric contraction of those muscles as the bar passes the knees. There are then a partial concentric contraction of the quadriceps and partial and isometric contractions of the trapezius muscles).

Many muscle groups and types of work are left out of the preceding analysis but the point should be clear. Different muscle groups are stressed in different ways by these exercises (not to mention the fact that different speeds of motion and motor skill complexity are involved). Therefore, it should not be surprising that identical set, rep and intensity patterns may yield different results on these different exercises. Once a coach or athlete is aware that differences exist, he or she can begin to search for the training stimuli that are optimal for each exercise and area of the body instead of searching for the universal training program that is optimal for all forms of weight training.

The Overall Challenge of the Training Stimulus

Measuring the training stimulus is perhaps the most difficult challenge for the coach and athlete. And the task cannot be accomplished without the participation of both parties. In many cases it is only the coach who is skilled at analyzing quantitative indicators of the training stimulus. However, only the athlete is in a position to report perceived effort (although the experienced coach will be able to estimate an athlete's perceived effort over time by observation of that athlete). The athlete and coach must always consider as many factors as possible in analyzing and planning training. Factors which cannot be measured easily precisely may exist nonetheless. The fallacy of ignoring what cannot presently be measured (or measured precisely) puts an athlete at peril in terms of his or her chances for success. The athlete and coach must work together as a team to optimize the training process.

The "SAID" Or Specificity of Training Principle

Next to understanding how intensity and frequency work together to create the training effect, SAID is perhaps the most fundamental and powerful concept of training. SAID stands for "specific adaptation to imposed demands." What does SAID mean? It means that the body's adaptation to the training stress is very specific to that stress.

At least some of the reasons for the specificity of the body's response to training are now understood on a scientific level, and Appendix II presents the science behind the principle. At this point it is sufficient to say that when a demand is placed on a muscle, that muscle reacts in a very specific way.

It is clear that the body responds to the speed of the movement; the direction of the movement; the direction of the force offered by the resistance encountered by the muscles during the movement; the actions of surrounding muscles; the level of the resistance it encounters; and to the frequency and type of the muscle action that occurs during the training session. For instance, if an athlete performs partial squat for sets of twenty repetitions in a slow manner, he or she will improve performance in partial squat in the range of twenty repetitions. There will also be an improvement in the athlete's ability to perform a single repetition in the partial squat, but the improvement is not likely to be as great as it will be in the partial squat for ten reps and even less in relation to the athlete's increased ability in the partial squat for twenty reps. Perhaps more importantly, the athlete's ability in the full squat may improve little, if at all, by mere training on the partial squat. The carryover in the training effect from a more limited range of motion to a fuller range of motion is incomplete (although the carryover from a full range of motion to a partial one is far more complete).

The SAID principle implies that if you want to become strong in a certain exercise, you must practice either that exercise or some other exercise that approximates it in the most important areas. In addition, you must practice the exercise at the same speed that you will when you perform and for the same number of repetitions. Naturally, the SAID principle suggests that you should perform the classical lifts in single repetitions with maximum weights; anything else is sub-optimal! Unfortunately, it appears that training is not that simple because of one final and powerful training concept: variability.

SAID Versus the Benefits of Training Variety

Despite the powerful and all encompassing influence of specificity in training, there is considerable evidence to suggest that variety in the training stimulus can contribute significantly toward an athlete's progress in training. The reasons for this phenomenon are not well understood. It has been speculated that the body's adaptive mechanisms react more dramatically to what they perceive as a "new" stimulus than to a form of stimulation that they have experienced before. While increased intensity is clearly a new stimulus in one respect, it appears that other changes in the training stimulus are significant as well. Psychological reasons have also been given for the usefulness of variety (i.e., variety is needed to keep that athlete interested in the training sessions). Finally, variety in training appears to help athletes avoid injuries that can result from continuous movement in the exact same "groove."

Variety can and does come in many forms in strength training. Athletes vary the speed with which they perform a given exercise. They vary the way in which they perform the exercise. For example, in doing a snatch, the width of the grip might be changed from workout to workout; the athlete might snatch the bar from the floor in one workout, from a "box" in another. (A "box" is a training device designed to raise the bar from the floor so that the athlete is concentrating only on a partial aspect of the pull.) Or the athlete might stand on a small platform that elevates the lifter and leaves the bar in its position on the floor (thus making the athlete lift the bar a greater distance than is normally the case). Set and rep patterns can be varied, as can the intensity of various workouts within the training day, week or month. The potential for variety is virtually as limitless as the imagination of the lifter and the coach.

There can be little doubt that variations in the training stimulus (at least in some training

dimensions) facilitate the training effect, but different trainers define and apply the principle of varying the training stimulus in different ways. At one extreme there are those trainers who will argue that variety is almost unavoidable in the training process and that it need not be planned. For example, if an athlete three days a week (e.g., Monday, Wednesday and Friday), some degree of variation is built into the workout because there are two days of rest between two of the sessions (Friday and Monday) but only one day between two of the sessions (Monday to Wednesday and Wednesday to Friday). Moreover, the athlete will not feel capable of performing at exactly the same level at every workout; therefore, the weights lifted will vary naturally, and there is no need for introducing variety beyond this level. Finally, it is argued that even if the athlete tried to perform identical training sessions, the body would vary in its capabilities from session to session. Consequently, training variety is unavoidable and need not be planned.

Trainers at the opposite end of the spectrum believe that no two workouts should be the same. They feel that a given exercise should never be performed in quite the same way in any two consecutive workouts (i.e., at least one of the variables of tempo, range of motion of the bar, grip width, etc., should change every workout). They of course feel that the weight on the bar should vary, as should sets and reps.

There are some very influential trainers at both ends of the spectrum. Sigmund Klein, an outstanding athlete in both bodybuilding and weightlifting in the earlier part of this century and a trainer for more than fifty years, is reported to have followed a similar weekly workout program for nearly fifty years. The Bulgarian coach Abadjiev, acknowledged by many in the sport of weightlifting to be one of the most outstanding coaches of all time, has dramatically reduced the variability of exercises in the workouts of the Bulgarian team over the last twenty years, to the point that the Bulgarian team was reportedly performing only six exercises in their training (snatch, C&J, power snatch and power clean, and front and back squats) by the late 1980s). In addition, the Bulgarians of that period limited their reps almost exclusively to singles, with some occasional doubles. Weights varied in accordance with what the athletes were capable of on a given day and training session (of which there were typically several per day), with between two and three exercises. But in every exercise and training session the athlete attempted to lift as much as possible. (There were differences in the overall loads lifted by the athletes in different parts of the year and a light or, "unloading," week was scheduled every fourth week of training.)

Trainers on the other side of the debate about variability also have a long history. Bob Hoffman, one of the founding fathers of American weightlifting and the greatest promoter it has had thus far, advocated variety in training more than fifty years ago. He recommended heavy and light days, varying reps within the workout and across the week, varying the number of days of training per week and changing the exercises performed (sometimes using bars, other times using dumbbells, etc.). In more recent years, Vorobyev and Mevedyev of the former Soviet Union, both former World Champions in weightlifting and successful coaches of USSR World Championship teams, have advocated a great deal of variability in the training process. Variations in exercises, tempo, the intensity of workouts within the week, within weeks of the month and within months of the year are all recommended. Closer to home, Curt White, one of America's most outstanding lifters in the 1980s, told me that when he was at his peak in lifting, he never did two workouts in the same way (grip width and the height of the bar were just two of the variables he preferred to manipulate).

Who is correct? Apparently both systems have merit. How could this be? For one thing, as was indicated above, no matter how much you try to avoid it, there is variability in all training unless you refuse to add weight to the bar when you can and train every day on the same exercises at the same pace, etc.. In addition, there will always be some variety in an athlete's training because the athlete will not be able to handle the same weights every day (although this could be avoided by lifting sub-maximal weights every day). However, if you do not vary the training at all, training loses its distinction from work. A manual worker who works on an assembly line assembling the same amount of items every day is the quintessential example of the person who has the same workout every day (except that even these workers have days off and vacations during the year). What occurs is an adaptation to the work early in the worker's career and then stagnation due to a lack of change in the stimulus for the rest of his or her career. It is believed that this stagnation in the work process plays a role in the development of overuse injuries, like lower-back pain and carpal tunnel syndrome. This is probably because the work load is not varied with the body's needs and because not making an effort to develop the muscles beyond the level required by the work precludes overcompensation (which might lead to a point where the work actually presents less of a stress to the body). Only by exercising like a worker can a trainee fail to progress, and such training would certainly be the exception to the rule.

The advocates of extreme variability no doubt have the advantage of fostering psychological interest among their lifters through the constant variety in the training. In addition, stimulating the body in a constantly changing way may well elicit a degree of adaptation that is greater overall than the one that would be achieved by a lesser variety in the training. However, there are disadvantages to a great deal of variety as well. Consider what the concept of specificity of training tells us. It says that the closer the training is to the requirements of competition, the more effective it will be in terms of the carryover effect. Therefore, while the organism of the athlete who trains with great variety may be more broadly adapted to a greater number of stimuli than the trainee who utilizes less variety, it may also be true that much of that adaptation is wasted (i.e., it cannot be applied to the athlete's sport).

Another concern is that a great variety in training can expose the lifter to injury because he or she has not adapted to the rigors presented by a variation in exercise style or a particular workload. Another issue is one of the inability to measure and understand the effects of all of the variations that are being applied. For example, when a lifter makes a sudden improvement, is it due to a change in the workload or to the change in the pattern of exercises or to a combination of both elements? It will be difficult, if not impossible, to assess this when the variety of the workouts is extreme because there will be no discernible patterns in training. Therefore, one of the great benefits of training (the learning that it can provide about a particular lifter's response to various training stimuli) is lost or at least compromised.

Much of the confusion and controversy with respect to the issue of variability may stem from a failure to appreciate the concept of variability on psychological vs. a physical level. The human mind is capable of seeing patterns within very complex and only subtly interacting events. An athlete or trainer can see a given exercise within the context of a workout, a training week, a month, a year or even a series of years. The ability to conceptualize is man's greatest distinguishing characteristic as a species, but our bodies and their sense organs are not unlike those of many other animals. What the mind may not see as a great deal of variety, the body may well experience as a radical change.

The body does not know that Monday is a medium day, Wednesday a light day and Friday a heavy day. It only travels along its path of making an adaptation to previous stimuli or to maintaining its equilibrium until it bumps into a change in the degree of stimulus that it encounters. If that change involves a lower level of stimulus than the body has previously encountered, it may merely ignore that stimulus, because it is still responding the a prior one of greater strength. If the body simply maintaining its current level of adaptation, a lower level stimulus may simply be added to the muscle's "memory banks" in a way that says to the muscle, "there continues to appear to be no reason to maintain your current level of adaptation, because no stimuli of sufficient strength to justify it have been encountered recently." Therefore, any change in the level of stimulus is registered as such by a body that cannot see that what it is encountering is all part of a pattern. Therefore, a variety that may not seem as rich as what the mind can conceive may be more than sufficient to keep the body moving along the way to progress toward maximal strength.

In summary, it is obvious that some degree of variability in the training stimulus is required if the body is to engage in the process of adaptation. However, some degree of variation is almost unavoidable in the training process. Moreover, if the training is planned carefully on the micro level, there will always be variability because the coach and athlete will always be attempting to maintain a balance in developing in athlete's technique, strength and power. That balance can only be maintained by regularly adjusting the workout plan to fit the needs of the athlete at that point in time, since relative needs nearly always shift over time. In addition, the good coach will always be endeavoring to stimulate the body to progress, while keeping the risk of trauma to the athlete's body at a minimum. This generally entails substituting exercises like pulls and squats for the competitive lifts, at least occasionally. Finally, if the athlete is varying the reps and sets done in his or her workouts as well as the weight on the bar, considerable variability is taking place in this area as well. Therefore, variety in training will arise out of good workout planning as an effect rather than a cause. As long as the variety used in the training process can be understood to form a specific pattern of some kind, the trainer will be able to compare that pattern to the ones that have already been attempted with that athlete and thereby continue to better understand what kinds of training will benefit that athlete.

It should be remembered that the need for variability will itself vary with the athlete. Some athletes need more variety for mental as well as physical reasons. A trade-off exists between specificity and variability. The immediate applicability of any training effect sustained through practice that preserves a high degree of specificity is a powerful advantage. The extra stimulus of the training effect which results from variability may outweigh more specific training in some cases. Generally, if satisfactory improvements can be made with training that is highly specific, this is preferable. But an athlete who thrives on change may find too much regularity in a routine a prescription for stagnation. Such an athlete may find the more circuitous route of variety a more direct route to success.

Choosing Exercises for Weightlifting Training

The principle of specificity of training is never more important than in the choice of the exercises that an athlete employs in his or her training. In order for an exercise to be of assistance in the development of the special qualities that an athlete requires in order to perform a given event, that exercise must resemble the dynamic properties of the event to as great an extent as possible. All things being equal, training on the snatch and C&J will generate greater improvements in these lifts than training on any other exercises. Unfortunately, all things are not always equal. There is a wide variety of reasons why exclusive training on the classical lifts may not be optimal for a particular lifter, and this is where the rich array of "assistance" exercises which have been developed for weightlifting training can be very beneficial.

There are several areas in which specificity is of particular importance in terms of exercise selection. These areas include: the relative amount of resistance that is encountered in executing the event; the speed with which the exercise is conducted; the tempo (cyclic nature);, the angles of the joints as they encounter resistance; the direction of the resistance; the muscles being used; the sequence in which they are used; and the positions in which the maximum force is applied. All of these characteristics must be considered in the selection and application of exercises for improving performance.

One overreaching rule in exercise choice is to avoid exercises which involve a technique that is in conflict with the technique of the classical lifts (e.g., a lifter would not want to employ an exercise that required a different order of muscle group contractions than those used in the classical lifts). Chapter 5 discusses the common exercise choices that the athlete and coach have at their disposal.

There are those in the weight training community who are strong believers in the notion that exercises which involve a smaller range of motion than a full lift (often called "partials") are more effective than those which involve a fuller range of motion. For instance, there are those who argue that training on partial squats will make an athlete stronger more quickly than training on full squats. While there can be no doubt that partial movements make a muscle stronger, there is also considerable evidence to suggest that partial movements tend to strengthen a muscle to a far greater extent in the partial range of motion than in the full. In contrast, training in the full range of motion makes the muscles stronger throughout the full range of motion (i.e., in the partial range as well). Therefore, full movements are generally preferred for building strength. If strength is especially required in a limited range of motion that is replicated by a partial movement, then training on that partial movement will have a positive effect on performance of the full movement. The particular mechanics of a given movement must be carefully analyzed before such a conclusion can be drawn. However, long practice has shown that partial movements can never substitute fully for full movements. They are only useful as an adjunct to full movements.

The Major Methods Of Exercise

One very important aspect of training specificity is the action of the muscles during an exercise. Are the muscles shortening, lengthening or remaining the same length (or some combination thereof) during the exercise? Is the muscle action rapid or slow? If an exercise involves more than one kind of muscle action, is the transition from one kind of action to another rapid or gradual? In the section that follows, we will discuss the common methods of resistance exercise performance and some of the benefits and limitations of each.

Concentric Contractions Or Actions

Concentric contractions or actions, more than any other type of muscle action, are the basis for weightlifting performance. They are the primary focus of this chapter. It is the concentric action of the hip, leg and back muscles that lifts the bar during the pull. Concentric contractions involve shortening the muscles to move some kind of resistance. It is clear, both empirically and experimentally, that an athlete can improve strength dramatically and speed substantially by training concentrically. It is also clear that flexibility is generally helped and certainly not hindered by training concentrically through a full range of motion. While concentric muscle actions are of the greatest import for weightlifters, several other kinds of resistance exercise are important as well.

Eccentric Contractions Or Actions

Eccentric contractions or actions occur when a muscle generates tension by resisting a force and lengthens during this process. When a bar is lowered after being lifted overhead, the muscles of arms, shoulders, legs, hips and back are acting eccentrically. A contraction during the lengthening of the muscle may sound like a contradiction in terms, and that is why many scientists prefer to use the term "action" to describe muscular activity (muscles that are lengthening cannot literally be contracting). During an eccentric action a muscle is not relaxing as it is lengthening. In fact, the tension in a muscle that is lowering a weight can be greater than the tension that occurs while a weight is being raised. The muscles are working and working hard during an eccentric action. One

phenomenon that suggests the intensity of the muscular effort taking place during an eccentric action is that such actions generate more muscle soreness than any other kind of muscle actions, although the reasons for this are not entirely clear.

Eccentric contractions have been found by some researchers to be as effective as concentric contractions for developing a muscle's strength and size. More and more research is suggesting that the combination of concentric and eccentric training is more effective in eliciting strengthened size improvements than either type of training alone. For many years trainers have suggested that lowering a weight slowly will give the trainee as much benefit as raising it, and the research seems to support this notion. Fortunately, it is possible to perform both styles of training while performing most exercises since most exercises with weights involve both forms of contraction (at least when repetitions are done). The classical lifts of weightlifting and related exercises cannot be fully performed eccentrically, although the lifts themselves do involve some very powerful eccentric muscle actions (e.g., catching the weight in the squat or partial squat position of a snatch or clean). Therefore, some eccentric exercise is critical for the conditioning of the weightlifter. But lifters who practice the classic lifts and many of the associated exercises that will be explained later in this book will probably find that the eccentric contractions that normally take place during the performance of these exercises are adequate for their overall eccentric training needs.

There are trainers who recommend doing some sets of exercise in a totally eccentric fashion. Since an athlete can normally lower considerably more weight than he or she can lift, advocates of the system recommend using some number of pounds or some percentage over the athlete's best lift (e.g., 120%) and performing several reps, lowering the bar as slowly as possible in good exercise form. Naturally, the lifter should be sure to have good spotters to help him or her get the bar back up between reps and to catch the bar if any unforeseen event should occur. (There is more danger in exclusively eccentric training than in concentric-eccentric training because the lifter is handling more weight than he or she could possibly lift. There is also some risk to the spotters in that they are helping the lifter to lift some heavy poundages and often find themselves in awkward mechanical positions (e.g., leaning over a bench or standing behind a lifter in a squat position, often not directly over the bar).

Some lifters love eccentric contractions (or negatives, as they are sometimes called) because they build their confidence with heavier weights. However, there is no evidence that concentric contractions are superior in terms of building strength, and there are no weightlifting or powerlifting champions who have trained primarily by eccentric muscle actions. Therefore, training exclusively, or even primarily, by eccentric contractions appears to be a poor idea.

The reduced safety associated with maximum eccentric training diminishes its appeal, and the lifter who uses such training extensively may find that his or her popularity declines as an army of assistants must be recruited for each training (though this problem, in itself, is surely not a reason to abstain from such training). Another negative aspect of eccentric contraction is that it is difficult to measure (e.g., Did you really lower the bar as slowly as you did last time?). Still another problem is injury from the trauma of eccentric contractions. Finally, the angles of force and the tempo of its application are so important in lifts like the snatch and C&J that it seems doubtful that eccentric contraction would have a great deal of carryover into their performance (even if a lifter could emulate eccentrically the motions involved in the classic lifts).

Given all of these issues, the practice of lowering the bar slowly after performing concentric contractions (at least of some reps or sets) makes eminent sense. The lifter need not handle as much weight in the eccentric contraction as in pure eccentric training because the muscle will already be fatigued from the concentric portion of the contraction. There will be economy in terms of training time when an athlete mixes eccentric with concentric training. Outside of such training, there seems to be little need for most weightlifters to perform specific training with eccentric contractions.

Isometric Contractions

Isometric exercise consists of exerting force against an immovable object. More force can be developed during an isometric action than through any other kind of muscle action because the object against which the force is being exerted does not move (i.e., zero velocity is developed). Scientists have discovered an inverse relationship between the force that a muscle can generate and the velocity of the object against which the force is applied ; the lower the velocity of the object, the greater the force that can be generated against it.

Isometrics became very popular in the 1950s and 1960s, when it was widely accepted that one six-second contraction a day could yield significant strength gains under certain circumstances. This was appealing to the general public in that it suggested that in only a few minutes day, with limited equipment, a person could remain "fit." (In those days the notion of aerobic fitness had not been introduced, and the concept of specificity of fitness was not widely understood.).

Subsequent research has provided much illumination with regard to the subject of isometrics. It is now understood that one contraction a day may have little or no training effect (particularly if it is not a maximum contraction). The greater the contraction time during a workout (whether from sustaining contractions longer or doing repeated contractions) the greater the correlation with the degree of strength increase. (However, the muscles will become overtrained if too many contractions are performed.) Total contraction times of 15 seconds to 120 seconds have resulted in good strength improvements, although total contraction time of more than 30 seconds does not seem to have any additional benefit. Training every day has generally been found to be more beneficial than training less frequently. However, most of the research done in this area has been done with one exercise at one joint angle. Perhaps the subjects in such studies would have had quite different results if other exercises and/or joint angles had been included. For instance, if the athletes with longer duration of contraction had done more exercise for the same muscle in other positions, perhaps their results would have fallen off more than athletes using 30 seconds in a specific exercise. (Of course it is possible that athletes training longer would have had better results.)

Another major finding in the area of isometric training is that such training is very specific to the joint angle at which it occurs. There will be some strengthening at angles somewhat greater or smaller than the angle at which the exercise occurs (perhaps 15° or 20°), but not nearly as much at angles further away (although there is some evidence to suggest that more contraction time in training will increase the likelihood of carryover into other joint angles). Most of the research with respect to training isometrically at one joint angle indicates that little or no improvement in speed of muscle contraction occurs as a result of isometric training. It is nevertheless possible that had the training occurred at more than one joint angle, the results in speed might have been better. As is the unfortunate case with so many exercise fads, once isometric exercise lost some of its luster, it was totally abandoned by many trainers. Such trainers ignore certain fundamental facts. First, isometric exercise may be the most effective means of improving strength at a particular angle. Since there is a point in virtually all exercises at which the perceived effort required to move the weight is greater than at other points, concentrated exercise at these "sticking points" or slightly earlier in the movement can improve performance. Second, there is a point in most exercises (particularly in the snatch, clean and jerk) at which the athlete wishes to exert maximum force. If the athlete's strength in those areas is trained in a specific manner, special improvements can be expected to occur. Third, isometrics can be practiced outside the gym with little equipment, which makes them ideal for an athlete who needs to travel a great deal or who has

133

difficulty in getting to the gym and wishes nonetheless to continue his or her strength training.

It should be noted that a number of competitive lifters who have applied isometrics diligently in their training have had excellent success. During the 1960s Lou Riecke and Bill March both established world records in weightlifting (Lou in the snatch and Bill in the press), and Peter Rawluk broke a number American records in the snatch. All three men employed isometric contractions extensively (although not by any means exclusively) in their training. There are those who today argue that other factors accounted for the success of these men; these other factors were often available to their competitors, yet they still made records with their methods. One of the major differentiating characteristics in the training of these men was their use of isometric contractions. Does this mean that these same lifters would have not had greater success using other training methods? Certainly not. (In fact, Lou Riecke relied on standard pulls more than isometric pulls to achieve his world record snatch.) On the other hand, it is not appropriate to dismiss the success that they enjoyed through the use of isometric training.

How were isometrics applied by those who had success with them? In very general terms, they all practiced isometrics several times a week. They all trained at two or more angles in each exercise. To my knowledge, none did repeated sets in any one position in one training session, but all exerted maximum force in each of the positions and on each of the days when they did train. In addition, all of these men did exercise with the weights quite strenuously one day a week (occasionally more often).

It is my belief that isometrics can be practiced to good effect at positions such as the one where the bar is just below the knees in the pull and when it is at the point of beginning the final explosion in the pull and the jerk. In general I believe that isometrics are more effective for training the pull and the muscles that hold the bar overhead than they are for training the muscles involved in performing the squat. This should not be surprising when you consider that isometric contractions of certain large muscle groups are a key factor in maintaining correct body positioning during the pull, and in holding the bar overhead.

Isokinetic Exercise

Isokinetic exercise involves the performance of exercise at a constant speed. The exercise devices upon which it is performed are designed to maintain a constant speed, regardless of how much effort the athlete expends. The end result is supposed to be a training effect over a range of motion greater than with other forms of exercise.

Strength gains have been reported using a wide range of isokinetic exercise repetitions, speeds and resistances. Intermediate speeds (approximately one second to complete a full range-of-motion exercise) seem to have the greatest carryover to other speeds. In general slower speed training improved performance at slower speeds and faster speed training at faster speeds (specificity at work), although faster speeds tended to have more carryover into slower speed training than the reverse (specificity at work again). Overall, isokinetic exercise has not been found to be any better or worse than other forms of training in terms of increasing strength or muscle size.

One of the problems with isokinetic training with respect to competitive lifters is its limited carryover. Because the velocities and patterns of motion achievable when exercising isokinetically are not the same as those which are encountered while performing the classical lifts, it is doubtful whether isokinetic training would ever be of significant value in training for these lifts (at least not with today's equipment). In exercises like squats and deadlifts, the potential for successfully utilizing isokinetics is greater.

In the past, the inability to measure the degree of effort that an athlete was applying in exercising isokinetically made programming difficult and motivation hard to maintain. (Visible results are a key motivator for athletes engaged in resistance training.) Today many isokinetic devices have gauges that measure effort in various ways, so these machines have overcome these problems to a degree.

Variable Resistance Exercise

During the 1970s and 1980s variable resistance training was greatly ballyhooed. Remarkable gains in strength and muscle size were reported early in the use of this kind of exercise, but most of the "evidence" was generated by the promoters of the equipment on which the experiments were conducted.

Variable-resistance training devices use various mechanical means to alter the resistance that a trainee encounters when he or she exercises. These machines supposedly make an exercise equally difficult throughout the range of movement of each exercise. While this is their objective, careful evaluations of variable resistance machinery have revealed that most, if not all, do not accomplish their intended purpose.

Independent research has been unable to confirm that variable-resistance training confers any special benefits on its practitioners, although it seems to be just as effective as any other means of progressive resistance in terms of generating gains in muscle size and strength. The problem with variable-resistance exercise from the standpoint of the serious powerlifter or weightlifter is that the carryover of any strength gained on a machine to the execution of competitive lifts is likely to be very limited. Resistance does indeed vary when an athlete is performing the actual competitive lifts. It is important to an athlete's performance that these changes in perceived effort be encountered regularly, if not exclusively, in the athletes training.

Compensatory Acceleration

Dr. Fred ("Dr. Squat") Hatfield, World Champion powerlifter, world record breaker, highly respected weight training theorist and author of many excellent publications on bodybuilding and powerlifting, has coined the phrase "compensatory acceleration" to describe an approach to exercise in which the lifter moves the weight as quickly as possible throughout the range of motion (slowing it up a little at the end of the movement to avoid a jolt to the joints involved). Fred's contention is that by exerting as much force as possible throughout the lift, the athlete will incur a training effect at a wider range of joint angles than if he or she merely fought hard at the most difficult point of the lift and did just enough to complete the lift after that.

This concept is akin to isokinetics in that there is an effort to stress the muscles equally throughout the range of motion. In isokinetics the effect is achieved by maintaining the tempo of the movement throughout. With compensatory acceleration there is an effort to maintain the level of tension in the muscles by pushing harder and faster as the perceived effort of the exercise declines. Maintenance of this tension is not strictly possible because an athlete cannot exert as much force against an object that is moving quickly as he or she can against an object that is moving slowly. However, the effort to exert more force will surely increase the tension in the muscle to a higher level than would have been achieved otherwise. The result should be a more profound training effect from the same exercise. Moreover, what is lost in terms of uniform muscle tension relative to isokinetics is probably more than made up for in the more natural pattern and tempo of the movement relative to an isokinetic one.

At least one recent study which compared isokinetic and fixed-mass training in the leg extension showed that the fixed-mass training regimen (which essentially used the concept of compensatory acceleration) was more effective than isokinetic training. In the study each subject trained one leg isokinetically and the other using compensatory acceleration. The leg using the latter method not only had a higher one-rep maximum, but it also developed more strength throughout the range of motion than the isokinetically trained leg.

For purposes of weightlifting, compensatory acceleration was practiced by competitive weightlifters long before the term was used. Many lifters lift the bars as quickly as possible throughout most or all of the range of motion whenever they are pulling or jerking. However, some weightlifters do not apply the concept of compensatory acceleration to advantage when they are training or performing assistance exercises such as the squat. For example, many lifters do not attempt to explode out of the bottom position in the squat and very few move quickly near the finish of the squat. If a lifter were to drive through to nearly the top of the squat with as much speed as possible, he or she would be training the explosive power of the legs in the 1/4 to 1/8 squat position, as well as strength in the deep to perhaps the 1/3 squat positions (where the greatest effort in doing full squats is normally expended).

Again, the major caution that must be applied when using compensatory acceleration is to stop exerting maximum force at maximum speed at the very end of the movement, where such force could cause: a) the joints to hyperextend; or b) the bar to jump off the body and then crash back down and/or the body and bar to come off the floor and return with a violent impact.

Plyometrics

Plyometrics, or "shock training" (as it was referred to in the former Soviet Union), involves an eccentric contraction immediately followed by a concentric one. There are many examples of plyometric activities in sport. Running, for example, is essentially plyometric, as muscle groups are repeatedly eccentrically contracted and then immediately explode into a concentric effort. When a weightlifter performs dip and drive in the jerk, a plyometric movement is taking place. Perhaps the most strenuous example of plyometric training is the depth jump. In this exercise an athlete jumps down from a height, generally ranging from .5 m to 1 m, and then immediately rebounds up into a maximum height vertical jump.

Plyometric training is believed by some to increase or at least to utilize better the reactive capabilities of the muscles (both the use of the stretch reflex, which acts to contract a muscle more forcefully after it has been stretched, and the "elastic" properties of the muscle, which store some of the downward force exerted on the muscles before they contract concentrically).

Plyometrics have gained significant popularity in strength coaching circles in recent years. The practice is not as widespread in the weightlifting community. This may in part be due to the tendency for plyometrics to lead to injuries of the muscle-tendon units that are involved and because so much of ordinary training on the classic lifts involves a plyometric component.

Some lifters have reported improvements from using plyometrics, but many champions have never used them at all. It is probably too early in the existence of this kind of training for us to draw any conclusions regarding the effectiveness of plyometrics for weightlifters. However, in my view, great caution must be employed because of their potential for injuring an athlete.

Very Slow Training

There are some coaches of weight training who advocate the performance of very slow repetitions when a lifter is doing resistance training. The theory behind this method of exercise performance is that slow movement increases the degree and duration of muscle tension during an exercise so performed. Very slow performance (several seconds to perform a single rep) also minimizes or eliminates use of elastic capacities in the muscle and the reliance of velocity generated during a certain part of an exercise's range of motion to assist continued motion during a subsequent stage in the motion. On occasion this style of exercise performance may stimulate strength gains. However, such a training method precludes the development of power and strength at the same time in the way that explosive lifting and exercise styles such as compensatory acceleration do. Therefore, the lifter would be well advised to use the very slow exercise style only on occasion and in combination with more traditional methods of training. However, used in this way, such methods can be effective.

Electrostimulation

Up until now, this chapter has been devoted to training methods which involve the use of voluntary muscular contractions. This focus has been intentional. All sports involve such contractions, and one of the key challenges for the athlete is to learn how to control his or her muscles in the most effective way.

The scientific literature does contain references to the use of external muscle stimulation for the development of muscle strength. Some reports indicate that the use of muscle stimulation has been effective in terms of increasing muscle strength. However, there is little to suggest that such means are more effective that voluntary stimulation. Even if it were established that electrostimulation was a more effective means of developing strength than the use of voluntary contractions, it would be unlikely that such strength would be fully transferable in terms of weightlifting performance. Other research and empirical evidence suggest overwhelmingly that joint angles, velocity, direction, and motor control all play such a vital role in the effective use of strength that it seems highly unlikely that external stimulus could be as effective. Moreover, so many muscles are involved in weightlifting in so many ways that an electrostimulation workout might take as long as a regular one in order to reach all of the affected muscles.

It should be noted that some athletes that I have known who experimented with electrostimulation have developed tendinitis. Their belief was that the tension that was created by the electrostimulus was so great that it overran the body's ability to adapt.

The method of electrostimulation shouldn't be dismissed out of hand, however. Some elite athletes have reported success with it. For example, Derrick Crass, 1990 National Champion in the 90 kg. class, associated a significant increase in his leg with the use of electrostimulation. Nevertheless, when the overwhelming theoretical evidence does not support an approach, when the approach has injured some athletes and not much is known about its application, the athlete and coach would be well advised to proceed with caution if they choose to experiment with electrostimulation.

Comparing the Effectiveness of the Major Methods of Exercise

All of the forms of resistance training discussed above stimulate an adaptation in the muscles and nervous system such that greater and greater resistance can be overcome in the style of training being employed. The evidence is that there will also be a carryover from the strength developed through one form of resistance training into the ability to perform other types of resistance exercise. That carryover is enhanced by at least some practice at the other form of exercise. It is also clear that the principle of specificity of training applies very heavily in the area of resistance training. For example, those trained isometrically show a great increase in strength measured isometrically and a far smaller increase in strength measured concentrically. Similarly, those trained concentrically show a great increase in strength measured concentrically but a lesser change in strength measured isometrically. To develop the greatest possible amount of all around strength, the most sensible way to train would be to mix the methods. The principle of variability in training also points toward the use of different kinds of training, at least occasionally.

There is significant empirical evidence and some experimental evidence to suggest that the carryover from concentric, and especially free-weight, training to other forms of strength expression is greater than from other kinds of training to concentric strength expression. There is also a greater likelihood that a lifter who trains with free weights will develop the muscles that stabilize the prime movers during a given exercise more extensively than with other forms of resistance exercise. So much more research, both scientific and empirical, has been done in the area of concentric training that it is far easier for the trainee to move toward the optimization of the training process using concentric contraction training than it is if the athlete is training in other ways. Finally, in the sport of competitive weightlifting, strength is measured almost exclusively by concentric means (although some eccentric and isometric contractions occur during both lifts). Therefore it is obviously sensible for the trainee to spend the majority of his or her time training the muscles concentrically (with the eccentric training that is associated with concentric training because the lifter lowers the bar in addition to raising it). This does not mean that the other forms of training should necessarily be ignored. It simply means that these methods of training should be used only as an adjunct to more conventional free-weight training. These other methods of training may be especially useful when it is clear that a particular deficiency in the lifter's strength warrants special attention, or when some variety in the training is desired.

Other Important Training Variables

Guidelines Regarding Repetitions

Practical experience and some scientific research tell us that to achieve maximum strength, one to five repetitions per set are the most effective. A lifter can surely get stronger with repetitions in the six to twenty range. Bodybuilders who train at such repetition level can and do become strong. However, such high levels of repetitions do not seem to be the most effective way to gain strength. Moreover, with repetitions in the six to twenty range, considerable growth in observable muscular size tends to accompany any growth in strength. This is desirable for a bodybuilder, but it is not as desirable for most weightlifters and powerlifters. This is because the majority of the latter two types of athletes compete in weight classes, where strength accompanied by unnecessary muscle size is a disadvantage. Higher repetitions seem to develop the other factors that relate to muscle size in addition to muscle fiber diameter and strength. (The factors referred to earlier in the fallacies section of this book are explained in greater detail in Appendix II.) For athletes interested in increasing muscle size and strength to maximal levels, a combination of repetitions in the higher and lower ranges (but rarely more than six and almost never more than ten) seems to work best. It should be noted that, for reasons similar to those discussed above, careful selection of exercises is important if the only the muscles used in the events being trained are to be isolated. It makes no sense for a lifter who is concerned with competing in the snatch and C&J to add five pounds of muscle to his or her chest when such added size and any accompanying strength are of no functional use in performing those lifts.

Lower repetitions are not only the most effective means of developing maximum strength with minimum gains in muscle size; they also tend to be safer. Muscle fatigue, ligament stress and neurological fatigue (which lead to errors in technique) all seem to be minimized with lower repetitions. In addition, when performing exercises that involve considerable skill and explosiveness as well as strength, muscle fatigue tends to set in more rapidly and is accompanied by a deterioration in motor skills. Therefore, when training on the competitive lifts, there is a tendency to keep the repetitions low (one to three) and to virtually never exceed five reps.

In general, the fallacy of assuming that observable muscle size is related to strength has led most trainees to overvalue muscle size. The public tends to be far more impressed with an athlete whose muscles look large than with the athlete whose muscles are simply strong. Just as people tend to look at the trappings of "success" as being synonymous with success itself, they look at muscles as being synonymous with strength. Some people are devastated when they discover that fancy cars and clothes do not make them feel any happier than more functional or modest expressions of financial success. Similarly, the person who is really seeking strength can be disappointed to find that dramatic strength gains have not been made despite a large increase in muscle size. In effect, he or she is carrying around a lot of extra muscle, without a concomitant increase in muscular ability. To the most serious strength devotee, looking strong can be pleasurable, but being strong is sublime. Your rep patterns will to a great extent determine which road you take in this area; because of individual differences some athletes may experience substantial muscular growth doing only singles, and others may experience greater gains in strength than in size even when performing relatively high reps.

Performance of Reps

The snatch and clean, at least when they are performed in competition style, begin from a dead-stop position. While there are a number of ways to have the body move in preparation for lifting the bar from a dead-stop position (as discussed in the section on technique), there is really no way for the resistance of the bar to cause a pre-stretch or rebound effect in terms of muscle contraction.

In contrast, exercises like squats, which require an eccentric contraction before the lift actually commences, permit the athlete to enjoy certain "rebound" effects that can assist in the lifting of the bar. When the athlete is performing reps in exercises that begin from a dead stop, a rebound effect can be generated when the bar is being returned to the platform just prior to the commencement of the second or later reps. For example, the bar normally rests on the platform between reps in the clean or snatch, but when using the rebound method the athlete merely touches the floor or rebounds slightly from it and goes into the next rep. Advocates of this method feel that it develops a more explosive and natural rhythm for the exercise. They argue that the elastic energy of the muscles is being utilized along with voluntary effort when using this method. Skeptics argue that since any muscular rebound is precluded in competition, learning to use it and improving its function will have no carryover effect to the classical lifts.

There is some truth to each position, so the best advice is to use the rebound technique intermittently, interspersing it between some reps, some sets or different workouts.

It is important to distinguish between muscular, connective tissue and mechanical rebounds and the positions in which the rebounds take place. Virtually all of the tissues in the human body have a certain degree of elasticity (the ability of matter to be deformed and then to automatically resume its original shape). Skin, muscles and connective tissue are particularly capable in this area. Muscle tissue has a second form of elastic quality which arises from the ability of muscle to contract more forcefully after having been stretched. This characteristic arises out of the neurological and contractile properties of muscles acting in concert. Finally, to objects which the body may apply force (such as a bar) can have significant elastic properties as well (as was discussed in Chapter 1). The thinking athlete uses all of the elastic properties in concert in order to maximize his or her performance.

In achieving a muscular rebound, the lifter activates the muscles with a conscious effort to explode after the eccentric portion of the lift has ended. If the athlete makes no such effort and passively relaxes the muscles before making an upward effort, it is likely that more of the rebound effect is derived from connective tissue. This happens both because the volitional contraction of the muscle is reduced or eliminated and because such a lifter is likely to reach a more extreme position during the eccentric movement than he or she otherwise would, thereby placing more stress on the tendons and ligaments of the joint.

As a general rule, weightlifters should attempt to move the bar as quickly as possible without giving up good technique (especially avoiding premature contraction of any muscle group). Exerting maximal effort throughout the full range of upward lifting motion in the classical lifts (and all but the very end of the movement in such exercises as the squat) will yield the greatest gains in strength and power.

Before leaving the subject of repetition performance, we will touch upon a few of the commonly used methods for increasing the intensity of a given set or rep of exercise. Bodybuilders in particular, use a variety of training methods that has the objective of delivering additional stress to a muscle after it has reached the point of being unable to execute a full rep with a given weight. The theory behind these methods is that the extra stress of continuing to exercise after the muscle has failed will stimulate the muscle to new levels of adaptation. One of the most popular of these techniques is known as "forced reps." As was mentioned earlier in this chapter, forced reps involve the execution of an exercise until a lifter fails (or knows he or she has reached the last rep he or she can possibly perform) and then performs one or more additional reps, with a training partner providing just enough assistance to let the athlete finish the extra reps.

There are serious questions about the forced reps technique of training. The first question is whether stimulating a muscle after it has already failed will indeed cause that muscle to improve faster than it otherwise would. Surely squeezing out extra reps will make the muscle feel more "pumped," but there is a real question as to whether that pumped feeling is associated with the stimulation of extra growth. No scientific studies in this area have proven the efficacy of forced reps. Of course, trainers are often far ahead of research scientists in terms of pointing the way toward better means of training. Many of the top bodybuilders in the world today believe in the intermittent use of forced reps as a means of generating an unusual training stimulus.

Although forced reps may have proven to be effective for at least some trainers who are seeking maximum muscular size, the value of forced reps in strength development is far more questionable. To my knowledge no evidence that forced reps speed the development of strength exists, and a pump is surely not a prerequisite for strength gains. Moreover, there are several negative aspects of forced reps for strength trainers. One negative aspect of forced reps is that they can endanger the health of the athlete by pushing the muscle past the point where a properly executed rep is possible. Such a level of fatigue can easily lead the body to a state in which an injury may occur. In addition, the assistance of the helper can come at an angle that keeps the weight from moving in its normal direction, which will necessarily preclude any significant strength building effect.

Finally, from what I have observed, most training partners find it difficult to assess the amount of assistance a lifter needs in order to complete the lift. Helpers tend to get excited when assisting with the forced reps, compounding their tendency to offer more help than is truly needed. Too much help obviates any benefit that can be derived from the forced rep. Too little help will allow the weight to travel downward. If this happens quickly, the lifter and/or helper can be injured. Even if it happens slowly, when the helper sees the problem and applies some assistance, the weight is nearly always out of its normal groove, thereby virtually negating any value from the forced rep. The mere presence of the helper causes many athletes to put out less because they know that the helper will make up the deficit. When the lifter knows that no assistance is available, there is a tendency for that lifter to dig down deeper into his or her reserves in order to avoid a miss. "Assisted reps" are a variation on the forced rep concept that has become popular with many.

Cheating is another variation on the forced reps theme in the sense that the athlete is going on to do more reps than are normally possible. Instead of using a training partner to perform additional reps, the lifter relies on some form of cheating motion to compete a rep that would otherwise be impossible to perform. The cheating principle avoids the drawbacks that a helper can present (as pointed out above in the discussion of forced reps), but there are still problems with the method.

One problem is that the cheating method can become a habit to the point where it becomes the lifter's predominant method of performing the exercise. Another drawback is that the use of a cheating motion may actually prevent the training of strength in a needed range of motion because the cheating muscles can take over the primary effort of that portion of the lift. Occasionally the lifter will cheat regardless of how hard he or she tries not to. This is difficult to avoid completely when a lifter is pushing to the maximum in certain exercises. However, planning to cheat and having an occasional rep on which it occurs are completely different, and the former is to be avoided for the reasons mentioned.

"Burns" are still another method of making the body work a little longer and harder than it does normally. It consists of doing partial reps, either by lifting the bar as far as possible from the starting position or not letting it return all the way from the finished position and doing some partial reps.

The "multipoundage" system consists of doing as many reps as possible with a given weight and then stripping some weight off the bar so that a few more reps can be done (sometimes this bar stripping is repeated one or more times).

In short, forced reps, cheating, burns, the multipoundage system and similar methods are all based on the premise that extra stress after the point of normal failure has value. The value of these methods for building muscle size may be very real. Their value for lower rep training and for strength building in general is subject to considerable doubt. When the risks are balanced against the possible gain, it cannot be recommended that a lifter employ any of these methods on a widespread basis for building maximum strength. For that purpose, maximum and sub-maximum unassisted lifts in strict form are king.

Optimal Rest Between Reps

The earlier discussion of sets and reps outlined the means of distinguishing between them. As with so many things in weightlifting, there is disagreement among trainers about the optimal rest intervals. With regard to reps, some trainers advocate the immediate succession of reps, doing them in a rhythmic fashion so that there is virtually no line between the completion of one rep and the start of another. Other trainers advocate that the repetitions be performed with as little rest as possible between them (i.e., just enough to maintain concentration) but in a relatively deliberate fashion. These trainers feel that such an approach preserves the essential pattern of exercise (i.e., why use a virtual rebound if that is not a part of what one will experience in the competitive lift itself?) and properly emphasizes each separate rep (each rep performs the dual functions of training the muscle and of fatiguing it so that maximal effort will be experienced during the set).

Still another group of trainers feels that reps should each be done even more deliberately, with on each rep being treated as a single unto itself; they believe that at least several seconds of rest should be used between reps so that the athlete never feels a "pump" in the muscles or fatigue sufficient to hinder the technique applied to the exercise. In this kind of training, as with the second method described, the natural movement pattern is preserved. The major difference is that by using a little more rest between reps, the athlete may be able to experience more maximal or near maximal efforts in one set; the athlete may experience a rep that is near maximum, but through an extra few seconds of rest still another rep can be managed; had the other rep been attempted almost immediately, the athlete would have failed. Advocates of this method feel that more maximal efforts can be crammed into fewer sets, making for more intense workouts.

The choice between these approaches should be based on the athlete's reason for performing the exercise. For a less explosive athlete, the first method might build some speed and fluidity into the athlete's motion. The chief drawback of this method is that it can get the athlete mentally and physically accustomed to an exercise technique that cannot be used in competition (e.g., a rebound of the bar off the floor). Rebounding that is too wild can also expose the lifter to a higher risk of injury and can lead the lifter to pick up technical flaws.

The second method is the most conventional and should probably be the one used most often as it does preserve the proper exercise technique and the fatiguing purpose of performing repetitions.

For the athlete who seems to lack the ability to really "grind out" a rep (to put an all out effort into an exercise and to fight for the completion of each rep, no matter how great an effort is required), the third means of executing reps might teach such tenacity, rep by rep. This latter method would also be useful on a day in which the athlete was interested in incurring an absolutely maximal training stimulus.

The main drawback of doing reps of any kind is that as the muscles tire after each rep, the athlete can be exposed to a slightly higher risk of injury than with singles; fatigued muscles are more likely to break form, and a tired lifter is more likely to break concentration. Therefore, this method is to be avoided in the snatch and clean and jerk. (Due the deterioration of skills that can occur, most lifters avoid reps higher than two in the C&J and higher than two or three in the snatch, clean or jerk; the Bulgarians do singles almost exclusively in all of their major exercises.) Higher repetitions should also be avoided when doing exercises like the deadlift, not only because the loss of form can result in the body's falling into a poor mechanical position, but also because the strain of the bar can be transferred from tired muscles to ligaments, further increasing the chance of injury.

Guidelines Regarding Sets

Optimal Rest Between Sets

Researchers and trainers alike generally agree that intervals of two to five minutes or more are needed for a complete recovery between sets of weight training exercises of high intensity. The optimal rest between particular exercises with particular loads is a function of several variables: the intensity of the training effort,, the nature of the exercise being done, the number of repetitions being performed and the purpose of the exercise.

When an exercise is performed at a high level of intensity, it places a greater strain on the energy transport system of the muscles and on other systems of the body than does exercise of lower intensity. Therefore, the rest periods required between sets of such exercise will be greater than the period that is required when exercise of lesser intensity is performed. The ultimate example of this difference is that in cyclic exercises with relatively low intensity (such as rowing) the muscles are able to repeat muscular efforts at the same level for long periods without rest. When an all out effort in a snatch or a C&J is made, two minutes or more will be needed to recuperate between lifts.

The nature of the exercise being done affects recovery time in that exercises done at greater velocity (i.e., exercises in which the duration of the effort is brief) generate less fatigue than exercises done with a slower velocity and longer duration of effort. For example, the athlete will tend to recover more quickly from a set of heavy snatches than a set of heavy squats.

Sets done with low reps, even if the intensity is high, tend to require less rest between them than sets with higher reps. The reason seems to be that one rep, no matter how difficult, does not tax the energy transport system of the muscles very much. In contrast, doing reps fatigues that system further when it has not had time to recuperate from the earlier rep(s). The body then gets into a deeper energy deficit and takes longer to recover from it. Consequently, a single might take only two minutes to recover from, while a set of five might require five minutes.

Finally, the purpose of the training will determine the amount of rest that is taken between exercises. Weightlifters, whose usual objective is to build the maximum possible strength and the power to move heavy loads as quickly as possible, will generally want to rest between sets until breathing and the heart rate return to a relatively normal level (these measures will always be elevated somewhat during a workout) and any sensation of fatigue in the muscles disappears. Bodybuilders seek a sense of muscle fatigue ("the pump") and they will attempt to do their sets with enough rest to recover a good share of muscle capacity but not so much as to lose the pumped feeling altogether. For athletes who are required to perform while their bodies are in a fatigued state (e.g., wrestlers), performing their sets at small intervals so that the weight training session resembles the competitive session will probably be of benefit. Similarly, the competitive weightlifter will, at least occasionally, want to take shorter than optimal rest between exercises in order to prepare for the possibility that in competition he or she may be called upon to perform with little rest between lifts.

It should be noted that while the guidelines provided above are appropriate for most "mainstream" training methods (in terms of the intensity of the training) there are some approaches to training that challenge these rules. For instance, powerlifting coach, Louie Simmons, relies on a training method for the competitive powerlifts (bench press, squat and deadlift) that employs low intensity (60%), a high number of sets per workout session with the highest intensity load of the day (8), low reps per set (2) and little rest between sets (45 seconds). Louie indicates that most of his top lifters (and he has many) follow such a program with great success and are able to handle maximums in a competition without any heavy attempts in training whatsoever (although his athletes do go heavier and train more conventionally in their assistance exercises—the use of assistance exercises is discussed further in Chapter 5). Obviously, Louie's approach relies on brief rest periods to deliver the training effect (as compared with high intensity per set or rep).

In summary, the amount of rest taken between sets can follow some general rules, but the specifics of the type and purpose of the training being performed are as important as the general rules for determining the method to be applied for a specific athlete and situation.

Are Multiple Sets Better Than One For Weightlifting Training?

Performing multiple sets with the heaviest weight that is lifted in a particular exercise during a given training session is a very common training practice. In contrast, many athletes warm up to a maximum weight for the day and either end their training on that exercise for the day, or reduce the weight to perform a final "warm down" set or sets. Surprisingly, in today's weight training circles, there is a rather heated debate going on between the advocates of performing one heavy set of each exercise in a particular workout and those who believe in performing multiple sets with ones top weight of the day (and performing lots of sets per exercise overall). Naturally, there are many trainers who take a position somewhere in between these extreme positions. Examining this issue in some detail can help to clear up much of the confusion that exists regarding this issue, because much of the debate takes place because the theorists in each school are arguing from different contexts. They would have far less to disagree about if they agreed on some ground rules for their discussions.

At one end of the one set versus multiple set spectrum there are a number of influential advocates of what is often termed the "one set to failure" school of training (e.g., Mike Mentzer and Arthur Jones). Under this system, the trainee performs one or two warm-up sets and then attacks the heaviest set of the day. With that weight, the athlete continues to perform repetitions until he or she actually fails to perform a repetition; many advocates of this system recommend doing some "forced" reps (reps that are performed with minimal assistance from a partner once the point of failure has been reached with normal reps) and/or some eccentric contractions after failure occurs with regular reps.

The one set to failure theorists argue that the training stimulus derived from one all out set will be sufficient to foster continuing improvement in a muscle's strength and/or size and that any additional sets performed, while providing no further stimulus for the body to improve (i.e., it has already been stimulated to the maximum by the first set) will actually have a detrimental effect on the body caused by overwork.

At the other end of the spectrum are those who recommend performing several warm-up sets and then several sets with the heaviest weight to be lifted for the day (some advocate the use of weights that are challenging for the number of reps performed as the athlete warms up—at least after the first set or two, in a "pyramiding" approach—described later in this chapter). These theorists believe that an athlete can only stimulate a maximal training effect with multiple sets.

To the surprise of some, advocates of each approach (and many that are in between the extremes) have had great success in some cases and a lesser degree of success in others. What can explain this apparent contradiction?

To begin with, there are no contradictions. Whenever one encounters what appears to be a contradiction it is appropriate to check the premises that are leading to the apparent contradiction. In those premises, and/or the reasoning from them, one will find a flaw that has lead to the apparent contradiction.

In this case, many of the advocates of each side of the one set/multiple set controversy overlook important differences in their premises. For example, when each side talks about the optimizing the training effect they often fail to recognize that any training effect is multidimensional. You can't simply train for increased muscle size without influencing other capabilities of the organism, such as its contractile capabilities, its ability to recruit muscle fibers and the strength of its connective tissue. To say that one system has "the" optimal training effect fails to address the questions "Effect on what?" and "With what affect or cost to other capabilities?"

For instance, a one set to failure bout of exercise may create a training stimulus, but several sets performed in such a way may create an ever greater training stimulus. However, if the performance of several sets damaged so much muscle tissue that the body will not be able to recover from the effort for an extended period of time, the benefit of the extra training stimulus may be counterbalanced by the lack of an ability to recover from the training session. However, if an athlete needs to have the capability of performing several maximal sets in competition, the performance of one set during training may not generate a sufficient training stimulus for the athlete to be optimally prepared for the demands of a competition.

So how does one address the one set/ multiple set dilemma? One must look at the full expanse of what one is trying to accomplish in training—in our case training for weightlifting competition.

First, there is now scientific evidence that more muscle fibers are activated on a maximum set of five reps than on a maximum single. From this it follows that a maximum set of high reps is more likely to stimulate a maximal training effect than a maximum single. Since weightlifters need to perform relatively low reps in training (and especially in competition) they will typically need to employ more sets to achieve their ends than someone who is performing five, ten or twenty reps in a set.

Second, it is not clear that one set to failure does provide the optimal training stimulus for a give athlete. Repeating sets undoubtedly increases the training stimulus and athletes vary in their ability to recover from a training session. Those differences in recovery rates suggest that some athletes may benefit from a greater training stimulus (or a greater frequency of administering the same stimulus) than other athletes. Obviously, there is a point where more training does not increase the training stimulus (the body is simply as stimulated as it can be by a given bout of exercise).

Third, the mental and emotional effort of performing a truly maximal set may be so much for some athletes that training to failure in every workout is simply wears them down over time. Such athletes may benefit from performing multiple sets with a lesser load (which will provide a training stimulus without subjecting the athlete to too great a mental and emotional strain— another important training concept that I learned primarily from Mark Gilman).

It is clear that performing too many sets, particularly if they are done to absolute failure at every workout represents a waste of time that will eventually lead to overtraining.

For purposes of weightlifting training, multiple sets can help to develop skill in recruiting muscle fibers for all out efforts, and this skill is an important component of strength development. Just as massed study cannot replace properly spaced study periods for purposes of long term retention of learned material, one set cannot duplicate multiple sets in terms of the learning process that the latter entails. This is particularly true of complex movements like snatches and C&J's, where skill at the overall movement as well as in exerting force is an important asset to the lifter.

Another consideration in the training of weightlifters is that multiple sets build the endurance needed for an athlete to withstand the rigors of competition. Weightlifting is an anaerobic activity requiring little cardiovascular fitness, but a competitive weightlifter must have the ability to perform maximum efforts over a period of hours (during much of which the athlete may be resting and handling sub-maximum weights). Performing multiple sets in training can help to develop this ability.

Still another consideration is that having both the one set to failure and multiple sub-maximal set

approaches in ones training arsenal permits the athlete to go with the flow of the body's natural wisdom and cycles. There are some days when the lifter simply does not feel up to an all out effort. Nevertheless a lifter can have a very productive workout by handling lighter weights and doing multiple sets.

Finally, the trainee can train several aspects of a muscle's adaptive capacity by performing several different kinds of sets in the same workout (e.g., performing both high and low reps). This is obviously impossible without multiple sets.

How many sets should be performed for optimal strength gains? At least four variables influence the answer to this question. The first variable is that of intensity. The more intense an effort in a given set, the smaller is the number of sets that can be performed with the same intensity. An absolutely all out effort that results in a personal record may be impossible to duplicate in the same workout (and it is probably unproductive to try to do so).

The second variable is that of the number of reps performed in the set. Single efforts, no matter how intense, can nearly always be duplicated in subsequent sets (except perhaps the effort to attain a personal record that requires an athlete's complete psychological, emotional and physical reserves). Higher reps exhaust the athlete more completely and make repeated sets at the same intensity almost impossible. An all out set of twenty reps is a hard act to follow.

It should be noted that, as a group, the Bulgarians are at the extreme edge of those who believe that multiple maximum sets are beneficial. One of the reasons is that they train on singles, which permits more sets to be performed than if sets with higher reps are employed.

As a sort of rule of thumb, you often see athletes performing as many as five to ten singles with a weight that is difficult but not an all out maximum in training. Athletes who perform doubles generally perform from five to eight sets. When the reps rise to three, athletes rarely perform more than six sets, and three to five sets is closer to the norm. When reps rise into the four-to-six range, athletes perform as few as one and as many as five or six sets, but three sets is probably the median load handled. Naturally, all of the above are a function of the proximity of the load to the athlete's maximum. The closer the load to that maximum, the lower the number of sets is likely to be.

The third variable is the muscle groups involved in the effort. Certain muscle groups appear to recover more quickly from set to set than others. It is generally more difficult to perform repeated sets with maximal effort in the squat than in the military press. In addition, multiple maximal sets in the squat will fatigue the body far more overall than multiple sets of presses.

The last issue is the degree and length of muscle tension developed during the repetitions of a set affect the number of sets in which maximal efforts can be performed. Generally, the greater the tension that is developed in the muscle and the longer it is maintained, the more difficult it is to repeat sets at the same level of performance. It is easier, at least on a physical level, to repeat an all out effort in the snatch than in the squat. This is particularly true if the squats are performed in a slow fashion in both the ascent and the descent.

Only by considering all of these factors in combination can an athlete or coach estimate the training stimulus that will be generated by a given bout of exercise. By balancing these factors a athlete can generate improvements with multiple or single heavy sets.

Some Additional Issues With Regard to Intensity and Volume

The Training Workout Versus the Testing Workout

During training the objective should be to cause the appropriate mechanisms of the body to adapt to the stress being imposed by the training, which means that the stimulation applied must be sufficient to generate a training effect. At the same time the training should not be so stressful as to over run the body's ability to recuperate from and adapt to the training.

A training effect can generally be achieved at a level of training well below one that would over run the body's ability to adapt to stress. That is, there is normally a significant range of training stimulus between the minimum that can influence the body to change and one that can over run the body's ability to adapt. The objective of training should be to strike a balance between stimulating the maximum amount of adaptation and endangering the body's defenses. There should obviously be an attempt to achieve the former while avoiding the latter.

However, while this should be the overall objective of training (and in theory an athlete should be able to progress at the maximum rate by staying at the lower end of the training range), there are times when it is necessary and desirable to put the body and mind to the ultimate test, to push the mind and body toward the upper edge of the training range. It is not always possible to measure an athlete's progress without pushing him or her to the maximum. This is because an athlete can feel that certain weights are becoming easier to lift yet there has been no improvement in the athlete's maximum capacity. Why? When the athlete handles sub-maximum weights, they can be made to feel easier by a little extra concentration, a little more emotional excitement or a little

different technique. These variables tend to be eliminated as everything is taxed to an absolute limit with maximum weights. It is true that the lifter may fail to be able to marshal maximum concentration, emotional excitement and optimal technique at the time of the maximum effort, but then the athlete usually can recognize this kind of deficiency more easily than he or she can specify the level of effort that he or she is exerting with a sub-maximum weight.

The second reason why testing is important is related to the first. Only a maximum effort can reveal deficiencies in the athlete's preparation, whether it is psychological, emotional, or physical. Once revealed, these performance deficiencies can then be addressed in planning the next training sequence.

Finally, the ability to perform at a maximum level is a learned ability. It involves a combination of the abilities to recruit the maximum possible number of muscle fibers, to achieve the appropriate level of emotional arousal, to execute a skill on demand and to overcome natural inhibitions so that the body can be pushed ever closer to its limits. These qualities cannot be learned completely at less than maximum performance levels. As a consequence, there is the need to have testing or control workouts.

Perhaps the most important reason for the testing workout is to provide the athlete with the satisfaction that can only be derived from doing his or her personal record (PR). Improvements in an athlete's PR are the biggest single reason to train. Only the personal satisfaction that comes from making PRs can fuel the athlete's mind with the drive that is needed to achieve ultimate success. Therefore, maximum efforts in training are an important key to progress.

Although maximum days are important to a lifter's progress, absolute maximums often involve the athlete's working on his or her "nerve." That is, many athletes become very emotionally aroused while performing the maximum efforts. Training too often in such a state can deplete the athlete's nervous energy and make it harder for the athlete to recuperate from his or her training sessions. As a result, the number of training sessions in which the athlete's emotional energy is used in order to make the lifts he or she attempts must be carefully managed. Some coaches go so far as to say that an athlete should never use a significant amount of emotional arousal in training.

It is my belief that athletes who are able to lift maximum weights with great frequency in training have learned to lift with little emotional arousal. Such lifters are often able to train at high levels of intensity because they are not taxing their bodies and minds with emotionally draining workouts. This is a desirable ability for an athlete to have as it permits the athlete to work at high levels of intensity more often than an athlete who becomes emotionally charged to lift maximum weights. However, the athlete who becomes very excited while lifting maximum weights must recognize this fact by not going to maximum levels as often.

Limits in Training Versus Competition

There have been many athletes in weightlifting history who have been able to consistently lift more in training than in competition (some as much as 10+ kg. more on each lift). The true training prowess of such lifters has often been exaggerated because of a failure to note advantages that were taken in training relative to competition (e.g., the use of straps or training at a body weight well above the competition limits). At the other end of the spectrum, there have been athletes who have been unable in the gym to approach the lifts they could do in competition. Consider the example of Lou Riecke, the American world record holder in the snatch during the 1960s (147 kg. at 82.5 kg.). He reportedly never snatched more than 125 kg. in training prior to his record breaking performance. Similarly, Tommy Kono reported training alone at times and under such conditions that he was able to do 10% to 15% more in competition.

Having experienced both of the relationships of competition lifts to training lifts mentioned above, I can easily understand both circumstances. It is obvious that progress can be made by lifters with either training situation. The important thing is for the lifter to be aware of the factors that contribute to both kinds of relationships and to understand which ones are at work at which times. Athletes who are not able to do this will experience dramatic fluctuations in the relationships they have between training and competitive lifts, often with disastrous results in terms of predicting their competitive performances.

Perceived Versus Absolute Training Intensity

There is often a substantial difference in perceived versus absolute training intensity. In a given training session, an athlete may feel that he or she is lifting a maximal weight, but that weight may be far less than the lifter's recent best. Absolute intensity and the perceived intensity of effort required to lift a given weight can even change within one training session (after an athlete has performed an exhausting effort he or she might repeat an all out effort, although the same level of performance might not be achieved. In such a case the athlete's level of perceived effort is sustained from set to set, but the actual performance in terms of weight lifted or reps performed may decline. Some trainers believe that perceived effort should guide the training process while others believe that absolute intensity is key.

The Bulgarians are great believers in the perceived effort concept and have built much of their training of champion weightlifters around the concept of perceived maximums. The level of actual intensity at which each athlete will work in each training session is determined by that athlete's level of performance in that workout. Under this approach the athlete works up to a maximum effort during each training session and in each exercise. Once the weight that requires that effort has been identified, the athlete will perform repeated lifts with it. Often singles with the maximum for the session are interspersed with sets that are 5 kg. to 20 kg. lower.

For instance, an athlete might work up to a maximum in the snatch attempting a difficult lift as many as 3 times to establish a maximum for the workout. Then the athlete might reduce the weight by 10 kg. and perform 2 sets of 2 reps with that weight. Then the weight might be increased by 5 kg. and a single might be performed, followed by a single with the established maximum (again allowing as many as 3 attempts to make that maximum weight). Finally, the lifter might lower the weight 20 kg. and perform 2 repetitions, increase by 10 kg. again and perform 2 to 3 sets of 2 reps with that weight and then once again attempt the maximum weight for the day (again permitting as many as 3 attempts in order to make that weight). Alternatively, the lifter might work up to a maximum, then drop down by 5 kg. and perform for 2 singles and then drop down another 5 kg. to perform 3 singles. This pattern of working up to and around a maximum for repeated sets might continue for 2 to 3 weeks, after which the athlete would have an "unloading week" in which he or she would perform lower sets with 10 kg. and 20 kg. less than the maximum instead of 5 kg. and 10 kg. below. This method of training, with or without the in between lower intensity sets, is often referred to as the "method of maximal efforts" because the athlete is always functioning at his or her maximum at the time.

At times the Bulgarians use a method called "the method of utmost efforts." In this method the athlete works up to a maximum and then makes repeat efforts with that weight until it is not possible to make another single. An athlete might repeat his or her efforts with a maximum for six to ten singles without any reduction in weights between sets. The Bulgarians would regard a weight that could be repeated for more than six to ten sets as one that did not require an all out effort.

Frequency of Training

Frequency of training is one of the biggest areas of disagreement among coaches and athletes. It is interesting to note that many of the proponents of a particular frequency, refuse to see the possibility that some other schedule might be as effective (or even effective at all).

At one end of the scale, we have the Bulgarians. It is well known that today most Bulgarian lifters train six or more days a week and at least two times a day, sometimes three or more times in a day. These two or three daily sessions are not necessarily "split routines" (routines in which the same number of exercises that would have been done in one long workout are spread over several shorter workouts). Instead, at certain times in their training cycle the Bulgarian lifters may well snatch and C&J up to a maximum in the morning and then come back in the afternoon and/or evening to do the same thing. This concept of several maximum workouts a day, performed five or six days a week, is practically inconceivable to many Americans, yet it is well documented.

At the other extreme are the adherents of one day a week. Working out once a week workouts on a particular body part or exercise is still popular in the powerlifting community, and some quite famous and successful weightlifters have exercised in this way in the past. For example, Bob Bednarski, former World Champion and world record holder, did some of his exercises only once a week and often only one exercise a day (although Bob generally did related exercises twice a week, such as military presses on Monday and competition style presses on Saturday). Some of the athletes who have trained a particular exercise only once a week have made remarkable progress and reached the very highest levels of achievement in athletic competition. In fact, there have even been a number of reports on strength athletes who have reached very noteworthy strength levels training less frequently than once a week. Obviously, the human body has an ability to get stronger within a wide variety of frequency in terms of stimulation. The more important factor appears to be that a given bout of exercise provide a stimulus of sufficient strength to cause the body to begin and sustain the adaptive process.

Virtually all trainees find that they are unable to improve their performance in a given exercise unless they perform that exercise, or a related one, at least once in a period of one week to ten days and most require two training sessions across such a period of time. For example, for most trainees, improving squatting strength requires back squatting twice a week. Alternatively, he or she could back squat once and front squat once (i.e., perform related exercises). However, a program of jumping once a week and squatting once, or performing leg extensions once a week and squatting once would be unlikely to lead to a significant increase in the squats of many lifters over time (or at least not as great of an increase as would have occurred had the exercise been practiced twice).

At the other end of the spectrum, it would be difficult to demonstrate that it is necessary to perform a given exercise more that three times a week in order to improve at a maximum rate (although related exercises may be done daily).

There are some good arguments for and against training a given group of muscles more than three times a week. There can be little doubt that from the standpoint of pure skill, more frequent and correct practice aids in the development of better motor skills than less frequent training. More frequent workouts may also present an advantage in terms of the neurological basis for strength.

There does not appear to be a strong basis for the necessity of training every day in order to develop the size of the muscle fibers. Overall, the evidence that daily training is required for maximum strength gains is quite scanty. There have been some studies that suggest more days are better, but such studies generally used the same routine every training session, were of relatively short term duration and involved trainees with limited experience. If the intensity of the training stimulus had been increased for those exercising fewer days, would they have gained just as quickly? Would training every day have led to fatigue over the long haul? It is difficult to know, but the very notion that there is a need for light and heavy training days gives credence to the idea that daily training may not be a requirement. There is little evidence that any significant detraining occurs before forty-eight hours. There is no evidence that the training effect generated from a fairly vigorous workout wears off within forty-eight hours, and the full effects may not be felt for several days or even a week or more. Daily workouts may actually assist in the recuperation process from periodic intense workouts; a moderate workout done on Tuesday might help an athlete to recuperate from a heavy workout on Monday so that a heavy workout can be done again on Wednesday, whereas two days of complete rest might have been necessary had the Tuesday workout not been done. The majority of high level athletes train every day (or at least six days a week).

Even though most top athletes train daily, are there arguments against daily training of the same muscles via the same or similar exercises? Yes. You could argue that training every day fatigues the muscles and connective tissues and that such training will lead to injury over time. The annals of rehabilitation and occupational therapy are filled with stories of workers who "exercised" daily and ended their careers crippled by their jobs. Was insufficient time to recuperate the reason? Another argument against training every day is that such training may simply be a waste of time. It may also be a hindrance to the recuperation from heavy workouts. Once a stimulus is presented to the body, any further stimulus may be ignored, may interfere with the body's response to the first stimulus or may add momentum to adaptations that have already been initiated by a previous bout of exercise. No one knows the complete story in this area, even on a short term basis (the long term effects of doing too much exercise are not clearly understood). On a practical level, I have known very few people who trained regularly and suffered from underwork. I have known many more who suffered from overtraining and injury; the split is about 20% undertrained to 80% overtrained, if not 10% and 90%.

Arguments for infrequent training include giving the body time to recuperate fully between workouts, and erring on the side of undertraining surely poses less of a threat to the immune system (which can be compromised by overtraining). Of course, infrequent training can be taken to extremes as well. For example, with too much rest the body begins to detrain. The longer the rest the greater the detraining effect. Moreover, the detraining effect is not an even one. In all likelihood, the ability to train (the work capacity of the muscles) will decline before strength does. Therefore, even if one could retain any strength gains stimulated by previous training for three weeks, failure to train for such a period would compromise the body's ability to perform work. The result would be a great stress on the athlete's body when the athlete next trained. This stress might preclude the athlete from doing the kind of workout that might be necessary to generate a training effect during the next workout (or the body might spend so much of its adaptive energy rebuilding its ability to train after such a workout that it would have none left over to adapt to the stimulus to further develop its strength). Moreover, a muscle that gets fatigued easily, as a detrained muscles always will, is more susceptible to injury.

There is another category of daily training that can be recommended on a much less qualified basis: training every day but on different exercises and/or different muscle groups. It is common practice for bodybuilders to "split" their routines by body part. For example, a bodybuilder may do many exercises that affect his or her leg muscles one day and exercises that affect the upper body on another day. Or the legs and back may be worked one day, the chest and arms another.

Many bodybuilders use a "double split," exercising one muscle group per workout, but doing two muscle groups a day. There is some scientific and considerable empirical evidence which suggests that distributing training sessions in this way is beneficial, in that it permits the trainee to focus more concentration and energy on each workout, thereby achieving better results than are available through one longer session.

Similarly, there would doubtless be a benefit if weightlifters could practice in this fashion,. Unfortunately, the "whole body" nature of weightlifting exercises makes it difficult, if not impossible, to work only some muscles at each workout. However, there can be significant differences in the emphasis of a lifter's training from day to day. For instance, the development of the pull might be emphasized one day and the squat or jerk on another day. In such a case many of the same muscles are being trained each day but to a very different degree and in different ways. That is what I recommend to the athletes I train.

Building Volume Over Time

The need to increase the volume of a lifter's training over time in order to continue to stimulate a training effect is virtually accepted as axiomatic by many lifting coaches. These coaches believe that it is impossible to achieve the very highest results with anything less than staggering volumes of work. Although I subscribed to such a notion early in my career, I have come to believe that such thinking is simply false. In my experience, absolute intensity needs to increase as the athlete reaches higher and higher levels, but volume may even need to decrease (certainly not increase) once the lifter has reached a high level. A growing number of theorists who seem to share that view. Recent publications by noted Soviet and Hungarian theorists, as well as some recent work by American researchers (such as Costill) point in this direction.

There is no doubt that an increase in volume is one powerful tool in the arsenal of the athlete and coach. In many instances, increased volume itself will lead to an increase in results, but other means for increasing results are often more effective overall than a sheer increase in volume. When volume is increased, it must be done carefully and in an undulating fashion (the volume is increased for a time and then decreased back to a level just above what that lifter was handling during a previous period of low loading). A sharp and unremitting increase in load is almost always a recipe for disaster in the advanced lifter (an might be a lifter who has trained with very small loads and for whom the increased load is still well within that athlete's recuperative powers).

Whenever volume is increased substantially, there may be some unwanted costs attached to the increase in results that arises out of that increase in volume. First, the lifter may find it difficult to retain strength gained through increased volume should there ever be a need to reduce the volume again. Second, the increase in volume may itself lead to a virtually permanent state of borderline overtraining, in which the lifter rarely improves after the first (or first few) surges in volume. Third, training at a high volume tends to predispose the body to overuse injuries, injuries which can slow progress and even threaten a career. Fourth, high volumes require considerable training periods and rest periods. Such periods are available to athletes who live under the conditions of professional athletes. Unfortunately, these conditions are difficult for weightlifters to achieve, especially by lifters who are striving to reach high performance levels for the first time (and therefore have not been able to secure any special means of financial support that permit a limited work or school schedule). It cannot be emphasized enough that the effect of extra training time on a person's life is not limited to the time allotted to the training itself. That extra training also generates a greater need for relaxation and recuperation, a need which, if left unsatisfied, will retard progress.

Therefore, while increased volume can be a useful training variable, it should not be overly relied upon to achieve championship results. Fortunately it does not have to be. The history of American weightlifting is made up of stories of athletes who achieved literally world class results while holding regular jobs and/or attending school on a full time basis. Such stories are not limited to American lifters of the 1940s and 1950s (who, some allege, did not have as much competition as the lifters of today). For example, Mark Cameron, Jeff Michels and Cal Shake are all Americans who came within approximately 10 kg. of the world records in the snatch or C&J in their weight classes at the peak of their careers during the 1980s. None of these athletes lived as true professional athletes for any significant period immediately prior to those accomplishments (though they did not generally have what would be considered exhausting work schedules).

What are the limits to training volume? There have been reports of athletes performing as many as 50,000 reps a year in all of their weight training exercises combined (which for weightlifters translates to approximately 20,000 to 25,000 sets, or as many as 2,000 sets a month, 500 a week or more than 80 sets a day with 6 training days a week). Are there lower limits? I know of at least one World Champion who did approximately 1/12 of that workload, or perhaps 2,500 reps a year! Now, probably neither extreme is good for most lifters, and something a lot closer to the lower level than the higher is probably best for most of them. But I would argue that such a determination should be based solely on the lifter's particular needs, and that attention to counting aggregate reps verges on the inconsequential.

The lifter needs to do enough snatches and related lifts to improve that lift. Similarly, the lifter needs to do enough cleans to improve the clean, enough jerks to improve the jerk and enough squats to improve the squat. However, there may be little relation between the requirements for each, because the reasons and methods being used to develop each lift will tend to be different for different periods in time. Measurement of total volume is certainly important as an indicator of the overall stress that is being placed on the organism. Sudden, significant and persistent increases in volume can surely lead to overtraining and injury. Monitoring volume can serve as an early warning mechanism for overzealous athletes and coaches.

But to seek volume for volume's sake or to rely on volume as the key indicator of the training stimulus is almost always a mistake. The subject of volume will be covered in much greater detail in Chapter 6.

The Tolerance for Error Can Be Both Small and Great in Terms of the Training Effect

As we have seen, there are a wide variety of training variables that can be manipulated and combined to stimulate strength improvements in the weightlifter. Since we do not yet fully understand the mechanisms by which the strength of voluntary muscle contractions is increased, we cannot fully explain why so many methods of strength training succeed while others are less successful. The many available techniques of training tempt some trainers to conclude that "any method works as long as you believe in it," or "any method works if you get enough rest." The truth is that there can be a very wide range of techniques that work, but there can also be a very narrow difference between success and failure.

For example, I have seen a lifter who had been stuck at one weight in the squat for several months suddenly improve merely by increasing by 2.5 kg. the weights used during medium workouts. Similarly, I have seen lifters who were failing to progress on a given program . see improvements when they reduce the average weight lifted by 2.5 kg. How can a mere 2.5 kg. (1% to 1.5% of the lifter's maximums in the cases cited) make such a difference? Apparently, these lifters were just at the threshold of overtraining or undertraining, and the slight change tipped the balance in favor of positive adaptation.

The lesson in this has two parts. First, lifters should never become discouraged by a failure to improve. A lifter can fail to progress for a very long period and suddenly experience a turnaround merely by discovering a training factor that needs to be corrected. Wrong training methods can lead to total stagnation, and even regression, for years at a time. Then suddenly, a change can be introduced, and progress can begin anew. A surprising number of coaches and athletes repeat the same workouts with no signs that the workouts are effective, concluding in the end that the workouts are correct and the lifter unworthy. In point of fact, the standard of a good workout is whether it causes the athlete to improve.

The second lesson to be learned is that because the response to training is so individualized, research on many subjects can never hope to identify the ideal workout. To be sure, large scale studies can point the athlete and coach in a particular direction, but they cannot substitute for individual experimentation (which is the focus of a section on "Mills Methods" later in this chapter).

A Few Closing Remarks on Monitoring the Training Effect

Once a coach or athlete understands the concept of the training effect and how that concept applies to his or her training for strength, power or flexibility, he or she must embark on the path of discovering what training methods work him or her. There are two contrasting paths in that search. One path leads a lifter away from the truth and the other toward it. The path away involves following training methods blindly and without question or being misled by someone's version of "science." The path toward discovery involves learning how to differentiate truth from fiction. In this section on the training effect, we will spend some time on each of these areas. First, we will examine methods of logical inference that can be invaluable to the lifter in his or her search for sound training methods. Then we will look at the problem of relying on pseudoscience.

Faulty Interpretations of Practical Experience and Scientific Research

It is a practical dilemma of human life that we are forced to act without complete information on most subjects. Information has a price, as does inaction. In the interest of saving time and other scarce resources we all learn to make inferences about life on the basis of very limited exposure to all of the available data. While this ability has been at the root of an incalculable number of mankind's advances in knowledge and technology, improper inference has also led to many of the greatest tragedies that mankind has ever known. Prejudice, witch hunts, purges and the slaughter of millions of people have all resulted in the main from man's propensity toward hasty generalizations. So it has been with respect to uncovering the secrets of strength as well.

Throughout the history of strength, the thinnest shred of evidence for the effectiveness of any method of training has led to mass movements in the direction of some silly notion that was then regarded as "the" training method. There was a movement toward isometrics some years ago, then it was variable resistance and then isokinetics. Each was heralded as the advance that would change the face of training. In recent years there has been a focus on the "secrets" of the coaches and athletes in the former Soviet Union. Exotic food supplements, restoration methods and plyometrics are just some examples of these supposed "secrets." The results have been indigestion, lighter wallets and sore knees, but only limited advances in the way of a contribution toward safe and effective advances in the realm of training for strength gains. (This is the fault not of the many serious and honest Soviet sports specialists but of the hucksters who seek to make a quick buck out of these "secrets".) There seems to be an attitude among a small but vocal minority of coaches that can be described as follows: "Here is something new that I can try. It has a wisp of plausibility and will make me appear to be on the leading edge of training technology. Best of all, no one has yet had the time or money to disprove the theory. In the meantime, no will notice my general ineptitude as a coach with all of the commotion that I can create with the application of this new theory."

It is bad enough that lay people jump to the conclusion that because a great champion drinks a certain brand of cola while competing, or crosses his eyes while concentrating, therein lie the secrets to that athlete's success. Perhaps some reasonable person can talk the hasty generalizer out of his or her conclusion by pointing out that the champion in question may either present an unusual case or that the behavior observed was not a cause of that athlete's success. Unfortunately, when a training "insight" has reportedly been developed in the "scientific community," it is often regarded as sacrosanct (especially among nonscientists, who will then quote the study for the rest of their natural lives). Scientists themselves are trained to be very careful about making hasty generalizations. They realize that for the effectiveness of a given training regimen to be proven (more properly in terms of today's scientific thinking, for it to avoid being disproved), it must be performed under conditions that eliminate psychological variables on the part of the subjects and those who are performing the test (e.g., in a double blind study). In addition, the experiment must be one that has been repeated by other scientists with similar results. Popularizers of scientific research need not be bound by such constraints; they merely rush the results to press, along with a generous supply of speculation (which they couch in scientific terms and present as scientific fact).

Two examples in this area should suffice. One example is presented in Chapter 6 in the opening discussion of the section on "periodization". In the case of periodization, some very preliminary data were used to make enormous generalizations about training. The result is a lot of people blindly periodizing their training without even understanding the concept, assuming that it has been "proven" effective by the scientific community and by champion athletes. See Chapter 6 for further information.

A second example can be given with respect to the subject of plyometrics. Some years ago plyometrics (particularly the version known as "depth jumping") were introduced in the Soviet Union (some argue that they were actually developed in the United States first). Although defined differently by different authors, depth jumping consists of jumping from a height and then rebounding up as soon as possible. Various heights are advised, and some authors suggest that weight should added to the body of the athlete to add to the downward impact. Sources within the Soviet Union, such as noted speed strength expert Yuri Verkhoshansky, are relied on for scientific support of the training method. However, if you go to the source, the support for the theory becomes clear. In Verkhoshansky's own book Fundamentals Of Special Strength- Training In Sport, published in 1977 (a book devoted to the development of power for sport in general, not to the development of strength or power for the sport of weightlifting in particular), he gives very high marks to what he calls the "shock method" of developing strength (which is essentially depth jumping). When he discusses depth jumping, he states that the effect of such jumps on explosive strength is "exceptionally high" and that "they have no equal in comparison to the other means of strength training." He then goes on to mention a number of studies performed in the 1970s to support this contention.

However, the one study that he actually describes is a study involving track and field athletes. These athletes reportedly did a series of 475 depth jumps over a twelve week period in comparison with the control group (who did 1,472 general "push-offs," which he describes as squats, jumping and hopping with a bar loaded to various percentages of maximum). The former group demonstrated greater improvements in "reactive ability." Did the athletes benefit from the depth jumping? Very probably. But is it possible that they benefited from simply doing less training overall (the author even mentions the benefit of being able to improve results with less effort)? Or because the kind of bar training done was normally ineffective anyway? Or because variety had been introduced into the athlete's training? Or because the athletes snuck in a little bar training on the side? We certainly cannot tell from the description of the study, and it is probable that given the construction of that study, the answers would not be forthcoming by analyzing it. However, the key point here is not whether further analysis or a greater understanding of the material would support the conclusions reached by the author. The key is that one must know when the data provided is insufficient relative to the conclusion reached. If this is so, the reader should regard the author's conclusions not as knowledge but rather as educated speculation. Such speculation may be valuable and may indeed prove to be correct, but it has not been scientifically proven, and there is a major difference between speculation and proof.

A reference to using plyometrics in the training of weightlifters was made in the Soviet Union's 1982 Weightlifting Yearbook. In an article called "Speed-Strength Preparation in the Pre-Competition Stage," Deniskin, Verkhoshansky and Medvedyev explain a study that they performed with respect to "depth jumping with a rebound." They indicate that the purpose of the study was to compare the effectiveness of such "shock training" with the traditional methods of training highly qualified weightlifters in the pre-competition stage. The fact that such a study made the Yearbook and that no similar studies are mentioned in the article suggest that this may have been the first study of its type on weightlifters.

The study involved only fifteen lifters, ranging in ability from Class I to Master of Sport. All of the lifters followed what was considered to be a conventional kind of program. However, the control group did an average of 929 lifts and lifted an average of 114 tons, while the experimental group did 786 lifts and lifted 90 tons. The reduction in the number of lifts and total tonnage lifted was accomplished by reducing the number of squats performed by the experimental group. The experimental group did 310 depth jumps in addition to their lifting. The experimental group performed far better on the competitive lifts than the control group, and they did far better with respect to speed strength tests as well. The article concludes that depth jumps are useful in preparing for competition; that they are superior to traditional preparation with a bar; that the optimal dosage of jumps in a workout is four sets of ten reps and that the optimal number of jumps overall is 310; that the training volume can be decreased when jumps are used; and that such jumps should be done three times a week for four weeks before a competition. It is hard to believe that statements about the optimality of sets and reps, as well as total jumps, would be made on the basis of one study that did not even compare different set, rep and total jump configurations. Perhaps there were earlier studies that pinpointed the correct number of total reps, or perhaps this is just an example of hasty generalization. In either case, there is no way for the reader to tell. Could such scanty evidence have spawned a trend here in the United States? It appears so. Again the value of plyometrics may be as great as is claimed, or even greater, but this has yet to be proven scientifically.

It is interesting to note that in A System Of Multi-Year Training In Weightlifting, a major work about training weightlifters published in 1986, Medvedyev references one previously unlisted article that supposedly "corroborated" the effectiveness of "shock" methods. There is no mention of any studies that verify the research presented in the study that appeared in the 1982 Weightlifting Yearbook In addition, Medvedyev issues repeated warnings that such jumping should only be utilized up to three times a year, that squats should be reduced to compensate for the addition of the jumping, that depth jumping is only an adjunct to overall training and that caution must be used in its application. This suggests to me that at least some injuries may have occurred after the 1982 article was published. I have certainly seen them in the United States.

It is interesting to note that some more recent Western research suggests that there may be some real value to plyometric training. The benefit may lie in the stimulation and refinement of the body's stretch-shortening cycle (which is discussed in Appendix II). However, this does not mean that there is only one way to improve the performance of that cycle, that similar exercises weightlifters already perform (e.g., the dip for the jerk) don't elicit the same or similar training effects, or that it would be worth the risk for weightlifters to incorporate plyometrics into their training.

The lesson to be learned is not to accept the word of the experts without question, to read the original research and to realize that we are far from having arrived at "the" answer to it all in the realm of training human beings for athletic competition. Moreover, biological individuality strongly suggests that there never will be one "best" method of training for us all. Rather, each athlete, aided by the experience of other athletes, coaches and sports scientists, will have to discover (through the process of careful experimentation) what works best for him or her.

The Lifter's Best Friend: Mill's Method of Difference

Scientists have come to rely almost exclusively on highly sophisticated statistical methods in their research. Athletes and coaches are often precluded from using such techniques in evaluating training approaches because they lack a knowledge of statistics, the necessary computational equipment for statistical analysis or an adequate "sample" from which to draw conclusions from their experiments. This does not mean that a scientific method cannot be used to evaluate training methods. It merely means that a non-statistical method must be used instead of a statistical one. One such approach is Mill's method of difference.

Mill's method of difference was developed by the nineteenth century philosopher John Stuart Mill. Although he is probably best known for his theories in the area of ethics (i.e., utilitarianism), Mill was also regarded as one of history's great logicians. While some of Mill's logical methods were rightfully criticized by later philosophers, he did formally identify several key methods of reasoning that are as essential today as they were when he first worked them out. These are: the method of agreement, the method of difference and the methods of concomitant variation and residues. The employment of these methods to analyze and plan training is one of the best ways ever discovered to improve performance.

When we use the method of agreement, we look for a common factor that is present in all cases in which an effect occurs. If your squat improved appreciably at several points in your training relative to other times, it is appropriate to see whether a single factor was present during all of the periods during which outstanding improvements were made (e.g., an extra day of training or, more likely, an extra day of rest)). If such a factor is uncovered, it suggests that this specific factor is capable of causing extra improvements. It may not be the only factor that can cause improvements (there may be many others that you have not even tried yet), but it is one that apparently works for you. Such a factor is said to be sufficient but not necessary (it is sufficient to cause an event but it may not be necessary, because changes in other factors might lead to the same result or might compromise the result in some way).

The method of difference is applied by removing a single factor from training while holding everything else constant, then observing the result. If a particular effect disappears each time a specific factor is removed from ones training, it demonstrates the importance of that factor. The effect that disappears may be positive in nature (e.g., improvement) or negative (e.g., an inflammation of the knee). The method of difference tells us only whether a factor is necessary to cause a given result, not whether it is by itself sufficient to cause the outcome (i.e., other factors may be necessary as well in order to generate that outcome). The squat workout on Thursday may be working only because the lifter squats on Tuesday and Saturday as well (i.e., because Thursday is an extra day).

Unfortunately, many training factors cannot be evaluated using only the methods of agreement and difference. This is because matters of degree affect results (e.g., it may be that only an extra heavy day of squatting leads to improvements, not simply an extra day of any level of training intensity). We characterize differences in degree as quantitative not qualitative. The methods of concomitant variation and residues help us to identify quantitative differences.

The method of concomitant variations works by measuring the quantitative change in an effect associated with a difference in a believed cause. The correlation can be either positive or negative, weak or strong. A correlation does not, in itself, prove sufficiency or necessity. It simply demonstrates that given the presence of all of the other factors, variations in A are sufficient to cause variations in B. When the method of concomitant variations is used, it also does not tell one whether a cause is direct or indirect or guarantee the direction of the cause (A may be causing B or B may be causing A). Only if you understand the nature of qualitative relationships can you use the method of concomitant variations to measure the value of a constant in those relationships.

The method of residues can help us to identify an unknown factor or to quantify a known one. For example, if we know that a certain effect is partially a result of factor A and partially a result of factor B, we know that any remaining effect that is unexplained by A and B (the residue) is due to still another factor, factor C. A weightlifting analogy exists in the area of technique. Some years ago, when they were analyzing bar velocities, sport scientists from the Soviet Union realized that the velocity of the bar at the point when the lifter began the squat under in the jerk could not fully explain the ultimate height that the bar reached. This led them to further investigation which led to the discovery that other influences which occurred after the final explosion phase contributed to the upward rise of the bar.

In Mill's methods only one variable is manipulated and/or studied at a time. This is critical in order for Mill's powerful methods of reasoning to be effectively applied. Yet it is commonplace in weightlifting training to vary many factors at a time, thereby making it very difficult for the coach or athlete to determine which factor is responsible for which effect. Rather than changing the percentage of one's maximum, the number of reps in a given set, or the number of sets performed in a given workout, it is commonplace to change them all at once. And as if three changes were not enough, the number and nature of exercises done in a workout and the number of training sessions performed in a week are often changed as well. The problem of identifying effects becomes even more complicated because each change in a factor may have not only its individual effect but also effects which arise out of the interaction of each factor that changes. The result is the virtual assurance that it will be impossible for anything to be learned from experience about that particular lifter's reaction to a specific training response.

It is hard to imagine anything that would retard long term progress more than the failure to learn from experience. A lifter who does not is condemned to a career characterized by random changes in training variables, leading to a chaotic career marked by random results.

Some lifters, recognizing the difficulties posed by changing factors, respond by never changing anything at all. They suffer the same fate as the random trainer ; they never learn much about their own body's response to training. In addition, it is likely that even if they are to be wedded to a training method that happens to be successful for them from the start, they will be destined to have a very limited career.

Alternatively, if lifters and their coaches systematically varied only one training factor at a time, learning would take place far more rapidly, and the critical business of discovering the optimal training factors for that lifter would proceed as quickly as possible. It is true that manipulating one variable at a time can be an arduous process. Using such a method can require months and even years to explore certain variables effectively. Judgment and experience will enable the coached athlete to select the variables that are most likely to yield results and to reduce experimental time, so there is no substitute for such judgment. However, even when an experienced eye is not present, systematic variations will ultimately bear fruit. In contrast, the decision to alter many training factors simultaneously may be justified for a variety of reasons, but such a practice will hamper the athlete's progress in understanding which factors are leading to which effects.

Some Common Training Patterns

There is a virtually unlimited number of possible set, rep and intensity patterns that can be performed in a given workout. However, some popular general patterns have emerged over the history of weight training, and several of them will be examined here.

Multiple Sets With Similar Rep Patterns

The most common approach weightlifters use in their training is to perform the same (or a very similar) number of reps per set on a particular exercise for the duration of the training session. For example, a lifter who plans to perform five repetitions in the squat on his or her heavy sets of the day would perform approximately five reps on each of the warmup sets as well. Alternatively, an athlete who expects to perform heavy singles might warm up with doubles on the early sets and perform singles on the heavy ones, so the reps performed are similar but not identical for the duration of the training session.

Athletes and coaches who believe that a certain number of reps are the most beneficial for a particular workout generally reason that if doubles are what they intend to do at the end of the workout, it is doubles that they should perform most of the way up (or at least on most of the heavier sets of the training session)

There are several other repetition patterns that are also used in the training of weightlifters, though not nearly as often as the multiple sets with similar reps pattern.

Pyramiding

One of the longest lived and most widely used training systems ever developed is the pyramid system. First appearing at least fifty years ago (then often referred to as the "heavy and light system"), this training approach involves the use of medium (six to ten) and low (one to five) reps in the same workout. The most common way in which this is done is (after warming up with lighter weights) to begin with a weight that permits a medium number of reps and then to add weight and reduce reps as necessary to complete additional set. For example, after warming up with a couple of sets of ten repetitions with weights that can be done rather easily, the lifter might begin with a weight that is fairly challenging for ten repetitions, then move up to a weight that is difficult for eight repetitions and perform those eight repetitions. The lifter might then move on to a near maximum effort at six repetitions, followed by a limit set of four reps and then a limit set of two reps. Those interested in developing strength tend to start "higher" in the pyramid (perhaps at five reps with a heavy weight and then drop perhaps one rep per set while increasing the weight until they have worked up to a heavy single). This is sometimes called a half or partial pyramid (because the lifter starts halfway up the pyramid in terms of reps). Those mainly interested in gaining muscle size might only do the bottom half of the pyramid (starting with ten or twelve reps and only working up in weight until they get to five or six reps). Those interested in gaining size and strength would tend to follow a procedure closer to that of the first example.

There are many other variations on the pyramid theme. Some trainees use a "reverse" pyramid. After warming up thoroughly, these lifters first take the set that will have the heaviest weight and the lowest number of reps. Then the weight is reduced and the reps are increased, working down the pyramid. This approach enables the athlete to attempt the heaviest weights when he or she is the "freshest" and then to go for a maximum pump with an all out set to exhaustion. (When the lifter works from the bottom of the pyramid and performs an all out set of high repetitions, the athlete's ability to perform well with subsequent sets at higher weights and lower reps is generally compromised to a significant extent.)

Still other weight trainers work up the pyramid in the normal way, but they recommend finishing the training on that exercise with one or more sets at either end of the pyramid. For example, those interested in the development of strength rather than size might do extra sets of doubles upon reaching the top of the pyramid, thereby spending more time at the top of the pyramid than anywhere else. Bodybuilders might go back down the pyramid for one or more maximum sets with lighter weights and higher reps. Even some trainees who are primarily interested in strength feel that a final pumping or flushing set (one that permits perhaps eight to twelve reps all out) is beneficial, although I cannot recommend this procedure unless this last set is performed with a resistance that requires less than an all out effort on the last reps.

The primary advantage of the regular pyramid is that the athlete is able to warm up and to train different rep patterns at the same time. The primary disadvantage arises out of the balance between weight and reps with the lighter weights in the pyramid. If the athlete really goes all out on the medium weight, high rep sets, it is unlikely that there will be much left for the heavier sets (the athlete will be too pumped or fatigued to handle really heavy weights on the low rep sets). If the athlete takes it too easy on the higher rep sets, there will be little training effect from those rep patterns. Therefore, virtually no high level weightlifter's train using the traditional pyramid system (even for their pure strength exercises, like squats high reps are never performed on the classic lifts because of the deterioration in technique that performing such exercises for high repetition sets causes).

The reverse pyramid has the advantage of enabling the athlete to attempt the heaviest sets while still fresh and to do justice to those sets. Then the athlete can move down and push relatively hard on the higher rep sets. As a rule the higher rep sets will take more out of the muscles than lower rep sets in terms of the athlete's ability to perform further sets at a high level. Therefore, overall, the advantages of the reverse pyramid outweigh the advantages of the regular pyramid (with the main drawback of the reverse pyramid being the extra time required to warm up for weights at the top of the pyramid). Nevertheless, few (if any) champion weightlifters utilize reverse pyramiding in their training.

The half pyramiding schemes make the choice between the regular and the reverse pyramid less of an issue because there is less difference in the fatiguing effects of six as opposed to ten reps, or two as opposed to five reps, than there is in rep patterns at the top and bottom pyramid. Bodybuilders are more likely to perform pyramids at the bottom (higher rep portions) of the pyramid, while weightlifters remain at the high end of the pyramid if they pyramid at all (which they rarely do).

Regardless of the variations on the pyramiding theme, its chief feature is the belief of the trainee that performing multiple rep themes in the same workout will develop multiple muscle qualities (strength, endurance and size) at the same time. There is considerable merit in this notion, in the sense that training is very specific to the quality being trained, and detraining occurs very quickly. If the athlete is training to develop several muscle capacities at once, all of them can be addressed in the same workout by using the pyramid. However, there appears to be a limit to the body's adaptation energy at any one point in time. It is unlikely that the body can adapt simultaneously to its maximum potential in terms of developing size, strength and endurance. Therefore, the trainee who is interested in maximal development in a particular area needs to recognize that lesser results in another area will need to be accepted. However, for many trainees, mixing high and low reps in the same workout will provide a nice balance of muscle qualities. For the serious competitive weightlifter, working reps near the top half of the pyramid (i.e., one to five reps) will be more fruitful (with sets of four and five reps reserved for pure strength exercises such as squats and reps in the classical lifts limited to three, and performed primarily for singles and doubles). Pyramiding can also be useful when a lifter needs a change in pace.

It must be remembered that reps above two or three in the classic lifts can have a negative influence on technique. In addition, one heavy, high rep set during a warm up period can so fatigue the muscles that performance on later sets and reps is compromised. Finally, the weightlifter is interested in developing the greatest possible strength and power capability available from a given muscle. There is no value in increasing a muscle's size if the increase is due to the development of tissue that does not directly contribute to the generation of strength and power (which occurs when high repetitions are used in training).

Pyramiding Over a Series of Workouts

Some trainers recommend a different kind or pyramiding: working up the pyramid over a series of weeks. The underlying principle is that a foundation of muscular endurance and size is formed with medium reps and then that base is converted into strength and power by training with lower reps in ensuing weeks. Some trainers refer to this as a kind of "periodization" (a concept that is discussed at length in Chapter 6.

For example, the trainee might begin twelve weeks before a competition (or a planned workout in which a personal record was contemplated in a particular exercise). The first two weeks of the cycle might consist of three sets of ten reps with a weight that was fairly comfortable for that number of reps (i.e., more than ten reps— perhaps twelve or even fifteen—could have been done on each set in an all out effort). The following week the tens might be continued, but with a weight that would only allow eleven or twelve reps if the lifter really pushed. In the third and fourth weeks, the weights would be pushed up still further, and the athlete might perform three sets of eight reps (with a weight that would permit the athlete to do ten reps on an all out basis in week three and only nine reps in week four). By weeks five and six the reps would drop to six, and the athlete would be working with a weight that might allow an extra rep on the first or second set but that required a nearly all out effort by the third set. In weeks seven and eight the reps might drop to five or four with weights challenging enough such that no further reps would be possible on most sets. In weeks nine and

ten the reps would drop again into the two-to-three range, and in the last two weeks the lifter would be performing only doubles or singles with heavy weights. Normally, the heaviest weights would be handled approximately two weeks from the last day of the cycle; some trainers advocate only a week's rest from a very heavy effort, and some like as many as three or more.

As with the regular pyramid, there are many variations in the long term pyramid scheme. Some lifters like to increase the sets done as the reps decline, so that in the early weeks three sets of ten reps are done; when six reps are adopted, the sets might increase to four or five. At three reps or less, the lifter might do five or six sets. The theory here is that higher reps are more fatiguing and lower reps less, so therefore sets can be done when fewer reps are performed in each set. As a consequence, more sets are possible and desirable with fewer reps.

Still another approach involves a light and heavy day within the pyramiding cycle, with the rep patterns described above used on one (heavy) training day and another rep pattern and/or different weights used on the other (generally lighter) day (e.g., a regular pyramid, or three fixed sets of eight or ten reps with a lighter weight than is being used on the other training day).

Although this kind of pyramiding is often used, particularly in the powerlifting community, it does not appear to be the most effective way to train year round. One reason is that the premise of size and endurance serving as the foundation for strength has really never been proven to be superior to other, more conventional methods of strength development. Clearly, there are many athletes who have gotten very strong never having done higher reps and never having developed great muscle size (in many Eastern European countries high reps are virtually never done). Another consideration is that with the body's propensity toward specificity of training and rapid detraining, there is little reason to believe much of the capacity developed earlier in the cycle will remain by the end of the cycle if at least some training on the same number of reps is done. Similarly, the ability to perform low reps will be reduced after several weeks of training with higher reps only. Further, if the weights lifted early in the cycle are too light, the body will lose some strength during this light training period. Then its adaptive capacities will tend to be overwhelmed by successive weeks of very heavy training later in the cycle. In addition, if the athlete starts with relatively heavy weights too early in the cycle (even if higher reps are done), he or she will undoubtedly be overtrained before the end of the cycle is reached and will never reach the weights that have been planned.

Therefore, in the main, the lifter is likely to get the maximum benefit from a cycle that has the following characteristics: a) whatever the range of reps included, the lifter never goes more than a couple of weeks without doing at least one set of reps in both the higher and lower ranges (thereby retaining some of the training affect developed at both ends of the range, assuming that maintaining such an ability is important); b) the cycle is relatively short, between two and six weeks; and c) during any cycle, no more than four to six weeks pass between maximum or near maximum all out efforts with reps in the lower range if strength development is a key concern. The only exception to this rule would be when an athlete is coming back after an extended layoff from training or from an injury, in which case a special comeback or rehabilitative cycle should be used. Such a cycle would be tailored to the length of the layoff, the nature of the injury and the athlete's condition at the time of resuming his or her training.

Super Sets and Pre-exhaustion Systems

Super sets consist of doing two exercises with little or no rest in between. The most popular method is to use opposing muscle groups in the paired exercises (e.g., doing leg curls and leg extensions one after the other). Another version is to work the same overall muscle group from different angles (e.g., doing presses in front of and behind the neck in successive sets). Pre-exhaustion training is similar to the second form of super sets, except that the principle involved is to tire a muscle that is not normally fully taxed during a multiple muscle group exercise, so that it will be stressed more fully while the lifter is performing the multiple-muscle-group exercise. For example, performing leg extensions immediately prior to squats has been advocated as a method of placing more emphasis on the quadriceps muscles than on the back and hip muscles during the squat(because the quadriceps muscles are already fatigued when the squat is begun).

The first method of super setting discussed above has yielded good (though not superior) strength gains for the paired groups of muscles and the use of super sets may save time overall for strength trainers. However, such sets have no demonstrated value when one is performing exercises that involve many muscle groups that overlap between exercises (like snatches and squats). Instead, they are likely to be very detrimental to the technique of a lifter because fatigued muscles cannot perform motor skills as effectively as those which are not.

The latter method of super setting (performing similar exercises in immediate succession) is not dissimilar to cheating and burns, etc., in the sense that it is a means to continue to work a muscle group that has already been fatigued. To the extent that the second exercise resembles the first, the effect is similar to having done one set with more reps and should have a relatively similar training effect. To the extent that it is different, the super set is not fully accomplishing its purpose of introducing extra fatigue into the muscle.

Pre-exhaustion has pros and cons similar to those of the latter form of super setting. In addition, the fatiguing of a single muscle before performing another exercise involving the same muscle as well as others poses a special hazard. If the pre-exhausted muscle causes the second exercise to be performed in an unusual style, an injury can result. Moreover, the action of a pre-fatigued muscle will be different than it would have been if it were fresh. Even if this posed no threat of injury, this difference in the action of the muscles tends to limit the value of the sets performed after pre-exhaustion (because of the principle of specificity of training). Consequently, the second form of supersetting and pre-exhaustion training cannot be recommended for serious strength training and is definitely not recommended for the Olympic lifts (because pre-exhaustion methods can literally destroy an athlete's technique in those lifts).

Circuit Training

It is generally acknowledged that in order for the body's cardiovascular system to be trained, the heart rate must be elevated to a certain threshold and then sustained at that level for at least several minutes. (Until recently the rule of thumb was twenty minutes, but new research has suggested that elevating the pulse to the target level for three ten-minute sessions a day may exert just as profound a training effect as one thirty minute session.)

Resistance exercises, such as those done in weightlifting, can surely raise the heart rate, but the rest that weight trainers normally take between sets allows the heart rate to return to a near normal level. However, an elimination or significant reduction of the normal rest between sets can convert weight training to a cardiovascular exercise by sustaining the heart rate at an elevated level over time. Thus far, research suggests that such training is not as effective, in certain respects, as more common forms of aerobic exercise (e.g., running and cycling). The difference seems to be that the use of the same muscles throughout the exercise period has a greater stimulative effect on the heart and lungs than training with varied exercises that activate different muscle groups. Nevertheless, circuit training can be a useful way to train both the anaerobic and aerobic capacities of the body simultaneously. This can be a good time-saver for the busy trainer. However, the result of such training on muscle size and strength and on the body's aerobic capacity will not be as good as if separate training of these capacities were undertaken. The value of such training for the athlete seeking maximum strength is almost nil (as is any extensive anaerobic training, though some moderate aerobic training may be useful, or at least not harmful, to the progress of the strength seeker). Circuit training while performing the Olympic lifts is clearly unwise, since such training will almost surely undermine the weightlifter's technique. However, moving from set to set as soon as the lifter has recuperated adequately from the previous set will result in some benefits to the cardiovascular system.

Cycles

The weightlifters and coaches of today generally see each workout as a part of a broader plan or "cycle" in which the athlete will perform a sequence of workouts over a period of time (rather than performing a series of unconnected individual workouts, or workouts in which the same intensity is employed). The underlying premise of this kind of process is that each workout builds upon the prior ones to reach a better outcome than would be achieved by training at the same level each workout or training totally in accordance with ones whims of the day. Much more will be said regarding this longer term view of training in Chapter 6, In this chapter, we will simply try to create a sense of what cycling is about, especially as it applies to training on a particular exercise.

The Diminishing Reps Per Set Strength Cycle

During the 1980s a special kind of strength building cycle became quite popular, particularly in United States powerlifting circles. Proponents of the system have referred to it as "periodization" or "cycling" (among other labels). These terms have very different meanings in the context of training on the Olympic lifts. The basic principle is to vary the repetitions performed in training over time, typically a period of six to twelve weeks. The objective is generally to reach peak performance for a single rep maximum at the end of the cycle.

Several concepts underlie the diminishing rep cycling approach. First, there is the concept of the need for variability in training. A constantly changing rep scheme provides the body with differing kinds of stimulation at all times during the cycle. Second, the varying rep structure of the routine emphasizes the development of different factors in muscle strength at different times. The advocates of the diminishing rep cycle argue that higher reps tend to stimulate hypertrophy, while lower reps tend to develop neural components of strength and power. Third, the sequencing of the repetitions is designed to build the body's strength factors in a logical fashion. The cross section of muscle fiber that is believed to set the outside limits of a muscle's ability to generate force is first increased. Later in the cycle the athlete focuses on the expression of the strength potential that lies in newly developed muscle mass.

Although the recommended procedures vary somewhat from author to author, reps performed are normally in the eight-to-ten range at the beginning of the cycle and in the one-to-two rep range at its conclusion (which is generally just before a major competition or all out day in training). It is also common to have one heavy day a week (on which the diminishing rep scheme is scrupulously followed) and one lighter day on which the reps never go below the three-to-five range, and the lifter exercises at a considerably lesser level of effort. In some variations of this method, the lighter day remains at a fixed weight and repetition scheme throughout the cycle. In all of those cycles the amount of weight lifted on the heavy day increases significantly across the cycle as the reps diminish.

The diminishing rep approach is intuitively appealing, and there is at least one study that has suggested that this approach is more effective than a standard fixed rep approach (however, the study was only six weeks long, and it compared the diminishing rep cycle with a relatively ineffective kind of fixed rep workout scheme). Moreover, a very large number of high level powerlifters have used it with considerable success.

There is little doubt that the diminishing rep approach can be more effective than a lifter's merely coming in the gym to do three sets of five reps to failure two or three times a week. It may be more effective than a cycle in which the lifter maintains fixed reps but increases the amount of weight lifted each week. However, the reasons for its relative effectiveness may not be those cited by many of this method's advocates.

For instance, it may be true that training variety can serve to stimulate improvement, but it has not been established that variety in repetitions, or at least the variety that is embodied in the broad range of one to eight or ten reps, is an effective form of variety. In fact, that is rather unlikely. Since different repetition schemes are likely to cause very specific and very different adaptations in muscle tissue and function, it is unlikely that there is a great deal of transfer between the effects of training schedules with very different repetition patterns. The smaller the difference, the greater the transfer and the smaller the degree of variability attributable to the difference in reps. If the mere change in the number of reps per set is not responsible for strength gains under the diminishing rep system, one possible reason for the improvements that have been noted is that the total number of reps performed decreases during the cycle, while intensity increases (a popular method of peaking in Eastern Europe but there the reps per set do not vary nearly as much across the cycle).

Serious criticisms can be made of the concept of emphasizing the development of different capacities during different phases of training. For example, it is not at all clear that the kind of extra muscle development that takes place during training that emphasizes hypertrophy can be utilized for strength enhancement; the increase in gross muscular size that is stimulated by higher repetition training may not reflect proportional growth in the muscle's components that are responsible for increases in absolute strength levels. Moreover, if the extra muscle development that was acquired during the higher repetition phase was applicable to strength generation, it would be likely that the removal of the special hypertrophy development stimulation via higher reps would lead to a detraining effect (a reduction in the extra size previously gained) during the subsequent lower repetition period of the cycle. Therefore, while this kind of cycling shouldn't necessarily be dismissed, it should not be accepted as "gospel."

The Diminishing Total Reps Peaking Cycle

The most popular strength development cycle used in weightlifting is the method of diminishing the number of total reps but increasing the average intensity of the reps that are performed during a training "cycle" (a series of training sessions that are viewed in combination to generate a particular training effect). This is typically accomplished in several ways. First, the number of reps per set is decreased. The reduction is less severe than in the diminishing reps per set system (e.g., the cycle might begin with an emphasis on two or three reps per set and end with the emphasis on singles, although some sets with four to five reps and some singles might be performed throughout the cycle). Second, the number of sets is often decreased somewhat as well, especially if the number of reps per set does not change much during the cycle. Finally, the number and variety of exercises are often diminished (the closer the competition, the greater is the emphasis placed on the competitive and closely related lifts).

As with the diminishing reps per set system, this approach has its positive and negative aspects. Variety in terms of reps per set and exercises performed is present during the cycle. Diminishing the overall work load enables the lifter to take advantage of the body's adaptation capabilities. The body is stimulated to adapt early in the cycle (by a large workload). Such adaptation may indeed be occurring during the period of large workload, but the body is unable to express the adaptation because of the continued stress of the workload itself. When the workload is diminished, the body has an opportunity to complete any unfinished aspect of the adaptation process, and its energy

stores are replenished. The result is that the body in able to express its new higher level of adaptation with a higher level of performance.

The negative aspects of the diminishing total reps cycle are several. First, the period of higher workload and the period of diminished workload may each be longer than required to cause an optimal adaptation. If so, time is being wasted during the cycle, and the desired result may not occur when it is planned. Second, the body may be overtrained at certain points in the cycle and undertrained in another. This can unnecessarily expose the lifter to injury, both because of the overtraining and because of the rather large swings in the content of the training over the long term. Finally, a significant change in the exercises themselves can place a significant strain on the body's adaptational apparatus. If an exercise is beneficial, it is important that it be included, at least to some extent, throughout the training period, lest the positive adaptations that it generates be lost at the later stages of the cycle when its effects are most needed. The exceptions are exercises which teach or emphasize a specific skill (one which is later preserved in the practice of the classical lift itself).

A Better Cycle

It is my belief that the drawbacks of the diminishing total reps cycle can be overcome and most of its advantages retained by employing a fundamentally different form of cycle. This can be done through what I term the "reciprocal mini cycle." The differences between it and more conventional cycles are numerous and, in my view, quite significant.

The first difference is that the basic exercises in the cycle remain the same, but their frequency and emphasis shifts during the cycle. As was suggested earlier, if a conditioning exercise is worth doing, it is worth doing all of the time, at least to a certain extent. If it is not included with some regularity in the lifter's training, the lifter is exposed to a conditioning risk when the exercise is added and to detraining risk when it is omitted. The second difference is that all of the reps that are normally performed in a cycle are performed throughout the cycle, though the emphasis may change. Here again, the premise is that if a certain rep pattern is worth doing it is worth doing, at least to some extent, all of the time. The reason is essentially the same as the one given for maintaining exercises. The third difference is that workouts with high volume and lower intensity and workouts with high intensity and lower volume and other variations alternate throughout the cycle. The principle here is to enjoy the benefits of alternating periods of high load with those of high intensity but to keep those periods short enough so that the benefits of both can be enjoyed throughout the year, indeed throughout the training month.

A simple example of how such a cycle can be applied to the squat follows (see Table I). I developed the cycle routine over a period of years, and it proved to be very beneficial in building my leg strength and that of a number of United States lifters who have used it (ranging from the novice to high level lifters). It is a three week cycle with weekly heavy workouts (some have found a two or four week variation, with heavy days spaced anywhere from 5 to 11 days to be more effective). All percentages shown are for the number of reps indicated (e.g., if the athlete's best set of 5 reps is 100 kg, he or she lifts 85 kg. for 3 sets of 5 reps on Tuesday's workout). The 101% shown on the third Saturday really symbolizes the lifter's attempting a new personal record by 2.5 kg. In the table, percentages appear first, reps second and sets third; if there is no third number shown for that day, only one set is performed after the warm-up sets of squats. Warm-ups are not included, but the athlete generally warms up with several sets, the last being approximately 90% of the heaviest weight that will be handled on that day. In this particular variation of the cycle, back squats are performed on Tuesdays and Saturdays, front squats on the Thursday workouts of the first two weeks (front squats are omitted during the third week).

Within each week the above routine achieves variety in terms of volume, intensity and exercises performed. There is also some variation between weeks one and two and considerable variations (in volume, intensity and exercises) between weeks two and three. Nevertheless, the longest intervals between exercises is two weeks (i.e., between front squats in weeks two and one), and both rep schemes (threes and fives) are generally worked once a week. The variations are significant enough to cause adaptations at a consistent rate, yet not so great as to threaten the body with too much change at once or to permit detraining to occur. In my experience, it is possible to perform two to four cycles of this type in succession with considerable success. In between such multiple cycles one or two heavy or light weeks can be placed, depending on the needs and responses of the individual lifter.

There are of course many other variations of this method. Some lifters will require the use of higher percentages than those shown above, and others will require lower ones. Some athletes will benefit from longer rests between heavy workouts, and others will benefit from shorter rests. The

same lifter's needs may change over time. (I found that I needed ten days of rest between heavy workouts when I was in my 40s, where a week had been fine during my teenage years and my 20s.)

The preceding description is merely intended to serve as a starting point from which the athlete and coach can begin to experiment. The foundations of the reciprocal mini cycle are: a) maintaining the exercises throughout the mini cycle by varying their frequency; b) performing more total reps on lighter days and fewer total reps on heavier days; and c) varying the number of reps per set to a certain degree but not in a dramatic way (and always maintaining the number of reps in the strength and power building range).

The Intuitive Trainer, or the Purely Natural Cycle

A number of outstanding strength athletes and/or coaches have advocated training "intuitively." The definition of intuitive is not widely agreed upon. To some lifters, it means that the athlete works out in accord with what he or she feels like doing on certain day. This "do what you feel" method extends from the exercises selected to the amount of weight lifted to the number of sets that are performed.

The argument made for the intuitive method is that your mind and body know what is best, so set them free to have their unconscious way. Such a system may work for a lifter whose unconscious has been programmed by years of analysis of training methods and the body's reaction to them, but for the lifter who is not as experienced or whose mind has not been programmed in a positive way, intuition can be a disaster. Moreover, much in the same way that a person walking in the woods without a compass or other external directional guide will tend to walk in a wide circle, the trainer who has not been fortunate enough to have enjoyed steady success may find himself or herself walking in a circle of stagnation or even destruction without a plan (though a flexible one). In my experience, there are few, if any, lifters who will find this method to be truly beneficial. However, there is a modified version of the intuitive method that can be used very successfully. It can be referred to as the "structured natural cycle."

A Structured Natural Cycle

Many successful athletes and coaches train in accordance with a somewhat structured yet "natural" and somewhat intuitive cycle; they

TABLE 1

	Tuesday	Thursday	Saturday
Week 1	Squat 85% x 5 x 3	Front Squat 90% x 3	Squat 90% x 5
Week 2	Squat 85% x 3 x 5	Front Squat 90% x 3	Squat 90% x 5
Week 3	Squat 85% x 5 x 3	No Front Squat	Squat 101% x 3 or 5

157

designate the exercises and appropriate number of sets to be performed in a given workout but leave the highest weights to be lifted on a given day as a variable to be determined by the lifter's condition that day.

A number of very successful United States lifters from the 1950s and 1960s employed this kind of approach in their training. For example, World and Olympic champion Issac Berger would work up in each of the lifts by performing singles and making 5 kg. jumps during each workout. Once he reached his maximum for that day, he would generally move on to the next exercise. Sometimes, after a miss he would lower the weight by 5 kg. and, if successful, would try to work up to a heavier weight again.

As was mentioned earlier, the modern Bulgarians have a more strenuous variation of this procedure. They have the lifter warm up in each exercise and reach a limit or near limit for the day. Then a series of five to six lifts with that weight might be performed. Alternatively, the lifter might do one lift at that weight, then a lift with 5 kg. to 10 kg. less, then go back up to the original high for the day and repeat that process several times. In this way the lifter is assured of making several lifts with the maximum for the day, whatever that maximum happens to be.

Jim Williams, the lengendary bench presser of the 1970s (he succeeded with more than 700 lb. in the gym but narrowly missed it in competition), devised a program that reportedly involved an interesting variation of the natural cycle. He came into the gym approximately five days a week looking for a personal record in the bench press. He would work up over the course of a few sets, with the last being in the area of 90% of his maximum. If that went well, he jumped to a personal record weight and made an attempt. If he was successful, he noted this and resolved to try for more in his next workout. If the attempt failed, he came back to it the next day or at most two days later. By using this method Jim was testing his limits each day (with the 90% weight) but never pushing to the maximum unless a record seemed possible.

These natural cycling methods are clearly not for every athlete, particularly not for those who have a strong tendency to overtrain or undertrain if left to their own designs. However, they are evidently very effective for some athletes and may hold a real promise of training optimization for those athletes who are able to adjust to the routine.

Examples of Classic Strength Training Methods

We have thus far presented the basic building blocks of the training complex. The challenge for the coach and athlete is to apply those concepts in concert and in the real world. It is one thing to select the appropriate number of reps for the lifter's purposes, to perform those reps in the appropriate manner (e.g., explosively and concentrically), to select the appropriate exercises and to perform those exercises through the appropriate range of motion and at the correct range of intensity. It is quite another thing to develop a program that works. A coach can prepare a program in which, in general terms, everything is well designed. Despite this, the athlete who uses the program may make no progress and may even regress. Coaches and athletes must design programs that not only make sense on a conceptual level, but that also cause particular athletes to improve. That is the true test of coaching ability.

Devising training programs that work is no simple process. As was noted earlier, every athlete is at least somewhat different from every other. It is rare for the same athlete to react to the same program in exactly the same way every time he or she uses it because the athlete's adaptability and overall conditions of training tend to change over time. Therefore, the wise athlete and coach build upon sound training principles through the process of individualization and do not blindly copy the exact methods of other individual athletes.

However, as a starting point, the coach and athlete may find it useful to examine some specific training routines that have actually been used by athletes and coaches with success. These programs represent only a small sample of the kinds of programs that exist. They are approaches designed to increase strength and power in a specific exercise. They do not represent complete training programs, which are discussed in a later chapter.

Unfortunately, the weightlifting literature of Eastern Europe is relatively sparse when it comes to describing the training programs of individual athletes or exercises. Perhaps this is because the collectivist tendencies that existed for so many years in Eastern Europe worked against the notion of presenting individual results. Another possible reason is that coaches and athletes are not eager to share the precise details of the training methods that they follow in an environment in which weightlifting is essentially a professional sport.

In addition to failing to present the programs of individual athletes, the literature of Eastern Europe rarely presents the specific content of workouts on an exercise-by-exercise, set and rep basis. It may be reported, for example, that an athlete performs a total of 2,000 reps in a given month and that 10% of those reps were accounted for by squats. We may further be told that the average intensity of that month was 100 kg. and that there were so many reps performed in each of several zones of intensity. We may even be told of the rep and exercise distributions across a week or month, but there will be no detail regarding the sets and reps performed in each exercise and intensity. This information has some value, and a significant amount it will be presented in Chapter

6. In this chapter we will discuss some of the exercise routines that have been employed by some of the strongest athletes of the past, primarily those of the Western world. These programs have been selected because of their availability, their effectiveness for a significant number of athletes and their applicability to conditions found in countries in which weightlifting is not a professional sport.

John Davis's Multiple Set of Low Reps

John Davis' was one of the greatest lifters ever to touch a bar. The fact that he won eight straight World Championships and two Olympic Games would certainly establish John's special place in weightlifting history. But when you consider that John's career was interrupted by World War II, his achievements are truly unbelievable. He won the last World Championship in 1938 and seven more championships after the war, beginning with the first one held in 1946 . How many more championships might John have won in the eight years between championships?

During his workouts John favored and ultimately popularized a training system that was founded on the performance of eight sets of two repetitions with a fixed weight. While the program of eight sets of two was far from the only one John used, he felt the stimulation received from performing many sets with a fixed weight was very beneficial. He attempted to use the same weight for two or more workouts a week and adjusted the intensity by his feelings on a given day and the style of exercise performance. For example, if he were pressing and the weight he normally used felt heavy, he would permit himself to cheat a little in order to perform the required number of sets and reps. When the weights started to feel lighter, John would increase the amount he lifted in that exercise.

John typically lifted well within himself in training (he was generally able to lift from 10% to 15% more in a competition than in training). Therefore, while he was training with more or less the same weight in every workout, that weight represented a sub-maximal load (perhaps in the 85% to 90% range. This kind of program, while very simple, has been highly effective at generating strength gains in many athletes over many years.

The Hepburn Method of Building on Reps

Doug Hepburn of Canada won the Heavyweight (now the Superheavyweight) class of the 1953 World Weightlifting Championship. Doug was not a powerful giant from birth. In fact, he was born with a club foot, which, though surgically repaired early in his life, left him with a partial disability in his leg. Despite his handicap, Doug built himself into one of the strongest men who ever lived, and not always under the best of training conditions.

One of his favorite training concepts was to try to make some progress at every workout, but not necessarily by adding weight to the bar. Instead, Doug felt that he could always add something to his training. He could add weight to one or more of his sets or he could add a rep or a set with one rep, just as long as progress of some kind was made. The Hepburn concept involved consistent but somewhat undulating increases in intensity because for a given series of sets and reps the lifter was always handling his or her best (or nearly so) and was adding to that. Hepburn was gradually modifying the training stimulus, exercise by exercise, in order to assure improvement. For instance, he might be adding to his total tonnage in the squat on a given day by adding a set or rep. However, the following workout he might actually drop a rep or set but increase the weight on one set, thereby decreasing the volume but increasing an element of intensity.

This addition of weight, reps or sets on the heavy sets of the training session not only led to ever increasing stimulation for the muscles but presumably its gradual nature also gave the body time to adapt. In addition, it provided the lifter with three invaluable psychological benefits: a) an enormous sense of confidence that arose out of establishing small goals for each workout and repeatedly achieving those goals; b) the enthusiasm that arises out of making continual progress; and c) the enhanced commitment that arises out of an increased sense of self worth and enthusiasm (which in turn leads to more progress, more confidence, more enthusiasm, more commitment and so on).

One example of the Hepburn program is to begin training with a weight that the lifter is able to lift for five sets of three reps. During each workout (the program assumes that there will be three training sessions a week on the exercise for which it is being used), the lifter adds one rep to one of the sets until after five such increments the lifter is performing five sets of four reps. Then the lifter adds one more rep each week until five sets of five reps are executed. At this point the lifter increases the weight being lifted and returns to performing five sets of three reps. Then the entire cycle is continually repeated with heavier weights as the athlete's strength progresses.

I have used the Hepburn approach with considerable success on the squat and press. However, it does appear to lead to a state of overtraining after several cycles. This tendency can be mitigated by making a change in the program after a few cycles, by having a lighter workout once a week or by performing the program only twice a week.

Paul Anderson's Training Programs

Paul Anderson was a true legend of weightlifting, and deservedly so. He rose to championship levels in a phenomenally short period of time (he was exceeding world weightlifting records within three years of commencing serious training for the sport). During the 1950s he established records in the squat, push press and some other exercises, records that arguably still stand today. He was most famous for his prodigious squatting ability.

Paul described his basic squat program in the November, 1964, issue of Muscular Development. He said that he would squat three times a week, using a similar program each day. For each workout he would load the bar to a weight that he could perform fairly easily for three repetitions. Then, across a period of many hours (with very long rests between sets, during which he often drank a quart of milk), he would perform numerous sets with this weight. Although he made tremendous progress on this program, he reported that his progress was so rapid that after a while the weights he was handling felt very heavy on his shoulders. Therefore, he began to perform some quarter squats with weights heavier than those he was able to full squat. Using this approach, he soon became accustomed to supporting very heavy weights on his shoulders quite comfortably.

After a while Paul's progress on this program ceased. He decided to change his program radically by performing sets of ten reps for a time. This change in his program stimulated new progress for a time.

Another program change involved the concept of progressive movement (gradually increasing the range of motion used in an exercise). In order to implement this idea, Paul dug a hole in the ground that was deep enough to allow him to step in the hole and to have his waist approximately at the level of the ground. He would roll a bar over the hole and proceed to perform quarter squats. He would begin with a weight that was approximately 100 lb. above his best performance in the full squat and would perform twenty to twenty-five reps with this weight for two sets. This program would be performed every day. Approximately 3" of soil would be added to the hole every third day, and the number of repetitions that were performed per set would be reduced by three. After Anderson had gotten to a point at which he was moving the bar as far as possible for two reps, he would rest for two to three days and then try for a maximum squat. He reported a significant improvement in his squat following such a program.

Still another program that Anderson favored involved the extensive use of eccentric training. He recommended sets of three reps in the squat with weights well in excess of the lifter's best squat. During those sets, the athlete would resist downward force applied to the bar by spotters (who offered extra resistance at the easiest point in the squat and assistance in recovering from the bottom position after each rep).

Sometimes Paul would mix repetitions when he trained, performing early sets in the workout for ten reps, following those sets with a heavy set of three reps and then finishing with a set of ten reps. One of his favorite programs involved performing alternating sets in the full squat and the quarter squat using a pyramid kind of program. He would finish the workout with a three sets of one-legged squats.

Paul suggested linking several very different routines together in succession. For example, he recommended beginning with a program that involved three sets of ten reps in the squat. Then, after several weeks, the lifter should move to a program with a core of three sets of three reps with heavier weights. A third routine called for performing quarter and full squats in alternating sets. A fourth program consisted of alternating sets of full squats, quarter squats, full squats and one-legged squats while standing with the squatting leg on a bench. (This entire sequence would be performed three times in one workout.)

Paul had similar programs for the pull and press. His unique idea for training these latter muscle groups (lower back and arms and shoulders) was to invert the body while exercising (he would perform deadlifts in a decline bench with a pulley and would do handstand presses to build his pressing power). Paul believed that one of the reasons he had progressed more rapidly in the squat than in the pull or press early in his career was that during the squat blood was drawn to the legs, but in the press or pull it was being drained away from the area while the exercises were being performed. By inverting the body, Paul was increasing the blood supply to the area being exercised, and he believed that this improved his rate of progress. (While no scientific evidence has yet been developed to support this theory, Paul apparently achieved better results from his inversion program then when he trained more conventionally.)

Anderson never reported with any degree of precision on the loads he actually lifted, but several things are clear regarding the Anderson approach. One point is that he believed in significant work with sub-maximum loads. Those who saw Paul train always reported that he appeared to be lifting within himself. He was not performing set after set with grinding effort, but he did often perform many sets over the course of a day. Second, he believed in the use of partial movements and eccentric contractions as an adjunct to full movements (but he always cautioned that at least some of a lifter's training should always be on the full movement). Third, he believed in variety in training and in changing the program regularly. Fourth, and perhaps most importantly, he believed in

Table 2

Workout	Week 1	Week 2	Week 3
1	75%x5x4/80%x5x3	80%x5x3/75%x5x4	75%x3x4
2	85%x5x5/90%x5x1-4	85%x5x6/85%x3x5-6	85%x3x3/80%x3x3*
3	60%x3x4	60%x3x4	60%x3x4\65%x3x4

* An extra set can be added here if the athlete tolerates it well.

experimenting. Paul never had a real coach. He devised his own programs through trial and error, and most of the time he had no idea what the rest of the world was doing. While he may have wasted time with programs that more experienced lifters and coaches might have told him would never work, he was not burdened by the baggage of slavishly adhering to whatever training program was in fashion at the time. He created programs that worked for him, and the reward was some of the greatest performances in weightlifting and powerlifting history.

Two Soviet Squatting Routines

While reports on exercise specific training programs and exact percentage loads by exercise are rare in the Eastern European literature, both the 1974 and the 1976 USSR Yearbooks (annual publications that for many years presented some of the most interesting research and analysis in the Soviet literature) presented specific programs for improving an athlete's squatting strength. The 1974 version of the squat routine constitutes a significantly more modest load than the 1976 version. Both claim to have produced excellent results for the athletes who used them, but in my experience the 1974 version is more effective for most athletes.

It should be noted that apart from the differences between the squat routines in terms of the severity of the exercise, the 1974 version of the program appears to be meant as a steady training approach for the athlete, while the 1976 version is intended more as a squat specialization routine that is to be performed when the loading that the athlete is employing in other exercises has been diminished.

The 1974, program, which was reported on by V. Maslaev, employed a three week cycle, with loads being very similar and heavy during the first two weeks and then lighter during the third ("unloading") week. Under this program the athlete squats three times a week (See Table 2). In the first workout of the week, the weights range from 65% to 75% of maximum for three to four sets of five repetitions. The second workout employs weights that are 75% to 85% of maximum for five to six sets of five reps. The third workout in the week is the lightest, with the weights lifted being 60% to 65% of maximum for three to four sets of three reps. Maslaev suggests that if the athlete accepts the prescribed load comfortably during the first three week cycle, the intensity of the heavier days of the first, or the first and second weeks, can be increased.

In all workouts the athlete performs a warm-up set in the squat with 50% to 55% of that lifter's maximum. (In the heavier workouts—ones which involve a weight in excess of 80%—an additional warm-up set with 65% of the lifter's maximum is performed.) The table that follows depicts the pattern of the heavy sets for each training session. Where a slash appears in the table, the load described before the mark is the basic program that Maslaev prescribes, and the load that appears after the slash mark is the one he suggests if the lifter finds that he or she can accept a load greater than that provided by the basic program. This second set of loads would be attempted during the second three week cycle that the lifter performed.

The routine displayed in the table can be modified in a number of other ways. The athlete can perform three heavier weeks in a row and follow that with two unloading weeks. An athlete who has particular trouble with recovering from the clean (even though his or her back squat may be 25% or more in excess of his or her clean, a level of leg strength normally considered to be adequate in relation to the C&J) can substitute front squats for back squats during the unloading week.

Maslaev suggests that the above routine be followed during the competitive period, but he recommends that the reps performed on the heavy sets be reduced to three and the weights lifted during the unloading week be reduced to the 60% to 75% range. During the last squat workout, which he suggests be carried out two to three days before the meet, the athlete should lift 65% to 75% of maximum for two to three sets of three reps.

Maslaev also makes a number of other interesting points. He suggests that while the above routine constitutes a considerable training load for an athlete who performs 1,000 reps a month in all exercises combined, it should be continued until satisfactory results in the squat have been achieved. He also notes that the actual loads lifted depend not on the total load lifted by the athlete but on the athlete's individual work capacity. Therefore, the selection of the proper loads depends on the athlete's own individual characteristics. He also suggests that advanced lifters can improve their squats by from 20 kg. to

Table 3

Workout	Load	Workout	Load	Workout	Load
2	80%x3x6	8	80%x6x6	14	95%x3x3
4	80%x4x6	10	85%x5x5	16	100%x2x2
6	80%x5x6	12	90%x4x4	18	105%x1

30 kg. (with the lighter lifters improving more in terms of total kg. and the heavier athletes improving by a larger number of kg).

In the 1976 version of the squat program, the loading pattern is somewhat simpler than in the program that was explained in 1974. Essentially, lighter and heavier loads are alternated (a lighter workout is followed by a heavier one). As in the 1974 program, squats are performed three times a week. But the program runs for six weeks rather than three, and a maximum (105% of the lifter's previous best squat) is scheduled for the concluding workout in the six week series.

The warm-up sets (at least those that are listed in the program) consist of one set of two reps with 70%, followed by a set of two reps with 75%. After these two sets, the lifter moves on to the heaviest load of the day. As has been indicated, lighter and heavier workouts are alternated, but unlike the 1974 program, the weights lifted on the lighter days of the 1976 program remain the same throughout the program. All odd numbered workouts (the first, third, fifth, etc.) are performed with a weight that constitutes 80% of the lifter's maximum. That weight is lifted for six sets of two reps. In contrast, the even numbered workouts show an increasing level of intensity throughout the program. (See Table 3.)

As you can see, both the volume and intensity of the heavy day increase in weeks one to three: the volume by virtue of the total number reps performed and the intensity by virtue of the number of reps per set. (The more reps performed, the greater is the intensity, as measured by the effort that is required to perform the lifts.) In the fourth through the sixth weeks, the intensity of the heavy days increases in terms of absolute intensity, but the number of reps performed diminishes.

I know a number of lifters who have tried the 1974 or 1976 squat routines. Several have reported success with the 1974 program, but I have never met a lifter who has completed the 1976 routine as written (i.e., reached a 105% squat at the end of the sixth week). Most lifters using this latter program report improved performance during the early weeks of the routine, but most are overtrained by the second half of the cycle. Lifters who have modified the program by beginning with weights 5% to 10% lighter than are called for under the program have had success with it.

Why this difference in success rates between the programs? Despite their superficial similarities (e.g., both routines have three workouts a week and weeks with differing loads), these programs are

structurally quite different. Detecting these differences is simpler if we match the lengths of the programs by simply repeating the 1974 program for a second three week period, so that we have two programs that run for six weeks. Under the 1974 program the athlete is only performing one heavy squat workout a week, while under the 1976 program a heavy workout is performed every four to five days. The 1974 program provides for an unloading week after two heavy weeks (two such weeks in every six week period), whereas the 1976 program has no unloading weeks (although it could be argued that the first two weeks are essentially unloading weeks because no weights above 80% are handled and those sets are performed with no more than five reps).

Perhaps the greatest difference between the programs exists in the number of truly heavy workouts that occur across a six week period. Under the 1974 program there are no workouts that could be considered absolutely all out. Four workouts with 85% of the lifter's maximum are performed, and both programs require the athlete to lift that 85% load for sets of five reps. Most athletes can perform 85% of their maximums for five repetitions without an all out effort (some athletes can lift as much as 90% of their maximums for five repetitions). However, the athlete is called upon to perform repeated sets with 85% (five to six sets in all), so for most lifters, this workout will be quite strenuous. Looking at this program then, we can say that most athletes would be challenged by the four truly heavy workouts across the six week period (probably to the point at which a training effect would be generated). As result, progress could be expected.

In the 1976 workout plan the athlete handles a comparable load to that of the 1974 program on the first heavy day of the fourth week and then is required to perform 90% for four sets of four reps in the second heavy workout of that week. For some athletes (those who can perform five reps with 90% of their maximum) this will constitute a difficult but manageable workout. For other athletes (those who can normally perform only three reps with 90%), this workout would require a personal record effort on the first set and then would require the athlete to repeat that performance for three more sets. This would constitute a Herculean effort for such athletes, one which might exhaust their reserves for some time. However, there is little time to rest, as four to five days later the athlete must perform three sets of three reps with 95% of the lifter's maximum. For virtually all lifters this would represent a record breaking effort (since few if any lifters can perform even one set of three reps with 95% of their maximum). Repeated sets with 95% would truly push the athlete to new performance heights but would also probably break down the athlete's muscles to the point where they might require several weeks to recuperate fully. If the lifter survives such an effort, four to five days later the athlete must cope with a perhaps even more challenging prospect: a workout in which the lifter must lift his or her previous best for two sets of two reps. Such a workout would constitute approximately a 5% performance improvement for most lifters. Four to five days later the athlete must repeat this level of effort with a single 105% of maximum effort.

The most obvious problem with the 105% day is that since the lifters has had so many heavy workouts over such a short period immediately preceding that workout, the lifter is probably exhausted by the time he or she reaches this last workout in the program. The only situation in which this would not be true is one in which the athlete had actually improved his or her abilities to the point at which the load lifted did not constitute as heavy a load as the percentages lifted would imply. (If the athlete's abilities had actually improved by 5% by the end of the fourth week, the 90% of previous best workout would only amount to 85%, a weight that could be handled comfortably for four sets of four reps. Similarly, the 95% workout performed four to five days would only constitute 90% of load, which could surely be performed (though not easily) for three sets of three reps.

But very few lifters indeed can improve by 5% in a matter of weeks, and certainly such a rate of progress could not be sustained over several six week periods in succession. Therefore, this latter program constitutes an overload for most athletes, and that is why they do not progress as hoped. The athletes who begin their programs at a level 5% lower than is prescribed by the program have had far greater success because they are performing within their capabilities for a greater portion of the cycle.

Ed Coan's Squat Program

Ed Coan is considered by many to be the greatest powerlifter competing today and one of the greatest of all time. He excels in all three lifts but is particularly well known for his squatting and deadlifting strength. He recently produced a series of three video tapes (one each on the squat, deadlift and bench press) which explain his technique and training methods. (See the Bibliography for further details.) Ed's program calls for squatting once a week, working up to one set with the heaviest weight that he will handle that day. He will also perform one set each of leg extensions, leg curls, one-legged leg presses and seated calf raises.

Although Ed does not believe in expressing his workouts in percentages, the following table summarizes the percentages of the maximum weight that Ed hit in training two weeks before a major competition and at the competition itself (the actual weight squatted at the competition was 975 lb.).

These percentages may appear a little hard to understand at first glance (they hover around 80% for the first few weeks, decline and then rise steadily through the rest of the cycle). However, there is a hidden factor: Ed does not use knee wraps or a supportive suit during the first four weeks of the program and only uses wraps for the second four weeks. The supportive suits and wraps worn by powerlifters can increase squatting performance by 15% to 25%. Therefore, the first four weeks of Ed's routine are rather strenuous. Those weeks are followed by several weeks of gradual build up in intensity. Then intensity remains rather high during the last few weeks (with the weight on the bar and the number of reps decreasing over those weeks).

Ed performs deadlifts and other forms of heavy back work several days later. No other leg work is performed for the balance of the week. Although Ed only squats once a week, his routine has certainly been effective for him. It may not be a suitable program for weightlifters, but it certainly provides food for thought for those who argue that an athlete can get strong only by squatting every day.

A Final Word on Strength Programs

The programs presented above merely scratch the surface of the rich array of approaches that champion lifters have used to gain strength. They are meant to provide concrete examples of the principles that have already been discussed (and to show how some of those principles have been violated and strength gains have come nonetheless). It as not always necessary for all of

Table 4

Week 1	77.4%x3	Week 7	83.1%x5	Week 13	95.4%x3
Week 2	79%x3	Week 8	85.1%x5	Week 14	97.4%x2
Week 3	80.5%x2	Week 9	87.2%x5	Week 15	100%x1
Week 4	82.1%x2	Week 10	89.2%x5	Week 16	84.6%x5
Week 5	79%x5	Week 11	91.3%x5	Week 17	100%x1
Week 6	81%x5	Week 12	93.3%x3		

the training factors to be applied perfectly in order for improvements to be make. Nevertheless, applying the proper principles leads to even faster and more consistent improvements. Unfortunately, the final word on which factors are most significant has yet to be written. In the meantime we can all enjoy the challenge of building strength with our own experience, judgment and ingenuity as our guide.

Special Training Considerations For Developing Power Together With Strength

Generally speaking, the weightlifter who increases his or her strength will also experience an increase in the power that he or she can generate when lifting heavy weights. This is particularly true in the exercises on which the athletes trains regularly. However, if no specific effort is made by the athlete to develop power at the same time he or she is training for strength, improvements in strength will be grossly disproportional in relation to improvements in power. This is not a desirable situation for a weightlifter. Weightlifters need great power as well as great strength. In fact, when they are performing the classic lifts, weightlifters develop the highest power outputs that have ever been measured by sports scientists.

The major factor responsible for the power outputs that weightlifters generate is the strength they possess as a result of their specialized training. (When two athletes are equal in terms of their speed capabilities, the stronger athlete will be able to move a heavy weight faster, thereby generating greater power.) Another important factor which contributes to the strength capabilities of weightlifters is their constant focus on producing large power outputs when they train and compete. It is possible to lift a heavy weight without generating a very high power output if that weight is lifted very slowly. Even when a lifter produces a very large force when lifting, lifting at a slow speed assures that the power values developed by the lifter will be relatively low. In contrast, if the athlete wishes to perform a snatch or C&J, he or she must move the bar fast enough to be able to move under the bar and catch it on the shoulders or at arm's length. This requires moving a heavy bar with speeds of as great as 2 meters per second. The amount of the weight and the speed of the bar combine to yield a tremendous power output.

Although a strong athlete may have the potential to move heavy weight at a relatively high speed, that athlete will not be able to do so unless he or she has practiced moving the bar as quickly as possible. Merely exerting the effort to move a heavy weight quickly will train the athlete to develop higher power outputs. However, if an athlete never attempts to move the bar as rapidly as possible, he or she will not be able to utilize his or her strength to its maximum potential in terms of generating power outputs.

Weightlifters learn this fact by a process of trial and error, so most of them attempt to move the bar as explosively as possible in most of the exercises that they perform (except for "remedial" exercises that are performed to prevent or rehabilitate injuries or correct strength imbalances). Recent research has confirmed the validity of this approach. What research and experience also suggests is that varying the speed and the load in a lifter's training increases the rate at which the athlete develops power..

Specifically, if a weightlifter lifts a weight that is lighter than his or her maximum in the snatch, the lifter can lift the bar faster than when lifting a maximum weight. Practicing with lighter weights seems to improve the lifter's ability to move a heavier weight more rapidly. Similarly, selecting a weight that is somewhat in excess of the athlete's maximum snatch and attempting to lift the bar as rapidly as possible can enable the athlete to move his or her current maximum weight faster (thereby increasing the lifter's effective maximum). Therefore, training with both heavier than maximum and lighter than maximum loads can improve a lifter's performance in the actual lift as long as the athlete attempts to move whatever weight he or she is lifting as rapidly as possible. The application of this approach will become obvious as exercises and programs for developing all of a weightlifter's capabilities are discussed in later chapters of this book.

The case is similar with respect to actions that involve the sudden reversal of direction. When a lifter performs a jerk, he or she bends the knees and then reverses direction to drive the bar upward. The lifter could slowly bend the legs, even pause when the legs are bent as far as the lifter wishes, and then drive the bar upward. However, the athlete is able to enjoy the benefits of a mechanical and neuromuscular "rebound" if the reversal of direction occurs quickly.

If the athlete practices a rapid reversal of the downward action he or she generates in preparation for driving the bar up, that athlete will become more proficient at reversing direction and at generating upward force after doing so. Consequently, the athlete will be able to make better use of the available mechanical and neuromuscular rebounds and thereby generate a greater upward thrust against the bar (ultimately jerking more). This is the principle underlying the practice of plyometrics, a subject which has already been touched upon in this chapter and which will be developed further later in this book.

As a general rule, the athlete who is strong relative to the amount of power that he or she can generate needs to devote more time to moving lighter weights faster in his or her training and to moving heavy weights ever faster. The athlete who generates as much power as his or her strength permits must work on developing more basic strength. However, once an athlete has exploited his or her inherent ability to generate maximum speed with a heavy weight, only increases in strength (while maintaining the ability to generate the greatest power possible with a heavy weight) will improve the athlete's performance in weightlifting.

This is a special condition of weightlifting, where only a certain bar speed is required to give the athlete time to move under the bar. Achieving faster speeds with a given weight may make lifting that weight easier, but it will not directly increase the amount an athlete can lift. Only lifting a heavier weight at the required speed will increase the athlete's competitive result. This is in direct contrast to weight throwing events (e.g., the shot put and discus) in which the weight of the implement remains the same and the objective is to move the weight ever faster so that a greater distance can be covered by the weight when it is released

Before leaving the subject of power development, it is appropriate to mention a second important factor in power generation: proper technique. Technique is important on at least two levels. First, the athlete who employs the proper mechanics when lifting will utilize his or her strength and power capabilities in the most effective way (i.e., the athlete will use most appropriately the levers that his or her body supplies to impart force to the external object of interest, the bar). Second, the athlete who contracts his or her muscles in the most effective sequence will maximize the power that he or she can generate with those muscles (i.e., the athlete will use his or her muscles in a way that will move his or her body levers with the largest possible amount of force and speed that his or her muscles are capable of generating).

Developing Flexibility For Weightlifting

Introduction

In the sport of weightlifting there are two opposite schools of thought with respect to the subject of flexibility. There are those who ignore the subject altogether. They view flexibility as a fixed physical quality, such as adult height or eye color. The range of motion that a person is capable of, they say, is essentially dictated by that person's "conformation." The best that an athlete can hope for is to work with what has been given by nature. This is a most unfortunate point of view, both because flexibility is quite amenable to training and because a lack of flexibility can lead to injury and/or to the utilization of faulty technique. Faulty technique can itself cause injury and, perhaps even worse, enormous frustration. (Frustration can be even worse than injury because it has unnecessarily ended far more lifting careers than injuries ever have.)

At the other end of the flexibility spectrum are those who worship flexibility and see it as the answer to all human problems, whether physical or mental. They spend incredible periods of time stretching, often concentrating on areas of the body that are totally unrelated to weightlifting. They take the greatest pleasure in assuming contorted positions and challenging others to duplicate their feats. They ignore the hazards of stretching a joint to the point of doing damage to it, whether directly or indirectly (the latter by enabling the joint to assume a weak mechanical position during the performance of a lift). They ignore the waste of time and energy that their stretching programs lead to.

In reality, weightlifters need to be quite flexible in a number of areas of their bodies. A study done at a recent Olympiad found weightlifters to be among the most flexible of all athletes, second only to gymnasts. Flexibility is necessary for the athlete to be able to assume certain functional positions while imparting force to the bar (or preparing to do so) and to receive the force of the bar (as in the low squat or split position). There is absolutely no substitute for adequate flexibility, and it is virtually pointless for an athlete to embark on the process of learning weightlifting technique if he or she does not possess the requisite flexibility. If an athlete attempts to do this, the result will be the enormous sense of frustration, arising out of a lack of ability to execute a lift properly, as well as exposure to injury. Exposure to injury occurs because weightlifting technique is entirely functional in nature. While good technique is a pleasure to watch, its basis is not aesthetic but mechanical. The positions that are assumed while lifting with proper technique are designed to assist in the application of maximal force to or the receipt of maximal force from the bar. Faulty technique results in assuming less than optimal mechanical positions, which places undue stress on the body and therefore can expose it unnecessarily to injury.

Flexibility training can have one further beneficial effect for the weightlifter, that of preventing and treating injuries. There is considerable evidence that inadequate flexibility increase the likelihood that an athlete will be injured, and many athletes and clinicians have reported the value of stretching in treating tendinitis and low back pain and in rehabilitation from a wide variety of musculoskeletal injuries. Stretching and its relation to injury treatment will be addressed later in this chapter. We will begin with a discussion of the nature of flexibility.

Functional Flexibility for Weightlifting

A limited number of good general texts have been written on the subject of flexibility. Some of these are listed in the Bibliography. Our focus in this chapter will be on the specific areas of the body that require flexibility in order to perform the classical lifts of weightlifting and on how to develop that flexibility to an optimal level. We will begin with a discussion of the general principles of developing flexibility.

Muscles Are the Primary Focus of Proper Flexibility Training

Virtually all of the tissues in the human body have the ability to undergo a certain degree of deformation when force is applied to them (i.e., a change in shape or size) and to be restored to their original condition without suffering any damage. Both the amount of force applied to the body and the size of the area over which it is applied affect the stress that is experienced by the tissue receiving the force. "Elasticity" is the scientific term used to describe the capacity of a tissue to return to its original size or shape after it has been stretched. The relationship of a tissue's length after stress has been applied to what it was before the stress is called its "strain." A tissue's elastic limit is the smallest stress that causes a permanent strain when applied to a tissue (a condition in which the tissue will return to its original length once the stress is removed). This permanently stretched condition is also referred to as "plastic deformation."

While it is possible to stretch all of the soft tissues of the body (e.g., muscles, tendons and ligaments), muscle tissue has by far the greatest potential for increasing its length. Moreover, muscle is also the tissue most likely to increase in flexibility without being damaged the process. When tendons and ligaments are stretched past a certain point, they actually lose elasticity (the ability to return to normal length) and strength. Stretched ligaments can seriously undermine the stability of a joint and therefore are to be strictly avoided (which is possible through careful stretching). Laxity in joints has been implicated in certain kinds of injuries as well as in the development of arthritic conditions.

Muscles are under tension in their natural state (a muscle removed from the body shortens approximately 10% independent of any contraction), but like tendons and ligaments, they can be overstretched, although this is not as common an occurrence as stretching a tendon or ligament. Muscles have a far greater ability to adapt to flexibility training by developing a permanently greater range of motion without losing the ability to contract to their original length or to contract with maximal force. Muscles are able to do this partly because they are capable of growing longer by adding sacromeres, which are the sub-units of muscle fiber which run in series throughout the length of the fiber. (This characteristic of muscle tissue is explained in more detail in Appendix II, which covers some of the scientific bases of sport performance.) Therefore, the proper focus of flexibility development is on increasing the length and flexibility of the muscles.

Research suggests that the type and duration of a stretch and the temperature of the tissue that is being stretched influence the amount of elongation that results from a stretch and whether a tissue's elongation is permanent. Higher force and shorter duration stretching relies primarily on elastic deformation while lower force and longer duration stretching leads to a monoplastic deformation. Tissue with a higher temperature will stretch more than tissue with a lower temperature when the same amount of force is applied. The tissue itself will have a lower tensile strength when it has been heated, but the potential for injury that arises out of such weakness is believed to be overcome by an increase in the extensibility of the tissue when it has been warmed. Finally, there is less weakening in the structure of a tissue that is stretched when it is warmer. In addition, when elongation is maintained as the tissue cools, the degree of plastic deformation will be greater than when no force is applied to the tissue during cooling.

A muscle that is stretched rapidly and then held will gradually lose its tension over time. This process is referred to as "stress relaxation." When a constant force is applied, a muscle will slowly lengthen through a process called "creep." The tension that develops when a muscle is stretched is known as the muscle's "stretch response" (a response that results from the properties of the muscle and not from any involvement of the nervous system). This is contrasted with the "stretch reflex," which is a reaction within the central nervous system to the stretch.

There is a trade-off between the force used to generate a stretch and the degree to which a muscle that has been stretched retains its position. When a low level of force is applied to a muscle, it requires a greater length of time for a muscle to reach a given muscle length than when a greater force is applied. However, when the force applied is removed, the muscle stretched with the lower level of force retains a greater degree of its length than the muscle that was stretched with a greater force. There is a similar relationship with respect to the plastic (i.e., permanent) deformation of muscle, with lower levels of force leading to greater degree of plastic deformation.

When connective tissue is permanently stretched, it loses some if its tensile strength. This occurs to a lesser degree when the tissue has been stretched with lower force at greater duration than with higher forces for shorter durations. When stimulation is applied to muscle, nerves within the muscle discharge at a rapid rate. As the force is maintained, the rate of discharge decreases.

It should be noted that normal growth and maturation can affect flexibility. For instance, during periods of rapid bone growth, such growth can outpace corresponding increases in the range of motion of soft tissues. A common example of this is diminished flexibility in the hamstring muscles of young people whose legs have quickly grown longer during a growth spurt.

The Specificity of Flexibility

As with so many physical qualities, flexibility is specific. There is no correlation between the flexibility of one joint and another. People who are flexible in one area of their body are not necessarily flexible in another. Consequently, while one athlete may be flexible in most joints and another may be inflexible in most joints, most athletes will be somewhere in between these extremes (i.e., flexible in some joints and inflexible in others).

Types of Stretching

There are several methods of stretching. For many years, the most popular method was "ballistic" stretching. This method of stretching involves repeatedly swinging or bouncing through a full range of motion. Rapid toe touches or high kicks are examples of the ballistic approach.

Ballistic Stretching

Ballistic stretching has been criticized because of its supposed potential for causing injury and its allegedly lesser value in improving range of motion relative to other forms of stretching. Few carefully controlled studies comparing the incidence of injury when using ballistic as opposed to other kinds of flexibility training are available.

It seems plausible that if rapid force is applied to stretch muscles beyond their normal range of motion, injuries can result. (Many injuries, after all, occur when the musculotendonous-tendon unit is forced to go through a greater range of motion, or the same range of motion under a greater load, than was previously experienced.) However, this is generally not the precise pattern that occurs when ballistic stretching is performed. Most often, a greater range of motion is achieved only gradually, through successive repetitions of the stretching exercise.

My guess is that injuries that have occurred during ballistic stretching have most often been the result of overdoing the activity or have been due to a predisposition to injury because of prior activities. During a ballistic stretch, momentum can push a muscle through a greater range of motion than is normal, and this can have a positive

training effect. However, when the momentum is too great, the overload can cause damage instead of improvement. In addition, an athlete who initiates a workout with ballistic stretching may not notice a slight injury, or predisposition to injury that has developed during or following a previous workout, until it is too late (i.e., until after further damage has been done).

Static Stretching

"Static stretching" is a stretching method that came into vogue in the 1970s. When using this method, the athlete slowly moves toward the full range of motion in a given position but stops short of the point where significant pain is felt. The position is then generally held for twenty to thirty seconds, with the range of motion gradually increased as the muscles relax (some trainers recommend that the stretched position be held for as long as sixty seconds). When an athlete uses this method of stretching he or she often uses some form of externally applied force to reach and hold the stretch position; for example, when sitting on the floor with the legs straight and moving the torso forward to stretch the hamstrings, the athlete may place the hands under the legs and then use the arms to pull the torso toward the legs.

There is no doubt that this form of stretching can increase flexibility substantially. However, many athletes have not been satisfied with the results that they have attained exclusively through static stretching, and some feel that this kind of stretching has overstretched their ligaments and actually aggravated certain injuries. At least one recent study that compared ballistic stretching with static stretching found that muscle soreness and the levels of creatine kinase (an indicator of muscle damage) were higher with static stretching than with ballistic stretching.

PNF Stretching

A third approach, called "fatigue stretching" or "proprioceptive neuromuscular facilitation" (PNF), generally involves the use of a partner. While there are a number of varieties of PNF, perhaps the most popular variant is one in which the athlete assumes a starting position for the stretch which is similar to that used in static stretching. While in this position, the athlete pushes (isometrically) in the opposite direction of the stretch, against resistance supplied by the partner, for four to six seconds. Then the athlete stretches further than the original stretched position (which is made relatively easy by the relaxation that takes place in the muscles that were just isometrically contracted). This process is generally repeated two more times in one set. Another example would be a stretch in which the lifter sits on the floor with the legs straight and stretches to touch the toes with the hands. The athlete's partner places his or her hands in the middle of the athlete's back, and the athlete pushes back against the partner's hands (the partner resists so that the athlete is performing an isometric contraction). Then the athlete stretches further toward the feet and when the furthest position had been assumed (without significant discomfort), the athlete holds that position for several seconds and then pushes back against the partner again. This process is repeated one or two more times. Fatigue stretching generally will permit the athlete to assume a stretched position that is more extreme than would have been possible with a simple static stretch.

Still other common approaches to stretching are: passive, passive active, active assisted and active methods. Let us look at how each type would be applied to the same exercise that was used to illustrate the PNF technique. A passive stretch involves a partner pushing the subject's torso toward his or her legs, with the subject neither resisting nor assisting. In a passive-active stretch the partner pushes the subject's torso as close to the legs as possible and then removes his or her hands while the subject tries to maintain that position by using the abdominal muscles and other muscles that pull in the opposite direction of the muscles being stretched. In an active-assisted stretch the athlete brings the torso toward the legs as far as he or she can and then relies on a partner to push the torso closer to the legs. In an active stretch the athlete performs the stretch without any externally applied assistance. Most of these varieties of stretching are performed in essentially a static manner (i.e., with the most extreme position reached during the exercise being held in a static fashion).

The selection of a stretching method should be determined by the purposes of the flexibility training that is being undertaken and the capabilities of the subject who is undertaking the training. A person who is weak in the muscles that work opposite the muscles being stretched to achieve a good position for stretching will benefit from passive stretching (which is why this type of stretching is so often used by physical therapists and others who are working with subjects who are ill or injured). The primary drawback of passive stretching is that it tends to increase the subject's passive range of motion but not necessarily his or her active one. This is troubling because there is some evidence that the larger the difference between a person's active and passive ranges of motion, the greater the risk of injury. (Interestingly, full-range-of-motion strength training appears to influence a person's active range of motion.) Consequently, athletes should not be encouraged to rely on passive flexibility training to improve their flexibility for their sport.

A New Method of Stretching: "Active Isolated"

One final method of stretching deserves some attention. Referred to as "active-isolated" (AI), it has gained in popularity among runners in recent years. It shows significant promise for improving flexibility in a manner that avoids the most of the drawbacks of ballistic or static stretching.

When using AI training, the athlete stretches his or her body as far as possible and then assists himself or herself to go further, until a point of mild irritation is achieved. That position is held for two seconds or a little less. The athletes then returns to the starting position, relaxes for two seconds and repeats the exercises. Two sets of eight to twelve repetitions are generally performed in this manner, often at the beginning and end of the workout. Using the exercise that was previously used to illustrate the other kinds of stretching as an example, an athlete doing this seated hamstring stretch would bring the torso toward the legs as much as possible. The athlete might then place the hands underneath the thighs and use the arms to pull the torso closer to the legs (alternatively, the athlete would place a rope at the bottom of the feet and pull against the rope to bring the torso closer to the legs). This stretch would be held for two seconds or a little less, and then the athlete would relax and let the torso return to a relaxed position (even as far back as the floor). After relaxing for two seconds in that position, the athlete would repeat the stretch (for up to eleven more repetitions). Many athletes who have found passive stretching to be painful or ineffective have benefited significantly from AI stretching.

I have found this stretching method to be very useful for increasing a weightlifter's flexibility in very weightlifting specific areas. For example, an athlete might increase his or her flexibility in the low squat position by squatting down with a fixed pole or railing in front of him or her. The athlete would squat down to a comfortably low position, grasp the railing or pole and use it to push himself or herself into a lower position, which would then be held for two seconds. The athlete would then stand up from the squat, squat down again and repeat the stretch.

The Importance of Combining Stretching Methods

In recent years research has begun to suggest that none of the traditional stretching methods may be optimal for athletes. Ballistic stretching may have some risks and may not be especially effective in improving flexibility. Static and fatigue stretching may have limited carryover value to actual athletic events, because these events generally require flexibility under dynamic conditions (i.e., relatively rapid movements into the most extreme positions required by the sport in question). Some studies have shown that the range of motion (ROM) achieved by static stretching may not be achieved when the stretch is performed quickly.

Other studies have shown that a slow, controlled, intermittent force of given intensity develops ROM faster than a static force of similar intensity. In view of the specificity and the limitations of each of the forms of stretching, it appears that a complex (i.e., combination) of flexibility training methods is likely to yield the greatest and most functional improvements in flexibility for the sport of weightlifting (and most other sports). And the complex should always include some dynamic flexibility training.

Training for Increased Flexibility

Like all training that addresses physical qualities related to weightlifting, flexibility training must be carefully designed. Above all, it must not be neglected. While flexibility work requires less time and equipment than other kinds of weightlifting training, there is often a tendency among lifters to perform their weight workouts but to neglect flexibility work. At the beginning of the workout, there is a desire to get to the lifts, and at the end the athlete is anxious to get to the showers and on to the other aspects of life. If the athlete does too little flexibility training, the desired improvements will not occur. But, as with all forms of training, fatigue and injury can result if too much training is performed.

Flexibility will not improve unless a given part of the body is required to move through a range of motion that is greater than usual (i.e., the flexibility training stimulus must reach a certain threshold). A second principle is that the stimulus must be administered frequently enough so that the muscles involved have not lost the training effect that has occurred before the stimulus is applied again. Finally, the duration of the stimulus is an important contributor to the training effect. All things being equal, the longer a stimulus is applied, the more profound will be the training effect.

Any number of combinations of these factors (range of motion, frequency and duration) will achieve results, but some element of all three factors is necessary to generate a training effect. Obviously, the greater the degree to which all three factors are present, the greater the training stimulus, but there is a limit to the amount of stimulus that can be responded to at one time, and any excess stimulus is likely to lead to overstress and injury rather than improvement. Athletes who overdo their flexibility training (particularly when they go from performing little such training to performing a great deal of it) often experience significant soreness in the connective tissues (which sometimes causes those who most need

such training to give it up). Therefore, care must be exercised in formulating the program.

The athlete must find the types, intervals and intensities of flexibility training that yield the best results for him or her (in conjunction with other training). He or she must identify the areas of the body and the positions which require the most attention in terms of his or her flexibility training. Once a desired level of flexibility has been attained, the athlete must work to maintain flexibility at an adequate level and must do so regularly. But there is no need to go much beyond the range of motion that is actually required.

An approach to flexibility training that can generally be recommended is to use static stretching or AI stretching to enhance flexibility in key muscle groups. This is particularly true when the athlete is attempting to increase flexibility in the extreme positions required of weightlifting that have already been described. However, after various specialized stretching exercises have been performed, the lifter should always endeavor to achieve the desired range of motion in the exercises related to lifting. For example, after stretching to achieve a good squat position, it is always a good idea to do a few sets of squats with the empty bar or a small amount of weight in order to stress the adoption of a correct position in an exercise that is closely related to the lifting movement itself.

A good general procedure for static stretching is to assume the position for the stretching exercise (after a general warm-up or after a workout) and then to move to a point in that exercise in which mild tension or resistance is felt. That position should then be held for from several to approximately thirty seconds while the athlete concentrates on relaxing the muscles being stretched. During this period the athlete should experience a lessening of tension in those muscles. If this does not occur (or if the athlete experiences sensations of pain, burning or quivering of the muscles being stretched), he or she should ease off the stretch to assume a slightly less extreme position. Once a feeling of relaxation has been achieved, the athlete should attempt to stretch a little further, until a feeling of moderate tension has once again been achieved. This position should be held for ten to sixty seconds while the athlete "fine tunes" the experience. He or she should be striving for relaxation and a slightly greater range of motion. If there is too much tension, the purpose of the exercise will be defeated. Too little effort to stretch to the lower edge of discomfort will result in the training effect not being realized.

The appropriate method for AI stretching has already been discussed. I have generally had better success with this method than the static stretching method, but both methods have their place.

When performing flexibility training, it should always be remembered that in weightlifting the need for flexibility (as opposed to strength or speed) has its limits. Flexibility is required to attain correct lifting positions, but flexibility beyond that can result in the overstitching of joints to the point where ligaments are placed under unnecessary stress. A squat position that is so low that the buttocks touch the floor may be interesting and dramatic, but the lifter may also overstretch the knee joints in such a position and make the recovery to the standing position exceedingly difficult. Consequently, the value of training to assume such a position is highly questionable. (Obviously, the athlete who naturally assumes such a position accepts this and arranges his or her technique so that somewhat less extreme positions are assumed while lifting.)

Similarly, an athlete should generally strive to attain sufficient flexibility in the elbow joint to straighten the arm fully. This enables a lifter to support weights comfortably overhead. But an arm that goes any further than such a position tends to be less stable than one that can only fully straighten. This subjects a lifter to unnecessary risk of injury to the elbow. Therefore, any training to achieve fuller range of motion on the part of a lifter who has achieved adequate flexibility would be wasteful and perhaps risky.

Permanent Versus Short Term Increases in Flexibility

When an athlete performs flexibility exercises prior to a workout, the primary purpose is to generate an acute increase in flexibility that will be utilized during the workout. Post-workout flexibility work is often employed as a means to facilitate the athlete's cool down process and to reduce the tension that can follow a strenuous workout. While both of these purposes are laudable, flexibility exercise of the kind described may not fully serve the purposes of the athlete with a flexibility problem: to cause a permanent increase in flexibility.

If the flexibility work performed by the athlete pre-workout is of sufficient intensity, duration and frequency, it can lead to some permanent changes in flexibility. However, such a vigorous pre-workout stretching session cannot be recommended for at least two reasons. Such stretching is believed to pose certain risks because muscles and connective tissues that have not been fully warmed up are not as supple and are therefore more prone to stretch related damage, than muscles that are fully "warm." In addition, some athlete's report an uncomfortable "overstretched" feeling when they perform very significant pre-workout stretching. Significant post-workout stretching is generally preferable to extensive pre-workout stretching, but athletes often neglect such stretching.

The athlete whose flexibility is inadequate in some area must train for a permanent increase in the range of motion of that area. That training must be consistent and specific and must provide an adequate training stimulus. The athlete's progress needs to be monitored carefully to determine whether the training is having the desired effect. Generally, for permanent changes in flexibility to be attained, the athlete will need to train at least once a day, preferably twice a day or even more. Less frequent training will generally not produce optimum results. Care needs to be taken with respect to the intensity of the training. Stretching for the purposes of achieving a permanent change in range of motion should not be painful. Pushing far enough to cause an increase in flexibility will generate a certain degree of discomfort, but outright pain must be avoided for two reasons. One reason is that such pain can signal damage to the area being stretched (especially if the pain is felt in the joint itself or in the connective tissues around it). Another reason is that pain can actually hinder the training process by causing tension in the muscles that are being stretched; proper stretching causes tension in the muscle being stretched, but if the tension is not overdone, the muscle will eventually achieve a relaxed state while it is being stretched. Stretching to the point of significant pain can delay or prevent this relaxation process.

Specificity of Training

It should not be surprising to discover that the muscles develop flexibility following principles that are similar to those used when training to develop strength. There is a specific adaptation to imposed demands. This specificity seems to apply to the range, direction and rate of motion. For example, as was suggested earlier, if flexibility is developed through passive stretching (using some external force to move the joint through its range of motion), the athlete will tend to demonstrate substantial improvements in passive stretching, but improvements in active stretching performance will tend to be significantly smaller. The terminology of flexibility recognizes these differences in that the term "static flexibility" refers to the range of motion that a person can achieve without any emphasis on speed, while "dynamic flexibility" is the range of motion that a person has in normal physical activity (i.e., at normal or rapid speed).

The Requirements of Flexibility in Weightlifting

In order to understand the nature of the flexibility required in weightlifting, we need to look at the positions that require the greatest degree of flexibility. These are the positions in which the joints of the body must assume angles that are close to the limits of the normal body's range of motion. In weightlifting these positions tend to occur at the liftoff position in the pull at the bottom of the dip in the jerk (although flexibility problems here are unusual) and at the position in which the weight is received in the squat or split. As a general rule, if a lifter can assume the proper positions at these points in the lift, then his or her flexibility is adequate to the task of lifting maximum weights. If the athlete's flexibility is inadequate to assume these positions, the athlete will be inhibited in the performance of the lift in question by a lack of flexibility.

The Starting Position of the Pull

As is discussed in Chapter 1, when the athlete assumes the proper starting position in the pull his or her knees are bent at an angle of between 45° and 90°. The athlete's shins are inclined well forward over the feet. The arms are straight and the lower back is arched. The chest is expanded outward and the shoulders are back slightly but not up. Many fledgling lifters are not able to assume this position, or if they are, experience significant discomfort in doing so. If that is the case, the lifter needs to practice flexibility exercises that are conducive to achieving the proper starting position.

While each muscle can be stretched separately in hopes of achieving the desired level of overall flexibility, perhaps the most effective way of training to achieve adequate flexibility in the starting position is to have the lifter lower a bar or stick to the lowest possible point at which a proper position can be maintained and then to use static or AI stretching techniques to reach a lower position with the bar without "rounding" the back or sacrificing the correct position in any way. Once the proper position can be assumed comfortably, the lifter should progress to the point where he or she can achieve a proper starting position with the bar at a lower position than is assumed at the point of lift off. This is accomplished either by having the lifter stand on a slightly raised (e.g., 1/4" to 3/4") platform or having the lifter use plates that have a slightly smaller than normal diameter. The weight need only be enough to help pull the lifter into the necessary position and allow the lifter to maintain balance (e.g., 20% to 40% of his or her best in that lift). However, the lifter should not support the weight for an extended period during a static stretch of this type. Rather, the weight should be resting on some support (the platform or blocks), and the lifter only applies sufficient force against the bar to maintain the desired position. The lifter can also practice lifting from this stretched position, increasing the weight of the bar until the lifter is deadlifting or pulling more from this stretched position than he or she is able to snatch or C&J. This exercise will serve the dual purpose of maintaining adequate flexibility and building strength for starting the bar off the platform. See

Chapter 5 for a more complete description of this exercise.

The Low Position in the Snatch

Perhaps the best way to develop flexibility for the low squat position of the snatch is to practice overhead squats with the empty bar or a very light weight. The lifter can descend smoothly, pause in the bottom to achieve the best possible low position and then return to a standing position.

Squat style lifters begin this exercise with the feet in the same position that is used in the low squat and then the lifter merely descends. Split style lifters begin the exercise with the feet in the forward and aft positions that are assumed in the deep split. The lifter then balances on the ball and toes of the rear foot and the flat foot of the forward foot. Finally, the lifter allows the forward leg to bend and the knee to travel forward as he or she descends into the full split position.

It is important to have the coach correct the lifter's position in the bottom. This is because any failure to assume a correct position is often due as much to a failure to balance the tension and relaxation of various muscle groups as it is to an actual lack of flexibility. The coach will therefore instruct the lifter to "arch the back" and to "push the knees forward." If there is no coach, a mirror can serve as a proxy for the coach's instructions by giving the lifter visual feedback regarding his or her positioning. In cases where the lifter needs to be able to see his or her positioning from the side, two mirrors can be used in combination to provide such a perspective.

For many lifters, several weeks of such practice will be sufficient for the lifter to assume the correct position with some effort (it may take several months or longer for the position to actually become relatively comfortable).

Perhaps the most common difficulties that new lifters experience in learning the squat snatch position are keeping the arms locked (i.e., absolutely straight) while in the low position and keeping the bar just behind or in line with the back of the head while in that position. The coach can help by supporting and/or helping the lifter to balance the bar in the deep position, gradually lessening the degree of assistance as the athlete becomes surer of his or her position. Most lifters perform this exercise much more effectively when they turn the arms, so that the insides, or crook, of the elbows are facing forward and upward rather than just forward.

The Low Position in the Clean

The principles described for the snatch apply to the clean as well. In this lift the bar is placed on the lifter's shoulders, and the lifter descends into the squat or split position. Here, as in the snatch, the lifter will try to keep the back arched. There will be more of an emphasis or keeping the torso upright in the clean than in the snatch. Perhaps the most common difficulty the athlete will encounter will be that of keeping the elbows up while the hands are grasping the bar lightly. Here again the coach's hand, and/or the mirror, can provide the lifter with invaluable feedback. It should be noted that many lifters will have difficulty keeping the bar in contact with the shoulders when there is no weight on it, but if the lifter is having trouble keeping the bar on the shoulders with 50 or 60 kg. then some special training will likely be required in this area (the goal should be to support even the empty bar comfortably on the shoulders)

The Low Position in the Jerk

In testing flexibility for the jerk, two positions should be considered: the bar resting on the shoulders in preparation for the jerk and the bar overhead in the lowest position at which the lifter will receive the bar in the jerk (in this latter position the bar should be slightly behind the rear of the head and the arms fully straightened). If the lifter has difficulty with supporting the bar comfortably in either of these positions he or she will need to practice achieving the correct positions daily, at least until the requisite flexibility is attained.

When Practice In the Extreme Positions Is Not Enough

While many lifters will find that the kind of practice described above will be sufficient for them to develop the flexibility required for correct weightlifting technique, a significant number of athletes will require specialized flexibility training in at least one muscle group in order to bring that area up to par with others. It is important to engage in such training at the outset of weightlifting training before the lifter begins to lift heavy (for him or her) weights. As was noted earlier, attempting to lift maximum or near maximum weights before adequate flexibility is achieved is an invitation to learning faulty technique and to injury and frustration. Even light technique work in the full classical lifts should not be performed until at least some flexibility has been attained (athletes may perform partial versions of the classical lifts that do not require them to assume extreme positions, e.g., power snatches from the hang position).

The advantage of specialized flexibility training is that the athlete can focus on the specific area or areas that require particular attention. The disadvantage is that when flexibility training is specialized, it can provide a lesser degree of specificity. Consider a situation in which a lifter is unable to raise his or her elbows high enough in the low position of the clean. Let us assume further

that it has been hypothesized by the athlete, after a careful monitoring of muscle tension, that lack of flexibility in the rear deltoid may be the primary reason for trouble. The athlete may perform a number of exercises to stretch the rear deltoid and make considerable progress in those exercises yet experience very little improvement in raising the elbows while actually lifting. How can this happen? It can happen because the lifter has failed to improve his or her flexibility in the specific way that it is used during the performance of the lift. It can also happen because the tension that was felt in the rear deltoid was actually caused by tension occurring elsewhere in the arm and shoulder complex (such as in the biceps).

For optimal performance in weightlifting the lifter needs to be able to raise the elbows high enough and to do so quickly, while the body is moving into and then sitting in a full squat position. In short, the rear deltoid must relax quickly and in concert with contractions and relaxation of other muscle groups, each group having varying degrees of influence on the action of the rear deltoid. Consequently, the relaxation of the rear deltoid must take place under a very specific set of conditions, conditions which may not be simulated when the muscle is stretched separately. Therefore, the closer the athlete comes to emulating the actual positions and conditions required during the activity, the more likely it is that the necessary degree of flexibility will be achieved.

To continue the example, the lifter is likely to develop the desired degree of flexibility if practice is undertaken while the lifter is in a full squat position and he or she attempts both to activate the muscles needed to raise the elbows and to relax the rear deltoid. During such practice it is very helpful if the coach assists the lifter in understanding which muscles need to be relaxed and which need to be contracted. Learning which muscles to tense and which to relax can be as important as the actual flexibility training. The coach can do this by referring to the muscle, pointing to it or touching it to assure that the lifter understands the muscle that is being referred to.

The same principles can be applied to the development of the flexibility required in any of the extreme positions of weightlifting that were referred to earlier in this chapter. The lifter attempts to assume the required position. The inhibiting muscles are identified, and an effort is made to relax those muscles while contracting the antagonists to those muscles (the muscles that move the body in the opposite direction of the muscles that are being stretched). An example would be the lifter's lowering a bar or stick progressively closer to the starting position in the pull while keeping the chest out and the lower back arched.

The athlete may also benefit from stretching movements which isolate the muscle or group of muscles that inhibit the desired movement, and such exercises can and should be experimented with. However, in most circumstances, the lifter will benefit less from such exercises than from the same amount of effort applied to stretching in positions that simulate the extreme positions assumed when performing the classical exercises.

Common Sites of Flexibility Problems

A lack of flexibility can occur in virtually any area of the body, but there are several areas in which flexibility problems seem to arise most often in the beginning weightlifter. These areas are: pectoralis major and minor, shoulders (both in terms of rotation and in the ability to position the arms to the rear of the head while they are outstretched above the head), elbows in both the most flexed and extended positions, illiosoas muscles, adductors, quadriceps, hamstrings and ankle joints. Special exercises can be used to improve flexibility in each of these areas, but as noted earlier, care must be taken to integrate the flexibility achieved by special exercises into functional flexibility for the weightlifting events.

Supplemental Flexibility Exercises That Can Be of Assistance to Weightlifters

While the exercises that will be of the greatest help to weightlifters in attaining the flexibility to execute the classical lifts properly have already been explained, special assistance exercises can be used as an adjunct to these exercises in order to facilitate the lifter's progress toward the attainment and maintenance of adequate flexibility in specific areas of the body. These special exercises can help in several ways. First, they can provide additional flexibility training to supplement the training on the lift related stretches that have already been discussed. Second, because they generally require little equipment or utilize equipment that is readily available outside the gym (e.g., walls, ropes and broomsticks), the lifter is able to practice them more often than the exercises that are performed in the gym. Third, these exercises can be used to isolate a specific area that may be especially troublesome for a particular lifter.

It is beyond the scope of this text to present an exhaustive list all of the flexibility exercises that may be of use to the weightlifter. Instead, we will describe a few of the most effective and most often needed flexibility exercises. The reader who does not find these exercises to be appropriate is encouraged to consult one of the books on flexibility listed in the Bibliography. These books contain a myriad of other exercises. Readers should select the exercises that appear to be appropriate and then test the results in terms of functional changes

in flexibility in the most extreme positions assumed while performing the Olympic lifts.

The rule that the flexibility trainer must always bear in mind is that any exercises performed must be carefully designed to increase range of motion in movements that are specific to weightlifting. In order to assure the appropriateness of any flexibility exercise and to gain the maximum benefit from using it, it is useful to carry out the following procedure. After doing two to three sets of any flexibility exercise, the lifter should assume the lifting position that the flexibility exercise being performed is intended to improve. If the exercise in question is really of value, the lifter should detect some degree of improved comfort and/or range of motion in the lifting position. If no improvement is noted, the exercise should be practiced again in the same or a subsequent workout. If no improvement (even of a minor nature) is noted at this point, the exercise in question may not be of great value. When the flexibility exercise is useful, the immediate application of the new flexibility assists the lifter in making that improvement functional (i.e., useful in performing the Olympic lifts).

The exception to this rule occurs when an exercise is useful but the newly achieved flexibility created by the exercise cannot yet be expressed in the lifting position in question because of a lack of flexibility in other areas.

The five exercises that I would recommend for those who need added flexibility training are: shoulder dislocates with a stick, Achilles tendon stretches, quadriceps stretches, elbow stretches in the power rack and squatting against the wall.

Fig 15 shows the mid-point in the shoulder dislocate. In this exercise the athlete begins by gripping a stick with a snatch grip, or wider, with the stick held on straight arms above the head. The stick is then lowered behind the lifter, while the lifter maintains straight arms, until it comes in contact with the rear of the body. If the lifter cannot keep the arms straight during the first rep he or she should widen the grip. With a wide enough grip the movement should be reasonably comfortable to perform. The lifter should continually endeavor the perform the exercise with a narrower grip each time it is done (beginning with a wide grip and moving the hands a little closer with each rep). With practice the lifter should be able to perform the exercise with something close to a clean grip (I've actually seen some lifters do it with the hands together or crossed over one another—but such extremes are unnecessary). This exercise gives the lifter flexibility to hold a snatch overhead comfortably in the low snatch position.

Achilles tendon stretches are done facing a wall or other fixed surface. The athlete places the toe up against the wall and the heel as close to the wall as possible. Then the knee is bent and pushed forward toward the wall. The higher the toe on the wall and the more the knee moves forward the greater will be the stretch on the Achilles tendon. This exercise helps the lifter to squat more comfortably with the knees forward of the toes (see Figure 16). The Achilles tendon is one of the hardest areas to stretch, so patience is needed here.

Quadriceps stretches enable the lifter to squat more comfortably. There are a number of ways to perform the exercise but the one which probably puts the least pressure on the knee joint and the most on the quadriceps muscle is the version shown in Figure 17. The lifter pulls the ankle up and rearward to develop a stretch on the quadriceps muscle.

Elbow stretches in the rack are performed as shown in Figure 18. The lifter sits in the squat position, with the hands around the bar. An assistant pulls up on the elbows as shown, to stretch them out. PNF stretching is particularly effective in this exercise. The athlete should not be satisfied until he or she can assume the position shown in the photo without undo discomfort. It important for the lifter to learn to relax the biceps during this stretch. Many lifters actually contract the biceps during this exercise (in an effort to bring the lower arm closer to the upper arm). Doing this is counter productive because tension in the biceps makes it harder for the lower arm to fold back against the upper arm. I've seen short men with 20" arms get their elbows up very well—its not an issue of arm size but of practice and selective relaxation.

Squatting against the wall is another exercise which helps the athlete to squat with the hips close to the ankles while keeping the back arched (see Figure 19). The key here, as it is in all stretching, is to relax (in this case the legs) completely. Ironically, when athletes are eager to stretch further they will often create tension that prevents the greatest possible range of motion.

These are just a sample of the exercises that athletes may find useful as the work to achieve the flexibility required to perform the classic lifts effectively. It is not necessary for every athlete to perform these exercises or to perform flexibility training at all. That need is dependent on the individual. If your quadriceps are so flexible that you can touch your buttocks to the floor in a full squat there isn't much point in stretching them further (you may even increase your risk of injury to the quads). You'd be better served by learning the lift with your feet close enough that your buttocks are partially supported by the calves in the bottom position than by engaging in further flexibility training. In contrast, if you lack the requisite flexibility to perform any of the classic lifts, training to improve your flexibility in the areas that are deficient is critical

Summary

The reader who has reached this point in the text has learned the elements of proper technique, how technique can be learned and how to create a training stimulus for improving strength, power and flexibility. Now that we have discussed the methods an athlete and coach can employ to develop technical skills and train the body to improve its strength, power and flexibility, it is time to examine the equipment that is at the weightlifter's disposal to enhance his or her performance.

Figures 15-19 — Supplemental Flexibility Exercises

Fig. 17

Fig. 16

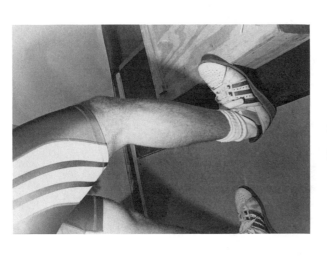

Fig. 19

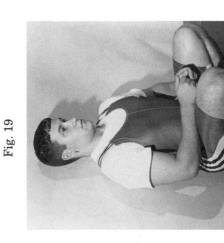

Fig. 15

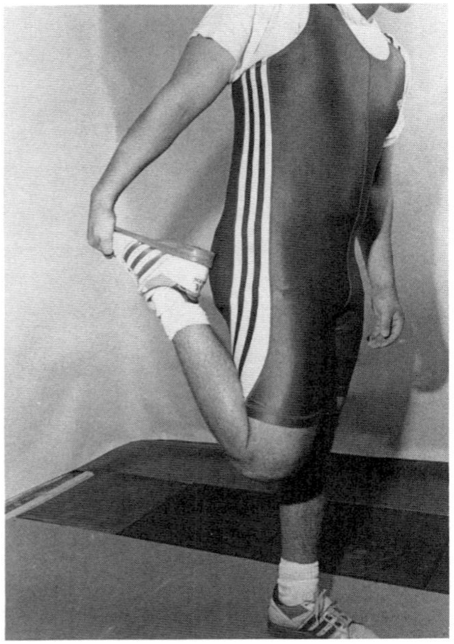

Fig. 18

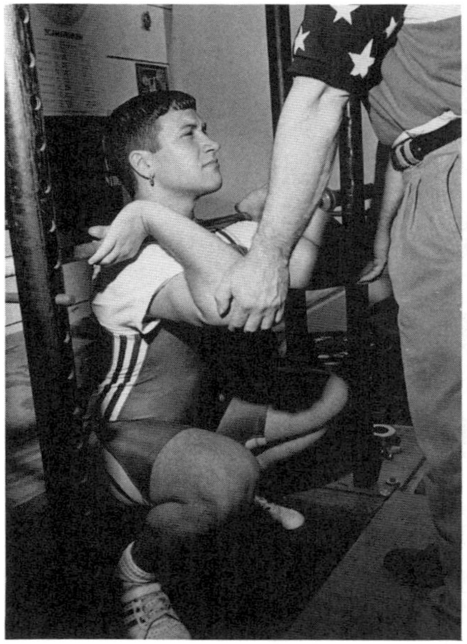

These and other supplemental flexibility exercises can be useful for the athlete who has special difficulties with attaining the flexibility needed for efficient weightlifting.

John Davis, who was undefeated in World and Olympic competition from 1938 through 1952, had very little of the equipment that is available to modern weightlifters.

176

CHAPTER 4

Selecting Weightlifting Equipment And Using It Safely And Effectively

Weightlifting is not an expensive sport to get a start in. You need some basic personal equipment, and then you need a gym in which to train. Most people already own, or can very inexpensively make, whatever personal equipment they require. When it comes to a training facility, you can either join an appropriately equipped gym (if you are lucky enough to live near to one) or buy some equipment, build some other equipment and start your own gym.

One other very important resource for weightlifting is human in nature: a coach. I started lifting without a coach, but did have limited coaching at certain points in my career. There are athletes who have won World and Olympic titles with very little in the way of coaching support. But lack of guidance from an experienced coach or lifter is certainly a drawback (although a bad coach can certainly be more destructive than no coach at all).

This book was written, in part, to help those who want to begin in the sport without anyone who can "show them the ropes." If you study it thoroughly, you will begin with far more knowledge, at least in certain areas, than have many experienced athletes and coaches. Nevertheless, feedback is important, and no book can give you that.

If you cannot find local coaching, or if you are a person who would like to start a weightlifting club, you should consider taking at least the Club Coaches' course that is offered by the US Weightlifting Federation. The instructors are for the most part well experienced and generally adhere to the curriculum developed by the USAW. Even the limited exposure given to the student in this affordable weekend course can be invaluable for the athlete or coach who is just getting under way. The USAW also offers more advanced courses for coaches who wish to further develop their skills in coaching.

In this chapter we will discuss the kinds and purposes of personal equipment. We will also

discuss how to select a gym or how to create one, and how to become an official club of the USAW.

Personal Equipment

There is a certain amount of personal equipment that every weightlifter should use or at least own (so that the equipment is available on an immediate basis should the need arise). Other items are optional or are needed only by athletes in particular situations. Some items are used only in training, other items are typically used only in competition and still others are used both in training and in competition. We will cover all of these items in this section. There will also be tips on how to select and maintain your equipment.

Lifting Suit

All lifters are required to wear a weightlifting suit (also known as a "singlet") in competition, The suit looks very much like the one that is used in wrestling competition (see the sequence photos in Chapter 1 for examples of lifting suits). It covers at least a portion of the lifter's hips and all of the waist and then emerges into suspender like shoulder straps.

It the past, weightlifting suits were not permitted to cover a substantial portion of the lifter's thighs. Recently the technical rules of weightlifting were modified to permit suits to cover the thighs down to a point just above the knees. This is a significant advantage for lifters because longer length suits protect the lifter from abrasions that can arise as a result of contact between the bar and the lifter's thighs. In addition, if the suit is made of the appropriate material, it can lessen the friction that is normally created between the bar and the skin of the thighs during the pull. This lessening of friction facilitates the upward progress of the bar during the pull. Longer suits (which cover the thighs) are becoming available, and lifters are permitted to wear bicycle shorts under their suits to create the same effect as a longer suit.

The material used in the weightlifting suit is stretchable and non-supportive (in contrast to the highly supportive "super suits" that are used in powerlifting to increase the lifter's ability to rise out of a squat). A supportive suit is not specifically proscribed by the rules, but it would be inappropriate. Freedom of movement and speed in descending into a full squat position are of great importance to the weightlifter. The negative aspects of a constraining garment would outweigh any advantages it might offer in terms of support.

Since the weightlifting suit is not supportive, it has no function in training. It is therefore rarely worn except in competition. An exception to this generalization is the workouts immediately prior to competition. Some lifters like to accustom themselves to the feel of the suit and lifting the bar with it on prior to competition day. Most lifters find this unnecessary, but others feel it essential.

For a description of the specific requirements of a competitive suit, please see Appendix 1 (Figs. 15-19 of Chapter 3 display a modern suit).

Sweatsuits and T-Shirts

In terms of training gear, a sweatsuit, or at least sweatpants, is the stock in trade of most lifters. Scientific evidence about the value of maintaining a feeling of warmth during training (or at least avoiding a feeling of being cool) is limited, but virtually any veteran of the game will tell you that they feel more comfortable, more flexible and more ready to lift when they are warm. Since the legs, hips and lower back are the foundation of high lifting performance, most lifters wear sweatpants to keep the legs warm.

In addition to providing warmth, sweatpants serve an important protective function for most athletes. As noted in Chapter 1, virtually all technically proficient lifters experience contact between the bar and their bodies at some point in the pull (usually on the thighs and/or hips, but sometimes on the shins as well). Such contact can abrade the skin, particularly when it is repeated many times during a workout. Wearing sweatpants assures that most of the abrasion will occur against the pants and not the skin.

Sweatpants must be made of a stretchable material. Weightlifting involves dropping into a low squat position frequently, and the material used in the sweatpants must be quite flexible in order to handle such an extreme range of motion without tearing. In addition, it is important that the movement of the lifter must not be constrained in any way.

Perhaps the best material for sweatpants is a heavy, stretchable nylon knit. Nylon stands up very well to the abrasion of a bar, and the texture of the material is such that the bar will glide easily along the legs or hips of a lifter wearing it. A heavy nylon knit also offers sufficient insulation to keep the lifter warm.

The modern nylon or Spandex tights are not particularly suitable for weightlifting because they are so thin that drafts easily penetrate the fabric and because they do not protective athletes from bar abrasion as well as thicker pants. They are nonetheless popular due to their availability, variety and price. The lightweight nylon of these pants is more acceptable in warmer climates, but their lack of abrasion resistance does not make them a first choice.

Old fashioned cotton sweatpants are comfortable and warm, and they will suffice if they are large enough to allow for freedom of movement without tearing, but they will not last as long as heavy nylon. Polyesters and blends are generally not as resistant to abrasion as nylon, so they will not generally last as long.

Sweatshirts, usually of the long-sleeved variety, are often worn in cooler weather. They are not as common when the weather is warm or the gym is well heated.

Instead, the typical lifter relies on a T-shirt. Such a shirt helps the athlete to retain some body heat, absorbs perspiration and protects the lifter's skin from abrasion when the bar is placed on the shoulders, whether behind or in front of the neck.

Cotton is best for T-shirts because it offers more friction to the bar than a cotton/polyester blend and also absorbs perspiration better. When a sweatshirt is being worn throughout the workout, a pullover cotton shirt is preferable for the same reasons that give a cotton T-shirt the edge.

Historically, T-shirts that are to be worn in competition have not been permitted to display anything except the lifter's club name and logo (in competitions through the national level) or the symbol of the national federation (internationally). Wearing the official competition T-shirt in that particular competition has normally been permitted as well.

In a pinch, a shirt with an illegal logo or name can normally be worn inside-out. T-shirts that are used in competition cannot have sleeves that extend further than halfway down the arm. Collars are not permitted in competition either (the normal round or V-neck collar is permissible, a turtle neck or dress shirt collar is not).

In recent years the rules regarding advertising and logos have been modified in various ways to permit greater freedom, but this is still an area of substantial flux. Consequently, the lifter would be well advised to avoid ostentatious displays of manufacturer names and logos on lifting uniforms and T-shirts unless these garments have been examined and approved by the referees and technical controller of the competition. (More information regarding the technical rules of weightlifting appears in Appendix I.)

When the sweatshirt is to be worn intermittently in workouts and competition (e.g., the lifter likes to perform an actual lift with only a T-shirt but likes to keep warm between sets with the sweatshirt) a zippered sweatshirt jacket is more practical. This feature is particularly useful in a sweatshirt that will be used during warm-ups at a competition when the shirt must be removed to lift on the official competition platform. The sweatpants that are used in warming up at a competition should also be built to facilitate easy removal. The lifter will often want to wear the pants between attempts in the competition, when nerves are frayed. At such times a garment that is easy to put on and off will be much appreciated.

From time to time sweatsuits made of rubber (or some other material that is used to induce heavy perspiration) come into vogue. These suits are generally a terrible idea for training. Dehydration is a natural tendency in training, one that must be combated with an adequate intake of fluids during the workout. A rubber suit increases the tendency to dehydrate, so it should be avoided in the main. It should also be noted that wearing such a suit does not induce a permanent weight loss of any kind. The one exception to this advice is the lifter who is using the suit to facilitate a temporary weight loss in order to make weight for a competition. In such a case the suit may be used in the last workout or two (assuming such workouts are taking place a day or so before the competition. (Weight loss through dehydration—a subject that is treated in more detail in Chapter 8—should take place only during the last twenty-four to forty-eight hours before the competition, or later.)

Socks

Socks should be worn in training and competition. Lifting shoes are too expensive to be destroyed by sweat, and the lifter will generally be more comfortable with good athletic socks. The socks used in training should be absorbent and warm. Many lifters like long socks, because of the added protection they afford against abrasion of the shins. The only limit on the socks that are worn in competition is that they may not go over the knee or touch any knee wrap that the lifter uses.

Briefs and Shorts

Although there is no evidence that athletic supporters prevent hernia (which, contrary to popular belief, are rare among lifters) or any other injury, many male weightlifters feel more comfortable wearing them or some kind of brief that offers support. Most men and women wear some kind of brief under their lifting suit. Such a brief is handy during the weigh-in, makes most

athletes feel more comfortable and, in the unlikely event of a shift in the suit or a split seam during a lift, the brief will serve to maintain a level of privacy for the lifter. In addition, wearing a support brief will make it more comfortable to pull the bar close to the body.

Some athletes wear shorts over their lifting suit in competition and/or sweatpants in training. This is permissible in competition as long as the shorts fit the body closely (baggy gym or boxer shorts are not permitted). Some referees interpret the rules as requiring that the shorts be worn under the uniform. The nature and purposes of bicycle shorts has already been discussed.

Sport Bras

Most women lifters I know wear a sport bra during training. While not absolutely essential, such a bra offers support and tends to flatten the breast tissue somewhat, which most women find comfortable and which can make it easier to keep the bar close to the body during the pull.

Straps

A piece of equipment called the "strap" has become an important adjunct to the training of a weightlifter. The strap consists of a strong strap or belt like material that is typically made of leather, cotton or nylon. The strap material is generally between 3/4" and 1 1/2" in width. The strap describes a circle around the lifter's wrist and then is wrapped once around the bar from the back, around the bottom, around the front and over the top of the bar (i.e., one full revolution). The strap, in effect, secures the lifter's wrist to the bar, thereby assisting the hands in holding the bar and assuring the grip.

The best material for the strap is nylon or a synthetic of similar strength. Seat belting or the strapping material used for mountain climbing is ideal. A wide strap that is fairly thick distributes the force of the bar over a larger surface area of the wrist than a thinner strap, and it is several times stronger than a thinner and narrower strap made of the same material. Leather is to be avoided because it becomes brittle with age and exposure to perspiration. Cotton simply does not have the strength of nylon and, like leather, can deteriorate over time with exposure to perspiration.

There are two basic types of straps: open and closed. The open strap is simply a length of strapping material (typically 12" to 15"). When it is used, the center of the strap is placed over the wrist with the wrist in a palms-down position. The ends of the strap are then crossed over one another to form a sort of asymmetrical and elongated X (the top portion of the X is shorter than the bottom section). The top of the X is placed against the wrist and the longer side of the X is wrapped around the bar inside the lifter's hand. The material of the strap encircles the bar once, with the remaining part of the strap hanging free.

The second kind of strap is one that is sewn together. Here the lifer makes a loop with one end of the strap. The loop is structured so that the short end of the loop goes under the lifter's wrist and attaches to the rest of the strap; the end of the strap is nearest the lifter and the long end of the strap hangs outside. This is done on both hands so that the loops go in opposite directions on each hand.

The open type of strap is easy to make (all you need is the material). It is also easily adjustable to the hand and wrist sizes of different lifters. Should a lift be missed while the lifter is wearing such a strap, it is easy and safe to release an open strap, as long as it has not been wrapped around the bar more than once. In that case the strap typically unwraps from the bar, and the X opens up as well (a closed strap only unwraps). The major disadvantages of open straps relative to closed ones is that they are somewhat more difficult to fasten and somewhat more likely to come apart when that is not desired.

Closed straps are stronger and surer overall, but they do carry a hazard that open straps do not. The lifter who uses open straps is cognizant of securing the strap so that it does not open on each set (sometimes each rep). The lifter who uses closed straps can become so confident that an unwanted opening will not occur that he or she does not even give it a thought. If such a lifter becomes overconfident, he or she may fail to check the straps regularly, and when a breakage does occur it will come as a total surprise (an unexpected loss of grip can result in an injury). Such a possibility can be almost completely eliminated by taking two precautions with a closed strap. First, have it sewn with the strongest thread available (a shoemaker is generally the best person to do the sewing). Have the shoemaker sew both a square around the strap and an X inside the square. This should provide ample strength. Then check the strap before every workout. Make sure that the thread that holds the strap together is intact. At the first sign of wear or a breakage of any thread, have the straps re-sewn. Examples of open and closed straps appear in Fig. 20—the closed strap is furthest to the left and the open one is next to it).

One variation on the closed strap is the adjustable closed strap. Such a strap has a small loop at one end just large enough for the unlooped end of the strap to fit through. When the unlooped end is passed through the looped end, a larger loop (like that of the conventional closed strap) is formed. That loop is pulled tight to fit the lifter, and then the strap is used is the same way as the normal closed strap.

Whether you are using an open or closed strap, check the material thoroughly at the beginning of every workout. It only takes a few seconds. At the first signs of any tear in the strap or any significant wear, make a new pair. Even the smallest tear in a strap weakens it dramatically and makes it subject to a complete tear at the next explosive effort. Lifters who have not had the experience of having a strap break in mid-pull often dismiss the risk of such an occurrence. Any lifter who has had the experience is unlikely to forget it or ever to overlook the importance of strap maintenance.

Other than regularly checking the strap, the only maintenance that is required of straps is to wash then occasionally. Such washing will not affect the strap's life very much, but your workout partners will really appreciate your consideration.

Lifting Belts

Virtually every weightlifter or would be weightlifter (and many people whose work involves some kind of lifting) owns a lifting belt. Ask any person who owns a belt why he or she is wearing it, and they will say "to protect the back" or "for support." There is probably some truth to these answers, but a more truthful answer for most people is that they saw someone else doing it— not the best reason.

Serious lifters should wear a belt selectively. There is no need to wear a belt for every exercise, and many world records have been in made in weightlifting competition by lifters who were not wearing belts. Going without a belt in the snatch is actually quite common among lifters of all levels.

There are at least four reasons for a competitive weightlifter to wear a belt. First, the belt itself can offer some level of support (i.e., to the extent it resists bending, it can provide some physical force against which the body can exert a force). Second, the lifter can exert some outward force against the belt with the muscles of the torso (primarily the abdominal muscles), helping to achieve rigidity in the torso. Recent research has demonstrated that the combination of these two effects can provide some support for the spine. Two smaller advantages are that the belt can help to keep the area that it covers warm and that the pressure of the belt can help to remind the lifter to maintain the correct position of the spine and the proper degree of tension in the lower back muscles.

With all of these advantages, why would anyone not wear a belt? For one thing, most of the advantages to wearing a belt are not highly significant. For example, a belt can support the spine, but a lifter who trains properly, has a solid spinal structure and employs proper technique may not have an overwhelming need for added spinal support (though extra support is always welcome, at least with very heavy weights).

Those who do not wear belts argue that the belt can interfere with their pulling motion. This could occur if the belt actually provided a physical obstruction to the upward progress of the bar or by led to a conscious or unconscious reluctance to pull the bar close to the body (for fear of hitting the belt). Actually hitting the belt could be a disaster, but fear of hitting it could have a more profoundly negative influence over the long term than a one time accident. In my own case, I did hit the bar against my belt early in my competitive career, and I never again wore a belt in the snatch or C&J.

Many lifters take a moderate approach to wearing a belt. They wear it on certain exercises that can be particularly stressful to the spine (e.g., repetition squats and jerks) but do not wear it when doing other exercises. Other lifters may not wear the belt with lighter weights (on the premise that some lifting without a belt will build more strength in the muscles that support the spine).

The rules of competition prohibit the lifter from wearing a belt that is more than 12 cm wide. Therefore it is unwise for the lifter to practice with a belt that is any wider (at least on a routine basis while performing the classical lifts). The belt may be as wide in the front as it is in the back. To the extent that it is, the belt will be more supportive overall. However, a belt that is as wide in the front as it is in the back is more likely to be caught on the pull. Consequently, very few lifters wear a belt with such a design.

Weightlifting belts have traditionally been made of leather. In recent years, belts made of synthetic materials have become popular and widely available, While there is nothing wrong with synthetics in theory (they are likely to stand up to perspiration more effectively), I believe that leather has the advantage at present. Leather eventually conforms closely to the lifter's shape. It is relatively long lasting and is available in a wider variety of styles than synthetics (although the synthetics will probably soon catch up in this area). Regardless of the fabric being used, the buckle of the belt should be as flat and unobtrusive as possible. There are some belts that are manufactured with a buckle on the side. This makes it less likely that the belt will get in the way. And a recent development in belt design is a padded back that includes an air "pump" so that the belt can be adjusted to conform to the physique and preferences of the lifter.

Generally, a belt will be of the greatest use in exercises that involve placing the bar overhead with a clean grip (e.g., jerks and clean grip presses) or exercises in which the bar is placed behind the back, like back squats. These exercises tend to place more downward and backward pressure on the spine (and are therefore more likely to lead to a hyperextension of the lower back) than exercises like snatches and pulls.

One other minor item to consider when selecting a belt is ease of release. All things being equal, it is a plus if a belt is easy to release, particularly when the belt is new. New belts tend to be quite stiff and can be difficult to take off once they have been tightened to the maximum. I had the experience of purchasing the thickest and stiffest belt I have ever seen shortly after I began in weightlifting. I was training alone in my basement on the first day I tried it. In honor of the new belt, I decided to attempt a record press. I was so psyched up getting ready for the press that I tightened the belt with great ferocity. When the set was over, my adrenaline level quickly subsided, and when I tried to take the belt off I could not pull it far enough to free the buckle, even though I gave it several efforts. By this time I felt my circulation being restricted and my breathing being constrained by the belt. There was no one home, and there was nothing nearby with which I could cut the belt. Realizing that the rest of my workout was doomed and that several minutes or hours of discomfort (if not something worse) awaited me if I failed to free the belt, I psyched up as if preparing for a record lift and gave it my all. Some skin was sacrificed, but the belt buckle just barely wiggled free. Needless to say, I wore the belt more loosely on succeeding sets and never tightened it to the maximum unless assistance was available (at least until the leather became "worked in" a little and was easier to handle). See Fig. 21 for an example of a weightlifting belt.

Weightlifting Shoes

A pair of weightlifting shoes is perhaps the single most important item of training equipment that a weightlifter can own. Shoes are required by the technical rules; they provide the lifter with vital support and can be used to incline the lifter's feet at the perfect angle. A weightlifter's shoe does not have to listed as such by its manufacturer in order for it to serve that purpose. Similarly, merely calling a certain shoe a weightlifting shoe does not make it suitable for the purpose. There are several important qualities that make a shoe suitable for weightlifting.

Composition of the Sole and Heel

The ideal weightlifting shoe offers firm support to the foot. This means it has an arch support, a flat bottom and good side-to-side stability. The composition of the sole should be such that is has a slight degree of give under substantial impact, but the sole and mid-sole should not be soft at all (e.g., running shoes are completely unsuitable because of the soft rubber used in the insole). Since weightlifting places considerable force on the foot a good rule of thumb is that if you press your thumbs toward one another (one at the heel inside the shoe and one opposite that thumb on the heel outside the shoe) and feel anything more than the slightest compression, the material is too soft (leather soles typically compress a little less than is ideal).

The bottom of the sole needs to provide some traction, but not too much. Leather and composition soles are generally unsuitable, as they tend to be too slick when they touch against a wooden platform. Rubber soles with treads, nubs or rubber spikes offer too much traction and can cause the foot to "catch," a potential disaster. Relatively hard rubber with just the slightest texture is best. The sole should be flexible enough to allow the lifter to rise on the toes easily and the lifter to place either foot back in the split and rest comfortably on all five toes.

Certain shoe designs have inherent weaknesses. For instance, the standard Soviet shoes have some excellent features, but unless the leather sole has been replaced or overlaid with rubber, they can offer slippery footing. Similarly, during the late 1970's and early 1980's, a major shoe manufacturer's product caused many lifters to complain of knee pain when they started wearing those shoes and several lifters tore their quadriceps tendons shortly after beginning to wear those shoes (a rare injury in weightlifting). Did the shoes cause the knee pain or injuries? In my opinion, they were at least partly responsible. The reason may have been the heel angle or the fact that the wooden heel transmitted more than usual force to the leg, or it may have been a coincidence. The manufacturer, which has had a long history of making excellent shoes for weightlifting and a host of other sports, stopped making that model a number of years ago, and no problems have been reported with the models made in recent years; most lifters love them.

Thickness of the Sole and Height of the Heel

All things being equal, the thinner the sole of the shoe, the higher the bar sits in relation to the lifter when it rests on the floor and the easier it is to lift the bar from the floor. Too thin a sole will not provide the lifter with much in the way of support or stability, so there is a trade-off here.

The height of the heel can be an important feature of a weightlifting shoe. Most lifters find a heel of between 1/2" and 1 1/4" to be best for them. Generally speaking, a higher heel will allow the lifter to maintain a more upright torso in the squat position and to maintain a slight arch in the lower back in that position as well. However, a higher heel will tend to place more stress on the knee, and a little more effort is required to get the knees out of the way during the pull. A lower heel tends to place a little more stress on the hips and lower back. Some very flexible lifters are able to lift with no heel at all, and a few lifters with flexibility problems have used heels higher than 1 1/4". Most lifters will do well to stay within the 3/4" to 1" range. Note that the heel heights given refer to the heel in comparison with the lowest part of the sole,

and they include the height that may be added to the heel by layers of material on the inside of the shoe at the heel only.

One final point about heels. Do not change their height by any substantial amount without allowing some time for the body to become adjusted to the new height. Any change in a lifter's heel places different stresses on the body. Even if the change is a beneficial one overall, the lifter's muscles, joints and nervous system have to develop a new sense of equilibrium. I once increased the height of the heel in my weightlifting shoe by less than 1/4". With my first heavy squat workout I developed a tendinitis in the knees that lasted for months. On a later occasion, once the inflammation had subsided, an adjustment to a similar height was accomplished very gradually without any knee problems. A gradual change can be made either by changing the height in steps, or by using the new shoes or heels in some workouts and not others, on the early sets but not the later ones in the workout or in certain exercises and not others. Then, over time, the full time use of the new shoe is phased in.

Support for the Foot and Ankle

It is important for the weightlifting shoe to support the foot and ankle effectively. In order to accomplish this, the design and use of the shoe's upper must be just right. For example, the athlete may feel the need for some ankle support in the low squat position. However, if the shoe has a high-top design and is laced tightly around the ankle while the shin is at a 90° angle to the foot, the movement of the lifter's ankle can become constrained as he or she descends into the squat position. Alternatively, if the lifter tightens the laces with the shin in a position in relation to the floor that simulates the squat position, support will be available where needed without constraining movement into the squat. A strap over the arch can help to keep the foot in place in the shoe when the lifter's foot is stopping quickly by using a frictional force on the bottom of the foot (i.e., when one foot is placed forward in the split jerk)). This prevents the foot from traveling forward in the shoe and colliding with the toe box (an uncomfortable and destabilizing phenomenon). Laces that cover most of the length of the shoe can serve the same purpose (because the laces can be tightened to hold nearly the entire length of the foot securely against the sole of the shoe).

Weight

A shoe that provides support and stability will necessarily weigh more than a ballet or gymnastics slipper. However, the heavier the shoe, the more weight and inertia it has, and the more difficult it is for the lifter to move the foot quickly. Weightlifting is a sport in which split seconds are very important. Therefore, the lifter wants the lightest shoe which can supply the support and stability required (particularly if the lifter moves the feet significantly in the squat or split under). See Fig. 21 for two examples of weightlifting shoes.

Fig. 20

Tape

Every lifter should carry some porous, surgical type adhesive tape. The porous variety of cloth tape is usually preferred by lifters because it adheres well to the skin and offers enough friction when a lifter places pressure on it to give the fingers a good grip over the tape. Non-porous tape tends to be more slippery, and non-allergenic tape tends not to adhere to the skin as well as standard surgical tape. (Obviously, if the lifter has a medical need for non-allergenic tape, it must be used or the lifter must avoid using tape at all.)

Surgical tape has a variety of uses. It can be used to hold the end of a supportive wrap (such as a knee or wrist wrap) closed. It can be used to provide support to a joint such as the ankle, or to hold a bandage in place. Tape can even be used for such utilitarian purposes as covering the center knurling of a training bar that is irritating the necks of the lifters who are using it.

Perhaps the most common use of tape by weightlifters is to protect their hands. It is not uncommon for lifters to tear a callus on their hands (though it is generally unnecessary, as is discussed in Chapter 11). It is also common for the bar to abrade a certain spot of skin on the palm or finger, so that the lifter suffers some pain or is in danger of causing some additional damage to the skin by continued training. Finally, some lifters know that they have certain spots on their skin that tend to split when enough pressure is applied to that area; taping such an area prior to the workout or before doing a given exercise can prevent such damage. Therefore, taping has become a part of standard workout preparation for many lifters. More information about the use of tape will be provided in Chapter 11.

Many lifters regularly wrap their thumbs with one layer of tape to protect the skin of the thumb when a hook grip is being used. I like to do this in training and in warming up for a contest. I remove the tape before my snatch attempts on the theory that the smaller diameter of the untaped fingers will make for a stronger hook grip and will avoid any possibility that the tape giving way could compromise my grip during a competitive lift.

Most lifters agree that the most versatile kind of tape is the 1" variety. However, many lifters prefer a 2" or 1/2" width. To some degree the choice is related to the kinds or uses that will prevail for a certain lifter. Otherwise it is simply a matter of personal preference.

Special varieties of tape are designed to serve specific purposes. For example, Johnson & Johnson makes a tape called "Elastikon". This tape is like an "ace" elastic bandage, except it has adhesive on one side. The premise of its use is that the elastic bandage is kept in place indefinitely. I do not like this kind of bandage because of its permanence (except for lightly wrapping the thumb). If a lifter wants to wear elastic bandages while lifting, he or she should be sure to loosen or remove the bandages between sets to permit free circulation. (The exception to my reservations about prolonged use of elastic type tape would be when it does not fully encircle a limb or joint, as when strips of tape running the length of the Achilles tendon are used to support it.) Naturally, specialty tapes like the non-porous variety can be helpful when a lifter needs to keep a certain area clean and dry.

Lifters should become familiar with the rules regarding use of tape in competition (see Appendix 1). There is nothing wrong with using taping procedures in training that would be inappropriate for competition, as long as the lifter has a plan for using legal taping during the competition and as long as the lifter gets at least some practice with legal tapes in place.

Talcum Powder and Other Lubricants

Some lifters use talcum powder and similar substances to lubricate their thighs, so that the bar does not lose a great amount of its upward momentum when it touches their thighs during the explosion phase of the pull. The talc is also used to prevent the bar from abrading the thighs when it makes contact with them during the pull. In training, neither of these needs is significant because the lifter generally wears warm-up pants. However, some lifters like to train without such clothing, particularly before a major competition, in order to better simulate meet conditions.

Talc and other such lubricants are illegal under the technical rules of the sport. Officials feel that lubricated thighs give the lifter an unfair advantage. In addition, there is a safety concern over the use of lubricants. A lubricant may be transferred from the lifter's thighs to the bar, undermining the lifter's grip. Alternatively, the lubricant might fall to the platform, making for a slippery lifting surface.

Despite the prohibitions regarding its use, talc and similar substances (some with an oil base) are employed by lifters on a relatively widespread basis in competition. Naturally, if a light layer of talc is applied sparingly, it is difficult to for any observer to see. Talc is easy to detect if an official touches the powder, but touching a lifter's thighs before each attempt is far from routine. In addition to the problem of detecting talc easily (particularly when it is applied without the technical controller seeing it), some officials overlook it on the premise that many lifters use it and that there is some need for it. Such discretion is not given to the officials under the technical rules, but it is often exercised nonetheless.

Some lifters use the chalk (magnesium carbonate) that they use to assure their grip on the bar on their thighs as well. It is hard to understand why, since chalk is not a lubricant; rather, it tends to increase friction between the bar and the skin unless it is used in very large amounts. It is obviously preferable to learn to lift without talc. A lifter who is able to do so is protected in competitions where the lubricant rules are strictly enforced, and it protects all lifters from unnecessary slippage of the grip or feet.

The most sensible approach to the lubricant question is simply to take advantage of the new technical rules and employ a lubricant that is legal (i.e., a singlet that covers the thighs or bicycle shorts made of a low friction material). The lifter is then well within the rules, the thighs are protected from abrasion, other lifters are protected from lubricants on the bar or platform and a lubricant does not have to be applied throughout the competition.

Magnesium Carbonate (Chalk) and Rosin

Chalk is an invaluable tool for the serious weightlifter. Chalk on the hands can help the lifter to grip the bar securely and to prevent the bar from sliding on the shoulders when it is cleaned, or during the dip for the jerk. Chalk should be applied in the following way. If the lifter applies chalk to the neck and the front of the shoulders (i.e., where the bar will rest during the recovery from the clean and the dip for the jerk), that area should be dried (if necessary) before the chalk is applied. Then the chalk should be applied to the lower front of the neck and to the front of the shoulders. Next, the chalk should be applied to the entire thumb (front, sides and back). This is best accomplished by applying the chalk liberally to the palms and the insides of the fingers and then inserting the thumb into a lightly closed hand and twisting the thumb back and forth inside the closed hand to assure that the thumb has been coated. Finally, if needed,

some additional chalk can be applied to the hands and fingers to assure that the entire inside surface of the hand and the thumb are dry and coated with a thin layer of chalk.

Chalk is usually stored in a specially constructed "box" that is approximately at the height of the lifter's waist. Although some rather elaborate designs have been developed for chalk boxes, there are only two basic needs. First, the box should be carefully sealed, so that it is dustproof. Chalk dust is very fine and can get through nearly any porous surface or small crack. If you want to keep the gym clean and to conserve chalk, a fully sealed or one piece box is a must. (Most professionally built ones are extruded from a single piece of metal or plastic so that there are no seams for the dust to seep through.) Walls that are 3" to 6" high help to assure that the chalk will stay in the box (higher walls tend to make the box uncomfortable for the lifter to use). Many professionally built boxes are circular and have a narrowed mouth, or look like an ellipse with two holes in the top (one for each hand). This minimizes the scattering of chalk dust. When applying chalk, it is important to stay over the chalk box. This will keep the area clean and save chalk. (Though chalk tends to increase friction when applied to the skin, it can actually act as a lubricant when it is on the varnished surface of a gymnasium floor.) The other important design issue is that the inside of the box should be as smooth as possible. There should be no sharp corners, protruding fasteners or rough surfaces. When such things are covered with chalk dust the lifter will not be able to see them and a wound to the hand can occur.

Some lifters like to apply rosin to the undersides of their shoes to prevent slipping while on the platform. This is generally a good idea, and is vital when a lifter's footwear is prone to slippage (e.g., for example, when the lifter is wearing leather-soled shoes and the platform surface is smooth wood). The rosin box should be large enough to accommodate the largest foot comfortably. Its walls need only be 2" to 4" high, because rosin is not as likely to become airborne as chalk.

Knee Wraps

The knees are not the body's most stable joint, and the knee joint is exposed to considerable stress in weightlifting. Proper training will help to condition the knees to accept that stress comfortably. However, some lifters do experience soreness in the knee and/or the muscle-tendon unit of the quadriceps and patella structure from time to time during their careers. Many such lifters feel that knee wraps provide some relief from this discomfort. Knee wraps are also worn by lifters without any discomfort, on the premise that the wraps will provide some support for, and stability to, the knee joint.

I have serious reservations about the wisdom of using knee wraps, particularly when the lifter is performing the classical lifts. There are many aspects of wrapping the knee that are not well understood. For example, many lifters who have knee soreness report diminished discomfort in their knees when they use the wraps. Is that reduced discomfort a consequence of the support offered by the wrap, or could it be that the wrap interferes with pain impulses in some way, relieving any pain but merely disguising the underlying condition? Do wraps actually stabilize the knee, or does the pressure they apply merely give the athlete a sensation of greater stability while compromising the free movement of the tendon?

Another concern that I have is that the lifter who uses wraps creates a kind of wedge behind the knee joint when the lifter is in the deep squat position. Much as an object lodged in a hinge can "spring" (i.e., destroy the integrity of) a hinge, can an obstruction behind the knee damage the knee? It seems highly probable.

Naturally, if the athlete is performing exercises that place stress on the knee but in which "bottoming out" in a very deep squat can be avoided (such as when doing power cleans or squats), the use of wraps does not present a danger to the integrity of the joint. In such a case, the use of wraps can actually aid in the athlete's recovery from tendinitis of the quadriceps or patella tendons.

My recommendation is to avoid using wraps if you do not have any knee discomfort or pathological instability. If you must use them, try to avoid it on the classical lifts. If you must use them on the classical lifts, try to minimize any bunching of the wrap behind the knee and make sure that the hips, thigh flexors and adductors are absorbing as much of the impact of receiving the weight as is possible.

There are several varieties of knee wraps. One type is the one piece elastic sleeve that fits over the knee and usually covers a distance of 8" to 10" from the upper calf to the lower thigh. This type of wrap, though popular because of the convenience of simply slipping it on, makes little sense to me. If the wrap is loose enough to be worn continuously, it is probably not providing even the limited support a knee wrap can offer. If the wrap is tight enough to provide some kind of support, it is too tight to be worn throughout a competition. Some lifters find this type of wrap useful for keeping the knee warm. If this is the case, the wrap should be as loose as possible while maintaining contact with the knee. If warmth is the objective, the lifter may well find that a neoprene sleeve is more effective than an elastic and cloth one.

During the 1960s the eight-time World and two-time Olympic Champion Tommy Kono developed knee problems. He discovered that wearing a piece of the leg portion of an old skindiving wetsuit around his knee kept it warm and comfortable during a workout. He brought his idea to the attention of other lifters and to Bob Hoffman, owner of York Barbell . Bob and his lifters loved the idea, and by the late 1960s Hoffman was manufacturing knee and waist bands made of neoprene and distributing them widely. These bands provide a feeling of warmth that can be soothing to a sore knee or a stiff back (some lifters wear the waist band under the erroneous assumption that it will assist in "spot" reducing the waist). Neoprene wraps were made illegal in competition in the early 1970s and so fell into disfavor, but recent changes in the rules have made them legal once again. If this part of the lifter's costume provides comfort, there is little harm in using neoprene. However, the lifter should guard against using neoprene that is too thick around the knees in order to avoid the hinge destabilizing problems discussed later in this section.

Another variation of the sleeve type of wrap is the sleeve with stabilizer bars on the outside and inside surface of the knee. These supports were designed to prevent lateral knee motion (especially for the person with slack ligaments). They are not legal in weightlifting competition, and the support bars are not normally designed to permit the lifter to assume a full squat position. Therefore, they cannot be recommended for the typical lifter. The only exception to this rule would be the lifter who is rehabilitating himself or herself from an injury, wants lateral knee support during limited workouts and is not intending to perform classical lifts.

A second major kind of knee wrap is the "ace" bandage (which takes its name from the dominant brand of that kind of wrap). The ace bandage is a combination cloth and elastic wrap that is typically between 2" and 6" wide and 6' long. Because of its construction, the bandage can normally stretch to nearly twice its original length. The greater the stretch, the greater is the force that is applied by the wrap to the surface (like a rubber band that is stretched before it is wrapped around someone's finger).

To prepare for the wrapping process, the lifter normally takes one end of the wrap (the end without any fasteners, if fasteners are part of the wrap, otherwise either end) and begins a rolling process with each layer on top of the preceding one (akin to rolling up a rope or hose). In order to use the bandage, the lifter generally begins with one end taking a turn around the upper calf. When the wrap has gone approximately a little more than a full turn around the knee, the end is held in place by the second layer, which somewhat overlaps the first. From that point, the lifter begins to wind the wrap around the knee in a sort of spiral fashion, with each layer just overlapping the one below, so that there is no bare skin between the spiraling levels. When the end of the wrap is reached, it is normally tucked inside the last spiral to hold it in place. During the entire wrapping process, the lifter pulls fairly energetically on the wrap so that it is well stretched as it is wrapped around the knee.

Powerlifters have developed a thicker version of the ace bandage, one that has a greater resistance to being stretched. That wrap is usually called a "super wrap." Its advantage is that is offers greater support and tension. Its disadvantage is that its thickness places a thicker wedge behind the lifter's knee in the deep squat.

If someone is going to wear a knee wrap, the ace or super versions are more likely to provide support than the sleeve type. In addition, the ace and super wrap permit the removal between sets, which is a great help in terms of maintaining normal circulation. Therefore, if you are going to use a wrap for support, the ace or power type has the edge. For pure warmth and convenience, the sleeve type is superior (for this purpose, it should only be snug, not very tight). To the extent that at least some training can be performed without the wrap, this is advisable, particularly when the knee is asymptomatic.

Fig. 20 depicts the sleeve (at far right) and "Ace" (furthest to the rear) types of knee wraps.

Wrist Wraps

Most lifters train and compete without any special form of wrist support. It is not uncommon for beginners to experience some discomfort in the wrists when overhead lifts are performed. This is particularly true when doing exercises that place pressure on the wrists for a sustained period. Examples of such exercises would be the overhead squat or front squat, in which there is some stress on the wrists for the entire set (in the latter case this is generally only true when the lifter is tight in the arms and shoulders and therefore cannot rest the bar comfortably on the shoulders). Generally, this discomfort disappears or greatly diminishes after several weeks of the commencement of a training or the addition of a new exercises that places stress on the wrist.

A small number of lifters will find that overhead lifting does irritate their wrist joints, whether because of a genetic predisposition to wrist problems or because of a prior injury of some kind. Such lifters must take care to avoid developing a chronic problem in this area. A combination of careful loading, adjustments in technique, special exercises to strengthen the wrists (such as wrist curls) and wearing wrist supports selectively can help the lifter to avoid this eventuality.

A larger group of lifters will experience an occasional minor sprain or inflammation in the wrist area. It is in these circumstances that lifters turn to wrist wraps for temporary support so training can continue (although the other methods mentioned for the treatment of more chronic wrist problems may be required as well).

There are two basic types of wrist wraps. One type is like a belt or sleeve. This wrist support typically has snaps, straps, Velcro, or other method of fastening it around the wrists. It can be made of a stretchable material, a sturdy cloth or leather.

The second type of wrist support is actually wrap like in nature. It is wound around the wrist in layers. The material used in such wraps is generally a sturdy cloth of the stretchable type (e.g., an ace bandage). Sometimes tape is used for this purpose.

The general rule for such supports is that they cannot cover an area more than 10 cm in width or extend into the hand, and there cannot be more than one material used in the support. For example, the lifter cannot make a wrap from cloth and then wrap one or more layers of tape around the cloth. A recent exception that has been made by some referees to the two substances rule is that a thin foam "tape prep" is permissible to protect the skin under tape. One further restriction on the wrist supports is that they may not contain any rigid wrist support in addition to the support offered by the wrap of sleeve itself. For example, an elastic sleeve type of support may not have metal or plastic supports sewn in.

My experience and that of most lifters I know has demonstrated that the least beneficial kind of wrist support is one made of stretchable material. To the extent that it stretches, it does not provide support and it interferes with the circulation going to the hands, so it needs to be removed between sets. Another poor choice is tape. Tape is supportive and does not affect the circulation adversely if it is not applied too snugly at the outset, but the degree of snugness cannot be adjusted once it is applied. In addition, tape cannot be conveniently removed and replaced if it loosens during the workout or competition.

Many lifters like wraparound wrist supports made of cloth. These are commonly worn by boxers (although boxers often extend the wrap into the hand itself). These wraps are wound snugly around the wrist while the hand is in an open position with the fingers spread. The open hand position helps to prevents the lifter from making the wraps too tight, assuring adequate circulation and freedom of movement with the wrap in place. If the wrap is made just right, the lifter can actually make it tighter before a set by twisting it in the direction of the wrap, and loosen it by twisting the other way after the set.

My personal favorite, and a favorite of many lifters that I know, is a leather, belt like support (which I wear only when a wrist is acting up in some way). Leather tends to be the strongest and most rigid of the support materials that is used on the wrist. Such supports are typically held on the wrist by two straps that are made like belts, so that they can be tightened to the desired degree. This easy adjustability makes it a simple matter to loosen and tighten the supports between sets (See example in Fig. 20—rear right of photo).

Perhaps the single most important element in making wraps work well is assuring that the upper portion of the wrap (the portion closest to the hand) is properly positioned. There are two considerations that affect proper placement: the degree of support required and the need for freedom of movement. Generally, the closer the top of the wrap is to the hand (even to the point of extending somewhat up the hand) and the tighter the wrap is at that point, the greater the support it will provide for the wrist. Of course, the higher and tighter the wrap, the more it will restrict the motion of the wrist. Snatching, jerking, and particularly cleaning require that the wrist be permitted to flex, so that the top of the hand can fold back toward the forearm. If the movement of the wrist is restricted too much, the lifter will be unable to move the hand and wrist properly when lifting. This increases the likelihood of injury, decreases performance and can negatively influence technique (in the case of the clean it can be downright dangerous). Because of the need for wrist flexibility in the clean, I do not recommend that any athlete wear wrist wraps while performing the squat clean.

A good rule of thumb to employ in supporting the wrist is to allow range of motion to the point just before significant discomfort is experienced. If that point is much different from the one that is normally assumed while lifting, the lifter should seriously consider abandoning the competitive lifts altogether while the wrist is healing and emphasizing strength building and other forms of conditioning that do not place the wrist under significant strain.

Fig. 21

Hip Pads

Some lifters make very hard contact with the bar in the area of the hips near the pubic bone when they are pulling. This is far more common in the snatch than in the clean. A lifter need experience a direct hit on the pubic bone only once to realize that this is a movement to be avoided in the future. One way to do that is to change the width of the grip so that the bar makes contact with the hips or thighs at a slightly different position. Another solution is to modify the style so that the contact is less severe (the drive from the hips should be primarily upward and should not emphasize a forward thrust, as many who emphasize hard contact with the hips tend to do). However, when neither of these options is appropriate, the lifter may find that the use of padding in this area while training is useful.

Some lifters place a handkerchief or other similar material in their briefs. Others use a piece of dense foam rubber. The rules of competition are not completely clear in terms of using such an aid. Certainly, the rules do not recognize a pad as being permitted, although they do not specifically prohibit its use. Most officials would probably interpret the rules to mean that a pad is not permitted, on the premise that nothing may be worn under the uniform. The lifter who uses a pad must then face the problem of getting used to something in training that will not be used in competition, or using something that can lead to a problem during the competition if it is discovered.

One solution for lifters who do make hard contact with the hips is to use a pad during the early warm-ups when most bruises occur (because of the unusually high speed with which that lifter and bar are moving, relative to the speed achieved with heavier weights), and then to remove it for the last warm-up or two and while lifting on the competition platform.

Soap and the First Aid Kit

Soap would hardly be considered a specific piece of lifting equipment since everyone, lifter or not, uses it (we hope). Nevertheless, two specific kinds of soap can be beneficial to the lifter. One kind is an antiseptic soap, which the lifter can use to clean the occasional abrasions that occur during training and competition. The other kind of soap is one that dries the skin by removing oils and similar substances from the skin's surface. Using such a soap immediately prior to a competition can assist the lifter in assuming a secure grip. Having soap available is particularly important when the lifter applies a rub or other substance that is slippery before the competition.

Pernox is the brand name of a soap that has drying and abrasive ingredients. It is made primarily for acne patients and is available in most pharmacies. Pernox or some similar soap is ideal for cleaning any natural oils and other slippery substances from the hands prior to a competition.

A standard first aid kit is a useful item for a lifter to have in training and competition. Cuts and abrasions are not uncommon events, and it is important to treat such injuries promptly in order to avoid discomfort and infection.

Gloves

Nowadays, whenever you go to a gym or store that sells equipment to the "weightlifter" (really weight trainer), a selection of gloves (generally of the fingerless type) can be seen. Gloves have become popular with trainees for three basic reasons. First, many people want to avoid the skin irritation and resulting calluses that lifting barehanded causes. Second, gloves, like any other piece of equipment tend to make you feel like part of the "crowd." Third, some people actually believe that gloves will improve their grip and hence performance. (When chalk is banned, as sadly it is in so many gyms today, gloves may actually be a viable way to improve the grip.)

Gloves, at least those that are commonly available today, have no value for the serious competitive weightlifter. While they are now permitted in competition, they do not assist the grip overall in the competitive lifts. Moreover, it is important for the lifter to develop some toughness in the skin to withstand the rigors of practice and competition. Therefore, if you are using gloves, phase them out; if you are not, do not start.

In the event that a lifter has an injury to the skin of the hand, gloves may provide protection until the injury heals. It should be noted that gloves do increase the possibility of a sudden slip of the grip, which can be a disaster for the lifter. Therefore, I do not recommend using them.

The Well Equipped Gym Bag

Every lifter should carry a well equipped gym bag to all workouts. The ideal bag is large enough to carry all of a lifter's equipment with some room left over. Bags with pockets at both ends and along the sides permit the lifter to keep needed items separated from one another and easier to find. (It can be quiet tedious to locate your straps if you have a great deal of personal equipment and it is all mixed together in a bag with one large section.) Handles that go completely around the bag offer more support and tend to lead to a longer lasting bag. A shoulder strap makes the bag easier to carry (particularly if you have a long walk to the gym).

A lifter should include most of the items of personal equipment that have already been discussed in his or her bag. Assuming a lifter wears sweats to the gym, the only essential item is a pair of shoes. Few lifters wear lifting suits or use talc in training (the latter is unnecessary and can present a real hazard for everyone who trains on the same

platform), but most lifters consider straps and a belt near necessities. Briefs and sport bras follow in popularity. Carrying tape is a good idea, even if you do not ordinarily use it, because it is likely to be needed from time to time (lifters hate others who are always "borrowing" items like tape). The same can be said of a first aid kit.

Carrying chalk is always a good idea as you never know when it may run out at your gym (if they supply it at all). It is also a good idea to store it in a container that is sturdy and has a strong seal (such as Tupperware). Storing chalk in plastic bags or frail containers will inevitably lead to the need to clean a very dusty gym bag one day.

Carrying a set of wraps for the knees and wrists, as well a something that can be used as a hip pad is a sound precaution as these items will then be there should you need them. Bathroom tissue, at least in your car, is still another useful item to have. Gloves are only necessary if you use them regularly (which I do not encourage). Even when your skin is irritated, applying tape (as discussed in Chapter 11), is generally preferable to using gloves.

There is one other item that arguably always belongs in a lifter's gym bag (an item that always gets a chuckle when I mention it but then a nod of agreement—bathroom tissue). Biological urges can crop up at any time and it is comforting (mentally as well as physically) to be prepared. It is not uncommon for lifters to have sudden urges to use the restroom during competition, whether due to nerves, a change in diet because of weight reduction or a strange new geographic location. Nothing is more disconcerting than running to the restroom before an attempt, under pressure of time, only to discover that the last occupant used all of the paper. Having your own supply can provide security and comfort so that these routine matters remain in the category of routine. Lifters who are traveling abroad will often discover that the quality of paper available in other countries is quite inferior to the "cottony soft" varieties that are available in the United States. Therefore, having your own paper can be a welcome blessing. Naturally, if you are training at home or in a well equipped gym this may not arise an issue, but being prepared is never a mistake.

A further discussion of the items that should be carried to a competition is included in Chapter 8. Some of the items listed there should be considered for inclusion in the daily gym bag as well.

Gym Equipment

Bar

Perhaps the single most important piece of weightlifting equipment is the bar. It is the only piece of equipment that the lifter is in contact with while lifting. If you are buying equipment for the first time and money is an important consideration, do not skimp on the bar. A good bar will last three to ten times longer than a poor one.

Many good bars are made in the world today but many bad ones are made as well, so the lifter needs to be very careful when selecting a bar for the special purpose of Olympic-style weightlifting. Unfortunately, there are no established standards for measuring the quality of a bar (though there are "official" dimensions for the bar established by the International Weightlifting Federation). Nevertheless, there are some guidelines that can be used in evaluating bars.

Good bars share at least the following characteristics:

1) They are perfectly straight and are made of a steel that will flex somewhat under a load but will not take a permanent bend even after considerable use. The quality of the steel used in the bar is the chief determining factor of the bar's resiliency, and high quality steel is expensive. If the manufacturer skimps on the quality of the steel, the bar will not have a good "spring" and will not remain straight for a long period.

2) They meet all contest specifications with respect to dimensions. Many bars that call themselves "Olympic" do not actually conform to the rules (see the rules section for exact specifications and get the specs from the manufacturer before you buy).

3) The bar will turn freely but will not "spin" too much. One convenient way to test whether the bar turns freely enough is to place it on the platform with several large plates on each side. Then try to spin the bar with your hand or foot. (You might be thrown out of a Soviet gym for using your food because touching the bar with the foot is considered by the Soviets to be disrespectful to the bar.) The bar should revolve easily but should not continue to spin more than a revolution or two after the turning force of your hand or foot has been removed from the bar. If possible, have an athlete clean or snatch the bar and hold it for perhaps ten seconds. If the plates continue to turn around the bar for more than a few seconds after it has been lifted (a rare problem) they can create a gyroscopic effect. This phenomenon makes it more difficult for the lifter to control the bar when it is lifted (particularly in the snatch). This places unnecessary stress on the lifter's joints.

4) The "sleeves" of the bar (the larger areas on either end of the of bar on which the plates are loaded) are fastened to the bar in such a way that they will not loosened when the bar is dropped. There are a variety of methods to secure the inside collars and the sleeves to the bar. Eleiko uses a series of snap rings that fit in grooves that are machined into the bar or sleeve. York Bar fits a "collar" inside the sleeve with pressure and heat. The sleeves are held in place with an outside round nut that is screwed onto the bar and then held in place by a set screw that goes into an indentation in the bar or through a hole drilled all the way through the bar. There are a number of other designs that will work as well. However, all successful designs that I have seen incorporate either some means of distributing the force and vibration that is imparted to the bar when it is dropped (like the Eleiko design) or multiple means of fixation (like the York bar). What does not work is a simple bolt (or nut) that is screwed into (or onto) the end of the bar (a very popular design for inexpensive bars made today). These bars may hold up for bench presses or squats, but they are simply destroyed by Olympic lifting.

5) The plates fit snugly on the bar. If the plates are too loose, they will tend to slide when they are lifted, necessitating the use of collars whenever lifting takes place. To test the plates, place the bar on the floor with one plate loaded on each side. Push the bar sideways to each side. If the plates do not remain nearly at a 90° angle to the bar, they are too loose.

6) The "knurlings" (the textured areas on the bar) foster a secure grip without being so coarse as to cause the toughened skin of a trained lifter to tear unnecessarily. The knurling is made by cutting tiny diagonal grooves into the bar at right angles. If the grooves are too deep, the bar becomes like a rasp and tears the skin on the hands, the shins and the thighs. If the knurling is not deep enough, the lifter cannot achieve the maximum security in his or her grip. Virtually all bars have a knurling that begins at a width a little narrower than the average lifter's shoulders and extends to the inside collar of the bar. Some manufacturers knurl several inches of the bar at its center as well (this is actually part of the International Weightlifting Federation's specifications). This serves to prevent the bar from sliding on the lifter's shoulders in the clean of the dip for the jerk. However, many lifters find that such a knurling abrades their necks in the clean. Therefore, athletes have been known the place tape over the center knurling for training purposes.

Some bars are plated with chrome, nickel or even gold. The plating certainly improves the appearance of the bar but not its performance. Bars that are located in areas in which rusting is a problem will tend to avoid rusting for a longer period if they are plated.

There are only two American made bars that I can recommend for Olympic-style weightlifting. (There may be others that are suitable, but I have not encountered them.) One is manufactured by the York Barbell Company and is their "Olympic Standard" model (they do have a less expensive model that is designed more for weight training than for weightlifting).

The York organization has been a supporter of weightlifting in this country for well over half a century, and their bars have been used extensively in national and international competition. York has had some problems with quality control at times, but over the long term the performance of their bars has been good. Moreover, York has had a history of being a reliable organization with a reputation for standing behind their products. If a problem of any kind occurs, my experience has been that they will rectify the situation promptly. The York Olympic Standard bar reasonably priced and is widely available (York has reportedly developed a more "upscale" model of their bar which has bearings in the sleeves in order to make the bar spin more smoothly than the Standard bar, but I have not sampled one of these bars as of press time for this book).

Mav-Rik is another company that has been in the business for more than a quarter of a century. They make several reliable bars. Their top of the line bar is guaranteed in writing never to bend (a unique guarantee in the industry). Maverick has had some problems with meeting competition specifications at times, but I am assured that their bars are up to specs today. If this is a concern with Maverick or any other manufacturer, obtain a written set of specifications in advance of the sale.

The bar that most lifters regard to be the premier bar in the world today is manufactured by the Eleiko Company of Sweden. The Eleiko bar has unique spring to it. That spring aids the lifter in the jerk and helps to absorb the shock of receiving the bar in the clean. In addition, the springy nature and strength of the steel used in the Eleiko bar make it virtually impossible to bend it permanently in normal use. Eleiko bars spin freely so that the lifter experiences little resistance in turning the bar over at the top of the snatch or clean pull. In fact, the bar turned too freely at one time, causing a gyroscopic effect (a problem that Eleiko corrected many years ago). Eleiko bars are tested like no other. The top of the line (competition) Eleiko bar is more expensive than many bars that are out there, but it is a lifetime investment for the lifter and an excellent value for a gym because of its durability. Eleiko has recently developed a "training" bar that retains many of the important characteristics (including the steel) of the competition bar but is significantly less costly.

Buyers of Eleiko in the America's have the added bonus of sales as service support from Dynamic Fitness (see the Bibliography of this book for further information on York, Mav-Rik and Dynamic Fitness).

There are a number of other manufacturers who make high quality barbells (such as Uesaka of Japan), but in my opinion, none of these matches Eleiko's overall quality.

All bars should be cared for by lubricating them with grease every few months and by wire brushing them at least every few weeks (using a brass brush cleans chalk and other foreign matter from the bar but will not abrade the bar). Bars should never be left in a loaded state on a rack of any kind between workouts because doing this can cause the bar to assume a permanent bend. Ideally, the pins of any power rack or the forked portions of squat or other racks that are used to support the bar should be covered with rubber or some other material that is softer than the steel of the bar. This will protect the knurling of the bar from being smoothed out by contact with another hard surface. Such a material will also serve to absorb some shock when the bar is returned to the pins.

Perhaps the worst insult to a bar is loading it with one large diameter plate and then many small diameter plates (particularly 10 kg. plates) and dropping it. When a bar so loaded is dropped, all of the impact must be absorbed by the large plates and the small area of contact that such plates have with the floor. In addition, when the downward motion of the bar and the large plates is stopped by the contact of the large plates with the floor, the entire downward force of the small plates must be absorbed by the bar instead of the floor. This places stress on both the surface of the bar's sleeve and the bar itself. The greater the number of small plates and the greater the weight of those plates, the greater the pressure. A number of gyms have eliminated the use of small diameter plates of 10 kg. or more. Their equipment will surely enjoy longer life as a result.

In general, the heaviest available plates should always be used in loading the bar and the use of small plates should always be avoided (except when they are needed to achieve the appropriate weight). This not only protects the equipment but also simulates meet conditions, conditions in which the largest available plates are always used.

Plates

Many varieties of plates are used for weightlifting, The most common kind are made of cast iron. Many champions have been developed by training with such plates. Today lifters prefer "bumper plates." These are plates that have a core of steel or other metal surrounded by rubber or a resilient plastic. Bumper plates protect the platform if they are dropped, and they reduce noise in the gym. Bumper plates are not absolutely essential for the lifter, but they do make life a lot easier and purchasing them is highly recommended.

York, Mav-Rik and Eleiko all make quality bumper plates that will last a long time if they are treated properly (Eleiko makes a training bumper plate and a competition plate, the former being less expensive and designed specifically to withstand daily use).

It is generally a good idea not to mix brands of bumper plates because they have different degrees of resiliency, and the plates will tend to absorb differing levels of strain. It is also considered less than ideal to use the bar of one manufacturer with the plates of another because of differences in the fit between the plates and the bar and differences in the resiliency of the plates (although most good brands work quite well with one another).

Some manufacturers may make different plates for training and competition. In such cases it is generally wise to purchase the training version for daily use and leave it to competition organizers to purchase the competition model.

Collars

Collars are used to hold the plates on the bar in a certain position. Inside collars are fixed to prevent the plates from sliding along the bar toward the lifter and to present the lifter with consistent conditions (i.e., spacing) in terms of gripping the bar. Outside collars are removable so that plates can be loaded on the bar in any combination and then locked in position. It is a good idea to use collars at all times to prevent any movement of the plates, but in reality collars are seldom used when athletes train with high quality bars; in they are always used in competition. During training lifters find that placing collars on the bar and tightening them for every set becomes rather tedious. Since the bar is lifted in a balanced fashion in most cases, the plates seldom shift significantly during any given lift, particularly when the plates fit the bar snugly. If the lifter is doing several reps, the need for collars is increased because even a slight shift on any given rep will tend to cause the plates to shift further on the next rep. This tendency develops because the bar is beginning in an unbalanced state and such a bar will tend to be lifted in an uneven manner (i.e., one end of the bar will be higher than the other). The plates on an uneven bar tend to shift when the bar is lifted or replaced in the platform.

Although lifting without collars on the bar cannot be recommended, most lifters have little problem with not using the collar for low rep exercises in training, particularly when weights that are comfortably below the lifter's maximum are used. However, if the lifter does go without collars, special care should be taken that no one is injured if the plates shift or even fall off the bar during or immediately after the lift. The lifter who is not using collars must be alert, so that if any shifting of the plates is sensed, he or she will immediately return the bar to the platform.

Platform

The weightlifting "platform" is the special surface the weightlifter stands upon while performing Olympic lifts and related exercises. It is the only other piece of lifting equipment that as import as the bar. The platform serves the function of providing the lifter with a stable, level and relatively smooth surface upon which to stand and perform the lift. It also protects the flooring below the platform.

There are essentially two kinds of platforms: competition and training. The dimensions and composition of competition platform are governed by the technical rules of the sport (see Appendix I). The dimensions are designed to give the lifter adequate room to perform the lift, and the composition rules are intended to assure that the lifter has an appropriate surface on which to perform the lift.

In general it is not necessary to train on a platform that has competition dimensions. Most lifters confine their movements during a lift to an area less than 5' in length and a few inches longer that the bar in terms of width. Therefore, a platform that is 8' by 8', or 3 m by 3 m (the European standard), is perfectly adequate for training purposes (as compared with the 4 m by 4 m that is required in competition).

Wood provides an ideal material for a platform. It is hard enough to offer a solid surface against which the lifter will press with his or her feet during the lift. Yet it is not so hard that it does not give at all on impact (as compared with a material like concrete, which gives far less).

An excellent platform can be made by using two by fours that are placed on end (the 2" side down) or four by fours bolted together with steel rods. The underlying structure is then normally covered with at least one layer of plywood in order to assure that the surface of the platform is even. When an 8' by 8' platform is used, the center of the platform (front to back) is normally covered with a solid sheet of plywood; then another sheet is split lengthwise into two 2' by 8' pieces so that the lifter has a seamless sheet of plywood on which to stand when lifting and two "runners" outside that sheet on which the bar is placed. A further improvement can be made by using masonite with the screened surface turned up as a final layer. Masonite seems to offer a nearly perfect amount of friction to the lifter's feet. Slippage is virtually eliminated by the texture of the screened surface, but the screening does not present so much friction that the lifter's foot will "catch" or be difficult to move when the feet are brought closer together (such as when recovering from a split or squat).

It is common for the outside runners (or at least the center 2' to 4' on either side) to be constructed of rubber instead of plywood. The rubber surface helps to absorb the shock of the bar when it is dropped and spares the plates as well. Such rubber is not necessarily ideal for the entire surface of the platform because the lifter's feet may catch on it even if it is of a fairly hard composition. Soft rubber in the center of the platform (where the lifter stands) is completely unacceptable because the lifter's feet will sink into the surface. This creates both a lack of stability and a depth from which the lifter's foot needs to be lifted before it can be moved (an extremely unsafe situation).

However, when a hard rubber surface becomes fairly smooth and a little dusty, it generally permits a lifter's feet to move freely enough for it to be acceptably safe. An alternative and inexpensive platform design consists of two sheets of 4' by 8' plywood (3/4" in thickness) placed side by side. There should be at least two (preferably three) layers of plywood. The top layer should have the seam between the two sheets of plywood running from front to back. The layer underneath should have the seam running side to side. This kind of design is easy to assemble and quite durable (although it will not distribute the force of a falling bar quite as well as a design that includes a layer of long boards). If rubber runners are to be used, they should be the same thickness as the plywood or a multiple of it (e.g., twice as thick). If they are the same thickness as the plywood, the top surface of the platform can have one sheet of plywood with its 8' length running from front to back and 2' by 8' lengths of rubber running along either side of the center plywood.

The wood of any platform should be secured with screws or threaded rod. It should never be glued together. Glue tends to create a platform that cannot withstand long term stress. Generally the glue will not give way, but the wood will break at the points of the greatest stress. Moreover, gluing a platform will make disassembly impossible. This can create problems if the platform should ever have to be moved. Even worse, if certain areas of the platform become damaged while others remain intact (a virtually inevitable development), gluing prevents the easy disassembly that enables you to replace or move the damaged boards, thereby dramatically extending the life if the platform.

A surface of hard rubber under the entire training platform, regardless of its construction, will help to protect the underlying floor as well as the lifter's joints. When the platform is being erected for competitions, some sort of covering with a slight amount of give will serve to protect the surface of the floor from damage from the platform and make it more likely that you are invited back to that venue.

Squat Racks

There will be many instances in which a weightlifter will want to suspend the bar at approximately shoulder level in performing a certain exercise. The "squat rack" permits a lifter to suspend a bar at the appropriate height, and therefore it is a vital piece of equipment for any gym (unless the gym is equipped with a power rack, which is described below). Squat racks are generally adjustable in height. There are two basic types: movable and step racks,

Movable racks are preferred by many lifters because they can be placed on and removed from the platform whenever desired. This permits the lifter to perform on a platform with no obstructions when snatches, clean and jerks and pulls are being performed. When the racks are needed for squatting, jerks from the rack or some other exercise, they can be placed on the platform. If the lifter should miss a lift after having taken a weight from the rack, it can be harmlessly dropped to the platform.

These racks generally consist of a base at least 12" square, a steel pipe or rectangular tubing (which forms he upright of the rack) and V- or U-shaped area at the top of the upright into which the bar is placed. Better racks have an extension of the Y or U at the rear so that it is difficult for the athlete to step through or overshoot the racks when replacing the bar on the racks.

Step racks are fixed and can be used for squatting and a few other exercises. They typically consist of two railing like structures with several rungs or steps 6" to 12" in depth and arranged at successively lower levels from the back of the rack to the front. Several uprights support each railing. The railings are placed so that each is several inches inside the inner collars of the bar. These railings are usually connected with lengths of flat iron that are placed at the back of the rack at the top and the bottom. The last step nearest the front of the rack is generally deeper than the rest (at least 18") and is set at a level just below the point the bar would reaches if the lifter performs a back squat to the lowest depth possible. This step, among other functions, serves as a mechanical spotter for the squat.

When the athlete uses such a rack for squatting, he or she places the bar on a rung that facilitates easy removal of the bar from the rack. To squat, the lifter faces the rear of the rack and straightens his or her legs to raise the bar from the support. He or she then steps backward to a position in which the bar is over the middle of the lowest rung of the rack. The squat is then performed. Should the lifter miss a squat, he or she merely relaxes a little and lets the bar come to rest on the lowest rungs of the rack. The steps at higher levels accommodate lifters of different heights and lifters who wish to perform exercises in which the bar begins at various levels.

One important caution that must be observed pertains to the grip, whichever kind of rack is being used. The lifter should be sure that the width of his or her grip is narrow enough so that if the bar is replaced on the rack (or dropped in the event of a miss) the hands are well out of the way of the bar. A safety rack can easily become a dangerous threat if this rule is not observed.

Fig. 34, in Chapter 5, which shows the front squat, also displays a set of squat racks.

Power Rack

A power rack supports a barbell at a wide variety of heights. Power racks have two pairs of vertical "uprights" (one on either side of the lifter). Horizontal holes are drilled into each pair of uprights at the same level so that a steel rod or "pin" can be passed through the uprights (front to back). These pins support the barbell. The holes are generally drilled at intervals of 2" to 3".

The earlier versions of most power racks had only a few inches between the paired uprights (i.e., from to back, referred to as "depth"), with the pairs of uprights having a distance between them of 3' to nearly 4' (i.e., the inside width). Because the depth of such racks is small, high quality steel pins that are 5/8" in diameter can support as much as a half ton on well constructed racks (assuming the weight is not dropped on them). More recent designs have a far greater depth than the original versions of the power rack, typically between 2' and 3'. This permits lifters to perform certain exercises (like squats) that may involve some forward and backward motion and considerable vertical motion inside the rack. In such a case, a short pin or hook is be used to support the bar at the starting point of the exercise. A set of pins that are longer than the depth of the uprights are placed just below the lowest point the lifter will assume during the lift. Then, if the lifter misses, the bar will be "caught" by the racks and the lifter can safely and easily move out from under the bar (see the bottom of Fig. 22 for an example of such "safety" pins).

In terms of materials used to construct a power rack, there are a number of choices. Many beginners build their own racks with the uprights made of wood. Racks that are made of four by fours, with holes drilled no closer than 3" and pins 5/8" in diameter or more, will comfortably support weights of up to a quarter of a ton or even more. Steel is recommended for heavier weights, and by the time such weights are needed, it is best to purchase a commercial rack. The buyer should look for uprights constructed of 2-3" steel pipe or tubing with walls that are at least 1/8" thick. The pins used should be at least 5/8" in diameter (for shallow racks, 6" deep or less), 1" for deeper racks.

If the bar is to be lowered from its initial position on the rack during the exercise, it should be supported in that initial position on a set of short pins or hooks that make it easy to remove the bar and step a short distance back in order to clear the pins. The pins should have a nut, washer or other "stopper" on the end furthest from the rack so that the bar cannot roll off the support accidentally (see the upper area of Fig. 22 for an example).

There are several important guidelines for using power racks. As with other kinds of racks, care must be taken to assure that the hands or any other part of the body do not get between the bar and the racks. The pins should always be longer and stronger than required for the weights being used so that there is a margin for error should the pins move or should the weights be dropped forcefully on the pins. The uprights themselves should be securely fixed to the floor or a heavy platform at the bottom and to the wall or overhead rafters on top. Always use two sets of pins. The first set supports the bar. The second set catches the bar when the lift can't be completed (in a shallow rack the second set of pins is placed immediately below the first in the event the first set is dislodged or otherwise fails). Holes should be drilled no closer than every 2"—closer holes will weaken the rack (removable 1/2" layers of plywood can be placed within the rack to achieve other relative bar heights, should such precision be required). Fig. 22 illustrates a deep power rack.

Fig. 22

Jerk Boxes

A piece of equipment that has become popular in Europe in recent years is the jerk box. One box is used to support each side of the bar (the plates rest on the box). The boxes are typically designed so that their height can be adjusted for lifters of different height. The bar rests in a position just below the position assumed by the lifter at the lowest point in the dip for the jerk. The lifter bends the legs into a partial squat in order to remove the bar from the rack and then straightens up to a standing position.

Jerks are performed in the same way that they would be from any rack. The advantages of the jerk boxes are: a) the lifter does not have to walk away from the racks in order to perform the jerk; b) if a miss should occur, there is no need for the lifter to replace the bar on the rack again; and c) when the lifter is doing reps, he or she simply steps out from under the bar after locking out each rep, permitting it to be caught by the blocks in a proper position for the next rep. Care must be employed in using such racks since it is possible for an off center jerk to cause the plates to miss the blocks entirely, so that the bar falls on the blocks instead. If this occurs, the bar can catch the lifter's fingers against the block, causing a serious injury. At least one European lifter has lost a portion of a finger in this way.

Pulling Blocks

There are a number of advantages in performing lifts, pulls and deadlifts with the bar at a starting position above the floor. Blocks serve to raise the bar to a higher level. There are a number of designs for blocks, each with advantages and disadvantages. For example, the larger a block is, the safer. This is because the bar is less likely to miss the block when it falls. On the negative side, a large block is harder to move and store.

All blocks should be wide enough (approximately 16") to support all of the plates on a fully loaded bar. (They should be spaced widely enough so that they are a few inches inside the inner collars of the bar on either side.) The distance front to back should be at least the width of the plates (45 cm) if it is unlikely for any forward or backward motion of the bar to occur in the course of the exercise (e.g., if only pulls and deadlifts are to be performed). If classical lifts are to be done from the boxes, a length of at least 24" is preferable. As was stated earlier, oversized dimensions serve to give the lifter a margin for error if there is a miss.

There should be "stoppers" just inside either end of the block to keep the bar from rolling off. Strips of wood or rubber at least 1/4" thick will serve this purpose (rubber tends to stand up better and protects any bumper plate that is dropped on it). The stoppers should run nearly the width of the blocks. With a little thought, blocks can be constructed so that they are stackable.

Some blocks are constructed of solid planks of wood. Others are constructed of plywood placed on top of two by sixes that have been positioned on edge so that they form a rectangular frame with several braces or cross members inside. Several pieces of plywood can be laminated together to form a block as well. It is a good idea to use plywood or some other wood that is resistant to splitting, especially on the top layer of the box. Placing a layer of rubber in the surface of the box is also advisable as it will both preserve the life of the block and help to protect the surface of bumper plates that fall on the block.

Perhaps the most popular height of blocks is approximately 6" to 7". This height places the bar just under the knees of most lifters. As was

suggested earlier, two or three blocks can be placed one on top of the other so that varying heights can be achieved. Alternatively, blocks can simply be made at different heights to achieve different purposes. This is probably the preferred approach, but it requires considerable storage space for the different types of boxes. A set of blocks is displayed in the picture of the athlete who is cleaning from the blocks in Chapter 5.

A Block To Stand On

In addition to raising the height of the bar by placing it on blocks, lowering the bar in relation to the lifter by raising the lifter's body is also useful. This is normally done by the lifter's standing on a raised surface. The ideal surface would simply be the length of a training platform (e.g., 8' to 10') and the width of the portion of the platform on which the lifter stands (3' to 4'). The height of the surface would be between 1" and 4" (generally at the lower end of this range—i.e., 1" to 2").

Unfortunately, a platform as large as the one described above would be difficult to move and would take up considerable storage space. Therefore, most lifters settle for a block that is approximately 2' long (front to back) and 4' wide. Power snatches and cleans, squat lifts and pulls can be performed with relative safety on such blocks, but split lifts cannot (they require a platform that is at least 4' long). However, when lifts are performed, the lifter must be careful to remember that he or she is on a smaller surface and that there is not as much room to run and adjust as on a full-size platform. Therefore, no attempt should be made to "save" a lift by quickly moving the feet under the bar when standing on a block.

It is best to make the raised platform out of solid wood, but if a hollow box is used, the builder should be sure to place supports within the block so that there is ample support for the bar, the lifter and the combined forces that develop during the lifting process.

Using "The Ropes"

From the 1930s through the 1950s, one of the most highly regarded weightlifting coaches and theorists in the United States was Charles Ramsey. A successful businessman, world traveler and student of famous strongman Maxick, Ramsey was a pioneer in many aspects of weightlifting training. One of his innovations was the use of a pair of ropes as a supportive mechanism for a bar so that the bar could be lifted from varying heights. Such ropes have many of the same uses as a power rack, but offer some interesting advantages over the power rack.

Each of two ropes are arranged to hang vertically at a point just inside the inner collars of the bar (spliced loops in the rope are used to connect the ropes to the bar). The ropes are supported by two pulleys on either side of the bar. These pulleys are supported by a single "I" or "H" beam that is placed across the top of two "A-frame" structures that are similar to the supporting structure of a child's swing (the pulleys are attached to the beam by means of pipe clamps). The A-frame structures must be placed such that they are at least a foot wider than the weightlifting bar it will support. This assures that the bar will be in no danger of contacting the supporting structure in the event of an off balance miss. In addition, the base of the rack must be substantially wider than any possible forward or backward travel of the bar during the lift.

The far ends of the supporting ropes are secured to a chain via clamps and snap hooks which are attached to the A-frames on each side are used to secure the chain to the A-frames. The links in the chain permit the ropes to be secured at virtually any height when the chain's links are fixed to the A-frame.

When using the ropes, the lifter sets the bar at a height that is appropriate to begin a particular exercise. As soon as the bar is lifted, slack is created in the rope, permitting nearly complete freedom of movement in the bar. If the lifter misses, he or she need only step out from under the bar pushing away with the arms. The bar will then be caught by the ropes. Some of the most popular exercises that were performed with the ropes were jerks, hang snatches and cleans and partial presses and squats of all types.

In order to assure safety when using ropes, it is important that the rope be several times stronger than is necessary to stop the falling bar (considering the mass of the bar and the degree to which it is accelerated by the force of gravity). The rope, its loops an its clamps need to be in a good state of repair so that they are at full strength. The loops must be small enough so that they will not slide easily over the inside collar and it will not slide out inadvertently. Finally, the lifter must not attempt to save the bar by running forward or back. In such a situation, when the bar is released, it will begin a pendulum like action around the support, causing the bar to swing dangerously.

Although rarely used today, Ramsey's ropes offer an interesting and versatile training aid for the lifter who has the space and the initiative to build them.

Grip Development Devices

A number of grip development devices are on the market today. Many of them are effective, but none of them are effective if they are not used regularly. Chapter 5 explains the various grip exercises that can be done with and without these devices.

There are two fundamental types of exercise approaches. One emphasizes development of the holding or isometric type of strength. The other involves the use of concentric contractions (i.e., closing the hand against resistance). Holding types of exercise are generally practiced by using devices commonly available in the gym. These consist of holding the bar itself, holding plates, lifting dumbbells and barbells with thick handles (e.g., 2" diameter) and rope climbing, or chinning on hanging ropes. In doing these exercises the lifter merely endeavors to hold the grip against greater resistance or against the same resistance for a longer period.

Some athletes favor holding a weight for long periods (fifteen seconds to one minute). Others hold a more difficult resistance for two seconds to twelve seconds. I prefer the shorter holds with heavier resistance because less strain is placed on the joints of the fingers. I once won a pinch gripping contest at our gym by holding a given form of resistance for a longer period than anyone else (seventy-five seconds). When I released the resistance, the joints of my fingers ached for several minutes, and it took weeks for the joints to fully recover. Needless to say, that was my last effort at an extended period of pinch gripping.

Exercises that involve closing the hand typically use plates or heavy springs for resistance. Years ago, Iron Man magazine publisher Peary Rader offered V-shaped grippers with different strength springs that offered resistance at the bottom of the V. Today those kinds of grippers are available only from IronMind Enterprises. IronMind offers other kinds of gripping devices as well (see Bibliography for further information).

My favorite spring type gripper is the "Super Gripper," which is still available through Iron Man magazine and Iron Mind Enterprises (see Bibliography for addresses). It comes with two springs that can be moved along the length of the gripper to vary the resistance. I have added two additional springs (which is not recommended by the manufacturer) and have experienced no failure of the device despite years of use. The adjustability offered by this device, as well as its smooth operation, make it a pleasure to use (a plate loading grip device and the Super Gripper are shown in Fig. 23.

Fig. 23

Benches

Although bench presses are hardly a staple exercise for the Olympic lifter, having a bench in a weightlifting gym is a good idea. The most versatile type has a hinge near one end that permits it to be converted from a flat bench to an incline bench with a seat (see Fig. 44 in Chapter 5), enabling the lifter to exercise the pressing muscles at a variety of angles. If a lifter trains alone or in a gym where there are an ample number of power racks, the benches need not have uprights attached, because the power rack can be used to support the weight.

Whenever a bench is purchased, it is a good idea to get a heavy duty one. This means one with steel at least 1.5" in diameter supporting the bench, a heavy board (at least 2" thick) supporting the back and high density foam padding. Such a bench will offer long life and safety and is well worth the additional cost.

Height Gauge

A device that is not used in most gyms as frequently as it should be is the height gauge. As its name suggests, a height gauge is designed to measure the height that is achieved by a lifter's pull, or at least to determine when a given target has be achieved. Most height gauges are free standing on a base that is 1' or more in diameter. An upright that has holes drilled in is every inch or two is supported by the base. A hinged or spring loaded device protrudes from the upright at a 90° (i.e., parallel to the floor). The purpose of the spring is to enable the protrusion to freely travel higher should the bar rise above the target height (leaving the base and upright of the gauge undisturbed).

A simple and ingenious version of the height gauge has been developed by Tommy Kono. Squat racks are placed a couple of feet in front of and behind one end of the bar. A stick is placed on the weight holder of the squat racks at the target height for the pull. One end of the stick is secured to one of the squat racks by a rubber band. When the bar hits the stick, the end of the stick that is not secured by the rubber band is free to move upward while the other end of the stick remains in contact with the rack and pulls the other end of the stick back into its place on the rack after the rep. When using the gauge, the lifter places it so that the protruding measurement device is above one end of the bar, outside the plates. It is set at the height necessary for the lifter to snatch or clean the bar. Then the lifter endeavors to hit the protrusion in order to demonstrate that the proper height, or more, has been achieved.

Care must be taken in setting the bar to the desired height. It is easy to assume that the target height is equal to the bar height that must be achieved by the lifter in order to snatch or clean the bar. This may not be true for many lifters. The reason is that the action of the lifter during the pull and the actual lift are different. In the pull there is no necessary break in the pulling motion so that the squat under can be performed. In addition, the force transmitted to the bar by the lifter is not equal to the reaction force to the squat under. These offsetting actions, and a series of others sometimes result in differences in the height that must be achieved in the pull and the lift. In some cases the lifter will need to pull a weight higher in the pull than in the lift in order to have a hope of succeeding with the lift. Other lifters do not have to pull the bar as high. Only experimentation will tell.

A height gauge assures that the height of the bar is being measured correctly. The more traditional method (having the lifter pull the bar to his or her chest or waist) is not a reliable measurement method because the degree of leg bend and torso position, as well as the actual height of the bar, have an effect on the apparent height of the pull.

The other caution in measuring with the height gauge is that a gauge like the one described above will measure the height reached by the top of the sleeve of the bar. When the lifter is lifting, he or she is pressing up on the underside of the bar itself. There is a difference of approximately 1" and 1/2" between these heights, and this must be taken into account when any measurements are made. Fig. 24 depicts a height gauge.

The Training Facility

In some respects the ideal place for a lifter to train would be a large gymnasium, similar to one used for indoor basketball. Such a gym has a high ceiling and plenty of room, and it simulates the arenas in which many competitions are held. Unfortunately, lifters rarely have the luxury of such surroundings, and, in reality, most of such

Fig. 24

space would be wasted much of the time. Much smaller spaces are normally all that is available (and truly needed). Lifters should know that most of the great champions in weightlifting had access to only very modest quarters during most of their careers, and this did not prove to be a hindrance of any consequence. In fact, some champion lifters have trained in conditions that were unbelievably Spartan. Lack of adequate heat, space and optimal equipment has never stopped the lifter who was determined to become a champion.

The minimal space required for optimal lifting training is a floor space at least 10' in length and 9' in width (9' by 12' if you are training with others, so that they have a place to sit or stand). There must be sufficient overhead space for the lifter to lift the bar and the largest plates to arm's length with the feet and arms at shoulders' width. A little extra height is needed to allow for the thickness of the platform the lifter will stand on. For the average lifter (5' 8"), a ceiling height of 7' 6" is necessary and 8' or more is better (since the height of the platform will reduce the usable overhead space of the facility). Since the bar is 7' from side to side, a 9' width gives room on either side for some adjustment and spaces to store the plates at the sides of the platform. The 10' length gives the lifter some space to adjust forward and backward for a lift that is somewhat out of position (1' in the front and back of an 8' platform).

When space permits, having at least one platform that is competition size (4m by 4 m) permits club competitions to be held under official conditions.

When platforms are set side by side, there should be at least 18" between them. This allows for plates to be stored flat between the platforms when they are not being used. In such close quarters the lifters must be taught to drop the bar

before the plates are off the platform and never to chase the bar off the platform. The platform must be kept free of any plates that are not loaded on the bar. In this way the lifter knows that as long as his or her feet are within the confines of the platform, there is no danger of tripping.

The gym should be a pleasant place to spend time. Therefore, it should be kept clean and well ventilated, at a comfortable temperature and without drafts. There should be adequate light, though glare is to be avoided. Noise should be kept to a minimum. The music of the bars dropping, plates rattling, feet landing, coaches instructing and athletes encouraging one another are all that should be heard.

Some lifters say that listening to music helps pass the time in the gym. My feeling is that if you are just passing time, you should not be in the gym. Every set and every rep should have a purpose and should merit the lifter's full concentration. Listening to music can be both calming and inspirational, but calming should be reserved to pre- and post-workout sessions and inspiration to private pre-meet listening sessions. Moreover, music can make it difficult for the athlete to hear a coach's instructions.

When warm-ups and low intensity remedial exercises are being performed by all athletes and all of the athletes can agree that a certain kind of music is desirable, it may be appropriate to permit its use. However, it is generally better to have athletes who prefer to listen music at such times to use headphones. If this is done, special caution must be employed to assure that lifters who are disassociated from the sounds around them are not in a position to fail to hear a warning when some form of danger approaches them (e.g., another athlete who is trying to save a mispositioned lift).

Placing instructional posters, sequence photos and appropriate still photos around the gym can be inspirational and informative. References to upcoming meets and existing club and personal records can provide inspiration and focus as well. It is also a good idea to have at least one platform that has vertical and horizontal lines around it. Such lines provide an excellent background against which to measure the movement of the bar and the lifter when lifts are being performed. Having such lines on the platform as well can also be useful (as long as they do not affect the surface of the platform). They are an asset for video analysis as well as the coach's visual analysis. .

Starting A Club

One of the best ways to get a lifting program under way is to start an official USAW club (even if you have only one member to start). It is easy and inexpensive to do (it currently costs $50 for an annual membership). As an official club you will receive recognition from the USAW in the form of a certificate. You' will also receive the USAW's magazine <u>Weightlifting USA</u> . This magazine helps you to keep up with events in United States and world weightlifting. Information on selection criteria for international events is published regularly, as are meet results, coaching tips, profiles of athletes and clubs and information on products that are of use to athletes and coaches. In addition, club status makes you eligible to compete as a team in USAW competitions, to hold official competitions (upon receiving a formal sanction from the USAW) and to receive various awards and incentive programs sponsored by the USAW. USAW individual memberships and club membership are two truly outstanding values in weightlifting today.

As you can see, it does not require a lot of money to begin training for weightlifting competition. From several hundred to several thousand dollar in equipment and access to a modest physical facility in which to put it will do, and equipment properly used can last a lifetime.

Managing Risks

Our Litigious Society

We live in a litigious society. This fact is the source of great controversy today. Some people feel that litigation is far too widespread in our society, and many blame lawyers. This is far too simple an explanation. Lawyers certainly have personal values and powerful economic incentives that foster litigation, but juries that award damages where there is little or no fault, legislators who create a climate for legal claims and those victims who seek instant riches through the courts are at least as much to blame for our current litigation woes. It should be recognized that much good has been done by reasonable lawsuits that were successful. Entire industries have been motivated to alter unreasonable practices when losses suffered in court have caused companies to re-examine their standard ways of doing business.

Regardless of the merits of liability awards and legal reform, today's coach faces more legal responsibility than ever before. This fact, along with the relatively amateur nature of weightlifting, makes it especially appropriate for coaches to be extremely careful regarding the well being of their athletes. But there is an even more important reason for the coach to be concerned with an athlete's well being. The moral and the practical are the same thing. There is no advantage to be gained by any coach who places his athletes on the edge of disaster on a regular basis. Eventually, injuries will occur, the coach's athletes will suffer (along with the coach's reputation) and the coach's success will thereby be undermined. If a coach

regard the health and well being of his or her athletes as a foremost consideration out of common decency, the practical arguments for doing so are overwhelming.

How can a coach minimize his or her liability? One step is to get adequate training as a coach. Another step is to become familiar with first aid techniques. Still another step is to emphasize safety in all of its dimensions and to minimize liability risks. Safety should be a primary concern in teaching technique, in equipping and operating a gym and in developing a training plan.

Minimizing Liability Exposure

All gyms in which anyone other than the owner and immediate family trains regularly should consider taking some steps to limit their liability for training accidents and injuries. Every coach should secure some form of liability coverage. Such coverage is available through a variety of organizations. Knowing he or she is protected from lawsuits can offer valuable peace of mind for the coach. Remember that anyone can sue you. They may or may not be successful in such a suit, but merely defending yourself can be extremely expensive. Having insurance which covers you for defense costs as well as any losses is extremely important.

A second step is to secure releases (unless you are an employee or official volunteer of a facility that itself takes such measures) from all athletes with whom you work. No release, no matter how well drafted, can protect the coach from being sued or being held liable for negligence, but it can reduce the likelihood of such an occurrence. It is also advisable to secure a medical release indicating that the athlete is free to engage in strenuous exercise. If the athlete does not choose to secure such a release, you should at least go on record as having recommended an examination and medical permission to participate.

The most important step for the coach to take is to practice safety in its every facet and to inculcate the importance of safety in all of those he or she coaches. Negligence must be avoided at all times and be replaced by vigilance. Negligence can be defined as the failure to take action that an ordinary and prudent person would have taken under similar circumstances. To be found guilty of negligence, a person must have had a duty to act in a certain way and the victim of negligence must have suffered damages. For example, in a recent case a football player who suffered a paralyzing neck injury sued on the basis that he was not taught proper tackling techniques and neck strengthening exercises, things he argued, the prudent coach would have taught his players.

There are several kinds of negligence, all of which are unacceptable. Malfeasance involves acting in a manner that is deliberately injurious to another person (e.g., taking the bench out from underneath an athlete who is doing bench squats). Misfeasance is attempting to do something but doing it incorrectly (e.g., incorrectly teaching someone a lifting technique). Nonfeasance is the failure to do something that should have been done (e.g., when the end of the bar is loose and the coach permits an athlete to try a limit lift without tightening it securely, resulting in an injury when the bar falls apart during the lift). Obviously all forms of negligence must be avoided for moral and legal reasons. Some hints for doing this and for promoting general safety in the gym our outlined in the next section of this chapter.

Safety and Conduct Guidelines

Every gym should have safety and conduct guidelines which are communicated to each lifter and enforced. These guidelines should include an emergency procedure (see Chapter 11) for some information on first aid guidelines). It is best to communicate both in writing and orally. Where demonstrations or illustrations are appropriate they should be provided to all new athletes. Rules should apply for visitors as well as athletes. Two rules are foremost: stay out of the lifting area and avoid distracting the lifters. When anyone is actually lifting, they should be given the respect and attention of the other lifters (both to show support for the performer and to assure that others are aware of any dangers that the lifter may pose to them (e.g., by running toward them with the weight he or she is lifting). The gym is not a place for horseplay. Silence should be observed immediately before a lifter begins a lift.

Gyms should have a first aid kit available along with the entire contents of a competition or gym bag that have already been discussed.

In addition to the safety consideration already mentioned, there are a number of other general safety practices that merit mention here.

1) When changing the plates loaded on a bar that is on a rack, remove weights from racks symmetrically (one plate at a time, with equal amounts on each side, particularly when removing plates that are 10 kg. each or more).

2) The weight room should always be maintained in good order. Plates, personal equipment, dumbbells, etc., should not be left in the area in which a weight will actually be lifted. Plates in particular should never be lying where the bar may fall.

3) Overcrowding in the gym should be avoided; the risk of injury increases significantly as the gym becomes more crowded. Lifters should always be able to stay a safe distance from one another while lifting. When an athlete is performing on Olympic or related lift, no one else should be on the platform. When the lift being performed requires a spotter(s), no one but the spotter(s) should be near the lifter.

Each piece of equipment should be spaced far apart so that other there is room for athletes to walk between the equipment safely (otherwise athletes should refrain from doing so).

4) Use collars unless you have a bar on which the plates fit quite snugly, and especially in areas of high humidity. (Chalk can be added to the sleeve of the bar on high humidity days to reduce the phenomenon of plates sliding along the sleeve.)

5) Chalk should be used to assure the grip, even when using straps.

6) All weightlifting equipment should be checked regularly and maintained in a state of good repair. A seriously bent bar, or one that does not revolve freely, can be a hazard. Any piece of equipment that is showing any signs of wear should be replaced promptly. Pushing too far with worn equipment simply is not worth the risk. If the gym compromises, it should only be in terms of aesthetics. Worn paint never hurt anyone, but a worn cable on a machine or a broken collar has done so many times.

7) Proper weightlifting shoes should always be worn. If the athlete has leather-soled shoes (not recommended), he or she should apply rosin to the shoes before any attempt that will involve significant foot movement. Rosin may be appropriate even with rubber-soled shoes if the platform is not providing good traction for the lifter.

It should be noted that there is a fine line between adequate traction and too much traction. Inadequate traction leads to slipping (which can lead to missed lifts and injuries). However, if there is too much traction (friction) between the lifter's shoes and the platform, the lifter's feet can stop too suddenly. This can cause the lifter to lose his or her balance, to misposition his or her feet, or to be injured by the trauma of too sudden a stop. Excess traction can occur, particularly with textured rubber matting and shoes that have a rubber sole that is made to grip the surface of the platform.

8) Athletes should always face any racks from which weights are to be taken and replaced. In this way the athletes see where they are going at the end of the lift.

9) Athletes should dress properly in clothing that is stretchable, closely fits the body and is appropriate for the temperature in the gym, although wearing full length training pants is encouraged in order to avoid abrasions to the thighs and shins while pulling. Lifters should not wear jewelry (particularly on the neck) or hats while lifting. Jewelry around the neck can catch the bar on the way up or down and injure the lifters. A hat with a brim can be dislodged by the bar when lifting. Other kinds of hats can also become loose and fall to the platform or interfere with a lifters vision, so they should be avoided.

10) Lifters should always double check any weight they are about to attempt to see if it has been loaded correctly (and evenly to the correct weight). The best communication between an athlete and others can still result in a mistake, and it is not uncommon for athletes to mis-load their own lifts. We have always had a saying at Lost Battalion Hall (the gym in which I have done most of my training over the past thirty years) that if a lifter attempts a weight that has been loaded improperly by someone else, it is the lifter's fault and not the loader's. The loader is helping. It is the lifter's obligation to assure that the weight is correct (this is true in a competition as much as it is in the gym).

11) Lifters should be encouraged to maintain their own equipment carefully. Shoes deserve special attention (worn or loose heels or soles can be very dangerous). Straps that are frayed can break when a lifter explodes in the pull and lead to an injury. Belts that break in mid-lift can be a hazard as well. Again, faded sweat pants never hurt anyone, but functional features of equipment must be maintained at the highest level.

Keeping the Lifting Platform Safe

The surface upon which weights are lifted (the platform) is one of the key components of weightlifting safety. It must be kept clear of everything other than the lifter and the bar during the classical and related lifts.

Plates must be kept off the platform. An athlete can trip over them during, before or after a lift. In addition, they pose an extra hazard should the lifter drop the bar or replace it on the platform heavily. In such a case, contact with a plate could cause the plate to flip into the air, injuring the athlete or someone else nearby. Alternatively, the bar could rebound horizontally from the plate after hitting its edge (a fast moving bar of this type can again injure the athlete or anyone standing nearby). Even in the best case, contact with another plate can damage a bumper plate unnecessarily.

Any racks, blocks, chalk boxes and similar equipment should be stored a distance of several feet from the athlete when not in use. In this way, if an athlete should "run" off the platform in attempting to save a lift, there is some margin for error before the athlete or bar contacts one of these objects.

When a lifter replaces the bar on the platform, he or she should be aware that the force of the bar's rebound can be considerable (especially when the bar has bumper plates). Many a lifter has sprained a finger or wrist by dropping the bar or replacing it heavily with the hand positioned directly over the bar. The lifter can avoid this risk by not replacing the bar too heavily, by keeping hands and wrists well behind the bar when it lands and by

permitting the hands to break contact with the bar altogether just before it contacts the platform.

The platform should always rest on a completely stable surface. It should be absolutely level and flat, with nothing protruding from the platform at any point (i.e., there must be nothing for the lifter to catch his or her feet on while lifting). The surface of the lifting platform should always be kept clean of anything that could possibly cause the athlete to slip.

The Use of "Spotters"

As a safety precaution, it is generally recommended that weightlifters request "spotters" when they are using a near maximum weight in an exercise that places the body between the bar and some other piece of equipment (including even the floor). The need for a spotter is greatest in situations in which a miss will result in the lifter's being unable to replace the bar on the support from which it was taken at the start of the lift or in which the lifter cannot easily permit the bar to fall safely to floor in the event of a miss. For example, a spotter is critical in the bench press because the body is between the bar and the bench upon which the athlete is lying, because the lifter who misses a bench press will be unable to replace the bar on the rack from which it was taken at the outset of the exercise and because the lifter cannot easily let the bar fall to the floor in the event of a miss. The squat is another example of an exercise is which spotters should be employed (although it is generally far easier to drop a weight backward during a squat than it is to set out from under a missed bench press).

Spotters are not generally used or recommended when an athlete is performing one of the classic lifts or closely related movements for several reasons. One reason is that it requires a great deal of skill and timing to "catch" a bar that is missed in one of the classical lifts. This is because the bar always descends after reaching its highest point in a snatch or C&J before the athlete is able to "fix" the bar. Therefore, in most instances any spotter would have to allow the bar to fall and only interfere after the bar had, in his or her judgment, fallen too far—a very difficult thing to do. If there is one spotter on each side of the bar, it is unlikely that a bar that is moving quickly will be caught at the same time by both spotters. This poses a risk to the spotters and the athlete.

Another problem is that the spotter would have to stand so close to the lifter that he or she might be endangered by the athlete's movements or could pose a risk to the athlete (by interfering with the movement of the bar). Perhaps the most compelling reason for offering no spot in the classical lifts is that the athlete who has been properly trained is able to let the bar fall safely to the platform whenever a miss occurs. There is rarely a need for a spotter when an athlete has been tutored in how to miss. The most common exception to this general rule of not spotting the classical lifts occurs when an athlete is a complete beginner and the coach wants to permit the athlete to feel the proper positioning of the bar without fear. In such situations, the weight being lifted is light enough for a single spotter (usually the instructor) to control the bar quite easily.

There are two fundamental types of spotters: human and mechanical. Human spotters are more common and versatile and tend to be more readily available, but they also tend to be less reliable. We will address the use of human spotters first.

Human Spotters

While spotters are vital for some exercises, all things considered , no spotter than is better a poor one. Therefore, it is important for spotters to follow appropriate guidelines in their work.

There are three basic configurations of human spotters: the one, two and three person spots.

The one person spot typically consists of having the spotter place his or her hands near the middle of the bar or near some part of the body (usually the torso) of the lifter being spotted. With a two person spot, one spotter stands on either side of the exerciser, just outside the end of the bar being lifted. A three person spot (which is normally used only when two spotters are not confident they can handle a given weight in the event of a miss) combines the one person and two person spot.

There are several fundamental rules that all spotters should observe, The first rule is that spotters should never touch the bar or lifter while the athlete is attempting to make a lift and still has a reasonable chance of success. There are many definitions of "reasonable" in this context, but the one that I have found to be the most reliable is the point at which the upward progress of a bar has ceased and it has actually begun to descend. For instance, if a lifter is attempting to stand up from the squat position, he or she may move the bar very slowly at the most difficult point of the lift. The bar may even stop very briefly before continuing its ascent. However, once the bar begins to descend, the lift is essentially over, and the lifter should be assisted. (I have never witnessed an athlete make an all out effort at a maximum squat, begin to descend and then recover successfully; I have seen athletes lose their balance with a submaximum weight and then recover successfully after descending, achieving the proper "groove" or activating a muscular rebound and then attempting the squat a second time.) Therefore, spotters should not intervene unless one of three things happen: a) if the upward motion of the bar begins to reverse its upward motion (lifts can still be made after a bar stops, but a lifter is virtually never able to raise a bar back up again, once its

upward motion has been reversed; if the spotter renders assistance as soon as the slightest bar drop is detected, intervention will occur before the bar picks up significant downward velocity and any danger of injury arising is minimized); b) if the lifter asks for help with a pre-agreed word like "take" or some non-verbal indication of a need for help (spotters must be aware of what signal a lifter will give when he or she wishes to ask for assistance); or, c) if an obvious accident has occurred or the spotters are all aware that an accident is about to occur, and the lifter either does not know it or is too disabled or too frightened to ask for help.

If the spotter renders assistance as soon as the slightest bar drop is detected, intervention will occur before the bar picks up significant downward velocity, and any danger of injury arising will be minimized. Intervening any earlier means that an attempt which the lifter might have completed unassisted has been interfered with. Since it is generally agreed that maximum muscular effort and tension are major factors in training progress, the overanxious spotter will deprive the athlete of the training effect that he or she so dearly strives for. However, delaying assistance beyond the earliest point at which the bar begins to descend exposes the lifter to unnecessary risk.

When the spotter jumps in prematurely during a one person spot, the worst case is normally that the lifter will have missed the opportunity for a good set. With a two person spot, a premature catch on the part of one spotter can be disastrous to the lifter, the other spotter or both. Hence it is very important for the spotters to agree on when the bar will be caught, and they should always be watching each other as well as the bar, to assure that an uneven catch will not occur. It is also important for the lifter to continue to try to lift the bar (unless he or she is injured). A lifter should never leap out from under the bar unless the spotters have been given fair warning. Any lifter who does so is not respectful of the spotter's well being and is therefore not deserving of a spot. All parties should agree to criteria to indicate when the attempt is over (e.g., when the lifter asks for help) unless there is an obvious emergency. Obviously, all parties should know the exact nature of the exercise being performed, the weight that will be attempted and how many reps the lifter is striving to achieve. (Spotters should always check to be sure that the weight has been loaded properly; this is the primary responsibility of the athlete, but an extra check has never hurt anyone and has often helped.)

A second rule is that wherever possible the spotters should only touch the bar or other form of resistance (although never the plates), not the lifter. It has unfortunately become common for spotters to touch the lifter instead of the bar in many gyms. This is dangerous for several reasons.

201

One reason is that when the lifter is touched, it can cause him or her to lose balance, effective positioning under the bar or concentration, all of which can lead to a disaster. Another problem is that a touch to the lifter's body can cause the lifter to lose the position of the body or the rigidity of a body part, also a disaster. Still another problem is that touching the lifter ignores the fundamental purpose for a spotter—to protect the lifter from the bar. That function is not being performed very well when the lifter is being effectively held under a bar that he or she has failed to lift. Perhaps the worst form of spotting is the variation in which the spotter touches a lifter's limbs (e.g., the arms in the bench press); such a spotter can exert uneven pressure on the two separate limbs, causing the lifter to lose control of the bar. Therefore, the spotter should always attempt to spot the bar, not the lifter. If the body must be touched, it should almost never be on the limbs, but rather, wherever possible, the torso.

A third key to safe and effective spotting is to make sure that the direction of the resistance is changed as little as possible by the spotter(s). Every effort should be made to lift the bar in the direction in which it would have otherwise gone. Pulling the resistance out of line with what the lifter expects can cause the lifter to lose balance or the ability to exert force (because the resistance moves outside the lifter's "base of support," a concept that is explained in Appendix II). This phenomenon endangers the lifter and the spotter(s). Agreement between the lifter and spotter(s) regarding the exact nature of the assistance the spotters will provide (e.g., assistance in replacing the bar on the rack or only in the event of a miss) further reduces the chance of something untoward happening during the lift.

There are also some important rules for the spotter to observe on the premise that self-protection comes first. It may seem heroic for a lifter to dive under a bar to save another lifter, regardless of the risk. Such a spotter forgets that under extreme (and extremely rare) conditions of real danger to the lifter, he or she is that lifter's only hope, a hope that fades if the spotter is injured. To assure his or her safety, the spotter should make sure that his or her hands are never placed between the bar or plates and any support that is being used (e.g., a rack in the case of the bar, the floor in the case of the plates). That way, if the lifter should collapse and the bar fall, the spotter will not get caught in the middle. When two spotters are working, both should stand just outside the ends of the bar, so that if the bar falls, it falls on their extended hands, not their bodies.

Mechanical Spotters

Mechanical spotters, such as a lower set of pins in a power rack, the training ropes described earlier or the lowest level in a step rack can be very valuable spotters. They prevent injury by catching the bar before it can harm the lifter without intervention from any person. They permit an athlete to train alone in relative safety.

There are at least four cautions that should be observed when an athlete is using a mechanical spotter. One caution is that the spotter must be up to the task. Flimsy or unstable racks that do not have the surplus capacity to safely stop a bar as it falls (as compared with a bar that is carefully placed on the rack) must not be relied upon. A second caution is that the spotting device must be set at the appropriate height. If it is too low, it will not provide adequate protection, and if it is too high, it will not permit a full movement. A third caution is that the lifter must be absolutely sure to keep his or her hands clear of the points at which the bar is likely to contact the supports in the event the lifter is unable to complete the lift.

Finally, mechanical spotters are not meant to have the bar dropped on them. They are made to stop the downward progress of the bar when the lifter settles down into them after realizing that the lift cannot be made. Dropping a bar on a spotter may damage the bar or the spotting device. More importantly, it may rebound from the support, causing injury. In an emergency, a good mechanical spotter will hold up to having a bar dropped on it, but that is not its primary purpose. Therefore, mechanical spotters are not intended to be used to spot the classical lifts. To my knowledge, the only devices that have ever been developed for that purpose are the "ropes" that have already been described in this chapter. Even they should be built with a very large safety margin, be used only sparingly and never be completely relied upon.

Mechanical spotters generally take the form of a pair of supporting surfaces placed below the lowest point the bar is expected to reach during the exercise. Step racks and power racks that have uprights which are placed far enough apart for the lifter to exercise inside the uprights (i.e., racks with a depth of a foot or more—Fig. 22 depicts such a rack) are common examples of mechanical spotters. The key cautions to be observed when using mechanical spotters is to set them at a height that is below the lowest point that is reached in the normal lift (a higher position can cause the bar to bounce and control to be lost). A position that is too low can fail to protect the lifter. (An inch or two below the lowest position is usually enough; for a lift like the bench press, where the body is between the bar and the bench, anything more than an inch below may be too much.) The final caution is that the lifter should be sure that the hands are always held well away from (usually well inside) the spotters. As was suggested earlier, mechanical spotters can be your best friend when they are used properly and judiciously.

When an Accident or Injury Occurs

Despite your best efforts, accidents and injuries will occur from time to time. If an injury occurs, your first concern should be the welfare of the injured athlete. First aid procedures (some of which are outlined in Chapter 11) should be followed immediately. Once first aid has been administered and the athlete has been properly attended to, the incident should be documented (date, time, nature of accident, witnesses, procedures followed). Have the physician and/or emergency personnel who treat the patient verify your report. Obtain statements from the witnesses and the injured athlete (these should be dated, signed and verified by impartial witnesses). Contact your attorney and liability carrier to explain the occurrence. Make no statements to legal representatives of the injured party without your own representation. Obtain a medical release for a return to activity when the injured athlete returns to the gym.

The USAW includes limited athlete accident insurance in its membership fee. There is also liability coverage for meet directors. Further information on coverage can be obtained from the USAW National Office at (719) 578-4508.

Summary

Vigilance regarding safety, and the selection and maintenance of personal equipment, gym equipment and training facilities will go a long way toward assuring high performance and safety in weightlifting. In the next chapter we will examine how some of the equipment that has been discussed in this chapter can be used to perform exercises that a weightlifter can use to facilitate the development of strength, power and technique for the competitive lifts.

Assistance exercises were important tools that Yuri Zacharevich used to become the dominant 100 kg. and 110 kg. lifter of the 1980s.

CHAPTER 5

Assistance Exercises For The Snatch And C&J

There is certainly no question that a lifter can improve his or her competitive lifts very substantially by doing nothing but those lifts. In fact, a significant number of World Champions has done little more than the snatch and C&J in practice, and some modern coaches argue that such training approaches the ultimate in weightlifting preparation.

In contrast, there were World Champions in the 1950s and 1960s who rarely trained on the Olympic lifts once they had developed their style (which in some cases was extremely crude). While there have been no reports of recent World Champions who have not practiced the Olympic lifts at all in training, there have certainly been a significant number of world class lifters who have spent only a small percentage of their training time on the "classic" lifts (i.e., the Olympic lifts performed exactly as they are in competition). There have also been some outstanding Master's Program lifters (athlete's aged thirty-five and above) who have been successful with hardly any heavy training on the classic lifts. With the rich array of exercises that can be used to improve performance in the snatch and C&J, this should not be surprising.

Can any lessons be learned from the champions about the use of assistance exercises? With a little study, it is relatively simple to identify some underlying principles. First, all champions spend at least some of their training time on the competitive lifts, typically a minimum of 15% to 20% of overall training time, and sometimes as much as 60% to 80%. It seems that everyone must practice their trade, the classic lifts (perhaps with the exception of some older lifters who have been doing the lifts for a generation or more). Second, no champions have become great training on the lifts alone. At least some assistance work seems to be required, particularly in terms of leg strengthening exercises like the squat. Third, it is obvious that a rather broad range of exercise mixtures can yield high level results. Fourth, the blend of exercises often changes over a lifter's career as the lifter's needs change. Fifth, while it is probable that even the greatest champions are doing some unnecessary things in their training, it is also quite likely that at least some of those champions are champions <u>because</u> they have discovered the optimal blend of classical lifting practice and assistance exercises for <u>them</u>.

The aim of this chapter is to acquaint the reader with most of the assistance exercises that are used in the training of weightlifters and to help the athlete and coach sort out the good exercises from the bad (yes, there are some assistance exercises that are simply bad, because they are dangerous and/or almost totally ineffective) and the appropriate exercises from the inappropriate. (An exercise may be effective yet completely inappropriate for a given lifter, at least at a certain point in that lifter's career.)

What is an Assistance Exercise?

An assistance exercise is any exercise, other than the classic snatch and C&J, that can improve performance (directly or indirectly) on the snatch and C&J. The reason for this distinction is that even the snatch and C&J themselves can be assistance exercises, if they are done in an unconventional (for that lifter) way. For example, a lifter might practice jerking with a pause at the bottom of the dip. The purpose of the pause might be technical (e.g., to teach the lifter better control during the dip). Alternatively, a pause at the bottom of the dip might be used as one of a variety of techniques to strengthen the lifter's legs in order to facilitate a better drive in the jerk. Such a practice would convert the jerk into an assistance exercise (as compared with doing the jerk with a tempo that is normal for that lifter).

The General Purposes of Assistance Exercises

Assistance exercises, by their very nature, are exercises that emphasize some different aspect of the lift or the muscles that perform that lift or de-emphasize something that the classic lifts include. In general, these exercises fall into three categories: exercises that improve some aspect of technique; exercises that improve some aspect of functional strength and/or power; and exercises that are used to prevent or treat injuries by strengthening a specific area of the body. As the various exercises are presented below, we will discuss both their nature and purposes. Naturally, many exercises have more than one purpose.

Four Cautions About Assistance Exercises

Assistance exercises are methods of assisting development in the classical lifts. They are not an end in themselves. If they are used appropriately, they can be one of true foundations of long-term progress. However, the hazard of overemphasis on assistance exercise must be avoided.

It is common for an athlete to take a liking to a certain exercise because he or she is good at it, finds it pleasurable to do, or sees it as the key to correcting some deficiency. While it is very important for an athlete to develop enthusiasm for any exercise that he or she must do and there is no limit to the value of such enthusiasm, love of an exercise must not be permitted to influence unduly the overall composition of the lifter's training in terms of the exercises performed. The content of workouts must be determined by an athlete's relative needs and objectives at given stage in his or her development. Exercises should not appear in the regimen solely, or at least primarily, because the athlete likes them. If a rational planning process has been used to determine the overall content of the lifter's training program, then the lifter's enthusiasm can and should be completely released in training.

A second point to consider in employing assistance exercises is that the principle of the specificity of a training effect must always be considered. In this respect, it is generally true that the closer an assistance exercise is to a classical lift in terms of tempo, the nature of the motion, the tensions required to complete the exercise successfully, etc., the more direct the benefit to the classical lift will tend be. It is therefore important to consider that while an assistance exercise is selected because it has a somewhat different emphasis from a classical lift, a movement that is too far afield from the lift itself is likely to have little, if any, positive effect on performance in that lift (although there may be other reasons to do the exercise).

A third but important point to consider with regard to assistance exercises is that doing an exercise for the first time something of a shock to the body. The greater the difference between the assistance exercise and other exercises that have been practiced in the past, the greater the shock. If the exercise is very different from what has been practiced before (e.g., if the range of motion is greater, or the body or the resistance is in a different position when it exerts force), it ought to be treated like an entirely new exercise; the lifter ought to train on that exercise somewhat like a beginner. That means doing one or two sets of the exercise during the first few training days, doing the exercise only two or three times a week, starting light and progressing gradually over time. If the exercise is very close in nature to what the lifter has been doing or involves a shorter range of motion, there is less need for caution, although it never hurts to exercise moderation at first. There tends to be a long period of progress when exploring the limits of a new exercise if the resistance is increased gradually. That path of progress can be shortened or virtually eliminated (or an injury can result) when the athlete starts that exercise with near maximum or maximum weights or increases the weights he or she is using too rapidly.

Many a trainee has been forced to abandon an otherwise valuable exercise because he or she became injured doing it (particularly at the early stages in which the exercise was included in their routines) or because they injured the muscle(s) and/or joint(s) stressed by that exercise soon after it was included in is or her routine. These kinds of injuries occur primarily because the stress imposed by the new exercise (no matter how positive in nature overall) combined with the stress imposed by exercise(s) already being performed by the athlete prove to be too much for the muscles and/or joints to handle. When adding a very new exercise to a training program, it is wise to heed the advice of the two-time World Champion and former Olympic team coach, John Terpak: "make haste slowly."

A fourth and final caution to be observed when doing assistance exercises is the need for spotters while doing some of those exercises. Spotters are used to prevent a missed lift from falling on a lifter or to help a lifter who cannot complete a lift to return the resistance to its starting position. As was suggested in the previous chapter, spotters are not recommended when performing the classical lifts or their variations, such as the power or partial versions of those lifts (once the lifter learns how to miss, something a lifter should begin to learn on day one). Nevertheless, some assistance exercises (e.g., squats and bench presses) require the use of spotters for safety's sake. As was suggested in the previous chapter, these exercises are generally the ones in which the body is between the bar and the platform or supporting devices (such as benches) when the lift is being performed.

The Wide Array Of Assistance Exercises That Is Available

In discussing specific exercises, the following approach will be followed. The popular name(s) of the exercise will be provided, the purpose(s) of performing the exercise will be explained and a description of how it is to be performed will be given. Finally, an evaluation for the effectiveness of the exercise as well as any special dangers that can arise in doing the exercise or that, in the author's opinion, make the exercise not worth doing will be provided. The exercises are grouped by type, not by the lift to which they apply. For example, the power snatch, power clean and power jerk are all grouped together because the principles behind them are more or less the same, even though each assists a different lift. Whenever such grouping occurs, the exercises in the group may refer to an earlier exercise or assume the description of the first exercise in the group has been read. Therefore, it is important to read the description of the first exercise in the group before reading any of the others. It should noted that the amount of space that is devoted to an exercise is in no way related to its value.

Direct Variations Of The Classic Lifts

We will begin the list with exercises that are generally considered to be closely related to the classic lifts and that are generally included by Eastern European coaches among their volume counts for classic and related lifts.

Cleans

Purpose(s): Cleans are often performed without the jerk in order to facilitate practice on the clean. This is particularly true when the lifter wishes to do repetitions in the clean, since performing repetitions in both the clean and the jerk is very fatiguing. Cleans are also done alone when the lifter's clean is lagging relative to the jerk, or when the lifter prefers to work somewhat different muscle groups in different workouts (e.g., the pulling muscles one day and the jerking muscles the next, even though there is some overlap).

Description: The same as for the clean part of the C&J, which was explained in detail in Chapter 1.

Effectiveness: Performing cleans alone can be very effective and should be a part of virtually every lifter's training, at least at some periods

during the year. However, doing cleans separately (to the exclusion of C&J's) immediately before a competition can lead to unhappy results as the lifter may find it difficult to prepare mentally and physically for the jerk after doing the clean.

Jerks from the Racks or Stands

Purpose(s): The reasoning for performing jerks separately is much the same as for performing cleans by themselves. Jerks from the rack are particularly important for the lifter who is not able to consistently jerk what has been cleaned, because always practicing the jerk after the clean leaves the lifter in a fatigued state. While it is true that the lifter will always be in such a state during competition, it is also true that learning is enhanced by practice when the athlete is not fatigued, so at least some jerking by itself should be performed by certain lifters.

Description: The exercise is performed in the same way as it is after the clean, except that the athlete lifts the bar from supports which hold the bar somewhat below shoulder level when the athlete is standing. The supports (generally referred to as "racks") should be set at a height that will allow an inch or so clearance from the rack when the lifter straightens his or her legs with a loaded bar. The lifter should generally face the rack(s) when doing any exercise involving the rack(s).(The main exception to this rule occurs when a lifter is performing jerks from the rack with limited platform space; in such a case the lifter may want to face away from the rack and step forward to prepare for the lift so that there is more space in front than behind, since more jerks are missed forward than behind.) This permits the lifter to see where he or she and the bar is going when the exercise is over (a time when the lifter is more likely to be fatigued and in a hurry, as compared to when the bar is removed from the rack). The lifter should also be sure that he or she has backed away a sufficient distance so that even with the deepest split, there is plenty of clearance from the rack should the bar fall forward during a miss. The uprights of the rack(s) should also be placed widely enough so that the very widest of splits, and even some sideways adjustment, can be performed by the lifter without approaching the racks. Most lifters find that they can jerk more from the racks than after a clean; 5% to 10% more is a normal range. However, some superior jerkers can handle as much as 15% to 20% more, and a very small number of others cannot do as much from the rack as they can after a clean. (Such lifters simply do not feel as comfortable and/or motivated when they take a bar from a rack without cleaning it first.)

Effectiveness: Same comments as for the clean. It should be noted that in order to emulate the feeling of cleaning before the jerk without engaging the pulling muscles, some lifters have found that performing the jerk from the rack after a front squat (or even two or more reps in the front squat) is helpful. This preserves the advantage of being somewhat fatigued and in a physical position that is similar to the position the lifter would be in after the clean. But it does cause the lifter to lose the advantage of being "fresh" immediately before attempting a jerk.

Jerk Behind the Neck

Purpose(s): This exercise is used primarily to teach the lifter to place and hold the bar well behind the head when it is in the overhead position. It can also be used to teach certain aspects of jerk technique when the lifter finds it difficult to hold the bar in front of the neck because of flexibility problems or injury. Lifters with faulty jerk technique may be able to handle 10% to 20% more in the jerk from behind the neck than the regular jerk from the rack. Better jerkers will not see as much of a difference and may even jerk less from behind the neck.

Description: The bar is placed on a rack and the lifter faces the rack, lowering the body and bending the head forward or sideways enough to place the bar on the shoulders behind the neck. Placing the elbows forward of the bar in this position simulates the arm position the lifter has prior to a normal jerk, but it introduces the risk of the lifter dropping the bar backward from the shoulders while dipping for the jerk or catching it at the shoulders after jerking it (which cannot be recommended). Having the elbows positioned well behind the bar will prevent any bar slippage but will place the arms in a very different position from the one that is used in the classic jerk. Therefore, a more moderate elbow position, one with the elbows nearly under the bar, is best for most lifters.

Effectiveness: Although Soviet coach Medvedyev has reported that this exercise has one of the highest correlations to the jerk of any assistance exercise, I have found this exercise to be of limited value for most lifters. It is best used when a lifter is having trouble keeping the bar behind the head while it is overhead. Jerks from behind the neck are not particularly effective for correcting a lifter's tendency to dip forward or to drive the bar forward. In fact, they can worsen the problem, because the lifter can dip forward and/or move the head forward during the dip and drive and still manage to get the bar behind the head in split position (lulling the lifter into thinking that these faults are not significant). The jerk behind the neck can be a relatively dangerous exercise, because if the lifter does not exercise perfect control while lowering the bar, the bar can come into forceful contact with the rear of the cervical or thoracic vertebrae, causing a bone bruise, or even (in rare cases) a fracture. It can be a useful

teaching tool in the jerk for lifters who have trouble holding the bar comfortably in front of the neck (until the lifter's flexibility improves and the bar can be held comfortably in that position).

Power Snatch

Purpose(s): The power snatch is used primarily to develop pulling power for the snatch. Since the lifter does not have to lower his or her body significantly after the pull, the movement is simpler than a full squat snatch. The power snatch therefore places less stress on the nervous system than full snatches, and therefore maximums can typically be achieved more frequently in the power snatch than in the classical snatch. Stress on the knees and hips that arises out of assuming a low squat position in an explosive manner is less than in the squat snatch, as is stress on the shoulders, wrists and elbows. The exercise is also useful for the beginner because it is simpler than the squat snatch and because it is a motion that can be practiced by a lifter who is too stiff to assume a low squat position while the lifter is building the flexibility to execute the full squat.

Description: The bar is pulled in the same way as in the classical snatch. The legs are bent somewhat to catch the bar overhead. There is some controversy over how much a lifter can bend his or her legs and still be performing a power snatch (as opposed to a full or squat snatch). Some feel that anything deeper than a quarter squat position is too low, others term a snatch to that position as a "flip" snatch. However, most lifters agree that when the lowest part of the thigh (the underside) is not parallel with the platform, the lift is a power snatch (Fig. 25 depicts the low position of a power snatch).

Effectiveness: The power snatch can be a very

Fig. 25

208

effective means of improving a lifter's pulling power. As indicated above, it can be a useful exercise for the beginner. It can reduce the stress on the nervous system of the more advanced lifter and can provide variety. In addition, some research suggests that practicing movements at a faster than normal tempo carries over well to movements at a somewhat slower tempo, and the power snatch fits that description admirably (because lighter weights are used in the power snatch than the full snatch, and they can be moved faster).

However, despite the benefits of power snatches, there are a number of cautions to be observed when prescribing them. First, the lifter must be sure to place the feet in a position identical to that used for a squat snatch when the bar is caught in the partial squat position. One technical error that must be guarded against in the power snatch (and any other "power style" lift) is jumping the feet under than the position that is used in the full lift. A wide stance is artificial and places unusual stress on the knee joints. The simplest way to avoid this error is for the lifter to think of vigorously replacing the feet in the same position as they would be placed for the squat lift. Too many lifters "float" under the bar in the power style exercises. The issue here is not simply a matter of replicating the classical lift in every way possible (an important consideration), but enabling the lifter to comfortably lower his or her body into a full squat position when the bar has not been pulled to sufficient height for a power snatch.

Second, when doing power snatches, the lifter has a tendency to stop the downward motion of the body as quickly as possible in order to be "credited" with a power snatch. Such stopping short can place significant strain on the knee joints, particularly the muscle-tendon unit of the quadriceps. Over time this can lead to tendinitis or even to more serious tendon damage in some lifters. Therefore, the lifter should be encouraged to gradually reduce the speed of bar when it is caught in a position lower than a quarter squat, even if this means "riding" the bar down into a position that is lower than an acceptable power snatch. This does not mean that the lifter goes under the bar slowly, but, rather, that he or she does not attempt to stop very short once he or she has locked it out. It also means that if the power snatch causes discomfort, its use should be limited.

Third, the lifter must make every effort to pull the bar in a way that is similar to what is done when squat snatching. That is, the lifter must not get into the habit of delaying the explosion phase of the pull or remaining in the extended position too long, lest an artificial pulling style, relative to the pull timing that is used for the squat snatch, be cultivated.

Power Clean

Purpose(s): Similar to the power snatch discussed above.

Description: Similar to the power snatch.

Effectiveness: The same advantages and cautions apply to the power clean as to the power snatch, except that in the power clean, the stresses applied to the body in stopping short are even greater, so even greater care should be used when employing this exercise. This is not as much of an issue for athletes who are practicing power cleans as their sole weightlifting exercise, but it is more significant when the power snatch, power clean and power jerk, along with full lifts and squats, are all being performed. When performing power cleans, the lifer must be especially careful to catch the bar with the torso in a vertical position (never leaning back) and the elbows high. Sloppiness in these areas can make power cleans a far less safe exercise.(Fig. 26 illustrates a power clean).

Fig. 26

Power Jerk

Purpose(s): The purposes for doing the power jerk as opposed to the split jerk are similar to the purposes of the power snatch and power clean versus the squat version of those lifts. However, it requires as much or more shoulder flexibility to power jerk effectively as it does to split jerk. Therefore, the usefulness of the power jerk for lifters with shoulder flexibility problems is doubtful.

Description: The method of performance is similar to the classic jerk in that the lifter dips and drives the bar in the normal way, but after the explosion phase the lifter simply jumps the feet slightly sideways and generally turns the toes out somewhat to end in a foot position that is similar to

209

the one used for squat lifting, except that the legs are not bent to as great an extent. Most lifters bend the legs less in the power jerk than in either the power snatch or power clean because it is somewhat difficult to control the bar in a position where the lowest part of the thighs are just above parallel. But many of the best power style jerkers do go this low (see Fig 10 in Chapter 1).

Effectiveness: The power jerk can be an effective means for improving jerking power, teaching beginners certain aspects of the jerk and providing variety for the more advanced lifter. However, for a number of reasons, the power jerk is not as valuable an assistance exercise as the power snatch or clean. First, there seems to be less direct relationship between performance in the power jerk and the split jerk than there is between performance in the power snatch or power clean and their respective squat styles. Most lifters are able to power snatch or clean between 80% and 95% of their best lifts in the squat position. (Lifters can usually power clean a little more in relation to their clean than they can power snatch in relation to their squat snatch.) The range for the power jerk is considerably wider, probably 80% to as much as 100%, and whatever the relationship for a particular lifter, it tends to remain stable over time or even more. (Some few lifters can power jerk more than they can split jerk.) A second reason for the lesser effectiveness of the power jerk is that the complexity of a low power jerk is greater than that of a low power snatch and clean. Third, except for the rare squat jerker, there is no possibility for a transition from a low power jerk into a classical jerk, as there is for a low power snatch or clean.

Muscle Snatch or Snatch Stretch

Purpose(s): The muscle snatch is used to improve a lifter's pulling power: to teach the lifter to keep the bar close to the body throughout the pull; to help the lifter learn to keep the elbows above the wrists (as compared to behind the wrists) for as long as possible during the pull and the squat under; and to teach the lifter to push out with the arms after the action of the legs and back in the pulling motion has been completed. Most lifters can muscle snatch between two-thirds and three-quarters of their best classic snatch.

Description: The muscle snatch is pulled in the same way as the classic snatch, except that after the lifter reaches a fully extended position at the end of the pull, he or she maintains the elongated position of the body. The feet return to a flat-footed position while the arms work to pull the bar close to the body but the legs are not rebent as they are in the power snatch (they remain straight after the 4th stage of the pull and the feet assume a flat-footed position). Finally, the arms are turned from a position with the palms facing rearward of the pull to the palms-up position, and then the arms

push up until the bar is at arm's length. The lift is generally viewed as having been successful if the lifter is able to get the bar to arm's length without a noticeable "pressout" of the arms (a situation in which the momentum imparted to the bar by the pulling muscles ceases and the bar either slows noticeably or the lifter uses the arm extensors and shoulders to press the bar to arm's length).

Effectiveness: The muscle snatch can be effective for all of the reasons indicated above. It can also be a helpful exercise when the lifter is injured in some way that permits the pull to be performed but causes pain when the bar is caught in a full or partial squat position. Its disadvantages are that is teaches the lifter to lock the body in an extended position after the explosion phase of the full, a very different movement pattern than is required during the actual lift. In addition, while the lifter is presumably taught the value of pulling with the elbows above (rather than behind) the wrists and pressing up on the bar, slow motion analysis of high caliber lifters clearly indicates that such lifters do allow the elbows to travel behind the bar once the explosion phase of the pull has been completed and that there is no significant pressout of the arms at the finish of the snatch. (The elbows are behind the bar, not under it, until the very finish of the pull and any pressing motion that takes place is for a very short distance; it is more of a "lockout" than a "pressout"). Finally, some lifters get into the habit of leaning back and pressing out considerably at the finish of this exercise, which is both poor technique and stressful on the lower back.

Muscle Clean

The muscle clean is virtually nonexistent in the training of weightlifters. There is no pressing motion at the finishing point of a clean, and any attempt to clean without rebending the legs tends to lead to a lean back of the torso when the weight is received on the shoulders and a "reverse curling" motion with the arms. These are serious technical errors that can lead to injury of the back and/or wrists and to the development or maintenance of poor technique.

Push Press

Purpose(s): This exercise is the rough equivalent in the jerk of the muscle snatch. It is used to improve the jerk drive imparted by the legs and the elastic qualities of the bar and to teach the lifter to push up on the bar sharply after the leg drive. The exercise permits such practice with virtually no stress on the knee joints when the bar is received overhead. Most lifters can push press between 70% and 80% of their best jerk.

Description: The dip and drive are performed in the same way as during the classical jerk. At the end of the leg drive, the body is lowered to a flatfooted position while keeping the body vertical and the legs in a locked position. The arms are used to press the bar as rapidly as possible to arm's length and behind the head in a position that is the same as the finished position in the jerk.

Effectiveness: The push press can be useful for improving both leg drive and pressing power for the jerk. It can also teach the proper use of the arms in the jerk. However, the lifter must guard against a number of tendencies that can hurt his or her technique. One problem is that the arms can begin a pressing motion too early (during the dip or explosion phases). A second problem is that because the legs are not being rebent after the drive, there is a tendency for the torso to lean back. This is absolutely inappropriate for jerking. Finally, in order for the lifter to get the bar to arm's length as quickly as possible, there is often a tendency to push the bar straight over the head, or even slightly in front of the head, which is generally a position to be avoided in the jerk.

Dead Hang Snatch or Snatch from a Standing Position (SFSP)

A Note On Nomenclature and History: Dave Sheppard taught me this exercise about thirty years ago, and he had been using it on himself and many of America's top lifters for about twenty years prior to that. Dave called the exercise the "dead hang snatch." Later that name began to be used to refer to a pull from any position in which the lifter did not return the bar to the floor after a previous lift but did pause for a moment in that position above the floor. Today, the term "snatch from a standing position" is more common. Dave Sheppard may have been the leading performer of all time in this exercise (he surely was in his day). He was able to dead hang snatch 255 lb., dead hang clean 350 lb. and drop jerk (the equivalent exercise in the jerk) 350 lb. in his prime. These lifts were done with no assistance from the legs, so they are truly amazing achievements.

Purpose(s): The SFSP is sometimes used to teach the lifter to finish the pulling motion with the trapezius muscles and an explosive rise on the toes. However, its primary purpose is to teach the lifter to move very quickly under the bar and to do so instantaneously after having explosively contracted the trapezius muscles while rising rapidly and only slightly on the toes.

Description: The lifter stands with the body fully erect and the legs and arms straight. The trapezius muscles are relaxed, but the shoulders are back. The lifter explosively shrugs the shoulders and rises on the toes, then instantaneously moves under the bar into the full squat position (the lifter should not bend the torso forward or bend the legs prior to the shrug and the rise on toes). The lifter must focus on an explosive pull followed by a very rapid jump under and

pressing out on the arms. Very light weights are used at the outset, but ultimately the lifter ought to be able to handle 60% to 75% of his or her best lift in the classical snatch, though this is not necessary to derive major benefits of the exercise.

Effectiveness: The dead hang snatch can be very effective in teaching a lifter to go under the bar quickly. For the advanced lifter, it affords the opportunity to work at maximal speed in low positions with weights that do not tax the joints as much as maximum classic lifts. The effectiveness of this exercise is improved when incorporated into the regular lift as soon as possible (even in the same set).

Dead Hang Clean or Clean from a Standing Position

Purpose(s): Same rationale as for the dead hang snatch.

Description: Same basic approach as in the snatch, except that the lifter emphasizes a fast and high elbow whip while going under the bar.

Effectiveness: The dead hang clean can be very effective in teaching an explosive finish to the clean and a lightning like elbow whip. It is probably the most beneficial exercise of the standing snatch-clean-jerk group and should be in the arsenal of all lifters, at least periodically.

Drop Snatch Or Snatch Balance

Purpose(s): Teaches the lifter to move rapidly under the bar into the low snatch position and to maintain his or her balance in that position. It also enables the lifter to condition the body to supporting the bar in the low snatch position without having to handle maximum weights in the snatch itself.

Description: The lifter places the bar on the shoulders behind the neck (usually after taking the bar from a rack and stepping back several steps), then explosively drops into the full squat position while pushing up with the arms to catch the bar at arm's length. Many coaches advocate a slight upward drive with the legs to get the bar moving before dropping under. Obviously, more weight can be handled in the latter style. Many lifters are able to handle weights in excess of their best snatch (especially after giving the bar a preliminary leg drive) after they have practiced the exercise for a time.

Effectiveness: This exercise can be of help to both the beginner and the advanced lifter and should be included in the routine from time to time, particularly in any periods in which the lifter is doing many pulls but not many snatches. Doing reps can be dangerous due to the possibility of the bar hitting the rear portions of the vertebrae while it is being returned to the shoulders.

Drop Clean

This exercise is virtually never practiced. It would effectively involve jumping into a full squat position with the bar on the shoulders in front of the neck. This would place more strain on the joints in the low squat position than would ever be placed on them by a clean. Therefore it is not recommended. Lifters who wish to condition their bodies for receiving the bar in the clean merely need to do occasional back and front squatting with a rapid descent into to the full squat from about the half squat position.

Drop Jerk or Jerk from a Standing Position

Purpose(s): Same rationale as for the drop snatch.

Description: The lifter presses up with the arms in order to move to bar off the shoulders and then moves explosively into the split position. Some coaches advocate a slight leg bend to help get the bar moving.

Effectiveness: Like the drop snatch, this exercise can teach rapid movement into the low position. The weights used are not as heavy as those used in the classical jerk so the load on the joints is not as great. The drawbacks are that arm movement is encouraged while the bar is resting on the shoulders—not something that occurs during an actual jerk—and that the athlete can also have a tendency to split backward somewhat. Therefore I would not categorize it as a highly effective exercise for most lifters.

Snatching or Cleaning from the Hang or from Blocks

An entire series of assistance exercises for the snatch and clean consists of these exercises done from levels other than the floor. Sometimes the exercises are done with the bar placed on a pair of raised surfaces called "blocks" (described in Chapter 4), between which the lifter stands. At other times the lifter will lift the bar until he or she has reached a standing position (a deadlift) and then lower the bar to the desired starting height for the exercise. One final variation is for the lifter to lift the bar from a lower position than is normally required to begin the lift. This is accomplished either by having the lifter stand on a raised surface or by loading the bar with smaller plates than are normally used in competition.

The merits of performing lifts from various heights will explained below. The list of exercises always refers to a lift from a block, but the same basic principles apply to lifting the bar from the hang at the same position. While the advantages of pulling from certain heights pertains more or less equally to a pull from the block or from the hang, there are some differences between pulling from the hang and from the floor.

When an athlete pulls from a block there is an opportunity to prepare mentally for the lift while the bar is in a weightless state. The lifter can proceed at his or her own pace, so concentration can be facilitated relative to lifting from the hang (in which the bar is tiring the body as the lifter waits to begin the lift from the hang). The strength of the grip, in particular, is saved when the lifter pulls directly from a block as compared with a pause in the hang position, especially when the lifter is doing reps.

There are advantages to pulling from the hang as well. One advantage is that the lifter is less likely to assume an artificial position in the pull from the hang than from a block. For example, some lifters who are using blocks will place the bar in direct and forceful contact with the shins when they are pulling from a position with the bar just below the knees and will position the shoulders directly above the bar as well. In contrast, when performing the classical lifts, the bar should not be in contact with the shins (or at least should touch them very lightly) and the shoulders should be well in front of the bar when the bar is just below knee level. The lifter's position tends to be more natural when pulling from the hang below the knees.

Another advantage of pulling from the hang is that the lifter has three choices in the execution of the lift. The lifter can lower the bar and attempt to catch a muscular rebound when reversing direction. Alternatively, the lifter can lower the bar to the desired position, pause briefly and then perform the lift. A third alternative is for the lifter to lower the bar, pause for several seconds and then execute the lift. This first method of hang pulling will tend to promote the lifter's ability to activate the muscles quickly and explosively in reaction to the pulling muscles that have been previously stretched (i.e., the "reactive" capability of the athlete). The second method is the most common and is the one that most closely emulates pulling from a block that is in the same position. The final method can be used to strengthen the muscles isometrically in the pause position and to give the lifter some mental toughness because it requires the lifter to explode while in a slightly fatigued state.

A final advantage of the hang pull is that the safety factor is as great for it as it is for the classical lift. When the lifter lifts from a block, there is always the chance that the block will break when the bar is replaced, or, if the lift is missed, that the bar will be deflected towards the lifter or an observer (i.e., the bar may hit the corner of the block, or one block and not the other, on the way down).

Similarly, in comparing lifts with small plates with lifts while standing on a raised surface, when the lifter stands on a block or raised platform, there is always the chance that the block will break, the lifter will step off the block, or that the bar will fall on the block and be deflected. When the lifter lifts with small plates, there is always the danger that a missed lift will injure the lifter (since the normal clearance between the platform and lowest position of the bar with competition size plates is not sustained). Naturally, when the lifter is performing pulls from differing positions instead of the lifts ("pulls" are discussed later in this chapter), the difference in the safety factor with blocks and hang lifting is diminished due to the smaller likelihood of a "miss."

It should be noted that while the explanations below pertain to the classical lift, several of the exercise variations described earlier can be done from the blocks or from the hang (i.e., muscle snatch, power snatch, power clean). This is also true of the "pulls" that are described later in this chapter. Fig. 27 shows the starting position of a clean from the blocks.

Fig. 27

Snatch from Below the Knee

Purpose(s): The snatch from below the knee can be used to teach the lifter proper positioning of the bar and body during the crucial amortization phase of the pull. It can also be used to teach the lifter to emphasize the final explosion in the pull because momentum from the second stage of the pull cannot be relied upon. Finally, pulling the bar from a position higher than the floor lessens the load on

the athlete's legs and lower back. When an athlete is injured or fatigued in either or both of those areas, pulls from a block can be of great help.

Description: Bar height can vary, but the bar is typically placed on blocks that raise it to a position just below the lowest part of the knee when the athlete is set to begin the pull (i.e., the bar is at the top of the shin). The shoulders should be in front of the bar, the bar should be just slightly in front of or lightly grazing the shins. The legs should be nearly as straight as they get during this phase of the pull (i.e., in the same position as they would be if the bar had been lifted from the floor to that position). It is generally a good idea to pull the bar from the blocks in a relatively controlled manner, using the legs only at the first instant (i.e., not attempting to straighten the torso as the bar comes off the block) and then accelerating as the bar begins to move from the block. In the hang version of this exercise, the bar is typically deadlifted from the floor and then lowered to a position below the knee. Alternatively, it is placed on a rack or block in front of the lifter, at a position just below the lifter's finished deadlift position. Then the bar is lifted from the rack, and the lifter steps back several paces to lower the bar and begin the exercise.

Effectiveness: The snatch from blocks or hang below the knee can be helpful for the reasons discussed in the "Purposes." There are two cautions that should be observed when exercising from this position. First, the pull must ultimately be performed as one motion. Too much practice in the segments may actually hamper development of proper technique in the classical movement. This is a particularly important issue for the lifter who pulls rather quickly from the floor to the knees. Second, it is possible for the lifter to assume a starting position for this exercise that is different from that which is assumed during the classical lift. Naturally, when this occurs, the carryover value will be diminished. The most common version occurs when the lifter sits back on heels as the bar is lifted from the blocks and positions the shoulders directly above the bar (they should be slightly forward of the bar). Pulling from this position does not approximate the position achieved when the bar is lifted from the floor, and most lifters straighten the torso too early and lean back too much at the finish of the pull when they commit this error in commencing the lift. Fig. 28 shows the starting position of the snatch from below the knees).

Fig. 28

Clean from Below the Knee

Purpose(s): Similar purposes to the snatch from this position.

Description: Similar to the snatch from this position.

Effectiveness: The effectiveness of lifting from this position tends to be somewhat less it is in the snatch. This is because most lifters rely on developing almost continuous acceleration from the floor in their cleans (while many do not in the snatch). Pulling from the blocks provides no such opportunity for near continuous acceleration, so the timing in the clean from the blocks tends to be different from its classic counterpart. (The exception to this rule would be the lifter who pulls slowly from the floor and relies on the final explosion in the clean pull to achieve adequate bar height and speed.) However, this style of lifting does reduce the stress on the legs and back that normally arises out of lifting the bar from the flood. It can therefore be useful for specific teaching purposes. I have known some lifters who felt they benefited from performing this exercise from the hang with a rapid turnaround from this point to that at which the bar is lowered (so that the elastic capacity of the muscles is utilized). This exercise can have value, but it should be used sparingly, if at all, for most lifters.

Snatch from above the Knee

Purpose(s): The snatch above the knee is used to teach the lifter to achieve a powerful final explosion in the pull. It is also used with beginners to simplify the process of learning the pull.

Description: The bar is typically placed in a position that is approximately one-third up the thigh (some lifters place the bar even lower, closer

to the top of knee). The shoulders are generally placed directly above the bar as it leaves the block.

Effectiveness: There is probably no single position in lifting that can improve a lifter's final explosion faster than this exercise. Unfortunately, the exercise carries with it one great danger. Because the lifter must rely totally on the final explosion of the pull to impart all of the bar's speed, there is a tendency to lengthen the explosion phase of the pull (i.e., for the lifter to assume to an excessively elongated body position at the finish of the pull by stretching too high on the toes and remaining in that position for too long a period). This results in the lifter's moving too late under the bar and taking too long to move under the bar, both serious technical flaws. In addition to extending the body excessively and/or remaining in that position longer than necessary, some lifters tend to start with the shoulders behind the bar and the balance toward the heels and then to rotate the torso backward too much in a futile effort to pull the bar for a longer period. Therefore, this exercise, while potentially effective, must be used with great care and must be intermingled with the full lift or pull. Recent research performed by Marchenko in Eastern Europe suggests that performing this exercise (and its counterpart in the clean) builds more explosive power than any other variation of the lift and that pulling from the hang with an immediate reversal of direction is the best way to build the lifer's "reactive" capabilities.

Clean from above the Knee

Purpose(s): Similar to the snatch.

Description: Similar to the snatch but the bar is typically lowered to a position that is just above the knee.

Effectiveness: This exercise tends to be somewhat less effective than its counterpart in the snatch, because of the greater importance of the velocity generated in earlier phases of the pull in the clean, as compared to the importance of early velocity in the snatch pull. The exercise can still have value in certain circumstances, since there is surely a need for an explosive finish to the clean, but the exercise should be used more sparingly for the clean than the snatch. In addition, even greater care must be taken to ensure that the lifter does not overextend the body or stay in the extended position too long.

Snatch Standing on a Block or with Small Plates

Purpose(s): Whether the lifter stands on a raised surface or lifts a bar with plates that have a smaller diameter than those that are used in competition, the purpose of the special equipment is to lower the height of the bar in relation to the lifter when the lift is commenced. Performing snatches from this position strengthens the starting position of the snatch by requiring the muscles involved to go through a greater than normal range of motion. It also can be used to teach a lifter not to rely too much on the start of the pull for imparting acceleration to the bar, because performing the pull while standing on a raised surface tends to place the body in a less favorable position from which to start (making it more difficult for the lifter to begin the lift explosively). Lifting while standing on a block can also teach a lifter to wait longer before commencing the amortization and final explosion portions of the pull, teaching patience during the second stage of the pull. (This applies to lifters who prematurely contract certain muscles groups as soon as they separate the bar from the floor, or even earlier.)

Description: The lifter stands on a surface that is raised 1" to 2" above to the platform. (Some lifters use a platform as high as 4", but this is unusual and is not generally recommended.) The lift then begins in the normal way, except that lifters who normally begin their pulls with an explosive effort should begin this style of lift more slowly than usual, because the joints and muscles are in a less favorable position to overcome the weight and inertia of the bar than when the bar is started from the normal position. The lifter should make an extra effort to maintain a sound and functional position for the joints as the bar is started from the floor. Essentially, the legs are bent more than usual so that the lifter can reach the bar. The angle of the back relative to the floor, the arch in the back and the chest out position normally used to start the pull must be maintained (generally more difficult to do from this position than from the floor, so special emphasis must be placed on this point).

Effectiveness: This exercise can be effective for the purposes described above. However, it should be used sparingly for the snatch, because the normal starting position for the snatch is rather extreme, and strength in the pull from the floor is relatively less important in the snatch than in the clean snatch. In addition, lifters are somewhat less likely to contract muscles prematurely, or to accelerate the bar prematurely, in the snatch than in the clean.

Clean Standing on a Block or with Small Plates

Purpose(s): Similar to the snatch.

Description: Similar to the snatch.

Effectiveness: This exercise tends to benefit performance in the clean more than in the snatch. Strength in separating the bar from the floor is a more important factor in cleaning than in snatching. Premature contraction of muscle groups and improper sequencing of the acceleration are more common problems in the clean than in the snatch.

Varying the Grip When Lifting

Most variations of the snatch lifts mentioned above and some variations of the clean (e.g., snatches, power snatches, muscle snatches, snatches from different heights and power cleans) can be done with a grip that is anywhere from several inches wider than a normal snatch grip to one that is narrower than the normal clean grip. (Some old-time strongmen even did snatches with the arms crossed, which surely cannot be recommended.) There is value in sheer variety. Muscles are stimulated at a slightly different angle, and the challenge of a different exercise can give a psychological boost to the lifter's training. However, any grip variations are typically restricted to the preparatory and transition phases of training in order to assure that technique is honed to a perfect and consistent groove before important competitions.

I am not a big advocate of the general use of grip width variations. They have the potential for changing a lifter's technique for the worse and they can lead to injury for the lifter who is not conditioned to do them (particularly the snatch with a wider than normal grip, squat cleans with a wide grip and squat snatches with a clean grip). The risk of injury can be greatly reduced if the variations are practiced often enough to condition the lifter to use them, and then often enough to maintain that condition. Unfortunately, if this is done, lifts with varying grips are probably using too much of that lifter's training time.

There are several special circumstances that can make extensive practice with a different grip worthwhile. The lifter who is injured and finds that a different grip does not aggravate the injury may find the variation vital. A lifter who has a problem with technique can sometimes benefit from the practice of a variation. For example, the lifter who has a habit of extending the body too far in the snatch and/or holding the extended position for too long can be helped by the power clean with the wide grip. Because the lifter needs to get immediately into catch position after the pull and the height of the pull is close to that of a squat snatch, practice of the wide grip power clean can help the lifter to improve upon the structure of his or her snatch pull. (It is even helpful to alternate the wide grip power clean with the snatch on occasion.)

Varying Speed While Lifting

Some coaches advocate varying the tempo of the exercises done in training. For example, the lifter might practice snatching with a lighter than maximum weight and executing the pull, or parts thereof, faster then normal speed. Alternatively, the lifter might go through the pulling motion in the snatch at a slower than normal speed. One rationale for lifting at different rates of speed is that there is some evidence of a superior training effect emanating from training at various speeds. One reason for pulling faster is to increase the lifter's speed. One reason for pulling slower is to increase the tension in the lifter's muscles, which is thought to lead to a greater increase in strength. These arguments have merit, but there are hazards to varying the pace of the lift too much. If a lifter's technique and timing are good, practicing the same lift at different tempos can lead to a deterioration in that technique. I believe that the advantages of varying speed can be enjoyed without having to practice the classical lifts themselves at varying speeds. The lifter can achieve greater speed in the pull or jerk thrust by practicing power snatches, cleans and jerks. Slower pulls and more muscle tension can be achieved through practice pulls with heavy weights and deadlifts and shrugs. There are enough differences between these exercise and the classical lifts that the nervous system is likely to be able to retain them as different patterns of movement in its memory banks and not to confuse the power snatch or snatch pull with the pull for the squat snatch.

Assistance Exercises Related To The Classic Lifts

The assistance exercises that are presented in this next group are related to the classic lifts and can have a direct effect on performance in those lifts. However, they are generally not considered to be close enough to the classic lifts to account for them (in terms of training volume and intensity) in the same way as the lifts that were presented in the previous section.

Snatch Pulls

Purpose(s): To develop pulling power and certain aspects of pulling technique without having to perform the lift itself.

Description: Snatch pulls are essentially a snatch without the squat under phase (i.e., the first four stages of the pull are performed but the last two stages are not). Pulls can be done from the floor or from the hang or boxes of various heights (i.e., essentially in the same variations that were presented above for the snatch). There is general agreement that when performing a pull the lifter should endeavor to emulate as much as possible the pulling technique that is used in actual lifts. There is, however, considerable disagreement about how to accomplish such an emulation.

Some lifters attempt to complete all of their pulls with an explosive effort and a follow through with the body to a fully extended or elongated position. This finished position generally finds the lifter with his or her heels raised somewhat from the platform, the body stretched vertically as much as possible, shoulders up and arms bent with the

elbows above the bar or slightly to the rear of it. On occasion some lifters who employ this style of pull attempt to hold this elongated position momentarily (some lifters actually pause noticeably with the body supported on the balls of the feet and the toes). Other lifters employ this technique but attempt never to bend the arms, which results in the appearance of an explosive snap of the shoulders at the end of the pull, as the upward momentum of the bar generated by earlier stages of the pull is slowed by a collision of the bar with the straight arms of the lifter. Still other lifters achieve a fully extended position and then lower their bodies by rebending the legs (which results in the bar's traveling higher in relation to the lowered body, though not necessarily relative to the floor).

Another group of lifters attempts to achieve a maximum explosive effort in the pull before reaching the extended position and then more or less let the bar travel further on the basis of its momentum (rather than attempting to increase bar velocity and height even further by a follow through). Some of the lifters in this group even attempt to "check" any follow through into a fully extended position by intentionally never completely extending their bodies after executing the final explosion at a position with the bar near the tops of the thighs.

Effectiveness: Pulls can be a very effective way of improving power and technique in the snatch. As was noted in Chapter 2, some Bulgarian coaches actually teach the pull by having the lifter practice high pulls instead of partial or full versions of the classic lifts. This method appears to have considerable merit.

Pulls place much less strain on the nervous system than does a snatch from a similar position. They also place less strain on the body when the lifter is slowing the descent of the bar after it has been pulled because the downward motion of the bar is amortized over a longer distance than in the snatch. There is, of course, little strain of the arms and shoulders because the bar is never lifted over the lifter's head. Since the overall movement of the pull is less complex and does not require as much movement of the body as a snatch, the lifter does not become as fatigued while doing a pull as while doing a snatch with the same weight. This is particularly true when a lifter is performing repetitions. If a lifter wishes to exploit the advantages of higher reps (up to five reps) to develop his or her pull, then pulls are the means of choice. (Maximum sets of five, or even three, reps in the classic snatch cannot be recommended except in special circumstances, while such reps in the pull can be used to great benefit in terms of strength and power development.)

In terms of the style used in the pull, there are different theories behind each of the styles mentioned above. The lifters who practice pulls to a

fully extended position feel that one of the functions of the pull is to teach the lifter to extend explosively and completely. Since the lifter need not worry about descending under the bar in the pull, the exercise affords the lifter the opportunity for total concentration on the final explosion phase of the pull and the opportunity to achieve a full follow through position after the final explosion (which, advocates of this style believe, would occur as a natural product of the pull, were it not for the pressing need of the lifter to catch the bar overhead after the explosion phase of the pull has been completed). Lifters who pause in the extended position feel that this exaggeration of the follow through will carry over into the performance of the lift and cause the lifter to pull a little more forcefully and extend a little more completely than he or she otherwise would. The lifters who bend their arms at the top argue: "The arms eventually bend during the squat under phase of the lift, so why not at the end of the pull?" and/or, "The arms help to pull the lifter under the bar at the end of the snatch, so why not use the pull as a means to strengthen and educate the arms for doing this?" The lifters who keep their arms straight at the top maintain that the arms never bend except in the

squat under phase of the pull, so maintaining straight arms helps to avoid the fault of pulling too much with the arms during the final explosion phase of the pull. Fig 29 depicts the near finished position of a pull in which the lifter will fully straighten the body and not bend the arms at the finish. Fig. 30 shows the lifter remaining in the stretched position and permitting the arms to bend as the bar rises (but the arms are not being used to pull the bar up to this height).

The lifters who attempt to complete their final explosion before the body achieves a fully extended position, either to minimize the extension of the body or even to check it, argue that such a style resembles the lift more than an extended body pull. Such lifters are concerned that by extending the body in the pull too much they will get into a pattern of having too much of a follow through in the lift itself, giving them less time to squat under the bar and accomplishing little in terms of adding height to the pull. On balance, I find the latter arguments more compelling. More lifters extend too long than fail to finish their pulls. Moreover, practicing a greater and longer extension than is used in the lift may lead to poorer timing in the lift itself. However, as in so many aspects of weightlifting, the use of the pulls and the style employed must be individualized. For example, the relatively rare lifter who is having trouble achieving proper extension of the body may benefit from practicing pulls that emphasize extension of the body. The lifter who tends to overextend may benefit from actually checking the extension while practicing the pull. There is certainly no one correct way for performing pulls, but there is at least one major wrong way to do so. Any deviation from the normal pulling style (that which is used for the lift) during the first four phases of the pull is a bad idea. What the lifter does after that is much more of an individual issue. Therefore, one of the keys to successfully using this exercise is to make sure that the lifter is using the same tempo that he or she uses during the lift.

As was the case with snatches from the hang or boxes, lifters tend to benefit from practicing partial snatch pulls because they focus on the crucial amortization and final explosion phases of the pull, but the same cautions that were noted for partial snatches must be noted here as well. Using a height gauge for all types of pulls can be helpful in assuring that the lifter is pulling hard and not just "going through the motions" when performing pulls. Height gauges are discussed in Chapter 4.

Clean Pulls

Purpose(s): Similar to the snatch pull.

Description: Similar to the snatch pull.

Effectiveness: Essentially the same arguments as in the snatch pull. Clean pulls from the floor tend to be more useful than clean pulls from the higher positions because of the greater importance of the second and third stages in the pulls of most lifters during the clean relative to the snatch.

Combining Pulls and Lifts

Purpose(s): To tax the pulling muscles beyond the point that is feasible while doing the lift alone. Alternatively, to give the lifter practice in some aspect of the pull or the thrust of the jerk before doing the actual lift.

Description: When the lifter is adding the pull to the lift as a means of continuing to train strength after the lift has been completed, the pull(s) are done following the lift(s). This is not a common method of training, but some lifters feel that by doing a pull after a lift they are more likely to use lift-like technique while doing the pull. They may be right.

The more common use of the pull and lift (or jerk thrust and jerk) combination is to have the lifter experience some phase of the pull first, without having to worry about completing the entire lift. After doing one or more pulls (or jerk drives) with the correct focus, the lifter does a complete lift.

Effectiveness: Pulls done immediately after a lift are an effective way to increase strength and to do so by the same pattern of movement that is used in the lift itself (although most lifters prefer performing one exercise at a time). In addition, if this pattern exercise is used on the last set in which the lift will be attempted, the lifter can move right into pulls after the lift has been performed. If successive sets of the lift and pull combination are performed, particularly if several reps in the pull are employed, the lifter's pulling muscles can become so fatigued that the technique used on the lift can be compromised.

The process of performing a pull or jerk drive before performing a lift tends to be the more useful version of this exercise. The pull or dip for the jerk becomes, in effect, a partial practice lift. It is then hoped that this "practice" technique will carry over into the lift when it is performed almost immediately thereafter.

Consider two examples. I was recently working with a lifter who persistently dropped the elbows at the low point of the dip for the jerk. She tried dipping once or twice without dropping the elbows before attempting an actual jerk. There was a nearly immediate improvement in her technique in the actual jerk. In another case a lifter was having difficulty not using the arms prematurely in the clean. Performing a couple of reps in the clean pull with straight arms before attempting a clean enabled this lifter to perform cleans with straight arms immediately thereafter.

Naturally, the lifter eventually needs to learn to do the lift correctly without the preliminary motion, but doing the lift properly with the help of that "warm-up" motion can often help the lifter begin to experience the lift done correctly, an important step in reaching ultimate mastery.

For the more advanced lifter, the pull and lift combination can still be used to help the lifter focus on some aspect of the pull before doing the lift. The pull and lift combination exercise should certainly not be the foundation of a lifter's classical lift and pull training, but it can be a helpful adjunct to the overall development of each of these exercises.

Snatch Deadlifts

Purpose(s): To strengthen the pull from the floor and to teach the lifter proper positioning and timing of the bar and body in the first, second and third stages of the pull.

Description: Same as for the snatch or snatch pull. Because a heavier weight is handled in this exercise than in the snatch, a special effort must be made to maintain proper positioning, timing and balance during the execution of the lift. Some athletes lift the bar until they are standing fully erect at the end of the deadlift. Other athletes lift the bar until it reaches a position similar to that achieved at the end of the third stage of the pull.

The primary purpose of the latter method is to assure that the lifter achieves a proper position for the beginning of the fourth stage of the pull. Many lifters find that by pausing in such a position they are able to "feel" and thereby learn it more quickly and deeply.

Effectiveness: Snatch deadlifts can be a useful adjunct to the snatch for the purposes described above. One caution that should be observed when doing any kind of deadlift is to limit the number of repetitions. I do not recommend ever doing more than five reps. Fives should only be done with submaximal weight (at a minimum, there should always be room for another rep or two after the fifth rep). Threes or lower reps should be the more common rep pattern, especially for maximum efforts. This is because the muscles of the lower back generally fatigue first in the deadlift (before the hip extensors). When the back muscles are fatigued, additional strain is placed on the ligaments of the spine (which are already heavily loaded during normal weightlifting training). This additional strain places the spine at an elevated risk of injury; it is not worth the risk when lower reps and better control can yield essentially equal benefits.

Clean Deadlifts

Purpose(s): Same as for snatch deadlifts.

Description: Similar to the snatch deadlift except that the starting position of the clean is assumed instead of the starting position of the snatch. The lifter needs to make even a greater effort in the clean deadlift than in the snatch version in order to maintain the body in the same position as in the clean throughout the deadlift.

Effectiveness: There seems to be a greater carryover from this exercise to the clean than from the snatch deadlift to the snatch. One reason is that a strong initial pull in the clean is generally more crucial to its success than an energetic initial pull is for success in the snatch. Another reason is that the clean pull is slower than the snatch pull, so an exercise that is performed slowly has more carryover to the clean than the snatch. A variation of the deadlift that was very popular up through the 1950s is called the "hopper" deadlift. There are several variations of the hopper deadlift, and some special equipment is required to perform some of those variations. The essence of the hopper is that the bar is rebounded from the floor (or other surface). It was thought that this rebounding motion improved the lifter's explosiveness and strength. Many practitioners of the hopper swore by its benefits. To my knowledge, no modern study of the exercise has been performed. There seems to be at least some theoretical support for the idea that the elastic qualities of a muscle along with its strength can be enhanced by performing a movement like the hopper. However, there is some

question as to whether such training would carry over into the static start that most lifters use in the lifts or to the explosion at later phases in the pull. Both of these propositions seem doubtful, but the exercise may be of some value for lifters who need more explosiveness in the second stage of the pull. Moreover, bouncing the bar against a support would cause the lifter to lose at least some of the effect of the pre-stretch on the muscles that execute the pull because the support absorbs some of the downward force of the bar.

Lifters who employ deadlift training should always be careful to employ a position virtually identical to that used in the lift and to limit deadlift training to only a few sets and one or two training sessions a week (the lower back becomes easily fatigued from this exercise).

Halting Snatches, Cleans, Jerks, Pulls and Deadlifts

Purpose(s): Halting lifts (lifts with a pause at one or more points during the exercise) are used to teach the lifter certain crucial positions that are assumed during the execution of the lifts. They are also used to strengthen specific positions in the pull, typically the positions that lifters find to be the most difficult. As is noted in Chapter 3, one of the primary benefits and limitations of isometric contractions is their tendency to improve performance in a range of motion that is near to the position in which the isometric is performed. This can be a drawback when the lifter is attempting to strengthen the full range of motion with isometrics, but it can be an advantage when the lifter wishes to target a narrow segment of the lift. Typically, the lifter finds the greatest difficulty in the pull during the start (when both inertia and the weight of the bar need to be overcome) and when the bar is approximately at the level of the bottom of the knee.

Description: The lift, pull or deadlift is performed in the same way as its non halting counterpart, except that on one or more reps in a set the motion of the bar is halted on the way up and/or on the way down. Perhaps the most common position for a halt in the snatch, clean, pull and deadlift is just below the lifter's knee. Another popular position is just after the bar clears the floor. In the jerk a popular position is at the lowest point in the dip; another is at the lowest point of the split. The halt is normally sustained for two to six seconds. It is important to maintain correct position during the halt.

Common faults while performing this exercise are to permit the back to round or relax somewhat during the halt and to shift the body to a position that is different from what the lifter normally does during that phase of the pull. For example, the lifter might raise the torso to a straighter than normal position while pausing at the knee. This is a far easier position for the lifter to sustain, but unless the lifter halts in the same position that is used during the pull, the results will tend to be poor.

Another variety of the halting deadlift and/or pull is one in which there are multiple halts during the exercise. For example, one variety of multiple position halt popular some years ago was performed with a halt just below the knees on the way up. A second halt was effected at the top of the pull (the fully extended position), another was done at the knees on the way down and a final halt took place just above the floor.

Effectiveness: The deadlift version of this exercise can be very effective in building pulling strength at points in which the pull is most difficult. It is particularly useful for the clean. The best results are normally obtained with weights that are between 100% and 120% of the lifter's best clean or snatch at the time. Handling more weight, while entirely possible, tends to cause the body's positioning to break down. Doing classical lifts and pulls with a halt can bring some variety to the training, but the down side is that they can adversely affect the timing of the pull. Despite its drawbacks, this type of exercise can be useful in teaching the lifter to assume proper positions in the lift or pull and to be patient and confident enough to actually achieve those positions while doing the pull at normal speed.

Halting pulls, particularly in the snatch, are a favorite of 1994 World Champion Robyn Byrd-Goad and her coach, John Coffee. Robyn used these pulls very effectively in preparing both for the snatch World Records that she established and the World's Championship that she won. John has used the exercise successfully with a number of his other athletes in addition to Robyn.

In the jerk, the pause at the bottom of the dip can be used to teach the lifter proper depth, proper voluntary muscular effort in the drive (explosion phase) of the jerk and proper position of all of the joints and body segments at the point of beginning the explosion phase of the jerk. Pausing in the split can teach the lifter the importance of landing in a well balanced and strong position. A variety of this exercise that I have used with success is to perform jerks inside a power rack with pins set at the height the bar would achieve if it were caught in a low split position. Then I take the bar from a set of pins positioned just below the lowest point in the dip and rise to a standing position. The jerk is performed in the normal way, except that once in the low split position, the bar is sustained for several seconds before recovering from the split and letting the bar fall to the shoulders at the same time. The placement of the pins prevents too high a thrust in the jerk and forces me to assume a low and well balanced split. When I first tried the exercise, I had trouble controlling weights that were even 33% of my maximum. Eventually,

however, I was able to handle with consistency weights that were approximately 85% of my maximum standard jerk from the rack. By that time my precision and control in the split position of the jerk had improved significantly.

The multiple stage variations of the halting style have the advantage of utilizing isometric contractions in multiple positions, thereby strengthening more than one range of motion in the pull. They are generally not effective for teaching technique.

The disadvantages of these exercises are that not all of the positions trained will need to be strengthened and that extreme fatigue during the movement can cause the lifter to assume positions unlike those used during a lift. Undue fatigue can even expose the lifter to injury. Therefore, multiple stage halting pulls and deadlifts need to be designed carefully and used sparingly and with caution if they are to be beneficial.

Partial Deadlifts and Pulls

Purpose(s): Partial pulls are performed for the same reasons as regular pulls, except that they are meant to focus on certain aspects of the pull, similar to the way regular lifts from the hang and blocks are used. Partial deadlifts are performed with the purpose of strengthening a particular phase of the deadlift, to train around an injury that precludes a full deadlift or to reduce the load on the legs that is created by pulling from the floor while permitting the muscles of the lower back and hip extensors to be worked. In order to enjoy the full benefits of this exercise, the athlete must maintain an arch in the lower back and minimize the curve of the upper back (i.e., mimic the position assumed during the pull).

Description: Partial pulls are performed in a fashion similar to regular pulls, except that the bar is started from a block or the hang (see the section on snatches and cleans from the hang or boxes for a fuller explanation of this kind of movement).

Effectiveness: Partial pulls are a good way to bring variety into training and to focus on specific areas of the pull. The same cautions that apply to hang lifts and lifts from the blocks apply here as well. Partial deadlifts can be an excellent way to train the back and hips. They resemble the good morning exercise in many respects, but they are superior in most cases. This is because consistency in the angle of the back at the bottom of the deadlift can be assured by always pulling from the same height with the body in the same position (there is always a question of whether someone has done a "full" good morning). From a safety standpoint, if a strain is felt in the back on the deadlift, the bar can be dropped immediately. In contrast, getting rid of the bar in the good morning is not as easy. From a technical standpoint, the lifter can assure that the position of the body and the balance on the feet in the lift can be emulated in the partial deadlift much more easily than in the good morning, and this must be done. In my experience the most useful version of this exercise is the clean deadlift from below the knees. Former world record holder in the C&J Frank Capsouras relied almost exclusively on this exercise for improving his pulling power in the clean.

Pulls and Deadlifts Standing on a Block or with Small Plates

Purpose(s): Similar to regular pulls and deadlifts, except that the strengthening and technical benefits are derived in the context of the overall purpose of a pull or deadlift rather than a lift.

Description: The lifter begins the lift while standing on a block or using small plates. This use of small plates tends to be impractical for the advanced lifter because the weights being handled are hard to fit on the bar.

Effectiveness: In terms of technique and strength, pulling from this position can certainly offer benefits similar to those mentioned in the discussion of lifts while standing on a block. The higher the block, the more difficult it is to assume a correct starting position (i.e., with the lower back arched, the upper back flat, the chest out, etc.). In the snatch this problem is greater than in the clean. Deadlifts from this position place a great load on the back, hips extensors and legs and can therefore build considerable strength in these areas. However, really pushing the deadlift from this position has its hazards. Because it is more difficult to assume and maintain the proper position of the back when deadlifting from this position, there is some risk of lower back injury. Therefore, when practicing such lifts, great care needs to be taken to assure that: a) the muscles are gradually accustomed to the load, and b) that proper position is scrupulously maintained (which implies that the athlete is flexible enough to perform the exercise with perfect technique). If the lifter loses this position, he or she will lose much of the value of the exercise and may risk lower back injury.

Good Mornings

Purpose(s): To strengthen the lower back muscles and hip extensors. In some variations the exercise can also be used to build explosive power in those same muscle groups and the leg extensors.

Description: There are several variations of this exercise with a few common characteristics. The bar is placed behind the lifter's neck, resting on the rear of the shoulders and trapezius muscles at the start. With the body in a standing position, the torso is then moved forward and down into the lowest position of the exercise; the athlete then returns to the starting position.

Perhaps the most popular variation of the good morning is one in which the back is maintained in essentially the same position as during the pull (lower back arched and the upper back with only the normal curve). The torso is inclined forward and the legs are bent until the lifter assumes a position similar to the one that is achieved when the lifter is beginning the amortization phase of the pull (i.e., the legs are only slightly bent and the back is at an angle similar to the one used in the early stages of the pull from the floor). Some lifters attempt to bend forward even more, until the torso is approximately parallel to the floor. The lifter then rises up to a standing position, while maintaining an arch in the back.

A second variation of the good morning is similar to the one described above, but the lifter attempts to perform the exercise as rapidly as possible; as the lifter nears completion of the exercise, there is an explosive extension of the legs and even a rise on the toes.

A third major variation is one in which the lifter lowers the torso until it is well below parallel with the floor (some lifters go to the point where the torso is upside down, or the body is in a near "jackknife" position). In this variation the lifter allows the back to round in the low position, but the legs are maintained in a nearly locked position throughout the lift.

A fourth variation involves performing the good morning while the lifter is seated on a bench. This version of the exercise places the legs and back of the lifter at a much smaller angle than does any other variation of the exercise. Therefore, an extreme stretch is placed on the adductor muscles, the hip extensors and the lower back muscles. In some ways this position resembles the one assumed by the lifter who lifts the bar from the floor while standing on a block with a snatch grip, except that there is no strain on the knees or leg extensors. Fig. 31 illustrates the low position of the most popular version of the good morning.

Effectiveness: I am not a big fan of the good morning exercise, not so much because it is inherently ineffective or unsafe, but rather because it falls short of partial deadlifts in both of these regards, for the reasons set out in the discussion of the partial deadlift. All of the benefits of the first version of the good morning that was discussed above can be secured from the partial deadlift from below the knees. The explosive version of the good morning can be emulated by partial pulls and/or deadlifts with a finishing shrug. The partial pulls or deadlift and shrug have the advantage of training the trapezius muscles as well as the lower back and leg extensors. Moreover, all the appropriate muscles can be trained in concert and in the same sequence that occurs during a normal lift. Finally, there is some danger that in the explosive variation of the good morning the spine and knees can be traumatized when the lifter

221

comes down from the explosion position (the bar itself can also crash against the neck and shoulders). These risks are greatly diminished or eliminated in the pull. The benefits of the good morning using full range of motion can be obtained through the stiff-legged deadlift with less risk (again the bar can be easily dropped while doing the stiff-legged deadlift).

The good morning shines when a lifter has injured the arms and the shoulder girdle. Here, good mornings can be used to load the lower back and hip extensors while the shoulder girdle and arms are recovering. I do not recommend the seated version of this exercise because of the extreme positions that it requires the lifter to assume and because of the difficulty in getting rid of the bar in the event of an injury or miss.

Fig. 31

Stiff-legged Deadlifts

Purpose(s): To strengthen the leg flexors, hip extensors and lower back. This exercise can also be therapeutic for some lifters with lower back injuries.

Description: There are two basic variations of this exercise. In one variation the lower back is kept arched and the upper back flat. The bar is raised from the platform with the legs nearly straight. The bar is then lowered back to the floor or as near as the lifter can come to the floor while maintaining proper back positioning. As soon as the bar touches the floor, it is usually deadlifted once again. This process is then repeated until the set is completed. At its lowest point, the lifter's torso typically reaches a position parallel to or somewhat below the platform.

In the rounded back variation, the bar is lowered to a deeper position than in the straight back version. It is very common for the lifter to stand on a block when doing this variety of the exercise, so that a deeper position can be obtained. Normally, the neck rounds forward with the body so that the head is down by the time the lowest position is reached.

Effectiveness: Stiff-legged deadlifts can certainly strengthen the leg flexors, lower back and hip extensors. If they are done with the lower back in an arched position and the upper back relatively flat, the strength developed will have significant carryover into the snatch and clean pull. Doing the exercise with a rounded back will also strengthen the leg, hip and lower back muscles (the latter in a concentric manner, as compared with the isometric manner applied when pulling and in the flat back stiff-legged deadlift). However, during the performance of this version of the exercise, there is enormous pressure on the spine in a position that is not identical to the lifts. To me this represents a significant risk with only a modest benefit. Therefore, I do not recommend doing heavy stiff-legged deadlifts with a rounded back, but there are some athletes and coaches who believe in them.

There is one special situation in which rounded back stiff-legged deadlifts have been found by some lifters to be beneficial: when they are performed with light weights and are used to stretch the lower back muscles. Please see Chapter 11 for a description of how this potentially risky version of the stiff-legged deadlift has been employed effectively by some lifters. Fig 32 displays the low position in the stiff-legged deadlift.

Fig. 32

Stiff-Legged Lifts and Pulls

Purpose(s): To place added stress on the hip extensors and back muscles while placing less stress on the leg extensors.

Description: The lifter assumes a position similar to the one used while doing the classical lift or the conventional pull. The main difference in the execution of the stiff-legged version of the lift or pull is that the legs are placed in a nearly straight position at the outset of the exercise, and they maintain that position until the final explosion phase of the pull is completed.

Effectiveness: This variation of the classical lift and pull will strengthen the lower back and hip extensors, perhaps to a greater extent than conventional lifts and pulls. However, the coordination of these movements is so different from those of the conventional lifts that the carryover of any strength so developed to the conventional lifts tends to be disappointing. One negative aspect of this difference in coordination is that when the legs are unavailable in the final explosion of the pull, the lifter will tend to lean back with the torso at the finish of the pull in order to apply force for a longer period. This serious technique flaw presents a risk to the lower back, so it should be scrupulously avoided. In addition, pulling in the stiff-legged position can place so much additional strain on the lower back and hip extensors and put them through so much larger a range of motion than is normally experienced by the lifter that injuries or overtraining of these areas can occur when the exercise is first introduced. Therefore, any stiff-legged lifting and pulling need to be introduced gradually. Given these overall limitations, it appears that the stiff-legged lifts and pulls should be used sparingly, if at all.

Split and Squat Recoveries and Supports

Purpose(s): To strengthen the shoulder girdle and arm extensors for purposes of fixing and holding a snatch or jerk overhead. To teach a lifter the proper positioning of the bar in relation to the body when the bar is overhead.

Description: There are several variations of this exercise, all of them utilizing a power rack or similar equipment. When the lifter is training the split jerk, the bar is typically set on a power rack at a height that is equivalent to or slightly below the lowest position the lifter is likely to reach while jerking. The lifter then assumes the split position under the bar (either by jumping into it as he or she would when jerking or by simply placing himself or herself under the bar in a split position). When the lifter is doing a "recovery," the lifter recovers from the split position as he or she would after reaching such a position in the split jerk (i.e., the front foot is brought back toward the lifter first,

and then the back foot is brought forward under the lifter). When the lifter is merely doing a support, he or she pushes up with the legs enough to get the bar to clear the pins supporting it in the rack. The bar is then generally supported in the split position for two to six seconds and then is returned to the rack.

In the squat variation of the support, the bar is set at a height approximately equal to or slightly below the lowest point in the power jerk. In the rare case of the lifter who actually uses a full squat in the jerk, the bar could be set at the lowest position that is assumed in that style of jerking. If the lifter is doing an actual recovery, he or she stands up from the low position with the bar over head, much as would be done if the lifter were recovering from that position in the jerk (overhead squats would probably be just as effective or more so). If the lifter is doing a support, the bar is raised enough to clear the pins and then held for three to six seconds. Another variation of the exercise that permits the lifter to handle heavier weights and reduces the stress on the legs, hips and back involves setting the bar so that the lifter need only to descend into a one-quarter or one-eighth squat in order to get under the bar with the arms straight,. The lifter then recovers from that position.

Recoveries and supports with the arms in a snatch position are not practiced as often as they are for the jerk. One reason is that the lifter who practices sufficient snatches, and/or overhead squats, and related exercises will rarely experience difficulty in supporting a snatch overhead. In addition, few power racks are set wide enough for the lifter to assume a snatch grip while inside the rack. (Even if the pins are a little wider than the lifter's normal grip, some margin must be available so that if the lifter loses his or her balance, and/or shifts the grip somewhat during the exercise, the hand will not be caught between the rack and the bar when it is returned to the rack.) Lifters with collar-to-collar grips will, of course, never have a rack wide enough to accommodate their grip.

One solution to that problem for the lifter who is doing supports is to position the bar off-center in the rack (with the bar's inside collar touching one pin). Depending on the rack, this position often permits the lifter who does not use a very wide grip to assume a snatch grip. This is done by placing one hand on the bar inside the rack (on the side of the bar that has its inside collar against the rack's pin) and placing the other hand outside the rack but inside the collar of the bar on the other side. This method cannot be used if there is not adequate clearance for the hands, so that even if the lifter shifts the body or the hands during the exercise, the hands will not be pinched when the bar is lifted or returned to the rack. Whenever this variation of the exercise is done, spotters should always be used to assure that the lifter is in no danger of pinching the hands at any point in the movement. Fig. 33 illustrates the split support.

Fig. 33

Effectiveness: This group of exercises is not very important for the average lifter and therefore are not part of most lifters' regular training programs. However, when these exercises are applied selectively in specific circumstances, they can be very useful. A lifter who has trouble with his or her armlock and with holding a bar overhead can use supports to strengthen the arm extensors and shoulders (although regular presses and partial presses can be effective for this purpose as well). Perhaps the major effective use of the recovery and support exercise is to teach the lifter the proper positioning of the body and bar in the jerk.

For most lifters, the greatest benefit will come from using moderate weights (70% to 90% of the jerk) and emphasizing correct position. This is because the lifter who is having trouble holding weights overhead is rarely experiencing the problem purely as a result of a lack of strength. An improper arm position is almost always at least one contributing factor. By using heavy weights and emphasizing the amount lifted, the lifter is almost assured that improper positioning will continue. With more moderate weights, the lifter can use the exercise to experiment with different arm and shoulder positions (e.g., the bar further behind the head, the crook of the elbow turned slightly toward the front of the lifter and the shoulder blades pulled together). When the lifter is using a small enough weight to relax somewhat and to focus on form, maximum benefits can be derived from these exercises. Once proper positioning has been learned, heavier weights can be used occasionally.

Supports and recoveries can also be very useful for the lifter who is resting or rehabilitating certain areas of the body that would otherwise preclude practicing the jerk. In addition, they can be helpful to the lifter who wishes to condition the body for a change in style, before actually beginning to use that style. An example would be a lifter who is planning to switch legs in the jerk (i.e., reverse the legs placed forward and back) or one who wishes to learn to place the bar well behind the head in the jerk, instead of in front of the head or directly over it.

Jerk Drives and Front Quarter Squats

Purpose(s): To increase the power that the lifter can generate in the amortization and explosion phases of the jerk and, to a certain extent, the final explosion of the pull. These exercises are also used to improve the technique of the lifter in the dip and drive of the jerk.

Description: These lifts are typically performed in one of two ways. One is to take the bar from a rack, step back and the perform the jerk drive or partial squat. In the other variation the lifter begins the exercise from a position that simulates the lowest point in the lifter's dip for the jerk and then returns the bar to the pins of the rack (or at least touches them) between reps. When the drive is performed, the lifter attempts to emulate the explosion phase of the jerk (and the amortization phase as well, if the bar is lowered before the drive). After the drive there is no attempt to move the feet, so that once the bar reaches its maximum height, the lifters catches the bar at the shoulders (absorbing the shock by bending the legs with the torso held upright) or on the pins of the rack.

When a lifter practices the jerk drive, the most common mistake is to extend the body too far at the top of the drive and to get the majority of the power at the end of the drive. This may result in a higher drive, but it also causes the lifter to learn improper timing of the most powerful part of the jerk drive and creates a significant downward shock to the body if the weight is caught at the shoulders. Maximum power must be applied when the legs are still well bent, not at the point where the lifter in on the toes and reaching up with the arms.

In the front quarter squat, heavier weights are used, and the speed of the jerk drive cannot be achieved (although the lifter generally attempts to drive the bar with as much speed as possible).

Effectiveness: Jerk drives and front quarter squats can increase a lifter's strength and power output in the jerk drive. As noted above, this will only occur if the timing of the maximum power output is correct. In quarter squats the point of maximum effort is almost automatically correct because the greatest strain is felt at the start of the lift (which is close to where maximum power is to be applied in the jerk). Both exercises can be used to teach certain aspects of technique, such as proper depth in the dip, good arm, leg and torso position in the dip and correct balance and proper timing. However, these exercises are not mainstays in the training of most lifters because of the difficulty of truly mirroring the style of the jerk. In the case of the jerk drive, lifters must avoid the exercise because it is quite unpleasant (and potentially dangerous) to catch a weight at the shoulders once it has been driven up.

Overhead Squats

Purpose(s): To improve the strength of the arms and shoulders and the lifter's balance and position in the full squat snatch.

Description: The exercise begins with the bar held on straight arms with a snatch grip and the lifter in a standing position. There are two ways to get the bar into position. One is to set the bar at a height and in such a position on the power rack that the bar can be removed from the rack with a slight bend of the knees. The lifter then steps well back from the rack, so that if a miss or loss of balance occurs, the bar will not bounce against the rack, but, rather, will fall safely to the floor. The other method of getting the bar to the proper starting position is to power jerk it from behind the neck.

Once the bar is overhead, the lifter carefully lowers himself or herself into a full squat position. It is helpful for the lifter to fix the eyes on one position throughout the squat (the position that would be used when doing the squat snatch). The lifter should also think of pushing up and pulling out on the bar. The greatest difficulty in balancing the bar will typically be experienced during the first third and last third of the squat. It is also a good idea for the lifter to pause for a second or two at the bottom of the squat in order to improve his or her balance, position and strength in the low squat position. It is a good idea for the lifter to have spotters when this exercise is performed, but not for the purpose of catching the bar if the lifter should miss (unless protecting the floor of the gym is a primary concern). When a miss occurs, it is better for the lifter to push himself or herself away from the bar (as is done when missing a snatch)

rather than having the spotters catch the bar. However, the spotters can be used to great advantage when the bar is returned to the rack or to the shoulders of the lifter. In the former case the spotters can guide the lifter back to the rack and assure that the lifter does not pinch his or her hands between the bar and the rack. In the latter case, the spotters can ensure that the bar does not fall heavily onto the shoulders of the lifter at the end of the set. Alternatively, the lifter can step forward and let the bar drop. The only time a spotter should be used for the squat itself is to assist the rank beginner find the correct position for the bar and to prevent a miss in the low position (the latter problem should go away as soon as the athlete is taught how to miss).

Effectiveness: The purposes cited above can all be accomplished using the overhead squat. The exercise can help the beginner build confidence, balance, position and strength. For the advanced lifter the exercise can be of great help when the lifter wishes to take a break from practicing the classical lifts but wishes to maintain conditioning in the arms and shoulders and still be in control of the bar in the squat position.

Front Squats

Purpose(s): Front squats are used primarily to strengthen the legs of the lifter for the recovery from the low squat clean position.

Description: The exercise begins with the lifter taking the bar from a rack and assuming the same position that he or she will be in at the end of the clean. From there the lifter lowers himself or herself smoothly into the full squat position and then recovers immediately to the starting position. Every effort is made to keep the torso erect, the upper back straight and the lower spine slightly arched throughout the lift. The feet are always kept flat on the floor during this and all other versions of the squat. Squatting on the toes places undue strain on the knee joints and gives the lifter only a very small point on which to balance. The lifter should try to descend in a controlled but smooth manner and should avoid crashing into (i.e., dropping in a completely free fall without any control on speed) or rebounding out of the full squat using the joints. (He or she should feel the muscles doing the recovering instead.) However, it is generally a good idea for the lifter to attempt to explode up from the bottom of the squat with as much power as possible. This effort will build power in the squat but will not place as much stress on the joints as crashing into, or bouncing up from, the bottom position.

Variations of the squat include the squat with a slow descent, the squat with a pause at one or more positions in the descent, the squat with a pause at the bottom and the squat done more quickly than usual (in the descent, the turnaround into the

recovery and/or during the ascent). Fig. 34 shows
the low position in the front squat.

Fig. 34

Effectiveness: Front squatting is a highly
effective method of strengthening the legs for the
recovery from the clean and can also be used to
condition them to catch the weight in the clean
position. With proper training and mechanics in
the pull, the lifter will be able to pull very heavy
weights to the shoulders while in the clean.
Without diligent training in the squat, the lifter
will find it difficult, if not impossible, to recover
from the full squat position. Moreover, a difficult
recovery makes it less likely that the lifter will
have sufficient energy left for the all important
jerk. Therefore, dedicated training in the squat is
essential.

Squatting slowly, or with one or more pauses
during the descent, is aimed at both taxing the
muscles eccentrically and pre-fatiguing the leg
muscles on the way down, so that the recovery
becomes more difficult. Squatting in this fashion,
as well as squatting with a pause at the bottom, is
also meant to reduce or cancel the use of the elastic
qualities of the muscle during the recovery. It is
important to use the same foot position in this
exercise as in the clean and to keep the torso
vertical and the spinal curves in a normal position
while squatting (i.e., do not permit the back to
round).

Performing squats with a faster than normal
descent trains the elastic qualities of the muscles
as they pertain to the recovery from the squat and,
to a certain extent, conditions the body to absorb
the shock of catching the bar in the clean. Too
much can place undue strain on the joints and the
muscle tendon units of the legs, so practice of this
version of the front squat must be carefully
controlled. Nevertheless, for the lifter who does not
perform the squat clean very often, the fast front
squat can maintain and improve the conditioning
of the leg muscles, so that they can absorb the
impact of the bar at the bottom of the clean and use
their elastic qualities to the greatest advantage.

Back Squats

Purpose(s): Back squats are used to develop
strength in the legs and hips, and, to a lesser
extent, the lower back. Most lifters can squat from
120% to 140% of their best C&J.

Description: The bar is placed on the top of the
rear deltoids and the trapezius muscles. The head
is held in a vertical position, the upper back is as
straight as possible and an arch is maintained in
the lower back. The elbows are placed behind the
bar, the hands grip the bar firmly with a grip that
is a few inches wider than shoulder's width (some
lifters feel more comfortable with the hands placed
even wider). The method of descent described for
the front squat is followed. Many lifters find it
helpful to look up (at least slightly) while
recovering. This helps to keep the back tight and to
prevent the lifter from leaning forward during the
recovery from the squat position. Fig. 35 depicts
the low position in the back squat.

Effectiveness: Many coaches have called back
squats the "king" of the assistance exercises.
Former junior world record holder Victor Schreiner
only half jokingly calls the squat "the basis for life
on earth as we know it." More strength has
probably been built by more weight trainees
(whether competitive weightlifters or not) using the
squat than any other single exercise, and those
who have overlooked the squat in favor of exercises
like the bench press have failed to develop the full
power of the body's strongest muscle groups, the
legs and hips.

Squats are essential for weightlifters. If the
lifter is to succeed, they must practically become an
obsession. Squats are very hard work, and the
amount of development the lifter achieves in them
is almost directly proportional to the conscious
effort that the lifter applies while doing them. It is
difficult to recruit all of the muscles of the legs, and

Fig. 35

only profound concentration and volitional effort will both teach the lifter how to recruit those muscles and train them. Paul Anderson, former Olympic champion and one of the strongest men who ever lived (if not the strongest) built most of his legendary power through highly specialized training on squatting. He once said that, contrary to popular belief, he disliked squatting. However, he became convinced early in his career that squatting would be the key to his success, so he learned to like every set, not for the experience but for the knowledge that every set marked step toward the success he strove for and achieved. Others would do well to learn from Paul's example. This is not to say that training the squat should ever take precedence over the classic lifts, but it should take precedence over most other assistance exercises unless a lifter has surplus squatting strength (i.e., can squat with much more weight than is necessary in order for him or her to stand up easily from the low squat position in the clean).

One caution should be observed when doing the squat in general and the back squat in particular; spotters should always be used when heavy weights are being attempted. It is true that if a lifter misses a squat, he or she can always push the bar backward and jump forward out from under the bar, thereby letting it fall to the platform. There is some risk in this procedure, however. The bar can scrape against the lifter's torso as it falls or become caught on the lifter's belt (thereby exerting a significant downward force on the lifter). A less likely scenario is one in which the lifter loses his or her balance or is injured as he or she descends into, or recovers from, the squat position. In any of these situations, the use of spotters helps to prevent the worsening of any misfortune. Spotters are especially important for the back squat because of the bar's position behind the head of the lifter. This position makes getting out from under the bar more difficult than in other varieties of the squat. (When a lifter is doing an overhead squat or front squat, pushing the bar forward and jumping back permits him or her to get rid of the bar relatively easily.) As is the case with most versions of squatting, bench squatting should be performed with the torso as upright as possible, the curves of the back in a normal position and with the feet in the same position that is employed during the execution of the squat clean.

Partial Squatting

Purpose(s): Partial squatting is used to improve the strength and power of the legs in other than the full position. As noted earlier, the partial front squat can be used to improve the jerk. The partial back squat can be used for the same purpose; it can also strengthen the legs in the finishing position of the pull.

Description: The bar is typically placed on a rack at or just below the height the lifter wishes to focus on in terms of building strength and power. One common position for performing partial squats is the half squat (a position in which the bottom of the thighs are just above parallel with the floor). Another common position is the quarter squat, in which the legs are bent at an angle of approximately 150°. When performing partial squats it is important to keep the torso absolutely upright or inclined very slightly forward (never backward) and to keep the knees directly over the front of the feet in the starting position (as compared with outside or inside of the feet - i.e., if the toes are pointed out from the center of the body at a 45 degree angle, the thighs and knees should be at a similar angle to the center of the body as well).

Effectiveness: The carryover from full movements to partial ones is far greater than any carryover from partial movements to full ones. In addition, the half squat can place a great deal of strain on the back as the lifter attempts to struggle up from the half squat position. (This is a very difficult position for the legs, so there is a tendency to let the torso incline forward, so that the angle of the legs can be increased, thereby placing significant stress on the lower back.) When the torso is inclined to a greater degree, there is a greater than normal strain placed on the lower back. Quarter squats can place a significant strain on the muscle-tendon unit at the front of the knee. I have injured my lower back doing half squats and my knee doing quarter squats (and I have seen others do the same on a number of occasions), so I am not the greatest fan of either of these exercises. Partial squats can have their place for certain special strengthening purposes, but they should be used sparingly. They tend to yield better results when they are done quickly with sub-maximum weights (for power more than pure strength) as long as you don't permit the bar to crash back down on the body significantly after exploding up. In no event are partial squats a viable substitute for full squats (which for weightlifters means squatting as low as possible while maintaining good back position and, of course, not hitting the floor with the buttocks.

Remedial Exercises For Strengthening Specific Muscle Groups

Exercises that strengthen muscles that are directly or indirectly involved in the classical lifts are often referred to in the weightlifting literature as "remedial" exercises. The carryover value of these exercises, in terms of performance on the classic lifts, tends to be small or nonexistent. However, it is thought that performing these exercises helps to balance the strength of an athlete's muscle groups and to prevent injuries. Remedial exercises also offer a means for maintaining the condition of a muscle group without placing the same stress on the body as when executing the classic lifts and closely related exercises.

Lunges and Related Exercises

<u>Purpose(s):</u> Lunges are used to strengthen the legs in the split position and as an occasional substitute for, or adjunct to, squats.

<u>Description:</u> Lunges can be performed in a number of ways. The bar can be placed behind the neck in the same position as for back squats. It can also be placed on the lifter's shoulders in front of the neck and at arm's length overhead in a snatch position (where it becomes the equivalent of overhead squats or split snatchers). Regardless of where the bar is placed, the lifter begins the exercise by stepping forward far enough with the front foot so that the feet are positioned properly in order to descend into the low split position. (Depending on the depth of the lunge, more than one step may be required to accomplish this.) The lifter then lowers the body by bending the forward leg while maintaining a straight position with the rear leg. The torso remains in a upright position, with the upper back flat and the lower back slightly arched. The head is up and fixed on a point that will be slightly above eye level in the full split. In recovering, some lifters follow the same pattern as when recovering from a split while lifting (front leg a large step and then back leg a smaller one). Other lifters take two or even more steps back with the front leg until they have recovered to a point where one step forward with the best foot will complete the recovery process.

Still another variation of the exercise is to place the bar on the floor and then to have the lifter step over the bar and descend into a split position, so that the hips and upper body are directly over the bar. The lifter then lowers the body sufficiently to grasp the bar with the hands. The athlete then raises the bar as high as possible with the legs. Obviously, in this latter technique, the lifter is prevented by the bar from recovering to a standing position. Lifters who perform this variation of the lunge often place the feet on elevated surfaces, so that the depth that they are required to achieve in the split in order to grasp the bar with the hands resembles the very lowest split position it is possible to achieve. Fig. 36 shows a fairly low position in the lunge, although flexible lifters can go lower than this (and split lifters must).

<u>Effectiveness:</u> Lunges are very useful for strengthening the legs in the split position. Needless to say, they are nearly as important for split style lifters as squats are for squat lifters. For the majority of lifters (who only split in the jerk, and not very low at that) the exercise is of less

import, but it has some value nonetheless. It can be used to condition the legs for the split and to prepare the lifter for the eventuality of a lower than normal split on some occasion. Lunges are especially useful when a lifter is not practicing the split jerk for a time (e.g., when specializing in the

Fig. 36

power jerk off-season), enabling balance and conditioning in the split position to be retained.

Regardless of the variation of the exercise used, it is a very good idea to practice lunges with alternating legs. When the lifter practices the actual lift, he or she will always put the same foot forward and the opposite foot backward. While this is desirable from the standpoint of skills, it places uneven strains on muscles and joints that were built to be used symmetrically. In addition, the spine is subjected to an uneven strain. Practicing lunges only with this leg position will tend to accentuate the problem. Using both legs in an alternating fashion promotes balanced conditioning. Bud Charniga, a former top ranked lifter American lifter with an M.A. in physical education, Eleiko dealer, noted translator of Soviet publications, owner of Dynamic Fitness and one of the most knowledgeable coaches in the United States today, advocates a greater volume of lunges using the arrangement of the legs opposite to that normally used in the jerk and/or split. He believes that extra lunges on the leg opposite to the one that is used in the jerk even out the stress on the body. I believe there is great merit in Bud's advice.

Leg Presses

<u>Purpose(s):</u> To strengthen legs and hip extensors.

<u>Description:</u> In the most common kind of leg press today, the athlete sits on a small seat that is

228

at or close to floor level with the back supported by an incline bench with an incline of approximately 45° to the floor. The legs then push on a platform that is forward and above the lifter (the resistance slides along supports that are typically at approximately a 45° angle to the floor). The back remains stationary and the feet are pushed away from the body.

Effectiveness: The vast majority of weightlifters never do this exercise, but I know of at least one national level Olympic lifter and one high level power lifter who have partially substituted leg pressing for some squatting and deadlifting. No lifter has ever built great squatting power without practicing the squat. However, the leg press can provide some variety for the athlete. It can also be used to increase the leg flexibility of some lifters and can permit others to work around certain injuries to maintain some leg strength.

Leg presses are normally performed with the lifter either lying on his or her back or sitting in a specially designed seat with a rigid back. The feet are placed on a surface that is attached to the resistance being applied in performing the leg press. The leg press machine is constructed in such a way that the legs must be well bent (often to the point of the knees touching the lifter's chest, or nearly so) in order for the feet to be placed in a flat position against the resistance at the outset of the exercise. The lifter pushes against the resistance with his or her legs until the legs are straight. The bar is then returned to the starting position.

Step Ups

Purpose(s): Similar to lunges except that a more extreme low position is achieved with respect to the front leg, and the strain on the back leg is reduced. Consequently, the step up might be looked upon as a bridge between the squat and the split.

Description: The bar is typically placed on the shoulders, behind the neck. The lifter places one foot on a block that is approximately at the level of the lifters mid-thigh (although higher and lower blocks are often used). The back leg is relatively straight. The lifter pushes off the back foot to generate some momentum and then pushes up almost entirely with the front leg to lift the lifter and bar onto the box. The opposite leg is put backward for the descent, and the lifter lowers himself or herself to the starting position and performs a rep with this opposite leg. This process is repeated for the appropriate number of reps on each leg. Figure 37 displays the starting position in the step up.

Effectiveness: The front leg is worked in a deeper position in the step up versus the lunge. There tends to be a greater stress placed on the hip extensors as a result. Step ups have been touted as a replacement for the full squat, but I doubt that the step up will ever be accepted by the serious weightlifter or weight trainer as such. One of its weaknesses relative to the squat is that it is harder to ensure that performance is uniform and that the unevenness of the stress that is placed on the legs will not simply mimic the stresses that are part of the squat. This does not mean that the exercise may not have value when done in conjunction with squats (i.e., as a substitute for squats only in some training sessions). It simply means that the "jury is still out" with respect to its effectiveness and safety. Of course for those looking for an excuse to avoid the squat, the step up offers a wonderful "loophole" to escape the full squat exercise that is dreaded by so many trainees because of its strenuousness. However, if the experiment does not work, the big loser will be the trainee.

Hatfield or Safety Squat Bar Squats

Purpose(s): To strengthen the leg and hip muscles in the same way as squats but without as much strain on the lower back and with less skill in execution than the regular squat

Description: A special bar with a padded "yoke" built into it supports the plates on the athletes' shoulders, eliminating the need to hold onto the

Fig. 37

229

bar. Instead, the lifter holds the uprights of a power rack for balance while performing this version of the squat. Because of the positioning of the load and the assistance provided by the uprights of the rack, most lifters can use significantly more weight in this form of the squat than the regular squat. Though invented by someone else, this bar's use was popularized by "Dr. Squat," Fred Hatfield.

Effectiveness: Fred Hatfield swears by this piece of equipment, and I have known a number of powerlifters who believe that it has helped them to a degree. I have known some Olympic lifters who have experimented with it but none who have reported material improvements in their squats. This exercise may be of some value as a means of introducing variety into a lifter's squat training, but this version of squatting will never replace full squatting for Olympic lifters.

Leg Extensions and Leg Curls

Purpose(s): To strengthen the leg extensors (leg extensions), leg flexors (leg curls).

Description: The leg extension is most frequently performed while seated on an bench that is specifically designed for leg extensions and leg curls. In the most common version the upper legs are supported by the bench and the lower legs hang over the edge of the bench, so that the upper and lower legs are approximately at a 90° angle to one another. Resistance is provided by a bar that hangs on a rigid set of "arms" attached to the bench (the bar is normally set at the level of the lifter's ankles). The lifter straightens the leg and typically pauses, at least momentarily, before lowering the bar to its starting position.

Leg curls are typically performed while the lifter is lying face down on a bench designed for the leg curl exercise. Both the lifter's torso and upper legs are supported by the bench. A bar is attached on either side to the bench through a set of rigid arms. The lifter places the rear of the ankles beneath the bar and then curls the lower legs toward the buttocks, going as far as is possible. Machines designed for the performance of standing leg curls also exist today.

Effectiveness: Leg extensions and leg curls are very popular in rehabilitation circles and health clubs. They are effective for strengthening the muscles they are designed to strengthen, but they are not very useful for improving a lifter's performance in the classical lifts or the squat. Because of their popularity in rehabilitation circles, leg extensions are often erroneously used to "rehabilitate" the knee from such conditions as quadriceps tendinitis. There is evidence doing leg extensions can help quad tendinitis and some evidence that it can hurt (by irritating the inflamed tendon even more).

In fact, the evidence is building that leg extensions are more stressful to portions of the knee joint than squatting. The leg extension can be useful in rehabilitating an injured knee that is not ready for squatting or for maintaining some strength in the leg extensors when squatting is precluded for a time due to injury. The leg extension can also be used for "quad setting," which can be used to rehabilitate the knee of a lifter affected by chondromalacia (see Chapter 11 for further details).

Leg curls are used to train the leg flexors directly. They are of little or no use in improving performance in the classical lifts or the squat. There is a school of thought in sports medicine that believes uneven strength in the opposing muscles of the legs could be the cause of some knee injuries (especially in sports which generate high velocity leg movements, such as sprinting). As a consequence, on the premise that their leg extensors had become much stronger than their leg flexors (through the practice of the classical lifts and squats), a number of lifters began to practice leg curls. I have met few people who felt that they benefited from leg curls (either in terms of weightlifting prowess or injury prevention/rehabilitation). This may be because during weightlifting exercises, the leg is never straightened forcefully against little resistance (as it is while running). A second reason for the weak results may be that many of the exercises performed by lifters (e.g., full squats and pulls from the floor) do train the leg flexors, at least to an extent and in a limited range of motion. This does not mean that a given lifter may not find practicing leg curls or similar exercises beneficial. It simply means that for the majority of lifters the benefits are not clear.

Hyperextensions and Glute-Ham Exercises

Purpose(s): To strengthen the muscles of the lower and middle back, the foremost of which are the spinal erectors (the muscles that hold the spine in a rigid position during the pull). Also to strengthen the buttocks and hamstrings in certain positions.

Description: The lifter lies face down on a high bench with the hips, or the legs and hips, supported by the bench (the torso, from about the bottom of the waist up, extends beyond the bench). The legs are held in place by a sturdy strap or bar that is placed over the ankles (or by another lifter who usually sits on the exerciser's ankles). The lifter lowers the torso until it is nearly perpendicular to the floor (see Fig. 38a), then raises the torso until the shoulders are at the level of the hips or slightly higher level (see Fig. 38b). (In the glute-ham variety of the exercise the lifter continues to raise the torso further by bending the legs.) Naturally, the equipment used to support the

Fig. 38a)

Fig 38(b)

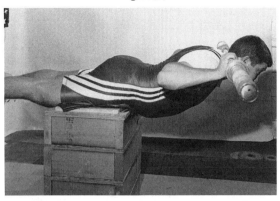

lifter's lower body during this exercise must be high enough off the ground so that when the lifter is in the low position, the head is well clear of the floor. When the exercise is performed against resistance, as it should ultimately be, a bar is placed behind the neck of the lifter.

Effectiveness: The hyperextension will strengthen the spinal erector muscles (especially the lower area of these muscles), the hamstring and the gluteus muscles. The hyperextension's value is somewhat limited by its limited effect on these muscles. In addition, the tensions experienced in the legs, hips and back are not very similar to those experienced during the pull. This is because the greatest stress on the spinal erectors during the pull occurs when the angle between the legs and torso is the smallest (i.e., during the second and third phases of the pull). In the hyperextension the greatest effort of the spinal erectors occurs when the back in nearly in line with the legs.

The hyperextension can be of value for general conditioning, for rehabilitation and when the lifter is injured in such a way that regular pulls are precluded. It can also help lifters who have trouble keeping the spine rigid when lifting.

When performing hyperextensions, the lifter should be very careful to assure that the strap or bar (or the partner) holding the legs is very sturdy. It must be remembered that during the hyperextension the head of the lifter is between the bar and the floor. If the feet become loose, an injury could result. It is also important to assure that the bench be sturdy, stable and attached to the floor (or weighted in some way). Significant force is created outside the base of support of the bench when the hyperextension is being performed with weights. Therefore, there is a tendency for the bench itself to become upended if it is not weighted at the opposite end or fastened down. I prefer straight benches to the specially designed benches that support the hips because the former tend to support the knees more.

Obviously, the glute-ham exercise requires that the knees bend at the end of the motion so it

cannot be performed on a conventional high bench. Some lifters truly believe in this latter exercise, but I have not detected any dramatic benefits from its use.

Calf Raises

Purpose(s): To strengthen the muscles that extend the foot in rising on the toes.

Description: In its most common variation, the bar is placed on the shoulders, behind the neck. The lifter rises as high on the toes as possible and then lowers the body to the starting position, using only the calf muscles. The torso and knees are kept straight throughout the exercise.

Effectiveness: In the 1960s and 1970s a great emphasis was placed on the importance of rising high on the toes at the top of the pull. This follow through in the pull was regarded as a key to proper technique. With the today's styles, there is less of an emphasis on rising on the toes. Therefore, the need for specially strengthening the calf muscles has been somewhat diminished, and so the need for this exercise (if there ever really was one) has declined. It is rarely, if ever, included in the routines of top lifters.

Sit-ups and Other Exercises for the Midsection

Purpose(s): To strengthen the midsection (abdominals, external obliques, etc.) of the lifter so that the spine is well supported and to maintain some balance between the muscles that run along the front and sides of the torso and the muscles of the back.

Description: There are three main variations of the sit-up: sit-ups with the legs straight, sit-ups with the knees elevated and partial sit-ups. Sit-ups with the legs straight are the traditional version of this exercise. The legs are braced and the torso is lifted from the floor by curling the head and neck up toward the chest, lifting the torso from the floor until the lifter is at a 90° or greater angle to the floor.

231

Fig. 39   Fig. 40

In the bent-knee version, the feet are placed flat on the floor and the knees are elevated. This reduces the stress on the spine but still utilizes the hip flexors during an extensive portion of the exercise, though to a lesser extent than the regular sit-up. The partial sit-up typically ends when the head and shoulders are lifted from the floor. It is the only version of the sit-up that exercises the abdominal muscles alone (or at least primarily). This is because the only function of the abdominals is to flex or curl the trunk to its greatest extent; once this has been accomplished, the act of raising the torso is performed by the hip flexors.

Another exercise that is popular for strengthening the abdominals and hip flexors is the leg raise. When doing the leg raise, the lifter lifts the legs (which are typically kept straight) towards the torso. The most popular variation of the exercise is for the trainee to lie on the floor or a bench and to lift the legs from a position in which they are in a straight line with the torso up to a point where they are at a 90° angle with the torso and then return them to the starting position. A more advanced variation, one that places more stress on the abdominals and hip flexors and less on the back, is the hanging leg raise. In this version the lifter hangs from a chinning bar or from straight arms on parallel bars and raises the legs until they are parallel with or higher than the ground (sometimes pausing in that position before returning to the starting position).

An easier variation of both the regular and hanging leg raise is the bent-knee leg raise or frog kick. In this exercise the knees are bent as they are lifted toward the torso. The lifter pulls the knees as close to the torso as possible before returning to the starting position.

Both the straight and bent leg variations of the lying leg raise can be combined with the sit-up, so that the legs and torso are lifted toward one another at the same time. This combination exercise is more strenuous that either exercise done alone and is a time saver because more muscles are trained at once. Fig. 39 depicts the combination crunching sit-up and bent knee leg raise while Fig. 40 illustrates the hanging leg raise.

Side bends and twists are the most popular forms of exercise used to strengthen the obliques, although they are often done incorrectly. Twisting while standing with an evenly loaded bar is virtually a waste of time because the only resistance applied to the obliques is the inertia of the bar (a relatively small resistance). Twisting while leaning forward places much more pressure on the lower back than on the obliques, and it places the spine in a position that make it vulnerable to injury. Twisting while standing erect with the bar unevenly loaded is far more effective in terms of loading the obliques on the opposite side and is safer than the lean forward style.

Side bends are typically done with dumbbells of equal weight in either hand. Unfortunately, these equal weights essentially cancel one another out in terms of the added resistance they supply during the side bend itself. Side bends with a weight in only one hand are much more effective in terms of stressing the oblique (though they may place more strain on the spine than the two arm version).

An exercise that is better than the side bend in terms of stress on the obliques, and one that probably exerts less stress on the spine, is the side hyperextension. This exercise is performed with the athlete lying on his or her side on a bench with the torso overhanging the end of the bench. The torso is lowered as far as possible toward the floor and then is raised as high above the legs as possible. Naturally the legs must be firmly supported by a strap or by the hands of another lifter.

Effectiveness: It is important to strengthen the abdominal and oblique muscles for the reasons above. Sit-ups with the legs straight strengthen the hips flexors as well as the abdominals. They place the greatest stress on the spine of any of the three versions of the exercise. Nevertheless, it is my opinion that they can be useful for the Olympic lifter, because many of the movements that a lifter makes involve a coordinated effort of both the abdominals and the hip flexors. Both muscle groups need to be strong.

The two other variations of the sit-up can be used to strengthen the abdominals while placing less strain on the hip flexors and spine. Such exercises have their place and it is a good idea to mix the versions of the sit-up. Sit-ups can aggravate groin, back and certain knee problems (the latter is especially true of sit-ups done with bent knees).

Leg raises are also a good exercise for the lifter, but they should be done in the hanging style as soon as the lifter can master it. This both loads the abdominals more strenuously and appears to reduce the pressure on the spine (relative to standard leg raises). The bent-knee version of the leg raise is a good cooling down exercise for the lifter in that it stretches the spine. Resistance should be added to hanging leg raises whenever possible.

As mentioned earlier, combined leg raises and sit-ups are a good exercise and a time saver. The main disadvantage of the exercise is that it is difficult to increase the load after the exercise has been mastered with no added resistance (the lifter would have to add resistance to the feet and shoulders, probably an uneven one).

Properly performed twists and side bends can both be used to strengthen the obliques, but in my opinion the side hyperextension is the exercise of choice for strengthening the obliques. (In some cases this exercise unloads pressures (in/on) the back as well.)

Once the athlete is past the beginning stages of these exercises, doing them without weights is virtually a waste of time. Lifters practice sit-ups to strengthen their abdominal muscles. Muscles do not get stronger without progressive resistance. In addition, high reps are ineffective in the sit-up. There is nothing special about the abdominal muscles. Low reps make them stronger without building undue mass. Reps in the six to twenty range will tend to build size and strength, and reps that are much higher will tend to build endurance.

Presses and Dips

Purpose(s): Pressing and dipping movements are used to strengthen the arm extensors and shoulders. Dips strengthen those same muscles as well as the pectoral muscles of the chest.

Description: There are five common variations of the press: the military press, the press behind neck, the seated press, the bench press and the incline press. Any of these variations of the press can be practiced with a wide (snatch like) or narrow (clean width) grip. The narrower grip places more stress on the arm extensors than on the shoulders. A wider grip places more strain on the shoulders than on the arms in the overhead versions of the press and more stress on the chest muscles in the bench press. The clean grip is the grip most frequently used by Olympic lifters when they press because it promotes more overall muscular development and because most lifters feel they need arm and shoulder strength more for the jerk than the snatch, Both the military press and press behind the neck should be done with the torso perfectly upright. There must be no leaning back with the upper body. Leaning back places undue strain on the spine and simply lessens the strengthening effects of the press at the desired angles.

The military press is usually begun by taking the bar from a rack. The exercise is then commenced with the bar resting on the shoulders in front of the neck. The elbows are generally held in a lower position than they are for the clean or front squat (near the front of the chest). From here the lifter pushes up with the arms, keeping the bar close to the face and with the elbows traveling in a position that is neither alongside the body nor in front, but, rather, between these points. At the end of the motion, the bar should be well behind the head in a position that simulates the finished positions of the jerk. Fig. 41 illustrates the middle position in the military press.

The press behind neck begins with the weight behind the lifter's head. It is then pushed to arm's length with the arms while maintaining the position of the bar behind the lifter's neck. Here the elbows move primarily sideways and up. For many lifters, starting the bar from behind the neck places undue strain on the shoulders (much more than the military press), and the lift does not stimulate the starting position of the jerk. Fig. 42 depicts the middle position in the press behind neck.

The seated press can be performed either behind the neck or in front. The lifter normally sits on a bench after taking the bar from the bench supports or those of a rack. The press itself is performed in the same way as the standing version. One variation of the exercise is with the lifter in a full squat position instead of sitting on a bench. The lifter simply presses up from that position (the snatch grip is generally used in this exercise). Sometimes lifters perform a cheating version of this exercise by bouncing up with the legs a little as the press commences in order to give

Fig. 41

Fig. 42

the press a little start. (This lift is typically begun with the bar resting behind the neck.)

The bench press is performed while the lifter is lying in a supine position on the bench. The bar is normally taken from a rack that is attached to the bench. The lifter then lowers the bar to the chest at a point just below the nipples and pushes the bar up to straight arms. When the bar travels up, it is pushed gradually toward the lifter's shoulders, so that it is traveling in a slight backward curve throughout the lift. The elbows are neither at a 90° angle to the torso of the lifter nor against the lifter's sides, but, rather, in between those two positions. Fig. 43 illustrates the starting position for the bench press (after the bar has been lowered to the chest).

The incline press is performed on a bench that is normally set at between 45° and 60° in relation to the floor. It is executed in much the same way as the bench press, except that the bar is lowered to the shoulders or the top of the chest instead of the lower part of the chest. Figure 44 captures the incline press just after the athletes has begun to

Fig. 43

Fig. 44

press the bar up from the chest and shoulders.

Dips are normally performed on parallel bars. The lifter begins by pushing the body up on the bars, so that the upper body is above the bars, the legs are hanging below the bars, and the arms are straight and supporting the entire weight of the body. The palms are pointed down and are generally facing the body. A dip begins when the body is lowered by allowing the arms to bend, and it continues until the shoulders are at the same horizontal level or are below the level of the elbows. Then the lifter pushes the body back up to the starting position. During the exercise the body is kept as motionless as possible (e.g., the legs hang straight down and do not swing). Fig. 45 shows the low position in the dip (some athletes do go lower but doing so seems to increase the risk of injury to the shoulder).

Effectiveness: All forms of pressing will develop the strength of the arm extensors and some portions of the shoulders to a certain degree. In the days when the sport of weightlifting included the

234

Fig. 45

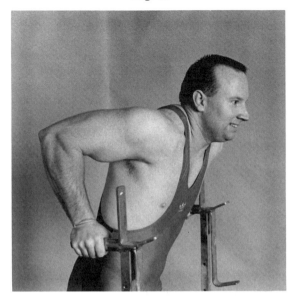

overhead press, all lifters spent a great deal of their training time practicing the press and hence building great strength in the arms and shoulders. I never saw a dislocation of a shoulder in those days, and shoulder injuries, in general, were extremely rare. It is my belief that the extensive pressing that weightlifters practiced at that time was at least partially responsible for that extremely low injury rate. Today's lifters still have strong arms and shoulders as a result of practicing the snatch and jerk, but their strength through the full range of motion is not as great. While shoulder injuries are still relatively rare, we do see a significantly higher incidence of them since the press was eliminated from competition. I believe it is important for all lifters to practice pressing as a protective measure and to develop well rounded (i.e., full range of motion) strength in muscle groups that are important in performing the classical lifts.

The pattern of movement in the military press resembles the pattern of arm movement during the snatch and jerk to a greater extent than any other pressing movement. Therefore, in terms of protecting and strengthening the muscles involved, the strength it develops should have the greatest degree of carryover to the lifts,. They should be the cornerstone of any lifter's press training.

The press behind the neck stresses the lateral aspect (outside portion) of the shoulders more than the military press. Some lifters rank it before the military press as an arm and shoulder strengthening exercise, and others disagree (I am one). It is probably a good idea to at least some training on both exercises.

The seated press is intended to be a stricter version of the military or press behind the neck, one that supposedly places less strain on the spine because the lifter cannot lean back while doing it.

It has been my experience that seated presses can place more strain on the back than the standing version. This is partly because in the standing version, if the lifter does lean back, it is possible and likely that the lifter will let the hips travel forward as well, limiting the arch in the spine itself and thereby placing less pressure on the spine than during the seated press. The lifter also has a greater ability to move the body overall in response to a loss of balance, etc., in the standing version. In the seated press the hips are fixed on the bench; when the lifter braces the back in order to press the bar up at a difficult point in the press, the only way the shoulders can be lowered is to arch the spine. The only way to correct for a loss of balance is to shift the hips around on the bench. In addition, most lifters find it more necessary to tense the muscles of the lower back to maintain torso position in the seated press than in the standing version. For all of these reasons lifters may experience more back problems in performing seated presses than the standing versions, but the incidence of injury is very low if either exercise is performed properly.

When a lifer has an injury that prevents the lower body from supporting weight, the seated press can be used to maintain strength in the shoulders and arms, but the standing version of the press is far superior for the healthy lifter.

The versions of the press that are done with the lifter sitting in the full squat position are meant to simulate what the lifter experiences during the snatch. While on the surface this may appear to be true, a closer analysis reveals that this argument is not as strong as it sounds. When the lifter is snatching, the bar is in front of the head and shoulders during most of the motion, including the squat under, It is only as the lifter descends into the low position of the snatch that the arms begin to press up and back. It is true that the torso is leaning forward somewhat since the lifter is sitting in a full squat position, and the resulting body angle during the press is different from that which can be achieved when standing; this difference may have some carryover value to the snatch. However, pressing while sitting in a squat position places the knees in a stressful position for the entire set. When stress is placed on any joint for an extended period, the muscles surrounding that joint tend to fatigue and relax, placing greater stress on the ligaments. Overall, the practice of pressing while in a squat position may have some value, but it should not be the primary pressing exercise for a weightlifter.

The bench press is probably the most popular pressing exercise in the world today. This is probably because it is easy to learn, it is one of the lifts used in powerlifting competition and it develops more upper-body muscles than perhaps any other single exercise. The main advantage that the bench press has over the standing presses discussed above is that it develops the chest muscles, as well as the arm extensors and shoulders. The chest muscles are impressive to the general public and are viewed by many as one of the measures of an athlete's strength and development (right behind the arms).

For the weightlifter (and for most athletes), the bench press is definitely a second-rate exercise. Since it develops the chest muscles, a group of muscles that are virtually useless in lifting a bar overhead, the weightlifter who practices bench presses extensively develops unnecessary muscles (and hence unnecessary muscular body weight), which can push the lifter up a weight class or make it harder to reduce to a lower weight class. Another disadvantage of the bench press for the weightlifter is that it exercises the shoulders in a less well rounded fashion than the overhead press. The anterior deltoid is greatly stressed in the bench press, and the lateral aspect of the deltoid is far less stressed (if at all). Overhead pressing utilizes a wider range of shoulder muscles in positions that resemble the snatch and jerk more closely.

One final major disadvantage of the bench press lies in the safety factor. While most weight training exercises are very safe in comparison to other athletic activities, the bench press is one of the more hazardous (though it is still quite safe overall). One danger of the bench press is that its starting position is the one in which the body is the strongest (i.e., with the arms in an extended position). If the lifter cannot complete the exercise once the bar has been lowered, or the lifter otherwise loses control of the bar, the body is caught between the bar and the bench that supports the lifter. Because of this position, the lifter cannot merely move the body out from under the bar and let it fall harmlessly to the floor (as in the squat, for example). Moreover, a bar that does fall can actually fall on the neck or face of the lifter. This problem has led to a number of injuries and even some fatalities over the years (making it the only exercise with weights that I know which has directly caused fatalities). For this reason, spotters (or mechanical substitutes) should always be used when performing the bench press. However, even with spotters, bench presses have caused a significant number of shoulder injuries and tears in the pectoral muscle, particularly when performed with a wide grip.

Since heavier weights can be handled in the bench press than the overhead versions, it has been argued that the arm extensors are more strenuously worked near the lockout position in the bench press than in the overhead press. This may be true, but the difference in the position in which the arms are stressed makes it less likely that a carryover to the Olympic lifts will occur. Moreover, if the lifter wishes to train the strength of the arm extensors near the lockout position (a good idea for the lifter who has trouble locking out or supporting

a weight at arm's length), partial presses that begin a few inches below the lockout position are likely to be far more effective. With all of the disadvantages associated with the bench press, the Olympic lifter would be wise to avoid it, or at least to keep its use to a limited level. Most athletes will find that standing and incline presses more closely parallel the movements required in their sports as well.

Incline pressing is a cross between bench pressing and overhead pressing. The higher the incline, the closer it is to the overhead press in terms of the muscles it loads. It is therefore better for the weightlifter than bench pressing, but is not quite as useful as overhead pressing. For the lifter whose lower body is injured, the incline press can be used in conjunction with the seated press to maintain upper-body strength. The incline press has the advantage of placing less stress on the spine than the seated press, so the lifter can really push this exercise to the limit without putting much strain on the back.

Dips work the arms extensors, shoulders and chest muscles through a full range of motion and consequently were favored by many lifters for strengthening these muscles when the press was part of weightlifting competition. They have since fallen into general disuse. Overall, this appears to be a good thing. While dips are a very effective exercise for strengthening the aforementioned muscles, the extreme range of motion and the angles at which force is exerted place an enormous strain on the shoulder joint. More than one lifter has suffered a career-ending (or at least damaging) injury while doing the full version dips. Since other pressing movements are safer and as effective for the purposed of the Olympic lifter, dips are to be avoided. At a minimum, when they are done, the athlete should lower the shoulders no deeper than to the level of the elbows. This method of dipping will load the arm extensors significantly but will tend to lessen the strain on the shoulders and pectoral muscles.

Grip Work

Purpose(s): To strengthen the grip for the snatch and clean.

Description: There two basic varieties of grip work: grip work that provides resistance to the act of closing the hand (concentric grip work) and grip work that provides resistance to the act of maintaining the hand in a closed position (isometric grip work).

In the first category of exercises are those that employ spring type hand grippers, hand grippers that use weights for resistance and exercises that entail squeezing an object that has a certain amount of give (like a ball). In the second category are exercises like pinch gripping (holding the edge of a plate(s) in the hand), lifting, pulling or

236

deadlifting without straps or without a hook grip and holding a weight in the hand after a partial deadlift (particularly with one hand at a time).

Effectiveness: Gripping exercises are among the exercises most neglected by lifters. This is an incredible omission when you realize that in weightlifting, perhaps more than any sport, the grip is vital to performance. Remember that in the snatch and the clean, it is the hands that transmit the force created by the leg, hip muscles to the bar. Except for thigh contact during the pull, the hands are virtually the only parts of the body that touch the bar.

Every lifter, whether they are have large hands or small, whether they have a strong grip or a weaker one, should practice some gripping exercises. If the lifter practices an ample number of lifts without straps and/or without a hook grip, it may be possible for such lifts to fulfill the lifter's need to train the grip isometrically, but this is unlikely. Why? As most lifters know, the hands tend to become abraded by the bar before the muscles in them, or the muscles of the legs hips and back, have had their full complement of training. Grip work, when properly done, need not cause any material increase in abrasion to the skin of the hands, yet it can measurably strengthen the hands. Isometric grip work is probably the more important of the two methods of grip strengthening.

The lifter can practice isometric grip work by holding a smooth (non-knurled) bar while deadlifting with a hook or regular grip. Partial one arm deadlifting (lifting the bar from a position a few inches below the completed deadlift position) and holding at the finished position for a few seconds are excellent variations of isometric grip strengthening. Pinch gripping is a poor substitute for such lifting because the fingers are in a different position from that used to encircle the bar and because the joints or the fingers can be placed under great stress while they are in a hyperextended position (which can damage the finger joints). Isometric gripping of any kind should be of very limited duration (i.e., three to six seconds). Holding the contraction any longer does little to improve the training effect and can place greater than normal stress on the ligaments and cartilage of the fingers, thereby exposing them to injury.

The lifter should also do some concentric grip work to build more well rounded strength in the grip. As noted above, there are a number of exercise devices that have been developed for this purpose (see Chapter 4). The main caution to observe when using these devices is to try to maintain the arm and hands in the same position as when lifting (i.e., with the arm straight, sometimes with the wrist bent as it is with a wide grip). In addition, try to do the exercise as strictly as possible. I once saw a gentleman who claimed to have one of the strongest grips in the world demonstrating his prowess on a gripping machine. He loaded the machine to approximately 300 lb. and lifted the resistance 2" or more. However, the careful observer was able to see that the fingers merely held the resistance during the lift. The lifter's body was doing most of the lifting (as the lifter leaned back during the lift). No doubt, the demonstrator's grip was far stronger than normal, but his feat did not require anything close to the level of gripping ability that the typical observer might have thought. Therefore, try to be strict, and at a minimum be consistent in the way you practice your grip work. No matter what, do some grip work.

Upright Rows and Shrugs

Purpose(s): Upright rows are used to strengthen the arm flexors, shoulders and trapezius muscles. Shrugs are used almost exclusively to develop the trapezius muscles.

Description: The upright row is commenced with the body in an upright position, the bar hanging on straight arms and the palms facing the rear of the lifter. The arm flexors are then contracted and the elbows are raised. This process normally continues until the bar has reached the height of the neck, whereupon it is returned to its starting position. The bar is kept close to the body throughout the motion. It is customary for bodybuilders and weight trainers to employ a grip narrower than shoulder width when performing this exercise. When weightlifters use it, they generally assume either a clean or a snatch grip. When weightlifters use the snatch grip, some continue to lift the bar until it is at arm's length. Weightlifters normally use light enough weights in this exercise so that they are able to "pull" the bar to arm's length without having the "press" it out at the finish (i.e.,, without having to turn the palms up and press up with arm extensors and shoulders to any significant degree). Some lifters perform this version of the upright row while sitting in a chair.

The shrug is begun in the same position as the upright row. From that position, the lifter attempts to elevate his or her shoulders to the highest possible position (i.e., shrugs his or her shoulders). The arms remain straight and the bar remains close to the body. There are several variations of the shrug. One consists of pulling the shoulders back as well as up. Another variation is to pull the shoulders straight up and then to pull them back after the highest possible elevation has been achieved. Both of these variations are used in an effort to activate both the part of the trapezius and other back muscles that pull the shoulders back and the portion of the trapezius that pulls the shoulders up. Still another variation, one that is used by injured lifters, is the shrug on an incline bench. In this variation the lifter lies face down on the bench (which needs to be an incline bench without a seat). The bar is handed to the lifter who then performs the shrugs. Fig. 46 depicts the regular grip shrug.

Fig. 46

A final variation, one that is popular with Olympic lifters, is often called the "power shrug." The power shrug is performed by starting in the normal position for a shrug, but then allowing the torso to incline slightly forward of the vertical position and/or to bend the legs slightly. Then the bar is shrugged at the same time as the torso is straightened and/or the legs are extended. Both the snatch and clean grips are used in the power shrug.

Effectiveness: Upright rows do strengthen the arms, shoulders and trapezius muscles. However, much of this strengthening occurs in positions that are unlike those assumed when the lifter is performing the classical lifts. Consequently, the carryover value to the lifts tends to be small. In addition, upright rows have been known to irritate the shoulders, occasionally leading to a shoulder injury. With the limited benefits that upright rows offer and the potential for injury, they cannot be warmly recommended. The exception is when a lifter has a lower-body injury that prevents more conventional training. Then the upright rows can be used to maintain some conditioning in the muscles involved.

The conventional version of the shrug, or the versions in which the shoulder are pulled back as well as up, has not been very effective in improving the pulling power of weightlifters. This is probably because the position in which the standard shrug is performed is not quite like the position that is used when the lifter is actually pulling. In addition, as was noted in Chapter 2, practicing a portion of a skill that involves several muscle groups by isolating one muscle group does not have much

carryover to the normal movement. Better results have been obtained with the power shrug using the legs, hips and lower back or the pull from the high blocks or high hang. These motions resemble the pull, both in terms of the positions assumed and the coordination of the muscle groups producing the power. When lower-body or back injuries prevent the use of power shrugs and pulls, the regular shrug can be used as a means for maintaining condition in the upper-back muscles. In such a case the versions of the shrug that involve both upward and slight backward shrugging of the shoulders tend to be more beneficial. The shrug performed on an incline bench places virtually no strain on the legs or back of the lifter and therefore can be very helpful for the injured lifter who wishes to maintain as much condition as is possible. These shrugs (shrugs with a bar held on the shoulders behind the neck exercise the trapezius muscles when a bar cannot be held in the hands. (The invention of this exercise is attributed to J.C. Hise, a nationally ranked heavyweight weightlifter during the 1930s who was also an early advocate of concentrated training on the squat.)

Bent-Over Rowing Exercises

Purpose(s): To strengthen the rear deltoids and the upper-back and middle-back muscles.

Description: There are many variations of the rowing motion. Perhaps the most common is the bent-over row. In this exercise the lifter typically grips the bar with the hands in a position that is between the snatch and clean grip. The torso is nearly parallel to the floor and the legs are slightly bent. There is an arch in the lower back and the upper back is flat, or nearly so. The lifter then pulls the bar up to the chest, using the arm, shoulder and middle-back muscles. In the "cheating" version of this exercise, more force is often generated against the bar by straightening the back somewhat at the outset of the movement. Performing bent-over rows with the standard cheating method places a significant strain on the lower back.

The version of the bent-over row that I recommend is one that Dave Sheppard has advocated for years: the one arm bent-over row. In this exercise the lifter places the arm opposite the arm to be exercised on a bench that is directly below it. That arm is straight (or nearly so) and is supporting the torso. The torso is held parallel to the ground or somewhat more upright, and the legs are nearly straight. The lifter then grasps a dumbbell that has been placed directly beneath the arm to be exercised. The lifter performs the row by pulling the dumbbell toward the chest without any added help from the lower-back or hip muscles. Fig 47 illustrates the one arm bent over row.

Fig. 47

Effectiveness: When done with heavy weights, the basic version of the bent-over row can actually be used to strengthen the pulling muscles of the back. In fact, years ago an article in <u>Strength and Health Magazine</u> by their outstanding writer and lifter Bill Starr advocated this exercise as the pulling exercise for the off-season. I know several lifters who used Bill's off-season routine (rows, squats and bench presses) with success. Most lost very little on their lifts over a period of a few months, and one nationally ranked lifter of my acquaintance actually broke his all time record in the clean shortly after resuming more conventional training after being on Bill's routine for approximately three months.

When the bent-over row is done in stricter fashion or with one arm in the manner described above, it strengthens the muscles indicated in "Purposes." These muscles all play an important supporting role in the snatch and C&J. When done properly (really pulling the shoulders back), the bent-over row can help the lifter to get the chest out and shoulders back during the early stages of the pull.

Curling

Purpose(s): To strengthen the biceps muscles of the arms (the arm flexors).

Description: There are many variations of the curl, but the chief categories are: a) with the palms up; b) with the palms down; or c) with the palms held midway between the up and down position. In all variations the arm begins in a straight position and then is brought to a fully flexed position. The palms-up version (easily the most popular) builds the biceps most directly. The palms-down version builds the forearms more and the biceps less, and the in-between version, of course, has an in-

between effect. The latter version, often called the "Zottman" curl, is probably more closely related to weightlifting movements than any other version of the curl, yet it is the least frequently practiced (it can only be reasonably performed with dumbbells). Figure 48 illustrates the middle position in the standard barbell curl and Fig. 49 shows the middle position of the Zottman curl.

Fig. 48

Fig. 49

Effectiveness: Curling exercises are probably the most popular exercise done with weights. The public loves big biceps, and curls are surely the way to get them. Unfortunately, the biceps are nearly useless for the weightlifter. Therefore, like the bench press, the curl develops muscles that are

239

unnecessary and adds body weight where it is not needed.

In some cases a lifter may find it useful to perform curls in order to stabilize the elbow (e.g., in cases in which the lifter's elbows tend to hyperextend when the bar is held overhead and/or the lifter feels discomfort in the elbows during of after snatching). However, if this is the case, the reps should be relatively low and the emphasis should be placed on building strength, not size. The hand positioning in such a case will depend on the area to be strengthened.

Other "Isolation" Exercises

Isolation exercises are done with machines or free weights and are designed to focus exclusively on one muscle group. Exercises like hyperextensions and leg extensions are examples of isolation movements.

Isolation exercises have very limited value for the competitive weightlifter. When power is applied in crucial areas of weightlifting, it virtually always involves the activity and coordination of multiple muscle groups. Muscle groups that are exercised in isolation generally show limited transfer of their improved strength when they are combined with the action of other muscles during the actual classical lift in which they play a role. In addition, the kind of motion through which the joints and muscles are taken while doing the isolation exercise is rarely the same or even similar to what occurs during the actual lift (e.g., the muscles involved may be the same, but the point at which they experience maximum resistance and the positions of the other muscles that support the prime movers during their efforts are rarely in the same). Therefore, the overall results that have been attained doing such exercises have not been very favorable. Naturally, in cases where the actions and tensions produced by the major muscle groups involved in a given movement are replicated, the carryover is likely to be more favorable.

Isolation exercises can be helpful for purposes of rehabilitation and to strengthen areas that are clearly lagging in development relative to other areas of the body. However, in order to be effective, the isolation exercises must be carefully designed and executed.

There are literally many thousands of resistance exercises that we have not covered in this chapter. However, most of them are either variations of the exercises that have been presented or are isolation exercises that are not of consequence for most competitive weightlifters. However, these exercises may serve particular needs, and there are a number of sources if the reader wishes to learn more about them. One of the best is Bill Pearl's Keys To The Inner Universe (see the Bibliography for more information).

Resistance Exercises Performed With Machines

Many exercise machines have been created with the purpose of providing the lifter with resistance while exercising one or more muscles groups. In most cases the machine is constructed so that movement can only take place in one direction. In addition, the machine may be constructed in such a way that only the muscles which move a certain bone are activated during the exercise, while the muscles that normally stabilize other bones during such an action are not brought into play (e.g., the shoulder muscles act to stabilize the upper arm when a standard bar curl is performed), but those muscles may not be active when a curl is performed on a machine. Therefore, exercising with a machine generally requires less skill than lifting a "free" weight. This can be an advantage if the stabilizing muscles are injured or the athlete lacks skill in using them .

A wide variety of progressive resistance machines exists. Machines have been designed to exercise virtually every major muscle group in the body. From the standpoint of the exerciser, machines generally have the advantages of: a) being relatively easy to adjust (in terms of the resistance applied); b) requiring no spotters; c) requiring little coordination to use; and d) in some cases providing relatively constant resistance throughout the full range of the exercise. There are so many kinds of machines available today that it is beyond the scope of this book to describe even a small portion of them. A machine vendor or owner or gym instructor can be consulted about which machine does what (although such reports may be unreliable because these people may have been poorly trained or misled by the manufacturers of such equipment).

Generally speaking, the results obtained by lifters who have used machines in an effort to improve their lifting ability have been poor. There are a number of reasons for this, all of which are related to the principle of specificity of training explained earlier in this book. The pattern of movement that is experienced with a machine is rarely (if ever) the same as that experienced with free weights, especially when doing the classical lifts. Even if the pattern of movement experienced using the machine were identical to the movement used with the bar, the muscle tensions applied by the lifter at various points while in the machine based exercise would not be the same as those applied while using the bar. This could be because the angles of resistance are not quite the same as those experienced during the exercise when it is done with a bar, because little or no tension is required of the muscles that normally hold the bones that are stable in place during the exercise or because the effort required during the bar version of the exercise provides quite uneven resistance while the machine's resistance is more constant.

One other consideration is that the lifter is not required to maintain his or her balance to the same extent while using a machine as when a bar is being lifted or to coordinate the motion of the resistance (as is necessary with a free weight). As a result, when the normal movement is experienced, the lifter perceives a very different sense of motion, and the carryover from what was done with the exercise machine is limited.

Machines can be helpful to the lifter who is in a process of rehabilitation or who needs to strengthen a specific muscle group that is not easily exercised with free weights. (For example, concentric contraction of the hamstring is easily accomplished using a leg-curl machine but is not as easily accomplished using free weights.) In most cases however, the lifter will benefit far more from using a bar than from using a machine. This is probably true for powerlifters, bodybuilders and general weight trainers as well (especially those weight trainers who are trying to improve their abilities in a specific sport).

More General Conditioning Exercises

Sprinting and Jumping

Purpose(s): To increase the speed and explosive power of the lifter.

Description: Weightlifters who practice sprinting generally the limit the distances practiced to forty to fifty yards or less. The practice of sprinting is typically conducted during the preparatory phases of lifting training, and such training is usually eliminated well before any major competition.

The most common forms of jumping that are in a lifter's training are the standing broad jump, the vertical jump and the jump onto a horse or box. When doing broad jumps it is fairly common for the lifter to string several jumps together into a series of "bounds." Vertical jumping is done from a standing position, typically with one or both arms overhead at the finish. In jumping onto a horse or box, the lifter stands at a distance of approximately one foot from the object onto which the lifter is jumping (the distance varies with the size of the lifter and his or her jumping style). The lifter then jumps onto the box, typically landing in a full squat position.

Effectiveness: Sprinting and jumping have long been popular with many weightlifting specialists as a means to increase the speed and explosive power of their athletes. But the use of such exercises remains controversial. Most elite athletes, champions and world record holders do little or no sprinting. Only some perform any jumping. Some

of those who jump swear by its value. The research evidence is far from conclusive.

I tend to come down on the side of the doubters. The concept of specificity of training and a significant amount of research suggests that training at velocities that are very different from those that are experienced during the event does not have much carryover value. Clearly, the speed obtained by the lifter while he or she is loaded by a heavy bar is far less than the speed attained while the athlete is sprinting or jumping (except when a lifter squats under the bar, and specific drills for going under the bar quickly may be useful for the lifter). In addition, sprinting and jumping can often lead to injuries. Moreover, the kinds of injuries that are sustained are often those that have a direct negative effect on the performance of the lifter and can have long-term negative consequences (e.g., strains of the muscle tendon units of the groin and knee are not uncommon and are very problematical for the lifter).

A final point to consider with respect to sprinting and jumping raises a major question with respect to the value of these activities. Several years ago, a coach of a major United States international weightlifting team encouraged team members to perform some sprint drills before a major competition. During one of these drills, one of the best lifters on the team pulled a groin muscle. The injury almost cost the athlete an important international title, and the injury has recurred a number of times since. There was absolutely no reason to have a lifter over the age of thirty (when joints tend to become more fragile), who had never trained on sprints, perform such a drill, particularly before a major championship.

Most coaches would agree that sprinting and jumping should be reserved for the preparatory cycle of the lifter's training. However, if this is true, how much carryover value can be expected on the day of the competition weeks or months later. To me there is a real question about any activity that cannot be carried on until very close to the event. (Remember that the training effect of most activities—other than skills—tends to wear off very rapidly.) To the extent that rapid reaction is a skill, a period of learning followed by occasions for "brushing up" on the skill may be useful. But I believe that the skill is better learned specifically while practicing.

Plyometrics

Purpose(s): To increase the power outputs of lifters, particularly in a movements that involves an eccentric contraction immediately followed by a rapid concentric contraction (e.g., the amortization and explosion phases of the pull and the dip and explosion in the jerk). Plyometrics are believed to accomplish this by training the athlete to better utilize the elastic and speed-strength qualities of

241

his or her muscles and nervous system so that the athlete can reverse direction and generate maximum force rapidly following that reversal in direction. This capability is particularly important in executing the third and fourth phases of the pull and jerk (the adjustment/amortization phase and the final explosion phase).

Description: There are many variations of plyometrics, from push-ups with a rapid descent followed by an immediate and explosive push to the finished position to depth jumps (perhaps the most well known version of plyometric training). In this latter exercise the athlete typically walks off a box that is from .5 m to 1 m in height, lands flat footed on both feet (with the feet in the same horizontal line) and immediately jumps upward as quickly and as high as possible. Placing a slightly shock absorbing and non-slip material where the lifter will land reduces the risk of injury.

The literature of Eastern Europe has included many articles and books which contain advice on preparing for competition, and there is a growing body of information on the subject provided by authors in the United States. Yuri Verkhoshansky, a Soviet researcher and writer, is credited with being one of the developers of plyometrics. He would probably describe what he developed as training methods which increase the "speed-strength" of an athlete, with an emphasis on training which improves the athlete's performance during the "stretch-shortening cycle" of muscle contraction (a cycle in which a muscle undergoes a stretch immediately prior to shortening , as when an athlete dips and explodes upward in the jerk). Although the training modalities recommended by Verkhoshansky include sprints and conventional and special jumps, the training innovation for which he is most widely known is "depth jumping" or "shock training." Verkhoshansky recognizes both the effectiveness and the strenuousness of depth jumping and therefore recommends that athletes perform it only twice during the classic annual training cycle in which there are two major competitions at different points in the year. Those two times are during the latter half of the competitive period. According to Verkhoshansky, if depth jumping is performed during the preparatory period, it should be terminated five to ten days away from the competition.

Verkhoshansky recommends that depth jumping be performed for three sets of ten repetitions two to three times a week and that the load of squats be reduced to compensate for the added training stress of the depth jumps during the training period in which depth jumps are used. As was suggested earlier, repeated admonitions in the Soviet literature against doing depth jumps too often suggest that poor results and possibly injuries (a number of serious injuries have been reported in the United States) have resulted from too much of what many coaches consider to be a good thing. So, apparently depth jumps can be easily overdone (particularly by weightlifters whose training contains similar movements with high loads).

Effectiveness: There is considerable debate regarding the effectiveness of plyometrics. A number of studies have demonstrated improvements in power outputs as a result of plyometric training. However, these studies have not addressed the question of whether the improvements made are essentially one time phenomena that will not be repeated. That is, once the athlete has learned to execute the stretch-shortening cycle efficiently, will there be substantial improvements from practice thereafter, or can the improvements be sustained by application to the sport involved?

The larger questions facing weightlifters are: a) whether such results can be obtained by the practice of the classic related lifts, and b) whether the risk of injury as a result of performing such highly stressful exercises such as depth jumps is too high, considering the results. My belief at this time is that the answer to both questions is affirmative. The classic lifts are inherently plyometric in nature, and it is unlikely that any dramatic additional results will be attained through the use of plyometrics. Moreover, because the classic lifts themselves involve plyometric aspects, performing additional plyometric training carries with it a significant risk of generating injuries from overuse.

If the lifter wishes to try plyometric training, it should be limited to one or two periods of several weeks during the year, the amount and intensity of the training should be carefully limited (e.g., do not jump from a high box and do not perform many sets and reps) and the load in similar exercises should be reduced in order to reduce the risk of injury. When practiced in this way, plyometrics can aid the lifter in decreasing the time it takes for that lifter to achieve maximum force and improving his or her power output. However, once the athlete has learned this lesson, very moderate practice of this type or mere practice of the lifts should be enough to retain the benefits of plyometric training without running the risk of overdoing such training in combination with classic lift training.

Aerobic Exercise

Purpose(s): To improve the efficiency of the heart, lungs and the aerobic efficiency of the athlete.

Description: Aerobic exercise is virtually any exercise that can raise the athlete's heart rate above a certain targeted level and sustain it for a period long enough to cause a training effect. For many years, it was thought that a training effect would only occur if the heart rate were elevated for twenty minutes or longer. More recent evidence suggests that two to three shorter periods may also be effective, as long as the total period of elevated heart rate is twenty minutes across the day. The most common forms of aerobic exercise are brisk walking, jogging, bicycling, swimming, rowing, continuous calisthenics (also known as aerobics), stair climbing (stepping) and cross-country skiing.

Effectiveness: There can be little doubt about the health value of aerobic training, particularly for older adults. In addition, aerobics can be used to burn calories, thereby helping to achieve or maintain an ideal body weight. However, for the weightlifter who has a minimal level of body fat and whose objective is maximum performance in weightlifting, aerobic exercise must be strictly limited. To be sure, aerobic exercise at a moderate level (three or four times a week, for twenty minutes at a time) will do no harm and may actually be of benefit (a body in better overall condition tends to recover more quickly from workouts). However, it is also fairly certain that aerobic activity that goes much beyond those limits is not beneficial for a number of reasons. (Research and practical experience both support his view.)

One negative aspect of strenuous aerobic training is that it expends the body's limited performance and adaptive energies on an activity that has little or no carryover value into Olympic lifting performance. An athlete only has so much time and energy to train and to recuperate from that training. The serious athlete cannot allow that valuable energy to be dissipated in activities that will not directly benefit his or her sport. Significant aerobic exercise may even prevent the use of certain muscle fibers for purposes of strength and power development.

Another drawback of aerobic exercise is that it stimulates the body to adapt its muscles and energy supply in ways that are counterproductive for strength and power athletes. An athlete who performs extensive aerobic exercise actually works against these strength and power development goals. (see Appendix II for further details.)

Still another problem with excessive aerobic activity is that such activity can cause trauma to the athlete's joints. Olympic lifting places substantial stress on the joints. This stress need not have a negative effect on the athlete. In fact,

there is evidence that such stress causes the body to adapt in a positive way, making the joints even stronger and more resilient. However, if other activities place strain on the body as well, the chances of injury can increase substantially. This is a particular risk with aerobic exercises that involve high impacts with a hard surface, such a running. Problems can also develop with exercises like rowing, which places a significant strain on the back—an area that is already stressed by Olympic lifting.

Finally, there are environmental risks attached to certain aerobic activities. For example, one trip while running, one slip on the ice in winter, or one collision with a motor vehicle at night can be a career-ending incident for a weightlifter. While these risks may be minor, they do exist. If an athlete is injured in training for his or her primary sport, it is a terrible thing, but at least it involved a necessary risk. To be hurt doing a supplementary activity is truly tragic.

On balance, a moderate level of aerobic exercise can be beneficial to the lifter and should not be encouraged. However, any aerobics should be limited, extremely safe and non-traumatic.

Summary

Assistance exercises can be valuable tools for the development of the weightlifter. They contribute variety and emphasis to the athlete's training. Assistance exercises differ greatly with respect to their effectiveness and safety, so they must be carefully chosen and carried out. It is clear that all of the possibilities have yet to be exhausted with respect to assistance exercises. If the lifter invents one that is helpful and is not dangerous, its use should surely be encouraged and expanded.

Now that the issues of proper technique, the development of strength, power and flexibility, the equipment used by weightlifters and the assistance exercises that can be useful in a lifter's training have been explored, we are ready to discuss a critical performance factor: the development of a training plan that puts what you have learned thus far to use.

Careful planning helped to give David Rigert the strength, skill and courage to win an Olympics, 6 World Championships and establish 65 World Records.

CHAPTER 6

Putting It All Together: Developing The Training Plan

In preceding chapters we have discussed proper technique and its foundations. We have covered the topics of learning proper weightlifting technique, building strength and power, developing flexibility, training the mind, selecting equipment and choosing exercises to assist the weightlifter in improving his or her performance in the classical lifts. Having been given the "raw materials" that form the building blocks of training a champion weightlifter, the reader is now prepared to study the all important process of integrating these resources into a training plan and creating a workable plan for the optimal development of individual weightlifters.

Creating the Training Plan

In this chapter we will deal with such issues as warming up for a workout, the proper sequence of exercises, the use and misuse of periodization and cycling, combining complex means to improve performance, the value of short- and long-term planning, diagnosing needs and many other aspects of workout construction. However, we will avoid any emphasis on what seems to be obligatory for most books on bodybuilding, powerlifting, weight training and weightlifting: the "cookbook" workouts for beginners, intermediate lifters and advanced lifters. Overall, any use of "one-size-fits-all" workouts should be avoided, because lifters of all levels vary so much in their needs that illustrative workouts are almost useless in terms of practical application to real athletes. It is true that lifters with similar levels of experience have many needs in common. For instance, all beginners will need to learn proper technique, and that only occurs with a great deal of practice. But the question of just what is practiced and how can only be answered precisely on the basis of each lifter's specific situation.

Similarly, more advanced lifters should not merely copy the training program of any particular champion. Some actual training programs of weightlifting champions will be presented in this chapter, and there is no doubt that such programs provide very useful examples of planning concepts that have already been presented to specific athletes in particular instances. But the reader will be explicitly warned that a coach or athlete should not merely adopt such programs wholesale.

This chapter will provide a survey of the principles and guidelines for planning that have evolved in the weightlifting world. Such information can serve as a valuable starting point for coaches and athletes as long as they understand one overarching principle: the guidelines being presented are not rigid rules to be applied blindly. Rather, they are a foundation on which the coach must build in order to reach the optimal training plan for each individual athlete. If coaches and athletes understand the principles and techniques of planning and can see how they are applied, the problem of developing their own programs should present no insurmountable challenges (although training design is always one of the great challenges in coaching, even for coaches of great experience and ability).

Before we begin an actual discussion of training plan design, it is important to set forth some underlying principles. Bill Bowerman, the legendary coach of the great University of Oregon track and field team, has identified three "cornerstones" of training in any sport: moderation, consistency and rest. By moderation, Bowerman does not mean that an athlete should not train hard. High level performance can only be achieved through excruciating effort. However, in the overall context, training must not be so extreme that it leads to a loss of motivation, overtraining or injury, the three biggest threats to any athlete's performance. A champion must be completely dedicated to his or her training and must exert heroic levels of mental and physical effort during some phases of training and competition in order to reach elite levels of performance. Sport must come first in the athlete's life. But the athlete who is always on the brink of injury or overtraining, one whose training is all consuming and leaves no time for anything else in life, is bound to falter at some point, losing valuable training time and, perhaps, a career.

Consistency, Bowerman's second cornerstone, is absolutely essential. An athlete cannot reach the elite level without a fanatical adherence to his or her training schedule (though schedules can and should be modified in accordance with an athlete's reactions to training). Helter skelter training does not work in the long run; consistency is key. Not surprisingly, consistency goes hand in glove with moderation. The athlete whose training does not adhere to the principle of moderation will not be consistent in his or her training. An injury will occur, an illness will come up or a loss of motivation will arise and the need for "a break" will emerge. Consistency will be breached, and the athlete's overall performance will ultimately suffer. On the other hand, the athlete must let nothing get in the way of executing the properly designed training plan in its entirety.

Bowerman's last cornerstone, rest, is the forgotten side of training. Without rest, the athlete will not recuperate from his or her training, which is to say that no training occurs. Contrary to popular belief, younger athletes need even more rest than fully mature (though not "master" athletes). It is during rest that recuperation and adaptation take place. If athletes and coaches had half the respect for rest that they do for exercise, levels of performance would soar, and incidents of overuse injuries and overtraining would be rare.

Bowerman's three cornerstones make sense only when they are added to the fundamental training principles of overload, specificity, reversibility and individuality. These principles have already been discussed in this book, but they bear repeating here. If exercise is to generate a training effect, it must overload the body, providing a greater stimulus than that which has previously been applied to the athlete. To be effective for purposes of training, exercise must be strenuous enough to constitute an overload. However, not just any overload will do. The training stimulus must be specific to the qualities that the athlete wishes to develop. For instance, a weightlifter can perform a certain exercise to "get the back strong," but if the exercise does not stress the same back muscles in the same way that they will be taxed when he or she is performing the classical lifts, such training will contribute little to competition performance. Reversibility means that any adaptation gained will be lost unless a training stimulus of sufficient magnitude is applied often enough. Just as the body is capable of positive adaptations to increasing demands, it is capable of negative adaptations to decreasing demands (i.e., detraining).

Finally, training is an individual process. No two individuals will have precisely the same needs in their training and no two individuals will be equally stressed by the same training stimulus or respond to it in precisely the same way. The same training program may work for two different athletes, but it will never work in exactly the same way for both, and it will almost never be optimal for both. Therefore, it is vital that training programs be individualized.

The Essence Of Planning

Planning an athlete's training is in some respects akin to filling an article of luggage with only the items essential for a trip. The luggage itself presents a size constraint, but the variety that is possible in terms of what is packed in the luggage enables the traveler to meet his or her needs and to exercise a great deal of judgment during the packing process. In addition, the experienced traveler knows that by packing carefully, much more can be fit in than if he or she merely throws items randomly into the bag. Similarly, the coach can place a wide variety of training modalities within the constraints of a training time that an athlete has at his or her disposal. Therefore, the skill of the coach at designing the program will permit the athlete to "fit" more of what is valuable within the training period. (The training time available is always constrained by the athlete's energy level, his or her recuperative powers and other needs in the athletes life.)

Given the limitations that exist with respect to the training process, the first questions the effective planner must ask are: "What are we trying to accomplish during the period of training for which the plan in being created? What qualities of the athlete are we trying most urgently to improve?" Unless the planner explicitly addresses these fundamental questions, the training plan will be too haphazard to provide maximum benefit to the athlete.

In establishing the objectives for the training period, it is particularly useful for the coach to consider the four important categories of athletic qualities: mental, emotional, physical and neurological. (The latter term is loosely used to identify subconscious aspects of human behavior that have their basis in the nervous system but which cannot, at least with present methods, be measured objectively.) Within the mental qualities are the processes and content of the lifter's mind (what the lifter is focusing on and what kind of activity the lifter is undertaking). The athlete can learn to control the direction, width and depth of his or her focus as well as the actual content of the conscious mind. As a result, processes such as visualization of the execution of cognitive skills are under the direct control of the conscious mind and can be improved with practice and effort.

Developing an athlete's emotional qualities involves improving the ability to generate and control certain emotions. Athletes need enthusiasm, desire and a certain level of arousal in order to perform optimally. They must never permit a negative (from the standpoint of its affect on performance) emotion to intrude into consciousness during the performance of their events. Practice outside and inside the gym can assist the athlete in controlling his or her emotions during at least a limited period of intense effort.

The physical qualities required for weightlifting are, of course, multifaceted. The most important are: strength, power, speed, flexibility, the endurance to perform the work of training and the ability to accept the stress of training and lifting maximum poundages.

The neurological capabilities of the athlete include the ability to exert force rapidly and maximally (within the constraints of the athlete's physical abilities) and the ability to move efficiently and consistently (motor skill). These qualities are developed by a combination of physical work and mental effort and they embody the mind/body link.

The effective training plan must be designed to help the lifter improve (or at least maintain previous improvements) in all of these areas. If the coach were not constrained by the athlete's training time, he or she could attack all of the athlete's needs at once. But since a constraint always exists, the primary challenge facing the coach is to establish priorities (in view of the athlete's objectives) and resolve conflicting demands to arrive at a training content that will optimize the lifter's improvement in the areas that are most urgently targeted for improvement. The coach must carefully consider what to place within the training period, recognizing that by careful "packing," the coach can optimize the nature and strength of the training stimuli, so that the athlete will get the maximal possible results out of the resources at his or her disposal.

The tools at the coach's disposal are the exercises that the coach prescribes, the volume and intensity achieved in those exercises, what the athlete is thinking about while the training is being performed and what the athlete does during and after training sessions in order to recuperate from his or her workouts. (The latter subject will be discussed in later chapters of this book.)

The Fundamentally Cyclic Nature of All Planning

Where do you begin in designing a training plan? Do you begin by creating an annual or even longer plan and fill in the framework for even shorter periods (e.g., year to month to day)? Or is it better to begin at the workout level and build outward into the long term plan? To answer that question we will examine first the two prevailing, and in many ways contradictory, approaches to planning. Then we will examine a radically different

approach, one that I will argue represents a significant improvement over either of the others. However, before we examine the two opposite approaches to planning, let us look at the root of all planning: the training "cycle."

While athletes and coaches may disagree on the degree on the nature and importance of the training plan, what cannot be denied is the fundamentally cyclic basis of any plan. Any planner must see a plan as a "cycle" (even if the concept of a cycle is only implicit to that person). For example, even the most "intuitive" planner says, in essence, "I will do snatches today because I feel I need them." But why does the planner think this is so? Generally, because he or she has not done snatches in a while and feels ready to perform them effectively, or because the need to perform at a certain level on an upcoming day suggests that snatches should be performed today. In other words, this planner is placing today's training session in the context of what has been done in the past and/or what will be done in the future. Viewing a training session as part of a training unit consisting of today's workout and past or future ones is the essence of a training "cycle," because a cycle is nothing more than training done over a period of time that is viewed as unit. As soon as someone says "I do snatches every day" (or every other day, or once heavy and once light in a week), that person is acknowledging the existence of a cycle of some sort, the cycle consisting of whatever time period he or she has identified.

The ability to develop training cycles that are of optimal length and content is perhaps the single greatest key to progress in weightlifting. Unfortunately, ideal cycles have never been developed for all lifters, nor can they ever be. Individual differences between the genetic makeup of athletes, their backgrounds in training, the techniques that they use, the degree of mental and emotional effort that they apply in their training, their outside activities and many other factors affect their reactions to training. Therefore, while uniform cycles can be developed for and applied by all athletes, the degree of benefit that different athletes will derive from the same cycles will vary.

Although there are no cycles, short or long, that are optimal for all athletes, some very useful guidelines can enable the lifter to achieve the greatest rate of progress possible through proper cycling. Nevertheless, the journey of discovery that is entailed in individualizing the cycling process and planning and executing its many steps is the responsibility of each athlete and his or her coach. This continuous journey of discovery is one of the many things that makes weightlifting a wonderfully exciting and rewarding sport.

Now that the foundation of planning (the concept of the cycle) has been presented, let us examine the evolution of the planning process (from early experimentation to short term planning to long term planning philosophy) that dominates training today. Then we will look at some means for improving on what many coaches are doing today as well as avoiding an oversimplified view of the planning process.

The Evolution of Early Planning

In the early years of the development of weightlifting as a sport (during the latter part of the ninth century and the first half of this one), there were no established "seasons" for weightlifting. Because weightlifting was generally considered to be an indoor sport (although some notable competitions, such as some of the early Olympic competitions and some famous exhibitions, were held outdoors), there was no reason to schedule major competitions at a specific time in the year or day. In addition, because weightlifting was considered a developmental sport, many athletes trained year round to improve their abilities, without a particular competitive outlet for their new abilities in mind. Other athletes introduced seasonality into their training, perhaps reducing their weight training when outdoor activities tended to be most feasible and pleasurable (e.g., during the summer).

Early trainers noted that they could not perform at their best every day and that some form of fatigue seemed to be at the root of their poor performance. As a result, the concept of training every other day was born. On the basis of some understanding of anatomy and the observation that certain exercises were "felt" more in certain areas of the body than in others, the causal link between exercise selection and improvements in the appearance and performance of certain muscles of the body was noted. Because some responses to training occur rather quickly (e.g., fatigue, muscle soreness and improvements in strength performance) early training schedules were often derived from observation of those responses and on the premise that the ideal training regimen would lead to a straight progression in training (i.e., that if the proper level of stimulus was provided, the body would simply improve continuously). For instance, if a particular improvement was noted after the addition of an exercise to the lifter's workout or a change in routine, it was assumed that this was a "good routine" for that purpose. If not, the new program and/or training regimen were discarded or modified.

Trainees who decided to train every day noticed that while performance varied from day to day, they could train every day as long as there was no attempt to perform at the same level every day. Alternatively, they noticed that they could train and perform well on successive days if different exercises and/or different parts of the body were exercised on successive days. Early trainers also noted that after a certain period of time on a particular program, progress seemed to slow or stop, and sometimes the trainee seemed to take a step backward. This phenomena was referred to as a period of stagnation or "staleness." Athletes in this state were typically advised to change their routines and/or to improve their general health habits so that the body's recuperative powers would be improved (e.g., athletes were urged to improve their diets, to get more rest and sleep and to avoid excessive alcohol consumption). Another popular suggestion was to stop training for a week or two and then to resume.

In addition to encountering periods of stagnation, athletes noticed that they had a tendency to overtrain before pending competitions and that extra rest before competitions was beneficial in many cases. Therefore, while many athletes trained in much the same way all year round, they learned to estimate their abilities as the competition approached by "trying themselves out" on the competitive lifts. They adopted the practice of taking a few workouts with smaller workloads and lighter weights in the days immediately prior to the competition to assure that they would appear for the competition in a rested state.

When the approaches described above are viewed in the aggregate, they comprise a relatively complete approach to short term planning and program design. If done properly, combining these training concepts can be quite effective. This is because all workouts are planned within a time span that permits reasonable predictions of performance, the workouts can be well balanced across a series of days and weeks and the reactions of the athlete tend to be monitored very closely, with modifications being made as needed. Some truly great champions have been produced using this kind of planning. And although it has fallen out of favor today, there is much to recommend this approach.

While the mainstream of thinking about the training process in the middle of this century was characterized by the principles and practices outlined above (many of which are still as valuable today as when they first emerged), some athletes discovered that despite their adherence to those training methods, their training and competition performances were often quite unpredictable. Some of these variations from expectations can be attributed to purely human factors and to chance, but others can be traced to shortcomings in the nature of short term planning.

One shortcoming of short term planning is that it fails to take advantage of workout sequences that can build toward a certain result over a rather extended period. Consequently, exclusive reliance on short term planning can make it difficult for some lifters to peak reliably for major competitions because the conditions that lead high performance at a given competition are not established early enough in the training process. Another shortcoming of short term planning is that its proponents tend to analyze training results only from a short term perspective. Such analysis can overlook longer term factors that influence performance.

In an effort to address the shortcomings of short term planning, coaches and athletes began to search for approaches to training that would yield better and more predictable results. That search took two basic paths, and the influence of those who explored those paths is still with us today (as are many of the short term planning concepts pioneered by early experiments in weight training).

"Intuitive Approaches To Planning"

One direction of exploration was in the area of abandoning all planning. Some coaches and athletes had concluded that virtually all planning was futile, reasoning that all training should be performed on the basis of how the athlete feels emotionally and physically on a given training day (the so called "intuitive" training concept).

In this approach the workout is established as the lifter goes along. In the most extreme cases the lifter's and/or coach's intuition on a given day governs everything. The athlete lifts in accordance with his or her "feelings." A workout might begin with a few snatches because someone else in the gym is doing them and they look like fun. Then, because the snatches do not "feel" very good, the lifter proceeds to cleans. The cleans go well, so the lifter does many sets. The squat racks are already set up as the lifter is finishing the cleans, so he or she moves on to squats. And so the workout continues.

Advocates of this approach argue that it represents the most advanced training method possible because it is based on how the athletes feels, which to their way of thinking is all that counts. What is wrong with such an approach? Perhaps nothing if the lifter is highly skilled, usually "feels" like working on his or her weak points, has an impeccable sense of when to rest and when to push hard and does not have to perform successfully on any given day (i.e., the lifter is not a competitive athlete). How many lifters out of the thousands I have observed or with whom I have trained over many years have satisfied all of these criteria? None. Does that mean that such lifters do not exist? No. It merely means that such lifters are the exception rather than the rule and that therefore the purely intuitive approach cannot be recommended for the vast majority of lifters.

The lifters I have known who make the best use of intuitive training are veterans who have spent so many years studying the sport and their bodies that their "intuitions" have been highly developed by a lot of thought. This is certainly not the norm, not even for such knowledgeable veterans. Even for

these highly advanced weightlifting "sages," completely intuitive training is not likely to be the most effective coaching strategy, because these veteran lifters cannot feel what is going on in a pupil's body as they can in their own.

The obvious weaknesses of failing to plan at all were apparent to most coaches and athletes, so accepted the "purely intuitive" branch of training for very long. In view of the perceived shortcomings of short term and intuitive training, many athletes and coaches turned to what seemed to them to be the only authentic alternative: long term planning.

The Dominant Philosophy of Beginning with a Long Term Plan and Filling in the Details

Long term planning is the dominant planning approach to high performance weightlifting training today (at least if you believe the weightlifting literature). It became popular in Eastern Europe in the middle of this century and is now employed all over the world. (The coaches and athletes in the United States were probably among the last to embrace long term planning, but its popularity has increased dramatically in recent years.)

In this approach the coach creates a long term plan or model of lifting development for an athlete. On the basis of this framework or foundation, the coach then progresses to planning ever shorter time frames in order to fill in the details of the plan. The coach begins on the level of the "macrocycle" (a period that is generally one year but can be as short as several months or as long as several years). Once the macrocycle has been created, the "mesocycles" are planned. Only occasionally calendar months, these training "months" are generally twelve periods of four to five weeks each that fit into a twelve month period. Finally, "microcycles" are planned (the weeks within each mesocycle and the individual workouts within each week).

In its most extreme and ineffective variety, this kind of "top down" planning relies almost completely on models developed from statistical analyses of lifters at various levels to establish the content of the training plan. The results of the statistical analysis are often modified by the creator of the workout models to conform to his or her judgment of how the model workouts should look.

For example, the coach might say that it will take six years for the talented athlete to develop to the international level. At that level, the average lifter might be doing 18,000 reps a year (in all exercises combined) distributed over 500 workouts. A typical beginner might be able to handle 5,000 reps in a year across 200 workouts. Therefore, a plan is made to increase the lifter's load to the appropriate level over a six year period. To fill in the first year's plan, the coach might rely on some statistic and/or recommendation by an expert that beginners spend 35% of their time on general physical training, another 45% of their time on the classical exercises and 20% of their time on strength work.

In planning the training, the coach might be guided by a study or book that recommends three training cycles a year with a specific distribution of loads and monthly training emphases. Many published guidelines break the monthly training sessions into weekly ones and the weekly ones into daily workout plans. Using these guidelines, the novice coach can supposedly duplicate the entire planning process of the most highly successful coaches down to the smallest detail.

Such workout planning is a joy for busy coaches. It is simple and almost purely mechanical in nature. Moreover, if a long enough plan is created, the coach need only do planning on occasion. In fact, virtually the entire process can be computerized, making the work of the coach nearly effortless once the "master plan" has been programmed. The coach decides how many reps are to be performed in a particular month, then multiplies the guideline percentages of reps allocated to each exercise by the aggregate number of reps that month in order to determine the number of reps to be performed in each exercise that month. A similar procedure is then followed in assigning the reps to weeks and particular workouts and in determining the distribution of reps into various "zones" of intensity. Underlying the overall plan is generally some preconceived rate of progress toward a certain training load as one of the objectives for that athlete

The shortcomings inherent in the kind of long term planning procedure described above are numerous. However, let us identify five of the most severe faults of the process.

First, the statistics or theories generally used to create the basis for such planning are gathered from individual lifters and then combined (unless a specific group of lifters was experimentally placed on the same program). Therefore, the average figures so accumulated do not represent the actual workout pattern of <u>any</u> particular lifter (i.e., the average athlete in the group studied is training as described but no particular athlete is training in exactly that way). Unfortunately for the statistician, the differences between the programs of individual lifters may account for at least a portion of the success of those programs, and it is possible that none would have had as much success if he or she had performed the "average program."

To clarify this point, consider a situation in which the jerk training of 1,000 high level lifters was studied. Let us assume that 10% of such lifters employed the power style of jerk in competition and that the remaining 90% used the split style of the splitters, 30% had jerks that were strong relative to

their cleans (i.e., they virtually never missed jerks after cleaning a weight). Those lifters spent 50% of their time split jerking and 50% power jerking. The other 70% of the splitters spent 90% of their training on the split jerk and 10% on the power jerk. Those who used the power jerk style in competition spent 90% of their time power jerking and only 10% split jerking. The average allocation of split and power jerk training among these 1000 lifters was 71% to the split jerk and 29% to the power jerk. It is obvious that such an allocation was not successful for the splitters or the power jerkers. Nevertheless, a gross statistical analysis could lead to the conclusion that the 71% to 29% distribution of split jerks to power jerk is desirable (because elite lifters have such a ratio), when in fact a very different ratio was favored by the superior jerkers in this group (the lifters really worth emulating).

It could be argued that the problem with the statistical approach described above lies not with the approach per se, but with the lack of skill of the person collecting the data. If that person were insightful enough, the correct allocation of exercises would be discovered (e.g., by focusing on the good split jerkers versus the bad). But even with more sophisticated analyses, the problem does not go away. It might be true that, as a group, the better jerkers allocated their split and power jerks 50:50. But it might also be true that, within that group, one-third did no power jerks at all and that the remaining two-thirds of the group had a 75:25 ratio of power jerks to split jerks. Therefore, the 50:50 spilt was not used by anyone. In reality, the "secret" of the better jerkers might simply have been that they identified the pattern of jerk practice that was most effective for them early in their careers.

A second and related problem with the top-down planning process is that it can miss the entire rationale for what coaches and athletes are doing in the gym at any particular moment. To clarify this point, let us consider a business analogy. Suppose a business analyst was sent to study the activities of the world's most successful microchip manufacturer and noted in careful detail every measurable activity occurring within the manufacturing facility across a year (or even a series of years).

That analyst might say that each chip requires one hour to make. Of that hour, ten minutes are spent in each of six stations along the production line. There are a total of 1,000 workers, 10% of whom are managers, 10% are sales people, 10% are maintenance people, 5% are in shipping, 5% are in receiving and the rest (60%) are actually involved in the direct manufacturing of the chips. In further observing the managers, the recorder might note that they spent ten minutes of every hour on the phone, twenty minutes in meetings, ten minutes writing memos, ten minutes on benefits and compensation issues and ten minutes talking about what they were planning to do on the weekend and other personal matters. Would a fledgling microchip manufacturer who established a factory that had all of the above characteristics have any chance of becoming world class in chip manufacturing? Obviously not. In order to understand the business, a new manufacturer would have to understand how and why things were, how procedures evolved, which were necessary and which a matter of chance or the preferences of the employees. The new manufacturer would also need to understand the present conditions in his or her marketplace and the characteristics of his work force, suppliers, customers and owners in order to have any chance of succeeding.

Thinking that you can model training plans blindly is as misguided as thinking that you can observe the operations of a factory and simply start up a successful replica. This does not mean that the trips Japanese manufacturers made to American companies while they were learning to be world class competitors were not valuable, even critical, to their success. But if the Japanese had merely tried to duplicate what the Americans were doing, they would have never become the formidable competitors in international business that they have become. The same applies to Soviet scientists or American coaches who rely on statistics gathered about the champions.

The third major problem with basing exercise prescriptions on average workouts is the fallacy of applying laws derived from large numbers to individual cases. For instance, it is true that highly trained mathematicians who are specialists in applying statistical data to real world situations can accurately calculate life expectancies on the basis of a population's age and sex. So successful are such mathematicians (called actuaries) at their mortality projections that hugely successful financial enterprises (insurance companies) have been built on the basis of the predictions that they make. However, the prognostications of actuaries are only accurate in the aggregate. No matter how skilled the actuary, no matter how perfect the data upon which the actuary bases his or her projections, a prediction of the age at which any specific individual will die is totally outside the realm of the power of statistics.

Similarly, even if we know that 60% of the lifters in a very large population got stronger doing three sets of five reps with weights that were 80% of their respective maximums than they did with five sets of three reps with the same weight, we could not say that it is _any_ more likely for a specific lifter to benefit from one alternative than another. We can only say that if we train a large enough group of lifters with a weight that is 80% of their maximum, more of them will benefit from three sets of five reps than five sets of three reps.

The fourth major fallacy of top-down planning is its underlying premise that any truly effective long term plan can be made under normal circumstances. The process of training the human organism is highly complex. Many bodily systems interact during the training process (e.g., the central nervous system, the muscular system and the endocrine system). Training can affect each system, and each system can affect the others. Moreover, the mind can affect these systems and vice versa.

For instance, a lifter's values and mental focus can influence the training effect his or her body receives from a given bout of exercise, and the body's reaction to the training can influence a lifter's values and mental focus. With so many interactions, it is impossible to predict the ultimate outcome with real accuracy, even across a time span as short as several days or weeks. Making accurate overall predictions with respect to an athlete's progress over a period of months or years is absolutely out of the question, and making predictions of development in specific areas is even more futile (e.g., technique may not develop as quickly as had been expected, or strength gains in one area of the body might easily outpace all expectations).

A related problem with long term planning structured around peaking for a particular competition is that the length of the various cycles is established by the competition schedule rather than the lifter's long term needs. For example, a lifter can have a technique or strength deficiency that will require many months of specialized training to correct. In such a case, interruption of the lifter's technical education with the high intensity lifts that are generally used to prepare for a competition may actually hinder the lifter's progress. Nevertheless, a coach who blindly follows the long term plan would dutifully schedule the competitive preparations required by the season's contest schedule, thereby damaging the lifter's long term optimization of his or her capabilities.

The final major problem with long term planning is that it tends to put the workout schedule on "autopilot" for too long. Many long term planners tend to create the plan and then never really monitor and modify the plans as needed. Moreover, because the athlete is not often tested against maximums in the classical lifts in many long term training plans (especially those that are based on the principle of long term periodization), such plans can go very wrong long before any problem is discovered.

Does this mean that long term planning of any kind is a waste of time? Not at all. Long term planning can establish a valuable framework for shorter term planning. It can place short term planning within the context of the competitive schedule and assure that any short term training plans consider the overall developmental objectives that a coach may have (e.g., in terms of reaching certain volume objectives).

A long term view can also serve as a powerful analytical tool for determining training effectiveness, because some of the effects of training are cumulative and an analysis of long training periods permits the analyst to gain a full picture of the training process. However, the limitations of long term planning that have been cited must not be overlooked by anyone who uses it; good coaches never do.

In this chapter we will examine periodization, the dominant method of long term planning. Periodization is an invaluable training concept. Moreover, it forms so much of the framework of today's planning (and the training analyses in Eastern Europe) that it is important to gain a thorough understanding of its elements to appreciate fully training planning as it is done by many coaches today.

Periodization Of Training (Soviet Style)

In essence, periodization involves dividing the training process into periods which have different goals, lengths and training contents. The classic model of periodization suggests that training should be planned across the span of several months or years and should move from the general to the specific in preparation for major competitions. Specifically, the training of an athlete should be divided into distinct phases or "periods," each having an objective of eliciting a certain response. In most periodization models, training is divided into three periods in the following order (although there are often subdivisions within these periods): preparatory, competitive and transitional.

The preparatory period is generally several weeks to several months (although for very young athletes it may last for a period of years). It tends to focus on general aspects of physical conditioning, injury rehabilitation and the correction of technical flaws. Naturally, the content of the training varies with the sport, but the general principle is that a larger quantity and variety of training are done during the preparatory period than during any other period.

In the sport of weightlifting, the tendency during this period is to do fewer of the competitive lifts and more of the lifts that are similar to them (e.g., power snatch and hang snatch) and to emphasize the development of strength and perhaps particular areas of technique in which the lifter is deficient. Some trainers emphasize developing the more general athletic characteristics of the athlete during this period (e.g., through running and jumping). There is also a tendency to perform more repetitions in exercises

during the preparatory period than in the competitive period and thereby to have a lower absolute intensity (i.e., weight on the bar) in training, at least on the same exercises. (The plan often calls for an even lower absolute intensity than would otherwise be necessitated by the greater number of repetitions per set.) The objective of this period is not only to develop special qualities in the athlete which will ultimately enhance performance in competition, but also to provide mental and physical variety in the training stimulus.

During the competitive period of training, the athletes begin to approximate more closely competitive conditions in training. In weightlifting training the competitive period of training focuses more on the competitive lifts than on assistance exercises (at least relative to the mix of these exercises during the preparatory period). Technique is emphasized, repetitions tend to be lower (so the average weights lifted tend to be higher in each exercise) and competitive lifts make up a greater share of the total lifts that are performed. Here the emphasis is on preparing the athlete in every way for an upcoming major (for that athlete) competition, which is typically timed so that it falls at the end of the competitive period. During the competitive period there are often trial or "control" competitions, which are designed to permit the athlete to practice performing under competitive conditions with the typical aim of having the athlete's peak performance occur at the final competition of the competitive period.

Finally, there is the transitional period. As its name implies, it is a period of transition to a new preparatory period of training. Its purpose is to assure that the athlete has both mentally and physically recuperated from the rigors of the competitive cycle so that the preparatory phase of training can begin once again. During this period any nagging injuries that may have developed during the competitive period are attended to, and physical activities of a general nature tend to be undertaken. Exercises related to the athlete's sport are not necessarily discontinued (although they are reduced in terms of the overall volume and intensity of the training effort). These transitional periods may be as long as a month or two for very young athletes, but they decrease in length as the athlete matures. (High level athletes rarely have more than two consecutive weeks a year of such training.)

In trying to explain the conceptual underpinnings of the classic periodization model, some coaches have described the model as consisting of a period of preparation, followed by a period of adaptation and climaxing with the application of the new capabilities which have developed as a result of the adaptation. While this all sounds reasonable, there are many training approaches, other than the classic periodization model, that are in concert with the notion of preparation, followed by adaptation, followed by application. As a consequence, the classic periodization model is not without its critics.

During a recent IWF-sponsored symposium in Olympia, Greece, Bulgarian professor Dimitar Gjurkow proposed a change in the nomenclature and characterization of long term planning. First he proposed that the concept of an annual cycle be "doubted" when it is not connected to a sport that has seasons, because each training cycle within the year (he suggests three a year) is based on the prior cycle more than it is the annual plan. Gjurkow argued that the concepts of preparatory and transitive periods are inappropriate. He maintained that the transitive period is not the end of one but, rather, the beginning of a new one (a beginning that a lifter would not undertake if he or she was not planning to continue his or her career). He also asserted that the term "preparatory" is a misnomer because all training amounts to preparation for competition. It is difficult to disagree with any of these criticisms of the classic periodization model.

Gjurkow recommends the following cycle structure. First, there is a "period of active rest" (the former transitional period). Second, there is a period of "recuperation" (or the gradual resumption of more conventional training), during which the lifter is once again acclimating to the normal training load. Third, there is the basic training period (formerly the preparatory period). Finally, there is the pre-competition phase (formerly the competitive phase). Unfortunately, while Gjurkow's proposed new labels appear reasonable at first, there are at least as many problems with his proposed periodization terminology as with the existing nomenclature. For example, why refer to a period as one of recuperation (an obvious reference to a prior period from which one is recuperating) when the recuperation period involves reconditioning the body to accept the higher training loads? Similarly, why call the period immediately before the competition the pre-competitive phase when in fact all of the training performed prior to the competition (active rest, recuperation and basic) is in some sense pre-competitive? Perhaps the terms active rest, reconditioning, training and peaking would be more appropriate to explain Gjurkow's proposed periods.

I have not introduced Gjurkow's proposal to advocate it or to refute the existing terms or concept of periodization. Rather, the point is to show that the preparatory, competitive and transitional periods are not "carved in stone" as the only way to plan or to reference what is going on in the periodization concept. The concept easily allows for many variations (although the richness of the possible variations has not yet been fully explored).

This concept of focusing on different aspects of training during different periods of the year (or even over an athlete's career) has probably been around for hundreds, if not thousands, of years. The form has changed and has been greatly refined during the second half of this century, and particular emphasis on this kind of training has manifested itself over the last thirty years. Today, it is virtually dogma. To question it is considered radical. But in my opinion it is high time to be a radical with respect to the concept of periodization.

One reason to question the classic periodization model is that, for all of its popularity and acceptance, the efficacy of periodization (as characterized by the traditional three cycles discussed above) has never been proven. It is true that most of the world's top athletes use it, but then so do many of the world's worst athletes. Just as the fact that most of the "qualified" doctors in the Western world once cauterized wounds with hot oil or bled their patients with leeches did not mean that such procedures were medically effective, so use of the classic periodization model by many coaches and athletes does not prove its efficacy.

This is not to say that periodization does not work. It is just that such training (as it is currently structured by many trainers) has not been proven to be the most effective training method. Nor is it based on a clear and unambiguous foundation of underlying scientific theory. (Hans Selye, often alluded to as the philosophical father of periodization, would probably have laughed if he had heard that his theory gave specific support to a particular form of periodization, although his work, and other knowledge that we have of the training process certainly suggest that some form of variation in training loads over time is appropriate.) In addition, there are no proven theories of biological rhythms that support periodization as it is performed today.

Again, this is not to say that periodization is not an effective means for training athletes. Rather, the intention of this discussion is to convey the idea that there is no reason to believe that periodization (at least as it is most often practiced) need be accepted as a given of training in the way that concepts like specificity of training or overload are today. (The concept of variability of training probably should have a status similar to that of the concepts of overload and specificity when it comes to workout planning.)

Another reason for questioning the effectiveness of the standard version of periodization is the proven principle of specificity of training. If muscles are trained most effectively with exercises and techniques that most resemble those of the events in which the athlete will compete, why is it necessarily beneficial to spend long periods avoiding or de-emphasizing those exercises or techniques? There may be reasons (I cannot think of any), but they have certainly not yet been fully developed or proven. For instance, it has never been proven that a large volume of training necessarily leads to better long term development of strength (i.e., that a foundation of large workloads necessarily leads to the potential for tremendous strength development). If such a theory were true, we would have only to search for the ditch diggers and other manual laborers of the world (who have devoted their lives to one large volume, preparatory period) and give them some competitive training.

Since strength training fits into a category of adaptation that requires frequent repetition of a stimulus to maintain or enhance the training effect, there is no basis for assuming that a capacity developed earlier in the training cycle will be sustained at an appropriate level to contribute to performance at a later stage in the cycle. (Detraining occurs rather quickly.) This is particularly true if the capacity developed during one period is not trained during a subsequent one. Again, this is not to say that having "periods" in training is a mistake, merely that periods as they are widely known and applied today should not be considered sacrosanct.

Another reason for questioning the efficacy of the classic periodization model is the enormous practical evidence that coaches who use periodization have collected (even if they themselves do not always see the importance of that evidence). One brief example should serve to support my point. I can recall hearing a very well known and respected coach lecturing on training methods some years ago. During the course of his presentation, he stressed the importance of a more or less classic approach to periodization. He spent much time explaining how the complex structure of his program was necessary in order for his athletes to achieve their absolute peak condition during the most important competition of the year. In a very minor reference during his presentation, he indicated that every athlete in his program made all of their personal best lifts during the preparatory period. Apparently, it had never occurred to this coach to question the value of his competitive period despite the fact that his athletes never made improvements in performance during such periods!

Why has today's version of the periodization concept been accepted so widely and seemingly without much question? There are at least several reasons, some of them good and some of them bad. One reason is that some forms of periodization work better than many forms of short term planning. Another reason is that variety is often appreciated by athletes in training. Performing the same exercises over and over can become monotonous. Periodization can offer a welcome break from the monotony, so athletes tend to like it.

Periodization can also make the process of planning an athlete's training easier. A coach does not need to do as much analysis of an athlete's training when its effectiveness is not tested very often. In addition, anyone can do broad brush planning and call it periodization. It is simple, easy and foolproof; to make an impressive plan, just pile on the volume and exercises during the preparatory period and cut things back during the competitive period, and you will have a plan that looks good on paper.

Still another reason for the acceptance of periodization is its natural fit within competitive seasons and the idea that it assists the athlete in peaking, because all training appears structured (appropriately) around the competitive season.

Finally, as we suggested earlier, the concept of periodization has supposedly been given scientific support by the theories of Hans Selye (a man whose identification of the "general adaptation syndrome" was considered a breakthrough in biological science). In essence, Selye found that when a very wide variety of stressors are applied to the body, the body responds in the same general way. First, there is an alarm stage in which the body reacts to the stressor in order to minimize its negative effects on the body. Then the body goes through a stage of resistance in which it attempts to adapt to the stressor. Finally, if the stressor is strong enough and is not withdrawn, the body's defenses and adaptive capabilities may be overrun, and a stage of exhaustion in which the body succumbs to the onslaughts of the stressor, occurs. Brilliant as it might have been, Selye's work gives only very limited support to the idea of periodization. If the body cannot withstand continual stress, then stress must be applied at intervals. This much Selye's work suggests. But to claim that Selye's work supports preparatory and competitive periods and the like or that it even suggests the use of a macrocycle is more than a "stretch" of Selye's theory; it is a nearly complete "leap of faith."

Research in Eastern Europe has reportedly supported the use of various periodization models, and supposedly a scientific rationale for a specific version of periodization has been supplied by research in the West. For example, a number of weight training experts have pointed to a 1981 study by Stone, et al., as "proof" that periodization is superior to conventional forms of training for building strength. In the study Stone's group compared the effectiveness of three sets of six repetitions in several exercises with a program which involved decreasing the number of reps over the training period while increasing the weight lifted. Better results were achieved, particularly in certain exercises, by the group that used "periodization." However, there are several reasons to be careful in interpreting the results of such a study.

First, the study only continued for a period of six weeks. What would have happened over longer periods (like the months or years that it takes to develop high strength level or complete a full blown periodized training plan)? What would have happened if the non-periodization athletes had trained using one set or three reps or a pyramid of alternated light and heavy workouts? Would they have performed better than the athletes doing the periodization? Does merely cutting reps and increasing the weights constitute periodization as it is currently understood? The answer to all of these questions and many similar ones is: "We can't say for sure."

This is not to say that the Stone study was not pathbreaking or useful. It was, after all, probably the first study that attempted to compare a training model used by many weight trainers with any form of periodized training. And it is surely to be commended for that effort. However, I am sure that neither Dr. Stone nor his colleagues would agree that their study (nor the few similar and limited studies that followed) "proved" the effectiveness of periodization. Rather, they would probably say that such studies suggest that such training methods may have promise and bear further study (and they might, on a personal level, adopt these methods in their training of athletes). Nevertheless, the popularizers of periodization would have us believe that the book has been closed on this subject and that whatever version of periodization they espouse represents the last word.

There does appear to be much truth in the periodization concept (as there is in many concepts that do not necessarily represent the "final solution"). For one thing, variety can indeed be a valuable training stimulus (on psychological and physical levels), and variation in the intensity of training is clearly very important in assuring long term progress). Periodization is also supported by the fact that when a lifter performs resistance training in an effective manner, at least two major physical capacities can be improved. One is physical strength and the other is work capacity. These two qualities are related, but the extent and nature of that relationship is not fully understood. Training to improve either quality clearly stresses the body's adaptive capabilities. If an athlete is training both qualities and then reduces the training on one, there is a period during which the body, now able to devote its adaptive recuperative energies to developing one quality, seems to spurt ahead in the development (or at least the expression) of that quality. Moreover, the other quality enjoys a period during which it is sustained at its previous level (partly because it takes some time for the training effect to be lost and partly because whatever other training is continued, it has some effect on maintaining that quality as well).

A parallel can be drawn here with the case of the injured athlete who, during the period of resting the injured area, often reports a sudden spurt in the capabilities of a non-injured area. The body is suddenly expending its entire adaptive energy to that one area with resulting progress. However, this process seems to be of a limited duration. After a time the body adapts to the new overall demands placed on it, and progress returns to a more normal rate (especially if the athlete concludes that his or her newfound energy can be applied with benefit by increasing the amount of training that the athlete does on the injured area). Unfortunately, during the process of truly long term periodization, the advantages that arise out of the body's growth spurt when focusing on fewer capacities may be long gone by the time the cycle ends.

In summary, the concept of periodization has significant merit, but the classic periodization model is seriously flawed. However, revised models of periodization can be very useful. As is the case with so many aspects of coaching, the "devil is in the details" (as are the keys to all successful planning). The real question is: "What kinds of training variations work best, and how can long and short term planning be effectively integrated?" In the sections that follow, we will focus on an extension of the concepts of planning and on the many details that make for successful planning. We will begin by looking at the "Macrocycle, the starting point of long term planning models." However, before beginning the presentation of the macrocycle, the mesocycle and the microcycle, it is important to include a cautionary note.

Much of what is being presented in the next sections is a reflection of the current "state of the art" in training theory and practice, and this makes sense. When planning to enter any field of endeavor, it makes sense to look at what the top performers are doing. It would, after all, be foolish to ignore the lessons that have been learned through arduous trial and error by the leading members of the field (e.g., practicing athletes and coaches in the field of weightlifting). But it would be equally foolish to assume that everything the champions (or their coaches) do has been learned by trial and error (i.e., is based on sound personal experience), or that the quality of every athlete's experiences and the evaluation of those experiences have been the same. More often than not, the established "wisdom" in a given field is a combination of science, rigorous clinical experience (i.e., in the gym), working hypotheses, that have been accepted as sensible, pure imitation of other athletes and unconscious actions. There is no way to tell one from the other by mere observation. Even questioning the athlete and/or coach involved is not reliable, because they may be unable or even too embarrassed to provide entirely accurate explanations of their rationales for doing what they do.

The great breakthroughs that have been made in weightlifting training, and in all other fields of human endeavor, have been made by those who were willing to question and improve upon existing "knowledge." In contrast, the great blunders and follies of human history have been made by those who ignored existing knowledge. Therefore, challenging the existing body of knowledge for the sake of the challenge is a serious mistake, rivaled only by accepting everything the "experts" in a given field have to say because they are experts. The key to navigating successfully between these two potentially disastrous alternatives is to discover the basis for the beliefs that are currently held and the degree of certainty that can be properly assigned to the veracity of each belief. If the beliefs can withstand careful scrutiny, their basis can be described as "scientific" in the broadest meaning of that term. If all the known facts support a particular theory, and none contradicts it, it is appropriate to apply it until and unless contradictory evidence emerges. If the degree of certainty in a given training method or technique the belief is relatively high, then spending a great deal of time questioning that method may be fruitless.

In contrast, if the theory is not scientifically based, no particular weight should be attached to it, regardless of who generated it or who follows it. Scientific in this context does not necessarily mean proven in a laboratory but, rather, established by carefully manipulating variables in a clinical (i.e., real world) setting. If the degree of certainty that can reasonably be attached to a given method lies between those two extremes (i.e., between contextual certainty and mere speculation), the belief may properly be regarded as only provisionally accepted and subject to further consideration and testing. (That may not be a priority if the issue under consideration is not currently causing a problem or is not a significant limiting factor in an athletes progress.)

To give just one example of a provisional belief, consider the notion of studying the physical characteristics of weightlifting champions to assist in the selection of future weightlifters. Such study may indeed ultimately reveal some fundamental characteristics that are shared by all of the subjects and are not common in the general population, but for the most part the characteristics identified so far either do not appear to be very exclusive or may have been developed by training. True genetic advantages (or at least insurmountable disadvantages) have not as yet been revealed by the relatively crude methods that we currently have at our disposal. It must be remembered that even when apparently distinguishing features between champions and also-rans have been identified, they may well have been the result of previous selection (particularly when those features are less than universal in nature). In such a case the characteristic identified might be necessary but not sufficient, or sufficient but not necessary, to develop a champion.

In order to increase the likelihood that a fundamental trait has been identified, a study would have to test non-weightlifters as well as those who have trained seriously and failed to achieve satisfactory results. Even such a study would not approach certainty, because those sampled had been successful or not at the then prevailing level of training knowledge and practice; perhaps other training and/or nutritional methods would have helped the poorer performers to equal the results of today's better performers.

This is not to say that there are no traits that give certain athletes advantages over others; there most certainly are. The point is that we do not currently know very much, and the claim that we are has probably caused as many potential champions to be missed as to be selected (and this does not consider the psychological damage some of these spurious theories may have done to potential champions). Consequently, we must be very careful to assure that we do not fall into the self-fulfilling prophesy: look at the champs, see how they train and what traits they possess, then merely repeat the selection of such people and apply the same training methods (i.e., look for people who tolerate the prescribed training instead of optimizing the training of each of each athlete). Therefore, the reader is encouraged to evaluate what follows with a critical and active mind instead of merely digesting all of it as "gospel."

The Macrocycle

The classic macrocycle can be defined as a unit of training that includes at least one (or more) of each of the three training periods (preparatory, competitive and transitional). Macrocycles can be from several months to several years in duration, but cycles that are longer than a year are generally viewed as two or more macrocycles, one built upon the other.

For many years it was virtually an article of faith in workout planning that the macrocycle should consist of a year or more. Most sports (including weightlifting) have some kind of annual cycle. An athlete wants to "peak" at the most important competition of the year, and he or she certainly cannot maintain the very highest level of performance year round. Therefore, why not plan training in accordance with an annual structure (or, in the case of athletes who are involved in Olympic sports, in four year cycles)?

The most obvious answer is that it is difficult to predict an athlete's response to training across a period of several months, let alone several years. Most coaches who have actually tried to apply very long term plans soon discovered this through hard experience. This does not mean that all long term planning is futile. It is actually be a very useful tool in the arsenal of the coach who wishes to optimize the planning process, but it is clearly not sufficient.

In recent years, there has been a somewhat subtle but significant change in the thinking of many coaches who use classical periodization in their training planning. It is a change in a direction I consider to be very positive. That direction has been away from the very long term planning on at least two levels. The first is that of the planning horizon itself. Four year plans, at least for advanced level athletes, have been losing favor, as the recognition that such plans are very tentative at best has broadened. The second level of change in the macrocycle has been in the lengths of the cycles within the long term plans; they tend to be shorter today. An annual plan with one preparatory, one competitive and one transitional period is fast becoming a thing of the past. An annual plan which encompasses two, three, four, or even more such cycles has become more and more common.

Those who cling to the traditional long term planning concept may argue that only the content and not the concept of long term planning has changed with the advent of shorter cycles. of course, this is not truly the case unless the coach refuses to consider the results of each cycle prior to the athlete's beginning the next cycle. If the coach does rethink each cycle after the close of the prior one, then the athlete is no longer carrying out one long term plan but, rather, a series of shorter term ones in which the results of each affect the design of the succeeding ones (although an effort may be made to remain within the framework of an annual plan as well).

Within the context of training cycles, there has also been a movement toward reducing the degree of difference in the content of the training that takes place across the cycles. While with long cycles the content of the training at two different stages of the cycle tends to be very different, within short cycles the differences in the content of the training during the preparatory and competitive cycles tend to be a matter of degree more than kind. There is simply no time for the lifter to change content dramatically within short cycles.

It is now rather widely acknowledged that very high level athletes require greater variety in the loads that they lift from workout to workout than do lower level athletes, while periods of significantly lighter loads are not generally performed for any significant length of time by advanced athletes. High level athletes simply cannot afford to go without a training stimulus for any extended period of time.

While some of these changes in periodization practice may not have been the result of a completely conscious intent on the part of cycle planners as they moved from longer to shorter cycles, the effect has been the same. Moreover, I believe that these have, for the most part, been positive developments that have a very sound theoretical and practical basis. The body readily adapts to imposed exercise stress. It also responds nearly as well to lack of exercise stress (by detraining). There is also a relationship between the length of the period during which training occurred and the length of the period for which an adaptation is retained. The longer the period of training, the greater is the tendency for the training effect to be preserved.

Therefore, if during an exercise cycle a certain training effect is generated, that effect will not be preserved to any significant degree months (or even weeks) later, unless the lifter continues to apply (at least occasionally) a stimulus similar to the one that created the training effect. For example, if the lifter engaged in cardiovascular training from October through December during an old style yearly cycle, there would be virtually no remaining training effect during the competitive cycle in the period from June through August(unless the lifter continued such training through most of the competitive period). The primary exception to this rule is in the area of learning. Learned capabilities, such as concepts of how to perform a lift, motor skills, and probably the ability to recruit muscle fibers, are likely to be partially, if not fully, retained for extended periods with little or no continued rehearsal.

Therefore, designing cycles with the intention of building a physiological capability and then assuming that this new capability will be retained during a future period in which no continuing training for that type of capability takes place is virtually pointless. In order to avoid any detraining effect, the training that developed a given capability must be continued, at least on a maintenance basis, up to the point (or nearly so) at which it will be needed. This is why a change in training emphasis can be useful, but a change in the kind of training done is likely to be less so.

This is not to say that a lifter may not require regular breaks from the normal training stimulus, so that the body can have a respite to recuperate from training stress. Special training modifications may be required if the lifter becomes overtrained or injured. But such an "active rest" should be seen as a period during which recuperation is taking place, not a period during which conditioning is being done for some competition six months away.

The design of annual cycles can vary significantly from coach to coach. The structure of an annual cycle also tends to vary with the developmental level of the lifter (a point that will be discussed in greater detail in the next section of this chapter). The general pattern is to identify several competitions during the year and to build cycles around those competitions, so that there is a preparatory period with generally higher volumes, more exercise variety, and higher repetitions per set. During such a period, there is an emphasis on strengthening the athlete, improving the athlete's condition and correcting specific technique flaws. The athlete then moves into a competitive phase during which intensity is gradually increased and volume of training is decreased. There is greater emphasis on the classical lifts and a reduction in the repetitions per set during this period. Immediately before the competition, both intensity and volume fall as the athlete attempts to "peak" for the day of the competition.

After the competition (if it is a very important one in the overall plan), the athlete generally has a period of training (the transitive period) in which the volume and intensity are relatively low in comparison with the rest of the year. The objective here is to give the athlete a period of active rest (i.e., light activity), during which any injuries have an opportunity to heal, any overtraining will have a chance to resolve itself and the athlete can have a break from the training stimulus. In this way the athlete can enter the next preparatory cycle refreshed and enthusiastic about the challenges which lie ahead.

Analysts in the former Soviet Union have performed extensive research in the area of periodization as it applies to weightlifting and have developed a number of guidelines for the content of preparatory and competitive periods. These guidelines include suggestions for variations in the monthly loads, the monthly intensities and the exercise content of months within the competitive and preparatory periods. These guidelines have been further refined to the point where they are specific to the athlete's level of development. Therefore, before presenting any of the recommendations that have been made with respect to the content of various training periods, let us look at the stages that is exist in a typical athlete's career.

Plans for Long Term Development

In the past several years, a great deal of attention has been paid in the weightlifting literature of Eastern Europe to the subject of the long term development (i.e., over a period of several years or more) of young athletes. This approach to planning must be contrasted with what was being done under some of the older periodization models, which tried to apply long term plans to mature athletes. Plans for long term development are not very long macrocycles because they are presenting a sequence of development that will not be repeated within the career of the same athlete. (They are not cycles at all but, rather, a plan for a developmental process.)

Authors Medvedyev, Dvorkin, Roman and Gjurkow, to name a few, have presented plans for the long term development of young weightlifters. Extracts of their methods will be presented here in order to acquaint the reader with some of the thinking that is going on in this area. In order to gain a more complete understanding of what these and other theorists have to say regarding the long term development of young weightlifters, the reader is encouraged to read their original works (which are listed in the Bibliography).

The reader is also encouraged to cast as critical eye on all of the systems presented, because while they each have many very sensible elements, they also have many aspects which can and should be brought into question. More importantly, any multi-year system suffers from the same shortcoming that any system of long term training has; no trainer can anticipate the response any individual athlete will have to any system, even in the short term. Any system that presents a long term plan necessarily increases (exponentially) the likelihood that the system will fall out of sync with the lifter's needs at some point (a point which I am sure most of the developers of multi-year systems would concede).

My purpose in presenting these systems is not to say that any of them can or should be followed as written. Rather, the systems are presented for the purpose of suggesting what some of today's thinking is with regard to the general direction of a young lifter's development and how many of the theorists of Eastern Europe (and by extension many other parts of the world, including the United States) view this issue. My purpose is also to point out that young athletes should never be expected to follow the training methods of advanced lifters without a long period of careful preparation.

Because so much of the material that follows provides programming guidelines that are related to the "classification level" of the athlete, let us explain the classification levels that were established in the former Soviet Union. These standards provided a total for each weight category and were established for each Olympiad; the standards did not change from 1988 to 1992. Athletes received various incentives for achieving each level (with the greatest incentives reserved for those who reached the highest levels). The standards ran from Class III (the lowest) to Master of Sport International Class (MSIC, the highest classification). Competitors in the latter class were considered ready to challenge the best in the world (although, due to the competitiveness of weightlifting in the former Soviet Union, an athlete could make the MSIC standard and still never be able to represent the Soviet Union in a World or European Championships. A table summarizing the classification standards for Classes II through MSIC appear in Table 1.

Table 1
CLASSIFICATION STANDARDS EMPLOYED BY THE FORMER
SOVIET UNION: 1988-1992

Class	MSIC	MS	CMS	I	II
Category					
52	240	205	180	172.5	155
56	265	220	200	190	170
60	285	240	220	202.5	182.5
67.5	320	270	245	227.5	202.5
75	345	290	260	245	220
82.5	365	310	280	262.5	235
90	385	325	290	275	247.5
100	400	340	310	287.5	257.5
110	415	350	320	297.5	
Super	430	360	335		

In his book A System of Multi-Year Training in Weightlifting, A. Medvedyev, former World Champion and coach of the Soviet National Team, outlines his vision of the development process of the typical high level weightlifter. Medvedyev's highly structured long term plan for an athlete's development reflects two processes that are taking place in the athlete at the same time: maturation and adaptations to training. This is because his plan assumes that most athletes will begin their specialized training at roughly the same age. (Selection of athletes is assumed to take place at around the age of twelve, and actual specialized training is expected to begin between the ages of thirteen and fourteen.) Consequently, athletes are maturing and adapting to training at the same time; if an athlete were to begin several years later, the training effect would take place, but the maturation would have essentially been completed.

It should be noted that although both Medvedyev and Bulgarian sources talk about athletes beginning their training in the prepubescent period, R. Roman, in analyzing a group of 131 highly qualified weightlifters who competed between 1979 and 1982, found that the average age of starting weightlifting was fifteen, plus or minus two years. (Athletes in lighter weight classes began training as late as age nineteen). Therefore, although this relatively small sample cannot be considered conclusive, it would appear that "ideal" starting ages and actual starting ages may be quite different, even in Eastern Europe.

Medvedyev divides the developmental process into four general stages: beginner/selection, educational training, formation of sport mastery (or, as he refers to it, "sport perfectioning") and the achievement of high sport mastery. The beginner stage generally lasts for one year or more and emphasizes general physical preparation (general conditioning of the athlete via such activities as running, jumping, playing soccer, etc.), teaching the fundamentals of technique and evaluating the mental and physical qualities of the athletes.

During this stage the coach is also trying to develop the athlete's love for the sport, a love that will be needed to see the lifter through the training that must occur if the athlete is to achieve true sport mastery. General physical training comprises approximately 40% of total training time at this stage, as the development of general physical qualities is being stressed.

The second or educational phase lasts for a period of approximately three to four years. During this time the young athlete passes through several classification levels, until the athlete has reached the level of Candidate Master of Sport (CMS). In the educational phase, the development of correct technique and precision in executing that technique is emphasized, while the volume of training is steadily increased and an ever increasing portion of the athlete's training is devoted to specialization on weightlifting (and progressively less to general physical preparation).

The third stage of development represents true specialization on weightlifting training and is designed to raise the performance of the athlete to the Master of Sport level and beyond. It generally requires up an additional two to three years for the athlete to reach this stage of development. Developing the very highest levels of technical skill and strength and power is emphasized during this period. General physical training drops to an insignificant level as full sport specialization takes place.

It is at the end of this stage that athletes enter the critical high sport mastery level of development and future champions emerge and go on to success on a national and international level.

Overall, Olympians typically require three to four years to reach the Master of Sport level, five to ten years to make the national team. (The average is seven years, with lighter lifters reaching a high level faster than heavier lifters.) R. Roman found that the rate of progress of record holders and other highly qualified athletes was similar during the first four years of training, but that those who

Table 2

Period:	Prep	Comp	Prep	Comp	Prep	Comp
Classification:	II-III	II-III	I & CMS	I & CMS	MS	MS
Exercise:						
Snatch	10	10	9	9	8	8
Snatch Related	10	10	11	12	12	13
Clean	7.5	7.5	6	6	5	5
Clean Related	9.5	9.5	9	9	8	8
Classic Jerk	7.5	7.5	7	7	6	6
Other Jerks	3.5	3.5	5	6	7	8
Front & Back Squat	27	27	23	23	20	20
Other Squats	15	15				
Snatch Pulls			7	5	8.5	5
Clean Pulls			5	6	10	12
Pressing & Other Remedial Exercises (e.g., Good Mornings)	10	10	18	17	15.5	15
Avg. # lifts/mo.	1250	900	1650	1200	2100	1500

achieved higher results continued their rapid rate of progress in the fifth year, while the other athletes began to experience slower progress at that point. The number of years that a lifter requires to reach the highest levels of development is related to the age at which the athlete began training and to the size of the lifter. Athletes who are lighter in body weight and start later in life generally require fewer years to reach their potential than the average athlete. In contrast, athletes who begin at a young age and who will ultimately lift in the heaviest weight classes take longer to develop.

Although smaller athletes generally reach their highest levels of performance earlier than heavier athletes, there is a trade-off in this advantage. Progress tends to level off for athletes in the lightest weight classes after twelve years of training, but in the heaviest weight classes this does not tend to occur until after fifteen to sixteen years. Athletes who move up a weight class after six or seven years (or sooner) improve their results substantially (from 20 kg. to 50 kg. on average) and extend the period during which progress occurs.

Soviet research suggests that during a lifter's development to a high level of ability, the athlete increases both the volume and intensity of his or her training. Both the total weight lifted in training sessions and the average weight on the bar increase. After this period of rapid development, the total volume lifted tends to stabilize or even diminish, while the intensity of the training continues to increase (in terms of average weight lifted, not necessarily in terms of percentages of maximum lifted or number of reps performed in the maximum and submaximum repetition zones).

Some research performed in the USSR indicates that an increase of 3.5 kg. in the average weight lifted (assuming a relatively fixed mix of exercises) yields a 10 kg. improvement in the total. While the correlation here makes sense, there is a question regarding the causal link. Is the athlete able to lift more in the total because the average training load has been increased or because his or her capabilities have improved?

In 1980 Roman recommended a distribution of lifts among exercises based on the athlete's classification, with differences in distribution during preparatory and competitive periods (see Table 2). For example, a 10 in the row labeled "snatch" means 10% of the lifter's total training volume should be devoted to snatches).

It can be seen in Table 2 that differences in the distribution of exercises during the preparatory and competition periods are zero for lifters in lower classifications. These differences become more pronounced (though never large) for more advanced athletes. However, it can be seen that significant differences among lifters in different classifications occur with respect to exercise distribution and total reps.

Lifters in the lower classifications spend approximately 20% of their training time performing the snatch and snatch related exercises, and fully half of that time is spent performing the classic snatch during the competitive and preparatory periods. For Class I and CMS level lifters the ratios of classic snatches to total snatch related exercises decline to 45% and 43% respectively during the competitive and preparatory periods. (For MS level lifters, the ratios are 40% and 38%.) Roman indicates that less qualified athletes spend 44% of the time they devote to cleaning to the classic clean itself, while highly qualified athletes spend only 38% of their time doing classic cleans.

In contrast, lower level athletes spend 68% of the time that they perform jerk related exercises in the classic jerk, with highly qualified athletes

Table 3

Classification:	Beginner	III-II	I & CMS	MS	MSIC
Volumes:					
Preparatory	1100-1300	1000-1500	1300-2000	1500-2700	1300-2500
Competition	900-1000	750-1050	950-1450	1100-1900	950-750

spending 46% of their time on the classic jerk (and a slightly lower percentage of their time during the competitive period). Lifters of higher qualification tend to spend a little more training time doing high pulls, with proportional reductions in other lifts. They also spend less time on the clean and jerk and more time doing separate cleans and jerk and related exercises. Subsequent studies have supported distributions of training loads similar to these, although some writers suggest performing more snatch pulls and fewer clean pulls.

The average monthly loads (in terms of numbers of repetitions performed) recommended by Medvedyev for Novices, Class III, II, I, Candidate Master of Sport (CMS), Master of Sport (MS) and Master of Sport International Class (MSIC) are, respectively: 700, 900, 1000, 1100, 1250 and 1700. (He acknowledges that individual differences can lead to variations from these recommendations by as much as 40%.) These average loads vary with the period of training. During preparatory and competitive periods, respectively, loads are approximately: 1000/700 for Class III; 1200/900 for Class II; 1400/1000 for Class I; 1600/1100 for CMS; 1800/1200 for MS; and 2000/1300 for MSIC. Fluctuations in monthly volume (as a percentage of average volume) tend to be similar among athletes in different classifications but fluctuations in the absolute number of reps are larger for more highly qualified athletes. The number of lifts performed tends to be higher than the averages presented above for athletes in lighter weight classes and lower for athletes in heavier weight classes. Relative intensities also tend to be higher for athletes in the lower body weight classes, but heavier lifters seem to achieve the same training effect with smaller relative intensities.

The number of lifts in the highest zones tends to be small for beginners and peaks at the MS level. The highest level athletes (above MS) show a decline (relative to the MS level athletes) in the highest number of lifts in the maximum and submaximum zones.

On the basis of 7,000 reps in the first year of training, Medvedyev recommends an annual growth in loading of from 10% to 30% during the first 7 years of training. This would lead to loads in the seventh year of between 12,400 and 33, 800 (the former if loads grow by 10% each year and the latter if they grow by 30% each year). It should be recognized that loads will not necessarily increase by the same percentage each year and that attempts to force the loading up excessively are likely to result in the lifter's failing to reach his or her true potential (for reasons such as overtraining and/or the development of overuse injuries).

The range of annual reps that a coach tries to achieve is in part a function of the coach's training philosophy with regard to management of the training effect. Some coaches strive to apply maximum stress to their athletes primarily when they have reached a state of supercompensation. (The coach permits the athlete to train at lower levels of intensity following a maximum or near maximum effort, so that the next bout of maximum stress occurs when the athlete has adapted or overcompensated and is prepared to perform at a higher level.) Other coaches favor applying successive training stresses to the body before it has fully recuperated from a prior stress. Here the notion is that successive stresses before adaptation occurs will have a stronger cumulative effect in terms of invoking an adaptive response in the athlete's body. A coach who subscribes to the full recuperation approach will not train his or her athletes as hard and will have more easy days than will the coach who believes in the value of cumulative stresses.

During the transition period training is reduced substantially. Total breaks from bar training of from two to eight weeks a year are permitted (with beginners tending to be at the longer part of the range and more advanced lifters at the shorter). These rest periods tend to be coordinated with the length of the macrocycle (a six-month cycle will result in breaks during two transition periods, while an annual cycle will provide one longer break). A light "unloading" week is generally provided every one to two months.

As an example, consider the monthly volume arrangement that Roman suggests for athletes of various classifications shown in Table 3.

Roman has also offered a plan for athlete development with the monthly load distributions linked to the athlete's level of development as shown in Table 4. (The C which appears after the number of lifts in some months symbolizes a competition month, while a P symbolizes a preparatory month and a GPP symbolizes a month of general physical preparation).

Table 4

Classification:	Beginner	II & III	I & CMS	MS
Month:				
1	1150/P	1100/P	1350/P	1900/P
2	1250/P	1300/P	1500/P	2100/P
3	1200/P	900/C	1650/P	1500/C
4	1000/C	1250/P	1200/C	2000/P
5	500/GPP	900/C	1000/C	1400/C
6	1100/P	1500/P	2000/P	1200/C
7	900/C	750/C	950/C	1600/P
8	1100/P	1250/P	1500/P	2100/P
9	900/C	900/C	1650/P	1500/C
10	450/GPP	1250/P	1200/C	1600/P
11	450/GPP	900/C	1000/C	1100/C
12	Active Rest	Active Rest	Active Rest	Active Rest

It can be noted that the load is smaller during the second half of the year than during the first half. (Roman suggests that the lifter is becoming fatigued from the large load employed during the first half of the year and can only withstand smaller loads during the second half.) GPP indicates that the focus of the month's training is on general physical preparation (e.g., non-barbell conditioning exercises and remedial exercises, although some athletes use the bar during such a period).

In depicting the development of the elite athlete, Medvedyev uses a somewhat different method. He offers a table that summarizes the athlete's development on the basis of somewhat different parameters than those used by Roman (see Table 5).

In his book Weightlifting And Age, L.S. Dvorkin has made recommendations for training athletes aged 11-16, as shown in Table 6.

In training the young athlete, Dvorkin recommends two-hour workouts three times a week for the first 6 months. In the first of those workouts, 36 minutes is devoted to training with the bar (18 minutes each of snatching and squatting). In the second workout the athlete

Table 5

Indicator	Begin-ner	Educational Training				Sport Perfectioning			High Sport Mastery	
Classifica-tion	Begin-ner	Nov-ice	Class III	Class II	Class I	CMS	CMS	MS	MS	MSIC
Ages	12-13	13-15	14-16	15-17	16-18	15+	16+	17+	18+	18+
Training Hrs/Week	6	8	12	16	20	24	28	32	36	36
Annual # of lifts in 000s*	4-5	6-7	7-9	9-11	11-13	13-15	15-17	16-19	17-21	20-25
Annual # 90% + Snatches & C&J's (clean and jerks counted separately)	100-200	100-200	200-300	200-400	200-400	300-400	300-600	300-600	300-600	400-700
Relative intensity in Snatch & C&J exercises in %s	60-70	60-70	65-75	73-77	73-77	73-77	73-77	73-77	73-77	73-77
Annual # of competi-tions	3-4	3-4	4	5	5	6-8	6-8	6-8	6-8	6-8

* For beginners the number of lifts do not include any lifts less than 50% of maximum on the snatch and C&J, lifts under 60% are not included for all other categories of lifters.

Table 6

Age:	11	12	13	14	15	16
Percentage of Training Time Spent in Gen. Phys. Prep./Specialization	20/80	30/70	40/60	50/50	60/40	60/40
Percentage of Training Time Spent in Various Zones of Intensity						
50%-59%	40	30	10			
60%-69%	50	30	30	20	10	10
70%-79%	10	40	50	60	60	50
80%-89%			10	10	20	30
90% and Above				10	10	10
Norms in terms of percentage of body weight young athletes can lift.						
Snatch	40	45	50	60	70	80
C&J	60	70	80	90	100	110

trains for 60 minutes with the bar (20 minutes each of the C&J, the overhead squat and the bench press). In the third workout the athlete also trains for 60 minutes with the bar (20 minutes each of power snatches, an isometric version of the squat and an isometric version of the bench press). During the period from 6 to 18 months of training, the total time of training increases by 40 minutes per week (the athlete is still training 3 times a week), and the amount of time spent with the bar increases to approximately 3 hours a week. During the 18 to 24 months, total training time remains about the same, but the time spent lifting increases to just over 4 hours per week.

How does the distribution of training loads across zones change as the athlete matures and improves his or her abilities? When the strongest lifters in the Soviet Union were studied in 1980, it was found that, on average, 19% of their training was with weights in the 50% to 60% range; 28% of their reps were in the 61% to 70% range; 34% were in the 71% to 90% range; 15% were in the 81% to 90% range; and 4% were in the 91% to 100% range, with a total of 500 lifts being performed in the classic lifts in one month. This load distribution reveals that the majority of lifts are in the middle zones, with fewer lifts being performed at the upper or lower zones. However, Soviet researchers have noted that there are significant differences among lifters in the distribution of loads. Some perform more lifts in the middle and lower zones and fewer in the higher zones, while others perform more lifts in the higher zones and fewer in the lower zones.

The tables that are often used to depict changes in an athlete's training programs as the athlete matures and becomes more accomplished can omit other important changes that are taking place in the athlete's training regimen. For example, in addition to changing the monthly loads as an athlete develops, Medvedyev also believes in changing the number of exercises the athlete employs in his or her training. Early in the educational training phase, lifters practice up to 23 exercises. The number of exercises is gradually increased to 37 by the fourth year of training, 52 in the fifth year, 62 in the sixth year, 70 in the seventh year, 79 in the eighth year, 84 in the ninth year and to more than 100 exercises after that.

While the number of total lifts is increasing substantially during this growth in the complex of exercises, the number of lifts in the classical exercises is falling both as a percentage of the total lifts and in absolute terms. For example, Medvedyev talks about a Class II lifter who performs approximately 9000 lifts a year, spending 7% of his or her time on the classic snatch and 12% on the clean and/or jerk. By the time that lifter has reached the stage of high sport mastery, he or she may be performing more than 20,000 total repetitions, but may be spending only 2% of his or her training time on the classic snatch and an equal amount of time on the C&J. However, the time devoted to exercises related to these lifts (snatches and cleans from the blocks or jerks from behind the neck) is growing dramatically, to the point where they comprise approximately 30% of the training load. According to Medvedyev, methods are changed every three weeks to prevent staleness and to maintain a constant level of stimulus.

In starting an athlete, Medvedyev recommends only the snatch and snatch related exercises and squats be performed during the first week of

Table 7

Period	Preparatory			Competitive			Transitional		
Reps	1-2	3-4	5-6	1-2	3-4	5-6	1-2	3-4	5-6
Class II - CMS	29	55	16	47	48	5	17	51	32
MS and MSIC	16	56	28	27	60	13	10	55	35

training. Jerk related exercises are focused on during the second week, and in the third week the clean is the primary exercise.

According to Medvedyev, another change that should occur as the athlete develops is a shift in the training time that the lifter spends on various repetition patterns (see Table 7). The table suggests that the amount of time a highly qualified athlete spends doing higher repetition sets should grow as the athlete becomes more advanced.

It should be noted that Medvedyev would have to be considered at the extreme end of the coaching spectrum in terms of the training variety that he recommends. In contrast, by the end of his coaching career in Bulgaria, Ivan Abadjiev would have to be considered at the opposite end of the spectrum in terms of training variety (recommending essentially the power clean and power snatch, the classical exercises and front and back. squats and very low repetitions on all sets in an athlete's training).

Some of the most interesting differences in training during the preparatory and competitive periods take place with respect to reps with weights 90% and above, so let us spend some additional time in the analysis of what some of the weightlifting literature has to say regarding training in this important area (one in which coaches often differ with respect to their exercise prescriptions). Studies of high level athletes in the former Soviet Union have shown that they perform 10 to 60 lifts a month with maximum and submaximum weights (90% and above) in the average training month. While some of these variations in the total such reps performed are attributable to differences in loading on the same exercises (e.g., the classical lifts) and in the allocation of those maximum efforts across exercises, a greater share is attributable to differences among athletes in the distribution of high intensity efforts among exercises.

For the majority of athletes, 90% and greater

efforts in the snatch tend to outnumber such efforts in the C&J by a factor of two to one. (There is speculation that as more athletes separate cleans from jerks in their training, a growing trend at least among some coaches, the number of lifts in these combined exercises may come closer to the number of snatches performed, and the overall number of 90%+ efforts in the clean and jerk will increase.) Overall, many of the athletes who perform more attempts with 90%+ weights do so in non-classical exercises.

Regardless of how many 90%+ reps athletes perform in an average training month, significant variations in the number of maximum and submaximum efforts occur among months, and those differences are related to the period of training. A number of studies have suggested that the number of 90%+ lifts tends to be limited to twenty to thirty during the preparatory period but rises to forty to sixty during the competitive period. Maximums (100% efforts) are typically attempted once or twice a month (but usually not closer than eighteen days before a competition, a minimum of ten to fourteen days out).

Robert Roman recommended that the distribution of loads (in terms of the percentage reps in each intensity zone) during the preparatory and competitive periods be structured as shown in Table 8.

It should be noted that athletes in higher classifications are attempting a smaller number of 90% weights because lifters of lower classifications appear to thrive on more maximum and near maximum attempts than do the highest level athletes. It appears that the number of such attempts follows almost a flattened bell curve distribution in that athletes require and perform few heavy attempts early in their careers, then progressively increase the number of such attempts as their skill and conditioning improve. Ultimately, a large number of maximum attempts are not well tolerated, and the athlete reduces the number (see

Table 8

Zones	Up to 70%	70-75%	80-85%	100+
Periods				
Preparatory	25	30	40	5
Competitive	20	25	42	13

Table 9
Total Number of Lifts Per Month at 90% or More of Maximum In All Exercises

Period:	Preparatory	Competitive	Transitional
Level:			
Class II	56	44	20
Class I	44	56	32
CMS	20	28	12
MS & MSIC	20	28	8

Tables 9 and 10).

This philosophy would seem to conflict somewhat with the approach of the Bulgarians, who require even the highest level athletes to perform many maximum and near maximum attempts.

The distribution of attempts across zones of intensity for the classic lifts and pulls, as recommended by Medvedyev, appears in Table 11 (Table 12 provides a similar distribution for squats).

In addition to the number of lifts in each zone and the number of lifts with 90% or more of maximum, another indicator that is used in

exercises and therefore have a greater ability to handle higher average weights. In such a case the value would be more a reflection of a training trade-off (volume for intensity) than a message of the training stimulus.

In an article in the 1984 Weightlifting Yearbook, N.R. Tonyan and V.G. Grigoryenko proposed what they consider to be a more precise measure of overall training intensity and a better indicator of what to expect in terms of competition results. They believe that the athlete's results in the snatch or C&J (separately) can be predicted using the following formula: (The Average Weight Used in the Snatch or C&J and related exercises) X

Table 10
90% and Greater Lifts per Year in the Classic Exercises

Level:	Class II	Class I	CMS	MS & MSIC
Exercise:				
Snatch	176	165	100	87
Clean	56	59	28	35
Jerk	203	205	99	86
Total	435	429	227	208

Eastern Europe is the Ki (coefficient of intensity) value (often simply referred to as the Ki value). It is calculated using the following formula: (Average Weight Used During Training X 100) / Total in the Biathlon = K_I.

Most athletes have Ki values in the 35% to 41% range, but there has been little evidence of any close relationship between successful performance and the Ki value. Perhaps this is because the content of the athlete's training can have such a profound influence on this value. For instance, the athlete who performs many pulls and squats will tend to have a higher Ki value than will an athlete who performs many classical exercises and does a limited number of pulls and squats. In addition, that same athlete might be able to obtain similar results by training with a different content (e.g., a higher proportion of classical lifts). Therefore, the Ki value would be of little use in evaluating the athlete's training. Similarly, an athlete may tend to use low reps in his or her training of the classic

$100* / 2 K_I$. (*The snatch includes the snatch, snatch from the hang and snatch from the blocks; the C&J includes the C&J, clean, clean from the hang or blocks and the jerk or power jerk from the racks.)

T. Ajan and L. Baroga, in their book, Weightlifting: Fitness for All Sports, suggest that intensity measures can be refined by dividing volume measures by the athlete's body weight in order to reflect the influence of body weight on the ability of an athlete to execute a certain load in training. The limitation of such a method is that it relies upon there being a linear relationship between body weight and the capabilities of an athlete. This is clearly not the case; there is a relationship, but it is not nearly that simple. However, although such relationships may not be linear across wide spreads of body weight classes, they may be stable within weight classes, and therefore, this approach can be useful within that context.

Table 11
Classic Lifts and Pulls (Snatch/Clean)

Zones:		60-65%	70-75%	80-85%	90-95%	100%
Exercise	**Classification:**					
Classic Snatch and C&J	Class II	9/8	51/42	29/37	11/12	0/1
	Class I	7/4	56/45	28/39	8/11	1/1
	CMS	10/9	61/53	25/33	4/5	0/0
	MS/MSIC	16/11	63/55	19/31	2/0	0/3
	Zones:	70-75%	80-85%	90-95%	100-105%	110%
Snatch and Clean Pull	Class II	0/6	26/36	41/40	36/20	3/4
	Class I	0/17	24/34	33/26	39/19	4/4
	CMS	0/23	31/36	32/23	31/13	6/5
	MS/MSIC	0/20	25/38	37/24	32/13	6/5

Having looked at the prescriptions that have been offered regarding the macrocycle, it is now appropriate to examine what analysts have had to say about the mesocycle. However, before doing so, it is worthwhile to take another look at the developmental process of weightlifters from a somewhat different perspective.

Physiological Changes That Are Taking Place During the Developmental Process

The perspectives on long term planning that have already been presented will enable the planner to see the "big picture" of an athlete's entire career. However, viewing the long term development of the weightlifter primarily as a process that involves a gradually increasing training load, greater sport specialization (through a wider or narrower selection of bar exercises but also through a diminution of non-weightlifting related exercises) and improved results can be somewhat limiting. Therefore, a more detailed analysis of what is going on during the developmental process can help the coach to understand that process.

Table 13 identifies the important physical characteristics of the weightlifter and describes the kind of development taking place during the various stages of the elite lifter's career.

As can be seen in Table 13, only certain qualities improve to any significant degree after the beginning and intermediate stages of the lifter's career. Those qualities are strength from

hypertrophy of the contractile elements of muscle tissue, power derived from the athlete's ability to produce more force (the strength based component of power) and skill. Muscular hypertrophy in the contractile elements of muscle tissue results from the continuing training stimulus that arises from an increase in absolute intensity and a continued supply of the nutrients that facilitate muscle growth. As strength increases, power output does as well, because the lifter can move a heavier object at the same speed as he or she could move a lighter object before (although the athlete may not be able to move a lighter load materially faster than before). Continued practice yields continued, albeit ever smaller, increases in skill (even musicians who have been playing the same instrument for thirty years can detect new levels of skill as they continue to practice).

In contrast, increases in muscle strength and power due to neural factors are more difficult to continue over time. (There is also a change in the character of the improvements as earlier gains stem more from the ability to recruit muscle fibers into concurrent action, while later improvements come more as result of better coordination of the actions of certain muscle groups and overcoming the natural mind/body inhibition against maximal muscle contractions.) The changes that take place in a lifter's training over time dovetail nicely with these neurological improvements. Early training emphasizes lighter weights and proper technique, which permits the athlete to gradually learn to

Table 12

Zone %:	50-55	60-65	70-75	80-85	90-95	100-105	110
Level:							
Class II	13/3	28/8	27/28	30/32	2/16	0/12	0/1
Class I	14/3	27/11	21/31	35/31	3/16	0/7	0/1
CMS	22/5	28/11	25/40	22/26	3/10	0/6	0/2
MS&MSIC	22/4	30/13	25/39	20/25	2/10	0/8	0/1

Table 13

		Developmental Stage		
	Beginner	Intermediate	Advanced	Mature
Quality Developed				
Strength - Neurologic Basis	Significant increase in the ability to recruit and coordinate the action of muscle fibers	Continued increase in ability to recruit and coordinate while overcoming disinhibition against maximal contractions	Slight refinements in ability to recruit and continued reduction in disinhibition	Maintain improvements in ability to make maximal voluntary efforts in muscle contraction
Strength - Contractile Proteins	Modest increase	Greatest increase	Continued increase	Slower increase (unless muscular bdwt. increases)
Power - Force Component	Modest increase	Greatest increase	Continued increase	Slower increase
Power - Rate of Force Development	Substantial increase	Modest increase	Very slight increases	Maintained
Speed	Substantial increase	Modest increase	Maintained	Maintained
Flexibility	Substantial increase	Modest and targeted increase	Maintained	Maintained
Endurance	Modest increase	Greatest increase	Some increase	Maintained or slightly reduced
Work Hardening	Significant increase	Continued increase	Maintained	Maintained
Lifting Skill	Significant increase	Significant refinement	Continued refinement	Continued but more modest refinement

exert force and to coordinate the action of the muscles in doing so. Later training incorporates more maximum and near maximum efforts which refine an athlete's ability to generate force and help the athlete to reduce inhibitions against the generation of maximum effort. This more strenuous training also stimulates the hypertrophy that forms the foundation for improvement in the later stages of the lifter's career. But this more strenuous training only occurs at a time when the athlete has been conditioned to accept a greater level of training effort.

Increases in flexibility are generally insignificant and unimportant after the early stages of a lifter's career because by that time adequate levels of flexibility have generally been acquired. Speed does not increase much because after a few years of training the lifter has learned to move as quickly as possible under the bar (although it is always important for the athlete to think of moving as quickly as possible under the bar throughout his or her career).

The need for the body to harden to the stresses of training generally presents no problem for the young athlete who is just beginning in weightlifting, because he or she is not strong enough to lift weights that could create overuse injuries (though an improperly supervised beginner may attempt to do so or may incur a traumatic injury from attempting a heavy weight before he or she is technically or physically prepared). In contrast, the concept of work hardening is particularly crucial to the athlete who is becoming a weightlifter after developing his or her physical qualities in another sport. Such an athlete is at particular risk for injury because his or her capabilities permit the athlete to handle relatively heavy weights and/or to withstand a training volume the ordinary beginner could not.

Anaerobic endurance increases as the athlete increases his or her training load. Such an increase is not necessarily required for an increase in the lifter's performance in every physical quality, but an overall increase in endurance permits the lifter to increase the amount of training he or she can effectively perform and thereby allows the lifter to address more training needs within a given period of time.

Finally, the "work hardening" process is one by which the athlete's body adapts to the loads involved in lifting and is able to handle them more easily. For example, when certain stresses are placed on the joints, the tissue in those joints responds by toughening and adapting to that stress. The importance of this process cannot be overstressed. An athlete can only withstand the demands of weightlifting if his or her body has been given the chance to adapt to the training loads that are imposed by weightlifting. If the athlete tries to handle heavy weights before the body has had a chance to adapt to the stresses of the sport, injuries can result. The most wonderful aspect of the work hardening process is that the body adapts rapidly to a modest increase in load during the early stages of training. (It is highly receptive to the stimulation that modest loads provide.) Then, as greater training demands become necessary to further stimulate improvements, they are gradually increased in undulating fashion, with lighter and heavier loads being alternated to permit stimulation and recuperation.

Classic examples of athletes in this situation are powerlifters and weight throwers who decide to make the transition to weightlifting. Powerlifters have often become very strong by practicing their sport. Even with very inefficient weightlifting technique they are sometimes able to lift some fairly heavy weights in the classic lifts. Such weights would not present undue stresses to an athlete who had reached that level through the practice of weightlifting, but to the athlete who has no such background the stresses may be more than the athlete can tolerate. They may experience joint pain or injury as a result and blame weightlifting for their problems. The reality is that they have bypassed an important element of the training process and are suffering as a result of that, not because weightlifting is inherently tough on the joints. Similarly, a weight thrower may have developed considerable strength through the weight training that he or she performed. Such an athlete may have even performed partial versions of the classic lifts (e.g., power cleans) in his or her training. A skilled and powerful athlete of this type may be able to handle some fairly heavy weights in the classic lifts their first time out. But the joints of these athletes are generally not prepared to handle such stresses. For instance, while the weight thrower may have developed considerable pulling power via the power clean, his or her knees are not accustomed to the stresses of the full squat position. The athlete can pull a heavy weight to the shoulders in that position, but his or her knees are not conditioned to the task. The end result can be injury.

Therefore, athletes who are engaging in competitive weightlifting for the first time need to go through at least a modified version of the development process in order to harden their bodies to the stresses of weightlifting. (This as also true of a weightlifter who has taken a long layoff from the sport; such an athlete may still remember how to lift a fairly heavy weight, but he or she is not in condition to do so.) If they do go through the development process, they are on the way to becoming a weightlifter. If they do not, they are running a high risk of suffering an injury just when they were beginning to appreciate what a truly wonderful and unique sport weightlifting truly is. The primary value of understanding the kinds of development that can and should take place over time is to use this knowledge in designing training programs for the various stages of an athlete's career. For example, because increases in flexibility and skill are possible and appropriate during the early stages of training, it is important to emphasize development in these areas in the programs of beginners.

Having examined the developmental process in further detail, let us now return to the subject of planning and consider the conventional wisdom with respect to the planning of training during the mesocycle (the next unit of training after the macrocycle).

Guidelines for the Amount of Volume a Lifter Can Tolerate

One of the basic rules of weightlifting training (or any other kind of training) is that it must reach a certain threshold of volume in order to have training effect. Beyond that minimum threshold, increases in volume can increase the training effect, up to a point. After that point has been reached, further increases in volume or intensity will not increase the training effect proportionally and, if the volume of training is pushed to extremes, it will tear the body down so much that regression will occur instead of progression. Therefore, while an increase in training volume will stimulate an increase in strength, increasing the training volume is neither the only nor necessarily the best way to achieve improved performance.

Although pushing an athlete's training volume up simply for its own sake (as compared with accomplishing other specific ends by that volume) is seldom a good idea, it is interesting to see where others have been in this regard and what the limits in human ability seem to be in this area. Studies of the volumes handled by elite athletes have been done in many Eastern European countries, particularly the former Soviet Union and Bulgaria (where volume, and many other aspects of weightlifting, may have been pushed further than in any other country in the world).

Clearly the direction of training loads from the 1950s through the 1970s (and, is some cases the 1980s) was in an upward direction. For instance, one study done of Soviet National Teams showed an increase from an average of just under 9,000 reps a year in 1964 to an average of 21,000 reps a year in 1980. In 1972 the average member of the national team trained from three to five times a week, but by the latter half of the 1980s the average number of training sessions had increased to twelve times a week (with most days in the week having multiple training sessions).

At the extreme upper end of volume, average monthly training loads in excess of 4,000 reps (or approximately 50,000 reps a year) have been reported by some high level athletes. (Lifts with weights that are less than 50% or 60% of maximum are not being counted in those totals; some coaches who report lower numbers of reps per year do not count weights that are less than 75% or 80% of the athlete's maximum.) Average monthly loads of up to 3,000 reps per month have been proposed by a number of highly regarded coaches in recent years as a sort of standard for high level athletes. (Some coaches see such levels as representing upper limits, while others see such levels as standard objectives.) Many elite athletes have thrived on average loads of between 1,000 and 2,000 reps per month. (The actual load in a particular month can be as little as half, or as much as double, the average monthly load for a given year.)

It should be noted that some lifters have performed at the elite level with far lighter loads. For instance, Robert Bednarski, 1969 World Champion and many time world record holder, trained at a volume somewhere in the area of 2,000 to 3,000 reps a year at his peak. Clearly, Bob was at the lower end of the volume spectrum while being at the upper limits of the success spectrum.

Indeed, few athletes can train effectively at the upper or lower load levels mentioned above. The vast majority will benefit from training loads that fall between the extremes cited, and each lifter will have a range within which he or she can function most effectively. This tolerable range can be increased over time if the lifter gradually trains himself or herself to accept a larger load (e.g., increasing the overall load 10% to 30% a year with variations among monthly loads being maintained or increased). An athlete's tolerable range of loads can also decline because of aging, injury, cumulative fatigue or if the lifter reduces his or her load and sustains it at that lower level over time. The key point to remember is that the relationship between performance and loads tends to be quite limited (except at the extreme ends of the ranges, where training volumes beneath the lower limit will fail to elicit a training effect and volumes beyond the upper limits will lead to overtraining and injury). More is not necessarily better. and it can often be worse.

One final point with respect to loads bears mentioning. First, there has been speculation in the international weightlifting community that the training loads that were handled in the 1970s and 1980s, when anabolic steroid use was at its peak, cannot be achieved under today's era of drug testing. Therefore, there has been considerable discussion in recent years of training with lesser loads (especially with lower volumes).

The Cuban approach once again demonstrates that there are many ways to "skin" the proverbial cat.

The Monthly Cycle or Mesocycle

The mesocycle that fits within a training macrocycle is generally a training "month." In athletic circles, a month usually consists of four weeks, but some athletic "months" have as few as three or as many as six weeks. Planning on the basis of actual calendar months is virtually unheard of, because most coaches construct their months out of seven-day training weeks (such weeks fit into 4 or 5-week "months" but not into most calendar months).

The placement of a week into the wider framework is essential for effective workout planning. An athlete who repeats the same training week to week is destined for sub-optimal results. It is appropriate neither to attempt maximums every week nor to train at sub-maximum levels week after week. Training sessions with maximum weights and/or large numbers of lifts with near maximum weights simply cannot be repeated week after week. Training week after week with weights that are well below maximum (at least for the number of reps being performed in a given set) will not lead to optimal rates of improvement (except in the case of the beginner).

Different coaches recognize these facts in different ways. When the Bulgarian team trained under the guidance of Abadjiev, he reportedly most often prescribed three weeks of heavy training followed by an "unloading" week of lower volume and intensity. Most of the programs described in the mainstream literature of the former Soviet Union have far more variety from week to week than Abadjiev's, with intricate patterns of loading and intensity which are often repeated in successive months. Medvedyev has indicated that most of the weekly variations in loads center around the following distribution (each number represents the percentage of the month's total load lifted in that week): 35/28/22/15. Naturally, significant variations from such a distribution are recommended by Medvedyev and other authors.

For instance, one common variant is to increase the load from week to week in a four week cycle. So, for example, 14% of the month's load might be lifted in the first week, 25% in the second, 29% in the third and 32% in the fourth week. Therefore, the first week is akin to an unloading week in terms of volume. Weeks two through four are progressively more difficult.

Another variation begins with a relatively low week of loading (e.g., 14%) and then achieves relatively high loadings in the second and third weeks (e.g., 31% in each week), followed by a medium load in the fourth week (e.g., 24%). A third alternative would be to have a small load in the first week (e.g., 14%), almost double the load in the second week (e.g., 26%), increase it further in the third week (e.g., 36%) and then drop off in the fourth week to a load lighter than that lifted in the second week but higher than that of the first week (e.g., 24%).

While quite different in terms of loading patterns and differences from week to week, these approaches do not exhaust the possibilities. They merely illustrate patterns that have been used with success with many athletes. It is important to understand that individual athletes will respond differently to these variations in loading and that the appropriate pattern will depend on the content of the training (e.g., exercises and intensities used) as well as the individual characteristics of the athlete. Therefore, the planning of weekly loads within training months is a challenging aspect of developing the training plan.

In his 1986 book The Training of the Weightlifter, R. Roman suggests that the six most common patterns in the distribution of weekly loads within training months are: a) those that have the highest loading during the first week in the month and then gradually diminish the load during the rest of the month; b) those that have the highest load in the second week of the month with the third and fourth weeks being lower; c) those that have the highest load during the third week, the second highest in the first week and smaller loads in the other weeks; d) those that have a maximum in the first week, nearly as much in the third week and lower amounts in the other weeks ; e) those that have the highest load in the second week, the next highest in the fourth week and the lowest in the first and third weeks; or, f) those that have maximum load in the fourth week, the next highest in the second week 2 and the lightest loads in the first and third weeks. Some examples of monthly loading distributions expressed as percentages of the month's total load are presented in Table 14. (The notation used in the "load structure" indicates the week with the greatest load first and the week with the next largest load next: e.g., 4-2 means the fourth week is the one with the largest load and the second week is the one with the next largest load.)

Roman indicates that for competition months, load variants such as 2-3 or 3-2 in addition to the load structures shown in the above table can also yield favorable results.

While coaches have had success with these and other loading patterns, considerable judgment is required in order to select the proper loading patterns for individual athletes and particular circumstances. For example, if an athlete has recently had a month with a particularly high load, the coach may wish to assure that the first week of the next month is not a maximum week and that maximum loads are not undertaken until at least the second week and perhaps as late as the fourth week in the month.

It is generally believed that, both from the workout and weekly perspectives, a large load produces a training effect, a medium load maintains a training effect that has already been achieved and (at least in the short term) a small loading permits for supercompensation when the body has been previously subjected to large loads. If used continuously over the longer term, small loads lead to detraining.

It must be remembered that the volume, intensity and exercise prescription typically vary within the overall months because different months represent different periods in the macrocycle. Consequently, it may happen that no two weeks within an annual period are identical in terms of volume, load, or even exercises performed, even though the relative loads and intensities within the weeks of the different months may be similar or even the same. (For example, the month's load may be distributed in such a way that 30% of the total load is lifted within the first week of two different months (A and B). but the actual load lifted in the first week of month B may be 10% or 20% different from the load that is lifted in the same week of month A, because the overall load in month B is significantly different from that of month A. Moreover, a high volume week in a low volume month may employ a lower volume than a low volume week in a high volume month.

In order to better compare weeks in different training months and periods, A. Medvedyev has suggested a method for characterizing all weeks regardless of when they occur in the annual training cycle. A "minimum" week has a training content of up to 75 repetitions; a "small" week 76 to 210; an "average" week 211 to 345; a "large" week 346 to 480; a "very large" week 481 to 615; a "maximum" week 616 to 750; and a "stress" week in excess of 751 reps. The annual distribution of the above weeks recommended by Medvedyev is: 2, 11, 21, 13, 3, 1 and 1. Although Medvedyev does not mention it, this categorization of rep loads seems to be appropriate for athletes of a specific level, perhaps CMS. This is because the beginner who is performing only 7,000 reps a year would find even the "average" week depicted above to be a very large load, given his or her average training load. In contrast, for the athlete who is performing 24,000 reps a year, an "average" week's training load would have to be in the "large" to "very large" range for the athlete to reach 24,000 reps in a year.

Table 14

Load Structure	Week 1	Week 2	Week 3	Week 4
Preparatory Period load structures:				
4-2	21	28	17	34
3-1	27	18	32	23
2	20	35	27	18
1-3	32	19	27	22
2-4	22	33	18	27
2	23	32	26	19
1	31	27	23	19
Competitive Period load structures:				
1	36	28	28	12
3-1	29	25	35	11
2	28	33	26	13
1-3	32	26	29	13

Under Medvedyev's loading scheme, more than 40% of the lifter's training is spent with average loads (there are nearly two such weeks in every training month). There is one small and one large week in most training months, and 87% of the weeks in the year fall within the small to large loading range. Weekly loads in the very large to stress range are incorporated only every two months. This is not to say that loads are distributed on this average basis evenly across the year. On the contrary, two weeks of minimal loading might occur in one month because the lifter is taking his or her annual "vacation" away from lifting. In another period of training, two weeks of very large or greater loading might take place in two contiguous months, and then no such loads might occur in two other months. The annual loading distribution merely summarizes the variations in the loads among weeks across the span of a year.

It is my view that most athletes and coaches tend to conform unnecessarily to the notion that the length of the mesocycle is most appropriately four weeks. While their psychological and cultural backgrounds make planning around a seven day week reasonable (though not necessary) choice for most coaches and athletes, there is far less reason to conform to a four-week notion of the mesocycle. In my experience, many athletes benefit from training with mesocycles of three weeks, and some thrive on cycles of five or six weeks, or even longer. Moreover, the same athlete will often benefit from mesocycles of differing length across a year.

The only way to discover an athlete's optimal mesocycle length (and it will vary within the same athlete with different training contents and as a result of other external factors, such as amount of time spent relaxing, etc.) is through trial and error, by observing the athlete's responses to various patterns of weekly and monthly loading. My suggestion is to begin with the shortest cycle (perhaps three weeks) and to try various patterns within such a cycle. Then the coach can expand out to four-week patterns and then try five- and six-week patterns if no great success has been enjoyed with shorter cycles.

More often than not, the coach will discover one cycle length that is generally the most beneficial for each athlete (considering the typical content of that athlete's training) and then he or she can plan around that cycle. However, the coach will also tend to discover that different cycle lengths can be used with success but that the content of the training within the cycle will vary with its length. For example, a given athlete may seem to benefit from a three-week cycle that has a relatively high load but moderate intensity in the first week, a higher intensity but lower volume in the second week and a higher intensity with the same volume in the third week. That same athlete might benefit from three consecutive weeks of high intensity training with the same volume, followed by a week of lower intensity and volume. Knowledge of such patterns permits the coach not only to provide variety in the athlete's training (e.g., by using a three-week cycle at times and a four-week cycle at others) but also to peak his or her athlete properly, even when a competition does not happen to fall along a classic four-week mesocycle.

The Weekly Plan or Microcycle

The formulation of a weekly plan or "microcycle" is one of the most fundamental and important kinds of planning that takes place in weightlifting training. It is within the training week that the coach must become truly specific with respect to the exercises that will be performed within which training sessions.

There are three basic ways to fill in the volumes and intensities on the weekly and workout levels. One approach is what I will call the "classic

271

periodization" method, because it is an extension of the long term periodization concept. Under this method the loads (the total number of repetitions) of the monthly mesocycles and weekly microcycles are filled in on these basis of the repetition numbers that were included in the macrocycle plan. Then the coach fills in the framework of load with various exercises, sets and reps to meet the overall loading objectives. During this process the coach considers whether each month falls within the preparatory, competitive or transitory periods. A greater variety in exercises and repetitions is employed during preparatory months, greater specialization on the classical lifts occurs during the competitive period and general physical preparation may be emphasized during the transitory period.

Given those overall planning constraints, the coach will generally emphasize a relatively greater variety of exercises in a week that calls for a large load than during a week with a smaller load. In addition, more sets per exercise and more reps per set will tend to be performed during such a week. This means of structuring the training has the advantage of offering the athlete great variety in his or her workouts, in that the widest range of training factors changes from week to week. This classic periodization method tends to be favored by many Soviet theorists and coaches, though there are many Soviet specialists who take issue with such an approach.

A significantly different approach to varying loads across months and weeks is to determine the exercises that will be performed first and then to leave those as a relatively fixed factor throughout a given training period. Then the sets and reps within various training periods are varied in order to achieve the appropriate loading. There is much to commend this "fixed exercise" planning approach. First, a limited number of exercises closely related to the classical lifts are typically performed. Employing exercises that are outside of that group has the advantage of creating training variety but the offsetting disadvantage of lack of transferability to the classical lifts. Second, when exercises are not performed on a regular basis, detraining with respect to those exercises tends to occur. When that exercise is later resumed, a renewed training effect must occur. Constant detraining and retraining can place a significant strain on the body's adaptive capabilities. Moreover, it is unlikely that a long term positive adaptation will occur from such training, except, perhaps, in terms of skill development.

Still another advantage of the fixed exercise prescription is the assurance that exercises that are regarded as important will be performed throughout the training cycle, making it more likely that the performance of those exercises will be mastered. Finally, fixing the exercises eliminates one major variable in the exercise-

training experiment. Since the coach varies only the volume and intensity of training (not the exercise content), there are fewer things to consider when assessing the effects of a particular training program. Consequently, it will be easier to differentiate between effective and non-effective volume and intensity configurations.

The great Bulgarian national coach of the 1970s and 1980s, Ivan Abadjiev, favored a relatively fixed exercise regimen. Moreover, the range of exercises performed by the Bulgarian national team narrowed over Abadjiev's career to just six by the end of the 1980s (snatch, clean and jerk, power snatch, power clean and jerk, squat and front squat). Abadjiev appeared to reduce the variety in the other aspects of the training cycle over time as well. He also increased his reliance on multiple workouts per day.

The third main approach to filling in volumes and intensities for months and weeks can be called the "exercise based" method. Under this method, which is preferred by Medvedyev and others, the coach relies on the scope of the exercises included in the lifter's training as the primary means for varying volume. During periods of high volume, a wide variety of exercises are included in the lifter's training. During periods of lower volume, the number and variety of exercises is diminished. Many coaches believe that variety itself is conducive to the development of weightlifting performance, and varying exercises (in addition to varying volume and intensity) is one of the most powerful ways to create variety in training.

Naturally, all of the methods described above are interrelated. The classic periodization planner is generally using both the classic periodization and fixed-exercise methods of varying volumes and intensities, because there are generally at least some intervals in the training plan during which exercises remain fixed and only reps and their intensity vary (whether those intervals are within a week or a month). Similarly, although the fixed-exercise practitioner may maintain the same exercises in the lifter's training for extended periods, those exercises may be changed from macrocycle to macrocycle (as Abadjiev did when he reduced the number of exercises in his arsenal over time). Finally, a coach who favors exercise variety must cast an eye toward volume and intensity constraints, so that the number of exercises selected for each training interval fits within the longer term plan.

It is my contention that none of the approaches described above is ideal because each subordinates the exercises themselves (arguably the most critical training variable) to other variables. The periodization planner subordinates exercise choice to the constraints of the overall plan and uses exercise variety as a means to accomplish the overall periodization process. The fixed-exercise planner assumes that an ideal complex of exercises exists for most or all lifters. The exercise based planner focuses on the need to provide variety with the underlying assumption that variety itself is perhaps the key training variable.

A more effective alternative is to use exercise selection as a means to induce specific ends in terms of technical mastery and the development of physical capabilities rather than as a fixed set of optimal or necessary exercises or as a means to achieve training variety. This concept will be discussed later in this chapter.

Regardless of the method used to arrive at the exercises that will be performed in a given training week, once objectives for exercise frequency and volume have been tentatively established for that week, they must be fit into a plan of some kind for the individual days within the week. For example, if an athlete is supposed to perform snatches three times a week, the next step is to determine on which days the snatches will be performed. Generally speaking, it is advisable to spread the exercise relatively evenly across the week. Therefore, it might be useful to snatch on Monday, Wednesday and Friday (as compared with Monday, Tuesday and Wednesday). Motor skills tend to be better developed when practice is distributed across several days than when it takes place on successive days. In addition, there is the issue of building strength and maintaining conditioning. Strength is better developed and maintained when workouts are spread relatively evenly across the week than when they are concentrated into one portion of the week.

None of the above suggests that a planner must slavishly space workouts as much as possible across a week. At times an athlete may benefit from hard practice in the same lift on consecutive days This is particularly true when the emphasis is on developing a skill. An athlete may have achieved a technical breakthrough on a given day and the trainer may wish to reinforce the new skill by daily practice until the skill has been well reinforced. This may be the case even when continued practice leads to a short term reduction in performance because of fatigue (as long as such fatigue is not leading to a breakdown in the skill being practiced or is not increasing the risk of injury).

The trainer also needs to be aware that the weekly plan, while often convenient, is not necessarily optimal. There are a number of psychological and cultural reasons to adhere to a weekly schedule, and many athletes prefer a weekly schedule. For example, athletes who are working full time may prefer to perform their most arduous workouts on Saturday because they feel most energetic when they have not had to work prior to training. Many athletes prefer Sunday as a day of rest because of family responsibilities or religious practices.

However, not all athletes find themselves in the same position relative to the week. For some athletes Sunday may be the best day for a heavy workout. Others may find an afternoon workout less pleasant than an evening one. Some may find that Monday may be a "down" day after a long weekend of social activity, whereas others may find that Mondays are a great day after a restful weekend.

A coach should also bear in mind that there is certainly no rule of nature that dictates a seven-day week for society in general or for athletes in particular. In fact, I have known many athletes who have found another cycle optimal for them. At times that has applied to me.

Many bodybuilders follow a program which involves training for two or three days consecutively and then resting for one day, regardless of where that takes them in the week. There are those who would argue that bodybuilding and weightlifting are unrelated and that one offers no model for the other. However, I would argue that bodybuilders have gravitated toward such programs at least partially because their training tends to be far more individualized and less institutionalized than the training of weightlifters. It must be remembered that the vast majority of weightlifters (at least before the fall of communism around the world) trained under a system in which weightlifting was a job and weightlifters were coached by professionals. Few professionals (whether coaches or athletes) like to work seven days a week or to have variable hours and workdays. Therefore, it follows that traditional work week patterns crept into the training patterns of athletes who trained under professional conditions.

The lesson to be learned here is that the traditional weekly cycle will be beneficial for many athletes, but variations within weekly cycles should be addressed athlete by athlete, and the coach and the athlete should always be willing to consider that a seven-day week may not be optimal.

Many coaches like to plan a week so that there is a similarity in the load and intensity of all exercises done in a given day (or in training session within the day). As a result, Monday may be a day of moderate load and intensity, while Tuesday might be a day of similar load but higher intensity. Such a coach needs to make a decision regarding the number of heavy or peak days there will be in a week. Some coaches favor only one truly heavy (maximum or near maximum) day a week, while other believe that two or more are necessary. Generally, such a coach will plan the week around the heavy day(s), filling in with medium, light and rest days as appropriate.

In contrast, other coaches hold the view that various days in the weekly cycle do not need to be uniform in terms of their treatment of different exercises. For example, Tuesday might be a light day in the snatch but a heavy day in the squat and a medium day overall in terms of volume and intensity. In fact, many coaches believe that one of their most powerful coaching tools is the ability to structure different training sessions so that one exercise or kind of performance can be emphasized on one day while another kind can be stressed on another. (This concept can be applied to the mesocycles as well, so that while certain weeks have larger loads than others, the intensity and/or load in a particular exercise may be substantial even during a week that has a modest load overall.)

For those who prefer the kind of microcycle that treats loads and intensities relatively uniformly for each exercise on a given day, research and training practices in Eastern Europe provide a great deal of guidance. Many coaches and writers have made recommendations for varying the training load across a week. The way in which the load is distributed depends on the phase of the periodization cycle in which the lifter is training. For example, in his book A System of Multi-Year Training In Weightlifting, A. Medvedyev notes that athletes who are preparing for a competition must follow a special pattern of loading within the pre-competition week in order to assure that they are fully rested and prepared. He cites A. Vorobyev's recommendation that an athlete restrict the load lifted in the week before the competition and that there be only three to four training sessions in that week. If the athlete trains three times, he or she might handle 55% percent of the week's load in a training session six days before the competition, 30% of the week's load in the second training session of the week and 15% of the load in the last training session before the competition. In contrast, for non-competitive weeks, Medvedyev recommends variations such as: large/small/average/small/large (for a week with five training days) and large/average/large/small or large/average/above average/small (for weeks with four training days). For high level athletes who have large overall training loads and are training six days a week with two or more sessions per day, he recommends patterns such as: large/medium/large/small/medium/large, or large/large/small/medium/large/large.

Roman has suggested that a small day is one with 50 reps or fewer; a medium day has 51 to 100 reps and a large loading day has more than 100 reps. These guidelines tend to be more accurate across a wider range of athletes than Medvedyev's weekly loading categories mentioned above. Athletes at lower levels tend to perform fewer workouts per week than more advanced athletes. Nevertheless, the athlete who is lifting only 7,000 reps a year and is training three days a week averages less than 50 reps per workout. Clearly, all of those training sessions cannot be viewed as small loading days for that athlete.

In terms of the arrangement of loads within a week, Roman suggests the following patterns, which vary with the number of training days per week (S = a small load, M = a medium load and L = a large load):

3 days a week: S,L,S; M,L,M; L,S,L; or L,M,L

4 days a week: S-R, L-R, M, S; L-R, M-R, L, M; L-R, M-R, L, S; M-R, M, S; M-R, L-R, M, S.

5 days a week: M, S, L-R, M, S; M, S, L-R, M, M; S, L, S-R, L, S; M, S, M-R, M, S.

6 days a week: S, M, S, M, S, M; M, S, L, S, M, S; M, L, S, M, S, M; M, M, S, M, S, M; M, S, L, S, M, M; S, L, S, L, S, M.

Chenryak has developed guidelines for the distribution of weekly loads based on the number of training days per week. If an athlete is training 3 times a week, he recommends a pattern of 24/28/48 in terms of the percentages of the week's load that are lifted in a given day. For athletes who train 4 times a week, he recommends a pattern of 15/22/28/35. For athletes training 5 times a week, he recommends a distribution of 13/15/15/27/30.

As varied as these load patterns are, they only scratch the surface. Weekly loading patterns have an almost infinite potential for variation. In addition to an enormous range of possibilities for alternating or repeating light, medium and heavy days, there is also a great potential for variation in the structure of the days themselves. For instance, a coach may have found that the medium, light and heavy pattern in training days works very well. However, with a little experimentation, the coach might discover that a somewhat heavier medium day followed by a somewhat lighter light day is equally beneficial. Moreover, if the trainer looks beyond the period of a week into the interrelationship of training sessions in different weeks, he or she is likely to find that weekly variations that recognize variations in prior and subsequent weeks are more beneficial than weeks that are treated more like separate units within a training month.

For coaches who structure workouts in a pattern that is outside the traditional seven-day week, there are even more potential variations in the pattern of weekly loading (especially when the training week is longer than seven days).

The important thing for the coach to remember is that the same weekly cycle will not necessarily work in the same way for every athlete and that the response of the same athletes to a given weekly cycle may change over time. In addition, the same athlete may have different optimal cycle patterns and/or lengths for different exercises. This is because of the unique responses of different athletes to the same exercises, because different exercises affect different body parts to varying degrees and because the recuperation rates of those body parts can vary. This does not imply that a

Table 15

Period One	12-14 Years Old	14-16 Years Old	16 Years & Above
Month One Total	60	70	90
Initial Week	15	18	22
Basic Week	20	23	30
Stressed Week	15	17	23
Test Week	10	12	15
Month Two Total	70	80	114
Initial Week	17	20	26
Basic Week	23	26	40
Stressed Week	18	21	30
Test Week	12	13	18
Month Three Total	80	90	105
Initial Week	20	22	23
Basic Week	25	30	38
Stressed Week	20	23	28
Test Week	15	15	16

coach may not have a basic weekly cycle that applies to most athletes under most conditions. It does imply that the basic weekly cycle may have to be varied for different athletes so that each can optimize his or her training (or at least that relative volumes and intensities in particular exercises may have to be manipulated so that recuperation patterns in different exercises are brought more closely into line).

Other Approaches To Periodization

Bulgarian Periodization Methods

The literature regarding Bulgarian training methods is far more sparse than that on Soviet methods. Most of the sources of information on Bulgarian training methods are lectures given by Bulgarian coaches or reports by coaches and athletes who have emigrated to Western countries from Bulgaria. These lectures and reports paint a picture of lifting cycles which are quite different from those reported in the literature of the former Soviet Union. For example, the Bulgarians work harder (more intensely) and have less variety in their exercises and in their monthly and weekly loads than the Soviets.

When Angel Spassov (the renowned Bulgarian coach who has worked with many high level athletes and lectured on weightlifting training throughout the world) visited the United States in late 1980s, he indicated that annual monthly training loads in terms of tons varied with the age and developmental stage of the athlete. The materials he distributed during his 1989 lecture tour indicated that for ages twelve to fourteen,

monthly loads (in terms of metric tons) were: 30, 60, 70, 80, 65, 75, 85, 70, 80, 90, 10 and 10 (the latter two months represent summer vacations for young Bulgarian athletes). For ages fourteen to sixteen, the monthly loads increased to 40, 70, 80, 90, 80, 90, 100, 90, 110, 100. There was one month off, and competitive weeks followed the fourth, seventh, tenth and eleventh months; hence only ten "training months" were listed. For athletes ages sixteen years and above, the monthly loads were 50, 90, 115, 105, 105, 130, 120, 120, 150, 130 and 85. Athletes up to the age of eighteen were given one month off a year (after that there was only one week off), and competitive weeks followed the same pattern as for the fourteen to sixteen year olds (after the fourth, seventh, tenth and eleventh months). For both the fourteen to sixteen year olds and those sixteen and older, the eleventh month of the year was considered a competition month.

Table 15 summarizes Spassov's guidelines for the weeks that fall within a three-month training cycle, categorized by age.

Within the monthly cycles, weeks follow the patterns which are associated with age as well. For example, in a sixty ton month performed by twelve to fourteen year olds, the weekly loading pattern is: Week I, 15 tons; Week II, 20 tons; Week III, 15 tons; and Week IV, 10 tons.

Another Bulgarian coach, Dimitar Gjurkow, has expressed the progressive loading of young athletes in a somewhat different way. He explains that Bulgarian youngsters do not compete in weightlifting up to age fourteen, but they typically begin their training for weightlifting between the ages of ten and eleven. Their training progresses as shown in Table 16.

Warm-ups remain at fifteen minutes in duration throughout the development of the lifter.

Therefore, at ages ten to eleven, the warm-up comprises 25% of the training session, but by age seventeen it has diminished to 10% of the workout. In contrast, the portion of the workout spent in performing the competitive lifts begins at 10% (six minutes) and increases to 45% (sixty-seven minutes), while the portion of the workout spent on strength training increases from approximately 5% of the workout to 40% (i.e., from approximately three to sixty minutes). In terms of hours per year, the program is summarized in Table 17.

The snatch and C&J are the competitive lifts. Squats, front squats, power snatches, power cleans, power jerks (in front and behind the neck), lifts from the blocks and pulls are considered basic strength exercises. Abdominal exercises and other

and increases 100 tons per weight class until they reach 2500 for athletes in the 108 kg. and superheavyweight categories. The number of maximum attempts is 1400 per year for athletes in the 54 kg., 59 kg., 108 kg. and superheavyweight categories; 1450 for athletes in the 64 kg., 70 kg. and 99 kg. categories; and 1500 for athletes in the 76 kg. to 91 kg. categories. Sets or lifts to refusal are 450 for the 54 kg. to 70 kg. and 99 kg. and above categories, with 460 such sets being performed by athletes in the 76 kg. to 91 kg. categories.

As a group, Bulgarian trainers are probably more committed to distributing their workload across the day than trainers from any other country. They typically arrange the training plan

Table 16

Training Stage:	Age	Trning Wks/Yr.	Wrkts. /Week	Wrkts. /Year	Avg.Wkt. Minutes	Annual Hours
Non-Competitive	10-11	42	4	168	60	168
	11-12	42	5	210	75	263
	12-13	42	5	210	105	368
	13-14	42	5	210	135	473
Sport Perfectioning	14-15	46	6	273	135	621
	15-16	46	6-7	300	135	675
	16-17	46	7-8	345	135	776
Top Class	17+	46	9-11	460	150	1150

forms of remedial exercise are categorized as all around strength exercises.

Gjurkow also provides guidelines for what he suggests are the key measures of training content. They are: total tons lifted (1 ton = 2205 lb.); the number of attempts made at maximum weight; and the number of attempts to refusal. (These are relatively high rep sets—as many as 10 reps— in which the athlete lifts the weight as many times as possible until he or she reaches a point of failure.) The number of lifts in these parameters varies with the body weight of the lifter. Tons lifted per year begin at 1700 for athletes in the 54 kg. category

so that there will be at least three to four days a week with two training sessions. This practice is common throughout Eastern Europe, but the arrangement of these training sessions by the Bulgarians tends to be different. They believe that the time devoted to a particular exercise should be from thirty to sixty minutes (with forty-five minutes the most common training period). They will then often rest for thirty minutes between exercises, performing two to four exercises per session. For example, during the late 1980s when a number of Bulgarian coaches were conducting seminars abroad, one of the programs presented is

Table 17

	Warm-ups		Competitive Lifts		Basic Strength		Remedial Strength		Other Sports	
Age	%	Hrs	%	Hrs	%	Hrs	%	Hrs	%	Hrs
10-11	25	42	10	17	5	8	10	17	50	84
11-12	20	53	10	26	10	26	10	26	50	132
12-13	14	52	15	55	15	55	10	37	46	169
13-14	11	52	20	95	20	95	10	47	39	185
14-15	11	69	25	155	25	155	10	62	29	180
15-16	11	75	30	202	30	202	10	68	19	128
16-17	11	86	35	271	35	271	9	70	10	78
17+	10	115	45	517	40	460	3	35	2	23

depicted in Table 18.

The arrangement of the exercises is not always the same (e.g., sometimes the lifters begin with the lifts instead of squats). The loading and intensity are varied by the height of the maximum lifts for the day, the number of times the athlete goes up and down during the workout and the amount by which the athlete diminishes the weight from the maximum for the day for his or her other sets. (This process was explained in greater detail in Chapter 3).

At least two reasons are given for this arrangement of the training sessions. The first is that spreading the training over the day gives the athlete the greatest opportunity (because of rest periods) to perform at his or her best in more of the exercises performed. The second reason offered is that, according to research performed in Bulgaria, blood testosterone levels become elevated during a training session, but the peak testosterone level achieved during training falls by the end of one hour. A greater number of training sessions permits testosterone levels to be elevated more often, and this facilitates greater progress in training. (Higher testosterone levels have been associated with greater improvements strength and muscle mass.) It should be noted that this exact pattern of testosterone elevation during training sessions has not been reported in the Western literature.

At least one of Abadjiev's leading athletes (a former world champion and world record holder) has opined that the evolution of Abadjiev's training methodology owed as much to social as to theoretical reasons. According to this athlete,

Abadjiev had difficulty controlling the behavior of his athletes when training sessions were conducted only once or twice a day. No matter how hard such training sessions were during the day, the athletes always found a way to "relax" during the evenings and often into the wee hours of the morning. Needless to say, these periods of relaxation often involved activities that were not truly restorative in nature and deprived the athletes of much needed rest and sleep. As Abadjiev expanded the training to include multiple daily sessions (separated by from one-half to several hours), these training sessions, along with other activities of daily living (e.g., eating and bathing), "pedagogical" lectures on training and competition and other organized activities sometimes extended from 7:00 A.M. to 10:00 P.M. With such a long and demanding day, even the most dedicated revelers found it difficult to muster the energy to do anything but sleep when their heads hit the pillow after the last training session of the day (particularly with the prospect of another grueling day ahead).

We may never know for sure how much of a role such considerations played in Abadjiev's thinking, but my source is convinced that it was the foremost consideration in his mind. The athlete supports his contention with the evidence that the athletes who did not follow his all-day program enjoyed similar, if not superior, results.

As was indicated earlier, the Bulgarians typically vary the volume within the training month (particularly in preparatory months) by having three hard (high volume and high intensity) weeks followed by an easy (lower volume and somewhat lower intensity) week. In addition, the overall loading between months varies, with some months being "unloading" months in which there are three weeks with relatively low volume and one maximum loading week.

The Bulgarian coach Gjurkow has argued against macrocycles of less than two months (because little training effect can be generated) or more than five months (because there is not enough opportunity for athletes to compete at a high level with long cycles). He suggests that when an athlete begins a training cycle after a period of active rest, two to four weeks are needed for the athlete to work up to training levels that are approximately 90% of the level previously achieved when that athlete was in peak condition. During this period the athlete emphasizes technique; by the end of this first phase of training, the athlete is working up to maximums for three to five reps. Over the next two months the volume (or at least the intensity) of the training is increased. During this period maximum efforts for as much as six to ten reps are used in some exercises, and repeated efforts at maximum weights are used as well. Then, two to four weeks before a competition, any maximum efforts in high repetition sets are eliminated. The last seven to eight days prior to

Table 18

Session One		
(M, W & F)	**Time**	**Exercise**
	9:00-9:30	Front Squat
	9:30-10:00	Break
	10:00-11:00	Snatch
	11:00-11:30	Break
	11:30-12:30	C&J
	12:30-1:00	Front Squat
Session Two		
(M, W & F)	4;30-5:30	C&J
	5:30-6:00	Break
	6:00-7:00	Snatch
	7:00-7:30	Front Squat
	7:30-8:00	Pulls
Session One		
(Tu, Th & Sa)	9:00-9:30	Squat
	9:30-10:00	Break
	10:00-10:45	Power Snatch
	10:45-11:15	Break
	11:15-12:00	Power Clean
	12:00-12:30	Front Squat
	12:30-1:00	Pulls

the competition, maximum efforts are excluded, and maximum weights lifted are approximately 10 kg. less than those that are normally lifted in training (as much as 20 kg. in non-competitive exercises).

It should be noted that while the Bulgarians do plan the volume of training to be performed during each workout, the methods mentioned above permit a very flexible approach to intensity. The intensity that the athlete can achieve during each training session is discovered as the athlete works up to the heaviest weight possible for that workout. A fatigued athlete will be unable to reach a very high level of intensity during his or her workout, but an athlete who has recovered from prior workouts can push himself or herself to the max.

The Resident Athlete Training Program at the Olympic Training Center in Colorado Springs

When Dragomir Ciroslan was hired as the coach of the Resident Athlete Training program in 1990 (he was subsequently elevated to the position of National Coach of the USAW), he structured a program that was based on the principles that he had developed as coach of the Romanian National Team. However, Dragomir soon modified his overall program for the conditions which exist in the United States and ultimately for the specific athlete. Moreover, he is constantly adjusting the training programs that he prescribes on the basis of the responses of the athletes and as his training philosophy continues to evolve.

In general terms, however, a brief description of the 1994 program follows. (Weights lower than 75% of the athlete's maximum are never counted in the loads used, and they are omitted in the figures presented below.) It should be noted that part of the annual plan for each lifter is based on that lifter's load during the previous year and his or her response to it.

If an athlete successfully handled an average of 1500 lifts a month in 1993, his or her load might be increased by 10% to 15% in 1994 (e.g., to 1700 reps). Such a load might be distributed as follows: Snatch, 135 lifts; C&J, 115 lifts; Jerk, 85 lifts; Jerk Behind Neck, 90 lifts; Front Squat, 300 lifts; Snatch Pull, 200 lifts; Squat, 300 lifts; Clean Pull,

200 lifts; Romanian Deadlifts, 150 lifts; and Push Press Behind Neck, 125 lifts. The athlete might perform a total of 400 reps in the first week, 500 reps in the second week, 350 reps in the third week and 450 reps in the fourth week. During the preparatory period, , the distribution of reps and exercises for a week with 350 reps might be as shown in Table 19.

At times (particularly during the early portions of preparatory periods), higher reps are emphasized, with the athletes performing five reps, or even more, in some exercises. At other times (especially during competitive months), singles are emphasized. There is a significant amount of training in "segments" (the Bulgarian practice of working up to a maximum in a particular lift for the day and then performing a number of sets at that level with intermittent sets that employ 5 kg. to 20 kg. less). According to Dragomir, this training structure permits the identification and then correction of technical errors (it also supplies a powerful training stress that increases an athlete's strength and power). Multiple sets with fixed weights are used, as are pyramiding and alternating sets with higher and lower reps.

Dragomir has developed his own training zones, which he finds more helpful for gauging training intensity and loads than those used by the Soviets. His zones are: 75% to 85%, 86% to 95% and 100%. He attempts to achieve a distribution of the training load in these zones of approximately 60/35/5, respectively. (The stress actually experienced by the athlete with weights in each zone is, of course, a function of the repetitions per set as well as the actual zone in which the training is performed.) When a lower rep week is done, work in the third zone is eliminated and reps in the second zone are reduced, so that such a week is truly an unloading week. In contrast, the fourth week is typically a stress week,, and the total number of reps in the two higher zones is increased. During the competitive period, loads are reduced, and the distribution of exercises is altered. More emphasis is placed on the classical lifts, and the number of pulls and squats is reduced.

Jumping is typically performed twice a week during such a period, and abdominal work is performed after nearly every workout, though the load performed in these exercises is not counted in

Table 19

Day:	Monday	Tuesday	Wednesday	Thursday	Friday	Saturday
Exercise:	Squat - 25	Fr Sq - 25	Squat - 35	Fr Sq - 15	Fr Sq - 35	Squat - 15
	Jk - 15	PP - 15	Sn Pl - 15	Remedial	Cl Pl - 25	Sn Pl - 15
	Sn Pl - 20	Sn - 15	Jk BN - 15	exercises	Hypers	C&J - 15
	Hypers	Cl Pl - 15	RDL - 20			RDL - 15
		Hypers	Hypers			Hypers

the overall load.

The 1994 training program has been significantly modified across the years and there is more individualization today than there was at that time.

For example, it was reported in the October 1996 issue of Milo Magazine that in the weeks preceding the Olympics at least one of the athletes from the Olympic Training Center trained only 4 days per week. On Monday mornings he would do squats, military or push presses and/or some snatch pulls. In the evening, he would perform heavy snatches and snatch pulls. On Wednesdays, he'd front squat and then military press, push press or pull. In the evening he went heavy in the C&J. Friday would be a replay of Monday's workout and Saturday he might do power snatches or power cleans. The emphasis was on being rested for the Games and this rest obviously paid off. Virtually all of the resident athletes had outstanding performances at the Olympics

Gayle Hatch's Training Programs for Blair Lobrano and Buster Bourgeois

Two of the hottest prospects in the American weightlifting scene are Blair Lobrano (who broke all of his Junior American records and took fifth place at the 1994 Junior World Championships and placed second at the 1997 National Championships) and Buster Bourgeois (who broke all of his Junior American records and placed eighth in the same competition at the age of seventeen). They are members of the Gayle Hatch Weightlifting Club. Gayle Hatch has been active as a weightlifting and strength coach for twenty years. His club has won the team competition at many Junior National Championships in recent years, as well as three Senior National Championships. Gayle has also had at least one athlete on three out of the last four United States Olympic teams.

He has honed his approach to training over many years of day-to-day work with young athletes. He bases his approach on the classic periodization model, with preparatory and competitive periods and mesocycles that are four weeks in length whenever possible. During each mesocycle there will typically be three weeks of heavy loading followed by one unloading week.

Six weeks before the 1994 Junior World Championships, Gayle shifted his mesocycle to three weeks in length, with two weeks of heavy loading followed by an unloading week. During the course of the year preceding the Junior World Championships, Blair Lobrano lifted a total of 21,000 reps with weights that were 75% of his maximum or more. Fifty-five percent of Blair's reps were in the 75% to 85% range, 40% were in the 90% to 95% range and the remaining 5% were in excess of 95% (more recently 55% of the reps have

been in the 75-87.5% range and 40% have been in the 87.5-95% range)

Buster Bourgeois' training was similar to Blair's, except that Buster's total number of repetitions during the year was significantly lower. The reason for this is that Buster was playing football during this period. For the twelve weeks of the football season, Buster reduces his training to two to three sessions a week. This enables him to maintain his conditioning both for football and weightlifting during the season.

Gayle's lifters perform segment work in the classic lifts. However, while they perform many singles, they do many doubles and triples as well. (Gayle feels that these reps are key factors in of strength development.) During the preparatory period, Gayle's lifters do a significant number of squats and pulls in sets of five repetitions.

Blair and Buster (when the latter was not playing football) trained nine times a week (six days, with two of those days having two workouts). They used a wide variety of exercises, including: the classic lifts, power snatches, cleans and jerks, overhead, front and back squats, snatch and clean pulls, jerks from the rack, push presses, jerk lockouts and recoveries, jerk drives, presses, Romanian deadlifts, step ups, single leg squats, hyperextensions, good mornings, abdominal work and jumps.

When Gayle's athletes move from the junior to the senior ranks, he believes in reducing the number of exercises they perform and focusing their training efforts more on the classic lifts and related exercises. There is a reduction of approximately 1000 reps in annual volume as a consequence of this change.

Gayle also believes in careful supervision of his charges. He observes virtually every workout, carefully adjusting the planned load for the condition of the lifters on that day.

While there is no doubt that the training programs that Gayle uses are effective, as an outsider looking in, I would have to say that much of the success that Gayle and his athletes have enjoyed stems from the attention that he devotes to the mental aspects of the sport. He inculcates a team spirit in his charges. His gym is steeped in symbols of the team's success. Gayle has had banners made to represent each of the approximately 40 national level championships (AAU Junior Olympic through Sr. National) which his teams have won. An athlete raised in such an environment cannot help but be awed by the tradition that he or she is joining. But Gayle does not overlook the importance of individual achievement. A variety of boards record the personal records and rankings of individual athletes. Who would not be motivated by the opportunity to change the numbers next to his or her name?

As is so often the case, the contributions that a great coach makes often extend beyond the reach of the athletes whom he or she helps directly. Denis Snethen, coach of the Wesley Weightlifters, the 1995 Men's Senior National Champions, says that he has patterned much of what he has done with his club after Gayle Hatch's program. What greater honor could there be than to be beaten by a team you inspired? Despite the honor, no doubt Gayle will be working to see that he is not "honored" by Denis' team too often in the future.

The Training Of The Greek Team Prior To the 1996 Olympics

The Greek weightlifting team had a spectacular performance at the Atlanta Olympic Games. Virtually all of the athletes on the team made personal records and many of those records were world records as well. As a team, the Greeks were physically and mentally well prepared and exhibited a tremendous team spirit, as well as a deep respect for coach Christos Iakovou.

Mr. Iakovou, was a excellent lifter in his own right (he placed 5th in the 1972 Olympics). He had been living in the US for a number of years when he was asked to return to Greece to prepare the team for Atlanta. It turned out to be one of the best investments the Greek Weightlifting Federation has ever made.

How did the Greek team prepare for the Games? After a two week transitional period of relatively moderate training during the last half of January, the team began what was the first of four competitive cycles prior to the Atlanta Games.

The four cycles were quite similar in terms of exercises employed (coach Iakovou agrees with the Bulgarians in terms of focusing on the classic lifts and squats as compared with having very complex exercise configurations and repetition arrangements). This can be seen by studying Table 20, which depicts the exercises employed by the Greek team during the first of the competitive cycles.

During the second cycle, morning workouts were added to Tuesday and Thursday (the same workouts as the first cycles' Monday and Wednesday workouts). However, during the second cycle, Wednesday morning and Saturday morning workouts were changed so that the athletes squatted first, then power snatched and power cleaned and finished with front squats. In addition, the optional exercise that was permitted for each athlete during the first cycle (e.g., a press or pull) on Monday, Wednesday and Friday afternoons was eliminated. Instead, the C&J was performed a 2nd time at the end of Monday's workout (so the workout sequence was: snatch, C&J, squat and C&J). In a similar way, the snatch replaced the optional exercise on Friday (the optional exercise was eliminated entirely from the Wednesday afternoon workout). Finally, a Saturday afternoon workout was added which included the snatch, C&J and front squat. The exercise pattern of the second cycle was essentially continued during the third and fourth cycles.

The athletes typically employed 6-7 sets of 2 reps as they warmed up and lifted loads in the 80-85% of maximum range during each workout. When snatches were performed for 2 reps the first rep was lifted from the floor and the second rep was lifted from knee level. In the C&J, when 2 reps was called for, the athlete did one clean and two jerks.

Weights 90% or higher were lifted for singles. Generally, once a lifter hit his maximum for the day the lift was repeated no more than once (it appears that as many as three attempts at a maximum were permitted). A finishing set with 5-10 kg. less than the maximum for the day was done after most exercises. The athletes took a 30 minute break between exercises in the middle of each workout.

The athletes tested their limits on the classical lifts, front squats and back squats in mid-February, mid-March and Mid-April (with unloading weeks preceding the March and April tests). The results of each test were used to establish goals for the next mesocycle.

In mid-April there were three weeks of loading followed by an unloading week. Then there were four weeks of loading followed by an unloading

Table 20

	Monday	Tuesday	Wednesday	Thursday	Friday	Saturday
Mornings	Squat		Squat		Squat	Squat
(10:00 AM-	Snatch		Snatch		Snatch	Snatch
12:30 PM)	C&J		C&J		C&J	C&J
	Fr. Squat		Fr. Squat		Fr. Squat	Fr. Squat
Evenings	Snatch	Snatch	Snatch	Snatch	Snatch	
(5:00 PM-	C&J	C&J	C&J	C&J	C&J	
730 PM)	Squat	Squat	Squat	Squat	Squat	
	Optional Ex	Snatch	Optional Ex	Snatch	Optional Ex	
		Fr. Squat		Fr. Squat		

week, then four more weeks of loading followed by a test in mid-July. Unloading weeks essentially had 9 workouts per week instead of 12 and all weights are reduced approximately 10 kg. from the prior week.

The mid-July test was approximately 10 days away from the competition and included a maximum in the front squat as well as in the snatch and C&J. Light days (approximately 60% of maximum) were alternated with heavy days after the 10th day. On the 8th and 6th days out the workout was similar to the 10th day except that the back squat and C&J were performed with 10 kg. less than the 10th day. The lifters worked up to approximately their starting attempts on the 4th day out and went relatively light thereafter until the competition.

It is important to note that throughout the training process the athlete had goals for each workout as well as the overall training cycle. Records were maintained for each athlete with respect to how he performed relative to goal is the snatch, C&J, squat an front squat. These were goals and it was not expected that every athlete would be able to perform at the level of the goal each day. There were often days in which the athlete lifted weights that were well below or above the goal (e.g., during the two months prior to the 1996 Olympics, Leonidis Sabinas lifted as much as 20 kg. more and as much as 10 kg. less than goal in the snatch on a given training day, but overall, he performed close to the daily goals throughout that training cycle). However, each athlete had something to strive for each training day and cycle. Careful goal setting obviously played an important role in the preparations of the Greek team for the Games.

Training Methods Employed In Cuba

During the 1960's and 1970's, Cuba emerged as a world power in weightlifting. Learning from their Soviet teachers very well, the Cuban coaches then added a number of their own "twists" to the Soviet methods, gradually forming their own unique approach over time. The Cubans have managed to dominate weightlifting in the Western hemisphere over the past two decades with a population and resources that are a mere fraction of what is available in the US - a great tribute to Cuba's coaches and athletes.

There has not been a great deal written about the Cuban training methods outside that country and virtually nothing outside Cuba and the former Easter bloc countries. Recently, some information has become available and it suggests a very well thought out approach to training.

The Cuban team trains in what is one of the largest, if not the largest, single facility designed for weightlifting in the world. With 60 platforms, it is a dream for the weightlifting fan (except that it

is hard to observe what is going on the entire facility from any one vantage point and there is no air conditioning despite the tropical climate).

The Cubans typically train nine times per week (twice per day on Monday, Wednesday and Friday and once per day on the alternate days - normally there is no training on Sundays). The morning workouts take place at 10:00 am and the afternoon workouts at 4:00 PM. The morning workouts are relatively light and short. They are followed by lunch and rest for a few hours (including a 2.5 hour nap). In addition, the Cuban athletes typically sleep between 8.5 and 9.5 hours per night. There is also an emphasis on relaxation after workouts through such activities as movies and lectures. Consequently, these athletes are well rested

Most training sessions are performed with weights that are approximately 80% of maximum. Such weights are typically lifted for sets of 3 repetitions. When an athlete uses 90% of maximum, he or she generally performs doubles. Two to four weeks before a competition the athletes will lift a maximum for a single.

When competitions are not imminent, the athletes will occasionally lift as much as 90% of maximum for three sets of three reps to load their bodies. Alternatively, they will go as high as 95% for a single (only on relatively rare occasions will a lifter attempt a maximum single in training). Straps are used during training most of the time (their use is discontinued approximately 2-4 weeks from a major competition.

The coaches prepare plans for each athlete for each workout. The athletes are free to go heavier than planned during the Monday, Wednesday and Friday workouts, but are expected to follow the plan exactly on the other days (to avoid overtraining).

Squats are generally performed only 4 times per week. Some other assistance exercises are also performed regularly (such as good mornings and high pulls), so the workouts of the Cuban lifters appear to be more varied than those of the Bulgarians. But the Cubans hardly fall into the Medvedyev camp in terms of variability of exercises. Certainly their system works well for them

Integrating Long And Short Term Planning

Many coaches rely on long term planning to form the foundation, filling in the details of ever shorter periods of training on the basis of the decisions that were made regarding the longer term plan. Other coaches plan only the next workout or week on the basis of the athlete's present condition. Yet neither of these approaches is optimal because both short and long term planning are necessary to achieve optimal results. Therefore the key to successful planning is to employ both methods. Many expert coaches who use the long or short term approach as their basis for planning learn to compensate for the deficiencies of the approach they use (the long term planner by making adjustments as he or she goes along to assure that the long term plan does not sacrifice the short term needs of the athlete, and the short term planner by assuring that any short term plan will fit into the longer term needs of the athlete). But such an approach relies on the "gut" of the coach to recognize when adjustments are made. The less experienced coach, or the more experienced one who does not wish to rely completely on his or her instincts to tell him or her when things are going astray, needs a more explicit method for resolving conflict between long and short term plans.

What method is there for doing this? Surely a coach cannot do both forms of planning at the same time. If short and long term planning are performed separately, how does the coach tie the results of both processes together? Moreover, when each method implies different training prescriptions, which method should have precedence? These are difficult questions, some of which cannot be answered scientifically. They are at the root of the art of coaching. Nevertheless, there are some important guidelines that help lead the coach through these difficult judgments. Three key processes underlie the effective coordination of long and short term approaches to planning: a) identification of the objectives of a specific period of training on the basis of the individual needs of the athlete; b) applying the techniques of long and short term planning in the proper sequence; and, c) using iteration between the long and short term perspectives to integrate them together into a unified and effective whole.

Set Objectives First

Before any training plan is formed, the athlete and coach must both understand and agree on the objectives they are trying to accomplish during a particular period of training and the hierarchy of those objectives. If it is believed that the athlete must reach certain training volumes in order to achieve success, that objective must be considered when the training plan is formulated. If is important to achieve specific results at certain points during the training period, that must be considered as well. The planner must also consider where the lifter is today and what his or her previous reactions to training have been. Then all of these considerations must be placed in a hierarchy of some kind. It is difficult to emphasize everything at once, and there will probably be a need to make some trade-offs among objectives, which can only be done effectively once priorities have been established. In setting objectives, the outline of the developmental process that was presented earlier should provide an appropriate framework for the long term aspects of the planning process. The short term perspective of the planning process should be founded on a different set of objectives, that of exploiting the greatest opportunities for growth that a given athlete has at point in time.

We have all heard the very wise adage that "a chain is only as strong as its weakest link." This is particularly true in the sport of weightlifting, wherein all of the necessary characteristics of the mind and body must be developed harmoniously in order for peak performance to occur. However, on reflection, I think that the "weak link" concept has a flaw. The flaw is not in the validity of the phenomenon that is being described, but, rather, in how it is framed. In the weak link analogy, the focus is on the negative: the weak. In reality, the focus should be just the opposite. It should be on the opportunity for rapid growth that is afforded by areas that have not attained as high a level of development as others.

To make this point clearer, consider the example of a lifter who is able to pull to the shoulders in the clean 5% more than he or she can stand up with. (The lifter can clean 150 kg. and pull to the shoulders 157.5 kg.). Let us further assume that this lifter can jerk nearly 8% more from the racks than he or she can pull to the shoulders (170 kg.). One way to view the situation is that the lifter is weak in the legs and must work harder (almost as a form of punishment) to improve his or her leg strength. The other approach is to look at the wonderful opportunity that is afforded by this lifter's situation. A concentrated effort on one area is likely to bring immediate and dramatic results in the lifter's total. In fact, no amount of effort in any other area can be as effective.

If the lifter improves his or her jerk, there will be no immediate improvement in the lifter's performance in the C&J, no matter how much improvement the lifter makes. In the clean the situation is only a little better. If the lifter improves his or her pulling power by 5% or 10%, the effect on the lifter's best clean is likely to be minimal. This is because most lifters can pull to the shoulders 10% to 20% more in the squat clean than they can power clean (the lifter described in this example is in this range, with a best in the power clean of 135 kg.). Therefore, even if the lifter improves his or her pulling power by 10%, he or she will not be able to power clean as much as he or she was able to squat clean initially. In fact, without improving leg power, the lifter would have to improve pulling power by nearly 13% (to a 152.5 kg. power clean) in order to clean more than before. (Somewhat less of an improvement in the pull might make the pull easy enough for the lifter to clean a little more in the squat style than before without any improvement in his or her leg power, because an easier pull gives a lifter a greater opportunity to position the bar and body optimally for recovery from the full squat position and to utilize the elastic qualities of the leg muscles in recovering from the low squat position.)

Therefore, instead of focusing on the negative and all it entails, the lifter should focus on the positive. The lifter should not necessarily, nor exclusively, be thinking that he or she is weak in the legs; rather, he or she should focus on the terrific opportunity that exists to improve his or her C&J by focusing on the legs. This may be a subtle difference, but it can have a very real effect on the psyche of the lifter. Some lifters become motivated by negative statements regarding their "weaknesses" and rise to the challenge to eliminate weaknesses. But many other lifters would benefit from the much more positive viewpoint of exploiting available opportunities for growth.

Regardless of whether you accept the "weak link" or "opportunities for rapid growth" perspective, the point is the same. The coach and lifter must identify the lifter's most urgent short term and address those aggressively through the short term planning process.

Once long and short term objectives have been set, it is useful in virtually all planning to follow a specific sequence that considers both the short and long term aspects of planning. However, regardless of how effective a specific sequence is, there is a need to perform planning "iterations" (i.e., to cycle back and forth from long to short term planning frameworks in order to modify each in view of the insights contributed by the other). That process is outlined in the next few sections of this chapter.

Next Take the Long Term View to Find Your Constraints

Once objectives have been set, it is useful to begin creating a long term perspective on the plan. One of the advantages of formulating a long term plan is the wide-angle perspective that it requires the planner to employ. Such a perspective makes it more likely that the planner will see the forest as well as the trees. Perhaps the primary virtue of establishing the long term plan first is that it provides important guidelines for the short term planning process, assuring that short term actions do not undermine the more important longer term objectives.

Taking the long view assures correct timing of certain types of training by placing all training in the context of ultimate goals and objectives. For example, an athlete may well benefit from altering his or her technique in the jerk. However, it is likely that the athlete will take several weeks to begin to perform the new technique properly and at least several months for the athlete to automate the process sufficiently for it to hold up with maximum weights. In such a case, the coach would

not undertake an effort to modify the athlete's technique if a major competition were three months away, a fact that the long term plan would make evident. Naturally, if there is always an "important" competition in three months, some adjustment must be made in terms of performance expectations for certain of those competitions so that the lifter's problem in the jerk can be corrected.

Taking the long view also enables the coach to establish a cutoff date, after which experimentation with the new technique must cease. If, under an initial plan, the intent was to learn the new technique over a period of six to eight weeks and then to automate it over a period of four to six months, the coach might well decide that if the new technique is not being performed correctly at the end of twelve weeks, the adoption of the new technique will be postponed until the athlete's schedule next offers a long break before any major competition. Alternatively, the athlete might decide to pass on the planned competition or to accept a lower level of performance in order to continue working on the new technique. Prior planning helps to assure that such decisions are made carefully and consciously, not out of desperation and at the last minute.

The long term plan can take the process described above a step further by enabling the coach to develop a sequence in the development of the lifter. For instance, the coach might wish to correct several elements of the lifter's technique in the jerk. However, the correction of one aspect requires the prior correction of another. The discipline of the long term planning process can assure that changes are conducted in the proper order and that the timing of the changes appears reasonable. The same sequential approach can be used in building up the training load that the lifter will handle each year (assuming that the coach believes that such a build-up is appropriate for the development of the athlete).

When an athlete uses a long term peaking process to prepare for a maximal effort (a form of periodization), the long view helps to assure that the peaking process will begin at the proper time.

One final advantage of beginning with a long term plan (or at least a long term perspective) is that it prevents a lifter's load and/or intensity being increased too fast and helps the coach to discover when those training variables are bumping up against the lifter's limits. If the coach thinks only short term, he or she can ignore the cumulative effect of training (e.g., failing to realize that a few more sets here and there can add up to a disaster over time or that the "random" occurrence of injuries is not so when the incidence is viewed from a longer term perspective).

It is easy for the coach or athlete who looks only at the short term plan to focus on what the athlete seems to require at the moment. If more snatches are needed, as many as seem to be needed to arrive at a certain result are added. However, if the coach does not take a longer term view, this can lead to week after week of heavy loading without any respite. Such a process can lead to overtraining and even injury, if the change in the lifter's added load is significant enough and continues for a long enough period.

In a sense, then, a training plan is much like a business plan. You do not make a plan because you expect things to conform exactly to that plan (if anything, you hope for an even better outcome). Rather, the purpose is to trace out what will happen if the "best guess" outcome occurs, as well as some better and poorer alternatives. In addition, you make a plan in order to establish goals for a given period. Finally, you use the plan as a reference point for making adjustments. If you define goals and sub-goals for a given period, then you can see how progress is being made along the way. You can then see whether more attention needs to be devoted to a certain area and whether things can be accelerated somewhat since goals are being achieved faster than was anticipated. You can also see whether the goals originally established are proving to be too optimistic and whether downward adjustments need to be made in order to protect the lifter from overtraining and injury and to increase the likelihood that later progress will get the lifter back on schedule.

This should not be interpreted to suggest that any plan can or should be expected to move forward smoothly. Training does not proceed in a straight line of upward progression, and it rarely moves in a precise upward progression punctuated by precisely recurring peaks and valleys. Rather, there are unexpected peaks and valleys, and overall progress at a certain rate is far from a given. This does not mean that the lifter should not seek a smooth progression. It is just that failure to proceed that way in the short term should not necessarily lead to a complete revision of the total plan (although significant deviations over time should).

Once Constraints Have Been Established, Focus Intensely on Short Term Planning

Once the bare bones, long term plan or "macrocycle" has been formulated, it is time to focus on short term planning. There are a number of ways to do this. Perhaps the most popular method is to work toward increasingly shorter time frames on the basis of the plan already established for a longer time interval. Using this approach, once the macrocycle has been planned, the coach fills in the details (volume and intensity) of the mesocycle; then volumes and intensities for the weeks within the mesocycles are established. Finally, the same process is followed for allocating volumes and intensities within the workouts that are planned for a particular week.

Within the broad framework supplied by the macrocycle and the general structure of the mesocycles (the period into which they fit and the loads that the athlete is expected to handle), planning should start with and emphasize the nature of the exercises the athlete will perform in the near term, chosen on the basis of the individual needs of each athlete. Why begin with exercise selection? Because the arsenal of exercises at the coach's disposal offers the broadest available means for influencing both the technical preparation and physical conditioning of the athlete (i.e., what the athlete will do is at least as important as how he or she will do it). After planning the exercises, the trainer must review the planned exercises from the standpoint of load and variety, then evaluate their likely effect to arrive at the final exercise prescription.

This too should be an iterative process, with the trainer first planning the exercise mix, then filling in the load planned for each exercise on the basis of what is needed to achieve improved results overall and in those exercises, then looking at the interrelationships between the loads that are contributed by the training on each of the exercises and assessing their likely effect on one another as well as their overall effect. Finally, noting that the work load is either too high or low, the trainer may go back to alter the load planned for certain exercises or to add or delete certain exercises. This process may be carried out several times, until the coach feels that the optimal plan has been formulated.

It is critical during this phase of planning to consider the individual athlete's characteristics and responses to training. Some lifters flourish under a constant variety of training stimuli. Changes in training days, venues and exercises are quite welcome to some athletes. Other lifters seem much more comfortable with and responsive to a regular pattern of training (e.g., light on Monday and Thursday, heavy on Tuesday and Saturday and medium on Wednesdays and Fridays). In addition, as was suggested earlier, the optimal length and nature of the various periods will vary with the lifter. Some will prosper with very long cycles, and others will benefit from periods that are half the normal length or less. Similarly, some lifters will benefit from periods that vary only in terms of emphasis, while others will respond well to rather major changes in exercises, volumes and intensity during various training phases.

Resolving Conflicts Between Short and Long Term Plans

At times apparent conflicts arise between the short and long term plans. When this occurs, a method for resolving these conflicts must be applied.

Perhaps the best method involves placing the problem into the specific context of the ultimate (long term) interest of the athlete, i.e., his or her career. By considering the likely effects of shorter and longer term training plans, a clearer picture is developed.

For instance, performing extra sets or heavier sets in the snatch during a given workout, or even over a series of weeks, may be beneficial when the coach and lifter seem to be "on to something." Perhaps the lifter has been working to correct a technique flaw for many months, or even years, without success. Suddenly a new approach is tried, and the lifter is making real progress in perfecting the new technique. If there are no important competitions around the corner and the load in snatches thus far has not been unusually high, there is likely to be no harm and much benefit in doing the extra snatches to reinforce this new technical breakthrough. On the other hand, if a key competition is pending or the lifter is already significantly overtrained, doing the extra snatches may conflict with the original objectives of the long term plan, i.e., performing well at an upcoming competition.

Resolving this conflict becomes easier when the coach and athlete consider career goals. If performance at the upcoming competition is truly critical (e.g., if it represents that lifter's likely last chance to make an Olympic team or to qualify for a special training camp in which any technique flaws stand a better chance of being corrected), then the opportunity to correct the lifter's flaws in the snatch may properly be subordinated to the need to prepare for the upcoming competition.

If the upcoming competition is not expected to play a particularly important role in the lifter's career (e.g., if the lifter is qualified to participate but is not expected to place high or has already attained a similar placement in the past), it may be more important to correct a major weakness which might significantly change his or her long term performance. In such a case, the true career interests of the athlete may be better served by exploiting the opportunity to make the technical improvement, even if that means changing the long term plan. Naturally, in making such a decision, the coach and athlete must consider a wide range of effects. If the lifter's work to improve his or her snatch technique were to result in a poorer performance at the Nationals, would that set the lifter's enthusiasm back so far that any benefit would be offset? Is the breakthrough likely to be substantial enough to justify forgoing peak performance at an important competition? Is there some way to maintain some of the benefits without placing performance in the competition at risk? Once clear answers have been secured, the coach and athlete are in a position to make a decision that will serve the best interests of the athlete.

Seeing the Sport of Weightlifting as a Triathlon: A Key to Effective Short Term Planning

All of the means for planning the training of a weightlifter share an underlying similarity: a focus on process. The coach who plans workouts on the basis of varying loads through complex means (i.e., intensities, volumes and exercises) is operating on the premise that cyclical variety will produce favorable results. Similarly, coaches who follow a fixed-exercise approach to planning and those who use variety in exercises as a means to vary an athlete's training are focusing on the process of varying loads or exercises as the chief means to improve performance.

A fundamentally different approach to planning the training of an athlete is to focus on the aspects of each competitive exercise that an athlete needs to improve in order to improve performance and then to focus on the athlete's improving performance in the most critical and/or most fundamental of those areas. A coach who employs this approach uses variations in loads, intensities and exercises to accomplish specific effects in terms of the performance of the classical lifts. Therefore, the individual needs of each athlete determine which exercises are required in a given series of workouts. The nature of these needs is determined by the lifter's developmental status (e.g., age, skills and physical conditioning). For example, for technical and conditioning reasons, a particular lifter may require more practice in the jerk in order to push the lifter's body to a new level of adaptation. These needs will be considered in selecting the exercises that are most appropriate for correcting the lifter's technical flaw(s) and in determining the load of those and other jerk related exercises in terms of training stress.

For purposes of planning a lifter's training, it is very helpful to regard the sport primarily as a triathlon consisting of the snatch, the clean and the jerk. The logic of regarding the snatch and the jerk as separate lifts is obvious. Regarding the clean and the jerk as two separate lifts is less common. For planning purposes, the clean and the jerk should be viewed as two distinct lifts, linked only by the fact that they are performed in immediate succession in the competition. While many of the same muscle groups are used in a similar way in all three lifts, there are many differences as well. The exact combination of muscles used in each movement of the clean and the jerk is different; so are the sequences of force applications, the joint angles that are traversed and the lines of force that are experienced by the athlete. Moreover, there are virtually no exercises which improve both the clean and the jerk in the same way and to the same extent (even the C&J itself). While it is vital for the lifter to practice the clean and jerk together, more progress can generally be made on the overall lift by placing a separate emphasis on the clean and the jerk in at least certain phases of training. In essence, the coach should identify what the lifter needs to do in order to improve his or her snatch, clean and jerk. The exercises, the load and the points to concentrate on should all be planned separately. Then, particularly before a competition, the coach should look for opportunities to combine the clean and jerk into one lift.

The only major exception to this mode of planning should occur when the lifter notably falters in either the clean or the jerk when they are performed together rather than separately. For example, the typical lifter who can comfortably jerk what he or she cleans in competition generally jerks 5% to 10% more from the rack (assuming that an equal effort is put forth in that exercise and in the C&J). If a lifter cleans 100 kg. and jerks 110 kg. from the rack, then fails to jerk 100 kg. after the cleans, that lifter probably needs more practice in the C&J. Such practice, if properly focused on the rapid and complete transition in the athlete's mental and physical preparedness from the clean to the jerk, should quickly develop optimal performance in both phases of the lift.

In using the triathlon perspective, the coach identifies the optimal training to be performed for each event, assuming that the other events will not be performed. (It is clear that in most cases a lifter who "specializes" in such a way will perform better in his or her specialty.) There is great value in understanding just what the optimal training routine will be for each classical exercise. This planning should be very complete and should consider exercise selection, the frequency with which particular exercises and workouts are scheduled and loading considerations (e.g., volume, intensity and number of repetitions per set). Once the coach has planned separately the training on the three lifts, he or she should then begin to look at the overall training sessions and consider how the lifts may complement or interfere with one another. For instance, a lifter may be experiencing difficulty with the second and third phases of the pull in both the snatch and the clean (for the same or different reasons). When planning the training for each lift, the coach may therefore create training programs that include a significant number of clean deadlifts standing on a raised platform and snatch deadlifts. When combined (as they will be in practice), these independently planned programs will place a large load on many of the same muscle groups in much the same way. This is likely to be counterproductive, especially when the change in loading from one to the next is substantial.

Faced with a situation in which exercise programs that were developed for each separate lift conflict with one another, the coach has several options. One is to emphasize only one of the lifts during the program. If it is determined that improving the starting strength and position of the snatch is more important at this time, the snatch might be emphasized and the clean deadlifts postponed to a later point in the training sequence.

A second approach is to employ both exercises but to use a smaller volume in one and a larger volume in the other, so that the combined change in volume and the resulting total volume are not too great. A third approach is to employ both exercises but to use a smaller volume of each than was originally planned, once again ensuring that the combined change in volume and the resulting volume are not too great. A fourth approach is to alternate the exercises for periods within the cycle; the snatch start might be emphasized during the first three weeks of a given cycle and the clean start during the next three weeks, and so on until the cycle is over. A fifth approach is to increase the training on both exercises but the to cut back to a smaller load after two to four weeks, so that the body has an opportunity to adapt gradually to the new stress level.

Once the relationships between exercises have been considered and adjusted for as necessary, the total load presented by the modified plan needs to be evaluated. Individual muscle groups are subject to the overstress from too drastic a change in training (with the unhappy consequence of overuse injuries). In addition, the total load imposed on the organism can have its own effects. If the overall load imposed on the organism is too great, the body can go into a state of overtraining with very negative consequences. (A discussion of overtraining is presented later on in this chapter.) Once the program has been adjusted to the proper level in terms of load, it can be implemented. But once implementation is under way, the coach must monitor the program's effects, so that adjustments can be made as needed.

How to Select Exercises: Balancing Specificity with Variety

Hundreds, perhaps thousands, of exercises have been used by weightlifters in an attempt to improve their performance. Some have yielded great benefits and others have actually led to a decline in performance. A wide array of widely used exercises, along with some general appraisals of their effectiveness, has been outlined in Chapter 5. However, generalized evaluations, regardless of their validity, will certainly not apply in all cases. An exercise that is usually effective may not be of help to an individual athlete at a particular point in time. Similarly, an exercise that is generally a waste of time can be helpful to a lifter at a given point in time. Therefore, special adaptations for particular circumstances, based on observation and experimentation, will often have to be made.

Some basic exercises which should always be included in a lifter's training. Unless the lifter is injured or taking an active rest, no week (and for some lifters not more than three or four days) should go by without the lifter's having done front and/or back squats, the classic lifts and/or power versions of them (e.g., snatches and/or power snatches). The only exceptions to this rule are when an athlete has injuries or physical limitations that preclude such frequency and when the athlete is in a phase of training that emphasizes recuperation from previous efforts, injuries or overtraining (e.g., during the classic transitional period). Otherwise, the aforementioned exercises are the lifter's stock in trade. Why?

The classic lifts define weightlifting. They are what it is all about. Athletes must practice their events, both for motor skill development and to condition the body to withstand the loads presented by the classic lifts. This certainly does not mean that a lifter needs to handle maximum and near maximum weights in these lifts all of the time. What it does mean is that at least some practice of a skill is required in order to maintain proficiency (and even more practice is needed to improve).

Why practice power snatches, power cleans and power jerks? They provide alternatives to the squat or split varieties of the lifts, and variety itself can induce a stronger training effect. Power style lifts are generally less taxing on the nervous system than the full lifts, so maximums can be attempted more frequently. Perhaps most importantly, they are performed more rapidly than the classical lifts (at least in the second through fourth stages of the pull). There is significant evidence to suggest that exercises performed at faster speed than the event normally requires help the athlete improve his or her speed in the event itself.

Back squats are regarded as hip and leg strength developers without peer. Front squats develop the body's capacity to stand up from the low position in the squat clean. An easy recovery tends to make the jerk more certain. One of the advantages of squatting is that it enables the lifter to concentrate on only one phase of the lift: the recovery from the low position in the squat. Another advantage is that the lifter can work with heavier weights than in the lifts themselves. Most lifters can pull to their shoulders in the clean less weight than they can front squat. Therefore, a maximum clean may stimulate the pulling muscles to a maximum, but the legs may not be fully challenged. Separate squatting can provide adequate stimulation to the leg and hip muscles.

Examining the reasons for each of the basic exercises leads to the basic principles for performing assistance exercises: a) to offer variety in the training stimulus and b) to stimulate certain adaptive responses more than others so that the overall training effect can be enhanced.

As noted above, there is evidence that variety itself can provide a stronger training stimulus than does training on a uniform set of exercises. The evidence for such a phenomenon is far from conclusive, but it is worth noting. The more important reason for variety stems from the mind and nervous system of the lifter. Some lifters will become very bored and/or suffer nervous system fatigue using an exercise program that repeats the same exercises. These lifters thrive on the stimulus of a new challenge and will tend to benefit from variety, if only because they will put more effort into training sessions that they find interesting.

The stimulation of better adaptations through more focused exercises is the other key reason for adopting them. A certain exercise may help the lifter to concentrate more on one particular aspect of a classical lift than the lift itself. Perhaps the simplest example of this would be practicing the jerk from the rack as opposed to the clean and jerk. When the lifter practices only the jerk, he or she is "fresh" when the practice is done, not tired or distracted by the clean. The lifter will be able to practice the jerk longer and harder than if the clean was performed before the jerk each time. This narrowing of focus is even more extreme when a portion of the lift is practiced (e.g., a clean from the dead hang). Here the lifter may concentrate only on the last three stages of the clean. If the lifter requires special attention in these areas, dead hang cleans may help. However, in order for the benefits of any kind of partial practice to be transferred, the lessons must be quickly integrated into the classical lift for which the assistance exercise is being done.

The advantages of a narrow focus can be applied to technique improvement, speed, power, flexibility or strength. The focus flows from the exercise and the way in which it is performed (including what the lifter is thinking while doing it).

Since the purpose of incorporating assistance exercises is to provide variety and special emphasis, these principles must guide exercise selection. If the athlete can perform only the basic exercises without being overcome by any undue feeling of monotony and has no special faults that cannot be corrected while practicing the classical lifts themselves, there may be no particular reason to do anything else (except squats and some remedial exercises designed to correct some muscular weakness). This is basically the approach that has been adopted by the great Bulgarian coach, Abadjiev, in recent years. A much more modest variation of this approach was also advocated by the famous Soviet theorist, Roman, in his later years. World Champion and world record holder Bob Bednarski of the United States was a great believer in sticking to the classical lifts and the squat, as is world record Holder and World Champion Antonio Krastev (even after leaving Bulgaria).

Bednarski had this approach to training ingrained in his mind by his coach, the legendary Joe Mills, but Bob was hardly a blind follower of Mills' theories. He made many changes in the Mills approach as he advanced in his career. Similarly, Antonio Krastev was exposed to Ivan Abadjiev's methods from an early age, but he was not reluctant to question a number of the Bulgarian coach's approaches quite vigorously (to the point of negotiating the right to devise his own training programs during his most productive years when he won his two World Championships and set his world records). Both of these tremendous athletes doubted the value of most of the exercises that athletes perform, and both rarely performed reps in either of the classical lifts (relying almost exclusively on singles and the classic lifts as their training mainstays).

On the other side of the theoretical spectrum we find coach A. Medvedyev and athletes such as the immortal V. Alexseev (eight times overall World Champion, twice Olympic champion and the most prolific world record makers in the history of weightlifting). Medvedyev has an absolute devotion to variety in training. He has focused on this subject in much of his research, and it is clear from his recent book, A System of Multi-year Training in Weightlifting, that he believes variety to be one of the major keys to success in weightlifting. In his book Medvedyev cites more than 100 exercises; the higher the athlete's level, the more important variety becomes, according to Medvedyev. In a similar way, Alexseev astonished more conventional coaches with his training methods because he so often performed assistance exercises and relatively high repetition sets fairly near to a competition.

In between these extremes is the more mainstream approach, which balances practice on the classic lifts with the performance of a limited group of "core" assistance exercises. For instance, in a number of studies performed during the mid and late 1970s, Soviet researchers found that high level athletes spent an average of 22% (a range of 18% to 27%) of their time performing snatches and snatch related exercises; 25% (21% to 27%) on the C&J and related exercises; 10% (8% to 12%) on the snatch pull; 10% (8% to 12%) on the clean pull; 22% (19% to 24%) on squats; and 11% (10% to 15%) on pressing and related exercises.

How can highly successful athletes and coaches disagree so much on these subjects? I believe that the answer lies in two directions: individual differences among athletes and trade-offs in the benefits that are and disadvantages of each approach.

There are two aspects of the issue of individual differences among athletes. First, athletes differ with respect to their needs. No two athletes have exactly the same strengths and weaknesses, and therefore, no two athletes should train in exactly the same way. Each must seek the training approach that will maximize results by addressing areas with the greatest opportunities for growth and by not permitting current strengths to become weaknesses. Second, athletes can have differing responses to the same training structure and load. Two athletes can train in the same way (as measured by external means), but those athletes will respond differently.

Individual differences aside, there are trade-offs among exercises in terms of their specificity and the degree to which they generate a training effect. The principle of specificity of training tells us that training on the classical lifts should have the greatest carry over to performance in competition. Practicing the classical lifts improves the athlete's skills in those lifts, and the training stimulus received by the body replicates the stresses that are received while competing. In contrast, a significant variety in a training stimulus can by its very nature induce a large training effect and overcome boredom (which may be the major limiting factor in the training of many advanced lifters). The question is where the optimal trade-off between specificity of training and variety in the training stimulus occurs in general and for each athlete.

Clearly there are a number of drawbacks to training solely on the classical lifts. Such training can have an uneven effect on the athlete because the classical lifts are so complex. For example, let us suppose that a lifter has trouble arising from the squat position in the clean even though he or she shoulders the bar with little difficulty. That athlete could practice cleans with weights that were difficult to stand up with, and over time that lifter's ability to stand up from the squat position would undoubtedly improve. Alternatively, the athlete could practice back and front squats and strengthen the legs. Most coaches would suggest the latter approach or some combination of the two. Few, if any, would suggest the former approach. That is because the lifter would be likely to get tired of pulling the weight to the shoulders and then standing up long before he or she had applied a maximum stimulus to the legs.

Similarly, an athlete who was trying to improve his or her pull might discover that skill and the desire to go under heavy lifts had waned before the pulling muscles had been stimulated enough to generate an optimal training effect. Practicing high pulls would provide a good solution for such a lifter. Interestingly, some great lifters rarely practice high pulls, and others rely on pulls as their chief means to improve their pulling power. How can this be? Obviously, those who train exclusively on the lifts are receiving their training stimulus in the pull from the practice that they do in the classical lifts. In the case of those who pull a great deal, the training stimulus is probably derived more from the pulls than from the classical lifts. Although the second group of lifters benefits from the greater number of pulls in terms of developing pulling power, in terms of specificity of training, they no doubt lack something when compared to lifters who perform more classical lifts.

At least two characteristics determine the benefits of an exercise for any athlete. One is specificity of training and the other is the magnitude of the training stimulus. These may seem identical, but in fact they are not. Let us examine these issues further to see why this is true.

Let us make a hypothetical comparison between the training stimulus generated by the snatch and the snatch pull for a particular lifter. Let us suppose that this lifter requires at least ten attempts at 90% or greater weights a month in the snatch in order to generate any kind of positive training effect in that exercise. (We will stipulate that this threshold rate of improvement is 0.5% per month.) Let us further suppose that this lifter would actually improve more if he or she performed more than ten such lifts, and that the maximum training effect for that lifter would be generated by twenty such lifts (0.75% per month). However, it is established that doing more than twenty lifts would actually present something of an overload for that athlete and his or her improvement would be smaller with loads in excess of twenty lifts a month at 90% or greater weights. This is because the lifter's nervous system becomes so fatigued by so many heavy attempts that he or she loses the ability to perform successfully in the snatch and because his or her joints become mildly sore when loads beyond twenty are performed (which hurts the athlete's performance and technique somewhat). Therefore, while the training effect from doing thirty maximum or near maximum snatches a month is increased to the level of 1% per month, nervous system fatigue and soreness actually diminish the lifter's performance by 2%. (This means that while the athlete's pulling power might be improved by 1% after one month of training with thirty lifts at 90% of maximum or more, performance would actually decline by 1%.)

Let us further suppose that a snatch pull, because of its failure to duplicate all aspects of the snatch, exerts a zero training effect on the fifth and sixth stages of this lifter's snatch and that even the pull during the first four stages of the snatch is only 80% replicated by snatch pulls. However, suppose this athlete can perform either twenty snatches or ten snatches and twenty snatch pulls with 90% or greater weights in one month with equal amounts of stress on the lifter's nervous system and joints. In such a case, the athlete would clearly be better off doing the latter program. The lifter would have a performance increase of 0.75% doing the first program and a performance increase of 0.9% performing the latter program. In the latter case, a .5% improvement would be generated by the ten snatches, and 80% of an additional .5% (or 0.4%) improvement would be generated by the twenty snatch pulls. (Twenty additional snatches would have added 0.5% to the training stimulus, but we assumed that snatch pulls were only 80% as effective as snatches in stimulating improvement in the first four stages of the snatch.) We are also assuming that a training stimulus to substitute for the deficiency of the pulls in training the fifth and sixth stages of the snatch could be found (such as overhead squats), or that the lifter had sufficient reserves in these two phases of the lift to forgo any training effect for some time before anything like maximum capacity in those stages was tested.

Since lifters vary in the amount of stress they experience from performing the classical lifts and in the amount of stimulus they receive from performing variations of those lifts, and since lifters differ in their relative strengths in different phases of the classical lifts, the same program can have very different effects on two athletes. However, carryover values and relationships among lifts often remain stable in the same lifter over the long term.

Perhaps the most effective way to judge the carryover value of various assistance exercises for a particular lifter is to keep records of the relationship between that athlete's performance in the classical lifts and his or her performance in various assistance exercises. Such records can help the athlete and coach judge the athlete's capabilities at a particular point in time. In addition, but changes in relationships can highlight progression or regression on the part of the athlete in certain respects (e.g., if the athlete's power clean and clean get closer over time, the change may signal a deterioration in the athlete's clean technique).

Frequency of Exercise Performance

Once the desired exercises for a given training period have been identified, the next task is to determine how often the exercises are to be employed (generally in a week but sometimes over a period of weeks). The week, or some grouping of weeks, is typically used in planning because of the general tendency for human activities to fit into a weekly cycle, but it should again be noted that for the athlete who can train on any day, the "week" may not follow the normal constraints of seven days. Many athletes have found that training intervals which do not fit into the traditional seven-day week are the most beneficial. For example, some lifters find that two days of rest between heavy training sessions are very helpful and that heavy to maximum training days (at least for certain exercises) can only be handled every six days. Such lifters find that six-day cycles of training (e.g., two days of rest followed by a medium or heavy training day, two days of rest and then a heavy or maximum training day) are the most effective. Moreover, the ideal "week" for different body parts or exercises may not be the same. Recovery rates from bouts of exercise vary with the muscle group(s) involved and the way in which those muscle groups have been stressed.

One way to deal with the varying recovery rates for different muscle groups or exercises is to let them fall where they may, so that a heavy day for the lower back muscles may sometimes fall on a rest or light day for the squat. On another occasion it will fall on the same day, on still another occasion it will fall on a medium day, etc.. Alternatively, the lifter may vary the amount of training performed with two muscle groups, so that recovery from one is either slowed or accelerated to fall into the same recovery pattern as another muscle group (e.g., the athlete can include more sets and/or apply higher intensity in one exercise than the other in order to slow down the recovery process for the muscle groups involved in that exercise). In this way, training days for two muscle groups will never conflict.

Once the exercises and the number of workouts to be performed during a given period have been established, the exercises can be fit into the workouts. It is generally advantageous to spread exercise sessions on the same exercise as much as possible during the period being considered. For instance, if a lifter squats twice a week, those workouts might be planned for Monday and Friday. If there are three squat workouts a week, Monday, Wednesday and Friday may make sense. If a lifter squats five times a week, Tuesday and Saturday workouts might be added, and if seven workouts are required, the lifter will squat once a day. These arrangements are generally more advantageous than squatting Monday and Tuesday when doing two squat workouts a week or three times Monday and twice on Wednesday when the plan is to squat five times in a week.

Similarly, if a lifter is planning to perform snatches from below the knee three times over a four-week period, he or she might perform them once a week (on the same day) for three weeks and then skip the fourth week, rather than doing them three times in one week and then forgoing them for the next three weeks.

There are three major exceptions to this rule. One is for situations in which the exercise planned is designed to teach a certain skill and then is to be phased out as the newly learned or improved skill is transitioned into a more classical exercise. In such a situation, snatches from below the knee might be performed frequently for a time and then be phased out in favor of snatches from the floor once the lifter had learned a targeted skill through practicing snatches from below the knee. Similarly, depth jumps might be used during one phase of training to improve an athlete's ability to rapidly express force immediately after a muscle has been stretched. Once that ability has improved, the exercise might be phased out for months or years because it is possible for the athlete to preserve the effects of such training through the practice of related exercises (e.g., the dip for the jerk and rapid amortization and recovery in the last stages of a squat clean). In lieu of totally phasing out an exercise, an athlete might perform it periodically or for just a few sets, in order to preserve the learning that occurred while that exercise was emphasized.

The second exception is a situation in which the conditioning effect of the exercise in question will be replaced later with another exercise that may be more specific to the classical exercises. This can occur when the number of workouts in the squat is decreased and the number of front squat workouts is increased. The third exception involves peaking for a certain performance. When an athlete is peaking, the reduction or elimination of certain exercises from the athlete's training in the final weeks before an important competition may help the muscular or nervous system of the athlete to recuperate in such a way that a noticeable improvement in performance is experienced. (The issue of peaking for competition will be discussed in greater detail later in this chapter.)

Planning for the Workout Day

The smallest realistic unit for planning the details of the workout is the day. An athlete may have none or several workouts in a day, but most coaches believe that there ought to be careful planning of the content of work within a day and that some of the most important relationships to be considered when planning a training program are those of the day.

There are several reasons for this. First, the athlete has only so much energy in a day. Second, there are daily physiological cycles which influence the quality of the work that can be performed. For most athletes, the best training periods are in the late morning, early afternoon and early evening. Few athletes are able to perform at their best immediately upon waking or just before retiring.

Considerations such as the time of day of the athlete's most important competition(s) and what the athlete does during the day (other than lifting) should also guide the planner in deciding which exercises should be incorporated into which workout in the day. Still another consideration is the kind of training the athlete has done thus far in the day. Naturally, if the athlete has performed a record squat, there is little reason to schedule more limited squats later in the day. Similarly, if a lifter has executed a large load in a given exercise early in the day, there would be little reason to do much, if anything, with that exercise later in the day.

In contrast, if the morning exercise session consists of light exercise, there is little reason to place any significant restrictions on the activities performed during the evening. In addition, the morning workout might have emphasized an exercise that was intended to promote performance in an exercise scheduled later in the day. For instance, the lifter might have been performing snatches from the blocks in the morning with an emphasis on placing the shoulders in advance of the bar as the bar approaches knee height. Snatches from the floor in the evening workout might pick up on that theme by having the lifter concentrate on reaching the same position that had been achieved during the morning's training from the blocks. (The athlete might even warm up for the evening snatch workout with snatches from the hang or from the blocks in order to reinforce the lessons learned in the morning's training session and to assist in the transition of that learning to the standard version of the snatch.)

The general pattern is to plan the most strenuous workout of the day and then to plan any other workouts around that one. Within such a workout, the progression is generally as described in the next section of this chapter (i.e., skills, speed, strength and endurance). In contrast, if only one exercise is to be pushed to a maximum in a given day, that exercise might be given precedence despite the general rule of order. For example, if the athlete intends to go for a squat record on a given day and no other maximum lifts are intended, the coach might wish to incorporate the squat relatively early in the training day and certainly early within the workout in which it will be performed.

The Workout Plan

Once the structure of the training day has been developed, the coach or athlete is prepared to determine the plan for each workout.

Basic Workout Structure

A basic structure for an individual workout based on experience and scientific evidence has evolved over the years. Prior to the start of the workout, many athletes perform some form of mental readying activities, a very advisable process (which will be discussed in Chapter 7). That process is followed by a physical warm-up, after which the body of the workout is performed. The workout concludes with a cool down period, which aims at restoring body temperature to the normal level and achieving a relaxed state (a process normally assisted by the workout itself). We will begin with a discussion of the warm-up phase of the workout.

Warming Up

The primary training effect that is derived from any workout session comes from the heaviest weights that are lifted in that session, and muscles can do only so much work before they suffer a temporary loss of work capacity as a result of fatigue. Knowing only these facts, an athlete might be tempted to begin his or her workout with maximum weights. Nevertheless, few coaches of weightlifting or weight training would advocate that a trainee lift his or her heaviest weights of a particular training session at the very beginning of the workout. The vast majority of coaches and lifters agree that at least some warm-p is necessary before attempting heavy weights.

Some coaches advocate a general warm-up which has the objective of raising somewhat the pulse rate and body temperature. This may be done with calisthenics, brief bouts of jogging (of the normal type or in place) and/or by emulating the lift to be performed with an empty bar or stick. Other coaches advocate warming up only with the exercise(s) that will be used early in the training session, beginning with as little as the empty bar but no more than 50% of what will be lifted that day. The lifter then works up gradually, increasing the weight on the bar to the heaviest weight of the day.

There tends to be a degree of transfer in the warm-p effect. If there has been a previous general warm-up, the need to warm up with the bar will typically diminish. (The transfer effect is more direct if the same muscles are used in the general warm-up as in the lift.) Similarly, if the lifter does several warm-up sets with the same light weight, there is a tendency to take fewer sets the rest of the way.

Exercise physiologists have not been able to agree completely on the scientific basis of or support for warming up, but most athletes and coaches agree that warming up is pleasurable and beneficial for both psychological and physiological reasons. There does not seem to be any point waiting for scientists to prove what trainees already know, although understanding the scientific basis would enable coaches to design the warm-up process more effectively. Younger athletes and those who have had no previous injuries tend to be more able to train without a warm-up than do more mature athletes and/or those who have suffered trauma to their bodies. For most Master lifters (thirty-five and over), there does not seem to be any choice about warming up; an extended warm-up is a must to get old joints moving freely and with minimal discomfort.

There seems to be growing agreement in the lay and scientific communities that vigorous stretching is not a good idea when the muscles and other soft tissues of the body have not been warmed up. Therefore, trainees should increase the range of motion gradually with each rep and/or set as they warm up, and no vigorous stretching should be performed prior to a general warm-up.

Some athletes have found that externally applied stimuli help them through the process of warming up. Some lifters like to have a vigorous and brief massage just before beginning their warm-ups (or a very brief massage in one or more areas of their bodies immediately before taking a heavy attempt, particularly in competition). As an adjunct to the warm-up process, other lifters like to apply liniment to certain areas of their bodies (usually to those areas that tend to be stiff or slightly painful until they are warmed up thoroughly).

As indicated above, the warming up process for a particular lift or exercise depends to an extent on what has preceded it. When a lifter is warming up for the exercise that is done first in the workout, he or she will generally start lighter and work up more gradually than when the second or later exercise of the workout is being performed. If a lifter is training a set of muscles that have just been used in another exercise, the warm-up period required can often be greatly reduced or even eliminated (depending on how closely the prior movement resembles the current one in terms of range of movement and the amount of weight handled).

Still another characteristic that can influence the length of the warm-up is the stage of development of the lifter. Beginners are often limited in their warm-ups for practical reasons. A lifter who intends to perform his or her heaviest set(s) of the day with 100 lb. might begin with the empty bar (which typically weighs between 25 and 45 lb. and then go to 65 lb. to 75 lb.) before lifting 100 lb.. An advanced lifter who intends to lift 400 lb. in his or her workout might begin with between 45 lb. and 135 lb. and work up in the following increments: 135, 225, 295, 345, 375 and 400.

While warming up, it is common for lifters to perform their earlier sets with higher numbers of repetitions and to reduce the number of repetitions as the workout progresses. For example, in the warm-up sequence for the advanced lifter described above, the lifter might do 135 lb. for 5 reps, 225 lb. for 4 reps, 295 lb. for 3 reps and 345 lb. for 2 reps, before doing singles with 375 lb. and 400 lb. This is done for at least two reasons. One reason is that each lift contributes to warming up the body, so that more reps warm it up more, to a point. Doing 10 reps or more with all but the very lightest of weights might "pump up" and fatigue the muscles, compromising the body's ability to lift heavier weights on later sets. Using 2 to 5 reps minimizes the fatigue and pumping factors yet accelerates the warming-up process faster than single reps. Therefore, by employing more reps during the earlier sets (rather doing sets of singles), fewer sets and less overall time may be required to warm up.

(However many lifters use only singles, except with the very lightest weights, and more than three reps are seldom used in the classical lifts—especially the C&J— even for warming up.) The alternative is to perform more sets and fewer reps (perhaps 2 sets of doubles with 135 lb. and 225 lb. in the previously listed workout sequence).

Regardless of the number of reps employed during the warm-up, that process takes some time. (The mind and body appear to need some time to get into "gear," although we do not fully understand what getting in gear means, and the amount of activity that athletes require to reach such a state of full readiness clearly varies from athlete to athlete and in the same athlete on different occasions.) Performing several sets of a given exercise and taking the cumulative time that they entail appears to be unavoidable in order to accomplish a proper warm-up.

A second reason sometimes given for varying the reps with the weight on the bar during an exercise session is to attempt to accomplish multiple ends within the same workout, through a technique called "heavy and light" or "pyramiding." (discussed in Chapter 3). It should be noted that this is not generally a sound method for training the classical lifts, as reps in excess of five are rarely used in the Olympic or related lifts (primarily because of the inevitable breakdown in technique which occurs on these lifts when fatigue sets in), and three is more commonly the limit, except with light to moderate loads. Moreover, for athletes who are interested primarily in development of strength (where hypertrophy is a means to the end of getting stronger, not an end in itself), a more effective approach is to work up to a maximum in a conventional way and then to reduce the weight after the heaviest reps have been completed in order to perform a final high rep set or sets.

One final issue that often influences the warming up process is the nature of the exercise that is being performed. The primary aspects that can affect the warm-up process are: the degree of skill required by the exercise, the range of motion involved in performing it and the speed with which the exercise is performed. For example, in an exercise like the military press, there is little skill involved, and while the military press is a relatively full range of motion exercise, it does not require as extreme a range of motion for most of the joints involved as an exercise like the parallel-bar dip or the full squat. The difference is that in the press, the range of motion through which the arms and shoulders are exercised is limited by the bar touching the shoulders (i.e., regardless of the flexibility of those joints, the bar is never lowered beyond the top of the shoulders). In addition, the stress that is placed on the joints that are relatively fully flexed at the start of the press (the elbows) does not reach a maximal level until the level of flexion in the elbow joint has been considerably reduced. In the dip or the squat, there is no inherent limit on the range of motion achieved except the flexibility of the joints involved (if the shoulders and elbows in the former and the knees and hips in the latter). The military press is also not inherently an explosive exercise. Many trainers encourage the lifter to push the bar up as quickly and explosively as possible while doing presses (and there is substantial evidence that such a method has advantages), but speed is not an essential part of the exercise. Since the press does not involve an unlimited range of motion or a great deal of speed or skill, it can generally be performed with a relatively limited warm-up, perhaps two to four sets. (An older or injured athlete may require more of a warm-up.)

In contrast, the snatch involves a great deal of skill and speed and a very full range of motion. There is a tendency to warm up more on such an exercise in order to prepare the joints and muscles for an all out and explosive effort and to fine tune the athlete's motor patterns. Because of the considerable motor skills involved in performing the snatch, there is also a tendency to use lower reps while warming up and training. (As indicated earlier, skills have a tendency to deteriorate quickly as the muscles become fatigued during the same set.) Therefore, more warm-up sets tend to be required in warming up for the Olympic lifts than in warming up for exercises in which higher reps can be used effectively. The common range of warm-up sets in the snatch would be three to five in the earliest sets and doubles and singles as the weight grows heavier (unless heavy sets of three reps were being performed, in which case the warm-up sets would typically never fall below two to three reps).

Regardless of the health and age of the trainee and the order of an exercise in the workout, the amount of warm-up varies greatly among trainees. Some employ one or two warm-up sets and others may use as many as eight or ten. The majority of trainees fall somewhere in between, with beginners typically taking fewer warm-up sets and the more advanced trainers taking a greater number before attempting their maximum weights of the session.

In an article in the Soviet 1985 Weightlifting Yearbook, R.A. Khairullin suggested that many athletes fail to perform optimally in competition because of inadequate warm-ups. The author then suggested the following warm-up sequence for the snatch: up to one minute of jogging; 5 to 6 calisthenic type exercises, each performed for 8 to 12 reps; and repeating a circuit of 3 to 4 exercises 4 or 5 times (e.g., snatch stretches for 6 to 8 repetitions with the empty bar, 5 to 6 good mornings with a plate held behind the head and 4 to 5 overhead squats using a plate instead of the bar as the resistance). Then the athlete performs 3 to 4 reps in the snatch stretch with 25% to 30% of

his or her best snatch. However, after the bar is brought to arm's length on each rep, the athlete lowers it to the shoulders behind the neck and then, while pressing up with the arms, descends into a squat position. With each rep the lifter goes lower and lower, until the full squat position is achieved on the last rep in the set. With 35% to 40% of his or her maxim, the athlete performs 3 to 4 power snatches (each rep followed by lowering the bar to the shoulders and then performing a drop snatch) and then finishes the set with 1 to 2 reps in the snatch from the hang above the knees. Finally, the athlete raises the bar to 50% to 60% of maximum and then deadlifts the bar to a point where it is one-third up the thighs, pauses and performs a snatch from the hang above the knees. After this preliminary warm-up has been completed, the athlete performs a series of 6 to 8 sets of classical snatching, with 1 to 2 reps on the earlier sets and singles thereafter, progressing up toward the athlete's first attempt.

Khairullin's concept in the C&J is similar, but the first set with real resistance is performed with a weight that is 40% to 50% of the lifter's maximum. With this weight the athlete deadlifts the bar to a position one-third up the thigh and, after pausing, performs a power clean. This is followed by 1 to 2 front squats and 2 to 3 push presses. The resistance is then increased to a weight which represents 50% to 60% of the lifter's maximum. With this weight the athlete performs a power clean, a squat clean from the hang above the knee, a push press and 1 to 2 classic jerks. At this point the athlete is prepared to begin a progression of 5 to 6 singles in the C&J up to the athlete's opening attempt.

While few athletes perform as extensive warm-up as that recommended by Khairullin (e.g., I have seen very few athletes, and even fewer of the top ones, jog before they lifted), there is much to be said for a fairly extensive warm-up. Non-strenuous warm-ups can do little harm and may do some good. I remember watching Vasili Alexseev warm up during his last World Championships appearance in 1978, and he began his snatches with 40 kg. Alexseev always believed in a thorough warm-up, and he had one of the longest and most illustrious careers in all of weightlifting. While that kind of career can surely not be attributed to thorough warming up, it surely did not hurt the great Alexseev.

One thing that I cannot recommend during the warm-up period is extensive stretching. Despite recommendations to the contrary in the current literature, I continue to see athletes begin their warm-ups with stretching. It has been well demonstrated that muscles and other soft tissues which are "cold" (98.6°) are not as pliable or ready to accept loads as muscles which are warmer following activity. Athletes who like to perform stretches before they lift should do ballistic or static stretches sparingly and only after they have done some preliminary exercises to warm up muscles and body. Moderate AI stretching is probably the most useful method for an athlete who requires pre-workout stretching to achieve adequate mobility. Regardless of the actual stretching method used, the warm-up should be carefully performed. Stretching after the workout is a better choice when the athlete is attempting to permanently increase his or her range of motion. When warm-ups prior to stretching are not performed, the athlete should proceed very carefully and gradually with any stretching.

As a sidelight, the reader may be interested to know that two-time World Superheavyweight Champion Antonio Krastev told me that he never saw any weightlifter in Bulgaria stretch (other than while performing warm-ups with the bar) before and after the workout. Further, he never saw any athletes, other than those from the Western countries, stretch extensively at the World Championships. He was astonished to see the amount of stretching that goes on in American gyms and found it ludicrous. In defense of the Americans, we have many more athletes who, because of lack of flexibility is specific areas of the body, would not have been selected for weightlifting in Eastern Europe: hence the need for many Americans to perform remedial stretching. Moreover, the mere fact that champions do or do not do something is no proof that their approach is best. However, Antonio's observation regarding stretching probably has some merit.

The Order and Number of Exercises Within the Workout

Once the coach has planned the exercises to be performed in a given workout, the exercises should be assigned to a specific order. The general rule for the ordering of exercises in a workout (following a general warm-up) are: skill building exercises first, speed development second, strength development third and endurance development last. The idea behind this arrangement is that new skills (or improvements to existing ones) are best learned when the mind and body are freshest. When it comes to conditioning, muscles which have been fatigued by strength and/or endurance training are less amenable to speed training than muscles that are in a relatively rested state. Endurance work clearly compromises the muscles' ability to contract maximally, hence its placement last in the workout. It also appears that speed and strength work have only a minimal negative effect on endurance, therefore the placement of endurance work at the end of the workout has only a minimal negative effect on performance in endurance exercises (if any are to be performed).

These general ordering principles are far from absolute. For example, master lifters (particularly mildly arthritic ones) often find that warming up with a strength exercise, such as squats, actually facilitates performance of the more skill dependent exercises like snatches. The squat warms up stiff joints and muscles and permits faster whole-body movements (such as the classic lifts) to be performed with less discomfort. In addition, some research in the area of motor skills suggests that a greater degree of learning takes place when the athlete is fatigued than when he or she is fully rested, perhaps because the athlete must focus more intently. However, tired muscles will perform less well than rested ones and bad habits can be developed when fatigued, so skill practice after an athlete is fatigued is not generally recommended, despite its occasional value.

The one aspect of the ordering described above that appears to be most universally true is that any endurance related exercises belong at the very end of the workout. However, since few lifters perform such exercises and there is virtually no reason to believe that they would have a significant positive effect on weightlifting performance, this is essentially a moot point in the training of weightlifters.

The skill, speed and strength ordering of exercises suggests that the classical and other exercises used for technique development come first and that strength building exercises, such as squats and pulls, should be performed later in the workout. It also suggests that any exercises such as plyometrics or jumping be performed after the classical lifts, but before the strength exercises, though in practice, jumps and related exercises are generally placed at the end or near end of the workout (they are certainly done before endurance work in done, if any is planned).

In addition to arranging the order of exercises within the workout, the coach must be cognizant of the limits on the number of exercises that can be performed. Obviously, the smallest number of exercises that can be performed is one, and there are athletes who do as many as a dozen exercises in a workout. The correct number of exercises that can be performed in a single workout is a function of the conditioning of the athlete, the athlete's state at the outset of the workout (e.g., fully rested or fatigued), the kinds of exercises that the athlete will perform and the number and intensity of the reps performed in each exercise. A well conditioned athlete who handles a large training load can perform more exercises in a workout than an athlete who is not as well conditioned. An athlete who is rested will be able to do more in a training session and do it more effectively than an athlete who is not rested. Similarly, if an athlete is performing his or her second workout of the day, he or she cannot expect to do as many exercises as if the first workout had not been performed.

The more complex and strenuous the exercises, the fewer the athlete will be able to perform. If the athlete is doing the classical lifts, he or she may not be able to perform more than two or three exercises within the workout. If the exercises are of a remedial nature (e.g., hyperextensions and abdominal exercises), multiple exercises may be performed without causing undue overall fatigue. A high number of reps in an exercise, particularly a high number of reps per set, will reduce the number of exercises an athlete can perform within one workout. An athlete who performs a few sets of one to two reps in each exercise may be able to perform many exercises in one workout.

Finally, the higher the intensity of the training in each exercise, the smaller the number of exercises that can be performed effectively within one training session. An athlete who takes several attempts at a maximum weight in a complex exercise will not be able to successfully perform many other exercises at the same intensity. (This is particularly true if the exercise expends a great deal of the athlete's nervous energy, as in a personal record in a classic lift, or involves a full-body effort, as in a maximum deadlift or squat.)

The most common range of exercises per workout is two to six, with the number varying both with the load intended for the workout and the considerations already mentioned. The coach or athlete will need to experiment to determine the average number of exercises that are most beneficial for each athlete and then adjust the plans for specific workouts.

When it comes to balancing the volume and order of exercises, the process is often interactive. Order can affect the volume that a lifter can perform in a given exercise; a lifter fatigued by a given volume of exercise will be able to do less volume in a subsequent exercise than when fresher, although a prior related exercise will also diminish the amount of warm-up required during a subsequent exercise.

Cooling Down

After the workout has been performed, the athlete will cool down (his or her body will return to a normal resting state). Stretching and moving about after a workout are good practices, as is making a conscious effort to relax (although often such an effort will be unnecessary, as muscular and nervous system fatigue tend to have a calming effect). Although research has yet to demonstrate any link between the exposure of an overheated body to cold temperatures, many athletes feel that restoring the body to its normal temperature before venturing out of doors is essential to avoid colds and similar illnesses.

If the athlete is interested in permanent improvements in flexibility, the cool down period is the best time in the workout to accomplish such aims. The muscles are warm, and they will not be called upon to contract forcefully until the next training session, so any stretching that is performed will tend to leave muscles in a relaxed and lengthened state.

Extensive flexibility work is not a good idea if pain in any area has been generated during the workout and that pain does not subside upon stretching. When a minor injury might have occurred during the workout, the athlete is well advised to postpone any vigorous stretching until the nature and extent of the injury is ascertained.

It is useful for the lifter to close the workout with some mental practice by reviewing successes and correcting any mistakes. Rehearsal aids retention, and mental rehearsal will at the very least help the athlete retain what has been learned on the cognitive (if not the motor) level. Lastly, some final notes regarding the workout and what was learned during it should be made in the training log at this time. (If the athlete does not carry the training log to the gym, those notes can be mental ones that will be recorded when the lifter returns home.)

Determining the Volume Devoted to Each Exercise Per Session

Once the coach or athlete has determined the identity and frequency of the exercises to be included in the lifter's training, the amount of training that can be devoted to each exercise is determined by a number of very practical considerations: a) the number of training sessions in which the exercise is included in a given training period (e.g., a week); b) the length of time devoted to each session; c) the total number of reps that will be performed and how those reps will be apportioned in terms of reps and sets; d) the proximity to the lifter's maximum of the weights lifted; e) the nature of the exercise; f) the amount of rest that is taken between reps, sets and exercises; g) the condition of the athlete and his or her inherent energy levels and recuperative powers; and h) the general constraints in the human organism that limit the number of maximum or near maximum efforts that an athlete can perform within a given time period. The most important of these factors are the number of reps per set, the rest between sets, the nature of the exercise and the proximity of the load to the athlete's maximum. The higher the reps and the closer to the athlete's maximum the load on the bar, the fewer the sets that an athlete will be able to perform at a given level. The more tension that is developed in the muscles during the exercise and the larger the muscles that are affected, the less able the athlete will be to repeat maximum performances.

If an athlete performs an all out set of twenty reps, it is doubtful that more than one additional set could be performed at a high level. If an athlete is performing five reps, the maximum number of sets with a weight close to the athlete's maximum for five reps is probably four to six (fewer if truly maximal loads are lifted on each set). With two to three rep sets, the athlete can generally perform six to eight sets with near maximum loads (for that number of reps) but may be able to do as many as ten sets or more when performing singles before fatigue really begins to hurt his or her performance. In exercises in which the bar is moving more quickly (e.g., the snatch), the athlete can often perform more maximum efforts. When the exercise involves slower motions (e.g., the squat), fatigue sets in more quickly. (An athlete may be able to generate five or ten really good attempts at a maximum weight in the snatch but will rarely be able to make more than one or two all out efforts in the squat.)

Generally, the more rest an athlete has between sets, the greater the number of maximum efforts that can be performed (as long as rests between maximums are not so long that the athlete cools down). The Bulgarian "segments" method of training that was described in Chapter 3 offers an interesting way of increasing the number of maximum efforts possible during a given training session. Under this system athletes perform one to six maximum efforts, then reduce the weight on the bar by 5 kg. to 20 kg. After this reduced weight has been lifted for one or more sets, the bar is raised gradually, or immediately, to the athlete's maximum. This process is sometimes repeated several times in a single session. The end result is that the athlete has been able to attempt maximum weights more times than if he or she had remained at the maximum weight until absolute fatigue set in. Whether this training method has special merit is a question that remains to be answered by further research, but on a very practical level it appears to have been an effective method for the Bulgarian lifters (although there have been reports that a significant number of lifters are lost due to injury in the Bulgarian program, perhaps as a result of these rigorous training methods).

Rest Intervals Between Exercises

From a physiological standpoint, the amount of rest taken between different exercises should not be similar to that taken between sets of the same exercise. However, most trainers recommend a somewhat longer rest between exercises than between sets of the same exercise because they feel that the change in the movement and thought patterns and the psychological value of breaks suggest that some additional rest between exercises is beneficial. The learning literature tends to agree that some "interference" skills building occurs when different skills are used one after the other. In addition, for psychological reasons (such as motivation), breaks are more appropriate between exercises than during them.

On a more physical level, a break between exercises makes more sense than a break between sets because too long a break between sets of the same exercise might require one or more additional warm-up sets, perhaps more overall work than was planned. There is customarily a warm-up for each new exercise, so the break between exercises creates little or no need for extra sets. The exceptions to this rule would be exercises like front squats performed after squat cleans or snatch pulls performed after snatches. When this kind of exercise sequence is used, moving directly into the next exercise can significantly reduce or even virtually eliminate the need for a warm-up in that new exercise

As with the other rest intervals described above, the guidelines for the rest intervals must be considered in the context of the purpose of a workout. Trainees interested in developing a high level of cardiovascular fitness (not in competitive weightlifting) may wish to move from one exercise to another with little rest in between (a technique known as circuit training). Bodybuilders pair two or more exercises in the "super set" fashion described in Chapter 3. Weightlifters may find this to be a time-saving arrangement of exercises when maximums are not being performed and the two exercises being done involve different muscle groups (e.g., squats and presses). Some trainers prefer to perform different exercises in entirely different workouts (even if there are several of these in one day) so that the athlete can devote his or her full attention to improving one exercise or group of muscles at each separate session. For most weightlifters who are doing more than one exercise in a session, three to ten minutes of rest between exercises will suffice.

Once the complex of exercises has been established, it is advisable to build the plan in the following order: from the microcycle (usually a week but conceivably more or less than 7 days) to the days within the week to the workout. After detailed plans for the week and the workouts have been formulated, the coach can revisit the general plan previously established for the mesocycle and determine how the short term plan can be reconciled with it and whether adjustments need to be made in the overall content of the mesocycle in light of exercise selection and content.

Once the final plan for the mesocycle has been established, the coach can review the next few months in the macrocycle to determine whether any adjustments can or should be made to those months. (Planning ahead by more than a few months is essentially futile because such plans will almost inevitably need to be changed considerably on the basis of the actual results attained earlier in that macrocycle.) At the completion of each mesocycle, the coach will want to review the balance of the plans in that macrocycle to determine whether any further adjustments need to be made.

The Process of Developing Training Programs: Three Examples

Having reviewed the training regimens of three champions, let us now turn to the programs that were constructed for particular athletes at somewhat lower levels of performance. The names and certain details of these cases have been altered or omitted in order to maintain the privacy of the athletes involved and to make the situations of greater general interest, but the essential accuracy of the examples has been preserved.

In each case, we will describe the state of the athlete prior to the implementation of the new workout plan. Then we will describe how a specific workout plan (i.e., a short term plan or microcycle) was created on the basis of that athlete's particular needs. Next we will show how the microcycle was integrated into the mesocycles and macrocycles. Finally, we will report on the results. This process should enable coaches to understand better how the principles presented thus far can and should be applied, enabling them to diagnose and prescribe for individual athletes who will have different problems, be in different training states and hence require different routines.

Alan Shrug is an eighteen-year-old lifter who has been training for three years. At a height of 5'8" and a body weight of 75 kg., his best lifts are a 102.5 kg. snatch and a 120 kg. C&J. Alan has been training five days a week, averaging 1,000 reps per month with weights 60% of his maximums or higher. He has been devoting 25% of his training time to the snatch and snatch related exercises and an equal amount of his time to the C&J. An additional 20% of his time has been devoted to the squat, another 20% to pulling exercises (equally divided between the snatch and the clean). The remaining 10% of Alan's time has been devoted to other auxiliary exercises (such as pressing, hyperextensions and abdominal work).

Alan has recently gone off to college, and his coach at home has suggested that he find a local person to help him there. Had he remained at home, his coach would have planned for a total load of 13,200 reps per year (an average of 1,100 per month). Because Alan's C&J is a little low relative to his snatch (his snatch is more than 85% of his C&J when the typical relationship is closer to 80%), his coach had planned to increase the amount of time Alan spent in the C&J and related exercises (the squat and the clean pull). As a result, Alan's time allocation with respect to exercises would have been as follows: snatch and related exercises, 22%; C&J and related exercises, 27%; squat, 22%; clean pulls, 12%; snatch pulls,

9%; and other exercises, 8%. Alan's coach would have woven these basic numbers into a periodized annual plan that would have had Alan peaking for the National Collegiate Championships in October of his sophomore year.

Alan's new coach Bob Thinker asks Alan for his training records for the past six months. After studying them carefully, Bob concludes that more specific tailoring of Alan's training would benefit him more than the overall plan outlined by his former coach. Alan's limiting factor in the C&J is primarily his leg strength. He can easily pull weights to the shoulder that he cannot stand up with, but even when he stands up with great difficulty he has no trouble jerking the weight. In the snatch Alan's limiting factor is a tendency to let the bar travel away from his body during the second stage of the pull. This results in inconsistency and inefficiency in Alan's snatch, and he often "swings" the bar forward and then back to various degrees during the final stages of his pull. While his 102.5 kg. snatch is high relative to his C&J, he is very inconsistent in the snatch due to his technical errors in the pull, often missing with weights of 95 kg. and above. (The day he snatched 102.5 kg. he missed 97.5 kg. and missed 102.5 kg. three times before finally making it.)

Given this information, Bob constructs a very different program for Alan than what his former coach had in mind. During the first month of Alan's new training program, he will perform fewer snatches than usual. (He needs some time to correct his technique, and merely performing more snatches at this early stage is likely to reinforce incorrect technique patterns.) However, the number of snatch pulls and deadlifts will be increased in an effort to focus on executing the second stage of the pull more correctly. In order to offset the additional work in the snatch, the number of cleans and clean pulls, particularly cleans and clean pulls from the floor will actually be reduced somewhat. The number of squats Alan will perform will remain the same, but there will be a change in the structure of his training. There will be fewer training sessions in the squat (three as opposed to five a week), but there will be more reps per set (an average of 4.5 versus the previous average of 2.5), and the intensity will be stepped up on the heavy days and reduced somewhat on the lighter days. This pattern of higher reps will help Alan build additional muscle mass as well as strength in his legs. (It is likely that he will ultimately compete at 83 kg. or even 91 kg., so building some muscle mass is a sensible process for this athlete.)

After performing an increased number of snatch pulls and deadlifts for several weeks (and correcting his technical problem while performing those exercises), Alan will begin to merge his snatches and pulls in some workouts. He will perform a pull followed by one or two reps in the snatch. The purpose of this is to permit him to "groove" the pull correctly while he is performing the pulls (when he has nothing to focus on but the pull) and then immediately to perform a snatch or two in the same groove). As Alan gains mastery in this compound exercise, he will begin to perform more snatches without the preceding pull, eventually returning to a point where most of his workouts in the snatch do not involve preliminary pulls. (Whenever he is having a problem with his technique in the pull, he will return to a set or two of pulls and then pulls with snatches, in order to regroove the pull properly.)

In terms of daily training sessions, Alan's workout plan for the first month of his training is summarized in Table 21 (the number of reps above 60% is shown for each exercise).

As was indicated above, over a period of weeks snatches will be emphasized more and snatch pulls and deadlifts less. It should be noted that snatch pulls will be performed with lower than customary intensity during this stage of Alan's training. He will perform many reps in the 85% to 90% range so that the tempo of the snatch can be preserved. (Remember that at this stage the pull is being used to build skills as much as to increase strength and power.) Most of Alan's squatting will be performed in sets of five reps in order to stimulate strength development and hypertrophy simultaneously.

Alan's new coach plans to increase the number of reps that Alan performs in the snatch and the C&J as the year progresses and into the following training year; in this stage in Alan's career he needs more practice in performing the classical lifts in order to perfect his technique. Over the next two or three years he must achieve true sporting perfection in his technical capabilities, while at the same time increasing his strength and power. The additional practice on the lifts will assist him in both of these areas.

A second case is that of John Power. John has been training for six years and has reached the Master of Sport level. At a height of 5'10", his body weight is 100 kg., and his best lifts are 155 kg. in the snatch and 195 kg. in the C&J. He is graduating from college shortly and will return to his home town to pursue a business career while continuing his weightlifting training. He will resume his training under his old coach Bill Sage; he began his career under Bill but trained under the guidance of Gregor Steel during his last three years in school. John's lifts took off during the first

year under Gregor's regimen, but progress slowed during the second year and stopped completely in the third, partially as a result of John's having to curtail his workouts because of minor but persistent injury problems.

John is becoming frustrated as he has not been able to advance to the international level of performance. In addition to a lack of progress, John has experienced some problems with overuse injuries to his knees. While he has had no problems that have required extended layoffs or surgery, he has chronic soreness in his knees. From time to time he has used anti-inflammatory medication to relieve these symptoms, but when the medication is stopped, the pain always returns. The pain, while never severe, is persistent and generally tolerable when John is fully warmed up during his workouts. He notices that his pain is most significant in the hours after his heavy clean workouts.

John's technique is good. He rarely misses lifts with below maximum weights unless he is particularly tired. His C&J has actually declined slightly over the past year as his practice of heavy C&J's has been hampered somewhat by his knee problems. John performs just under 22,000 reps a year in his training, or 1800 reps in an average training month. He trains six days a week, doing two workouts on three of his training days.

When John returns home, Bill Sage asks for his training records; after studying them at length, he suggests a very different path for John's future training. Bill states unequivocally that John's first goal must be to eliminate his knee pain. Bill reasons that if John is to C&J 220 kg. required to be internationally competitive, he is not going to do it with sore knees (and if his present course of training continues, his knees surely are not going to feel any better with heavier loads). At the same time, John needs to get much stronger if he is to compete on an international level. His technique can be marginally improved in terms of efficiency, but most of John's future progress will be derived from improvements in his physical capabilities (e.g., strength and power) rather than his skill.

During John's first month of training, Bill has him perform his normal volume of pulls and squats but restricts the intensity of his snatches, and particularly his C&J's, to 75% of maximum or less. Each classic lift is only performed once a week. Bill's intention is to permit John's knees to heal while at the same time maintaining John's

Table 21

Monday	Tuesday	Thursday	Friday	Saturday
Sn Pull - 15	Power Jerk - 15	Sn Pull - 12	Sn Pull - 15	C&J - 12
Sn Deadlift - 9	Power Sn - 12	Snatch - 12	Snatch - 15	Cl Pull - 12
Snatch - 12	Squat - 25	Clean - 10	Sn Deadlift - 9	Sn Pull - 15
Power Cl - 12	Press - 10	Fr Squat - 12	Press - 10	Squat - 15
Hypers	Ab Work	Hypers	Ab Work	Hypers

298

Table 22

Monday	Tuesday	Thursday	Saturday
Power Snatch - 10	Snatch - 18	Power Clean - 10	Snatch - 10
Snatch Pull - 15	Overhead Squat - 15	Clean Pull- 20	C&J - 15
Clean Pull - 15	Squat - 25	Snatch Pull - 20	Clean Pull - 20
Clean Deadlift -15	Snatch Pull - 20	Front Squat - 18	Overhead Squat - 15
Press - 10	Jerk - 15	Press - 15	Squat - 20

strength level. During this period, primarily as a result of the reduction of classic lifts that John performs, the total volume of John's training is reduced by a third (as are the number of training days) from what it has been in recent months. A sample week of training appears in Table 22.

In order to reduce the likelihood that John's knee pain will recur when John returns to more conventional training after his "healing" month, Bill takes several steps. First, he reduces the overall number of reps that John will perform during his workouts by approximately 15% overall (to an average of 1,500 reps per month versus his prior average monthly load of 1800 reps). The mere reduction in the overall volume of John's training should afford him some relief from his knee pain. The primary means of reducing the number of reps will be to decrease both the volume and the intensity of the classical lifts performed during workouts. Second, John will perform squats somewhat less often than he has in the past, and he will vary the intensity more than he has in the past. Finally, John will reduce the height of his heels slightly (by approximately 1/16"), which in his case will reduce the strain on his knee joints in the low squat position.

After one month, provided John reports no knee pain, he will move back into a more conventional program (i.e., somewhat higher intensity snatches and C&J's), although he will not return to his previous volume of training in the snatch and C&J for the foreseeable future, and the number of training days on which he squats will remain diminished relative to what he was performing before he rejoined his old coach. For example, he will perform one clean and 2-3 reps in the jerk in his Saturday workout, maintaining a more limited load in the exercise that irritates his knees most (the clean). He will also perform a few sets of light repetition lifts in the classical lifts several times a week (60-75% for 2-3 reps). This kind of training should serve to toughen his joints to the strains of

lifting without irritating those joints (later the load of heavier lifts may be gradually increased, although probably never to its former level).

John will increase his reliance on snatches and clean pulls as an important means of improving his pulling strength. He will commence using a height gauge when he pulls, so that he will have a way to measure his progress in those exercises.

Within three months after beginning his new training program, John makes personal records in both the snatch and the C&J. After stagnation for some time, he is overjoyed to make progress once again. He enjoys two additional dividends as well. His knee pain remains at bay. There are occasional twinges of pain, but they are minor and quick to go away. John has not needed any anti-inflammatory medication during the three months of his new training regimen. Finally, John feels more rested and energetic than he has in the past. He looks forward to each training session with greater enthusiasm than he has in years and even leaves his workouts feeling pleasantly fatigued instead of exhausted. And, as an added bonus, he has found very productive ways to spend the time that he has given up in the gym, such as relaxing and employing some restorative measures to enhance his recuperative powers (activities far more effective for furthering John's career than extra training would be).

John's weekly training plan during the second month back with coach Sage is summarized in Table 23.

Our third case involves Cindy Starter, a fourteen-year-old who has just been introduced to weightlifting. She fell in love with it after she attended her first competition with a friend. Cindy has been somewhat athletic throughout her life, having tried her hand at a number of sports, but she has never really trained seriously for any sport.

When she is introduced to coach John Bear, she says she wants to be a weightlifter like her friend, but she wants to know what her prospects for

Table 23

Monday	Tuesday	Wednesday	Thursday	Friday	Saturday
Snatch - 15	Jerk - 15	Power Sn - 12	Power Jk- 10	Power Cl - 12	C&J - 15
Clean - 15	Sn Pull - 15	Clean - 15	Snatch - 10	Snatch - 15	Cl Pull - 15
Squat - 20	Snatch Ddlft - 10	Frnt Squat - 15	Snatch Pl- 15	Squat - 15	Clean Ddlft - 10
Press - 10	Cln Pull - 15		Clean Pl - 15	Press - 10	Sn Pull - 15
Ab Work	Press - 10			Ab Work	Press - 10

success are. Coach Bear says that while there are certain physical characteristics that give athletes an advantage at the outset of their weightlifting careers (e.g., good flexibility and natural strength), the real determining factors in a weightlifter's success are the desire to excel and the discipline to go through the entire developmental process without skipping a step. He emphasizes the importance early on of developing sound technique and makes it clear that if Cindy wants to be a champion, she will have to focus her initial efforts on becoming a master technician. The coach explains that using light to moderate weights at the outset will increase Cindy's strength, while struggling with heavy weights will preclude her developing good technique and will not result in her gaining strength any faster.

During her first visit to the gym, Cindy is asked to observe the technique of the other lifters in the gym while the coach gives her some pointers on the fundamentals of weightlifting technique. Coach Bear then tests her flexibility in the extreme positions of lifting (the starting position in the snatch, front and overhead versions of the squat position and the overhead squat with a snatch and clean grip). Observing that Cindy has adequate flexibility in the elbows, legs and hips but is somewhat stiff in the shoulders, John demonstrates some exercises for increasing shoulder mobility and instructs her to perform those exercises at a moderate level every day.

John then shows Cindy how to miss. He emphasizes that knowing how to miss will prevent accidents and ultimately give her the courage to attempt even the heaviest of weights without fear, because she will know how to get out from under a missed attempt without injury. John then has Cindy perform several sets of eight to ten reps in each lift with a broomstick. In the snatch and the clean, the lifts are performed from a position at or above the knees. While Cindy is practicing the clean, John notes that a lack of resistance is causing Cindy to lift the stick far away from her body and to poorly time the exercise, so he has her perform two sets with a light bar, simply so Cindy can get the feel of some resistance. The coach corrects major errors in the broomstick lift after each set (sometimes after each rep if the error is gross enough). Cindy finishes her workout with two light sets of squats, a set of military presses, a set of abdominal exercise and some stretching for her shoulders. Coach Bear then tells her to return to the gym in two days and to bring a notebook for her training log.

In Cindy's second workout, she works again on missing (this time with a light bar after warming up with a stick). She is taught how to make notations in her training log. She performs each of the lifts with a stick (a light bar is used when a little more resistance is required). If the coach observes that Cindy seems to perform her snatches

and cleans more correctly from below the knee than above it, Cindy will spend most of her early lifting days practicing from that position. (While the hang position above the knees is the position most often taught at the outset, some athletes seem to perform more effectively with the bar beginning below the knee. Why force the lifter to practice a small segment of a lift when a larger segment of that lift comes more naturally?)

During these early training sessions, John places great emphasis on assuming the correct starting and finishing postures in each exercise. He also emphasizes the distinctions between what an athlete appears to be doing and what he or she is actually doing while lifting (e.g., the bar is not being lifted to the shoulders in the clean by the arms, rather the legs and back are throwing the bar and the arms are used to pull the body under the bar).

Because Cindy is so young and willing to work, her shoulder mobility training soon has increased her shoulder flexibility to the point that jerks with the bar well behind her head and overhead squats can be comfortably performed. She is taught the hook grip after a few training sessions and uses it on at least one lift per workout. Cindy is having trouble not using the arms prematurely in the clean, so John Bear decides to have her perform a few sets of clean pulls preceding her clean workouts. She then performs one or two reps in the clean pull immediately before each set of cleans (actually as the first rep(s) of each set of cleans). This kind of practice soon has Cindy performing her cleans with minimal unnecessary arm action.

During the early weeks Cindy's training is very flexible, as she and the coach experiment with different reps and styles of lifting (from the floor, the hang below the knees and the hang above the knees). Many teaching systems specify a certain order in the exercises that a lifter is taught at the outset, but John Bear bases the sequences taught on a general approach that he follows, modifying it for Cindy's abilities and her patterns of learning.

The order of exercises is also experimented with (some workouts begin with the snatch, while others start with the clean or the jerk). After several weeks a plan that will be loosely followed for a period if four weeks is created; this plan is summarized in Table 24. Each lift related exercise in this above program is performed in five to six sets of from three to five reps on each set with a very light resistance. But each assistance exercise (pulls, squats, presses and ab work) is limited to three sets of three to five reps. Moderate weights are used throughout, with the lifter being permitted to try a new higher weight every few workouts in each exercise. (Heavier weights are not permitted in more than two exercises per workout.) In no event is a true maximum effort attempted, only a weight that is more than that lifter has ever comfortably lifted before.

Table 24

Monday	Wednesday	Friday
Power Snatch & Overhead Squat	Power Cleans	Jerk From Racks
Clean Pull & Power Clean	Power Snatch	Power Snatch & Overhead Squat
Jerk From Racks	Power Jerk	Power Clean
Squat	Front Squat	Squat
Military Press	Press Behind Neck (Wide)	Military Press
Hypers & Ab Work	Ab Work	Hypers & Ab Work

In each workout (and usually for at least several training sessions in a row), the coach emphasizes one aspect of technique. The athlete may be doing many things incorrectly, but the coach selects the appropriate error to be corrected on the basis of the prioritization method that was discussed in Chapter 2. Once an error seams to have been corrected and that corrected behavior has stabilized for several workouts, the coach begins to address other errors. However, if an error suddenly appears through what seems to be a lack of attention, the error is corrected immediately, so that the lifter maintains the technique that she has already established.

Occasionally, Cindy is permitted to perform the clean and the jerk together, but at the early stages of learning, separating the two exercises is generally preferable. Some workouts with either the snatch or clean performed from the floor are done; all pulls are performed from the floor. Because Cindy seems to pull as correctly from the floor as she does from the hang in the clean, she is soon performing more of her cleans from the floor than from the hang. She is not performing her snatches as smoothly from the floor as she does from the hang, so some lifts from each position, as well as some sets in which there is a blend of both methods, will be done for some time. Every two to three weeks Cindy has an unloading week during which she does lighter lifts, performs fewer reps in each exercise, and emphasizes general physical preparation as much as lifting exercises.

A few comments on Cindy's specific case are in order. Because Cindy is a true beginner, Coach Bear bases his training regimen on a number of ideas that are worth making explicit. The first of these is individualization. On the day that any person decides to pursue a career in weightlifting, he or she becomes a "beginner." While most beginners share many qualities (e.g., the need to learn technique and the need to increase their strength), there will be many characteristics that make individual beginners different as well. One beginner may have a background in weight training and another may not. The lifter with a weight training background may be better conditioned for at least some forms of weightlifting training than the non-lifter but may have picked up some bad technical habits along the way or may

have developed uneven levels of strength in certain lifting areas.

One beginner may be more flexible in the shoulders and less flexible in the ankles than another. Therefore, in certain ways, there is no such thing as a fixed and optimal training plan for "the" beginner (any more than there is such a program for the lifter at any other stage of development). Nevertheless, meaningful guidelines for training beginners can be provided, as long as the coach recognizes the importance of adjusting any general approach to the individual needs, abilities and qualities of each beginner.

When a lifter first begins to train with weights, virtually any lifting that he or she does will have a training effect (at least with respect to that exercise). The biggest single mistake a beginner can make is to interfere by overworking with the adaptations that the body is trying to make in response to the training stimulus. Overwork leads to fatigue. A truly fatigued lifter is more likely to use poor technique, more likely to be injured and, perhaps worst of all, more likely to become discouraged about his or her training.

The special susceptibility of a new lifter to these problems arises out of three kinds of adaptation that are taking place simultaneously (at last two of which are related). At the outset of training, the body is developing the ability to perform a greater volume of work with less disruption to the body's systems, and it is adapting to the higher intensity of the work being performed. Developing both of these qualities (the ability to work harder and to lift more) seems to place a greater strain of the body's resources than training separately on one or another of the capacities (although there is always a significant degree of interaction between training both capacities). A third adaptation has to do with motor learning. The new lifter is learning to contract his or her muscles more rapidly and forcefully and to coordinate new patterns of movement. This learning places a significant stress on the athlete's nervous system. Care must be taken in planning the training of the beginner to assure that this combination of demands does not overcome the lifter's ability to adapt.

When it comes to building strength, I generally encourage the new lifter to begin training with one moderately difficult set of each strength building exercise that needs to be done. (The lifter should end the exercise when one to three additional reps could have been performed with considerable effort, i.e., each rep that is done should be performed smoothly and without assistance.) The use of a single set (after one or two warm-up sets) that entails a moderate effort (one in which one or two extra reps would probably be possible) gives the body a nudge in the direction of developing both its work capacity and strength. The number of workouts in which the "one set" routine is used depends on the age and overall condition of the athlete as well as the number of exercises the athlete is performing in the workout. Naturally, a young athlete who is well conditioned, perhaps from training for another related but non-weightlifting sport, is able to increase the training load relatively readily and may even be able to begin with more than one set. An athlete who has done weight training that included the exercise in question can of course perform more sets at the outset. An older athlete, particularly one who has been inactive for some time, might do well to keep training on one set per exercise for two or three weeks or even longer. Then the workout can be increased to two sets per exercise per workout, and then to three sets after two to three more weeks.

Prepubescent athletes can and should use even lighter loads than those described in the previous paragraph, both because caution in loading young athletes must always be observed and because Soviet research has shown that younger athletes actually improve more rapidly when they train with 70% weights than when they train with weights that are 80% to 90% of maximum (the mainstay for strength building in more mature and higher level athletes).

Many people feel that they are not doing enough when they do only one set of several basic exercises in their early workouts. They insist on doing more sets and more exercises and on prematurely increasing the weights used. The end result is often a classic case of overtraining or injury. The new trainee experiences this (generally after a period of ten days to several weeks) as a loss of interest in the training process, fatigue, constant soreness or an aching feeling in the muscles and/or joints and a general feeling of malaise. (These sensations are not the same as the acute pain of delayed onset muscle soreness, which generally first appears from several to twenty-four hours after a workout, reaches a peak at twenty-four to seventy-two hours after the workout and then goes away within from one to several days.) Many people quit at this point, concluding that weight training is not for them (that it hurts them, makes them sore, is too strenuous, etc.). They do not realize that by abandoning progressive resistance training they are thereby resigning themselves to a life of progressive muscle atrophy, weakness, unnecessary demineralization of their

bones and a loss of flexibility, all of which could have been prevented with regular exercise with weights. The decision to quit lifting weights may well be one of the most tragic they will ever make, and it was caused by a failure to follow the basic principles of proper conditioning. (This point applies to progressive resistance exercise overall, not only to the classic Olympic lifts.)

The appropriate training for beginners who are Olympic lifters is a special case. When an athlete is trying to learn a skill as well as to condition himself or herself (as is the situation when trying to learn to snatch or C&J), it is necessary to do considerable practice (i.e., many sets of the movement being learned). The ability of the beginner to handle multiple sets of Olympic lifts without undue strain on the body is made possible by several factors. One is that the athlete learning technique can use very light weights initially, thereby keeping bodily fatigue to a minimum while still improving motor skills. Second, since the snatch and C&J, particularly with light weights, are rapid movements, the muscles are not able to develop the degree of tension that they do when slow movements are performed. Therefore, some of the training and fatiguing effects of more strenuous resistance exercise (in terms of muscle tension) are avoided.

However, given the factors mentioned earlier, there is a limit to the number of sets a new lifter should perform. A trade-off can be made between the number of sets and the difficulty of the set. For example, if instead of using a weight that is moderately difficult, the lifter stays with a weight that is even easier, more sets and reps can be performed without overcoming the body's reserves. Even a new lifter might be able to perform three to five sets in the first few workouts in the classical lifts without experiencing any undue stress, if the weights are very light. The number of sets can be increased to four to six after several weeks, as long an most of the sets are light, but this should not be done in all exercises in the same workout. (Select one exercise per workout for several weeks and add a second exercise per workout after another several weeks for the increased number of sets.)

Beginners can use a stick to practice the lifts and complete as many as five to ten reps per set merely to learn the motion (once more resistance is added as time goes on, the reps will fall to the 2-5 range). Further, there is no need to use weights which are difficult in any way. Six sets of three to four reps with 40% to 50% can be quite useful for purposes of learning the skill associated with performing an Olympic lift. (For a further discussion of weight selection, see Chapter 2).

What kind of progress can an athlete expect to see? A correlation has been noted between the starting age of the athlete and the time it takes an athlete to reach the status of Master of Sport. For instance, one study performed in the former Soviet

Union found that athletes who began at age twelve typically required four years to reach the status of Master Of Sport. Athletes who began at twenty-one only required thirty months to reach that standard. Athletes in heavier weight classes take significantly longer, on average, to reach high levels of performance. It should be noted that while a champion lifter's rate of progress during his or her early stages of training is generally significant, even a lifter who may ultimately be outstanding can find it slow going in the early years as the search for proper technique and sound training methods is under way. Similarly, a lifter who starts at a relatively high level of performance and progresses rapidly early on can hit a "wall" quite easily if the foundations for future high performance were not carefully laid.

Although the case histories presented above are different, they share the same theme. The athletes had particular needs, and addressing those needs became the focus of the training plan. The fit within the long term plan was considered in each case, but the needs of the athlete, rather than the annual phase of training, governed what the lifter actually did in his training. (In Cindy's case, the long term plan is of no great significance except to assure that Cindy is not overloaded in her early training; competitions at this point are of no particular interest.) This distinction between setting priorities on the basis of some preconceived model or training progression and objectives and an individualized focus is crucial for the development of effective training plans.

What does it matter if the calendar lists an important competition if conditions for an individual athlete suggest otherwise? As an example I am forced the recall the case of an athlete that I knew whose schedule called for an important competition in the near future. He had incurred an injury a couple of months before this competition and relied on medication to try to relieve the symptoms. The medication helped, but the lifter was still bothered by the injury, which was to an area of the body that undergoes tremendous stresses during the performance of the classical lifts. Because the competition calendar called for it, the athlete decided to compete. He faced unexpected competition and was forced to attempt some near maximum weights in order to win the competition. On one of those attempts, he was injured seriously, and that injury changed the entire course of his career. In retrospect, that lifter surely recognizes that the "important" competition was not so very important after all.

There is a fine line between conjuring up an excuse not to compete or not to make an all out effort to perform well at a given competition and ignoring legitimate factors which should influence planning. When the intense pressure of preparing for a critical competition looms, it is easy to find an excuse or to ignore signals of impending disaster.

Careful judgment is the only tool the coach and athlete have to guide them through these difficult issues. But the first step in exercising such judgment is the recognition that the individual athlete's needs are for more important and relevant to making calls about his or her career than long term training models developed by theoreticians or statisticians. An individual athlete is not a statistic, and theories (critical as they are) must be tested and modified in the arena of reality. If either Alan or John had felt that a particular competition was important enough, training could have been arranged to accommodate the competition. However, what really counted in their training was that their weaknesses were effectively addressed by considering their needs rather than some preconceived notion of what they should be doing or what some idealized long term model of training suggests.

The Special Needs of Powerlifters and Other Strength Athletes Who Convert to Weightlifting

Athletes who have been engaged in strength training for a significant period of time (e.g., powerlifters and weight throwers) must employ a very special approach to training when they become weightlifters.

First, they must recognize that learning to be a skilled weightlifter will take years of work. There are no shortcuts to learning the skills of weightlifting–no matter how strong one is. The athlete who intends to convert to weightlifting must swallow his or her ego and accept the lot of a beginner (a very strong beginner with major advantages over the typical beginner, but a beginner in a number of important respects nonetheless).

Second, strong beginners face a challenge that normal beginners do not. They may actually be able to lift enough early on to injure themselves. A high strength level and lack of skill are a dangerous combination. It is not unlike teaching someone to drive in a Corvette, or skiing for the first time on an expert slope–accidents are likely to happen. Consequently, emphasizing the development of sound technique is even more critical for the strong beginner than the weak one.

Third, strong beginners are not in condition to lift heavy weights in the classic lifts. They would be making a mistake to attempt it–even if they had the technique and flexibility to carry it off. As was noted in earlier chapters, training is very specific. Only when the body is conditioned to accept a particular load (the speed, mechanics, intensity and volume of the loading must be prepared for) can it effectively handle that load without being overwhelmed.

The good news is that by training technique with light weights the athlete can both learn to lift properly and condition the body to accept the loads that the very strong athlete will ultimately be able to lift.

The smart strength athlete who is planning a conversion to weightlifting will do several things. He or she will find a good technical coach. The athlete will have his or her weightlifting flexibility assessed and will begin to work on any areas of deficiency immediately. The athlete will continue to train on the exercises that made him or her strong if they are related to the strength required for weightlifting. But those exercises will be modified as needed to be more specific to the classic lift.

For instance, if the athlete has been performing power squats (squats to a depth where the thighs are just below parallel to the floor, the bar is held on the upper back and a wide foot stance is generally employed), he or she will begin to do more squats with the bar high on the shoulders and the feet closer together than powerlifters do. This should be a gradual process where the athlete does only lighter sets in this manner for a time, gradually performing with heavier and heavier weights in the new style.

As the training weights on the classic lifts and related exercises increases, the other exercises should be gradually reduced, and, in some cases, be phased out altogether (e.g., wide stance squats and round back deadlifts can eliminated in favor of heavy close stance squats with the bar placed high on the shoulders and the lifter squatting as far down as possible).

Similarly, deadlifts, particularly round back and Sumo style deadlifts, would be phased out in favor of deadlifts in a position identical to that of the first three stages in the pull.

Muscles that have may not been trained in the past but that are important for weightlifting performance (e.g., overhead pressing) will need to be gradually added to the program. The athlete should begin with a small number of sets and moderate loads (perhaps threes sets, including warm-ups and finishing with a weight that is relatively comfortable in the last rep of the last set).

It will take several months for a strength athlete's skills and conditioning to prepare him or her for serious training on the classic lifts and related exercises. Even at that point, the athlete is advised to train like a beginner or novice. That is, training should only occur three or four times per week. Over time the training can be increased, but the lifter must not rush into daily heavy training because his or her body will simply not be up to the task. It will take years (at least 2-3) before the athlete is mentally and physically ready to demonstrate anything near his or her true maximum abilities in the snatch and C&J. This is not to say that they can't lift heavy weights even earlier but any such lifts will not be near their

ultimate potential (remember it takes a typical beginner 5-7 years to reach anything close to his or her potential, so the background that a strength athlete from another sport has can cut that time by as much as half).

I have heard a number of powerlifters and other strength athletes say that they "tried" weightlifting and it hurt their joints and I have witnessed it myself. But in every case I am aware of this has occurred because the athlete has not learned proper technique and allowed for proper conditioning.

It is only natural for the powerlifter or other strength athlete to want to "try himself or herself out" to see if he or she "has it". The truth is that no one "has it" and the only way to get "it" is to train for it. The athlete who wants to see if he or she is really strong should be content to perform some squats to a fairly low position with a fairly close stance, with the bar high on the shoulders and with no supporting gear. Such an athlete will learn respect for weightlifters who can take a squat with 600, 700, 800 or more pounds to the bottom. In some cases these relatively new athletes may demonstrate truly extraordinary strength. Even in that event, the new weightlifter will need to be content with that form of strength expression (and improving upon it) until he or she develops the skill and conditioning necessary to express his or her strength through the classic lifts.

Strength athletes should not be discouraged by the advice that has been provided above. If they prepare properly they will ultimately be able to demonstrate their abilities in the most competitive strength sport in the world. The strength training that they have done will make the road to the top shorter than it will be for most others. In addition, other skills that they may have developed while training for competing in other strength events (concentration, poise under pressure, good training habits) will all give them and advantage as they make the transition.

There is nothing I would like to see more than the best powerlifters and other strength athletes of the world develop the strength and skills needed to compete with the best in the world in weightlifting. This influx of new athletes into the sport of weightlifting will no doubt raise the competitive "bar" for everyone. But only the intelligent, dedicated and patient athlete making the transition from another weight sport to weightlifting will get the job done.

The Actual Training Programs of Three Champions

Having presented the concepts of programming, throughout this chapter, it is now appropriate to give some examples of planning in the real world, in the form of some workouts used by particular athletes. We will do that in two ways in this section of the chapter. First we will present some workouts used by three champion weightlifters. Then we will present programs that have been developed for somewhat lower level athletes on the basis of their individual needs. In the latter case the reader will have the opportunity, in effect, to look over the coach's shoulder as he constructs the programs, so that the reasoning underlying their construction can be understood. By seeing both of these real world applications of training principles, the reader should be in a far better position to construct his or her own program.

Many books on weightlifting and other sports include a series of sample or recommended workouts. Sometimes these are offered merely as very generalized examples of what full workouts look like. In other cases the workouts are somewhat more specific. For instance, they may be presented in such a way that there are workouts for athletes of different levels (e.g., beginner, intermediate and advanced). While these approaches can provide valuable concrete examples of the application of workout planning theories, they can and do lead to a number of serious misunderstandings. There is a tendency for readers to assume that these examples are the actual workouts that athletes should endeavor to perform. Sometimes authors intend this because they believe that they have developed "the ideal" workout and want others to use it. In other cases the reader assumes this, even though the author may caution against it. In reality, there is no ideal workout for all lifters, all lifters of the same level or even all lifters with the same strengths and weaknesses. As has already been discussed, different lifters react to the same workloads in different ways.

There are unquestionably universal principles of training that apply to all lifters. These principles have already been presented at length. The challenge for the coach and the athlete is to apply these principles properly. That is why we are providing examples, not off-the-shelf solutions. Before proceeding we will warn the reader once again that the programs being presented cannot be followed blindly. They are programs that were developed to meet the individual needs of the lifters and were based on the judgment of the lifters or coaches who formulated them at that time (which means that they may or may not have been optimal for those lifters at that time). The purpose of illustrating them is to show how planning principles have been applied rather than how they should be applied to you or your athletes, different individuals with different needs and abilities.

I have selected the programs of three lifters: two-time World Superheavyweight Champion, Antonio Krastev; the 1994 Women's World Champion in the 50 kg. category, Robin Byrd-Goad; and 1976 Olympic Gold Medalist, Lee James. The first two workouts are presented as they were told

to me, and the last one is presented as it appeared in the 1978-1979 issues of <u>Strength & Health</u>.

The Training of Antonio Krastev

Between the fall of 1991 and the fall of 1993, Antonio Krastev, two-time World Superheavyweight Champion and many time world recordholder and the man who snatched 216 kg., the greatest weight ever recognized by the IWF as a world record, trained in our gym in New York City. When he arrived, he had not trained for an extended period, and lifts of 120 kg. and 150 kg. gave him a great deal of trouble during his first workout with us. However, over a period of several months, he regained a significant amount of his former condition and was doing lifts of 185 kg. and 230 kg. Over the next year or so he trained irregularly because of job commitments and other issues which made training difficult. Then, toward the beginning of 1993, things settled down for Antonio, and he trained seriously through May of that year. At the end of that period, he performed lifts of 200 kg. and 250 kg. in training, equaled the snatch in competition, clean and jerked 235 kg. in the same meet and cleaned 245 kg. relatively easily, narrowly missing the jerk. In a matter of months, Antonio had worked himself into shape and very nearly lifted the highest total made in the world that year.

That Antonio Krastev is a remarkable athlete is obvious by his lifting ability. However, he credits much of his success to the training approach that he has developed over more than two decades in weightlifting. Unlike the other Bulgarian lifters of his day, Antonio constructed his own training programs when he did his best lifting (from 1985 to 1987 when he won two World Championships and set his amazing snatch record of 216 kg.).

When he was able to train full time in Bulgaria, Antonio trained six days a week, twice a day. His workouts were founded on the six exercises that the Bulgarian elite lifters of the mid and late 1980s performed: snatch, C&J, power snatch, power clean, front squat and back squat. However, Krastev also performed his version of a high pull approximately once a week with each grip. (His method of performing the pull consisted of lifting the bar in an identical fashion to the classic lift, with a very explosive effort at the finish of the pull but never bending the arms or permitting the bar to rise above the position in which his body was fully extended, leaning slightly back and on toes.)

In his morning workouts Krastev would typically perform the snatch and C&J plus some kind of squatting (he would often substitute a power snatch or power clean for the squat versions of those lifts). He worked up to a comfortable maximum in each exercise, training exclusively on single lifts. (Krastev rarely performs a double and never does more than two reps in any weightlifting related exercise in training.)

In the evening Antonio would again work up to maximum in both lifts and either the front or back squat. While he could not work up to his best lifts every day, he found that he could usually equal or exceed his best C&J once or twice a week and do the same in the snatch two or three times a week. His experiences were similar in the squat. In the pull Antonio would work up well in excess of his best lifts in the snatch or clean respectively, always emphasizing an explosive effort.

When he trained in the United States, Antonio modified his approach somewhat because he worked during most of his stay here. He therefore generally omitted the morning workout. He also introduced a greater degree of variability of volume and intensity into his training. His training was based more on how he felt on a given day. For example, in the spring of 1993, the day after he snatched 200 kg. for the first time in the United States, he came into the gym, worked up to a power snatch with 90 kg. and ended his workout. He felt that much was enough on that day. With respect to cycling, Antonio rarely varied the reps or exercises that he performed. However, during lighter months or weeks, he merely lifted at a lower level of intensity.

While much of Antonio's success can be attributed to the physical side of his training, much of his tremendous performance capabilities must be attributed to his mental preparation. To watch Antonio train is to experience a truly unusual level of intensity. While he relaxes between sets, when Antonio wraps his hand around the bar, he is all business. His concentration is awesome, and he prepares himself for every lift (light or heavy) in the same way in terms of focus. (He obviously becomes more aroused emotionally when he prepares for his heaviest lifts.)

When Antonio gets ready to lift, the observer feels that he would not notice if the building collapsed. This kind of focus not only pays off in terms of his ability to perform heavy lifts on a regular basis but also explains his consistency. Over the two years that I watched Antonio train, I did not see him miss more than a handful of lifts in either the snatch or the clean (and when he did miss it was with a maximum attempt). Moreover, his skill is so great that it is rare for him to have a lift that is out of the groove or requires any adjustment as he lifts. Virtually every lift is rock solid and is performed with exemplary efficiency and explosiveness.

During Antonio's peak, his best lifts were: a snatch of 222.5 kg.; a C&J of 265 kg.; a power snatch of 200 kg.; a power clean of 220 kg.; a squat of 410 kg.; a front squat of 310 kg.; a power jerk of 250 kg. (last performed in 1980 when his former coach Abadjiev had his lifters abandon them); and a jerk from the rack of 270 kg. (last done in 1981 when Abadjiev abandoned them as well).

The Training Program of a World Champion: Robin Byrd-Goad

November 25, 1994, was a magic moment in United States weightlifting history. For the first time since the Women's World Championships began in 1987, the United States had an all around world champion weightlifter: Robin Byrd (recently married to U. S. National Weightlifting Champion Dean Goad and now Robin Byrd-Goad). Robin has had a long and illustrious career in weightlifting, setting world records in the snatch in both the pre-1993 and post-1992 weight class eras and winning silver medals in World Championships on three occasions. Finally, in 1994 Robin received her greatest reward to date. She was the true queen of the 50 kg. division at last!

How did Robin prepare for the 1994 World Championships? The complete answer includes a decade of hard and intelligent training and a great deal of determination. But in terms of the immediate period prior to the 1994 World Championships, Robin has been gracious enough to provide me with her actual training log for the nine weeks prior to the event during which she worked herself into the best shape of her career. As it turned out, Robin was able to be conservative on the day of the meet and did not have to exceed her training bests in order to win (although she is fully capable of doing so when necessary).

During the period from nine weeks to one week before the competition, Robin trained five times a week on average, but her workouts varied from three to six days in a given week, depending on her energy level, the degree to which she felt recuperated from prior workouts and the available training time. Most of her training was done once a day, in part because of the demands of her employment as a teacher. (Unlike most competitors from other countries, Robin holds a full time job, proving that an athlete can work and still achieve championship performance levels.) Obviously, with the constraints on Robin's training, her workouts had to be highly efficient at generating results.

In her pre-competition training, Robin employed a total of fifteen different bar exercises: snatches. power snatches, snatches from the block, C&J's, jerks, power cleans and jerks, snatch pulls, snatch pulls from the hang, snatch deadlifts and shrugs, clean pulls, clean deadlifts and shrugs, stop squats, squats, front squats and presses. She averaged three exercises per workout but did only one exercise in some workouts and as many as five exercises in others. She spent nearly 25% of her training time performing C&J's and related exercises and about as much time performing snatches. A little more than 25% of her training time was spent performing snatch and clean pulls and deadlifts (with snatch related exercises of this type comprising a little more than half of the total number of reps), while another 17% was spent on squatting. The balance of her training was devoted to presses and other remedial kinds of exercises.

The single exercises Robin performed most often in her training were the snatch and the power clean and jerk, which she did a total of twelve times during her training sequence. Snatches and snatch deadlifts were next in terms of frequency, being performed eleven times each. C&J's and power snatches tied for third place with ten training sessions on each.

Robin performed jerks from the rack only four times during the training cycle. However, in one of her workouts, she jerked 105 kg., her all time best. She preferred snatch and clean deadlifts with a shrug about 3.5 to 1 over pulls with either grip and performed front and back squats with nearly equal frequency.

Robin would typically handle 95% to 100% of maximum in her deadlifts for three sets of three reps. Front squats were generally in the 95% to 105% range in relation to her C&J for two to three reps, while back squats were generally performed with from 122% to 132% for sets of two to three reps.

During the two training months prior to the World Championships, Robin did a total of approximately 1000 reps. She performed singles and doubles most often in the classic lifts and related exercises, rarely doing more than three reps in these exercises. However, sets of three reps were her most common pattern in squats and in pulls.

Approximately six weeks prior to her World Championships victory, Robin competed in a local competition as a sort of tune up for her World competition. At that competition, 3 kg. overweight, she made lifts of 82.5 kg. and 97.5 kg., actually trying an 85 kg. snatch. She made no special preparations for that competition, other than reducing her training load during the week preceding it. In the final week prior to the competition, Robin trained only twice. She performed the power snatch, C&J and a few jerks from the rack five days out. Snatches and C&J's with approximately 85% of maximum were handled during the last workout, which was two days before the competition.

Robin's workouts were curtailed a little more than they normally would have been before a competition, both because she had a long trip to the competition and because she had a kidney infection that nearly prevented her from competing at all. Only quick thinking on the part of her personal coach (and that year's Women's World Team coach), John Coffee, resulted in her getting the treatment she needed, permitting Robin to enjoy the most glorious moment of her career and the brightest moment in recent United States weightlifting history.

While he tends to maintain a low profile, John has coached more of the US's top women lifters than any other coach in the history of US weightlifting. His women have won more than ten National Championships and he has had more than one of his athletes on virtually every international women's team ever fielded by the US. The breadth of John's knowledge and success is often overlooked because of his unassuming ways, but he is truly one of the sport's unsung heroes.

The Training of Lee James

Lee James had a meteoric rise to weightlifting success during the mid-1970s. He took fourth place in the 1974 Nationals in the 82.5 kg. category but made the 1974 United States World Weightlifting Championships team through some very good fortune. In 1975 he took second at the U. S. Nationals and had good fortune second time as the champion, Peter Rawluk, was injured during the championship, and Lee got to represent the United States once again. He went on to win the Pan American Games that year and then really caught fire. He moved up to the 90 kg. class and over a period of less than a year added 20 kg. to win a silver medal at the Montreal Olympics.

Lee injured his knee in Montreal and, after wrestling with the problem for some months, finally had surgery in 1977. Many wrote him off after the surgery, but he fought back, setting American records once again, winning the Nationals in 1978 and looking as if he would be a real contender at the 1978 World Championships, which were to be held in the United States later that year. Unfortunately, disaster struck shortly after the Nationals, as Lee reinjured his knee once again; he was unable to lift at the World Championships and never fully recovered after that.

His post-injury program during 1977-78 is of particular interest because it shows how a lifter coped with an injury by reducing the number of classic lifts and relying on strength and power building exercises more than the classic lifts to restore him to his former competitive form and beyond. It must be remembered that Lee was already an established lifter with good technique when he embarked on this program, so the need for him to practice the classic lifts was not as great as it would have been for a lifter of less skill or experience. It should also be noted that Lee emphasized good technique during all of this strength building work so that his newfound strength could be converted to improved performance on the snatch and C&J as much as possible

In the latter part of 1977 and the first half of 1978, Lee trained on a program of four days a week

Table 25
Preparatory Period

Intensity Level	85%	95-100%	80%	70%
Monday (AM)				
Front Squat	5-2	3-1	8-4	16 (3 sets)
Snatch Shrug	8	6	12	18 (3 sets)
Monday (PM)				
Power Snatch	5-2	3-1	6-4	none
Good Morning	8	6	10	none
Press	5-2	3-1	8-4	none
Tuesday (AM)				
Squat	5-2	3-1	8-4	16 (3 sets)
Clean Shrug	10	6	12	18 (3 sets)
Tuesday (PM)				
Power Clean	5-2	3-1	6-4	none
Hyperextensions	8	6	10	none
Thursday (AM)				
Snatch Pull	5-2	3-1	6-4	none
Pull to Knees	5-2	3-1	6-4	none
Snatch Hang Pull	5-2	3-1	6-4	none
Thursday (PM)				
Snatch Shrug	8	6	12	18 (3 sets)
Jerk Support	10 seconds	5 seconds	15 seconds	none
Friday (AM)				
Clean Pulls	5-2	3-1	6-4	none
Pull to Knees	5-2	3-1	6-4	none
Hang Pull	5-2	3-1	6-4	none
Friday (PM)				
Squat	5-2	3-1	8-4	16 (3 sets)
Clean Shrugs	10	6	10	18 (3 sets)

and two workouts a day. The workouts were performed on Mondays, Tuesdays, Thursdays and Fridays, giving Lee the weekends and one day in the middle of the week to recuperate from his grueling program. He believed in focusing on one of the lifts each training day and hitting that lift from every angle. He then performed some kind of squatting exercise on each training day. On two of his non-training days he would do some jumping and stretching.

He followed the practice of setting up four-week mesocycles, with similar percentages lifted in each lift during each week. Reps performed were higher in the lower intensity weeks and lower in the high intensity weeks Table 25 depicts his workouts. The percentages shown on the table refer to the percentage of maximum that was lifted in the top set(s) of each training day that week. The "maximum" refers to the Lee's maximum for that exercise. For example, Lee did his pulls to a height gauge, so the percentage referred to in that exercise is of the heaviest pull that he could do correctly and touch the height gauge (when Lee snatched his personal best of 170 kg. his best snatch pull was 185 kg.). Percentages are all of the maximums for that exercise. Unless otherwise noted, each exercise was performed for seven sets

(Thursday's and Friday's shrugs were performed for five and four sets respectively).

Lee performed his shrugs up to 85% with no preparatory leg bend but with a rise on the toes and shoulders pulled as high and as explosively as possible. With weights above 90% he used some leg drive to assist in the shrugging motion. Pulls to the knee were performed standing on a 2" block with two-second pauses on each rep 2" above the floor, below the knees and again 2" above the floor on the way down. (He just brushed the floor between reps.) On the hang pulls Lee lifted the bar form above the knee. Good mornings were performed with the knees bent and the torso lowered to a position parallel to the floor. Abdominal work was done after the Tuesday and Friday workouts.

Approximately four weeks prior to a competition, Lee modified his workouts to focus on the competitive lifts. (See Table 26.) He reduced his training volume significantly through a reduction in reps and sets. He did singles in the classic lifts and began his pulls with three reps but reduced them to singles with the heaviest weights of the day. Front squats were reduced to five sets of three reps throughout this cycle and were eliminated entirely one week before the competition. Back squats were reduced to five sets of three reps two

Table 26
Competition Program

Monday	Tuesday	Thursday	Friday
Snatch	C&J	Snatch	C&J
Snatch Pull	Clean Pull	Snatch Pull	Clean Pull
Snatch Shrug	Front Squat	Clean Shrug	Squat

weeks before the competition. All exercises were staggered in terms of percentages from workout to workout (ranging from 70% to 100%). He would attempt a maximum C&J fifteen to twenty-one days before a competition and a maximum snatch approximately ten days out (trying to have seven days between the maximum training C&J and snatch). His focus during this period was on explosiveness and technique. Lee tended to move quickly through his workout, resting approximately 45 seconds between most sets (except for squats, where he typically rested for 2 minutes between sets).

Lee always felt that mental training was at least as important as physical preparation and that most less successful lifters got the results they did because of lack of mental training rather than poor physical preparation or genetic deficiencies. He feels that development of mind, spirit and heart is the most important factor in a lifter's success—a contention with which few people who have raised themselves to success in any endeavor would disagree.

The James workout approach would have to be considered atypical, but they have worked well for him and for some other athletes who have tried similar ones, modified for their own circumstances.

Peaking Methods

To this point, we have focused primarily on training to improve overall capabilities. In this section we will focus on training methods that will enable the athlete to express whatever abilities he or she has on the competition platform (i.e., to arrive at the competition in the best possible condition). This special training process is often referred to as "peaking."

As has been indicated earlier in this book, training is a process of applying a stimulus of sufficient strength to the body in order to cause an adaptation by the body. However, in order for the body to generate an adaptation, it must be given time. Applying another stimulus before the body has adapted to the first is unnecessary. Moreover, if another stimulus is applied before the body has adapted to the first, the body can be stressed to point at which its adaptive energies are diverted from the process of positive adaptation to mere maintenance. If unnecessary stimulation continues, the body can be overwhelmed to the point at which it regresses or becomes injured or

sick. Consequently, getting adequate rest is one of the keys to weightlifting progress.

Adequate rest can be even more critical before a weightlifting competition. There is a tendency for lifters to overtrain in preparation for a meet (primarily due to the need to prove to themselves that they are in top condition by repeatedly demonstrating that condition to themselves). A second reason is that stress arising out of concerns about the competition is often high just prior to that event. This extra stress can overwhelm a body that was otherwise in balance with regard to the relationship between rest and training. Therefore, extra rest immediately before a competition can assure that the body will be adequately rested on the day of the meet. It can also provide the added reserve that may be needed at a crucial moment in competition.

While extra rest is desirable, some lifters let the quest for extra rest accomplish the opposite of its intended purpose. Rest may help build the reserves necessary to handle stress, but if worry about rest itself becomes a stressor, little is accomplished by attempting to get extra rest. Lest the emphasis on extra rest become exaggerated, it should be remembered that a healthy athlete who has properly prepared for a competition will have the capacity to perform well, even if the rest he or she gets immediately before the competition is not optimal.

Proper preparation should build a lifter's reserves so that he or she will be able to prevail regardless of any last minute conditions. Several steps should be taken to accomplish this. First, the training volume should generally be reduced somewhat prior to a competition. Second, the lifter should set aside a little more time than usual for relaxation. Third, the lifter should also be sure to get adequate sleep. Finally, the lifter should attempt to reduce sources of stress. For example, the weeks before a major competition are not the ideal time to change jobs, cultivate new love relationships, confront major family problems or undertake any major changes in living habits.

Skill is required to combine these extra rest factors, and that skill consists primarily of proper timing. If extra rest begins too early and is too extreme, the athlete can actually begin to lose some of his or her adaptation to the training. If the rest begins to late, it will not have enough time to exert a full positive effect. Timing will vary among athletes and within the same athlete depending on that athlete's condition immediately prior to beginning the special energy conservation effort.

To determine proper timing, I recommend a "condition assessment" approximately six top twelve weeks prior to a major competition. Such an assessment is far from scientific, but it can be vital. During the condition assessment, the lifter should consider such issues as his or her present physical and emotional state and the career and family obligations that are likely to arise before the competition. If the lifter feels a little overtrained, this is the time to correct that problem. In contrast, if a lifter is undertrained or coming off an injury, it may be appropriate to plan a gradual increase in intensity up to the competition. If extra emphasis on some minor aspect of technique or strength needs to be applied, this is the time for this. If a significantly stressful event is anticipated, this is the time to consider how to reduce the level of such stress. Plan to make travel arrangements far enough ahead so that stress with regard to that process is avoided; five to six weeks before a major competition is a good rule of thumb. Repair or replace any personal equipment (e.g., get the heels of your lifting shoes fixed if they need it). Arrange things so that only unexpected events are likely to require any extra effort part as the competition draws closer.

In essence, the purpose of this planning session is to cause the lifter to pause and re-evaluate the situation. Perhaps more importantly, it allows the lifter to pause early enough to make meaningful corrections and preparations. The final aspects of the peaking process are planned during this phase.

There may be as many peaking methods as there are lifters, but most methods can be characterized in one of two ways: decreasing volume and increasing intensity or gradually increasing intensity and maintaining relatively stable volume. The first method is probably the more popular of the two, but both methods can work if they are tailored to the lifter. Elements of both methods are often combined. For example, volume can be traded off for intensity, and intensity can increase gradually. Naturally, circumstances can favor the use of one over the other.

Peaking by Reducing Volume and Increasing Intensity

Peaking for competition by decreasing volume and increasing intensity is typically part of a larger overall training plan based on periodization. The reduction in volume as the competition nears virtually guarantees that the lifter will be able to increase the intensity of his or her training without experiencing undue fatigue. Therefore, the athlete should be well rested on the day of the competition, even though he or she has made a relatively high number of maximum and near maximum attempts

in the classical lifts in the month(s) immediately before the competition. Additional assurance of arriving at the competition in a rested state is attained when the lifter further reduces the volume and intensity of training in the final days before the competition.

In order to use periodization for successfully when peaking, the coach must constantly monitor the progress of the athlete and make adjustments to the program as necessary. If the athlete enters the competitive period in a state of fatigue, the normal reduction in volume and increase in intensity during the competition phase will not peak the athlete effectively. If the athlete is performing at a very high level in the classical exercises during the preparatory phase, there may not need to be as long a competitive period as was originally planned. These and a multitude of other considerations must be factored in as the coach observes the lifter in training.

In addition to the information that has already been presented in this book, a significant amount of research has been performed in Eastern Europe regarding the preparation of an athlete for a major competition in the closing weeks before the competitive month. On the basis of such research, Robert Roman, the late writer from the former Soviet Union, provided a number of guidelines for preparing for competition in his works. In one of his later works, Roman suggests that athletes not attempt maximums in the snatch closer that seven to fifteen days from the competition. Weights 95% to 97% of maximum should not be lifted within six to twelve days of the competition, and weights 90% to 92.5% should not be lifted within five to nine days. In the C&J, he recommends no maximums within nine to eighteen days of the competition, no weights 95% to 97% within seven to fifteen days and no weights 90% to 92.5% within five to thirteen days. He believes that 94% of all heavy squats in the month should be performed during the first three weeks of the competition month and that all heavy clean pulls should also be done during those weeks. In the squat, he recommends that the athlete not handle weights in excess of 120% of the C&J ten to sixteen days prior to the meet, weights 110% to 117.5% eight to twelve days before or weights 100% to 107.5% six to ten days before. Finally, in the clean pull, he warns against handling weights in excess of 120% within eleven to nineteen days of the competition, weights 110% to 117.5% within nine to fifteen days and weights 100% to 107.5% within eight to twelve days.

In terms of pre-competition training, with the competition scheduled on the eighth day, the athlete should perform a total of seventy lifts on the first day at below average intensity. On the third day the athlete performs a total of fifty lifts, with the highest lifts reaching maximum levels of intensity, does a total of thirty-six lifts of moderate intensity on the fifth day and rests on the sixth and seventh days. According to Roman, athletes in heavier weight classes should employ a somewhat different pattern of preparation during the competition week, performing fifty lifts on the first day (hitting a maximum or near maximum in the snatch and a near maximum in the C&J). The athlete performs a total of sixty-five lifts with below average intensity on the third day, a total of forty lifts of moderate intensity on the fifth day and a total of thirty-five lifts of minimum intensity on the seventh day (the day before the competition). Athletes in higher classifications (up to the MS classification) tend to do more lifts at higher relative intensity, but there is a drop off in the number of lifts with athletes of even higher classifications. The athletes who achieve the best performances in competition tend to increase the number of reps that they perform in competition related lifts but reduced the number of classical lifts, the number of reps in the 70% to 79% zone and squats and pulls with weights exceeding 100%.

Maximums (100% efforts) are typically attempted once or twice a month (but usually not within eighteen days of a competition, never less than ten to fourteen days out). First attempts at weights in the C&J are generally performed up to eight days out from the competition, first attempts at the snatch four days out (give or take one or two days). In recent years some coaches have suggested heavy attempts be made even closer to the competition, but I do not find their arguments very compelling, and I think there are some very good reasons for not doing it.

At least one study conducted in the former Soviet Union suggests that there is a correlation between the distribution of the loads lifted in the four-week period prior to a competition and performance in the competition. It compared the preparation of two groups of lifters; one group repeated their training performances in the competition and the other improved upon their training performances in the competition. The lifters who failed to improve had a distribution of weights 90% or greater as follows: lifts with 90% to 92.5% of maximum comprised 56% of the total load of weights in excess of 90%; lifts with 95% weights accounted for 17%; lifts with 97.5% weights comprised 7%; and lifts with 100% weights constituted 20% of the load. In contrast, the lifters who improved did 65% of their lifts above 90% with weights that were between 90% and 92.5%, 20% of their lifts with weights 95% of maximum and 15% of their lifts with weights 97.5% of maximum; they made no attempts at 100% weights. Another study by Kuzmin, Roman and Rysin (published in the 1983 Weightlifting Yearbook) suggested that the number of lifts performed with 71% to 90% of maximum correlated with the results attained in competition but that lifts in the 95% to 100% range had no correlation. I have detected similar patterns

of performance in the athletes I have observed over the years.

Recommendations for the distribution of a month's load into individual weeks are different when there is an important competition at the end of a training month. A clear reduction in load takes place as the competition nears. For example, Medvedyev recommends one of three loading patterns in pre-competition months (with deviations plus and minus 2% to 4% for individual athletes): a) 26/35/23/16; b) 36/28/21/15; or c) 24/38/25/13. In his textbook Weightlifting, A. Vorobyev recommended the following loading patterns before a competition: 25/37/23/15, 36/30/21/13 or 25/38/25/12. He prefers the first variant. R. Roman recommends the following variants of weekly loading for a competition month: 36/28/24/12, 29/25/35/11, 28/33/26/13 or 32/26/29/13.

Although the weekly loading patterns that Medvedyev, Vorobyev and Roman suggest vary considerably, they have some common characteristics. The last week in the month is always the lightest in order to give the athlete rest before the competition, and, in all but one variant (Roman's second), the week with the largest load comes either in the first or second week. (The third week is always a medium week.) In my experience, older and heavier athletes tend to have the greatest success with a pattern like Medvedyev's second pattern, and younger and lighter athletes tend to benefit from his first pattern. However, in virtually every case the individual needs and circumstances of the athletes are the most important factors in selecting the arrangement of the loading.

Peaking by Gradually Increasing Intensity and Volume

When a lifter is out of condition because of an injury or a break in training, he or she can often peaking for a competition by gradually increasing intensity and volume. This method can be particularly helpful when there are only four to eight weeks to prepare for the competition.

Perhaps the most amazing application of this method that I ever witnessed was former National Champion and American record holder Peter Rawluk's preparation for the 1970 Philadelphia Open. Peter had just completed a term of service in the Air Force and had been stationed in Alaska until just before the competition. Training conditions were not the best in Alaska, and Peter had taken some time off from training after his discharge. He arrived in New York several weeks before the Philadelphia Open, looking like a shadow of his former self. His body weight was approximately 154 lb. (in peak condition he would weigh approximately 173 lb. and then reduce to 165 lb. for competition). Peter snatched 180 lb. on his first day of training, and it did not look very easy. (He then held the American record at 305 lb., a lift he had performed approximately six months earlier.) After snatching 180 lb., Peter confidently declared that he would break his American record at the upcoming competition. Those who were present to hear Peter's declaration were probably evenly divided with respect to their reactions to his statement; half doubted he would do it and the other half was sure he would not!

Peter trained steadily over the next several weeks, gradually adding both intensity and volume to his training during the first few weeks (after which the volume of his training remained at a more or less fixed level). His body weight increased steadily along with his strength, and by the end of his preparation he weighed a solid 173 lb. Incredibly, he managed to add 20 lb. to his snatch at each and every Saturday workout, until he reached 280 lb. a week or two prior to the meet. At the competition, he snatched 290 lb. He pulled an American record 310 lb. to arm's length, but the lift was slightly out of position and as he fought to hold it, he dislocated his elbow, missing the lift. Nevertheless, despite this setback, Peter's performance was a remarkable example of a lifter knowing just how to peak and having the confidence to execute a daring plan.

There are those who will argue that getting into condition so rapidly is what injured Peter Rawluk, and they may be correct. Injury certainly is one of the hazards of increasing volume and intensity at the same time. In addition, such a method can result in sudden exhaustion. (An increase in both volume and intensity provides a training stimulus that is so strong that it can overwhelm the body over a relatively short period of time.) Nevertheless, a well planned peaking cycle of this kind can be very useful for a lifter who is well rested and therefore well prepared to withstand several weeks of progressively increasing demands. If the weights handled at the end of the peaking cycle are not too close to the lifter's maximum, a gradual peak practically precludes being overtrained on the day of the competition.

Naturally, combinations and variations of both cycles can be effective. The general rules that I recommend, regardless of the peaking method that is used, are as follows:

1) Eliminate extremely heavy back work two to three weeks out from the meet. Any limit on good morning exercises, clean deadlifts and the like should be eliminated at this stage.

2) Eliminate extremely heavy leg work and pulls ten days to two weeks out from the meet. Limit squats and pulls at 100% or above (particularly clean pulls) should be eliminated.

3) Do no snatches or C&J's that require you to draw on your nervous energy ten days out from the meet. Allow no more than one miss at a weight. If you miss more than once on a given day, reduce the weight to a level at which you are certain of success and stop there, whether you make the lift or not.

4) If your nervous energy seems a little depleted during the last ten days before the meet, substitute singles in the pull up to your starting attempts for the snatch and clean lifts and do a few moderate jerks from the racks in one of your workouts five to ten days before the meet. This can do wonders for restoring your energy and desire to lift prior to the meet. Toward the end of his career, Tommy Kono used to train with bodybuilding exercises two weeks before the meet. He said such training kept his muscles strong and left him with a great feeling of freshness and desire to lift on the day of the meet. It should be noted that Tommy was _not_ unaccustomed to such exercises as they were often a part of his normal training.

5) Experiment with different last workout schedules. Some coaches believe that there are magic weights above which no one should go. This is more common among older coaches, and the most popular weight is 60 kg. This choice probably stems from the days when the only Olympic bar plate with a full 45 cm diameter was the 20 kg. plate. By going up to 60 kg., the lifter was able to simulate the height of the bar in relation to the floor when it is lifted in competition. These coaches also tend to recommend that the last workout before a Saturday competition be on Wednesday or Thursday, giving the athlete two or three days of complete rest. In contrast, many Eastern European athletes train the day before the competition with as much as 90% of maximum (though 75% to 80% is more common). The last workout will probably have little or no effect on the lifter's competition performance, unless it further tires the overtrained athlete, further conditions the undertrained athlete or causes an athlete to expend significant nervous energy.

6) Do not panic. The single biggest mistake lifters make in preparing for a competition is to place too much emphasis on performance immediately prior to a contest. They somehow come to believe that as they perform in training, so they will perform in competition. While the classical lifts actually performed in training are one indicator of what to expect in competition, they are only one indicator. If a lifter has to use every bit of nervous energy that he or she is able to marshal in order to make particular lifts in training, the lifter may be exhausted at competition time. In contrast, if a lifter manages only mediocre classical lifts in training but is well rested and strong, he or she may turn in an outstanding performance.

The moment of truth comes when that lifter realizes the most important aspect of preparation is not lifting the maximum weight in training in the classical lifts, but, rather, in assuring that he or she is rested enough to perform at his or her best on the day of the competition.

Pre-Contest Control Competitions

In addition to peaking programs designed to bring an athlete to maximum performance readiness on the day of a competition, special pre-meet workouts that are designed to replicate meet conditions are recommended by many coaches. In Eastern Europe, these are often referred to as "control" competitions. Such workouts normally take place in the training quarters, but otherwise the conditions are the same as in a competition. The lifters dress in their lifting uniform and warm up and compete on different platforms. Each lifter has three attempts in the "competition," and the time limits for attempts are the same as those in official competition. The purpose of the control competition is to give the lifters more experience and training under competition like conditions and to help the coaches select those athletes who are most likely to perform well.

A number of coaches in the United States have advocated variations of control competitions. For example, Bill Starr, a former editor of <u>Strength and Health</u> and still one of the most influential writers in the American weightlifting community, has written a fine little book on preparing for competition, called <u>Defying Gravity</u>. In his book Bill recommends what amounts to a control competition two weeks before the meet. According to Starr, the Olympic lifter should work up to heavy singles (singles or doubles for powerlifters) in each of the competitive lifts. The lifts should be performed in the same order as in the competition. Bill also recommends that the lifter train at the same time as the contest during the last two weeks, that he or she wear the same clothes and that other conditions of the competition be duplicated as far as is possible (e.g., not training in front of a mirror, having someone give referee signals and practicing longer with shorter rests between lifts than is normal).

I agree with the general notion of simulating meet conditions in training, but not without some reservations. First, some lifters adjust to competition so well and concentrate so effectively that such preparations serve no real purpose. This is especially common when training conditions are already similar to competitive conditions. Second, some lifters will become too excited by meet like conditions and will burn up excessive mental energy during and after control competitions.

But the single biggest mistake is relying on control competitions as a gauge of what can be expected in competition. Some coaches place great and unnecessary stress on the lifter during such a mock competition. The lifter with such a coach has two competitions to worry about: the control competition and the actual competition. Such lifters can burn up so much nervous energy during the control competition that they have nothing left during the competition itself.

Decisions about a given competition should never be based on the outcome of one training session, regardless of how much the conditions under which it is done resemble those of a competition. Decisions about contest attempts should be based on the overall level of pre-competition workout performance, the lifter's appraisals of those performances and conditions on the day of the competition. For example, if a lifter trains at a body weight 6% above the class limit and gets very excited in training, that lifter may be lucky to come within 10 kg. of his or her best training performances in competition. In contrast, a lifter who trains alone and finds it difficult to get "up" for a workout may routinely lift 15 kg. more on each lift in a competition than in the gym.

Modern weightlifting competitions are most often conducted in temperature controlled auditoriums and gymnasiums. However, on occasion, climate control can be lacking. When such a possibility exists, the athlete should prepare by training under the climatic conditions that are likely to prevail. If the climate is likely to be warmer than the one in which the lifter trains, the lifter can either turn up the heat in the gym during training or wear warmer clothing while training. When colder conditions are anticipated, the lifter can train at lower temperatures or wear a lifting suit instead of a sweat or warm-up suit in training.

Fatigue and Overtraining

The most common fatigue that a weightlifter experiences occurs during the performance of an exercise. The muscle tires to the point where additional lifts are difficult or impossible without some rest. If a lifter has not reached a state of complete exhaustion during a given set (i.e., has not made an all out effort), the lifter then finds that, with rest, the same amount of weight can be lifted for the same number of reps once again. Eventually, if the athlete continues to do set after set, a point will be reached where the same performance cannot be achieved on each set. The exact point where this occurs depends on how strenuous each set is, how much rest is taken between sets and the condition of the athlete. If the athlete continues to exercise at this point, performance will continue to decline.

At first the sensation of fatigue will be felt as a lack of muscular response. The athlete will push on the bar but it simply will not go as far or as fast as it did before fatigue began to set in. (If the cumulative reps performed are high, particularly in one set, the athlete will also begin to feel "pumped.") If the athlete continues to train, some pain will be experienced in the muscles, and, eventually the lifter will be virtually unable to move the bar through the full range of motion with the same load.

When a muscle works at a low enough level of intensity, the body is able to restore the muscle's function on an ongoing basis. The muscle does not necessarily become fatigued or trained to any significant extent (unless the duration of the activity extends well beyond what the athlete is accustomed to, in which case endurance is ultimately improved by the training effort). If the immediate ability of the muscle to maintain its steady state of performance is overcome, it will reach a state of fatigue as described above.

If the athlete rests sufficiently after a bout of exercise, the fatigue factors will be overcome, and full muscle function will be restored. If the stress applied during the exercise is sufficient (and not excessive), an adaptive response will occur, and the muscle will become capable of more work than it had been prior to the exercise.

While fatigue and adaptation are related, they are not synonymous. A bout of exercise can cause fatigue without stimulating much of an adaptation, and an adaptation can be stimulated without the lifter's experiencing a sense of fatigue (although a feeling of not being able to perform another rep will often be experienced). Recovery from fatigue is the body's automatic effort to restore the body to a state of equilibrium. Adaptation is the body's effort to reach a level of readiness for stress so that its equilibrium cannot easily be disturbed once again. The latter response is at the core of the training effect.

If the exercise stress in a given workout or series of workouts is carried to extremes, the muscle's ability to adapt to the stress can be completely overcome, and damage or injury can result. This point marks the dividing line between training and overstress.

Fatigue, no matter how extreme, falls within the body's responsive capabilities by restoring the body to a state of equal or greater functioning (with sufficient rest). When a state of overstress has occurred, full restoration of function will not occur. By the time recuperation has occurred, there will also have been a detraining effect. The muscle then recovers its ability to function, but that ability is less than it was before the exercise that fatigued the muscle was commenced. This specific and localized kind of overstress can be referred to as overtraining, but the term "overtraining" tends to be applied only to a more global or "full body" state.

When a combination of stresses reaches a certain threshold (whether through overstress being applied to multiple muscle groups or by other causes), the body's overall adaptive energy can be overcome, and systemic fatigue can be experienced. This generalized overstressed condition is commonly referred to as "overtraining." The athlete experiences both physical and psychological fatigue, and the body slips into an overall state of performance stagnation or decline. Ultimately, the body's capabilities can be so completely overcome that illness and/or injury result.

If an athlete carefully balances training and rest and sees to it that he or she never to outruns his or her adaptive capabilities, overtraining can be completely avoided. However, most athletes who are anxious to improve their performance never feel comfortable simply waiting to recover from their workouts. Instead, these athletes will forge ahead as soon as reasonable muscle capacity has been restored (even if adaptation, also known as overcompensation, has not occurred).

The phenomenon of overtraining is perhaps less well understood than many of the body's reactions to training. Researchers and sports specialists cannot even agree on what overtraining is. For example, at least five kinds of overtraining have appeared in the literature: monotonous, addisonic, basedowic, sympathetic and parasympathetic.

The "monotonous" variety of overtraining is different from the other four variations in that it appears to be more of a mental than a physical reaction to training. There are no physical symptoms associated with it. Rather, it has been defined as a cessation of progress (or even regression) and a loss of motivation. Therefore, it is questionable whether it is a form of overtraining at all. Boredom and a general loss of enthusiasm with training can result from psychological causes (such as a perceived loss in the connection between training and fundamental goals and values) and may have no physical basis at all. Such a phenomenon is not linked to the training load per se and therefore is not properly the subject of this chapter, except to the extent that variety in training can help an athlete avoid the experience of monotony. (Motivational aspects of training are discussed in Chapter 7). In contrast, an athlete can exhibit such symptoms as a result of burnout, a true state of overtraining in which so much stress has been placed on both the mind and the body that a physical and psychological reaction occurs.

The other four varieties of overtraining all appear to have a physical basis (although they may have a psychological causes as well). The addisonic and basedowic varieties of overtraining appear most often in the Eastern European literature, while the sympathetic and parasympathetic varieties tend to be more widely accepted and discussed in the West. (There are clearly many overlapping areas in these states, which is not surprising when different specialists are attempting to define the same or similar phenomena.)

Addisonic overtraining has been so named because the symptoms are allegedly similar to those of Addison's disease, in which there is a deficiency in the secretion of adrenocortical hormones. With such overtraining, athletes reportedly experience a slight overtired feeling, a low resting pulse rate and hypotension. Addisonic overtraining is thought to result from an overall overloading of the athlete, particularly in terms of training volume.

Basedowic overtraining is so named because of its apparent resemblance to Basedow's disease (a hyperthyroid condition). With such overtraining, the athlete reportedly experiences accelerated metabolic and heart rates, irritability and restlessness, an increased rate of perspiration and weight loss. Basedowic overtraining is thought to result from overloading with respect to intensity and/or mental stressors.

Sympathetic overtraining is reportedly associated with such symptoms as decreases in motivation, body weight and lean body mass and/or increases in heart rates, blood pressure and cortisol concentrations. Depression, insomnia and a depressed immune system are also symptomatic of such an overtrained state. The athlete who becomes overtrained in this way is likely to experience a feeling of chronic fatigue and a plateauing or regression in terms of performance.

Parasympathetic overtraining is reportedly associated with lowered heart rates and blood pressure, depressed physical and mental behavior, an increased requirement for sleep and a depressed endocrine response to stressors.

Are the types of overtraining mentioned above all encompassing? Do they overlap? Does it matter? It is likely that the definitions of overtraining are imperfect. They may include some nonessential symptoms and exclude some important ones. There is probably some degree of overlap between at least some of the types identified. In reality, overtrained athletes may experience most, or only one or two, of the above symptoms (in part because the bodies of different athletes are overcome to a different degree and in a different way by the overtraining). What is important here is to understand that there are systemic responses when the combination of an athlete's training, psychological and environmental stressors overcome the athlete's ability to adapt.

The most obvious and universal symptom of overtraining is a general and persistent decline in performance, especially in the classical exercises. Often the lifter will be able to force a reasonable result in the first or second exercises in the workout when the overtrained state is first detected, but the athlete will note a more rapid than normal onset of fatigue. Adequate rest, proper nutrition and a reduction in the stress levels to which the athlete is exposed are the only ways to recover from overtraining. (Restorative techniques, such as the use of saunas, whirlpool baths, massage can also be of some help in this area.)

Many trainers advocate training to achieve an overtrained state (I used to be one of them). They believe that overtraining is necessary to achieve results and that a certain amount of overtraining is beneficial. However, I would argue that training to a point of significant fatigue is beneficial to the

degree that it stimulates the athlete's adaptive capacities but that the best results are generated when training stops short of pushing the athlete into an actual state of overtraining. This means that the athlete is briefly subjected to a greater than normal training stress, but that stress is reduced before any signs of overtraining develop or, at least, at the very onset of signs of overtraining. Such a process stimulates but does not overcome the body's adaptive capabilities. Overtraining (in the overall and systemic context) may be one means to stimulate an adaptive response, but it is surely neither the only means nor the safest. In order for it to pay dividends, it must be handled by a very skilled trainer who has a very good level of communication with the athlete, so that reliable information on the athlete's actual and perceived states is available at all times.

In general, overtraining is one of the biggest threats to an athlete's success. It precludes progress and kills the desire to train. It can weaken the immune system, making the body more susceptible to illness. Further, it clearly exposes the body to the risk of injury, both directly and indirectly. The direct exposure is in the nature of overuse injuries. The indirect exposure is in the form of the weakened immune system, which is believed to predispose the body to injury.

Perhaps the worst aspect of overtraining is that while it has little or no positive effect on the organism (and presents all of the risks previously mentioned), often the only way that the athlete can overcome it expeditiously is to reduce the training load significantly and for a long period, a step that will preclude any progress until some time after the overtraining has been overcome it and a more normal level of training has been resumed. Therefore, athletes are generally well advised to avoid a true state of overtraining, particularly for a prolonged period. As with many aspects of life, hard work is a prerequisite for success, but those who work smarter are far more successful than those who simply work harder. There is such a thing as too much of a good thing!

The Training Log

All lifters should maintain a written record of all of their workouts in a sort of training diary. Many beginners and even some more advanced lifters apparently see no purpose in studying their past reactions to training, believing that they will always remember precisely what they have done in the past. They are completely mistaken. The study of a lifter's past training and his or her reactions to it is one of the most important tools that a coach and athlete have for improving future planning. After a lifter has performed hundreds or thousands of workouts, it will be virtually impossible to remember the details of each one. (Some lifters have trouble remembering what they did during their last workout.) So the training log is the lifter's means of preserving a near perfect memory of the lifter's entire career and is therefore in many ways his or her most valuable possession.

In a training log, it is typical to devote separate sections or pages to each workout, recording the date, day of week and the hour of the day of each workout. Many athletes enter notes on how they felt prior to and during the workout (e.g., "I felt tired emotionally but fine physically as I began the workout, but as the workout went on, I got excited watching Jack and Jill make personal records in the snatch, and the second half of the workout was done with great enthusiasm"). Others comment on their readiness to work out (e.g., "I came into the gym with my mind on other things—my misunderstanding with my boss—and I was tired due to having gotten only five hours of sleep last night"). Still other lifters include comments on their diet (e.g., "started taking an extra 500 mg. of vitamin C a day on Monday"). Most athletes record their body weights (usually at a consistent time each morning, before the workout, etc.) and include some commentary on any injury or illness that may have affected their performance.

Virtually all athletes who keep logs list the exercises done, generally in the order in which they were done, the amount of weight lifted on each set and the number of reps performed with each weight. The notation that I recommend is to list the weight lifted first, the number of reps done with that weight second and the number of sets done with that weight third. This approach is very logical in that if a lifter does a single rep and set with a given weight, he or she need only indicate the weight (the rest is understood). If the lifter fails with a given weight, he or she can merely show the weight with a line through it, showing that an unsuccessful attempt was made with that weight. I add a comment after the line to clarify the nature of the miss. (If I am doing C&J's and miss the jerk, I simply write "jerk" after the crossed off number; this reminds me that I attempted a given weight and that while I missed the jerk, I did make the clean.) If more than one rep is performed, the weight can be listed, followed by a times (x) sign and the number of reps performed. If more that one set of the same number of reps with that weight was performed, an additional times sign can follow the number of reps indicated, and that can be followed by an indication of the number of sets. Therefore, three sets of five reps with 100 kg. would be noted as follows: 100 x 5 x 3.

If the lifter takes his or her training log to the gym (a practice that I do not necessarily recommend because of the potential for leaving this critical record behind) and is attempting 100 kg., he or she can write down "100" before the attempt. If the attempt is successful, nothing further need be noted (unless the lifter wishes to make some comment on the lift). If the attempt fails, the athlete puts a line through the weight attempted and possibly a comment. If more than one rep is made on that set, the number of reps can be written down after the times symbol. If the athlete intends to do more than one single with a given weight and he or she makes the first single, any notation about this can be withheld until after the second set. If the next attempt is successful, the athlete can then add "x 1" to the number already written, followed by another "x." (If the athlete plans no further immediate attempts with that weight, he or she writes the number 2 following the last "x," indicating that two sets of single reps were performed). If the athlete intends to attempt at least another set, he or she can delay filling in the last number indicating the number of sets until all of the attempts at that weight have been made. (To keep track of the sets successfully done so far, the athlete can put two small check marks above the weight being attempted.) When an athlete is doing an uneven number of reps from set to set, it is easier to simply indicate the weight being attempted and then the number of reps done on each set, separated by commas (e.g., 100 x 3, 4, 5 means that 100 kg. was lifted for a set of three repetitions, then a set of four and finally a set of five reps). If any reps are missed on the three sets in the example, the athlete can write: "100 x 2 (did not stand up on the third rep).

This notation system enables the lifter to avoid having to make any corrections for unanticipated misses, and it gives the athlete information about any misses or successes that have occurred. Unlike the Soviet system, it also lends itself to recording in a spreadsheet like Lotus. The Soviet method of notation uses a structure similar to that of a fraction, with the weight or percentage of maximum being placed in the position of the numerator, the number of reps appearing as the denominator and the number of sets appearing to the right of the fraction like notation of weight and reps. For example, four sets of three reps with 100 kg. would be noted as following:

$$\frac{100}{3}\,4$$

Finally, the lifter should circle any set in which a personal record is made, whether that is the lifter's personal best for a single or a set of five reps. In this way it is relatively easy to locate records. (Lifters who have trouble remembering their personal records can list them, along with the date, in a separate section of the log.) The final section of the workout diary consists of comments about technique, ideas for improvement and other insights, such as explanations for poor or good performances. In general, you can never record too much, and most athletes record too little. Therefore, the extra space at the end of the log page or the section for a given day should be generous.

Once a month, the athlete should scan the workout book or diary, noting personal records, technique tips and training insights gleaned from the workout records for that month. These should be recorded in separate sections at the end of the diary. There should be sections for technique, training insights, psyching tools, injuries (hopefully you will never have one, but if you do, it is important to describe it, note the date of onset, when it stabilized and when it ended, as well as what you did to bring it to an end, e.g., rest, therapy, and change of exercise, etc.). As suggested earlier, there should be a personal record listing at the end of the book.

It is also a good idea to record things like the total training volume, reps per exercise by zones, etc. While the value of these measurements has probably been exaggerated by some trainers, they can be useful when employed as part of an overall program of monitoring and planning training. Such averages tell little about the all important microtraining process or the effectiveness of one workout scheme versus another, but they can help to explain why you suddenly feel like your body is falling apart or is not recovering from your workouts. (The training volume may have crept up by 20% in a relatively short time and with no intervening period of unloading to let the body have time to adapt; you may not be able to sense what has happened intuitively, but the training log helps to identify the problem through its monitoring of aggregates.) Capturing aggregate numbers also enables the coach or athlete to assure that he or she is proceeding in accordance with the overall training plan.

The ambitious and computer-literate athlete and/or coach may wish to enter data from all workouts in a data base like DBase IV, Data Ease or Paradox. This will take a little extra effort in terms of recording the workouts (i.e., identifying the necessary fields of information to be entered into the computer and then performing the entry process) but doing so will make analysis much easier to perform. Fortunately, there is an even easier way to track and analyze workouts today. It is called "Electronic Weightlifting Journal." The program, which was developed by Mark Gilman, runs on virtually any IBM-compatible PC. It enables athletes to record all of their workouts and then to analyze them in terms of a wide array of volume, load and intensity measures. The program can be purchased from Mark Gilman by writing to him at: 31 Park Lane East, Apt 3, Menands, N.Y. 12204.

Apart from the analysis on the quantitative level, a training log will give you the ability to analyze your training on an informal basis from any number of perspectives. You cannot possibly know how you will want to use all of the data when you enter it, but if it is all there and is relatively well categorized, you will be able to find what you need without too much wasted time and effort. For example, you may wish to find out how many times you have had a certain injury and if you were doing certain exercises when it occurred. First, you look for the listing of the injuries. Then you go to the actual workout records to see what exercises you were doing, beginning several weeks to several months before the injury. Perhaps you can find an exercise or group of exercises which uniformly preceded the injuries. Perhaps there will be a pattern in terms of training volume or how you said you felt for several weeks before. Perhaps you will find no pattern at all. However, the data is still there, ready to be analyzed from some other perspective or on the basis of some other hypothesis.

The importance of the training log cannot be overemphasized. By giving a lifter a good sense of where he or she has been, it can provide invaluable data upon which to base future planning. It has been said that a person stranded in the woods with no compass will very gradually walk in a large circle. Similarly, an athlete training without a log will find themselves making the same mistakes, repeating ineffective techniques and ineffective programs and mistreating recurring injuries. As the old adage goes: "those who do not learn from history are doomed to repeat it." Your training log is your insurance against that process if you record your workouts in it without fail and if you analyze them rigorously and regularly.

Summary

In this chapter we have presented the elements of programming the training of athletes from the beginning through the elite level. Conventional as well as more innovative planning approaches have been presented. By now the reader should have a good conceptual grasp of how to put together an effective training plan. However, only through practice in preparing, evaluating and modifying actual plans will the athlete or coach master the planning process. And no matter how effective the planner becomes, there is always more to learn and try out. This continuous process of programming, testing, revising the program and testing again is part of what makes weightlifting the mentally and physically challenging sport that it is.

The reader who has reached this point in the text has learned the elements of proper technique, how to create a training stimulus for improving strength, power and flexibility, how to select and use weightlifting equipment, what exercises can be used to improve weightlifting performance and how to combine all of this knowledge about technique and training into training programs that will generate continual improvement. Now it is time to address the development of the weightlifter's (or any person's) greatest key to success—the mind. Effective use of one's mind enables one to build a burning desire to succeed, to control emotions and mental focus and thereby to achieve the ideal performance state. Those are some of the topics covered in Chapter 7.

A sickly and underweight youth, Tommy Kono's towering integrity and indomitable spirit enabled him to become one of the greatest and most popular weightlifters of all time.

CHAPTER 7

Building The Mind Of A Weightlifting Champion

A person's mind is by far the most important factor determining his or her success in weightlifting, and virtually anything else in life. We will explore the proper use of one's mind in this chapter.

Why The Most Powerful Indicator Of Weightlifting Success Is Often Overlooked

One concept in vogue today with many "scientific" weightlifting coaches is that of "selection." Select athletes with the proper physical characteristics (e.g., an outstanding vertical jump and natural flexibility), the argument goes, and champions will almost inevitably grow from this talent pool. In essence, the athlete comes to the coach to find out whether he or she has "it." If the lifter does have "it," the coaching process begins. If not, the lifter is advised that the pursuit of weightlifting glory is futile, and it is suggested that his or her energy would be better spent in other endeavors.

This idea is flawed, tragically flawed, because it presumes a knowledge that we do not have. It is tragic because it has destroyed many weightlifting careers before they ever began. From a scientific standpoint, we are quite a distance from being able to test for the physical traits that are essential to weightlifting success. We can identify certain gross limitations that greatly hinder performance, but we rarely encounter limitations that are so great as to preclude success; nor have we identified gifts so substantial as to make success highly probable. This is partly because we have not identified all of the essential physical characteristics of a champion weightlifter. Our analytical skills and tools for evaluating such characteristics are still relatively primitive. There are so many factors that interact in the making of a high caliber weightlifter that it

is not yet possible to measure or fully understand their combined effects.

With regard to evaluating the potential of bodybuilders, 1992, 1993 and 1994 Mr. Olympia, Dorian Yates, has said: "I think the subject of genetics is a bit overrated.... I can't look at you and say that you have or haven't got the genetics for a 21" arm. No one knows until you've tried it." He is talking about a single quality: a person's ability to gain muscle size. The physical factors that impact on weightlifting performance are far more complicated; therefore, the ability to predict an individual's physical potential for weightlifting is even more suspect.

However, even if our ability to evaluate physical potential were at the near perfect level, we would find it difficult, at best, to predict success with a substantial degree of accuracy. The chief problem with any assessment based on physical characteristics is that such characteristics are not the only, or even the most important, determinants of a lifter's success. The key characteristics that we cannot measure are what is in the athlete's mind and what is popularly called the athlete's "heart."

If there is anything more important than body strength in weightlifting, it is strength of mind. If an athlete is to begin and to sustain an effective regimen of weightlifting training, a proper mental attitude is a prerequisite. Does this mean that the will conquers all, that the athlete merely needs to "want it" badly enough for success to be inevitable? Absolutely not. The mere act of wishing for something is far from enough to cause it to happen. Neither is "working hard" a guarantee of success (working smart <u>and</u> hard is critical). The mind <u>and</u> the body are needed for weightlifting success. They must act in concert. There must be no rift between thought and action.

As the great philosopher and novelist Ayn Rand said in defining her principles of ethics, there are three fundamentals that man (and woman) must hold as primary if he or she is to live a successful (i.e., moral) life: reason, purpose and self-esteem. Reason enables a person to proceed in accordance with reality, using nature as the means to success. Purpose is the goal a person selects through a process of reason. Once selected, it serves as a guide in the selection of steps for fulfilling that purpose, as a guide to <u>action</u>. Self-esteem is a consequence of acting rationally towards the achievement of the purpose one has set. A person who values and respects himself or herself will grasp the importance of his or her values. Such an understanding stimulates the mind to reason further, refining and devising additional means for achieving his or her purpose, the action toward which builds self-esteem, creating a sort of success spiral.

I would add one more element to Rand's group of three mental fundamentals: support. By support I do not mean the sacrifices of others to facilitate your success (though help from others may well be welcome under certain circumstances), but, rather, creating an environment that nurtures success. Establishing conditions and cultivating associates that complement your objectives can mean the difference between success and failure.

Having an academic or work schedule that permits quality training time and adequate rest is critical to achieving maximal progress, while work or school commitments that do the opposite can make success virtually impossible (although this does not mean that you cannot work or go to school while training). Similarly, having associates who are psychologically supportive of your efforts (even though they may not share your interest or involvement in the sport), can be of great help. In contrast, having associates who despise your sport, discourage your efforts and make light of your success at every turn is likely to have a negative influence on your progress. Support, therefore, has both physical and psychological dimensions.

It should be noted that some "scientific" weightlifting coaches who fully accept the importance of the mind in a weightlifter's success are undeterred from making prognostications regarding the probability of a lifter's reaching championship level. They will simply apply a mental test instead of or in addition to a physical one. In short, a personality profile will be substituted for vertical jumping ability as a means of assessing an athlete's potential. Unfortunately for this variant of prognosticator, no test has ever been devised which can identify the mind of a champion.

Numerous attempts have been made by sports psychologists to relate sports performance to various personality traits. The nature, definition and range of traits that have been studied and/or grouped to create some sort of personality profile or index vary considerably. Such attributes as assertiveness, motivation, baseline anxiety, social styles and self discipline have been studied. The overall outcome of such research has been that a wide variety of personality styles has been successful in athletics. It might be expected that an attribute such as motivation would be highly correlated with performance, but even athletes with limited motivation, as assessed by standard measurement tools, may be outstanding performers. This can be explained by motivations that are not measured by whatever instrument is being used, by a lack of complete candor or self understanding on the part of the athlete and by differences in perceived motivation when responding to questions in a laboratory as opposed to engaging in practice or competition.

Does all of this mean that the experienced coach cannot spot an athlete who has better than average physical and mental characteristics? Of course not. With careful observation a trained eye can certainly evaluate the current status of an athlete quite accurately. However, what the coach cannot predict with any level of certainty is how quickly and how much further any athlete can or will develop. The athlete is the only one who is in a position to know, particularly when it come to his or her mental capabilities. And while the athlete's predictive powers may not be perfect, there is no one else on earth who is in a better position to decide just how far he or she can go.

Perhaps the most important single reason that predictions regarding development (particularly mental development) have limited value is the fact that the mind of a champion can and must be built. The purpose of this chapter is to help the athlete in that process.

Philosophical And Theoretical Issues Relating To Mental Attitude

Can You Really Control What Happens in the World?

In order to be a champion, or to succeed in any major undertaking in life, you must have answered this question in a certain way, even if only implicitly. In the very briefest of terms, the answer to that question must be a resounding yes. But the reasons a person answers yes to that question are as important as the answer itself.

There are two rational and fundamental reasons to believe that success is possible and that its achievement is largely under your control. Those reasons are: a) that existence exists independent of consciousness; and b) that existence is benevolent, particularly to the person who acts rationally.

To say that existence exists independent of any consciousness is to say that the world outside any person is independent of what that person thinks of that world and that existence has its own immutable laws which cannot be altered by any consciousness. This does not mean that humans cannot alter the external world, merely that simply wishing for change is not enough. A person who understands that existence exists understands that action is required to succeed in life. Action must be taken to alter the external world or to alter the athlete's primary tools for dealing with that world— his or her own mind and body.

The notion that existence is benevolent toward humankind does not mean that existence has any ability or desire to think or to act on humankind's behalf. Rather, the idea is based on the assumption that if humans were not fundamentally suited to live in the world, they would not have survived and prospered as they have. By the nature of humankind and its relationship with the universe, success is not only possible, it is probable. Tragedy and disaster are not norms; success and happiness are.

Why are these beliefs so crucial to the underlying premise of a person's ability to control existence? A person who believes that consciousness itself influences reality (whether his or her own consciousness or some else's) will be reduced to merely willing that something change or waiting for some other will to exercise its power. Action, then, will be implicitly considered to be ineffective and, as a consequence, any hope of achieving control of personal destiny will be wiped out.

In a similar way, a person who believes that humankind has the ability to be happy, that the world is not out there just waiting to snuff out all initiative and pretenses at happiness, will see thought and action as worth undertaking because of his or her ability to control the course of his or her life. Therefore, an understanding of existence and an appreciation of humankind's fortunate place in it are the foundations upon which success is laid. If a person does not hold these premises, little can be done to achieve success in weightlifting or anything else.

Lest you conclude that the space taken above for establishing premises is unnecessary "philosophizing," you should consult the literature of sports psychology. Considerable research supports the notion that successful athletes believe in an internal locus of control for their successful actions (i.e., that they, not events beyond their control, are primarily responsible for the positive outcomes that they experience and that the causality of events is essentially stable). In contrast, athletes who are oriented to failure perform poorly when under stress. They internalize defeat. They get depressed and anxious at the first sign of failure. For instance, if things do not go as planned in a given competition or workout, their conclusion is not that they have been unable to perform on particular occasion but, rather, that they are "failures."

The athlete with a favorable self image and perception of his or her ability remains with activities longer. An athlete's view of his or her self-efficacy also affects the choice of an activity, the effort expended on that activity, the persistence exhibited in the activity and the appraisal of feedback. Finally, an athlete's self image influences the goals he or she selects. Those who see their ability as poor tend to select goals that are extremely modest (because of their lack of confidence and unwillingness to risk failure) or patently ridiculous (so that when they fail no one will see them as failures since no one could have succeeded at the task).

Athletes differ in their attributions (the factors they attribute to success or failure). Winners tend to make dispositional attributions (e.g., "I did not do A, therefore my performance suffered, but I can correct that in the future"). They then work to correct the cause of the unsatisfactory performance. Poor performers tend to make situational attributions (e.g., "the arena was too hot and the officials were unfair"). Such attributions may preserve the athlete's psyche in the short run, but they preclude true enjoyment of any success because such success must necessarily be attributed to external factors as well. In addition, such attributions imply that success is always contingent on a wide variety of factors that are outside the athlete's control, so why even try to control them?

In discussing the mental state of a person who is unable to differentiate effectively between things that are and are not under that person's control, Ayn Rand made the following brilliant observation:

> "Any small success augments his anxiety: he does not know what caused it and whether he can repeat it. Any small failure is a crushing blow: he takes it as proof that he lacks the mystic endowment. When he makes a mistake, he does not ask himself: "What do I need to learn?" He asks, "What's wrong with me?" He waits for an automatic and omnipotent inspiration, which never comes. He spends years on a cheerless struggle, with his eyes focused inward, on the growing, leering monster of self-doubt, while existence drifts by, unseen, on the periphery of his mental vision. Eventually, he gives up."

Your mental state and your view of the world are under your control, and they are the very foundation of athletic and all other forms of success.

Single Mindedness of Purpose

Bob Hoffman, the legendary promoter of weightlifting in the United States and worldwide, often said for a lifter to be the best in the world, weightlifting must come first. This is a true statement. It does not mean that weightlifting must be the only thing that you do or think about. It does mean that when any decisions are made in your life, the first question that must be asked is, "will this action hurt my weightlifting career?" If the answer is yes, that action should generally not be undertaken. The second question is, "will it help? " If the answer is yes, the action is probably the right one to take.

Now these questions need to be answered with a long term view. Looking for a job today may not help today's workout as much as a nap might, but having a secure job can help to provide the lifestyle that is necessary to train effectively in the long run. On the other hand, a job that will require considerable overnight travel is likely to interfere very materially with training over the long and short runs. Therefore, no matter how attractive it may be for other reasons, it is generally not the right choice for the competitive weightlifter. In today's competitive world, great success in weightlifting cannot be achieved by the athlete who treats the sport as a second or third priority in life; it must be number one, period.

Keeping priorities straight is not always a simple matter. Constant sources of inspiration must be sought to maintain a proper focus. These sources of inspirations may be people who you admire, your specific goals or various images that you bring to mind. It is also important to pause during the day to refocus on your objectives and to relax (avoiding any tension other than what is required to achieve your ultimate purpose). In the gym it is very helpful to have a coach and training mates who share your enthusiasm and objectives. Exchanging letters and phone calls with fellow lifters can be still another source of inspiration.

A top performer is unflappable in terms of the ability to focus on the most important task at hand and to commit to carrying out his or her plan.

Balancing Ambition and Patience

A prerequisite for championship weightlifting performance is a powerful ambition to succeed. The road to success is an arduous one, and only intransigent ambition can make success a reality.

Those who are ambitious are also often impatient to achieve success as well. This is only natural, as time is one of life's limited resources and therefore it is very important to use it efficiently. However, being overly impatient can be very detrimental to an athlete's progress.

It is true that an athletic career can sometimes be cut short by an injury or other circumstances and the idea of "saving" capabilities for a later date increases the risk that those capabilities will never be realized and/or displayed. But an equal possibility is that an athlete will place great pressure on himself or herself to achieve a given goal by a certain date when, in the grand scheme of things, a later date would have served just as well. An athlete's desire can be so great that it results in his or her attempting specific weights or training methods that are dangerously beyond the athlete's true capabilities. One key to weightlifting success is to find the proper balance between the essential qualities of impatience and patience, and the key to discovering that balance is rationality.

A rational person recognizes the difference between what is within his or her control and what is not. A weightlifter must be impatient to apply all of the techniques that are within his or her control in order to achieve success as quickly as possible. The athlete must never think, "I can put off working my squat until the weather gets colder and I feel more like training hard," or "I'll get my body weight under control after the holidays, so I'll overeat now." There is no time to waste in applying the measures that are needed for success. The successful athlete learns to apply his or her full desire to succeed to such areas.

On the other side there are some things that take time. They cannot be hurried beyond the body's maximal rate of adaptation. An athlete cannot break a personal record in the squat before the body has recuperated from its last maximal effort. Restoration techniques may speed recovery, but they can never eliminate adaptation time. To recover from a workout is one thing, to adapt to a new higher level of capability is another. Willing things to be different in this area is a positive waste of time; an athlete who tries and fails because of ignoring the constraints of the human body is always courting disaster through exposure to injury and constant frustration.

Similarly, the body can only recover from an injury over a sufficient period of time. Proper therapy can make recovery as rapid and complete as possible, but the time for recovery cannot be eliminated. To think, "if only I could eliminate recovery time I could be a champion tomorrow," is no less wasteful than thinking, "if I could only get gravitational pull to be suspended when I lift, I could outlift everyone."

In order to be a champion, the athlete must develop his or her strength to a champion's level. The proper technique must be learned before heavy lifts can be attempted. Therefore, the athlete can never say, "I'll deal with my technical faults tomorrow because I feel like going heavy today." Adequate flexibility must be developed before proper technique can be achieved. Therefore, the athlete can never say, "I'll work my flexibility tomorrow, but I feel like snatching today". Everything must be done in the proper order and measure.

In essence, the weightlifter must be absolutely impatient with any delay in taking the next steps that can possibly be made toward success; they must be taken today, at this hour and this instant. At the same time, infinite patience must be exhibited in the context of waiting until the prerequisite of each step on the road to success is completed. Each athlete is responsible for maintaining the delicate balance between what he or she is responsible for and what he or she cannot change. The most important patience of all is that of knowing that real patience is one of the most profound expressions of confidence in yourself and in reality. The proper principles, applied in the proper fashion, will lead to success. Unshakable confidence in the ultimate effectiveness of rational effort is the hallmark of a champion.

The Pluses and Minuses of a Positive Mental Attitude

There is a great deal of misunderstanding about the importance of a positive mental attitude when it comes to weightlifting (or anything else). Some argue that keeping a positive mental outlook is crucial for weightlifting success. Others argue that positive thoughts are unrealistic and that what is often referred to as a positive mental attitude (PMA) only leads to ineffective fantasy and eventual frustration. As is so often the case when there are two such points of view, the truth lies in another direction.

The will, or volition, is the prime mover in all of man's activities. It selects a goal, and it is capable of generating action toward the achievement of that goal. Therefore, the will is necessary, in fact crucial, to success. But the will is not sufficient for success. The mere act of wishing for something will not make it so. Existence is what it is, independent of man's consciousness. Frustration arises with various PMA programs, and they are quickly abandoned by many people, because a belief in the omnipotence of the will is cultivated by those to promote or attend the programs, and it is against that standard of omnipotence that the performance of a positive mental attitude is tested. Naturally, since no creature is omnipotent, the test is inevitably failed, and the tester comfortably (in the short term) retreats to a position of non-effort. Non-effort gives short term comfort because it reinforces the status quo. In reality, non-effort is a ticket to stagnation, regression and a lifetime of suffering.

In another sense the will is virtually unlimited in its power, and this is what the few rational and insightful advocates of a positive mental attitude are referring to, albeit often not in a thoroughly reasoned or very clear way. The will is unlimited in

its power to improve human existence, existence within the scope of what is possible to man ("man" refers to humans regardless of gender). What is possible to man is possible only because man exercises his (or her) volition. Man is able to choose to think and what to think about. When thought is applied toward rearranging the world in accordance with the laws of nature, the possibilities are limitless. Therefore, the adage "thinking will make it so" is more accurately stated as "thinking can make it so—if the thought process is rational and action in accordance with the results of that thinking is undertaken."

There is little question that the amount of effect you devote to achieving a given objective is highly correlated with the probability of success that you assign to that effort. If you think, "no matter how hard I try, I'll never do X," it is unlikely that you will work very hard to achieve X. Sometimes in life we are lucky enough to experience an event that causes us to dramatically revise our estimates of the probability of success (e.g., a "lucky" break during a competition). One important factor in making success happen is making those enthusiasm building "breaks" come more often. When you cultivate the habit of maintaining a positive mental attitude, you will experience an increase in the number of positive indications of success.

What is really happening is these cases is that your subconscious mind, programmed by your conscious mind's focus on the positive, is constantly processing information in search of solutions to the problems that you face in achieving your objectives. This leads to existential success, which contributes to the mind's belief that success is possible, which further programs the mind to look for more solutions, and so on.

For an example of how a positive mental attitude was actually applied by a champion with great success, consider the case of Bob Bednarski, the great American weightlifting champion of the 1960's and 1970's. Bob told me that when he was in his prime he had a strict policy of categorizing all input he received from others in one of two ways, positive or negative. If he sensed any negativism at all, he attached the label "negative" to it (which meant it was to be totally ignored). When positive input was received, he savored it, absorbed it and replayed it over and over. This absorption of positive statements served to build an overwhelming sense of confidence and enthusiasm, which led to a blazing desire to succeed and an unshakable confidence that success was to be his. This lead to actual success, and the process continued, leading to ever growing success.

It should be noted that Bob did not consider advice on correcting technique or training methods as negative or something to be ignored. Rather, he considered such constructive criticism to be very useful, indeed essential. What Bob was avoiding was the "gloom and doomers" who said things like, "Do not think about smashing world records, think about American records instead, and you won't be disappointed." or "You're too small to compete against the really big superheavyweights." (Bob began to chase superheavyweight glory in 1965, when he weighed a little more than 90 kg.. The then current world champion weighed in excess of 160 kg., and there were no weight classes between 90 kg. and superheavyweight. Bob reached his quest in dramatic fashion on June 9, 1968. Weighing approximately 115 kg., he made the heaviest C&J ever in the history of weightlifting, 220.5 kg., to literally shock the weightlifting world!).

The essence of an effective positive mental attitude relates to three interrelated concepts: a) any proper and positive attitude must have a rational basis; b) the focus of the mind should be on the positive; and c) there must be an underlying belief that thought is efficacious. Each of these concepts requires some elaboration.

To say that an attitude has a rational basis is to say that it recognizes the proper scope of human thought and action. If you say, "I am positive that the earth is flat, or that if it is not, wishing will make it so," you are dropping the context of rational thought. What you are really saying is that anything goes. You are denying or refusing to consider all of the evidence that is available, ignoring the nature of consciousness (the capacity of perceiving that which exists). But in reality, anything does not go, and as soon as you let your guard down long enough to see reality, the illusion of the fantasy form of positive thinking becomes obvious. Positive "thinking" of this kind is not thought at all but, rather, mere imagining of the metaphysically impossible.

Focusing the mind on the positive is not merely "seeing the good that exists in everything," because there are many things in which there is no good. Rather, focusing the mind on the positive pertains to turning your attention to what is possible and what can be done to overcome any obstacle or setback that you encounter. It has been argued that the value of positive thought is as much attributable to its ability to turn attention from the negative as it is to the positive thought itself.

Positive action is, of course, indispensable as well. Positive affirmations, such as "I like it" (when you are about to do something that you do not), "I am ready" (when you do not fell completely so) and "I will do it" (when you are not entirely sure that you will), have the effect of improving your confidence and, ultimately, your behavior as well. When your behavior improves, so will your confidence. In a similar way, acting the part of believing can ultimately affect belief itself. If you act as if you are confident, it is likely that you will begin to feel more confident. This is because the mind and body are inextricably tried together.

Regardless of the reason for its effectiveness, a focus on the positive is important. If your goal is to become the best weightlifter possible, any physical limitation that is encountered in that quest may simply redefine one aspect of what is possible, but it leaves the other avenues toward success open to the original objective.

For example, if you lose your hand, you cannot do a two hand snatch with two natural hands or snatch as much as you might have otherwise. But it does not preclude you from becoming the best lifter you can be or from enjoying the fundamental benefits of such an achievement. You could, after all, specialize in the one arm snatch or snatch with a prosthesis. Either would permit one to experience the joy of lifting. This example is a random one in the sense that its message applies to all kinds of challenges that a lifter might face, but it is a very real example in another sense. During the 1930s there was an athlete who was missing the better part of one hand and who nevertheless managed to place second in the U.S. Nationals and to be competitive on a national level for a number of years. This lifter, whose name was Tony Vega, took second place in the 1939 nationals against a full field of lifters with two complete hands.

How did he do it? It is hard to imagine the courage that such an undertaking required; to say that his focus was on the positive would be an understatement. On a physical level Tony Vega took the normal overhand grip with his normal hand and a reverse grip with the other hand (which had no fingers but only a partial palm and a thumb). The bar was supported at the juncture of the palm and wrist by curling the palm toward the wrist.. Vega would pull the bar with this grip and then turn his partial hand as he descended under the bar, catching it in the juncture of his partial palm and his thumb.

Not only was Tony Vega highly competitive, but his lifts were well balanced (i.e., the relationship between his press, his snatch and his clean and jerk were relatively typical). There was probably no one to teach Tony how to lift with a partial hand, and no allowances were made for him by the officials or competitors. I cannot even begin to speculate about the arduous struggle of trial and error he must have gone through to discover and perfect his unconventional technique. The misses that must have occurred due to the lesser degree of control that he had over the bar must have been staggering in number. The mental toughness that he must have possessed in order to persevere in the face of the "friendly" advice that he must have received from many (to the effect that he had better concentrate on doing something he had more of a chance of success with) is unimaginable. It is hard to find words to express my admiration for such an achievement or my gratitude for the inspiration he provided to so many with his obvious focus on the positive.

Another legend in weightlifting who gained his well earned reputation as much through his positive mental attitude as through his accomplishments is Norbert Schemansky. By the time Norb was in his late twenties, he had won Olympic gold and silver medals and a World Superheavyweight Championship and had set numerous world records. Norb had been plagued by lower back problems for much of his career and ultimately required spinal surgery (no picnic today, but an extremely risky procedure in the 1950s). He attempted a comeback after the first surgery and was injured again, requiring a second surgery. He was told after the second surgery that he would be lucky to walk again and that any further lifting was absolutely out of the question.

When Norb discussed his plans for a second comeback with Bob Hoffman (then the perennial United States World and Olympic team coach), Bob gave Norb four convincing reasons to forget about the idea. First, he was in his mid-thirties, too old to comeback. Second, he had already had two spinal surgeries, and even a young man could not come back from that. Third, he was never a large superheavyweight and was much too small by the day's standards (Norb may have weighed around 100 kg. when he was in his prime in the mid 1950s, and the top supers in the 1960s were in the 130 kg. to 160 kg. range). Finally, his press had historically been weak and by the day's standards was much too low to be competitive (the press was one of the three Olympic lifts then performed in weightlifting competition). Any one of those reasons was legitimate, and in combination they were devastating. Nevertheless, Schemansky used them as a spur to vault him toward success. He came back carefully, gained body weight and dramatically improved his press. By 1962, at the age of 38, he had regained his national championship, broken a world record in the snatch and taken second at the World Championship in a close battle with the reigning champion. Norb went on to win a bronze medal at the Tokyo Olympics at the age of 40. In so doing, he became one of the great legends of weightlifting and one of the greatest testaments to the power of positive thinking.

The final concept of effective positive thinking is confidence in the efficaciousness of the human mind. As was suggested earlier in this chapter, if you believe that we live in a universe that is out of our control or that tragedy is fundamental to human nature (despite a modern world replete with examples of man's efficaciousness and the norm of existential success), then there will be no desire to exert mental or physical effort. The result of such a belief will be a world where tragedy is the norm and where the world will seem out of control. In contrast, if you have the confidence to see that success is possible, is in fact the norm, then no amount of existential failure generated by

mechanisms beyond your control will cause you to give up the one thing that could change the failed state: rational (i.e., positive) thought. Positive here means thought with the understanding that action is possible and good. Positive thought and action are the keys to much of the happiness that is possible to humankind on this earth.

Harnessing Your Mental Powers

Goal Setting on a Macro Level

Goal setting is one of the most effective ways to build the enthusiasm and the mental attitude needed to became a success in weightlifting or in other areas of life. Sports literature is replete with stories of great performers who established ambitious goals from the outset of their careers, but goals are important in all walks of life. For example, a recent survey of Harvard Business School graduates found that graduates who had established specific goals for themselves upon graduation and regularly thereafter out-earned counterparts by a factor of three to one. Graduates who established written goals on a regular basis out-earned those who did not set goals by a factor of ten to one. Now, mere goal setting itself may not explain this difference in results (the types of people who write down goals may have other characteristics which are more significant contributors to their success than writing goals down), but the goal setting group would probably attribute a significant share of their success to having goals which were reviewed and acted upon on a regular basis.

Psychological studies have demonstrated that goals are more important factors in predicting behavior than perceptions of ability (although perceptions of self efficacy and perceived ability, along with past performance, are major indicators of future success). However, the nature of the goals that athletes choose are influenced by the fundamental motivators of the athlete. Those motivated by internal factors and mastery goals focus on process, while those who are motivated by external factors and outcomes focus on the product.

The kinds of goals that are being referred to here can be termed macro goals. Macro goals can be defined as long term goals and the intermediate steps that are identified as the stepping stones to those goals. For instance, a 64 kg. weightlifter who can C&J 100 kg. might set a long term goal of doing a double body weight C&J in the 70 kg. weight category (i.e., 140 kg). The athlete might then break the goal down by resolving to improve his or her C&J to 115 kg. at 64 kg, 125 kg. at 66 kg, 132.5 kg. at 68 kg. and 140 kg. at 70 kg. Or, the athlete might determine that to C&J 140 kg, his or her squat must be increased by 50 kg, his or her power clean by 35 kg, etc..

Psychological studies on goal setting have revealed that those who established goals related to mastery tended to establish challenging goals, to exert a high level of effort and to confront failure constructively. Those whose goals were related to outcomes (such as winning a particular competition) tended to attribute a greater role to external factors when they did not succeed.

While setting goals does not assure that the goal setter will achieve them, goals do apparently play a vital role in helping an athlete to keep objectives in sight. They also give an athlete the opportunity to experience the kinds of rewards along the way that are essential to maintaining an athlete's enthusiasm. Interestingly, those trained in setting performance goals rated effort as having a more important influence on success than ability.

By outlining an inspirational but realistic goal and then achieving it, an athlete accomplishes much more than taking a vital existential step toward success (as important as such steps are). The athlete also builds his or her confidence in his or her efficacy. In effect, the athlete concludes, "I am right for the world and for success, I have the power to establish goals in the real world and to accomplish them. I am in control of my destiny." These are powerful thoughts indeed. They are the thoughts of a champion.

Specific and difficult goals are more effective in eliciting improved performance than easy, moderate or "do your best" goals. Difficulty is more important than specificity, and combining them both with feedback yielded the best performance overall. Positively focused goals are best for new and difficult tasks. However, negatively focused goals (e.g., goals of making fewer mistakes) are more beneficial for perfecting learned skills.

Goals should be formulated both in terms of the long and short range. They should generally be specific, attainable, measurable and within your control, but there is an important role for more subjective goals as well. For example, an athlete may have an objective of a 200 kg. C&J and a 265 kg. squat. But he or she can also have an objective of maintaining his or her composure under competitive conditions. The latter goal is not as easily measured, but success can clearly be identified. A person who is able to maintain control in competition can directly perceive the feeling of such control, even if those feelings cannot be measured mechanically.

Once long term goals have been identified, the athlete needs to take stock of where he or she is at the present. Then the athlete needs to establish sub-goals that will be stepping stones to the major objectives that the athlete has established. These sub-goals need to be of two basic types. One type has to do with the steps of progression. If the lifter's objective is to C&J 200 kg. and he or she is doing 155 kg. at present, sub-goals might be set at 170 kg, 180 kg. and 190 kg. A second type of sub-goal is one that contributes to a more fundamental goal. To continue the example, the athlete might recognize that a 170 kg. power clean will be necessary in order to clean 200 kg. smoothly and therefore might establish a 170 kg. power clean as a sub-goal (along with further sub-goals in the power clean of 140 kg, 150 kg. and 160 kg).

Sub-goals can be set for technical improvements, body weight, body fat, mental performance and a host of other areas. While it is important for goals to be measurable in some way, it is equally important that the means of measurement conform to the quantity being measured. This is a particular challenge in the mental realm, but the challenge is not insurmountable. The athlete should have clear images of each of those sub-goals, so that they can be brought to mind on a routine basis. This will serve both to keep those goals in the forefront of the mind and to increase the motivation to achieve those goals.

Once the athlete has established detailed sub-goals, he or she must make plans for training to achieve them. When it come to goals for improving certain mental capabilities, the athlete can identify specific times of the day when he or she will attempt to think about a specific goal or to exercise a desired quality and then practice as planned. For example, having decided that he or she needs to develop patience, the athlete can decide to exercise patience with respect to each practice session and determine that, instead of rushing through a given exercise, he or she will perform it at a predetermined pace. The athlete can use a timer, a series of thoughts or some other mechanism to assure that the proper timing is being achieved. This effort can begin with one exercise, or some brief time interval, and then be extended. The important thing is to work toward achieving some progress at each session (even though progress may be uneven) and to continually build on the progress that is made. Regardless of the nature of the goal, feedback regarding its achievement is vital to success. Neither feedback without goals nor goals without feedback helps performance very much; both are vital.

Perhaps the most important thing to remember is that once goals have been established, the focus must be on the process of achieving those goals rather than on the goals themselves. Goals set the direction for effort. They help the athlete to select the means to achieve the goal and to direct attention away from negative or distracting thoughts, and they provide motivation along the way. But the process is the sport and the existential means for accomplishing the goal. Action is required to make a goal a reality, and it is that action which must be focused upon. This is where goal setting on a micro level is so effective.

Goal Setting on a Micro Level

Goal setting on a macro level is important for any weightlifter who wants to reach his or her full potential. Athletes who have long term goals tend to develop more complex and adequate strategies for achieving those goals than those who focus solely on the short term. However, there has been a tendency in the sports psychology literature to focus almost exclusively on this kind of goal setting to the exclusion of the all-important subject of goal setting on the micro level.

I would define micro goal setting as establishing goals which can be achieved in the immediate future, often during the workout in which the athlete is engaged. The need for these kinds of goals cannot be overemphasized. It is, after all, the achievement of immediate goals that makes the achievement of longer term goals possible. Moreover, only these micro goals are within an athlete's direct ability to control. Therefore, the failure to focus on this area is surprising.

It is my contention that every athlete should go into every workout with one or more micro goals. Generally speaking, these goals should be both quantitative and qualitative. For example, an athlete may have an objective of snatching 100 kg. for five singles in a given workout. Now, the athlete can meet such an objective by merely making the weight successfully. But the athlete could receive a much greater benefit from the workout if he or she had at least one other complementary objective as well. The nature of that complementary objective depends on the athlete's needs at the time.

For one athlete, the objective might be to pull each successive rep higher and higher. For a second athlete, it might be to move under the bar faster than ever before. For a third athlete, it might be snatching the weight without expending too much nervous energy. The possibilities are endless. Creating combined goals has the added benefit of making the workout more interesting and challenging for the athlete.

Goals can be created for even the most mundane tasks. An athlete who is doing five sets of five reps in the squat might, at least on certain occasions, find the task someone routine and daunting. Concentrating on doing each rep better than the one before can be of help, as can trying to "groove" each rep perfectly. But sometimes goals can be created simply for fun. For example, one famous swimmer reported that he was able to fend off the boredom of swimming endless laps in the pool by imagining that there was a pretty young lady at the end of the pool urging him on and ready to reward him with a kiss. This athlete was able to use this mental goal setting technique (striving for the kiss) to make his arduous workouts an otherwise pleasant experience. A weightlifter might use his or her imagination in a similar way or might visualize each snatch as the one needed to win the Olympic Games. The particular image is not important. What is important is that the athlete use the micro goal setting technique to get the most out of his or her workouts.

If an athlete has selected the right sport, the sport itself will provide tremendous motivation for the athlete to train for success. However, no matter how enthusiastic the athlete, there will be occasions when the athlete will regard some necessary form of training as boring labor. Many athletes slog through such feelings for hours, days, weeks, months and even years at a time. They accept the need to do the work but see little joy in it.

Many coaches feel that there is nothing inherently wrong with such an attitude, as long as the necessary work gets done. I disagree for two primary reasons. First, anything an athlete does not like will tax his or her mind unnecessarily, will create negative memories and associations with the sport and will tend to undermine enthusiasm and hence the quality of the workout experience. Perhaps more importantly, an irreplaceable opportunity of life will have been missed: the opportunity to enjoy what you are doing at all times.

It may not seem possible to someone who has not tried it, but there are an infinite number of ways to turn the most mundane workout into a challenge and a pleasure. The examples already provided should give you the idea, but it is up to every athlete to take the responsibility to create means of making all workouts a pleasure, a source of inspiration and satisfaction.

While short term goals are critical to success, there is a context in which they can be misused. If moment-to-moment performance is overemphasized, athletes can become discouraged by short term failures and can swing back and forth from elation to frustration on the basis of extremely short term feedback. The key to successful use of micro goals is for the athlete to use them for motivational purposes but not to place so much pressure on performance that he or she is in a constant state of anxiety or attributes too much to any one instance in which performance is not at the level desired. Remember that the purpose of short term goals is to enable the athlete to focus better and enjoy workouts more.

The Vision of Success: Building Desire

The starting point for building the overwhelming desire to achieve outstanding results in weightlifting (or anything else) is to set an objective that truly inspires, a goal that evokes a true passion. In order for the goal to do this, it must meet three criteria. It must be exciting.. It must be specific. And, it must be believable.

Excitement about the prospect of an achievement arises out of the perception that the goal is worth achieving, that its achievement will make one a happier person. The higher a goal appears in a person's hierarchy of values, the greater the desire to achieve it. If a goal doesn't excite you it is not likely that you will work very hard to achieve it.

Specificity is important because it is difficult to get truly excited about a goal, or fully focused on its achievement, if one is not specific about what one wishes. Clarity in a goal makes it much more real and inspiring. In addition, in order to achieve any goal you will need to make decisions and trade-offs regarding your actions toward you goal. If you goal is not clear in your own mind, making such decisions and trade-offs will be difficult if not impossible.

Finally, you must believe that your goal is possible to achieve because you will not strive with all of your ability to reach a goal that you believe to be impossible to achieve.

It is not uncommon for a person to experience a certain level of difficulty in placing various objectives within a hierarchy of values. This requires identification of the most powerful needs of your innermost self. This can be done in a number of ways. One of the most effective and direct methods is to consciously rank your values and objectives. You can begin by listing the things you want to accomplish in the short and long term. To determine the short term goals, you might ask, "If I had only six months to accomplish everything that I wanted to do in life, what would I do?" To identify your long term goals, you might ask, "Where would I like to be five or ten years from now, what would I like to have accomplished?"

A less direct approach, but one that can be very effective, is to attempt to recall the accomplishments in your life which made you feel the greatest sense of achievement. Think about what aspect(s) of those accomplishments made you feel the greatest satisfaction. These may be things that other people would overlook if they were reviewing your personal history, or they may be aspects of that history on which you may place much greater weight than others. For example, you might identify winning a race when you were eleven years old as one of your most fulfilling experiences. Others might conclude that the pleasure you derived arose out of the victory itself. To you, the primary thrill may have arisen out of knowing that you had performed your best on a day that you did not feel particularly well. The point is that you can use a personal inventory to identify the kinds of events that gave you the greatest sense of satisfaction and the specific aspects of those events that meant the most to you. While this kind of exercise will not help you to identify specific objectives in weightlifting, it will help you to understand better the kinds of achievements that will give you the greatest sense of fulfillment (e.g., lifting 200 kg. vs. winning a specific competition).

Forward projections or visualizations can also be used for values identification. See yourself achieving a number of things that you consider to be important. Then imagine those experiences of success and all of the things that accompany them. Think about which one of those things give you the greatest sense of accomplishment. By combining a review of history and future projections you will be able to identify recurrent themes. Certain kinds of thoughts and experiences will give you the most satisfaction. These should form the basis of your goals. Only by focusing on your core values (assuming that they are rational), can you plan to achieve the things that will truly bring you joy.

Out of this kind of analysis will also come another kind of conclusion, the identification of a sense of mission. A mission is a very fundamental kind of objective that a person forms. It states in the simplest and most concise terms a person's fundamental goal(s). It answers the question, "What kind of person do you intend to be when you have achieved your major objectives?" This is a more basic kind of goal than a specific achievement.

For example, your ultimate goal may be to make an Olympic weightlifting team. You may have a number of sub-goals along the way, including winning two national championships, setting several American Records and winning the Olympic tryouts. However, your mission might really be to compete with the best in the world at the biggest event in the world. Membership on the Olympic Team might be your means to accomplish this mission, but your real mission is to be on the platform with the best, to warm up with them, to give them some competition and to gain their respect as a member of their elite club. Consequently, if you made the team because some other athletes were injured and your own level of ability was not sufficient to be really competitive with the rest of the world, merely making the team might not fulfill your true mission, while a chance to compete with distinction at a particularly difficult World Championship might bring you closer to the accomplishment of your more fundamental goal. Personal missions are as different as people. Some people want to show that they can overcome some obstacle, to prove the "naysayers" wrong. Others merely like to pursue certain ends irrespective of what others think. The exact nature of what such a person might choose as ultimate achievement is secondary to the satisfaction he or she will derive from striving to achieve, and ultimately achieving, a challenging goal.

Once a person has identified his or her core values and basic mission, he or she is ready to establish goals that are really likely to generate excitement over the long term and to help that person become the best that he or she can be.

Although the perceived desirability of a particular achievement is the spark that can ignite a burning desire to succeed, it is not by itself enough to motivate a person to action. Many people spend much of their lives dreaming about a desired state of being. They can imagine the desired state and gain considerable satisfaction from that process of imagination. What separates these dreamers from those who achieve success (or at least attempt to do so) is the belief that appropriate action can lead to that desired state (or at least a state that is better than the current one). Those who act certainly do not believe that success is assured, but they do believe that they can make success happen. Such people have converted an imagined state into an actual object of desire.

Reaching your full potential in weightlifting requires an enormous expenditure of mental and physical effort. It requires an alignment of all aspects of life toward the achievement of your goal. Finally, your diet must be right, and you must receive adequate rest and relaxation. You must train assiduously. Total concentration must be applied to your lifting efforts. There may be some sports in which an athlete can let his or her mind drift during the training process, because the activity being performed is repetitive and relatively automatic in nature. Weightlifting requires complete focus and an awareness of what you are doing at all times. And, while weightlifting is a relatively safe sport, performing the activity at a high level requires courage. Hurling your body with blinding speed under a falling weight of several hundred pounds, to catch it at just the right moment, is not an activity for the fainthearted or the distracted. The dedication and courage to accomplish all of this exist only when you have achieved a burning, overwhelming desire to succeed.

To summarize, the process of building the champion's mind begins by visualizing the person you want to be. See the image of yourself as a future champion, a person who has all of the characteristics that you desire and will possess when you become the champion you want to be. Then identify the characteristics that you need to improve upon or dispense with if that ideal person is to be created. See the desirable characteristics emerging as dominant. Give the unwanted characteristics images and see yourself destroying them or throwing them away.

Work to increase your desire for the target characteristics and your distaste for any undesirable ones that you may currently possess. You will eventually find that you are almost automatically becoming the person you want to be. What you see when you close your eyes is what you can and must become.

The importance of developing a "no limits" mind set cannot be overemphasized. What you can conceive you can ultimately achieve (as long as it is not at odds with the laws of nature). The champion is energized by the image of success and is therefore capable of awesome deeds. Energize yourself with your vision of success and you will become capable of such deeds a well.

The Value of Visualization

Many people who have achieved great things in life have been surprised when their accomplishments were recognized. It is certainly true that a person's opinion of his or her abilities is often not a very accurate measure of those abilities. Moreover, wishing will not make it so. Believing something does not make it true, and imagining achievement of a certain objective does not guarantee that a person will achieve that objective. But it is also true that very few people have accomplished great things who did not first visualize themselves in some way having achieved their objectives. Visualization is clearly not sufficient to make a champion, but it may be necessary and there can be little doubt that it is helpful.

Why is visualization valuable? For one thing, it fuels the desire to succeed. Imagining a result can give you enthusiasm for that result. The more clearly you can imagine success, the closer you can come to experiencing the joy it will bring, and that can fuel the desire to achieve the goal in reality. Imagining yourself as a great champion you admire or as the end product that you aspire to can greatly increase your motivation and confidence. At least one major study of Olympic level athletes found that more successful athletes tended to imagine success and dream about it more than athletes who were less successful. There also seemed to be a relationship between the frequency of an athlete's imagining success and his or her commitment to their sport. Could it be that these athletes imagined and dreamed of success and were more committed to their sports because success was objectively more achievable for them than for other athletes? The study attempted to control for this variable, but it still found a relationship between imagining and dreaming about success and the achievement of actual success. It is therefore likely that imagination and/or dreaming had same effect on the success of these athletes.

In his Encyclopedia Of Modern Bodybuilding, the great bodybuilder Arnold Schwarzenegger says: "To be a champion, you have to have the mind of a champion and that mind is created step be step, just like the physique." I couldn't agree with Arnold more, and his words apply just as well to weightlifters, if you substitute "strength and technique" for the words "the physique" in his quote. Visualization is one of the important steps that Arnold alludes to. Visualize the person you want to be several times a day, put up pictures of your ideal or goal. These and similar actions will improve your ability to visualize success, and that, in turn, will increase your chances of achieving that success.

A second benefit of visualization is that it can return your focus to your real priorities. The vicissitudes of life can often cause attention and interest to be drawn away from what is truly important. The cause of such a diversion can be pleasant or unpleasant. A personal tragedy, such as the death or illness of a loved one, or a great opportunity, such as a chance at a better job or a better education, can divert attention from even a deep seated goal. Visualization cannot eliminate the diversion, but it can serve to bring your focus back to your goals, giving you the desire to balance that goal against the challenges that threaten to lessen or extinguish it.

A third application of visualization is that you can use it to play out mental struggles or physical or technical problems. For instance, you can visualize a fear and then see yourself throwing it away or destroying it. Or, you can visualize what you believe to be your true identity and see that as your "center," a place from which you control your thoughts, your body and your feelings. Then you can visualize your control center actively influencing all of these areas to achieve a positive effect (a positive feeling, a good thought, a desirable action) or to do away with an undesirable effect. Athletes who use visualization in this way often combine it with relaxation technique. (For example, if an athlete visualizes a situation in which he or she becomes too excited, he or she then uses a relaxation technique to reduce the level of anxiety and then continues the visualization.)

A fourth application of visualization is in "seeing" yourself as someone who is accomplished (either by imitating a particular person or by simply seeing yourself performing in an accomplished manner) as compared with accomplishing a particular thing. Just acting as if you are an accomplished person can cause you to adopt and exhibit certain behaviors characteristic of such a person and to ultimately become more accomplished.

Why would such an approach work? Many psychologists have argued for years that the mind cannot distinguish, at least not completely, between reality and imagination. If you imagine yourself succeeding at something, the subconscious mind processes that information as if it had really been experienced. A sufficient number of such experiences programs the subconscious mind in the same way the actual experience would.

The notion of programming the subconscious has been discussed for hundreds, if not thousands, of years, but one of the modern pioneers in this area was Maxwell Maltz, who published a book called Psycho Cybernetics in the 1960s. Maltz was

a plastic surgeon who noticed that it took most of his patients several weeks from the first time they saw their new appearance after surgery to accept fully that appearance and to see themselves as having the new look that they actually had achieved. Perhaps even more interesting was Maltz's observation that some patients who experienced dramatic changes in appearance never seemed to accept their new appearance. He then reasoned that if some of those who had experienced change could not see it, there was an aspect of belief that transcended reality (in terms of its effect on the mind). This led to the realization that the opposite situation could occur; the mind could be induced to believe that a change had occurred even when it had not. Maltz argued that suggestions made to the subconscious could effect such a change and that people could therefore actively cause mental change. Maxwell Maltz and many subsequent writers have made this point in many ways over the ensuing decades, and many who have tried suggestion feel that it indeed works for them. Obviously, believing that you are 7 ' tall when you are 5'6" will never make you taller, but believing you can do something that is actually within your capabilities can make you attempt it (when you never would have otherwise).

In recent years, visualization has expanded outward from the realm of the few athletes who seemed to have taught it to themselves to become an established discipline within which much work is being done. Scientists are studying the phenomenon intently. There is still a great deal more that we do not understand than we do, but ignorance is gradually giving way to insight. While it will probably be many years before we fully grasp how and to what extent the mechanisms of visualization work, we are learning more and more about how to make visualization effective. This is often the case with technology. We understand that something works well before we understand why it does.

One of the insights that we have developed regarding visualization is that visualization can clearly help an athlete learn the cognitive aspects of a sport faster than pure practice (as was indicated in Chapter 2, there is still considerable debate about whether visualization can be of value in the development of power or motor skills).

However, those who believe in the use of visualization or imagery to improve motor performance generally describe two distinct approaches to visualization. One method involves seeing yourself perform perfectly as an external observer would. For instance, you might see yourself mounting the platform, preparing to lift and then performing a perfect lift. As you gain ability in this area, you will be able to manipulate images more easily and to view the performance from every imaginable angle. This kind of visualization is used to primarily in improving confidence and motivation as well as skill. If you can see yourself performing well in your mind's eye, you can more fully accept that you will be able to duplicate this performance in reality.

The second major technique of visualization involves imagining a performance as you will experience it. Ideally, the athlete "experiences" all aspects of the performance. He or she imagines mounting the stage, feeling the steps up to the stage, seeing the arena and hearing the crowd. Then the lifter feels the lift being performed, from the visual experience to the feel of the bar to the feel of the entire movement and the applause afterward. (Focusing on response stimulus— how you feel—as opposed to pure performance— moving in a certain way—results in a greater degree of vividness in the experience, though the link between vividness and success has not been thoroughly established.) Elite athletes appear to use this kind of mental rehearsal to improve motor performance more often than the external-observer approach. While science has been moving cautiously in its evaluation of the effectiveness of such training, many outstanding athletes award a great deal of credit in terms of performance enhancement to such visualization.

These athletes "rehearse" technique mentally. Athletes who have a sense of how they feel at various points in a given movement appear better able to utilize the mental rehearsal technique. Some athletes use visualization to create the mental experience of executing a skill in slow motion (e.g., visualizing a movement five times in slow motion and then visualizing it ten times at normal speed). This ability can be developed if the athlete concentrates on generating a broad internal focus. In so doing, the athlete can develop a series of discriminative cues (indications of effectiveness in performance). Those cues usually involve the recognition of tension in various parts of the body, the orientation of the body in space and proper tempos of movement.

Imagery control and vividness seem to relate to performance (especially in the cognitive aspects of performance). Proponents of "psychoneuromuscular" theory believe that a small number of the neurons of the muscles that are involved in a given activity are activated during the visualization of such an activity. It is interesting to note that some studies have demonstrated similar degrees of improvement in certain tasks performed with the left hand between subjects who practiced with the left hand and those who practiced only with the right hand and performed mental practice with the left hand.

In order to be effective, this mental rehearsal should only take place when an athlete is not actively engaged in the activity; mental rehearsal and actual rehearsal cannot effectively take place simultaneously, although many athletes use mental rehearsal as a readying technique and as a

means of reviewing and remembering a good performance. In fact, there are many coaches and athletes who believe that a mental rehearsal immediately prior to the execution of a performance is absolutely critical to success.

The movement being mentally rehearsed should also involve a large enough segment of the activity to create a coordinated motion. In weightlifting this will generally be a full snatch or C&J (or at least a full clean or jerk) but occasionally may involve a more limited segment of the movement.

At least one successful gymnastic coach has reported great success in terms of skill development through the use of visualization. He had his athlete practice a particular vault through the lead-ups, concentrate on the trick, including tightening any muscles used during the trick in the proper sequence during slow motion visualization, and then hit a complex trick on their first try.

Rehearsal can be used to analyze technique as well as to practice it, by recalling actual past performances. An athlete can compare good and bad performances and try to identify differences in the feelings experienced during both. By so doing, he or she can develop the kind of discriminative cues referred to above. Such cues are a key to developing a sense of correct and incorrect technique. Using recall of how he or she feels during a movement can also help an athlete to learn the direction of his or her mental errors— what he or she is thinking when a problem arises (and when it does not).

Many aspects of a movement can be important, including balance, body positions, feelings and the sensations produced by the interactions between the body and the implements that are involved in the activity, and those can all be analyzed to an extent by a mental review of technique. This analysis can be conducted in sequence and in slow motion, making sure that all of the important points, whether identified verbally or through images, are called upon. After several times in slow motion, the athlete can then move into motion at the actual performance speed and repeat that several times. Before the rehearsal process, the athlete may be aided by a review of correct technique, whether via film, video, still pictures, or a list of performance points.

Before undertaking any mental rehearsal, the athlete should attempt to define carefully the reason for the rehearsal. Is it to improve skill, change his or her mental state during performance, or improve some other area of performance? Once the athlete has made this determination, he can she can focus on becoming attuned to the right cues for improving the particular aspects of performance that require correction, whether those cues involve arousal level, a certain element of technique or the need to explode harder. For example, mentally reviewing only technique while exaggerating a technical mistake can be an important tool for emphasizing the characteristics that differentiate good technique from bad or other performance determinants (although the vast majority of what an athlete rehearses should be good technique, not bad).

A number of studies on mental rehearsal have shown that actual practice and mental rehearsal appear to be more effective combined than either is alone. Perhaps this is because the combination serves to increase total practice time or because these different forms of practice activate learning in the nervous system in ways that complement one another. Some have argued that the chief benefit of mental rehearsal is that provides rest from physical practice that would have otherwise fatigued the athlete. It should be noted that actual practice with an implement but without the full context of the event (e.g., lifting an empty bar instead of a heavy weight) can be helpful. The lifter can do this in slow motion or in sequences, always moving to full motion and speed, at least by the end of the practice session (if not immediately after some slow motion efforts). Practice with eyes closed can emphasize kinesthetic sense. This can be done in one series of sets with eyes open and closed, or in alternate sets or in alternate reps. When focusing on feelings, it is useful to bring in one sense at a time until the fullest possible experience of the event is reached.

Apart from improving the performance of a skill, there is evidence that imagery may also be effective in regulating arousal. That issue will be discussed further in a later part of this chapter.

Some practitioners of medicine believe that visualization can be used to facilitate recovery from illness and injuries. The effectiveness of such visualization has yet to be established scientifically, but the issue bears further investigation. (There is no reason to believe that visualization and wishing for a cure have a direct effect on healing, but thinking about healing may help to mobilize the body's healing capacities in some way.)

One final note on visualization is appropriate. As is the case with virtually every other training method, it is not for everyone, at least not at all times. An athlete who becomes very emotionally involved during visualization can exhaust himself or herself with excessive visualization. Similarly, the athlete who finds that visualization in the days prior to a competition leads to added nervousness may opt to avoid it, as any gain in confidence or skill that may accrue as a result of such practice will be offset by losses from a depletion of the athlete's energy stores.

Mental Toughness: Sustaining Power

Weightlifting is full of exaltation and frustration. The weightlifter must control the latter in order to experience the former on a consistent basis. The first step in controlling frustration and developing an iron will to succeed is to differentiate between failure and a situation in which you do not succeed.

When a person strives to achieve great things, there will be many times that success will not be achieved initially. The first acrobat to do a triple somersault did not succeed in his initial attempt at this feat. In fact, he, and others before him, missed the triple many times before he succeeded. But when successful people do not succeed at a particular task, they analyze the unsuccessful effort, searching for its causes. They then plan out a corrective strategy and try again. And herein lies the difference between success and failure. The successful athlete views a miss as valuable feedback that demonstrates where he or she really is and what further steps are needed in order to achieve success. The unsuccessful athlete sees a miss as evidence that he or she has "failed."

Failure is a state of mind that arises when the person who has attempted something pronounces a personal judgment. Were the men who tried the triple "failures" because they did not succeed, or were they pioneers who helped to add to the knowledge of the field? Part of the answer depends on the specifics of each case (i.e., whether they were making rational attempts at the jump and whether information regarding their attempts was used by others in making their attempts). But the other part of the answer lies in a person's point of view. The person who is thinking rationally views all of those who are doing rational work in a given field as fellow contributors. The person who is thinking irrationally places an almost mystical value on the person who happened to achieve a specific result first. To be sure, the individual who is the first in some landmark area is to be applauded and revered. But such an achievement does not in any way diminish the achievements that others made along the path to that landmark.

In the case of the athlete who has suffered a loss, reasons for that loss can be discovered. The athlete may have failed to live up to his or her capabilities or may have met a superior opponent. In order to change the outcome, the athlete may need only improve his or her ability to perform at his or her best more consistently. If the opponent was superior, the person needs to take the steps necessary to improve his or her capabilities so that they exceed those of the opponent. In no event should a loss be automatically considered a "failure."

Thomas Edison is surely one of the greatest, if not the greatest, inventors of all time. By any standard his life was a monumental success. Yet Edison would have been the first to admit that he failed many more times than he succeeded when he worked in his inventions. What separated Edison from others who might have had an equal degree of genius was his dogged persistence in his work and his confidence that there was no limit to his ability to make a given invention.

Many of the productive greats in history have shared some common attitudinal threads. One was the view that time was the only opponent that could defeat them. Archimedes said: "Give me a long enough lever and I can move the earth." The great creators said, "give me enough time and I will find the answer to problem I am addressing." A second important attitude was the recognition that all limits are contextual. Four hundred lb.. was a great barrier in the C&J for many years. When it was finally achieved in official competition by John Davis in 1951, few could even imagine a 500 lb. C&J. Yet, in less than twenty years the 500 lb. barrier was broken, and a number of athletes were closing in on a 400 lb. snatch. Today, a 600 lb. C&J is in view, and a 500 lb. snatch does not seem impossible. Was a 500 lb. C&J possible with the diet, training methods and techniques and mental attitudes available to athletes in the 1950s? Probably not. And just as a 300 kg. C&J may seem out of the question today, some athlete will come along who can do it, most assuredly one who thinks he can.

Creators in every field, including many great athletes, have incredible mental toughness. That toughness stems from an ability to put aside any setbacks by addressing them squarely in terms of what current actions are available to overcome the obstacle and to focus on future success. Top performers have a way of seeing problems and stressful situations as exciting challenges which invite action. (When no action is possible at present, they are mentally filed away under the heading "problems that are to be dealt with as soon as conditions permit".)

Handling success in the proper way helps an athlete to develop mental toughness as much as handling lack of success effectively. In the case of the person who has succeeded in a given situation, he or she must identify the reason for the success. If the reason was that he or she performed up to potential, then that should serve both as positive reinforcement and a source of valuable information on how to perform at his or her best. If the victory was due mainly to the fault of an opponent, the athlete should realize that he or she will need to improve in order to achieve victory at the next competition. Alternatively, if the victory was due to a weak opponent, more challenging ones should be sought. There is nothing more ridiculous than an athlete's concluding he or she cannot lose because he or she is undefeated, when the real reason is that he or she has never met a suitable opponent. Such bravado is just as wrongheaded as the negative self-image of an athlete who loses and then declares himself or herself to have a permanent tendency to do so. Either mistake can lead to less serious training for the next competition.

You can increase your mental toughness by developing a vision of the success you wish to achieve, making a plan for that achievement and beginning to work the plan, while understanding that the specific methods for executing the plan may have to be modified many times before success is achieved. The effort required to succeed may be great, but if the plan was realistic to begin with, it can be achieved. The mentally tough athlete is the one who never forgets that principle.

The key to mental staying power is a proper perspective. As was suggested earlier, one aspect of such a perspective is the ability to focus on the positive (e.g., "now that I have tried, I can see what is keeping me from success, and I'll now use that information in order to improve my preparation for my next attempt). The second characteristic is to break the goal into manageable steps and to have the confidence to realize that the ultimate goal can be reached by taking each step in succession.

This last attitude is particularly important for sustaining enthusiasm when a lifter is making a comeback from an injury or illness or when the distance up is very long. For example, near the beginning of my career, after a couple of years of fairly hard training, I can remember becoming a little disappointed that I could lift only about half as much as the world record holders of the day. The world record, which I had a deep desire to break some day, seemed so very far away. Then I realized that each athlete who has achieved great heights has traveled the same path, and in blazing that path has made it easier for others to follow. The trick in traveling such a path is to conscientiously put one foot in front of the other and then to proceed step by step, both enjoying the journey and pausing to reflect on how far you have come. In the same way, when a person is making a comeback, there is a tendency to focus on how far he or she has fallen, to emphasize the distance that must be traveled again. However, the winning attitude is to realize that familiarity is likely to make the trip faster and surer the second time. Moreover, in taking the trip again, there is always the opportunity to savor the high points once again, to avoid the bad spots and to correct any errors that were made the first time out.

The mentally average athlete who confronts an unexpected and/or seemingly overwhelming obstacle says: "How am I ever to succeed in view of this setback? It's hopeless." In contrast, the champion says: "What a wonderful achievement it will be when I succeed despite this obstacle or setback." The average athlete sees the setback as an impassable obstacle and himself or herself as controlled by it. The champion sees the setback as a natural and ultimately unimportant event in his or her inexorable rise to success.

In the short term, as in a competition or workout, it must be remembered that performance is related to how you feel (e.g., if you feel well, you

335

are likely to perform well). Therefore, part of being mentally tough is developing the ability to create positive feelings regardless of circumstances. You must learn to say "stop" to negative thoughts, and to substitute positive affirmations and behaviors over and over. Alternatively, you can act determined and, in so doing, become more determined. Finally, you must also learn to focus on performance (i.e., that which is under your control) rather than pure outcome (e.g., placement in a competition on a given day, which may or may not be under your control).

Naturally, there is a physical side to mental toughness. Vince Lombardi's adage that "fatigue makes cowards of us all" is eminently true. The athlete must be in condition for the event. However, because of the limited number of attempts required of weightlifters in competition, physical fatigue is rarely a problem for the weightlifter who trains regularly . Occasionally, when a competition has many athletes at the same level, there may be such a long wait between attempts that an athlete's warm-ups can actually become fatiguing, but this is a relatively rare situation in major competitions. The primary means of avoiding fatigue during a competition is to avoid burning unnecessary nervous energy (a subject that will be covered in greater detail later in this chapter). When fatigue does develop, some athletes are comforted by the notion that their competitors are at least as tired as they are.

Still another strategy for improving mental toughness is to intentionally expose yourself to adverse conditions (in competition or training) and to overcome them. Each time you succeed in such a process, you build confidence and determination. An example of this kind of mental toughness training is to practice with distractions. Practicing in the presence of external distractions can teach you to ignore them and to calm any inner mental distractions that result from them.

Irrespective of the particular adversity that you overcome, the fact that you overcame it will be of great value to you. When the going gets tough, you can focus on how you have overcome adversity before and be inspired to rise to the occasion once again.

Plumbing Your Inner Resources

The legends of competition are replete with stories of athletes who "reached down" or "dug deep" to their innermost reserves of mental and emotional energy to snatch victory from the jaws of defeat. There is a great deal of truth to many of these stories, because there is often a narrow margin between the abilities of athletes who are at a high level, and extra effort can make the difference in an outcome. Therefore, even a small lapse in concentration or effort on the part of one competitor can cause one athlete to effectively cede victory to the other. Alternatively, a little bit of extra effort at a crucial moment can lead to victory over an opponent who is of fundamentally equal ability.

In certain respects, these issues arise less frequently in weightlifting than in many other sports, primarily because of the relatively closed nature of weightlifting competition (i.e., three attempts for each competitor in each of two lifts). Physical (or at least muscular) fatigue is therefore rarely an issue in weightlifting competition, and the need to mobilize resources to overcome fatigue is minimal. However, this does not mean that there is any less need to call upon other resources in a very profound way.

While a weightlifter's muscular energy will rarely be exhausted by competition, there is still fatigue to overcome. Nervous energy can be depleted by the rigors of the competition and a special effort may be needed to overcome this. In addition, inhibitions and fears must often be pushed back in order for the lifter to perform a lift that is a new personal record or requires an extraordinary effort in terms of the lifter's capabilities on that day. Finally, what weightlifting does require is a terrific intensity of effort, one that requires the full application of mental, emotional and physical capabilities. Therefore, there is often a critical need for the lifter to have the ability to dig deeply into his or her reserve.

In the short term, whether in the gym or in competition, there is often a moment where a competition is lost or the productivity of a workout lessened, when the lifter gives up with a thought that amounts to "I've lost the day so why continue?" or "this is just a "bad" workout, so I might as well just cruise, or even stop." Often, these thoughts are premature or, at a minimum, lead to a lesser degree of success than might have otherwise been achieved, merely because the ability to dig deeply into your resources and to overcome the short term thinking of a negative focus leads to a diminution in performance. It has often been said in coaching circles that the athlete who will not be beaten cannot be beaten. This is true on two important levels. First, as has been suggested, many competitions are lost by those who could have won, simply because that athlete lost his or her will or focus while an athlete of lesser absolute ability did not. Second, to the extent that an athlete will turn in the very best possible performance on a given day by "refusing to be beaten," that athlete will go away knowing that, regardless of the official score, he or she had a winning day.

Inner resources are also called upon in generating the resiliency to recover from adversity, the ability to pick up the pieces and move forward again when disappointment strikes. As was suggested in the previous section of this chapter, this challenge can arise on a short term basis, such as when an athlete is performing below his or her capabilities and/or expectations at a particular point in a competition. In such a case there is the temptation to "throw in the towel," to say, "I can't win, so why continue to put myself under pressure?"

The challenge to call upon inner resources can also be much more long lived when an athlete faces a serious illness or injury, when financial or personal problems divert his or her energy or when a loved one is suffering or has passed away. There may be a temptation to give it all up, to be overcome with that sense that you just cannot continue. Yet, as difficult as they are, these are all challenges that can and have been overcome. But they can be overcome only through the greatest imaginable commitment to the idea that the struggle must continue and that the greater the loss or the challenge, the greater its hidden affirmation of the importance and grandeur of a life lived for achievement. If a life is not lived in accordance with and in pursuit of important personal values, the momentary sense of loss at not achieving or sustaining these values will not be so strong. But values are worth living for; indeed, they are the only thing worth living for. Therefore, no matter what the setbacks, a life realigned toward achieving what is possible will soon begin to move toward achieving all the values that are possible to it. Learned helplessness is your only real barrier to long term self-control.

The Pain Barrier

We have all heard the expression "no pain, no gain." There is certainly some truth to it. Without mental and physical effort, improvement cannot occur. There is a certain pain threshold that we all must reach and exceed if progress is to occur. However, a distinction needs to be made between pain that is a symptom of damage and "pain" that stems from the discomfort of pushing yourself to new heights.

Pain is the body's basic means of telling the mind that the body is in danger. Whether the pain is a direct result of an external stimulus (e.g., intense heat) or represents a symptom (e.g., inflammation from damage to some tissue of the body), it is the body's signal that there is some direct threat to its well being that is not to be ignored. On the other hand, strenuous activity (e.g., training) will generate a reaction from the body that is designed to protect the body's state of equilibrium. The body will produce signals of distress (e.g., increased respiration and heart rates) to warn the athlete that the body's equilibrium has been disturbed. The successful athlete must be able to discriminate between the pain that signals injury and the discomfort that signifies effort. He or she must be attentive to the former and heed its warnings. He or she must

learn to characterize the latter as a state of stimulation and learn to seek those feelings because they are an indicator of the generation of a training effect.

Chapter 11 deals with the subject of injury. Injury aside, the dedicated athlete welcomes the signs of discomfort which are associated with the training effect because they are the sign that the training regimen being followed is strenuous enough. Without this kind of pain on appropriate occasions, there will be no gain.

The Fear Factor and the Most Common Fear: Fear of Failure

Fear is an emotion experienced by all higher animals including humans. In normal life and at normal levels, it serves a valuable, life protecting function. Fear reflects a person's automatic evaluation of a certain situation as a threat to his or her values. However, as with all emotions, fear cannot be relied upon as an indicator of actual danger. It is for the conscious mind to determine whether a given fear is truly justified. If so, the signal presented by fear should be heeded; if not, it can be circumvented.

Some people have an irrational fear of using their bodies, and this fear lessens the enjoyment that they could otherwise gain from athletics and other physical activities. In contrast, other people impulsively or obsessively misuse their bodies, ignoring signals the body gives and all reasonable safety precautions that should be taken while engaging in any activity. The correct balance is demonstrated by a third group of people who use their bodies without fear or abandon, enjoying the possibilities that are before them; this is the healthy model for most people, including weightlifters.

Some people have a fear of exerting themselves. Others may fear a certain competitor. Still others may fear making a certain movement or lifting a certain weight. In general terms, we fear the unknown, loss of identity, change and suffering.

In the properly trained and prepared athlete, most athletic fears are unfounded. Exertion per se poses no threat to an athlete's well being (assuming the athlete is not in ill health). Competitors cannot hurt you (at least not in weightlifting competition). An athlete who performs a particular lift skillfully is not apt to be hurt, and if the weight being tried is within the athlete's current capabilities, there is little to be feared from the weight. It is true that accidents can happen, but they are accidents (i.e., the unusual). And the vast majority of accidents, rare as they are, can be prevented by proper safety precautions (e.g., proper equipment and training methods, good technique and full concentration). Through proper mental and physical training, the barriers of irrational fear are progressively pushed back to the point where they are virtually non-existent and are not a major factor in performance. When you know what you are doing and have confidence in your abilities, fear comes under control.

Perhaps the most pervasive fear that athletes face is fear of failure (with its associated fears of embarrassment and loss of self-esteem). This is a very irrational fear because, as strange as it may sound, failure is generally good. It helps you to know your capabilities. Without it, it would be hard to know what your current limits truly were. Without it, you are unsure as to whether you are pushing yourself towards true limits. Failure can help you to know your weaknesses and to set about overcoming them. It is one of the most important feedback mechanisms that we have. Naturally, you should never intentionally fail, but failure per se is not to be feared or avoided; rather, success, in its full measure, should always be actively sought.

Irrational fear of failure keeps us from attempting something that is at our limits. It therefore inhibits progress. What is more, fear of failure can become a sort of self-fulfilling prophecy. The fear itself may keep you from performing at your best, causing you to fear to attempt more, which further fuels your fear. You must learn to focus on performance more than outcome, to learn to love the battle and the effort. In doing so, fear of the outcome will fade away as you become fully immersed in and dedicated to making an all out effort.

Another technique for handling fear is to create a mental image of the fear or its cause and then to find a way to mentally dispose of it (smash it, throw it in the garbage, blow it up, etc.). For example, you might envision fear as a certain facial expression and then visualize that image changing to a positive one or running away from you out of a fear that it can no longer influence you.

On the positive side, fear can actually help to motivate the athlete toward high performance, as long as it is not permitted to get out of control. Former undefeated heavyweight boxing champion Rocky Marciano reportedly feared losing so much (after experiencing defeat once as a amateur) that he was able to train religiously and fight courageously. Perhaps this was not the most pleasant way to live, but it surely kept Marciano in a state of fighting readiness.

Developing Mental Control

The Importance of Concentration

Concentration is the ability to focus full attention on a given task, to the exclusion of everything else (at least on a conscious level). The ability to concentrate is a key characteristic of an accomplished weightlifter for a number of reasons.

First, concentration helps the athlete to apply motor skills more effectively and consistently. Second, it improves strength and power performance significantly. Third, concentration can reduce fears and inhibitions, permitting the lifter to move under weights aggressively (i.e., without hesitation).

There is an important aspect of the application of concentration to the reduction of fears and inhibitions that I did not really appreciate fully until I had been both a coach and a high level lifter for many years. I was working with a national level athlete who had reached a sticking point in his lifting. One day, while we were analyzing his situation, he reported that in recent months all of the weights he was lifting felt heavy. Thinking that the cause was physical (i.e., fatigue), I reduced both the volume and intensity of his training. This seemed to have little effect. We tried several other kinds of physical interventions with an equal lack of success. In thinking about the problem one day, I began to introspect about the nature of the sensation of heaviness. It was after some thought that I realized the nature of this lifter's problem. It was not physical, not the result of a heightened sensitivity to the sensation of heaviness. Rather, this lifter's problem was a failure to focus on applying maximum effort to the bar. Since the mind can only truly focus on one thing at a time, when a lifter is focusing or an explosive effort, the conscious perception of the weight of the bar is diminished. The lifter who says that the bar feels heavy (barring a physical cause such as fatigue or overloading the bar) is really saying that he or she is not concentrating on applying sufficient force to the bar to effectively block out or reduce the sensation of the bar's weight. Correcting his mental fault was no easy process for this lifter, but once he understood the problem, he was able to work on refocusing his mind, and the problem did eventually disappear (or at least that is what he reported).

Still another benefit of concentration pertains to the psychic pleasure that can arise out of the act of extraordinary concentration on virtually anything. A certain feeling of calm and mind/body is experienced as a result of an act of concentration. Some people derive it from meditation, others from concentrating on mental work, and athletes experience it from a total focus on their activity. In my view, the athletic experience is the most profound of these experiences, perhaps because of the combination of mental and physical activity (the latter of which can have physiological effects, such as the release of endorphins, substances which have a calming and pain relieving effect on the body).

One final dimension of concentration needs to be discussed before we move on to a discussion of how you can develop concentration. That dimension is one of sustained concentration, even when you are doing something else. What I mean by this is a form of concentration that causes you never to lose sight of your primary objective. In order to succeed, you must be able to concentrate on other things and at the same time occasionally to question whether your efforts are appropriate to the overall purpose of what you are doing. This sustained level of staying in focus (really the single mindedness of purpose referred to in an earlier section of this chapter) must be carefully cultivated if an athlete is to reach his or her full potential.

There are a number of exercises and procedures that an athlete can perform in order to improve his or her concentration. They come from many disciplines. Yoga, for example, has many exercises which can improve concentration. One such exercise consists of sitting at one end of a darkened and quiet room and achieving a relaxed state (relaxation techniques are discussed in a later part of this chapter). The subject then stares at a lighted candle that has been placed at the other end of the room for a period of ten or twenty seconds, until the image of the candle's flame has been fully fixed in the subject's mind. (It is a good idea to shade the flame or wear sunglasses while doing this exercise to assure that the brightness of the flame does not harm the eyes). Then the subject closes his or her eyes and tries to see the image of the candle (which is automatically retained for a time) and to preserve that image as long and as sharply as possible. With time, the ability to retain the image and to exclude other thoughts will improve, as will the overall ability to concentrate at will.

Variations of this technique consist of using another prop, such as a ball or bar. The object is to examine it in detail, to look at it, to feel it and even to talk about it. Then one can think about how the object is actually used in the sport. The purpose of the exercise is to develop the ability to focus selectively, deeply and at will.

Another kind of concentration exercise consists of maintaining focus in the face of distractions. The subject first cultivates the ability to concentrate on something in a favorable atmosphere (such as the candle exercise described above) and then attempts to perform a similar exercise where there are more distractions (e.g., the noise of a radio or under rapidly changing conditions of light). This exercise may be even more helpful if it is done under actual training conditions (i.e., the lifter concentrates on his or her lifts even with distractions in the gym). A lifter who learns to concentrate under such conditions will be truly hard to rattle under meet conditions. Moreover, the confidence that such an athlete will develop regarding his or her abilities to concentrate under all conditions will pay dividends beyond those of mere concentration itself, as the athlete will feel in control at all times.

Still another powerful technique for gaining control of concentration is to learn to use any distraction or negative thought as an impetus to turn attention in another direction. For example, suppose an athlete has a habit of occasionally letting his or her mind drift to a fear of making a certain technical mistake. The athlete should then cultivate the habit of immediately turning his or her attention to a more positive thought or image (such as that of seeing the lift performed without such a mistake) and to making that new image stronger and more clear. The athlete should in effect couple the two items by association, so that the negative thought almost automatically leads to a focus on the positive one. If this practice is diligently cultivated, the lifter should have no difficulty eliminating the negative thought altogether or, at a minimum, eliminating its negative effects.

The result of mastering concentration is that the athlete learns to isolate himself or herself from virtually all stimuli other than the task at hand. Some athletes have described this as being enveloped in a "cocoon" that protected them from the distractions of the outside and inside worlds to leave them "alone" with the task to be performed.

Controlling the Direction of Attention

While concentration is the ability to focus attention, there is an entirely different aspect of attention control that needs to be addressed by the athlete. That aspect is the direction of attention. The direction of attention has two fundamental dimensions: a) the width of attention; and b) whether that attention is focused internally or externally.

Width of attention refers to how much the athlete is trying to take in. Attention can be narrow or broad. An example of a narrow attentional focus would be thinking about the feeling of the bar on the shoulders while preparing for the jerk. A wide focus would be observing the entire audience as you wave after a good lift. There are those who argue attention cannot be narrow or broad (i.e., that the mind has only one fundamental kind of attentional capability). Instead, they say, it is the size of the "unit" being focused on that varies (e.g., the field or the ball). However, regardless of its cause, attentional width does vary, and the existence of this phenomenon has important implications for athletes and coaches.

With respect to the internal/external direction of attention, an internal focus refers to instances in which a person focuses on himself or herself rather than the external world. An example of an internal focus would be an athlete's monitoring his or her sense of fatigue. An external focus would consist of observing the texture of the bar's surface.

In certain sports a broad external focus is beneficial. The quarterback in football needs this kind of focus when sizing up the flow of players on the field to determine to which receiver to throw a pass, or whether to throw a pass at all. Later on in the play, after the decision has been made to pass to a specific receiver, the quarterback requires a narrow external focus in order to deliver the ball to the receiver and to ignore the "footsteps" of the defensive lineman who is about to bring the quarterback to the ground (at least until the pass has been released).

In contrast, the weightlifter requires a more narrow form of attention throughout a lift. His or her attention may shift from an internal focus when the athlete is concerned with controlling his or her arousal. Then the focus (external) will be on lifting the bar. The ability to shift attention as required and to engage the appropriate width of attention is critical to athletic success. In order to develop this ability, the athlete must first learn the appropriate direction of attention and then learn how to control it so that the proper direction is attained. Only then can the powers of concentration take over to maximize the benefits of properly directed attention.

Attention control is a learned ability rather than a simple act of pure will. It requires practice. Many athletes are able to control the direction of their attention at will when they are relaxed, but stress and the anxiety it produces can seriously undermine the ability of most athletes to control their attention appropriately. This can result in the athlete's either being distracted from what should be the object of his or her attention or becoming so focused on one small aspect of reality that they miss the larger picture. Other athletes may actually be aided by anxiety, finding it difficult or impossible to narrow their focus sufficiently to the task at hand unless they are anxious. For the athlete who lacks the ability to narrow his or her focus, meditation (which is discussed later in this chapter) and mental rehearsal can help to improve ability in this area. For athletes who need to widen their focus, progressive relaxation, hypnosis and biofeedback (both of which are discussed later in this chapter) can be of help in attaining a state that is more relaxed and therefore more receptive to information. Mental rehearsal that involves shifting a narrow focus among many things can be used to simulate a broader overall focus, but ultimately the athlete must develop the ability to "see" the big picture.

Athletes who are too internally focused need to learn to attend to external cues lest they develop a level of ignorance with respect to the external world. In contrast, those with an external focus are more susceptible to "psych-out" techniques and distractions than are those who normally focus more internally.

As was noted above, the weightlifter's focus needs to be relatively narrow. However, it is possible for the focus to become too narrow. For instance, the lifter can be so focused on an explosive pull that he or she "forgets" to move

under the bar rapidly or to push up on the bar during the squat under. Therefore, the athlete needs to be able to focus relatively narrowly and to shift his or her focus appropriately as the lift progresses. The lifter must also be able to shift rapidly from an internal to an external focus, so that both the bar and the body itself are experienced. Ideally, the athlete will be able to experience the bar and body as one unit, with the bar being seen as an extension of the body, at least at certain points during the lift.

The width and direction of focus can be affected by the lifter's level of arousal and the instructions he or she receives. As arousal levels increase, attention tends to narrow. Therefore, a pep talk can narrow attention if it is stimulating. If the talk is so stimulating that attention is too narrowly focused on the right thing, it may not improve performance. Legendary football coach Vince Lombardi used his pep talks as a vehicle to narrow the attention of his players to two areas: believing in themselves and playing the game all out. Brilliant coach that he was, Lombardi did not seek arousal solely for its own sake; he looked for an appropriate focus as well.

Sport psychologist Robert Nideffer, one of the leading thinkers in attentional behavior and training today, has drawn broad applications for attentional control in everyday life as well as sports. For instance, Nideffer argues that by choosing what you attend to you can control anxiety and emotions and learn to relax. His focus is not on what causes a person to attend to the wrong things but, rather, the ability of humans to choose what to focus on and thereby control their emotions.

Controlling Emotions and Level of Arousal

The hallmark of the champion athlete, or anyone who must perform at a specific time, is the ability to control emotions. In this context control means creating the required emotional state whenever it is needed. Emotions can be a powerful energy source for peak performance, or they can inhibit, or even destroy, a potentially outstanding performance. The prerequisite for achieving an outstanding performance is to generate the appropriate emotion at the appropriate level of optimal performance.

For example, in many circumstances most lifters find that the positive emotions inspired by a desire to achieve a heavy lift are all they need to become highly motivated and emotionally charged enough to make that lift. But sometimes an added lift from emotional energy will be needed. For some lifters this added lift can be elicited by imagining the cheers and congratulations of the audience as they succeed. For others, motivation will come from an overwhelming desire to avoid the embarrassment of a loss. The important point is not what is needed to achieve the appropriate emotional state but, rather, that it is achieved.

The champion learns to control his or her emotions at will and to select the appropriate emotion for the job to be done. This ability arises out of the athlete's experience with various emotions and their effect on him or her, as well as an understanding of what triggers those emotions. For instance, the emotion of revenge can be a powerful motivator for an athlete if the notion of revenge arouses a powerful emotional state in that athlete. However, creating a desire for revenge only works if it does not evoke too extreme a response, if the desire for revenge can be satisfied by defeating an opponent on the platform and if the opponent actually acts in a way that elicits the desire for revenge (or the athlete can imagine such behavior to the point where the emotion is triggered).

Sometimes something spontaneous happens to activate the necessary emotion. I can recall lifting at the National Junior Championships for the second time in my career. I had placed third the first year and was favored to win in my second appearance. Things were not going well for a variety of reasons (most of which were exacerbated by my lack of skill and experience). My first two attempts in the snatch with a lighter weight than I had initially planned for my start had been missed for technical reasons. I was so dejected as I prepared for my third attempt that I might well have missed it. As I was contemplating my disappointment, I happened to glance over to the side of the platform and noticed that most of my competitors were looking on, including one who had delivered a minor insult to me earlier in the day. It then occurred to me that missing would cause this lifter, and some of the others, to rejoice at my faltering. I did not normally think of my competitors very much, but the thought of this angered me, causing me to come out of my depressed state. The result was a near power snatch on my third attempt and an easy victory after that.

When emotional states are not triggered by such fortuitous events, the lifter needs to be able to create his or her own emotional state by imagining the necessary triggering event. Joe Puleo, many time U.S. National Champion and American record holder and one of the top ranked lifters in the world at one time, told me about a technique that he used on occasion. In the earlier part of Joe's career, he found it very helpful to be mad at his competitors. He would sometimes go so far as to provoke his competitors to say or do something that he disliked simply to have a reason to be mad at his opponent. (I hasten to add that Joe is really a very nice fellow who did this all in the spirit of fun and good competition.) When Joe was competing against Mike Karchut, the first man to beat Joe in many years, he found it hard to get mad at Mike.

Anyone who knows Mike can understand this, because in addition to being one of America's all time great lifters, Mike is one of the nicest guys ever to mount a platform. No matter how he tried, Joe couldn't get mad at Mike, so he turned his attention to Mike's close friend and competition coach of many years, Lou DeMarco. While Louie is a close competitor to Mike for the title of weightlifting's nicest guy, Joe found that he could at least generate a mock anger toward Louie by imagining that Lou was saying negative things about Joe in an attempt to inspire Mike. Such thoughts were sufficient to get Joe's competitive juices flowing and helped him to perform at his best (even though it was only a mental game that Joe was playing with himself, one that never interfered with his friendly relationship with Lou and Mike outside of those few moments in competition).

Each athlete must learn not only what works for him or her but also under what precise conditions it works. For example, if an athlete is in a lethargic state, a minor level of fear might cause the athlete to increase his or her level of arousal to the point of performance enhancement. In contrast, an athlete who already dislikes an opponent and is prone to physical displays of his or her displeasure may get into a fight with another athlete if a high level of anger is induced.

The arousal level that a lifter achieves during a competition is the strength of the emotional energy that the athlete experiences. This is, to an extent, controlled by the nature of the emotion that is being experienced; some lifters will experience fear of failure as a weak or virtually nonexistent emotion, and others will find it to be so powerful as to have a very powerful effect on performance. But most athletes will experience the same emotions at different levels on different occasions.

Most athletes will feel a certain baseline level of arousal throughout most of a competition (although there will often be a difference between the pre-start, post-start and pre-lift levels of arousal), and that level will generally be too high or too low for purposes of optimal performance (although some athletes have a typical level that is just right).

To a point, performance depends on arousal level. The most widely accepted theory of the relationship between performance and arousal is the "inverted U" hypothesis. This theory says that performance improves rapidly with arousal level until it heats a peak zone (the top of the inverted U), then falls off rapidly as arousal continues to rise. A number of criticisms have been made of the theory (e.g., that anxiety is multidimensional and that somatic and cognitive anxiety has different effects on performance), but most athletes and scientists would agree that performance generally increases with ones arousal level, to a point. However, too high a level of arousal, or the wrong kind, can ruin concentration, technique and other aspects of performance (the more skillful the athlete, the less likely it is that high levels of arousal will disturb his or her performance). Similarly, too low a level of arousal can lessen an athlete's energy and desire for success. Even athletes who have achieved similar skill levels will manifest individual differences with respect to their ability to tolerate a given arousal level without a breakdown in technique. Some lifters will be able to maintain their skill while relatively excited and others will find that only a moderate level of arousal will lead to a performance breakdown. We simply do not understand enough about human arousal and its interaction with skill to provide definitive advice in this area, except to say that the athlete needs to monitor his or her own balance of arousal and skill to maintain that arousal at the proper level.

It should be noted that the arousal level employed by the lifter will tend to vary between training in competition and in competition between warm-ups and official attempts. For example, while warming up for the competition, the lifter will likely want to conserve energy for the actual competition, with arousal being only gradually elevated as the warming up progresses. Indeed, even during the lifter's first attempt (particularly in the snatch), arousal may be quite controlled in order to save energy and to execute as precise a movement as is possible. In contrast, the last lift in competition may be attempted with the highest level of arousal that is possible without causing a technique breakdown. This is because: a) that lift often demands all of the athlete's reserves; b) there is nothing critical to save energy for (particularly after the last C&J); c) the lifter will typically be relaxing for a time after the competition to rebuild his or her energy reserves; and d) there is generally no more important lift than one that is done in competition.

Lifters typically follow a similar pattern in training, so that their nervous energy is not necessarily expanded. However, in training, it is important to control arousal more carefully. Training in a highly aroused state with great frequency can lead very quickly to burnout and to undue training stress overall. If the athlete is to perform at an optimal level, he or she must learn to control his or her state of arousal at will. This can be accomplished by having mechanisms for calming down as well as getting more excited. Focused deep breathing, muscular relaxation techniques, meditation, listening to certain music or inspirational tapes, self-hypnosis and similar methods can serve to bring the lifter's level of arousal to the appropriate level. The lifter needs to become skillful enough in using such techniques that he or she can raise or lower his or her arousal level on command.

Regardless of the specific technique used by an athlete to bring his or her emotional state under control, it is far easier to do so before that emotional state has moved very far away from the desired level. It requires far less effort to bring an arousal level under control when it is only a little above the desired level than when it is dramatically above that level; the longer an unnecessarily high level of arousal is maintained, the greater the amount of unnecessary energy that is burned.

Athletes vary in their reactivity to circumstances within the competition, in the degree of control that they can generate and in the typical range and nature of their emotions during competition. Most lifters will find that they are either characteristically too highly aroused or too relaxed to perform at an optimal level (being too highly aroused is the more common problem). Therefore, they will generally need to regulate their emotional arousal either upward or downward. But an ability to do both can be critical, regardless of what a lifter's normal challenge is. My performance at the 1970 Junior Nationals was a case in point.

In 1970 I was nearing the end of my eligibility as a Junior and was finally in shape to accomplish what had been the biggest sub-goal of my lifting career for the previous four years: to establish Junior world records. I was lifting in the Junior Nationals (later renamed the American Championships). As I mounted the platform for my first attempt at a press (there were three lifts in those days, and the press preceded the snatch and the C&J), there was a great deal of pressure on me. My press was the heaviest starting weight in the competition, and it was approximately 7.5 kg. more than I had ever successfully attempted in competition (though I had made considerably more in training immediately before the competition). Only a handful in the audience thought I had any chance at success with that weight, but I knew that if I made it, my next attempt would be approximately 7.5 kg. more, enough to break the existing Junior World Record.

As I approached the bar, my arms suddenly began to tingle and the rest of my body seemed to go numb. As I prepared to grip the bar, these sensations worsened. It occurred to me that I was actually too aroused to make a successful attempt, a rare occurrence for me. At that moment, I paused, stepped away from the bar and breathed deeply, making a conscious attempt to relax. Then, after ten seconds or so, my level of arousal receded somewhat (though it was still quite high, as it always was in competition). I approached the bar once again, feeling more like my competitive self and made a successful attempt. And, several minutes later, I was successful with a new Junior World Record. Shortly after that, I faced a mental challenge of a different kind.

In those days the rules required that both the athlete and bar be weighed immediately after a world record (the athlete to assure that he was within the body weight limits of the class at the time the record was broken, and the bar to ascertain the exact weight of the bar fully loaded). The rules also required that the athlete be nude when weighing in. Even though I had another attempt in the competition, I had to wait for the bar to be weighed and subject myself to a stripped re-weigh as well. There were many people congratulating me while all of this was going on, and the temptation to relax and celebrate was enormous. Rather than fall victim to that temptation, I focused on my next attempt with 5 kg. more and worked to elevate my emotional state by thinking about what an achievement it would be to break my own record by a full 5 kg. and how important it was to lift as much in each lift as possible in order to pursue my ultimate goal of breaking the total record that day. These thoughts got me excited again.

There were those who reasoned that no additional attempts should be taken because I was still in close competition for the championship and still others who suggested a 2.5 kg. jump to increase my chances at a successful third attempt. My view was that my record had been lifted relatively comfortably and that if I missed my next attempt it would not be because of 2.5 kg. one way or the other but because of a technical error (which was just as likely with either weight). In addition, I was thinking about the record I wanted most that day—a Junior world record in the total—and I felt that an additional 5 kg. in the press would be a key to that. Therefore, I insisted on taking my third attempt and on taking it with the extra 5 kg, and I was successful with that weight. Moreover, I did go on to establish a new Junior world record in the total that day, partly due to my record spree in the press.

The point of the story is that if my mental approach had been different on the opening attempt or the third attempt, the greatest day of my weightlifting career would certainly never have turned out the way it did. Instead of three world records and a championship, I might have simply had a good day or failed to register a total at all. Here then is a real world example of the difference that being in control of your emotional and arousal states can make.

Anxiety Control

Anxiety generally serves to worsen athletic performance by compromising the athlete's ability to control his or her attention properly (although, as noted earlier, athletes who benefit from a narrowing of attention can actually benefit from the effects of anxiety, at least in this respect). Too much worry and anxiety can increase self-awareness to a point where it negatively affects

skills. Anxiety can also affect arousal, and that can have an effect on performance.

Athletes experience two levels of anxiety, their "trait" or baseline level and their "state" anxiety. Your baseline level of anxiety is what is with you most of the time, when there is no external stimulus to either raise or lower it. For example, some people are characterized as high strung and others as reserved. Trait anxiety is obviously a complex phenomenon, and its causes are not well understood, but it has been posited that people with characteristically high levels of baseline anxiety simply see more things as a threat than do people with lower baseline anxiety levels (and worry over worry is believed by many to be the single biggest cause of escalating anxiety). While a person's trait anxiety can change over time, such changes are not commonplace.

Some research suggests that high strung athletes (those with a high baseline anxiety level) tend to do better than those with a lower baseline level of anxiety in non-threatening situations, because anxiety seems to provide action energy for high strung athletes. The same research suggests that the reverse tends to be true in stressful situations. Highly anxious people appear more likely to become overly stressed and to react negatively to such situations. Obviously, these are merely tendencies, not absolute outcomes.

State anxiety has to do with the change in anxiety experienced as a result of being in a certain situation or thinking about a certain thing. (Anxiety in athletic competition seems to be experienced most profoundly by those who seek prestige through competition.) Both the degree and the nature of the changes that take place when anxiety levels are changed vary from person to person. Some people can move from a very relaxed state to a highly anxious one, others are at a fairly high or low baseline level of anxiety and suffer only a small change in that level under certain stressful conditions. In addition to individual differences in the level of response, different people experience different bodily reactions to anxiety. (For example, one person may experience significant tension in the neck muscles and another will have a greatly elevated heart rate, while still another will have both symptoms.)

One final major difference between people in terms of the way they experience anxiety is in their ability to sense changes in their anxiety level and its symptoms. Some people are very sensitive to any change while others can undergo major changes and barely notice it at all.

It has been argued by some sports psychologists that athletes who "choke" tend to be those with high trait and state anxiety and that a narrow and negative internal focus is usually present at the time of choking. Others argue that only cognitive anxiety at a very high level poses a threat to performance (such anxiety is characterized by worrying thoughts, a high level of self-awareness, an inability to concentrate and a high level of negative thoughts). Physical anxiety, which is characterized by such symptoms as cold hands, hyperventilation, butterflies and nausea, rarely has an ill effect on performance (though they are surely unpleasant phenomena).

In cases of high cognitive anxiety, it is possible that a strong external stimulus applied to the athlete will break his or her focus on internal negative thoughts and thereby bring the choking to a halt. A less radical approach is for the athlete to learn to think of other things when such a state arises. The sooner the athlete begins this process of diverting his or her attention away from the anxiety producing thoughts, the better.

Physical anxiety responds to a wide array of techniques, such as massage, yoga, biofeedback and sleep. Athletes who are prone to developing physical anxiety should experiment with these and other means of dealing with the problem in order to identify the methods that work best for them

Many psychological approaches to controlling trait anxiety focus on understanding its causes. This may make sense over the long run, but correcting such causes, assuming that they can be identified and corrected, can be an extremely long process. Moreover, the condition can actually worsen as this lengthy discovery takes place. A more practical approach for most athletes is to learn to redirect attention from worries and fears and toward a relaxed state and perfect performance.

In order to reduce anxiety, athletes use a number of techniques. They range from hypnosis to positive affirmations to relaxation and meditation; the aim is to enable the athlete to focus so fully on external things that he or she no longer worries about winning or losing.

One of the more direct techniques of dealing with performance anxiety, one that has been successful for many athletes, is systematic desensitization. Desensitization involves an athlete's creating an anxiety hierarchy. This is a series of situations which creates ever increasing levels of anxiety. For example, the athlete might say that entering the competition arena itself generates a low level of additional anxiety beyond his or her trait or normal level (this lowest level of additional anxiety is characterized by a 1). Getting ready to attempt a winning lift after being insulted by an opponent might produce the highest level of anxiety imaginable by the athlete (so it would be assigned a 10). The subject is taught a relaxation technique to enable that subject to control anxiety or tension. After some weeks of practice in this area, the desensitization process begins. First, the athlete is asked to relax and then describe, on a scale of 1 to 10, his or her current level of tension. The purpose of this procedure is to establish a baseline level of tension for that session. Then the

athlete is asked to imagine the situation that raises his or her tension only slightly (to the lowest of the elevated levels that was originally described by the athlete). The athlete is then asked to signify the level to which his or her tension has been raised by imagining this minor tension raising situation. If the athlete's tension has been elevated by imagining that situation, the athlete works at the relaxation technique that he or she has learned until the tension level is reduced to the baseline level for that day.

The development of the ability to control tension, even in this mildly tension producing situation, may take more than one practice session. Once the technique has been mastered, the athlete progresses to imagining the situation which produces the next higher level of tension and works on achieving baseline tension while imagining that activity. Eventually the athlete will progress to the point of achieving baseline level tension while imagining even the most stress producing situation on his or her list. That ability should enable the athlete to carry over the skill of achieving a relaxed state when the actual situation presents itself. Some researchers have suggested that mentally rehearsing in the relaxed state before going on to a higher anxiety provoking incident can be helpful in associating the ability to perform effectively after confronting the anxiety producing event and relaxing successfully. It is not uncommon for an athlete to require eight to sixteen sessions to reach a successful result with this method.

It is a wise practice for the athlete who is dealing with worries and anxiety to select a specific and consistent time and place in which to deal with negative thoughts. This time and place is used to deal with worry as a means to resolve problems. The idea is to worry intensely and then to stop after a specific time. The athlete resolve not to worry elsewhere and keeps a list of what to worry about so that there is no need to worry about failing to worry about the right things. The athlete uses the session to learn how and why he or she worries, reflects on whether there is a level of worrying that brings about the right state of arousal and learns how to control worrying so that he or she only worries to that level. (A person who cannot control worrying cannot use this readying technique). After the worrying session something must be done to take the athlete's mind off worrying. With some practice, many athletes will find that this approach will bring the problem under control.

A simpler approach to controlling anxiety is to have the athlete make every effort to focus on the process he or she will be performing rather than the objective and to avoid any thoughts about what he or she should not do. (For example, the athlete should never be thinking, "I'd better not get this weight too far in front"; a much better approach is to say, "I need to be sure that the bar is close to the body and that I explode upward during the pull.")

A coach can be a great help or a great hindrance to an athlete trying to manage or avoid anxiety. A coach who identifies poise as a value to be admired and developed early on can help an athlete immensely; inculcating in the young athlete the importance of playing within and for himself or herself will be invaluable to the athlete who is trying to control his or her anxiety level.

Exploring the Rich Potential of Our Complex Personality

We all have multiple personality traits. While psychologists tend to distinguish between personality traits (which are stable and dominant in behavior) and personality states (mental states that are more occasional and less dominant), this distinction is not terribly important to athletes (in terms of their effect on performance). We may think of some of those traits and/or states as desirable and of others as undesirable. However, with a little ingenuity we can often find strategies for using effectively nearly all of the rich range of personality traits/states that we possess.

For example, at times we may act bravely and at other times we may be timid. We may be very quiet most of the time but quite noisy at others. Often, within the behaviors that we have already exhibited, we can find those that are identical or at least similar to behaviors that would be highly beneficial in preparatory or competitive athletic situations. If so, we can then endeavor to increase the strength and frequency of the behaviors that are desirable and to do the opposite for those that are not.

Another useful strategy for utilizing personality traits and states is to try to identify appropriate uses for behaviors that are generally negative. For instance, communicating by shouting and waving your hands would be considered aggressive under most circumstances, but on the trading floor of a stock exchange it might be perceived as merely assertive or even reserved. Similarly, thoughts of embarrassing an opponent by delivering a public beating cannot be acted out, but thoughts of embarrassing an opponent via a sound "beating" on the weightlifting platform are well within the bounds of athletic behavior (though you might wonder why such a desire exists at all). Still another approach to employing behaviors in an effective way is to identify movements, thoughts or feelings that are useful but have not previously been used for athletic performance by the athlete.

One final note on personality traits. Your attitude toward them is nearly as important as the traits themselves in terms of their effect on your life. You tend to be influenced most by the traits with which you associate yourself, by everything which you recognize as being part of your "true"

personality. However, you tend to be better able to control "personalities" which you do not identify with yourself. Therefore, your attitude toward behavior that you exhibit can be as important as the behavior itself.

For instance, attitude that "I have made many mistakes and therefore I am tragically flawed" can lead to a lack of interest in controlling behavior and a tendency to focus on and accept further mistakes as being part of your nature. If instead you accept the error and recognize it as an error but take the attitude that you are "better than that," you are more likely to correct the mistake and to avoid making it again in the future. Naturally, you can make terrible errors and disassociate yourself from them as a defense mechanism (e.g., by saying, "that is not really me so I'll ignore it, no matter how prevalent the behavior becomes"). This, of course, can lead to a continuation of the same destructive behavior. But the former error is more common than the latter.

Pain Control

There are many psychological methods for dealing with pain available to athletes. Some center around relaxing the painful area and the areas surrounding it. Others involve diverting the athlete's attention away from the pain or using mental techniques to block the pain.

For example, visualization can be used to control pain. In order to apply the visualization technique an athlete might put his or her hand in cold water until it is numb and then visualize the cold of the water touching other parts of the body (i.e., injured areas). Another visualization strategy is to see the pain getting smaller or relaxing and letting it slip away.

Obviously, before making any effort at pain control, a person must be sure that the pain is not serving a necessary function (e.g., warning of an injury that could become worse with activity). Blocking out functional pain, though possible, can simply lead to the athlete's further. damaging an injured area However, when pain is not functional (i.e., it is not symptomatic of an injury or the injury cannot be exacerbated by continued activity), pain reduction techniques can be invaluable to the athlete. Before proceeding with the use of any mental (or physical) pain control techniques, it is critical to get medical clearance. Only a health professional can help determine whether a given pain is functional. See the Bibliography for books with further information on this subject.

Hypnosis

Some athletes have been found hypnosis a useful adjunct to their preparation for competition. Contrary to popular belief, hypnosis is not some technique of mental training that permits a person to accomplish superhuman feats. It merely enables the subject to reach his or her true potential when the achievement of that potential is blocked by mental attitudes or processes that the athlete may have acquired. For instance, a state of hypnosis will not give super strength, even if the hypnotist suggests to a fully hypnotized subject that he or she has it. It may enable a subject to apply more easily the strength that the subject already possesses, by removing any inhibitions that person may have about expressing that strength.

Hypnosis has four phases: induction of the hypnotic state, the hypnotic state itself, termination of the hypnotic state and the stage of post-hypnotic suggestion. The hypnotic state is induced by the hypnotist's ability to gain the subject's attention and to take the subject through a set of suggestions (e.g., your arms are getting heavier, you are feeling warmth, etc.) until the subject has achieved a relaxed state in which he or she gives the hypnotist his or her full attention.

Once the subject is in the hypnotic state, the hypnotist provides a series of directions that describe the way the subject will behave once a specific triggering word has been heard by the subject or a particular set of circumstances occurs during the post-hypnotic state. For example, for a lifter who is having trouble concentrating in competition, the hypnotist might say: "When you mount the platform in competition, everything around you will become quiet, you will feel alone with the bar and will be totally focused on making the lift until you hear the signal from the referees to put the bar down." The nature of the hypnotic suggestion itself is very flexible. Suggestion can be used to control pain, to improve concentration and to facilitate relaxation. Positive suggestions are generally the most effective.

Once the suggestion has been given, the hypnotist will explain to the subject that a certain procedure will be followed (e.g., "I will count backward from ten to one and when I reach the number one you will wake up"). At the end of that procedure the lifter will wake up feeling refreshed and remembering the suggestion for post-hypnotic behavior. The post-hypnotic suggestion can be effective for a period of minutes to a period of months, depending on the subject and the nature of the suggestion.

Naturally, the hypnotist must be careful in providing post-hypnotic suggestions. They must be very limited. Otherwise, the potential for triggering unwanted behavior can be significant. For example, if the athlete were merely told that he or she must block out everything else when he or she mounts the platform (failing to specify the competition platform), the athlete might not hear any instructions from the coach during training.

It is possible that a hypnotist could be helpful in competition itself to redirect the attention of a panicking athlete if the hypnotist could remain focused, break through to the athlete and redirect the athlete's attention.

While there are no scientifically precise figures on the susceptibility of the general population to hypnosis, it has been estimated that approximately 10% of the population can achieve the very deepest of hypnotic states, another 10% cannot be hypnotized at all and the rest fall in between these two extremes.

I have never experimented with hypnosis. I do know a number of athletes who have done so, and none of them have reported long term success in using it (admittedly, my sample is a small one). Nevertheless, the very concept of hypnosis bothers me for three reasons. First, it is meant as a means to place the mind on a form of automatic pilot in a certain situation. As was noted earlier, automatic pilot mechanisms can be triggered at inappropriate times and cause unintended effects. If hypnotic suggestions are designed with care, the likelihood of errors can be greatly reduced, but the risk can never be eliminated. Second, the point at which hypnotic suggestion will wear off is unpredictable. It could happen at the most inopportune time, and the athlete who relies on hypnosis is unlikely to have developed adequate coping skills for situations in which the suggestion has worn off.

Finally, the very notion of giving up control of his or her mind to another person is anathema to many athletes. One of the major benefits of sports is its ability to challenge the athlete to develop his or her own mental faculties. The sense of control over the mind and the ability to achieve a certain mental state at will contribute to a person's confidence and maturity not only in athletics but also in life. Relying on someone else to produce a certain mental state, no matter how beneficial, essentially precludes this kind of benefit. For most athletes it would be preferable to use the other techniques that are discussed in this chapter to achieve the benefits that could be achieved through hypnosis. Nevertheless, for the athlete who has a specific need that can be effectively met by hypnosis and who does not have the time or has been unable to develop his or her own approach to the problem, hypnosis can be a useful tool.

As is the case with many of the methods of mental and physical development in weightlifting, combining techniques is often more effective than any one alone. This can certainly be true in the case of hypnosis. For instance, consider the case of an athlete who is having difficulty relaxing before an event. The athlete has tried relaxation techniques and hypnosis, and both have helped to a point, but the athlete feels that a fully relaxed state has not yet been achieved. He or she might persist in perfecting relaxation skills or persist in hypnotherapy. Either path might very well lead to ultimate success. However, another approach would be to combine the two techniques by achieving a state of hypnosis, performing relaxation exercises in that state and then suggesting that the same state could be achieved post-hypnotically by saying a certain word or phrase. The result might be a faster and deeper state of relaxation than could be achieved in the same amount of time with either technique alone.

It should be noted than hypnosis can been used for analgesic purposes, but the cautions expressed in the previous section on pain control must be observed when hypnosis is used in an athletic context. If the analgesic effect is really powerful, it may disguise a real problem.

Self Hypnosis

Self hypnosis is generally a much more appropriate technique of mental preparation for the athlete than regular hypnosis. The problem of dependency on the hypnotist is obviated with self hypnosis. In addition, the problem of having the suggestion wear off is avoided because the athlete can reaffirm the suggestion on a regular basis.

In a sense, all hypnosis is self hypnosis, because the subject must believe to a certain extent in the process and the hypnotist before hypnosis can be induced. A good hypnotist should be willing to assist a subject in performing self hypnosis by including the suggestion that the subject can achieve such a state if he or she wishes.

An athlete is capable of inducing a state of self hypnosis without any intervention by a hypnotist. In fact, many of the techniques referred to earlier involve elements of self suggestion. The relaxed and focused states that are induced by meditation and progressive relaxation are essentially the same as those achieved by hypnosis. The difference is that with self hypnosis the focus is on the suggestions the subject is making to himself or herself. For example, instead of focusing directly on relaxing his or her legs, a subject might repeat the suggestion (really an inner statement) that his or her legs were relaxing. A sequence of statements suggesting relaxation and then falling ever deeper into a hypnotic state are the means to create a self hypnotic state. Once such a state has been achieved, suggestions are made for the post-hypnotic state, much in the same way that they are made by the hypnotist. (It is generally recommended that the suggestions be positive, that repetition be used in making the suggestion and that suggestions that lead to images of success supplement verbal suggestions.) After making the appropriate self suggestions, the subject suggests the process of emerging from the hypnotic state to a state of normal consciousness.

If the athlete has trouble achieving a relaxed state and maintaining the ability to make suggestions to himself or herself, a simple solution would be to record the entire process, from hypnotic induction to the suggestions to be made during the hypnotic state to suggestions for awakening from the hypnotic state. Then the recording could be played at the appropriate time and the athlete could be self hypnotized by the recording.

Biofeedback

Biofeedback is a process that involves giving a subject feedback on a bodily function that is not normally well perceived. Examples of this are the electrical activity that takes place in the brain (e.g., alpha and beta brain waves), blood pressure, blood flow and low levels of muscle tension. Feedback can help the athlete to understand how to control all of these things. The ability to control such processes might be achieved without direct feedback, but it would take far longer and would have to take place in a more indirect way (e.g., concentrating on slow breathing might cause the subject to relax, and that could lead to a decline in blood pressure). With feedback the athlete might learn about other thought processes and behaviors that might achieve the same result more quickly and certainly.

For example, "alpha brain" waves are associated with achieving a relaxed state. Without biofeedback the average person cannot appreciate when he or she is producing this kind of brain activity. He or she might indeed achieve the desired state with diligent practice of meditation, but that would be an effect of the meditation process, which might take a very long time to master without special feedback.

If control of a particular process or area of the body is important for an athlete, and other methods of control have not been successful, biofeedback may be worth exploring. However, specialized equipment and knowledge is required in order to apply biofeedback effectively. Therefore, an expert in this area needs to be consulted before biofeedback can be appropriately employed.

Achieving a Relaxed State at Will

It is very useful for an athlete to cultivate the ability to achieve a relaxed state at will. This ability can be helpful in many ways. First, it can help the athlete to control his or her mental and emotional state immediately before and during competition (an athlete who is too anxious and emotional will "burn out" before the competition is over). Second, it can help an athlete to sleep soundly before a competition. Third, it can enable an athlete to save energy prior to and during the competition. Fourth, a relaxed state is considered by many advocates of mental rehearsal to be a prerequisite for such rehearsal (although research in this area has not thus far supported that contention). Fifth, reducing stress may help to prevent and even to speed the healing of certain kinds of injuries. There are a number of means for achieving a relaxed state. We will outline four here. Others can be learned from some of the books that are listed in the Bibliography at the end of the book.

Perhaps the first relaxation technique that was written about extensively in Western literature was one developed by Edmund Jacobson in the early 1900s. That technique, called "progressive relaxation," consists of carefully and sequentially tensing and then relaxing various muscle groups. Jacobson believed that the contrast between tension and relaxation helped the subject to better sense a truly relaxed state. He also believed that if the body could achieve a thoroughly relaxed state, many bodily ills such as headaches, hypertension, and anxiety could be cured. Jacobson had considerable success in treating patients with his relaxation technique.

Briefly summarized, the Jacobson method begins with the subject lying in a supine position in a comfortable, quiet and darkened room, with the arms positioned at the sides. The subject concentrates on relaxing, permitting the body to sink into the bed or other surface upon which he or she is lying. The subject then creates very slight tension in the arms and sustains that tension for approximately ten seconds. Then he or she increases the level of tension somewhat and sustains than level for another ten seconds, concentrating on how that tension feels. Next the subject concentrates on gradually relaxing the same muscles and on how the process of relaxation and the relaxed state feel. This relaxation process continues for one or two minutes. This cycle of creating two levels of tension followed by a period of relaxation is repeated twice. On each successive cycle the subject attempts to achieve a deeper level of relaxation. The object is to be able to detect the very slightest levels of tension and to correct that tension. The three cycles of tension and relaxation are repeated for the muscles of the legs, chest, abdomen and face. Eventually, as the subject becomes more accomplished, the tension phases of the relaxation sessions can be eliminated. Ultimately, the subject will be able to relax completely in a very short period of time.

Another approach to relaxation is a technique called "autogenic training." It was first developed by Johannes Schulz in the middle of this century. Schulz's technique involves moving through a series of six steps. First the subject concentrates on creating feelings of heaviness in the limbs, then on creating a sensation of warmth. Next the subject attempts to regulate his or her heart rate and then focuses on breathing. In the fifth step of the process, the subject endeavors to develop a sensation of warmth in the abdomen. Finally, in the sixth step the focus is on developing a contrasting sense of coolness in the forehead. This combination of steps is expected to enable the subject to achieve a fully relaxed state, which he or she will be able to assume even more quickly with practice.

Much more ancient techniques of relaxation have come down to us through religious practices, yogis and martial arts practitioners. Their meditative states create a very relaxed condition. A number of researchers and theorists have attempted to abstract aspects of these ancient techniques in order to achieve the benefits in terms of relaxation and control of mental activity, without having to devote years to the discipline. One of these techniques involves deep and slow breathing while the subject is concentrating fully on the inhaling and exhaling. Sometimes this is accompanied by some physical gesture, such as placing one or both hands on the diaphragm or doing so and breathing in slowly, holding, exhaling to 4 counts and practicing with associating a word with the relaxed state.

A related relaxation method consists of repeating short phrases until you feel what is being suggested by those phrases (e.g., "I am relaxed"). Ultimately, one key phrase will be all the athlete needs in order to complete the entire relaxation process.

Still another technique which became very popular in the 1960s and 1970s is transcendental meditation (TM). Practitioners of TM were found to be able to lower their heart rates, blood pressure (especially if it was previously elevated), respiration and blood lactate levels through meditation. The TM technique involves the repetition of a sound (called a "mantra") over and over while the subject assumes an attitude of passive concentration. Ultimately, the result is the relaxed TM state.

In order to master any of the preceding relaxation techniques, it is recommended that the subject practice daily for approximately forty-five minutes (in the case of TM and the breathing techniques, TM trainers typically recommend two twenty to twenty-five minute sessions).

All of these techniques share the objective of relieving tension while at the same time focusing the mind inward and not on the external world. This combination of focused attention and physical relaxation seems to predispose the subject to a relaxed and receptive state of mind. From this "platform" of a relaxed state, the athlete directs his or her attention on the process at hand, whether that is near term physical performance, technique improvement, further relaxation, self affirmations or some other objective.

As was noted earlier, it is very worthwhile for an athlete to master at least one relaxation technique to the point of being able to enter a relaxed state nearly at will. With such an ability, the athlete can be relatively certain that he or she can bring his or her emotions under control when that becomes helpful prior to, or during, a competition. No athlete has an unlimited supply of nervous energy. Many years ago the great champion Dave Sheppard counseled me: "You must learn to turn your intensity on and off like a light switch." Cultivating the ability to save energy wherever possible is bound to pay long term dividends in the athletic arena as well as in other walks of life. The increased feelings of well being, higher energy levels and improved ability to concentrate that can result from mastering the art of relaxation are all laudable objectives as well. Ultimately, the athlete can learn to relax almost immediately, such as by taking as little as one breath while focusing on it completely (the mastery of which technique can be supported by practicing several times a day).

For the athlete who has not yet become skilled at relaxation, laughter can be a source of relaxation. This does not suggest that a good belly laugh before a big lift is beneficial. Rather, some mild humor well before the heavy lifts begin may serve to break unnecessary tension, such as the tension that can build up early in the process of waiting to warm up (building some humor into life is probably a good general health practice).

For athletes who have not developed the mental skills of relaxation, there are other approaches to relaxation involving physical stimuli. A mild form of exercise can assist the relaxation process, particularly if it does not tire the athlete, if the athlete is used to such exercise and if the exercise can cause or help the athlete focus on the exercise itself or on anything else that is calming to the athlete. Some recent research done with weightlifters suggests that a light training session the evening or morning before a competition may help some athletes to relax.

Flotation tanks can be a great source of relaxation, particularly if the athlete can learn to achieve a similar relaxed state by association after experiencing the tank a number of times. The problem is that such tasks are generally not available at the competition site (although a reasonable substitute might be created with a sleeping bag and portable audio equipment with earphones).

Naturally, relaxation, like anything else, can become too extreme. An athlete who is totally relaxed will not be able to perform at a high level. But this is rarely a problem for a competitive athlete. Just being at a competition is generally sufficient to get the athlete aroused enough to perform well.

One more comment needs to be made with respect to relaxation. A top level athlete, or a great achiever in any area of life, needs to develop the ability to relax merely to control his or her expenditure of nervous energy. No one can sustain a peak or even high level of energy at all times. There must be times for the mind and body to rest and recuperate from a state of full effort. Sleep is not enough for the competitive athlete. Relaxation must be built into daily activities as well. (It must also be remembered that stress has been correlated with illnesses and athlete injuries.)

Paul Anderson, the great Olympic and World Champion and one of the strongest man who ever lived (undoubtedly the strongest in certain respects), often noted the importance of rest. Early in his career, he reportedly lived by the rule that you should walk if you do not have to run, sit if you do not have to walk, lie down if you do not have to sit, and sleep if you do not have be awake. Similarly, the great bodybuilding champion Reg Park has reported that the fastest gains in his bodybuilding career came when he merely rested completely between workouts. Admittedly, these men followed these guidelines for limited periods, and few have a life situation that would permit them to emulate Anderson or Park. However, there can be no doubt that the ability to relax where possible and to save your energy for training will contribute significantly to your progress.

Relaxation need not mean a total vegetative state. It does mean a state in which the body is free of tension and anxiety, the emotional state is at a relatively low level and the mind is receptive to stimuli but not racing. You are clearly in control and comfortable overall.

Achieving the Optimal Performance State

Most people have experienced certain moments in their lives when their concentration seemed to be complete, when their confidence was high, when the importance of the task at hand seemed unusually clear, when success seemed inevitable, when achievement seemed effortless. This kind of state has been described variously as a condition of being totally focused, in the sweet spot, or in the "flow." In short, it is the ideal mental state at which to perform to full capabilities. One of the most important objectives of mental training and preparation is to be able to achieve such a state at will. Athletes who have been able to cultivate this ability are the small minority who are able to perform at their best regardless of the conditions. How can you achieve this ideal state at will?

Many athletes and coaches seem to feel that performing the activity that the athlete will be performing in competition is the best or only warm-up needed to perform at an optimal level. Other athletes need to feel ready before they can begin, and still other athletes need to consciously build the proper mental state as they warm up physically. Once an athlete understands what is needed to reach his or her optimal state, he or she needs to perform the actions that lead to proper readying on a consistent basis.

Many performers use rituals to prepare, especially those which are totally under the athlete's control and help to assure readiness. Rituals differ from superstitions in that they do not depend on something beyond your control and are not negative. Rituals can be calming, energizing or tied to performance (assuring all is in readiness). If an athlete wishes to try the ritual approach to preparation, the place to begin is to look at existing rituals and see if they work and, if so, how they do. Then the athlete can adopt the ritual specifically for purposes of preparation, instead of performing it irregularly. One technique is to use a "countdown" of external events to cue mental preparation. For instance, review your goals after the weigh-in. Then dress in a certain order, each clothing item triggering another readying thought. The first weight on the bar then triggers another thought, and so on.

Another approach is to create a readying spot (a place and/or time) for doing whatever is needed to perform at optimal level. In order to do this, the athlete should have approximately twenty minutes of uninterrupted time. During this time the athlete goes through a series of thoughts and/or action which place him or her in the optimal state.

Many athletes find rituals too lengthy and unnecessary. For such athletes, readying may simply involve finding his or her best positive image and then evoking it. This could be done through visualization. Alternatively, it could be the use of a nickname (such as "Mr. Comethrough") that evokes a positive image. Still other athletes merely need a key word or phrase to place them in an optimal state.

Every athlete derives his or her motivation from different sources and has different strengths and weaknesses with respect to achieving an optimal mental state. Therefore, each athlete will need to find his or her individual path to achieving the state of full readiness at will. The starting point for all athletes is to observe the internal and external causes of their thoughts, feelings and behaviors during workouts and competitions. Then the athlete needs to answer the question: "What leads to the good performances and what does not?"

For example, how did you feel during your finest hour(s)? at your moment of most complete and pleasurable relaxation? at your moment of greatest fear and loathing? at your most depressed and defeated? It is important to identify not only what you felt but also what led to those feelings. Including in your training log mental states and noting what events, thoughts and feelings were associated with ideal and poor mental states are invaluable practices. Understanding the conscious and subconscious judgments that triggered an emotional state is often just as important as understanding the events that lead to the evaluations that you made. This is because emotions are physical and mental reactions to your instantaneous value judgments. When you are dealing with emotional triggers, one approach is to remove an unwanted trigger or to incorporate a desired one. However, the other approach is to alter your valuations. Serious work done in this area can help not only to achieve an optimal state with greater consistency but also to avoid undesirable ones more frequently.

In order to achieve the optimal performance state, three major variables need to be observed and, ultimately, regulated: arousal, motivation and concentration. Arousal has been discussed earlier. It must be set at the optimal level, generally by bringing it up or bringing it under greater control. The athlete must learn to evaluate his or her sense of arousal and to regulate it, primarily through developing the ability to relax and to control focus.

Motivation is the desire to achieve the lift. It is a function of two things: the positive desire to perform the lift and the absence of fear (or, stated more positively, the presence of confidence). The lower the fear and/or the higher the desire, the greater will be the lifter's motivation to perform the lift. Desire comes from goals and the role that a given lift is perceived to have in the achievement of those goals.

The greatest motivation of all is a love for the sport and an associated desire to master it (an achievement orientation), but motivation can arise out of such factors as the desire to affiliate with others, the desire to beat others, the desire to affirm competence and the desire to gain approval. Positive affirmations can also help to build a desire to succeed.

While many athletes will almost automatically have the level of desire necessary to perform optimally, some athletes need a special effort to remind themselves of the importance of what they are about to do. Pictures, videos and inspirational notes or books can all serve to get the athlete on the right track in this regard.

Lack of fear stems from the confidence that a particular effort is reasonable within the context of the lifter's abilities and that, in the event of a failure, the ability to "bail out" safely can be counted on. More fundamentally, it stems from the feeling that you will perform well rather than a concern with competitive outcomes. The motivated lifter will feel an energy that cries to be released and confidence that success will be achieved. I have almost never missed a lift that I was highly motivated about. I have rarely made a maximum lift that I lacked confidence about making or lacked the burning desire to complete.

While proper arousal and high motivation are critical, concentration is the third critical factor. As has already been indicated in this chapter, concentration is the ability to focus completely on the task at hand and to focus at the correct level (i.e., neither too widely nor too narrowly). This state has been described by some as being consciously unconscious. What this means is that the athlete's attention is so completely focused on the task at hand that he or she is not consciously (i.e., conceptually) aware of that focus or of what his or her mind is doing. In a sense, the mind is still, in that it is virtually impervious to thoughts outside of its primary focus. In another sense, such a focus is extremely active because total attention is actively directed to the task at hand. However, the overall experience is one of mental (though not necessarily emotional) calm and extreme clarity of mental focus. As was noted earlier, this state has been described as being in a "cocoon" (the athlete is oblivious to any distractions to the point where the world outside the field of concentration seems to be powerless to penetrate the athlete's active attention). Some athletes are actually aided in achieving this state by consciously thinking of "nothing," of emptying their minds (this is often beneficial immediately before a lift is commenced).

This kind of concentration is vital in at least three respects. First, full concentration virtually assures the attainment of a correct level of arousal; it is difficult to be too relaxed or two anxious when one is focusing almost exclusively on performance. Second, full concentration makes it more likely that the skill at hand will be performed properly. Third, when an athlete is learning a skill (and learning never really ends), the ability to concentrate on how the body is performing the movement provides the most valuable feedback on the movement itself. (This does not mean analyzing every step on the conceptual level but, rather, fully experiencing and understanding the movement.)

Ultimately, by combining optimal arousal, motivation and concentration (and these three aspects of mental state are interrelated), the athlete achieves the ideal state of mind, which, when combined with a body that is well peaked, is capable of producing outstanding performance. The true challenge of competitive athletics, one that is only rarely met by an athlete, is to achieve such a state consistently and at will.

Those Who Can Help Your Mental Training

The Role of the Coach in Fostering the Mental Development of the Athlete

Coaches can play a great role in the development of the minds of athletes as well as their bodies. A coach cannot make or break an athlete's mind (the athlete, after all, has free will and may choose to be influenced by the coach or not), but the coach can certainly have a major influence on the mind of the athlete, particularly if the athlete is not evaluating what the coach is saying but is merely absorbing it. In my view the role of the coach in developing the athlete's mind can be at least as important as the role the coach plays in developing the athlete's body. My experience has been that coaches who are

truly effective long term motivators (not simply those who can arouse a lifter at a competition) are more successful than many coaches with superior technical skills who are poor motivators.

Research and practical experience have shed significant light on the role of the coach. It has been discovered, for example that positive feedback from the coach generally helped the athlete's perceptions of competence. The major exception to this rule was when the athlete was being praised for things that the athlete regarded as relatively easy. The explanation for such a phenomenon is that when the athlete is praised for easy things it implies that the coach thinks these easy things are actually challenges for that athlete; thus, what is actually communicated to the athlete is that these mediocre performances are all the athlete can hope to do. Positive feedback also generally helps the athlete's intrinsic motivation.

The quality of feedback is a very crucial determinant of its value. Feedback must pertain to legitimate criterion of performance and be appropriate to the level of achievement of the athlete. Information on how to perform well makes athletes believe that they can actually perform better.

Some coaches seem to foster an environment in which they are the sole source of wisdom. Those coaches seem to enjoy developing a cadre of athletes who are dependent on them. But coaches who emphasize the autonomy of the athlete tend to have athletes who are more intrinsically motivated and have better self-esteem. It is the age old story of teaching a person to fish as opposed to giving them a fish.

Children are often seeking different things from sports than adults. In addition to seeking pure achievement, they are also looking for affiliation, team competition, fitness and just plain fun. Their motives are typically multiple. Parental pressure can kill performance and the child's pleasure in that performance. Children must be permitted by their parents to find their own way in sports.

Behavioral modification is a psychological technique for changing behavior that employs the use of specific techniques that "reinforce" a given behavior (makes it more or less likely to recur). Behavioral modification essentially suggests that a coach employ some physical, social or economic reward to reinforce a desirable behavior. A rule of thumb for coaches is that 50% of their behavior should be positively reinforcing, 45% should be ignoring and 5% should be negatively reinforcing (punishment). The point here is not that half of the coach's time should be spent in reinforcing behavior and the other half in ignoring it but, rather, that the coach should not spend any significant portion of his or her time punishing athletes. Positive reinforcement is far more likely to result in good behavior than punishment. In offering positive reinforcement, praise should be progressively greater if performance is good. The coach should also reinforce consistency, which is an important behavioral attribute.

But the coach should also be aware that the continued use of external rewards can undermine an athlete's development of deep personal motivation. Athletes who are motivated primarily by their own desires prefer coaches who provide instruction and training. Athletes who participate because of external rewards (scholarships, trophies, etc.) are more likely to accept autocratic coaching styles.

Research and practical experience suggest that coaches generally receive the best results from positive feedback (e.g., encouragement, praise, positive suggestion). Despite this finding, many coaches deal with athletes with a constant stream of criticism. It is one thing to correct technique flaws as often as needed; it is another to attack an athlete's person. The former leads to progress and the latter to conflict and poorer performance. Some athletes seems to be able to perform well wherever they go, with or without help. Antonio Krastev and Naim Suleymanoglu are such athletes. They know themselves, their technique and how to train. Both have moved to new environments in which little coaching or a dramatic change in coaching occurred, and both could still perform. Other athletes who find themselves under similar conditions are lost. Clearly the former are better off than the latter.

Under competitive conditions, a coach can be of greater assistance in helping an athlete to relax when appropriate, to focus on the right things and to properly evaluate the athlete's performance. Anyone can be an athlete's friend when things are going well. The true coach and friend is there when things do not go as well.

When To Consider Getting Professional Sports Psychology Help

Virtually all of the techniques for improving mental performance that have been discussed in this chapter come under the heading of "self help." In most cases the athlete who is psychologically healthy psychologically will be able to conduct most of his or her own mental training. Even athletes who have psychological problems that hinder performance will be able to develop ways for dealing with those problems in training and competition by applying one or more of the rich array of techniques that have been described in this chapter. However, many athletes will find the assistance of a trained sports psychologist to be very valuable.

There will be some occasions when even psychologically healthy athletes (and many who are less healthy) will need assistance from a psychologist. The first indicator that you may need

professional help is doubt that you are handling a given mental problem properly. Some athletes find it difficult to identify their problems properly. They may simply not be able to understand the nature and origins of the problem, or they may constantly identify "the" problem, only to redefine it the next day or week. If you are having trouble determining what your problem is, some professional help may be useful.

Similarly, if you are having trouble determining what approach to take to solving a perceived mental problem, or if you have been working to resolve a particular problem for a substantial period of time without any real results, the advice of a professional may help (even if the only help provided is to reassure you that you are on the right track). An experienced sports psychologist may help you to understand better the training techniques that you have selected or may suggest one that is better suited to solving your problem.

Finally, if you have psychological problems that extend well beyond the athletic arena, professional help of a more general nature may be necessary.

While a discussion of such problems is well beyond the scope of this book, three general suggestions can be offered. First, it is rarely necessary for an athlete to resolve some or all of his or her overall psychological problems in order to be a successful athlete. Many champions have been able to achieve outstanding success while still harboring substantial psychological problems. The techniques described in this chapter will often enable an athlete to gain sufficient control of his or her problems during competition and training so that they pose no performance threat. Second, psychologists differ in philosophy, technique and style. The mere possession of some degree, license or certification does not mean that a psychologist is skilled in every area, or that the areas in which a particular therapist has skill will necessarily be useful to a given athlete. Just as an athlete must experiment with diet, exercise, rest and many other variables to achieve championship results, so an athlete who needs professional help may have to experiment with different practitioners and methods before success is achieved.

Third, do not permit yourself to become dependent on a particular therapist as "the sole solution" to your psychological problems. A good therapist will help you learn to deal with you own problems over time—not make you dependent on some guru for all of the answers to your problems.

A Closing Word on the Mind

While this chapter has been devoted to presenting the ways in which the mind can be used to improve weightlifting performance, it should be noted that the kind of mental development that leads to weightlifting success can offer many dividends in other areas of life. For example, concentration, a positive mental attitude and the setting and visualization of goals can all be as powerful outside athletics as they are within it. The heightened self-esteem and well being that can come out of weightlifting success tend to carry over into other areas in life. Knowing that you can achieve success in the world at something often opens up your minds to a myriad of new possibilities (this is particularly true of those who began with problems of self-esteem).

Note the relationship here. Mind and body work together. The mind sets the goals, the body achieves them. This gives the mind more confidence, which leads to further motivation and effort, which leads to existential success. The mind and the body are inextricably linked, as are thought and action. One is worthless without the other. In combination they enable man to achieve all the joy that is possible on this earth—and that is a great deal indeed. Life itself embodies a continuous effort to set, to achieve and to maintain values. The true measure of a life is not only the number or importance of a person's values but also the nature of their values and, perhaps most of all, the quality of the effort that they put forth toward the achievement of those values throughout their lives.

The legendary football coach Vince Lombardi often spoke of the pursuit of excellence as being the real key to success in sports and in life. Seek excellence, and happiness will follow out of the existential achievement that you will almost certainly enjoy. Perhaps even more importantly, happiness will arise from the sheer joy of knowing that you have committed to something and given it the best that you can give, the best within you.

Summary

The athlete's mind is the "prime mover" behind championship performance. The tools that have been provided in this chapter will enable the athlete to build the mind of a champion. Now that we have discussed the elements of training the mind and body for high performance, the next chapter will explore the all important issue of preparing for top performance in a competition. It is a great achievement to create the mind and body of a great weightlifter. Being able to express that ability when it counts is still another step toward becoming the weightlifter's weightlifter.

An intimidating competitor, Vasili Alexseev set more world records and won more World and Olympic Superheavyweight championships combined than any other athlete in weightlifting history

CHAPTER 8

Performing In Competition

Gaining strength, developing proper technique and cultivating a well trained weightlifting mind are all critical steps in building the ultimate weightlifter. However, the weightlifter who seeks to demonstrate his or her ability in competition and to receive official recognition for his or her achievements needs to learn special skills to prepare mentally, physically and strategically for competition. These skills are not necessarily developed solely by general weightlifting training. Rather, their development requires special attention.

Similarly, coaching an athlete in a weightlifting competition is very different from coaching an athlete in training. A coach can be very effective in the gym but relatively ineffective at competitions, and vice versa. As with the development of any skill, mastering the ability to coach an athlete in competition requires knowledge and practice. The purpose of this chapter is to provide the coach and/or athlete with the requisite knowledge for fostering high performance in weightlifting competition. It is up to the athlete and the coach to do the practice.

I ask that the athlete who is reading this chapter for his or her own information bear with the constant references to the "coach." Knowledge of the principles and practices discussed here is just as valuable for the athlete as the coach. Choosing one perspective (in this case the coach's) at the outset and maintaining it throughout made it easier to write the chapter with clarity, consistency and economy.

The Phases Of Competition Coaching: Pre-, During and Post-Competition

Competitive coaching can be broken down into three phases: pre-contest (from several months before the competition to the weigh-in); the competition itself (from the start of the weigh-in through the athlete's last C&J); and post-competition. (This last period begins after the outcome of the competition has been determined and can last from several hours to several weeks, depending on how long the coach and athlete are in contact after the competition.) Each phase has different requirements, and all three are essential if an athlete is to derive every bit of benefit from each competition.

The Pre-Contest Phase

A coach should have three major objectives during this phase. First, the coach needs to understand the conditions that will exist at the competition and get to know the lifter and his or her competitive needs. (The coach who handles a lifter in training as well as the platform has an advantage here.) Second, the coach must help the lifter perform at the very highest level possible on the day, in the context of that lifter's needs and objectives. If defeating the other participants (or at least as many as possible) is a major goal, the coach should find out as much as possible about the legitimate competition (i.e., the competitors who are within striking distance of his or her athlete) and then help the athlete to establish the proper framework in which to turn in the best possible performance against those athletes.

While the objective of defeating as many competitors as possible may seem to be automatic, this is often far from the case. In some competitions it may be appropriate for a lifter to ignore his or her competitors. A lifter may find himself or herself far better or worse than the other lifters in the meet. In that case, true competition is not possible, but a high performance by that athlete is possible. An athlete may have legitimate objectives in a given competition that have nothing to do with other athletes (e.g., making all six attempts, breaking personal records, developing the ability to concentrate fully in front of an audience). Of course, winning is the usual objective, but if the most successful coaches in every sport have one thing in common, it is their emphasis on performing well rather than winning. (Although Vince Lombardi was famous for his comment that winning in the only thing, his true emphasis with his athletes was on excellence and performing at their very best, as he knew that victory would surely flow from such a focus.)

Understanding the Primary Conditions of The Competition: The Rules of Weightlifting

Do you know which organization is recognized by the International Weightlifting Federation and the U.S. Olympic Committee as the national governing body for competitive weightlifting in the United States (and is probably "sanctioning" any competition your athletes are entering)? Do you know that you may not be able to join that organization (the USAW) on the day of a competition (though that is usually possible)? Do you know that you must enter a national level competition several weeks before it is held? Do you understand the way in which the competition will be carried out and what your athletes must wear when they compete? Do you know all of the infractions that can cause the referees to rule no lift?

The answers to all of these questions are in the rulebooks and/or Weightlifting USA, the bimonthly magazine published by the USAW. You must know the rules in order to be an effective coach. Appendix I provides a fairly extensive explanation of the USAW's rules, and every coach and athlete should study it carefully. Then you should send for a USAW rulebook and join the USAW as a coach, so that you receive the Federation's magazine regularly. Untold heartache and ill will in the sport of weightlifting have been caused by ignorance. Do not let your athletes be added to the long list of those who have learned the rules the hard way.

The rules of weightlifting are a marvel of comprehensives, economy and fairness. They have been carefully designed and modified over many years to make competitions run as smoothly and equitably as possible. But the best of rules are not perfect, and they certainly cannot overcome ineptitude on the part of those who enforce them. While most officials at USAW sanctioned competitions, especially on a national level, are highly competent, errors are occasionally made. But the few errors that go against an athlete are eventually matched by errors that are to his or her benefit. And it must be remembered that all officials of the USAW are volunteers. They perform their duties year after year because they love the sport, and they deserve your respect even when you do not agree with them.

Once you know the rules, you should teach your athletes those that pertain to performance of the lifts, and you should emphasize them even more before the competition. For example, lowering the bar before the referee's signal or dropping the bar after the signal are causes for disqualification of a lift. If I had a nickel for every time I saw this at a competition, especially one for new lifters, I would not be rich, but I would certainly be able to retire sooner.

Making a mistake in putting the bar down is an unnecessary and unnerving way to lose a lift. All lifters should practice lifting with mock referee signals during pre-competition training, and someone should remind the lifter to wait for the signal once the lift is at arm's length. Have the lifter put the bar down carefully, with both hands on the bar. (As the bar nears the platform, make sure that the wrists are positioned behind the bar—not directly above it—so that if the bar bounces, it will not jam the wrists.) Help the lifter develop the mental strategy of saying: "It was rough to get it up there so I'll savor the moment with it overhead for just a little while." The lifter will not go wrong with such an attitude as long as he or she does not make a habit of holding the bar overhead for an unnecessarily long period after receiving the down signal. Faulty replacement of the bar on the platform is just one example of a foolishly lost attempt. Knowing the rules will help prevent many other mistakes as well.

Getting to Know the Lifter

Getting to know the lifter is the first step in the pre-competition coaching phase. This is a particularly important process for the coach who has been appointed or requested to handle an athlete in a particular competition when he or she does not normally coach that athlete. For an athlete's personal coach, a much more abbreviated process is sufficient, but the process should not be ignored, no matter how well a coach knows an athlete. When "understanding" is totally implicit, there is always a great risk of being incorrect.

The earlier and more completely a coach gets to know a lifter, the better. Ideally, this is an ongoing process that spans the lifter's career. More often than not on the international scene, where one or two coaches serve an entire team, the process takes place over several weeks or months before the competition.

Tommy Kono is the best coach I have ever seen in this regard. When he is selected as a team coach, he immediately begins the process of getting to know his athletes. He solicits information about each athlete on special forms that he has developed for this purpose. Tommy contacts not only the lifters, but also their coaches. He begins a dialogue with the team, corresponding with them regularly. His communications combine inspiration, coaching advice and information about the trip and the destination. Tommy makes himself available by phone and/or written correspondence to all team members well ahead of the event. In addition, he tries to meet and work with as many of the lifters as possible prior to the competition. For example, he generally attempts to organize a pre-competition camp for the team. Once with the team, Tommy is all business. He is there for the team members at all times, giving as little or as much assistance as necessary. All of this is not surprising when you consider that Tommy has always been a thinking lifter and coach; with eight World Championships (including two Olympic Gold medals) and many international coaching assignments, he has "been there."

For a variety of reasons, circumstances can prevent any meeting of the coach and the athlete before the weigh-in. In such situations, it is possible to conduct an abbreviated version of the familiarization process described below after the weigh-in but before the lifter begins to warm up.

There are several components to the process of getting to know the athlete.

1. Begin building trust by showing respect. The proper role of a competition or "platform" coach is to help the athlete achieve his or her goals. This is particularly true when a coach is functioning solely as an athlete's competition coach (e.g., when the coach is serving an international team of athletes, most of whom he or she does not know). There is often a temptation for the coach to impose his or her values and judgment on the athlete. Coaches tend to like to take charge, and they are used to having their commands obeyed. In most cases this autocratic streak arises out of a sincere desire to help the normally younger and less experienced athlete. But in other sad cases, an autocratic style is the result of lack of confidence or outright egomania on the part of the coach. Such a coach would do well to remember that the bond of longtime friendship, respect and admiration that should exist between athlete and coach is born of mutual respect for individual values and sovereignty. Respecting other people's values (as long as they do not entail the initiation of force against others) is a prerequisite for such a relationship. Reasonable people can and do disagree, and the athlete has only one career, while the coach, at least vicariously, has many.

For example, if the coach feels that the greatest honor that a person can receive is to represent his or her country, but the athlete merely wants to do his or her personal best, the competition site is not the place to discuss or attempt to resolve such differences (if they need to be resolved at all). The coach should be there for one purpose and one purpose only: to help the athlete achieve his or her best performance in the context of his or her goals. Differences in opinion about those goals can and should be settled at another time and place.

Nothing will ruin an athlete's chances of success more completely than a challenge to his or her core values on the day of the competition or in the days and weeks immediately before it. Values are at the root of all motivation. Failure to grasp this concept has probably caused more of our poor international performances over the last twenty or thirty years than any other single cause (although I am happy to say that at least some of our coaches have learned their lessons in this vital area).

2. Observe the athlete. This step is both first in the familiarization process and the only one that must continue throughout the competition. Does the lifter appear to be physically, psychologically and emotionally fit to compete? The coach must be careful here to make evaluations within the context of that lifter. For example, for some athletes, 8% body fat can indicate a lack of condition. For other athletes, 12% body fat may represent the peak of lifting fitness. Some lifters can appear to be intense and focused when they have just withdrawn into a private mental turmoil. Others can seem to be nervous when they are "just right" for competition. The coach must learn how each lifter looks, talks and behaves when he or she is in varying stages of readiness. A coach who accomplishes this has taken one major step in the direction of effective competition coaching. When you know where your lifter is, you can make the crucial decisions about whether he or she needs to be brought up or down (in terms of arousal level) and whether his or her focus is correct. (All of this assumes that the lifter agrees and responds to external manipulations, which is not always the case.) In addition, observations of overall preparedness and the lifter's warm-up attempts help you to advise the athlete in the areas of technique, poundage selection, etc. Observation is clearly one of the coach's most powerful tools.

However, observation has significant limits, particularly when you do not know a lifter very well. For example, I have known lifters who get so worked up in the warm-up room that all of the weights they lift look very light. Then, when they get on the platform, they are too exhausted to perform. I have known others who exude confidence prior to the competition and right up through the warm-ups and then wither on the platform. Still others look tired and slow or sound so negative that you want to give it up. Then they go out and deliver a stellar performance. Even when you know a lifter quite well, you can be mistaken on a given occasion. So, observe your lifter carefully, but do not become overconfident in your ability to predict performance on the basis of pure observation. Observation is an important tool, not a source of omniscience.

3. Interview the athlete. Discuss feelings, desires, goals, past successes and training prior to the competition. Use open-ended questions (questions that require explanations) instead of

questions that can be answered with a simple yes or no. For instance, "can you tell me about the most important things that you'd like to accomplish in this competition?" is much better than, "do you want to win today?" Open-ended questions elicit more information and encourage a free flowing dialogue. Once a question has been answered, it is important to probe, requesting clarifications and elaboration.

Pose different scenarios and discuss what could or should be done in these situations. Psychological research has shown that people often think they are more certain of what they want or think than they really are. For example, if you ask a lifter if he or she wants to go all out, the answer might be yes. However, if you present a specific situation in which a famous lifter far above your lifter's ability shows up to compete, the athlete might be happy with personal records or taking second. Only proper questioning will reveal a clear picture of the athlete's values. Failure to clarify values is probably the single greatest cause for unnecessary suffering in competition. Starting with 25 kg. more than what is necessary to win and missing three times is not a problem if winning is not all important to that lifter in that competition. He or she is merely faced with the technical challenge of discovering what went wrong. If the lifter puts winning first, he or she would be very disappointed by an avoidable loss.

It should be noted that many, perhaps most, coaches will disagree with what has just been said. They will argue that "you always make a total first" or "you always go for the win first." It may be true that this is desirable for the majority of athletes, perhaps even more athletes than would ever admit it. But such principles are not immutable; they are not true for all athletes at all times. The purpose of careful questioning and discussion is to clarify the lifter's values and objectives, so that appropriate decisions can be made during the competition.

4. Review all known facts about the athlete. Gather and evaluate all of the information you can about that athlete's past performances. However, remember that while history can be very useful in making projections about the future, it does not necessarily determine the future. Therefore, gather information but do not form premature hypotheses.

5. Develop a preliminary idea of what can conceivably be accomplished at the competition and with what degree of certainty. Is winning reasonable? Placing? Making records? Making personal records? Improving the lifter's rate of success? Understanding these issues, along with the athlete's objectives, is the basis for formulating a strategy for that athlete in that competition.

6. Develop a strategy. The strategy must take into account the athlete's goals, his or her condition, the competition and the overall environment of the competition. The strategy should be a flexible plan of how to get the lifter from the warm-up room to where he or she wants to be after the competition.

7. Get to know the lifter's special needs. All athletes have psychological, emotional, physical and technical needs. Learn what a given lifter needs to see, hear and feel in order to be totally prepared to perform at the optimal level. Certain cues usually help. These may range from a technique reminder to an exhortation, a slap or simple silence. Learn what the cues are, and make sure they happen in the right sequence at the right time.

Making Weight

Every sport has its unpleasant aspects. For marathoners, its the potential for hitting the wall and the risk of dehydration. For skiers, it is the other skier who ventures out on a slope that he or she is not ready to ski (and who thereby endangers the competent skier). In weightlifting it is making weight.

It is the rare lifter who does not find himself or herself with the need to make weight at one time or another in his or her career. Making weight is somewhat unpleasant at best and sheer agony at worst, but there are some steps that can be taken to make it a more certain process and to minimize the discomfort the lifter experiences. The first rule is: do not try to reduce if you are too far away from the weight limit. Lifters vary in their ability to reduce their body weight. I have known lifters who could reduce their body weight by nearly 7% within the last few days before the meet, with little negative affect on their performance. But such lifters are rare indeed. Most athletes will notice a significant reduction in performance with a short term weight loss in excess of 5%, and some will be relatively intolerant to much of a weight loss at all. Research in the area of exercise physiology tends to support these informal observations. When weight loss through dehydration is overdone, it can lead to severe cramping and other very unpleasant symptoms and can actually become life threatening. Dehydration alone can pose a health threat, but changes in electrolyte balances can actually lead to heart arrhythmia (life threatening irregularities in the contraction of the heart muscle). When your heart cramps, you are in major trouble!.

There are essentially four ways to lose body weight: lose muscle size, lose fat, reduce the food and/or liquid in the body's gastrointestinal and urinary systems and dehydrate. Obviously, losing muscle size is undesirable for to a weightlifter in most instances. Muscles lift weights, and you need all of the quality muscle you can get. Virtually all methods of losing body weight can result in some degree of muscle loss, but the objective is to keep such a loss to a minimum (and careful training and diet will usually accomplish this). A diet adequate in protein and the stimulation of training will go a long way toward preserving muscle mass.

Losing fat is unquestionably the best weight loss alternative for the athlete. Fat lifts nothing, and a leaner athlete is generally more effective than one who has a higher percentage of body fat. Losing fat without losing muscle requires a long term strategy because quick weight losses are almost totally the result of dehydration. In fact, sudden and significant changes in diet can make the body more resistant to weight loss (as the body automatically reduces its metabolism rate to offset the drop in caloric intake). A combination of increased aerobic activity, reduced caloric intake (primarily by reducing the intake of fat in the diet) and careful training (in effect, to tell the body that muscle mass must be maintained) are all crucial accomplish loss of fat.

However, once body fat is reduced to its minimal level, the only way to lose further weight (without reducing muscle mass) is to is to resort to the last two means (emptying the gastrointestinal and urinary systems and/or generally dehydrating the body).

There is a practical way to reduce ones lean body weight by approximately 5% the week of the meet. Beginning on the Monday before a Saturday competition, monitor the diet to assure that no extra or unnecessary calories are taken in. The diet should be "tightened" a bit on Wednesday, so that on Wednesday and Thursday the overall caloric intake is 10% to 20% below normal. Beginning on Friday morning, the athlete should substantially reduce the quantity of food eaten (to less than 50% of normal). This serves to reduce the food in the body's digestive system and furthers the overall weight loss process. Watching the diet during the week and reducing the food intake on the day before the competition can cause the athlete to lose from 1/2% to 2% of his or her body weight.

Some lifters resort to laxatives at this point in an effort to clear the large intestine. This practice cannot be advised for several reasons. It is often difficult to predict the effects of a laxative. It is easy to take too much or too little. The effects of a laxative are difficult to modify. Once the laxative is taken, it will run its course. In contrast, more direct forms of dehydration can simply be controlled by stopping the process. Finally, a portion of the bodyweight reduction that results from a laxative comes from dehydration anyway, so it makes more sense to control hydration in some more direct and effective way.

Another bad idea is cleaning the lower intestine by an enema. Practitioners of this technique often forget that the large intestine can absorb water as well as expel it; a dehydrated lifter may simply absorb water. Some argue that just the right saline concentration in the enema solution will preclude

water absorption, and they may be right, but, there are better ways to accomplish a similar result.

Still another solution to the quick weight loss problem is the use of diuretics. Apart from the health risk that can arise from diuretics (e.g., over-dehydration, a loss of potassium), it is now illegal to use them prior to and during competition. Admittedly, many lifters found them to be quite effective in the past, but that is a moot point today.

Today, the most practical means for losing the last few pounds of body weight, are to limit the intake of fluids and increase the loss of water from the body by increasing the process of perspiration. Reducing fluid intake can be torture for some and just unpleasant for others.

An increase in the rate of perspiration can be achieved by increasing activity or by exposing the body to heat. Increased activity is generally not a good choice for the lifter, because it can lead to muscular fatigue. Body temperature (and hence perspiration) can be elevated by reducing the effectiveness of the body at eliminating body heat. This can be accomplished by insulating the body so that body heat cannot be dissipated (e.g., by wrapping the body in a blanket) or by exposing the body directly to heat through the mechanism of a sauna or steam room. The difference between a sauna and a steam room is essentially one of humidity; the latter has a higher humidity level. At any given temperature, the body will perspire more at a higher level of humidity. This is why a person can tolerate a much higher temperature in a dryer climate.

Why is the body sensitive to humidity? The reason is an indirect one, The body cannot react to humidity. Rather, it relies on perspiration as a means to cool itself. The evaporation of that perspiration helps to regulate body heat. In a higher humidity, perspiration does not evaporate as quickly, so the body responds by sweating more (as though the reason that cooling has not been sufficient is that perspiration has not been sufficient). The body's system has in effect been "fooled" by the higher humidity. Therefore, the choice between a sauna and a steam room may be more a matter of personal preference than effectiveness. The rate of weight loss is generally faster in a steam room, but the lifter may not be able to tolerate the heat of the steam room for as long a period. Eastern European lifters generally favor the sauna, which may be for cultural as well as effectiveness reasons.

A Bulgarian technique called "boiling" can be highly effective. I heard about boiling through Ben Green. Ben was a nationally ranked Olympic lifter for many years as well as a World Masters Champion in weightlifting. He has coached many national and international level weightlifters in his career, including several Olympians. He learned the boiling technique from Bulgarian coach Angel Spassov. The advantages of this method is that it is effective and convenient and requires no special equipment. The technique consists of submerging a lifter in a bathtub filled with hot water. Only the lifter's head remains out of the water. The water should be as hot as the lifter can tolerate it but not so hot that it burns the lifter's skin (though the skin will become very flushed during the boiling process). The lifter generally remains in the water for fifteen to twenty minutes (never beyond the point where the water cools off and the lifter is not sweating profusely or so long that the lifter begins to feel faint or light headed). For the sake of safety, the lifter should always be accompanied while being boiled. At the end of this period, the lifter is immediately wrapped in blankets to retain the heat that has been generated in the bath (the entire body, including the head, should be covered at this time). The body will continue to perspire in an effort to cool itself. If the boiling process is carried out in an effective manner, it is not unusual for the lifter to lose up to 1 kg. in thirty minutes.

Whether an athlete elects to use the sauna, a steam room, boiling, a combination of warm clothing and a heavy blanket or a reduction in fluids is a matter of preference and time constraints. Dehydration by fluid deprivation takes longer to work than the sauna or steam room. It is generally agreed that the less time the lifter is at the reduced body weight the better. Therefore, temperature generated weight loss is likely to be more effective than limiting fluids. However, each lifter is different, and each will have to find the proper blend of techniques.

As a lifter gains knowledge and experience about making weight he or she will become more proficient at it. Often the lifter will develop an almost uncanny ability to know where his or her body weight is. Nevertheless, frequent checks at the scale are always a good idea to monitor progress in this regard and to assure that the athlete does not overdo it.

One last point regarding making weight. If that is an important issue (and it is for most lifters), scout out the location of the scale(s) and other equipment (e.g., steam room). upon arrival at the meet site, If possible, get some help from someone who has already weighed in and immediately weigh in on the alternate or back-up scale to see if that scale has the same readings as the official one.

Even the best of plans can fall short when the pressure is on. No emergency measure can replace having an athlete at the target body weight before he or she goes to weigh in, but some quick fixes can get your athlete where he or she needs to be in a crisis. Urinating and defecating are two obvious ways of eliminating the last few ounces of body weight. Expectorating (spitting, into a cup please!) can also help. A quick rubdown with a dry towel can blot up the last bits of moisture, as can drying hair (hair absorbs moisture). When an athlete is very close to the necessary body weight and time is short, cutting the athlete's hair can do the trick. A car with the heater turned up or a hot shower can serve as a proxy for a sauna. Some lifters have even used a finger down the throat (though this technique cannot be recommended because of its health risks, and I have never known a lifter who has used it and performed his or her best).

Electronic scales prevail at major competitions today, and lifters are sometimes required to stand in a specific spot on the scale. With a mechanical scale, the lifter may find that standing in one place on the scale or leaning in one direction may have a slight influence on the scale's reading, enough help him or her make weight. There is nothing illegal about this (unless the referees have stipulated otherwise), and minimizing your reading is your prerogative. However, it is risky to rely on such a technique for making weight.

Preparing for Drug Testing—Don't Assume That You Are Ready

Most athletes know enough not to use anabolic steroids. Apart from the fact that steroids are banned from competition, there are a host of other reasons not to use them (many of which are addressed in other sections of this book). But today's drug testing at major weightlifting competitions covers many drugs other than anabolic steroids. Some such drugs (e.g., amphetamines) are obvious ones to ban because they may give one athlete an unfair advantage over another, but other banned substances are not as obvious. Beta blockers (which are normally used to calm the nerve impulses to the hearts of people with heart conditions), diuretics ("water pills") and some over-the-counter cold medications are examples of banned substances that have unpleasantly surprised many athletes. Even more surprising to many is the incidence of banned substances in many "herbal" preparations. Athletes who are completely committed to never using drugs and ingesting only "natural" substances may consume herbs that end up causing them to be suspended.

Ignorance is not regarded as an excuse by sports governing bodies, and the list of tragic cases of athletes who have been severely penalized for innocently ingesting banned substances unfortunately grows longer every year. The only way to combat this problem is to educate your athletes regarding banned substances and to remind them of this issue well before any competition in which they may be tested. Both coaches and athletes should become very familiar with the drug testing rules so that something unfortunate will never happen to them.

The coach must stress that the athlete should ingest no banned substance or any substance of uncertain origin or content (and should not listen to anyone other than doping control experts from the USOC, IWF or IOC). When there is any doubt, do not take the substance.

Dietary Considerations Before a Competition

We have already discussed the issue of dieting to make weight at competition. The issue of eating to maximize energy in training and competition will be discussed is some detail in Chapter 10. However, apart from considerations of making weight and consuming the nutrients that are optimal from a nutritionist's standpoint, there are practical considerations to assure that the athlete will be comfortable and focused on performing well during the competition (because poor or unusual dietary factors will distract the lifter). In my experience, there are three considerations that should determine a lifter's competition diet: 1) his or her normal dietary habits and inherent rate of digestion; 2) the degree to which the athlete's normal diet has been altered in order to make weight; and, 3) the amount of time available to the athlete after weigh-in and between the snatch and the C&J.

It is often a good idea to minimize any differences between what the athlete normally does and what he or she does on the day of the competition. A well balanced diet that is higher in protein and lower in fat than the typical American diet is generally a good idea for a lifter. However, if that is not the athlete's normal diet, the day of the competition is not the day to begin experimenting. Theoretically, a diet that is lower in fat and protein and higher in complex carbohydrates is best for competition, but such a diet should be experimented with before competition day.

The content of the diet is perhaps less important than the timing of food ingestion. Some people actually say they feel better lifting on a relatively full stomach. I prefer not to eat for several hours before competing, as a full stomach seems to sap my energy and gives me an uncomfortable feeling when I lift. Various eating intervals should be tried to learn what is most agreeable for each individual athlete. However, you should be aware that the content of the athlete's diet will affect his or her rate of digestion. Fats are digested most slowly, protein more quickly and carbohydrates most quickly of all. Therefore, a meal that is high in fat may feel as if it is sitting in the stomach for many hours, while a meal that is mostly carbohydrates may take only an hour or two to be digested. This is why the interval between the weigh-in and the competition and the interval between the snatch and the C&J can be significant. For instance, if there are only a few competitors in a weight class, the time between the snatch and the C&J may not permit the athlete to eat much of anything. On the other hand, if there is likely to be an hour and a half between an athlete's last snatch and when he or she begins to warm up for the C&J, some light eating may very well be in order after the snatch has been completed. If an athlete has really starved to make weight, it may be very important for the athlete to eat before a competition in order to regain his or her energy. If the athlete has been able to eat normally going into the competition, the effect of food hours before a competition will be less significant, so in such a situation it is probably better to err on the side of eating less than normal.

It is a good idea to experiment with the many athletic specialty drinks that are available today as an energy source during competition and workouts. While some of these drinks are not much more than water, sugar, flavoring and color, others offer a balanced mixture of simple and complex carbohydrates that can really assist the performance of some athletes. There is no substitute for reading the labels and experimentation. While some athletes can drink these preparations straight, many will find that cutting the drink with an equal volume of water makes it more beneficial and helps to prevent dehydration as well. In fact, dehydration will affect performance far more than lack of food. For this reason, the lifter should drink fluids at regular intervals (e.g., six to eight ounces per hour) rather than relying on the sensation of thirst (which may not be felt until significant dehydration has occurred).

Packing the Competition Bag

Successful meet preparation requires packing the gear that may be used by an athlete in competition. Many veteran lifters have bags that contain a seemingly unlimited number of items. They have often assembled these bags after being caught without something necessary at a crucial time. They are truly prepared.

You should not rely on the athlete to pack every item that he or she may need at the competition. Prepare two packing lists, one for the athlete and one for you. Between the two lists you should have every item on the following list (and anything you can think of that may help). Before you leave for the competition venue, make sure either you or the athlete has every item on the list.

I have found the following items to be useful.

1. Lifting Suit and T-Shirt. Many lifters like to pack two, in case one becomes soiled, damaged or perspiration soaked during the meet.

2. Lifting Shoes. Most athletes like one pair of athletic shoes for the general warm-up and lifting shoes for lifting. Some even have two pairs of lifting shoes (one for the snatch and one for the C&J). Still others bring an extra pair of shoes; this precaution is almost never necessary, but it is not a bad idea.

3. Extra Shoe Laces. The best practice is to change them before the meet if they even have small signs of wear and to have an extra pair. When the lifter is pulling those laces tight under stress, they will often break.

4. Lifting Belt. If the lifter wears one, make sure the leather or other material from which it is made is in good shape and that any stitching is sound.

5. Straps. It is not advisable to warm up with straps, but having a pair can be helpful when the warm-up is long or the skin of the hands has been torn up before the event. (And the lifter may want to train after the event.)

6. Wraps. Bring a set of all permissible wraps and extras of the ones that the lifter normally uses. (Even a wrap that he or she normally does not use can become necessary in the event of an injury.)

7. Chalk and Rosin. You might be surprised how many warm-up rooms run short. Occasionally the athlete will not like the chalk provided in the warm-up area, having his own can be a pleasure in such a situation. Rosin helps to keep the soles of the shoes from slipping on a platform that is too smooth or slick.

8. Sweats. Even if the lifter does not normally use them, having sweats will be useful if the competition site is cold.

9. A Long Robe Or Blanket and a Towel. Robes and blankets are easier to get on and off than sweats and warmer when that extra warmth is needed (whether because the arena is cool or to make weight unexpectedly). Towels have obvious uses.

10. Fluids and Electrolytes. Do not depend on their availability at the meet site. The ingestion of fluids is important in training, but the stress of a long competition and the dehydration that may precede it make fluid intake even more important. You should have fluids with and without carbohydrates so that the lifter can meet his or her fluid requirements under a wide variety of conditions. Electrolytes help to replace the minerals that have been lost during any pre-competition weight reductions.

11. Reminder Notes. A reminder list that provides technique pointers, suggestions about what the lifter should be thinking, a record of warm-ups and motivational sayings can be a meet saver. This list assures the athlete that nothing important will be forgotten.

12. Personal Items. Some athletes use certain item to calm, focus or inspire them during a competition. These can range from audio or video tapes to pictures or "worry beads." These items should be in the competition gear. Ideally, the athlete will not rely on anything but his or her own mind to prepare for the competition, but when a lifter uses an external aid it is important for it to be there, and the only way to assure that is to put it on your packing list.

13. Chewing Gum. Gum assists in expectorating when making weight.

14. Tape and Tape Spray. Tape can be used on the thumbs and anywhere else the lifter might need it during the competition. Tape sprays help tape to adhere better or be removed more easily.

15. Surgical Scissors. These are used to trim tape, bandages and torn calluses (even hair to make weight).

16. Tweezers. These are used to remove splinters and help trim torn calluses.

17. First Aid Kit. Tearing skin on the hands can occur occasionally, even if the lifter cares for his or her hands properly. Since some other kind of cut, abrasion or bruise may occur, the kit should include ointment with an analgesic (e.g., xylocaine). A callous board can also be useful. If one is going abroad, a prescription pain killer is a good idea in the unlikely event that a painful injury arises while you are abroad (bring the prescription and check local laws first to make sure the drug isn't illegal in the country your are visiting).

18. Chemical Or Other Ice Packs and Liniment. In the event of any strain or sprain, it is important to have cooling agents. Ice applied in combination with compression becomes a valuable first aid measure. Cold sprays can be helpful in the short term when ice is unavailable.

19. Smelling Salts. These are used to clear the head when and if necessary (some lifters find they provide a psychological boost before a lift). However, some recent medical evidence suggests these can be a very bad idea for someone with a heart condition.

20. Assorted Survival Tools. A compact "mess kit" (knife, fork, spoon, plate, cup and bottle and can opener) plus safety pins, pen, paper and calculator can all come in handy. A number of non-lifting medical items (e.g., anti-diahrreals) can also be helpful for travelers, particularly when they are going to foreign countries, but be aware that local laws may forbid certain drugs.

Traveling to and Adapting to the Competitive Environment

It is important for the lifter to become acclimated to the competition environment as quickly and as fully as possible. The first step is to get the athlete there. Make sure you leave early when you go to the airport and competition site. Plan to arrive at the site well before weigh-in. Make alternative travel plans. Professional travelers think nothing of booking more than one flight, or even more than one means of transportation (plane, train, auto, etc.) but be sure to notify the alternative means of transport as soon as you have made a final decision on how to proceed.

The complete weightlifter must be a professional traveler. Planning the trip—

scheduling, packing, selecting transport and accommodations— must be done with care. While the champion may be resilient, there is no point in creating unnecessary stress. A trip should be planned well in advance. Find out about the city and state or country to which you are traveling. If you are making an international trip, seek out the assistance of the team manager (if there is one), other athletes, or any one else who has been there. (Better still, find someone who lives there and is very familiar with conditions in the United States as well.) Get data on food and water, travel options and things to watch out for. Your local health department can normally supply this kind of information. If not, numerous travel books and other materials provide this information.

Two strategies are generally preferable when traveling a substantial distance or to very different living conditions. One is to come in as late as possible, the other is to arrive several days before the competition. The advantage of a late arrival is that the stress of travel will probably not have taken real effect (because there is usually a short lag in such effects). Performance at a higher altitude is generally best immediately after arrival or after five to ten days of adjustment. The time required to overcome jet lag depends on how many time zones have been traversed and in which direction, but its effects are not fully experienced immediately. Jet lag can be shortened considerably with some very specific dietary and sleeping pattern manipulations. (see Overcoming Jet Lag by C. Ehret & L Scanlon for further information.) A late arrival also reduces the likelihood of exposure to bad food or water and to extreme temperature conditions.

An early arrival enables an athlete to adjust to changes in the time zone, climate and altitude. There is also ample time to get to know local conditions firsthand and to visit the lifting venue. All of this can be an advantage. When arriving early after a long trip or a trip to an important meet, plan to arrive at least thirty hours ahead of the weigh-in. The expense of early arrival is its major disadvantage. A less common disadvantage is having more time for performance to collapse (under the rare circumstances in which conditions are so poor that adaptation is almost impossible, at least over the course of a few days or weeks). In the case of travel, as in the case of virtually everything else in lifting, everyone is a little different. One athlete will thrive on late arrival, and another will find is stressful. One athlete will become bored sitting around a site, while another athlete will find the travel interesting and restful. The athlete should be permitted to do what is best for him or her, even if it creates inconvenience or added expense; the value of success is priceless.

Here are some helpful tips for the lifter.

1. Try to bring some familiar things along on the trip. Something as simple as a well worn robe or familiar music can be extremely comforting in a strange place. If you are visiting a foreign country and bring something that requires electric power, make sure it will work under the voltage conditions there. (Inexpensive electricity converters are readily available."

2. Do not drink the water, do not brush your teeth with it and do not wash or rinse food with it unless you are absolutely sure that it is safe. This is not an issue in the United States, but when traveling abroad, it often is; if you are unsure, do not drink it.

3. Enter the competition early and document your entry. The reason for an early entry is to assure that the entry has been sent on time and received. I have seen athletes train hard for a meet, send in an entry and travel all of the way to the competition, only to be unable to lift because their entries were never received. Make sure this does not happen to you. Send all entries certified mail, return receipt requested. In addition, you should bring a copy of the entry so that you have further evidence that you entered. Minors should take at least one of three further steps. First, bring a second original entry (signed by a parent) to the competition. Second, call the USAW National Office (or meet director) to confirm that the entry has been received. Third, send a stamped, self-addressed envelope with a confirmation letter signed by the meet director, stating the entry has been received and is complete. These extra steps for the lifter who is a minor go beyond demonstrating that the entry was made on time. They also assure that the meet director has parental consent required for the athlete to compete.

4. Pack early and have a list. No matter how often you travel, there is always the possibility of overlooking something. Experienced travelers pack early enough to discover and replace missing items, and their lists assure that nothing vital is forgotten.

5. Carry critical items on board the carrier. Airlines and other common carriers are generally pretty good about getting your luggage to where you are going. However, there are occasional losses (temporary or permanent). Losing anything can be annoying, losing a favorite and irreplaceable item can be maddening, but losing your lifting shoes is a virtual disaster.

I vividly remember an incident that took place at my first Senior Nationals in Chicago in 1969. The airline managed to lose the luggage of one of my training partners, Gary Hanson. Gary had been a National Champion several times. He was in shape to win still another title, but when he arrived in Chicago, his luggage had not. Gary lost his lifting shoes, belt and suit. He managed to remain reasonably calm, and after some desperate scrounging around, to borrow some equipment that was adequate, although he didn't look like a fashion plate when he mounted the platform. It was a tribute to Gary's experience and character that he maintained his composure and went on to win the meet. If he did not learn a lesson, I surely did. I will never trust critical items to an airline or anyone else.

When you arrive at the site, check the following conditions.

1. The Platform. It can be smaller or larger than standard. In either case, the officials should be persuaded to draw a line around the platform indicating the official size. I have see lifters lose lifts at National Championships because they stepped over a line they did not know existed. Platform height can tell you if a lifter needs to be on his or her way there a little sooner. (a 5' elevation can result in a lifter needing a little more time to prepare to lift after he or she has mounted the platform, particularly if that lifter is very large.) The surface of the platform can provide traction or be slick. (In the latter case, get out the rosin you have undoubtedly brought along or get someone to clean things up before your lifter begins.) An early survey of the platform's surface can also help to identify problem areas(softness, unevenness) and whether or not the platform is level (if you brought your level). These things can be corrected before the competition begins, or perhaps the bar can be placed in a position that avoids the bad spots. Its too late when the athlete has tripped, slipped or unnecessarily lost his or her balance.

2. The Arena. How far is it from the warm-up room to the platform? The farther it is, the earlier the lifter will need to head for the platform, and the more you will need to bring along (for example, fluids, blankets, a chair). Is access too restricted? Too narrow an entrance can mean you need more time to get out to the platform and that you cannot sit there awaiting a lift. What is the temperature like? Do you need a blanket or a fan? Scout out a private place for your lifter to relax and to concentrate between attempts. Be aware that conditions can and do change before and during the competition. Think about what gap between attempts will make it reasonable to return to the warm-up area and what circumstances will preclude such a return. Help the lifter to spot points to focus on during the snatch, clean and jerk. It is usually a good idea to have the lifter come out to the platform to find his or her focal points and to become familiar with the surroundings before the competition begins. The main exception to this rule is the lifter who gets too nervous when he or she is exposed to the arena beforehand.

Pay particular attention to the warm-up area. Just before the warm-ups begin, set up a place that the lifter can call his or her own (with a chair, blanket, fluids, etc.) for the duration of the competition. A familiar spot (albeit a temporary one) can help the athlete psychologically and the coach (e.g., so that you do not have to look for your athlete when you come back from counting attempts).

3. The Barbell. Does it have the same dimensions as your training equipment? (Even the same brand can vary at times.) Is it smoother or rougher? (More or less tape or chalk may be needed if the difference is significant.) Will the bar on the platform be loaded with the same plates as the warm-up bars? (This is particularly important for athletes who are lifting weights that can affect the height of the bar from the floor, or where 25 kg.. plates can feel very different from 20s, 15s and 10s loaded randomly.) Is the bar bent? If so, get it replaced, or at least have the lifter pull with the inside of the bar bent upward. When the bar does not turn freely, there is nearly always a portion of its circumference through which turning is smoother. In such a case, the lifter should be sure to position the bar so that it will move freely when the bar is turned over as the lifter executes the squat under.

It is important to have the lifter check the bar before the competition for another reason. Lifters who do not check the bar before the competition often do so immediately before they lift. When a lifter waits to check the bar for the first time, there is little likelihood that some kind of coping mechanism can be introduced to remedy any unexpected discovery. Tardiness in examining the bar is somewhat foolish, but as long as the lifter confines the contact of the hands to the portion of the bar which he or she will grip, better late than never.

The real problem arises when the lifter touches the bar in a place other than the one where his or her grip is to be placed during the lift. This is because some lifters use a lubricant on their thighs when lifting (although it is technically illegal). That lubricant can be transferred from the lifter's thighs to the bar during the lift, making the bar slippery where contact was made. Should the lifter touch such a spot, some of the lubricant can be transferred to the lifter's hand and can negatively affect the lifter's grip. It is bad enough if this happens as a result of a lifter touching the bar where he or she actually grips the bar to lift, but it is a tragedy when this occurs as a result of touching the bar in an unnecessary place. Interestingly enough, the lifter's grip is rarely affected if the bar is touched only where necessary, because the thighs of the other lifters will rarely have touched the bar at the same point.

While it is important to gain some understanding of, and control over, the competitive conditions, you need to prepare your lifter for the human conditions that he or she may encounter at the competition.

Pre-Competition "Head Games"

Some athletes love to engage in behavior that they believe will "psych-out" an opponent. On balance, it is probably best to avoid such "head games." Weightlifting is one sport in which competitors can almost ignore each other completely without affecting their chance of winning. Psychological games can easily divert a lifter's attention from the real task at hand: lifting as much weight as in humanly possible on that day. Nevertheless, a knowledge of some basic ploys will enable the coach and the athlete to avoid being drawn in by an opponent's behavior.

The first principle to keep in mind in psychological warfare is that efforts to destroy an adversary imply respect for that opponent. If an opponent did not feel your athlete had a chance of winning, he or she would not attempt to achieve a mental victory. That fact alone should bolster your athlete's confidence. Moreover, the athlete who engages in psychological warfare is often its greatest victim. This is the psych-out artist's own fears and uncertainties convince that person of the efficacy of such emotions in defeating others. Just knowing that the competitor who is waging psychological warfare feels that an edge is necessary in order to assure victory over your athlete should give your athlete added confidence.

Here are some popular ploys in psychological warfare.

1. "I'm in great shape": This is usually based on a foundation of prior competitive performances, training performances, and/or warm-up room performances. This image can be further augmented by announcing a high starting attempt (then dropping it back to a more reasonable level later). The object of the game is to convince opponents that they have no chance. It is certainly true that such a method can work. The initiator of such an effort risks tiring himself out with all of his or her fussing. Failing to unnerve an opponent with these tactics can be unnerving in and of itself. In addition, having to drop back a starting poundage after setting it at an artificially high level can give opponents an unwanted morale boost.

2. "I'm in Poor Shape": This approach is less draining on the person who carries it out than the "great shape" approach. This "poor shape" approach is often augmented by submitting a low starting attempt but jumping the start up later. This method can, of course, lull an opponent into a false sense of security. On the other hand, giving the appearance of being in poor condition can give an opponent just the psychological boost he or she needs to overcome self-doubt and perform well.

3. "I'm uncertain": This approach has two variations. The athlete either claims not to know whether he or she is in shape or suggests that perhaps he or she will not lift today. This approach is often supplemented by showing up at the weigh-in at the last minute. This technique can unnerve opponents and can cause them to suffer mood swings. Of course, the surprise can often end up being on the one who utilizes this ploy.

4. "I'm aggressive and intense": Here the athlete roars around the warm-up room looking as if he or she were possessed. This can make an opponent wonder why he or she is not as intense. Fortunately, the bar is not influenced by such behavior, and a savvy opponent may be inspired to rise to the occasion instead of folding his or her tent early. In addition, acting out such a role can be tiring.

5. "I'm relaxed and confident": Here the athlete exudes an aura of confidence and/or friendliness. The opponent may then wonder, "why is he or she so relaxed and confident?" Moreover, who wants to beat such a nice gal or guy? Again, the bar is not cognizant of such behavior and it may backfire. For instance, the opponent may conclude that a laid back person is not be much of a threat and that nice guys finish last.

6. "Us against the world": This clever ruse manifests itself in a variety of ways, but its purpose is twofold. First, it is intended to undermine the opponent's confidence by identifying an apparently insurmountable obstacle to performance. Second, it enables the perpetrator to gain the confidence of his or her victim. The lifter might say: "The platform is slippery; how do they expect us to lift on it?" A comment like that can undermine an opponent's confidence and lull the opponent into thinking of the other athlete as a comrade rather than a competitor. Finally, it implies that something beyond any athlete's control is affecting everyone, making a lower standard of performance acceptable to all.

The keys to overcoming psychological warfare are to understand it and to avoid engaging in it, either as an initiator or a victim. If you understand it, you will not be intimidated. If you avoid engaging in it, you reduce the risks and save yourself some energy in the process.

The Actual Competition

There are two fundamental elements to coaching during the actual competition: helping your lifter perform as well as possible and helping your athlete to place as high as possible in the competition. The first element is taken care of by timing the athlete's warm-ups, helping him or her in selecting poundages, maintaining a focus on the strategy planned, providing the proper cues and continuing to help the lifter adapt to the environment. The second element is taken care of by observing your athlete and the opponents and by utilizing the rules of the game effectively to achieve an optimal outcome against the competition.

Determining the Number of Warm-up Attempts

The number of warm-up attempts required to perform effectively on the platform is a highly individual and situational issue. The lifter's physical condition, emotional state and habitual warm-up patterns will all influence the structure of the warm-ups. The situation that exists at the competition can have an influence as well.

Overall, there are two general (albeit weak) tendencies with regard to warming up. One tendency is for lifters to warm up too little rather than too much, particularly in the snatch lift. The second tendency is for a lifter to require more warm-up attempts in the snatch than the C&J.

Researchers in the former Soviet Union found that most lifters performed best in the snatch after several maximum attempts. While the research would have to be far more extensive before the findings could be regarded as conclusive, the results of this single study will strike many coaches and athletes as being intuitively sound. We have all witnessed the phenomenon of a lifter progressively improving during successive attempts with a heavy weight, or warming up a second time and performing better the second time around. (We have all witnessed the opposite phenomenon as well, although not as frequently.) Generally, if a lifter is not overtrained, grossly out of condition, or using significant nervous energy when warming up, it is hard to r warm up too much (the greatest risk is probably tearing a callus).

There are at least four reasons why a lifter's performance in the snatch seems to benefit from an extensive warm-up, especially relative to that needed for the C&J. The first reason is that athletes tend to develop less muscular fatigue with lighter versus heavier loads (e.g., in the snatch versus the C&J). A second reason is that more motor precision is needed to perform a snatch than a C&J, and precision tends to improve in successive trials. Third, the pressure on the athlete tends to be greatest during his or her first attempt on the competitive platform. An extra warm-up or two can give the lifter a little more confidence and take the nervous "edge" off (although burning off excess nervous energy by lifting is not as effective as learning to control that energy). Finally, the snatch is performed before the C&J in competition, so the body is already warmed up by the time the C&J begins (unless there is a significant break between the snatch and the C&J). We may not have a full scientific explanation for the need to warm up, but most lifters seem to benefit significantly from a thorough warm-up.

I am not a recommending that a lifter automatically extend his or her snatch warm-ups or that the warm-up period be any longer than is necessary to achieve top performance. It is merely a suggestion that if the effectiveness of a particular warm-up method has been less than desired and the warm-ups are conventional in length (i.e., consisting of five to nine sets), the lifter should probably consider a more extensive warm-up as a first effort at a remedy.

What guidelines can be given for the length of the warm-up? As with the range of training techniques that can generate strength gains, the amount of warming up that is necessary varies widely. Former World Champions Bob Bednarski and Pete George had two of the most limited warm-up approaches ever used in high level weightlifting competition.

Pete George often warmed up with 60 kg. when his planned starting attempt was approximately 100 kg. higher. Pete argued that the need for a warm-up was basically mental and that a thorough warm-up with a light weight prepared the body sufficiently for heavy attempts, while avoiding fatigue. (Pete's skill at mental preparation was legendary.) Bob Bednarski's warm-up habits were perhaps even more unusual. In 1968, when Bob did his immortal 486 lb. World Superheavyweight C&J record, he performed only one C&J of 325 lb. in the warm-up room. Bob then took his first attempt at 425 lb. and jumped directly to the historic 486.

About a year and a half later, Bob gave perhaps an even more amazing demonstration of warm-up brevity. Weighing in under the 110 kg. limit, he made a 217.5 kg. training C&J, a lift that exceeded the world record at the time. What made his lift so incredible is that Bob did not intend to C&J at all that day. He entered the gym planning to do only a few cleans. He took three or four attempts to arrive at 200 kg., which he cleaned relatively easily. In view of the easy clean, Bob decided to jerk the weight as well. The jerk attempt resulted in a miss, but that did not phase the indomitable Bednarski. He merely loaded the bar to 217.5 kg. and clean and jerked it handily!

I do not relate these examples to advocate such limited warming up. Few of us are as courageous or as talented as Pete George or Bob Bednarski. Moreover, these outstanding lifters might have performed even better had their warm-up methods been somewhat more conventional. But their stories do illustrate that very limited warm-ups can be effective for at least some lifters.

As was noted earlier, too brief a warm-up is more likely to be a problem than too much of a warm-up. While rare lifters like George and Bednarski perform exceedingly well with very limited warm-ups, I have never known nor heard of an advanced lifter who could lift his or her maximum without warming up (although I have known a number who have tried and come reasonably close). Among those who could perform at a very high level without warming up, I have never known one who said they felt better without any warm-up at all. Therefore, it is fairly clear that at least some warming up is preferable, if not absolutely necessary.

At the other extreme are lifters who employ warm-ups that would virtually exhaust the average lifter. For example, I have seen lifters perform competition warm-ups that included a long, hot shower, half an hour of stretching and calisthenics, five or six sets of snatches with the empty (20 kg.) bar and a gradual progression using sets of three to five reps until the lifter reached approximately 75% of maximum. This was followed by a progression to the lifter's starting attempt in 5 kg. increments.

Is there such a thing as warming up too much? Absolutely. A lifter who warms up excessively can reach a point of physical fatigue. Perhaps more importantly and more likely, such a lifter runs the risk of exhausting the nervous system and becoming emotionally fatigued. Under contest conditions, nervous energy is at a premium. Because emotions tend to heightened during competition, performing the same number of warm-ups as a lifter would in a typical training session can use up far more energy. Lifters who warm up less in competition than in training seem to sense that.

Two rather bizarre examples of approaches I have witnessed illustrate the two most common ways in which warm-ups can be excessive. One case was that of a lifter who suffered from a severe lack of confidence. He had "bombed out" of a number of competitions and was determined not to let it happen again. Since he felt unable to predict his competition performance on the basis of his training lifts, his plan was to warm up early and to try his opening attempt in the warm-up room. He reasoned that by so doing he would be sure of what he could do that day. While most lifters find that going all of the way up to their starting attempt in the warm-up room is both tiring and unnecessary, some lifters do find this approach effective. Unfortunately, this lifter had some trouble making the weight he intended to open with in the competition, so he lifted it several times just "to be sure he could do it." Finally, when he was sure, he confirmed that he would open as originally planned. That is when things began to unravel for this lifter. It seems that he had warmed up too early. As a result, he had to wait quite a while before being called to the bar. Consequently, he rested and warmed up again. By the time he got back up to his opener again, he was a little off and missed. Obviously upset at this turn of events, he attempted this weight several more times with mixed success. By the time he was called to the platform for his opening attempt, he was completely unnerved. His missed first attempt destroyed what little confidence he had left, and two more misses followed in close succession. While much of the blame for this lifter's unfortunate experience undoubtedly lies with mental failure on

his part, excessive warming up played a major role in the entire episode.

The hazards of excessive warming up are not limited to the mentally weak or inexperienced, as the story of multiple World Champion and world record holder will illustrate. This great champion from Eastern Europe was lifting in a meet in the United States. during the early 1980s. At this competition, he opened his C&J's within 10 kg. of the existing world record and lifted it quite comfortably. He then called for an attempt at the world record on his second attempt. Since there were only a few attempts between his first and second attempts, he probably could have simply rested between attempts. Instead, his coaches directed him to take a warm-up with 20 kg. less than his opener, which he did without much difficulty. This was clearly a judgment call by the coach, who was trying to balance the risk of his lifter's cooling off and of tiring himself unnecessarily. If ten experienced coaches had been faced with the same decision, five would have probably gone each way.

But this is not the end of the story. As soon as the lifter completed his warm-up, he was directed by his coach to take still another warm-up, this time with 10 kg. less than his opening weight. That struck me as excessive, both in terms of the weight being lifted and the short rest between warm-up attempts. I could tell by the lifter's expression that he agreed with me. The coach apparently caught his athlete's expression and motioned for the lifter to go ahead. As the lifter approached the warm-up bar, he was called to the competition platform for his second attempt, which gave him 1.5 minutes to get out to the platform and begin his world record attempt. Upon hearing the announcement, the lifter paused and looked up at the coach, obviously expecting the coach to rescind his previous order. Seemingly oblivious to what had transpired, the coach reiterated his order to take the warm-up. Now he and the lifter began to exchange some words of disagreement (all of this while the clock was running on the lifter). Finally, with about a minute left on the clock, the disputed warm-up was taken. The lifter then hurried out to the bar to make his attempt, which was unsuccessful due to an elbow touch.

The lifter was given a three minute rest, as he was to follow himself on the competition platform. I thought that with three minutes he might make his third attempt. But the coach was apparently not finished yet, He made the lifter go backstage and take still another warm-up. (If he was not warm after shouldering a World Record, I do not know how his coach came to believe that a warm-up with a lighter weight would make him so.) By the time the lifter got back to the warm-up area, performed his warm-up, and returned to the platform once again, he was clearly getting tired, and he missed again. Would this athlete have made a record if he had not been required to take those extra warm-ups? We will never know for sure. World records, after all, are as rare as they are wonderful. But surely those extra warm-ups did not help the lifter's chances for success.

What are some guidelines for warming up? The first principle is that the warm-up pattern should at least resemble the lifter's habits in training, except that while the lifter may vary reps in training, competition warm-ups should almost always be singles (except for the very early sets in the warm-up series). The athlete should experiment in training with different numbers of warm-up attempts and with differing rest periods between warm-up attempts. One of the fastest and surest ways to create muscular fatigue is to take too little rest between warm-up attempts. On the other hand, speeding up the warm-up tempo can hasten the warm-up process. The lifter must find his or her proper balance.

Most lifters will probably find that five to seven sets with weights 50% of maximum and above will be about right and that two to four minutes between attempts is a comfortable pace. The last warm-up should generally be 5% to 10% below the opener (toward the lower end in the snatch and the higher end in the C&J). Older lifters (i.e., 35 and above) and those with sore joints may require more warm-up attempts with lighter weights (up to 75%) before going on. Novices and those who are modifying their technique in some way may find that a longer warm-up, one with more sets and more gradual increases than the norm, is helpful. Even taking as much as the opener for the final warm-up, particularly in the snatch, may be helpful. This approach may also help athletes who have high anxiety levels when they prepare for their opening attempts. (This strategy can work against the lifter if he or she misses when warming up and then worries about the miss; other lifters feel more comfortable whether they miss or succeed in the warm-up room because they have at least "felt" their opening attempt there.) Those with well established technique and a tendency to burn up a lot of energy in the warm-up room should experiment with a shorter warm-up.

Warm Up Physically, But Let the Emotions Warm Up More Slowly

The importance of warming up physically without getting too emotional was brought home to me by a young boxer who trained at Lost Battalion Hall when I was a teenager. Although he and I rarely spoke, we developed a deep and mutual respect for one another on the basis of one simple shared value: total dedication to our sports. We both came early to practice and left late. We both relished the drills that no one else seemed to want to do. When a blizzard kept everyone else away from the gym or a summer heat wave made it sensible to shorten

the training session, we were there doing every last exercise. He became the best conditioned boxer in the entire program, and my lifting steadily improved. Slowly and methodically, we were becoming hot young prospects in our given sports. Then one day he stopped coming to the gym.

When I asked the boxing coach what had happened I received both a shock and a valuable lesson. The boxing coach told me that my young boxing friend had a serious weakness; he could not go the distance (i.e., fight effectively for the full duration of the boxing match). After two or three terrific rounds, he would become utterly exhausted and fall victim to the onslaughts of his opponents. He had became so distraught and frustrated over this problem that he quit the sport. I was astonished at this revelation. I even argued with the coach. How could my friend tire so quickly? He was in such fine condition. Yes, the coach said rather sadly, this young athlete was very well conditioned, but nonetheless, he tired quickly in competition. Why? He was unable to control his emotions. He became so excited early in the fight that all of his nervous energy was quickly depleted. Even the vast amount of conditioning work that he performed could not prepare him for that kind of stress. Apparently, training does not expand the capacity of the adrenal gland (or at least not to the same extent that it improves other capabilities).

I reflected on what the boxing coach had told me for days. Becoming fatigued during a competition (which consisted of three lifts in those days) was something that I sometimes experienced and had been unable to explain. In terms of work done, my workouts were generally more arduous than a competition, yet I rarely felt anything near the level of fatigue in the gym that I did after some competitions. What was worse, I sometimes felt exhausted going into a competition, even thought I had reduced my training prior to the competition in an effort to conserve energy. Obviously, the real need is to conserve nervous energy before and during the competition, Since there is some relationship between the expenditure of nervous energy and the amount of physical work that is done, it is useful to avoid warming up too much. However, an even more important method of conserving energy is emotional control, a subject that has already been discussed at length in Chapter 7.

Timing Warm-ups

Timing warm-ups is one of the competition coach's most important functions, yet it is one of the functions most frequently botched (and I have seen some of the top coaches in the world do it). In planning warm-up timing, it is best to write down all of the lifter's planned warm-ups, including stretching, free-hand exercises, meditation. etc.. Then the coach should back into the warm-up attempts. That is, he or she should determine the lifter's probable starting attempt, and then ask the athlete how many attempts on the platform he or she wants to elapse between the last warm-up and the opening attempt. (Most experienced lifters know this.) Some lifters may like as little as one attempt. (This is rare with today's one minute rule, because in most situations lifters only have to make their competition attempts; until a few years ago, two minutes were permitted.) Others prefer several attempts to catch their breath and get mentally prepared. Most lifters prefer two to four attempts (since the average time span between competition attempts is 1 to 1.25 minutes, two to four attempts equals two to five minutes). A lifter who "wraps" the knees or uses other protective/supportive equipment—tape, wrist wraps, etc.—will tend to be at the longer end of the range.

The advantage of linking warm-up attempts to the attempts taken on the competition platform is that if the competition attempts take more or less time than was expected, the lifter's warm-up timing is adjusted almost automatically.

Attempts can be converted to minutes, if necessary. As was indicated earlier, each attempt on the platform generally averages approximately 1 to 1.25 minutes (plus or minus fifteen seconds). The actual times vary from competition to competition and at the different times during the same competition based on such factors as the experience of each athlete; the pace set by the announcer, the leaders and the expediters; the distance from the warm-up room to the platform; and how tightly packed the competitors are in terms of proximity of weight attempts. As the competition unfolds, you can adjust the 1 to 1.25 minute estimate based on the actual progression of events.

It must be remembered that the timing of warm-ups can also be dependent on the availability of equipment. If there are several lifters on each warm-up platform, then each athlete may have to wait longer between warm-ups than is preferred (unless it can be arranged for that lifter to work on two warm-up platforms at once). If this is the case, adjustments may need to be made in warm-up timing.

Some coaches try to time warm-up attempts by counting the number of lifters taking any number of attempts before their lifter or weight then on the bar (keeping warm-up weights at the level of the competition bar). Unfortunately, knowing the number of lifters starting before your athlete is next to worthless, since each competitor can have from one to three attempts (the latter if he or she misses twice with a weight that is lower than the weight your lifter is attempting and elects to take a third attempt with that weight). Using a one minute average time per attempt and twenty competitors (none of whom jump their starts up),

there can be from twenty to sixty minutes before your lifter starts. Tracking the weight on the bar can be even more misleading than counting the number of lifters. The bar can take thirty minutes to move up 5 kg., or a few minutes to jump 25 kg., depending on how many attempts are being made with a given weight.

Only counting attempts offers anything of real value in terms of timing warm-ups (although even that exposes your athlete to fairly wide fluctuations in timing). Counting attempts accurately is a simpler process than many people think. Nevertheless, it does take some skill and practice to master. In weightlifting competition, each lifter is permitted to take three attempts in each lift. The competition begins with the bar loaded to the lowest weight called for by a lifter and then is raised to the next weight that has been called for once all of the lifters who wish to attempt a given weight have had an opportunity to attempt that weight.

Except in rare instances, even high level lifters have no more than a 12.5 kg. difference between their first and last (third) attempts. Male athletes in lighter weight classes and women rarely have more than a 10 kg. difference between their opening attempts and their third attempts because 10 kg. is as large an increase in weight (on percentage basis) as 12.5 kg. is for high level male athletes in the heavier weight classes. Consequently, it can be assumed that any lifter starting at least 12.5 kg. lower that your athlete will complete all three attempts before your athlete begins. (Remember that few lifters plan to jump 12.5 kg., and even fewer make the first two attempts that will enable the plan to be carried out.) Similarly, anyone opening with more than 7.5 kg. less than your athlete can be expected to take two attempts before your athlete starts. Anyone who starts 2.5 kg. to 5 kg. lower t will surely take at least one attempt before your athlete (unless they change their starting attempt, which some coaches have a habit of doing). When two lifters start with the same weight, the attempt number, the magnitude of the lifter's increase in weight from his or her prior attempt, and the "lot" numbers drawn before the competition determine the lifting order. Getting an initial count in the relatively conservative manner described above makes sense because it is better to be warmed-up a little early than not to finish a planned series of warm-ups. It is far easier and far safer to extend the warm-up sequence than to shorten it.

When you formulate your count of the minimum number of attempts your athlete is likely to have, you should also make an estimate of the maximum number of attempts. This is done by assuming that every lifter who starts before yours (except one who starts with the same weight) will take all three of his or her attempts before your lifter begins. Knowing the range from maximum to minimum (assuming that no one jumps or withdraws from the competition) lets you begin to focus in on what is likely to happen while still being mindful of what could happen.

In the United States, it is customary for the announcer to have one index card on his or her table representing each competitor. Each competitor's card will display that lifter's lot number and body weight and will have a place to show all of the attempts that the lifter makes. These cards are generally arranged in vertical rows, by the order of the competition (i.e., the lifter going next is at the bottom of the row and the lifter with the highest announced attempt is at the top of the row). When there are too many competitors to display in one row of cards, the cards may be sub-divided into two or three vertical rows. Coaches frequently check the cards as the competition progresses, modifying their count of attempts by estimating the number of attempts each lifter whose card precedes their lifter's will take before their lifter is called to the platform. For lifters who have not yet started, you can use the system described above. For lifters who have taken one or two attempts, you need to make an adjustment in your counting methodology.

Generally, any athlete can be expected to jump no more than 5 kg. between the second and third attempt in the snatch and no more than 7.5 kg. in the C&J. Therefore, any athlete taking a second attempt with jumps less than 5 kg. in the snatch or 7.5 kg. in the C&J can be expected to complete his or her third attempt before your athlete goes. Naturally, anyone taking a third attempt with any poundage below your athlete's will go first.

In international and national competitions, there may be an "attempt board" in addition to, or in lieu of, the index cards. This board lists each lifter's name, body weight and attempts called for and taken. During the course of the competition, a person stationed at the board notes changes in attempts and the outcome of attempts (generally putting a line through missed attempts and checking successful ones). These boards can be used to count attempts, but the coach must scan the entire board, mentally noting which lifters have completed which attempts.

When athletes are taking the same poundage, three rules establish the order of attempts. In order of priority, these rules areas follows.

1. Attempt Number: Those athletes taking first attempts go before those taking second attempts. Similarly, athletes taking second attempts precede athletes taking third attempts. If two athletes are taking the same weight on the same attempt, then the next rule applies.

2. Distance From Last Attempt: The athlete who makes the biggest jump from his prior attempt goes first. For example, let us assume that two lifters, A and B, are taking a second attempt with 100 kg.. Lifter A started with 92.5 kg. and lifter B started with 95 kg.. In such a case, lifter A will go first. If two lifters are attempting the same weight on the same attempt number and both lifters took the same weight on their previous attempt, the final rule applies.

3. Lot Numbers: The lifter with the lower lot number precedes the lifter with the higher lot number.

During the competition, the range between your count of the maximum and minimum number of attempts will tend to narrow in terms of absolute numbers. Nevertheless, timing becomes more critical as your athlete's turn approaches. For example, you might check the count again at 24, 18, 13, 9, 6, 4 and 2 attempts. At each checkpoint, try to establish a new maximum and minimum range as well as a "best guess." Have a warm-up strategy planned for either extreme of the range as well for your best guess. It has been said that success is 1% inspiration and 99% perspiration. In counting warm-up attempts, this ratio certainly applies. Knowledge of how to count attempts accounts for a small (though critical) part of the coach's success. The rest is attributable to the coach's willingness to get up from his or her chair and count.

When the athlete has warmed up too soon or is waiting between first and second or second and third attempts, a good rule of thumb to follow is that no more than five minutes should pass between attempts at the bar. If a lifter lacks confidence or looks too relaxed, an extra warm-up with the last planned warm-up weight may make sense. If everything is proceeding according to plan, something in the area of 80% to 85% of maximum is probably a good bet (anything lighter may have too different a "feel" for the lifter to adapt to when going to the platform, and anything heavier may cause fatigue or a miss and undermine a lifter's confidence). If a long (ten minutes or more) delay is anticipated, alternating 60% to 75% weights with 80% to 85% (or higher) weights can extend the warm-up period without creating undue fatigue. An experienced, confident and well coordinated athlete may be able to use weights that are 50% of maximum or less, but this is the unusual athlete, typically one who has used this method before.

Should your lifter be called before he or she is ready, there are three alternative responses: squeeze in an extra warm-up as your lifter is called; forget the last warm-up; or jump the lifter's attempt upward to get more time. Each approach has advantages and disadvantages.

Taking the extra warm-up can be a key to the necessary preparation for some lifters. On the other hand, taking an attempt and then moving to the competition platform can leave an athlete fatigued enough to lessen his or her chances of success on the platform. In addition, if the athlete is nervous about the situation, he or she may miss the last warm-up, leaving him or her both tired and worried. A general rule of thumb is that if you are caught relatively early in the warm-up process (when the lifter would normally have taken at least two or more additional warm-ups) and the lifter will have at least ninety seconds after the last warm-up to take his or her first attempt, it is a good idea to risk the extra warm-up attempt, particularly in the snatch.

Forgoing the last warm-up assures that the lifter will be fresh, though possibly quite worried and lacking some of the coordination necessary to lift maximum poundages. Overall, however, this second approach is better if the lifter would not be able to recover significantly from the warm-up attempt or is so close to an optimal warm-up that forgoing the last attempt will not cause a major problem.

Jumping the opener avoids the hazards of the first two approaches (unless jumping still means the lifter is next and the loaders are very fast in changing the poundage), but it can be devastating if the athlete is either not in good enough condition to raise the start or if he or she experiences excessive apprehension because the start has been raised. Naturally, the best solution to this dilemma is to make sure that your minimum attempt estimate is both accurate and as current as possible. One sign of a developing problem is when a number of athletes with higher lot numbers have listed openers 2.5 kg. to 5 kg. below that of your athlete. Since jumping openers is fairly common, attempts can suddenly evaporate in this kind of situation (just as they can easily multiply with unexpected misses).

Planning the Jumps Between Attempts

A general philosophy with respect to the size of the jumps that your lifter will take on the platform should be formulated before the competition begins. Large jumps (i.e., 7.5 kg. or more between the first and second attempts and 5 kg. or more between the second and third attempts) can work well when you have an athlete in uncertain condition, one who is not confident about opening attempts, one for whom 5 kg. to 7.5 kg. does not represent a large percentage increase in weight or one who is not lifting in close competition. Small jumps may work well for the consistent performer, particularly in close competition. Naturally, the decision here will affect the choice of a starting attempt. Special consideration needs to be given to beginners, especially in the lighter weight classes. For a lifter whose best C&J is 50 kg., a 2.5 kg. jump represents 10% of the lifter's best. For a lifter whose best is 250 kg., however, it represents only 1%. For most lifters, a jump of 10% to 15% or more is very difficult to handle. For the lifter at 50 kg., that is 5 kg. to 7.5 kg., but for the lifter at 250 kg., it is 25 kg. to 37.5 kg.. (This may seem like an obvious point, but one that is apparently not appreciated by at least some athletes and coaches.)

Selecting Poundages

The choice of a starting poundage also depends on factors other than the amount the lifter plans to jump up after the first attempt. What is the lifter trying to accomplish? How important is making a total? (To some, the cardinal rule in weightlifting competition is to make a total; to others, missing an opener or the weight they really want to make, perhaps a third attempt, is equally frustrating.) Another consideration is the purpose of the competition. On the day of a single tryout, making a total of any kind may be critical. The ability of the lifter relative to his competitors influences the decisionmaking process here as well. The dark horse has nothing to lose by taking risks, but the favorite may see no point in jeopardizing a victory.

How an individual approaches risk is crucial here. Some people prefer to go for broke on a second or even first attempt (though that is rarely an effective strategy). For these individuals, success means making the poundage they came to lift. Success or failure with lesser weights means little to them. However, even those who are willing to go for an all out attempt would be wise to consider the fact that a well done opener or second attempt is likely to contribute to success on a third attempt. Those who are erratic may reason that two or three attempts at a poundage increase their chances of making it. To others, building on success and ending with a good total, if not a personal record, are more satisfying. There is a wide latitude for choice here. The choices should be made well before the competition, before emotions run too strong, but should be adjusted as events unfold. For instance, if the plan for a personal record is obviously not going to work, just taking the place or competing well under the conditions that do exist that day will often offer some solace and very possibly a valuable experience.

Your evaluation (and the athlete's) of how his or her warm-ups and attempts on the platform and of what the competition is doing in the C&J (and in the snatch if there is a medal involved) should determine poundages. It generally makes sense to put in an opener at the lowest possible level (i.e., the worst case scenario). The lifter can always jump to the original planned opener if all is going well in the warming up process. Dropping the opener is far more difficult. In fact, it is impossible if the warm-ups have not been timed to enable the lifter to change his or her opener downward. (If another lifter has taken a second attempt with the weight your lifter would like have the bar reduced to or a lifter with a higher lot number has taken a first attempt, your lifter will not be permitted to attempt that weight.)

An athlete who is not a great competitor (i.e., one who is not positively influenced by the pressure to win or by knowing what a competitor is doing) or one who has complete faith in his coach may choose to give some input into poundages while leaving the final decision to the coach. Athletes who like to know what is going on and be more active in making choices may rely on the coach for input while making the final decisions themselves. A person's need for control is crucial here; ignoring this need can lead to a motivational disaster.

The coach can often bring a cooler head (though the opposite can certainly be true), a perspective on the overall strategy and the benefit of being an external observer of technique, speed, etc.. However, in the final analysis it is the lifter's life, and the coach must respect the individual's right to make decisions about his or her own career, regardless of the consequences. (No value gained by coercion is a true value.)

Throughout the competition the coach must help the lifter with proper cues and protection from the environment, whether its threats are well meaning meddlers, heat, cold, other competitors or anything else. The performance of a maximum lift is a magic moment, one that needs all of the nurturing a coach can supply.

Using Tactics to Win

Assuming the strategy prepared for the competition includes an effort to place as high as possible or to win the competition, proper tactics will aid considerably in that endeavor. The subject of tactics merits its own book. However, I will cover a few basics here. The first key to proper tactics is knowing what is needed to win. This may sound like a simple point, and in one sense it is. In some competitions, all you need to know is what an athlete's competitors have totaled and what they weighed. (When two lifters lift the same poundage, the lighter lifter places higher.) Nevertheless, even in major competitions, mistakes are made in this regard. In all instances it is necessary to know at least this much, and in some instances knowing only this will be enough.

The second key to tactics is evaluating what your athlete can reasonably be expected to lift as compared what his or her competitors can lift. Here the tactician needs to know his or her lifter as well as the competition. This is an art in itself. Knowing an opponent's best lifts, success ratios, etc. helps. Sizing up how he or she looks on the day is even more important. In my experience, coaches tend to significantly overestimate their abilities in this area. An instance at a recent National Championship amply demonstrates this point. A friend of mine, who happened to be a highly ranked national lifter some years ago, approached one of the United States' top ranked coaches, a man who is better known for his lack of coaching modesty

than his success with athletes. My friend proposed a simple wager. He said, "Mr. X, you are supposed to know a lot about lifting. Whenever an athlete approaches the bar, you indicate whether you believe that he will make the lift or not. I will simply wager the opposite." Mr. X readily agreed. At the end of a dozen or so bets of this kind, my friend was well ahead, and they called it a day. This experience appeared to shake Mr. X up a little, but not for long. He was soon heard to be claiming coaching omniscience once again (though not within earshot of my friend).

To use the information gathered in the two steps described above, you must accomplish two things: make the opponent attempt as much as possible in order to beat your athlete, ideally more than he or she really needs, , and make sure that your lifter attempts only what is needed to defeat his or her opponents.

As I mentioned earlier, an entire book could be written on the subject of tactics, and this book is long enough already. However, one anecdote illustrates the importance of good tactics so well that I feel compelled to tell it. I was coaching a training partner of mine at the National Championship one year. This two-time National Champion and former world record holder had an excellent chance to win another National Championship that day. His main competition was a lifter who had had an even more outstanding career, but who was not in his best shape on that day. These athletes were tied after the snatch, with my friend holding the lead on the basis of lighter body weight. My friend started first in the C&J with a relatively conservative 190 kg. (his official best was 12.5 kg. more). He cleaned this weight easily, jerked it to arm's length, and then lost it as he loosened up while recovering from the split (a most uncharacteristic thing for this particular lifter to do). He repeated with that weight on his second attempt and made it quite easily. His competitor made the same weight on his second attempt, though he looked shaky. My friend still held the lead on lighter body weight.

At this point, my friend asked for my counsel regarding his third attempt. I encouraged him to take 197.5 kg. or even 200 kg.. Suddenly the official coach of my friend's team, a coach with a considerable international reputation, appeared for the first time that day. (My friend and I represented different clubs even though we often trained together.) After listening to my advice, this coach recommended that my friend take no more than 195 kg.. When I asked him why he was suggesting 195 kg., he said he did not think my friend could make more than that.

I pointed out that what mattered was not what our charge made, but, rather, what he forced the other lifter to try (the more the better). I reasoned that if our lifter attempted and made 195 kg. on his third attempt, the other lifter would have to try

197.5 kg.. If our man missed 195 kg., the other lifter would still need only the same 195 kg.. In contrast, if our lifter merely tried 197.5 kg., whether he made it or not, the other lifter would have to take at least 197.5 kg.. Obviously, there is a limit to the strategy I was proposing; the attempt had to be believable. If our lifter called for 210 kg., the opposition would realize that our lifter was trying to "pull him along" and would probably not take the bait. However, our lifter's opponent could not be certain that such a strategy was at work if our lifter attempted 197.5 kg. or even 200 kg.. This was because of our lifter's previous best (202.5 kg. done the previous year) and his apparent fitness that day (190 kg. had not been unduly difficult). The official coach, apparently failing to comprehend my argument, replied: "I do not think he can make 197.5 kg. or 200 kg., so let's take 195 kg. and play it safe." He then essentially ordered my friend to take 195 kg.. He made a good attempt at that weight but failed. The opponent, thrilled at this turn of events, took 195 kg. and managed a hard fought and shaky success. Could he have made 197.5 kg. or 200 kg. ? We will never know because he did not need to try. A failure in strategy made his task easier than it should have been.

Implementing the tactical guidelines described above takes considerable skill if your athlete has only one or two competitors. When the number of competitors reaches three or four, true tactical virtuosity is required in order to make the best of each attempt. Beyond four opponents (who are close to your athlete's ability), it is almost impossible to cover all bets. Therefore, it makes sense to go back to fundamentals in such instances; squeeze every pound out of your athlete, and hope for the best.

When All Else Fails, the True Champion Prevails

No matter how well the lifter prepares for a competition, the unforeseen can occur. Over the years, I have seen competitions in which the heat was unbearable, or the cold had people shivering, an athlete came up with a minor but painful injury or illness, the officiating was poor or one of a hundred other things went wrong. Nevertheless, there are always some athletes who perform brilliantly when they are truly challenged. When adversity strikes, the athlete's character is truly tested. It is at this time that the true champion emerges. The true champion has learned to convert anger, stress and frustration into an overwhelming desire to overcome the bar and the competition.

As my father (a hero of World War II and better under pressure than anyone I have ever known) told me many years ago, in every disaster, those who lose their heads will lose the day. On the other hand, there will be those who face the worst bravely, who meet the most colossal threats with a cool head and are therefore in the best possible position to overcome them. These are the true champions and the true heroes.

Post-Competition

This subject is, in a very broad way, is covered by the rest of the book. The training and preparation for every competition should be partly a result of post-competition coaching and partly of a plan for future progress. However, in a narrower sense, post-competition coaching occurs when the coach who assisted the lifter at a given meet helps that lifter to make the competition a rich learning experience. Unfortunately, post-competition coaching is probably the most neglected, though perhaps the most crucial, aspect of competition coaching. This is especially true in situations where the competition coach does not work with the lifter year round.

Unless a lifter intends to retire after the competition, , that lifter needs to derive two things from competing:: motivation and a learning experience. Missing out on either of these benefits is the only true failure that can occur in a competition. In short, competitions that have led to desired results should be celebrated (psychologically and emotionally, not with an all night session of debilitating carousing). If there is no joy in success, there is no point in working for it. Joy is the greatest reward of a successful performance, and the drive to experience such joy again is one of the most powerful motivators. The athlete should also learn from success by identifying what went well and why. Even with success, there may have been certain aspects of the performance or preparation that might have been improved upon or could lead to future problems. Identify these areas and work to correct them. If the performance was essentially perfect, the goal should be to learn how to replicate it.

When a competition has not been as successful as planned, a great deal can be learned. Both the lifter and the coach need to focus on learning as much as they can, even if it is only that they have more to learn. Great motivation can come out of bad experiences as well as good ones. Pete George, one of our greatest lifters and a strong advocate of proper mental attitude, made this point better than anyone I know. In a series of articles in Strength and Health several decades ago, he mentioned four possible responses to not doing as well as one had expected in a particular competition: laugh it off; make excuses; get depressed and angry; or plan for future success, as your disappointing performance has just set the stage for a great comeback.

Obviously, the first three responses are not productive or pleasant. The fourth response is incredibly productive if it used properly. In fact, it is key to success in weightlifting and in life. Any experience you have can be interpreted and responded to in a number of ways. It is up to you to choose only the productive response, to rise to the challenge and return the better for having faced it.

Summary

Coaching for success in weightlifting competition is a skill like any other. It takes knowledge and practice to master the skill. It is my belief that any athlete can learn to perform up to his or her maximum potential in any competition. Great competitors are rarely, if ever, born that. They are made. It may take longer for some to learn how to achieve their potentials in competition, but everyone can learn. What it takes is the will to succeed and the willingness to pursue success in a rational way. It is my hope that all of you determine to undertake the effort and to do it rationally, for that is the most important key to your success.

Having taken the reader through the major elements of training and preparation for weightlifting competition, it is now time to address the issue of how considerations of age and gender can affect the training of weightlifters. That will be the subject of the next chapter.

The only overall World Champion produced by the US in the 1990s, Robin Byrd-Goad celebrates her victory at the 1994 Worlds Championships.

CHAPTER 9

Special Training Considerations For Women, Masters And Young Athletes

It should be evident to the reader by now that the underlying theme throughout this book has been that athletes need to be treated as individuals. There are a great many principles that apply to all weightlifters, but the application of those principles must be carefully individualized if each lifter is to achieve his or her true potential. If this focus on the individual athlete is maintained, any differences in the needs of athletes of different ages or sexes will be addressed almost automatically. If this focus on the individual athlete is not maintained, generalization with respect to the influences of age or sex on athletes will do very little to enable the coach to adjust the training of particular athletes in any useful way.

For example, it has been noted that the "average" woman has wider hips in proportion to the rest of her body than the average man. This difference causes the femur (thighbone) to angle in more from the hip to the knee joint in the average woman than in the average man. If this inward slant goes beyond a certain point, it is thought by some researchers to make the knee joint less stable. While this anatomical difference between men and women may be of some interest to the coach, it is of little value in the real world. This is because coaches coach not the average man or woman (there is no such person) but, rather, individual athletes who happen to be men or women. Among those individual athletes, there may be some women who have a femur angle that is sufficient to destabilize the knee. But there are men who have this same anatomical configuration as well and many women who do not. What is of real interest to the thinking coach is the contention that an excessive inward slant of the femur toward the knee joint may destabilize the knee. This possibility will alert the coach to watch for such a characteristic in all athletes, male or female, and to pay particular attention to the issue of knee

stability in any athlete, male or female, who exhibits this characteristic.

In this chapter, we will examine same of the special concerns and needs of women, younger athletes and more mature athletes. But it should be remembered throughout that we are dealing with statistical tendencies, not immutable laws of nature. As a result, the coach needs to be aware of the issues and how to deal with them, but he or she should not necessarily expect them in all cases. We will begin our discussion with an examination of women in weightlifting, then proceed to the special needs of children and conclude with an examination of the needs of more mature athletes.

Women And Weightlifting—A Great Match

Among the trillions of cells in the human body, only those of the reproductive organs result in physical differences between men and women. There are no significant sex related differences in any of the other organs of the body. For example, a pathologist cannot look at the heart or brain of a human and determine the sex of the body. There are no differences in structure, and any differences is size are related to body mass of the person (i.e.., the size of the heart of a man and woman with the same overall body mass is approximately the same).

The reproductive organs indirectly influence the appearance of males and females by producing certain hormones (testosterone in males and estrogen in females) which are responsible for the development and maintenance of "secondary sex characteristics." These characteristics include, but are not limited to, muscular and skeletal development and the arrangement and consistency of hair on the body. In terms of skeletal differences, women tend to have shorter, smaller and less dense bones, narrower shoulders, proportionally wider hips and "true" pelvis space (the space inside the pelvis) and smaller joints (except for the knee joint). Women also tend to have more pelvic tilt than men, with the consequence of a greater incidence of lordosis (an excessive curvature of the lower back) and resultant backache. The average woman has a slightly lower center of gravity than the average man, but that is more a function of height and body type than sex.

Women also have less muscle mass, more subcutaneous body fat (22% to 26% in young adult women and 13% to 16% in males of the same age), with extra deposits in the breasts, hips and buttocks. However, differences in the percentage body fat tend to be smaller among men and women in the same sport than in the general population.

Men and women also differ in their rate of maturation. Women tend to become physically mature earlier than men. For instance, women typically reach their full height and weight (an average of approximately 5'4 1/2" and 123 lb.) at age eighteen. Men continue to grow for about another two years, growing approximately 5" taller and weighing approximately 35 lb. more.

Women's bodies generally consume less energy. Part of this is due to the average differences in body size (larger bodies require more energy). Part of the difference in energy consumption arises because women generally have slightly lower basal metabolism rates than men (37 kilocalories per square meter of body surface per hour for women and 40 kilocalories for men). But this difference is probably due, at least in part, to the smaller lean body mass of most women relative to men of the same size (the metabolism rate increases in proportion to lean, or muscular, body mass).

Note that all of these differences exist between the average man and woman, not between a particular man and woman. Although women are generally shorter than men, particular man may be shorter than a particular woman. He may also have a greater percentage of body fat and be weaker than a particular women. That is why information regarding the average characteristics of a population is interesting but not especially enlightening to people who have to deal with individual athletes (which is virtually all of us).

Strength Differences Between Men and Women

Not surprisingly, research on strength has revealed that males are stronger, on average, than females. A similar conclusion has generally been reached by anyone who has observed men and women in everyday life. However, what is far more interesting is the equalities in strength that exist between men and women when comparisons are made with certain qualifications.

For example, there is no difference in the nature of muscle fibers. (Since muscle fibers grow with use, men typically have larger fibers because they have a greater tendency to use those muscle fibers.) There is also no difference in the distribution of muscle fiber types (i.e., fast versus slow twitch). Not surprisingly, given the similarity in muscle structure between the sexes, strength differences between men and women decrease when appropriate adjustments are made in the data being compared. For example, when differences in body mass are considered, the difference in strength levels diminishes considerably (i.e., the average body mass of men is greater than that of women, but strength differences between men and women with the same body mass is relatively small). Moreover, when lean (muscular) body mass is considered, the differences grow even smaller. (Women tend to have a higher percentage of fat in their bodies than men, so when straight body mass is compared, we are comparing athletes with different muscle masses.) In fact, when the strength of muscle with identical cross-sections is compared, the differences between men and women virtually disappear.

The most important implications of recent research are that the potential for women to hypertrophy and to gain strength with training appears to be similar to that of men. Differences in the apparent level of training response between men and women suggested by some early studies have now been attributed by some scientists to the crudeness of the experimental methods employed. For example, measuring the girth of limbs did not take into account a reduction in subcutaneous fat accompanied by a gain in muscle mass that may have produced no change in limb girth although hypertrophy occurred. The average woman may indeed begin at a lower level of strength and muscle mass than the average man (due in part to hormonal differences between men and women, e.g., in testosterone levels), but her potential for proportional improvement in strength is probably quite similar (i.e., the potential is very great) .

The implications of all of this are that, over time, women's performances in weightlifting are likely to grow much closer to those of the men than they are today. The women weightlifters of today have an opportunity to build on what the pioneers in women's lifting have already accomplished. What a wonderful opportunity for women embarking on their weightlifting careers today!

Other Physiological Differences Between Men and Women

Women undergo cyclic changes in their bodies as a result of their menstrual cycles. Premenstrual changes can include an increase in body mass and changes in such indicators as blood glucose, body temperature (an increase after ovulation, higher than average level during the luteal phase with a fall to normal levels at menses), heart rate (which increases during any period of temperature elevation) and breast size. While these changes occur to at least some degree in most women, the extent to which they occur varies considerably from woman to woman.

Approximately 50% of women regularly experience some degree of discomfort during menses and as many as 10% suffer incapacity for one to three days. The most discomfort/disability tends to occur between the ages of twenty and twenty-four, with symptoms tending to increase after the onset of menstruation and to decline gradually in the mid-twenties and thereafter. Do these monthly cycles in women's bodies cause performance changes? Most of the scientific literature suggests that these changes do not affect such physiological markers as maximum oxygen uptake or heart rate during exercise. Many women experience a greater degree of perceived effort in achieving the same performance during menses. However, in studies of elite athletes, as many women reported improved performance during menses as reported diminished performance. This may be due to higher than average motivation in these athletes or to the fact that women who have more moderate reactions to menstrual cycle are more likely to take up sport. It may also be due to a positive effect of exercise on PMS (a condition which has been reported anecdotally but which has not yet established by research).

Severe dysmenorrhea (painful menses can affect performance negatively. Primary dysmenorrhea (pain without macroscopically identifiable pelvic pathology) can often be treated very effectively with prostaglandin inhibitors (e.g., aspirin or ibuprofen). These drugs counter the elevated levels of prostaglandins which are thought to contribute to primary dysmenorrhea (by causing intense contractions of the uterus that lead to a diminished blood supply and resulting discomfort). The most successful treatment for PMS is an oral contraceptive (which contains progesterone and estrogen). However, many women find oral contraceptives unacceptable, because of the temporary infertility that they cause and/or because of their side effects. It has been argued that for women who need to control their menstrual cycle for a specific event, progesterone withdrawal (to bring on menstruation well before a major competition) is superior to delaying the cycle through the use of estrogen and progesterone, because a high concentration of these hormones can remain in the body during the event and possibly lead to fluid retention. Moreover, such hormonal manipulation should be limited only to important events because of the general inadvisability of tampering with natural body cycles.

There is little in the scientific literature to suggest that vigorous activity has negative physiological effects (although it may be extremely uncomfortable) during menstruation. For certain women, intense or prolonged training sessions may not be a good idea during this time in their menstrual cycles. Nevertheless, regardless of the results of scientific studies and surveys, the principle that was identified at the outset of this chapter needs to be followed. Individual physical, mental and emotional responses to menstruation differ from woman to woman. Therefore, the training and competitive efforts of each individual athlete must take into account her reactions. Some women may need to cycle their training in order to take into account their feelings during various phases of the menstrual cycle.

In a recent IWF sponsored seminar, a Chinese coach, Wenyuan Cao, indicated that while some of the women on the Chinese weightlifting team (which currently dominates women's weightlifting) train right through the menstrual cycle, others do indeed follow a training cycle that includes a significantly reduced training load during the first two days of menstruation. In addition to the intensity of the workout being lower and the load smaller, certain exercises, such as pulls from the floor and squats, are avoided. For the next two days the load is gradually increased, so that by the fifth day after the onset of menstruation, normal training has been resumed. Women who feel a diminished capacity to train during their menstrual cycle should make a point of emphasizing this to their coaches (whether those coaches are male or female).

Although some sport specialists have argued that women might damage their reproductive organs with the strain of athletic effort, there is no evidence of such a phenomenon (at least as long as the natural pelvic support offered by the body has not been seriously damaged by childbirth or some other phenomenon. Even in those cases, reports of any difficulty are minimal, if not non-existent, but a problem is at least possible. Actual experience has shown that the reproductive organs of males are more prone to sports injury than those of females.

The Relationships Between Training and Amenorrhea

Amenorrhea is the absence or suppression of menstruation. Training stress, weight loss and low body fat have been associated with amenorrhea, but these relationships are not consistent across all studies. To the extent that relationships do exist, they may reflect the effect of strenuous training on hormonal levels. For instance, the suppression of gonadotropin and female sex hormones has been linked to strenuous training.

It has been noted that when amenorrheic athletes reduce their levels of training and restore a normal caloric intake, menses typically resume within two months. It should be understood that the relationship between amenorrhea and athletic participation has been found in activities in which caloric expenditure is very high. Weightlifting training does not generally fit this profile (unless an athlete is training very hard for several hours a day). Even under such training conditions, the likelihood of amenorrhea occurring is probably small, unless the athlete is seriously restricting her diet as well as training very hard. Poor diet is also a known factor in amenorrhea (e.g., vegetarian athletes and those who severely restrict their diets are more likely to be amenorrheic than women who have a more normal diet and amenorrheic women are more likely to have zinc and iron deficiencies than women with normal diets). Psychological stress may be a contributing factor as well, but there is no scientific evidence of stress causing amenorrhea at this time.

To the extent that strenuous training affects the menstrual cycles of some women, it also seems to affect the various phases unevenly. For example, many athletes with apparently normal menstrual cycles may in fact have a short luteal phase of the menstrual cycle, which results in infertility. Moreover, this condition may progress to actual amenorrhea.

Amenorrhea is not something that should be ignored. Even if serious medical causes have been ruled out, amenorrhea itself has serious effects. Osteopenia (mineral loss from bones) is perhaps the most serious effect. Reduced estrogenic activity resulting from exercise that is too strenuous can lead to a failure to maximize bone density during the maturation process. In addition, such conditions as uteritis, atrophic vaginitis and endothelial atrophy have all been associated with amenorrhea. Some athletes may welcome amenorrhea as a convenient birth control method, but it should not be assumed that amenorrhea offers absolute protection against pregnancy. Pregnancies can and do occur in women who are amenorrheic.

Therefore, whereas amenorrhea is an unlikely consequence of even the most strenuous weightlifting training, any occurrence of it should be addressed by a health professional immediately. And if that health professional believes that the athlete's training may be the cause, the training load should be reduced.

Associations between diet and amenorrhea or eumenorrhea have been shown in a number of studies. For example, 82% of amenorrheic runners were vegetarians while only a small percentage of eumenorrheics were. Amenorrheic runners had a zinc deficiency (iron?).

The Effects of Athletic Activity on Menarche

Many young athletes experience late menarche (i.e., a late onset of menstruation). This is particularly true for those athletes who engage in sports which require a large energy expenditure and/or a low level of body fat and for athletes who restrict their diets significantly. This is not surprising when you consider the effect of these same factors on some women who are already menstruating. This kind of problem does not appear to be common among young women weightlifters, but those who artificially restrict their body weight to remain in a certain weight class are at risk (still another reason why this practice should not be encouraged in young athletes). Again, if it appears that an athlete is experiencing menarche, it is appropriate to consult with a physician to determine the cause and address it accordingly.

Pregnancy and Training

While most women who are in serious training for any sport choose to avoid pregnancy until their careers are over, some women do choose to bear children at some point during their athletic careers. These women are naturally concerned about their safety and that of their fetuses during training and competition.

Most of the work that has been done in the area of studying exercise and pregnancy has been done in endurance sports, such as running. The results of those studies have not yet led to the establishment of clear guidelines for exercise during pregnancy. The American College of Obstetricians and Gynecologists has taken what is considered by many to be a very conservative (and perhaps arbitrary) position with regard to pregnancy and exercise. They recommend that any strenuous activity undertaken by pregnant women not exceed fifteen minutes in duration, that exercise in a supine position not be undertaken after the fourth month, that the maternal heart rate not exceed 140 beats per minute, that the athlete's core temperature never exceed 38° Celsius (just over 100° Fahrenheit) and that activities which involve executing the valsalva maneuver be avoided altogether.

Many medical and sport science personnel who have been seriously involved in athletics take a more individualized and less conservative approach to exercise and pregnancy. They argue that the athlete's own level of discomfort is the best guideline for training modification. It should be noted that some researchers have argued that lack of activity may be the major cause of certain complaints associated with pregnancy, such as postpartum back pain. Experts agree that any symptoms such as vaginal bleeding or hypertension should be addressed immediately. As a general guideline, they argue that there should be no restrictions on activity for at least the first three to four months of pregnancy. In the fifth and sixth months, a reduction in activity is recommended, and only light activity is recommended in the last three months. It should be noted that many women have competed at high levels not realizing that they were pregnant with no apparent damage to the fetus.

The timing of the return to activity should be guided by the same rules that apply to any return to activity after a layoff. There should be a gradual return to previous levels of training volume and intensity with intermittent "unloading" weeks to give the body a chance to adapt and recuperate as it returns to top condition. A number of women have performed at record levels within a year or less after delivery. Most women can return to competition within five to six weeks after an uncomplicated delivery. C-sections will both sideline the athlete longer and contribute to a reduction in abdominal strength (at least in the short term).

It is not a good idea to take anti-inflammatory medications such as ibuprofen or aspirin while pregnant, as these medications can have an adverse effect on the fetus. Similarly, X-rays of the abdominal area during the early stages of pregnancy present a risk to the fetus. Some writers and medical personnel discourage swimming in the later months of pregnancy on the theory that the cervix may be partially exposed to the water at this stage.

With regard to weightlifting, no research on the effects of training during pregnancy exists. However, many time national champion, national record holder and World Championship medalist Sibby Flowers has competed while pregnant and returned to record breaking levels after delivering a healthy child. While the anecdotal evidence supplied by one person hardly provides a scientific standard for recommending training during pregnancy, a brief summary of Sibby's experiences may of great interest to readers.

Sibby discovered that she was pregnant in June of 1990, shortly after she had conceived. She continued training normally for the next two months and then, worried by her physician's apprehensions, discontinued her training in August and September. She resumed training at the beginning of October and continued to train through the early part of December. During this period she avoided exercises which caused strain in the abdominal area and avoided becoming overheated. She employed full squats with gradually diminishing weights during this period (lifting approximately 100% of her C&J in the earlier part of this period and reducing to approximately 70% by the time her training ceased in mid-December). She also gradually reduced the depth of her squats as the size of her abdomen

began to interfere with her ability to descend comfortably into the full squat. Presses were employed during this period to maintain upper-body strength, and dumbbell shrugs were employed to work the upper and middle back while avoiding any contact of the bar with the abdominal area. Sibby did not train at all in January and February. By that time, her body weight had increased a total of 56 lb., from her pre-pregnancy training weight of 102 lb. to 158 lb. Much of this weight gain was attributable to an unusual amount of water retention (when she was released from the hospital three days after her delivery, Sibby had lost 30 lb.).

Sibby delivered her baby via C-Section on March 3,1991, and began a very mild program of exercise within two weeks. By the third week after the delivery she was doing calisthenics, including sit-ups. Eight weeks after giving birth she lifted in the U.S. Nationals in the 48 kg. class (her body weight class prior to pregnancy had been 44 kg.). She managed lifts of 47.5 kg. and 60 kg., taking second in the competition and qualifying for the 1991 Olympic Festival, where she would have an opportunity to qualify for the World's Championships and 44 kg.. She had a harder time making weight there than ever before but managed to do so after a great struggle. At the Festival, she placed second with lifts of 50 kg. in the snatch and 62.5 kg. in the C&J. This qualified her for the World Championships, which were held in November of that year. At the World, Sibby broke American records in the snatch and total and placed second overall, only eight months after delivering her healthy baby boy, a remarkable performance and a tribute to Sibby's tremendous courage and desire to return to the platform. By the time her weight class was changed from 44 kg. to 46 kg., Sibby had raised the American records to 65 kg. and 80 kg.. Today, with the advent of the new weight class, she has already moved her personal bests even higher, and she expects to continue to do so in the future. Pound for pound, Sibby is in all probability the world's strongest mother (not to mention one of the world's nicest).

Sibby did report an episode of pain in her knees between the Nationals and the Olympic Festival. This pain was generalized in nature and quite uncharacteristic for her. It is known that during pregnancy certain hormonal changes increase flexibility in the pelvic area and perhaps in other joints as well. Sibby reported a feeling of joint laxity following her delivery, and she feels that this may have contributed to her bout of knee pain. It is of course possible that there were other causes of her pain, such as a return to vigorous training after an extended layoff. However, the issue of joint laxity merits further investigation. In the interim, coaches should be aware of the possibility of post-pregnancy joint laxity causing a problem.

Psychological and Social Conditions that Can Influence Women Who Are Weightlifters

While the physical differences between men and women are not sufficient (at least is most cases) to justify significant differences in their training, some women find that a commitment to a sport like weightlifting feels unusual. Because many cultures have not historically valued strength and muscular development among women, some women and men are still uncomfortable with women's weightlifting.

However, the world is changing quickly and for the better. Models and actresses who are the role models for so many young women are becoming far more muscular. Today, women's bodybuilding and fitness and strength shows are often more popular than their counterparts with male competitors. Women's weightlifting, which had its international debut about a decade ago, has become popular throughout the world, with approximately forty nations now being represented at the Women's World Weightlifting Championships each year. And it appears likely, that women's weightlifting will soon be an Olympic event, even though the organizers of the Olympics are mightily resisting the inclusion of new sports (whether males or females compete in them). (Men's weightlifting has of course been part of nearly every modern Olympic Games since their inception in 1896.) In the United States, one of the pioneers in women's weightlifting and the first country to hold a Women's World Weightlifting Championship (in 1987), the National Weightlifting Championships features nearly as many competitors in the women's division as in the men's division.

The challenge of getting stronger and more powerful, of developing the technique, flexibility and courage to lift great weights overhead is obviously as powerful an urge for women as it is for men, as it should be. Therefore, no one, man or woman, should feel the least bit self-conscious about wanting to become a weightlifter. On the contrary, men and women should feel proud to have chosen such a wonderful sport, one which can offer them a lifelong challenge and a lifetime of strength fitness to meet both the extraordinary and the daily challenges of living.

A Few Closing Words on the Differences Between Men and Women

At various times it has been argued that women can train harder or less hard than men. It has been said that women are more flexible than men and that they are more emotional. And these alleged differences only scratch the surface of those that have been claimed. However, other than differences in their reproductive systems, very few of the differences that have been reported have also been proven. Even when researchers have uncovered strong tendencies, they are merely tendencies and as such are far from universal. Since coaches do not coach tendencies or averages, they would do well to concentrate on individual athletes and their needs (and not project needs on the basis of gender alone). This does not mean that coaches should ignore differences between men and women, but, rather, that the focus should be on the individual athlete and his or her needs. It may be that the average woman is more likely than the average man to turn their knees in when they squat (placing extra strain on the ligaments of the knee). But whether a man or a woman does this, the coach must intervene to teach proper technique. It may also be that women are more flexible than man and that the typical woman therefore needs less flexibility work before she begins lifting. But every beginner, whether a woman or a man, needs to be tested with respect to his or her flexibility, and wherever there are deficiencies, they need to be corrected.

The same principles apply to all the characteristics of athletes. If a particular athlete has a smaller waist or smaller joints than is normal, it may be appropriate for that athlete to spend extra times with remedial exercises to strengthen these areas. If an athlete is so weak in the upper body that he or she can pull weights overhead in the snatch or drive them overhead in the jerk but has difficulty holding them there, that athlete's upper body needs to be strengthened. Such a need may be more likely to arise in a female lifters, but some females will require little in the way of additional strengthening in that area while some males will require much work. All weightlifters, regardless of gender, require individualization in terms of technique or training methods if they are to be as successful as they can be.

Weightlifting And Children

For decades, if not centuries or even longer, mankind has feared lifting heavy weights. Folklore regarding hernias, becoming musclebound and a host of other alleged risks has kept many who were interested in weightlifting at a "safe" distance. If parents and educators fear anything more than weightlifting, it is children who lift weights. Nearly hysterical fears regarding "stunted" growth, crippling joint injuries and even psychological damage have curdled the blood of many parents and adults who are responsible for children in any way. Yet the evidence suggests that such fears are wildly exaggerated relative to the real risks. Weightlifting is a far safer sport than most people think. Moreover, its risks, appear to be significantly smaller than those of more popular children's sports (such as football, basketball, soccer and gymnastics), at least on the basis of what has been observed in the United States. (The information from Eastern Europe, where weightlifting is far more popular than in the United States, appears to support a similar conclusion).

In many countries in Eastern Europe, physical education is far more structured than it is in the United States. Young children are observed for signs of the physical, emotional and psychological qualities that are believed to indicate "potential" for specific sports. Children who exhibit what is perceived to be unusual potential are channeled into sport specific preparation programs. The ages of children who are channeled into specific sports vary from locality to locality and from sport to sport. In weightlifting, the starting age for actual weightlifting training is generally between nine and eleven (although some countries select athletes as young as six or seven or as old as fourteen or fifteen). During at least the first six to twelve months of training (several years in the case of athletes who begin training at a very young age), the emphasis is on general physical conditioning and learning the basic technique of the two competitive lifts with a stick or light bar. Once a base of conditioning has been achieved, basic strength and technique development exercises are added to the program. Over the next one to three years, the young athlete's training becomes more and more sport specific and more and more intense. Therefore, somewhere between the ages of twelve and fourteen, most athletes have reached the stage of serious specialization and a limited focus on competitive results.

None of the Eastern European countries has thus far reported any ill effects attributable to such early specialization, and many have made claims of favorable effects on the health of athletes who undertake rigorous sport training as compared with their more sedentary counterparts. Of course, since only the best physical specimens are chosen for these programs, the evidence may be biased. In addition, a number of aspects of the Eastern European sports programs have been shrouded in secrecy and there is always the possibility that suppressed reports of damage to young athletes will ultimately come to light. However, the anecdotal reports of the many émigrés who have come to the United States and other western countries from Eastern Europe in recent years seem to support the notion that there are no apparent ill effects from early and carefully controlled sport specialization. In considering the possibility of hidden adverse effects on children it should be noted that while there is always an incentive to suppress information on illegal or advantageous practices (such as doping), there would seem to be little to gain by damaging youth. Few athletes excel at very young ages (this is particularly true in weightlifting). Therefore, if sport preparation were really dangerous to the health of young athletes, there would be little

advantage in continuing the practice, since the pool of healthy mature athletes would ultimately be reduced.

A number of medical and professional organizations in the United States, such as the American Orthopedic Society for Sports Medicine and the American Society of Pediatrics, have acknowledged that resistance training can have a positive effect on children (e.g., generating an increase in muscular strength and endurance). However, sports medicine specialists and coaches emphasize the need for careful workout planning, proper exercise technique and selection and adequate supervision. Most of these organizations discourage participation competitive events such as weightlifting and powerlifting and training with maximum resistance until an athlete has reached a certain level of physical maturity (e.g., The American Academy of Pediatrics suggests a "Tanner stage 5", which the average teenager reaches at approximately 15, regardless of sex but with significant individual variations). There have been many real world exceptions to this guidance (e.g., three time Olympic champion, Naim Suleymanoglu was setting World's Records at 15 and up until now, having won the 1996 Olympics at approximately age 30, has reported no ill effects from such early training).

Studies on prepubescent children that have lasted as long as six months have not been able to document a hypertrophy response to resistance exercise. Substantial strength gains documented in a number of these studies appear to arise out of training the nervous system to put forth stronger voluntary muscular contractions. Therefore, having prepubescent athletes exercise for the purpose of generating hypertrophy appears to be a questionable practice.

Growth and Maturation

When working with younger athletes, it is important not only to appreciate the different rates at which different athletes mature but also to realize that maturity takes place at differing rates in different parts and systems of the body. By understanding these issues, the coach is in a better position to adapt his or her training to the needs of young athletes.

More than sixty years ago, R.E. Scammon identified four growth curves for the human body. He developed these curves to depict the differences that exist in the maturation process in four general areas of the body. The most all encompassing curve, which he termed the "general" maturation curve, subsumed such characteristics as weight, most external dimensions of the body and most internal organs. This curve is characterized by rapid growth during a child's early years, a steady (but much slower) growth rate in the later years of early childhood and another dramatic growth spurt beginning in puberty, with growth slowing once again in the later teen years. In contrast, the curve which describes the maturation of the nervous system shows a rapid growth throughout the years of childhood, but then flattens out well before puberty, exhibiting only gradual growth through the teen years. Scammon's "genital" curve (which encompasses most primary and secondary sex characteristics) exhibits a rapid growth in the first few years of life, then a relatively flat period, followed by explosive growth at the onset of puberty. Finally, the "lymphoid" curve (which includes the lymph gland, thymus glands, the appendix and tonsils) grows throughout childhood, peaking between the years of eleven and thirteen (where it reaches a level approximately double that of adulthood), after which it subsides.

While some of the specific features of Scammon's curves have been brought into question by later research, the general principle that various systems of the body mature at different rates cannot be ignored. As a consequence, the knowledgeable coach must take into account the maturation process both in terms of the each athlete and in terms of the in the various characteristics of the athlete.

The maturation process is further complicated by the gender of the athlete. Gender influences the maturation process in different ways. For instance, females tend to mature faster in the area of motor performance. In contrast, males experience a more or less linear growth in strength until the ages of thirteen to fourteen, after which there is a spurt in strength development over the next several years. Females continue the linear growth in strength until the ages of sixteen or seventeen, after which growth in strength is negligible. The spurt in strength made by males at puberty is believed to be caused by the increased production of testosterone.

Power development appears to approximate strength development. An example is performance in the broad jump. Females improve linearly until about the age of twelve; from that point progress halts, and some regression often occurs. In boys, there is linear growth in performance until about the age of thirteen, at which point there is a spurt in performance.

Girls tend to be more flexible than boys at all ages.

Maturation is assessed in a number of ways. For example, the shape of bone, the degree to which cartilage has been replaced by bone and the union and/or fusion that occurs at the epiphyses are all indicators of skeletal age. The pattern of pubic hair and the development of the breasts and genitalia are indicators of maturation. Still further indicators are gross measurements and the percentage of adult height that has been attained. Finally, there are dental indicators of maturation, such as the presence of baby teeth and the degree to which calcification of the teeth has occurred.

These indicators tend to correlate with one another, but the correlation is not perfect.

The knowledgeable coach can use these indicators in several ways. First, they can suggest to the coach the physical age of the athlete as compared with his or her calendar age. Second, they suggest the sequence of activities in which young athletes should structure their training. Since athletes mature more fully and quickly in the area of motor skills than with respect to strength, it is appropriate to stress skill development rather than heavy poundages with young athletes. This emphasis fits well with other areas of maturation (e.g., cartilage which has not fully matured into bone is believed to be mere susceptible to injury than the bone structure that will ultimately develop).

Exercise Prescriptions for Children

There has been a concern within the medical community for many years regarding the practice of strenuous forms of athletics by young athletes. There is special concern with respect to prepubescent athletes and those in the early stages of pubescence. Most of this concern centers around the possibility of damage to growth centers and of outright traumatic injury. While conclusive evidence has not been developed in Western Europe and the United States, it appears that practice of weight training and weightlifting is relatively safe (more so than other sports, such as basketball and football, about which parents and medical authorities appear to have fewer concerns). In Eastern Europe, where the sport of weightlifting has been practiced by athletes as young as ten or eleven for many years, sports medicine authorities have generally detected no reason to restrict the activities of these athletes (as long as well established principles of employing proper technique and gradually increasing the training load over a period of years are followed).

In order to err on the side of caution, sports authorities such as the American Orthopedic Society for Sports Medicine, the American Academy of Pediatric Medicine and the National Strength and Conditioning Association have taken the position that weight training is acceptably safe if the young athletes follow certain guidelines. Among those guidelines are recommendations that are intended to limit the training stress that is applied to young athletes. For instance, one recommendation is that young athletes should never use weights in excess of what they can handle for at least six repetitions.

Unfortunately, recommendations of this type are rather arbitrary and may be inherently dangerous. The six-rep guideline appears to be based on the assumption that weights which an athlete can lift for at least six reps are well enough within that athlete's capabilities that an injury is unlikely. However, an athlete is at least as likely to hurt himself or herself on the sixth rep of a maximum set of six as on an attempt with a single rep maximum. This is because by the time the athlete has reached the sixth rep of an all out set, considerable fatigue has set in. Under such conditions, motor control deteriorates and stress is more likely to be transferred from muscle to connective tissue than when the muscles are "fresh." Neither of these conditions is conducive to safe exercise. A more reasonable standard would be that young athletes should never attempt weights that they cannot perform comfortably and that they should avoid high reps altogether on the Olympic lifts. They should never perform more than five reps in any Olympic or related lift, and reps this high should only be performed with weights that permit the last rep to be performed crisply and rather easily.

Research in Eastern Europe suggests that younger athletes can gain strength with far lower intensities than older athletes. In fact, high intensities appear to be counterproductive in terms of generating strength gains in youngsters (not to mention the threat of injury that they pose).

Injuries to athletes (young or old) usually result from pushing too hard and employing improper technique. Pushing too hard can occur either when athletes compete against their peers (particularly when these athletes are not well matched in terms of size, sex, maturity and experience) or when overzealous coaches and/or parents push athletes to their limits and beyond. Therefore, giving children or their supervisors the license to push to the maximum as long as the weight can be handled for six or some other number of repetitions can be at least as dangerous as permitting them to try single rep maximums.

In attempting a single rep maximum, errors and accidents can occur as a result of unrealistic expectations, fear, over-excitement, technical errors (which are more likely to occur with maximum weights) and the sheer stress of a maximum effort. But these same factors can contribute to failure in the later reps of a six-rep maximum attempt as well. And, as noted above, on such a late repetition there is the additional and significant risk factor of muscular and nervous system fatigue. Most bodybuilders use fairly high repetitions (six or more) in most of their training, and injuries among body builders on the later reps of high rep sets are not uncommon.

In training young athletes (and athletes of all ages) it is important to emphasize proper technique and gradual progression. The coach should never push or permit the young athlete to attempt any all out maximum, regardless of the number of repetitions. No attempt should ever be made at a weight that may be beyond the athlete's limit on a given day, irrespective of how much an athlete may have lifted in the past. It should be emphasized to the young athlete that the true measure of his or her success is technique perfection and gradual conditioning to the demands of high level performance, the foundation of all subsequent performance. Moreover, as was indicated in the earlier chapters of this book, research in Eastern Europe suggests than young athletes actually experience faster strength gains when they exercise with moderate loads than when they lift heavy loads.

Great care should be taken never to overtrain the young athlete. Patience should be exercised in eliciting the body's adaptive capabilities. Young athletes require their energy for growth and maturation as well as sports improvement. Exhaustion may divert such energy. In addition, an overtrained athlete is prone to injury and illness, both of which are to be especially avoided in young athletes. Finally, there is evidence (though it is not directly related to weightlifting) that heavy physical exercise over a sustained period can cause damage to growth cartilage, with resulting bone deformation, pain and/or disability. Joint pain should never be ignored in any athlete and this is doubly true in young athletes.

All young athletes should be carefully supervised in order to assure that proper training methods are applied, to teach them proper technique and to prevent their attempting lifts that are beyond their capabilities. Finally, all young athletes should be taught how to handle situations in which misses occur. As was noted in Chapter 2, one of the first things any lifter should learn is how to handle a miss safely. Once that is learned, the chances of any subsequent injury are greatly reduced.

As has been emphasized throughout this book, the coach should pay attention to the physical and mental characteristics of the athlete. While the maturation process takes place in all young lifters, the rate and precise character of the maturation process varies substantially from athlete to athlete. Athletes who are psychologically, emotionally or physically unprepared for weightlifting training should not be permitted to engage in such training regardless of their age. Those who are ready should not be arbitrarily restrained (though they should be rationally managed). That is, they should never be pushed, and their training should always emphasize proper technique and careful conditioning, but if the athlete demonstrates an ability to tolerate a little more (not necessarily heavier) training, there is no reason to discourage or forbid it, as long as the increase in training is gradual, periodic and carefully monitored.

Although it has long been feared that bone growth would be inhibited by weight training, there is a growing body of evidence that weight training has positive effects on bone growth. Little or no evidence developed in the United States suggests any negative effect of resistance training (or other exercise) on the growth of bones, and considerable evidence now suggests that bone density is improved through resistance training. Similarly, long term studies performed in Eastern Europe (at least those that have been widely reported in the West) do not indicate that resistance training adversely affects bone growth.

It is important to note that the "growth cartilage" of children is particularly susceptible to injury from trauma. This growth cartilage is located at three primary sites: the growth plate of long bones, the point of tendon insertion onto a bone and the joint surfaces. Severe damage to the growth plates prior to their ossification (late in puberty) is believed to interfere with further bone growth. Any or all of the growth cartilage sites can be damaged by a single trauma or by repeated smaller traumas (microtraumas), with damage (e.g., fractures) to the growth (epiphyseal) plate being perhaps the most common type of joint injury in children. Low levels of stress stimulate epiphyseal growth, but excess stress may suppress the development of epiphyseal cartilage and consequent endochondral ossification.

Growth plate fractures have been reported as a result of weightlifting by children. However, the majority of these injuries have occurred among unsupervised athletes who were lifting near maximal weights. Recent studies involving closely supervised resistance training among children suggest that the injury incidence among such children is quite low. While no serious research has been done in the United States with respect to weightlifting or powerlifting among children, work done in Eastern Europe suggests that with close supervision and carefully applied training loads, weightlifting is a relatively safe activity for young athletes (as long as the emphasis is on skill development and maximal and near maximal efforts are absent or strictly limited).

As has already been noted in earlier chapters, frequency, duration and intensity of training are the key variables which can be manipulated to manage the stress that is presented by training. However, these are certainly not the only variables with which the coach needs to be concerned, particularly as pertains to injury prevention and management in young athletes. In this area, technique and the selection of exercises require careful attention as well.

Adaptations in the functional performance of pre-pubescent athletes as a result of training appear to parallel those of adults. However, as was noted earlier, the ability of prepubescents to generate muscle hypertrophy appears to be significantly smaller than that of adults. Research on adults suggests that resistance training increases bone density and helps to prevent certain kinds of injury, but no such effects have yet been documented in children. (There has been very little research in this area at all.)

When training with children is being conducted under conditions that are not climate controlled, special care should be taken. Children have less resistance to short term changes in temperature, and they adjust more slowly to changes in climate. Therefore, this fact should be taken into account in all activities in which children participate.

Dietary restrictions are far more problematic in children than in adults. Children require adequate nutrition for growth and development. Dietary restrictions in order to remain in certain weight classes are definitely contraindicated. Some coaches who are anxious to push their athletes to high performance and/or to score team points encourage artificial weight control. This kind of behavior can undermine the athlete's growth and development and, hence, the athlete's long term potential.

It should be noted that the potential for increasing an athlete's muscle mass is never greater than during the athlete's late teens and early twenties. Consequently, artificially restraining increases in muscle mass during this period undermine the fulfillment of the lifter's potential in a way that can never be overcome.

It is important for coaches to realize that increases in the height and weight of young athletes during puberty may outrun increases in strength. Flexibility may also fail to keep pace with rates of bone growth. In addition, it will also take time for many young athletes to adjust their motor skills to changes in body mechanics that occur as a result of growth. Therefore, young athletes may undergo stages of increased awkwardness during the maturation process.

Adults who engage in large training volumes tend to suppress the effectiveness of their immune systems and therefore can be more susceptible to infections. This has not yet been studied extensively among children, but because infectious diseases often affect the young (and the elderly) more profoundly than adults, special care should be taken to avoid training loads that could adversely affect the immune system. Similarly, increases in cortisol (which are associated with stress) can stimulate collagen synthesis in the short term, but prolonged treatment with related compounds (gluccocorticoids) restrains it. This suggests that overstress may negatively impact collagen growth and synthesis.

Some of the keys to safety and effective training for youngsters are:

1. Never permit the very young athlete to attempt a maximum or near maximum weight;

2. Teach proper technique and require that such technique always be employed;

3. Inculcate a desire to learn proper technique at the outset;

4. Convey the message that overall progress will actually occur more rapidly if the athlete

trains with lighter loads than if he or she trains with heavier ones;

5. Emphasize that lifting without proper supervision in unacceptable and that weights are not toys;

6. Develop an understanding in the athlete that competition and attempting heavy weights at this stage are unimportant. What is important for the athlete is to lay a foundation of sound general physical preparation and perfect technique, so that championship poundages can eventually be lifted (this is the method used by the champions).

In summary, the following guidelines should be followed when training prepubescent athletes in the sport of weightlifting:

1. The training of young athletes should emphasize the development of general physical qualities and not overemphasize weightlifting.

2. Training should be limited in volume and intensity. (Beginners neither require nor benefit from excessive loading, and in children the risks of such loading make it even more important that moderation be stressed.)

3. The training load should be only gradually increased, and the increase should be cyclical in nature, so that there is an overall increase but high and low loads are interspersed throughout the training process.

Athletes should be carefully evaluated and monitored to identify those at increased risk for injury or those who have any negative reaction to training (e.g., delayed menarche). The biological, psychological and emotional age should be considered along with the chronological age in planning the training. In sports which have a relatively high incidence of certain kinds of injuries, athletes should be monitored and examined frequently to assure that no injury is being incurred. This is particularly important for those who have a physical characteristic which places them at increased risk. Careful instruction in technique and modification for individual needs are required in order to develop skills that are both safe and efficient for that athlete.

When training young athletes, the emphasis should be on the development of a love for the sport and for training. Such a foundation will carry a lifter much further than any physical capabilities that are developed through early training.

Weightlifting And The Mature Athlete

While weightlifting has not yet been widely accepted as an activity for more mature athletes, its popularity has grown dramatically over the past decade. Weightlifters participating longer and at higher levels than ever before as our understanding of the training process improves. Contrary to popular beliefs, you are never too old to begin or continue resistance training. Quite the contrary. The older one gets the more essential it becomes to train if one wants to maintain a satisfactory level of functioning. However, in order for one to cope with the aging process one must understand it.

Losses in Physiological Functioning with Aging

With aging come a number of physiological changes which influence an athlete's performance in training and competition. For example, the body's ability to regulate homeostasis (the maintenance of a relatively stable state within the body) declines. As a result, more time is needed to adjust to changes in activity levels, and more rest is needed to perform the same tasks. With aging, muscle fibers are lost (up to 30% of fibers may be lost by age eighty), and this loss occurs to a greater extent in white than in red muscle fibers. The remaining fibers lose tension, generating myofibrils, which leads to a reduction in muscle fiber diameter. ("Fast twitch" fibers atrophy earlier than "slow twitch" fibers.) There is a lower absolute maximum aerobic capacity and strength level as an athlete grows older, but most of this change can be explained by the change that is occurring in lean body mass. This loss of lean body mass may be the result of reduced synthesis of new muscle proteins, a loss of motor neurons (which contributes to atrophy) and reduction in the synthesis of acetylcholine (which reduces efficiency of muscle contractions).

The percentage of body fat in men tends to increase dramatically with aging, nearly doubling from age twenty-five to age seventy-five. Part of this change is due to in increase in fat deposits, but most of it is probably due a loss of muscle tissue. Women begin with a significantly greater percentage of body fat, but the change with aging is far smaller (approximately a 33% increase in the percentage of body fat), probably because they have less muscle mass (as a percentage of body mass)to lose.

Basal metabolism drops 1% to 3% each decade from age three through age eighty. After age thirty, this reduction in the metabolic rate is believed to be primarily due to the normal decline in lean body mass.

The losses in aerobic and anaerobic power that occur with aging are far smaller among people who exercise vigorously than those who do not. For instance, research has revealed that cardiovascular fitness and a number of other markers of aging are similar in highly trained women who are in their seventies and untrained women in their twenties. Therefore, it appears that many aspects of the general decline that is normally attributed to aging are due at least as much to a reduction in activity as to aging itself. It is believed that the gradual decline in skeletal and cardiac muscle tissue can be reduced by at least 50% if the athlete continues to exercise vigorously.

Exercise produces less of an absolute training effect in older athletes (although the rate of improvement experienced by older athletes can rival that of younger ones). Hypertrophy, strength increases and other physiological adaptations to training are still possible in older athletes with proper training. However, because the older person is starting with lower levels of physiological functioning, the absolute levels of performance he or she can expect to achieve are not a great as those of the younger athlete. But the greatest joy in training is improving and that is possible for healthy athletes of any age.

Training and the Mature Athlete

Weightlifters and other athletes often lose their commitment to their sport as they grow older (although this has probably been less true of weightlifters than most other athletes). However, with the advent of "masters" competitions for athletes who are considered to be too old to be truly competitive in the open divisions of their sports (typically athletes 40 and older, but younger in some cases) and the current fitness rage, many more athletes stay with their sports to rather advanced ages. (In the sport of weightlifting, masters competitions begin at age 35 and proceed in five-year age brackets, e.g., 35 to 39, 40 to 44.)

The human body tends to undergo significant changes during the aging process. But, perhaps to an even greater degree than in the process of maturation (which can vary from individual to individual), the rate and nature of the aging process differs, at least in some respects, from person to person. The complex effects of aging make training the older athlete a challenging process. The athlete who has responded in a certain way to training for many years can gradually find himself or herself reacting in quiet different ways as he or she ages. Some athletes will respond to those changes by redoubling their efforts, in hopes that extra effort will help them to outpace the aging process. Other athletes merely accept what they see as an inevitable decline and lose their commitment to continued progress. The more successful athletes will search for training modifications that will compensate for the effects of aging. In effect, the challenge of aging can trigger an entire new wave of creativity to address the altered responses to training that are brought on by aging. On the basis of my experience and that of others I have observed, it is clear that many lifters can perform far better than they think they can and for far longer if they make appropriate adjustments in their training. On the other hand, failing to heed the warnings that the body is providing about how it is being affected by aging

can lead to unnecessarily shortened careers, or at least make those careers far less pleasant.

Physiological changes due to aging lead to slower recuperation from training and slower recovery times from injuries and inflammations, decreased flexibility, stiffening of the joints and muscles in between bouts of activity and a greater likelihood of developing a wide variety of health problems. Increases in the time needed to recuperate from a heavy workout can be dealt with by performing heavy workouts less frequently. (As I indicated earlier in this book, in my younger days I could recuperate from a heavy squat workout in a week, while today I need ten days to recover from the same level of training stress.) Slower recovery times can be overcome by an increased use of therapeutic modalities and other restorative methods, but the most practical way of dealing with slower recovery rates is to plan your training even more carefully, so that overtraining and consequent overuse injuries are avoided.

Exercising care to avoid overtraining and fatigue prior to a competition is particularly important for the older athlete. Joints and muscles do not recuperate as rapidly from a maximum effort, particularly in the classic lifts. Consequently, the athlete must complete his or her heavy sessions further in advance of the competition than a younger athlete. Added rest will benefit the older athlete's nervous system as well as the athlete's muscles since many older athletes find it more difficult to get "up" to lift, and find their nervous systems take longer to recuperate from a maximal effort than it did when they were younger.

Mike Huszka, who tied for first and lost to the great Alexander Kurinov on bodyweight at the 1963 World's Championships (Mike represented the Hungarian team at that time but emigrated to the US in the late 1960's) has performed at a higher level for a longer time than virtually any other athlete in weightlifting history (he has also been a coach of some of the US's best lifters).

As a many time World Masters Champion and often the winner of the "best lifter" title as well, he has learned to adapt his training to the to changes that aging has imposed on his body. In a recent article in International Olympic Lifter magazine, Mike provided his advice on preparing for a competition as a Master lifter.

First, Mike suggests that an athlete must be fully recovered from his or her workouts prior to the competition by the day of the competition. According to Mike, arriving at such a state is dependent on what the athlete has done during the two weeks before the competition.

Huszka does not go above 70% of maximum in the classic lifts during the last two weeks before the competition. In his strength and power exercises, Mike uses between 80% and 90% of his maximum two weeks out of the competition, applying 80-100% effort on each lift. He feels that by performing his lifts with the greatest speed possible gives him a positive last minute training effect. The week before the competition, weights on the power exercises are reduced to 70% of maximum. During that week Mike performs power snatches and power cleans, military presses and squats with no training on the classic lifts at all. He does a significant amount of stretching before, during and after his workouts and continually massages his muscles during his workouts.

His last workout before the competition is three days out. During that workout he lifts only 40 kg. for 4-5 singles focusing on speed. Mike emphasizes that after 45 years in competition he knows what he can do and does not have to prove himself in training. For instance, he knows that if he can power snatch 70 kg. for 3 reps in training he can start with 90 kg. in the competition. Naturally, a good diet, appropriate supplementation, rest and relaxation all play a role in competition preparation.

It is interesting to note that Tommy Kono has advocated some training techniques that are similar to Mike's for older athletes. Tommy has indicated that toward the end of his competitive career, which came in his late thirties, he often rested from the classic lifts altogether for two weeks prior to competition, training on bodybuilding exercises instead. According to Tommy, these exercises maintained his strength but gave his nervous system a well needed rest and made him very hungry to lift at the competition.

I have had similar experiences in my training and, even relied on pulls and squats to maintain my strength before successful competitions when I was younger (heavy classic lifts took a great deal out of my nervous system so pulls and squats maintained the strength and power while giving my mind a rest).

Perhaps the most extreme case of using pulls and squats to prepare for a competition comes from Ben Green, who in addition to having coached some of the US's best athletes has been one of the top Master lifters in the world. Ben snatched more than 300 pounds for the first time in his life when he was 42 years of age. He had been training for about a quarter of a century to achieve that goal. Making a lifetime personal record at 42 (when one has trained since ones teenage years) is a remarkable enough achievement, but it is even more so when one considers that Ben snatched more than 60 kg. only once in his preparations for his record breaking performance. Instead he relied entirely on pulls to a height gauge in his snatch training.

Ben was unable to perform the classic lifts in training because of two knee injuries that he sustained while in college (they were unrelated to weightlifting). These injuries caused his knees to swell up whenever he did the competition lifts (or anything else stressful on the knees) so Ben was forced to develop his unique approach to training in order to continue to compete.

While Ben hardly advocates his program for other athletes, with enormous thought, dedication and courage, he arrived at a means for coping with his limitations. That is why Ben is one of the finest coaches in the US and why lifters flock to him for advice. If he figured out a way to perform at such a high level with few of the tools that are available to most athletes, imagine what he can do with athletes who have no such limitations.

Decreases in flexibility that normally occur with age can be dealt with by paying more attention to performing mobility exercises. A tendency to lose elasticity in the muscles and joints between sets can be dealt with by performing gentle mobility exercises or other light activity between sets of exercises with the bar. Health problems can be dealt with by seeking the advice of a health professional who is familiar with the challenges of activity for adults with health problems. Any athlete with arthritic, cardiorespiratory, neuromuscular, endocrine, metabolic or psychological disorders should exercise special caution when engaging in resistance training, and this is particularly true for the older athlete.

The older athlete is more prone to such disorders than the younger athlete and he or she may be unaware that such a problem exists. Therefore, the older athlete should have a thorough physical before beginning or continuing any strenuous exercise program. Should a limiting condition exist, a special program needs to be developed by a health professional who is trained in dealing with patients who have medical problems.

Summary

Women are just as strong, pound for pound of muscular body weight, as men, and they are just as capable of achieving success in weightlifting when they are matched with competitors who have similar lean body masses at same body weight (generally, other women). The desire to be strong and physically well developed is as "natural" for women as it is for men, but certain genetic differences between men and women (e.g., lower testosterone levels in women) will prevent most women from achieving the same degree of muscular development as most men. Therefore, women weightlifters will not look like men, but, rather, like strong women with firm and shapely muscles. There are no physical differences related to gender that make it inappropriate for women to lift heavy weights (except during pregnancy).

Athletes of any age and gender can enjoy and benefit from the practice of weightlifting. Pre-pubescent athletes should never train with heavy weights for medical (avoiding injury and any interference with growth) and practical reasons (young athletes improve their strength with light weights more quickly than they do when they lift heavier weights). Technique, safety and the development of overall athletic qualities should always be stressed with young athletes, and they should always be carefully supervised in their training.

Resistance training is more important for older people than younger people because only through such training can older people retain much of the strength and muscular development that they had in their youth. However, older athletes need to exercise more care in their training. Older athletes do not recuperate as quickly from their training. They are more subject to injury and slower to heal when they are injured, so they must be especially careful in observing the rules of proper programming. No one is too old to begin training, but no one can or should make up for years of inactivity by a sudden increase in activity. Older athletes need to go through the developmental process of training every bit as much , if not more so, as young athletes. Middle-aged and elderly people should only begin resistance training with the approval of their physicians. Those with health problems must adapt their training to their physical limitations with the help of the appropriate health professional.

Weightlifting has something for everyone, regardless of age or gender. Who, whether male or female and regardless of age, does not want to be strong and have well developed and shapely muscles? You can have all of that and more through proper training. You need only apply intelligence and effort to the training process.

A discussion of achieving top performance in weightlifting would not be complete if it did not cover the nutritional needs of athletes in general and weightlifters in particular. That is the subject of the next chapter.

Bob Bednarski used proper diet to increase his bodyweight from 198 lb. to more than 250 lb. and lift the greatest weight ever lifted overhead up until that time—a 220.5 kg. C&J in 1968.

CHAPTER 10

Nutrition And Weight Control

Discussions of nutrition in sport are generally full of facts and fallacies. Debates regarding the merits of various nutritional theories and ergogenic aids abound. Research in nutrition is advancing at a rapid pace and some of its findings have been able to resolve many of the controversies that have existed for years. Nevertheless, there are still many "gray" areas in the subject of nutrition, areas in which the facts are not fully understood. In this chapter, we will try to present some important nutrition facts, explode some fallacies and delineate some of the gray areas.

As is so often the case whenever approaches to performance enhancement are debated, there are at least two different schools of thought regarding nutrition. There are those who believe that most people, and even hard training athletes, receive perfectly adequate nutrition on virtually any diet. Their position is that "too much fuss is made about diet, almost any diet will do." Many outstanding athletes subscribe to this view. Indeed, I have known world class athletes who have performed at astonishing levels on diets consisting of little more than beer and fatty processed meats. Other athletes make incredible claims regarding the importance of diet, estimating that diet is responsible for as much as 80% of athletic success. Not surprisingly, many such athletes have an interest in selling a particular kind of food supplement that they argue is "essential" for success.

The reasonable approach for most athletes lies somewhere between the extremes. Athletes who have truly poor dietary habits are probably undermining the strenuous training that they do. Athletes who take every supplement known to readers of "muscle magazine" ads are probably doing little more than making supplement manufacturers successful.

There are a number of important and basic nutrition rules that apply universally and should be followed by all serious athletes. However, as has been stressed throughout this book, there are individual differences among athletes. We vary in terms of our genetic make-up, in the environmental influences to which we are and have been exposed and in the way in which we respond to what we experience. These individual differences influence the nutritional needs of athletes as much as other needs.

Some athletes appear to have very limited nutritional needs. They can prosper on intakes of certain nutrients that could lead to a deficiency in others. It is possible that their digestive systems are especially effective at extracting needed nutrients from the foods they consume. Perhaps their bodies adjust very easily to large swings in the availability of certain nutrients. Perhaps these athletes train at levels that are easily handled by their bodies, and, therefore, their nutritional needs are modest. Perhaps stresses that can increase nutritional needs (e.g., smoking and emotional stress) are not significant in the lives of these athletes, again minimizing their nutritional needs. Whatever, the reasons, these athletes might not benefit significantly from improvements in their dietary regimes (though a better diet surely would not hurt their performance and might well improve their overall health).

Other athletes may fall on the opposite side of the spectrum. They may not assimilate certain nutrients very well, their ability to adjust to variations in nutrient levels may not be strong, their training may stimulate substantial changes in their bodies and they may be affected by various stressors that increase their need for certain nutrients. These athletes will certainly benefit from special attention to their diets. Indeed, an improvement in diet may make the difference between achieving their athletic goals and not doing so.

Still other athletes have allergies or manifest other forms of intolerance to certain foods. Symptoms such as skin rashes, indigestion, diarrhea, asthma, nasal congestion or rhinorrhea (runny nose) and even joint pain can result when some athletes ingest certain foods. Even some nutritionally outstanding foods are not well handled by some people; when this occurs, athletes should adjust their diets accordingly. In some cases, this will mean changing the way in which a food is prepared (e.g., a raw version of a food may cause intolerance problems while the cooked version is well assimilated). In other cases it will mean that a certain additive or supplement is needed to aid digestion. (For example, people with lactose—milk sugar— intolerance generally lack a digestive enzyme called lactase; when lactase is added to their milk, they have no difficulty in digesting it.) Finally, some athletes must avoid certain foods altogether.

Over time an athlete who experiments carefully with his or her body will come to know his or her needs, including (to a certain extent) dietary . But while an athlete is learning, , a reasonable approach would be to provide the nutrients that the body needs and to err on the side of a little too much rather than too little.

At the very least, this means consuming a well balanced diet, perhaps taking a modest vitamin and mineral supplement and carefully balancing the intake of so called "macronutrients," such as proteins and carbohydrates. For certain athletes (e.g., for those who must increase their lean body mass), it also means selective manipulation of dietary variables.

For athletes who want every potential edge that nutrition may provide, there are many nutritional supplements that cam be helpful, at least to some athletes. In the balance of this chapter, we will attempt to address nutrition from the standpoint of athletes who are conservative with respect to nutrition as well as those who wish to be more aggressive.

Even those athletes who tend to ignore nutrition because they feel fine consuming whatever they now eat should realize that sound nutritional habits set the stage for lifelong health and therefore should be a primary concern of every athlete. With any luck, an athlete's career will span more than a decade and perhaps more than two (for athletes who compete as "masters," that career might span half a century or more). Sound nutrition cannot help but maximize the length of both career and life.

As with maintenance of personal equipment and mental preparation, the primary responsibility for proper nutrition rests with the athlete. The coach can help to build technique, strength and flexibility but he or she cannot supervise an athlete's diet. Only the athlete knows what he or she is consuming and what his or her true body weight is. Therefore, it is the athlete's responsibility to monitor progress in these areas.

Our discussion will begin with an examination of the basic facts and principles of sound nutrition. Later in the chapter we will focus on some aspects of nutrition that help weightlifters reach ideal body weight and minimize body fat and discuss the use of nutritional supplements to facilitate lifting performances.

The Essential Nutrients

It is important to understand the nature of the nutrients that are available to the body. There are more than fifty substances that are required by the human body. These essential nutrients can be grouped into six major groups: carbohydrates, fats, protein, vitamins, minerals and water. Although we will be examining many of the nutrients in these categories individually, it is important to bear in mind that nutrients work synergistically. This means that they act on a combined basis in the body and that they can interact with one another to have effects which are greater than any one nutrient could achieve on its own. Similarly, the lack of one important nutrient in the diet can limit the effectiveness of others that are present.

Carbohydrates

Carbohydrates are perhaps the most important nutrient for the production of energy. There are four basic carbohydrate categories: monosaccharides, which include glucose (the main carbohydrate in the body), galactose and fructose (fruit sugar); disaccharides such as sucrose (table sugar) and lactose (the most common carbohydrate in milk); polysaccharides, which consist primarily of starch (potatoes, beans, corn, bread, spaghetti and rice) and fiber; and fiber (which is found in most fruits, vegetables and whole grains).Carbohydrates in the first three categories are important sources of energy for the human body, particularly for the bodies of athletes. Carbohydrates in the fourth category, fiber, are the only ones that humans cannot digest to yield energy,) yet they appear to have an important role in the human diet. Dietary fiber deserves some special attention because it is so often absent or limited in American diets. There are two kinds of fiber: water soluble and insoluble. Insoluble fiber acts primarily in the large intestine, where it absorbs water and produces soft stools. Insoluble fiber is believed to play a role in preventing irritable bowel syndrome and diverticular disease. (Whole grains, particularly the bran portion of those fibers, are good sources of insoluble fiber.) Soluble fiber is found in such foods as apples and citrus fruits. (This kind of fiber has been associated with reductions in serum cholesterol and protection against colon cancer.) Nutritionists recommend that twenty-five to fifty grams of fiber be consumed every day. It is estimated that the average American consumes only 40% of that target level. Carbohydrates which can be used for fuel differ in their effects on the body. Some release their energy more easily and directly than others. Some have a more profound effect on blood sugar levels.

The most common means for categorizing carbohydrates is to place them in one of two classes: simple or complex. Simple carbohydrates fall into the first two of the carbohydrate categories mentioned above. Complex carbohydrates include carbohydrates in the third and fourth categories. Nutritionists have long used the classifications of simple and complex carbohydrates to explain at least certain aspects of the behavior of different carbohydrates in the body (e.g., simple carbohydrates are digested more rapidly than complex ones).

Another system of classifying carbohydrates, the "glycemic index." has emerged in recent years. The glycemic index is an indicator of how much a specific quantity of a particular food raises the blood sugar level in relation to some "reference" food (generally white bread or glucose). While glycemic indices are regarded as fairly accurate, variations occur within certain foods (e.g., the degree of ripeness of a banana can affect its glycemic index). Diabetics find the glycemic index of great value because they can use it to anticipate how particular meals are likely to change their blood sugar levels. Table 1 provides a list the glycemic indices of some common foods.

Lipids

Lipids are a group of fat or fat like substances that are insoluble in water. There are three basic kinds of lipids that are of significance in the diet: triglycerides, phospholipids and cholesterol. Triglycerides make up more than 90% of lipids ingested and are the primary non-carbohydrate source of energy in the diet. They generally yield energy more slowly than carbohydrates and are therefore considered to be a "slow burning" source of energy. Phospholipids generally make up a very small portion of the lipids ingested (approximately 2%). Nevertheless, they serve an essential role in the emulsification of triglycerides (which aids in their absorption by the body) and in facilitating the interaction of water soluble and non-water-soluble substances in the body. Cholesterol serves a vital role as a precursor of a number of important hormones, as part of nerve tissue and in the creation of the bile salts, which play a vital role in digestion. (Cholesterol can have negative effects on the body as well, some of which will be discussed shortly.) The body typically manufactures significantly greater amounts of both phospholipids and cholesterol than are ingested in the diet, but the composition of a person's diet can affect the amount of these lipids that the body manufactures (this is particularly true of cholesterol).

Triglycerides can categorized in at least two ways: by the length of the carbon chains that make up various fatty acids or by the categories of saturated and unsaturated fats. The length of the carbon chain that makes up a fatty acid is

Table 1

FOOD	GLYCEMIC INDEX
Whole Meal Rye Bread	89
Whole Grain Pumpernickel Bread	68
Macaroni	64
Rice (instant, boiled 1 minute)	65
Brown Rice	81
Corn Flakes	121
Porridge Oats	89
Oatmeal Cookies	78
Water Biscuits	100
Baked Russet Potato	116
Yam	74
Baked Beans (canned)	70
Chick Peas (dried)	47
Chick Peas (canned)	60
Soy Beans (canned)	22
Apples	52
Bananas	84
Fructose	26
Sucrose (table sugar)	83
Honey	126
Milk	44
Potato Chips	77

inversely related to its melting point and solubility. True short fatty acids are not part of a normal diet, but medium-chain fatty acids are found in such foods as milk, coconut oil and palm oil. Medium-chain fatty acids are absorbed by the body more quickly than long-chain fatty acids. Some research has suggested that medium-chain fatty acids are not easily converted by the body into body fat and that a diet unhealthfully high in medium-chain fatty acids may aid in fat loss.

Saturated fats are solid at room temperature and are derived primarily from animal sources (although vegetable sources of saturated fat include coconut oil and cocoa butter). Saturated fats tend to raise serum cholesterol levels (and the risk of heart disease) and appear to be risk factors in certain forms of cancer.

Unsaturated fats exist in a liquid form at room temperature. At least two fatty acids (linoleic and linolenic acids) are known to be essential to human nutrition and must be consumed regularly. These fats appear to pose less of a health risk than saturated fats, although some health experts believe that a high intake of unsaturated fats increases the risk of some kinds of cancer and certain other diseases.

The consumption of fat (especially in saturated forms) in the American diet is believed to be excessive. It is widely recommended that calories from fats comprise no more than 30% of the diet, and many nutritionists recommend an even lower level. It is generally recommended that one-third of this 30% be from saturated fats. Another third should come from polyunsaturated fats (sunflower, safflower and corn oil are good sources), and the remaining third should come from monounsaturated fats (olive, almond and canola oils are all good sources of these fats). If any of these unsaturated fats have been hydrogenated (e.g., converted into margarine), most of their value as unsaturated fats has been lost, and they behave much like saturated fats in the body.

Before leaving the subject of dietary lipids, a brief discussion of a related topic, serum cholesterol, is in order. Cholesterol has become a household word, one that most people fear. People often use the word cholesterol in discussing both dietary and serum (blood) levels of cholesterol, but there is a distinction. Dietary cholesterol typically accounts for only a third of the serum cholesterol levels of the body (the rest is manufactured by the body). Therefore, the mere control of cholesterol intake will not control cholesterol levels. Moreover, the association between dietary cholesterol and serum cholesterol appears to be weaker than was originally surmised. Instead, the serum cholesterol level and the level of triglycerides in the blood appear to be far more closely associated with the dietary level of saturated fats than with the dietary intake of cholesterol.

The interest in cholesterol initially arose when an association between total serum cholesterol and heart disease was discovered. It is now understood that the relationship between high density lipoproteins (HDLs) and low density lipoproteins (LDLs), or total cholesterol, is more important in predicting heart disease than total cholesterol levels. The higher the ratio of HDLs to either the LDL or total cholesterol, the better (a ratio of four or greater is considered to be a cause for concern, while ratios of three or below is considered good).

A number of studies have linked exercise to reductions in serum cholesterol and lipids, but the results in this area have not been universal. A more consistent result of exercise is in increase in HDL relative to LDL (considered to be a highly favorable response). While most studies conducted in this area have looked at aerobic exercise, evidence is mounting that weight training has the same effect.

Proteins

Proteins serve a fundamentally different purpose in the body than carbohydrates and fats. Although they can be an energy source, proteins contribute to the growth, rebuilding and repair of the tissues of the body. Consequently, proteins are often referred to as the "building blocks" of the body. These building blocks are of particular interest to those who are engaged in a training process (especially one that stimulates muscle hypertrophy), because proteins furnish the raw material that is used in the adaptation process.

Proteins are comprised of compounds called amino acids. More than twenty amino acids are used by the body for protein synthesis within the body. At least eight of these amino acids (isoleucine, leucine, lysine, methionine, phenylalanine, threonine, tryptophan and valine) are considered "essential" or "indispensable" for adult humans. At least three other amino acids may be essential for optimal functioning; we know that infants require histidine, and adults may require it in small amounts, while there is some evidence that arginine and taurine may be needed under certain circumstances. The body appears to be incapable of manufacturing the essential amino acids, at least in significant amounts. The body is clearly capable of creating the non-essential amino acids needed by the body out of the essential ones.

Many foods contain proteins, but not all foods are good sources of dietary protein. The percentage of protein contained in some foods is far lower than in others. (For example, a cake may contain egg whites— a very good source of protein— but the egg white may represent such a small percentage of the total calories that the cake would have to be considered a poor overall source of protein.) Another factor affecting the protein value of foods is the presence of all of the essential amino acids. Some foods, such as unsweetened gelatin, contain a high percentage of protein but lack one or more of the essential amino acids. Such proteins cannot be fully used by the body for one of their most essential functions, building and restoring tissue. Foods which contain all of the essential amino acids are said to contain "complete" proteins.

While the presence of all of the essential amino acids in foods may technically make a protein "complete," the body's ability to effectively utilize the protein in those foods depends on the amino acid balance (the ratios of the essential amino acids to one another) found in those foods. In order for the body to fully utilize all of the amino acids present in a food, these amino acids must exist in a very specific relationship to one another. The closer the amino acid balance in a given food approximates that perfect relationship, the higher the "quality" of the protein.

In severe cases of amino acid imbalance, the presence of one amino acid in excess of others can actually depress the growth rate or even lead to protein toxicity. (Methionine and tyrosine are the most toxic of the amino acids, and threonine is the least toxic in this context.) In these cases, the addition of another amino acid can significantly improve overall protein utilization. Finally, actual protein toxicity can occur when an excess amount of one or more amino acids exists.

Another factor influencing the body's ability to utilize ingested protein is their "bioavailability" (the degree to which the body is able to utilize them). A food may contain a certain amount of protein with amino acids in a certain relationship, but the body may not be able to absorb all of the proteins present. This may be because a given food contains chemicals which inhibit digestion of certain proteins. Food processing procedures (such as cooking) can also influence the degree to which proteins can be used by the body. For instance, heating proteins in the presence of certain sugars (like the heating of milk protein with milk sugar) can make lysine (one of the amino acids in milk) "unavailable" during the digestive process. Similarly, severe heating of any protein or severe treatment with an alkali can make lysine and cysteine unavailable. Finally, processes that can take place in stored foods can influence the availability of some proteins. For instance, certain kinds of oxidation can cause a loss of methionine.

Measuring the Quality of Proteins

Several indices have been developed to measure the overall biological values of proteins. Perhaps the oldest index involves measuring the constituent amino acids in a given food and grading the protein on the basis of the essential amino acid found in the smallest concentration in relation to animal or human needs. The problem with such an index is that it does not recognize that even foods completely lacking in one essential amino acid can promote slow growth and that foods vary in terms of their bioavailability.

In order to overcome these limitations, scientists have developed methods of evaluating the actual biologic effects of proteins on animals. Perhaps the oldest approach of this is the "protein efficiency ratio" or PER. The PER is derived from feeding proteins of various kinds (but equal in terms of the percentage of total dietary intake from protein) to young and growing animals. The scientists then observe the reactions of the animals in terms of weight gain per gram of protein eaten. A gain of 3 grams in body weight for each gram of protein eaten would yield a PER of 3.0, while a gain of .5 gram would yield a PER of .5. The main problem with the PER measure is that it tends to understate the value of lower value proteins. For example, in one study, casein had a PER of 2.8, while wheat gluten had a PER of .4. This suggests that casein is 7 times better than gluten in terms of protein quality. In reality, without any protein at all, the animal would actually lose body weight. Therefore, even a relatively low quality protein like gluten has a very positive effect in terms of arresting weight loss, and it actually contributes to a weight gain. Consequently, the true biological value of gluten relative to no protein at all makes it closer to casein in terms of its value to the body than using the PER measure would suggest.

An index called "biologic value" is currently the most widely accepted measure of protein quality. It measures the nitrogen (N) intake of proteins ingested and the output of N in the urine and feces and compares them with the same outputs on a zero protein diet. Any difference in the values of the N excreted in the zero protein diet and the amount excreted in the diet with a particular protein is presumed to be the amount that is not absorbed by the body. If equal amounts of two proteins (A and B) are ingested, and protein A does not increase the N excreted but protein B does, then protein A is considered to be superior to protein B.

Still another way to measure the quality of proteins is to compare the protein in the bodies of a group of animals after being fed a certain protein with the protein present in the bodies of a group of animals fed no protein. The protein gain in the bodies of the group fed the protein is compared to the amount of protein that they ingested, and the resulting proportion is called the net protein utilization (NPU). This gross measure has the advantage of reflecting the digestibility factor of proteins in that if two proteins are of equal value, and one is digested more effectively than the other, the better digested protein will have a higher NPU. Naturally, this also means that it will impossible to separate the influences of digestibility and inherent quality from one another if this measure is used exclusively.

Table 2 lists the NPU of some fairly common protein sources. Meat, fish and poultry have NPUs that are higher than any of the common vegetable sources of protein, but they are not as high as the values of eggs or human milk, which makes the NPU rankings similar to the PER's.

Table 2

Source	NPU
Eggs	94
Maize	51
Milk (human)	87
Milk (cow)	82
Millet	44
Rice	59
Soy	65
Wheat	48

The FDA has reportedly adopted a standard of protein quality called the Protein Digestibility Corrected Amino Acid Score (PDCAAs) for rating the quality of proteins. As its name suggests, this standard considers the amino acid profiles of various proteins and their bioavailability. The problem with the FDA's application of PDCAAs is that the highest permissible value will reportedly be , and that value will be the equivalent of soy protein. Therefore, even if egg, milk or some other form of protein is of superior biological value, it will not merit a higher rating.

It is not uncommon for manufacturers of protein supplements to select the protein quality measure on which their supplement performs best and then to claim the superiority of their supplement on the basis of that score. Buyers of such supplements should judge their value with this in mind.

It must be remembered that, regardless of the protein quality measure that is used, the profile of a diet that is optimal in terms of protein has significant individual variations. For example, there is evidence to suggest that growing children require more well balanced essential amino acids than adults. Overall protein needs are believed to decline with age, but the decline in the need for essential amino acids is more pronounced. Individuals of the same age and sex differ with regard to their overall protein requirements and their requirements for individual essential amino acids; these requirements may vary significantly within the same individual under different conditions.

Vitamins

Vitamins are one of the six categories of nutrients that contain no calories and are therefore not direct sources of energy. Vitamins are substances which the body needs to carry on its metabolic processes effectively. Inadequate amounts of specific vitamins lead to deficiency diseases, and excessive amounts of specific vitamins can have toxic effects (some vitamins, such as vitamins A and D, are far more likely to have such effects than others).

There are thirteen nutrients which are conventionally categorized as vitamins (various writers have argued for the inclusion of additional substances in this category). The thirteen accepted vitamins are: A, D, E and K (the fat soluble vitamins which can be stored in the fat deposits of the body), thiamin (B1), riboflavin (B2), niacin (B3), panthotenic acid (B5), pyridoxine (B6), biotin, folic acid, cyanocobalamin (B12) and C. The B vitamins and vitamin C cannot be stored by the body and therefore need to be consumed on a daily basis.

Minerals

Minerals are a second category of nutrients that contain no calories and are therefore not direct sources of energy. Minerals fall into two categories: macro and micro. The former are needed in large quantities on a regular basis. The macro-minerals are: calcium, chloride, magnesium, phosphorous, potassium, sodium and sulfur. Micro-minerals include: chromium, copper, fluoride, iodine, iron, manganese, molybdenum, selenium and zinc. This latter category of nutrients are needed in only very small amounts. (There is evidence that the minerals arsenic, boron, bromine, fluorine, germanium, lead, nickel, silicon, tin and vanadium are required in extremely small amounts as well.) It is believed that an adequate supply of most of the micro and macro minerals is obtained from diets that might be considered relatively poor from the standpoint of the presence of other nutrients. The only minerals which generally raise concerns with respect to the potential for deficiencies are calcium, iron (especially in female athletes), iodine, zinc and magnesium.

Nutritionists generally agree that one macro-mineral is consumed in excess in the typical American diet: sodium (commonly referred to as salt). Many foods contain substantial amounts of salt, and many people add salt to their foods as well. It is recommended that salt intake be no more than 1 gram per 1000 calories of food consumed (assuming a reasonable caloric intake).

Water and the Importance of Maintaining Proper Hydration

Although it is perhaps the single most important nutrient in the human diet, the importance of water is often overlooked by athletes. Nutritionists often recommend a dietary intake of six to eight glasses of water a day. (Virtually any fluid counts as "water" as far as the body's requirements for hydration, but substances other than water have different effects on the body.) However, the temperature and humidity of the air the athlete is training in, the mass of the athlete and the strenuousness of the activity can all affect an athlete's need for fluids. A hard training athlete can easily lose two gallons of water in a day through his or her lungs, skin and urine.

Maintaining the proper level of hydration is important for all athletes, but it is typically less of an issue for weightlifters than many other kinds of athletes. There are several reasons for this. For one thing, weightlifting training, particularly low repetitions with significant rest between sets, does not raise body temperature and metabolism as much as aerobic activities. Another factor is that weightlifting is an indoor sport. Because workouts often take place under temperature controlled conditions, the dehydration that can arise in extremely hot temperatures is generally not a problem faced by weightlifters. Finally, water is normally available at the workout site, and rests between sets provide ample opportunity for fluid replacement. Therefore, weightlifters generally find maintaining hydration to be relatively convenient.

Naturally, when a weightlifter faces the prospect of training in high temperature and humidity (particularly when temperature and humidity are both in excess of 70° Fahrenheit and 70%, respectively), in areas where no fluids are readily available, or after dehydration has already occurred as a result of weight loss, special care must be taken to avoid dehydration.

Some research has suggested that dehydration of as little as 2% of body weight is enough to negatively impact the cardiovascular and thermoregulatory systems and may have a negative effect on endurance. (It appears that larger reductions are required in order to affect strength, but reactions to dehydration vary with the individual, and some athletes may react negatively to small fluid losses while others continue to perform well after substantial losses.) Regular consumption of fluids (particularly water) during the entire workout, well before the sensation of thirst is experienced, is the key to avoiding dehydration.

After an athlete has intentionally dehydrated (e.g., when making weight), special efforts must be made to rehydrate through a conscious effort to consume fluids. Fluids with carbohydrate concentrations of 80 g to 100 g per liter of fluid are emptied from the stomach faster than plain water and so facilitate rapid rehydration, but if fluid replacement is more important than energy replacement and extensive amounts of fluids are needed in order to maintain or restore proper hydration, more diluted solutions are preferable in order to avoid excessive carbohydrate consumption. Guzzling water is not a sound approach to rehydration because it can lead to significant gastric discomfort (though consumption of up to 600 ml of fluid at one time may speed gastric emptying). Persistently sipping water at the rate of approximately 100 ml to 200 ml every ten to fifteen minutes is generally the most appropriate way to rehydrate.

Meeting Nutritional Requirements

Now that we have discussed the essential nutrients, we will look at how much of each is desirable (other than water, which we have already dealt with) and how to assure that you are meeting your requirements. For this purpose, nutrients can be divided into two broad and not necessarily mutually exclusive categories: nutrients which are the building blocks of the body's various tissues and/or help it to carry on its chemical activities (vitamins, minerals and proteins) and those which supply the body with energy (carbohydrates, fats and proteins). Proteins serve as both a building block and an energy source for the body but are typically more important as the raw material for growth and repair. We will begin by looking at recommended dietary intakes of vitamins and minerals.

RDAs, U.S. RDAs And The Vitamin and Mineral Requirements Of Athletes

Nutritional scientists have worked for many years to establish recommendations with regard to the daily intake of nutrients. Organizations concerned with public health in a number of countries (including the United States) have developed "recommended dietary intakes" for their populations. The World Health Organization of the United Nations has done this as well.

In the United States. the Food and Nutrition Board, a committee of the National Research Council of the National Academy of Sciences, has developed Recommended Dietary Allowances (RDAs). These RDAs have been designed with the objective of meeting the needs of the vast majority of the population. This was done by first estimating the needs of the average population. Variability in the need for each nutrient was then considered and statistical techniques were employed to project levels of each nutrient that would satisfy the needs of 90% of the population. A further increase was then made in the recommended nutrient levels to allow for individual inefficiencies in the absorption of nutrients. The net result of these steps was to reach a level of nutrient intake sufficient to meet the needs of 98% of the population (with a significant margin of error for the majority of the population). In order to make RDAs more accurate, specific RDAs have been developed for more than a dozen different populations, based on considerations of age and sex (e.g., infants under the age of six months, adult males aged nineteen to twenty-four).

RDAs should not be confused with U.S. Recommended Dietary Allowances (U.S. RDAs), which are derived from, but not identical to, the RDAs. U.S. RDAs have been used by the U.S. Food and Drug Administration in nutritional labeling.

While RDAs have been established for many nutrients, information regarding others was regarded as insufficient to establish specific RDAs. For many such nutrients, ranges of intake that are considered safe and adequate have been established. All RDA recommendations are expressed in terms of daily intakes, but it is not considered essential for the intake of each nutrient to meet such a standard each day, as long as the average daily intake of these nutrients does meet these standards over time.

There is a great deal of misunderstanding regarding RDAs. While they have been designed to meet the needs of the majority of the population, even the staunchest advocates of RDAs admit that they are not meant to be used as individual recommendations. They are public health tools which in reality say that if the overall population receives these levels of nutrients, then the overall population will not suffer from nutritional deficiencies. So concerned were scientists about the misinterpretations of recommended dietary intakes that the concept of RDAs replaced a previous concept that was regarded as less clear.

Prior to the advent of RDAs, nutritional standards called Minimum Daily Requirements (MDRs) were employed in the United States. The use of the term MDR was regarded as inappropriate because the levels of nutrients described were not guaranteed to meet the minimum needs of each person in any population. The more flexible concept of RDA merely says that the RDA of each nutrient is expected to meet the needs of most of the population.

There are a number of known conditions which affect nutritional needs. For instance, pregnancy and lactation increase the need for calcium, protein, iron, vitamin D and other nutrients, and post-menopausal women may have a greater need for calcium than younger women. A high protein diet leads to the excretion of more calcium than usual, so there may be a need for additional calcium in the diets of those with high protein

intakes. In short, there are many factors which can affect the need for various nutrients.

This distinction should not be lost on athletes. First, high level athletes, particularly hard training weightlifters, may not fit the category of the general population from a nutritional standpoint. They are subjecting their bodies to unusual levels and kinds of stress. Such populations are not addressed by the RDAs. Second, individuals, hard training or not, may have needs that are very different from those addressed by the RDAs. Studies performed on athletes do not suggest that doses of vitamins well in excess of the RDAs help performance, but individual differences may still make intakes in excess of RDAs useful for particular athletes. Of the nutrients studied, thiamin, riboflavin, vitamin C, vitamin E and iron (for female athletes) appear to be the nutrients that are the most likely to be needed in increased amounts as a consequence of training. As a reference, Table 3 displays the 1989 versions of the RDAs for males aged 19 to 24. This population segment has been selected because its values are

Table 3

Nutrient	Other Name	RDA	Athlete Dose[2]	Unit of Measure
Retinol	Vitamin A	1000/3333	3333-75000 IU	mcgRE/IU
Cholecalciferol	Vitamin D	10/400	400-600 IU	mcgRE/IU
Alpha Tocopherol	Vitamin E	10/10	200-1600	mg α-TE/IU
Phylloquinone	Vitamin K	70	same	mcg
Thiamin	Vitamin B1	1.5	40-600	mg
Riboflavin	Vitamin B2	1.7	30-250	mg
Niacin	Vitamin B3	19	100-1000	mg
Panthotenic Acid	Vitamin B5	4-7[3]	25-1000	mg
Pyridoxine	Vitamin B6	2	40-300	mg
Ascorbic Acid	Vitamin C	60	2000-16000	mg
Folic Acid	Folate, Folacin	200	400-1200	mcg
Cyanocobalimin	Vitamin B12	2	25-300	mcg
Biotin		30-100[3]	50-100	mcg
PABA	Para-amino-benzoic acid	none	25-500	mg
Choline		none	25-1000	mg
Inositol		none	25-1000	mg
Calcium		1200	1000-5000	mg
Magnesium		350	500-2000	mg
Phosphorous		1200	200-2000	mg
Iron		10	15-60	mg
Iodine		150	150-1000	mcg
Zinc		15	22.5-150	mg
Selenium		70	200-1000	mcg
Copper		1.5-3[3]	0-5	mg
Manganese		2-5[3]	15-100	mg
Fluoride		1.5-4[3]	none	mg
Chromium		50-200[3]	300-1000	mcg
Molybdenum		75-250[3]	50-500	mcg

the highest, overall, in the RDA tables, at least among the RDA categories that are most likely to apply to athletes (some of the RDA's for pregnant women are higher, but most pregnant women will not be competing in weightlifting.) The 1989 RDAs were the most current at the time this was written.

A number of writers and researchers in the area of athletic nutrition recommend that athletes (and even non-athletes) take much higher dosages of vitamins and minerals than those recommended by the RDA. Their logic is that the special stress of training creates special energy, rebuilding and growth needs. The ranges presented attempt to summarize the recommendations that have been made by some of the most popular of these authors.

Where "none" appears in a Table 3 column it means that the writers feel that no specific supplementation is required in this area because even a poor diet provides adequate amounts of this nutrient. See the Bibliography for some suggested reading in the area of vitamin and mineral megadosing.

When the evidence is considered insufficient by the creators of the RDA to formulate a specific RDA but they believe that a specific nutrient is required in some significant quantity, a Recommended Safe And Adequate Daily Dietary Intake (RDI) is often constructed; the recommendation is presented in a range instead of a specific number.

The issue of bioavailability (a measure of the amount of a given nutrient that can be absorbed from a specific food) was discussed earlier in this chapter in the section on proteins. The concept of bioavailability also applies to vitamins and minerals. Two foods may contain equal amounts of the same nutrient, but one may yield much more to the body during the digestive process. For example, only about 10% of the iron consumed is absorbed, with iron from animal sources being absorbed at a far higher rate than that from vegetable sources. The variations in the bioavailability of nutrients explain why erring on the side of extra nutrient intake appears to be a sensible practice, up to a point.

Nutrient Toxicity

Just as there are minimum requirements for optimum functioning, there are levels of nutrient intake that can impair functioning. It may be sound advice for an athlete to err on the side of extra nutrients, but that error too great, the risk of reaching a level of actual toxicity can become very real. In nutrition, as in almost everything else, there is such a thing as too much of a good thing. Fat soluble vitamins are the nutrients most likely to cause toxicity, and among them doses of at least ten times the RDA are needed to cause toxicity.

Energy Supplied by Proteins, Fats and Carbohydrates

Proteins, carbohydrates and fats are the only nutrients that supply the body with energy. The amount of that energy is almost universally measured by the kilocalorie, which is generally referred to as a calorie. A kilocalorie is the amount of fuel raise the temperature of a liter of water by 1° Centigrade.

The average person burns approximately 1700 to 2200 calories a day, but every person has their own rate of energy expenditure (metabolic rate). A number of factors affect the metabolic rate. Total body mass, activity level and lean body mass all affect the metabolic rate (the higher the body mass, lean body mass and activity level, the higher the metabolic rate). Lean body mass is more directly related to caloric expenditure than total body mass, so one strategy for losing body fat is to increase your metabolism by increasing muscle mass. Since increased muscle mass is generally desirable for weightlifters, this is a doubly desirable result.

Activity level also has an important influence on metabolic rate. Increasing activity level causes the body to burn more calories during training, and the level of caloric expenditure can remain higher for a number of hours following activity, burning still more calories. In addition, vigorous exercise speeds the movement of food through the digestive tract, and this speed of movement may decrease the absorption of certain nutrients, which may further contribute to weight loss.

Proteins, carbohydrates and fats are not equal in terms of the amount of energy they yield. Protein and carbohydrates each supply approximately four kilocalories of energy per gram. Fats supply nine kilocalories per gram, more than twice the energy yield of carbohydrates and proteins. This is one of the reasons that low fat diets are often recommended as a means of losing weight.

The Special Protein Needs of Athletes

For many years athletes believed that you ate muscle to build muscle. Strength athletes almost universally accepted the notion that meat (which generally consists of the muscle of animals), and plenty of it, was needed to enhance performance. There was much myth and some sense in this view.

Clearly, a pre-game steak (a meal that is relatively high in fat and protein) is not beneficial to athletes, particularly those who are involved in endurance sports. There are a number of reasons for this. Fat requires more oxygen than carbohydrates in order to be metabolized. Digestion of protein generates certain byproducts that are believed to hinder performance. Neither proteins nor fat are converted to energy as efficiently as carbohydrates.

For years modern nutritionists maintained that athletes required no more protein in their diets than the average person (the RDA for males aged nineteen to twenty-four is 58 grams per day) and that their only legitimate need was for increased calories, which were best provided by carbohydrates. Today research appears to support what many athletes have believed for years: that extra protein does seem to be of value for athletes, particularly those who are interested in building strength and muscle size. Nutritionists are slowly accepting the notion that extra protein may be beneficial to athletes in special situations (i.e., when muscle tissue is being broken down and built up as a result of intense training).

How much protein does an athlete need? Typically, prescriptions are related to body weight. Standard nutritional recommendations for the general public typically range of from .75 gram to .90 gram per kilo of body weight. This recommendation assumes that the average person uses a little less than .5 gram of protein per kilo of body weight per day. The recommended dietary allowances are in the .75 to .90 range because it is assumed that the quality of protein ingested will not be perfect (in terms of its composition and bioavailability) and that there is a need to provide for individual differences with regard to protein needs.

Recent research suggests that hard training athletes may want to establish target levels of 1.5 to 2.0 grams per kilo of body weight (perhaps even more for the athlete who is training very hard and seeking to facilitate hypertrophy). This level of protein intake appears to have little chance of doing any harm (unless an athlete resorts to a diet that is high in fat as well as protein). For athletes who are already at the limits of their weight classes in terms of muscular body weight, the 1.5 to 2.0 range indicated above, or even less, may be perfectly adequate. Not surprisingly, individual differences need to be recognized. Some athletes who consume as much protein as was suggested will neither feel well nor perform well. Athletes who are growing very fast may find that even more protein is needed. Each athlete needs to monitor his or her own reaction to protein in order to devise a dietary plan that will work. In addition, the same athletes may have different needs during different periods in their athletic lives. When the athlete is moving up a weight class and training to encourage muscle growth, more protein may be needed. When the athlete is training less rigorously or is maintaining his or her body weight, protein needs will tend to decline.

In most cases, the hard training athlete will be able to achieve needed protein levels without altering the percentage of protein in the diet (12% to 15% of calories is generally considered to be a good target range). This is because the athlete who is training very hard is typically ingesting more calories than one who is not. Consequently, the protein intake per kilo of body weight is automatically higher than it is for an athlete with a lower caloric intake. The exception to this rule may be the weightlifter who is training very intensely but with a relatively low volume of exercise. In this case, the caloric requirements of the athlete may not be very much higher than the caloric requirements of a relatively sedentary person. This weightlifter may need a higher than normal percentage of protein in his or her diet in order to achieve adequate levels of protein intake.

Dietary Assessment

There are several ways an athlete can assure that his or her diet is adequate. The most sophisticated is to plan a specific diet from scratch by analyzing the nutritional content of various foods and then combining them to assure adequate intake of each nutrient. There are a number of guides available today that provide information on the vitamin, mineral, protein, fat and carbohydrate content of various foods (see the Bibliography for further information in this area).

Another approach is to monitor your intake of food over a period of time to determine what you are already obtaining through your diet and then to make adjustments to the diet as appropriate. It is normally recommended that you monitor the diet for one week, or at least two weekdays and one weekend day.

In order to properly monitor your diet, it is necessary to determine the quantity of each food that is being consumed. This can be done by measuring the quantity of the food ingested, by reading the food labels or by closely estimating the quantity.

ADA Dietary Exchange Lists

While the ideal means for monitoring diet is to know the nutritional content of every food that is eaten regularly, a shorthand way to gain an approximate idea of dietary content is to make use of "Dietary Exchange Lists." These lists have been created by the American Dietetic Association and the American Diabetes Association. In an effort to enable those who must manage their diets carefully (particularly diabetics) to make simple substitutions among foods, a series of rough food equivalencies have been developed. Foods with similar protein, fat, carbohydrate and caloric contents are grouped together. If a dieter knows the identity of a reference food and the other foods that can be considered "equivalents," it is easy to achieve a target dietary content with a wide variety of foods. There are six exchange categories: milk, vegetables, fruit, bread (starch), meat and fat.

The list that follows provides some common dietary exchange items in the category of "milk." Full dietary exchange lists are available from the organizations mentioned above and in many books on nutrition. (See the Bibliography for further information.)

A Partial List of Milk Exchanges

Skim & Very Low Fat Milk: 1 cup of skim milk, 1 cup of non fat yogurt, 1 cup of low fat buttermilk

Low Fat Milk: 1 cup of 2% milk, 1 cup of low fat yogurt (these constitute one milk and one fat exchange)

Whole Milk: 1 cup of whole milk, 1 cup of whole-milk yogurt, 1/2 cup of evaporated milk (counts as one milk and two fat exchanges).

Four Basic Food Groups

Nutritionists generally recommend that a wide variety of foods be eaten. One way to get a proper balance of foods in their lives is to eat foods from each of the four food groups every day. The four groups are: 1) meat, fish and poultry; 2) milk and milk products; 3) bread and cereal; and 4) fruits and vegetables. Two daily portions of the foods in the meat and milk categories are suggested, while four daily portions of foods in the cereal and vegetable categories are recommended.

The concept of food groups is rather shallow because a person could eat a very poor diet while obeying the guidelines. (For example, you could eat four servings of high fat ice cream, two servings of french fries and two avocados and theoretically meet the guidelines despite having a very high level of dietary fat.) It is wise to t eat low fat varieties of the foods in these groups (particularly in the meat and dairy areas). Whole grains are preferable to processed grains because they generally contain more vitamins, minerals and fiber. You should avoid all foods prepared in ways that add calories from fat (e.g., by frying). At least one dark green vegetable and one fruit high in vitamin C should be eaten each day.

Nutritional Density

Nutritional density is a concept that has been introduced to make people aware that the same apparent volume of different foods (e.g., 100 grams) can have very different amounts of important nutrients. In some respects, foods which deliver large amounts of essential proteins, vitamins and minerals per 100 grams can be considered desirable because the person who consumes them gets a great deal of nutrition for the caloric value. (Densities also consider the fat content of foods, the single biggest factor in determining their caloric content.)

Some diets use the concept of density differently. They argue that the lower the density of a food (at least in terms of the caloric and fat density), the better. If a person consumes a similar volume of apple cake and fresh apples, that person will receive fewer calories from the apples, yet may feel as full. Consequently, a person who is seeking to lose weight may find it easier to do so if he or she focuses on foods with a large volume and a relatively small caloric value. In contrast, the hard training athlete who requires a large caloric intake may wish to ingest high density (though not necessarily high fat) foods.

Special Topics In Diet And Nutrition

The Ergogenic Application of Ordinary Foods and Nutrients and Special Ergogenic Substances

As has been noted in the earlier discussions of meeting nutritional needs, many people believe that athletes have special nutritional requirements because of their training. It should be reiterated that training should be distinguished from exercise. A person who engages in a routine form of exercise for the pleasure or benefits of that activity but does not attempt to increase the volume or loading of that exercise is not training in the sense in which most athletes and coaches use that term. Athletes are generally trying to improve their ability to function by stressing their bodies at progressively higher levels in order to force the body to make adaptations. In the case of weightlifters, most are trying to build functional muscle tissue (contractile proteins). Therefore, their form of activity is special. It may well be that this special form of exercise generates special needs for some or all nutrients. Research has not fully answered this question. While the jury is out, many athletes feel that it is a good idea to assure that they are getting extra amounts of the nutrients that their bodies require in order to assure the best possible growth from their training: hence the popularity among athletes of taking high doses of certain vitamins, minerals and proteins.

As long as these athletes stay well below the toxicity levels of the nutrients they consume, this extra nutrition should pose no problem. However, athletes should be aware that individuality works both ways. An athlete may have an individual requirement for certain nutrients, but he or she may also have a lower threshold for the toxicity of certain nutrients. Therefore, megadoses of nutrients are probably not a good idea. A sensible approach is to take some extra amounts of nutrients that are likely to have a positive effect and to monitor your response. If there is no response, the nutrient was probably in sufficient supply before the dosage was increased. If there is a positive response, the dosage can be maintained or raised to see if more is indeed better in this circumstance.

Scientific research in recent years has confirmed that intense exercise leads to the creation of substances called "free radicals" in the body. Free radicals are molecular fragments that damage the tissues with which they make contact. Certain nutrients help to minimize free radical damage. They include vitamins A (and Beta Carotene, a substance from which the body makes vitamin A at the rate of one unit of vitamin A for every six units of Beta Carotene), C, E, ubiquinone (also called. Coenzyme Q10), the mineral selenium and the amino acids L-glutathione and cysteine. The amounts of the vitamins A, C and E and selenium that were presented in the "athlete's dose" of nutrients earlier free radical damage. Coenzyme Q10 dosages between 30 mg and 60 mg are often recommended, and amounts of 1 g and 2 g of glutathione and cysteine, respectively, have been recommended by some writers. While the antioxidant or anti-free-radical advocates were considered crackpots for a number of years, a growing number of people in the medical profession are beginning to embrace the importance of nutrition in this area, so athletes would be well advised to pay attention to what is going on with respect to antioxidant nutrition.

Although the importance of consuming proteins with a balanced amino acid content has already been explained, there are some nutritionists who recommend taking one or a group of amino acids to accomplish specific ends. For example, some writers have suggested that ingesting a dose of the branch chain amino acids (BCAAs) before and after the workout can be beneficial. (The branch chain amino acids are leucine, isoleucine and valine.) BCCAs make up a disproportional share of the proteins in muscle tissue and are depleted during exercise to a greater extent than other amino acids. The logic of pre-workout ingestion of BCCAs is that these amino acids may spare the BCCAs found in the muscle tissue. (Some studies have shown improvements in performance with pre-workout ingestion of BCAAs; thirty minutes to two hours before training is generally recommended.) Ingesting BCCAs shortly after training helps replace BCCAs lost from the muscle during exercise.

Amino acids such as arginine, glycine and ornithine have all been shown to increase the body's production of growth hormone (sought after by strength athletes because of its anabolic effects). Unfortunately, injections of these substances have a more potent influence on growth hormone than oral dosage. In addition, the health risks of ingesting large amounts of these amino acids are not known.

Lactic acid builds up in muscles that are being exercised, and when it reaches a certain threshold, it inhibits muscular contractions. The ingestion of certain substances (e.g., sodium bicarbonate and sodium phosphate) to combat the build-up of acid has been shown to increase endurance, even in some short and high intensity events. Unfortunately, sodium bicarbonate in high doses causes diarrhea in many athletes, and both sodium bicarbonate and sodium phosphate contain sodium, large doses of which cannot be recommended.

Some athletes use a substance called carnitine in hopes that it will build their endurance, but it can have little effect on weightlifters. Ginseng (and a similar compound, eleutherococcus) and caffeine are believed by some to improve performance, but the former is illegal under USOC rules, and excessive doses of caffeine are also illegal, as is ephedrine (and herbs that have it, such as Ma Huang). Moreover, these substances could be expected to help endurance athletes more than weightlifters.

Trimethylglycine (TMG) and Dimethylglycine (DMG) have been identified by some writers as substances that enhance the delivery of oxygen to the muscles. The results of studies in these areas have been uneven. Inosine and creatine phosphate have both been cited as substances which can improve an athlete's endurance. A number of athletes that I know believe that these substances have helped them, but research has yet to confirm any positive effects.

Boron is a mineral that has been virtually ignored by nutritionists until recent years. It is believed that it serves an important role in the formation of certain hormones. Most people's diets probably contain adequate amounts of boron. But some sports nutritionists recommend supplementation in the range of 3 mg to 6 mg a day. Some claims have been made for the anabolic effects of larger dosages of boron, but they have yet to be supported by serious research.

GLA or gamma linolenic acid is a substance that the body needs in order to utilize the essential fatty acid called linoleic acid. Normally, gamma linolenic acid is created by the body from linoleic acid. However, older people suffer a decline in their ability to produce gamma linolenic acid, so some nutritionists recommend that older athletes supplement their diets with GLA.

D.L.Phenylalanine (DLPA) is believed to facilitate the release of endorphins by the body. Endorphins are the body's natural pain killers, producers of a natural high. Supplementation with DLPA may make an athlete with chronic pain more comfortable during training, but the question is whether DLPA masks the pain so that the athlete does more than he or she should.

There is some evidence that certain forms of fats have beneficial effects on health, though not necessarily on athletic performance. In particular, the fish oils, eicosapentanoic acid (EPA) and docosahexinoic acid, have been cited as doing everything from preventing inappropriate blood clotting to easing the pain of arthritis. There do appear to be positive health effects that are worth investigating. Monounsaturated fats, such as those that are found in olive oil, are also believed to have positive effects on health, including controlling serum cholesterol levels.

Anabolic Steroids and Their Risks

There is little doubt that anabolic steroids can improve short term muscle size and strength. On both a scientific and empirical basis, the demonstrations of steroid effectiveness when used in conjunction with proper diet and exercise have been substantial. Despite their effectiveness in enhancing short term strength gains, the serious American athlete does not even consider using them for several reasons.

First, they are illegal in weightlifting competition. Athletes who are found guilty of steroid use face a four-year penalty from the USAW for a first offense and lifetime suspension for the second. Testing now takes place at all major competitions in the United States before any American team leaves on a trip to an international competition and (for our top athletes) randomly throughout the year, upon forty-eight hours' notice. It is not practical for an athlete to attempt steroid usage, even if he or she is unconcerned about the health risks, his or her long term career in weightlifting or the moral issues of using steroids when other athletes are not.

Second, there are significant health risks associated with steroid use. While wild claims about steroid "causing" brain tumors and virtually every other ill known to mankind are unsupported by any scientific research, significant health risks have been identified. Use of anabolic steroids has been associated with elevated cholesterol levels, hypertension, serious degenerative changes in the liver and a number of other health problems. Some data also suggests that the long term use of anabolic steroids may increase risk of certain cancers and may make the tendons more subject to career threatening injuries.

For women, the negatives are even greater. Such side effects as a lowering of the voice, growth of new and coarser facial hair and other "masculinizing" effects of steroids are irreversible. (The extent of these effects is greater when an athlete uses testosterone as opposed to an anabolic steroid.) For most women, such physical changes are highly unwelcome.

Third, the use of steroids (other than under a physician's care for specific medical conditions) is a felony. An athlete who would not dream of using illegal recreational drugs could acquire a criminal record through mere possession of steroids.

Fourth, there are moral implications. Because most athletes, at least in the United States, are clean, the athlete who uses steroids maintains an unfair advantage over his or her opponents.

Finally, on a very practical level, it can be argued that the use of anabolic steroids actually impedes rather than supports long term progress. There are several reasons for this. Steroid use cannot be continued indefinitely. Whether because a test is imminent or for health reasons, use must stop at some point. When it does, a large share of the improvements that are sustained through steroid use are lost. This has obvious physical consequences, but the psychological consequences can be far worse. An athlete who uses an external aid for his or her strength necessarily becomes dependent on that aid. When it is not available, the athlete faces a major problem. If he or she believes that the drug is responsible for his or her success, the athlete's confidence will be greatly eroded when the drug is withdrawn. Many athletes whom I knew during the boom years of steroid use found it virtually impossible to be serious about training when they were not using drugs. In my view, this greatly undermined the effectiveness of their training when they were not taking steroids.

The opposite problem arises when the athlete ignores the effect that steroids may have had on performance. Such an athlete often attempts to maintain the very same volume and intensity of training as when he or she was using the drug. This results in overtraining and often in overuse injuries as well. The steady progress that an athlete can make year round, when steroids are not used, can make up for the larger, shorter term gains that a steroid user can enjoy.

The Time Factor in Nutrition

Just as training takes time to generate performance changes, so changes in diet often do not manifest themselves immediately. A dehydrated athlete may notice an improvement in performance within hours after rehydration has begun. Positive changes from other areas of dietary improvements may take weeks or months to manifest themselves. For instance, in the case of a sustained increase in the protein intake of an athlete whose body was deficient in protein, it will be some hours before the body begins to utilize it, several weeks before the increase is reflected in physical appearance and performance and several months before the full effects are manifested. This is because while the body is destroying and synthesizing protein constantly, the body requires several months to replace the majority of its proteins.

Therefore, an athlete who make appropriate dietary changes must give them a fair trial period before drawing a conclusion about their effects. While modifications in nutritional regimen need to be given time to work, the benefits of such changes certainly need not be accepted "on faith" forever.

405

True improvements in nutrition (as opposed to mere changes in diet) should show results.

Eating Disorders

The primary reason for eating is the necessity to ingest certain nutrients on a regular basis. Two other important reasons for eating are that people enjoy eating and eating can be a positive social experience. As long as the amount and type of food consumed are appropriate, there is certainly no reason not to enjoy what we eat. Unfortunately, some people use food in an unhealthy way (apart from eating foods that are in themselves bad for the body). These people either chronically overeat or undereat; both of these behaviors can be deleterious to health and even life threatening.

Obesity

Chronic overeating leads to obesity. Obesity has a number of definitions, but perhaps the most widely accepted one in the United States is a body-fat level of 25% or more in males and 32% or more in females. (Body fat is now used instead of height and weight as the primary means for identifying obesity, because it has been recognized that extra weight can be attributed to additional muscle as well as additional fat.) Obesity has been linked to a number of serious health risks, such as hypertension, blood lipid levels and glucose tolerance, as well as to a number of health conditions, such as heart disease, arthritis and certain cancers.

A number of reasons have been cited for obesity, including low activity levels, lack of knowledge or concern over caloric intake, early feeding patterns, hormonal problems (which are probably quite rare), variations in the way the body adapts to reduced caloric intake and other hereditary factors. However, no case of obesity can resist dietary treatment if that treatment persists for a long enough period of time, and an appropriate diet is maintained thereafter.

Body-fat levels can increase through an increase in the number of fat cells a person has or an increase in the size of those cells. The number of cells is not believed to increase in mature persons, so any gains in their body fat are attributable to a hypertrophy of their fat cells (the fat cells of obese people may be two to three times the normal size). Studies suggest that the periods during which a person is most susceptible to an increase in the number of fat cells are during the last trimester of pregnancy, during the first year of life and during the adolescent growth spurt. Exercise during the growth years appears to depress the growth of new fat cells.

Weight loss is attributable solely to a reduction in the size of fat cells. The number of cells cannot be reduced by dieting. Therefore, controlling the number of fat cells that a child develops appears to be important in avoiding obesity. Obese people can have five to six times the normal number of fat cells (which of course predisposes them to obesity).

In a sport like weightlifting, obesity presents an insurmountable obstacle to success in all weight classes other than the unlimited body weight classes, because an obese athlete would be giving up too much in terms of lean body mass to other athletes of the same body weight. Some successful weightlifters in these unlimited classes have been obese or nearly so, but they are the exception rather than the rule. A number of athletes have used a combination of diet and weightlifting training to overcome obesity, and a number of athletes have reported that the practice of weightlifting has led to a far more dramatic decrease in body weight than the caloric expenditures that have been traced to weightlifting training would suggest.

Anorexia and Bulimia

Anorexia and bulimia are two eating disorders which are believed to be on the rise in the United States. They are particularly prevalent in young athletes who are in sports that can involve or benefit from a restriction in body weight. Since weightlifting is one such sport, these disorders can be a problem for weightlifters. Fortunately for weightlifting, most athletes and coaches recognize that in increase in lean body mass is generally desirable in terms of the long term performance of an athlete and therefore do not artificially restrict solid bodyweight growth. Nevertheless, weight restrictions do exist, so coaches and athletes should be aware of anorexia and bulimia.

Anorexia is an obsessive focus on body weight which manifests itself in extreme attempts to reduce caloric intake and/or to expend energy (e.g., through exercise or pharmaceutical intervention). It is believed that the vast majority (approximately 90%) of anorexics are women. The incidence of anorexia in the overall population is believed to be extremely small (perhaps 1 in 10,000 to 100,000), but in selected groups the rate of occurrence can be quite high (e.g., 1 in 100 in middle class adolescent girls and as high as 5 to 20 per 100 among ballerinas).

Bulimia is also an obsessive focus on body weight, but, in contrast with anorexia, bulimia manifests itself through binge eating followed by a variety of techniques to offset the binge (e.g., vomiting, fasting, the use of laxatives and diuretics). These behaviors can have extremely negative effects on health. Burning of the esophagus and other areas of the upper digestive tract with stomach acid is a common result of vomiting. Mineral depletion and severe electrolyte imbalances can result from the use of diuretics and laxatives, particularly when they are used for a long time.

The incidence of bulimia is believed to be much greater than anorexia. Bulimics tend to be somewhat older than anorexics, and a higher percentage of men suffer from this disorder than from anorexia. Some studies have shown that as many as 30% of female and 15% of male athletes who are in sports in which weight control is important are bulimic. One study reported that as many as 75% of female gymnasts who were told that their body weights were restricting their performance resorted to techniques of weight control that are associated with bulimia. Because weightlifting is a sport in which weight control is important, bulimia is a potential problem. Coaches should be aware of this and should counsel athletes regarding the risks of bulimic behaviors.

Fasting and Short Term Reductions in Food Consumption

Many old time strongmen believed in the value of fasting occasionally (often one day a week). They believed this practice permitted the digestive system to rest and cleanse itself. More modern athletes, particularly in Eastern Europe, have also experimented with fasting or temporarily reducing food intake. The theory behind this practice is that a sudden and temporary reduction in caloric intake will cause the body to absorb nutrients more effectively after the fast.

Determining Your Ideal Body Weight

One key to weightlifting success is increasing your functional lean body mass or muscle mass. ("Functional" in this context applies to the ability of this increased mass to enable the athlete to generate greater strength and power.) Increasing muscle mass is one of the most important ways to foster strength and power development. However, muscle mass, as it is currently defined, is not necessarily directly related to strength, because the ultrastructure of muscle (and the performance related factors therein) is affected by the kind of training that developed the muscle mass, not merely the mass itself.

The ratios of various components in the overall muscle tissue of bodybuilders and weightlifters tend to be different in a number of respects, primarily because of differences in training methods. As a result, a mere increase in the external diameter of an entire muscle does not have a strict correlation with an improvement in strength. In fact, the correlation may be surprisingly low. However, when the nature of the training that leads to an increase in muscle mass is appropriate (i.e., it leads to an improvement in the functioning of the contractile elements of the muscle), such an increase will generally lead to an increased potential for performance. Therefore, weightlifters will benefit from an increase in muscle mass that was "honestly" attained through strength training. But how much of an increase in muscle mass (and body weight) is appropriate?

There has long been a search for the "ideal" height/weight for weightlifters. In fact, many coaches will look at an athlete and say something like "he will be a 91 kg. lifter some day," judging by the lifter's height and approximate level of maturation. A number of studies in Eastern Europe over the years to have tried to determine the relationship of height to weight in various weight categories. Such studies usually looked at elite athletes, calculated the average height of athletes in each weight class, presented a range which encompasses most athletes and then suggested that this was the ideal range. There is some value in such information in that it can give the athlete and coach guidance in terms of which direction (a bodyweight increase or decrease) is likely to yield the best results for that athlete. But these are only guidelines. Individual athletes may lift better if they are outside the normal range of height for a given weight class. In fact, some of the best weightlifters have competed in weight classes that would generally be regarded as outside the normal range for athletes of their height.

Yuri Vardanian, one of the all time great lifters from the former Soviet Union, was taller than most of his competitors in the old 75 kg. and 82.5 kg. weight classes. Many would have thought that he was too tall for either class. When Yuri increased his body weight toward 90 kg., he continued to be outstanding, but not as much as at 82.5 kg.. Similarly, Naim Suleymanoglu, arguably the outstanding lifter of the 1980s and certainly on of the greatest lifters of all time, is shorter than most of his competitors. Although he was outstanding in the old 52 kg., 56 kg. and 60 kg. weight categories, Naim was at his best in the latter class, in spite of the fact that at approximately 5' in height, he was shorter than many competitors in the lowest of these classes (52 kg.) and much shorter than his competitors in the class in which he was most outstanding (60 kg.).

How does an athlete find his or her ideal weight class? First, the athlete should realize that while most athletes find a "perfect" weight class for them, other athletes may be competitive in either of two weight classes or, on rare occasions, in more than two. Therefore, for many athletes, the ideal body weight is really a range, a range that may change somewhat over time. However, the importance of an athlete finding his or her best Bodyweight range must be emphasized. Many athletes spend considerable time (even a whole career) at the wrong body weight, with quite negative effects on their results.

In order to estimate his or her ideal range, the athlete must take into account present conditions and undertake careful experimentation. Important present conditions include the athlete's current age, height, gender, body-fat levels, total training time (how long he or she has been training seriously), total time at their current body weight, recent rate of progress, dietary habits and current lifting strengths and weaknesses. Because these considerations can affect the appropriate body weight for a particular athlete, let us examine each one.

Height: Although height is not a perfect predictor of ultimate Bodyweight category, it does form a basis for a target range. Clearly, the athlete who is 5' tall should not plan to be in the 99 kg. category and the athlete who is 6' tall should not expect to compete at 59 kg.. Table 4 summarizes Roman's recommendations regarding the relationship of body weight and height. (It is based on research regarding the heights and weights of elite level Soviet weightlifters in the old (pre-1993) body weight classes):

The information in this chart should only be used as a guide. All along the way, whether increasing or reducing body weight toward the estimated category, the athlete should be monitoring the situation carefully in order to determine whether the expected optimization in performance is occurring. The blind pursuit of a bodyweight goal is senseless. If the direction is correct, performance should reflect this relatively quickly. If the lifter is increasing his or her body weight, a gain of a few solid pounds should manifest itself with some strength gains. If, in contrast, fat is being lost, performance should remain relatively stable (unless too much bodyweight is being lost, or it is lost too quickly).

Age: An athlete must take into account his or her age as well as height when Bodyweight class estimates are being made. One reason is because age has a relationship to ultimate height. The athlete who is thirteen is not going to remain at his or her current height as he or she matures. Therefore, the athlete's likely adult height must be considered. One of the biggest mistakes that athletes and coaches make with young athletes is

to have then remain at too light a body weight for too long because there is little competition for the athlete at that body weight. Young athletes need to grow. Holding their weight back may actually prevent them from reaching their full height, but it will most assuredly prevent them from reaching their full muscle mass and strength potentials. Naturally, if a young athlete is carrying significant adipose tissue (fat), it may be appropriate to avoid a weight gain until the athlete becomes leaner at the same body weight.

In the case of older athletes, the age factor suggests that a lighter weight class may be appropriate as the athlete ages. Since loss of muscle mass becomes evident in many athletes by the time they reach their late forties or early fifties, it makes sense for the athlete to consider reducing his or her body weight at this time. Certainly such a weight loss makes sense for athletes in their sixties or seventies. The athlete who competes at seventy in the same weight class that he or she did at thirty is almost certainly carrying significantly more body fat than at that earlier age.

Gender: Individualization in the process of determining an athlete's ideal body weight should enable the athlete to adjust to any differences that can be attributed, at least in part, to gender. Nevertheless, it is useful to understand some of the tendencies that are related to gender so that a more accurate "fix" on a target body weight can be made. Women's physique differs from men's in ways that can influence the determination of an ideal body weight. First, women tend to have somewhat different relationships between performance and height. One consideration is their height in relation to their weight class. Women tend to be taller that men in the same weight class. This is because while their body fat percentages tend to be higher than men at the same body weight, their muscle mass tends to be smaller at the same body weight. More important, their muscle mass tends to be smaller at the same height. Therefore, they are taller in the same weight class. Another consideration related to gender is that women mature faster than men in most physical ways. For instance, a woman's mature height is achieved at an earlier age than a man's. A fourteen-year-old woman may not get much taller as an adult, but a male is likely to. Therefore, projecting the future weight class of a young woman is often easier than projecting the future weight class of a young man of the same age.

Bodyfat Levels: An athlete who carries substantial body fat should consider losing weight. Athletes differ with respect to the level of body fat that enables them to perform well. Some athletes can function very effectively with body-fat percentages as low as 5%. Others will feel weak at such a level and may feel more comfortable carrying 10% or even more. (Athletes in higher

Table 4

Bdwt. Category	Ht. Range (cm)	Ht. Range (inches)
52	142-148	55.9-58.3
56	146-152	57.5-59.8
60	152.5-157.5	60-62
67.5	158-162	62.2-63.8
75	162-166	63.8-65.4
82.5	166-170	65.4-66.9
90	169-173	66.5-68.1
100	172.5-176.5	67.9-69.5
110	175.5-179.5	69.1-70.7
110+	180-192	70.9-75.6

weight classes tend to carry higher levels of body fat with greater success, partially because the relationship of body weight and performance falls off after about 100 kg. in men, and at a much lower level of body weight in women. For men the level of lifting is not very much higher at 108 kg. than it is at 91 kg., and the level of lifting at 120 kg. is not very much higher than at 108 kg.. In the higher weight classes it appears that a modest gain in muscular body weight, even if there is a gain in body fat as well, leads to high enough performance to make the gain worthwhile. In lighter weight classes, changes in body weight tend to lead to more profound changes in performance.

Clearly, athletes (other than superheavyweights) who carry excessive levels of body fat are lifting against other athletes with larger lean body masses. They are thereby giving away a significant body weight advantage to those athletes. In addition, they are required to move their own body mass, which consists of a higher amount of non-functional tissue. The solution is to reduce their body fat while maintaining their muscle mass and to compete in a lower Bodyweight class. Alternatively, they can increase their muscle mass while reducing their body fat, so that they can lift in the same weight category but with a higher lean body mass.

Total Training Time in the Sport and Time Spent At Your Current Body Weight: These factors are important because after a time it appears that performance improvements become very difficult at the same body weight. A Soviet study done a number of years ago suggested that after seven to ten years of training, the only athletes who continued to improve significantly in terms of absolute performance were those who gained body weight. (Superheavyweights had the longest improvement curves.) Presumably, most of the neural and muscular training effects that can take place at a given body weight have occurred after a few years. The only way the athlete can make meaningful improvements after that (putting aside technique improvements) is to increase muscle mass and body weight (assuming the athlete was lean to begin with).

It is important to note that this assumes that the athlete's training has enabled him or her to gain maximum performance out of existing lean body mass. For many athletes this is a somewhat dubious assumption. In many athletes, progress stops because that athlete has reached the maximum performance of which he or she is capable using particular training methods. Different methods might well yield better results. In addition, athletes at any level of achievement often reach a point at which their level of performance meets their needs. Better performance would be valued by such an athlete, but not enough to for that athlete to make any substantial new efforts. Such an athlete may have decided that

performing at a certain level is satisfactory and then entered into a training mode that maintains performance but does not focus on improvement. This can occur either because the athlete has no serious competition or because he or she does not believe that performance at a higher level is a reasonable possibility.

In contrast, an athlete who is making an all out effort to progress, who has a low body-fat percentage and who has been at the same body weight for some time may do well to investigate a weight gain as a way to begin progressing again. If no progress has been made after a careful six-month effort to gain solid body weight (and at least several pounds of muscular body weight have been gained), the body weight increase was probably not a good idea.

Recent Rate Of Progress: This is an important factor in Bodyweight decisions because an athlete who is improving steadily at his or her current body weight rarely needs to consider a change in body weight. The old adage of "leaving well enough alone" applies. There is no particular need to explore weight gains if good progress is currently being made. However, as was noted above, if an athlete has been at the same body weight and lifts for an extended period, the possibility of increasing lean body mass should be considered. This is particularly true if a variety of training methods and technique improvement strategies have been exhausted and the athlete has sincerely been putting forth a maximum mental effort.

Dietary Habits: An athlete's dietary practices should be examined to determine whether an improvement in diet might enhance progress. A sub-optimal intake of protein, carbohydrates, vitamins or minerals could be hindering training and the adaptation that is taking place as a result. An excessive intake of fats, sugars, alcohol, certain drugs and sodium or of overall calories could be supporting an unnecessarily high body weight or undermining progress in some other way. All of these possibilities should be ruled out before other options are considered. In cases where the diet is found to be inappropriate, a change can lead to increases in muscle mass, reductions in body fat, more training energy and better overall health (all of which can occur without any change in gross body weight).

Current Lifting Weaknesses And Strengths: This is another factor which can influence the decision to modify body weight. An athlete who has a serious strength deficiency is likely to find a careful weight gain to be very beneficial. For instance, an athlete who is strong technically but is often unable to stand up from the low position in the clean is a prime candidate for a Bodyweight increase. Increases in body weight generally yield disproportionate gains in squatting strength relative to strength gains made in other areas of the body. Many athletes who have had consistent difficulty standing up from their cleans have remedied the problem through a weight gain.

Mark Cameron, one of America's greatest lifters in the old 100 kg. and 110 kg. categories (the first and still the only non-superheavyweight American to C&J more than 500 lb.) was a case in point. Mark was a pretty good lifter at 75 kg., but he regularly pulled in weights with which he was unable to stand. By the time Mark reached the 82.5 kg. category, he was an outstanding junior lifter, and the occasions on which he was unable to arise out of a low clean position were diminishing. When Mark grew into the 90 kg. category, he rose to national prominence on the senior level and was rarely, if ever, "pinned" in the full squat position. At 100 kg. and beyond, Mark reached a level of national dominance and medal contention at the World and Olympic competitions, and at this point, he generally stood out of his cleans quite easily.

In a contrasting case, my old training partner Joe Gennaro reduced his body weight precipitously to become one of the top lifters in the United States. Joe, pound for pound one of the strongest men I have ever known, began his lifting career as a superheavyweight. He placed second in the 1966 Teenage Nationals, weighing approximately 230 lb. at a height of approximately 5'4". The following year Joe reduced his body weight to 165 lb.. It was a drastic and rapid weight reduction, and Joe lost a great deal of strength in the process. But through dedicated training he was able to increase his strength to higher levels than he had possessed when he was 65 pounds heavier. He later increased his body weight to 181 lb., at which point he was truly one of the strongest men in the world in his day. Had Joe remained in the superheavyweight class he never would have been competitive is a senior lifter.

In summary, every individual athlete has a body weight range in which he or she is most effective. For some athletes that range is rather large. These athletes become competitive at a certain body weight and then, as their weight increases, increase their performance along with competitive standards. For every athlete, however, there is a point at which added body weight does not yield improved results, and another point at which a reduction in body weight results in disproportionate strength losses. Between these two extremes is the athlete's optimum body weight range.

Reaching premature conclusions regarding optimal body weight must be avoided. That range may be somewhat flexible. An athlete who has gained weight improperly (e.g., too quickly or with too great a gain in body fat) is likely to conclude that no benefit came from the gain. However, a more careful weight gain probably would have yielded far better results. Similarly, the athlete who has reduced through a crash diet and with limited training may have noted a precipitous fall

in strength, a decline which might be counteracted after the athlete trains for some time at the new body weight. Finally, an older athlete may find better relative performance in a lower weight class, because of an age related reduction in muscle mass.

Once an athlete has reached his or her ideal body weight, that weight should be carefully maintained. Binge eating and crash dieting are neither healthy nor performance enhancing.

Minimizing Bodyfat

For most weightlifters (i.e., all but the superheavyweights), minimizing body fat is an important issue. Since there are weight classes in weightlifting competitions, weightlifters strive for maximum functional muscle mass and minimum body fat, so that they do not have to compete with athletes who have the same gross body mass but a greater lean body mass.

Standard height and weight tables that apply to the general public are virtually worthless for the weightlifter, primarily because such charts do not take into account the muscle mass that weightlifters develop through their training. Of course, there are some people who claim the right to ignore standard heighten and weight guidelines because they have so much muscle when in reality their claim to extra muscle is wildly inflated.

Visual inspection of your body can be a useful method for recognizing changes in body fat levels, if these inspections take place under consistent conditions. However, the only precise way to measure body fat is to remove chemically all of the fat from the subject's body. Unfortunately, this requires that the subject be dead, an obvious drawback. Considering that drawback, several other approaches to assessing lean body mass include a skinfold test, underwater weighing, electronic impedance and some other means of assessing body fat in a direct or indirect manner.

Underwater weighing is considered the most accurate technique, but even it (and other similar methods) has the drawback of relying on statistics that were accumulated from populations that may not closely resemble the weightlifting population. Nevertheless, reasonable estimates can be made using this or the other techniques mentioned. Perhaps the greatest value of these methods is in helping the same person to measure progress over time. For instance, if an athlete loses 10 lb. pounds of body weight and his or her skinfolds remain essentially the same, this is not be considered a favorable sign. In contrast, a similar weight loss with a corresponding decrease in skinfolds suggests that the loss was primarily in body fat and not muscle.

Body fat can be important in certain circumstances; it insulates the body from the cold, protects the internal organs against trauma and supplies energy when food is unavailable. Most of these purposes are not significant in countries in which weightlifting is popular today. Exposure of the internal organs to trauma is not an everyday concern. Energy can be stored in the refrigerator instead of the waistline. A wide range of clothing is available to offer insulation from the cold (not to mention central heating, which precludes the need for insulation altogether).

Excessively low levels of body fat do present at least two other risks. One problem is that extremely low body-fat levels in women have been associated with amenorrhea (the absence or suppression of menstruation). Another problem, one that affects both men and women, is that as the body's fat stores decrease, the body is more likely to utilize its lean body mass (muscle) for energy and other metabolic purposes. Reducing body weight nearly always results in a loss of some lean body mass; the lower the percentage of an athlete's body fat, the more likely it is that this will occur.

Diet can have an important effect on both muscle mass and body fat, primarily because of its influence on the balance of caloric intake and expenditure. If an athlete wishes to decrease his or her body fat level, caloric expenditure must exceed intake. This can be accomplished by reducing caloric intake, increasing caloric expenditure or some combination of both. A rule of thumb that is used by nutritionists to explain the relationship of body fat and caloric intake is that one pound of fat equals 3500 calories. If someone wants to lose 1 lb. of fat, they must generate a caloric deficit of 3,500 calories.

It is likely that the distribution of calories among carbohydrates, fats and proteins (as well as overall caloric intake) has an influence on body composition. For instance, a reducing diet that minimized protein could be expected to result in a greater loss of lean body mass than one which maintained a reasonable level of protein intake. Some athletes seem to react favorably to a diet that reduces fat intake more than anything else while others seem to benefit from a low carbohydrate diet.

The average person burns approximately 1700 to 2200 calories a day (a person's size and activity level materially affect this figure). It is generally recommended that caloric intake not be reduced below 1200 calories a day (which yields a negative caloric intake 500 to 1000 calories a day for the average person). For the athlete, a negative caloric balance of these proportions may be achieved at a much higher level of caloric intake because of the extra calories that an athlete expends during and after exercise (exercises burn extra calories from minutes to hours after activity ceases). There are two primary reasons for not creating a caloric deficit larger than 500 to 1000 calories. One reason is that balances which are much lower are likely to

result in significant loss of lean body mass and actually pose a health risk to the dieter. The other reason for not reducing calories precipitously is that doing so can cause a reduction in the body's basal metabolism rate, which may offset, to a certain extent, the reduction in calories in the diet. (This is less likely to be a problem among hard training athletes than among more sedentary individuals, partly because a large share of the athletes caloric expenditure is not affected by a change in the athlete's basal metabolism rate.)

Most health authorities agree that the ideal weight loss goal is no more than 2 lb. a week, and a slower rate of weight loss is often recommended.

Diuretics (which are illegal under IOC, USOC and USAW rules), laxatives, rubber suits, saunas, vibrating belts and the like do not produce a permanent or healthy weight loss. Most of these techniques (other than vibrators, which simply make you feel better) merely dehydrate the athlete, which hurts performance, and, in cases of extreme weight loss, can result in serious illness or even death.

For the average, non-training person, merely reducing caloric intake is a relatively poor way to lose weight. It has been estimated that from one-third to one-half of the weight loss achieved solely by dieting consists of a loss of muscle mass. So a person who merely diets will become smaller overall, but the percentage of body fat that they carry may not change very much. Consequently, the person with a "pear" shape simply becomes a pear of smaller circumference, but the basic shape changes little, if at all. This is particularly true of the person over thirty, who is beginning to lose muscle mass as part of the aging process.

Exercising while dieting reduces the loss of lean body mass by as much as one-half or more. If a dieter exercises at a level of intensity sufficient to stimulate muscular hypertrophy, he or she will lose more fat than muscle during the weight loss process and may be able to avoid an overall loss of muscle mass altogether or even experience significant muscle hypertrophy, at least in certain areas of the body. Depending on the nature of the exercise performed and the diet undertaken, the net effect of diet and exercise may be a reduction in fat and an increase in lean body mass (muscle).

Some people fear that an increase in exercise will increase their appetite, offsetting any advantages they may gain from exercising while dieting. Studies have shown that light to moderate exercise over an extended period has no effect on appetite. More severe exercise conducted for a short period of time appears to suppress appetite.

During prolonged exercise, fatty acids extracted from the body's fat stores are used for energy (through a process called lipolysis), and the utilization of these stores can persist for a significant period after the cessation of an exercise bout. (Therefore, the effect of exercise on the reduction of body fat may go beyond what would be predicted on the basis of the extra caloric expenditure that took place during the exercises.)

In the case of a weightlifter who is training properly, stimulation toward hypertrophy (or at least the maintenance of muscle mass) is occurring continually. Therefore, a weightlifter may safely lose weight merely by decreasing caloric intake. Nevertheless, even for the weightlifter, increasing the energy expenditure through a certain amount of aerobic exercise may be more beneficial than merely cutting calories. However, there are limits to the benefits of aerobic exercise for weightlifters. Our current understanding of muscle physiology, as well as practical experience, tells us that extensive aerobic exercise beyond a moderate level will interfere with hypertrophy and strength improvements. Safe limits appear to be somewhat above the level of aerobic exercise that is required to maintain aerobic fitness (i.e., three weekly sessions which result in the maintenance of a target pulse rate for twenty minutes). On the other hand, training for distance running and similar endeavors appear to be out.

Athletes who lose substantial body weight (more than 10%) often notice the following pattern. During the early stages of weight loss, the rate of loss is rapid, and the effect on strength is small. This is one of the reasons that rapid weight loss prior to competition (primarily due to dehydration and a reduction of the volume of food in the athlete's digestive tract) often results in little diminution in performance. As the process continues, weight loss becomes slower, and the athlete often begins to notice a reduction in strength as the loss of body weight mounts. This decline in strength can become precipitous for athletes who are losing substantially more than 10% of body weight. Athletes have described this phenomenon as the "bottom falling out." Fortunately, this is a temporary phenomena for the athlete who persists. After strength bottoms out at approximately the point where weight loss stops (or shortly thereafter), it stabilizes and then begins to move in the direction of previous levels. Although strength may not actually reach those levels (that depends on how much body weight, especially lean muscle mass, was lost), athletes who stick with a sensible training program report a remarkable recovery of strength after some period of time (typically several months). Athletes who become discouraged too early may regain weight too soon or give up training in disgust when a little more persistence would have led to success.

Gaining Muscular Bodyweight

Many young athletes need to gain muscular bodyweight in order to reach their potential in weightlifting. There are four keys to this process: adequate caloric intake, adequate intake of protein,

a training stimulus sufficient to stimulate growth and avoidance of activities that tear the body down.

In order to gain weight the athlete must take in more calories than he or she expends. Calories can be increased by consuming a greater quantity of food and/or increasing its caloric density. Athletes who are trying to gain weight may need to eat in a way that would not be encouraged for the average person. This is not a license to eat candy bars and donuts all day. But most athletes will find that an increase in dietary fat (through increased milk consumption or and increase in fish and vegetable oils) will aid in the weight gaining process.

Protein has already been discussed at length, so we will not repeat that discussion here, but the athlete should be reminded that complete proteins are the building blocks for muscle tissue and particular attention must be paid to getting adequate protein when the weight gaining process is under way.

Exercise must be if sufficient volume and intensity to facilitate weight gains. Exercise creates the demand for muscle tissue and food supplies the needed material. Training hard without adequate nutrients may improve performance but it will not increase muscular bodyweight. Eating more without training hard will simply increase your bodyfat.

Measuring what you eat is at least as important when you are trying to gain weight as it is when you are trying to lose it. If you want to gain weight you may have to eat when you are not hungry simply to raise your caloric and/or protein intake sufficiently. This does not justify pure gluttony— weight must be gained slowly if it is to be truly effective. A gain of one or two pounds should be held for a while (at least a few weeks) in order to get the most out of the increase. Once a performance improvement has been noted, a little more weight can be added. Bloating up all at once will not yield the desired results. Sudden and dramatic weight gains are possible for bodybuilders who are "pumping" their muscles with high reps. But they are generally developing the kind of "showy" muscle that will be of limited help to the weightlifter, who needs every pound of bodyweight to be fully functional in terms of increased strength and power.

Finally, the athlete who is working to gain weight should minimize the stresses of life outside of training and get plenty of rest. In the earlier chapter of this book on mental preparation it was noted that when Paul Anderson was training for maximum improvements he would rather ride than walk, would rather sit down than stand and would rather lie down than sit up. Similarly, it was mentioned that former Mr. Universe, Reg Park, said that he made the greatest gains in muscular bodyweight in his life when he stayed in bed all day and got up only to train. These are extreme cases but they make the point that the body has only so much energy to support life and adaptation, Frittering that energy away with unnecessary activity, late nights out or mental stress will prevent the athlete from reaching his or her full potential, whether he or she is trying to gain weight or not.

Eating To Perform Well In Training And In Competition

Eating well is important for athletes at all times, but special approaches to eating can improve an athlete's performance in training and in competition. It appears that the effectiveness of certain nutrients in meeting the body's needs is determined not only by what you eat, but also by when you eat.

Eating in the Days Before the Event

It is advisable for the athlete to build up his or her energy stores prior to a competitive event. For the weightlifter, consuming a diet relatively high in carbohydrates the day before the event should be more than sufficient (this may not be possible for the athlete who is making weight).

Athletes who participate in endurance sports often engage in a special kind of diet and exercise regime designed to deplete the bodies glycogen stores and then to permit the body to overcompensate before the event. This process is called "carbohydrate loading." Carbohydrate loading is not believed to be beneficial for weightlifters because weightlifters do not expend a great deal of physical energy during competition. Moreover, carbohydrate loading tends to cause the athlete to retain additional water along with the extra energy stores. This additional weight will tend to slow an athlete down. Decreased speed of movement and increased body weight are both bad developments for weightlifters.

The Pre-Game Meal

It is generally recommended that the pre-game meal for athletic events consist primarily of a mixture of complex and simple carbohydrates but be low in protein and fat. Protein is harder to digest than most carbohydrates and generates more metabolic wastes. Fats are harder to digest than carbohydrates and require oxygen to assist in the digestive process. Fats also slow the rate of gastric emptying, the opposite of what the athlete desires. (Athletes generally want rapid digestion of their pre-game meal so that they do not feel full or bloated during the event.)

The pre-game meal is not as much of an issue in weightlifting as in other sports. This is because the competition itself does not require a great deal of physical energy, because foods and liquids are relatively easy to consume during the event and because weightlifters do not process a great deal of additional oxygen as a result of the competitive lifting process.

As was suggested in Chapter 8, a meal that the athlete feels comfortable with is probably more conducive to high performance than one that has been scientifically created for competition but with which the athlete does not feel comfortable.

When one eats and the amount that is consumed can be as important as what one eats. For example, I cannot eat for at least two (and preferably three or four) hours before a training session or competition. If I do, my stomach is very uncomfortable during the competition or training session. In contrast, I know other lifters who feel ready to lift after finishing a full meal. Each lifter must experiment to determine the best approach for him or her. It is best to work this out well before any competition, so that unpleasant surprises do not arise during the competition itself. When in doubt, it is generally advisable to have an empty stomach rather than one that is too full.

Dehydration is not normally a problem for weightlifters because most competitions are conducted in climate controlled conditions. If conditions of high temperature and humidity do exist, or the athlete has dehydrated to make weight, consistent fluid consumption should begin immediately after the weigh-in. The athlete should not rely on a feeling of thirst to precipitate fluid intake. Rather, fluids should be ingested at the approximate rate of 100 ml to 200 ml of fluid every ten to fifteen minutes, at least until the athlete's normal body weight has been regained (or the high temperature/humidity conditions cease).

Eating During the Event

Under conditions of forced rehydration, there will be a need to urinate frequently. Therefore, it is important to know the location and availability of restroom facilities and to provide ample time during warm-ups for any necessary visits to those facilities.

During the event it is important to maintain hydration and to occasionally supply the body with some carbohydrates (e.g., 25 g to 50 g every thirty minutes or so). This can be accomplished most easily by ingesting a cup of fluid that has a 6% concentration of carbohydrates every fifteen to twenty minutes. In this way both fluid and energy needs are satisfied at one time and in a form that is easy for the body to assimilate. A solution that is less than 5% carbohydrates will not supply significant energy, and one that is more than 10% carbohydrates can result in cramps, diarrhea and nausea, none of which is welcome at any time, but all of which are problematical during a competition. Solutions that are high in carbohydrates will also slow the process of gastric emptying. (Most fluid is absorbed in the body by the small intestine, so any delay in the process of gastric emptying is undesirable.) Sodium in concentrates of 10 m/Ml to 30 m/Ml speeds the absorption of fluids, and a fluid temperature of 6° to 12° Centigrade hastens the speed of gastric emptying. Cold fluids also help the athlete to reduce his or her body temperature in hot weather.

Fructose is absorbed and metabolized more slowly than other simple carbohydrates, so it may help to prevent the development of hypoglycemia (low blood sugar) during the event. Glucose polymers (complex carbohydrates that are digested more slowly than simple sugars) are considered by many nutritionists as an ideal muscle fuel during and after exercise. A mix that has a small amount (less than 10%) of fructose and a balance of more complex carbohydrates appears optimal.

Consumption of 50 g to 100 g of carbohydrates per hour of exercise is believed to delay the onset of fatigue. This is best done by sipping a solution with 5% to 10% concentration of carbohydrates during training, so that you are meeting fluid and carbohydrate needs simultaneously.

Post-Game Meals

There are two primary nutritional concerns immediately after an event is over: rehydration (if needed) and the replenishment of carbohydrate stores. Some research suggests that volumes of fluids in excess of 800 ml per hour cannot be effectively absorbed. Therefore, when fluid loss exceeds that level or dehydration has occurred prior to the event, replenishment of fluids lost during exercise must continue after the exercise or event is over.

Meals that are relatively high in both simple and complex carbohydrates are optimal for the replacement of carbohydrate stores. Because the body (particularly the muscles) has a great need for carbohydrate replenishment following exercise, it is believed that the replenishment of muscle glycogen (energy) stores is facilitated when carbohydrates are consumed as quickly as possible after exercise .Some protein intake assists the body in the repair of tissue that has been torn down during a particularly strenuous bout of training or competition.

Summary

Great performers in all walks of life agree that excellence is built upon attention to detail. Proper nutrition is one of those details, one that should never be overlooked. Training stimulates the body to rebuild itself to perform at a higher level. Sound nutrition supplies the body with the raw materials that it needs for the rebuilding process. Nutritional management also permits the athlete to modify his or her body weight and body composition as is appropriate, a true key to weightlifting success. Therefore, training without giving proper attention to nutrition is nothing less than foolish. On the other hand, relying on miracle foods for strength and Bodyweight gains is no less foolhardy. You need to use the right bricks in the right way in order to build the perfect house, but more bricks will not make the house more perfect: so it is with nutrition, restoration and the body.

No matter how careful or genetically gifted an athlete may be, it is likely that her or she will face the prospect of on injury some day. The next chapter deals with preventing, treating and training around injuries.

The first person ever to win 4 individual medals in 4 separate Olympic Games (one at age 40), Norbert Schemansky came back from two major back surgeries to set this World Record at 38 years of age.

CHAPTER 11

Preventing And Dealing With Injuries And The Use Of Restorative Methods

Injuries are the scourge of sport. At a minimum, they cause discomfort, which, apart from its obvious drawbacks, can have a negative influence on technique. More serious injuries can lead to a loss of training time. These losses of training time can greatly decrease an athlete's chances of success. In some cases, injuries can end a career (or even a life). Avoiding injury is therefore one of the cardinal rules for achieving championship performance.

Training for high level athletic performance and competition itself present certain inherent and sport-specific risks to athletes. Risk cannot be reduced beyond this level with our current level of knowledge. In comparison with many more popular sports, weightlifting is a relatively safe sport. While statistics in this area are far from complete, the incidence of serious weightlifting injuries appears to be significantly lower than in sports like football, basketball, gymnastics and wrestling.

In all of my years in the sport of weightlifting the severest injuries I have heard of include one coronary that occurred during a competition (in a lifter in his mid-forties who had a heart condition of which he was previously unaware), one spinal cord injury that resulted in partial paralysis (which appeared to be the direct consequence of the lifter's foot being caught on a faulty platform) and a few losses of finger tips (the latter when the fingers were positioned between a weight rack and a bar when the bar was lowered in an uncontrolled fashion to a weight rack or simply dropped on such a rack). Severe strain of major muscle-tendon units occur on occasion, as do elbow dislocations. Less serious joint and muscle injuries are much more common, but the frequency and severity of such injuries is lower than in many other sports. When you compare this list to the numerous head injuries, spinal cord injuries and compound fractures that occur in some of the more popular sports, the risk of weightlifting appears far smaller.

Despite weightlifting's safety record, the general public, and even many of those who train with weights or coach athletes who do, regard Olympic style weightlifting as the most dangerous of the weight sports. This is a somewhat surprising view considering that deaths caused by the bench press are reported with regularity, yet few people regard bench presses as unsafe, and many practice them with little or no instruction or supervision.

The risks inherent in any sport tend to be far lower than the actual incidence of injury. Weightlifting is no exception to this rule. The percentage of weightlifting injuries that are preventable is very high. In my opinion, weightlifting's relatively moderate injury rate could be reduced by at least two-thirds, and perhaps more than 90%, if proper precautions with regard to supervision, training, safety practices and equipment were followed. In addition, if injuries were treated properly and promptly, the entire problem of injuries would be still smaller.

The main purpose of this chapter is to teach you how to prevent injury and to minimize the severity and negative effects of injuries that do occur and to help you recuperate more effectively from training so that your risk of overtraining and injury is reduced. The reader should recognize that I am not a medical professional and I cannot give medical advice. You will find a listing of some very fine books on sports medicine in the Bibliography. If you sustain an injury, I urge you to confer with the appropriate medical professionals immediately. This chapter is not intended to substitute for their advice.

What I will attempt to do in this chapter is to tell you what I have learned about injuries through hard experience during more than thirty years of training for competitive weightlifting and a longer period of training with weights. While much of the advice that I will offer would be considered "mainstream," I will sometimes say things that are at odds with the views of the medical establishment. These opinions are based on my own experience and are merely offered to the reader for informational purposes.

Although we will discuss many kinds of injuries, the reader should not be led to believe that these are necessarily everyday occurrences in weightlifting. If you are around any activity for more than thirty years, you see many mishaps and injuries.

Preventing Injuries

The old adage, "an ounce of prevention is worth a pound of cure," certainly applies to sports injuries, though it might better be expressed as a gram of prevention being worth a kilo of cure. Pain, inconvenience, lack of function, loss of training time, destruction of technique and serious health risks are all reasons to avoid injuries. If these negative aspects are not enough to encourage coaches to treat this subject seriously, moral concerns over the well being of athletes and concerns over legal liabilities certainly should.

The importance of safety in teaching technique, in developing training plans and in a wide variety of other areas has been stressed throughout this book. Chapters 2 and 5 presented a number of important safety guidelines. We will not attempt to repeat those guidelines here. Instead, we will focus on other measures that can be taken to assure the safety of athletes. However, before we address some of those issues, let us look at one important preventive measure that should be taken even before an athlete enters the gym.

Having a Check-up Prior to Commencing an Activity

A check-up with a physician, preferably one who is knowledgeable regarding sports, is an important precaution before participation in any sport. A doctor can screen an athlete for any serious risk factors, answer questions and concerns that he or she may have about a particular activity and establish a "baseline" measure of the athlete's condition before he or she undertakes an activity. If the physician fully understands the activity in which the athlete intends to participate, he or she may be able to make recommendations that will enable the athlete to avoid injury.

The prospective athlete should be aware, however, that the advice offered by a doctor may be have limited value for at least two reasons. First, the doctor may not fully understand the nature of the activity the athlete intends to undertake. This is especially true of weightlifting. Many physicians are no more aware of the nature of competitive weightlifting than the general public. They do not understand the distinctions between the various weight sports. They also do not understand the techniques of weightlifting or the adaptations that

the body makes to the activity. Consequently, a very good doctor may not make sensible recommendations regarding weightlifting. This is not to say that a physician's advice should ever be ignored; anyone does this at their own peril. But it does suggest that athletes and coaches should educate the physician about their sport and understand that the physician's advice is based on his or her own understanding of that sport and the athlete's condition. That advice must then be carefully judged by the athlete (or, in the case of a minor, by the athlete's parents) and the coach.

A second consideration regarding doctors is that many of them are conservative by nature. The first rule followed by any physician is to "do no harm" (and malpractice worries make that rule even more important for physicians today than ever before). Cautious doctors may never recommend an activity of a vigorous nature for fear that if injury occurs during such an activity their patients may try to hold them responsible in some way.

The coach should encourage his or her athletes (and parents, where appropriate) to understand the sport and the risks of participation before they begin. Weightlifting may be a relatively safe sport, but participation in any vigorous sport can result in injuries, and athletes need to understand that. Once they do, they can make their own decisions regarding participation.

Some organizations which deal regularly with the issues of exercise safety, such as the American College of Sports Medicine, have developed guidelines for safe participation in moderate activity without having medical clearance. However, since competitive weightlifting is strenuous by nature, these guidelines do not apply. A check-up, or at least a discussion with your family physician about participation in weightlifting, is a prudent precaution for every fledgling weightlifter.

Safety Is Enhanced by Proper Coaching

Good coaching is one of the most important ways to prevent injury. Sensible training programs are the foundation of good coaching. Training programs must be tailored to the level of ability, condition, physical and mental limitations (if any) of each athlete. The implementation of the program should then consider the athlete's condition and external conditions on any given day, so that appropriate modifications can be made. Training for athletic competition often involves pushing athletes to levels which exceed their previous bests. But this should not take place every training session and should never be attempted when the athlete is fatigued, impaired by injury or illness, mentally unprepared or limited in some other way. In addition, athletes should never be pushed beyond their legitimate limits.

Fatigued and overtrained athletes are prone to injury. When a coach observes signs of fatigue or overtraining, he or she should act to correct the situation, particularly when the fatigued or overtrained state is severe enough to compromise the lifter's technique or ability to perform to a significant extent.

Another important foundation of good coaching is teaching proper technique. The coach should always emphasize sound technique first, including how to miss (see Chapter 2). Proper technique is not only efficient; it is also generally safer than poor technique.

Proper workout design is nearly as important as the proper design of the overall training plan when it comes to preventing injuries. A proper warm-up is essential. Lifters who attempt heavy lifts when they are "cold" are running an unnecessary risk of failure (if not outright injury). Exercises requiring considerable skill (such as the classic lifts) should generally be prescribed early enough in the workout so that the athlete is not in a fatigued state when they are being practiced. (This is especially important if the athlete is going heavy that day, which is one of the reasons for the guidelines for exercise order provided in Chapter 6.).

One final and very important aspect of injury avoidance is being reasonable in terms of poundage selection when practicing and competing. This does not mean that the lifter must be overly cautious or afraid to attempt new personal records. A willingness to extend yourself is one of the true keys to progress in weightlifting. Being reasonable does mean that the weight attempted on any given day should be within or only slightly beyond the lifter's capabilities. Assessing capabilities requires consideration of the lifter's current physical and mental conditioning, his or her skill level and readiness on a given day.

The lifter's overall condition dictates that lifter's potential at that time. It is evaluated on the basis of the athlete's recent performances in the classical lifts as well as the assistance exercises. For example, if the lifter can typically power clean 85% of his or her squat clean and that lifter has recently power cleaned 127.5 kg. , a 150 kg. clean is a reasonable projection. Alternatively, if the lifter always seems to lift 5% more in competition than in the gym, and he or she cleans 142.5 kg. in the gym, a 150 kg. clean in competition is again possible. Perhaps the lifter will do even better. On a day when the lifter feels really wonderful, a 155 kg. clean might be possible. But 170 kg. is surely not within the realm of possibility for that lifter at that time, and attempting such a weight would be foolish.

The lifter's readiness on a specific day is another important consideration. Our lifter with a 150 kg. potential in the clean may well have a day on which 130 kg. presents a challenge. On another day, 140 kg. may look good but 150 kg. is simply not reachable. On still another day 150 kg. will be achieved and on a truly great day an additional 5 kg. or even 10 kg. more may be possible. The coach will get to know how an athlete looks when near maximums are being reached, and the lifter will know how he or she feels. The coach can supply valuable external feedback to the lifter, and the lifter can supply valuable internal feedback to the coach. As an example of the latter, many lifters have the ability to regulate their output of effort so that they can make a given weight, but it will not look easy. Then they can add considerable weight to the bar and lift it with the same apparent degree of effort, merely by increasing their focus and arousal level. Only the lifter knows his or her internal mental state, and it is important for the lifter to be able to monitor and judge that state. The lifter must come to know how to distinguish great courage from wishful thinking.

The final consideration with respect to judging a lifter's readiness for a given weight is that lifter's degree of skill. Mature and skillful lifters are able to make large increases from one attempt to another without suffering a breakdown in technique. Less experienced and less skillful lifters and those who get so excited when they attempt a heavy weight that their technique deteriorates may not be able to make large jumps in weight. For beginners and intermediate lifters, the fundamental rule is that increases should be gradual (no more than 10% at a time when the lifter is at 80% of maximum or beyond and often less than 5%). In addition, no increase in weight should be permitted unless the lifter is performing the current weight with correct technique. Moreover, if an increase results in a significant breakdown in technique, a lesser weight should be taken next and then any increases should be made more gradual than they were the first time around.

Two Major Causes of Injury Only Athletes Can Control

Regardless of what the coach does to assure safety, athletes are generally the biggest contributors to their own injuries. The two most common of these causes are fighting mis-positioned lifts and failing to concentrate on what you are doing.

Fighting A Lost or Mis-positioned Lift

One of the most common and completely preventable causes of lifting error is fighting to make a lift beyond the point where correction is reasonably possible. I have witnessed many examples of this, but I'll offer only two.

I knew one national level lifter who suffered a severe ankle sprain when he tried to recover from the low squat position in the clean after both knees had fallen to the platform and while the weight was still on his shoulders. He should have dropped the bar forward as soon as there was one knee touch. With two knees down, the appropriateness of "dumping" the bar was obvious. Attempting to rock back to normal squat position was ludicrous, as this athlete soon discovered. Fortunately, he recovered fully from the incident, but I am sure that he regards that incident as one of his most foolish.

Another lifter I knew had a long and outstanding career in the sport (including many national titles, a silver medal in the World Championships and three Olympic teams). This lifter effectively ended his career when he fought to press out a snatch that was guaranteed to be turned down by the referees had he been able to press the bar to arm's length. The attempt to save the bar resulted in a torn triceps muscle that was never properly reattached. He continued in a heroic effort to resume his previous level of performance, but he was never able to accomplish this. His mistake had ended his career.

The athlete must learn when a weight can reasonably be saved and when it cannot. There is no point in fighting the latter kind of lift, especially in training. It may look impressive to bystanders when a lifter twists and turns, struggles and squirms to save a lift that is unbalanced, outside the lifter's base of support or not cleanly lifted. But a lifter is wrong to use this kind of performance to demonstrate a fighting spirit. Struggles against maximum weights are part of the drama of weightlifting, but when the bar is grossly mis-positioned, struggling is a major mistake. A lifter who heeds this advice is likely to have a far longer and more rewarding career than one who does not.

Lapses in Concentration

Lapses in concentration are a major cause of injury. A lifter may have good technique and good equipment and follow sound safety practices, but if he or she lets his or her concentration lapse, the risk of injury rises dramatically. Concentration is a learned skill. Lifters should always be urged to cultivate this skill. Loss of concentration due to distractions or other causes can cause problems. But most problems occur when the lifter has not learned to focus on the exercise at hand for the full duration of its performance. The lift is not over until the bar is at rest on the platform or on the support from which it was removed. The majority of the accidents I have observed in the gym over the years can be attributed to the athlete permitting his or her attention to drift to something other than the safe completion of the lift. For instance, a acquaintance of mine has been lifting for approximately thirty-five years. He has trained vigorously for most of that time and is quite knowledgeable regarding the sport (having achieved the status of an international referee).

This lifter has broken his foot twice in training because he was talking as he was unloading the bar and dropped a plate on his toe. He would be the first to tell you that neither accident would have occurred if he had been concentrating on what he was doing.

Understanding Injuries

There are two basic categories of injuries: acute and overuse. Acute injuries are caused by a single incident. Examples include dropping the bar on a part of the body or losing your footing on a slippery surface while lifting and spraining a knee as a result. Most acute weightlifting injuries are avoidable. Proper technique, appropriate equipment, proper supervision and safe lifting practices all serve to minimize the incidence of acute injuries.

Overuse injuries result from repetitive forces that lead to the destruction of a small number of cells (also known as "micro-trauma"). In general, the body can adapt itself at the cellular level to physical demands, but the adaptation process takes time. Any sudden change in demands imposed on the body can result in a breakdown of tissue that exceeds the body's ability to repair itself. If the complete repair or replacement of the cells damaged by micro-trauma does not have sufficient time to take place, permanent injury can result. The destruction of even a small number of cells per incident of micro-trauma has a cumulative effect.

The causal factors of overuse injuries are generally divided into two categories: intrinsic and extrinsic. Intrinsic causes include the athlete's anatomy and physiology. Examples of extrinsic factors include an overly ambitious training regimen, improper technique, environmental stressors or some combination of these factors. The dividing line between extrinsic and intrinsic causes is not always clear. For instance, a gradual increase in training volume may lead to an injury in one athlete and not another. What is the cause here? Intrinsic or extrinsic? The answer is that overuse injuries are caused by the interaction of intrinsic and extrinsic factors. Therefore, overuse injuries that are addressed early enough can often be overcome by altering the training, technical and/or restorative activity of the athlete.

In some cases, there is also a fine line between traumatic and overuse injuries. An athlete may take a false step and incur a back injury as a result. The immediate reaction is to blame the wrong step and classify the injury as a trauma. The reality may be that the lifter had unduly fatigued his or her back with prior overtraining and/or the use of a technique which placed an unnecessary strain on the back, predisposing it to injury. Along comes the misstep and the lifter interprets the entire incident as one of those "freak" accidents that sometimes befall athletes. While the lifter who has such an "accident" needs to analyze the reason for a technical mistake or misstep in order to assure that it does not occur again, time should also be taken to consider the possibility that prior overuse may have contributed to the injury. If that is believed to be the case, the lifter should work to correct that problem as well.

A similar mistake can be made in analyzing the cause of other injuries that have a rapid onset. A fairly typical case is one in which an athlete walks into the gym, begins to warm up and suddenly sustains a strained muscle. The easy conclusion would be to blame an inadequate warm-up or some minor technique fault in the lift during which the injury occurred. These may well have been the sole causes. However, a more likely scenario is that the lifter had actually sustained an injury in a prior workout which had thus far gone unnoticed. When new strain was placed on the body during the later workout, the full blown injury actually appeared. It is important to analyze each injury carefully, searching out all of the contributing factors. If a likely cause is discovered, the athlete can make appropriate corrections. If the lifter is fortunate, the injury will never recur. Should the injury recur despite those precautions, the lifter may need to strengthen the preventive measures that he or she took prior to the injury or to reexamine the original hypothesis regarding the cause.

Genetic and Acquired Predispositions to Certain Injuries

Two athletes can train in exactly the same way, live the same lifestyles and be exposed to the same stressors, yet one will develop an injury and the other will not. One reason is that athletes vary in their genetic makeup (one of the "intrinsic" factors alluded to earlier). Some athletes have inherited sturdier constitutions and have much more room for error. Evidence suggests genetic predisposition to certain kinds of injuries. In some cases this evidence applies to specific injuries (e.g., Achilles-tendon ruptures) and in other cases it is related to the body's overall tendency to have degenerative reactions to stress.

Athletes also differ because of the environmental influences to which they have been exposed. Proper training strengthens the body's reserves against injury, so an athlete who has been properly trained will have better resistance to injury than one who has not. In contrast, an athlete who has had previous injuries to a given area of the body, or one who trains improperly, may be more susceptible to injuring that area of the body in the future.

An example that might fall into either of these categories would be an athlete who had done extensive stretching. If he or she had stretched areas which were more likely to be injured due to a limited range of motion, he or she would now be more resistant to injury than an athlete with the same genetic makeup who had not practiced such stretching. In contrast, if stretching had been performed by the athlete in an improper way, it could have resulted in laxity in the athlete's ligaments, which could actually make the athlete more susceptible to injury.

Psychological Characteristics that Can Predispose an Athlete to Injury

Athletes who emphasize mental toughness in their approach to sports can predispose themselves to injury by overestimating their invincibility and minimizing real injuries until they have worsened to a relatively severe level. While mental toughness is a characteristic of virtually all top athletes, it must be properly channeled. A healthy athlete must be determined to perform at his or her best, whatever the competitive conditions, but only as long as he or she is healthy. Minor injuries that pose no potential for serious complications need to be ignored, even if they present significant pain (i.e., pain which is disproportionate to the risk).

In contrast, an athlete who has a serious injury, or the precursor of one, must act immediately to avoid further damage. All athletes must believe in their invincibility on one level. If the risks of injury are too firmly in mind, an athlete will not be able to concentrate on performance. But false confidence must not lead to inappropriate techniques or cause the athlete to ignore reasonable safety precautions or warnings of injuries.

The Body's Fundamental Reaction to Injury

To a certain extent, the body reacts differently to each injury. The area injured, the condition of the athlete prior to injury, the cause of the injury and a number of other factors all interact to determine the exact nature of the injury. Nevertheless, virtually all injuries which involve vascularized tissues (i.e., tissues with a blood supply) generate a fundamental kind of response called the inflammation-repair process. The body has a similar response to infection, thermal injury and chemical injury. The purpose of this response is to localize the injury, remove damaged tissue and begin the repair process.

The body's response to trauma occurs at the cellular level. Cell necrosis, which arises out of direct damage or hypoxia (lack of oxygen to the tissue involved,) triggers the inflammatory response. Interestingly, the degree of the body's inflammatory response is not highly correlated with the degree of damage generated by the injury.

Different kinds of tissue repair themselves in different ways. Tendons, ligaments and cartilage rely on the migration of reparative cells (e.g., fibroblasts and macrophages) to the injury site in order for the repair process to proceed. Bones and muscles, which are more amenable to repair than tendons, ligaments and cartilage, have resident pluripotential cells (called "myoblasts" in muscle and "osteoblasts" in bone) which facilitate the synthesis of new tissue.

The inflammation-repair process has three basic stages: inflammation, acute vascular inflammatory response and repair regeneration and, remodeling regeneration. The vascular response occurs immediately following the injury. There is a brief period of vasoconstriction (contraction of blood vessels) to control bleeding. Within minutes vasodilation (expansion of blood vessel's diameter) causes blood and cellular debris to contribute to swelling and the eventual formation of a hematoma (blood clot). Virtually concomitant with this vascular response, the body activates a substance called "clotting factor XII" in the plasma. This has the effect of increasing clotting, capillary permeability and edema (swelling) and attracting inflammatory cells, such as leukocytes (white blood cells) and macrophages to the injury site. Other processes taking place in the injured area serve to increase inflammatory activity even further. (This latter stage of the inflammatory response is believed to be unnecessary, or at least exaggerated, and is the target of today's more advanced anti-inflammatory drugs.) This additional inflammation and accompanying edema creates a zone of secondary injury which envelopes the primary injury site. Inflammation is indicated by heat, swelling, redness and pain at and near the site of the injury. However, there are conditions which generate pain without any discernible inflammation and conditions which generate inflammation unaccompanied by any significant level of pain.

From two days to six to eight weeks after soft tissue injuries, another category of cells called "fibroblasts" emerge at the injury site and aid in the repair of the wound and in the formation of collagen. Collagen is made up of large protein molecules that comprise a major share of bones, tendons and ligaments. (A similar process takes place in bony tissue, with cells called osteoblasts serving the same purpose as fibroblasts do in the soft tissues.) Capillarization (the formation of tiny new blood vessels) brings a blood supply to the new tissues. The collagen which forms in the early stages of this second phase of the inflammation-repair process is immature (e.g., quite soluble and relatively weak). Its strength increases at the latter stages of this phase of repair. In addition, substances called "myofibroblasts" cause a contraction of the wound (one reason for the reduction in soft tissue flexibility after injury).

The third and final phase of the inflammation-repair process sees the repaired tissue begin to approximate normal tissue as closely as possible.

The biochemical profiles within the cells return to normal levels at this time as well.

Chronic Inflammation

There are times when inflammation does not follow normal patterns. Inflammation can be disproportionate to the magnitude of an injury or can be caused when relatively minor stresses are applied to a particular tissue, leading to atrophy and degeneration of the tissues involved and to a chronic state of inflammation.

Non-steroidal anti-inflammatory drugs (NSAIDs) are often used to interrupt the chronic inflammation pattern. However, these drugs are not meant to be long term treatments for inflammation. Some research that is beginning to appear in medical journals suggests that NSAIDs may interfere with the normal healing process. They also do not seem to positively influence it in the long term. Although, therapeutic modalities such as cryotherapy, thermotherapy, ultrasound and electrical stimulation all appear to reduce inflammation and promote healing, none of these therapies is fully understood. Exercise is by far the most powerful therapeutic modality for restoring damaged tissue to normal functioning.

Psychological Reactions to Injury

Athletes who have a serious injury generally pass through several psychological phases in reaction to that injury. At first the existence of the injury is denied or at least not fully grasped. Then the athlete becomes angry and/or frustrated over the injury. This is generally followed by a period of depression. Eventually there is acceptance. Finally, the successful athlete begins the comeback process. The length and severity of each stage varies with the athlete and the circumstances, and some stages may overlap with others. Certain stages of this typical l sequence may be virtually non-existent in some athletes or in certain cases.

A coach or other advisor who understands these phases can attempt to support the athlete as is appropriate. In addition, he or she will not be surprised by what may seem to be curious reactions to the obvious (e.g., an athlete's denial of an obvious injury). The wise coach learns to flow with these stages, to offer help as needed at each phase and to facilitate the athlete's movement toward the final and most productive psychological stage, the one in which dedication to come back develops.

Specific Kinds of Injuries

There are many kinds of sport injuries, but the vast majority are musculoskeletal injuries which fall into a category called "soft tissue" injuries. Soft tissues are essentially those which surround the bones (e.g., skin, muscles, tendons, nerves and blood vessels). In addition, there are other kinds of injuries or ailments that affect athletes (e.g., fractures and syncope) and we will address some of these kinds of injuries as well.

Two Soft Tissue Injury Categories

There are two general categories of soft tissue injury: closed and open. Closed injuries involve damage to soft tissues without a break in the skin. Open injuries are all of those in which the skin is damaged.

Open Injuries

The four main types of open injuries are abrasions, lacerations, avulsions and punctures. Abrasions occur when the uppermost (epidermal) layer of skin and a portion of the lower (dermal) level of skin have been scraped or rubbed away. Lacerations are cuts, many of which extend beneath the level of the skin into and blood vessels, nerves and muscles. Avulsions occur when the skin is torn rather than cut. Punctures occur when a pointed object penetrates the skin (sometimes penetrating deep into the soft tissues).

The treatment for all minor injuries of the four types described above involves cleansing with soap and water, the application of an antiseptic solution or ointment and the application of a sterile gauze. Wounds that go beyond the level of "minor" because of the pain associated with them, the depth of the wound, or the surface area affected should always be referred to a physician.

Blood vessel injuries can occur whether injuries are open or closed. Injuries to very small blood vessels (capillaries) are generally not serious and can usually be handled by the body's natural defenses. Bleeding and swelling that result from damage to capillaries can be minimized through the application of ice and compression to the injured area. Damage to larger blood vessels, though not common in athletics, must be controlled immediately, as described in the later section on "First Aid." Severe bleeding is life-threatening. A person in whom severe bleeding is observed or suspected must receive immediate medical attention.

Whenever an injury has caused a blood loss, it is important for the protection of others using the equipment and facilities that the blood be cleaned up immediately. This can be done with any appropriate disinfectant (a common recommendation is the use of a solution that is one part bleach to one part water).

Closed Injuries

Closed injuries fall into the following categories: sprains, strains, nerve injuries and blood vessel injuries.

A sprain occurs when a ligament is stretched or torn but the joint which the ligaments supports is not completely dislocated. A strain is a rupture in a muscle or tendon. Because strains involve the muscle-tendon unit, they are characterized by pain only when the athlete actively moves or exerts force against resistance. Sprains are painful even when the joint at which they occur is moved passively., Moving an injured joint to test for pain upon passive motion can be risky, however, and is not recommended without medical supervision.

Strains vary in severity with the extent of the damage to the tendon or muscle. Both mild and moderate strains are characterized by spasming and pain at the injury site and sometimes a loss of strength. The difference between the two is a matter of degree. Both will heal in time (the mild strain in days and the moderate strain in weeks). Severe strains involve complete avulsion of all or part of a muscle. They are generally quite painful, frequently manifesting themselves as deformities which can be observed and/or felt when the area is palpated (examined with the fingers). Severe strains often result in a loss of function This loss of function is not always visible because synergistic muscles or other muscles in the same muscle group can permit the athlete to continue to move despite a severe strain.

Sprains are also graded by their severity. Mild sprains are characterized by stretching of the ligament without an actual loss of continuity in the fibers of the ligament. Moderate sprains involve some actual tearing of the ligament, generally accompanied by some degree of abnormal laxity in the joint. Severe sprains are characterized by an abnormal range of motion and an inability to use the limb normally because of the pain and/or the position of the joint. Severe sprains involve the complete avulsion of the ligamentous fibers. In all cases in which severe strains or sprains are even suspected, the areas involved should be immobilized, and prompt medical treatment should be sought.

A delay in medical treatment for severe strains and sprains reduces or eliminates any likelihood of a full recovery. I have known a number of high level strength athletes whose careers were ended by a delay in treatment of a severe strain. In some of these cases the athlete denied the extent of the injury and did not seek treatment until surgical repair was ineffective. In other cases the athletes were so strong and the muscles that surrounded the injured areas were so well developed that the doctors who examined them pronounced the damage to be "minor" and not requiring surgery for a full recovery. Examinations of weightlifters should be performed by medical people who are used to examining and treating athletes with significant hypertrophy.

Injuries to Cartilage

Cartilage is a tough elastic and smooth substance that is generally situated between and at the ends of bones. Cartilage contains no blood, nerve or lymph supply. Synovial fluid lubricates the movement of cartilage and cancellus or soft bone tissue beneath the cartilage helps to absorb shocks that are applied to cartilage and, ultimately, to bones. Cartilage does not normally repair itself well but is replaced after damage by fibrocartilage (which is not as strong or durable as normal cartilage). The knees are probably the joints of the body that are most prone to cartilage injuries, but such injuries are not uncommon in the hip and shoulder areas and can occur in any joint.

Nerve Injuries

The human body has a complex nervous system which consists of two subsystems: the central nervous system (the brain and spinal cord) and the peripheral nervous system (the nerves that innervate the muscles and the nerves that send information from the body to the brain). Blows to the head or spine and fractures and dislocations of the vertebrae can result in damage to the central nervous system. Such damage can be life-threatening and/or can lead to paralysis. Consequently, athletes who suffer head and/or neck injuries, especially those which result in a loss of consciousness or any sensations of tingling, numbness or paralysis in the limbs, should be treated as if cervical damage has occurred.

Damage to the peripheral nervous system generally occurs as a result of deep lacerations, severe sprains and dislocations and fractures of bones other than those of the skull and vertebrae. It should be noted that injury to nerves can also occur when there is severe or repeated compression. Damage to the peripheral nerves can be assessed by checking for motor function and sensation distal to the injury site (further away from the spine). If any evidence of nerve damage is discovered, the athlete should be immediately referred to a physician.

Contusion

A contusion is a soft tissue (e.g., skin, muscle and/or tendon) injury caused by pressure (usually a blow or collision). Contusions often result in obvious "black and blue" marks in the skin where the injury occurs, but internal contusions (which typically result from a soft tissue being compressed against a bone beneath it by an external force) can lead to less visible (though normally painful) damage.

Fractures

Any break in the continuity of bony tissue is considered to be a fracture. Fractures that involve penetration of the skin by bony tissue are called open fractures. All other fractures are considered to be closed. Open fractures often result in greater blood loss than closed fractures, and they expose the bone to the external environment. Therefore, as a group, open fractures are considered to be more serious than closed fractures.

Within the category of closed fractures are displaced and non-displaced fractures. Displaced fractures are generally characterized by some sort of deformity in the involved limb. Non-displaced fractures show no external evidence of their existence, other than pain, and X-rays are needed to diagnose such fractures.

Special categories have been created for fractures with certain characteristics. Comminuted fractures involve the fracture of the bone into more than two pieces. Stress fractures result from repetitive stresses, such as running. Weak or diseased bones can suffer fractures when they are exposed to stress well below the level that would normally be required in order to sustain a fracture. Fractures that occur under such conditions are referred to as "pathologic fractures."

Two kinds of fractures are associated only with children: greenstick and epiphyseal. In greenstick fractures the separation of the bone runs lengthwise through only a portion of the shaft of a bone. In epiphyseal fractures the "growth plate" is damaged. (See Appendix II for a further discussion of epiphyseal tissue.)

Tenderness at a certain point in the bone, deformity, inability to use the limb, swelling, discoloration ("black and blue"), exposed bone tissue, grating upon movement and unusual motion beyond the point where a limb would normally go are all signs of fracture and should be further investigated. Grating and unusual movement should never be tested for as they can cause further damage.

Dislocations

A dislocation is an injury to the joint in which the ends of the bones that are normally in contact at the joint are no longer in such a position. A fracture-dislocation occurs when, in addition to dislocation, one or more of the bones that normally meets at the joint is fractured near the joint. Most dislocations and fracture-dislocations are associated with a sprain of the ligaments that stabilize the joint. The signs and symptoms of a dislocation are: deformity of the joint, swelling, pain at the joint that is worsened by any attempted movement and loss of normal joint motion.

Tendinitis and Related Conditions

Tendinitis is an inflammation of the tendon due to overuse. Tenosynovitis is inflammation of the synovial sheath that surrounds a tendinous tissue.

Bursitis

Bursitis is the inflammation of the bursa sacs (sacs comprised of two layers of joint lining tissue with a thin layer of synovial fluid in between). Bursa sacs generally exist where a tendon would otherwise generate friction by contact with a bone, or where there would tend to be friction between skin and bone. During the inflammation, the amount of fluid in the bursa sac increases. Over time the walls of an irritated bursa can thicken and the nearby tendon can degenerate or become calcified.

Myofascial Pain

Myofascial pain is also known as fibromyalgia. It is a muscle response that can result from a trauma. The condition is characterized by the formation of myofascial "trigger points," which are cord-like or nodular and are associated with muscle spasms. Trigger points are often quite painful, especially when pressure is applied to them. There is a school of thought which says that this kind of condition and its resulting pain comprise much of the pain that athletes suffer (particularly when it is a response to chronic injury). Deep-fiber massage techniques have been used to break up these spasming areas. Direct injection of analgesics and anti-inflammatory agents are also used by some practitioners to treat this disorder. In order for such treatments to work, they generally must be accompanied by rehabilitative exercise and a restructuring of the athlete's training and/or technique to prevent a recurrence of the condition.

Syncope

Syncope is a transient loss of consciousness. I have never witnessed complete syncope in weightlifting competition or training. The reports of such occurrences in athletes lifting weights have generally been associated with serious medical conditions, such as heart disease, manifestations of which may have been brought to the surface by strenuous activity.

Weightlifters do occasionally suffer a near loss of consciousness during overhead lifting. The cause is not entirely understood, but it probably involves one or both of the following mechanisms: a) a reduction in the blood supply to the brain when pressure is placed on the carotid arteries, b) intrathoracic pressure increases as a result of performing the Valsalva maneuver (holding ones breath against a closed glottis), and, c) pressure on the carotid sinus, which can slow the heart rate (this latter theory was offered to me by a friend,

avid weight trainer and eminent surgeon, Dr. Herbert Perry). Such pressure can develop when the bar is held incorrectly at the shoulders. It most commonly occurs when the bar has been lifted to the shoulders in the clean. In this position, it is possible for the bar to place considerable pressure on the anterior surface of the neck. In virtually all cases, this phenomenon occurs when the lifter is recovering from the clean, or shortly after he or she has done so. On one or two occasions I have also seen this kind of reaction occur as a lifter struggles to hold a weight overhead while holding his or her breath for an extended period (almost certainly a result of cause "b".

Generally, the lifter senses a weakness and simply drops the bar forward. Often the lifter's body will shake and generally exhibit a loss of muscular control (which in many cases returns within seconds) and the lifter walks away. On other occasions the lifter will slump to the floor and display weakness and lack of muscular control for from several to perhaps ten or fifteen seconds. During this period the lifter is normally conscious but is often unable to speak for a very brief period and exhibits considerable muscular tremor. Recovery to near normal functioning is generally rapid. Indeed, I have seen lifters return to the platform within minutes of such an episode and succeed with the same weight that caused the episode.

I have experienced this phenomenon a number of times over the years. It is a strange sensation, because you maintain full awareness of what is going on but cannot control body tremors or sometimes speak to those around you, although you can clearly see and understand the concern on their faces. Within a few seconds, the episode is over. In every case that I have experienced the bar was mis-positioned on my neck and the onset of weakness was very rapid.

On rare occasions a lifter can very nearly lose consciousness and fall (generally backward) with the bar on his or her shoulders. As long as the bar remains in the area of the lifter's neck, there is enough space between the bar when it is resting on the platform and the lifter's neck to prevent any injury to the athlete. (Indeed, one of the reasons for the large diameter of the plates used in weightlifting competition is that the distance of the bar from the floor generally protects the lifter from injury.) The only potential for injury is be if the bar bounces toward the lifter's head or chest, or if the lifter's arms are somehow positioned between the bar and the floor when he or she falls. In the handful of situations in which I have seen such a thing, there has never been such an injury. In fact, the likelihood of a bump on the back of the lifter's head appears greater than damage from the bar.

To protect against any injury when a "fainting" spell occurs, the lifter should drop the bar forward and then go down on one knee as soon as any sensation of weakness is felt. Ordinarily a lifter can feel this coming on and can move away quite easily. The way to prevent this kind of problem is to learn proper positioning of the bar on the shoulders and sound technique. When this is done, the likelihood of this affliction occurring is quite remote. Those who experience this problem will need to experiment with bar positioning in order to prevent its recurrence.

Dealing With Injuries

Should you incur an injury, you must first minimize the damage through first aid and then, where appropriate, seek professional treatment. When the professional treating you agrees, the rehabilitation process must begin. That is the athlete's job, with the help of the coach and health professional where appropriate.

A basic pattern for rehabilitation is associated with any injury which causes a break in training. First, the athlete must restore the function of the injured area. Then that area must be reconditioned to withstand the specific demands of the sport. During this process the fundamental nature of the injury has a direct bearing on the way in which it is handled.

In the rehabilitation of acute injuries, the focus is on getting the athlete back into his or her previous regimen. The injury was an "accident" (i.e., it was not linked to an inherent weakness or training overload). Its causes are to be avoided in the future, but recurrence is unlikely.

Overuse injuries are a direct result of the athletes' pre-injury training and physical state. Therefore, the athlete cannot merely return to the status quo. Otherwise, it is quite likely that the injury will recur. Some change in technique, training, restorative techniques or some combination of these is needed to prevent the same overuse cycle from being activated once again.

Sometimes the change is a simple matter. If the cause of the injury was a sudden or significant increase in the volume and/or intensity of the athlete's training (the former being much more likely), the athlete can probably resume his or her earlier level of training, and the injury will not recur. If the increase in load was inadvertent, this may be an acceptable solution. If the increase in training load was considered critical to the athlete's continued progress, the coach can devise a new plan that is different in any of several respects. One difference could be the rate of advancement to the new load. If that rate is made more gradual the second time around, the athlete is likely to tolerate it better. Another change that can be made is to give the athlete more opportunity to rest between periods of applying the desired load. A third approach is to use a somewhat smaller load, one that is effective in eliciting a training response, but is not as demanding as the level achieved before the injury.

Another means for reducing the "effective" load is to address the stress on the injured area from the standpoint of mechanics. For example, the athlete might have a tendency to "crash" into the bottom position in the clean (since the bar is permitted to build up considerable downward speed before the lifter catches it at the shoulders). When the lifter's load of cleans was below a certain level, this error in technique did not result in injury. When the load of cleans was raised, the athlete's knees simply could not take it. Correcting this technique flaw will enable the athlete to handle a greater load without injury. Alternatively, the lifter may be lifting with shoes that have a higher heel than the lifter requires to assume proper lifting positions. In this case a lower heel might reduce the strain on the lifter's knee, permitting the athlete to train at the desired level.

The options open to the athlete and coach for dealing with overuse injuries are limited only by the coach's imagination. The one approach that is destined for failure is a return to the combination of training regimen, lifting technique and restorative patterns that led to the injury in the first place.

This is an important consideration when the lifter has even minor overuse injuries. Pain that is moderate, comes on suddenly, and then goes away quickly is generally not a cause for concern. It merely signals the body's response to a new stress. What should never be ignored is a pain in a soft tissue that lasts through several workouts. When it appears that in injury is becoming progressively worse (even if very gradually), it is time to act, before the problem becomes chronic. The solution is not simply to take an anti-inflammatory medication or apply some liniment and go on.

The First Key to Injury Management: First Aid

A detailed exposition of the general principles of first aid is beyond the scope of this book. There are many useful sources of information in this area, the most well known of which is the Red Cross. The Red Cross has local chapters across most of the United States. Most chapters offer training in first aid procedures, and the Red Cross has numerous publications that deal with first aid. There are many other excellent sources of information in this area as well. I encourage all athletes and coaches to become familiar with first aid procedures, including CPR. A knowledge of first aid can be useful in the gym, but its value extends far beyond that into everyone's daily lives.

Most states have "Good Samaritan" laws which protect people who respond to an emergency, as long as they act in a way that a reasonable and prudent person would. This would include not moving a person unless his or her life is threatened, asking a conscious victim for permission before providing care, checking for life-threatening emergencies before rendering further aid, summoning professional emergency care and continuing to provide care until more highly trained personnel relieves you. When you are assisting an injured or ill person, you should always use common sense and do the best you can; you should not attempt to render care beyond your level of training. Coaches and others who supervise athletes may actually have a legal responsibility to intervene on behalf of an injured athlete under certain conditions. That is why coaches should be knowledgeable in first aid techniques.

In evaluating any injury, the Red Cross suggests three steps. The following is a brief summary of their recommendations, but the Red Cross should be consulted for training in the application of first aid techniques.

1. Check the scene. Check the scene for signs of danger. If either the person injured or the person seeking to render first aid are in danger of further harm, all reasonable efforts should be made to deal with that continued risk. If the person is in the street, this will probably involve stopping traffic. If the person is in the gym, it will probably mean halting all activity in the area and removing any threats to the injured person. If the potential first aid giver would be in danger if he or she began to render aid, he or she is not be expected to commence first aid until that danger had been removed. If this is impossible under the circumstances, the would be first aid giver should move on to the next step in the first aid process.

In checking the scene, the first aid giver should make an assessment of what happened, determine how many victims there are and whether any bystanders can help. An injured person should never be moved unless he or she is in imminent danger of life threatening injury by remaining where he or she is, unless a person who may be more seriously injured is blocked by this person or unless proper care cannot be administered where the person is (e.g., the person is in need of CPR but is on a surface which precludes the administration of CPR). When a person must be moved, avoid any twisting or bending of the victim, particularly of the head and spine and any other apparent areas of injury (e.g., a broken bone).

2. Call for help. You should call the local emergency number (generally 911) or arrange for that number to be called, by asking a specific bystander. He or she should be ready to give the emergency service dispatcher the exact location of the injured person(s), his or her name, the telephone number of the phone from which the emergency call is being made, what happened, the number and condition of the victim(s) and what care is being rendered at present. If the emergency number in your area is not 911, or if some other

emergency procedure is in place at your facility, that emergency procedure should be posted prominently in the workout area.

If you are unable to elicit any assistance in calling for help and are capable of rendering urgent first aid (such as pressure to arrest severe bleeding), the Red Cross recommends that you render such aid for about a minute while you think about the location of the nearest phone. Then make the call as quickly as possible and return to the victim.

3. Care. Even a basic guide to first aid for life-threatening conditions is well beyond the scope of this book. The following conditions are considered to be immediate threats to life: choking, lack of breathing, lack of a pulse and severe bleeding. These conditions require immediate attention as they can lead to loss of life within minutes if left untreated. Whenever an injured or sick person is conscious, you should introduce yourself, tell the person how much training you have and how you plan to help (in the case of a child, get approval from a supervising adult). If the condition is serious, permission is generally implied if a supervising adult is not present. Once you agree to render first aid, you should continue to provide it until you are exhausted or help arrives.

First Aid for Fractures and Dislocations

First aid procedures for fractures and dislocations are similar. Assuming that an athlete's vital signs have been evaluated and are stable and any open wounds have been treated, fractures and dislocations should be splinted. Only if there is an immediate threat to an athlete's life should the athlete be moved before a splint is applied. Splinting reduces pain and movement, prevents the bones from doing any further damage to the soft tissues and reduces the likelihood that the bone will either restrict blood flow distal to the injury, or that excessive bleeding at the site of the injury will occur. If you do not know how to apply a splint. you should wait for someone who does before moving the victim.

First Aid for Sprains and Strains

When uncomplicated strains and sprains occur, the recommended treatment is represented by the acronym "RICE. " ("Uncomplicated" means only a strain or sprain, i.e., there are no other injuries to the athlete.) RICE stands for: rest, ice, compression and elevation (which are not necessarily applied in that order). Rest means stopping activity to protect the athlete from the possibility of further damage and to treat the injury.

Compression can be administered in a number of ways, the most common of which is probably the application of an elastic or "Ace" bandage, which is wrapped firmly, not tightly, around the injured area.

427

Ice is applied to the injured area to minimize internal bleeding, swelling and pain. Ice is generally applied for periods of twenty to thirty minutes every one to two hours. This process should continue for from twenty-four to seventy-two hours (depending on the severity of the injury). A small number of athletes have significant negative reactions to treatment with ice. Nerve damage and frostbite are the most common of these effects. To prevent such reactions, the athlete should be monitored regularly. Particular care should be paid in situations where major nerves are relatively close to the surface of the skin. The peroneal nerve that is located in the posterior of the knee and the ulnar nerve that is near the surface of the posterior of the elbow joint are two examples of nerves that are susceptible to nerve damage when ice is applied because of their proximity to the skin's surface.

Elevation (raising the injured area above the level of the heart, if possible) is another method, used in conjunction with compression and ice, to reduce inflammation and bleeding into the damaged tissues.

The Second Key to Injury Management: Proper Diagnosis

Many athletes have wasted considerable time unsuccessfully treating an injury that was misdiagnosed. Today's doctors often rely on technology, such as MRI, to diagnose injuries accurately, but not every injury merits a diagnostic procedure that can cost $1,000, and even such spending may leave the problem improperly diagnosed. Diagnosis is as much a problem of logic as of technology. If the doctor is skilled at applying diagnostic logic and the correct information about the onset and symptoms of the condition is reported to the physician, the probability of a correct diagnosis is greatly enhanced. Analytical thinking in combination with up-to-date technology is critical to diagnostic success.

Soreness Versus Injury

One of the most common areas of misunderstanding among beginning athletes involves distinguishing soreness from injury. Exposing muscles to unaccustomed stresses often results in a response by those muscles that is referred to as "delayed onset muscle soreness" or DOMS. DOMS is an apt term for this phenomenon; the athlete seldom feels much during a workout, but a very significant level of discomfort can be felt twelve to forty-eight hours later .

The cause of DOMS is not completely understood, but it is generally accepted today that DOMS is symptomatic of minor (and perhaps beneficial) structural damage to muscle tissue (not a build up of lactic acid in the muscle as was once believed). In fact, the presence of a particular enzyme (creatine phosphokinase, CPK) during such soreness is evidence of some breakdown in the muscle tissue, albeit to a far lesser degree than when an actual injury occurs. (The level of CPK is far smaller during a period of DOMS than after an actual injury.)

What is not understood is why there is a delay in muscle soreness (strains, after all, are typically evident as soon as they occur), and why the condition is not worsened by activity (soreness generally diminishes after activity). Clearly there is some fundamental difference between muscle soreness and muscle strains. How do you tell the difference? The pain from strains tends to be localized and is more often in the tendon, or the juncture between the tendon and the muscle, than in the muscle itself. Moreover, strains feel worse with activity, while DOMS generally subsides gradually as activity is undertaken. DOMS can be worked through, while strains cannot.

Another differentiating factor is that strains often occur in the overtrained athlete, while DOMS ordinarily does not. On the contrary, DOMS occurs in the athlete who is returning to activity after a layoff or making a significant change in the training load or in technique. Strains can occur for these reasons as well, but they tend to arise even more often in an environment of fatigue.

The Third Key to Injury Management: Proper Treatment

Once the exact nature of an injury has been determined, a treatment plan must be formulated. Initially the treatment will probably focus on minimizing the swelling, bleeding into the wound and inflammation (e.g., the RICE treatment described earlier). Once the injury has been stabilized, there will generally be an effort to mobilize the injured area in a safe manner (ultimately restoring it to its full range of motion) and to reduce any residual inflammation. This is generally accomplished through some combination of rehabilitative exercise (including stretching), and the application of therapeutic modalities (such as ultrasound and muscle stimulation) and sometimes through the use of anti-inflammatory medications. Once range of motion and strength have been restored to the muscle, the gradual return to activity commences.

The details of these steps will vary significantly with the individual and the injury. For a sprain of moderate severity in a joint that can be easily stabilized, activity may begin soon after the injury. When a tendon is actually torn, it can take a year for its full strength to be restored. In such a case, vigorous activity will be curtailed for an extended period, and the return to activity will be very gradual indeed.

During the entire process, the advice of the health professionals who are rendering treatment should be followed. The athlete should provide input and ask questions about the rehabilitation process, but the right professional should be able to do much to make the rehabilitation process as short and effective as possible. The right professional is one who knows his or her business and understands and has dealt with your kind of condition.

Unfortunately, some professionals do not provide the kind of guidance people need. They may say something very general, such as "do what you feel you can." This kind of advice is rarely specific enough. Yet even when pressed, some professionals are simply not able to articulate more detailed advice. They may know how to deal with a rehabilitation issue when they see it but be unable to provide advice prospectively or in terms of principles. This is particularly true when the athlete has reached a point of reasonably full function and now wishes to resume his or her training.

It is wise for weightlifters to develop a network of health professionals who can support them as needed. Orthopedists, physiatrists, chiropractors, physical therapists, nutritionists, sport psychologists, massage therapists and other health professionals can all be of help to the athlete, and the help they can provide goes well beyond treating injuries into the realm of preventing them. Health specialists who have worked with athletes have all seen the results of improper technique, unsound training methods and unsafe practices. It is good to benefit from their insights before a problem develops.

The difficulty in selecting appropriate professionals lies in determining whether they really have the knowledge that is needed. Professional credentials are important, but no credential guarantees competence or specific knowledge of your condition and sports activity.

Ideally, the health specialists you use should have experience with athletes, preferably athletes in your sport. They should at least have experience with your kind of problem. An orthopedic surgeon may be brilliant when working with knees but only mediocre with shoulders. Such a specialist may also be great with the scalpel, but tend to over-prescribe surgery and be weak in the areas of prevention and conservative treatment. Another orthopedic specialist may have the opposite strengths and weaknesses.

Do not be afraid to ask specialists about their experience in the area of your concern. Make your goals and concerns clear to them. (The approach may be very different if your goal is to return to competition for as many years as you can and not. merely to get around comfortably in retirement.) Discuss what they propose to do. Ask about the risks and benefits. Ask about alternative treatments and their risks and benefits. Ask for references from people who have had the procedure. Go to a medical library and do a little reading. The more you know, the better equipped you will be to make a judgment about the best treatment for you. It is important to bear in mind that when you have surgery, there is often only one chance to get it right, so the surgeon (and the procedure) must be selected carefully.

It is always a good idea to line up your network before you need it. When you are injured and in pain, you will be less likely to select the correct professional or to make the right decision about your course of treatment than when you can do so at leisure and with a cool head.

Avoid the Knife Whenever Possible

We have grown up in a generation that reveres the skill of the surgeon. Many of us to look to the surgeon the way we look to a mechanic. We expect the surgeon to rebuild, replace or reshape so that we can go on with what we want to do. There is no doubt that surgeons can work wonders, but the cases in which athletes are better than new for the experience of major surgery are rare indeed. Unfortunately, a significant number of surgeons believe that they can fix nearly anything, and this attitude is often communicated to naive patients. It must be remembered that surgeons do not earn what they consider to be a reasonable living unless they perform surgical procedures. A combination of true belief and economic incentives can make it nearly irresistible for some surgeons to recommend surgery.

Even the most medically necessary and the best planned and executed surgeries have their risks and failures. And the downside can be severe indeed. Therefore, it is wise for the athlete to avoid surgery whenever possible. Whenever a more conservative treatment is available, it is generally a wise idea to try it first.

There are important exceptions to this rule. One is the case of a complete avulsion of a muscle, tendon or ligament. When this kind of injury occurs, surgical repair is a must and the need for it is urgent. The probability of success in repairing a complete avulsion declines in a matter of days and plummets after a week. I have known many athletes who postponed surgery for such injuries and who have never been the same. In contrast, athletes who had the problem attended to quickly have made very successful recoveries more often than not.

Surgery must also not be avoided when a delay is likely to result in further damage. One example is the development of a bone spur (a bony outgrowth) in the shoulder. Such a spur can rub against the rotator-cuff tendons as the shoulder moves, actually cutting them. Over time the simple spur, which could have been removed arthroscopically at one point, causes a tear in the rotator-cuff tendons ,a far more severe problem than the spur alone.

The need to differentiate between injuries that require immediate surgery and those which do not underscores the importance of asking the kinds of questions that were discussed earlier. Only by understanding what will happen if nothing is done will the athlete be able to make the proper judgments. When in doubt (and even when you are not), get a second opinion and even a third. Doing so will increase your chances of a correct diagnosis, enable you to hear a prognosis from more than one person and give you more choice with regard to who will treat you. Also, it is important to talk to people who have had the treatment to determine how they feel about the result. Often the patient is a better judge of success than the doctor.

Training Through and Around an Injury

While an athlete is having an injury treated he or she may wish to inquire whether the injury can be "trained through" or whether training in the normal way will make the injury worse or delay the healing process. How do you determine whether further activity is likely to cause further damage or hinder the healing process? The first step is to ask the health professional who is diagnosing and/or treating you his or her opinion. In traumatic injuries of moderate nature, continued activity may be perfectly appropriate as long as the activity has no danger of further damaging the injured area (i.e., the traumatic event can be prevented from recurring). In the case of strains that are moderate or worse, continued activity will prevent the healing process from taking place. The stretching or contracting of an injured area may continually irritate the injured area. Athletes often have difficulty distinguishing tendinitis from a minor strain that can heal even with continued activity.

A rule of thumb that I have found useful is to have the athlete warm up thoroughly and progress to heavier weights. An injury that can be trained through will not get worse as weight is added. (Pain may increase somewhat from the lighter to the heavier sets, but then it will level off and may actually lessen with the heavier weights.) Such an injury will also not become more painful as the reps in a given set proceed. If the pain does worsen at heavier weights or with each passing rep, a rest must be taken in order for healing to occur.

Another important indicator of whether continued activity is safe is the post-workout experience of the athlete. If the injury has not worsened a day or two after a particular activity has been undertaken, or, preferably, it has gotten better, there is reason to continue. If, in contrast, the pain or other symptoms of the injury have worsened, the liniment is only a masking agent, and continued activity is contraindicated.

Aids to Training Through Injuries

There are essentially three approaches to training through injuries: to tough it out by training through the pain; to treat the pain with analgesics, anti-inflammatory agents and/or a variety of agents that reduce pain; or to provide mechanical support to the injured area. These approaches are not necessarily mutually exclusive.

The Errors In "Toughing It Out"

Toughing it out means continuing to train in spite of the pain as long as you have medical approval (which means the injury isn't likely to worsen as a result of training). The main advantage of this approach are that you can maintain your physical condition in spite of the injury.

The main disadvantages of toughing it out are twofold. First, as my friend and former National Superheavyweight Champion Jerry Hannan, used to say, "the problem with pain is that pain hurts." And Jerry had a point. No one likes pain.

But there is an even more important reason to avoid pain. An athlete in pain will generally not perform as well and may begin to make unconscious changes in his or her movement patterns in order to minimize the pain. This can have disastrous effects on technique, and many an athlete has suffered permanent damage to his or her technique by training through an injury.

Treating Pain with Analgesics and Anti-Inflammatories

Athletes who want to train through injuries generally do so with the assistance of analgesics or anti-inflammatory agents.. If the pain is non-functional, training under the influence of an analgesic is not the worst thing in the world, as long the analgesic does not affect the athlete's alertness or coordination.

Today more athletes who want to train through the pain use anti-inflammatory agents than analgesics. In the early days of sports medicine, physicians often relied on corticosteroids, such as cortisone, to treat inflammation. Over time, research began to suggest that long term use of cortisone preparations had a number of undesirable side effects. Moreover, the direct injection of cortisone into an injury site (such as an injured tendon) could cause a weakening of that tissue and thereby lead to a far more severe injury.

In recent years, non-steroidal anti-inflammatory agents (NSAIDs) have become increasingly popular for treating chronic and acute joint and related pain. Tens of millions, if not hundreds of millions, of people worldwide have been able to return to activity on a relatively pain free basis because of these drugs. Athletes have also benefited from the development of these drugs.

While the side effects of NSAIDs are far more mild than those of corticosteroids, they can still be serious, particularly when these drugs are used on a long term basis. Ulcers and related gastrointestinal disorders, as well as damage to kidney function, are just two examples of the negative effects of NSAIDs. With respect to the use of NSAIDs by athletes, the jury is still out to a certain extent. It is as yet unclear whether the use of NSAIDs, on balance, prevents or causes injuries. They clearly reduce pain and permit continued training and competition. There is no doubt that unnecessary inflammation is reduced when they are used. But there is the possibility that prolonged use may have a negative effect on the integrity of injured areas, particularly if continued training leads to progressive micro-trauma and to severe injury at some point.

It is my belief that relying on NSAIDs over the long term is not a good idea. Apart from side effects (the incidence of which tends to grow with the term of use), the use of NSAIDs permits many athletes to employ lifting techniques and training methods that are inappropriate for them by putting off the consequences. Had the NSAIDs not been used, the athlete and coach would have been forced to address these issues earlier and to treat the cause rather than the symptoms of the condition.

If lifting is causing the wearing away of cartilage in an athlete, should the situation be masked until an athlete has no cartilage at all by age thirty? What if an athlete develops a reaction to NSAIDs at twenty-five? What will that athlete do when age causes joint pain without strenuous activity? What is left in the physician's arsenal? To my way of thinking, having an athlete live on NSAIDs (i.e., use them long term) is akin to having a person daily re-infect an area and then rely on an antibiotic to treat the infection. The day will come when the antibiotic will be ineffective. At that point, the real trouble will begin.

All athletes will sometimes overdo things a little. In such cases, a substance that clears up temporary inflammations may be used to good effect if it is used in conjunction with modifications of training, technique and restorative measures designed to prevent a recurrence of the problem. Treating a symptom without treating the cause is a mistake of major proportions.

Topical Applications to Treat Pain

Many athletes like to apply liniments or other substances to the skin to ease the discomfort of aching muscles and other minor aches and pains. There is no doubt that liniments can reduce local pain sensations. How this is accomplished is not fully understood. The application of "hot" liniments results in skin irritation, which leads to an increase in the blood supply to the area. This generates a sensation of heat. The heat thus developed does not penetrate below the skin, so liniments are not actually "warming up" the muscles through any kind of increase in blood flow to the muscle. Nevertheless, the feeling of warmth in the area does result in a reduction or modification of any pain sensation in that area of the body and therefore may reduce muscle tension and any spasming that is occurring in the muscle.

As was noted earlier, a reduction in the sensation of pain can have both positive and negative aspects. If such a reduction results in an athlete's engaging in an activity that causes further damage, it is of course a negative. If the pain was causing the athlete's to favor the injured area (i.e., by contracting muscles that are not normally brought into play or inappropriately modifying technique to avoid pain), then reduction in pain has had a positive effect .

Certain kinds of pain are non-functional. Pain can be disproportional to the injury and can linger on after healing has occurred. When it is appropriate for an athlete to work through the pain (i.e., when it is unlikely that continued activity will cause any damage to the athlete) substances that minimize discomfort can be helpful.

Mechanical Aids to Training Through Injuries

In weightlifting parlance, "wraps" are strips of fabric with some kind of elastic material interwoven. They are generally quite strong and have a significant elastic pull when they are stretched. They are most often used to support the knees (a shorter and thinner version is often used to support the wrists), but they can be used to support and/or compress virtually every area of the body.

Lifters are divided in their opinions regarding knee wraps. Some athletes almost never use them (i.e., only on rare occasions to support acutely injured areas). Others athletes never attempt a heavy squat or C&J without them. There is no question that an athlete who is properly wrapped can squat more than one who is not. Powerlifters are quite aware of this difference, and no serious powerlifter would think of competing without knee wraps. There is also no question that the application of compression to an injured area can lessen the discomfort produced by that injury. In addition, wraps can provide extra warmth to the knees (which offers a number of benefits).

On the other side, wraps restrict a lifter's range and speed of motion. They can also place added strain on a joint in its most completely flexed position (the same way an object placed on a hinge can break a it). They may also reduce the training effect of the squat exercise in a certain range of motion because of the extra support they supply in that range.

It is my opinion that the disadvantages of wraps generally outweigh the advantages when used on a daily basis. If an athlete has no injuries to speak of and is using wraps merely to improve performance in an exercise like the squat, the use of wraps is generally best avoided. A healthy lifter will gain strength through a greater range of motion by training without wraps and will avoid the possibility of damage as well. Any added ability to stand up from a low squat position that is gained through the use of wraps is probably offset by the speed lost in the descent under the bar as a result of wearing the wraps. (If the lifter is able to gain control of the bar at a slightly higher position because of speed in the descent, it will enable that lifter to recover more easily.)

Even when an athlete is in pain, there are some strong arguments against the use of wraps. First, masking the pain may disguise the symptom of an injury sufficiently for the athlete to do further damage. Second, we do not know how wrap masks pain. Does the painful area actually receive some added mechanical support, or does the diminution of pain occur merely because the wrap interferes with nerve impulses?

Some elite level athletes who feel that the added support, warmth and power that is derived through the use of wraps more than offset any of their disadvantages. Those who believe wraps actually do provide needed support for injuries will come down on the side of using them, even perhaps as an injury prevention measure.

There is at least one situation in which the knee-wrapper school is probably correct. It was suggested to me by Ben Green. Ben recommended the application of a knee wrap to my upper thigh in order to compress the area in which I was experiencing discomfort from an old groin injury. This particular injury was acting up in a way that told me (based on past experience) that I was going to have to lay off for a time in order to permit the injury to heal. By modifying my workouts somewhat and applying the wrap, I was able to continue my training for several weeks (at which time the pain went away). Although I had suffered this injury on a number of occasions, I had never been able to train through it before. Ben has reported similar success with himself and a number of other lifters with whom he has worked, so this approach is clearly worth investigating.

A similar treatment for the knee would involve wrapping only the quad tendon (if it were sore) or only the patellar tendon. The latter procedure is often employed for patellar tendinitis or "jumper's knee." This technique involves the use of a thin layer of wrap or a brace specifically designed for this purpose. The wrap is generally applied just above the tibial tubercle. This kind of wrap presumably supports the patellar tendon perhaps,

by altering the mechanics of the pull on it. This combination of effects provides pain relief for some athletes and may reduce mechanical stresses on the tendon, thereby facilitating healing.

Training Around an Injury

In my judgment it is very important for athletes who cannot train through an injury to train around it as much as possible (i.e., to perform activities as close to those of the athlete's sport as they can without aggravating the injury). Remaining in training at some level has several benefits. One is that the athlete maintains at least some level of conditioning (or even improves upon it) during the break from normal training. In the case of a weightlifter, this might mean breaking a squat record while treating a shoulder injury. The time away from normal training may actually permit the athlete to improve upon a lagging area while another area rests.

Another benefit of continued training is that it maintains at least some of an athlete's overall ability to withstand training. A body that rests completely during an injury will lose not only function in the injured area but also some overall functional capacity as a result of inactivity.

Still another benefit of training around an injury is that activity which increases movement and blood flow into the area without irritating the injured area can actually promote healing and contribute to the rehabilitation process. Some trainers believe this is the single most important benefit of exercising while injured. Naturally the athlete must be careful not to aggravate the injury as he or she is training around it.

The final major benefit of continued training of some kind is psychological. The athlete who has a training regimen is likely to feel much more in control of his or her destiny than one who sits back and worries about when the injury will heal.

The only real limits that exist with regard to training around an injury lie in the creativity of the coach and athlete. Let me give you some personal examples. When I sliced a finger to the bone while doing an auto repair, the wound required a number of stitches to close. The doctor cautioned against bending the finger significantly for several days to avoid tearing the stitches. Since I had a heavy snatch workout scheduled for that evening, I created a splint for the damaged finger to prevent it from bending. With the splint I was able to maintain the finger in a straightened position. Using straps, I was able to snatch up to 95% of my best snatch at the time despite the mishap with my finger.

On a number of occasions, I have had injuries to an oblique muscle that made pulling, and especially squatting, quite painful. By wrapping a full size bed sheet, folded in thirds, tightly around my torso, I was able to squat with very heavy weights without irritating the injured area (although breathing during the squat was not easy).

In other cases, supporting the injured area is not enough. Exercises themselves must be modified. For example, squatting with a hip belt can work the legs without placing any strain on the upper body. Shrugging lying face down on an incline bench can provide exercise for the muscles of the upper back when the lower back is out of commission. J.C. Hise shrugs (shrugging with a bar on the shoulders) can exercise the trapezius muscles when the hands or arms cannot hold a bar for pulls or shrugs. In almost every case, where there is a will there is a way. The phenomenon of an injured athlete walking into the gym and merely watching others train should almost never happen.

It should be noted that all of these examples involve training around an injury rather than through it. When you train through, you continue to use the injured area. When you train around an injury, the injured area is not used during training; rather, it is taken out of the action by a mechanical aid or change in exercise.

There are exceptions to the general advice that injuries be trained around. Some injuries are to areas that are involved in so many movements that training, even on different exercises may aggravate the injured area. For instance, I had a groin pull that precluded my doing full squats or any lifting from the floor. I decided to train around the injury by doing partial squats and pulls from above the knees. It turned out that the combination of exercises that I performed did not worsen the condition. Unfortunately, performing this group of exercises absolutely prevented the injured area from healing. The result was an injury that lagged on for several months, when several weeks of more complete rest would have permitted complete healing in a matter of weeks and a much more rapid return to a full training load.

Similarly, there are times when an illness or injury places such systemic strain on an athlete that all of his or her resources are required merely for the healing process. In such cases medical advice must prevail. However, the athlete should work carefully with his or her physician to assure that a return to activity will be as rapid as possible.

Rehabilitative Exercise

No matter how skilled a surgeon, how complete a rest, how therapeutic a modality or how effective a drug, nothing takes the place of exercise in facilitating the recovery from an injury. After healing has taken place, the injured area must literally be remodeled so that it can withstand the rigors of training. In addition, the overall conditioning level of the athlete must be restored. Neither of these two important steps can take place without rehabilitative exercise.

Sometimes what is needed for rehabilitation is merely the same exercise which the athlete was prohibited by the injury from performing. (It should be added slowly to the training, as discussed earlier in this chapter.) In other cases special exercises are needed to strengthen, condition and restore the flexibility of the injured area. The advice of rehabilitation specialists should be sought when exercise of this nature is planned. However, the athlete must also consider the demands that will be placed on the area by weightlifting. Any program of rehabilitation must be designed with the ultimate need to perform the classical lifts in mind.

Returning to Training After an Injury

Once the health specialist has approved a return to training, you should move ahead without delay. In addition to following the advice of your health advisers, it is helpful to follow a number of principles when returning to training and competition. First, the comeback should be gradual. Very roughly speaking, comeback time should be equal to the time lost from training. If the injury interrupted training for three weeks, it should take three weeks get back into shape. This is far from a hard and fast rule. The time required for a complete comeback is affected by the what occurred during the break in training. If the athlete was in a cast for several weeks, it will generally take more than several weeks to come back. If moderate activity was possible during a training break of three weeks, it might take less than three weeks for the athlete to return to a full level of training.

A second rule is that the athlete should never do as much as he or she is able at the outset. My experience has been that an athlete who is left to do as much as he or she can may perform quite well on the first day because of being well rested. He or she may actually be surprised by the level of performance achieved. Unfortunately, while the injured area is fully rested, it is not fully rehabilitated and reconditioned. As a result, training at or near full capacity may overload the injured area, causing a reinjury shortly thereafter.

A much more sensible approach is to begin at something near the 50% level (even lower if the injury has lasted more than three weeks) and add approximately 10% per week to the program (i.e., 60% in the second week and 70% in the third week). It is important that both volume and intensity be increased gradually. A de-conditioned area of the body is out of condition with respect to both its functional ability and its ability to recover from a workout. Therefore, the reconditioning process needs to move ahead in carefully planned stages that are adjusted to the reactions of the athlete.

433

Larry Mintz, former National Champion in both weightlifting and powerlifting, had a very simple program that he used to come back from the numerous and serious injuries that he suffered during his career. He would always begin with the empty bar (e.g., 20 kg.). In an exercise like the squat (where his performance capabilities were typically in the 225 kg. to 260 kg. range), Larry would add approximately 20 kg. per workout until he neared his pre-injury level, then he would begin to go heavy only once a week (he typically squatted two to three times a week). Under this kind of program it would take Larry from several weeks to two to three months to approach a near normal level of performance. Using this kind of program he was never injured during comeback, and he always returned to his previous levels of performance quite successfully.

Do Not Test The Injury

Injuries vary considerably in terms of their healing time. The nature of the injury and the age of the athlete are the two major variables in this area. Very minor injuries to young athletes can heal effectively within a few days. The same injury might take weeks to heal in a master lifter. Major injuries can take from several months to a year or more to heal fully. All injuries require a minimum of time for the injury itself to be repaired. Therapy and other forms of treatment can speed up the healing process, but nothing can eliminate the time required for the healing process.

In this context, distinctions must be made between injuries and dysfunction and between healing time and time away from training.

Certain phenomena can lead to muscle dysfunction but not cause injury (i.e., significant damage to tissue). For instance, an athlete can develop a simple cramp in a muscle. The cramp may be painful. It may absolutely preclude any effective use of that muscle for at least the duration of the cramp. Nevertheless, if the cramp goes away rapidly, it may be possible to resume general activity immediately. Activity that directly stresses the muscle that cramped should probably be halted for a day or two. (Severe cramping may be symptomatic of, or a cause of, muscle damage, and more rest will be required when such damage occurs.)

Similarly, an athlete who makes a misstep while lifting can damage the ligaments of the knee. If the damage is minor, and care is taken to protect the injured area, it may be possible to resume activity very rapidly because normal training activity will not aggravate the injured area.

When a tissue that actively participates in an activity is damaged, the case can be completely different. If an athlete actually strains a muscle unit that is actively used during training, the injury cannot be trained through (i.e., that muscle cannot be stressed during the healing process). Any stress placed on the muscle will simply preclude the healing process or will delay it dramatically.

The simplest illustration of the time required to complete the healing process is what happens when you sustain a minor cut. The cut occurs, then there is bleeding, then there is inflammation. A scab forms at the wound area, it hardens and eventually falls away from the wound. This leaves an exposed area that is still not fully healed. If the cut was shallow, any visible evidence of the injury eventually disappears. If the cut was deep, a scar remains. In either case, the entire process takes time. Any interference with the healing process will slow or even halt its progress. Try to move the injured area and/or separate the skin at the wound site, and bleeding will continue. Rub the scab as it forms or before it heals to a certain point, and another will have to be formed in order to replace it. Subject the area under the scab to friction as soon as the scab has fallen away, and it will not heal as quickly as if it were left undisturbed. In a similar way, muscle-tendon injuries take time to heal. If the athlete stretches the muscle-tendon unit or requires it to contract beyond a certain threshold, the area will not heal quickly or properly.

It has been my experience that injured athletes are anxious to determine when an injury has healed sufficiently for training to resume. However, the very process of testing itself can further damage a muscle-tendon unit that in undergoing the healing process.

If you do not test, how do you know when training can safely resume? There are no surefire methods for determining when an injury has healed, but there are several guidelines. First, a judgment of expected healing time needs to be made at the time of the injury, based on its nature. My experience has been that athletes in their late teens to mid-twenties require about three weeks to recover from a moderate strain sufficiently for training to resume. In such cases pain during light activity disappears within a few days. There is then a temptation to resume heavier activity. If the athlete does so, pain will recur when the activity level reaches the area of 50% to 75% of maximum. Unfortunately, when pain is experienced once again, it is the sign of a slight reinjury. If the athletes continues to add weight in hopes that he or she can work through the pain, further injury will occur, often enough to start the healing clock all over again.

Apart from projecting the healing time required, the second major tool for the coach and athlete who are feeling their ways after an injury is to make the comeback gradual in nature. There is evidence to suggest that during the healing process muscles and tendons are at or near their weakest point immediately after pain disappears. The major portion of the healing has taken place, but the area needs to go through a sort of toughening process in order to prepare itself for normal activity. Much like a cut over a joint that must be moved at a certain point to assure that the area heals with sufficient flexibility, an injured muscle or tendon appears to respond favorably to moderate stress as the healing takes place. Too little stress and the injured area will not adjust itself properly to the stresses to come, too much stress and the area will not have a chance to heal. If the comeback is gradual, it will stimulate the necessary adaptations on the part of the injured area, but it will not step over the line into creating detrimental stress.

The third major strategy for regulating the comeback is to be aware of the way in which the body is adapting to the comeback stress. The way to work out this issue is to apply some stress and then watch for the body's reaction. For instance, let us assume that a lifter has injured a vastus lateralis muscle (one muscle of the quadriceps group). He or she has rested the muscle for ten days and feels no pain during light activity. The athlete decides to begin squatting again and works up to 40% of his or her pre-injury maximum for five repetitions on his or her first day back.

The athlete notices some discomfort on the third rep, and it worsens slightly on the fourth and then again on the fifth rep. The following day the athlete notices some soreness in the area. A day later, when the athlete squats again, he or she notices the same level of discomfort with the same weight, and the discomfort worsens with 55% of maximum. This scenario suggests that full healing has not occurred. Continued training at progressively higher intensities is likely to cause further damage, ultimately beyond the point of the initial injury. Unfortunately, further rest, perhaps three weeks this time, will be required.

In contrast, consider a slightly different case. The athlete rests for three weeks instead of ten days. During the first workout the athlete goes up to 25% of maximum. A very slight discomfort is felt on the lighter sets that were used as a warm-up, but the discomfort does not change with the heavier weight. Very little discomfort is felt the next day; in fact, the area feels a little looser and more functional than it did before the first workout. During the second workout less discomfort is experienced than during the first. By the time the athlete has reached 55% of maximum for five reps (in perhaps the fourth workout), the injured area feels " as good as new.)

Observe the difference in the two approaches. In the second method, 55% of maximum was not reached until about four weeks after the injury (as compared with two weeks in the first example). In addition, several preparatory workouts were used to "coax" the injured area into condition. In my experience, the second method is far more successful than the first. Whichever method is used, the athlete must pay attention to what the body is telling him or her. Failure to do so can convert a minor injury that should take a lifter a few weeks out of his or her way to an injury that wastes months of the lifter's time.

The Importance Of Mirrors, Video Cameras and Monitored Training When Returning to Activity

When an athlete is coming back from an injury or even trying to train through one, the input from mirrors, video cameras, training mates or coaches can be critical. There is a tendency for the injured athlete to favor the injured area. This can lead to technique errors that can cause injuries to other areas or to a decline in performance.

A mirror can be a valuable training asset as it permits the athlete to receive immediate visual feedback on his or her body positions. For example, let us assume that a lifter is coming back from a knee problem and is using the squat as a primary rehabilitation exercise for the knee and for the leg muscles. This lifter may have a tendency to shift his or her body away from the injured knee. Alternatively, the lifter might not permit that knee to travel forward over the toe in the squat position (while the healthy knee does assume such a position). A mirror can give the athlete immediate feedback about such behavior. More importantly, the lifter can use the feedback from the mirror to enable him or her to assume the correct position and then feel what the correct position is like. Videos and training mates can help in this regard, but they cannot give the same degree of immediate and precise feedback.

The drawback of the mirror is that the lifter will find it difficult use the mirror when he or she is moving fast. This is where the training mates, coaches and video camera can be used to good effect. Training mates and coaches offer the advantage of being able to view a lifter's technique from many angles and to compare what they are seeing to what they have seen in the past. They can also provide feedback instantaneously, so that the lifter can make immediate adjustments.

Videos necessarily provide more retrospective analysis than the feedback of coaches and fellow athletes. However, they have the advantage of permitting slow motion analysis and more objective comparisons with past performances than the human eye (if the lifter has a video library of pre-injury lifts).

Using all of these tools in combination will enable a lifter to resume successful activity as quickly and in as trouble free a manner as is possible. Therefore, the lifter should avail himself or herself of each one.

Common Injury Sites

Wrist

Wrist injuries are among the most common experienced by lifters. Because the wrist supports the entire weight of the bar in the snatch and jerk and part of the weight in the clean, it is placed under considerable stress during lifting. Generally, the wrists adapt to that stress over time and are easily able to support the loads encountered. Occasionally, traumatic injury to the wrist occurs when a lifter fails to get his or her elbows up in racking the bar in the clean. Broken wrists are not unknown (although they are virtually unknown among lifters who keep the elbows up). When a break occurs, it most often happens in the scaphoid bone, which is below the base of the thumb.

When a break occurs, it must, of course, be treated by a physician, who will place it in a cast. Once the cast is removed, the lifter will gradually be able to return to training, and recovery is generally complete (as is the lifter's dedication to keeping the elbows up when cleaning).

For more chronic kinds of injuries, lifters generally apply an elastic and cloth wrap (the "Ace" type bandage), a wrap made purely of heavy fabric (such as that used by boxers) or a leather wrist wrap that is somewhat akin to a belt. My preference is for the latter type of wrist support. It can be easily tightened when taking a lift and loosened thereafter. The support offered is substantial, particularly if the wrist support is placed high enough to be in contact with the base of the hand. Naturally, if the support is placed too high, it will inhibit wrist flexibility. This may be desirable when doing an overhead lift, so that the wrist is not placed in an extreme position and is well supported, but a wrist that is not flexible can affect performance in all of the lifts, most particularly when an athlete is "racking" a clean on the shoulders.

One other fairly common injury to the wrist is the ganglion cyst. When a ganglion occurs, the joint capsule has herniated, and a clear fluid fills one area of that joint capsule, causing a bulge. The bulge can be rather large and fairly hard to the touch. Sometimes the ganglion disappears spontaneously, at other times it requires surgical removal. If the ganglion is not painful and does not restrict the athlete's range of motion, there is no particular reason (other than aesthetics) to treat it. Before considering surgery for this condition, an athlete should consider two remedies used by a number of physicians and others to treat this condition: deep massage and a blow to the ganglion with a blunt but relatively hard object. Massage therapists who use deep massage techniques have been able to disperse the ganglions of a number of people I know. The process can be somewhat painful, but it can help some people.

The best way that I can describe the second method is through the experience of female athlete of my acquaintance. She had a ganglion and mentioned it to her doctor during an office visit. The doctor said, "let me look into this." He picked up a large medical book and suddenly smashed the spine of the book against the ganglion. It disappeared as if by magic. (I had a similar experience when a large ganglion that I had for years suddenly deflated when I was doing a particularly strenuous set of snatch pulls and the material of the straps I was wearing pressed against the ganglion with significant and sudden force as I exploded into the finish of the pull.)

Hand Injuries

By far the most common hand injuries among lifters are skin avulsions of the calluses that develop at the base of the fingers. The irritation of gripping the bar causes the callus to form. When it becomes thick, it is likely that the shearing force of the bar when it is gripped will cause the callous and the upper layers of the underlying skin to avulse from the lower skin layers in that area.

There is typically moderate bleeding and pain when such a tear occurs. If not treated immediately, the tear can become more severe. Proper treatment involves cleansing the wound, trimming away the excess skin, applying an antibiotic and covering the injured area with a sterile dressing. Subsequently, the area should be treated with an antibiotic ointment that keeps the area moistened as well as clean. The hand should remain mobile during the healing process so that the new skin accommodates the full range of motion.

As with all injuries, prevention is a better approach than treatment for torn calluses. Proper prevention involves removing the excess skin of the callus on a regular basis. This is easiest to do when the skin has been wet for some time (such as after a shower or bath). Most athletes use an emery board, emery cloth or pumice stone for this purpose. Some use a single edged razor blade to cut off the excess tissue, but this method cannot be recommended. Using a razor blade always presents the risk of incurring an unintended laceration. A callus razor is specially designed to remove only a thin layer of skin at one time and is a much safer choice than a regular razor blade.

It is important for athletes to be able to continue their training during such injuries, but it is also important to protect the injured area. Most of the taping procedures used by trainers are not suited to this purpose. Nearly thirty years ago a training partner of mine, Dr. Theodore Ritzer (today an eminent cardiologist), developed a taping technique to address this problem. I have modified the technique substantially, and, in my experience, it is by far the most effective taping technique for this kind of injury. Karl Faeth, trainer to many United States World and Olympic weightlifting teams, who spent his own time and money to be there for US athletes before the USAW could afford to pay for trainers to accompany its teams abroad, subsequently adopted the technique and used it with great success for many years.

The technique utilizes a piece of 1" surgical tape that is double the length of the athletes hand plus 4" to 6". A hole is cut or torn in the center of the length of tape, and the finger at the base of which the injury exists is threaded through the hole until the tape is snugly against the base of the finger. (The sticky side of the tape runs along the lifter's palm and the back of the lifter's hand.) The last 2" to 3" on either end of the tape are applied to the wrist, leaving enough slack on either end to permit the hand to move freely about the wrist without disengaging the tape. Finally, a length of tape is wrapped around the wrist to secure the two ends in their position on the wrist. This taping arrangement protects the injured area well and generally lasts for the duration of a workout. This method was not legal in competition for many years and so a more conventional taping method— tape wrapped around the hand— was used for competitive attempts. Recent revisions in the rules of competition now appear to permit using my taping technique. A number of lifters use a "liquid bandage" such as "Nu Skin" to treat this problem. "Nu Skin" is painful when applied, but it does form a protection layer over the injured area.

Another common problem is discomfort in the thumb when a lifter learns the "hook grip" (see Chapter 1 for a full description). During the process of becoming accustomed to this grip, it is not uncommon for the athlete to experience considerable pain (particularly immediately after the bar is released after a lift). The longer the lifter holds the hook and the heavier the weight, the more profound the discomfort. The athlete may also experience discoloration in the thumb (redness or "black and blue" marks). This is not unusual and does not present a problem unless there is significant swelling of the thumb as well, or the discoloration process continues at the same level from workout to workout. If either of these symptoms persist the lifter is overdoing it or (in extremely rare cases) may have actually done some significant damage to the thumb (something I have neither seen nor heard of, but which is at least theoretically possible). This discomfort can be mitigated by limiting the initial practice with the grip to just a few lighter sets and then gradually increasing the work load performed with the hook. In addition, most lifters find it helpful to wrap a single layer of tape around the thumb (with at least 1/2" of overlap in the ends of the tape, so that the tape can adhere to itself and thereby be more securely affixed to the thumb). This layer of tape (often two layers of 1" tape placed side by side with

a small overlap so that most of the thumb is covered) reduces the pain from the hook grip. It also protects the skin of the thumb from tearing or splitting when this grip is used extensively during a workout.

A common sense rule needs to be applied in adapting to the hook. If the hook is used too infrequently or for too short a period, the toughening process will not take place (or at least not fully). If it is used too much without letting the thumb toughen, the thumb will not have a chance to adapt. A good basic rule is that the athlete is proceeding too fast if any significant discomfort remains from one workout to the next. (Since a typical beginner is only training every other day or three days a week, the properly conditioned thumb should have adequate time to heal between workouts.)

The final hand problem that occurs with any level of frequency in weightlifting is direct damage from the bar. One example is when a lifter drops the bar from an open hand immediately before it hits the floor. In such a circumstance, the bar can rebound sharply and sprain a lifter's finger(s). If the hand is kept on the bar but the wrist is placed over the bar when it hits the platform, the wrist can be sprained. There are three preventive measures that you can take to avoid this problem. The lifter can lower the bar slowly and softly, so that no significant rebound occurs. The lifter can release his or her hands from the bar when the bar is far enough from the floor so that a rebound will not cause contact with the hands. Finally, the lifter can make sure that the grip is loose and that the hand and wrist are well behind the bar when it contacts the floor. In this case, any rebound will tend to be straight up, and the lifter's hands will be out of harm's way. If the latter technique is used, the lifter should make an effort to slow the bar's downward progress at the beginning of the lowering process, so that the full force of a drop from arm's length will not be realized. (A very sharp rebound can slap on snap the hand or wrist that is positioned to the rear of the falling bar fairly smartly if the full force of a drop is permitted to be generated.)

Injuries to the Arm and Elbow

Injuries to the arm are not common in weightlifting, and elbow injuries are only a bit more frequent. Of the arm injuries that do occur, the most frequent are biceps or triceps strains. The biceps strains appear almost exclusively in lifters who bend their arms prematurely or excessively in the pull. (The arms are properly used to help the body move rapidly under the bar once the squat under has begun, not to pull the bar upward during the earlier stages in the pull.) This injury occurs in lifters who use their arms inappropriately because they are attempting to lift with the arms at a time when the force that is being applied to the bar can only be withstood by the larger muscles of the legs, hips and back. (Biceps pulls are not uncommon among power lifters who bend their arms while deadlifting.) The only triceps injuries that I have ever seen resulted from a lifter's trying to press out a snatch that would never have passed the referee's scrutiny (because of the extent of the pressout). Therefore, a lifter should never press out or try to "save" a lift if the bar is significantly out of position and lower than is necessary to execute a clean lift.

Elbow injuries occur almost exclusively in the squat snatch position and then only to lifters who have elbows which hyperextend (continue to bend backward after the arm is fully straight). Lifters with this kind of "armlock" find it relatively easy to hold weights overhead once they have reached arm's length, but the hyperextended elbow does make them more prone to injury in that area. Such lifters should be careful not to overextend the elbows in the snatch and jerk as they lock out (particularly with light weights). They should never fight a snatch that is out of position, especially if they feel any stretching or discomfort in the elbow or the bar is too far to the rear. Finally, such lifters will find it useful to strengthen the muscles around the elbows, so that the joint is stabilized as much as possible. These lifter must also be very careful about finding a stable position in the snatch. Too wide a grip may place too much of a strain on the elbows as the angle between the lifter's arms and the bar grows smaller. On the other hand, a grip that is too narrow causes the lifter to twist the shoulder and elbow somewhat, making it more subject to injury. Often a minor change in grip width will significantly reduce the strain on the elbow joint.

It is particularly important to avoid elbow injuries in young athletes, because such injuries can damage the growth plates of the maturing athlete's arm, causing permanent problems with the joint and its maturation.

When an elbow does dislocate, rapid reduction of the dislocation is necessary to prevent permanent instability and reduce the likelihood of nerve and vascular injury. However, the reduction must be done by someone skilled in this area, and fractures at or near the elbow joint must be ruled out. Restoring mobility to an elbow that has been dislocated is a difficult process. Such an elbow injury rarely recurs, as a joint once injured does not normally return to the hyperextended position which first predisposed the lifter to the injury (except when the ligaments have not fully healed after the injury and no longer stabilize the joint properly, a very rare occurrence).

Lifters occasionally suffer nerve entrapments in the infraspinatus and supraspinatus muscles that surround the largest nerves in the arm. Surgical decompression and intensive therapy are sometimes needed to treat this condition, but more conservative forms of treatment are often successful.

Back Injuries

Spinal cord injuries are quite rare in weightlifting. I know of only one, and it reportedly occurred because an unevenness in the surface of the lifting platform caused the lifter's foot to become caught while he was moving under a jerk. The bar fell on the lifter, causing the lower spinal cord area to be traumatized by the bar and its force.

A much more common problem is low-back pain, which is caused by overstress on the muscles and/or ligaments that surround the spine. Such an injury generally causes a sharp pain when it occurs. The condition normally worsens over the ensuing hours, typically reaching a maximum level of discomfort twelve to twenty-four hours after the injury.

Low-back injuries can be quite painful and debilitating. However, if they are not accompanied by serious damage to a disk (which is usually the case), the problem tends to be more painful than serious. The symptoms of this problem are treated with ice, analgesics, spinal manipulation and, later, with any of a full complement of therapeutic modalities like ultrasound and electric muscle stimulation in order to break the considerable spasming of the lower-back muscles that typically accompany this injury. Subsequently, stretching and strengthening exercises are often performed. When the acute stage of muscle spasming is taking place, the athlete may find that his or her body is stooped over and pulled to one side (the most common kind of spasming occurs on one side or the other of the spine). If the lifter remains stationary for an extended period of time, particularly if he or she is sitting in a chair, the spasming will tend to increase markedly when the lifter tries to stand up.

I have had the misfortune of apparently inheriting a back that is very subject to this kind of injury (my father had a similar problem). My first lower-back injuries occurred as a child, long before I ever began lifting weights. I have tried virtually every treatment known for the problem. Spinal manipulation has been the most effective means of alleviating the acute pain of such an injury; therapeutic modalities have been somewhat less effective, and muscle relaxants have been almost worthless. Conventional static stretching of the lower back has helped on certain occasions, but at other times (especially when the pain was most severe), seemed to make the pain, and even the condition, worse.

There was a point in my competitive career when my back problem become so severe that I thought I was almost certainly finished (this was at age twenty-one). Over a period of a few weeks, I injured my back five times. Initially, reinjury only occurred when I tried to resume training, but later, minor things, like lifting a light sack of groceries, caused a recurrence. Spinal manipulation and other techniques offered temporary relief, but then another flare-up would occur. Static stretching seemed to have no effect.

Fortunately, I discovered a treatment technique which lengthened my competitive career dramatically. It has served me well in the more than twenty years since I discovered it. (interestingly, Tommy Kono independently found a similar approach to treating lower-back problems— which he described in the June/July 1974 issue of Strength & Health Magazine).

I present the technique not because I recommend it (it would make most orthopedic surgeons and rehabilitation specialists cringe in horror), but because it emphasizes the need for injured athletes to "find their own way" when conventional and even unconventional wisdom has nothing to offer.

I was near the peak of my career at this time, having cleaned a weight within 7.5 kg. of the world record in training several months before. All of my dreams of weightlifting success seemed to fade away as I could barely accomplish the activities of daily living. I was working in a health spa at the time and was extremely depressed over my latest episode of back pain. I literally could not touch my kneecaps with my hands without serious pain and spasming. Desperate would be too moderate a word to describe my condition. Then I did something "stupid" that turned out to be a career saver for me. In frustration, I decided that I was going to stretch my back forcefully to make it loosen up. In an effort to accomplish this, I lifted a 50 lb. bar from a rack with a clean grip and attempted to lower the bar without hesitation to as low a position as I could in a stiff-legged deadlift. By the time I got near my knee caps, I was in agony, but I continued to lower the bar to kneecap level and then returned to a standing position. Then I lowered the bar again, determined to go further than the previous rep. I did get about 1" further, but only with the same amount of pain as I had experienced on the first rep. I went on to do ten reps, and on the last one I managed to reach the mid-shin level. I then stood up and replaced the bar on the rack.

At this point a strange thing happened. I felt a release of the tension in the lower back and a sense of mobility and relaxation that I had literally not felt there for months. What a relief! Within about thirty seconds, the stiffness and pain returned, but I seemed to be on the right track. A few minutes later I did another set, this time reaching near my shoe tops with the bar (its small plates permitted this). The pain was virtually the same as on the first set, but I was going further.

This time it took perhaps two minutes for my back to seize up again after the set. I repeated this process for several more sets, and by the end of my session my back remained relaxed for about twenty

minutes and did not resume its full stiffness for several hours. The next day I could hardly walk from the soreness that had developed in my hamstrings from stretching the lower back so strenuously, but my back condition was dramatically improved. I continued to treat the back with several sets of stiff-legged deadlifts for the next couple of days, by which time my pain had practically disappeared. By the third day I resumed training and within a week was back at it nearly full force. My back problem was essentially cured.

In the years since, my injury has recurred, but the same treatment has always had the same effect. I now include stiff-legged deadlifts with an empty bar at the beginning and end of almost every workout. As long as I do them without fail, my back rarely troubles me. If I slack off my deadlifts for some reason, my back soon provides me with a "friendly" reminder that I had better not neglect it. Over the years a number of other lifters of my acquaintance have tried this "treatment," and most have had success.

Ordinarily, stiff-legged deadlifts would be considered perhaps the worst exercise for an athlete with an injured back. My explanation of its effectiveness for me and others who have tried it relates to the way in which the movement is executed. I perform the exercise with the head down, the bar so close to the body that it virtually touches the legs, the abdominals flexing lightly to support the weight and the weight very light (e.g., 20 kg.). In addition, I perform the descent into the low position at progressively lower levels with each rep. The pace is smooth but not explosive or jerky; neither is it very slow. I come up almost immediately after reaching the low point on each rep (though not explosively and there is no "bouncing"). This methodology seems to stretch the muscles of the lower back and help them to relax their spasm, while it (at least in my case and for others who have used this exercise) does not seem to damage the ligaments, disks or vertebrae of the spine. (Static stretching seems to transfer the stretch from the muscles to the ligaments as the position is held, and, at least in my case, makes the condition worse.)

I am not recommending this exercise to anyone. Anyone with an injury should follow conventional medical wisdom first. If conventional treatment does not work, some athletes may want to explore other approaches (the ones with the lowest degree of risk should always be tried first). In the event that such treatments fail, some athletes may want to explore other areas if they have a plausible treatment method and are willing to accept the risk of injury that may arise out of unconventional treatments. I was willing to take the risk and it worked out for me. In your case it might not, and you could be far worse off for the attempt.

It has been my observation that the stiff-legged deadlift and other exercises which stretch the lower back are not useful during the first twenty-four hours or so after the onset of an acute episode of lower-back pain (i.e., before the pain and spasming appear to have peaked and stabilized somewhat). At such a time, the entire area seems to be too unstable for the athlete to attempt to "retrain" the muscle so that is does not remain in a condition of spasm. I have had the experience of trying to do my stiff-legged deadlifts shortly after the onset of an acute episode and have done more harm than good.

The exercise described above should never be attempted when the athlete is experiencing numbness, tingling, pain radiating away from the injured area or any loss of sensation. These phenomena are symptoms of "disc" problems, and any extreme form of motion during a period when a disc may be injured can worsen the condition substantially.

Discs are structures that separate the vertebrae. They follow the shape of the vertebrae. They have cartilaginous outer and inner walls, with softer tissue between the walls. The disk can be damaged by stress in a way the causes the cartilage wall (particularly the inner one) to break, permitting the softer substance within the disk to "leak" into (press against) the spinal cord itself. Alternatively, the broken cartilage itself impinges against the spine, causing the pressure there as well. In either case, such pressure can lead to terrific pain and can compromise the functioning of the nerves of the spine. In my experience, non-weightlifters experience this problem more often than weightlifters (who, through proper conditioning and the use of good technique are well protected—though not immune—from traumatic disc injuries).

If the damage to the disk is not severe, conservative treatment can cause the disk to assume its natural shape, and normal functioning can continue. Surgical intervention may be required in more severe cases. Such intervention can range from the injection of an enzyme which dissolves the tissue which is impinging on the spine to the surgical removal of the damaged material, the complete removal of the disk or the "pinning" together of the vertebrae between which the disk was positioned before its removal. The results of such surgery range from virtually complete recovery to lifelong disability, so this kind of surgery should not be undertaken without careful thought.

Injuries to the neck and upper back also occur occasionally among weightlifters. The only kind of neck injury that I have encountered in weightlifters is similar to, but generally less severe, than the musculoskeletal low-back pain. Rather suddenly, the lifter experiences a sharp pain in the neck. The onset typically takes places when lifting with the head or neck twisted or flexed to one side or the other. (This is one reason why lifter should always look straight ahead and never

turn or tilt the head sideways while lifting.) On other occasions, the lifter awakens with stiffness and pain in the neck. The pain generally increases when the lifter turns his or her head to one side or the other. Heat and anti-inflammatories can help to relieve this problem, but in my experience, the most effective treatment is manipulation followed by range of motion exercises.

A second condition that occurs occasionally is a strain in the thoracic region of the back. The muscles involved can vary, but generally the rhomboids and/or trapezius muscles near the spine are affected. The onset is typically sudden, with the lifter feeling a sharp pain, most often while the arms are over the lifter's head. The pain is often worsened with deep breathing, turning or lifting the head and raising the arms over the head. Fortunately, the pain is usually far worse than the condition. If the lifter does not perform exercises that worsen the pain, the injury typically heals itself within a few days.

A third condition that is only rarely reported in weightlifters is "spondylolysis," a stress fracture of one or more vertebrae. It is not a very common occurrence among weightlifters, but it does happen on occasion. Such an injury can be difficult to detect by X-ray, so often a bone scan is required. When the diagnosis is confirmed, rest is indicated. Stretching and abdominal work are often recommended once the injury has healed enough to withstand the stress of these exercises (the former to relieve any tension that may have contributed to the injury and the latter to create better support for the spine and prevent a recurrence). Any athlete who develops this condition would be well advised to evaluate his or her techniques, as some modifications that will reduce the stress placed on the spine during lifting may well be possible and appropriate.

Spondylolisthesis is a forward displacement or slippage of one or more vertebrae. While it is reported only rarely in weightlifters, the most frequent site of its occurrence is at the juncture of the fifth lumbar vertebrae and the sacrum, but can occur elsewhere. Prepubescent athletes and athletes early in puberty are most often afflicted by the problem. It generally results from chronic lower-back strain (which should rarely occur as a result of training because athletes at this age should not be subjected to training of an intensity or volume that can cause it). Treatment is normally conservative, but care must be taken to avoid re-instituting the stresses that caused the problem, at least not before the athlete has had an opportunity to better prepare for such stresses the second time around.

Finally, fractures of the spinous processes can occur while weightlifting (and doing many other things). They result primarily when a lifter accidentally drops a weight on his or her back or when a lifter carelessly replaces the bar at shoulder level behind the neck after doing a behind the neck jerk or similar exercise. Such an injury, while painful, rarely leads to any instability in the spine, and an athlete is often able to continue to train as the pain permits. However, the decision to continue training should never be made until after a thorough diagnosis that assures the lifter there is no danger to the spinal cord as a result of continued activity.

Prevention of lower-back pain should take several forms. First, the back should not be subjected to sudden and severe changes in the loads it is subjected to. Such changes can occur as a result of technique modifications, the addition of exercises that load the lower back and increases in the training load from existing exercises that stress the lower back. A second measure is to strengthen the lower-back muscles specifically, with such exercises as hyperextensions and deadlifts. These measures can be useful, but the athlete who employs them must be careful to assure that these exercises are not merely adding to a load that is already causing excess stress. In such a case, the "cure" will worsen the condition.

A third measure is to assure that the lower back is not being unduly stressed by faulty technique. The most common example is the athlete who fails to retain the natural arch in the lower back (or loses this arch at some point during the lift). Once the arch is lost (particularly if this occurs when the back is in a position of significant stress) the ligaments of the back are vulnerable to injury on the micro or macro levels. The most dangerous positions for this to occur are at points when the lifter is applying great stress to the lower back. (For instance, as the bar is taken from the floor in the pull, as the bar passes the knees, or when the lifter is fighting through the "sticking point" in the squat.)

A fourth measure is to stretch the lower back, hamstring and illiopsoas muscles. The purpose of stretching the lower-back muscles is to remove any unnecessary tension in that area. Such tension can itself place pressure on the spine. In addition, this tension can predispose the back to injury, either by fatiguing the back muscles (which makes them more vulnerable to strain) or by predisposing them to the kind of spasming that leads to an actual injury. The hamstrings are stretched because tension and shortness there can pull the back out of its natural position, particularly when the athlete is moving, predisposing the lower back to injury.

The purpose of stretching the psoas muscles relates to their function. These muscles normally act as hip flexors. However, they can cause hyperextension or flexion of the lumbar spine under certain conditions. Consequently, if these muscles lose their flexibility or generate abnormal tension, they can worsen or even cause a back condition. Because the psoas is a primarily a hip

flexor, any exercise that extends the hip will stretch it. One example is the split position, in which the psoas is stretched on the side of the leg, which is placed posteriorly. An even simpler way of stretching the psoas is to straighten the leg and let the pelvis tilt slightly rearward while standing. This exercise has the advantage of being so simple that it can be done at any time of day.

A fifth measure is to strengthen the abdominal muscles and all of the muscles which surround the spinal column. Conditioning of these muscles strengthens the entire muscular "girdle" which supports the spine and protects it from injury.

Finally, the lifter should not overlook the importance of an appropriate bed and sleeping positions in the prevention and treatment of back problems. A lifter who sleeps on his or her stomach may find that this brings on or worsens back pain. A lifter's mattress should be firm and supportive (you do not want a bed that sags in the middle like a hammock, particularly if you sleep on your stomach), but a hard bed is generally not desirable either. Mattresses that were "as hard as a rock" were the fashion for a number of years. But now health professionals realize that a bed that is too hard can impair circulation and cause the spine and other joints and limbs to fall out of alignment while the person is sleeping. In order to avoid this, the upper layer of the bed should give enough to conform to the body's contours and offer contact and support to the entire body. (A layer of foam rubber on top of a more conventional and reasonably firm bed is often used today to deliver a combination of give and firmness.)

Shoulder Injuries

Serious shoulder injuries are not very common in weightlifting, but the incidence has been on the rise in recent years. It is the contention of some coaches that this increase in the injury rate can be attributed, at least partially, to the failure of many of today's lifters to practice shoulder strengthening exercises, such as overhead pressing movements. Up until 1972, when the press was eliminated from weightlifting competition, weightlifters practiced pressing extensively. At that time serious shoulder injuries were extremely rare. Perhaps the correlation is simply a coincidence, but I doubt it. I believe that most lifters would benefit in terms of performance and injury protection if they practiced more pressing.

Of the injuries that do occur, dislocations are occasional, and damage to the rotator cuff muscles and tendons also occurs. More often than not, these kinds of injuries result when a lifter attempts to save a lift that has drifted out of position. The awkward position of the weight places an unusual strain on the shoulder, and damage results. Such injuries can also occur when an athlete's shoulder joint is unstable (e.g., the glenoid capsule into which the humerus normally fits is shallower than normal). This predisposes such a lifter to a shoulder injury. Finally, lifters may be predisposed to such injuries because activities in which they have previously engaged (e.g., sports in which repetitive shoulder strain occurs, such as baseball pitching or handball playing) have damaged the shoulder joint.

A more common occurrence for the lifter is a sore shoulder, which tends to be an overuse injury. The athlete may have added exercises or repetitions in exercises that affect the shoulder, and resulting in overuse, or a change in technique may have increased the stress on the shoulder. Such a problem can be addressed by reducing the training load and/or modifying technique.

Shoulder injuries can be very slow to heal. One reason is that everyday activities can place stress on the shoulder joint. Even carrying something at your side can place a strain on the shoulder joint. Amazingly, even sleeping can trigger, exacerbate or irritate shoulder injuries. This is because many people have the habit of sleeping with one or both arms over their heads. An arm placed in this position for long periods can place serious strain on the shoulder joint.

I learned this the hard way when a slight shoulder injury turned into a long term problem that always seemed to be worse in the morning. Eventually, it struck me that when I woke up with my arm over my head, the problem was far worse that day. The healing process was facilitated when I began wearing a long-sleeved nightshirt to bed. Before retiring, I would pin the sleeve of the arm with the sore shoulder to the bottom of the shirt so that I could not pick up my arm while I slept. (Immobilization of any limb during sleep can aid in the healing process if you discover that sleep patterns are adversely affecting an injury.)

Many athletes who have shoulder problems find that certain exercises aggravate the shoulder joint. In my case it is dips. Performing dips on a parallel bar, or even supporting myself from such bars, places a strain on my shoulders that they cannot long endure. While many lifters used to swear by dips as an assistance exercise for the press, I know several who had career ending injuries from doing that exercise with heavy resistance. A number of lifters I have known have also injured their shoulders and/or pectoralis muscles doing bench presses.

Knee Injuries

Knee injuries (particularly of the overuse type) are fairly common in weightlifting. Many sports medicine experts would not be surprised by this statement because they have been taught that full squatting (which weightlifters practice with great regularity) is very dangerous for the knee joint.

I have yet to find someone who has sustained a knee injury from performing full squats correctly. (I have known some athletes who have hurt their knees doing partial squats and many who have inflamed their knee joints while performing heavy leg extensions.) There is no evidence that the ligaments of lifters who perform full squats are "lax" (i.e., have been loosened by that activity). In fact, there is some evidence that squatting may improve the congruity and stability of the knee relative to one that has not been trained by full squatting. (Squatting is beginning to gain some popularity in sports injury rehabilitation programs.) In addition, there is considerable evidence that ligaments become stronger with training, both because of adaptive changes in the composition of the ligament and because of changes in the architecture of the ligament (e.g., alignment of the fibers of the ligament with the stresses that it must withstand). Moreover, evidence is accumulating that "open kinetic chain" exercises (where the body is fixed and a limb moves, as in leg extensions) are far more stressful to the joints than "closed kinetic chain" exercises (where the distal end of the limb is fixed and the body moves, as in squatting).

Most weightlifters who do sustain knee injuries attribute them to an accident while lifting (e.g., catching a foot or twisting a knee) or to overstress. It is important to evaluate all knee injuries as soon as they occur. Serious acute knee injuries tend to be accompanied by considerable swelling in a relatively short period. When examinations are delayed beyond fifteen to twenty minutes, diagnosis can be hampered by such swelling.

It must be realized that the fundamental means which a lifter uses to impart force to the bar in the snatch, clean and jerk is the jumping motion with a heavy load. In addition, fixing a weight in the snatch or clean involves receiving considerable force in the low squat position. Even fixing a weight in the power snatch, power clean or jerk involves a sudden stop. All of this strain placed on the knee and the muscles that support it makes the knee joint susceptible to sprains and strains (with the latter being far more common than the former).

Tendinitis in the quadriceps and/or patellar tendons is perhaps the most common knee problem experienced by lifters. Overuse leads to irritation of the tendon. This can be a particularly difficult problem because of the constant use of this area during nearly any form of training on the competitive or related lifts. Perhaps the most conservative treatment for this problem is icing the tendon after the workout. A number of lifters have found that this treatment alone provides relief in a relatively short time, particularly if the workouts are modified to reduce any additional irritation to the tendon. This does not mean that training must necessarily stop altogether. Rather, the lifter must identify the positions and exercises that are the most irritating and reduce or eliminate them. For instance, the lifter may find that squats present no problem but that cleans do worsen the condition. In such a case, cleans can be eliminated for a time, and clean pulls and squats can be continued. This will maintain and even increase the lifter's strength, while permitting the inflamed tendon to heal.

Other treatments for the condition include stretching the quadriceps muscle group. There are two theories behind the stretching treatment. Each theory argues for a different approach to stretching. The first premise is that a low level tension in the quadriceps muscles is created by hard training. That tension is relieved by relatively gentle stretching. The relaxed state induced by the stretching enables the tendon to rest more fully and this causes or reduction in the inflammation of the tendon. The second theory is that lack of flexibility in the muscle-tendon unit leads to micro-trauma when extreme positions are assumed in the squat (i.c., low positions in which great pressure is placed on the tendon as the bar is fixed in the snatch and clean). If the muscle-tendon unit is stretched to assume a greater resting length, trauma to the tendon will be relieved.

I find the first theory more convincing than the second. Many lifters I know have noted that their tendons are irritated at least as much by movements that do not involve extreme positions (such as power cleans) as by movements that do. They have reported relief using gentle stretching that merely relaxes the quadriceps group.

Some lifters who have had the most flexible quadriceps muscles imaginable (i.e., athletes who could touch their buttocks to the floor quite easily in a full squat position), have had serious injuries to the quadriceps unit. Why would these highly flexible athletes suffer such injuries if flexibility were a protective element? This is not to say that flexibility is not important or that some athletes may indeed have an increased injury risk because of lack of flexibility. However, flexibility is clearly not a panacea.

For the athlete who wants to try stretching as a treatment for tendinitis of the quad or patellar tendons or other tendons, several cautions should be followed. First, a stretching program which relaxes the tendon should be attempted before one that seeks to increase the lifter's range of motion. Second, the lifter should warm up thoroughly; stretching a "cold" tendon can be a bad idea (particularly if the lifter is trying to increase its range of motion). Third, every effort should be made to stretch the muscle rather than the tendon itself (a tendon which is already inflamed can be further irritated by efforts to stretch it). This is not easy (and some would argue that it is not possible), because the muscle and tendon are connected, and stretching one necessarily involves stretching the other. However, the emphasis does seem to vary

with the position in which the leg is placed when the athlete stretches. Generally, if an athlete kneels on the floor and then sits back towards his or her heels, the stretch will tend to be felt most in the tendon. If, in contrast, the athlete curls the heel of the opposite leg part of the way toward the buttocks while standing on one leg and then reaches behind to grasp the ankle of that leg in order to stretch it, more pull will be felt in the quadriceps area. This is particularly true if the athlete pulls the ankle rearward while doing the stretch (as compared with pulling the heel towards the buttock). By experimenting with the different angles of pull, the lifter can find the one in which the stretch is felt most in the belly (middle) of the muscle.

Athletes seeking a relaxing stretch will often find that stretching to a point where there is some stretch and no discomfort and then holding that position for thirty to sixty seconds will provide a greater degree of relaxation than assuming a more extreme position. Others find that repeated stretches of much shorter duration (e.g., AI stretching) are far more effective. (Chapter 3 describes such stretching methods.)

The athlete must also pay careful attention to the effects of the stretching session. If the tendon feels more irritated after the session, then perhaps that method of stretching is not beneficial for that particular condition. As with all forms of training, the exercise used and its intensity and frequency need to be monitored in order to achieve the desired purpose most effectively.

Knee wraps are employed by some lifters to "treat" tendon pain. Some of the pros and cons of using knee wraps were presented earlier in this chapter.

Doctors often prescribe NSAIDs to treat this problem. If the inflammation is a one-time occurrence with a specific cause, the athlete can generally benefit from this kind of treatment. However, for truly chronic pain it is important to look at the fundamental causes rather than merely treating the symptoms with NSAIDs or any other palliative measure.

Injuries to the meniscus also occur occasionally as a result of a technique error that is made while the lifter is resisting the downward force of the bar (e.g., from the mis-positioning of the foot while catching a heavy clean). If the injury is minor, conservative treatment is sometimes effective. When the injury is more severe, arthroscopic surgery can be an effective treatment, and an athlete is often able to resume very limited training within a few weeks. Weightlifters should recognize that coming back from a meniscus injury in weightlifting is not as simple as coming back from such an injury in a sport like running, in which the knee is not put through its full range of motion. Comebacks are generally quite successful, but doctors who tell you that you will be back at your full level of activity in three weeks have probably never tried any squat cleans after having such surgery.

Young athletes sometimes develop a condition called Osgood-Schlatter's disease. This a growth disorder at the site of the tibial tuberosity. The problem presents itself as swelling, tenderness and pain in the patellar tendon at that site. The condition tends to improve with maturity, but it can be quite a problem for some lifters, and it warrants careful medical monitoring and attention so that it does not become a long term problem.

Chondromalacia patella is another condition that can affect the knees of lifters. This injury involves a deterioration of the cartilage of the under-surface of the patella where it is in contact with the femur. The onset of chondromalacia is generally somewhat gradual (the lifter feels it progressing over at least a series of workouts). Typically, the athlete feels pain and/or stiffness and pressure in the area under the patella. The pain is normally worsened when the lifter is in a full squat position or taking a weight from the floor in the clean or snatch. My experience has been that conservative treatment is more effective in treating this condition than surgery. Few lifters, if any, have come back from surgery on this area.

Some years ago, I developed a fairly serious case of chondromalacia patella. Two surgeons recommended surgery but a third told me that if he (or anyone else) operated, it was unlikely that I would every lift heavy weights again. Instead, he recommended that I try an arch support in my shoe to alter the position of my feet t. More important, he recommended that I change my way of squatting to keep my shin nearly vertical when I squatted. (This involves sitting back with the squat rather than permitting the knee to travel well forward of the foot in the squat position.) I also avoided or temporarily eliminated the classic lifts and anything else that seemed to irritate the knee (deadlifts with a close or frog-leg foot position bothered my knee). This conservative method of treatment took nearly a year to lead to a complete recovery. That is an awfully long time. But some people I know who had the surgery at the same time that I began my more conservative treatment never came back from the surgery. While my performance never reached pre-injury levels, there were other reasons for that. (My knee healed almost completely over time.)

It has been my experience that a lifter's shoes can have a significant influence on knee problems. Some years ago a major shoe manufacturer came out with a new model of weightlifting shoes that looked great. Many lifters bought them, but within a year's time I saw several of those lifters suffer a complete quad-tendon rupture (something I had never seen in all of my years of lifting). Two of my friends suffered the same injury wearing these shoes. I bought a pair, and within few days I experienced a sharp pain in my quad tendon while doing relatively light snatches. When I changed back to my old shoes, the pain went away, and it has never returned in that way. Were the shoes responsible? If so, why were these shoes a problem? No one knows for sure. The manufacturer has long since discontinued them. Perhaps it is just a coincidence that just after distribution of these shoes stopped, the incidence of quad-tendon rupture fell precipitously, to the point where it is once again rare in the United States.

The real point of the story is that when a lifter changes his or her shoes, it takes time to get accustomed to them. Unless you are sure they are identical to the ones you have been wearing, do not begin using them full time all at once. Wear the new shoes for a few warm-up sets and then do the rest of the workout with the old shoes. Over a period of a week or so, work up to doing one exercise with the new shoes. Over a period of several weeks, phase them in to the entire workout. This process is particularly important when the height of the heel on the new shoe is different from the old shoe.

Generally, lower heels place less stress on the knees but more stress on the hips, back and shoulders (the latter when one is snatching). But this is not universally true. Some knee conditions improve when a lifter wears a higher heel.

As long as the lifter acclimates to a new shoe gradually, he or she will rarely encounter any serious problems. However, if knee pain has its onset shortly after new footwear has been introduced, the effect of the new shoes is worth investigating.

Pubic Bone Bruise

In the modern style of pulling, the bar often comes into vigorous contact with a lifter's thighs or hips. In the latter case, contact with the body at the level of the pubic bone can actually cause a bone bruise in that area. This rarely occurs with heavy weights, as the speed of the lifter and the bar are simply not enough to generate very hard contact. But when lifters are warming up, the contact can be very hard indeed. For most athletes, the solution to this problem is to widen or narrow the grip slightly, so that severe contact exactly on the point of the bone is avoided. Caution must be exercised to assure that the use of a slightly different grip does not cause the lifter to damage his or her technique in any way.

Some lifters who make violent contact with the pubic bone protect the area with some form of padding. The rules of lifting are somewhat vague in this area. Wearing any supportive device under the lifting costume is clearly prohibited by the rules. However, it is not clear whether a pad which protects the pubic area (e.g., a sponge or folded handkerchief) is supportive. Therefore, an athlete who wears a pubic pad should be aware that he or she might be challenged by an official in competition.

Should an injury occur, a combination of padding and a slight grip change can permit the lifter to continue to train. For most lifters, a rapid restoration of old technique patterns will occur as soon as the injury is healed and the old grip is resumed. The greater risk is generally in the athlete's continuing to train in pain. Such a process may cause further damage and will almost certainly be injurious to the lifter's technique. In an effort to avoid pain, the lifter is likely to slow the explosion down, bend the arms or do something even worse from a technical standpoint. The net result may be some permanent damage to technique. This is why training in pain is a major mistake for most athletes and why training around the pain makes so much more sense.

Groin Pull

The groin pull is a fairly common injury among weightlifters. It can arise either as a result of overuse or a sudden slip. The latter most often occurs when the lifter is in or is moving into the split position. If the lifter's back foot does not land on all of its toes, it can twist toward the inside edge of the foot. In this position, much of the strain on the back leg is taken up by the ligaments of the knee and the adductors of the leg (as compared with the quadriceps and hip flexors, which absorb most of the strain when the foot is correctly positioned on the toes). Such a position places the groin and knee at risk. Many groin pulls have occurred as a result of this position.

The other major cause of a groin injury is overuse. The athlete must realize that the adductor muscles are strongly activated during the back squat and the pull from the floor. When the athlete is increasing the load on these exercises significantly, there is always the risk of overstressing the adductors. This is especially true when the athlete has added or increased the load of deadlifts, pulls, deadlifts or lifts while standing on a raised platform (especially when they are done with a snatch grip). When these kinds or changes are made and the back foot turns in the jerk the risk of a groin injury increases substantially. Because the adductors are involved in so many movements, a complete rest is sometimes needed in order to clear up a difficult groin injury (along with taking steps to reduce the causes of overuse once the athlete does recover from the injury).

Abraded Shins

It is not uncommon for an athlete to abrade his or her shins with the bar while pulling. In a sense this can be viewed as a result of a technique error because when an athlete pulls correctly the bar only grazes the shins. Nevertheless, it is not uncommon for athletes, even those with good technique, to abrade the shins occasionally, particularly if they are training with a bar that has a sharp knurling. Wearing full sweat pants generally protects and athlete from abrasions. When they do occur it is important to treat the abrasion as one would any such injury.

In terms of recovering from the injury, it is important to give the shins extra protection while they are healing. A band aid applied to the injured area that is covered with tape is generally more than enough protection. Coupling the bandage with wearing full sweatpants should definitely be sufficient. If it is not you definitely need to take a look at your pulling technique. Constant abrasions are evidence of attempting straighten the back too early in the pull and of having the balance too far to the rear during the start of the pull.

Injuries to the Ankle and Foot

Injuries to the ankle are quite rare in weightlifting. Since most ankle injuries in sport result from twisting the foot or ankle while running or jumping, this should not be surprising. Despite the relatively low incidence of ankle injuries, some weightlifters are comforted by the perception of ankle support afforded them by a high- top athletic shoe, but many (if not most) prefer the freedom of movement that is available from a low-top shoe.

Naturally, supportive taping for the ankle should be considered if an ankle injury occurs, but care must be taken not to restrict the movement of the ankle that permits the knee to move forward over the foot while squatting. Restrictions in this area can cause uneven positioning of the legs and consequent changes in positioning in other areas of the body. This can result in injuries to those other areas.

The only injuries to the foot that occur often enough in weightlifting to be worth mentioning are the result of a lifter's dropping the bar or a plate on his or her foot. In one very unusual case, an athlete dropped a jerk behind himself, failed to step forward out of the way and kept the rear foot on its toes. In this case the heel of the foot was high enough for the bar to make contact with it. The result was a broken bone in the lifter's foot, which was painful and cost that lifter valuable training time. It could have been entirely avoided by the lifter's getting out of the way as the bar fell.

The more common injuries occur as a result of a plate falling off a bar that is supported by a rack or the a lifter dropping the plate while his or her foot is directly under the plate. In all instances these injuries are the result of carelessness or faulty equipment. Weight training is a relatively safe activity when it is practiced with care, but no activity is completely safe if a participant becomes careless. The athlete should avoid dropping any weight, especially when there is anything underneath it (e.g., a plate, a foot, another lifter), and should always pay attention to what he or she is doing when handling any weight.

Non-Surgical and Post Surgical Treatments for Injuries

There are a wide array of techniques for treating injuries without surgery or following surgery. The most important form of non-surgical treatment—exercise—has already been discussed. In this section we will examine a variety of non-surgical or post surgical treatments for injuries. Medicine has developed many therapies (also known as modalities) to assist in the healing of injuries. A complete description and analysis of these modalities is beyond the scope of this book. There are many texts which ably describe the full range of therapeutic tools, their mechanisms of action (at least as far as they are understood today) and the ways in which they are used. In this section we will merely touch upon the major categories of modalities.

Massage

Massage has been used by athletes for thousands of years. There is no doubt that sore and aching muscles are comforted by massage. Other soft tissues, like tendons, can also respond favorably to massage. Massage can be divided into at least two categories: massage that is designed to improve circulation, remove metabolic wastes, etc., and massage that is designed to break the pain cycle.

The former type is more common. Most of this kind of massage is performed by the masseur's full hand and generally consists of stroking and light "percussive" techniques. Such massage generally produces relatively pleasant sensations. It causes no harm (unless it is applied to an injured or infected area), and it does appear to promote the healing process. Athletes who have access to massage are therefore wise to take advantage of the opportunity. Athletes who are not as fortunate may be able to utilize mechanical substitutes, such as vibrators and whirlpool baths. While probably not as effective as skilled human hands, these modalities can achieve positive results.

Massage that is designed to break a pain cycle is an entirely different animal. It is generally relies on the application of considerable pressure to specific areas in which pain is mostly deeply experienced. The pain which results from such treatment can be excruciating. Practitioners of this kind of massage use thumbs, knuckles, elbows and even foreign objects to apply pressure to areas of the muscle and/or tendon that are regarded as responsible for an athlete's pain and disability. The theory behind this form of massage is that pain is often non-functional. It can persist after any injury, and the pain itself can cause non-functional muscle

contractions (.e.g., contractures) which themselves cause pain, leading to still further pain causing contractions. By applying pressure to the "trigger points" of pain, the contractures in these muscle-tendon areas are broken along with the cycle. (Otherwise, contractures can lead to changes in circulation and metabolism, which lead to further contractures, which impact circulation and metabolism in a vicious circle.)

Many athletes swear by these painful treatments. My experience has been that they can be useful under certain circumstances. Therefore, athletes who are experiencing chronic muscle pain may find such massage worth a try, particularly if alterations in training loads and technique and careful stretching have already been explored in an effort to address the problem.

Massage directed at breaking the pain cycle is best administered by trained professionals who specialize in this kind of treatment. However, some athletes will find that they are able to self-treat if the location of the injured area lends itself to self-treatment and the athlete receives the proper training.

Spinal and Joint Manipulation

Chiropractors, osteopaths, physical therapists and other medical professionals use spinal manipulation, and, to a lesser extent, manipulations of other joints to alleviate a variety of musculoskeletal ills. On the basis of my experiences, and those of other athletes who I have known, I have no doubt that manipulation can be very useful for treating certain kinds of conditions, particularly back and neck pain. No one, including its practitioners, fully understands the mechanisms through which manipulation works. The most common explanation is the theory of "subluxations," which essentially says that minor misalignments of the joints, especially the spine, can cause pain and loss of function. Manipulation presumably realigns the area in which the subluxation exists and thus corrects the condition.

Some practitioners carry the theory of subluxations much further. They attribute virtually every human ill to pinched nerves which result from subluxations. To many true believers, germ theory and other explanations for disease which have been scientifically demonstrated to be true can merely be ignored. These extremists even ignore evidence that is provided by their own theory. For example, subluxations of the spine have been blamed for disorders of the eyes, even though the nerves of the eyes travel directly to the brain, with no involvement with the spine. The errors made by the manipulation extremists do not alter the effectiveness of this treatment in certain circumstances, however.

Manipulation is clearly contraindicated for people with certain vascular problems, fractures of the bones that are being manipulated and some with "disc" problems. Reputable practitioners of manipulation are aware of these limitations and do not proceed when they exist. Patients should also be wary of manipulators who claim cures for such ills as cancer, infections and the like.

Because of their aversion for the use of drugs and surgery, many chiropractors and osteopaths have become very knowledgeable in areas of injury treatment that practitioners of surgery and/or drug therapy never bother to explore, but this is not universally true. Therefore, health practitioners need to be judged as individuals and not solely on the basis of the degree or license that they hold.

Cryotherapy (Cold Therapy)

Most therapeutic modalities use thermal energy to change the temperature of injured tissue and thereby facilitate the healing process. In the case of the application of cold, the purpose is to minimize damage to injured tissue.

When tissue is injured, much of the damage that occurs (particularly in the surrounding areas) results from oxygen deprivation (circulation that has been compromised by the injury leads to a lack of oxygen in the area). The application of cold reduces the temperature near the injury site and slows the metabolism in that area, reducing the area's need for oxygen and hence the damage that is done to it. The application of cold also causes vasoconstriction, which reduces the severity of the body's inflammatory response. Finally, cold tends to reduce pain (by reducing the excitability of nerves) and spasming at the injury site. Ice massage, the application of ice packs, immersion in cold or ice water and spraying with vapocoolants (such as flouro-methane) are all means to generate cooling of the tissues.

Because of its analgesic properties, cryotherapy is often combined with exercise during the rehabilitation process, because therapeutic exercise can be undertaken with less pain after or during the application of cold. However, such exercise should only be performed under supervision, because the presence of cold can mask protective pain and permit the athlete to exceed his or her capabilities. But when used properly, cryotherapy can be helpful in permitting an athlete to work through non-functional pain (such as when breaking adhesions, scar tissue that inhibits motion) to restore function.

Thermotherapy (Therapeutic Heat)

There are a wide variety of therapeutic modalities designed to generate heat within the injured area. In order for therapeutic heat to be useful, it must cause an increase in molecular activity. When the level and penetration of heat is too small, it will not lead to any improvement in the healing process. If the heat is excessive, actual damage to tissues can occur. The action of heat and the relative benefits of heat from different sources are not fully understood. The benefits of heat include improvements in tissue and joint flexibility, reductions in pain and spasming, reductions in swelling and cellular debris in the injury area and an increase in the blood flow in the area.

Thermotherapies include: moist heat packs, whirlpool baths, infrared radiation, fluidotherapy, contrast baths, shortwave diathermy, microwave diathermy, continuous electromagnetic energy ultrasound and phonophoresis. All of these therapies have their strengths and weaknesses, but some are clearly more effective than others. However, effectiveness can be offset by lack of availability and the athlete needs to balance these considerations. If the athlete can apply moist heat packs several times per day but can only travel to a therapist for ultrasound treatment once a week, the former treatment (though less effective than ultrasound) will prove to be more effective for that athlete. In most cases a combination of therapies will work more effectively than any single one.

Electrotherapy

While not used as widely as thermotherapies, electrotherapies are gaining in popularity. Electrotherapies involve the conduction of an electrical current through a particular tissue or group of tissues. Electrical impulses vary in shape, direction, amplitude and duration. Their primary effects are to modulate pain and to stimulate contraction of muscles. The mechanisms of pain relief are complex, but it is sufficient to say that electrical current can be very effective in controlling pain, which has an associated benefit of assisting the muscle to relax and freeing it from the pain/contraction cycle that was discussed earlier in this chapter. The stimulation of muscle contractions can avoid atrophy in muscles that have not been exercised, pump blood and other fluids through the muscle, strengthen muscles and reeducate them to contract after injury or surgery. Perhaps the most common form of electrical device for pain control is the transcutaneous electrical nerve stimulator (TENS).

A more experimental use of electrical current is in the stimulation of the healing process in bone and soft tissues. Here the electrical current is of a very low level that cannot be detected by the senses, but it alters the electrical activity in individual cells. This kind of device used for this purpose is referred to as a microcurrent electrical current neuromuscular stimulator (MENS).

Low Power Lasers

Lasers have long been used in certain types of surgery and other medical treatments that typically involve the destruction of unwanted tissue. Today the use of lower power lasers is being

447

experimented with in hopes that they will be able to stimulate collagen synthesis, destroy microorganisms, increase vascularization and decrease inflammation and pain.

Acupuncture and Acupressure

Acupuncture is founded on the premise that there are a series of "meridians" that run through the body. Points on these meridians are associated with pain in various areas of the body. By inserting needles into these points, pain can be relieved in the related areas. The Chinese, who developed the practice, believe they have identified thousands of these points.

There is evidence that these points do have some different characteristics than other areas in the body (e.g., electrical resistance is lower at acupuncture sites than other areas of the body), but there is no evidence that the explanation the acupuncturists have posited are accurate. However, there is significant clinical support for the idea that the pain reducing effects of acupuncture are real (whatever their cause).

Acupressure is the application of massage techniques to the points that have been identified by acupuncture (and generally pinpointed by the therapist as a source of pain). Pressure is applied to the appropriate area with a finger, elbow or other probing device. The degree of effectiveness of the treatment is generally positively related to amount of discomfort that it causes. Relief generally lasts for at least several minutes to several hours, and many athletes have reported a relatively permanent form of relief after one or a series of treatments.

Therapeutic Uses of Flexibility Training

Thus far we have focused on the use of flexibility training to permit the lifter's body to assume functional positions in executing the snatch and C&J. There is at least one additional purpose for doing stretching exercises. That reason is therapeutic.

Sports medicine specialists have found at least four major reasons for an athlete to practice stretching. First, stretching can be used to restore the flexibility to a muscle that has been restricted in terms of its motion and/or been damaged in some way. If a joint has been immobilized (e.g., placed in a cast), it loses strength, size and flexibility rather quickly. After the cast is removed, the athlete often needs to work just as hard to restore the range of motion to the joint and muscles involved as to restore the strength and size of the muscles. This requires flexibility training.

A second reason for stretching is to break up the spasming that is caused by certain types of injuries or muscle malfunctions. If a muscle is damaged, it will tend to spasm, and that spasm is part of a protective mechanism. It is not appropriate to stretch a muscle that has been damaged until sufficient healing to the damaged tissue has taken place. Premature stretching ruptured muscle or tendon fibers can undermine or preclude proper healing and thereby prolong the recovery process. However, a muscle that has gone into a state of spasming after an injury will tend to remain in the spasmed state (or at least a state of abnormal tension)longer than necessary. In fact, muscle tension can generate pain, and that pain tends to foster the continuation of the tension, creating a vicious cycle of pain, tension, more pain and more tension.

When sufficient healing has taken place, stretching will help break up any spasming, interrupt the pain/spasm cycle and restore the muscle to its normal level of functioning.

It has been demonstrated that stretching exercises can relieve muscle soreness and cramps. When a stretching stimulus is applied to a sore or spasmed muscle, the symptoms tend to be relieved faster than through pure rest. The mechanism of this relief is not well understood, but the effectiveness of the procedure has been well established on a practical level. Similarly, stretching the muscles of the lower-back often helps to relieve the lower back pain that arises from spasming muscles and serves to prevent the recurrence of this pain. Proper stretching for this condition can be more effective than medication (i.e., muscle relaxants) in controlling unwanted muscular tension.

A third therapeutic reason for stretching is to relieve tendinitis. A number of athletes and sports medicine specialists have reported that the careful and sustained stretching of a muscle that is attached to a tendon exhibiting the symptoms of tendinitis tends to relieve the symptoms of the tendinitis for many sufferers. When stretching to relieve tendinitis, care must be taken to assure that the force of the stretch is felt in the muscle and not the tendon; stretching that is felt at the site of a tendon can make the tendinitis worse. The athlete will need to experiment with the position of the joint and the effort applied to the stretch in order to attain a stretch that is felt in the muscle and not the tendon. Most often this occurs when the muscle is stretched only to the point of a slight tension followed shortly by a sense of relaxation and then the relaxed state is maintained without attempting to increase the range of motion. Here again, no one seems to fully understand the mechanism involved in stretching the muscle attached to the ailing tendon, but this technique does help many people. (It is believed that such stretching lowers the degree of resting tension in the muscle and that in turn relieves unnecessary stress on the tendon.)

It should be noted that when stretching for therapeutic purposes, the type, frequency and intensity of the flexibility training that is applied should be guided by two considerations. The first and most important consideration is the advice of the physician, physical therapist or other health professional who is treating the injury. A second consideration is the response of each individual to any flexibility training. While health professionals have access to research and practical experience that helps them to prescribe effective exercise programs, the unique needs of each individual need to be considered as well. People heal at different rates and have different pain tolerances, and different interpretations of instructions.. Consequently, responses to exercise therapy need to be observed and considered in making prescriptions. The patient's input and analysis are therefore critical.

A fourth therapeutic reason for stretching is to restore the original length of muscle tissue that has shortened in response to overuse. Overuse of any muscle group can cause the muscles of that group to assume a shortened position in their resting and active states. This shortening can lead to weakness, discomfort and a greater potential for injury. Regular stretching can help relieve these symptoms (though the athlete would be well advised to treat the cause of the overuse condition as well as the shortened condition of the muscle itself). An example of this is the shortening of the psoas muscles that can take place during the process of training. This shortening can lead to an accentuation of the curvature of the lower back (i.e., lordosis). Stretching the psoas muscles (by lying on your back and flattening the arch of your back, then lifting one knee up while other is flat in floor) can relax the psoas muscles and take the pressure off the lower back..

It is interesting to note that clinicians have discovered that stretching several times a day can prevent capsular contraction but that overdoing it can worsen the condition. This finding offers both a further therapeutic application of stretching and further evidence of the importance of exercise dosage in relation to the results obtained. It explains why one arthritic patient might complain that stretching made them worse, another might notice no significant improvement and still another might obtain significant relief through the use of stretching exercises.

One final therapeutic benefit of stretching is psychological rather than physiological. Stretching can contribute to a relaxed mental as well as muscular state.

Food Supplements and Derivatives

Nutritional aids to recuperation and adaptation have already been discussed in Chapter 10. In this section we will briefly touch on some nutritional approaches which some athletes believe have been of benefit to them in dealing with injuries

Promoters of "health foods" are always claiming that they have discovered "the cure" for a wide range of illnesses and injuries. Laboratory and clinical support for such claims is often scarce, and many of these treatments have little or no value, but some may be of help to some athletes under certain conditions. Since most of these treatments are relatively safe, there is little harm in trying them (as long as their use does not result in the avoidance of more proven approaches). It is worth mentioning a few substances in this context simply to give the reader a sense of what is out there.

It must be remembered that there is an entire medical and drug industry that benefits solely from the use of prescription drugs and especially brand name drugs that are under patent protection. There is no financial incentive for these companies to promote the used of natural alternatives which cannot be patented. This does not mean that there is a "conspiracy" to destroy the health food industry, but it does mean that some very worthwhile therapies may not be heavily promoted because it is difficult to make a profit selling them.

As an illustration, in just one area, the treatment of joint injuries, several athletes I know have reported success with a specific substance after experimenting with many others that they found to be of no value. I know several athletes who feel that a dietary supplementation of manganese has helped them with joint problems that they had been experiencing for some time (tendinitis in particular). Karl Faeth, trainer for many United States world and Olympic weightlifting teams, reports that his arthritic joint pains virtually disappeared when he added cod liver oil to his dietary regimen. Giselle Shepatin, many time National Champion and American record breaker swears by the use of a pine bark derivative called "pycnogenol." The use of the enzymes bromelain and papain (pineapple and papaya derivatives, respectively) to treat injuries has been accepted by many in the medical community for years. There is some evidence that grape seed extract can be helpful is this regard as well. Finally, the "popular" health literature in recent years has been promoting the use of glucosamine and chondroitin sulfate as two agents that can relieve joint pain and possibly help to regenerate soft tissues.

There are even some externally applied non-traditional restorative and/or therapeutic methods which some athletes believe have been of value to them. For instance, a number of athletes have reported relief from soft tissue injuries through the use of natural "poultices" (e.g., tincture of arnica or linseed oil poultices). Practitioners in a wide variety of natural-medicine disciplines have their own formulas for treating athletic injuries, and most of these treatments can do little harm as long as they are not substitutes for clearly needed treatments like casts or surgery.

Herbs, vitamin and mineral supplementation and a variety of food derivatives may work for some and not others. You will find some books which discuss natural remedies for a wide variety of afflictions in the Bibliography.

Mental Factors in Treating Injuries

Chapter 7 discusses a number of techniques that can be used by the injured athlete to maintain performance. Mental rehearsal is just one example of a method that can be used by an injured athlete.

A more controversial approach to applying the mind's power in sport is the use of positive affirmations and visualization to promote healing. Some people believe that visualizing recovery will actually improve the athlete's self-healing powers. They argue that direct physiological reactions to thought aid in healing. Others believe that the proper mental attitude improves the functioning of certain bodily systems so that healing may be promoted in an indirect way.

A more certain effect of visualization and similar techniques is that the athlete's anxiety declines because he or she believes that something positive is being done for the injury. An athlete who is becoming confident that he or she will make a successful comeback is more likely to do the right things in terms of treatment and rehabilitation.

"Chronic" Conditions That Go Away

When I was in my very early twenties, I developed rather severe bursitis and general inflammation in my knees. It came on as a result of overuse but then persisted over an extended period (even after a layoff and careful comeback). I became quite concerned and began to wonder how much longer I could continue my training with such a painful condition. Visions of my knee joints turning to "powder" at the age of twenty-five danced in my head. When I mentioned the problem to my friend, many time national champion, American record holder and silver medalist at the World Championship, Phil Grippaldi, his response surprised me. He told me that he had had such a condition for some time several years earlier. It came upon him rather suddenly, remained for several months and then just disappeared, never to return in anything like its initial severity. My problem lasted longer than Phil's, but one day it did indeed go away, and it never returned in anything like its previous severity.

Over the years, I have noticed a similar phenomenon with respect to other injuries. No matter how intractable an injury may seem, it can suddenly go away as quickly as it arrived. However, in my experience, this is most likely to happen when the athlete is willing to experiment with changes in training methods and lifting techniques. An injured lifter is often changing a number of variables at the same time when suddenly an effective combination comes along.

Spontaneous remission is far rarer. Such remission never occurs with respect to a strain of a major muscle group. Strains simply require rest in order to heal. This rest must be followed by or coordinated with a period of careful reconditioning.

My advice to any lifter afflicted with a chronic problem is to keep training around the injury and experimenting with treatment. Eventually, the right combination of treatment and training modification is likely to be developed. Virtually no injury should ever be accepted as permanent.

On the other hand, no injury should ever be ignored or masked with anti-inflammatory agents while the lifter continues with his or her training unabated. Such an approach to injury has the potential to turn a chronic injury of manageable proportions into a career ending tragedy.

It should be remembered that many lifters have gone on training at some level for years while nursing a particular problem and then discovered a solution to it. A lifter should neither give up prematurely nor delay addressing an injury in any way.

Restorative Measures

While some athletes are as attentive to recuperating from their workouts as they are to the workouts themselves, they are clearly in the minority. Many athletes train hard but fail to get adequate sleep and rest. Others have an improper diet or a highly stressful life outside of sport. Some athletes abuse drugs or alcohol.

Part of what it takes to be a great athlete is a feeling that you are virtually unstoppable, that achievement of your goals is inevitable. Because of this attitude, some athletes say, "I can drink all night, or dance all day or drive my car at 100 miles an hour because when the chips are down, I will always come through and avoid disaster." Unfortunately, while confidence is generally a great virtue, it is absolutely destructive when it is taken to an irrational level.

One area in which smart athletes gain an edge over their competitors is in the careful use of restorative methods. Restoration takes place on several levels. During the workout it takes place between reps and sets as the pause between lifts permits the body at least partially to rebuild its energy stores. Athlete recuperate from their training at different intervals, depending on the capability that is being restored (e.g., the majority of ATP stores are replenished within minutes of the end of a heavy set of exercises). In the hours immediately after the workout (and, if the workout was very long and strenuous, in the days that follow it), the body further replenishes its energy stores. (Glycogen stores require several hours or even days in order to be fully restored following a very long and exhaustive exercise session.) Proper nutrition and adequate rest between lifts and workouts, facilitate this process, and these issues have already been covered in earlier chapters. However, there are still other levels of restoration that need to be addressed.

A third level of restoration involves the adaptation that the body makes to training stress. Tissues are broken down in training . Those tissues and a variety of waste products need to be removed from the muscles and other tissues, and the body must deploy healing agents to the cells that will enable them to remodel in a way to enable them to better tolerate similar stresses in the future. (In this sense it is impossible to separate training from restoration because a training session can be both depleting and restorative.)

A fourth area of restoration takes place within the athlete's nervous system. Both the athlete's volitional and automatic nerve functions can be temporarily diminished following intense training, so the nervous system also requires time to recuperate.

Perhaps the most powerful restorative method available is a regular and well balanced schedule. Training at one hour on one day, and at a very different hour on another, sleeping at odd hours, eating irregularly and other such changes in the daily schedule place significant stress on the athlete and are therefore to be avoided.

Dietary agents (which have already been discussed in Chapter 10), a variety of mental and physical activities and a number of externally applied agents are believed by some to be restorative. The effects of some have been better documented than others, but we will mention a significant number here in order to convey the range of things that are used in the hope of improving restoration processes.

In terms of externally applied treatments, there are steam rooms and saunas, hot and cold alternating showers, bathing in mud or mineral water and being swatted by birch branches. All of these techniques are believed to stimulate the removal of wastes from the body and/or to facilitate the relaxation that is itself a means for improving recuperation.

On a psychological level, there are a number of methods which are believed by some to restore function. Simply sleeping and relaxing are perhaps the most popular measures. Socializing, enjoying various forms of entertainment, pedagogical sessions, eating in pleasant surroundings, hypnosis, autogenic training, going outdoors, hiking in naturally beautiful areas, lying in flotation tanks and listening to certain kinds of music or the sounds of nature: all can be psychologically restorative. Research regarding the use of these modalities is rather limited, but on an intuitive level we recognize the need for relaxation

and change when it comes the brain and the rest of the nervous system. Most athletes will need to experiment to see which methods seem to benefit them most. Many athletes will find that any one method loses at least some of its beneficial effect after a while. Consequently, for these athletes, alternating techniques will often be beneficial.

The athletes and scientists of the former Soviet Union and its allies devoted significant attention to the use of restoration methods. They employed electrostimulation with a variety of amplitudes, frequencies, intensities and duration to facilitate recuperation (rather than restricting the use of these therapies to injured athletes, which is the typical practice in the West). They used barometric pressure chambers to reduce the pressure to a specific area of the body (e.g., an injured limb), which is believed to increase circulation and tissue temperature and thereby stimulate recuperation in that area. Larger chambers were used to permit athletes to breathe oxygen under pressure, another measure that is believed by some to facilitate recuperation. Most high level teams had masseurs who worked on athletes daily to help restore function to tired and aching muscles.

Because these methods were used so widely, specific protocols were often developed for their use. For instance, one author spoke of taking a sauna for ten minutes, moving to progressively higher benches in the sauna over a period of minutes (the higher you go, the hotter it normally is). The athlete was advised to remain in a horizontal position during most of the stay in the sauna but then to place the legs in a vertical position for the last two to three minutes, presumably to prepare the athlete to walk out comfortably (i.e., without feeling lightheaded). Sauna temperatures of just under 200° Fahrenheit were generally recommended.

In addition to formulating specific guidelines for the employment of restorative methods, Soviet coaches also factored them into the developmental process and the training schedule. For instance, local healing measures (such as massage) might be used more during the competitive phase and more general recuperative methods (such as the sauna) might be used more heavily during the preparatory phase of training. Similarly, showers and massage might be used after the morning workout (indeed massage might be used during the workout), but more fatiguing methods, like the sauna, might be reserved until after the last workout of the day. Some authors have even suggested that restoration methods not be applied immediately after very heavy training for fear that these measures might in some way interfere with the training effect the strenuous workout was designed to create.

The stage in an athlete's career might influence the kinds of methods to be used in the restoration process of specific athletes. Beginners would clearly need more instruction on the principles of weightlifting, while more experienced lifters might focus on the more physical and psychological aspects of restoration. Author and coach Medvedyev has even suggested that recuperative methods be assigned a volume across the training year (e.g., 8.5 to 166 hours for a particularly modality and .5 to 2.5 hours of restorative activities a day, 10 to 12 hours a week).

Some would argue that athletes who employ optimal training methods and technique should not need massage or any other restorative technique in order to train and compete effectively because their training schedule will include adequate time for recuperation. However, such arguments are not completely convincing. If an athlete could recuperate from training more rapidly, he or she could presumably adapt more often within the same time period than another athlete who is not employing special recuperative techniques. In addition, training is seldom so perfectly structured that in athlete can be injury and pain free at all time. There will be occasions when even the best-laid plans result in an athlete's overdoing it somewhat. When slight excesses do occur, restorative techniques can be a vital mechanism to help the athlete return more quickly to normal levels of training.

Finally, it should be noted that some athletes who have reduced their training loads to the minimum level at which progress can be sustained or conditioning can be maintained and who have developed the least stressful techniques available, may still develop rather persistent aches and pains as they age (physiologically and in terms of their years in the sport). For such athletes, various restorative measures may be able to lengthen their careers significantly.

Summary

Weightlifting is a relatively safe sport. Proper training methods, sound technique and adherence to safety rules greatly reduce any risk of injury. The athlete who avoids injury takes an important step toward top performance. When injuries do occur, they must be treated promptly and effectively in order to minimize any loss of training time and function. The causes must also be analyzed in order to minimize the chances of a recurrence. A proper approach to the issues of injuries will help an athlete to have a long and healthy career.

THE RULES OF WEIGHTLIFTING

Many athletes, and even some coaches I know, seem to say, "I'm not going to worry about the rules, I'll just do good clean lifts and let the referees worry about the rules." Unfortunately, people with such an attitude are exposing themselves to unnecessary disasters that can arise out of a failure to pay attention to the rules. During more than thirty years of involvement in the sport of weightlifting, I have witnessed national and international level coaches make unbelievably basic errors with respect to the rules. These mistakes have actually cost athletes championships, a terrible tragedy.

Pay attention to the rules so that such things do not happen to you or your athletes. Besides, by learning the rules thoroughly, you may begin to appreciate the admirable logic, fairness and downright elegance that have been built into the rules of weightlifting by the many wise people who have contributed to the sport over the years. Yes, there are occasional inconsistencies and/or oversights in the rules, and sometimes they do not seem to be fair. But, overall, weightlifting rules are a wonderful achievement, still another reason to admire the sport of strength so much.

Before learning the technical rules, it is useful for the athlete and coach to understand the possible sources of rules that can affect a given competition. While the "rule book" is adhered to quite closely in the vast majority of circumstances, it is helpful to get a sense of who might influence those rules and in what respects.

The Organizations Which Govern Weightlifting

Five organizations influence the rules of weightlifting competition in any country in the world. They are (roughly in order of their overall influence): the International Weightlifting Federation (IWF); the individual National Weightlifting Federations; the International Olympic Committee (IOC); the Olympic committees of individual nations; and the organizing committees of specific competitions.

The International Weightlifting Federation (IWF)

The IWF is the organization that governs the sport of weightlifting internationally. It was founded in 1905. The IWF is recognized by the International Olympic Committee and the General Association of International Sports Federations as the international governing body for all sports involving weights lifted on a bar. The mission of the IWF is to organize and control weightlifting internationally, to develop friendship and cooperation among nations, to assist in the development of national federations, to resolve disputes among national federations, to set up the rules of weightlifting, to control international events, to supervise continental and regional federations and to verify all world records in the sport of Weightlifting.

The IWF does not permit any political or religious demonstrations at its events and is committed to making no distinction between continents, countries or persons on the basis of race, color, religion or politics. Its official languages are: Arabic, English, French, German, Russian and Spanish. English is the working language. (English is the language used in the IWF's publications and at meetings, and whenever a dispute arises with respect to the rules of the IWF, the English text governs.) Within the IWF, there are six "continental" federations: African, Asian, European, Oceana, Pan-American and South American. Each of these continental federations holds its own championships and has distinct representation in the IWF, but most of the day-to-day operations in the sport of weightlifting take place at the IWF level or within the national federations.

The IWF Congress is the highest authority in the IWF. Each country has two delegates (of their nationality or citizenship) to the IWF Congress and one vote. No member of the electorate may vote by proxy. The Congress meets annually at the World Championships. Every four years, generally at the Olympic Games, there is an Electoral Congress, which elects officers (President, General Secretary and six Vice Presidents) and the Executive Board members (eight members who, together with the officers of the IWF and the six Presidents of the Continental Federations, comprise the Executive Board) and considers changes in the Constitution and Rules of the IWF. Only one member per country is permitted on the Executive Board.

The IWF has four standing committees that carry out many of the functions of the IWF. With the exception of one committee, the Auditor Committee, all have ten members and a President (who is selected from among Executive Board members). The committees are:

Technical Committee. This committee appoints officials for the World Championships (the Executive Board does this at Olympic Games), considers questions regarding the technical rules, prepares courses and exams for referees, sets policy on the equipment used in competitions and proposes modifications to existing rules.

Scientific and Research Committee. This committee studies and questions training methods, lifting technique and methods to involve youth. It prepares materials, conducts clinics, takes a position on the technical rules from the standpoint of the coach and (along with the Technical Committee) judges equipment.

Medical Committee. This committee safeguards the health of the athletes, advises competition organizers on health matters, supervises medical services and facilities at competitions, supervises doping control, appoints doctors on duty, collects data on weightlifting's effects on the body and helps to educate the public on the health values of weightlifting.

Auditor Committee. This committee consists of three members elected by the Congress of the IWF. Its responsibility is to audit the books of the IWF once a year, to report on that audit and generally to advise the IWF on financial matters.

At any international competition, the IWF has direct and complete control over the running of the competition. The IWF also controls the domestic competitions of its national federation members to a significant extent. If the way in which a national federation operates (e.g., the way in which it administers the eligibility of athletes or conducts competitions) conflicts with the norms established by the IWF, that national federation faces the prospect of sanctions from the IWF. Such sanctions range from fines and suspensions to expulsion from the IWF. While the IWF recognizes that local conditions (e.g., the availability of officials and equipment) may make absolute compliance with all of its standards impossible, it does require reasonable adherence to its rules if the results of

competitions within a given national federation are to be recognized as official and if the athletes of a given nation are to be permitted to compete internationally at IWF events.

All things considered, the IWF is a remarkable example of what can be accomplished through the peaceful cooperation of nations. With rare exceptions, the IWF has managed to recognize the diverse interests of many people and to fuse a worldwide coalition of people who are dedicated to the advancement of the sport of weightlifting. The current address of the headquarters of the IWF is: IWF Secretariat, 1054 Budapest, Hold u. 1., Hungary. Its mailing address is: 1374 Budapest, Pf. 614, Hungary. The telephone number is: (36-1) 131-8153; (36-1) 153-0530; Fax: (36-1) 153-0199.

The National Weightlifting Federation of Each Country

Each country that is a member of the IWF has a single organization that is recognized by the IWF as the national governing body for weightlifting in that country. In the United States the organization recognized by the IWF as the sole governing body for weightlifting is the United States Weightlifting Federation (USAW).

Since the IWF recognizes the USAW as the governing body of weightlifting in the United States, it looks to the USAW, as it would to any national governing body, to give permission to its athletes who wish to compete internationally. Competing internationally without the permission of the athlete's national federation can expose an athlete to suspension by that federation. Before going on to describe the other three organizations that can affect weightlifting rules, let us take a closer look at the USAW.

The Organization Of USA Weightlifting (USAW)

The USWF was incorporated in 1979 (and started doing business as the USAW recently), but it had a prior history for more than fifty years as the Weightlifting Committee of the Amateur Athletic Union. (A law called the Amateur Athletic Act of 1978 resulted in many sports governing bodies in the United States becoming autonomous.) The purpose of the USAW is to encourage, improve and promote amateur weightlifting in the United States., The USAW exercises control over the administration, eligibility, sanctioning authority, representation and rules of competition for the sport of weightlifting in the United States.

The membership of the USAW consists primarily of local weightlifting committees (LWCs) throughout the United States. These committees consist primarily of the officials, administrators and coaches who work to operate the sport of weightlifting at the local level. Each committee must permit athlete representation with voice and vote on their committee. The jurisdiction of LWCs generally approximates the boundaries of a given state, but there are significant exceptions (e.g., New York State has two LWCs, one covering the northwestern part of the state and the other covering the southeastern part of the state, including New York City and the greater metropolitan area). In contrast, the states of Georgia and Alabama combine in one LWC.

Each LWC is entitled to send at least one administrator delegate representative (elected by all members of the LWC) and one athlete representative (elected by the athletes in the LWC) to the National Federation. Each of these delegates has a voice and vote within the National Federation. LWCs with at least fifty registered athletes are entitled to two delegates in each of the two categories and LWCs with 100 or more registered athletes are entitled to three delegates.

The National Federation has one annual meeting (additional special meetings can be called), normally held in conjunction with the U. S. National Championships. The National Federation is the highest authority in the USAW.

Some athletes take their voting rights for granted and do not participate at the National Federation level. Other athletes realize that all of the athletes in the USAW had only one vote within the National Federation until 1982 and that it required a substantial battle for the athletes to attain a more balanced voting representation. These athletes are careful to exercise their franchise, recognizing that they have more of a say in their chosen sport than do athletes in virtually any other sports governing body in the United States today.

The National Federation must approve any changes in the USAW's by-laws and elects the Officers and Board of Directors of the USAW (in summer Olympic years). The Officers of the USAW are: President, First Vice President, Second Vice President, Secretary and Treasurer. The Secretary is appointed by the President; all other Officers are elected. The Board of Directors of the USAW consists of eleven members and all of the Officers of the USAW (with the exception of the Secretary). Three of the members of the Board must be athlete's representatives, who are elected by the athlete's representatives from each LWC in an Athlete's Congress, which is held before each annual meeting of the National Federation. The other five Board members are elected in summer Olympic years by the National Federation at their annual meeting. (Prior to 1978 there was no athlete representation on the Board of Directors.)

The Officers of the USAW are given very limited powers by the Federation's by-laws. The Board of Directors has the sole authority to govern the USAW between meetings of the National Federation. In addition to making some policy decisions and managing the operations of the USAW year round, the Board of Directors is the final decisionmaker in the selection of athletes, coaches and referee nominees for international events. The day-to-day affairs of the USAW are carried out by its National Office. (The National Office is located at: U.S. Weightlifting Federation, One Olympic Plaza, Colorado Springs, Colorado, 80909, Telephone (719) 578-4508), Fax (719) 578-4741.) The day-to-day affairs of the USAW are conducted under the direction of the USAW's Executive Director (ED). The ED and his or her staff are paid employees of the USAW and have no role in its governance. Their mission is to carry out the instructions of the National Federation, the Board of Directors and/or the Officers of the USAW, within the guidelines provided by the by-laws.

The Federation makes every effort to be fair and open to its membership. It has formal grievance procedures both to discipline and to protect the rights of athletes, officials, coaches and administrators within the sport. The Federation's books and records are available for review by any member of the Federation during normal business hours (upon that member's giving due notice to the Federation's Secretary).

The USAW has a number of sub-committees that parallel those of the IWF in certain respects. As in the IWF, there is a Technical Committee, a Coaching Committee (which resembles the IWF's Scientific and Research Committee) a Medical Committee and a Finance Committee (which is somewhat similar to the IWF's Auditor committee). There are also a number of other committees, among the most active of which are the Women's Committee and the Master's Committee. Special committees are also appointed from time to time. A foundation created by the USAW manages the funds that the USAW holds in trust for the sport of weightlifting. At this time the funds that are on deposit in the foundation are comprised, in the main, of the proceeds from the 1984 Olympic Games. A portion of the earnings derived from these funds is used to pay for the ongoing programs of the USAW, while the remainder is used to grow the funds on deposit, so that future earnings will at least partially keep pace with inflation and maintain purchasing power.

In order for an athlete to compete in an event organized under the auspices of the USAW, that athlete must be a member of the USAW. In order to gain membership to the USAW, an athlete may either apply directly to the National Office of the USAW in Colorado Springs or through that athlete's LWC. The current annual membership fee is $20.00 ($10.00 for Juniors aged twelve to seventeen and $25.00 for Masters thirty-five and above). Membership in the USAW allows an athlete to compete in any competition organized by the USAW (for which he or she is otherwise qualified). It also secures limited medical coverage against injuries at competitions and entitles the athlete to receive Weightlifting USA, the official publication of the USAW.

When athletes register with the USAW, they are permitted to designate which registered club they wish to represent. (They may also choose not to represent any club and compete in an "unattached" status.) Any club representation extends for the duration of the registration, unless an athlete requests a change in affiliation. In making such a change, an athlete must obtain the permission of his or her LWC (which is generally given as a matter of course) and must be registered in an unattached status for at least four months. (This prevents an athlete's switching from club to club from event to event.) When an athlete relocates to another LWC, he or she has the choice of continuing to be registered within the original LWC (maintaining his or her club registration) or transferring to the new LWC. When a transfer is desired, the athlete surrenders his or her USAW registration card to the original LWC and applies for a transfer. The transfer application is then submitted to the new LWC, which issues, free of charge, a new card to the athlete. The effective date of that new card is the date on which the transfer application was submitted. The athlete is permitted to represent a club in his or her new LWC once he or she has been in an unattached status and has resided in the new LWC for at least four months. (The new LWC can waive some or all of the waiting period if the change in the athlete's residence took place for reasons beyond the athlete's control.)

All competitions organized under the auspices of the USAW must be sanctioned by the USAW. Sanctions can be applied for on the LWC level or directly from the National Office. The appropriate fee must accompany the application for sanction, as must a draft of the entry that will be used for the competition. Obtaining a sanction for a competition assures that any performances made therein will be recognized as official by the USAW. In addition, it secures liability coverage for the sponsor of the event and assures the athletes competing that their amateur status will be protected and that their medical insurance coverage will be in force during the competition.

In order for an athlete to represent a club in USAW competitions, that club must be registered with the USAW. Applications for club membership should be presented to the LWC in which the club operates. Renewals of club memberships can be handled either on the LWC level or through the National Office.

The International Olympic Committee (IOC)

This is the organization that controls the Olympic Games. While the IOC tends to have little effect on the rules of competition for weightlifting, it can influence the structure of weightlifting competition in the Olympic Games in a very general but important way. The IOC determines what events will be held at each Olympic Games, how many medals will be awarded in each event, the maximum number of athletes that will be permitted to represent each country in the various events, the doping or drug control policies that will be employed with respect to competitors in the Games and the definition of an "amateur" athlete that will be used for purposes of the various events in the Games. (Amazingly, the definition of an amateur is not identical for all sports, although the use of the word amateur is rapidly disappearing.)

Since the Olympic Games represents only one competition in four years, many people might be surprised to learn that the IOC's influence is important in all non-Olympic weightlifting events. However, such an influence becomes understandable when you consider the enormous prestige that is associated with being an "Olympic" sport. This prestige has led the IWF to treat the Olympic Games as the most important event on its international calendar of events (although the annual World Championships that are held by the IWF are considered to be of virtually equal importance by most weightlifting aficionados). Consequently, the IWF does not wish to stray too far in its rules for other competitions from the event that is held at the Olympic Games, lest such straying cause observers to conclude that the sport is not the same as the Olympic one or cause competitors to develop techniques that cannot be used in the Olympic Games.

The Olympic Committee of Each Country

These are the organizations that are charged by each nation with fielding that nation's Olympic Team. (The Olympic Committee of the United States also fields a team for the Pan American Games, a competition which includes North, Central and South America.) In the United States this organization is called the United States Olympic Committee (USOC). This organization affects the USAW in three major ways. First, it must approve the means that the USAW proposes for the selection of the Olympic Team. Second, the USOC oversees certain procedures that affect an athlete's eligibility for competition, such as the doping or drug control procedures that are employed before and during competitions. Third, the USOC provides substantial financial support to many of the sports governing bodies in the United

States (including the USAW). As a result, while the USOC has little direct influence on the way competitions are organized by the USAW, the USAW is always mindful of the USOC's spheres of control, and it wishes to be closely aligned with the rules of the USOC.

The Organizing Committee of a Particular Competition

The rules of the IWF and of the national federation under whose auspices an event is held (if the event is not an international one) are overwhelmingly dominant in the operation of any competition. However, the governing bodies of the sport, recognizing the limited resources of many of the organizations that hold events, do permit some latitude in the interpretation of the rules for some events. For example, in the United States it is permissible for the organizing committee of the competition to forbid the competitor from letting go of the bar before it reaches the floor and once the lift has been completed. (The IWF rules permit the lifter to let go of the bar once it passes the waist.) The purpose of this flexibility is to permit the meet organizer to protect the facility, where necessary, from any damage that might result from unnecessary dropping of the weights. IWF rules require the use of an electronic scale to weigh the athletes and bar before the competition. In competitions below the national level, organizing committees are often permitted to use mechanical scales (though such scales are expected to be accurate).

A Word about Amateurism and Eligibility

The concept of amateurism (competing and training without financial reward) has been controversial virtually since it was introduced more than a century ago. Over the years many tragic stories have unfolded because of an athlete's failure to protect his or her amateur status. Today it is accepted by most sports authorities that the notion of amateurism has become virtually meaningless. In recognition of this, most sports governing bodies have relaxed or eliminated their standards regarding amateurism. The latest IWF rulebook states, "There are no financial considerations with regard to an athlete's eligibility." The USAW and USOC are moving in a similar direction with their rules.

During this transition period as amateurism is completely phased out, athletes who are in a position to receive substantial monies for their athletic performance of commercial uses of their name would be well served by consulting with the National Office of the USAW before any questionable activities are undertaken or agreements are made.

The basic reasons for which an athlete can lose his or her eligibility to compete are:

a) fraud;
b) receiving compensation for athletic services;
c) presenting oneself as a representative of the USAW while competing or exhibiting athletic skills at unsanctioned events or against ineligible athletes;
d) permitting someone other than the athlete ;
d) failure to compete in an event for which the athlete has been entered without a bona fide excuse (such as illness or injury);
e) refusal to testify before or respond to questions raised by an LWC;
f) unfair dealing in connection with an athletic competition or ungentlemanly or unladylike conduct (e.g., using profanity in the competition area or obstructing the progress of a competition);
g) indebtedness to the athlete's club;
h) use of a substance (e.g., drug) banned by the USAW, the USOC, the IWF or the IOC.

Persons other than athletes can be suspended from the USAW for directly or indirectly helping or allowing any athlete to participate in an unsanctioned event without warning the athlete of the consequences, aiding or abetting an athlete in the use of banned substances or acting in a way that can lead to the athlete's losing his or her eligibility to compete.

Ingesting banned substances (described below under "Doping Control") is by far the most common way today's athletes become ineligible for competition. You may think you know what kinds of drugs are banned. Do not depend on it. Even the most innocuous over-the-counter drug or health food may contain a prohibited substance; learn the rules of doping control.

It has been said that an Olympic gold medal in any sport can make an athlete a millionaire. Therefore, taking a chance with your athletic status can prove to be a very costly mistake. However, few if any athletes who have competed at the Olympic Games, or even at a far lower level, would exchange the enormous joy that they have experienced through participating in their sport for any amount of money. To sum it up in the vernacular, when you are faced with the temptation to do something that threatens your eligibility in any way, "don't even think about it." More accurately, think about it long and hard; a wrong decision could be something you will regret for the rest of your life. Get the proper advice before you act.

The Technical Rules Of Weightlifting

Now that we have identified the organizations which can affect the rules of the competition, let us look at those rules in detail. It should be noted that while every effort has been made to interpret and summarize the technical rules of weightlifting accurately, the athlete and coach should never rely on the interpretations in this book, both because they are only the author's interpretation and because rules change from time to time. Always consult the official rules and the officials for a given competition for definitive interpretations.

In the presentation of the rules that appears below, IWF rules are always explained first. Where the USAW rules are different, those specific differences are noted in the appropriate places.

The Competitive Lifts

The IWF recognizes two events, which must be done in competitions in the following order: a) the two hands snatch (snatch), and b) the two hands clean and jerk (C&J). The overall winner of any weightlifting competition is the athlete who lifts the highest combined amount of weight in the snatch and C&J (i.e., the heaviest weights successfully lifted in each event are combined). This combined score is called the "Total." While awards are given at major competitions for each event as well as the Total, recognition in the sport of weightlifting goes to the athlete who lifts the greatest total weight in competition. When a weightlifting aficionado speaks of the "World Champion" in weightlifting, he or she is speaking about the winner in the Total.

Because there are two events in weightlifting competitions, and the ultimate scoring of the competition is dependent on the highest amount of weight lifted by the athletes on a combined basis, a weightlifting competition is often referred to as a biathlon.

In the snatch, the bar is pulled in one explosive motion from the floor to full arm's length overhead. In order to make the lift easier to perform, athletes typically bend or spread their legs quickly while the bar is rising in order to catch the bar at arm's length. The combined attributes of great strength and blinding speed are needed to accomplish this challenging event effectively.

In the clean and jerk (C&J), the bar is also lifted to full arm's length overhead. However, although it is considered one event, the C&J is really two lifts that must be completed one immediately after the other. In the clean, the bar is raised (pulled) in an explosive motion from the floor to a point of rest approximately at the level of the shoulders. (The rules permit lifting the bar within a zone from the chest above the nipples to a position above the shoulders, as long as the arms

are in a fully bent position with the bar resting on the hands in the latter case.) If the bar has been lifted in one continuous motion to a level of the shoulders or below, it may not be moved from the original position at which it made contact with the chest or shoulders in preparation for the second (jerk) part of the overall lift. However, if the bar was originally cleaned to a position above the shoulders, it may be lowered to the shoulders, but no lower. After the clean but before the jerk, the lifter may unhook the thumbs if a hook grip was used in the clean (a "hook" grip is explained later in this appendix), and/or change the width of the grip. In order to make the lift easier to perform, athletes typically bend or spread their legs quickly while the bar is rising in order to catch the bar on the shoulders.

The second part of the C&J, the jerk, consists of bending the legs and then extending both the arms and the legs to bring the bar to full arm's length over the head in one explosive motion. In order to make the lift easier to perform, athletes typically bend or spread their legs quickly while the bar is rising in order to catch the bar at arm's length. Since the athlete is lifting the bar in two stages in the C&J, heavier weights can be lifted in the C&J than in the snatch.

As a practical matter, bending and/or moving the legs to catch the bar is a required aspect of the snatch, the clean and the jerk. Aside from being sound practice from an efficiency standpoint (the bar does not have to be lifted as high if the body is quickly lowered), it is virtually impossible for the bar to be lifted in a continuous motion (i.e., without a significant and visible change in speed) unless the body is quickly lowered just before the lift is completed and just as its upward velocity is slowing down.

Shared Characteristics of The Snatch and the C&J

The snatch and the clean and jerk share a number of characteristics in terms of the requirements for correct performance. For example, in both the snatch and the clean and jerk, the bar is placed horizontally in front of both legs (i.e., the plates or discs on both sides of the bar rest on the platform at the same level as the bottom of the lifter's feet). The bar is gripped with the palms down and the fingers encircling the bar from the palms to the tips of the fingers in a counterclockwise direction. The thumbs may be placed at virtually any position on the bar. For example, they may follow the counterclockwise direction of the rest of the fingers or may encircle the bar from the other side in a clockwise fashion. In addition, the thumbs may be placed alongside or under the fingers (the latter position is called a "hook" grip, a method of gripping the bar which is discussed in detail in the section of this book on technique). As the bar is lifted from the floor in both the snatch and the clean, it may slide along the legs and lap at any point.

Both the snatch and jerk are considered completed when the bar has reached its fullest extent or arm's length overhead, the legs are straight and the lifter is motionless in a position where the bar, trunk and feet are on the same line. (If you were directly above the athlete looking down, you could see that the bar, the lifter's trunk and the lifter's feet were all parallel.) Once this position has been achieved, the referees will give the lifter both a visible and audible signal that the bar may be returned to the platform. The clean part of the C&J is considered completed when the feet are on the same line, the legs are straight and the bar and lifter are motionless. The lifter may attempt to jerk the bar any time after such a position is reached.

As was indicated earlier, in order to make the lifts easier for the athlete, it is permissible for the lifter to lower the body by bending the trunk and legs and/or moving the feet. This typically involves the lifter's going into a full squat (i.e., deep knee bend) position with both feet flat on the floor. Alternatively, some lifters lower their bodies by jumping one foot forward and the other backward, while bending the front leg into a squat like position and keeping the back leg straight, or nearly so, with the weight of the back leg balanced on the toe. (The position resembles that of a fencer, except that the front leg is bent into a deeper position, and the back leg is balanced on the toe, with the foot parallel to and to one side of the front foot. This is called a split position.

Once an athlete has reached the lowest point in his or her squat or split position and has caught the weight, he or she may recover to a full standing position with the feet in line (i.e., if you were observing the lifter from either side, one foot would not be in front of the other), in his or her own time, taking as many attempts to rise from the lowered body position as he or she wishes. Rocking, bouncing, twisting and moving the feet are all permissible in an effort to straighten the legs and put the feet in line. The only limitation on the movement of the feet while lowering and recovering from the lowering of the bar is that the feet may not travel outside the confines of a designated lifting area called the "platform."

General Rules for All of the Lifts

A number of general rules apply to both the snatch and the C&J.

1. Any snatch or clean which reaches the height of the knees is considered an attempt, even if the lift goes no further than that position. (If the lifter decides not to make that particular attempt before the bar reaches the height of the knees, he or she can replace the bar on the platform and try the lift again, time permitting.) Only one attempt at jerking the bar is permitted after each clean. Any perceived failed attempt at jerking the bar (e.g., lowering the body or bending the knees) will be considered an attempt. In addition, the lifter may not deliberately oscillate the bar to gain an advantage in the jerk (i.e., both the bar and the lifter must be motionless before the start of the jerk).

2. When the bar is lowered from arm's length after the referee's signal, it must travel in front of the lifter and cannot be dropped. Under international rules, the lifter may release his or her grip once the bar has passed the level of the waist. In domestic competitions, releasing the bar once it has passed the height of the waist is only permissible if rubber bumper plates are being used and then only if the meet director permits it. (Otherwise both hands must remain on the bar until it is returned to the platform.) In addition, the bar must be replaced within the confines of the platform (i.e., the plates of the bar must touch down within the confines of the platform). It is permissible for the bar to bounce or roll outside the confines of the platform area, after the plates have touched the area inside.

3. If the athlete cannot, due to an anatomical limitation, fully straighten his or her arm(s), this fact must be reported to all three referees and the jury before the start of the competition). They will then interpret lifting the bar to "the fullest extent of the arms" rule in the context of that lifter's ability to extend the arms with no weight.

4. The use of grease, oil, water, talcum or similar lubricants on the thighs is prohibited, and the athlete may not arrive in the competition area with any substance on the thighs. ("Chalk"—magnesium carbonate— may be applied to any part of the body in view of referees.) Most lifters at least touch their thighs with the bar when they are lifting the bar in the snatch or clean; many lifters slide the bar along, the thighs or hips; lubrication helps during this process, perhaps unfairly. However, the main reason for prohibiting the use of lubricants is to protect all lifters from having to perform with a slippery bar and/or on a slippery lifting surface. If an athlete has been called to the platform and a lubricant is detected, the athlete will be required to remove the lubricant before making his or her attempt with that weight; the clock continues to run during this period, which means the remaining time the athlete has for making an attempt may expire before the lubricant can be removed, causing the forfeiture of that attempt. Therefore, using a lubricant is a risky business.

Incorrect Movements for All Lifts

In addition to the incorrect movements mentioned above, the following movements are not permitted in either lift.

1. Pausing, even briefly, during the raising of the bar to arm's length in the snatch or jerk (during the raising of the bar to the vicinity of the shoulders in the clean). This prohibition includes the motion called "pressing out," which invariably involves a momentary slowing or stoppage of the bar's upward progress and maintaining the body in a stationary position while using the arms and shoulders to raise the bar. all lifters push or press out on the bar as it goes overhead in the snatch or jerk, but when either lift is timed properly, the body is being lowered while the bar is still going up (as a result of momentum that has developed earlier in the lift). Therefore, the motion of the arms is so fast that there is no visible "press out," and the lift is considered to be correctly performed.

2. Touching the ground with any part of the body other than the feet (e.g., the knee in the low split position, the buttocks in a deep squat position). Some officials have even argued that if a part of the lifters attire (other than the shoes) makes contact with the ground, the lift is not good. This requires some judgment. Clearly a lifter's buttocks (which are usually covered by a lifting suit) cannot make actual contact with the ground; only the lifting suit can. But what if the lifting suit is very loose fitting and does make contact with the ground? You are at the mercy of an official's judgment and ability to see the difference between your buttocks and the suit. The moral of this story is to see that your costume is close fitting.

3. Incomplete extension of one or both arms in the snatch or jerk: the bar must go in one continuous motion to arm's length on both arms at the same time.

4. Rebending the arms once the bar has been lifted to arm's length at any point prior to the down signal. (Once bar has gone to arm's length, it must stay there.) It is permissible to turn the arms at the shoulder in an effort to control the bar overhead, but no unlocking of the elbows is permitted. (Inexperienced officials sometimes have trouble differentiating between these two kinds of movement, but generally there is no problem in this area.)

Incorrect Movements Particular to the Snatch

During the raising of the bar, the wrists may not turn over before the bar passes the top of the head. (i.e., the palms may not flip from their downward facing position while the bar is pulled from the floor to an upward facing position before the bar passes the top of the head). This rule is another way of preventing "press out." (In the case of the snatch, this could occur if the lifter were unable to

get the bar to arm's length in one motion and tried to push it the rest of the way; the lift would then become something closer to a C&J than a snatch.) In reality, the press-out rule described above would, by itself, prevent turning the palms up too early in the lift, but lifting the bar directly to arm's length is so crucial a feature of the snatch that the officials want to make sure that everyone understands that only one movement is permitted.

Incorrect Movements Particular to the Clean and Jerk

In catching the bar on or above the chest or shoulders, no part of the elbow or upper arm may touch any part of the athlete's thighs or knees (e.g., when the athlete catches the bar in a deep squat position, the elbows can be in close proximity to the knees). The reason for the rule is to prevent the athlete from using the knees or thighs to lift or support the bar and to protect the athlete from incurring an injury to the wrist (which can result when a lifter does not strive to keep the elbows well up while he or she is in a low squat position).

Participants in the Competition (or Classes of Competitors)

Deeply rooted in the sport of weightlifting is the concept of competition among athletes who have an equal opportunity for success. Consequently, differences in the physical size, sex and age of competitors are recognized by having weight classes and separate competitions for males and females as well as for athletes who are younger or older than the prime competitive ages (i.e. very roughly twenty to thirty-five). However, athletes who are older or younger and women are often permitted to lift in "open" competition (i.e., competitions that are not specifically limited to competitors of a certain type or to residents of specific geographic areas) if they are able (in terms of their lifting ability). Participation in Senior World Championships and Olympic Games is restricted to those competitors who are age sixteen or older. To be eligible for the Junior World Championships, athletes may not be older than twenty nor younger than fifteen. The IWF has a special way of defining age, which is described later in this explanation of the rules.

Women's Competitions

Because there are far fewer female than male competitors in weightlifting and because women's weightlifting has a shorter history than men's, there are fewer competitions organized for women than for men. However, there are women's competitions right up to the World Championship level, so women can compete at any level. (There is a growing movement to get women's weightlifting into the Olympic Games, but thus far, tragically, the IOC has resisted this effort This is truly one of the greatest injustices in Olympic sport, and hopefully it will be corrected at the Sydney Olympic Games in 2000.

The United States has been one of the pioneering countries in this aspect of the sport, conducting the first national championship in women's weightlifting in 1981 and hosting the first World Championship for women in 1987. The opportunities for women in the sport of weightlifting are exciting and improving all of the time.

The Weight Classes

Physical size in weightlifting is measured by body weight. On an international level and within most national federations (including the United States), the body weights of competitors and the weights that they lift are recorded in kilograms (abbreviated as "kg.").

The weight classes used in weightlifting competition have been changed a number of times over the years. For example, from 1977 through 1992, the weight classes for men were (the upper limits being expressed in kg.): 52, 56, 60, 67.5, 75, 82.5, 90, 100, 110 and 110+ (or Superheavyweight). The women's weight classes began at 44, went to 48, then were identical to the men's classes, except that the last weight class before Superheavyweight was 82.5 kg..

In 1993, after much study, the weight classes were changed by the IWF. At that time, drug testing within the IWF was becoming more stringent and it was felt that it would be difficult for athletes to surpass the performances of the past under the new rules. Creating new weight classes permitted athletes to establish new records in an era of greater drug testing. The new classes (for men) were: 54, 59, 64, 70, 76, 83, 91, 99, 108 and 108+. The women's classes began at 46, went to 50 and then were identical to the men's, except that the last weight class before Superheavyweight was 83 kg..

Effective January 1, 1998, the weight classes have been changed once more. This time the reason is that women's weightlifting has been accepted into the Olympic Games of the year 2000. In return

adding women to the Olympic program, the IOC has asked the IWF to reduce the number of weight classes for men and women, so that the number of competitors will not increase by 90% (which might have happened had the old total of 19 weight classes for men and women combined been added to the program—as compared with the 10 weight classes that had been contested in the Games in the past).

As of 1998, there are fifteen weight classes overall—eight for men and seven for women. These weight classes are displayed in the table that follows (the upper limits of each weight class are shown in pounds in parentheses, rounded down to the nearest quarter pound, for readers who are more familiar with pounds):

No athlete can compete in more than one weight category during any competition, even if it is held across several days. In addition, it is required that competitions be held in order of the weight classes, lightest to heaviest. This allows a competitor who is over the weight limit in a given class to compete in the next higher one, assuming he or she has met the performance qualifications in that higher weight class. For example, if the qualifying total for a given men's competition is 230 kg. for the 69 kg. class and 250 kg. for the 77 kg. class, , an athlete who has totaled 250 kg. in the 69 kg. class can compete in either class (It should be noted that while an athlete who makes a total in one weight class is presumed to be capable of making that same total in a heavier weight class, it is not presumed that an athlete who has made a total in one weight class will suffer a specific degree of performance reduction if he or she moves to a lower weight class—so if an athlete has totaled 250 kg. while lifting in the 77 kg. class, it is not assumed that he or she can make 230 kg., or any other total, at 69 kg.).

Age Group Competitions

There are generally two kinds of age group competitions: Junior and Veterans (the latter group is also known as Masters in the United States). Juniors are those athletes who are 19 or younger. For competitions other than the World Masters competition, Masters are generally those athletes who are 35 or older. Masters compete in five year

Men	Women
56.00 (123.25)	48.00 (105.75)
62.00 (136.50)	53.00 (116.75)
69.00 (152.00)	59.00 (130.00)
77.00 (169.75)	63.00 (138.75)
85.00 (187.25)	69.00 (152.00)
94.00 (207.00)	75.00 (165.25)
105.00 (231.25)	75.00+ (165.25+)
105.00+(231.25+)	

Table 1

Table 2

Place	International	National (US)	Other (United States)
1	28	12	6
2	25	9	4
3	23	8	3
4	22	7	2
5	21	6	1
6	20	5	0
7	19	4	0
8	18	3	0
9	17	2	0
10	16	1	0

age brackets as follows: 35 to 39, 40 to 44, 45 to 49, 50 to 54, 55 to 59, 60 to 64, 65 to 69, 70 to 74, 75 to 79, 80 and above. (At the World Masters competition the 35 to 39 age group is deleted, and there is only one age groups above age 70.) Some experimentation always seems to be occurring with respect to age groups, so the above outline of ages may quickly become outmoded.

The way in which age is measured in weightlifting competition is special. Ages are defined as the age of the competitor on January 1 of any year. For example, those lifters who are classified as Juniors in any given year are those athletes who are age nineteen or younger as of January 1 of that year. This kind of measurement may seem to be strange, since at a Junior competition held late in the year many competitors may have an actual age of twenty. However, in many countries of the world ages are still only recorded in an approximate fashion (e.g., by year, or by year and month), and IWF officials, who are expected to verify age prior to international competitions were having great difficulty obtaining the exact age of competitors. As a consequence, in an effort to make the lives of its officials more pleasant and to avoid wrangling over the date of a particular competition within the year, the IWF has adopted this standard for all age related competitions.

Junior Competitions

Junior lifters have the same weight classes internationally as older males. In U.S. Junior National Championships, there are two age brackets: seventeen and under and eighteen to twenty. In the latter bracket the classes are the same as for older competitors. In the under seventeen category, there is no 108 kg. class, only 99.01 kg. and above. However, there are generally two additional body weight classes for the men (up to 46 kg. and up to 50 kg.) and one additional class for the women (up to 42 kg.). Junior competitions are occasionally held with other age and body weight groupings (e.g., with two-year age groups). Athletes must be at least twelve years of age in

order to compete in USAW sanctioned competitions.

Masters Competitions

At present the Masters have an Open World Masters competition, but it has not been officially recognized as a World Championship by the IWF; nor are world records for Masters recognized by the IWF. Part of the reason is that the IWF officially recognizes fewer age groupings than do organizations within continents and nations. There is also no doping control of the type of that the IWF requires of its high level events. The relationship of the IWF and the Masters group continues to be in a state of transition, so rules are modified with some frequency.

Team Competition

Although weightlifting is primarily an individual sport, a team element of the competition is recognized at most competitions. Each athlete may score a certain number of points for his or her team on the basis of placement in the competition.

Internationally, at World and Continental Championships and competitions at Continental, Regional and other organized Games (such as the Pan American Games), a country may enter a team with as many as ten athletes (nine for the women) and two reserves (three for the women) distributed in any way the country wishes, except that no country may enter more than two competitors in any weight class. In the Olympic Games three reserves are permitted to each country. Nationally, other policies are permissible. (In the United States the policy tends to be the same for national competitions but is generally left up to the discretion in the organizing committee of other championships.) Whatever the policy, it should be stated in the entry blank for the competition or, at a minimum, at the time of the drawing of the lots prior to the competition. Naturally, with the new number of weight classes (effective January 1, 1998) it can be expected that team sizes will be reduced proportionally.

Team Scoring

Individual team members receive team points on the basis of their placement in the competition. Point scoring for various competitions is as follows:

At international competitions, the point scores are reduced by one point per place for each place after 10th, so fifteen points are awarded for 11th place and one point is awarded for 25th place (no points are awarded after 25th place).

the World Championships and most other international competitions, and at U.S. National Championships, competitors are awarded team points for their performance in the snatch and C&J as well as the total. (For example a lifter in the World Championships who won the overall championship and each of the individual lifts as well would earn a total of seventy-eight points.) If individual medals are awarded for the snatch and C&J in American competitions other than the U.S. Nationals, team points must be counted in the same way. Otherwise, points are only counted for overall placements.

Equipment Used in Weightlifting Competitions By Athletes

There are essentially four kinds of equipment in use at weightlifting competitions: the barbell, the competition platform where all lifts are performed, the personal equipment used by the individual competitor and the system jointly used by the athletes, coaches, officials and spectators to follow the flow of the competition. We will examine each one in detail.

The Barbell

The bar has three basic components: the bar; the discs which comprise the bulk of the weight of the overall bar in most cases (they are usually called "plates" in the United States); and the moveable or "outside collars" of the barbell (often simply called the "collars"). The discs come in a variety of weights and are round. They have a round hole in the center just large enough so that the plate can fit on the bar.

The bar itself consists of a round steel bar with several components attached to it. At either end of the bar there are "sleeves." A sleeve is a hollow piece of round metal similar to a pipe. Its inside diameter is larger than that of the bar (so that it can fit over the bar). The plates that are placed on a bar actually rest on the sleeve. Between the outside surface of the bar and the inside surface of the sleeve, there is usually some sort of bearing (a mechanical device whose purpose is to enable the bar to turn freely in the lifter's hands when the bar is being lifted). Free movement of the bar facilitates the lifting of the bar. (Too much freedom can cause the plates to spin rapidly around the bar while it is being lifted, causing a gyroscopic effect

and making the bar more difficult and even dangerous to lift; this is a rare circumstance.)

The athlete grips the bar between the sleeves while lifting. The innermost portion of each sleeve has a section of metal (called the inside collar of the bar) that is larger than the diameter of the rest of the sleeve and larger than the hole in the plates. Its dual purpose is to protect the lifter by making it impossible for the plates to get any closer to the lifter than the inside of the sleeve and by making it impossible for the sleeve itself to move in toward the lifter.

The bar has several roughened (or "knurled" areas). These areas of knurling help the lifter to grip the bar, or to keep the bar from sliding on the chest when it is cleaned.

Specifications For The Bar:

The use of separate men's and women's bars, with different specifcations, began officially in 1997 (a bar with the specifications of today's men's bar had been used for men and women prior to 1997). The use of a gender specific bar is currently required at National and International competitions. The USAW permits some discretion in the use of the ladies bar at local competitions because many meet directors do not have access to a ladies bar at this time. In fact, women in the US resisted use of the ladies bar altogether because they felt that a bar with different specifications was not necessary for women (they'd been using the men's bar for more than a decade without difficulty). The Women's Committee if the USAW opposed the new bar because they felt it would form an artificial basis for a separation of men and women in competition and, in the short term, could reduce the competitive opportunities for women (e.g., a meet director forced to use a separate bar for men and women and faced with the prospect of a small number of women competitors relative to the men might simply opt to not run a women's competition, when in the past he or she might have done so as a matter of course because the same equipment could be used).

The bar(s) used in competition must meet the following overall specifications (women's specifications are shown is parentheses where they are different):

a) Weight: 20 kg. (15 kg.); a kilo equals 2.204622622 pounds, so the men's bar weighs just over 44 lb.—the simple way to convert kilos to pounds is to double the kilos and add 10%, so one doubles 20 kg. to reach 40 and adds 10% (4) to reach the weight of the bar in pounds (44);
b) Length: 2200 mm (2010), which is just over 86.5" with a tolerance of plus or minus 1 mm;
c) Diameter of the bar: 28 mm (25 mm), which is just over 1.1") plus or minus .03

Table 3

Weight (kg.)	Color	Diameter (mm)	Weight Tolerance
25	Red	450	+.1%,-.05%
20	Blue	450	+.1%,-.05%
15	Yellow	450	+.1%,-.05%
10	Green	450	+.1%,-.05%
5	White	None	+10 g, -0
2.5	Black	None	+10 g, -0
1.25	Chrome	None	+10 g, -0
.5	Chrome	None	+10 g, -0
.25	Chrome	None	+10 g, -0

mm on the smooth (non-knurled) part of the bar;

d) Diameter of the sleeve: 50 mm (just under 2 ") plus or minus .2 mm;

e) Distance between the inside collars: 1310 mm (just over 51.5") plus or minus .5 mm;

f) Width of the inside collar, including the collar of the sleeve (whether in two pieces or one): 30 mm (1.18 ") plus or minus 1 mm;

g) Knurling: In order to facilitate the grip and the positioning of the hands on the bar, the bar must be knurled. The latest IWF rulebook does not specify the positioning of the knurled and smooth parts of the bar, but the prior IWF rulebook and the current USAW rulebook indicate that for the men's bar they are to be arranged as follows (beginning with the inside edge of the inside collars): a smooth area just inside each inside collar measuring 5 mm, then knurled areas on either side measuring 190 mm each, then smooth areas of 5 mm each, then knurled areas of 245 mm each, then smooth areas of 150 mm each and finally one knurled portion at the center of the bar measuring 120 mm (there is no specific mention of such requirements for the ladies' bar).

While the IWF insists that these measurements be adhered to, it is not uncommon for a bar that does not precisely meet these specifications to be used in competitions, even to be approved by the IWF. (Officials in weightlifting competitions are absolute sticklers about the weight of the bar being lifted— it must always equal, if not exceed, the weight announced—but there is often some latitude given in terms of some measurements, especially regarding the width of the knurled and smooth sections of the bar.) Therefore, the wise lifter always measures the bar he or she will be lifting in a competition to assure that his or her grip width will be the same as in training.

Specifications For The Plates. There are strict specifications about the weight, size and color of the plates that are used in competitions (see Table 3):

It is required that all discs have a clear indication of their weight. The 450 mm discs must be covered with rubber or plastic. (This is to protect the surface on which the lifters are performing from the shock of the bar being dropped; generally such rubber or plastic is an inch or more thick around the outside diameter of the plate, where most of the impact of dropping the weight is concentrated.) The tolerance on the size of these large discs is plus or minus 1 mm. There is no size requirement of the discs that are 5 kg. or smaller (of course they may not be more than 450 mm), and they may be made of pure metal. The diameter of a plate that weighs 5 kg. or less is generally considerably smaller than 450 mm.

It is permissible to use 2.5 kg. or 5 kg. plates that measure 450 mm in American competitions through the national level. Such plates must comply with the IWF's weight tolerances for a regular 5 kg. plate and the size tolerances for any 450 mm plate. If such plates are not furnished by the organizer of the meet, but are brought to the competition by an athlete or coach, the plates are impounded by the officials to be weighed. Once the officials have approved these plates, if they are used by their owner, they must also be available to any other competitors who wish to use them during the competition. If the owner should refuse their use to others who require them, the attempts of any athletes who used the plates are forfeited. Obviously, the purpose of this rule is to prevent a lifter who owns a set of 5 kg. plates from gaining a competitive advantage over one who does not (the lifter who lifts on plates with a larger diameter does not have to lift the bar as far and does not have to bend down as far to reach the bar—which are generally advantages).

The Collars. Outside collars are placed on the bar for every attempt that is made with the bar in competition. The combination of inside collars built into the sleeve of the bar and outside collars locked tightly on the bar for each attempt prevents the weights from shifting during the attempt and assures that the bar will be in balance. Each of the collars weighs 2.5 kg. (plus 10 g. or minus 0 g.). Therefore, the bar and collars alone weigh 25 kg. (or a little more than 55 lb.). Whenever the weight on the bar is announced in competition, it includes the 25 kg. weight of the bar and the collars. In the USAW, "spring collars" are permitted up to the point where regular collars can be placed on the bar. (For example, when the athlete is attempting the minimum of 22.5 kg. that is permitted in competition, it would consist of the bar and 1.25 kg. plates with spring collars, the minor weight of which is not included in counting the weight on the bar.)

Loading The Bar In Competition

In competition, the bar is always loaded in a very specific way. The heaviest plates possible are always used first in loading every weight For example, if a lifter requests 105 kg., the bar will be loaded with a pair of 25 kg. plates first and then a pair of 15 kg. Another rule is that the heaviest possible plate that can be loaded and still not exceed the weight to be loaded is always used first, then the next heaviest set of plates that can be loaded without exceeding the weight desired is loaded, etc., until the desired weight is achieved. In our example, a weight of 105 kg. could have been achieved by loading a pair of 20 kg. plates and two pairs of 10 kg. plates. However, the rule of loading the heaviest possible plates in succession would have been violated. (The heaviest possible plate that can be loaded and still not exceed 105 kg. is 25 kg.; once the 25 kg. plates are loaded, the next heaviest set of plates that can be loaded without exceeding 105 kg. is the 15 kg. plates.)

The final rule in loading the bar is that the plates must be placed on the bar in such a way that the referees can read the numbers indicating the weight of each plate. As interpreted under the current rules, this means loading the first set of plates on the bar so that the numbers indicating their weight are turned in to face each other. (Many discs are made so that the weight is only shown on one side; if the weight is indicated on both sides of the plate, its placement obviously does not matter.) The next set of plates loaded on the bar, and every set of plates loaded thereafter, are loaded so that the number that indicates the weight of the plate faces out.

The Platform

The third piece of competitive equipment is the platform. All lifts in competition must be executed on the platform. As indicated earlier, both the lifter and the bar must remain within the platform's confines while the lift is being made. No one but the lifter is permitted on the platform while a lift is being attempted. Between attempts, the only other people permitted on the platform are the loaders (to load the bar to the necessary weights and to clean the platform or bar as required) and the officials (to check on the condition of the platform or the bar if there is a reason to believe that either is not functioning properly).

The platform must be square, measuring 4 m on each side. When the floor around the platform is similar in coloring to the platform, its top edge must have a different colored line around it that is at least 150 mm in width (so that the lifter can easily see when he or she is at the edge). The platform can be made of wood, plastic, or any solid material and may be covered with a non-slippery material. Its height must be between 50 mm and 150 mm (from just under 2" to just under 6"). On a practical level, there are three additional considerations involved in creating an acceptable platform. First, the platform must be absolutely flat. Nothing should ever protrude from the platform's surface. While lifting heavy weights, lifters almost invariably move their feet in order to lower their bodies to catch the weight overhead or on the chest. If the platform is not flat, the athlete can catch a foot with disastrous consequences. Proper weightlifting technique and conditioning make the sport very safe, but when a lifter is handling heavy poundages and moving quickly, a sudden severe twist or stop, which would generally be caused by an uneven platform, can result in a serious injury.

A second requirement is that the platform not be too smooth (i.e., slick). A slippery platform can be just as dangerous as one that is sticky or has something protruding up from it. That is why the rules permit covering the platform with a non-slippery material.

A final practical requirement is that the platform be level. Lifters train on level surfaces and they generally have a heel on their shoes in order to assure balance and proper positions while lifting. Even if a platform is off by a small amount, it could affect substantially the performance of the athletes.

In the United States, it is difficult to obtain materials for the platform that are in metric dimensions (e.g., wood that measures 4 m). Therefore, platforms are often oversized, with a border of tape or paint to mark the platform's boundaries. Under such conditions the outer boundaries of the platform are always the outside edge of the tape or painted line. The lifter's foot and/or the bar may not be placed outside the outer edge of the paint mark or tape.

The Lifter's Costume

There are very stringent rules in weightlifting competition concerning the athlete's uniform. So stringent are the rules that there is an official whose primary responsibility during the competition is to assure that no part of any lifter's costume is inappropriate. Moreover, when an element of the costume is found to be illegal, the officials may require that the athlete remove the offending piece of his or her uniform while the time that the athlete has to complete his or her lift is elapsing. This can be unnerving (if not disastrous) to the athlete, so any equipment that might raise a question on the part of the officials (rightly or wrongly) is to be avoided.

There are four primary reasons for the strict enforcement of the lifter's dress code. First, the referees need to see the limbs of the body very clearly in order to judge the performance of the lifts properly. Second, the officials want to be sure that no athlete obtains any unfair advantage over his or her competitors by virtue of some supportive capability beyond what is specified in the description of the uniform below. Where no written rules exist with respect to some aspect of a lifter's uniform, some examples of acceptable equipment are given. Where there is no specific rule regarding a portion of the uniform, the lifter is well advised to emulate what is widely accepted. When a lifter deviates from accepted standards, there is always a chance that an altercation of some sort may develop with the officials (who are only human and who may be confused and frustrated when some unusual item appears). Third, every effort is made to protect the health and safety of the athletes in competition. Parts of a lifter's costume that could be used as a means of support could also present a danger to the athlete. The rules pertaining to the athlete's costume are formulated in part with this kind of protection in mind. Finally, the officials want to assure that the athletes present a relatively aesthetic appearance to the audience. The following items are the required and/or permissible parts on a lifter's costume.

Required Equipment: Every athlete is required to wear a lifting suit and shoes in competition:

Lifting Suit. Every lifter is required to wear a one-piece or two piece, close fitting, collarless weightlifting suit that does not reach the knees or elbows (the suit must cover the trunk of the lifter). In no event may the lowest part of the suit make contact with any knee wrap or bandage the athlete may be wearing (most weightlifting suits look similar to the suits that are worn by amateur wrestlers.) In IWF competitions the athlete may, on each piece of their outfit, wear a trademark of a product or the symbol of a sponsor with a maximum size of 500 cm.^{2}. (USAW rules permit only a competition logo, club emblem or LWC emblem on the T-shirt, but nothing is indicated in the USAW written rules regarding other pieces of an athlete's costume.) Men's suits generally cover at least to the bottom of the buttocks (while the athlete is standing), and male athletes have been criticized and even made to change uniforms if they were wearing anything shorter. Women have been permitted to wear suits that are cut relatively high on their thighs in recent years.

For at least the past 20 years I have advocated the adoption of a lifting suit that permits the full leg to be covered. The recent rule allowing the suit (or a pair of leotard or bicycle type trunks) to extend to a point just above the knee is an improvement over the mid-thigh style that prevailed for many years. However, there is no good reason why a suit that runs the length of the leg should not be permitted .

In the days of the press, and when split lifting was popular, it was essential for the officials to be able to view the athlete's legs clearly. (Bending the knees in the press was prohibited, and touching the platform was a common fault in the low position of the split clean or snatch.) Today the need to observe the legs of the athlete has diminished (although the officials still need to see that the legs are straight prior to the jerk and after the snatch and jerk have been completed). In addition, the fabrics available for athletic costumes have evolved to the point where tight fitting yet flexible garments are commonplace. It would now be a simple matter to manufacture a lifting suit that covered the legs as well as the torso yet allowed the officials to see the athlete's every move (particularly if it were required that any bandages on the legs be worn over the costume). Such a uniform would keep the athlete warm between attempts (without the athlete's having to put on and remove sweats or warm-up clothes). It would eliminate the occasional debates over the length of the lifting suit. It would further diminish the likelihood that athletes would use any illegal lubricants on the thighs. Finally, it would protect the athletes from abrasions on the lower legs. What would be lost by using a full- length suit? A quaint but outmoded, traditional appearance.

Shoes. Shoes may be nearly any shape and made of any material or combination of materials. The soles and heels of the shoe may be of any height or thickness. There may be a strap over the instep, and the area around the heel of the foot may be reinforced with an extra thickness of leather. However, the heel of the shoe cannot taper outward from top to bottom, and no part of the sole can protrude more that 5 mm from the upper at any point (i.e., the shoe cannot be materially wider at the bottom than at the top). The upper of the shoe may not be higher than 130 mm from the top of the sole and heel.

Permissible Additional Personal Apparel Or Equipment. In addition to wearing the required equipment described above, the athlete may wear any or all of the following additional equipment.

T-Shirt. A T-Shirt may be worn under the lifting suit; it may have a logo or the emblem of the National Federation of the athlete (the emblem of the club, the LWC or competition in national and local competitions) but no advertising. (Small and unobtrusive trademarks are generally permitted but need not be.) The shirt may not have a collar or sleeves that cover any part of the elbows.

<u>Undergarments.</u> The use of conventional undergarments (i.e., athletic supporters for men, brassieres for women and briefs for both sexes) is permitted as long as they are worn under the lifting suit and do not extend beyond it.

<u>Trunks.</u> Trunks may be worn over or under the lifting suit, but they should be close fitting (e.g., bicycle type shorts). The rules regarding length are the same as those for the lifting suit. (A T-shirt and trunks may <u>not</u> be substituted for the weightlifting suit; they may only be worn in addition to it.)

<u>Socks.</u> Socks of any color or material are permitted, but they may not be long enough to touch or cover any part of the knee or any knee bandage that the lifter may be wearing (i.e., there must be some skin visible between the bottom of the knee bandage and the top of the sock).

<u>Belt.</u> A belt may be worn over the costume of the lifter. It may be up to 120 mm in width and of any thickness. There are no specific limitations on material, but leather is accepted without exception, and most fibers are accepted as well. A belt made of rubber would surely invite some objections from the officials, as might a belt made with supports of steel or plastic within it.

<u>Bandages and Plasters.</u> Bandages and/or medical plasters may be worn on the knees, wrists, hands, fingers and thumbs. They may be made of gauze, medical crepe or leather (although leather is normally only used on the wrists). Athletic adhesive tape and "Ace" bandages are included in this definition. Bandages on the hand may not cover the tips of the fingers and can be attached to the wrists but not to the bar. No bandages are permitted on the shins, thighs, trunk, arms or elbows (in the event of injury to the skin of the shins, plasters may be applied to that area). Only one type of bandage may be used on any one section of the body. For example, an athlete may not wear both an "Ace" bandage and a leather strap on the wrist or wrap the wrist with a bandage and encircle it with surgical tape. (Tape would be acceptable if it was used only to keep the bandage around the wrist and did not completely encircle the wrist.) In addition to the three types of bandages described above, a one-piece elastic or rubberized knee cap may be worn but it may not be reinforced in any way. There is no limit on the length of any bandage, but the width of the skin that is covered by a wrist bandage is limited to 100 mm, while the maximum width for the knee bandage is 300 mm (there must be some gap between the bottom of the lifting suit and the top of the any knee bandages). Fingerless gloves of the type worn by cyclists (which may extend only to the first joint of the fingers and may not touch any plasters applied to the fingers), or palm guards of the type worn by gymnasts may be worn.

If an athlete has been called to the platform because a correction must be made in his or her costume, the officials decide whether the clock is to be stopped while the correction is made. If the infraction appears to be intentional, the jury will usually permit the clock to continue to run, which can cause a lifter to run out of time and to forfeit an attempt before the costume can be corrected. Therefore, when in doubt about some item of costume, check with officials first. Do not wait until you are called to the bar. It is never illegal to wear any piece of costume or equipment before coming out to the platform to make an attempt, so that is the time to find out for sure whether or not something is permissible. Unless required to do so by the officials, lifters may not make any change in their outfits while they are on stage (e.g., they may not remove or change the position of any parts of their costumes).

Other Official Equipment of the Competition

In order for the officials of the competition to properly supervise it, they require certain equipment. At major international competitions such as the Olympic Games, World Championships, Continental or Regional championships (e.g., the Pan American Games), the following equipment is required.

Electronic Light System

All major competitions are conducted using an electronic light system with four major components.

1. <u>Two Sets of Decision Lights.</u> Each set of decision lights has three white and three red lights placed horizontally (in a way that reflects the placement of the three referees who adjudicate the lifts). White lights signify a good lift and red lights no lift. One set of decision lights is placed so that the competitors are able to see it and the other set is placed so that the audience can see it. The decision lights are designed so that they only light up once all three referees have made their decisions with respect to a given lift.

2. <u>Three Referee Control Boxes.</u> Each of these switch boxes must have two push-buttons, one connected to that referee's white decision light and the other to that referee's red decision light. In addition, each box must be capable of generating an audible signal to the referee (such a signal is used by the jury that oversees the performance of the officials to signal a referee that they wish to discuss something with him or her).

3. <u>One Control Panel.</u> This panel is placed on a table in front of the jury. It includes a small set of lights that are similar in appearance to the decision lights, except that each light goes on as soon as a referee has made a decision, instead of lighting after all three referees have made their decisions regarding a lift (as the full-sized decision lights normally do). In addition, the control panel

has a device that permits the jury to signal one or more of the referees to come to the jury table.

4. One Down Signal. This signal device emits both an audible signal (normally a loud buzzer) and a visible one (normally a light) which tell the lifter that the bar should be returned to the platform. The down signal must be placed on a stand in front of the platform so that the lifter can easily see it while the lift is being performed.

Scale

The official scale which is used to weigh the competitors must have a capacity of at least 200 kg. and must be precise to at least 10 g. The actual body weight registered must be recorded, to an accuracy of 10 g. At major international competitions, a second scale identical to the first must be placed near (but not in the same room as) the official scale. This helps the lifters reliably control their body weights before they go to weigh in officially. (At national championships a backup scale like the one required at major international events should be furnished.) The scale used in any competition must have been certified within one year of the competition. Records are never accepted unless the weights have been weighed on a certified scale. Therefore, any lifter who anticipates breaking a record of any kind should always check with the meet organizer well before the competition to make sure that a certified scale will be available for the competition.

Clock

At IWF competitions there must be an electronic clock which can: count "down" from at least fifteen minutes to zero; indicate ten second intervals or less; give an automatic audible signal thirty seconds before the end of a lifter's allocated time to make on attempt; and display time simultaneously in the competition and warm-up areas. The clock must be operated by a qualified official.

Forms

The following forms must be available for the running of the competition: a weigh-in list, competitor cards, competition protocols, a certification of the weight of the bar that will be used in the competition, record protocols, passes for the warm-up area and doping control forms.

Attempt Board

The attempt board is used to keep officials, athletes and the audience aware of the progress of the competition. It displays the name of the lifter who is currently making an attempt, the weight that is being tried and what attempt number that represents (i.e., first, second, third or fourth attempt outside the competition for a record). The attempt board must be constructed so that it is easily readable and placed so that it is easily seen.

Scoreboard

The scoreboard must be prominently placed in the competition area. Its purpose is to record and display results in specific weight categories (i.e., classes). It must have the start or "lot" numbers of each competitor; the competitors' names in order of lot number; the body weight of each competitor; the athlete's country (in international competitions) or club (in national or local competitions); spaces to display the three attempts made by the athlete in each of the lifts (shown in a way that enable the observer to determine whether each attempt was a good or no lift); the total made and the place obtained by the athlete.

Record Board

The record board is also placed prominently in the competition area. It displays the current records in the category and at the level of competition being contested, and sometimes higher level records. For example, at the World Championships the record board would show the current world records in a given weight class since there are no higher records. However, at the U.S. National Championships the record board might show the meet record (the highest lift ever recorded at that championship), the American Record (the highest lift ever recorded by an American) and the World Record. The record board also shows the name and country of the record holder. (In national or local competitions it might show the club of the record holder.)

Warm-up Area

A warm-up area near the competition area must be provided for the competitors. It must be equipped with chalk, platforms and barbells appropriate for the number of competitors. It should have loudspeakers that are connected to the competition announcer. There should be counterpart of the scoreboard, time clock and official's decision lights in the warm-up area, so that athletes and coaches can follow the progress of the competition

Special Requirements for Equipment at Major International Competitions

At major international competitions the following electronic equipment is required: two scales, a digital clock, referee decision lights and an attempt board. In addition, any other equipment that helps to improve the running of the competition (e.g., computers).is recommended.

Operations of the Referee's Light System

Each lift attempted in competition is judged by three referees. One of the referees (called the chief referee) sits facing the platform. He or she is positioned approximately 6 m directly to the front of the platform's center (or 4 m from its front edge). There is one side referee to either side of the chief referee. The side referees sit just slightly closer to the front edge of the platform and approximately 6 m to the side of the chief referee. This positioning permits each referee to view the lift from a somewhat different perspective. This contributes to the fairness of the officiating; a movement that looks like a fault from one position (but is not) can be seen from other angles by the other referees, increasing the likelihood that a correct decision will be made. Similarly, a fault that is difficult to detect from one angle will perhaps be seen from another. In addition, seating the referees in this manner permits the chief referee to observe the actions of the side referees (not required when an electronic light system is in use, but critical when the referees use their hands or red and white flags to signal a fault in a lift).

All three referees have equal authority in judging a lift. (The center referee is called the chief referee due to his or her leadership role in other areas; these functions will be discussed later.) A majority decision of the three referees (i.e., at least two out of three) determines whether a lift is judged a "Good Lift" or "No Lift." The referees' job during the performance of a lift is to scrutinize it carefully throughout to assure that it is properly performed. They are to press one of the buttons on their control boxes as soon as a lifter has properly completed a lift and become motionless with the bar, torso and feet in one line (in which case the referee presses the white button) or any fault which disqualifies the lift is observed (in which case the referee presses the red button). Once at least two referees agree either that a fault has been made or that the lift has been properly completed, the audible and visible down signal will be triggered. (Once two of the referees have made a decision, the remaining referee receives an intermittent audible signal from his or her control box, signifying the need to make a decision.) After the down signal is given but before the decision lights appear, the referees have three seconds to reverse their decisions. (This gives the referees a chance to alter a decision when they have signaled "down" by pressing their white lights only to see the lifter return the bar to the platform in an illegal manner, e.g., by dropping the bar.) The decision lights appear only when all three referees have made their judgment. The decision lights remain on for at least fifteen seconds, so that all competitors, officials and the audience can see the decision.

The Structure Of A Competition

All competitions have at least four major phases: the drawing of the lots, the weigh-in, the competition itself and the victory ceremony. At major international championships there is also a technical conference (which includes the drawing of the lots), an opening ceremony and a closing ceremony. Each of these phases will be described below.

Technical Conference (also the Drawing of the Lots)

The technical conference is held one day before the first day of most major international competitions. (For games, such as the Olympic or Pan American Games, the conference may take place one or two days before the first day of the competition.) At lower level competitions the conference (or drawing of the lots at local competitions) must be held in "due time" before the competition (early enough to be completed before the weigh-in begins). The time of the technical conference must be stated on the entry or invitation to compete in the competition. At the technical conference a final list of the competitors must be provided by each country or club that enters a team. (The athletes' names, the category in which they plan to compete, their dates of birth and best official totals must be given.) After the conference the names of the competitors cannot change. The competitors entered in a given category can be placed into to two or more groups, based on their best official totals, by the Competition Secretary. (Those with the highest totals are placed in the "A" session or group, those with the next highest totals in the "B" group, etc.) At the technical conference referees for each group and category are appointed, as are jury members, technical controllers and doctors on duty. Information on the program of the competition must be given at the technical conference (any special rules that will apply, etc.). In addition, lot numbers are drawn for each competitor. (These are retained throughout the competition, even if the competitor lifts in a higher weight class.) The lot number decides the order of the weigh-in. In local competitions (domestic competitions that are not national championships), lot numbers are generally drawn fifteen minutes prior to the beginning of the weigh-in for the first group of competitors. (Sometimes it is done fifteen minutes before the weigh-ins of each group of competitors who will lift together.)

In national and international championships each weight category, or sub-group thereof, generally lifts separately. At non-championships or at local competitions, different weight categories often perform at the same time, but separate scores are kept on the competitors in each weight category, so that athletes actually compete only against those in their own weight category.

The Weigh-In

The weigh-in is the period during which athletes are weighed in order to establish their official body weights for a given competition. The weigh-in begins two hours before the competition starts in the categories for which the weigh-in is being held. It lasts for one hour. The room where the weigh-in takes place is equipped with an official scale, a table and chair for the Competition Secretary and all necessary competition forms. During the weigh-in the chief referee operates the scale, with both side referees verifying the weight of the athlete. The Secretary records the body weight indicated by the referees. The competitor must be accompanied by a representative of his country; at domestic competitions where the athlete has no coach, this is not required.

Weigh-ins are held in private, with one athlete weighed at a time, and the body weights of all of the athletes are disclosed only after all athletes have been weighed. Competitors can be weighed nude or in their underwear, at their discretion (women are weighed only by women). In international competitions, only the IWF President, General Secretary, the Presidents of the Medical and Technical Committees and the Technical Controller of the category being contested are permitted in the weigh-in room (in addition to the parties mentioned earlier). Competitors are called in order of their lot numbers (any athlete who misses his or her turn is entitled to be weighed next after his or her return to the weigh-in area). In domestic competitions the identities of the officials conducting the weigh-in may vary, but there will generally be more than one referee to verify what is happening.

Each competitor must provide proof of identity in the form of a passport or ID card which he or she presents to the Secretary. (In the United States a registration card showing membership in the USAW generally serves as both proof of identity and eligibility to compete in a USAW sanctioned competition, but an extra ID is always a good thing to have. Junior lifters who have any expectation of breaking any age- group records should always have an original birth certificate with them; photocopies are not acceptable as proof of age. An athlete can only weigh in once, unless his or her body weight exceeds or falls below the limits of the category (in which case he or she may be reweighed as many times as necessary, up until the end of the weigh-in period, in order to achieve a body weight within the prescribed limits). As a practical matter, reweighs are generally only permitted once every competitor has been weighed at least once. Because many athletes are anxious to eat and ingest fluids immediately after they weigh in (so that they will

have as much time as possible to absorb what they have ingested) and because officials often have much to do after the weigh-in, athletes may sometimes feel rushed during the weigh-in process. They should cooperate with the officials and realize that dispatch is often necessary.

After the time limit on the weigh-in expires, lifters whose body weights are too low for the category are eliminated. Athletes whose body weights exceed the limit are permitted to compete in the next weight category if three conditions are met. First, the athlete must equal or exceed any qualifying standard (a minimum total made in official competition) that is required in order to lift in the next higher category. Second, the athlete's body weight must fall within the body weight limits of the next category when the weigh-in for that category takes place. Third, there can be no more than one competitor from that athlete's country entered in the higher category in which the athlete wishes to compete. As a general rule, an athlete who makes a total in a given weight category is expected to be able to equal that total if he or she performs in a higher weight category. However, it cannot be presumed that the athlete's total will go up if the athlete competes in a higher weight category. Similarly, it cannot be assumed that an athlete will be able to equal a total made in a heavier weight class if that athlete reduces his or her body weight. (Nor can it be assumed that the athlete's total will go down in a way that is proportional to the lifter's change in body weight when he or she reduces body weight.)

Once an athlete has been weighed, the athlete, or the athlete's representative, is required to tell the Competition Secretary what initial attempts in the snatch and C&J are planned. (The athlete or coach is permitted to change these first attempts twice after making their initial declaration.) Two changes in second and third attempts are also permitted once a competitor officially provides such attempts.

The first attempts planned by the athlete are recorded, along with the athlete's body weight, on a weigh-in sheet (a form specifically designed for recording body weights and other important information collected from the competitors at the weigh-in). Then the athlete, or the athlete's representative (e.g., a coach), is required to initial the sheet, signifying his or her agreement with the body weight and starting attempts recorded by the Secretary. Before the beginning of the weigh-in (or as a practical matter, during it) one team official of each national federation or team gives the Secretary the names of the team officials who will accompany the athlete to the warm-up area. (Separate passes are given out for each body-weight category that is contested.) If there is more than one group per weight class, passes are given out for each group. (Often the formality of providing a list of names is waived, and the team

470

official simply asks for a specific number of passes for each category.) If a country or team has only one athlete in a category, that country or team is permitted to have four passes (two at domestic competitions). If there are two athletes, five passes are permitted (three at domestic competitions).

It is very important that weigh-ins be conducted as scheduled. Athletes who arrive early are not permitted to weigh in before the official beginning of the weigh-in, and those who are late are not accommodated (although they will sometimes be permitted to lift as extra lifters whose lifts cannot count toward any awards given in the competition). This is because the officials want to assure that all lifters have an equal chance to weigh in. (Lifters who weigh in early could eat more before the competition, those who weigh in late have the advantage of knowing what the others in the class weigh.) In addition, the officials are often on a tight schedule and need the time before and after the weigh-in to prepare for the competition.

The Presentation

Fifteen minutes before the beginning of the competition in each group or category, all of the athletes line up in order of lot number and march onto the stage or the area just behind the platform that will be used for the competition. (This is often done ten minutes before the competition in the United States.) Each athlete is then presented to the audience. Once all of the athletes have been introduced, they leave the platform together to warm up. Following the departure of the athletes, the officials for that category or group march on stage and are presented. The referees, technical controller and the doctor on duty are all introduced. The jury members and Competition Secretary are also introduced, but they are presented in their places (where they will be during the competition), not on stage. After all of the officials have been introduced, those who are on stage march off together and assume the positions that they will occupy during the competition.

The Competition

The competition organizers appoint enough "marshals" to assure the proper progress of the competition (in terms of the order of the attempts taken by the competitors and the progression in the loading of the bar). The marshals work under the supervision of the Competition Secretary. The marshals use competitor cards in their work. These cards resemble index cards. They have the athlete's name on them (and generally the athlete's body weight and lot number as well). They also have spaces to record each of the three attempts an athlete requests on each lift. (Most cards have three lines for each attempt: one for the first weight the athlete requests and the other two to record the two changes to which the athlete is

entitled.) In theory, the marshall asks the athlete/coach to write his or her attempts on the card. (This procedure is particularly important at international competitions, where language differences between the marshall and the athlete or coach could cause errors to be made if verbal communications were relied upon.) It is then the marshall's responsibility to relay the athlete's request to the speaker.

Depending on the level of the competition and the equipment available, the attempts chosen by the athlete are then communicated: to the Competition Secretary or the appointee of the Secretary, if such person is situated near the speaker or directly to the speaker (if the Competition Secretary or the Secretary's appointee is not seated near the speaker at the competition). Communication can take place by personal contact between the speaker and the marshall, by telephone or intercom or by a video camera. After each attempt, the marshall asks for the athlete's next attempt. In theory, the marshall should wait for the athlete/coach to decide. In practice, particularly if the officials feel that the competition may be delayed if competitors take too long to make their decisions, the Competition Secretary may inform the lifters that a specific increase (generally 2.5 kg.) will be assumed from the first to second and the second to the third attempts (unless the athlete misses a second or third attempts, in which case a repeat with the weight is generally assumed). Since athletes still have a right to make two changes in poundage, such an approach on the part of the speaker is generally not objected to, and it does tend to make the competition move forward with fewer delays.

In national competitions, it is not unusual for the marshalls to actually write in the weight the athlete requests, instead of having the athlete or coach do it (remember that in such situations language is generally not a barrier.) At local competitions, where there may not be any marshalls, the lifter or coach often must communicate their attempts directly to the speaker. (Even in international competitions, it is always permissible to communicate your attempts directly to the speaker in order to save time.)

One or more appointed speakers announces the name of the athlete, the athlete's country or team, the weight of the bar and the attempt number for every attempt made in the competition (i.e., whether it is a given athlete's first, second or third attempt). The speaker also notifies the next competitor that he or she is next (in the United States it is customary to refer to the next athlete up as "on deck" and to announce the lifter who will follow after that as in the "hold" or "hole."

During the competition the bar is loaded with progressively heavier weights, beginning with the lightest weight to be attempted in the competition of that class or group. The weight on the bar can never be reduced after at least one lifter has either actually attempted to lift the bar or has been called to the bar and has thirty seconds or less remaining on the clock to make his or her attempt. The only exception to this rule is when some kind of error by the officials has caused a lifter to miss taking an attempt at the proper time. Reducing the bar is never permitted as a result of a mistake by a lifter or the lifter's coach. Therefore, it is the responsibility of the lifters and coaches to follow the progress of the loading of the bar and to be ready to make an attempt when the weight he or she has chosen is on the bar and that athlete has been called to the bar. (An athlete is only entitled to be called to the bar once for each attempt he or she has requested.) Only multiples of 2.5 kg. can be asked for during the competition. Consequently, a lifter is required to increase by at least by 2.5 kg. after any successful first or second attempt.

One minute (sixty seconds) is allowed for an athlete to make his or her attempt with a weight once he or she is called by the speaker to the bar. This call does not take place until the bar has been loaded to the weight requested by the lifter, the bar has been positioned properly on the platform by the loaders (generally at the center of the platform with the bar parallel to the front edge of the platform) and the loaders have left the platform. It should be noted that the lifter or coach can request that the bar be placed to the front or rear of center; such a request should properly be made of the Technical Controller, the official responsible for seeing that the bar and platform are positioned and working properly during the competition. An attempt in this context means that the bar has been raised at least to the height of the athlete's knees by the time the clock has run down to zero. If, following his or her attempt, an athlete requests another attempt and is called to the platform next, that athlete is given two minutes (120 seconds) to make his or her attempt.

For all attempts, there is a warning buzzer when the clock has counted down to thirty seconds remaining. No changes in weight are permitted after the thirty second warning, and the athlete cannot take more than the remaining 30 seconds to begin his or her attempt (get the bar at least to the height of his or her knees). Therefore, once the clock has reached the point where there are 30 seconds remaining, the lifter has used one of his or her attempts, regardless of whether he or she actually attempts to lift the bar during the time remaining.

If a lifter requests a change in the weight on the bar and, as a consequence, another lifter is called, the lifter who requested the change will be given sixty seconds to make his or her attempt when he or she is called back to the platform. In contrast, when a lifter requests a change in the weight on the bar and remains on the platform, the clock is stopped while the weight is being changed. The clock begins again at the point of elapsed time once the weight requested has been loaded.

In international competitions between individuals or teams in which athletes in different weight categories are competing at the same time, competitors may lift alternately (with the lifter attempting the lighter weight starting first and the same order being maintained throughout the competition on that lift).

Once the speaker has announced (at the request of the athlete or the athlete's coach) that a competitor has decided to decline an attempt or to withdraw from the competition, the decision cannot be reversed. During any competition held on a raised platform or stage, no one but the jury, officiating referees, speakers and technical officials (e.g., the Technical Controller, the official operating the clock) and competitors in the specific group or category are permitted around the platform or stage.

The Order of Calling the Lifters for Their Attempts in the Competition

During the competition lifters are called to the platform to make their attempts in a very orderly fashion. A thorough understanding of this ordering method is essential if an athlete is to time his or her warm-ups so that he or she will be at a peak when called to the platform.

Four factors are considered in determining the order of competitors. They are, in order: the weight on the bar, the number of the attempt (i.e., first, second or third), the differences between the previous weights attempted by each lifter and the current attempt and the lot number of the athlete.

As was explained earlier, the bar is loaded progressively in weightlifting competition. Consequently, all athletes who are attempting 100 kg. make their attempts before those making attempts with 102.5 kg. Therefore, the order of calling by the weight on the bar makes perfect sense.

When more that one athlete is attempting the same weight, the second rule of ordering comes into play. The second rule, calling by attempt number, requires some further explanation. Why should athletes who are taking their first attempts with a given weight go before the athletes who are taking their second attempts? One explanation is the athletes who are taking lower attempts have been waiting to begin the competition longer than those athletes who are taking their second attempts. (This logic applies to the third rule of order as well.) Another reason is that the athlete with the higher attempt has fewer chances to assure a place than the athlete taking a lower attempt. Therefore, if the athlete taking a third attempt were forced to perform before the athlete taking a second attempt, the athlete taking the third would have no chance to make his or her only remaining attempt with a weight that was likely to defeat the opponent with the greater number of remaining attempts.

If two athletes are attempting the same weight and the attempt number for each athlete is the same, the third rule of order is applied. The third rule of order says that the athlete who has the greatest weight differential between attempts goes first. There are perhaps two underlying premises that give rise to such a rule. First, the athlete who took the lower weight on a previous attempt has had longer to rest. Therefore, that athlete should be more able to perform at something near an optimal level, or at least closer to it, than the athlete who has performed more recently. The second premise is that if both athletes who are taking a certain weight have waited far longer than either needs to recuperate from their prior attempts (and may even be "cooling down"), the athlete who had been waiting longer should have the opportunity to go first.

If two athletes select the same poundage, both are taking the same number attempt and each has increased the weight being attempted by the same amount from their previous attempts, the order of lifting is decided by the lot numbers that were drawn at the technical conference. The concept behind this rule is that if no order can be decided by the requirements of the competition and the rational interests of the competitors, then a choice should be made on a random basis, with each athlete having an equal chance. Moreover, it should be noted that a lower lot number has both advantages and disadvantages for the athlete. During the weigh-in a lower lot number means that an athlete has an opportunity to weigh-in sooner and to eat and drink to regain any lost body weight before the competition begins. During the competition, if there has been a long wait between attempts, the athlete with the lower lot number goes first, perhaps increasing his or her chances of success. Offsetting these advantages is the (on balance) greater advantage of going after your competitor and having the final opportunity to make any strategic adjustments that such a later position in the order permits.

There are those who argue that there is one instance in which the second rule of order can have a minor negative effect on the athlete taking the lower attempt. This athlete could miss a first attempt with a particular weight, and an opponent could be waiting for a third attempt with the same weight. In that case, the athlete who is repeating has only two minutes to prepare, because that athlete is following himself or herself. It is possible that if the athlete taking a third attempt were required to go first (i.e., if the current third rule of order became the second), the athlete waiting would have a longer wait; such a practice would speed up the progress of the competition. While the progress of the competition would be hastened by a reordering of the second and third rules, the athlete repeating his attempt would not necessarily be any better off. An alert opponent could take his or her attempt almost immediately, and then the athlete repeating might have little more than one minute between attempts (the time it took the athlete making the third attempt to take his or her attempt and the sixty seconds the repeating athlete would then have to make an attempt). Therefore, with the two minute rule, the officials assure the repeating athlete a two minute rest, instead of the prospect of a little more than one minute or two, depending on the behavior of the other athlete. All in all, the rules of order are wise indeed. They are just part of the commitment that the sport of weightlifting has to fairness in competition.

In all weightlifting competitions sanctioned by the IWF or USAW, there is at least a ten minute break between the snatch and C&J. This period allows the competitors to warm up for the C&J and enables the officials to take a break. At major international competitions and at some other competitions where individual awards are given for the snatch and C&J, there is an awards or "victory ceremony" between the snatch and C&J (and again after the C&J). In the United States, individual awards for the snatch and C&J are required only at the U.S. Nationals. The nature of the victory ceremony is discussed later in this section. When there is such a ceremony, the time required to complete the presentation is generally added to the required ten minute break.

If an athlete does not make any attempts in the snatch (the first lift contested), that athlete is permitted to C&J. Any individual awards and/or team points attributable to that athlete's C&J will count. Similarly, an athlete who has no score in the C&J, but who has had at least one successful attempt in the snatch, is eligible to receive any appropriate individual award or team points on the basis of his or her performance in the snatch. However, any athlete who fails to make a successful snatch or C&J cannot receive any individual awards or score any points toward the total (even in the unlikely event that the weight lifted by an athlete in the snatch or C&J alone was greater than a total made on both lifts by another athlete).

When two or more competitors lift the same weight in either lift, the athlete who had the lighter body weight at the weigh-in is placed higher in that lift. If two athletes have the same score on either lift and weigh the same, the lifter who did the lift first during the competition is placed higher. Similar rules apply to the total.

The Officials of the Competition

I have heard the comment more than once that there are more officials than athletes in some competitions. While this is rarely the case, a rather large number of officials is required to run a weightlifting competition properly. However, athletes and coaches should remember that virtually every official present at any competition is a volunteer. No official receives any remuneration for the act of officiating (although the travel and room and board expenses of some officials are paid for at some major events). Although the officials may appear cold and menacing to some athletes, they are all dedicated to a single proposition: that athletes are entitled to a fair and expeditiously run competition. Lifters and coaches would do well to remember this fact the next time they become frustrated with the officiating at a particular meet. Criticism, where appropriate, need not be withheld, but it may never be communicated to the referees during the competition. If an athlete or coach believes that a referee has made a serious technical mistake (not merely an error in judgment, but an action in clear violation of the technical rules, such as permitting a lifter to lift in the wrong order or with the wrong weight), this mistake can be brought to the attention of the jury during the competition. (The functions of the jury will be explained later on in this appendix.) After the competition, once the officials have stepped down from their official responsibilities, most are willing to discuss their decisions freely (though they are not required to do so). Such discussions can often help a lifter to clear up a misunderstanding with respect to the rules and to prevent a repetition of such a misunderstanding.

There are generally two or more layers of official authority to oversee the competitions. This multi-level approach assures the proper application of the rules.

Officials at international competitions can be easily identified by their required dress. The referees, doctor on duty, jury members and Technical Controller must all wear a blue jacket with an IWF badge on the pocket (at national championship events or below, the officials are expected to substitute the emblem of their national federation), a white shirt, an IWF tie and gray trousers. The Competition Secretary and timekeeper generally wear similar attire as well. In very hot weather, with the permission of the jury, the jacket may be removed. The uniform of the continental federations may also be worn at Continental Championships, and at the Olympic Games only the official uniform of the Olympics may be worn. Since the referee's uniform is quite formal, it is often modified at competitions below the national level. Nevertheless, as will become obvious as the description of officials proceeds, it is always easy to spot referees by virtue of their location and functioning at the competition.

In a broad sense the scorekeepers, scoreboard attendants, loaders, timekeeper (the person who operates the official clock that times each lifter's attempt), announcer and marshalls are all officials

of the competition. However, when the rules speak of officials, they are generally referring to officials who can and do exercise considerable judgment during the competition, as contrasted with those who administer the event (the six categories of officials that were mentioned above). There are five categories of officials who render judgments at most major competitions: jury, Competition Secretary, Technical Controller, referees and doctor on duty. When there are not enough officials present to fill all of the required positions, certain functions are combined to assure that all important tasks are attended to there are always three referees, however.

Jury

The jury is the highest level of authority at weightlifting competitions. Its function is to assure that all technical rules are followed, with a particular emphasis on the performance of the referees. The president of the jury is able to signal one or more of the referees during the competition, via the referees control box, to come to the jury table. After warning a referee of some mistake in officiating during the competition, the jury may, by a unanimous vote, replace a referee who is making what are considered to be incompetent decisions. The impartiality of referees cannot be questioned, but if a mistake is made involuntarily during the competition, the referee is given an opportunity to explain it.

At major international competitions all members of the jury must be Category I international referees (the highest category in the world). All members of the jury must be from different countries. Before Olympic and World Championships two juries are appointed to serve on alternate days. At Olympic and World Championships there are five members of the jury, one of whom is appointed president of that jury. Reserves may also be appointed.

After the competition jury members submit opinions of each referee's performance on forms that are collected by the Technical Controller (TC). The results are summarized and registered by the TC and the General Secretary of the IWF.

When a decision contrary to the technical rules has been made by the referees, the jury can, by a unanimous vote, grant an additional attempt to the athlete. Despite its level of authority, the jury can never reverse the decisions made by a referee, although they can relieve a referee of his or her duties if they feel that it is appropriate to do so. In addition to granting an extra attempt to the athlete when the decisions of the referees are subject to question, the jury and Competition Secretary (in conjunction) may grant an extra attempt to the athlete when there has been an error in loading the bar or if the weight has been incorrectly announced. For example, if the bar has been loaded evenly on both sides and to an increment of 2.5 kg., but is lighter or heavier than requested by the lifter, the lifter may accept a successful attempt and be credited with the weight actually lifted. If the lifter refuses to accept an improperly loaded or announced weight, the competitor is automatically granted another attempt with the weight originally requested. It the bar is not loaded evenly, there is a change in the bar (e.g., some plates come loose and change position during the lift) or the platform becomes disarranged, the competitor/coach may request an additional attempt (which request the jury may agree to grant). If the bar is not loaded to an increment of 2.5 kg., another attempt is automatically granted.

Regardless of the conditions at the competition, it is the responsibility of the athlete and coach to follow the progress of the competition and to be ready to lift when appropriate, even if there is a failure on the part of the speaker to call the athlete to the platform at the proper time. However, when the warm-up area is so far from the platform and communications between the speaker and the warm-up area are so poor that the competitors and their coaches cannot reasonably follow the progress of the competition and the speaker fails to call the competitor at the proper time, the bar can be reduced in order for the competitor to take his or her attempt with the weight actually called for.

The jury must be located in a position where the jury members' view of the lifter is clear and unobstructed (yet is similar in vantage point to that of the referees). Typically their position is between the chief referee and either side referee and somewhat further away from the platform (so that they can easily observe both the lifter and all three referees). Before the competition the referees' cards and those of the TC are placed on the jury table. After the competition it will be noted on the TC's and referees' cards (referred to as "licenses" by the IWF) that they officiated in that competition. This is important to the referees because they must referee in a certain number of competitions each year in order to maintain a current referee's license.

Competition Secretary

A Competition Secretary (CS) is appointed for all competitions. The CS is responsible for the running of the competition in cooperation with the jury and the TC. At World Championships, the General Secretary of the IWF (GS) is the CS. The CS verifies the list of competitors and, if necessary, divides them into groups according to the best results they have supplied. The CS also draws lots for each competitor at the Technical Conference, records the body weights of each athlete during the weigh-in and issues warm-up room passes for the personnel who will assist each athlete during the competition. During the competition the CS supervises the order of the lifting and registers any new records made during the competition, including any records made on extra attempts.

Technical Controller

The Technical Controller (TC) is appointed to assist the CS in supervising the running of the competition. In international competitions the TC must hold a Category I international referee's card. At World Championships the Technical Committee appoints the TC, and at the Olympic Games the Executive Board appoints them (two per category). In other international games or tournaments, they are appointed by the official IWF delegate. The TC attends the weigh-in to assist the CS in verifying the identity of athletes, as well as registering the names and body weights of the athletes. The TC is responsible for checking all of the competitive equipment (e.g., platform, bar, scales, electronic referee lights, clock, warm-up room and other facilities) as well as the costumes of the athletes and officials. The TC also assures that only the accredited number of team officials accompany athletes near the competition area. The TC is responsible for seeing that while the athlete is on stage, no one (including the TC) is seen in that area by the audience and/or any TV cameras. The TC controls the cleaning of the platform and bar, if required. He or she also assists the Doping Commission, if requested. At the end of the competition, the TC collects the referee inspection forms from the jury and gives them to the CS for recording.

Referees

The main task of the referees is to adjudicate the lifts done during the competition. Every referee at international competitions must hold an IWF referee's card issued to him or her at the national federation's request. No referee may officiate outside his country without an IWF license.

In order for a referee to receive an international license, he or she must have first been a national referee for at least two years and must be proposed by his or her national federation. (The USAW will only propose the promotion of referees who are considered to be "active" within the USAW; "active" means that the referee is officiating in at least two USAW competitions a year.) The referee also must have a complete knowledge of the IWF technical rules and must demonstrate that knowledge in an exam organized by the IWF or in an IWF authorized exam organized by the national federation.

There are two categories of international referees, Category II and Category I. Category II international referees are permitted to officiate at international tournaments, regional games and continental championships. Category I referees are permitted to officiate at all events that Category II referees are able to officiate in, as well as the Olympic Games and the World Championships. Category I referees are also able to serve on the jury or act as a TC at international competitions.

A chief and two side referees are appointed to each category or group at all competitions under IWF rules. Before the competition referees ascertain, under the guidance of the TC, that the competition equipment is in order and that the competitors weigh in within the limits of the category during the weigh-in time.

During the competition the referees ascertain that the weight on the bar agrees with that announced by the speaker. They also assure that no one but the lifter touches the bar during the execution of a lift and that only the lifters or loaders move the bar to a new position on the platform prior to making an attempt at a lift. If the TC asks the loaders to move, adjust or clean the bar or platform, the clock is stopped until the loaders finish. If the lifter moves the bar to a position where the view of a referee is impaired, that referee may move to a point where the lift can be observed correctly, after which the referee returns to his or her normal position in order to render a decision. The referees also assure that any record disks available for use during the competition are on the chief referee's table.

Electronic lights are used at major international competitions. If there is a malfunction in these lights or they are unavailable, the chief referee gives a "down" signal by saying "down" and at the same time motioning downwards with the arm. White lights signify a decision of "good lift" and red lights signify a decision of "no lift." Small white and red flags can substitute when lights are not in use; the appropriate flag is raised to signify the referee's decision. (When flags are unavailable, the referee gives a "thumbs up" signal for a good lift and "thumbs down" for no lift.) When there are no decision lights to generate a down signal, the side referees signify their recognition of a fault during the course of a lift by raising either hand. If two referees agree that a fault has been committed, the chief referees gives both the visible and audible down signal. Where there is no TC, the referees must do the TC's job as well as their own. Referees may not receive any documents concerning the progress of the competition and must abstain from any comments on any lift. In addition, they must not attempt to influence the decisions of other referees during the competition. After the competition the referees sign the official score sheets of the competition, protocols, record certificates, etc., and collect their referee cards (which have been noted and signed by the jury president).

At World Championships or Olympic Games, two referees from the same country may not judge the same category. Three months before the World Championships, each national federation may submit names of two Category I referees. The Technical Committee selects from this list of referees. The number of referees to be selected is based on the committee's knowledge of the extent of the program of the championships. National federations are advised of the appointment or non-appointment of their candidates. The referees selected are assigned to categories or groups by the Technical Committee at the site of the championships before the competition begins. Referees for the Olympics are selected by the Executive Board, based on names submitted by the national federations six months prior to the Games.

Timekeeper

At all international events a timekeeper must be appointed. The timekeeper must be a Category I or II referee.

Doctors on Duty

At major international competitions, doctors are appointed to be on duty in each body weight category. These doctors are to be present from the weigh-in to the end of doping control for that category. They are expected to know and to use available medical facilities, to cooperate in taking samples for doping control, to be prepared to render care for injury or illness, to cooperate with team doctors and to advise coaches, officials and athletes on the possibility of continuing the competition after injury. The doctors authorize the application of additional plasters or bandages during the competition. At World Championships there are to be two doctors on duty at the same time (if necessary, team doctors may assist doctors on duty). At the Olympic Games only IWF appointed doctors can be doctors on duty, two per category.

At all World Championships and the IWF World Cup competition, primary medical care of all competitors and officials for any disease or injury that occurs during the event must be furnished. A properly supplied medical room must be made available at the competition. Primary care should also be available twenty-four hours a day. The cost of such care must be borne by the organizing committee for the event (though the organizing committee can arrange for reimbursement from the insurer of any competitor or official whom it treats). When there is any doubt about whether the injury or illness for which treatment has been requested actually commenced during the event, treatment must be provided initially, and the issue can be brought to the attention of the IWF Medical Committee for further consideration (the competition organizers are not expected to bear the cost of treatment for chronic medical conditions, or those which existed prior to the event).

This aforementioned procedure is recommended for continental championships and games as well. At national events there is often a doctor on duty during the competition hours. If there is no doctor available, procedures to evacuate the athlete to a nearby medical facility are arranged.

Special USAW Rules Regarding Officials

When there are insufficient Category I referees at a competition in the United States,, the members of the jury are selected from available Category II referees. At other than national championships, the functions of the jury may be carried out by the highest ranking official when an insufficient number of qualified referees is available. In the absence of such an official, a committee of LWC referees will serve this function. (The meet director may never serve such a function, except as a member of the LWC committee.) Said committee is appointed by the senior LWC official present.

Opening, Victory and Closing Ceremonies

At World Championships there is an Opening Ceremony in which all participating teams or appointed members of those teams parade in alphabetical order, on the basis of the name of the country (with the exception of the host country, whose team or representatives appears last). Speeches are the made by various officials and the national flag of the organizing federation and the IWF flag is raised while the national anthem of the organizing federation is played. Guest speakers leave the stage, then the flag bearers and teams (or appointed members) march out. The ceremony can be followed by entertainment provided by the organizing federation.

Following the conclusion of each lift in each category, there is a Victory Ceremony. The names of the first six place winners are announced. The three medal winners and officials presenting medals march to the area of the platform. The speaker announces the name, country and result of the champion (who mounts the highest step, which is in the center of the podium). The speaker then announces, in succession, the winner and the presenter of the silver and bronze medals, and the winners mount the podium to the right and the left, respectively, of the champion. The national anthem of the champion is then played, while the national flags of the winners are raised (in the same positions, right to left, as the winners on the podium). The medal bearers, athletes and officials, in that order, then walk out. The victory ceremony is to be carried out with due solemnity, with the participants marching in and out to music; at some competitions a similar ceremony is carried out for the winners of the team competition.

There is also a Closing Ceremony at the conclusion of the World Championships during which the flag bearers of the participating teams mount the stage and form a semi-circle. The President of the organizing federation then makes a speech, the IWF President replies and declares the championships closed. The national flag of the organizing federation and IWF are lowered, while the anthem of the organizing federation is played. The IWF flag is brought to the IWF President. The guests of honor leave the stage and then the flag bearers march out.

Doping Control

Doping control, or drug testing, is recognized by all governing bodies of amateur sport as the key to maintaining a positive image for sport and assuring that all athletes compete on a level playing field (i.e., guaranteeing that no competitor has an unfair advantage due to the use of performance enhancing drugs). With regard to the sport of weightlifting, the IOC, IWF, USOC and USAW may all conduct drug testing both in and out-of-competitions. Doping controls are always part of major international weightlifting competitions, and virtually all national championships (i.e., Senior, Junior, American and Collegiate) and other designated competitions. Before each event the governing body decides the extent of testing (e.g., the frequency and timing). Competitors can be tested more than once in a given testing period. A seriously injured athlete may be excused under certain conditions.

Since several organizations can carry out the testing and each is continually improving upon their techniques, no precise description of every aspect of the testing can be given in this text. However, there are some shared characteristics of virtually all testing procedures, and these will be outlined in this discussion.

Doping control is always performed by urinalysis. Specially appointed doping control personnel generally obtain the urine samples and assure their safe transport to the laboratory. A variety of doping and other officials may be present during the sample taking. The athlete is always permitted to be accompanied by a representative of some kind. Women take samples from women and the same is generally true for the men. It is often required that the athlete be nude while producing the sample, or at least disrobed enough to permit the doping control representative to observe that the sample is being properly produced (e.g., it is the athlete's own urine and the athlete is not adding anything to it). The athlete chooses a container and produces 100 ml of urine of the proper concentration and pII value to be of use for testing (if the first sample is inadequate, additional samples are taken, until a satisfactory one is produced). The athlete then divides the urine between two identical bottles (after selecting those bottles). These bottles will serve as sample A and B (the need for two bottles will be explained shortly). The doping controller then seals the bottles, and they are transported in a refrigerated state to the testing laboratory.

Athletes are informed in writing, sometimes on the entry and sometimes via a letter or form, of the requirement that they be tested. At a competition there are generally escorts who accompany an athlete immediately after the competition to an area provided for doping control. In international and national competitions there is a provision for athletes to attend a press conference prior to reporting for testing. In the United States the athlete is permitted to attend the press conference for 60 minutes before reporting to the testing area. Analysis of the sample is carried out in a laboratory approved by the organization that is conducting the testing. When the IWF is doing the testing, it may allow some or all of the samples taken to be tested at a laboratory in the host country.

Results are communicated during the event if they are available at that time. Once a positive test occurs on an A sample, the athlete or the athlete's federation is generally given an opportunity to protest and thereby to have the B sample tested with a representative of the athlete present (often the analysis of the B sample is automatic). Only after the B sample has been determined to be positive are the results announced. The competitor is then disqualified from the competition, and a sanction is imposed on the athlete. Such sanctions generally range from a suspension of several months to two years for the first offense and from two years to lifetime for the second offense.

The governing bodies take the issue of drugs in sport very seriously. Therefore, when there are patterns of abuse in a given sport, the IOC reserves the right to implement sanctions against the entire sport. Similarly, when a number of athletes from a particular nation are found to be positive on their drug tests, the IWF may take action against the entire national federation. For example, the IWF may fine or suspend any national federation which has three or more athletes who test positive for any banned substance in one year.

The actual list of banned substances has grown over time; several hundred are listed by the IOC today (and many more substances in the same classes of drugs are being banned, even if they are not specifically listed). This list is frequently updated. The major classes of banned substances are: central nervous system stimulants, anabolic steroids (which includes the natural hormone testosterone), narcotics, beta blockers and diuretics. While these may appear to be fairly "heavy" drugs, some relatively innocuous ones appear on the list, including many over the counter medications like cold remedies and even some

health foods (e.g., certain herbs). To be safe, athletes should not take any drug or unusual food supplement of any kind several weeks to several months before testing, unless they have consulted with the organization conducting the test to be sure whatever substance they are taking is not banned. Claims of ignorance after the fact are viewed dimly and rarely result in any reduction in the penalty and never in the restoration of an award.

The USOC maintains a toll free "hotline" to answer any questions you might have about the legality of a particular substance and/or how long it might take for such a substance to clear your system. The current number is (800) 233-0393. Be sure to have a description of the ingredients in the substance in question available when you call. The USOC also publishes a helpful booklet. Drug Free, which provides a considerable amount of information about the USOC's drug testing program.

The USAW has a special out-of-competition drug testing program which requires that the top ranked athletes in the United States be subject to drug testing with no advance notice (those who wish to compete internationally must apply to be part of this drug testing program at least 6 months prior to the competition in which the athlete intends to qualify for an international competition) The athletes in this program are simply summoned to be tested, or are approached by a testing crew and asked to submit a sample immediately. The purpose of the program is to assure that athletes do not take banned substances (such as anabolic steroids)while in training and then stop taking them some time prior to a competition in order to "clean up" for any competition testing.

Gender Testing

Gender testing is required for women before they can compete in any international event. Once a women has passed a gender test, the results are centrally registered by the IWF and a gender card is issued to the athlete. Thereafter, the athlete need not submit to gender testing again; she can merely present her gender card as proof of eligibility for the competition.

The Procedures for Creating World and Other Categories of Records

The IWF recognizes two kinds of world records for men: Junior and Absolute (which may also be set by Juniors) in each of the weight classes. Similar categories of records are also maintained on the national level (they are called American Records). Records in all of the aforementioned categories are recognized individually in the snatch, clean and jerk and the total. World Records (WR) are ratified by the IWF when they are set at World Championships, international competitions and national championships that are included on the IWF Calendar of Events for a given year (providing doping control under the guidance of the IWF is carried out and the athlete making the record is tested). Three international referees must adjudicate WRs in the same way as they do international competitions. To be registered, a record must exceed the previous record in any individual lift by at least 500 g and in the total by 2.5 kg. (fractions of 500 g on the individual lifts are rounded down to the next 500 g, and fractions of 2.5 kg. on the total are rounded down to the next 2.5 kg.). The weight of the bar on which the record is to be made must be verified prior to the competition. After the record is set, a written report (i.e., record form) must be signed by the referees, affirming on their honor: the validity of the lift, the name of the athlete, the athlete's body weight, the weight of the bar, the type of lift (e.g., snatch), the place the record was set, the date and name of the competition and, for Junior records, the athlete's year of birth. The report must sent to the IWF General Secretary for registration and verification.

Records set during the competition that are not in increments of 2.5 kg. are credited for purposes of the athlete's placing in the competition at the nearest lower 2.5 kg.. Only competitors entered in the competition may attempt records outside the competition (additional athletes cannot be brought into the competition only to break records). As soon as any new record is established on an individual lift, a lifter who wishes to break the record must do so by at least 500 g (2.5 kg. for a total record). A lighter competitor cannot claim a record by equaling a record previously established, even if it was established in the same competition. At the Olympic Games or Continental Games, Olympic or Continental Records (i.e., records for that competition) in both individual lifts and the total can only be attempted in 2.5 kg. increments. World Records (Continental or Regional records) on the individual lifts can be attempted at the Olympics in increments of 500 g (with the athlete getting credit for the next lower 2.5 kg. increment in the scoring of the competition). In establishing and ratifying records at any competition, the principle involved is that only records of that competition or higher may be set and ratified with less than 2.5 kg. increments. (For example, at a National Championships, a 500 g increment could be requested in order to break a national record, but such an increment would not be permitted for a lifter trying to break a state record of his or her own state.)

For United States records, all referees must be at least National Level referees (except that one referee may be a referee undergoing testing to become a National Referee).

Qualifying to Lift in Various Competitions (or "How Can I Get To The Olympics?")

Because weightlifting is a measurement sport (i.e., performance is measured by objective means), the procedures for qualifying to lift in various events are quite straightforward. For example, for competitions up to the national level conducted by the USAW, there are qualifying totals (minimum totals that lifters in each weight class must achieve in order to qualify). Typically, a qualifying total must have been made within a year of the event in question and no later than approximately one month before the event in question (a performance made in that same event the prior year is generally counted). In addition, all totals must have been made in events sanctioned by the USAW. The totals do not change much from year to year and are always announced at least two or three months prior to the event (often much earlier).

To compete in a USAW sanctioned event, an athlete must be a USAW member. To enter a particular competition, the athlete must request an entry blank from the meet organizer. He or she then completes the entry, signs it (in the case of a minor, the signature of a parent or guardian is required) and sends the entry, along with the required fee, to the meet director. Although some meet directors accept entries on the day of the competition, most have a cutoff date that is anywhere from one to three weeks before the event and for national events the cutoff as approximately one month before the event; be sure to mail your entry in plenty of time. It is always a good idea to send the entry certified or registered mail with a return receipt so that you will have proof that the entry was received.

To qualify for international events, an athlete must be selected by the Board Of Directors of the USAW (or its designee). The qualifying total must be made in a competition which has drug testing (in a given year, the specific competitions to be used for selection purposes are generally announced in the official publication of the USAW—Weightlifting USA). In addition, it is generally required that an athlete has been participating in the USAW's out-of-competition drug testing program for at least six months prior to the date on which the qualifying total was performed.

For many years there were no established standards for selecting athletes to represent the United States in international competitions like the World Championships or Olympic Games (or, if there were, the athletes were never told about the standards in advance). The athletes were simply told that a "tryout" would be held on a given day. The athletes then did their best to impress the selection committee on that day. The selection group, after viewing the event, would sit down together to pick the team. Often standards were established as the selection meeting progressed. One member of the committee might say, "athlete A should go because he is younger and has greater long term potential for our country than athlete B." Then another selector might counter, "athlete B should go because he is older and this may be his last chance to represent the United States, while athlete A will have his chance again next year." Still another selector might say, "athlete C should go because although he has not performed well today, he has a history of having done well in the past." Finally, another selector might say, "I do not feel sure who we should select, why not have another tryout?" Needless to say, such discussions made for very long selection meetings. Far worse, they led to frustration and bitterness on the part of the athletes, who never knew what the selectors might be looking for on a given day.

Today, after many long battles to make selection standards more objective, the situation is far better. The USAW now generally selects athletes for international competitions in an exemplary manner, one that other sports would do well to emulate. Minimum qualifying standards are normally announced months in advance. Contingency plans for what will happen if too few lifters qualify are also announced. There is often more than one tryout, so if a particular athlete who is superior happens to be injured or otherwise indisposed on the day of a tryout, he or she may be given another chance (but all lifters know on what basis this will be done). Are the current methods perfect? No. Do the selection people occasionally modify standards for unusual circumstances? Yes. But the pre-announced standards tend to be more objective and all-encompassing with each passing year.

Summary

As can be seen from this discussion, the rules of weightlifting can seem fairly complex at times. Nevertheless, those rules, which have arisen through many years of trial and error, are designed to make the sport as fair as possible. Do not be intimidated by the rules, but do not ignore them either. Championships have been tragically lost by athletes and/or coaches who were ignorant of the rules. Get to know the rules, and they will become just one more tool to assure weightlifting success. As a first step in that process, become a member of the USAW. As a member, you will be able to participate in the USAW's activities such as rules and coaching clinics. You will also receive Weightlifting USA, the official publication of the USAW, which will keep you informed regarding current rules, USAW policies and procedures. So join today by calling (719) 578-4508.

A Short Course In Anatomy, Physiology, Mechanics And Biomechanics

It is not necessary to be an expert in anatomy, physiology, mechanics or biomechanics in order to be a weightlifting champion or a successful coach. If you have read the rest of this book, you have learned a great many scientific principles which apply to the sport of weightlifting without delving very far into their formal underpinnings in the more general sciences of anatomy, physiology, mechanics and biomechanics. I have known many successful athletes and coaches who had no formal or informal training in any of these general sciences, although all are quite familiar with many of the weightlifting-specific scientific principles that were presented earlier in this book and have at least an intuitive grasp of the more fundamental areas of sport science. No doubt you can be equally successful without further pursuit of subjects like physiology and biomechanics.

However, athletes and coaches who have achieved outstanding performance without such knowledge have been successful despite a lack of training in these areas, not because of it. It is difficult to fully understand some of the most basic principles of weightlifting training and technique without a grasp of the scientific bases of sports performance, at least those which pertain most directly to weightlifting. Therefore, in order for an athlete to live up to his or her potential, he or she should know some of the key concepts in these areas. Such knowledge is even more essential for the coach and/or the athlete who is self-coached. Space constraints, the essential purpose of this book and the availability of books which cover sports science thoroughly make it inappropriate to address more than the basics here. Those interested in further developing their understanding of sports science and their analytical skills with respect to weightlifting may wish to go well beyond what is presented in this section. The Bibliography of this book offers suggested readings for those who do wish to build

further on the foundation that this section provides.

The Interrelationship Of Anatomy, Physiology And Biomechanics

Weightlifting is primarily concerned with imparting force to a projectile called a bar (although receiving force from and sustaining force against a bar are also of great importance). Those who perform and analyze weightlifting are of course interested in how the application of force can be accomplished most effectively. The effective application of force to a bar (or anything else) is influenced by a number of factors, and many of these factors fall within the realm of different branches of the sport sciences.

For instance, general principles relating to the motion of a projectile, the application of force and the use of energy fall within the purview of mechanics, a subdivision of the science of physics. Biomechanics applies the principles of mechanics to the specifics of human movement. Anatomy tells us about the structure of the body, including the nature of the tools (e.g., levers) that the human body gives us for producing and moderating the effects of forces. Muscle physiology tells us how our muscles function in order to move the levers of our body (the bones) and produce force. We will examine each of these subjects separately in some detail.

In some cases the discussions of different disciplines will overlap. For example, in examining the bases of muscular contraction (an area of physiology), it is necessary to understand the ultrastructure of muscle tissue (an area of anatomy). Therefore, an aspect of anatomy will be discussed in the physiology section.

This point should serve to remind the reader that all of aforementioned disciplines, as they pertain to sport, are highly interrelated. In fact, a branch of scientific study called kinesiology has evolved as a result of the need to integrate biomechanics, musculoskeletal anatomy and neuromuscular physiology in order to understand the movement of the body. Therefore, you should always be mindful that what you learn in one part of this section of the book needs to be integrated with what you learn in another. Perhaps more importantly, what you learn in this section of this book needs to be integrated with what you learn in the others if its value is to be maximized in terms of weightlifting performance.

Physiology

Human physiology is a vast subject. Today we understand so much about the way that our bodies function that a person who spent his or her entire life studying physiology could probably not learn it all, and yet there is still a great deal that we do not know. In the discussion that follows, the focus will be on muscle physiology, the aspect of physiology that impacts most strongly on weightlifting. It is assumed that the reader has some basic knowledge of other areas of human physiology. If you do not, the Bibliography lists some resources for further study in this area.

Muscle Action as the Basis for Human Movement

Virtually all internally generated human movement is caused by what are conventionally referred to as muscular contractions. A number of researchers have recently argued that the term "action" is preferable to "contraction" because while a contraction implies a shortening, the term contraction is used to describe muscles that are shortening (concentric contraction), lengthening (eccentric contraction) or remaining the same length (isometric contraction). Physical movements of the kind used in sport are caused by the contraction of a specific kind of muscle, called skeletal or striated muscle (as compared with the cardiac muscle which powers the heart and the "smooth" muscles that support certain internal organs and functions of the body).

The Structure and Action of Skeletal Muscle

What we commonly refer to as a "muscle" is really a complex unit of contractile tissue that is surrounded by a connective tissue called the epimysium or fascia. Within the fascia are bundles of muscle cells called fasciculi, each of which is covered by a connective tissue sheath called a perimysium. Within the fasciculi are typically 100 to 150 muscle cells or fibers. Within those muscle fibers are bundles of units called myofibrils, which

run the length of the muscle fiber. Inside the myofibrils themselves, arranged in series (lengthwise, end to end), are entities called sacromeres. A sacromere is the smallest functional unit within a muscle (i.e., the smallest entity that

Figure 50

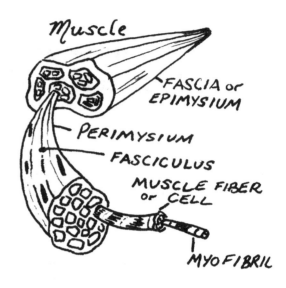

can contract).Fig. 50 depicts the progressively smaller components of the muscle.

While the mechanism of contraction is not fully understood, a rather well developed explanation of how muscles contract has emerged. Called the "sliding filament theory," it has undergone considerable amplification and clarification since it was first advanced by Huxley several decades ago.

Sliding filament theory can be explained as follows. Within a sacromere are "strings" of protein called filaments, which come in two varieties, thick and thin. The thick filaments are made primarily of a protein called myosin, and the thin filaments are made primarily of a protein called actin. These actin and myosin filaments run lengthwise in the sacromere, parallel to one another. Myosin filaments are typically two to three times the thickness of actin filaments, but the actin filaments outnumber the myosin filaments by a ratio of two to one. Fig. 51 depicts a cross section of the sacromere that highlights the arrangement of actin and myosin fibers.

Hundreds of myosin molecules make up each myosin filament. Each myosin molecule is made up of two identical sub-units, each shaped somewhat like a golf club and arranged with the "shafts" of these golf club shaped units intertwined. Within a myosin filament, these molecules are arranged with the shaft portions parallel to one another but staggered lengthwise, so that the heads of different molecules are nearer or further from the center than the heads of other molecules.

482

Fig. 51

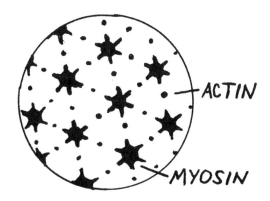

The molecules are further arranged such that half face one direction and the other half face the opposite direction. The result is that the club-head-shaped portions of these molecules are at either end of the filament and the shafts shaped ends meet in the center of the filament. Therefore, the center portion of the myosin filament appears thinner and contains less protein than either end of it (see Fig. 52).

The club-head-shaped portions of the filament are referred to as its "cross-bridges." On each cross-bridge there is a site at which it can bind to a corresponding site on an actin molecule and another site called the myosin ATPase site. This latter site is capable of binding with the chemical ATP (which is the only direct source of energy for muscular contraction) and breaking it down into adenosine diphosphate (ADP) and inorganic phosphate (Pi), yielding the energy which is utilized by the myosin cross-bridges during the actions that they perform during contraction .

Actin molecules are essentially spherical, each with a site at which it can bind with a myosin

Figure 52

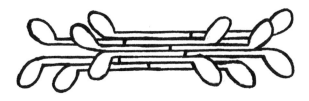

molecule. (At rest these sites are prevented from coming in contact with the binding sites on the myosin cross-bridges by proteins called tropomyosin and troponin.) The actin molecules are arranged like two strings of "pearls" twisted together to form an actin myofilament (Figure 53). These myofilaments attach at either end of the sacromere to a structure called the "Z-line," a connective tissue which separates myofibrils from one another at their ends (really a disc-like structure), so that the Z-lines connect (without direct contact) the ends of actin filaments of adjoining sacromeres and help to maintain their orderly arrangement.

Figure 53

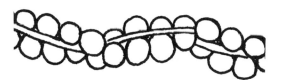

When viewed from the side, sacromeres appear to organize themselves into several segments or "bands." The schematic diagram in Figure 54 depicts in conceptual, if not visually accurate, terms the arrangement of these bands.

Within each sacromere in a relaxed state (schematic (a) of Figure 54), there is a significant gap between actin myofilaments (called the H-zone or H-band). The H-band contains the central, non-cross-bridge portion of the myosin filament and may contain some of the cross-bridges at either end of the myosin filament. The areas called the I-bands contain only actin filaments. The areas called A-bands contain the entire length of the myosin filament and the portion of the actin filament that overlaps either end of the myosin filament. In the center of the A-band is an area referred to as the M-line, which is believed to serve the function of holding the thick myosin filaments together in a vertical stack (much as the Z-lines help to maintain the order of sacromeres) ;like the Z-line, the M-line is really three dimensional in nature.

During contraction the binding sites on the cross-bridges of the myosin filaments make contact with the binding sites of actin filaments. This releases the energy stored during the breakdown of ATP, causing the cross-bridges to perform a swiveling or stroking action toward the center of the sacromere, pulling the actin filaments closer to the center of the sacromere (schematic (b) of Figure 59). At the same time ADP and Pi are rapidly released by the myosin filament. This frees the ATPase site so that it can attach to another ATP molecule (which occurs at the end of the stroking motion). The new ATP molecule is split by myosin ATPase, creating energy for the myosin cross-bridge to "stroke" once again. The attachment of ATP to the myosin site occurs before the cross-bridge link between myosin and actin is broken.

After each successive stroke (a process which results from "reloading" or "recharging" the cross-bridge with an ATP molecule), the cross-bridge returns to its original position, where it contacts another site closer to the end of the actin filament. In order for a complete shortening of the sacromere to take place, this process of attachment, stroking, detachment and repositioning of the cross-bridges must take place repeated times. In many cases, , relaxation (a chemical reaction which covers the actin binding sites with the two proteins that interfered with actin/myosin connecting before the contraction) occurs before maximal shortening is achieved.

Figure 54

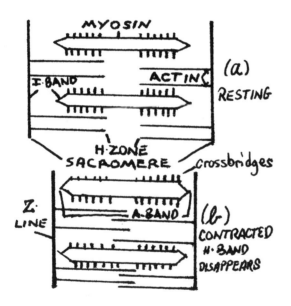

The attachment and detachment process takes place in an asynchronous fashion (i.e., with different cross-bridges in the same filament attaching at different times) so that there is a continual shortening of the overall sacromere. (If all cross-bridges went through the same part of this cycle at the same time, the actin filaments would

slide back to their original position during the period of no contact between the actin and myosin filaments.) It should be noted that the result of this asynchronous action within the sacromere is a smooth contraction of the whole sacromere.

As a result of the contraction or sliding filament process, the H-band becomes much narrower and may even disappear as the actin filaments are brought closer to one another. In addition, the width of the I-band at either end of the sacromere decreases. Neither the actin nor the myosin filaments themselves changes in length during contraction. Therefore, the width of the A-band (which is equal to the length of the myosin filament) remains the same throughout the contraction.

Contractile machinery comprises approximately 80% of muscle-fiber volume. The balance of the fiber volume is comprised of tissue that supplies energy to the muscle or is involved with the neural stimulation of the muscle.

The Neural Basis for Muscular Action

Contractions of skeletal muscles are caused by impulses or "action potentials" that are delivered to the junctions between specific kinds of nerves (called alpha motor neurons) and muscles. Because the process of muscle contraction involves the combination of neural and muscular activity, it is often described as neuromuscular in nature.

An alpha motor neuron consists of a cell body (or "soma") with numerous short projections called dendrites. The dendrites carry impulses to the cell body. Extending from one side of the neuron is a long projection called an "axon", which connects the alpha motor neuron to the muscle fibers that it innervates. The axon is almost fully covered with a white, fatty substance called myelin. Myelin insulates axons from other axons and dendrites in the same nerve. Small gaps in the myelin covering are called the "nodes of Ranvier." These breaks speed transmission of impulses along the axon as the impulses are actually able to "jump" from one node of Ranvier to another.

As the axon nears the muscle, it loses its myelin sheath and divides into many terminal branches. Each branch, or terminal, enlarges into a knoblike structure called a terminal button. That button fits into a small depression in the muscle fiber called the motor end plate), which delivers the contractile impulse to the muscle fiber itself. Figure 55 depicts an alpha motor neuron.

Figure 55

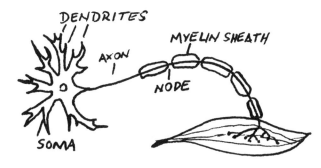

The speed with which the impulse travels along an axon is influenced by two primary factors: whether or not the axon is covered by myelin and the size (diameter) of the axon. Alpha motor neurons, which are large, myelinated (meduallated), neurons, can carry nerve impulses as fast as 120 meters per second. (Non-myelinated neurons that are very small carry nervous impulses at a speeds as slow—relatively speaking—as .5 meter per second.) There are no significant differences in speed related to gender, and these speeds remain relatively stable between the ages of twenty and forty, after which the speed begins to decline gradually.

One alpha motor neuron may control as few as several and as many as a thousand or more muscle fibers. However, each muscle fiber is innervated by no more than one neuron. The fibers controlled by a given motor neuron are distributed throughout the muscle.

All of the fibers stimulated by the same neuron tend to be similar in their physical, biochemical and ultrastructural characteristics, i.e., they are of the same muscle fiber "type." (An explanation of muscle fiber types and their properties will be presented later in this section.) This suggests that innervation has an influence on the properties of muscles (indeed some experimental evidence exists to support this notion).

A neuron and the muscle fibers that it innervates are referred as motor unit, the smallest contractile unit that is under neural control. Motor units vary in the frequency with which they can generate impulses (i.e., in their "firing rates"). The motor units of small muscles reportedly fire at rates between nine and fifty pulses per second, while the motor units of larger muscles have a narrower range (from thirteen to thirty pulses per second).

An accepted principle of muscle action is that either all or no fibers within a motor unit contract. This is referred to as the "all or none" principle. While the all or none concept is generally true, some researchers have argued that under certain conditions an impulse delivered by given neuron

may not activate all of the muscles it innervates. (A stimulus may not be of sufficient strength to activate some of the least irritable fibers in a motor unit because certain fibers may be compromised in their functioning by such factors as fatigue or limited circulation.)

Within a muscle, motor units vary widely in their maximum performance-potential and specific tension (the tension per unit of cross-sectional area that a muscle can develop).

When a muscle generates a sustained contraction of moderate or less than moderate effort, it avoids becoming fatigued by two forms of asynchronous recruitment of motor units (i.e., recruitment at different times). First, units that innervate the same types of muscle fibers will be recruited at different times, so that some are resting while others are working (this process is not possible at higher loads because more units are activated to contract simultaneously under the higher load). A second form of asynchronous recruitment of motor units occurs when fibers that are more fatigue-resistant are recruited before fibers that fatigue rapidly. It has been observed that during sustained voluntary contractions there is a dropout of active motor units and a recruitment of fresh fibers with similar but slightly greater thresholds of activation.

There is evidence that fatigue during fast and powerful activities may occur first at the neuromuscular junction. When neuromuscular fatigue occurs, the motor neurons cannot manufacture acetylcholine (a chemical which effectively transmits neural stimulation to the muscle) fast enough to maintain chemical transmission of action potential from the motor neurons to the muscles.

There is also a phenomenon referred to as central or psychological fatigue which occurs when the central nervous system (CNS) can no longer activate motor neurons. Fatigue, discomfort, boredom or lack of sleep may bring on CNS failure. The individual and combined influences of these mechanisms are not well understood.

The Chemical Basis for Muscle Action

While the preceding discussion of the neural basis for the stimulation of muscle contraction emphasized the "electrical" nature of that process (e.g., by discussing the effect of nerve impulses that are electrical in nature), chemical processes within nerves and muscles form the basis for the generation and transmission of electrical impulses. Therefore, it is now appropriate to discuss some key chemical processes that lead to muscle contraction. It should be noted that while the discussion focuses on activity within the muscle, similar processes occur within the nerve to maintain the neural activity there.

485

All living cells have the capacity to maintain the charged ions of different chemicals in a separate and electrically unbalanced state (ions are atoms that have greater or fewer electrons than electrically balanced atoms). In the case of muscle cells in their resting state, sodium ions ($Na+$) in the fluid outside the cell exist at a much higher level than on the inside (the opposite is true for potassium ions - $K+$). Overall, the outside of the cell is positively charged relative to the inside. This state of electrical imbalance is maintained in part by the permeability (or lack thereof) of the cell membrane (a covering that exists in some form around all types of cells) to $Na+$ and $K+$ ions and is referred to as a "membrane potential."

As mentioned earlier, neurons and muscle cells meet at a point called the neuromuscular junction. There is a small space between the axon ending and the motor end plate at that junction, but it is too large for a direct transfer of the electrical impulse in the nerve to the end plate. Therefore, a chemical transmitter called acetylcholine (ACh) is required to accomplish transmission. When the terminal ending of the axon is simulated by a nerve impulse, it releases ACh into the gap between it and the motor end plate of the muscle, effecting transmission of the nerve impulse to the muscle. The mechanism of that transmission process is described below.

The release of ACh into what is referred to as the "synaptic space" between the motor neuron and special receptor sites on an area called the motor end plate of the muscle cell membrane triggers a change in the ion permeability of the muscle cell membrane. Sodium flows into the muscle cell and potassium flows out, the latter slightly later and more slowly (the amount and duration of this process, known as depolarization of the motor end plate, is determined by the amount of ACh released). As a result of this ion exchange, the inside of the cell becomes positively charged for a short time and the exterior becomes negatively charged, generating a small electrical current called an action potential. When depolarization occurs at the motor end plate, local current flow occurs between the depolarized end plate and the adjacent resting cell membrane in both directions. (The neuromuscular junction is generally located in the center of a muscle fiber, so impulses must travel outward from it in order to reach the entire fiber.) The action potential that is thereby transmitted throughout the fiber causes it to contract.

A contraction that is the result of a single nerve impulse is referred to as a "twitch." Single twitches of a muscle fiber are too short and weak to be of any practical use, and they do not normally occur. Functional tension is generated by multiple twitches in the same muscle fiber and contraction by multiple muscle fibers.

An action potential lasts only one to two msecs (msecs), and it is not until approximately three msecs later that muscle contraction commences. That time interval is known as the latent period (during this latency period, the muscle is unable to respond to another contraction stimuli). It takes approximately fifty msec (from the time that a muscle commences its contraction) for the muscle to reach its maximum tension (this contraction time varies considerably with muscle-fiber type). It takes a slightly longer period for the muscle to relax, so that the overall time of contraction and relaxation is approximately 100 msecs.

It should be noted that the chemical ACh plays another key role in muscle contraction. When ACh is released into the muscle, it causes a chemical reaction that alters the two proteins that, at rest, cover the binding sites on the actin filament (points at which the myosin cross-bridges can attach). The cross-bridges then make contact (there is some debate within the scientific community over whether this contact is direct or is mediated in some way).

The entire process that links excitation to contraction is referred to as the excitation-contraction coupling process.

Muscle Fiber Types

All muscle fibers are not the same. At least seven different types of muscle fibers have been identified, and some researchers believe there may be even more. In humans, only three muscle fiber types have been detected in significant quantities: Type I (also known as slow twitch, slow-oxidative or red fibers); Type II A (also known as fast twitch, fast oxidative or white fibers); and Type IIB (a second variety of white or fast twitch fiber often referred to as a fast-glycolytic fiber). The differences between Type IIB fibers and Type I fibers are more significant than those between Type II A and Type I fibers.

Fast twitch (FT) fibers are better suited for anaerobic activity than slow twitch (ST). Relative to ST fibers, FT have a higher myosin ATPase activity rate (which results in a faster rate of energy release in the muscle). FT fibers shorten and relax more quickly than ST fibers, which enables the former to deliver more power than ST fibers with the same cross-sectional area. FT fibers also have a lesser degree of capillarization than ST fibers (which causes their paler or "white" color relative to ST fibers). FT fibers are larger in diameter than ST fibers because of the greater presence of actin and myosin in the FT fibers. ST fibers have more intramuscular triglyceride stores (a source of energy);more myoglobin (a substance which facilitates the use of oxygen to create energy—subject discussed in some detail later in this appendix—and gives these muscle fibers their red color); more aerobic enzyme activity; greater capillary density; and greater mitochondrial density than FT fibers. (Mitochondria are responsible for manufacturing approximately 95% of the ATP that exists in muscle tissue.) The characteristics of FT fibers make them highly sensitive to fatigue, so they are best suited for generating a large force over a short duration. Type II A fibers have good aerobic and anaerobic qualities, but Type II B are good anerobically and poor aerobically.

Fast oxidative (Type II A) fibers have high ATPase activity like fast-glycolytic fibers, but a high oxidative capacity like slow oxidative fibers. They can maintain a contraction longer than fast glycolytic fibers and contract faster than slow oxidative fibers. ST fibers have capacity for long-term, low-intensity work ,so they are better suited for aerobic activities.

Motor units appear to have homogeneous fiber types, but muscle fibers from different motor units are mixed within muscles. FT fibers have significantly larger neurons than ST fibers, so they are activated with more difficulty and only after ST fibers have been activated, but the speed with which nerve impulses move down their motor neurons is greater. FT fibers are typically brought into play either by the effort to move a heavy load or the need to move an object faster than is possible through the use of ST fibers alone. There is a positive correlation between a muscle's recruitment threshold (the point at which it is activated to contract) and its twitch tension (the degree of tension that it develops with a single twitch).

It should be noted that the speed with which muscle fibers contract varies. The average contraction time (time from the onset of a contraction to the point at which maximum tension in achieved) of a skeletal muscle is approximately fifty msecs, but there is more than a threefold difference between the contraction time of the fastest and slowest muscle fibers. Therefore, while an FT fiber may be activated later than a ST fiber, the former may complete its contraction at the same time as a slower fiber because of the differences in contraction speed.

Although the general order of muscle fiber recruitment is influenced by fiber type, the order of recruitment of particular fibers within fiber types is influenced by the nature of the motion that is undertaken. In fact, fiber-recruitment order appears to be fixed for a particular movement. For example, the recruitment order of particular muscle fibers in the hamstring muscles may be different for a leg curl than for a leg press, even if the tension developed in performing both exercises is identical.

Most muscles combine all three types of fibers, the percentage of each being correlated with the type of activity for which the muscle is specialized. For example, a higher proportion of slow oxidative fibers are found in the back and legs (which often contract at low intensity for long periods in resisting gravity). In contrast, fast glycolytic fibers dominate in the arm muscles. The distribution of FT and ST fibers varies among individuals as well as muscles, with most people having a fifty-fifty split. However, there can be very significant differences in the distribution of muscles types, presumably making some individuals better suited to certain activities.

Factors Influencing the Force Produced by Muscles

Despite the "all or none" principle of motor units, graduations in the force (i.e., tension) generated by motor units can be achieved by differences in the rate at which nerve impulses are generated by the neurons in those motor units (their "rate of firing"). Single twitches of muscle fibers occurring in rapid succession lead to stronger levels of contraction until fatigue begins to occur. This phenomenon of successive single twitches resulting in stronger contractions is referred to a "treppe."

The frequency of firing can also affect the tension generated by a muscle because of differences in the speeds of neuronal firing and muscle contraction. Specifically, an action potential and the latency (rest) period that must occur before another action potential can be generated is far shorter than the period of muscle contraction and relaxation (a few msecs for the former and more than 100 msecs for the latter). Therefore, as soon as a few msecs after a muscle is stimulated by a neuron to contract (i.e., well before the point of full or peak contraction from that impulse has even been reached), a new impulse may stimulate the muscle to contract again. As long as the new impulse arrives soon enough, it will stimulate the muscle fiber to contract before it has fully lost the tension generated during its previous twitch. This causes the muscle to achieve a higher level of tension than it did as a result of the first twitch.

The increasing tension that results from the muscle's receiving a stimulation to contract before relaxation has occurred is called summation. Summation continues as long as impulses of sufficient frequency are received by the fiber, until the fiber reaches its maximum level of tension, a state called tetanus (this normal state of maximum tension should be distinguished from the pathologic state of tetanic contraction that can result from a tetanus infection). It has been reported that the forces developed in muscle fibers as a result of summation are as much as four times greater than the forces that can be generated by single twitches. (The phenomenon of summation can occur in an entire muscles as well as in single fibers if stimulation is sufficient to make all muscle fibers achieve tetanus simultaneously.)

Within the ultrastructure of the muscle, tension increases when the thin actin filaments within the sacromere are brought closer together as a result of greater cross bridge cycling. With tetanus the maximum number of cross-bridge binding sites remain uncovered so cross-bridge attachment and, consequently, tension development, are at their peak.

The force developed isometrically by muscle fibers appears to be relatively independent of the fiber type but closely related to the cross-sectional area of the muscle fiber. However, since slower fibers tend to have smaller diameters, they tend to exert lower levels of force. Moreover, since ST fibers have slower speeds of contraction (ST fibers require 90 msecs to 140 msecs to contract, while FT require only 40 msecs to 90 msecs), their power output tends to be lower even if they can exert force equal to that of a given FT fiber.

The physiological cross-section of a muscle can be estimated by dividing the a muscle's volume by its fiber length. Overall muscle size varies with the size of the individual muscle fibers within it and, to a lesser degree, by the genetically determined number of those fibers.

In addition to the differences in force that muscle fibers generate as consequence of their size and the rate at which neurons stimulate them, graduations in force are achieved by differences in the number of units that are stimulated to contract at any given time. The more units that are stimulated to contract, the greater is the force that is developed. Normally the impulses that stimulate different motor units are not simultaneous (asynchronous). When a rapid and maximum effort is required, the impulses that travel to many or even all motor units may occur simultaneously. Finally, additional muscles may be brought into play to supply extra force under extreme conditions.

The firing rate of each motor unit increases gradually as effort increases while the recruitment of more units represents a greater change. Consequently, the rate of firing is probably utilized for more precise changes in force and the number of units recruited is more suited to extreme changes in force.

Even a relaxed muscle has some tension, or tonus, which is due to a baseline level of neural activity. Muscles used more often tend to have more tonus. Muscles used while held in shortened position develop tonus in that position (as do the muscles that oppose the action of those muscles).

All Muscles Have an Optimal Length for Generating Force

Apart from neuronal influences, the force with which a muscle fiber can contract is influenced by the length of the muscle fiber at the onset of the contraction. Each muscle fiber has an optimal length at which maximum force can be achieved (though that force may not be fully reflected externally, due to mechanical constraints). This optimal length occurs at the point at which there is maximum cross-bridge formation. When the muscle length is greater, the actin filaments cannot make contact with as many sites as when the muscle is at its optimal length. (At 70% more than the optimal length—which can only be achieved in a laboratory—there is no overlap of the myosin filaments by the actin filaments.)

When the muscle is at a shorter than optimal length less tension can be developed for several reasons. First, the chemical processes taking place within the muscle are so altered that fewer actin sites are uncovered (the reasons are unknown). Second, thin filaments from opposite ends of the sacromere overlap one another, reducing the number of actin sites exposed to the cross-bridges. Third, the myosin filaments touch the Z-lines, impeding further shortening. The most extreme forms of these reactions to muscle shortening occur only in a laboratory setting.

Under normal circumstances the optimal length of a muscle is its relaxed length. Moreover, under normal conditions, a muscle cannot achieve more than a 30% shortening or lengthening beyond its normal length (and these are the outside limits). At such extreme points, the ability of the muscle to contract is lessened by about 50%.

Activity within the ultrastructure of muscle tissue appears to have an effect on the muscle's resistance to injury as well as the work it can perform. It has been determined experimentally that the amount of energy that can be absorbed by a muscle before failure is greater when a muscle is active than when it is inactive.

It should be noted that in practice differences in the mechanical resistance offered due to the position and nature of the body levers involved (i.e., bones and soft tissues being moved by the muscle's action) are more influential in determining the force generated externally (the "strength curve") for that part of the joint motion than changes in the lengths of the muscles that are acting. The resistance offered agonist muscles (muscles that cause a lever to move) by antagonistic muscles (muscles that can pull the lever in the opposite direction) can have an important influence on the practical expression of strength as well. Consequently, a decrease in the resistance encountered by the muscles, a change that occurs as the as a joint angle increases, generally outweighs the decrease in the ability of the muscle to generate tension, with the result that the ability of the muscles to express its force externally increases. An example would be in the extension of the arm. More weight can be lifted at the end of the extension than at the beginning, even though the triceps muscles that are responsible for the motion are at a relatively weak point when the arm is nearly extended.

The Force-Velocity Curve

The maximum velocity of a muscle's contraction occurs when there is no resistance (i.e., when velocity is constrained essentially by the maximum rate at which cross-bridges can be formed and broken). The maximum speed of contraction appears to be unaffected by the number of cross-bridges that are interacting with actin filaments at any given point in time (because, unlike strength, speed of contraction is relatively stable over a wide range of muscle lengths). In contrast, maximum force develops at zero velocity (i.e., during an isometric contraction). It is presumed that the force-velocity curve is caused by a slower rate of cross bridge stroking under loaded conditions. This relatively smooth relationship between force and velocity pertains to entire muscles (see Fig. 56, in which the vertical axis represents contraction velocity and the horizontal the force of contraction).

Fig. 56

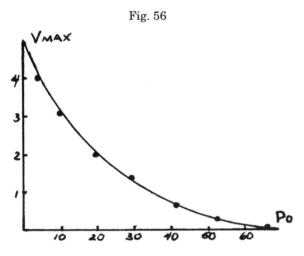

For single muscle fibers, the force-velocity relationship is more complicated. Instead of one smooth curve or relationship between force and velocity, there are two distinct curves located on either side of a break-point at approximately 75% of the muscle's maximum isometric force (Figure 57). A muscle fiber begins to lengthen when the force applied to it reaches its maximum isometric force (i.e., an eccentric contraction begins). Only when the force applied to a muscle reaches approximately 40% to 50% more than the muscle's maximum isometric force does the speed of the eccentric lengthening of the muscle become great. At forces less than the maximum isometric force, the muscle shortens (the smaller the percentage the maximum isometric force the faster the shortening). At the point of maximum isometric force, the force and velocity relationship becomes nearly flat, and there is little change in velocity with a fairly wide range of force change. This zone

of stability is what gives muscles the capability to be relatively stable when loads are high, such as when you walk down stairs.

Differentiation in the kinetic properties of muscles extends below the fiber level because the maximum speed of shortening (Vmax) and force-velocity relation vary from one part to another along the same fiber. (Variations in Vmax within a fiber may be as large as among different fibers in the same muscle, with Vmax generally falling near the distal ends of the muscles, essentially the points furthest away from the body's center.) A muscle's ability to produce force declines quickly as a muscle shortens, but this depressant effect on the strength of contraction falls over time, so that after about a second, a muscle that has shortened to a certain point is able to exert about the same force as a muscle that began contracting at that point.

Fig. 57

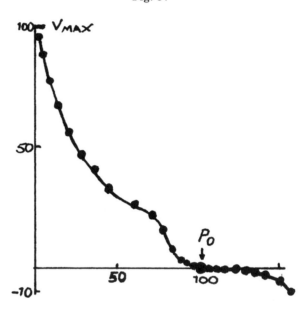

A fall in a muscle's ability to produce force as a result of fatigue is associated with a much smaller decline in the muscle's stiffness, so it is thought that the decline in force is due only partially to fewer cross bridges attaching. The major factor is believed to be a reduced force-output of the individual bridge (there is also a reduced speed of recycling of bridges during fatigue). All three of these effects are probably due, at least partially, to the accumulation of the breakdown products of ATP with continued muscle action.

The Arrangement of Muscle Fibers Within a Muscle

Muscle fibers can be arranged in a number of different ways within a muscle. There are two main kinds of arrangements: fusiform (longitudinal) and penniform. Fusiform muscles have their fibers arranged essentially parallel to the surface of the muscle and to the pull of the muscle when it contracts. Penniform muscles are arranged diagonally with respect to the pull of the muscle when it is contracted (Figure 10).

Fusiform muscles tend to have smaller cross-sections than penniform muscles. As a consequence, fusiform muscles generally contract with less force than penniform muscles. However, the arrangement of muscle fibers along the direct line of pull in fusiform muscles enables the overall muscle to shorten more rapidly and to a greater extent (in relation to their length) than penniform muscles.

Penniform muscles tend to have larger cross-sections than fusiform muscles, but their diagonal arrangement within the muscle causes them to give up some mechanical efficiency in terms of generating force. But less efficiency in generating force is more than offset by the greater number of fibers that can be brought into play by such muscles.

The Nature and Function of Connective Tissue

As s noted above, muscle tissue is infiltrated and surrounded by connective tissue (e.g., the epimysium which covers an entire muscle). The thickness and strength of these connective tissues that surround muscles and their component parts vary significantly from muscle to muscle. Such variations probably explain, at least in part, the different findings with regard to the physical properties of muscle tissue.

Most skeletal muscles merge into a connective tissue (called a tendon) at either end. It is the tendon that connects the muscle to the bone (at a juncture called the aponeurosis). The load that a tendon can sustain is influenced by the size and shape of that tendon, the speed with which any loading is applied to the tendon and any training effect that activity has had on the tendon. In normal activity, tendons are stressed at only a fraction of their limits, but very rapid and unexpected stresses (such as a slip while bearing a load) can overstress a tendon, causing it to rupture. This is one reason why proper conditioning, technique and equipment are so necessary for safe athletic activity.

Elastic Components of Muscle and Their Relation to Function

Muscles appear to have at least three interdependent elements which contribute to force generation: a contractile element (CE), a series elastic component (SEC) and a parallel elastic component (PEC). The CE functions through the sliding filament theory that was described above.

The series elastic component (SEC) is connected in series with the contractile element of the muscle

(i.e., along the length of the muscle). It acts like a spring within the muscle in that its function is related to tension development in the entire muscle-tendon unit, particularly when the muscle shortens from a previously stretched position. It is believed that both the tendinous tissues of muscle and the cross-bridges of the muscle fibers themselves contribute to the SEC. The SEC is capable of receiving the energy delivered by the contractile element and/or external forces and then returning that energy.

The PEC is comprised of connective tissue and is believed to be a major source of the opposing forces encountered when trying to elongate a passive muscle. It runs parallel to the CE and/or its line of pull. One of the functions of the PEC appears to be preventing a non-active CE from being damaged when external forces exert a sudden pull on it. It is believed to be activated when a muscle stretched. The PEC is also thought to contribute to the resting tension or tonus that is exhibited by muscles.

When a person is standing or moving slowly, the contractile element is a key factor in the movement. At higher speeds, contractions are generally immediately preceded by lengthening (negative) work. As a result, the muscles are stretched, and energy is stored in the elastic and viscoelastic components of the muscle (then released during an immediate shortening contraction). This entire cycle is known as the stretch-shortening cycle (SSC).

The extent to which elastic (not total) length-changes in a muscle-tendon unit are due to changes in tendinous tissue length can vary from less than half to as much as 90%. At least part of this difference can be attributed to significant differences between muscles in the share of the total length of the muscle-tendon unit made up of tendinous tissue.

The extent to which tendinous tissues change in length is rather limited. Researchers have estimated that increases in the length of tendinous tissues at low force levels range from 2% to 4%. When the forces on tendons are low, a small change in force can have a relatively great effect on tendon length. As force levels increase, the relative change in tendon length decreases significantly. However, regardless of the degree or change in tendon length, tendons can return a significant share of the energy that is applied to them if the rate of change in the force applied to the tendon is high enough. It is interesting to note that at long muscle lengths, the loss of power due to loss of cross-bridge overlap (and the concomitant decline in contractile capability) that results from the lengthening of the muscle appears to be more than offset by tension from stretching passive connective tissue.

Potential energy stored in elastic tissues that have been stretched is released when the force being applied to the elastic tissues is decreased; the faster the decrease, the faster the realization of the potential energy. Stored tendon energy can cause high velocities and power output without imposing those same velocities on muscle fibers. Therefore, as a consequence of the action of the elastic components of muscle, at a given velocity of shortening of the muscle-tendon complex, the muscle fibers can shorten more slowly than the overall complex. For example, during the end of the vertical jump push-off, more power is delivered by the tendon than by muscle fibers of the gastrocnemius and soleus (because a lowering of muscular force at this point permits the release of elastic energy).

When an active muscle-tendon unit is subjected to large changes in force, the unit acts eccentrically and a concentric contraction immediately follows; the degree of energy return from the unit muscle-tendon unit is relatively high. Such a sequence is often referred to as the stretch-shortening cycle (SSC). During the SSC, changes in muscle length are very small during the stretching phase, even though there is a very sharp increase in force. This suggests that the conditions presented by this kind of activity favor the use of short- range muscle stiffness to activate the SEC.

Different forms of muscle action have different mechanical efficiencies, and the velocities of stretching and shortening influence these efficiencies. The loading conditions during the start of an action from a static position are different from those during an SSC. This difference apparently leads to different mechanical efficiencies (ME) for the actions that result.

The ME of concentric exercise decreases with increasing shortening velocity. The mechanical efficiency of eccentric muscular contractions tends to be quite high and generally increases when mechanical work increases. The mechanical efficiency of eccentric contractions is improved with an increasing stretch velocity. In concentric contraction, electrical activity within the muscle, energy expenditure and mechanical work all change proportionally during slow muscle actions as effort increases. As velocity increases, the relationships between these activities change. The initial force peak becomes higher with fatigue, and the subsequent reduction of force becomes more pronounced. In addition, the contribution of reflexive action to sustaining repeated stretch loads is improved.

During an isometric contraction, the total length of the CE and SEC is constant, but the CE shortens and the SEC lengthens. The effect of the SEC is that the build up of force at the lever takes longer than it would be if only the CE existed. As force falls, the length of the SEC declines as well. In situations where the CE force falls rapidly, the contribution to the shortening velocity by the SEC is much greater than that of the CE.

It is a well-known physiological principle that stretching a muscle (up to a point) before it is contracted increases the force that the muscle can generate. Part of the advantage of pre-stretching can be understood from the perspective of the elastic components of muscle (e.g., in the enhanced recoil after a pre-stretch of the muscle). However, another reason for the increased force of contraction that follows a pre-stretch lies in the reflexive characteristics of the neuromuscular system, a subject that is addressed in the next section of this appendix.

Proprioceptive Receptors

The brain receives information from the muscles that enable it to control the actions of those muscles on a subconscious level. This information is provided by two special kinds of sensory organs, called proprioceptive muscle receptors. One type of muscle receptor is the golgi tendon organ. These organs are made up of afferent fibers entwined within the bundles of connective tissue that comprise the tendon. (Afferent neurons carry impulses from receptors in the body to the central nervous system, the system comprised of the brain and spinal chord.) These neurons respond to tension in the tendons that is created by the muscles to which they are attached. When the tendons are stretched, they cause the golgi tendon organs to be stretched as well, causing the afferent fibers to fire (the frequency of that firing being directly related to the tension that is developed). This information is sent to the brain, and at the same time, by means of interneurons (special neurons that connect afferent and efferent neurons), to the efferent alpha motor neurons of that muscle, thereby inhibiting its action. (Efferent neurons receive information from the central nervous system.) The sensory neuron of the golgi tendon organ also connects with the antagonists (the muscles that oppose, i.e., have a pull opposite to that of the muscle which in generating tension in the tendon the golgi tendon organ is monitoring— the agonist) and can cause the antagonists to contract, opposing the action of the agonists. This combination of effects on the acting muscle and its antagonists helps to protect the tendon of the acting muscle from overly high and potentially injurious tension.

The second kind of muscle receptor is known as a muscle spindle. A muscle spindle is a group of specialized muscle fibers known as intrafusal fibers. These fibers are contained within spindle-shaped connective tissue coverings that run parallel to normal (extrafusal) muscle fibers. The central or control area of the muscle spindle is non-contractile in nature, but it is sensitive to being stretched, while its ends are capable of contraction.

Each muscle spindle has its own afferent and efferent nerve supply. The afferent neuron has two types of sensory endings. Both of these sensory endings terminate on intrafusal fibers (i.e., muscle spindles). They serve as muscle-spindle receptors that are activated by a stretch. The primary endings are wrapped around the central portion of these intrafusal fibers. They detect both the change in length that takes place in the muscle and the rate at which that change occurs. The secondary endings are arranged at the end portions of many of the intrafusal fibers and are sensitive solely to length.

Muscle spindles have an action which is virtually the opposite of golgi tendon organs. When a muscle is stretched, the afferent neuron endings send an impulse to the spinal chord, synapsing directly on the motor neurons that reside in same muscle, causing contraction of the muscle and other muscles which cause the same movement. At the same time other neurons inhibit contraction of antagonist muscles. This overall reaction, known as a stretch reflex, resists any passive change in muscle length, so that the optimal resting length of the muscle is maintained. The best-known example of such a reflex is the "knee-jerk" reflex in the patellar tendon. The stretch can be and is used in athletics to maximize muscle power-outputs (as when the foot is planted in jumping events).

The efferent neuron of a muscle spindle is known as a gamma motor neuron. Gamma motor neurons initiate contraction of the muscular end regions of intrafusal fibers. Simultaneous activation, or "coactivation," of the gamma motor neuron system together with the alpha motor neuron system occurs when reflex and voluntary contractions and remove the slack from the muscle spindle fibers as the entire muscle shortens, permitting these receptor structures to maintain their sensitivity to stretch over a full range of muscle lengths. Gamma stimulation triggers simultaneous contraction at both ends of the intrafusal fiber, removing any slack from the central region. The extent of the gamma activity in a muscle being voluntarily contracted depends on the anticipated distance of the shortening that occurs.

The Influence of Hormones on Muscle Function

There are a number of hormones which are considered anabolic (i.e., have a muscle-building effect). Among these are growth hormone, insulin and insulin growth factors, testosterone and thyroid hormones.

The level of anabolic hormones appears to be affected in a positive way by resistance training. While mere elevation of these hormones has no discernible effect on strength and functional muscle growth, their presence, in combination with the stimulation of training, apparently has growth- and strength-building effects. Testosterone and growth hormones (the latter through the mediators of the insulin growth factors) appear to enhance growth, while insulin itself appears to protecting against the breakdown of protein in the body rather than to enhance its production. The effects of testosterone may be as much due to neural factors and to the influence of testosterone on the transition of muscle fibers from slower to faster as to any anabolic effect. The effects of thyroid hormone are secondary in nature (stimulating anabolism indirectly).

Certain hormones, such as glucocorticoids (particularly cortisol), are believed to have anti-anabolic or catabolic (i.e., muscle-wasting) effects. Both anabolic and anti-catabolic factors contribute to overall growth.

In a completely different category are hormones that appear to have an acute effect on performance (i.e., have an immediate and positive effect on strength), such as those from the catecholomines category (e.g., noradrenaline and adrenaline). Their role on muscle growth is not well understood, but through their ability to increase the strength of contractions, they may increase the stimulation from training (although the release of such hormones at too high a level and too often may have a negative effect on growth by fostering the development of an overstress condition).

The balance of anabolic and catabolic factors in the body is subject to change. Factors such as training, rest, general health, nutritional factors, aging and stress all have an influence. This is one of the reasons why a healthy lifestyle is so critical for the athlete.

Energy for Muscular Contractions

There is only one fundamental source of energy for muscular contraction: ATP. As was discussed in the section on the bases for muscular contraction, when an ATP molecule binds to myosin at the ATPase binding site, it permits the detachment of the myosin cross-bridge from the actin myofilament at the completion of the power stroke and the resetting of the cross-bridge in its original position, where a new connection to the actin filament can occur. The ATP molecule is then split by myosin ATPase, releasing energy for the power stroke of the cross bridge. The energy for the chemical process which reset the neuron for another stimulation of the muscle fiber is derived from the breakdown of ATP.

A very small amount of ATP is stored in muscle tissue, perhaps enough for as much as one to a few seconds of maximum muscular effort. Therefore, ATP must be supplied to the muscles on a continuing basis if activity is to continue. There are three means of generating ATP: the breakdown of phosphocreatine (PC); glycolysis; and oxidative phosphorylation (the citric acid or "Kreb's cycle" and electron transport). The latter process requires oxygen in order to occur and is referred to as aerobic, while the first two sources of ATP, which do not require oxygen to occur, so are called anaerobic.

PC, like ATP itself, is stored within the muscle (a rested muscle contains about five times as much PC as ATP). When an ATP molecule releases energy, it is broken down into adenosine diphosphate (ADP) and phosphate (Pi). When PC is broken down, the resulting energy is used to recombine ADP and Pi into ATP. ATP can be formed within a fraction of a second from the breakdown of CP. ATP stores remain fairly constant early in contraction, while creatine phosphate stores become depleted. ATP and the PC used to replenish it are exhausted in thirty seconds or less of all-out work. Although PC stores cannot provide energy for long-term work, they have the advantage of being immediately available and yielding a larger power capacity than other energy sources.

Also stored in the muscle is glycogen, a sugar molecule whose breakdown produces energy for the formation of ATP and a substance called pyruvic acid, which is ultimately converted by the body to lactic acid . This process is called anaerobic glycolysis.

An accumulation of lactic acid in the muscles causes pain in nerve endings during exercise. (Lactic acid accumulation was once thought to be the source of delayed onset muscle soreness, the soreness which people often experience twenty-four to forty-eight hours after a bout of exercise, particularly when they have not trained for some time, but this has not proven to be the case.) A lactic-acid buildup also makes the interior of muscle cells more acidic, which interferes with a number of chemical processes of the cell, including ATP formation and the chemical process that exposes actin filaments and permits cross-bridging. These combined effects, along with energy depletion, are believed to contribute to muscle fatigue. (The intensity of a given exercise as well as the type of muscle fiber influence the actual onset of fatigue.) Consequently, the energy provided by glycolysis has limitations. However, glycolysis can produce more energy than ATP-PC (though not as much per unit of time). It is a major source of energy in all-out exercise bouts lasting one to three minutes.

The production of ATP can occur aerobically through the process of oxidative phosphorylation mentioned above. Through oxidative phosphorylation the body metabolizes carbohydrates, fats and proteins to create energy (protein is normally used for energy only during starvation and long, intense, exercise bouts). The body's use of carbohydrates and fats is in large part determined by the nature of the activity that is being undertaken. Carbohydrates are utilized more extensively when work is intense; utilization of carbohydrates is nearly 100% at maximum work levels, assuming carbohydrates are available. The body uses fats as its primary energy source during activities of low intensity and long duration.

When the body metabolizes the carbohydrate glycogen using oxygen, the pyruvate released does not form lactic acid but, rather, through an extended series of chemical reactions called the oxidative phosphorylation, ATP, carbon dioxide (CO^2), which is expired via the lungs and water. In order to be metabolized, fats go through a process called beta oxidation and then through the oxidative phosphorylation process, yielding, as do carbohydrates, water, CO^2 and ATP.

The amount of aerobic energy that the body can produce depends on the amount of oxygen it can obtain and utilize in a given unit of time (which is typically measured in terms of the liters of oxygen per minute that the body can process). During exercise the amount of oxygen that the body processes is increased through faster and deeper breathing, a faster heart rate, the diversion of blood to the exercising muscles and hemoglobin releasing more oxygen to those muscles. In addition, some muscles have a large supply of myoglobin, a substance similar to hemoglobin (a molecule that binds with and transports the majority of the oxygen in the blood). Myoglobin can store small amounts of oxygen, but its most important role is in increasing the rate of oxygen transfer from the blood into the muscle fibers.

The aerobic method of energy production cannot produce enough energy for maximum efforts, but it can supply a virtually unlimited amount of ATP over time and is a very efficient energy source. (The breakdown of one glucose molecule by this aerobic mechanism yields thirty-six molecules of ATP as compared with only two molecules of ATP when glycolysis is the mechanism for supplying energy.) However, it should be noted that aerobic energy-production is the indirect source of anaerobic energy-production as well. On an intuitive level, the athlete can appreciate this by the heavy breathing that takes place after a bout of intensive exercise. This breathing is used to replenish ATP, PC and glycogen stores. The restoration of ATP takes place over several minutes. This rate of restoration is often explained by the concept of a "half-life" of restoration. It is estimated that half of the ATP depleted by an all-out bout of exercise is replaced in approximately twenty seconds. Half of the remaining half is restored in another 20 seconds, so that 75% of the stores are restored at approximately forty seconds, and virtually full restoration occurs within several minutes. The rate of restoration is slowed if activity which depletes ATP is undertaken during the restoration period. Therefore, sufficient rest between heavy bouts (e.g. sets) of exercise is needed in order to maintain performance at a high level.

The glycogen energy source is replaced while breathing gradually returns to normal after heavy exercise. During this process lactic acid converts back into pyruvic acid, part of which is processed through oxidative phosphorylation to create ATP. The balance is converted back into glucose by the liver (most of that glucose is converted to glycogen, which is stored in the muscles and liver). The half-life of lactic acid restoration is approximately twenty-five minutes. Light activity helps to remove lactic acid accumulation faster than rest (part of lactic acid is aerobically metabolized to supply some of the needed ATP to perform the light activity). Therefore, light activity is good between bouts of intensive exercise sets if rest periods are at least several minutes. (This presupposes that the activity being undertaken is one of sufficient duration to require energy from lactic acid in the first place.) Full restoration of the energy derived from this source can take several hours. The restoration of the glycogen stores utilized during extremely long exercise bouts can take days.

Part of the increased oxygen uptake that continues after exercise is attributable to the general metabolic influence of exercise. For instance, the release of certain catecholomines during exercise increases oxygen consumption, as does the increased rate of chemical reactions that takes place in the muscle as a result of the local increase in muscle temperature.

It must be remembered that each of the body's three energy systems is in use at all times, with one or another of those systems being the dominant source of energy at any given point in time, depending on the nature of the activity that is being performed and the availability of various energy stores in the body.

Anatomy

Human anatomy is an extremely complex subject. However, the gross anatomy of the structures that cause athletic movement (the muscles, connective tissue, bones and joints) is far simpler, though still complex. In this section we will examine the basics of human anatomy as they pertain to athletic movement.

The Development and Anatomy of Human Bones

At birth most human bones are fairly soft or cartilaginous in nature. As a child ages, the soft tissue is replaced by bone through a process called ossification. Ossification takes place in certain areas earlier than others. For example, the skull ossifies relatively early in life, but most long bones do not complete the ossification process until the late teens. Ossification also occurs in some bony protuberances, such as the tibial tuberosity (the small protrusion at the top of the shin).

There are approximately 200 bones in the human body that are involved in movement. These bones are generally divided into four categories: long, flat, short and irregular.

Long bones are the key components of human limbs and digits. Their primary purpose is to serve as levers. The largest portion of long bones is the dense shaft or diaphysis. At either end of the bone are areas called epiphyses, which have a larger diameter than the diaphysis. The epiphyses have a more porous or spongy inner area than the diaphysis and then a thin outer layer of denser bone. In the area at the ends of the bone where their bony surfaces come in contact with other bones to form a juncture or joint, there is a thin layer of articular cartilage. The cartilage here serves to cushion the shock when bones are pushed toward one another and also reduces the friction between the bones. Except where cartilage is present, a fibrous membrane called the periosteum covers the bone. It functions as a place for muscles and their tendons to attach to the bone. The ossification of long bones begins in the diaphysis and progresses to the epiphyses. Special areas called the epiphyseal plates lie between the epiphyses and diaphyses of immature bones. These areas gradually ossify with age. (As a child grows, new cartilage is created which is ultimately converted to bone through the ossification process.) This process of ossification takes place in other areas of the epiphyses as well. (It also takes place in the other types of bones, but the sites and patterns of ossification are somewhat different.) Growth in the bone's width and length continues until the ossification process is complete.

The scapula, ilia and ribs are examples of flat bones. These bones protect the internal organs that they at least partially cover. They also provide a large area at which muscles can attach. Their composition tends to be like that of the epiphyses (e.g., spongy on the inside with a denser outside layer).

The carpal bones of the wrist and the tarsal bones of the ankle are examples of short bones. These bones are composed of spongy bones with a thin outer layer of more compact bone. They have a more blocky shape than long bones.

The irregular bones are not paired like the long, short or flat bones. Examples are the pubis and the vertebrae. These bones have an irregular shape and typically serve particular purposes, such as protecting a certain area of the body or supporting the body.

Bones have three essential components: minerals (nearly half of the bone's total volume, primarily calcium compounds) and organic matter (nearly 40%, primarily collagen). The remainder of the bone's volume consists of fluid-filled spaces of various shapes. The organic factors give bones their strength, and the mineral components supply rigidity.

494

Anatomy of the Joints

There are three basic kinds of joints: diarthrodial (synovial), amphiarthrodial (cartilaginous) and synarthrodial. Diarthrodial joints permit movement in a variety of ranges and directions. Examples are the knee and shoulder joints. During their movement, diarthrodial joints are stabilized by a combination of factors. Their shape has a strong effect, with one end of the bone designed to fit into or to move smoothly along another. The ligaments that surround the bones hold them together so that movement in the correct groove is facilitated. Finally, the tendons and/or muscles that are in contact with the joint guide the action of the joint, maintaining the joint's integrity.

Amphiarthrodial joints permit a relatively small degree of movement. Typically a layer of fibrocartilage separates the bones. When movement occurs, it occurs primarily through the deformation of the cartilage. Ligaments connect these rather tightly to one another. The joints between the vertebrae and the sacroiliac joints are examples of this kind of joint.

Synarthrodial joints do not move; the bones merely merge together at these joints, joined by fibrous tissue that is essentially a continuation of the periosteum. Cranial sutures are examples of synarthrodial joints.

The ligamentous tissue that encloses the joint forms what is called an articular capsule. The thickness of that capsule varies within the same joint and among joints. A synovial membrane within the joint secretes a lubricating and shock-absorbing substance called synovial fluid into the articular capsule.

Tendons connect muscle to bone. They are often enclosed by cylindrical sheaths of connective tissue that are lined with a synovial membrane.

Two other kinds of tissues serve to absorb shock and facilitate movement at the joint. One is a fibrocartilage pad that rests between the bones. Examples are the discs between the vertebrae and the menisci of the knee. A second kind of shock absorber is the bursae sac. These soft, pad-like tissues are filled with synovial fluid. Both the bursa sacs and the articular capsule contain a relatively modest amount of synovial fluid under normal conditions. However, in the event of an injury to the joint, the amount of fluid can increase several fold or more. A common example is "water on the knee."

Directions of Human Movement

Scientists have adopted specific terms to describe human movement. Many of these terms are relative in nature. For example, the term superior is used by anatomists to describe some part of the body that is higher than or above something else. To say that your head is superior to your feet is true when you are standing, but not when you are lying down. Therefore, in the study of anatomy, a reference position to which all other positions are related has been established. This position, called the anatomical position, is used as a reference for understanding the direction of human movement. The anatomical position is assumed when the body is standing erect, facing the observer with the arms at the sides, palms facing forward. It is in relation to this position that anatomical movements and locations are described.

For instance, since the term superior means higher or above another structure, in the context of the anatomical position, the portion of the upper arm that is nearest the shoulder is said to be superior to the portion of the upper arm that is nearest the elbow. Inferior has the opposite meaning (in this case, the portion of the arm nearest the elbow is inferior to the portion nearest the shoulder). Lateral means farther from the mid-line of the body, and medial means closer to it. When the arm is raised sideways, it is said to be moving laterally; when it is lowered it is moving medially. Proximal means nearer to and distal means further away. Anterior is nearer to or in front of the body, while posterior is nearer to or behind the body. Finally, superficial means nearer the surface, and deeper means further away from the surface of the body.

Anatomically, all motions of the joints are measured from stipulated zero degree starting positions. For example, when the arm is completely straight, the elbow is said to be at the zero starting position (i.e., $0°$). At full flexion, the elbow is at an angle of approximately $150°$. Movement from the zero starting position to the fully bent position is called flexion. Movement back to the fully extended position is called extension. When the arm continues its extension past the point where it is straight and moves until the arm goes past the zero position it is said to be hyperextending. (In many people, such movement is not possible without injury, but in some people a hyperextension of as much as $20°$ can be comfortably attained.)

Movements are measured from Movements are also described in reference to three planes, imaginary flat surfaces, like thin boards, that pass through the body. The transverse plane is a horizontal plane passes through the body parallel to the ground (the mid-transverse plane divides the body into superior and inferior halves). The sagittal plane passes through the body from top to bottom, perpendicular to the ground, dividing it into right and left sides (the mid-sagittal plane divides the body into right and left halves, although right and left are not anatomical terms). The final plane, the frontal plane, is also vertical and perpendicular to the ground, but it divides the body into anterior and posterior sections (the mid-frontal plan divides the body into equal anterior and posterior halves).

Finally, movement can be described in terms of three axes that can be viewed as rods running through the center of the body. The transverse axis is like a rod running through the body from side to side. The anterior/posterior axis is like a rod running through the body from front to back. The longitudinal axis is like a rod running vertically through the body from top to bottom.

When movements are described, they often refer to the plane through which the body part is moving and the axis about which it is moving. Figure 58 depicts planes and axes.

General Kinds of Joint Actions

Joints can perform a number of actions. Many of these actions are quite universal in that they can be performed by a number of joints; others are functions limited to only one type of joint. The actions of joints and a definition of those actions are listed below.

Flexion: Flexion is a decrease in the angle between two bones or groups of bones. It occurs in the sagittal plane around the body's transverse axis. Flexion occurs when the palm is raised toward the shoulder in the anatomical position. Here, when the lower arm is raised to a position parallel to the ground, the angle between the bones of the upper and lower arms has decreased from approximately 180° to 90°.

Extension: Extension is the opposite movement to flexion (e.g., the arm being straightened from a flexed position). Extension takes place in the same plane as flexion and around the same axis, but there is an increase in the angle between two bones when extension occurs.

Abduction: Abduction is moving away from the body's (or body part's) mid-line. Movement generally takes place in the frontal plane around the anterior/posterior axis. (Some examples of exceptions are the hands and feet, in which

abduction takes place when the fingers and toes are spread apart.) Abduction occurs when the leg is raised sideways (laterally) from the anatomical position.

Adduction: Adduction is the opposite movement to abduction (e.g., the leg being lowered after having been raised sideways).

Elevation: Elevation occurs when body parts are moved to a superior position. Elevation occurs when the shoulder girdle is raised to a superior position.

Depression: Depression is the opposite movement to elevation.

Rotation: Rotation is a turning about the longitudinal axis. Rotation occurs when the head or trunk is turned from left to right or right to left. For the limbs, rotation is described as medial when the anterior surface of the limb is turned toward the mid-line of the body (inward or medially). Lateral rotation of the limbs is the opposite of medial rotation.

Supination: Supination is a special form of movement pertaining to the lower arm. In the anatomical position the arm is supinated (the palm is facing forward). The natural stance of humans is with their palms facing inward and to the rear. By rotating the forearm laterally (outward) from the natural position, the anatomical position is assumed.

Pronation: Pronation is the opposite of supination. Rotating the forearm medially (inward) from the anatomical position to a more natural position is an example of pronation.

Inversion: Inversion is lifting the (inner) medial border of the foot inward and upward.

Eversion: Eversion is the opposite of inversion. It consists of lifting the lateral (outside) border of the foot.

Dorsiflexion: Dorsiflexion is lifting the foot toward the shin (the starting or normal position of the foot is considered to be at an angle approximately 90° to the shin).

Plantarflexion: Plantarflexion is pointing the foot downward or rising on the toes.

In addition to the movements described above, there are also combinations of movements, such as circumduction (moving the joint in a circular direction). However, these terms merely describe some combination of simpler joint motions when they are executed in a specific sequence.

The Actions of Specific Major Joints

Joints vary considerably in their ability to move. Some joints are capable of only one basic kind of motion, while others can execute a variety of motions. The major joints and the movements of which they are capable are listed below. Types of motions are listed in the table that follows. The names of the motions have been abbreviated, but

Figure 58

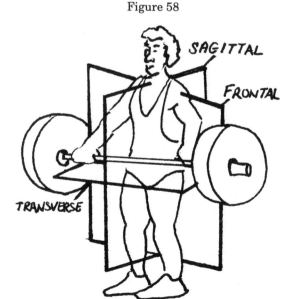

they appear from left to right in the order in which they were introduced in the preceding section.

Abbreviations of Headings: Flx = flexion, Ext - extension, Ab = abduction, Ad = adduction, Rotat = rotation, Elv = elevation, Dep = depression, Sup = supination, Prn = pronation, Inv = inversion, Ev = eversion, Dor = dorsiflexion, Pln = plantarflexion.

Abbreviations Within The Table: X indicates that both movements in the heading occur at that joint, H = hyperextension, Z = horizontal flexion, R = radial and ulnar flexion, and L = lateral flexion.

1. The scapula, or shoulder blade, can move if there is movement at the sternoclavicular articulation as well. The scapula can abduct, moving laterally, away from the spine, in conjunction with a movement known as a lateral tilt (adduction being the opposite movement). Elevation occurs when the shoulder blades are lifted (which occurs primarily in concert with the hunching forward of the shoulders). Upward rotation occurs when the arms are raised forward or to the sides and the scapulae are lifted, with the superior portion of the scapulae tilting inward and the inferior portion moving outward, creating an inward tilt of both scapulae from top to bottom. One final kind of motion, upward tilt, occurs when the shoulder joint is hyperextended.

2. In addition to flexion and extension (in which the arms are raised forward and upward about the transverse axis and down and back, respectively), the shoulder joint is capable of hyperextension (when the arm is moved rearward from the anatomical position) and horizontal flexion and extension. The latter two movements can be described in the context of the arm beginning at a point where it is held parallel to the ground and out to the side of the body and then moved medially, inward across the chest (flexion) and outward back to position at the side of the body (extension).

3. The shoulder can also rotate medially and laterally.

4. The wrist is capable of hyperextension (raising the posterior of the hand toward the posterior of the forearm in the anatomical position); radial and ulnar flexion (the outside—thumb side—portion of the hand raised to the outside of the forearm and the opposite side of the hand raised toward the inside of the forearm, respectively, in the anatomical position); as well as normal flexion and extension (raising the palm toward the anterior of the forearm and returning it to the anatomical position, respectively).

5. The vertebral joints are capable of lateral flexion to the left or right, as well as rotation to the left and right (when the head and/or shoulders turn to the right). Flexion is movement forward and down from the anatomical position, and extension is the return to that position.

6. The lumbarsacral joint permits pelvic tilt forward and backward.

7. The hip joint permits rotation medially and laterally.

Basic Muscular Anatomy

As was noted earlier in this section, there are approximately 600 muscles in the human body. However, there are far fewer muscles that have a significant effect on athletic movements in general and on weightlifting movements In particular. In this section we will limit our attention to depicting the shapes and locations of the major muscle groups that were identified above. Two illustrations of the muscles of the human body that most affect weightlifting performance appear in Figures 59 (a) and (b) Figure (a) shows the major muscles of the body as viewed from the posterior of the body. Fig. (b) shows a view from the front. By observing these muscles and relating them to their functions in joint action (see the discussion on pages 499-500), you should be able to gain a functional understanding of muscle anatomy.

Table 1

Actions	Flx/Ext	Ab/Ad	Rotat	Elv/Dep	Sup/Prn	Inv/Ev	Dor/Pln
Joints							
Shoulder Girdle		X	U&D[1]	X			
Shoulder Joint	X, HZ[2]	X	M&L[3]				
Elbow	X						
Radioulnar					X		
Wrist	X, HR[4]						
Vertebral Column	X, HL[5]		X				
Lumbosacral	Pelvic[6]						
Hip	X, H	X	M&L[7]				
Knee	X						
Ankle							X
Intertarsal						X	

Fig. 59 — Anatomy Of Major Muscle Groups

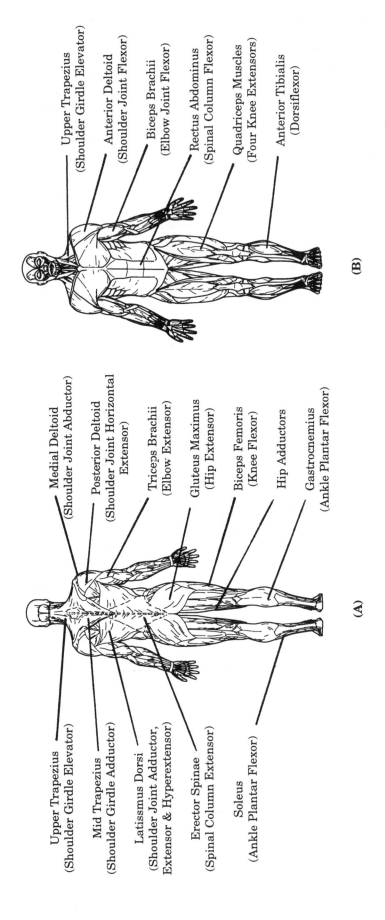

Upper Trapezius
(Shoulder Girdle Elevator)

Anterior Deltoid
(Shoulder Joint Flexor)

Biceps Brachii
(Elbow Joint Flexor)

Rectus Abdominus
(Spinal Column Flexor)

Quadriceps Muscles
(Four Knee Extensors)

Anterior Tibialis
(Dorsiflexor)

(B)

Medial Deltoid
(Shoulder Joint Abductor)

Posterior Deltoid
(Shoulder Joint Horizontal
Extensor)

Triceps Brachii
(Elbow Extensor)

Gluteus Maximus
(Hip Extensor)

Biceps Femoris
(Knee Flexor)

Hip Adductors

Gastrocnemius
(Ankle Plantar Flexor)

Upper Trapezius
(Shoulder Girdle Elevator)

Mid Trapezius
(Shoulder Girdle Adductor)

Latissmus Dorsi
(Shoulder Joint Adductor,
Extensor & Hyperextensor)

Erector Spinae
(Spinal Column Extensor)

Soleus
(Ankle Plantar Flexor)

(A)

Muscles Are Differentiated by Their Function in a Given Movement

A muscle that shortens, thereby causing a joint action is a mover or agonist for that movement. Some muscles are agonists for more than one action, and many have one or many actions on each of two or more joints that they happen to traverse. For example, the biceps brachii causes elbow flexion, radioulnar supination and several shoulder-joint actions. Muscles that are the most effective for a particular movement are often referred to as prime movers. Those which are less effective are termed assistant movers. Those muscles which assist the prime movers can vary according to the circumstances.

A category of muscles called emergency muscles are called into action only when exceptional force is needed. (Motor programs do not always activate all of muscles that can help to execute a particular movement; in fact, the opposite is the case, which is why motor skills must be developed.)

Antagonists have the opposite effect of the agonists of the same joint. (The hamstring muscles are antagonists to the leg extensors in the extension of the leg.)

Fixators or stabilizers support a bone, anchoring it in a given position. This provides a firm base from which a prime mover can exert its pull.

Synergists, or neutralizers, act to prevent or counteract actions of other active muscles that are unwanted. There are two categories of synergists: "helping" and "true" synergists. Helping synergists are two muscles that both cause a certain joint action. However, each has its own secondary action which is antagonistic to the other. An example of such muscles are the external obliques. These muscles act as spinal flexors while at the same time acting to cause flexion in their own direction. (Any actual flexion in either direction is counteracted by the actions of each oblique working against the other.)

True synergy only occurs in opposition to a muscle that acts across two or more joints. The true synergists act to preclude joint movement at one of the joints crossed by the multi-joint muscle by contracting statically. For example, when the fingers are closed to made a fist, a group of true synergists (the wrist extensors) act to prevent the muscles that flex the fingers from generating wrist flexion at the same time.

Skeletal muscles can also be categorized as spurt or shunt muscles. Spurt muscles impart the majority of their force across a bone instead of along it and thereby foster movement. Shunt muscles impart most of their force along the bones. This force has a tendency to stabilize the joints by pulling them toward one another. Many muscles act on more than one joint. In such a case the muscle is typically a spurt muscle relative to one joint while acting as a shunt to the other. A good example is the biceps brachii muscle. It serves as a spurt muscle at the elbow and a shunt muscle at the shoulder. There are even certain muscles that serve both functions at the same time (with certain fibers within the muscles acting as shunt muscles and other fibers acting as spurt muscles). In addition, the action of a particular muscle (or a portion thereof) as a shunt or spurt muscle is not fixed. The role of the muscle can change when the direction of movement changes.

Major Muscle Groups

Although the human body has approximately 600 skeletal muscles, there are only about seventy-five muscle pairs that are responsible for most skeletal movements and posture maintenance. The combination of muscles that causes a given movement at a particular joint is referred to as a muscle group. Such a group takes its name from the joint at which the movement takes place and the kind of movement it causes. For example, the muscles that are primarily responsible for flexion of the spinal column are referred to as the flexors. Those muscles are the external oblique, internal oblique and rectus abdominus. The following is an alphabetical list of the major joints of the body, along with the names of the major muscle groups which are responsible for the movements of those joints and the muscles that are considered to be the prime movers in those joints.

Ankle

Plantar flexors: gastrocnemius and soleus
Dorsiflexors: tibialis anterior, extensor digitorum longus and extensor peroneus tertius

Elbow

Flexors: brachialis, biceps brachii and brachioradialis
Extensors: triceps brachii

Hip

Flexors: illiopsoas, pectineus, retus femoris
Extensors and Hyperextensors: gluteus maximus, semitendinosus and semimembranosus
Abductors: gluteus medius
Adductors: adductor brevis, adductor longus, gracilis, pectineus
Lateral rotators: gluteus maximus, obturator externus and internus, gemellus superior and inferior, quadratus femoris and piriformis
Medial rotators: gluteus minimus and gluteus medius

Intertarsal

Inverters: tibialis anterior and tibialis posterior

Everters: extensor digitorum longus, peroneus brevis, perioneus longus and peroneus tertius

Knee

Flexors: biceps femoris, semimembranosus, semitendinosus
Extensors: rectus femoris, vastus medialis, vastus lateralis and vastus intermedius

Lumbosacral

Forward pelvic tilters: iliopsoas
Backward pelvic tilters: rectus abdominus and internal oblique

Radioulnar

Pronators: pronator quadratus, pronator teres and brachioradialis
Supinators: supinator, biceps brachii and brachioradialis

Shoulder Girdle

Adductors: serratus anterior and pectoralis minor
Adductors: mid trapezius and rhomboids
Upward rotators: lower and upper trapezius and serratus anterior
Downward rotators: pectoralis minor and rhomboids
Elevators: levator scapulae, rhomboids and upper trapezius
Depressors: lower trapezius and pectoralis minor

Shoulder Joint

Flexors: anterior deltoid and clavicular portion of pectoralis major
Extensors: sternal portion of pectoralis major, latissmus dorsi and teres major
Hyperextensors: latissmus dorsi and teres major
Abductors: middle deltoid and supraspinatus
Adductors: latissmus dorsi, teres major and sternal portion of pectoralis major
Lateral rotators: infraspinatus and teres major
Medial rotators: pectoralis major, subscapularis, latissmus dorsi and teres major
Horizontal flexors: pectoralis major and anterior deltoid
Horizontal extensors: infraspinatus, latissmus dorsi, teres major, teres minor and posterior deltoid

Spinal Column

Flexors: rectus abdonminus, external oblique and internal oblique
Extensors: erector spinae
Hyperextensors: erector spinae
Rotators: internal oblique, external oblique, erector spinae, rotators, multifidus
Lateral flexors: internal oblique, external oblique, quadratus lumborum, mutlifidus and rotators

Wrist

Flexors: flexor carpi radialis and flexor carpi radialis
Extensors: extensor carpi ulnaris, extensor carpi radialis longus and brevis
Abductors: flexor carpi radialis, extensor carpi radialis longus and brevis
Adductors: flexor carpi ulnaris and extensor carpi ulnaris

One-, Two- and Multi-Joint Muscles

Many muscles influence only one joint movement. That muscle contracts alone or in conjunction with other muscles, and there is a resulting movement or stabilization at a particular joint.

In other cases a muscle passes over two or more joints, acting on both whenever it contracts. Some multi-joint muscles, such as the group of muscles referred to as the hamstrings (the semitendinosus, semimenbranousus and biceps femoris), act to cause movement at the joint in opposite directions. (These muscles both flex the leg at the knee and extend the thigh at the hip.) Other multi-joint muscles cause flexion in the same direction at all of the joints that they cross (e.g., the flexors of the fingers).

None of the multi-joint muscles are capable of causing complete movement in both joints on which they act at the same time. One result of this limitation is that the contraction of one muscle group can cause another to contract (e.g., when the hamstrings act to extend the hip, they cause a contraction of the knee extensors).

The action of multi-joint muscles has been classified in two ways: concurrent and countercurrent. Simultaneous extension of the hip and knee joints is an example of concurrent movement. When this kind of motion occurs, the muscle groups lose tension at one end and gain it at another. (In hip and knee extension, the knee extensors lose tension in the knee area but gain tension in the hip area.)

In countercurrent movement, one of the multi-joint muscles shortens at both joints while its antagonist lengthens, gaining tension at both its ends. For example, if the knee is extended and the hip is flexed at the same time, a kick is executed.

The Influence of the Angles at Which Muscle Force Is Applied

The angle between a muscle and the bone to which it applies force has in important influence on the degree to which muscle contraction generates movement in the bone. The smaller the angle between the muscle's line of pull and the bone to which force is being applied, the larger the movement in the bone. For instance, when the arm is fully straight, the angle between the elbow flexors and the radius and ulnar bones is small. At

500

this point, even a small contraction of the elbow flexors generates a relatively large movement in the forearm. At the end of the curling motion, when the angle between these muscles is far greater, a given distance of muscle shortening results in a much smaller movement at the forearm.

From a mechanical standpoint, the most efficient angle for the application of muscle force to a bone is 90°. This is true because in such a case the force of the muscle is being applied fully to rotating the lever about the joint. At angles larger than 90°, at least some of the force applied by the muscle can pull the bone away from the joint, dissipating some of the efficiency of the force. At angles below 90°, at least some of the force exerted by the muscle is used to pull the bone in towards the joint. This action of the muscle stabilizes the joint, but it increases the frictional force that is generated by the joint, lowering the efficiency of the muscle's force.

Training Effects

Training has a profound influence on performance. Some portion of the training effect is attributable to learning. Another portion is due to changes that take place in composition of muscle tissue and its functional capabilities. But the effects of training are not limited learning to use muscles effectively or to changes in muscle tissue itself. Bone and connective tissue are capable of adapting to the imposed demands of training as well. While such changes generally do not have a significant direct effect on short-term performance, they do affect performance profoundly in the long term by influencing the ability to sustain stress without injury.

Training Effects on Muscle Tissue

Specific kinds of training can apparently cause a conversion among FT sub-types of fibers (e.g., Type IIB and Type IIA), but the available evidence does not suggest that Type I and II fibers are interconvertible. (Experimentally, the switching of motor neurons supplying fast and slow fibers has resulted in the gradual reversal of the speed with which the fibers contract.) It has been suggested that, on a practical level, the transformation from one muscle fiber type to another is impeded by a number of natural conditions. In the case of the transformation of slow twitch into fast twitch fibers, any transformation stimulated by training may be countered by the use of the trained muscles for postural reasons. (The low intensity and long-term kind of muscle action that is needed to maintain posture stimulates the slow-twitch qualities of the muscle, perhaps offsetting any stimulation for those muscles to transform into FT fibers.) The transformation of FT fiber types to ST is probably impeded by the fact that considerable effort is required in order to reach the threshold

necessary to activate the FT muscles often enough to transfer them to a slower type.

Training appears to selectively hypertrophy muscle fiber types. Most of hypertrophy is due to increases in the diameter of fast glycolytic fibers. For example, one study of bodybuilders found that their Type II fibers were 58% larger than normal while their Type I fibers were only 38% larger. In weightlifters and powerlifters, hypertrophy is probably even more selective in favor of Type II hypertrophy (because of the emphasis of these athletes on low-repetition training). It should be noted that an increase in the diameter of the muscles fiber is caused primarily by increased synthesis of actin and myosin filaments, which leads to a greater opportunity for cross-bridge interaction and hence an increase in contractile strength.

Training with maximal and near-maximal weights may lead to the recruitment of the high-threshold neurons that are not normally within the realm of voluntary control (heavy training may also cause an increase motor unit firing rates). FT fibers (particularly type II B) are rarely recruited, but when they are, hypertrophy of them is relatively rapid. ST fibers appear to grow less easily. Partial splitting (hyperplasia) of muscle fibers (not myofibrils) is observed in surgically overloaded muscle but little evidence of such an occurrence in live human muscle exists. Nevertheless, hyperplasia through a lengthwise split of an enlarged muscle fiber may occur to some small extent with unusual levels of training stress.

Endurance training can increase the amount and size of mitochondria, the muscle's ATP-synthesizing capacity, as well as capillarization within muscle tissue. Resistance training generally has no effect on the ratio of capillaries to muscle fibers, but capillary density within a muscle falls as hypertrophying muscle fibers comprise a greater share of total muscle. Bodybuilders who employ high reps in their training may be an exception to this rule (for these athletes the capillary density may not change).

It takes time for the influences of training to cause a change in the composition of muscle fibers. The half life of contractile proteins has been estimated to be seven to fifteen days. This is the time it takes for half of the contractile proteins to be synthesized (with synthesis taking place in FT fibers faster than it does in ST fibers). Therefore, the training effects on muscle tissue cannot begin to take widespread effect for several weeks.

Muscle fibers can adapt to stresses placed on them by increasing in length as well a girth (the former by adding sacromeres in series to the same muscle fiber). For example, the immobilization of muscles in a shortened position will result in a decrease in the number of sacromeres along the fiber in series (immobilization in the lengthened position has the opposite effect). It appears that length has a greater effect than tension on the number of sacromeres.

The Response of Muscle Tissue to Immobilization

It is well known that the immobilization of a muscle leads to atrophy (a decrease in the size) of that muscle. That atrophy is due in part to a decrease in the diameter of muscle fibers. However, a number of less obvious changes in muscle tissue typically take place during immobilization as well. For instance, when a muscle is immobilized in a shortened position, there is an increase in the ratio of collagen to muscle fiber; both decrease, but muscle tissue decreases faster. There is also a loss in the number of sacromeres in series within the muscle.

Electrical stimulation of an immobilized muscle can reduce the loss of serial sacromeres and minimize or eliminate the change in the ratio of muscle to collagen. Immobilization in a lengthened position also helps to reduce the loss of sacromeres and any change in the ratio of muscle to collagen. Atrophy is also mitigated by stretching (which can increase protein synthesis as well as the number of sacromeres is series). One study showed that stretching a muscle for fifteen minutes every forty-eight hours was enough to sustain the ratio of muscle to connective tissue at the same level. Stretching or stimulation alone showed signs of activation in slow fibers and the suppression of activity in the genes of fast fiber types. (Naturally, any of these activities might be dangerous to the tissues that were intended to be protected during immobilization so they should not be attempted without the permission and supervision of the physician who ordered the immobilization.) Once immobilization has been terminated, it takes several weeks for sacromere numbers to return to normal.

It should be noted that similar effects occur when a muscle is simply not used, , though they far less severe. Size decreases are partly due to reduction in the actin and myosin content of muscles that are used less often or less intensely.

After damage to a muscle, myoblasts (a small population of undifferentiated cells that reside close to a muscle's surface) can fuse to form a large multinucleated cell that then assembles the structure of a muscle. When an injury is extensive, this process cannot replace all of the lost fibers, and the remaining fibers may hypertrophy in order to compensate for the net loss of muscle tissue.

Training Effects on Bones and Connective Tissue

The bones and connective tissues of the body respond to stresses from the loads that are placed on them. The quality and quantity of the loads determine the body's response (e.g., an extreme stress can lead to an immediate fracture of otherwise healthy bone tissues, while a repetitive loading somewhat below that level can lead to stress fractures and stress at a still lower level can induce positive changes in bone tissue).

Electrical effects are probably responsible for the link between the mechanical deformation of bone tissue and that tissue's cellular adaptation response to that deformation. Dynamic strain appears to have a greater effect than static on adaptation. The thickness of bones is affected significantly and positively by training in general, and by resistance training in particular. The bone density (mineralization) of weightlifters is the greatest of all athletes. However, particularly strenuous training by an athlete with an immature skeleton may delay collagen maturation in connective tissues, slow the rate of long bone growth and/or negatively affect bone mechanical characteristics. Training which begins prior to middle age and continues into an advanced age appears to affect positively bone mass and mineralization. The effects of training commenced at middle age or later are not fully known at this time but the prospects of a positive effect appear to be good.

Exercise increases the maximum load which the tendons and ligaments can withstand before they separate from bone tissue. Exercise also increases collagen synthesis, but this synthesis is matched by degradation as a result of the stress of the exercise. However, overload leads to an increase in the number of fibroblasts in the tendon (fibroblasts are cells that aid in the formation of connective tissue). Overall, there is evidence that this process of synthesis and destruction leads to the development of stronger connective tissue. Training also appears to maintain tendon strength and integrity with aging. Despite the fact that circulation within collagenous fibers is limited, cyclic compression of these fibers apparently enhances the synthesis of collagen and perhaps meniscal fibrocartilage as well.

Activation of the SSC seems to provide neural training and metabolic stimuli to muscular tissue, specifically the loading components related to stiffness regulation, especially in explosive type force production. For example, after plyometric training, subjects preactivated their leg extensors earlier, before the impact of the landing, adding to the possibility of increased power during the breaking phase.

Finally, different forms of exercise produce different patterns of neuronal discharge to the muscle fibers. As was noted above, neural stimulation has an influence on muscle structure.

Physics And Mechanics

Mechanics is the branch of physics that deals with forces and their effects on objects. Kinematics is the subdivision of mechanics that studies the nature of motion. Kinetics studies the causes of motion. Biomechanics is the subdivision of the science of mechanics that deals with the application of the laws of mechanics to living organisms. Knowing certain principles of mechanics can help us to understand a number of principles of optimal technique, such as how best to impart force to the movement of projectiles like bars.

On one level the principles of mechanics can be used to analyze a number of the most fundamental aspects of force delivery. For example, you can say that in order to lift a bar of a specific weight to a certain height, you must impart a force of x over a period y in direction z. At a more fundamental level you can say that certain levers (e.g., the bones of the legs and spine) must pass through the certain angles with a given angular velocity in order to impart the force necessary to lift a bar (assuming there is solid contact between the levers and the bar. At a still more fundamental level, mechanics can be used to determine the amount of force with which the muscles of the legs and back must contract, and for how long a period, in order for the levers comprised by the bones and joints of the legs and back to be moved at the velocity required to lift the bar in the appropriate way.

A discussion of some of the basic principles of mechanics follows. That discussion will avoid the mathematical aspects of mechanics, but will attempt to cover relevant concepts in sufficient detail so that the reader will be able to understand both the concepts and how to apply them to the sport of weightlifting.

Some Basic Definitions Used in the Science of Mechanics

We will begin our discussion of the laws of mechanics with some key definitions. These definitions are important because the science of physics uses certain familiar words in a special ways as well as some unfamiliar words.

Kinds of Motion

There are four basic kinds of motion: linear, angular, curvilinear and general. In linear motion (also referred to as translation), all parts of a body move the same distance in the same direction and at the same time. Examples would be a box being pushed along the floor or a bar being pulled from the floor.

In angular motion a body moves along a circular path around a central line that is perpendicular to the plane of the motion. An example would be when plates of a bar are being spun around the bar. Angular speed is measured in terms of the angle traversed by an object in a given time interval. Because of this means of measure, all points on the rotating object are moving with the same angular speed, although the points on the object that are further away from its center are moving through a greater linear distance and at a faster linear rate than points that are closer to the object's center.

In curvilinear motion an object moves in a curved path but does not necessarily rotate as it does so. An example would be the movement of a ball swung on a string.

General motion is a combination of two or more motions. The combination might be motions of the same type (e.g., two angular motions) or of different types (e.g., an angular motion combined with a linear motion). General motions are the most common motions that we encounter. An example would be a weightlifter descending under a bar in the jerk. Roughly speaking, the lifter's center of gravity and overall body are moving in the same direction, at the same speed and at the same time. The lifter's legs are rotating about the hip joint as one is moved forward and the other rearward to assume a split position. On the leg that is being moved forward, the lifter's foot is undergoing angular motion about his or her knee joint as the front leg is being bent in stepping forward and at the same time undergoing linear motion from the position at which it began (under the lifter's torso) to a position well ahead of the lifter's torso.

Scalars and Vectors

In the language of mechanics, motion can be described in two basic ways. One way is to consider only the magnitude of a motion and not its direction. An example of such a means of description is the term distance. Linear distance describes how far an object has traveled in a straight line, but not its direction. (An automobile that has gone one way between two cities that are 100 miles apart has traveled the same distance as an auto that has made a round trip between two cities that are fifty miles apart.)

Similarly, angular distances are measured by the number of degrees of angle through which an entity has passed. (For example, a pendulum that has swung forward 45° from its starting point, returned to its starting position and stopped, has traveled an angular distance 90°, as has a pendulum that has swung forward 90° and stopped at that position.) Any description of motion which is comprised only of a one-dimensional measure is termed a scalar quantity.

Another means of describing motion is to consider magnitude and direction. Linear displacement is a measure of motion that consists of a straight line between the beginning point of the object's travel and its end point and an indication of the direction of that motion (e.g., 10 miles, north). Continuing the example of the automobile presented earlier, the auto that travels 100 miles north of its starting point and stops has undergone a displacement of 100 miles. In contrast, an auto that has traveled 50 miles north and then 50 miles south along the same line has undergone a displacement of 0 miles.

Angular displacement is the angle between an object's initial and final positions. Continuing the earlier example of the pendulum, the pendulum that has traveled 45° forward and then the same number of degrees back has undergone a displacement of 0 ° while a pendulum that has swung forward 90° and stopped has undergone a displacement of 90°. Descriptions of motion that include magnitude and direction are referred to as vector quantities.

Speed and distance are scalar quantities, while velocity, acceleration and displacement are vector quantities. Vector quantities have a distinct advantage over scalar quantities, in that the information they contain permits predictive calculations.

For instance, two vector quantities, such as the velocities of two objects before they collide, can be added to determine their combined effect, or the resultant vector. Consider a situation in which a bar is traveling at a speed of 2 meters per second vertically when it collides with the thighs of a lifter (which impart a forward horizontal velocity to the bar of 2 meters per second). The bar will move forward away from the lifter, at a 45° angle from the vertical at a speed of 2.828 meters per second. In a similar fashion, the horizontal and vertical components of a given vector can be calculated.

Speed. Speed in physics is defined as the rate at which a distance is covered. For example, linear motion (motion in a straight line) might be expressed as 50 mph or 30 meters per second. Speed is called a scalar quantity because it expresses a quantity in only one way. Speed measures only a rate of motion; no particular direction is implied. Since speed is by nature an average quantity (the distance that is covered by an object over a given interval), it technically has little to say about how fast an object is moving at any given point during the interval being considered. When scientists wish to address the speed of an object at a specific point in time and motion, they refer to its instantaneous speed (a term which is much closer to what most people mean when they talk about speed in conventional terms).

Velocity. Lay persons often use the terms speed and velocity interchangeably, but to physicists, velocity and speed have very different meanings. Speed is purely a rate of motion. Velocity is speed in a specific direction (e.g., 50 mph, north). Velocity is called a vector, or directed quantity, because it is described by its direction as well as the rate of motion. Since velocity is measured in the two dimensions of speed and direction, it will change if either the speed or direction of an object changes (an object traveling at the same speed that changes direction has changed its velocity). Both speed and velocity are used to describe linear motion, motion in a continuous direction.

Angular Speed and Velocity. When experts in mechanics speak about the rate of angular or rotational motion (movement in a circular path around a central line) they measure such motion in terms of the angular distance or displacement. For example, the speed of a rotating wheel might be described as 10° per second. While all points on such a wheel are moving through the same number of degrees of angular motion in the same interval, different points on the wheel are traversing different linear distances during the same period. Specifically, the further a point is from the center of the wheel, the greater its linear speed (the more distance it is covering in the same period).

Newton's Three Fundamental Laws of Motion

During the 1600s one of the greatest geniuses in the history of science identified many of the most important laws of physics. His name was Isaac Newton. Newton single-handedly developed an astonishing number of physical laws that continue to serve as the basis of the science of physics to this day. Among his many discoveries and insights, perhaps the most influential laws that Newton conceived were his three laws of motion: the laws of inertia, acceleration and reaction.

Newton's First Law of Motion: The Law of Inertia

The law of inertia (also known an the law of conservation of motion) states that a body at rest, or a body moving with a constant velocity in a straight line, will remain in that state until it is compelled to change its state by an external force acting on it. In short, all objects that are in motion have a tendency to remain in that same motion and all objects that are at rest tend to stay at rest. This tendency or property of objects is referred to as inertia.

The concept of inertia seems counter to our everyday experience, because we constantly encounter two forces that counteract the inertia of moving objects: friction and gravity. Friction acts to reduce the rate of motion of objects, and gravity acts to increase their rate of motion in the direction of the gravitational pull. However, in the absence of those two forces, objects once set in motion would remain in motion at the same speed and in the same direction (without the force of gravity, objects at rest, whether in space or on a solid object, would tend to remain in place).

Mass. The inertial property of an object is influenced by the number and type of atoms that an object contains. We measure an object's inertia with a concept known as mass. A kilogram is a measure of mass. Mass is a constant property. Regardless of whether an object is located on earth, on the moon or in space, its mass, its tendency to resist a change in motion remains the same.

Weight. In contrast to mass, weight is a measure of the gravitational force that the earth (or another celestial body) exerts on an object. The force of gravity does vary with the body exerting it (e.g., the moon versus the earth) and the distance of the object on which the force is being exerted from the surface of the object which is exerting the gravitational pull. Therefore, objects may weigh six times more on the earth than the moon (as a result of the earth's greater gravitational force relative to the moon), but the tendency of an object to remain in constant velocity motion (its inertia) is the same on the moon as on the earth (essentially because the makeup of the object's atoms does not alter when its location changes). Moreover, even objects in space that are far enough away from the earth to be considered weightless still have the same tendency to remain at constant velocity as they did on the earth, the same inertia (they simply are not affected by gravity and inertia). Weight is a product of mass and gravitational acceleration (g) and is measured in pounds or newtons (which weigh slightly less than a quarter of a pound).

Since the gravitational force that the earth exerts on an object at any point on the earth's surface is proportional to the object's mass, there is a fixed relationship between the mass of an object and its weight at that point on the earth's surface (although the relationship actually changes slightly over the surface of the earth, because not all points on the earth's surface are an equal distance from its center). It is because of this relationship that we speak of converting pounds (a measure of weight) to kilograms (a measure of mass or an object's inertia) and use kilograms as a proxy for weight, even though, at least to a physicist, a kilogram is a measure of mass. However, as noted above, the weight of an object will be one-sixth as much on the moon as on earth, while the mass of the object will remain the same. Therefore, while an object with a mass of 1 kg. weighs a little more than 2 lb. on the earth's surface, it will weigh about a third of a pound on the moon's surface, because of the moon's weaker gravitational pull on an object with the same mass.

It should be remembered that although mass and weight have a fixed relationship to one another at any given point on the earth's surface, they are really separate properties. That is, when lifting an object (e.g., a bar) from the earth's surface, the force exerted on that object must be great enough to overcome both the weight of the object and its inertial tendency to remain at rest. (If the force of the upward lift and the weight of the object are equal, the object will not move; it will merely achieve a virtually weightless state in which motion up, down or sideways takes an equal amount of force, the force required to overcome the object's inertia.) Ignoring any effects of friction, the act of moving a bar in a purely horizontal direction involves overcoming only the inertia of the bar and not its weight.

Perhaps we can come closest to directly experiencing the inertial property of an object on earth when we begin to push an object suspended from a string or slide an object on a nearly frictionless surface. For example, imagine the effort that it would take to push an object with a smooth surface across a surface covered with the slickest ice that you have ever experienced versus the effort that would be required to lift that object. The former gives a sense of an object's inertia (although only an approximation, since there is still some friction even on the slickest of ice).

Newton's Second Law of Motion: The Law of Acceleration

The law of acceleration states that, for bodies of constant mass, acceleration is proportional to the force that causes it and takes place in the direction that the force acts. What is acceleration and what is force?

Acceleration. Acceleration is the rate of change in velocity. It is normally expressed in terms of an amount of change in velocity that occurs in a given interval. For example, an object that falls toward the earth in a vacuum moves toward the earth 32 feet per second faster with each passing second (i.e., it is accelerating at a rate of 32 feet per second, per second, which is also expressed as 32 ft/sec^2). Therefore, if the object falls from a resting position, it will have reached a downward velocity of 32 feet per second by the end of one second and 64 feet per second at the end of two seconds. Objects that are stationary and those that are moving at a constant speed, are both undergoing zero acceleration, because their rate of motion is not changing over time. Acceleration can be positive or negative (negative acceleration is often referred to as deceleration). Acceleration only occurs when a force acts on an object (in the example of acceleration in an object falling to earth, gravitational pull is the force that causes acceleration).

Any object that is moving in a curved direction is constantly accelerating, because it is always changing its velocity. (Velocity is a function or speed and direction, and from the perspective of a straight line, the direction of an object moving in a curve is continually changing direction .) Therefore, an object that is moving in a curved direction must have a force acting on it. In contrast, linear motion at a constant velocity can occur in a frictionless and gravityless world (such an object would not be accelerating because it would be moving in the same direction and at the same speed).

Force. Force is a quantity that has a tendency to change the motion (i.e., the speed or direction) of an object. Force will always cause a change in velocity (acceleration), unless there is an equal or greater force that resists the acceleration. For example, if an athlete tries to lift an object that weighs 200 kg. by applying a force equal to 100 kg., the object will not move because it will exert an equal and opposite force of 100 kg.. It is only when the upward force applied to the object exceeds 200 kg., plus the inertia of that object, that it will accelerate (i.e., move upward) from its resting position.

Without a force of some kind acting on a object, it can experience no acceleration. Force is a function of mass and acceleration (mass x acceleration = force). Therefore, if two objects of unequal mass are to be accelerated at the same rate, more force will be required to accelerate the object with the greater mass. If two objects with the same mass are to be accelerated at different rates, the one that is to have a greater rate of acceleration will require more force. Similarly, if the force applied to an object is increased, so must its rate of acceleration, and if an equal force is applied to two objects, the object with the greater mass will be accelerated less.

The actual reaction that a force creates results from the magnitude of the force and the direction in which the force is applied. A force that is directed through the center of a body (centric force) causes that body to translate (i.e., to move in a linear fashion). An example would be an upward force applied to the exact center of a boulder that was larger than the forces of inertia and gravity combined (such an upward force would cause vertical translation of the boulder).

A force that does not act through the center of an object is known as an eccentric force. Such a force causes translation and rotation at the same time. An example would be a person applying upward force to one side of a boulder. If that force is of sufficient magnitude, the boulder will rise and rotate at the same time.

A combination of two forces acting in opposite directions is known as a couple. An example of a couple would be a person pushing down on one side of a boulder while pulling up on the other side. In such a case the upward and downward translatory effects of the forces applied by the person to the opposite sides of the boulder would be canceled. However, the rotational effects of the forces applied would combine to yield a purely rotational force and, consequently, a purely rotational movement.

Forces can also be categorized by another measure of effectiveness. Static force acts on an object but does not produce motion because of the counterbalancing force that it encounters. Dynamic force is one that causes acceleration because it is not completely counterbalanced.

Newton's Third Law of Motion: The Law of Reaction

The law of reaction states that for every force exerted by one body on another, there is an equal and opposite force exerted by the second on the first. In essence, there is always a pairing of forces, with those forces really being interactions between two objects that occur simultaneously or not at all. A force never acts in isolation.

The mass of each of two objects upon which equal forces are acting determines how much acceleration each experiences as a result of the contact with the other force. For example, if a baseball collides with the earth, the baseball and the earth exert an equal and opposite force on one another, which tends to accelerate the other in the opposite direction. However, the force received by the earth is insufficient to overcome its inertia, so that the earth's position is unaffected (it undergoes no acceleration, no change in motion, as a result of the contact. In contrast, the baseball is accelerated significantly away from the earth's surface because the force it encounters easily overcomes its inertia.

Newton's Three Laws of Motion Have Implications for Angular Motion

Newton's laws of motion, as described above, apply to linear motion. However, these laws all have counterparts that apply to angular motion. For example, Newton's first law of angular motion says that an object in angular motion will tend to remain in motion as long as it is not acted on by some force. This is because rotating bodies have their own version of inertia which is referred to as their rotational inertia or moment of inertia.

An object's moment of inertia is a function of its mass and the distribution of the mass around the axis of rotation. The greater the mass of the object and the greater its distance from the axis of rotation, the greater is the object's moment of inertia. For example, the arm has a greater moment of inertia when it is extended than when it is bent (because in the extended position the mass of the arm is distributed further from the shoulder joint). Similarly, the extended leg has a greater moment of inertia than the extended arm because the mass of the leg is greater and the leg is longer (so that mass is distributed further from its axis of rotation--the hip joint—than the arm is from its axis of rotation—the shoulder). An arm with weights held in the hand has a greater moment of inertia than an empty hand. Such an arm requires more force to move and more force to stop because of its greater moment of inertia.

506

The quantity of motion experienced by an object in angular motion is referred to as its angular momentum. Angular momentum is the product of the object's rotational inertia and its angular velocity.

Torque is a measure of the eccentric force that causes (a torque produces angular acceleration). Torque is a function of the force applied to an object that is being rotated and the perpendicular distance from the point at which force is applied (the axis of rotation). Shorten the resistance arm and you reduce the torque.

Newton's second law of angular motion states that the angular acceleration experienced by a body is proportional to the torque causing it and takes place in the direction in which the torque acts. Finally, Newton's third law of angular motion states that for every torque exerted by one body on another, there is an equal and opposite torque exerted by the second body (if both bodies have the same axis). Examples of the latter are the dancer who moves the feet counterclockwise and the hands in a clockwise direction when jumping. This is because when a body is in the air, if the angular momentum of any part of the body is changed, the angular momentum of another part must also change so that the total remains the same.

Other Concepts of Motion

Momentum

While the force required to move an object at rest (ignoring the influence of gravity) is only that needed to overcome its inertia, the force needed to change the motion of a moving object is different. In order to stop the motion of a moving object, one must overcome the quantity of the object's motion. That quantity is referred to as the object's momentum. Momentum is a product of the object's mass and its velocity. The faster an object is moving or the greater its mass, the greater its momentum. Therefore, if two objects are moving at the same velocity, the object with the greater mass has greater momentum. Similarly, if two objects have the same mass, the object moving with greater velocity has greater momentum.

The principle of momentum explains why when a larger automobile collides with a smaller automobile that is moving in the opposite direction, the occupants of the smaller vehicle tend to be more severely injured. Both vehicles are brought to a stop, but the larger vehicle is brought to a stop over a distance (which affords the occupants some opportunity to decelerate over time), while the smaller vehicle suffers a reversal of its direction (a much more rapid deceleration).

The law of conservation of linear momentum says that in any collision or interaction between two objects, the objects exert an equal and opposite force on each other for the same period and have equal and opposite changes in momentum. This means that if one object's momentum increases by a given amount, the other object loses an equal amount. The combined momentum has not changed; it has only been transferred. (If we know how much one object's momentum has changed, we know how much the other's has changed as well.) However, in the case of the automobiles given above, the heavier auto had more momentum to begin with, so even though its loss of momentum was equal to that of the lighter vehicle, its change in motion was smaller.

Impulse

An impulse is the average force exerted by a body in a given direction. The impulse is a function of the net force and the time over which a force is applied. The following equation expresses the impulse-momentum relationship: Momentum = Mass x Velocity.

The left side of the equation is the impulse of a force (a force that acts for a finite period versus those which act continuously, such as gravity). The impulse momentum principle says the impulse force is equal to the change in momentum it produces. The pressure is the average load supported per unit of area. (Very large loads or forces can be harmless, depending in the area over which it is distributed.) That is why objects are decelerated over distances and why protective equipment distributes its force over a wider area.

Impact

Impact occurs when two bodies collide. Whenever an impact occurs, the bodies which come in contact either remain in contact or separate. The velocity at which any separation occurs depends on the velocity of the impact and the elasticity of the objects (elasticity is the property that causes a body to return to its original shape).

The elasticity of a given entity can be described by its coefficient of restitution (COR), a constant that expresses the relationship between the velocity of impact of that object and its velocity of separation after impact occurs. It is derived by dividing the speed of an object after a collision with its speed before the collision. An object with a high coefficient of restitution returns a large share of the velocity it had prior to impact. An object with a low coefficient of restitution returns only a small share of its velocity prior to impact. If an object moving in a purely downward direction were to impact with the hard surface of an immovable object and separate with the same speed at which it had been moving immediately prior to impact, it would be said to have a coefficient of restitution of 1 (the maximum, which has never been observed experimentally). Rubber balls, such as basketballs, have a fairly high COR (NBA basketballs have CORs in the .76 to .80 range), while a ball made of cast iron (such the shot used in shot putting) has a relatively low COR.

The velocity with which a basketball bounces when it impacts with an inelastic surface is influenced by the ball's vertical force, any horizontal force component that the ball has when it impacts with the floor (including spin) and the friction of the ball against the floor.

When two free bodies collide (e.g., two basketball players jumping for a ball), the greater the velocity of player A prior to impact, the greater the velocity of player B after hitting player A. The greater the mass of player B, the less that player's velocity will change as a result of impact. Finally, the greater the coefficient of restitution of player B, the greater will be that player's force of separation upon contact with player A.

Work . Work is a function of the force applied to a body and the distance through which that body moves in the direction in which the force is applied. In terms of the science of mechanics, an athlete holding a weight overhead is performing no work, even though he or she is exerting considerable effort. When the object against which force is applied is raised, positive work is being performed. When such an object is being lowered, negative work is being performed.

Power. Power is the rate at which work is performed. It is determined by dividing the total work accomplished by the time it took to perform that work.

Energy. Energy is the capacity to do work. Energy can take many forms (e.g., mechanical, electrical and heat). Moreover, different kinds of energy can be transferred to one another. Mechanical energy can take several forms. It is the energy a body possesses as the result of its motion, of being pushed or pulled out of its normal shape or its position relative to the earth's surface.

Kinetic Energy. Kinetic energy is the energy an object possesses because of its motion, which can be the energy of translation or rotation. The kinetic energy of an object is determined by the object's mass and speed. Strain energy is the work capacity that results from that entity's being out of its normal shape. (The timing of movements associated with the development of strain energy and its release have an important relationship to the technique of many sports, including weightlifting.) Potential energy is determined by an object's position in relation to the surface of the earth. All things being equal, the farther an object is from the surface of the earth, the greater is its potential energy.

Virtually all work consists of transforming one form of energy into another. Lifting an object gives it potential energy (stored energy that can be later released). In an elastic collision, energy is transferred from kinetic to elastic and then back to kinetic. It is rare for kinetic energy that is turned in to elastic energy and then back to kinetic energy

not to lose some of that energy in the process (energy that is "lost" has really been transferred to friction or heat). The coefficient of restitution is a measure of a object's ability to return the kinetic energy it receives.

When an upward force is imparted to an external body (e.g., when a projectile is launched), the more the reaction force against the ground exceeds the weight of the object, the greater the upward acceleration will be. The longer the period and distance of acceleration, the greater the height that body will reach.

In jumping, an upswing of the arms just as the legs leave the ground transmits force from the shoulder muscles that are lifting the arms to the ground. This increases the launching force. Therefore, a faster upward thrust of the arms as a lifter splits in the jerk will cause the body to descend under the bar more quickly, and a fast and forceful rearrangement of the feet in the split-position stop will impart upward force to the bar (assuming that the arms and torso are in a position to transmit that force). This faster and more forceful rearrangement of the feet will place more stress on the body than a slower and less forceful movement, but it will also result in the athlete being able to fix the bar with the body in a higher position, which places less stress on the body, one of the many technique trade-offs in weightlifting).

Some Basic Principles of Levers

Torque is the principle behind a lever. A lever consists of a fulcrum (a pivot point) and a rigid object called a lever arm (the moment arm). The force that is applied to the lever arm of a lever is typically referred to as F and the force arm is referred to as FA. Gravity or some other force that opposes the action of the lever is referred to as R, and the resistance arm is referred to as RA. All things being equal, the longer the lever, the greater the torque it can exert.

There are three types of levers. A type I lever is one in which the force is applied on one side of the fulcrum and the resistance arm is on the other. The classic example is the seesaw. In the seesaw, the fulcrum is the point at which the seesaw pivots (the crossbar at the seesaw's center). A child who sits on one side of the seesaw represents the resistance (R) and the length of the seesaw between the second child and the fulcrum represents the resistance arm (RA). An adult on the opposite side of the seesaw who wanted to raise that child up from the ground would represent the force (F) being applied to the lever and the portion of the seesaw between where the adult applies the force and the fulcrum at the center of the seesaw represents the force arm (FA).

If the child were to merely sit with his or her feet on the board the force required to lift the child would be equal to that child's weight and inertia (seesaw riders normally sit with their feet on the ground rather than the board so that they can push against the ground to assist the person on the other side who is doing the lifting). If the child were to move closer to the center of board, he or she would shorten the resistance arm. This would reduce the force required to accomplish lifting the child. If the adult applied force to the lever at a point that was further from the fulcrum than the child on the opposite side, less force would be required to lift the child than if the distance of the adult and child from the fulcrum were the same.

When the force arm of a lever is longer than the resistance arm, it is said to create a mechanical advantage relative to the resistance arm. The greater the length differential of the force arm over the resistance arm, the greater the mechanical advantage of the force arm and the smaller the force needed to overcome the resistance. But a mechanical advantage comes at a price. A greater resistance can be overcome, but the distance moved at the shortened resistance arm is smaller than the distance moved by the lever arm. Pliers and crowbars are common examples of tools which assist workers by creating a mechanical advantage.

In a type II lever, the force arm and the resistance arm are on the same side of the fulcrum but the force is applied further away from the fulcrum than the resistance. Using our seesaw example, if the adult moved to the same side of the seesaw as the child but was positioned behind the child, he or she would be using a type II lever to lift the child. A wheelbarrow is a common example of a type II lever. In this case, the axle of the wheel represents the fulcrum, the load in the wheelbarrow represents the resistance and the force is applied to the handles of the wheelbarrow, which are placed behind the load.

In the type III lever, the force and resistance are also on the same side of the fulcrum. The difference between type II and III levers is that in the latter the force is applied closer to the fulcrum than the resistance. In the case of the seesaw, the adult would be positioned on the same side of the seesaw as the child but would be closer to the fulcrum than the child (i.e., between the child and the fulcrum). In such a case, the adult would be at a mechanical disadvantage in that he or she would have to apply a force greater than weight and inertia of the child in order to lift the child. The closer the adult was to the fulcrum, and the further child was away, the more difficult it would be to lift the child. However, for any distance the force arm was moved by the adult, the resistance arm would move a greater distance. Therefore, while a type III lever reduces the effectiveness of a force applied to it, it amplifies the distance over which force is applied.

This principle is of great importance in human movement. It enables muscles which are capable of exerting force over relatively short distances to cause skeletal movements many times larger (although rather large forces developed in the muscles generate much smaller forces at the ends of the bones upon which they act). Most of the muscles that are responsible for major body movements are in the type III category. One example is the biceps brachii, one of the muscles responsible for elbow flexion. In the case of arm flexion (such as when performing the curl), the elbow joint serves as the fulcrum, the radius and ulna form the bulk of the resistance arm, with the bar comprising the resistance. The biceps brachii is one of the four muscles responsible for elbow flexion. It attaches to the radius at a point near the elbow joint and is one source of the forces that are responsible for elbow flexion. The distance from the elbow joint to the point at which the biceps brachii attaches to the radius represents the force arm. This attachment point is far closer to the fulcrum than the resistance (as is the case for all four of the elbow flexors). The result is that a relatively large force generated by the elbow flexors is translated into a much smaller force at the end of the resistance arm, but a relatively short distance of contraction by the elbow flexors generates a large range of movement at the end of the resistance arm.

It is interesting to note that, technically, when the bar is being lowered in the curl exercise, the elbow flexors act to resist the force supplied by the bar. Therefore, the distance from the point at which the elbow flexors attach to the elbow joint is the resistance arm, and the distance from the elbow joint to the bar represents the force arm and the bar comprises the force. This is true for all eccentric actions.

The discussion of levers thus far has implicitly assumed that the force and resistance applied to a lever occur at an angle of 90° to that lever. In such cases the lengths of the force and lever arms are simply the distance from the point at which force or resistance is applied to the fulcrum.

The muscles in the human body are not typically acting in a direction that is perpendicular to the lever arm. This does not change any of the principles of levers, but it does change the way in which the length of the true lever- and resistance-arms are calculated. For instance, the true force arm of a human lever is the length of a line perpendicular to the line of pull of the muscle that intersects with the fulcrum (represented by the joint around which motion is occurring), which is generally far shorter than would intuitively be assumed.

Given the nature of levers, it should not be surprising that under certain circumstances, one of the objectives of sports technique is to shorten the lever arm as much as possible so that the muscle tension required to perform a given movement is minimized. In other cases the objective is to maximize the lever arm so that any distance of muscular contraction is multiplied as much as possible. The result is that the movement in the lever arm will be great and the acceleration created by that lever arm will occur over a long distance. In fact, many sports rely on this principle of amplification of distance to enable the participants to launch projectiles great distances. The golf club, for example, effectively lengthens the arms of the player, thereby converting a relatively small distance of contraction of the muscles that move the club to a much greater movement of the club head, which causes the golf ball to travel a great distance.

The Concept of the Center of Gravity

The concept of the center of gravity bears some discussion here because it is not typically explained well in the literature of weightlifting (if it is explained at all). In such literature an object's line of gravity is often mistakenly referred to as its center of gravity. In certain contexts these concepts are quite similar, but they are not the same. A line of gravity is essentially one dimensional, whereas the center of gravity is three dimensional. Lines of gravity are the focus of most weightlifting analysis (at least partly because they are much easier to determine). We will explain both concepts, beginning with the concept of the line of gravity.

As was noted in the discussion of anatomy, the body has three principle planes: 1) the mid-frontal plane, which divides the body into its anterior and posterior sections; 2) the mid-transverse or horizontal plane, which divides the body into superior (upper) and inferior (lower) halves; and 3) the mid-saggital plane (which runs the length of a body from top to bottom, dividing its right and left sides). These planes also represent the lines of gravity for the object in each of these dimensions, the line of gravity being the point at which the object would be balanced if it were supported there. In objects that are symmetrical in every plane and homogeneous in composition, such as perfect solid spheres or cubes, the location of these three planes can be easily calculated from the external dimensions of the object. For objects that have more irregular shapes (such as the human body) the determination of the object's mid planes is normally done experimentally by finding where it balances objects in each of three directions.

For every position in which an object is placed, a line can be drawn through the object to a point where it would be balanced if it were supported at that point. This is referred to as the line of gravity for that position of the object. For example, consider a statue of a human. We could determine the mid-frontal plane of the statue by placing it on a sharp edge running side to side and determining the point at which the statue was balanced (i.e., had no tendency to fall forward or backward). Similarly, we could identify the statue's mid-

saggital plane by balancing it on a sharp edge that ran from the front to back of the statue perpendicular to its sides. If the statue were placed in a prone or supine position on the sharp edge, its mid-transverse plane could be found by determining its line of gravity in that position. The point at which all three of these planes intersect is the center of gravity of the statue.

The center of gravity of a bar is relatively easy to locate because of the essentially spherical and symmetrical nature of the bar. Since the plates and bar are round and evenly balanced, one line of gravity runs through the exact center of the bar (viewed from either side), dividing the front and rear portions of the bar. Another line of gravity runs vertically through the center of the bar when it is viewed from the front or back, dividing it into right and left sides. A third line of gravity runs horizontally, parallel to the ground, and through the center of the bar, dividing it into upper and lower halves.

The center of gravity (COG) of the lifter is far harder to determine than the COG of the bar, because the lifter's COG is influenced by the position of the lifter's body and the anatomical proportions of the lifter. For example, an average male standing in an erect (e.g., anatomical) position has a center of gravity at a point that is approximately 55% of his height, and an average female has a her COG at about 54% of her height, approximately in the middle of the body when viewed from the front of back and from either side. If a person raises his or her arms above the head, the center of gravity of that person will rise. If a person moves only his or her right arm laterally, that person's center of gravity shifts to the right slightly. If a weightlifter strengthens his or her legs regularly, the mass of the athlete's legs will tend to increase in relation to the lifter's overall weight. In such a case the center of gravity of that lifter will be lower than it was at the outset of the lifter's career.

Much analysis of weightlifting technique involves the vertical lines of gravity run through the lifter or the bar when both are viewed from the side. These lines represent the mid-frontal planes of the bar and the lifter (the lines that divide the front from the back, the anterior and posterior aspects, respectively). This emphasis is appropriate because the horizontal level of the line of gravity (the mid-transverse plane) is not as crucial as the vertical one in the performance of the lifts (although the horizontal line of gravity is of some significance in weightlifting and is crucial in other sports). Similarly, the vertical line of gravity of the bar and athlete from side to side (the mid-sagittal plane) is assumed to remain the same during the performance of a lift (although this is not always a valid assumption). Hence, there has been little, if any, analysis of the actions of either of the latter two gravity lines.

In addition to analysis of the movement of the mid-frontal planes of the bar and the athlete, the analysis of weightlifting technique concerns itself with the single line of gravity that runs through the lifter and the bar combined, that is, the point at which, if the lifter and bar were viewed as one entity, where the lifter and the bar would be in balance along the mid-frontal line of gravity. Many Eastern European weightlifting analysts believe that the lifter and bar should be viewed as one system, and they do so in much of their analysis.

From an analytical standpoint, the center of gravity is important because if the action of a force passes through the COG, the force produces a linear motion in that object. If the force is off center (i.e., is an eccentric force), it produces angular acceleration (change in motion) as well as linear motion. It is also important because the center of gravity has an important influence on the stability an athlete and the athlete-bar system.

To remain balanced, an object's line of gravity must remain within the area of its base of support. An object's base of support is generally the perimeter of the portions of an object that are in contact with the earth. For instance, to determine the base of support of a human standing upright, we could draw a line around the outside of the person's feet and connect the distance between the person's feet with straight lines (i.e., trace a straight line from the rearmost point on each heel and from large toe to large toe). The area within those lines would be the person's base of support. (In reality, the base of support is slightly smaller than this, because the majority of a person's support is produced by the area between the ball of the foot and the middle the heel ; the toes provide only limited support, as does the back of the heel.) Using this method, we can see that the wider the feet, the larger the person's base of support would be laterally (i.e., from side to side). In addition, a person with longer feet would have a larger base of support from front to back.

The lower an object's center of gravity in relation to that object's base of support, the greater the force that is needed to upset the object. A simple example of this characteristic is the difference in the force it takes to upset the balance of a stick four feet long and one inch square when that stick is standing on end rather than lying on its side. If the stick is standing on end, it is extremely unstable, because the center of the stick (.5" from its surface) must remain over a narrow (1" square) base of support. Any movement in excess of .5" forward, back or to either side, brings the stick's center of gravity outside that base. When the stick is on its side, its base of support is quite large, with the center of gravity being a full 2' from either edge of the stick. Only a very large movement in the stick with respect to its length could cause it to become unstable.

Similarly, when a lifter is in a deep squat position, he or she has greater stability than when standing (even though the lifter may find it easier to sustain balance in a standing position because he or she is able to move his or her base of support more easily than when in a squat position).

Understanding the concept of the center of gravity will help the coach to identify the causes of an athlete's or a barbell's movement (e.g., the athlete is jumping forward) and how any inappropriate movements can be corrected.

The Motion of Projectiles

A projectile is a body that has been launched into the air. Once a projectile has been launched, it is acted on by air resistance and gravity (the former a negligible factor in weightlifting and the latter a critical factor). Whenever a projectile is in flight, its horizontal velocity (ignoring any effect of the friction contributed by air) is a constant throughout its flight. The horizontal distance the projectile travels is determined solely by the time it remains in flight before the pull of gravity returns it to the earth. Gravity exerts a constant downward acceleration on any projectile of 9.81 meters per second each second. A projectile that is rising rapidly loses speed at the rate of 32 feet per second.

The Action of Friction

Friction is a force which acts tangential to the points of contact that are made between two bodies opposing their motion. It occurs whenever one body moves, or tends to move, over the surface of another. The extent of friction experienced between two objects is influenced by the nature of the surfaces that are in contact (this is expressed as the coefficient of friction of that kind of surface) and the force that is holding the two surfaces together. The greater the coefficient of friction and the force holding the two objects together, the greater will be the resulting friction.

Athletes take various measures to increase and decrease friction, as appropriate for their events (or at least as they believe is appropriate). For example, magnesium carbonate placed on the hands increases the friction of the hands against the bar, thereby making the grip more secure for the weightlifter and gymnast. In contrast, lubricants applied to the thighs of weightlifters (though currently illegal) are used to reduce the friction between the bar and the athlete's thighs during the pull. This not only enhances the force that an athlete can transmit to the bar during the pull; it also reduces the possibility of contact between the bar and the lifter causing an abrasion of the lifter's skin . (On the down side, such lubricants can make the bar and/or platform slippery, one of the reasons the use of lubricants is prohibited.)

Summary

This appendix has provided more information regarding physiology, anatomy and mechanics than most coaches possess. Many coaches have been quite effective with far less knowledge of these branches of science. However, if you carefully connect what you have learned in this section with the practical information that has preceded it, you cannot help but improve your ability as a coach. Just as the actual practice of weightlifting will provide a coach with insights about the sport that could never be gained by merely reading about it or coaching it, knowing the science that underlies the principles of weightlifting technique and training can give a coach insights that mere coaching can never provide. Therefore, it is well worth the effort to digest this information.

Training On The Snatch And Clean And Jerk:

A Key To Athletic Excellence

Readers of this book will by now understand that weightlifters are unquestionably the strongest and most powerful athletes in the world. But their athletic abilities do not end there; they are amazingly accomplished in a number of other areas. They exhibit more joint flexibility than all other Olympic athletes, except for gymnasts. Elite Olympic style weightlifters can also run faster than all but the fastest sprinters and jump higher than all but the best high and broad jumpers. (For example, Yuri Vardanian, World and Olympic weightlifting champion, could reportedly high jump 7' without any special preparation in jumping.) These abilities are quite amazing when you consider that Olympic style weightlifters do not train them extensively, if at all (other than the training that arises directly from their practice of the Olympic lifts).

The Unique Value Of Olympic Lifts For Athletes

The truly remarkable abilities of Olympic style weightlifters are certainly due in part to genetic qualities of these athletes and to their outstanding physical condition. However, they are also due in no small measure to the kind of training that weightlifters do: performing the snatch and the clean and jerk (C&J).

Almost any form of resistance training can improve an athlete's strength, but the snatch and C&J are unique in their ability to develop strength and explosive power at the same time. And the benefits of practicing the Olympic lifts are hardly limited to developing strength and power. Here is a partial list of other added benefits:

1. The mere practice of the Olympic lifts teaches an athlete how to explode (to activate a maximum number of muscle units rapidly and simultaneously). Part of the extraordinary abilities of the Olympic lifters arises out of their having learned how to effectively activate more of their muscle fibers more rapidly than others who are not so trained (in addition to having developed stronger muscles).

2. The practice of proper technique in the Olympic lifts teaches an athlete to apply force with his or her muscle groups in the proper sequences (i.e., from the center of the body to its extremities). This is a valuable technical lesson which can be of benefit to any athlete who needs to impart force to another person or object (a necessity in virtually every sport).

3. In mastering the Olympic lifts, the athlete learns how to accelerate objects under varying degrees of resistance. This is because the body experiences differing degrees of perceived resistance as it attempts to move a bar with maximum speed through a full range of motion. These kinds of changes in resistance are much more likely to resemble those encountered in athletic events than similar exercises performed on an isokinetic machine (which has a fixed level of resistance or speed of resistance throughout the range of motion).

4. The athlete learns to receive force from another moving body effectively and becomes conditioned to accept such forces.

5. The athlete learns to move effectively from an eccentric contraction to a concentric one (through the stretch-shortening cycle, the cycle that is activated and trained through exercises that are often referred to as plyometrics).

6. The actual movements performed while executing the Olympic lifts are among the most common and fundamental in sports. Therefore, training the specific muscle groups in motor

patterns that resemble those used in an athlete's events is often a byproduct of practicing the snatch and C&J.

7. Practicing the Olympic lifts trains an athlete's explosive capabilities, and the lifts themselves measure the effectiveness of the athlete in generating explosive power to a greater degree than most other exercises they can practice.

8. Finally, the Olympic lifts are simply fun to do. I have yet to meet an athlete who has mastered them who does not enjoy doing the Olympic lifts. While making workouts enjoyable may not be the primary objective of a strength coach, it is not an unimportant consideration in workout planning. Athletes who enjoy what they are doing are likely to practice more consistently and to be more highly motivated than athletes who do not enjoy their workouts as much.

Case Studies of Athletes Benefiting from Olympic Lifting

Other than the abilities of Olympic style weightlifters, is there any proof that practicing the Olympic lifts actually helps athletes? There is an enormous number of examples of athletes who have benefited dramatically from practicing the Olympic lifts. Presenting these cases would require a very large book. I will provide just three examples to make the point. I have chosen those particular examples because they come from athletes who participate in sports which would not normally be expected to benefit very much from ordinary weight training.

Steve Bedrosian recently retired at the age of thirty-nine after a very successful career as a professional baseball pitcher, most recently as relief pitcher for the Atlanta Braves. His career had very nearly ended five years earlier. When he was thirty-four, Steve lost some of the feeling in two of the fingers of his pitching hand. As a result he had lost the ability to pitch effectively and was forced to take a year off in an effort to rehabilitate his hand. Many baseball experts felt that after this kind of setback his career was over. It was at this point that he met Ben Green, athletic director at the White Oak Athletic Center in Newnan, Georgia (Ben's accomplishments as a weightlifter and coach were discussed earlier in this book). Ben put Bedrosian on a program of Olympic lift training during his year off. After six months of such training, Bedrosian added eight miles per hour to his fast ball and was able to dunk a basketball (something he had often tried but had never in his life been able to do). Steve made a triumphant return to the mound during the 1993 season.

A second example is professional golfer Cindy Schreyer. She was introduced to the Olympic lifts by Ben Green in 1993. After approximately eight months of training, Cindy increased her drive by a full forty yards, a staggering improvement for a

person already highly skilled at golf. Cindy won her first PGA tournament shortly after this dramatic improvement in her drive occurred..

Derrick Adkins was a sophomore at Georgia Tech when he began to work with Lynne Stoessel-Ross, then the school's strength coach. Lynne has been a national champion and a national record holder in weightlifting and has represented the United States in the Women's World Weightlifting Championships. She has a strong academic background in physical education, having earned a Masters degree in that field. She currently works as and educator and strength and conditioning coach in Lubbock, Texas. Derek had already reached the international level as a 400 meter hurdler when he began training with Lynne in 1990, having won the Atlantic Coast Conference championships and placed sixth at the World University Games. His best time was 49.53 seconds. In less than a year of training on the Olympic lifts, he shaved nearly a second off his already outstanding time (reducing it to 48.6 seconds). An injury sustained during an unfortunate running accident hampered his training for more than a year after that. However, after recovering from his injury and resuming training on the Olympic lifts, he reduced his time by another .9 seconds and went on to win the U.S. Nationals and the Goodwill Games. More recently Derek won the 1996 Olympic Games in Atlanta.

Needless to say, if a baseball player, a golfer and a hurdler have benefited so much from practicing the Olympic lifts, football players and other athletes who participate in sports in which power is acknowledged to play a more critical role can enjoy and have enjoyed even more direct benefits.

Only Dedicated Athletes Will Gain Benefits from Practicing the Olympic Lifts

In order to enjoy the myriad benefits that arise from training on the Olympic lifts, there is a significant price that every athlete must pay. He or she must commit to learning the requisite skills. Most weight training exercises can be learned in one session, and the athlete's technique can be refined to the point where the athlete can train with little supervision (with regard to technique) in a few practice sessions. In contrast, mastering the Olympic lifts requires a deeper understanding of the mechanics of the movements (which are somewhat complex). Moreover, considerable practice under supervised conditions must take place before competency is attained. People who say that the Olympic lifts are dangerous are very wrong in most of their arguments, but they are correct in one very important sense. The Olympic lifts can be dangerous if an athlete does not learn how to perform them properly. An athlete who is not willing to learn proper technique is better off not practicing the Olympic lifts at all.

Teaching And Learning Weightlifting Technique

The processes of teaching and learning, in general and as they apply to weightlifting, are discussed at length in Chapter 2. A simplified sequence can be described as follows.

Before the learner attempts to perform a certain movement for the first time, he or she should be given the idea of the movement through the use of films, demonstrations and verbal descriptions of how to move and why. Once an understanding of the movement has been acquired, the learner is ready to attempt it. This can be done unassisted or through guided movement (the instructor physically assists the learner to move his or her body through the correct pattern of motion). A variation is to have the learner "walk through" (perform the movement at a slower speed or do only some aspects of the movement) while focusing on what he or she is feeling. (Asking for some explanation of what is being felt or experienced tends to cause the learner to focus more fully during the walk through.) In the case of the Olympic lifts, the beginner should do this with a broomstick or bar.

Once an athlete has a basic grasp of what is to be done, he or she can begin to learn the skill. There are two fundamental requirements for learning a motor skill (a skill of physical movement): practice and feedback about the practice. This means the person must consciously direct his or her nervous system through the required movement, and the person must experience feedback with respect to the success of that effort. At first the coach is the primary source of feedback, but ultimately performers themselves learn to supply much of their own feedback. This process can be facilitated by having learners give the coach performance estimates (the more multifaceted the better).

It is clear that mental practice (visualizing the desired performance) is very effective for beginners. It enables them to plan (i.e., anticipate their motion). Mental practice also helps the beginner to run through any cognitive elements involved in the task and to think through what might be done in a variety of circumstances. The evidence regarding the benefits of mental practice among more advanced athletes is more equivocal (though many advanced athletes are firm believers in mental practice).

Coaches often suggest that new skills be learned in parts. In order for such a process to be effective in learning the Olympic lifts, the learning sequence must have the following characteristics:

1. the segment practiced must be similar to the performance of that segment during the lift;

2. the sequence practiced must involve all activities that are being executed simultaneously during the actual task;

3. practice in parts must eventually be combined into the full movement;

4. the segments practiced must involve the most difficult or weakest (for that athlete) part(s) of the lift.

The Selection of Reps When Learning Technique

There are differences of opinion among coaches about what the optimal number of reps is for learning technique. Some coaches advocate the use of three to five repetitions, or more, and others believe that singles—doubles at most—are best for learning.

A reasonable principle to employ when deciding on the number of reps to use is to consider the load to which the lifter will be subjected. If a lifter is using a light bar to experiment with a particular aspect of technique (e.g., foot position in the split or balance in the low position of the snatch) there is no reason why the lifter cannot perform three to five reps or even more, as long as the athlete does not feel real muscular fatigue by the last rep of set and form is not deteriorating as the reps progress (which is generally possible only when an empty bar or stick is being lifted).

Once the lifter has gone past the early stages of learning, with its frequent need for experimentation and correction, two different approaches can be suggested for further perfecting technique. The first approach is preferred by the Soviets and the second by the Bulgarians (though neither uses one approach exclusively).

The first approach is to perform doubles with approximately 80% of the lifter's maximum and three to four reps with 65% to 70% of the lifter's maximum. Using this method, the athlete gets many practice efforts handling a weight that permits him or her to focus on proper technique and to "feel" a mistake.

The second method is to stress the use of singles with perhaps 85% to 90% of the lifter's maximum. Singles permit the load to approach maximal levels more often, levels at which the patterns of movement, tempo and force application all resemble most closely those to be used in maximum efforts. Singles also permit greater precision in movement, the ultimate objective of technique mastery. Higher reps are certainly employed for warm-ups, for variety and in assistance exercises to stimulate muscle growth, but singles form the foundation for the advanced lifter while performing the classical exercises (the snatch and C&J).

Whichever version of training is used, the power versions of Olympic lifts permit higher reps because they are simpler and less strenuous than the competitive lifts. Simpler versions of the lifts (pulls and hang lifts) tend to permit higher reps to be performed, but reps in these exercises should never exceed five if any real resistance is being used.

Most lifters will find that a combination of approaches is quite effective, but some may favor one method over another. Great lifters have been produced using both methods.

The Selection of Weight When Learning to Lift

It is always appropriate to begin teaching the lifter how to perform the Olympic lifts with a stick or empty bar. There are some aspects of the lift that will be impossible to experience without a loaded bar, but some of the basic patterns of movement can be amply modeled with minimal resistance.

Once the athlete has grasped the basics of the movement with the empty bar, he or she can begin to add weight gradually. The perfect weight for learning provides the athlete with enough resistance to feel how the bar is responding to technique variations. If the weight is too light, the lifter cannot feel any resistance and hence any difference between efficient and improper application of force. At the same time the weight must be light enough so that the lifter does not have to worry about making the lift. Such worries force the athlete to put technique on autopilot and hope for the best, instead of permitting the athlete to focus on the process with the assurance that success will occur as long as he or she performs the movement correctly.

The correct weight is relatively easy for the experienced coach to see, but the newer coach may need guidelines. First, the weight should not be flying all over the place (e.g., way in front of the lifter on one rep, behind on another). Second, the lifter should not be able to perform more than five to eight reps with the weight (and the lifter should never do more than three reps with a weight that can be made for five reps and five reps with a weight that can be lifted for eight when he or she is learning proper technique. The athlete should look nearly as fresh on the last rep of the set as on the first. If there is a noticeable slowing down or a declining precision with later reps in the set, the weight is too heavy for that number of reps (so either the weight or the number of reps should be reduced).

The good news is that the athlete can improve his or he power with virtually any resistance in the beginning. It is not until later in the lifter's training that heavier weights are needed in order to generate a training effect. Therefore, heavy weights in the beginning are both counterproductive to building technique and unnecessary for building strength and power.

It will generally take an athlete anywhere from several to a dozen or more workouts to exhibit basic technique in the Olympic lifts done in power style. It will take several months for the lifter to handle near maximum weights with sound technique, and such efforts should occur only on occasion (e.g., every two to three weeks). Any progression in weight should stop whenever the athlete's technique begins to deteriorate. The athlete should return to a lower weight that can be lifted properly at that stage.

Again, this presents no problems in terms of the athlete's enjoying the benefits of the Olympic lifts because improvements will come at first through handling only very modest weights.

The Importance of Gradual Conditioning for Weightlifting

The advice given in the preceding sections with regard to moderation in loading applies as much to the amount of weightlifting training that an athlete performs as to the amount of weight lifted per rep. The athlete must be permitted to adapt slowly to his or her weightlifting regimen. Extensive training at the outset is counterproductive both because it well not stimulate significantly faster improvements and because it exposes the athlete to unnecessary risk of injury. The overarching principle that should be used in setting up resistance training programs for athletes is that such programs are designed to assist the athletes in improving their performance in their chosen sport—they are not performed in order to make the athletes weightlifters. Athlete's will receive approximately 80% of the benefit that they will get from weightlifting training out of the first 20% of the loading that they apply (e.g., if 10,000 reps of training per year were expected to yield maximum results for a given athlete, the first 2,000 reps would probably confer approximately 80% of the benefit of the 10,000 rep load. Naturally, with this much lower level of training effort, the athlete would have far more energy to practice his or her primary sport and would minimize the prospect that his or her weightlifting training, in conjunction with practice of the primary sport, would lead to overtraining or to an overuse injury.

So begin with a very low load (a few sets each of a handful of exercises) and add gradually as needed to arrived at the ultimate training level—which should be a relatively moderate overall load.

Following these guidelines will enable the athlete to gain the greatest benefit from his or her weightlifting training with the minimum of risk.

Teaching Technique

Now that basic principles of motor skill learning and repetition and weight selection have been addressed, let us look at some examples of their practical application in teaching an athlete how to perform the Olympic lifts. The Soviet, Bulgarian and USAW teaching sequences are discussed in Chapter 2. However, it has been my experience that none of these approaches is optimal for every lifter. When weightlifting is taught in classes, the teacher needs some unified approach (such as one of those already discussed). However, when a coach has the luxury of one-on-one or small group training, optimization of technique training occurs when the teaching sequence is individualized.

Individualization is best accomplished by considering several issues. One is the athlete's current capabilities. It may be theoretically preferable to teach the snatch first (as many Soviet coaches argue), but a lifter who does not have the shoulder flexibility to hold the bar over head comfortably or who has a sore wrist is likely to have trouble learning to snatch first.

Another consideration is an athlete's initial grasp of the lifts. Most beginners grasp one of the lifts more quickly than the others. Moreover, some athletes find it easier to perform different segments of the lifts than others. For example, I have seen athletes who pull more correctly from the below the knees than above their knees the first time they try. It seems sensible to use such information as a basis for planning the early learning sequence rather than to adhere to one prescribed sequence or another. If a lifter is able to perform a more complete movement better than a smaller segment the first time out, why follow the smaller to larger segment sequence?

The intelligent coach will select one reasonable teaching sequence as his or her basic method of teaching an athlete the Olympic lifts but will be flexible enough to modify the sequence for an individual athlete.

Basic Errors in the Lifts

Five basic kinds of errors can occur when executing the two Olympic lifts and their variations. They are errors of: balance, body positioning, relative muscle tension, timing, and effort. While these errors can occur at virtually any stage of a lift and in nearly any combination, almost every fault in weightlifting technique can be traced to one or more of these five mistakes. If you can learn to identify and address these mistakes, then you are well on your way to perfecting your technique or your coaching. These errors are discussed at length in Chapters 1 and 2.

Special Safety Considerations for the Olympic Lifts

The overall issue of safety in the gym is covered in Chapter 4 (as well as in Chapters 1 and 2, which discusses how to teach proper technique and Chapter 5, which discusses assistance exercises). Practice of the Olympic lifts can be quite safe when performed under proper conditions, but the opposite can be true when care is not taken. Therefore, all coaches should study Chapters 1, 2, 5 and 6, and talk to experienced weightlifters when they set up an Olympic lifting program. The coach should pay particular attention to the space requirements of Olympic lifting, the characteristics of a good platform, the care of the gym equipment and the athlete's personal equipment. Athletes must also be taught how to miss, how to lower the bar and when and how to drop the bar.

Practice Enhances Safety and Makes Lifting Fun

Practicing the Olympic lifts or some variation of them will yield benefits that are virtually unattainable through any other method. However, the Olympic lifts require effort for the coach and the athlete to learn. The principles and tips provided in this chapter and in earlier parts of this book will help the coach and athlete to understand and apply the Olympic lifts, but there is no substitute for experience and for watching advanced performers of these lifts. There are many sources of video instruction available on the Olympic lifts, and the coach or lifter is who is interested in learning to perform them is well advised to study such instructional materials

Individualizing Technique for Each Athlete

It is important to individualize technique for each athlete. Individual athletes have different physiques and degrees of flexibility and are comfortable with different patterns of movement. Technique optimization is discussed at length in Chapter 1, but some of the more basic areas of technique individualization are discussed in this section as well. For further detail, please refer to Chapter 1.

Hand Spacing for the Snatch

Optimal hand spacing in the snatch is dependent on a number of factors, and there are trade-offs in the various grip widths. One simple technique for estimating a proper grip width is to have the lifter hold the bar with straight arms while pushing the chest out and pulling the shoulders back but not up. Next the lifter should bend forward slightly at the waist (with the back arched) and bend the thighs several inches. The lifter then adjusts the width of the grip so that the bar contacts the top of the thighs or the crease of the hips (the area where the most solid bar contact will occur during the pull of most lifters).

Once a reasonable starting grip width has been established, lifters will want to make modifications as needed. Some lifters will notice that with a normal snatch grip they will have difficulty maintaining an arched back when they lift the bar from the floor. Since a correct starting position is important, the lifter who finds himself or herself in this situation should either become more flexible or narrow the grip. Alternatively, an athlete may find that a wider grip enables him or her to hold the bar overhead more comfortably. Only some amount of experimentation and trading off of advantages will yield the optimum grip for that athlete.

Hand Spacing for the Clean

The common advice given to the beginning lifter with respect to grip width in the clean is that the grip should be "shoulder width." This generally means a grip that is wide enough so that the inside of the hand is just outside the shoulders when the bar is resting on the lifter's shoulders. Individual grip widths vary from approximately 16" to 26" between the insides of the hands (with most lifters being between 17" and 22"), although some international level lifters have used grips that were even wider or narrower.

A narrower grip (up to the point of being shoulder width) generally makes it easier for the lifter to start the bar from the floor. It also tends to make bar contact with the thighs, and the body in general, steadier during the lift. Most lifters find it easier to place their elbows in a high position when they receive the weight on the shoulders in the clean with a narrower grip.

A wider grip generally enables the lifter to pull the bar slightly higher and to contact the thighs at a higher point during the pull (which some lifters prefer). In the end overall comfort and performance considerations will lead the lifter to the optimal grip for him or her.

Hand Spacing for the Jerk

Most lifters use the same grip for the clean as for the jerk (i.e., a width between 16" and 26", with most lifters using a grip in the 17" to 22" range). A narrow grip in the jerk generally places the shoulders and elbows in a stronger and more stable position. However, with a wider grip, the bar does not need to be lifted quite as high, and many lifters, particularly those with tight shoulders, feel that with a wider grip they can get the bar further behind their heads and rotate their shoulders to a greater degree (a position considered to be more stable by most lifters). As with other technique issues, the trade-offs between techniques will need to be considered and experimented with.

Foot Spacing for the Pull

The final explosion in the pull is like a jump in many ways, so it has been argued that placing the feet in a position that in conducive to jumping may well be the best position for executing the final explosion in the pull. This is generally a position in which the feet are approximately hip width.

However, some lifters will find it hard to assume a correct starting position in the pull with the feet so placed. Their flexibility and body proportions may cause them to round their backs, to raise the hips faster than the shoulders or to make some other important error in the start of the pull if they place their feet in a jumping position. If a lifter has trouble finding a strong and reasonably comfortable starting position for the pull, widening the stance and/or turning the toes out more than usual may help. Something may then be given up in the explosion, but it may be worth giving up in order to gain a correct and secure starting position.

Foot Spacing for the Jerk

Most lifters assume a foot position in the jerk that is similar to the one they use in the pull (i.e., usually about hip width, with a minor turning out of the toes). This position may promote application of maximum force during the explosion phase of the jerk, but some lifters will find this position ineffective.

For example, in the jerk some lifters have a tendency to lean forward at the torso when they are dipping with a jumping stance. This can often be corrected by shortening the lifter's dip and asking the lifter to focus on a strictly vertical dip. Despite these efforts, the lifter may still persist in dipping forward. In such a case many lifters will find it easier to keep the back in an arched position and to dip straight with a wider and/or more turned-out foot position. If the lifter uses such a position, something may indeed be given up in terms of the power developed in the drive, but improved control over the direction of the drive may well make such a loss acceptable.

The Length and Speed of the Dip for the Jerk

Athletes generally lower the bar between 8% and 12 % of their height during the dip for the jerk. Athletes whose dips are at the longer end of this range tend to lower their bodies a little more slowly than those who have a dip at the shorter end of the range, and they take longer to reverse direction from the point at which they lower the body and bar to the point at which they commence the thrust.

Trial and error will help each athlete determine the best dip depth and speed for him or her. However, several guidelines will help make the process of optimization easier. First, the athlete should begin by dipping in a relaxed "free fall" kind of rhythm. The lifter should attempt neither to dip forcefully and quickly nor to resist the downward pressure of the bar; he or she should simply relax somewhat and let the dip happen. Second, the athlete must never dip so fast that the bar separates from the shoulders or deviates from the straight dip (a dip in which the bar moves in a strictly vertical fashion). Third, the dip should never be so low as to cause the lifter's legs to quiver or wobble as they are bending or reversing direction into the thrust. The athlete should be able to reverse direction abruptly and to drive upward without any visible loss of control. Fourth, the upward drive itself must be explosive.

Some Other Important Areas of Technique

There are many important areas of technique, but several stand out for their importance to athletes who employ the Olympic lifts (or variations thereof) in their training. They are: assuming a correct starting position; correct positioning and applying maximal effort during the final explosion phase of each lift; moving under the bar rapidly after the final explosion phase; moving with the greatest possible speed consistent with maintaining control; maintaining a stable and balanced position during the dip and thrust of the jerk; and finding a focal point. Chapter 1 should be studied to assure that a proper grasp of these elements of technique is acquired.

Securing The Grip in the Snatch and Clean

Maintaining a secure grip while performing the snatch and clean is important. Dry hands which are free of oil and other lubricants are a must for practicing any variety of the snatch or clean. Weightlifters apply chalk (magnesium carbonate) to their hands before virtually every set of snatches or cleans to dry their hands and to increase the friction between their hands and the bar. Athletes who train on the Olympic lifts should adopt this policy.

Athletes who wish to strengthen their grips will find that practicing the Olympic lifts with the regular "overhand" grip (fingers wrapping around the bar from the front and the thumb alongside the fingers coming from the back of the bar) has a grip strengthening effect.

Some lifters attempt to perform the snatch, clean, jerk and any pressing movements they do with a "thumbless" grip. In the thumbless grip the thumbs go around the bar in the same direction as the other fingers (instead of in the opposite direction as in the regular grip). Advocates of this style feel that it makes their position stronger and more comfortable overhead and places more strain

on the gripping muscles of the hand while the lifter is pulling. The thumbless grip cannot be recommended because it is far more likely that the bar will slip completely out of the hand when pulling with such a grip than with a normal grip. This can even happen while pressing or jerking with a thumbless grip (although it is very rare).

A special means of gripping the bar called a "hook" grip is the greatest method ever developed for improving a lifter's ability to grip the bar securely. Consequently, it is used by virtually every lifter of high caliber. The technique of the hook consists of wrapping the thumb around the bar from the rear and then placing the first and second (and sometimes even the third) fingers of the hand around the thumb and the bar from the front of the bar. It is considered normal for the lifter to experience considerable discomfort, even significant pain, when first using this grip. Ordinarily the pain peaks just after releasing the hook. During or after the workout the lifter may also notice a discoloration on the thumbs (ranging from red to "black and blue") which is caused by minor internal bleeding that may occur as a consequence of the pressure of the bar and fingers compressing the thumb against the bar. Both the pain and any discoloration will pass, typically after a few weeks. The only residual effect will be a more secure grip.

If the fingers develop a significant soreness that continues unabated from one workout into the next during this working-in process, the lifter should slow the breaking-in process. This is done by performing only some lifts with a hook or skipping a workout with the hook to allow the soreness to lessen. Many lifters find that wrapping a layer of surgical tape around the thumb before the workout lessens any irritation to the skin of the thumb. Illustrations of the various grips described above appear in Chapter 1.

Athletes who are engaged in sports in which grip strength is of little consequence (or who prefer to exercise their grips separately) may wish to use lifting "straps." These straps secure the grip and permit the athlete to focus completely on working the leg, hip and back muscles without being limited by a fatigued grip. Straps are illustrated and discussed in further detail in Chapter 4.

When a lifter uses straps it is important to encircle the bar only once; the straps should not be longer than is necessary in order to wrap around the bar once (as shown in the illustration of straps that appeared earlier in the book). Wrapping the straps around the bar additional times makes it difficult to release the straps in the event of a missed lift (important in avoiding injury from a falling or bouncing bar). It is also important to make sure that the straps are in good condition and are strong enough to sustain the heaviest loads the lifter intends to use. Any strap that has even the smallest tear in any part of its stitching or material should be discarded immediately. Breaking a strap in mid-pull is at best a very unpleasant experience. At worst, breaking a strap can be dangerous. Therefore, never use a weakened or damaged strap.

The Proper Position for "Receiving" the Bar in the Olympic Lifts

When a bar is "caught" in any of the Olympic lifts, several rules apply. First, the lifter's torso must always be rigid and vertical (a slight forward lean is generally fine as well, but no backward lean of the torso should be permitted). Second, the legs act as shock absorbers. They absorb the downward force of the body and the bar and should always "give" a little when the force of the bar is received. Third, the feet should generally be placed a little wider than shoulder width, with the toes turned outward somewhat. The feet should never be placed so wide that the lifter cannot comfortably lower himself or herself into the full squat position without moving the feet, but they are generally in a wider position than was employed by the lifter during the first four phases of the lift.

In the snatch and jerk the elbows should be fully extended while the athlete pushes up and tries to "stretch" the bar somewhat. Most lifters find it helpful to think of bringing the shoulder blades together somewhat. Proper tension in the arms and shoulders is essential for controlling the bar and protecting the joints of the shoulders and elbows. If the muscles are relaxed, the bar can be dropped unnecessarily (even after it has achieved the proper height and speed to be "caught" by the lifter in the low position).

In the clean, raising the elbows high and with substantial speed, as well as positioning the body as described above, are the keys to receiving the bar's force effectively. The bar should be positioned well back on the shoulders, resting lightly against the neck.

Use of the Power Clean, Power Snatch and Power Jerk by Athletes

In the early chapters of this book, we explored both the elements of proper technique and how technique must be learned. Athletes who wish to train on the Olympic lifts as a means to improve athletic performance need not delve into all of the intricacies of technique development. A concentration on the basics will be sufficient. Moreover, most athletes will gain the majority of the benefits that are available from training on the Olympic lifts by learning three more simple versions of the competitive Olympic lifts that were discussed in Chapter 5, the power snatch, the power clean and the power jerk. Not only are these variations easier to learn than the classic Olympic

lifts, but they also require less flexibility to perform than the competitive lifts.

The power styles of the Olympic lifts are learned relatively easily by most athletes. However, there are common and serious mistakes which must be guarded against by the coach. (The errors discussed below are in addition to those which were discussed in Chapters 1 and 2).

In the power snatch, the most common error is to "press the bar out" when it is nearly at arm's length overhead. When a snatch is performed correctly, the bar should almost "snap" overhead. There should be no visible press-out with the arms. An athlete who is pressing out is either pulling too long and using the arms at the end of the pull (instead of "throwing" the bar with the legs, hips and back and then rapidly descending into a partial squat); not bending the legs sufficiently when catching the bar; using too much weight; or some combination of the above.

In the power clean the most common mistakes are: catching the bar on the upper chest instead of on the top of the deltoids (shoulders); not having the elbows up (which causes the force of the bar to be received by the wrists and arms instead of the shoulders, torso and, ultimately, the legs); leaning the torso back to catch the bar, a mistake which exposes the athlete to a heightened risk of lower back injury; not bending the legs sufficiently; using too much weight; and any combination of the other mistakes.

In the power jerk the most common mistakes are: pressing the bar out at the top of the lift (instead of having the arms "snap" to a full lockout position; leaning back while trying to catch the bar at arm's length; not descending low enough in the squat; or some combination of the above.

A final mistake common to all three power style lifts is spreading the feet too wide in the partial squat position. Spreading the feet wide is a quick way to lower the body and thereby increase the amount of weight that can be lifted. However, a wide foot position is a major mistake for several reasons. First, it places great rotational strain on the hips and knees, which can lead to injury. Second, a wide stance can also contribute to muscle strains, particularly in the groin. Third, a very wide stance precludes the athlete from sinking into a deeper squat when that is necessary to control the bar. Finally, practice of such wide stance lifting practically precludes later learning of the full squat style of lifting, should the athlete ever choose to do so.

The Use of Partial Lifts

The power snatch and power clean from the floor can be performed effectively by most athletes with considerable practice. However, some athletes will find it extremely uncomfortable or even impossible to assume a correct starting position in the pull (the most common cause being a lack of flexibility). Athletes with this problem may wish to work on their flexibility until a proper starting position can be assumed. Other athletes may wish to forgo lifting the bar from the platform altogether. In either case such athletes can gain many of the benefits that accrue from training on the snatch and clean and jerk by doing partial versions of these exercises, either from the "hang" or from "boxes."

When a lifter wishes to perform these lifts from the hang, he or she can deadlift the bar from the platform to the hang position. Alternatively, the lifter can remove the bar from a stand or block that has been set just below a finished deadlift position, step back from the stand and assume a hang position.

The two most common hang positions are with the bar held just below the knee and just above the knee (essentially the ends of the second and third phases of the pull, respectively). These starting positions tend to make the lift simpler (by removing stages of the lift), and they require less flexibility to assume.

The lifter can also lift the bar from special "boxes" which are placed on either side of the lifter under the plates of the bar. These variations of the Olympic lifts are discussed in Chapter 5, and the construction of the boxes that are used in performing lifts from the boxes is described in Chapter 4.

When performing these partial lifts, care must be taken by the lifter to position himself or herself in a way that mimics the positions that would be assumed at comparable stages in the full lift. Lifters, especially new ones, have a tendency to deviate from normal lifting positions when lifting from the hang or blocks. By far the most common deviation is for the lifter to have his or her shoulders further back than is appropriate (i.e., when pulling from below the knees, making the error of having the shoulders directly over or behind the bar, or when pulling from just above the knee, having the shoulders behind the bar).

Lifters who pull from a position with the bar above the knees enjoy the benefits of mastering the final acceleration stage of the pull (the stage in which the greatest power is developed). Pulling from below the knees enables the lifter to train the stretch-shortening cycle and the final explosion as the knees rebend and the lifter then explodes upward.

The Use of Pulls

Another Olympic lift related exercise is a "pull." As was explained in Chapter 5, this is an exercise in which the lifter executes all but the fifth and sixth stages of the snatch and clean. The lifter simply performs the final explosion phase of the pull and then stops. Some lifters remain in a position with the body fully stretched at the end of the exercise, permitting the bar to rise up along the body (they then lower the bar in a controlled manner). Others lifters permit the legs to bend, or the legs to bend and the torso to incline forward somewhat as the bar reaches its maximum height.

Regardless of what is done at the finish of the exercise, many of the benefits that accrue from practicing the Olympic lifts are derived from pulls as well. Athletes who want to minimize any trauma to their bodies when they "catch" the bar in full squat of power position, yet who wish to gain many of the benefits of practicing the Olympic lifts, will find pulls to be very useful. Learning to pull is far easier than learning to power clean or power snatch (in fact, Bulgarian coaches use pulls as a means to teach their beginners the first four stages of the snatch and clean).

Athletes with knee or other joint problems may be able to perform a pull with little discomfort, even though a power clean or snatch might aggravate the injury. Athletes who simply are not willing to devote the effort necessary to learn the Olympic lifts may find that pulls are a valuable substitute. However, even pulls must be practiced and performed correctly.

If athletes intend to perform pulls exclusively, they will generally find it beneficial to use some sort of fixed device to measure the height of the pull (see the section on the height gauge in Chapter 4). Using a marker on the body as a means of measurement is not recommended because the marker can move (if the athlete touches the chest with the bar is it because the bar was pulled to chest level or because the chest was lowered by bending the legs or torso?).

Measurement is important because it is difficult for the athlete to know whether he or she is progressing unless the height of the pull is measured (this is unnecessary in the power snatch or clean because the exercise itself effectively measures the height of the pull). In this context, progress will occur both in terms of improvements in explosive power and in technique.

For athletes who are both unable to execute their lifts from the floor or to catch them overhead or on the shoulders, pulls from blocks or the hang position offer an avenue for obtaining some of the benefits of practicing the Olympic lifts. Pulls are discussed more fully in the chapter on assistance exercises.

Summary

Athletes can greatly benefit from practicing the classic weightlifting events and related movements. But the benefits outweigh the risks only if the weightlifting movements are performed correctly and if the loads lifted are gradually increased to the desired level. If an athlete is not willing to learn proper technique, or to progress slowly in terms of loading, he or she is better off not practicing these exercises. The good news is that heavy weights and many sets are not required to make good progress in the early months of training. Learn carefully, progress slowly and you will maximize the considerable benefits that can be derived from weightlifting training.

Good luck and good explosiveness!

APPENDIX 4

Selecting An Athlete And Selecting A Coach

Any thinking person who seeks a high level of achievement in a given field endeavors to maximize his or her access to the resources that will improve the probability of achieving success. In athletics the most important resources are clearly human. Athletes look for the best coaches to guide them to successful performance. Similarly, successful coaches look for talented and dedicated athletes so that they can work with the best "material." While it is entirely appropriate for athletes and coaches to seek the best people to work with, the quest to find the perfect coach or athlete can become an obsession. The athlete with such an obsession grimly pursues the coach who has the "secret" that will unlock the door to championship performance. Some coaches shamelessly woo the athlete who has the ability to make the coach a winner and prove that coach is as good as any other.

When the coach or athlete spends too much energy in this kind of search, it diverts the seeker's attention from the crucial task at hand. In the case of the athlete, that task is proper training. For the coach that task is learning and developing the optimal training methods for his or her athletes.

Many coaches who focus on learning about the sport they coach and communicating what they have learned to their athletes realize that the greatest joy in coaching comes through such a process. These coaches derive their primary satisfaction in coaching from seeing their athletes progress rather than from the levels of performance that their athletes achieve. Other coaches are more focused on the trappings of success: the number of championships their athletes have won and the international teams they have made. There is certainly nothing wrong with striving to compile the most outstanding record ever achieved by a weightlifting coach. The inspiration that a coach can gain from such a goal may drive that coach to heroic efforts which benefit both him or her and the athletes with whom the coach works. But some coaches are so concerned with scoring

high on external measures of success that winning at any cost becomes their primary focus. These coaches may go to great lengths to recruit athletes to their teams so that they can win championships. They may even resort to unfair practices to get the job done. There is little doubt that a great recruiter can often outperform a great coach in terms of championships won (though not in terms of satisfaction gained from coaching or the appreciation that athletes will show them for their work).

Recruiting makes it possible for a relatively mediocre coach to have a winning team and for a terrific coach to have a mediocre record when it comes to producing winning teams (particularly in an individual sport like weightlifting). This does not mean that a good coach will never produce good athletes, quite the contrary. A good coach will always produce his or her share of champions. Indeed, you cannot truly reach the highest level of coaching unless you have worked with some top athletes (because only advanced athletes present the challenges that are needed to hone coaching skills to the ultimate degree). However, the good coach will not rely on recruiting for his or her success, but, rather, will focus on perfecting his or her skills and maximizing the performance of his or her athletes.

Athlete Selection

Different coaches apply different approaches to athlete selection. Some coaches go after the "finished product," attempting to induce champions to join their clubs. In other cases recruiting takes place on the beginner level. Here the coach relies on various techniques of screening to identify athletes who are believed to have the greatest potential to become champions. Screening or selection of athletes has been virtually automatic for many years in sports that are popular among athletes. In these sports the coach has many more athletes who wish to be a member of the team than he or she can coach or use to field a team. The coach therefore selects from the athletes who are interested those who appear to have the greatest potential for success.

In sports that rely heavily on natural ability, such as sprinting and jumping, athletes who do not show any special aptitude for the sport at the outset are simply not going to reach a high level. For instance, speed can only be improved to a very limited degree by training. If an athlete does not display at least good running speed at the outset, he or she will not become a champion sprinter.

Coaches who are involved with sports in which developed qualities are the key to success have a much harder time selecting athletes on the basis of their inherent capabilities. How does one determine an athlete's ability to be a marathoner or a champion bodybuilder by examining an untrained person? Training plays a huge role in the success of athletes in these sports. While a naturally muscular person with a high percentage of fast-twitch muscle fibers will have an edge in bodybuilding and a naturally lean person with a high percentage of slow-twitch muscle fibers may have an advantage in marathoning, so much is determined by the training that such athletes do and their reaction to that training that predictions of success at the outset are virtually impossible. Relatively skinny beginners have blossomed into Mr. and Ms. Americas, while relatively stocky athletes have become successful distance runners.

Success in weightlifting depends far more on training than it does on natural talents. I have seen athletes start their careers physically strong and then improve their strength very little. I have seen other athletes begin their careers in a weak and emaciated state and then go on to become champions. I have seen athletes who were flexible and grasped the way in which the lifts are to be performed almost as soon as they were shown the technique of the classic lifts who went on to be mediocre technicians. Other athletes who had flexibility limitations that prevented them from achieving correct positions at the outset, and/or who seemed entirely uncoordinated when they tried to perform the lifts for the first time, have gone on to become excellent technicians. Because of the vital role that desire and proper training play in an athlete's progress in weightlifting, it is hard to predict an athlete's future success on the basis of his or her beginnings. Predictions of an athlete's success in weightlifting are particularly difficult because success depends on so many qualities (e.g., strength, power, speed, flexibility, skill and determination). Any effective selector of weightlifters would therefore need to assess an athlete's present ability and potential for future progress in each of these areas, something no one has been able to do to date.

Why have the selectors experienced such difficulty? The primary reason is that there are several major problems with the concept of screening tests. The first problem is that "tests test what tests test." While scientists and coaches (and other people involved in choosing who is most likely to be successful in a certain role) have probably been developing tests for a wide variety of general human capabilities for thousands of years, the vast majority of such tests have been found to be extremely specific. Performance on one test has little or no correspondence with another test that supposedly measures the same quality.

For example, in the psychological realm, there are no truly effective general intelligence tests. I.Q. tests test specific verbal and mathematical skills that are used in academic environments. Such tests may indeed be good indicators of academic success, but they do not fully or directly assess intelligence (let alone define it).

Similarly, there are no general tests that can predict skill, strength or flexibility in any area of the body that is not tested. Even the areas of the body that are tested can only be tested very specifically (e.g., a test that requires concentric contraction of the muscles measures their concentric capacity but does not do a great job of measuring their eccentric capacity). Even if the selector could predict whether the athlete could ultimately perform at a high level in each of these areas, few athletes would score consistently on most of them. Even those who appeared to have better overall physical potential would still present the single biggest unknowns to the selector: will the athlete put 100% effort into becoming a champion, and will he or she remain in the sport long enough to reach his or her potential?.

The second problem with selection tests is that no test can measure the single biggest factor in an athlete's success: desire. Sports history is filled with stories of athletes with modest beginnings who went on to become champions. In Bulgaria World Champions and world record holders Yanko Rusev, Naim Suleymanoglu (then of Bulgaria) and Antonio Krastev all fared relatively poorly on the standard tests that Bulgarians use to select athletes. Antonio once told me, "I can't jump from the floor onto a low desk, but I can move under a snatch very fast." And so he can.

Had the testers been given ultimate power, the world might have been deprived of one of the greatest clean and jerkers that it has ever seen (Rusev), the man who snatched the heaviest weight ever accepted as a world record in the sport of weightlifting (Krastev) or one of the greatest weightlifters ever to grace the weightlifting platform (Suleymanoglu). If these athletes had believed the testers, surely they would never have achieved the successes that they did. While those who support selection will argue that there are motivational advantages to telling a lifter that he or she has talent, they overlook the devastating effects of telling an athlete he or she has no talent, particularly when the grounds for making such a statement are shaky at best.

If their lack of reliability regarding what they claim to test and their failure to measure the most important factor in weightlifting success are not enough to discourage selection, the realities of modern weightlifting should suffice. In the United States, and probably soon in the rest of the world, the issue of selecting an athlete is no longer a major one. Selection implies the ability and desire to choose from among options. In the United States we generally do not have the luxury of choosing our athletes. Rather, they choose weightlifting, and we are happy to have them because they do.

Most coaches who truly love weightlifting for weightlifting's sake do not have any great desire to choose athletes. They are coaching because they love the sport and wish to help others discover its wonderful virtues, not solely because they want to produce champions. Most coaches are truly motivated by the desire to help an athlete be the best he or she can be. That, after all, is the ultimate challenge and the ultimate satisfaction in weightlifting and in life.

One last point with respect to athlete selection needs to be made. It pertains to the total misuse of the process. Most coaches who employ testing may legitimately think that such a process saves them and prospective athletes a great deal of time and energy. Unfortunately, a small number of coaches (usually inexperienced ones who claim to possess a great deal more knowledge than they do) is preoccupied with the issue of selection. This preoccupation may be an indirect expression of a lack of confidence in their skills. To protect their egos, these coaches have convinced themselves that there is no difference between coaches, that all are equally impotent in their ability to build champions and that all coaches rely on the roll of the dice for selection. If talented athletes come to them, they will be successful; if not, they will be doomed to an unrewarded struggle. Unfortunately these beliefs often rub off on their athletes.

Coach Selection

The selection of a coach is a topic that has rarely, if ever, been covered in a text on weightlifting, yet in many ways it is a much more appropriate subject for consideration than the selection of athletes. The athlete always has the option of coaching himself or herself if the availability of high quality coaching in his or her geographic area is poor. Therefore, the athlete always has a choice (even if it is not to use a local coach or to use no coach at all).

There are two main sets of criteria in evaluating a coach. One set is objective and the other is subjective. When using objective criteria, the athlete merely evaluates whether the coach has the full range and necessary depth of coaching skills to take that athlete to the level he or she wishes to achieve. If not, the athlete may not be able to rely on that coach alone to achieve his or her objectives. This is not a condemnation of that coach; nor does it mean that that particular coach should not be accepted. All coaches have areas in which they are weaker than others.

The purpose of the athlete's judging the coach in this way is to understand the nature and extent of the coach's strengths and weaknesses. Then the athlete can find a way to compensate for the coach's deficiencies. This can be done through supplementary coaching advice, by helping the coach to improve and/or self coaching in the areas in which the coach is deficient.

Subjective issues can lead to intractable clashes with the athlete even though they do not necessarily reflect a weakness on the part of the coach. For example, if a coach regularly criticizes an athlete and, at least in the athlete's view, rarely employs positive feedback, the athlete may find the experience of working with that coach to be a negative one overall, even if the coach possesses considerable technical skill. In contrast, the same coach may be perceived by another athlete as constantly presenting challenges. The relationship that such an athlete finds with such a coach can be very positive. A reserved athlete may be uncomfortable with a bombastic coach, while an outgoing and emotional athlete may be uncomfortable with a coach who is quiet and low key. Often these differences in personality can be overlooked by both parties and a successful coach/athlete relationship can be formed in spite of them, but this is not always the case.

Obviously, the ideal situation is one in which a coach serves an athlete's objective and subjective needs. When this is not possible, the athlete and coach may wish to subdivide responsibilities. For example, a give coach may have a good training facility and a good eye for technique problems. On the other hand, the coach may be weak in the areas of programming and motivating the athlete. In this situation the athlete may train with that coach and carefully heed the coach's technical advice but ask another coach to write his or her training program. In addition, he or she may look to other athletes to provide encouragement and motivation in training. This kind of an arrangement has worked well for many athletes.

In another situation a coach may be wonderful in training but may not be at his or her best in competition. This coach may seek the help of other coaches at competitions but may perform all other coaching responsibilities.

How do you tell a good coach from a bad one? There are several things to consider. First, what kind of results has the coach gotten? Has the coach been successful in building champion athletes from day one? How many athletes has the coach brought from the beginning all the way along in their careers (coaches with large teams and/or very successful athletes may have actually coached the athletes they take credit for to a very limited extent)? What are the qualities of the lifters that coach has developed (excellent technique, performance consistency, healthy bodies)? Second, does the coach prescribe the same program for everyone and then put the athletes on autopilot, expecting them to perform the workout without deviation, regardless of results? Or does the coach individualize training programs for the needs of the athlete? Third, and least important, does the coach have some credentials in terms of education or coaching ranking conferred by some independent organization?

Having a formal education in some scientific area that is related to weightlifting (e.g., physiology of exercise or biomechanics) is useful, but the relationship between such knowledge and success as a coach is limited at best. Many credentials do not mean much, because they can be acquired in a number of ways. For example, the USAW has some international level coaches who are extremely knowledgeable and who have learned their trade through many years of unstinting effort in the gym. There are other coaches who have achieved such a level through the grandfathering of undocumented relationships with athletes and/or their availability to accompany athletes with whom they had no relationships on unimportant international trips.

In contrast, there are coaches who have consistently developed some of the best athletes in the country who have never achieved the international ranking because of some formality that they have never gone through with the USAW.

This is not meant to be a criticism of the USAW, which has done many good things to foster the development of good coaches. Rather, it merely demonstrates that most ranking, credentialing and licensing systems are flawed and that they cannot be relied upon as the sole or even primary consideration when selecting a coach, a physician or any other professional.

Summary

In closing, it should be noted that while there is nothing wrong with athletes selecting coaches or coaches selecting athletes, both parties must realize that weightlifters and weightlifting coaches are both rare commodities in the United States. Moreover, most lifters and coaches are involved in weightlifting because they love the sport, and they are working to the best of their ability and in good faith. Therefore, we all should be careful about criticizing the abilities of any coach or athlete of good character and should welcome participants in either activity with open arms. Finally, athletes who change coaches should always remember the time and effort expended on their behalf by any coach who has helped them, or even honestly tried to do so; athletes should always be grateful for that help.

Its Up To You Now!

When I began weightlifting, useful information about this fascinatingly complex and rewarding sport was rather difficult to obtain. The only books on weightlifting readily available in English were Bob Hoffman's fifty page book, <u>Guide to Weight Lifting Competition</u> and <u>Weight Lifting and Weight Training</u>, by George Kirkley, both published in 1963. Each of these books provided a lot of information in a concise fashion, but neither gave the neophyte or more advanced lifter the information required to even begin to reach high levels of weightlifting performance.

Translations of Eastern European literature were generally unavailable at that time (and original works were very difficult to obtain). Sports training techniques used in the Soviet Union were virtually regarded as state secrets, so lectures in technique and training methods were rare occurrences. The fledgling weightlifter could gain access to a steady flow of information on the sport by reading <u>Strength & Health</u> magazine. However, as valuable as <u>Strength & Health</u> was, a reader had to study it for a number of years before gaining any reasonable knowledge of the sport.

Information on weightlifting is more widely available today than it has ever been. Today translations of Eastern European training manuals are available, and coaches from Eastern European countries are coaching and lecturing throughout the world. The coaching courses that were begun by the USAW in the 1980's and courses provided by organizations that certify strength coaches and other physical instructors can give the beginner substantial useful information regarding weightlifting and weight training.

However, there has never really been one comprehensive source of weightlifting information beyond the beginner's level. I hope that this book has filled that gap. Whether you are an athlcte, or a beginning to intermediate level coach, if you have studied the material in this book and have grasped its essentials, you have learned a great deal more about the principles and practices of weightlifting than most beginners and many advanced athletes and coaches know. But a conceptual understanding is not enough to enable you to become or coach a champion. Now you must apply what you have learned on a conceptual level to real athletes. Only then will you begin the process of understanding and refinement which will ultimately lead to true mastery of the material, to an approach that is uniquely your own and to a training philosophy that is firmly grounded in reality.

This book was written to help everyone who wants to become a weightlifter or a coach of weightlifters, regardless of their level of aspiration. But most of all it is written to those very few of you out there who have the dedication and the greatness of spirit to pursue the most fantastic goal in all of sport: to be the best in the world. Which of you wants to become champion of the world or lift a weight that no man or woman has ever lifted before? Which of you wants to be the next to make weightlifting history by setting the standard that all who follow must strive to improve upon? Human achievement is the grandest spectacle on this earth, and the world record is one of the clearest and most glorious displays of such achievement.

A special message goes to the United States lifters who read this book. This is not because I necessarily favor the lifters of the United States over all others. I admire all weightlifters, from whatever country, as athletes and individuals. But I am an American and very proud to be a citizen of a country that has taught more people about the values and possibilities of freedom than any other country in the history of the world. And while Americans lead the world in many areas, they face a special challenge in the sport of weightlifting.

For years we American athletes were hamstrung by amateur rules that few of our competitors followed. Then there was the period of the great "psych-out", a period when the minds of many America's most promising lifters, athletes who were great and destined to be greater, were converted to self-doubting and self-pitying shadows of their potential selves because they believed that the former Eastern bloc countries knew weightlifting "secrets" that they could never learn. Now that the myth of superior science in Eastern Europe has been destroyed and the Westernization of the former Soviet Block countries has led to the disbanding of many of the sports science centers that were doing serious scientific work, that fear should be largely behind us. Instead there is a new psychological threat to United States weightlifting.

The United States has an anti-drug policy that makes us the envy of all athletes around the world who want to compete without drugs. But this has lead to the idea that we cannot win until the rest of the world follows suit. Nothing could be further from the truth. Drugs help performance in certain respects. No reasonable person can deny that. But they hurt performance in many other areas by having negative effects on an athlete's general health, by requiring only intermittent use (as compared with proper diet and training methods, which can and should be used continually) and by undermining an athlete's confidence on the day of competition when he or she must perform at his or her best without drugs.

Regardless of the benefits of drawbacks or using drugs, the limits of human achievement in weightlifting have not been reached. No one knows how much more is possible. Drugs are a way of improving performance but there are many others. It is obvious that many people have forgotten that fact.

But I know that there are some of you out there who have not, some who are ready to face the greatest challenge ever taken on by a competitive weightlifter: defeating athletes who are taking drugs without using them yourself. Those of you who believe it is possible are halfway there.

The last American male to set a senior world record in weightlifting was Robert Bednarski in September 1969. I was the last American male to set a junior world record when I made a junior world record in the total on May 16, 1970. The last American woman to set a world weightlifting record was Robyn Bird, who set a world record in the snatch on April 4, 1994. The last American male to win a World Championship was Joe Dube in 1969. The last American woman to win a World Championship was Robin Byrd-Goad in 1994. There has never been an American Junior World Champion (there was no Junior World Championship in my day).

So this is where we stand today. Robin Byrd-Goad is looking forward to winning more World Championships and setting more world records now that she has taken some time off to become a proud mother. But who will take the torch that she proudly carries when her career is over?

I have not talked to Bob Bednarski or Joe Dube about this subject lately, but I think I can speak for them when I say that after more than a quarter of a century, we are getting tired of holding our torches and long for some young American men to take them from us. We want dearly to hand off to a new generation. Who will be the new American world champions and world record holders?

More than sixty years ago the United States found itself in a similar situation with respect to men's weightlifting. European lifters dominated world weightlifting, and there were no American world record holders or world champions. Then along came an American named Bob Hoffman, who gathered some of America's most promising young lifters of the time in the small town of York, Pennsylvania. Those who could not come to York he touched through a wonderful magazine called Strength & Health. In York and throughout the nation, he inspired American lifting to heights that it had never seen before.

Among the group of lifters that Bob Hoffman gathered in York was a young man named Tony Terlazzo. Tony was a very talented athlete physically, but his greatest asset was his ability to project human capabilities into the future and to realize that all lifters, including the Europeans he was trying to catch, could lift more than they did and that no one was lifting 100% of his or her potential. Tony boldly resolved to come closer to his full potential than others who had preceded him and thereby become the best. The result, as they say, was history. Tony became an Olympic champion and the first world champion that the US had ever produced, and he established a number of world records in the process. In so doing, he not only brought great glory to himself and the United States, but he also showed the way to a host of young American lifters who went on to make their own records, win their own championships and establish the United States as a real power in world weightlifting.

I hope that this book will provide at least some help to those special few of you who have the greatness of vision to see that you can be the next world champions and world record holders, the best in the world and the best who ever lived. I want to shake your hands on the day that you are victorious. You will be the first of a new breed of American lifters who will lead a new American era. The challenge and the opportunity belong to you. I salute you and wish you great success!

Writing this book has been a learning process for me as I have had to place a structure around the principles and techniques that I have learned to apply almost subconsciously over the years. The writing process has led me to develop new ideas, to integrate existing knowledge and to identify conflicts in my thinking and to resolve those conflicts. In a sense I will never finish this book. I know far more about weightlifting now than when I started and would write it somewhat differently if I had it to do again (and I will do so in future editions). But I will never be able to catch up on paper to where I am day to day. Nevertheless, you have to stop somewhere, at least for a while, and this is where I will stop. For now.

I will close with a message to all of you fledgling athletes out there who desire to become weightlifting champions. This book has been dedicated to those of you who will accept the challenge of becoming the greatest weightlifters in the world. The doomsayers will tell you that you do not have the talent or the resources of your competitors abroad, that the deck is stacked against you on drug testing or that you should not reach for the stars because you might be disappointed. Do not believe any of it. If you want with all your heart to become a champion, let no one stand in your way. Dream of it, plan for it, train for it, live for it and become the champion you can be. Being the best that you can be and the glorious journey towards that achievement will bring rewards that are greater than any you may have ever imagined. Good luck and great success in weightlifting, the most glorious sport ever conceived by the mind of man or woman!

Annotated Bibliography

Ajan, Tamas, Chief Editor. *International Weightlifting Federation Handbook 1997-2000*. Budapest: International Weightlifting Federation, 1997. The "bible" of international weightlifting. Includes the most up-to-date rules available for international weightlifting as well as information on the governing bodies of all nations and publications of the IWF. This book is "required reading" for all athletes and coaches - you must know the rules of the game.

—- and Lazar Baroga. *Weightlifting: Fitness for All Sports*. Budapest: International Weightlifting Federation, 1988. Dr. Tamas Ajan has been General Secretary of the IWF for more than 20 years. A longtime sportsman, trained as a physical educator, he was General Secretary of the Hungarian Weightlifting Federation from 1968-1983. Dr. Ajan, in partnership with the IWF President, Gotfried Schodl, has guided the IWF through troubled years when weightlifting was threatened with being eliminated from the Olympic program and has recently succeeded in having women's weightlifting approved as part of the 2000 Olympic Games, at a time when the IOL is seeking to reduce the number of athletes competing in each sport. Dr. Baroga, placed 5th in the 1964 Olympic Games, coached the Rumanian weightlifting team for 8 years and has been head of the Rumanian Weightlifting Federation since 1964. He became a member of the IWF Executive Board in 1980. These two men have collaborated to produce a very comprehensive book on weightlifting that describes: the physical and mental qualities of weightlifters, many weightlifting and weight training exercises for weightlifting and other sports, a wide range of training techniques, the process of developing training programs, how to develop good technique, restorative methods, and how to measure and record training progress. The book also has many detailed programs for weightlifting training. The Ajan/Baroga book offers a very different approach from many of the Soviet training manuals on a number of levels and should be in the library of all serious athletes and coaches.

Alexander, R. McNeill. *The Human Machine*. New York: Columbia University Press, 1992.

Alter, Michael. *Science of Stretching*. Champaign, IL: Human Kinetics Books, 1988. Perhaps the most comprehensive book on stretching for sport that is in print. Contains information on the theory and practice of effective stretching.

Amberry, Tom. *Free Throw*. New York: Harper Perennial, 1996. This small book contains more practical information on perfecting sports technique and one's mental approach to a game than anything else available. Written by the world's record holder in basketball free throws, a man who set the record when he was in his 70s.

American Academy of Orthopedic Surgeons. *Athletic Training and Sports Medicine*. Park Ridge, IL: American Academy of Orthopedic Surgeons, 1991.

American Red Cross. *Community First Aid & Safety*. St. Louis, MO: Mosby Lifeline, 1993.

Anderson, Bob. *Stretching*. Bolinas, CA: Shelter Publications, 1980.

Anderson, Paul. *Secrets of My Strength*. Vidalia, GA: Paul Anderson, 1970. Provides insights into the kind of creative thinking, hard training and careful dieting that made Paul great (no, he wasn't simply born strong). Paul may well have been the strongest man who ever lived (at a minimum he dominated his era in a way that no one before or since has dominated theirs).

—-. *Power By Paul*. Vidalia, GA: Paul Anderson, 1974. More tips on the development of strength and power from Paul but with a greater emphasis on the lifts performed in powerlifting competition. Paul Anderson was a prolific thinker and writer in addition to operating his Paul Anderson Youth Home, which is still being run by his wife, Glenda, and other members of the family. The Home's address is: P.O. Box 525, Vidalia, GA 30474. Paul's books include: *A Greater Strength* (his autobiography), *The Home: Society's Pacemaker, A Parental Guide* (a guide to nurturing children from a man who helped raise many children across a period of more than 30 years), *Weights And Sports* (a guide to weight training for sport), *Forty And Rising* (training for those age 40 and above), *Father And Son* (father and son weight training), *Youth And Strength* (when and how a youngster should train), *Kook Letters* (actual letters Paul received over the years), *How It Is* (some of Paul's poetry), *200 Years As I See It* (Paul's views on the US's 200th anniversary). Paul also recorded a number of cassette tapes and a video has been made about his career. These items and others can be obtained from his Home at the address provided above.

Arnheim, Daniel and William Prentice. *Principles of Athletic Training, 8th ed.* St. Louis, MO: Mosby-Year Book, Inc., 1993.

Baker, Gene, ed. *Coaching Manual, Vols. I-III.* Colorado Springs: USAW, [1980?].

Balch, James, F.and Phyllis A. Balch. *Prescription for Nutritional Healing*. Garden City Park, New York: Avery Publishing Group, Inc., 1990. A complete and up-to-date book on the wide range of nutritional approaches that are available to deal with many common medical problems.

Barnholth, Lawrence (with Lewis Barnholth and Peter George). *Secrets of the Squat Snatch*. Akron, OH: American College of Modern Weight Lifting, 1950. Larry, together with his brothers Lewis and Claude, created the American College training facility. That modest (physically) facility produced two World Record holders (brothers Peter and Jim George) and many national level lifters over the years. The Barnholth brothers were known for building the character of their lifters as well as their bodies. *Secrets* was the first (and perhaps only) book ever written on the squat style snatch. It was prepared at a time when the squat style was viewed as acceptable but was still widely questioned by many coaches (today it is overwhelmingly dominant). Larry presents a step-by-step-system for learning to use the squat style in the snatch and much of his advice is as useful toady as it was nearly 50 years ago.

Bloomfield, John, Timothy Ackland and Bruce Elliot. *Applied Anatomy and Biomechanics in Sport.* Carlton, Victoria, Australia: Blackwell Scientific Publications, 1994.

Boff, Vic. *Feats of Strength.* New York: Super Strength Publishing, 1979. A classic on how to perform impressive strength feats from a man who has been doing them for decades, in addition to watching some of the best in history perform.

———. *The Bodybuilder's Bible.* New York: ARCO Publishing, Inc., 1985. Vic covers a great deal of territory in this book that addresses a broad spectrum of the bodybuilding world. Vic uses the word "bodybuilding" in its traditional sense of improving health along with increasing muscle size.

Boompa, Tudor. *Theory and Methodology of Training: The Key to Athletic Performance, 2nd. ed..* Dubuque, IA: Kendall Publishing Company, 1990.

Bowerman, William and William Freeman. *High Performance Training for Track & Field.* Champaign, IL: Leisure Press, 1991. Bill is one of coaching's greats, and his fundamental principles apply to all sports, not only track and field events.

Brancazio, Peter. *Sport Science: Physical Laws and Optimum Performance.* New York: Simon and Schuster, 1984. A fascinating look at how a physicist sees various sports.

Cahill, Bernard and Arthur Pearl, eds. *Intensive Participation in Children's Sports.* Champaign, IL: Human Kinetics, 1993.

Carper, Jean. *The Brand-Name Nutrition Counter, rev. ed.* New York: Bantam Books, 1985. Lists the nutritional contents of a wide variety of foods (includes protein, fat, carbohydrate and caloric counts. as well as some key vitamins and minerals).

Casadei, Marino and Alain Lunzenfichter. *1896-1996: 100 Years of Olympic Weightlifting.* Budapest: International Weightlifting Federation, 1996.

Chandler, J. and M. Stone, eds. *USWF Safety Manual.* Colorado Springs, CO: United States Weightlifting Federation, 1990.

Charniga, Andrew, "Bud", Jr. *Variability Incorporated Into the Training of a Qualified Athlete: A Case Study.* Thesis submitted in partial fulfillment of the requirements for the Master of Education Degree in Physical Education, 1981. University of Toledo, OH. The author (a national level competitor) analyzes the effect of variability on his own performance.

Charniga, Andrew, Jr. trans. & comp. *Weightlifting Training and Technique.* Livonia: Sportivny Press, 1992. A selection of articles from a number of sources in the former Soviet Union from the leading US translator of Soviet books on weightlifting.

Coan, Ed. *The Squat.* Quads Gym, 745 North Torrance Ave., Calumet City, IL, 60409 USA. (708) 862-9779. Videocassette. Ed is one of powerlifting's true immortals, having won 10 world championships and having set scores of world records. Ed is also one of the game's true gentlemen. He has produced a series of video tapes that take you through each of the three lifts in powerlifting competition and describe Ed's training approach as well (not to mention permitting you to observe Ed do some fantastic lifts). If you are interested in powerlifting, you can learn a lot from Ed.

Colgan, Michael. *Optimum Sports Nutrition: Your Competitive Edge.* Ronkonkoma, NY: Advanced Research Press, 1993.

Diana, Sam. *Jim Williams: Powerlifting's Greatest Bench Presser.* [Scranton, PA, 1990].

Dintiman, George and Robert Ward. *Sport Speed.* Champaign, IL: Leisure Press, 1988.

Dvorkin, Leonid. *Weightlifting and Age: Scientific and Pedagogical Fundamentals of a Multi-Year System of Training Junior Weightlifters.* Trans. Andrew Charniga, Jr.. Livonia: Sportivny Press, 1992.

Faeth, Karl, ed. *Sports Medicine Manual.* Colorado Springs: USWF, [1986?].

Fleck, Steven and William Kraemer. *Designing Resistance Training Programs.* Champaign, IL: Human Kinetics, 1987.

Fodor, R.V. *Winning Weightlifting.* New York: Sterling Publishing Co., Inc. 1983.

Fox, Edward. *Sports Physiology.* Philadelphia: Saunders College Publishing, 1979.

Frankel, Victor and Margareta Nordin. *Basic Biomechanics of the Skeletal System.* Philadelphia: Lea & Febiger, 1980.

Frantz, Ernie. *Ten Commandments of Powerlifting.* Aurora, IL: Ernie Frantz, [1985?].

Freeman, William. *Peak When it Counts: Periodization for American Track & Field, 2nd.ed.* Mountain View, CA: Tafnews Press, 1991.

Gallwey, Timothy. *The Inner Game of Tennis.* New York: Random House, 1974.

Garfield, Charles. *Peak Performance: Mental Training Techniques of the World's Greatest Athletes.* Los Angeles, CA: Jeremy Tarcher, Inc. 1984. Presents a number of good approaches to improving one's mental performance.

George, Peter. "The Psychology of Weightlifting." *Strength & Health Magazine.* November and December 1961. Written by a World and Olympic champion, these articles are two of the very few (and the very best) published on various aspects of mental preparation for training and competition. Pete is widely remembered for being one of the earliest successful squat style lifters and for high performance at an early age (he very nearly won the Olympics at age 18). But he is also remembered for his ability to lift record weights with limited training (due to his intense studies in college and dental school while he was competing), for lifting maximum weights after warming up with 60 kg. and for the intensity of his mental preparation for a lift (Pete paced back and forth behind the bar working himself into a focused frenzy before each lift). Consequently, he knows of that which he speaks. See also the listing for Larry Barnholth above (who Pete collaborated with to create "Secrets of the Squat Snatch").

Glenney, Judy. *So You Want To Become A Female Weightlifter.* Farmington, NM: Glennco Enterprises, 1989. Judy, multiple-time national champion and American recordbreaker, a true pioneer in women's weightlifting and the first female athlete ever to be inducted into USAW's Hall of Fame, takes you through the basics of weightlifting from her special perspective.

Harder, Dale. *Strength & Speed Ratings*. Castro Valley, CA: Education Plus+, 1994. In this book Dale pulls together the best performances in history in track & field, weightlifting, powerlifting and various other tests of strength and power. In addition, he often presents summaries of the progress of records over time and lists records for athletes of various ages and bodyweights. If you want to compare what you or other athletes can do in relation to the best who ever lived, this book is for you (the book has been updated since 1994).

Hatfield, Frederick. *The Complete Guide To Power Training*. New Orleans: Fitness Systems, 1983. Fred has been a prolific thinker and writer on powerlifting and bodybuilding for many years. A former editor of *Muscle & Fitness*, widely published in the strength field and one of the founders of the International Sports Sciences Association (ISSA), this was Fred's first complete statement on training. He has added to what he wrote here in his subsequent books and articles, but for straight information on powerlifting training for strength this is still one of the best books around (even if it may be a little rough in terms of format relative to Fred's later works). Fred "Dr. Squat" Hatfield is a very original and creative thinker who proved many of his theories on his own body. His 1000+ pound squat when he was over 40 and barely above the 242 pound class still stands as one of the world's all-time great strength feats (and his 500+ pound bench after two rotator cuff surgeries can't be far behind). There isn't anyone who can't learn something from Fred.

——. *Ultimate Sports Nutrition: The Scientific Approach To Peak Athletic Performance*. Chicago: Contemporary Books, Inc., 1987. Here Fred focuses his fertile mind on nutrition.

——. *Power: A Scientific Approach*. Chicago: Contemporary Books, Inc., 1989. Updates much of the material in Fred's earlier *Power Training* book in a more elegant format.

——. *Hardcore Bodybuilding: A Scientific Approach*. Chicago: Contemporary Books, Inc., 1991. Fred's observations on bodybuilding.

Hay, James and J. Gavin Reid. *Anatomy, Mechanics and Human Motion*. Englewood Cliffs, NJ: Prentice Hall, 1988.

Hepburn, Doug. *Super Strength*. Vancouver, Canada: Doug Hepburn, [1994?]. Doug has some original ideas on training, a number of which contradict current wisdom. But few can quarrel with how effective they have been for Doug (who built himself up from an average-size youth to become the world's strongest man for a time) and others.

Hepburn, Doug. *Strength and Bulk*. Vancouver, Canada: Doug Hepburn, circa 1994.

Herring, George. *The Natural Cycle "Float Method"*. Pamphlet circa 1980.

Hernandez III, Gaspar. *Cuban Training Tape*. P.O. Box 131 Tranquillity, NJ 07879. Gaspar made this tape during a recent visit to Cuba. It provides some interesting footage of the Cuban training hall and a few of their top athletes training, along with Gaspar's narration (which supplies information on the training methods of the Cuban team).

International Weightlifting Federation. *Proceedings of the Weightlifting Symposium*, Siofok, Hungary: Budapest: International Weightlifting Federation, 1989.

Hill, Napoleon. *Think and Grow Rich*. New York: Ballantine Books, 1937, 1960. Undoubtedly the most well known book on personal achievement ever written in the English language (and translated to many others). Hill became a legend in this field by delivering an inspiring message during the Great Depression in the US and his advice is still very useful, whether you want to lift big weights or make money. While many have copied and tried to improve upon Hill, it is hard to find a better work than this one.

—— and W. Clement Stone. *Success Through a Positive Mental Attitude*. New York: Pocket Books, 1977. Written primarily by Stone (a long time associate of Hill's and builder of a the multi-billion dollar Aon Company) with the cooperation of Hill. This is the classic book on the importance of a positive mental attitude in the achievement of anything in life. Valuable for the weightlifter as well as the businessperson.

Hoffman, Bob. *Guide to Weightlifting Competition*. York, PA: Strength & Health Publishing Co., 1963.

——. *Functional Isometric Contraction, 2nd ed*. York, PA: Bob Hoffman, 1964. Bob was the power behind American weightlifting when it was at its zenith and he has crammed a great deal of useful information in this short book on training for weightlifting.

——. *Weightlifting, 3rd, ed*. York, PA: Strength & Health Publishing, 1963. A wonderful history of US weightlifting combined with training advice.

Horn, Thelma. *Advances in Sport Psychology*. Champaign, IL: Human Kinetics Publishers, 1992. Offers an advanced academic look at sport psychology. Technical but very informative.

Jones, Lyn. *USWF Coaching Accreditation Course: Club Coach Manual*. Colorado Springs: USWF, 1991. This book, as well as the two other books in the series, were written primarily to supplement the coaching certification courses offered by the USWF/USAW. There is useful information in all three books, but they are not designed to stand alone without the instruction offered by the course lecturers. Coaching weightlifting is a hands-on activity, so attending a USWF course is an important way to learn the basics of weightlifting coaching. Information on the USWF course schedule is available from their National Office (see listing in the "Resources" section below).

——. *USWF Coaching Accreditation Course: Senior Coach Manual*. Colorado Springs: USWF, 1991.

——. *USWF Coaching Accreditation Course: Regional Coach Manual*. Colorado Springs: USWF, 1996.

Kelley, David. *The Art of Reasoning*, 2nd. expanded ed.. New York: W.W. Norton & Company, Inc., 1994. A terrific college text on logic and its applications to everyday life.

Kirkley, George. *Weight Lifting and Weight Training*. New York: ARC Books, Inc., 1963.

Kirschman, John. *The Nutrition Almanac*. New York: McGraw-Hill, 1984. One of most complete books written on nutrition for the layperson, with a great deal of information regarding the use of a wide variety of vitamins and other food supplements.

Komi, Paavo, ed. *Strength and Power in Sport*. Oxford: Blackwell Scientific Publications, 1992. An excellent collection of scientific articles on strength and power science, theory and practice. Perhaps the most complete scientific work available in one volume.

Kono, Tommy. "ABC's Of Weightlifting." *Strength & Health Magazine*. Various issues from the late 1960s through the o mid 1970s. Tommy won 2 Olympic Games, took a silver medal in his third Games, won 8 World Championships and set 26 World Records across 4 weight classes during his career. He was head coach for the Mexican weightlifting team at the 1968 Olympics, the German team for the 1972 Olympics and has coached US men's and women's team at many international events. Tommy has also excelled as a writer about the sport and as a photographer of weightlifting. His series of articles in *Strength & Health* magazine, as well as many other articles written of the magazine over the years, contain a wealth of information for the athlete and coach (Strength & Health -*S&H*- magazine was "the Bible" for weightlifters worldwide from the 1940s through the 1970s). In his ABC series Tommy covered technique, injury prevention, training methods and more. If you can find Tommy's articles (and lots of others in S&H), you'll be well rewarded for the effort.

———. "Quality Training." *Strength & Health Magazine*. June 1968. In one of the seminal articles written on weightlifting during this decade, Tommy focuses on the importance of quality versus quantity in training. More is not always better (it is often not better) and Tommy suggests that one can lift some huge weights with limited training if that training is high in quality (and in this article he offers suggestions on how to improve the quality of your workouts). As athletes and coaches often race one another to prove that they (or their athletes) train harder than the next athlete or team, Tommy offers a "reality check" in terms that focus everyone on the ultimate goal - to lift more in competition rather than put in more training time or effort.

Kraemer, William and Steve Fleck. *Strength Training for Young Athletes*. Champaign, IL: Human Kinetics, 1993.

Kubik, Brooks. *Dinosaur Training: Lost Secrets of Strength and Development*. Louisville, Kentucky. Brooks Kubic, 1996. Brooks has some interesting ideas on training and his advice on preparing mentally for a training session is excellent.

Kuc, John. *John Kuc Speaks On Powerlifting*. Kingston, PA: John Kuc, 1982.

Lamb, David. *Physiology of Exercise: Responses and Adaptations*. New York: MacMillan Publishing Co., Inc., 1978.

Laputin, Nikolai. *Managing the Training of Weightlifters*. Trans. Andrew Charniga, Jr.. Livonia: Sportivny Press, 1989.

Lear, John. *Weightlifting*. Wakefield, West Yorshire, UK. EP Publishing, Ltd., 1980.

———. *Skillful Weightlifting*. London: A&C Black, 1991.

Loehr, James. *Athletic Excellence: Mental Toughness in Sports*. Denver: Forum, 1982.

Lukacsfulv, Agnes and Ferenc Takas, eds. *Proceedings of the Weightlifting Symposium: 1993 Ancient Olympia/Greece*. Budapest: IWF 1993.

MacDougall, J. Duncan, Howard Wenger and Howard Green, eds. *Physiological Testing of High Performance Athletes, 2nd ed*. Champaign, IL: Human Kinetics, 1991.

Mevedyev, Aleksei. *A System of Multi-Year Training in Weightlifting*. Trans. Andrew Charniga, Jr.. Livonia: Sportivny Press, 1989. Describes Medvedyev's approach to training weightlifters, which is very much oriented toward a high level of variability and long-term planning. A very worthwhile exposition of this kind of approach.

———. *A Program of Multi-Year Training in Weightlifting*. Trans. Andrew Charniga, Jr.. Livonia: Sportivny Press, 1995. Provides specific examples of training programs for lifters across their careers.

Mihajlovic, Vladan. *80 Years Of The Weightlifting In The World And Europe 1896-1976*. Budapest: International Weightlifting Federation, 1977. A wonderful book that has all of the world and Olympic Games results during the years covered, as well as the progress of world records.

Mihajlovic, Vladan. *Weightlifting Results: Part II Names, Numbers, Facts*. Budapest: International Weightlifting Federation, circa 1983.

Murray, Al and David Webster. *Defying Gravity*. 1964. A pioneering book on analyzing snatch technique.

Nadori, Laszlo and Istvan Granek. *Theory and Methodological Basis of Training Planning With Special Consideration Within a Microcycle*. Ed. and trans. Tibor Hartobagyi. Lincoln, NE: NSCA, 1989.

Nideffer, Robert. *The Inner Athlete: Mind Plus Muscle For Winning*. New York: Thomas. Y. Crowell Company, 1976. One of the earliest books on sports psychology and still one of the best.

Nugent, Daniel. *Turning Iron Into Gold: How To Succeed As A Personal Trainer*. New York: The Biomechanic Properties, 1995. Phone (718) 217-7506. Most weightlifters need to earn a living outside weightlifting and one of the best ways to do so is to become a personal trainer. Dan's book takes you through many of the important aspects of embarking on such a career in a very concise and to the point manner. The author is a personal trainer, and physical educator and a trainer of personal trainers.

1974 Weightlifting Yearbook. Trans. Bernd Scheithauer, Stanford University, 1975. To my knowledge the first such yearbook translated to English. This and all of the yearbooks that follow are interesting compilations of weightlifting theory, practice and analysis.

1980 Weightlifting Yearbook. Trans. Andrew Charniga, Jr.. Livonia: Sportivny Press, 1986.

1981 Weightlifting Yearbook. Trans. Andrew Charniga, Jr.. Livonia: Sportivny Press, [1984?].

1982 Weightlifting Yearbook. Trans. Andrew Charniga, Jr.. Livonia: Sportivny Press, 1984.

1983 Weightlifting Yearbook. Trans. Andrew Charniga, Jr.. Livonia: Sportivny Press, 1984.

1984 Weightlifting Yearbook. Trans. Andrew Charniga, Jr.. Livonia: Sportivny Press, 1987.

1985 Weightlifting Yearbook. Trans. Andrew Charniga, Jr.. Livonia: Sportivny Press, 1987.

Onuma, Kenji. The Japanese Frog Style. *Strength & Health Magazine*. May and June 1969. This was the first (perhaps the only) article describing the theory and practice of the frog-style pulling technique.

Orlick, Terry. *In Pursuit of Excellence: How to Win in Sport and Life, 2nd. ed*. Champaign, IL: Leisure Press, 1990.

O'Shea, John Patrick. *Scientific Principles And Methods Of Strength Fitness*. Corvallis, OR: OSU Bookstores, Inc., 1966. One of the very earliest and best books on strength training written by an academic who was also a weightlifter and all-around athlete.

———. *Quantum Strength Training*. Corvallis, OR: Patrick's Books, 1995. This book picks up where "Scientific Principles..." left off. Pat crams a lot of information into this book, covering the principles of developing training programs, the principles of sport science, proper technique, how one can integrate one's knowledge of training into sport-specific training and how to modify the training plan as one ages. You can tell from reading this book that the author was not only on top of the research in his field but has practiced what he has preached as well.

The Parliament of the Commonwealth of Australia. *Drugs in Sport: An Interim Report of the Senate Standing Committee On Environment, Recreation and the Arts*. Canberra, Australia, Australian Government Publishing Service, May 1989. Provides one of the best summaries of the history of drug use in sport that is available and, along with the companion volume that follows, documents the reportedly deplorable situation that existed in the Australian Institute of Sport with respect to employees involved in the promotion of drug use, especially in the sport of weightlifting.

———. *Drugs in Sport: Second Paper of the Senate Standing Committee On Environment, Recreation and the Arts*. Canberra, Australia, Australian Government Publishing Service, May 1990.

Pearl, Bill. *Keys to the Inner Universe*. Bolinas, CA: Physical Fitness Architects, 1979. Bill self-published this classic nearly 20 years ago and it still stands an the most complete explanation of weight training (though not weightlifting) exercises that has ever been published. Bill, one of the greatest and strongest bodybuilders or all time (and a real gentleman who remains in great shape to this day), both illustrates and explains the performance of hundreds of exercises, often comments on their benefits, and assigns a level of difficulty. If you want to know how to perform any bodybuilding exercise, Bill's book is the place to go. The book also contains information on nutrition, putting together a routine and a multitude of other subjects - its a true classic.

Pearl, Bill and Gary Moran. *Getting Stronger*. Bolinas, CA: Shelter Publications, Inc., 1986. This book focuses more on training than "Keys...". It describes many important training principles so that one can understand how to devise a program for his or her own needs. Specific programs are provided for bodybuilders of all levels and for the practitioners of sports from golf to wrestling.

Peikoff, Leonard. *Objectivism: The Philosophy of Ayn Rand*. New York: Penguin Group, 1991. The first truly comprehensive book on the Objectivist philosophy - a philosophy of great appeal to the reasoning mind.

Pick, J. and Becque, M. *Percent Activation of Two Quadriceps Muscles During the Squat Exercise in Trained Individuals*. Paper presented at the National Strength and Conditioning Association Conference in New Orleans in June of 1994. Reported in abstract form in the Journal of Strength and Conditioning Research, Vol. 9, #3, August 1995, pg. 194.

Platz, Tom. *Pro-Style Bodybuilding*. New York: Sterling Publishing, Co., Inc., 1981.

Raiport, Grigori: *Red Gold: Peak Performance Techniques of Russian and East German Olympic Victors*. Los Angeles: Jeremy P. Tarcher, Inc., 1988

Rand, Ayn. *Atlas Shrugged*. New York: Penguin Group, 1957, 1985. The novel that made Rand famous as a philosopher as well as a novelist and spawned the development of a comprehensive and widely studied philosophy—Objectivism.

———. *The Fountainhead*. New York: The New American Library, Inc., 1943, 1971. The book that made Ayn Rand a famous novelist and captured millions of fans. Still a strong seller after more than 50 years.

Rasch, Philip. *Kinesiology and Applied Anatomy*. Philadelphia: Lea & Febiger, 1989.

Reid, David. *Sports Injury Assessment and Rehabilitation*. NY: Churchill Livingstone, 1992.

Roman, Robert. *The Training of the Weightlifter, 2nd Ed..* Trans. Andrew Charniga, Jr.. Livonia: Sportivny Press, 1988. Roman was one of the great Soviet sports thinkers and this book is a great way to get acquainted with him.

Roman, Robert and Midkat Shakirzyanov. *The Snatch , The Clean and Jerk*. Trans. Andrew Charniga, Jr.. Livonia: Sportivny Press, 1982. Offers some terrific analyses of weightlifting technique.

Rothenberg, Beth and Oscar. *Touch Training For Strength*. Champaign, IL: Human Kinetics, 1995.

Sanders, Barbara, ed. *Sports Physical Therapy*. Norwalk, CT: Appleton&Lange, 1990.

Sandler, Ronald and Dennis Lobstein. *Consistent Winning: A Remarkable New Training System That Lets You Peak On Demand*. Emmaus, PA: Rodale Press, 1992.

Schmidt, Richard. *Motor Control and Learning: A Behavioral Emphasis, 2nd ed*. Champaign, IL: Human Kinetics, 1988. A very comprehensive text at the graduate level. Challenging reading but worth the effort.

Schodl, Gottfried. *The Lost Past*. Trans. Aniko Nemeth-Mora. Budapest: International Weightlifting Federation, 1992. Mr. Schodl has been President of the IWF for more than 20 years. He and Tamas Ajan have worked together to guide the IWF to a higher world profile, to Olympic success and toward becoming one of the strongest sports federations in the world in terms of drug testing. One of weightlifting's most outstanding historians, Mr. Schodl has gathered together some of the great stories and statistics of weightlifting history into this volume. If you are a weightlifting history buff, you have to own this book.

Schodl, Gottfried and Alain Lunzenfichter, eds. *From Alexseev to Zubricky:100 Years' Weightlifting Medals 1891-1991*. Budapest: International Weightlifting Federation, 1992. In this book Messrs. Schodl and Lunzenfichter have captured key statistics on individual lifters across the last 100 years. A unique work that summarizes the accomplishments of athletes from Alexseev to Zubricky.

Schwarzenegger, Arnold. *Encyclopedia of Modern Bodybuilding*. New York: Simon and Schuster, 1985. Arnold is world-renown for his acting, bodybuilding, business and charity efforts. He is a quality guy who always tries to deliver value to his audience. He has succeeded in this book quite admirably. While many stars will put their name on something merely to extend their "empires." Arnold has delivered the most complete single volume on bodybuilding that has ever been published. It's a great place for the beginning and intermediate bodybuilder to start and can teach some advanced bodybuilders a few things as well.

Seno, Bill. *Pushing For Power: In Powerlifting and Sports*. IL: William Joseph Seno, 1984.

Selye, Hans. *The Stress of Life, rev. ed.* New York: McGraw-Hill, Inc., 1976. The book that started all the talk about "stress" and its effects on our lives. Its message has often been misinterpreted by the popular press. This book lets you hear it from the source.

Sherwood, Lauralee. *Human Physiology, 2nd ed.* Minneapolis/St.Paul: West Publishing Company, 1993.

Shils, Maurico, James Olson and Moshe Shike. *Modern Nutrition in Health and Disease, 8th ed. Volumes 1 and 2*. Philadelphia: Lea & Febiger, 1994.

Simmons, Louie. *The Squat Video*. Westside Barbell Club. 1417 Demarest, Columbus OH, 43228. Tel: (614) 276-0923. Longtime powerlifter and coach of many powerlifting champions, Louie Simmons runs this very active powerlifting club. Louie has produced several very interesting video tapes on his unique training system. I don't agree with everything Louie says, and his tapes can be a little rough on production value at times, but Louie's enthusiasm and creativity shine through. His approach is certainly worth a look. Whether you agree with it or not, you can't help but come away from the experience of watching one of his tapes without some new thoughts of your own as well as a sense that there continues to be a great deal of room for innovation in weight training. Louie also has an interesting line of equipment, some of it of his own design.

Starr, Bill. *The Strongest Shall Survive*. Washington, DC: Fitness Products Ltd. , 1978. Bill was the editor of *Strength & Health* magazine for a number of years and was a national level lifter as well in both weightlifting and powerlifting. He provides sound training advice in his hallmark style - which is as entertaining as it is informative. Bill is his own man and bases his advice on what he knows from experience.

——. *Defying Gravity: How To Win At Weightlifting*. Wichita Falls, TX: Five Starr Productions, 1981. Even more entertaining than *The Strongest...*", this book packs more information on how to compete successfully than almost anything else around. In addition, it entertains the reader with inside stories of the athletes Bill knew during his York days and after that. You have to love Bill's writing style and his message.

Stone, M.H., O'Bryant, H. and Garhammer, J.A. *A Hypothetical Model for Strength Training*. Journal of Sports Medicine and Physical Fitness (21:336 342-351, 1981).

Strossen, Randall. *Super Squats: How To Gain 30 Pounds Of Muscle In 6 Weeks*. Larkspur, CA: Randall J. Strossen, 1989. In this compact volume Randy has gathered together information on the one exercise that will give a person who is willing to work hard more results than any other. Other writers have written about high rep breathing squats before, but Randy put it all together and with this volume assures that the bodybuilding benefits of squatting won't be forgotten.

Strossen, Randall. *Iron Mind: Stronger Minds, Stronger Bodies*. Nevada City, CA: Iron Mind Enterprises, 1994. A compilation of Randi's articles that appeared in a well know bodybuilding magazine over a period of several years. This book contains practical advice on handling a wide range of mental challenges in this book.

Tesch, Per. *Muscle Meets Magnet*. Stockholm, Sweden: PA Tesch AB, 1993. The first large scale attempt to evaluate the way in which various exercises stress particular muscles using an MRI.

Ungerlander, Steven and Jacqueline Golding. *Beyond Strength*. Dubuque, IA: Wm. C. Brown Publishers, 1992.

United States Weightlifting Federation, Inc. *Official USWF Rulebook 1994*. Colorado Springs, CO: United States Weightlifting Federation, Inc., 1994. Soon to be updated, this is the most current rulebook available that describes the rules of the USWF/USAW. Every lifter and coach should own and read this book so that they know the rules of the game. Rudy Sablo, former national-level lifter, a coach, an administrator and for many years the head of the USWF's technical committee, has long been the force behind the USWF rulebook. He, along, with Jack Hughes (former national champion and another incredibly dedicated referee), have trained and tested virtually every referee now practicing in the US. While their contribution has often been overlooked, there are those of us who realize how important their life's work has been to the sport.

Verkhoshansky, Yuri. *Fundamentals of Special Strength-Training in Sport*. Trans. Andrew Charniga, Jr. . Livonia: Sportivny Press, 1986.

——. *Programming and Organization of Training*. Trans. Andrew Charniga, Jr. Livonia: Sportivny Press, 1986.

Vorobyev, Arkady. *Weightlifting*. Budapest: International Weightlifting Federation, 1978. One of the first and best true textbooks written on weightlifting by one of its great champions.

Vorobyev, Arkady, *Heavy Athletics*. Moscow: Fiziculture i Sport, 1988.

Webster, David. *Preparing For Competition Weightlifting*. Huddersfield, UK: Springfield Books, Ltd., 1986

——. *The Iron Game: An Illustrated History of Weightlifting*. Irvine: John Geddes (Printers), 1976. A splendid history of the sport that contains pictures and references difficult to obtain from any other source. If Dave hasn't "seen it all" he has seen most of what has been accomplished in weightlifting and now you get to share what he knows.

——. *The Development of the Clean & Jerk*. Circa 1966. One of the pioneering analyses of the technique of the Clean and Jerk. Dave was perhaps the first person to write about the "double knee bend".

————. *The International Research Training Plan Parts I & II*. Circa 1966. One of the earliest expositions of periodization in the Western literature.

Wells, Christine. *Women, Sport & Performance: A Physiological Perspective, 2nd. ed.* Champaign, IL: Human Kinetics Books, 1991.

Wells, Katherine. *Kinesiology: The Scientific Basis of Human Motion*. Philadelphia: W.B. Saunders Company, 1971

Willoughby, David. *The Super Athletes*. South Brunswick & New York: A.S. Barnes and Company, 1970. One of the great historians of the Iron Game and other sports as well, Willoughby has put together the most complete collection of strength "best performances" ever assembled. This book is a treasure but is unfortunately long out-of-print. If you see a copy buy it without hesitation. It will provide hours of reading pleasure and give you a new appreciation for athletic performances of every kind, but particularly for the feats of the strong men and women who have made strength history.

Wirhed, Rolf. *Athletic Ability: The Anatomy of Winning*. New York: Harmony Books, 1984.

Yates, Dorian and Bob Wolff. *Blood and Guts: The Ultimate Approach to Building Muscle Mass*. Woodland Hills, CA: Wolff Creative Group, 1993. 6 time Mr. Olympia, Dorian Yates is one of history's greatest bodybuilders and a very strong one inaddition. His simple and clear messages on training and dedication to one's craft transcend the bodybuilding world. Following his guidance would make anyone a success in any area of life.

Yessis, Michael and Richard Turbo. *Secrets of Soviet Sports Fitness and Training*. Don Mills, Ontario: Collins Publishers, 1987.

Zatsiorsky, Vladimir. *Science and Practice of Strength Training*. Champaign, IL: Human Kinetics, 1995. A very interesting and imaginative work by one of today's best thinkers and reseachers on this subject, especially in the area of training for increased power.

Organizations and Publications Of Interest To The Weightlifter

The Association of Oldetime Barbell and Strongmen. 4959 Viceroy St., Suite 203, Cape Coral, FL 33904. Vic Boff, President. Weightlifter, bodybuilder, strongman, "polar bear," health food store owner, writer, and more, Vic has done it all in the iron game and is one of the true "keepers of the flame" for strongpersons worldwide. A friend of many of the game's greats (like Bob Hoffman, Sigmund Klein, John Grimek and Milo Steinborn), he started his association more than a decade ago with an annual birthday party for Sig Klein in a restaurant in Brooklyn. Now there is an annual dinner at New York's Downtown Athletic Club (home of the Heisman Trophy) honoring great weightlifters, bodybuilders, strongmen (or women), administrators and/or promoters. Vic also publishes a newsletter regarding the association's events and the whereabouts and accomplishments of the iron game's members. Perhaps most importantly, he is everywhere and anywhere promoting the benefits of resistance training and physical culture, discouraging the use of drugs in sport and life, and supporting his members. Whether it's advice for an iron game entrepreneur, flowers for a funeral, or simply a phone call to see how a forgotten member is doing, Vic is there, generally without anyone else knowing it. Vic's association and his movement should be supported, as he brings the factions in the game together while at the same time acting as the voice of reason and a focus on health in an era that has often supported performance at any cost.

Bruce Klemens. 139 Longwood Lake Road, Oak Ridge, NJ 07438, USA.. Bruce was a dedicated weightlifter whose interest in photography developed into a lifelong avocation. Bruce has probably photographed more weightlifters over al longer period of time than anyone in recent weightlifting history. His library of photos includes most of good and the great on the national (US)

and international scenes for the past quarter century. If you are looking for a weightlifting photos contact Bruce.

Crain's Muscle World. 3803 North Bryan Road, Shawnee, OK, 74801-2314. Tel: (405) 275-3689. Ricky Crain, a many-time world and national powerlifting champion who continues to break master's powerlifting records today, runs this company. He offers a wide range of equipment, books and videos that are often hard to obtain elsewhere. My experience with Ricky's services has been very positive.

Denis Reno's Weightlifter's Newsletter. 30 Cambria Road, West Newton, MA 02165, USA. Denis has been an athlete, coach, official, administrator, meet director and all around promoter of weightlifting for many years. He began publishing his newsletter in the 1970s and it has become a leader in its field in terms of furnishing the quickest printed meet results. Denis includes a lot of his own opinions and publishes many letters to the editor. His publication includes national and international results in serves as a forum for the exchange of ideas in weightlifting. Denis says what he thinks and this has made him unpopular in certain circles, but his devoted readership knows that most of the time he is right on the money. The sport needs independent voices such as Denis's. $24 US, Canada $26, Europe $32 and the rest of the world $37 for the year.

Dynamic Fitness. PO Box 510505 Livonia, MI 48151 (313) 425-2862. The exclusive distributors for Eleiko Sport equipment and Adidas weightlifting apparel in the US, this company has been serving the serious weightlifting and weight training community (individuals and institutions) for more than a decade. If you are in the market for weightlifting shoes, need a weightlifting suit or want to purchase Eleiko equipment anywhere in the Americas, Dynamic Fitness is your answer. Owner Bud Charniga has run the company (as well as Sportivny

Press, which publishes many of the books that were listed in the bibliography) from day one. A supplier to professional and college weight rooms, as well as the individual consumer, Bud's knowledge of the sport, reputation for honesty and dedication to service is as outstanding as the companies he represents. And when you deal with Dynamic Fitness you are dealing with the owner, a former national-level lifter who personally trains on and tests everything he sells. Behind the scenes, Bud has promoted the sport of weightlifting for many years as an athlete, coach, translator, athlete's representative to the USWF, meet director (he has personally run two fine national championships) and lecturer. He has donated equipment to the USWF's/USAW's training center and Colorado Springs, advertised in USA Weightlifting at times when no one else has, and loaned equipment to countless meet directors of national and local competitions. He does a great deal more behind the scenes to support weightlifting that he would be angry at me for revealing - so I will not. I will simply say that he is one of weightlifting's' true friends. More information on Eleiko equipment appears is Chapter 4.

International Olympic Lifter (IOL). PO Box 65855, Los Angeles, CA 90065. $28.00 per year. Founding editor and publisher, Bob Hise Sr., was an independent thinker who used IOL to provide his special view of weightlifting, how to live it and how to train for it. His recent death has placed the magazine in the hands of his son, daughter-in-law and grandson who have vowed to keep up the tradition.

Iron Man Magazine. 1701 Ives Avenue, Oxnard CA, 93033. $29.97 per year. This magazine was started by Peary and Mabel Rader in Nebraska in 1936. Peary offered a truly independent voice in the iron game for more than 50 years. During the 60s he published another magazine called *Lifting News* which was devoted completely to weightlifting and powerlifting. Mabel Rader was the first female national-level referee in the US and was the first chairperson of the AAU's women's weightlifting committee. She ably presided over women's weightlifting as the first national championships were organized in 1981 and continued to work toward the growth of women's lifting until she handed leadership of the committee over to Judy Glenney's able hands. *Iron Man* is currently published by John Balik. It contains a wide range of articles on training, nutrition and other subjects of interest to bodybuilders and weight trainers. John presents the views of many qualified authors with widely varying opinions in a way that will stimulate you to think. The magazine occasionally carries articles on weightlifting.

Iron Master. Editor Osmo Kiiha. 4456 West 5855 South, Kearns, UT. Osmo's unique publication generally features a chapter length biography of an Iron Game great along with a number of other interesting articles and classifieds. No one spends as much time on a biography written for a periodical as Osmo and it shows in the quality of what he publishes. When you contact Osmo to subscribe, be sure to ask for a list of any back issues that may be available. In them, you'll find information on the greats of strength history that you simply can't get from any other source.

Mav-Rik. 3602 Eagle Rock Blvd. Los Angeles, CA 96005. Bob Hise Sr., referred to in the listing of IOL above, started this company as an alternative to York Barbell. Athlete, coach, administrator and tireless

promoter of the sport, Bob always supplied a helping hand to a weightlifters in need and gave far more help than he was ever given credit for. I can recall asking Bob for permission to use his gym after a long day of work during a business trip to California. He not only gave me permission, but he came out to his gym at midnight to watch every lift I did. Mav-Rik is now being run by Bob's son Bob Hise III, his daughter-in-law Sherry and at least one of his grandchildren. See Chapter 4 for a description of some of the equipment produced by Mav-Rik.

Milo: A Journal For Serious Strength Athletes. Iron Mind Enterprises, Inc. PO Box 1228, Nevada City, CA, USA 95959. Tel. (916) 265-6725, Fax: (916) 265-4876. $29.95 per year in the US. There is no magazine today that covers as broad a spectrum of the strength sports as *Milo*. From weightlifting to stone lifting, Milo addresses it all. There are fine meet reports, excellent biographies, training and technique guidance and a host of other information of interest to lovers of strength worldwide. *Iron Mind* also offers an unusual catalogue of unique items designed for weightlifters and others who admire strength and its history (books, videos, equipment, etc.).

Muscle & Fitness. The flagship publication of the Weider organization, this magazine presents the bodybuilding scene along with many articles of general interest to weight trainers and others interested in fitness. Joe Weider and his brother Ben are to bodybuilding what Bob Hoffman was to weightlifting. They have tirelessly promoted bodybuilding for decades and have contributed immensely to its becoming a worldwide phenomenon. The popularity of weight training has been greatly enhanced by the efforts of the Weiders. Few remember that Joe began his career as a weightlifter and he maintains and interest in the sport to the current day.

Muscular Development. The very well-known health food company "Twin Labs," purchased this publication for the York organization some years ago. They offer a diverse magazine with some very knowledgeable contributors. This magazine ranks among the best for general information regarding resistance exercise and nutrition.

Powerlifting USA. PO Box 467 Camarillo, CA 93011. One year subscription $31.95 in the US. *Powerlifting USA* has for more than two decades been "'the" powerlifting magazine in the world. Editor Mike Lambert does an admirable job of maintaining neutrality among the many (sometimes warring) powerlifting federations in the US and worldwide. He covers meets very promptly and accurately with some great lift by lift descriptions of what went on. There are also numerous articles on how to train and eat, as well as biographies of the greats of powerlifting, along with those who are up and coming. In addition, there is some nice historical material from time to time. Mike has also published some very nice articles on Olympic lifting. I wish that we had a counterpart to this magazine for weightlifting - no doubt it would help to increase the popularity of the sport (as Mike's magazine has surely done for powerlifting).

Sportivny Press. See *Dynamic Fitness* listing above.

USA Weightlifting (USAW) and Weightlifting USA. One Olympic Plaza, Colorado Springs, CO 80909 (719) 578-4508, www. USAW. org. USA Weightlifting is the governing body for the sport of weightlifting in the US. You need to be a member of the USAW if you want to participate in competitions sanctioned by the USAW. *Weightlifting USA* is the quarterly publication, of the

USAW. The magazine provides information of vital interest to all competitive weightlifters in the US. Includes the latest rules, policies and procedures of the USAW, some articles on training and biographical material, extensive meet results and other items of interest to pure weightlifters. The magazine comes as part of membership in the USAW. Membership in the USAW is a must for the serious weightlifter or coach and it is a terrific value as well. Your membership dollars support the sport in this country while keeping you informed at the same time.

World Weightlifting: Official Magazine of the IWF and AIPS Weightlifting Commission. $35 US. IWF Secretariat, 1374 Budapest Pf. 614 Hungary. The official magazine of the IWF, this publication covers the world scene in a way that nothing else does. Includes meet results, biographies of the champions, messages from Messrs. Ajan and Schodl and a lot of other information. It also offers some of the best pictures in the sport (especially the poster that is inserted in each issue). No weightlifter, coach or fan of the sport should be without a subscription to this magazine.

York Barbell Company. PO Box 1707, York, PA, 17405-1707. Tel: (717) 767-6481. York Barbell was started and managed by Bob Hoffman for half a century. At one time it was probably the leading barbell and health food company in the world. Through his flagship magazine, *Strength & Health* (as well as numerous other publications), Hoffman popularized weightlifting and weight training for sport and created millions of believers in weight training around the world. He did more than any other person to make the US a power in world weightlifting from the 1930s through the 1960s and the importance of his influence can be appreciated only by studying what happened to weightlifting in the US in the years following Bob's loss of vigor and ultimate death. York Barbell has changed management several times since Bob's death. Its current owner, Vic Standish, has recently revamped York's product line. A discussion of York's bars and bumper plates appears in Chapter 4. York's "Hall of Fame" (located in York, PA) is unique, with its many pictures and exhibits from the history of the Iron Game, and its special focus on weightlifting history in the US. It's worth a visit if you are ever near York. York has also sponsored the activities of the USWF/USAW for many years, establishing the company as loyal friend of weightlifting

INDEX

539

time factor in, 405-6

—O—

oligomeric proanthocyanidins. *See* grape seed extract
ornithine, 404
ossification, of bones, 494
Ohuchi, Masashi, 59-60
overtraining, 245-6, 314–5, 419, 517
    Basedowic, 314-5
    monotonous, 314
    Parasympathetic, 315
    Sympathetic, 315
oxygen under pressure. *See* Restorative measures

—P—

papain, 449
Park, Reg, 5, 349, 412,
parallel elastic component (PEC), 490
peaking methods, 309
    peaking by reducing volume and increasing
        intensity, 310
    peaking by gradually increasing intensity and
        volume, 311
    using pre–competition "control competitions", 313
Pearl, Bill, 5, 240, 534
penniform muscles, 489–490
periodization
    Soviet style,
        the macrocycle, 252–8
        the monthly cycle or mesocycle, 269–71
        the weekly plan or microcycle, 271-5
    Bulgarian periodization methods, 275-8
    other approaches to periodization, 278-81
Perry, Herbert, 425
physiology, muscle. *Seealso* muscle
    energy for muscular contractions, 492–4
    factors influencing force production in, 487–8
    muscle action as the basis for human movement,
        482
    muscle fiber types *(see* muscle fiber types)
    neural basis for muscle action, 485–6
    optimal length for generating force, 488–9
plans, training. *See* training plans
Podlivayev, B., 23–4
positive affirmations. *See,* mind, controlling
positive mental attitude (PMA). *See* mind, theoretical
    issues
power, 8, 113–4, 138, 508, 513
    specialized training for the development of, 164-5
powerlifters and other strength athletes, the special
    needs of those who convert to weightlifting, 303-4,
    516
prepubescent and pubescent athletes, training of,
    exercise prescriptions for children, 384-7
    growth and maturation, 383-4
projectiles, motion of, 511
proprioceptive muscle receptors, *See,* golgi tendon
    organ and muscle spindles
psychoneuromuscular, 333
pubescent athletes. *See* prepubescent
Puleo, Joseph, 343
    pycnogenol, 449
    pyramiding *See* strength training variables

—Q—

qualifying to lift in competitions. *See* rules,
    organizations which govern weightlifting
qualitative analysis, 98 100

—R—

Rader, Mabel, 537
Rader, Peary, 197, 537
Ramsey, Charles, 194-5
Rand, Ayn, 322-3, 534
Rawluk, Peter, 134, 307, 311-24
reciprocal mini cycle, 156–7
recruitment of muscle fibers, 485, 488, 501
records, establish world and other kinds. *See,* rules,
    technical, world records
rehabilitative exercise, 433
Reno, Denis, 536
repetition. *See also* selection of repetitions in teaching
    technique
    definition of, 121–122
    guidelines of number of reps over and under 90% of
        maximum, 264-5
    number of and guidelines for training children, 384–
        5
    optimal rest between, 139-40
    patterns used in popular training methods, 151-8,
        501–2,
    performance of, 137–9,
    specificity of, 129-130
restorative measures, 450-2
Riecke, Louis, 136, 146
RICE, 427-428
Rigert, David, 244
Ritzer, Theodore, 436
Roman, Robert, 23, 28, 66, 69, 84-5, 258–264, 270,
    310–311, 408, 534
Ruchames, Daniel, xxiii
rules,
    eligibility
        a word about amateurism and eligibility, 457
        age group competitions, 461-2
            junior competitions, 462
            masters competitions, 462
        qualifying to lift in various competitions, 479-80
    equipment used by athletes in competitions,
        barbell, 364, 463-7
        lifter's costume, 465-7
        platform, 364, 465
    other official equipment of the competition, 467-9
        attempt board, 468
        clock, 468
        electronic light system, 467
        forms, 468
        operations of the referee's light system, 469
        record board, 468
        scale, 468
        scoreboard, 468
        special requirements for equipment at major
            international competitions, 468
        warm-up area, 468
    officials of the competition, 473
        competition secretary, 469, 470, 471, 474, 475
        doctors on duty, 476-7
        jury, 474-5

545

547

—U—

unloading, 129, 144, 161–2, 261, 269, 277-281

—V—

Vardanian, Yuri, 54, 407, 513
vectors, *See* motion, kinds of
Vega, Anthony, 326
Verkhoshansky, Yuri, 149, 242, 535
volume, 124, 146–7, 260–4, 267–78, 295-6, 310-14, 420, 426, 516
Vorobiev, Arkady, 69, 535

—W—

weight, definition of, 505
weight, making (reducing for competition). *See* competition, coaching prior to
weight, ideal bodyweight. *See* bodyweight
weight, gaining muscular bodyweight. *See* bodyweight
weightlifting and children, *See* prepubescent athletes, training
weightlifting and the mature athlete,
    losses in physiological functioning with aging, 387-8
    training and the mature athlete, 388-9
weightlifting, as a means for improving athletic performance,
    case studies of athletes benefiting from Olympic lifting, 514
    only dedicated athletes will gain benefits from practicing the Olympic lifts, 514-5
    unique value of Olympic lifts for athletes, 513-4
    using of partial lifts, 520-1
    using of pulls, 521
    using the power clean, power snatch and power jerk, 520
weightlifting, definition of, 1
weightlifting, fallacies regarding, 3-13

weightlifting, why lift?, 1
Weightlifting Encyclopedia,
    approaches to reading, 14–5
    contacting the publisher of, 549
Weightlifting USA, 198, 356, 456, 479, 480, 537
    Weissbrot, Morris, xxiii, xxv
Williams, James, 158, 531
world records, procedures for establishing. *See*, rules, technical
women and weightlifting—a great match, 377-8
    amenorrhea, relationships between training and, 379-80
    differences between men and women,
        a few closing words on the differences between men and women, 382
        in strength , 378
        other physiological differences, 378-9
    menarche, the effects of athletic activity on, 380
    pregnancy and training, 380-1
    psychological and social conditions that can influence women who are weightlifters, 382
work, 508 (*see also* volume)
work hardening process, 269–70
workout, planning a. *See* training, workout plan

—X—

Xugang, Zhan, 56

—Y—

Yates, Dorian, 4–5, 321, 536
York Barbell, iv, 185, 189, 538

—Z—

Zacharevich, Yuri, 204
Zatsiorsky, Vladimir, 536
zone, 125-7, 263-5, 278, 311

Contacting the Publisher

Ordering Information

Additional copies of this book may be obtained from your local bookstore. Alternatively, you can order additional books directly from the publisher at the following address:

A is A Communications
P.O. Box 680
Whitestone, N. Y. 11357-0680
USA

Please include a check or money order in the amount of $34.95 US payable to: A is A Communications ($29.95 for the book plus $5.00 for shipping and handling). NY State residents must add 8.25% sales tax ($2.47 per book for a total of $37.42 per book, including shipping and handling). For orders from outside the US add $5.00 to the standard US shipping and handling charges—for a total of $39.95 US.

Suggestions

We would welcome any suggestions that you may have for improving the next edition of this book or for related publications, in printed, video or electronic formats. We also invite you to ask any questions that you may have regarding the information provided in the book. Please send any questions or suggestions to us at the aforementioned publisher's address, via e-mail or by visiting our web site:

Web Site: www.wlinfo.com

E-mail address: input@wlinfo.com

Although the volume of communications we receive does not permit us to respond directly to the sender, we can assure you that your input will be considered in subsequent additions of this book and in the development of other publications from A is A. In addition, we expect, from time to time, to provide clarifications of material that we publish on our web site. We may also publish answers to frequently asked questions and/or those we feel will be of general interest. Thanks in advance for your help in making us more effective communicators.